Algebra 1

Concepts and Skills

McDougal Littell
A HOUGHTON MIFFLIN COMPANY

Evanston, Illinois • Boston • Dallas

About Algebra 1, Concepts and Skills

This book has been written to make algebra concepts and skills understandable to all students. The course focuses on the key topics that provide a strong foundation in the essentials of algebra. Lesson concepts are presented in a clear, straight-forward manner, supported by frequent worked-out examples. The page format makes it easy for students to follow the flow of a lesson, and the reading and vocabulary tips in the margins help students learn how to read the text. Checkpoint questions within lessons give students a way to check their understanding as they go along. The exercises for each lesson provide many opportunities to practice and maintain skills, as well as to apply concepts to real-world problems.

ISBN: 0-618-05051-5   123456789–DWO–04 03 02 01 00

Internet Web Site: http://www.mcdougallittell.com

About the Authors

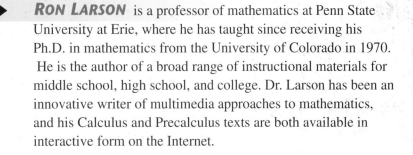

▶ **RON LARSON** is a professor of mathematics at Penn State University at Erie, where he has taught since receiving his Ph.D. in mathematics from the University of Colorado in 1970. He is the author of a broad range of instructional materials for middle school, high school, and college. Dr. Larson has been an innovative writer of multimedia approaches to mathematics, and his Calculus and Precalculus texts are both available in interactive form on the Internet.

▶ **LAURIE BOSWELL** is a mathematics teacher at Profile Junior-Senior High School in Bethlehem, New Hampshire. A recipient of the 1986 Presidential Award for Excellence in Mathematics Teaching, she is also the 1992 Tandy Technology Scholar and the 1991 recipient of the Richard Balomenos Mathematics Education Service Award presented by the New Hampshire Association of Teachers of Mathematics.

▶ **TIMOTHY D. KANOLD** is Director of Mathematics and a mathematics teacher at Adlai E. Stevenson High School in Lincolnshire, Illinois. In 1995 he received the Award of Excellence from the Illinois State Board of Education for outstanding contributions to education. A 1986 recipient of the Presidential Award for Excellence in Mathematics Teaching, he served as President of the Council of Presidential Awardees of Mathematics.

▶ **LEE STIFF** is a professor of mathematics education in the College of Education and Psychology of North Carolina State University at Raleigh and has taught mathematics at the high school and middle school levels. He is the 1992 recipient of the W. W. Rankin Award for Excellence in Mathematics Education presented by the North Carolina Council of Teachers of Mathematics, and a 1995–96 Fulbright Scholar to the Department of Mathematics of the University of Ghana.

All authors contributed to planning the content, organization, and instructional design of the program, and to reviewing and writing the manuscript. Ron Larson played a major role in writing the textbook and in establishing the program philosophy.

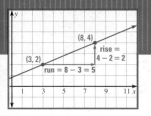

▶ REVIEWERS

Pauline Embree
Mathematics Department Chair
Rancho San Joaquin Middle School
Irvine, CA

Diego Gutierrez
Mathematics Teacher
Crawford High School
San Diego, CA

The reviewers read and commented on textbook chapters in pre-publication format, particularly with regard to classroom needs.

▶ TEACHER PANEL

Courteney Dawe
Mathematics Teacher
Placerita Junior High School
Valencia, CA

Dave Dempster
Mathematics Teacher
Temecula Valley High School
Temecula, CA

Pauline Embree
Mathematics Department Chair
Rancho San Joaquin Middle School
Irvine, CA

Tom Griffith
Mathematics Teacher
Scripps Ranch High School
San Diego, CA

Diego Gutierrez
Mathematics Teacher
Crawford High School
San Diego, CA

Roger Hitchcock
Mathematics Teacher
Buchanan High School
Clovis, CA

Louise McComas
Mathematics Teacher
Fremont High School
Sunnyvale, CA

Viola Okoro
Mathematics Teacher
Laguna Creek High School
Elk Grove, CA

The Teacher Panel helped plan the content, organization, and instructional design of the program.

CALIFORNIA CONSULTING MATHEMATICIANS

Kurt Kreith
Professor of Mathematics
University of California, Davis

Don Chakerian
Professor of Mathematics
University of California, Davis

The California Consulting Mathematicians prepared the *Mathematical Background Notes* preceding each chapter in the Teacher's Edition of this textbook.

CHAPTER

1

Connections to Algebra

Getting Ready

CHAPTER

2

Properties of Real Numbers

CHAPTER 3

Solving Linear Equations

CHAPTER 4

Graphing Linear Equations and Functions

CHAPTER
5

Writing Linear Equations

CHAPTER

6

Solving and Graphing Linear Inequalities

STUDENT HELP

Study Tip *324, 330, 337, 338, 342, 343, 344, 348, 349, 350, 356, 362, 363, 368, 369*
Skills Review *340*
Reading Algebra *323*
Writing Algebra *325, 331*
Vocabulary Tip *367*
Keystroke Help *374*
Test Tip *380*

APPLICATION HIGHLIGHTS

Music *321*
Astronomy *325, 359*
Mercury *327*
Fly-fishing *338*
Mountain Plants *343*
Steel Arch Bridge *346*
Water Temperature *352*
Poodles *357*
Fireworks *365*
Nutrition *371*

INTERNET

321, 327, 332, 337, 340, 346, 347, 349, 359, 365, 369, 371, 372, 374, 381

CHAPTER 7

Systems of Linear Equations and Inequalities

STUDENT HELP

APPLICATION HIGHLIGHTS

INTERNET

CHAPTER

8

Exponents and Exponential Functions

CHAPTER

9

Quadratic Equations and Functions

STUDENT HELP

APPLICATION HIGHLIGHTS

 INTERNET

ASSESSMENT

CHAPTER

10

Polynomials and Factoring

CHAPTER
11

Rational Expressions and Equations

ASSESSMENT

STUDENT HELP

APPLICATION HIGHLIGHTS

INTERNET

CHAPTER 12

Radicals and More Connections to Geometry

Contents of Student Resources

Pre-Course Test

DECIMALS

Skills Review
pp. 759–760

Find the sum, difference, product, or quotient.

1. $3.4 + 6.005$ **2.** $27.77 - 18.09$ **3.** 23.7×13.67 **4.** $9.744 \div 0.87$

FACTORS AND MULTIPLES

Skills Review
pp. 761–762

Find the greatest common factor of the pair of numbers.

5. $8, 28$ **6.** $36, 42$ **7.** $54, 81$ **8.** $50, 150$

Find the least common multiple of the pair of numbers.

9. $6, 7$ **10.** $10, 15$ **11.** $24, 38$ **12.** $12, 36$

Find the least common denominator of the pair of fractions.

13. $\dfrac{1}{2}, \dfrac{7}{10}$ **14.** $\dfrac{5}{8}, \dfrac{6}{7}$ **15.** $\dfrac{5}{9}, \dfrac{7}{12}$ **16.** $\dfrac{11}{20}, \dfrac{15}{32}$

FRACTIONS

Skills Review
pp. 763–766

Find the reciprocal of the number.

17. 12 **18.** $\dfrac{3}{16}$ **19.** $\dfrac{9}{5}$ **20.** $2\dfrac{1}{3}$

Add, subtract, multiply, or divide. Write the answer in simplest form.

21. $\dfrac{3}{4} - \dfrac{1}{4}$ **22.** $\dfrac{1}{2} + \dfrac{1}{8}$ **23.** $\dfrac{6}{7} + \dfrac{5}{9}$ **24.** $11\dfrac{1}{4} - 2\dfrac{5}{8}$

25. $\dfrac{1}{2} \times \dfrac{6}{11}$ **26.** $\dfrac{7}{11} \div \dfrac{3}{5}$ **27.** $\dfrac{4}{15} \div \dfrac{8}{3}$ **28.** $4\dfrac{1}{8} \times \dfrac{2}{3}$

FRACTIONS, DECIMALS, AND PERCENTS

Skills Review
pp. 768–769

Write the percent as a decimal and as a fraction in simplest form.

29. 7% **30.** 26% **31.** 48% **32.** 84%

Write the decimal as a percent and as a fraction in simplest form.

33. 0.08 **34.** 0.15 **35.** 0.47 **36.** 0.027

Write the fraction as a decimal and as a percent.

37. $\dfrac{9}{10}$ **38.** $\dfrac{4}{5}$ **39.** $\dfrac{7}{8}$ **40.** $\dfrac{11}{20}$

COMPARING AND ORDERING NUMBERS

Skills Review
pp. 770–771

Compare the two numbers. Write the answer using <, >, or =.

41. 138 and 198

42. 781 and 718

43. 8.4 and 8.2

44. -7.88 and -4.88

45. $\dfrac{5}{12}$ and $\dfrac{3}{4}$

46. $\dfrac{3}{6}$ and $\dfrac{4}{8}$

47. $\dfrac{5}{3}$ and $1\dfrac{1}{2}$

48. $16\dfrac{2}{3}$ and $16\dfrac{7}{8}$

Write the numbers in order from least to greatest.

49. 47, 74, 44, 77

50. 80, 808, 88, 8

51. 0.19, 0.9, 0.49, 0.4

52. $-6.5, -5.4, 6.4, -6$

53. $\dfrac{5}{8}, \dfrac{4}{7}, \dfrac{3}{5}, \dfrac{1}{2}$

54. $\dfrac{9}{7}, \dfrac{6}{4}, \dfrac{5}{4}, \dfrac{6}{13}$

55. $1\dfrac{5}{9}, 1\dfrac{3}{4}, \dfrac{13}{11}, \dfrac{7}{5}$

56. $-16\dfrac{1}{4}, -15\dfrac{1}{9}, -16\dfrac{1}{8}, -15\dfrac{2}{3}$

PERIMETER, AREA, AND VOLUME

Skills Review
pp. 772–773

Find the perimeter.

57. a triangle with sides of length 18 feet, 27 feet, and 32 feet

58. a square with sides of length 4.7 centimeters

Find the area.

59. a square with sides of length 13 yards

60. a rectangle with length 7.7 kilometers and width 4.5 kilometers

Find the volume.

61. a cube with sides of length 19 meters

62. a rectangular prism with length 5.9 inches, width 8.6 inches, and height 1.2 inches

DATA DISPLAYS

Skills Review
pp. 777–779

63. The list below shows the distribution of gold medals for the 1998 Winter Olympics. Choose an appropriate graph to display the data. ▶ Source: International Olympic Committee

Germany 12	Norway 10	Russia 9	Canada 6
United States 6	Japan 5	Netherlands 5	Austria 3
South Korea 3	Finland 2	France 2	Italy 2
Switzerland 2	Bulgaria 1	Czech Republic 1	

MEASURES OF CENTRAL TENDENCY

Skills Review
p. 780

Find the mean, median, and mode(s) of the data set.

64. 1, 3, 3, 3, 4, 5, 6, 7, 7, 9

65. 17, 22, 36, 47, 51, 58, 65, 80, 85, 89

66. 5, 23, 12, 5, 9, 18, 12, 4, 10, 21

67. 101, 423, 564, 198, 387, 291, 402, 572, 222, 357

DECIMALS

Skills Review
pp. 759–760

Find the sum or difference.

1. $14 + 7.1$

2. $11 - 0.003$

3. $19.76 + 48.19$

4. $73.8 - 6.93$

5. $10.2 + 3.805 + 1.1$

6. $7.2 - 3.56$

Find the product or quotient.

7. 17×3.9

8. 6.08×3.15

9. 15.2×5.02

10. 0.019×0.27

11. 45.28×16.1

12. $26.01 \div 5.1$

13. $7.03 \div 1.9$

14. $21.84 \div 0.84$

15. $0.0196 \div 0.056$

FACTORS AND MULTIPLES

Skills Review
pp. 761–762

List all the factors of the number.

1. 12

2. 41

3. 54

4. 126

Write the prime factorization of the number if it is not a prime number. If a number is prime, write *prime*.

5. 54

6. 60

7. 35

8. 47

List all the common factors of the pair of numbers.

9. 16, 20

10. 24, 36

11. 28, 42

12. 60, 72

Find the greatest common factor of the pair of numbers.

13. 8, 12

14. 10, 25

15. 15, 24

16. 24, 30

17. 36, 42

18. 54, 81

19. 68, 82

20. 102, 214

Find the least common multiple of the pair of numbers.

21. 9, 12

22. 8, 5

23. 14, 21

24. 24, 8

25. 12, 16

26. 70, 14

27. 36, 50

28. 22, 30

Find the least common denominator of the pair of fractions.

29. $\dfrac{5}{8}, \dfrac{5}{6}$

30. $\dfrac{5}{12}, \dfrac{7}{8}$

31. $\dfrac{7}{12}, \dfrac{9}{20}$

32. $\dfrac{5}{6}, \dfrac{8}{15}$

33. $\dfrac{3}{4}, \dfrac{15}{28}$

34. $\dfrac{9}{11}, \dfrac{8}{13}$

35. $\dfrac{5}{6}, \dfrac{20}{27}$

36. $\dfrac{17}{40}, \dfrac{27}{52}$

FRACTIONS

Skills Review
pp. 763–766

Find the reciprocal of the number.

1. 8

2. $\frac{1}{16}$

3. $\frac{9}{5}$

4. $3\frac{4}{7}$

Add or subtract. Write the answer as a fraction or a mixed number in simplest form.

5. $\frac{7}{12} - \frac{1}{12}$

6. $\frac{1}{8} + \frac{3}{8}$

7. $\frac{9}{10} + \frac{3}{10}$

8. $\frac{5}{15} - \frac{2}{15}$

9. $\frac{1}{3} + \frac{2}{9}$

10. $\frac{17}{20} - \frac{3}{5}$

11. $\frac{1}{6} + \frac{5}{8}$

12. $1\frac{2}{3} - \frac{8}{9}$

Multiply or divide. Write the answer as a fraction or a mixed number in simplest form.

13. $\frac{3}{5} \times \frac{1}{2}$

14. $\frac{2}{3} \times \frac{3}{8}$

15. $\frac{3}{5} \times 1\frac{1}{2}$

16. $2\frac{2}{3} \times 3\frac{3}{8}$

17. $\frac{2}{5} \div \frac{4}{5}$

18. $\frac{2}{3} \div \frac{8}{9}$

19. $5\frac{1}{4} \div \frac{7}{8}$

20. $4\frac{4}{5} \div 1\frac{1}{3}$

Add, subtract, multiply, or divide. Write the answer as a fraction or a mixed number in simplest form.

21. $\frac{2}{3} + \frac{5}{6}$

22. $9\frac{3}{8} - 5\frac{1}{4}$

23. $8\frac{2}{5} + 5\frac{3}{8}$

24. $\frac{4}{5} \times \frac{1}{4}$

25. $1\frac{2}{3} \div 1\frac{1}{4}$

26. $5\frac{3}{8} \times 3\frac{3}{4}$

27. $\frac{1}{4} \div \frac{1}{5}$

28. $1\frac{2}{3} - \frac{3}{4}$

FRACTIONS, DECIMALS, AND PERCENTS

Skills Review
pp. 768–769

Write the percent as a decimal and as a fraction or a mixed number in simplest form.

1. 8%

2. 25%

3. 38%

4. 73%

5. 135%

6. 350%

7. 6.4%

8. 0.15%

Write the decimal as a percent and as a fraction or a mixed number in simplest form.

9. 0.44

10. 0.09

11. 0.13

12. 0.008

13. 1.6

14. 3.04

15. 6.6

16. 4.75

Write the fraction or mixed number as a decimal and as a percent. Round decimals to the nearest thousandth. Round percents to the nearest tenth of a percent.

17. $\frac{3}{5}$

18. $\frac{5}{8}$

19. $\frac{17}{25}$

20. $\frac{11}{12}$

21. $5\frac{1}{5}$

22. $2\frac{1}{4}$

23. $3\frac{1}{16}$

24. $8\frac{3}{7}$

continued from page xxi

COMPARING AND ORDERING NUMBERS

Skills Review pp. 770–771

Compare the two numbers. Write the answer using <, >, or =.

1. 13,458 and 14,455

2. 907 and 971

3. -8344 and -8434

4. -49.5 and -49.05

5. 0.58 and 0.578

6. 0.0394 and 0.394

7. $\dfrac{15}{16}$ and $\dfrac{9}{10}$

8. $\dfrac{13}{20}$ and $\dfrac{1}{4}$

9. $\dfrac{9}{24}$ and $\dfrac{3}{8}$

10. $7\dfrac{1}{4}$ and $7\dfrac{1}{5}$

11. $-2\dfrac{11}{16}$ and $-3\dfrac{2}{9}$

12. $18\dfrac{2}{3}$ and $18\dfrac{5}{8}$

Write the numbers in order from least to greatest.

13. 1507, 1705, 1775, 1075

14. 38,381, 30,831, 38,831, 30,138

15. $-0.019, -0.013, -0.205, -0.035$

16. 6.034, 6.30, 6.33, 6.34

17. $\dfrac{1}{2}, \dfrac{2}{7}, \dfrac{5}{11}, \dfrac{5}{8}$

18. $\dfrac{4}{5}, \dfrac{3}{4}, \dfrac{3}{7}, \dfrac{4}{9}$

19. $-\dfrac{4}{2}, -\dfrac{2}{3}, -\dfrac{4}{3}, -\dfrac{3}{2}$

20. $\dfrac{3}{8}, \dfrac{5}{4}, \dfrac{7}{9}, 1\dfrac{4}{7}$

21. $1\dfrac{3}{5}, \dfrac{7}{5}, \dfrac{5}{3}, 1\dfrac{4}{5}$

22. $15\dfrac{5}{9}, 14\dfrac{2}{3}, 14\dfrac{5}{7}, 15\dfrac{5}{8}$

PERIMETER, AREA, AND VOLUME

Skills Review pp. 772–773

Find the perimeter.

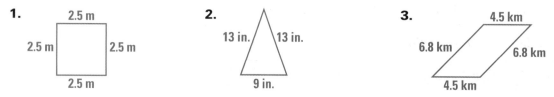

1. 2.5 m, 2.5 m, 2.5 m, 2.5 m

2. 13 in., 13 in., 9 in.

3. 4.5 km, 6.8 km, 6.8 km, 4.5 km

4. a rectangle with length of 12.5 centimeters and width of 11.6 centimeters

5. a regular pentagon with sides of length 19 feet

Find the area.

6. a square with sides of length 1.67 yards

7. a rectangle with length 1.4 inches and width 2.8 inches

8. a triangle with base 15 centimeters and height 10 centimeters

Find the volume.

9. a cube with sides of length 34 feet

10. a rectangular prism with length 18 meters, width 6 meters, and height 3 meters

11. a rectangular prism with length 6.5 millimeters, width 5.5 millimeters, and height 2.2 millimeters

DATA DISPLAYS

Skills Review
pp. 777–779

In Exercises 1 and 2, use the table shown below. Hurricane categories are determined by wind speed, with Category 5 the most severe.

U.S. Mainland Hurricane Strikes by Category from 1900–1996					
Category	One	Two	Three	Four	Five
Number	57	37	47	15	2

1. The data range from 2 to 57. The scale must start at 0. Choose a reasonable scale for a bar graph.

2. Draw a bar graph to display the number of hurricane strikes by category.

In Exercises 3 and 4, use the table shown below.

U.S. Mainland Hurricane Strikes by Decade from 1900–1989									
Decade	1900–1909	1910–1919	1920–1929	1930–1939	1940–1949	1950–1959	1960–1969	1970–1979	1980–1989
Number	16	19	15	17	23	18	15	12	16

▶ Source: National Hurricane Center

3. The data range from 12 to 23. The scale must start at 0. Choose a reasonable scale for a histogram.

4. Draw a histogram to display the number of hurricane strikes by decade.

Choose an appropriate graph to display the data. Draw the graph.

5.

Reported House Plant Sales for One Week				
Type	Violets	Begonias	Coleus	Orchids	Cacti
Number	90	46	39	70	60

6.

Republicans in the Senate by Congress Number						
Congress	100th	101st	102nd	103rd	104th	105th	106th
Republicans	45	45	44	43	52	55	55

▶ Source: *Statistical Abstract of the United States: 1999*

MEASURES OF CENTRAL TENDENCY

Skills Review
p. 780

Find the mean, median, and mode(s) of the data set.

1. 1, 3, 7, 2, 6, 3, 7, 9, 4, 7

2. 16, 19, 15, 17, 23, 18, 15, 12, 16, 7

3. 10, 48, 86, 32, 58, 73, 89, 39, 59, 27

4. 53, 54, 53, 45, 45, 44, 43, 52, 55, 55

A Guide to Student Help

▶ *Each chapter begins with a Study Guide*

CHAPTER PREVIEW
gives an overview of
what you will be
learning.

KEY WORDS
lists important new
words in the chapter.

READINESS QUIZ
checks your under-
standing of words and
skills that you will use
in the chapter, and
tells you where to
go for review.

STUDY TIP
suggests ways to
make your studying
and learning easier.

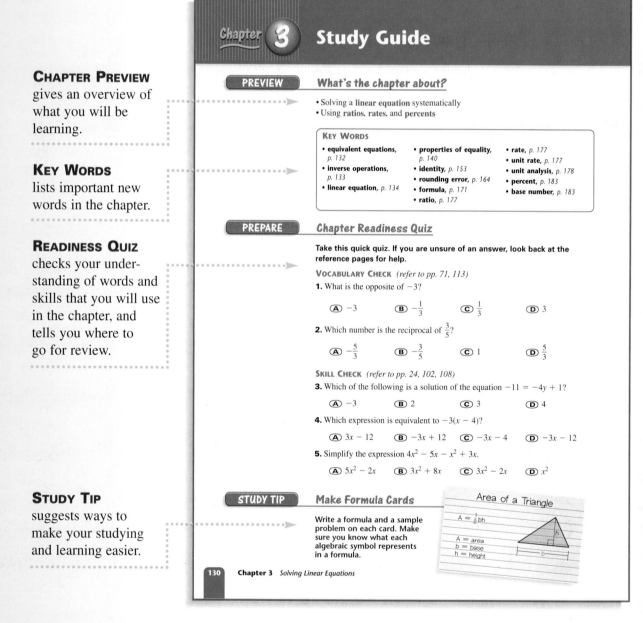

Chapter **3** **Study Guide**

PREVIEW **What's the chapter about?**

• Solving a **linear equation** systematically
• Using **ratios**, **rates**, and **percents**

KEY WORDS

• **equivalent equations**, p. 132	• **properties of equality**, p. 140	• **rate**, p. 177
• **inverse operations**, p. 133	• **identity**, p. 153	• **unit rate**, p. 177
• **linear equation**, p. 134	• **rounding error**, p. 164	• **unit analysis**, p. 178
	• **formula**, p. 171	• **percent**, p. 183
	• **ratio**, p. 177	• **base number**, p. 183

PREPARE **Chapter Readiness Quiz**

Take this quick quiz. If you are unsure of an answer, look back at the
reference pages for help.

VOCABULARY CHECK *(refer to pp. 71, 113)*

1. What is the opposite of -3?

    Ⓐ -3 Ⓑ $-\frac{1}{3}$ Ⓒ $\frac{1}{3}$ Ⓓ 3

2. Which number is the reciprocal of $\frac{3}{5}$?

    Ⓐ $-\frac{5}{3}$ Ⓑ $-\frac{3}{5}$ Ⓒ 1 Ⓓ $\frac{5}{3}$

SKILL CHECK *(refer to pp. 24, 102, 108)*

3. Which of the following is a solution of the equation $-11 = -4y + 1$?

    Ⓐ -3 Ⓑ 2 Ⓒ 3 Ⓓ 4

4. Which expression is equivalent to $-3(x - 4)$?

    Ⓐ $3x - 12$ Ⓑ $-3x + 12$ Ⓒ $-3x - 4$ Ⓓ $-3x - 12$

5. Simplify the expression $4x^2 - 5x - x^2 + 3x$.

    Ⓐ $5x^2 - 2x$ Ⓑ $3x^2 + 8x$ Ⓒ $3x^2 - 2x$ Ⓓ x^2

STUDY TIP **Make Formula Cards**

Write a formula and a sample
problem on each card. Make
sure you know what each
algebraic symbol represents
in a formula.

Area of a Triangle

$A = \frac{1}{2}bh$

A = area
b = base
h = height

130   **Chapter 3** *Solving Linear Equations*

▶ Student Help notes throughout the book

STUDY TIPS help you understand and apply concepts and avoid common errors.

MORE EXAMPLES indicates that there are more worked-out examples on the Internet.

READING ALGEBRA guides you in reading and understanding your textbook.

Student Help

▶**READING ALGEBRA**
Order is important for subtraction. "4 less than a number" means $y - 4$, not $4 - y$.

SKILLS REVIEW refers you to the pages where you can go for review and practice of topics from earlier courses.

Student Help

▶**SKILLS REVIEW**
For help with writing fractions in lowest terms, see p. 763.

Other notes included are:

• **WRITING ALGEBRA**
• **KEYSTROKE HELP**
• **TEST TIP**
• **LOOK BACK**

SIMPLIFIED EXPRESSIONS The distributive property allows you to *combine like terms* by adding their coefficients. An expression is **simplified** if it has no grouping symbols and if all the like terms have been combined.

Student Help

▶**STUDY TIP**
In Example 2 the distributive property has been extended to three terms:
$(b + c + d)a = ba + ca + da$

EXAMPLE 2 Combine Like Terms

Simplify the expression.

a. $8x + 3x$ **b.** $2y^2 + 7y^2 - y^2 + 2$

Solution

a. $8x + 3x = (8 + 3)x$ Use distributive property.
$= 11x$ Add coefficients.

b. $2y^2 + 7y^2 - y^2 + 2 = 2y^2 + 7y^2 - 1y^2 + 2$ Coefficient of $-y^2$ is -1.
$= (2 + 7 - 1)y^2 + 2$ Use distributive property.
$= 8y^2 + 2$ Add coefficients.

Student Help

▶**MORE EXAMPLES**
More examples are available at www.mcdougallittell.com

EXAMPLE 3 Simplify Expressions with Grouping Symbols

Simplify the expression.

a. $8 - 2(x + 4)$ **b.** $2(x + 3) + 3(5 - x)$

Solution

a. $8 - 2(x + 4)$
$= 8 - 2(x) + (-2)(4)$ Use distributive property.
$= 8 - 2x - 8$ Multiply.
$= -2x + 8 - 8$ Group like terms.
$= -2x$ Combine like terms.

b. $2(x + 3) + 3(5 - x)$
$= 2(x) + 2(3) + 3(5) + 3(-x)$ Use distributive property.
$= 2x + 6 + 15 - 3x$ Multiply.
$= 2x - 3x + \mathbf{6 + 15}$ Group like terms.
$= -x + 21$ Combine like terms.

Checkpoint ✓ **Simplify Expressions**

Simplify the expression.

3. $5x - 2x$ **4.** $8m - m - 3m + 5$ **5.** $-x^2 + 5x + x^2$

6. $3(y + 2) - 4y$ **7.** $9x - 4(2x - 1)$ **8.** $-(z + 2) - 2(1 - z)$

108 **Chapter 2** *Properties of Real Numbers*

HOMEWORK HELP tells you which textbook examples may help you with homework exercises, and lets you know when there is extra help on the Internet.

Student Help

▶**HOMEWORK HELP**
Extra help with problem solving in Exs. 34–39 is available at www.mcdougallittell.com

VOCABULARY TIPS explain the meaning and origin of words.

Student Help

▶**VOCABULARY TIP**
Equation comes from a Latin word that means "to be equal".

Connections to Algebra

▶ How much does it cost to rent scuba diving equipment?

APPLICATION: Scuba Diving

Scuba divers must be certified divers and must use scuba equipment in order to breathe underwater. Equipment such as wet suits, tanks, buoyancy compensator devices, and regulators can be rented at a cost per day at many sporting good stores.

Think & Discuss

The table shows the cost per day for renting a regulator.

Number of days	Rental charge
1	12.00×1
2	12.00×2
3	12.00×3
4	12.00×4

1. You decide to rent a regulator for 4 days. What is the rental charge?

2. Use the pattern in the table to predict the rental cost if you rent a regulator for 10 days.

Learn More About It

You will learn more about the price of renting scuba equipment in Exercise 24 on page 53.

APPLICATION LINK More about the prices of renting scuba diving equipment is available at www.mcdougallittell.com

What's the chapter about?

- Writing and evaluating **variable expressions**
- Checking solutions to **equations** and **inequalities**
- Using **verbal** and **algebraic** models
- Organizing data and representing **functions**

> **KEY WORDS**
>
> - **variable**, *p. 3*
> - **variable expression**, *p. 3*
> - **numerical expression**, *p. 3*
> - **power**, *p. 9*
> - **exponent**, *p. 9*
>
> - **base**, *p. 9*
> - **order of operations**, *p. 15*
> - **equation**, *p. 24*
> - **solution**, *p. 24*
>
> - **inequality**, *p. 26*
> - **modeling**, *p. 36*
> - **function**, *p. 48*
> - **domain**, *p. 49*
> - **range**, *p. 49*

Chapter Readiness Quiz

Take this quick quiz. If you are unsure of an answer, look at the reference pages for help.

VOCABULARY CHECK (*refer to pp. 3, 9*)

1. Which of the following is *not* a variable expression?

(A) $9 - 4y$ (B) $10 - 4(2)$ (C) $2x + 3$ (D) $2m + 3n$

2. Which term describes the expression 7^3?

(A) power   (B) exponent   (C) base   (D) variable

SKILL CHECK (*refer to pp. 772, 770*)

3. Find the perimeter of the figure.

(A) 30 feet   (B) 60 feet

(C) 120 feet   (D) 200 feet

[figure: rectangle labeled 20 ft (top), 10 ft (left), 10 ft (right), 20 ft (bottom)]

4. Complete the statement $0.5 > \boxed{?}$.

(A) $\dfrac{1}{4}$ (B) $\dfrac{1}{2}$ (C) $\dfrac{3}{4}$ (D) $\dfrac{3}{2}$

Keep a Math Notebook

Keeping a notebook will help you remember new concepts and skills.

Keeping a Math Notebook

- Keep a notebook of math notes about each chapter separate from your homework exercises.
- Review your notes each day before you start your next homework assignment.

1.1 Variables in Algebra

Goal

Evaluate variable expressions.

Key Words

- variable
- value
- variable expression
- numerical expression
- evaluate

How many miles has a race car traveled?

A race car zooms around the Indianapolis Motor Speedway at 180 miles per hour. In Example 3 you will find how many miles the car will travel in 2 hours.

ASSIGNING VARIABLES In algebra, you can use letters to represent one or more numbers. When a letter is used to represent a range of numbers, it is called a **variable.** The numbers are called **values** of the variable. For example, the distance traveled by the race car in the picture above can be expressed as the *variable expression* 180*t*, where *t* represents the number of hours the car has traveled.

A **variable expression** consists of constants, variables, and operations. An expression that represents a particular number is called a **numerical expression.** For example, the distance traveled by the race car in two hours is given by the numerical expression 180×2.

Student Help

▶ **WRITING ALGEBRA**
The multiplication symbol $\times$ is usually not used in algebra because of its possible confusion with the variable *x*.

EXAMPLE 1 Describe the Variable Expression

Here are some variable expressions, their meanings, and their operations.

VARIABLE EXPRESSION	MEANING	OPERATION
$8y$, $8 \cdot y$, $(8)(y)$	8 times y	Multiplication
$\frac{16}{b}$, $16 \div b$	16 divided by b	Division
$4 + s$	4 plus s	Addition
$9 - x$	9 minus x	Subtraction

Checkpoint✓ Describe the Variable Expression

State the meaning of the variable expression and name the operation.

1. $10 + x$ **2.** $13 - x$ **3.** $\frac{x}{16}$ **4.** $24x$

EVALUATING EXPRESSIONS To **evaluate** a variable expression, you write the expression, substitute a number for each variable, and simplify. The resulting number is the value of the expression.

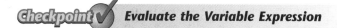

| Write expression. | $\longrightarrow$ | Substitute numbers. | $\longrightarrow$ | Simplify. |

EXAMPLE 2 **Evaluate the Variable Expression**

Evaluate the variable expression when $y = 2$.

Solution

EXPRESSION	SUBSTITUTE	SIMPLIFY
a. $5y$	$= 5(2)$	$= 10$
b. $\dfrac{10}{y}$	$= \dfrac{10}{2}$	$= 5$
c. $y + 6$	$= 2 + 6$	$= 8$
d. $14 - y$	$= 14 - 2$	$= 12$

Checkpoint ✓ *Evaluate the Variable Expression*

Evaluate the variable expression when $x = 3$.

5. $7x$ **6.** $5 + x$ **7.** $\dfrac{12}{x}$ **8.** $x - 2$

The variable expression r times t can be written as rt, $r \cdot t$, or $(r)(t)$.

RACE CARS The fastest average speed in the Indianapolis 500 is 185.981 miles per hour set by Arie Luyendyk, shown above.

EXAMPLE 3 **Evaluate rt to Find Distance**

RACE CARS Find the distance d traveled in 2 hours by a race car going an average speed of 180 miles per hour. Use the formula: distance equals rate r multiplied by time t.

Solution

$d = rt$	Write formula.
$= 180(2)$	Substitute 180 for r and 2 for t.
$= 360$	Simplify.

ANSWER ▶ The distance traveled by the race car was 360 miles.

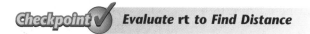

Checkpoint ✓ *Evaluate rt to Find Distance*

9. Using a variable expression, find the distance traveled by a car moving at an average speed of 60 miles per hour for 3 hours.

EXAMPLE 4 Find the Perimeter

GEOMETRY LINK The perimeter *P* of a triangle is equal to the sum of the lengths of its sides:

$$P = a + b + c$$

Find the perimeter of the triangle in feet.

c = 17
a = 8
b = 15

Solution

❶ **Write** the formula. $P = a + b + c$

❷ **Substitute** the side lengths of 8, 15 and 17. $= 8 + 15 + 17$

❸ **Add** the side lengths. $= 40$

ANSWER ▶ The triangle has a perimeter of 40 feet.

Checkpoint ✓ Find the Perimeter

10. Find the perimeter of a square with each side 12 inches long.

EXAMPLE 5 Estimate the Area

GEOGRAPHY LINK The area *A* of a triangle is equal to half the base *b* times the height *h*: $A = \frac{1}{2}bh$. Use this formula to estimate the area (in square miles) of Virginia.

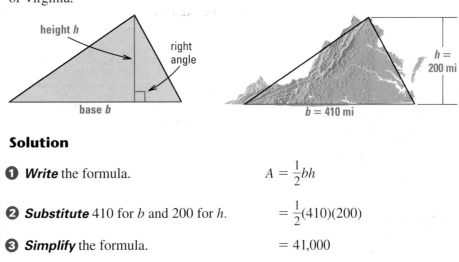

height *h*
right angle
base *b*
h = 200 mi
b = 410 mi

Solution

❶ **Write** the formula. $A = \frac{1}{2}bh$

❷ **Substitute** 410 for *b* and 200 for *h*. $= \frac{1}{2}(410)(200)$

❸ **Simplify** the formula. $= 41{,}000$

ANSWER ▶ The area of Virginia is about 41,000 square miles.

Checkpoint ✓ Find the Area

11. Find the area of the triangle in square meters.

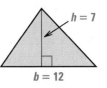

h = 7
b = 12

Guided Practice

Vocabulary Check | **Identify the variable or variables.**

1. $y + 15$ **2.** $20 - s$ **3.** $\dfrac{b}{10}$ **4.** rt

5. Complete: You __?__ an expression by substituting numbers for variables and simplifying. The resulting number is called the __?__ of the expression.

Skill Check | **State the meaning of the variable expression and name the operation.**

6. $\dfrac{5}{c}$ **7.** $p - 4$ **8.** $5 + n$ **9.** $(8)(x)$

Evaluate the variable expression when $k = 3$.

10. $11 + k$ **11.** $k - 2$ **12.** $7k$

13. $\dfrac{k}{33}$ **14.** $\dfrac{18}{k}$ **15.** $18 \cdot k$

16. **Geometry Link** Find the perimeter of each triangle.

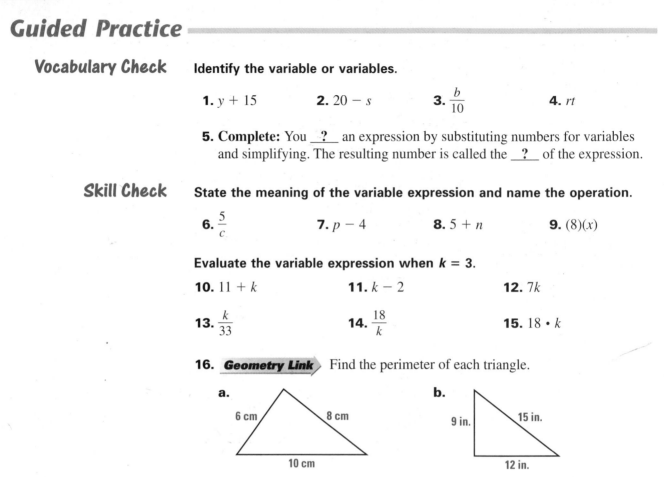

a. 6 cm, 8 cm, 10 cm

b. 9 in., 15 in., 12 in.

Practice and Applications

DESCRIBING EXPRESSIONS Match the variable expression with its meaning.

17. $y + 8$ **18.** $y - 8$ **19.** $\dfrac{y}{8}$ **20.** $8y$

A. 8 times y **B.** y divided by 8   **C.** y plus 8   **D.** y minus 8

EVALUATING EXPRESSIONS Evaluate the expression for the given value of the variable.

Student Help

▶**HOMEWORK HELP**
  Example 1: Exs. 17–20
  Example 2: Exs. 21–32
  Example 3: Exs. 33–39
  Example 4: Exs. 40–42
  Example 5: Exs. 43–46

21. $9 + p$ when $p = 11$ **22.** $\dfrac{1}{2} + t$ when $t = 2$ **23.** $\dfrac{b}{7}$ when $b = 14$

24. $\dfrac{d}{12}$ when $d = 36$ **25.** $(4)(n)$ when $n = 5$ **26.** $8a$ when $a = 6$

27. $12 - x$ when $x = 3$ **28.** $9 - y$ when $y = 8$ **29.** $10r$ when $r = 7$

30. $13c$ when $c = 3$ **31.** $\dfrac{18}{x}$ when $x = 3$ **32.** $\dfrac{63}{k}$ when $k = 9$

Student Help

▶ HOMEWORK HELP

Extra help with problem solving in Exs. 34–39 is available at www.mcdougallittell.com

33. DRIVING DISTANCE You are driving across the country at an average speed of 65 miles per hour. Using an appropriate formula, find the distance you travel in 4 hours.

FINDING DISTANCE Find the distance traveled using $d = rt$.

34. A train travels at a rate of 75 miles per hour for 2 hours.

35. An athlete runs at a rate of 8 feet per second for 5 seconds.

36. A horse trots at 8 kilometers per hour for 30 minutes.

37. A racecar driver goes at a speed of 170 miles per hour for 2 hours.

38. A plane travels at a speed of 450 miles per hour for 3 hours.

39. A person walks at a rate of 4 feet per second for 1 minute.

Student Help

▶ SKILLS REVIEW

The perimeter of any geometric figure is the sum of all its side lengths. To review perimeter and area formulas, see p. 772.

Geometry Link Find the perimeter of the geometric figure.

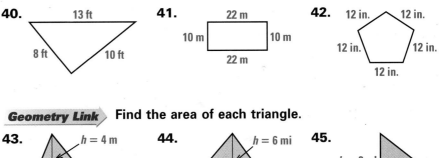

40. 13 ft, 8 ft, 10 ft

41. 22 m, 10 m, 10 m, 22 m

42. 12 in., 12 in., 12 in., 12 in., 12 in.

Geometry Link Find the area of each triangle.

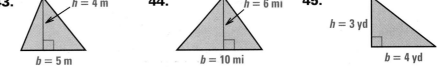

43. $h = 4$ m, $b = 5$ m

44. $h = 6$ mi, $b = 10$ mi

45. $h = 3$ yd, $b = 4$ yd

46. Geography Link To find the area A of a rectangle, you multiply the length times the width:

$$A = \ell \cdot w$$

Use the formula to estimate the area of Wyoming.

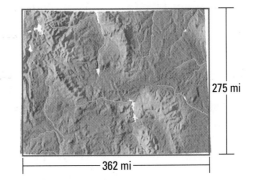

275 mi

362 mi

47. CHALLENGE A *tsunami* is a huge fast-moving series of water waves that can be caused by disturbances such as underwater earthquakes or volcanic explosions. If a tsunami is traveling at a speed of 500 miles per hour across the Pacific Ocean, how far has it gone in 15 minutes? *HINT:* Convert 15 minutes to hours.

EXAMPLE **Unit Analysis**

Writing the units of measure helps you determine the units for the answer. This is called *unit analysis*. When the same units occur in the numerator and the denominator, you can cancel them.

Use unit analysis to evaluate the expression. The letter *h* is an abbreviation for hours, while *mi* stands for miles.

a. $(3 \text{ h})\left(\dfrac{25 \text{ mi}}{1 \text{ h}}\right)$

b. $(90 \text{ mi}) \div \left(\dfrac{45 \text{ mi}}{1 \text{ h}}\right)$

Solution

a. $(3 \text{ h})\left(\dfrac{25 \text{ mi}}{1 \text{ h}}\right) = 75 \text{ mi}$ Cancel hours.

b. $(90 \text{ mi}) \div \left(\dfrac{45 \text{ mi}}{1 \text{ h}}\right) = (90 \text{ mi})\left(\dfrac{1 \text{ h}}{45 \text{ mi}}\right) = 2 \text{ h}$ Cancel miles.

Student Help

▶ **STUDY TIP**
When you divide by a fraction, you multiply by the reciprocal. See Skills Review, p. 765.

48. Evaluate the expression $(4 \text{ h})\left(\dfrac{60 \text{ mi}}{1 \text{ h}}\right)$.

49. Evaluate the expression $(80 \text{ mi}) \div \left(\dfrac{20 \text{ mi}}{1 \text{ h}}\right)$.

Standardized Test Practice

50. MULTIPLE CHOICE How many miles does Joyce travel if she drives for 6 hours at an average speed of 60 miles per hour?

Ⓐ 66 miles   Ⓑ 180 miles   Ⓒ 360 miles   Ⓓ 420 miles

51. MULTIPLE CHOICE The lengths of the sides of a triangle are 4 centimeters, 8 centimeters, and 7 centimeters. What is the perimeter of the triangle?

Ⓕ 7 cm   Ⓖ 16 cm   Ⓗ 19 cm   Ⓙ 28 cm

Mixed Review

OPERATIONS WITH DECIMALS **Find the value of the expression.** *(Skills Review p. 759)*

52. $32.8 - 4$ **53.** $3.98 + 5.50$ **54.** $0.1(50)$

SIMPLIFYING EXPRESSIONS **Simplify the expression without using a calculator.** *(Skills Review p. 765)*

55. $\left(\dfrac{30}{10}\right)(5)$ **56.** $(60)\left(\dfrac{2}{12}\right)$ **57.** $\left(\dfrac{3}{15}\right)\left(\dfrac{5}{6}\right)$

Maintaining Skills

ADDING DECIMALS **Add.** *(Skills Review p. 759)*

58. $2.3 + 4.5$ **59.** $16.8 + 7.1$ **60.** $0.09 + 0.05$

61. $1.0008 + 10.15$ **62.** $123.8 + 0.03$ **63.** $46 + 7.55$

64. $0.32 + 0.094$ **65.** $6.105 + 7.3$ **66.** $2.008 + 1.10199$

1.2 Exponents and Powers

Goal

Evaluate a power.

Key Words

- power
- exponent
- base
- grouping symbols

How much water does the tank hold?

How much water do you need to fill a fish tank? You will use a *power* to find the answer in Example 5.

An expression like 2^3 is called a **power**. The **exponent** 3 represents the number of times the **base** 2 is used as a factor.

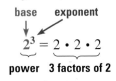

base   exponent

$$2^3 = 2 \cdot 2 \cdot 2$$

power   3 factors of 2

The expression 2^3 means "multiply 2 by itself 3 times." The numbers you multiply are factors. In general, $a^n = \underbrace{a \cdot a \cdot a \cdot \ldots \cdot a.}_{n \text{ times}}$

EXAMPLE 1   Read and Write Powers

Express the power in words. Then write the meaning.

EXPONENTIAL FORM	WORDS	MEANING
a. 4^2	four to the second power or four squared	$4 \cdot 4$
b. 5^3	five to the third power or five cubed	$5 \cdot 5 \cdot 5$
c. x^6	x to the sixth power	$x \cdot x \cdot x \cdot x \cdot x \cdot x$

Student Help

▶ **READING ALGEBRA**
Note that x^1 is customarily written as x with the exponent omitted.

Checkpoint ✓ **Write the Power**

Write the expression in exponential form.

1. 3 squared   **2.** x to the fourth power   **3.** s cubed

EXAMPLE 2 **Evaluate the Power**

Evaluate x^4 when $x = 2$.

Solution

❶ **Substitute** 2 for x.　　　$x^4 = 2^4$

❷ **Write** out the factors.　　　$= 2 \cdot 2 \cdot 2 \cdot 2$

❸ **Multiply** the factors.　　　$= 16$

ANSWER ▶ The value of the power is 16.

GROUPING SYMBOLS Parentheses ( ) and brackets [ ] are **grouping symbols**. They tell you the order in which to do the operations. You must do the operations within the innermost set of grouping symbols first:

First multiply. Then add.　　　　**First add. Then multiply.**

$(3 \cdot 4) + 7 = 12 + 7 = 19$　　　$3 \cdot (4 + 7) = 3 \cdot 11 = 33$

You will learn more about the order of operations in the next lesson.

EXAMPLE 3 **Evaluate Exponential Expressions**

Evaluate the variable expression when $a = 1$ and $b = 2$.

a. $(a^2) + (b^2)$　　　　　　　**b.** $(a + b)^2$

Solution

a. $(a^2) + (b^2) = (1^2) + (2^2)$　　　Substitute 1 for a and 2 for b.

　　　　　　　$= (1 \cdot 1) + (2 \cdot 2)$　　　Write factors.

　　　　　　　$= 1 + 4$　　　Multiply.

　　　　　　　$= 5$　　　Add.

b. $(a + b)^2 = (1 + 2)^2$　　　Substitute 1 for a and 2 for b.

　　　　　　　$= (3)^2$　　　Add within parentheses.

　　　　　　　$= 3 \cdot 3$　　　Write factors.

　　　　　　　$= 9$　　　Multiply.

Checkpoint ✓ **Evaluate Exponential Expressions**

Evaluate the variable expression when $s = 2$ and $t = 4$.

4. $(t - s)^3$　　　　　**5.** $(s^2) + (t^2)$　　　　　**6.** $(t + s)^2$

7. $(t^2) - (s^2)$　　　　**8.** $(s^2) + t$　　　　　**9.** $(t^2) - s$

In Lesson 1.3 you will learn several rules for order of operations. One of those tells us that $2x^3$ is to be interpreted as $2(x^3)$.

Student Help

▶**READING ALGEBRA**
Notice that in part (a) of Example 4, the exponent applies to x, while in part (b), the exponent applies to $2x$.

EXAMPLE **4** **Exponents and Grouping Symbols**

Evaluate the variable expression when $x = 4$.

a. $2x^3$ **b.** $(2x)^3$

Solution

a. $2x^3 = 2(4^3)$ Substitute 4 for x.

$ = 2(64)$ Evaluate power.

$ = 128$ Multiply.

b. $(2x)^3 = (2 \cdot 4)^3$ Substitute 4 for x.

$ = 8^3$ Multiply within parentheses.

$ = 512$ Evaluate power.

Exponents can be used to find the area of a square and the volume of a cube.

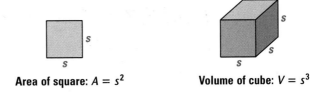

Area of square: $A = s^2$ Volume of cube: $V = s^3$

Units of area, such as square feet, ft^2, can be written using a second power. Units of volume, such as cubic feet, ft^3, can be written using a third power.

EXAMPLE **5** **Find the Volume of the Tank**

FISH TANKS The fish tank has the shape of a cube. Each inner edge s is 2 feet long. Find the volume in cubic feet.

Solution

$V = s^3$ Write formula for volume of a cube.

$ = 2^3$ Substitute 2 for s.

$ = 8$ Evaluate power.

ANSWER ▶ The volume of the tank is 8 cubic feet.

2 ft
2 ft
2 ft

 Find Area and Volume

10. Use the formula for the area of a square to find the area of each side of the fish tank in Example 5. Express your answer in square feet.

Exercises

Guided Practice

Vocabulary Check   **Complete the sentence.**

1. In the expression 3^7, the 3 is the __?__.

2. In the expression 5^4, the 4 is the __?__.

3. The expression 9^{12} is called a __?__.

4. Two kinds of grouping symbols are __?__ and __?__.

Skill Check   **Match the power with the words that describe it.**

5. 3^7 **A.** four to the sixth power

6. 7^3 **B.** three to the seventh power

7. 4^6 **C.** seven to the third power

8. 6^4 **D.** six to the fourth power

Evaluate the variable expression when $t = 3$.

9. t^2 **10.** $1 + t^3$ **11.** $4t^2$ **12.** $(4t)^2$

Practice and Applications

WRITING POWERS   **Write the expression in exponential form.**

13. two cubed   **14.** p squared   **15.** nine to the fifth power

16. b to the eighth power   **17.** $3 \cdot 3 \cdot 3 \cdot 3$ **18.** $4x \cdot 4x \cdot 4x$

19.   **Geometry Link**   A square painting measures 5 feet by 5 feet. Write the power that gives the area of the painting. Then evaluate the power.

5 ft

5 ft

EVALUATING POWERS   **Evaluate the power.**

20. 9^2 **21.** 2^4 **22.** 7^3 **23.** 2^6

24. 5^4 **25.** 1^8 **26.** 10^3 **27.** 0^6

Student Help

▶**HOMEWORK HELP**
Example 1: Exs. 13–19
Example 2: Exs. 19–39
Example 3: Exs. 40–45
Example 4: Exs. 46–51
Example 5: Exs. 52–57

EVALUATING POWERS WITH VARIABLES   **Evaluate the expression for the given value of the variable.**

28. w^2 when $w = 12$ **29.** b^3 when $b = 9$ **30.** c^4 when $c = 3$

31. h^5 when $h = 2$ **32.** n^2 when $n = 11$ **33.** x^3 when $x = 5$

34. 8^6 **35.** 13^5 **36.** 5^9

37. 12^7 **38.** 6^6 **39.** 3^{12}

EVALUATING EXPRESSIONS Evaluate the variable expression when
$c = 4$ and $d = 5$.

40. $(c + d)^2$ **41.** $(d^2) + c$ **42.** $(c^3) + d$

43. $(d^2) - (c^2)$ **44.** $(d - c)^7$ **45.** $(d^2) - d$

EXPONENTIAL EXPRESSIONS Evaluate the expression for the given
value of the variable.

46. $2x^2$ when $x = 7$ **47.** $6t^4$ when $t = 1$ **48.** $7b^2$ when $b = 3$

49. $(5w)^3$ when $w = 5$ **50.** $(4x)^3$ when $x = 1$ **51.** $(5y)^5$ when $y = 2$

52. INTERIOR DESIGN The floor of a room is 14 feet long by 14 feet wide. How many square feet of carpet are needed to cover the floor?

53. VOLUME OF A SAFE A fireproof safe is designed in the shape of a cube. The length of each edge of the cube is 2 meters. What is the volume of the fireproof safe?

54. ARTISTS In 1997, the artist Jon Kuhn of North Carolina created a cubic sculpture called *Crystal Victory*, shown at the left. Each edge of the solid glass cube is 9.5 inches in length. What is the volume of the cubic structure?

CRITICAL THINKING Count the number of cubic units along the edges of the cube. Write and evaluate the power that gives the volume of the cube in cubic units.

55. 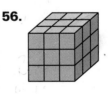   **56.** 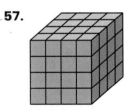   **57.**

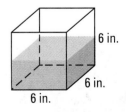

ARTIST Jon Kuhn used mathematics when creating the cubic sculpture *Crystal Victory*. The solid glass cube is made of lead crystal and colored glass powders.

CHALLENGE You are making candles. You melt paraffin wax in the cubic container shown below. Each edge of the container is 6 inches in length. The container is half full.

58. What is the volume of the wax in this container?

59. Each edge of a second cubic container is 4 inches in length. Can this second candle mold hold the same amount of melted wax that is in the candle mold shown at the right? Explain your answer.

6 in.

6 in.

6 in.

60. Design a third cubic candle mold different from the one given above that will hold all the melted wax. Draw a diagram of the mold including the measurements. Explain why your mold will hold all the melted wax.

61. MULTIPLE CHOICE Evaluate the expression $2x^2$ when $x = 5$.

(A) 20   (B) 40   (C) 50   (D) 100

62. MULTIPLE CHOICE One kiloliter is equal to 10^3 liters. How many liters are in one kiloliter?

(F) 10   (G) 100   (H) 1000   (J) 10,000

Student Help

▶ **TEST TIP**
Jotting down the formula for the volume of a cube will help you answer Exercise 63.

63. MULTIPLE CHOICE Sondra bought this trunk to store clothes. What is the volume of the trunk?

(A) 9 ft   (B) 9 ft^2

(C) 9 ft^3 (D) None of these

3 ft
3 ft
3 ft

Mixed Review

Geometry Link Find the perimeter of the geometric figure when $x = 3$.
(Lesson 1.1)

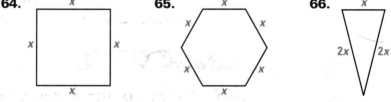

64. x, x, x, x **65.** x, x, x, x, x, x **66.** x, $2x$, $2x$

EVALUATING EXPRESSIONS Evaluate the expression for the given value of the variable. *(Lesson 1.1)*

67. $9j$ when $j = 5$ **68.** $6 + t$ when $t = 21$ **69.** $\dfrac{b}{2}$ when $b = 18$

70. $25 - n$ when $n = 3$ **71.** $c + 4$ when $c = 24$ **72.** $(7)(r)$ when $r = 11$

73. $\dfrac{24}{s}$ when $s = 8$ **74.** $3m$ when $m = 7$ **75.** $d - 13$ when $d = 22$

Maintaining Skills

SIMPLIFYING FRACTIONS Simplify. *(Skills Review p. 763)*

76. $\dfrac{4}{8}$ **77.** $\dfrac{10}{2}$ **78.** $\dfrac{15}{10}$ **79.** $\dfrac{6}{20}$

80. $\dfrac{8}{14}$ **81.** $\dfrac{18}{21}$ **82.** $\dfrac{8}{6}$ **83.** $\dfrac{27}{3}$

84. $\dfrac{25}{15}$ **85.** $\dfrac{21}{7}$ **86.** $\dfrac{3}{24}$ **87.** $\dfrac{28}{4}$

ESTIMATING Estimate the answer. Then evaluate the expression. *(Skills Review p. 774)*

88. $2.5 - 0.5$ **89.** $0.3 - 0.03$ **90.** $10.35 + 5.301$

91. $3.71 + 1.054$ **92.** $2.1 - 0.2$ **93.** $5.175 + 1.15$

1.3 Order of Operations

Goal
Use the established order of operations.

Key Words
- order of operations
- left-to-right rule

How many points ahead are you?

You are playing basketball. You make 8 field goals and 2 free throws. Your friend makes half as many field goals as you and no free throws. You will find how many points ahead you are in Example 5.

ORDER OF OPERATIONS In arithmetic and algebra there is an **order of operations** to evaluate an expression involving more than one operation.

ORDER OF OPERATIONS

STEP ❶ First do operations that occur within grouping symbols.

STEP ❷ Then evaluate powers.

STEP ❸ Then do multiplications and divisions from left to right.

STEP ❹ Finally, do additions and subtractions from left to right.

EXAMPLE 1 Evaluate Without Grouping Symbols

Evaluate the expression $3x^2 + 1$ when $x = 4$. Use the order of operations.

Solution

$$3x^2 + 1 = 3 \cdot 4^2 + 1 \qquad \text{Substitute 4 for } x.$$
$$= 3 \cdot 16 + 1 \qquad \text{Evaluate power.}$$
$$= 48 + 1 \qquad \text{Multiply 3 times 16.}$$
$$= 49 \qquad \text{Add.}$$

Checkpoint✓ *Evaluate Expressions Without Grouping Symbols*

Evaluate the variable expression when $x = 2$. Use the order of operations.

1. $2x^2 + 5$　　　**2.** $8 - x^2$　　　**3.** $6 + 3x^3$　　　**4.** $20 - 4x^2$

LEFT-TO-RIGHT RULE Some expressions have operations that have the same priority, such as multiplication and division *or* addition and subtraction. The **left-to-right rule** states that when operations have the same priority, you perform them in order from left to right.

EXAMPLE 2 Use the Left-to-Right Rule

Evaluate the expression using the left-to-right rule.

a. $24 - 8 - 6 = (24 - 8) - 6$ Work from left to right.

$= 16 - 6$ Subtract 8 from 24.

$= 10$ Subtract 6 from 16.

b. $15 \cdot 2 \div 6 = (15 \cdot 2) \div 6$ Work from left to right.

$= 30 \div 6$ Multiply 15 times 2.

$= 5$ Divide 30 by 6.

c. $16 + 4 \cdot 2 - 3 = 16 + (4 \cdot 2) - 3$ Do multiplication first.

$= 16 + 8 - 3$ Multiply 4 times 2.

$= (16 + 8) - 3$ Work from left to right.

$= 24 - 3$ Add 16 and 8.

$= 21$ Subtract 3 from 24.

Student Help

▶**STUDY TIP**
You multiply first in part (c) of Example 2, because multiplication has a higher priority than addition and subtraction.

A fraction bar can act as a grouping symbol: $(1 + 2) \div (4 - 1) = \dfrac{1 + 2}{4 - 1}$.

EXAMPLE 3 Expressions with Fraction Bars

Evaluate the expression. Then simplify the answer.

$\dfrac{7 \cdot 4}{8 + 7^2 - 1} = \dfrac{7 \cdot 4}{8 + 49 - 1}$ Evaluate power.

$= \dfrac{28}{8 + 49 - 1}$ Simplify the numerator.

$= \dfrac{28}{57 - 1}$ Work from left to right.

$= \dfrac{28}{56}$ Subtract.

$= \dfrac{1}{2}$ Simplify.

Student Help

▶**SKILLS REVIEW**
For help with writing fractions in lowest terms, see p. 763.

Checkpoint ✓ Use the Order of Operations and Left-to-Right Rule

Evaluate the variable expression when *x* = 1.

5. $4x^2 + 5 - 3$ **6.** $5 - x^3 - 1$ **7.** $\dfrac{2x}{x^2 - 1 + 5}$

USING A CALCULATOR You need to know if your calculator uses the order of operations or not. If it does not, you must input the operations in the proper order yourself.

EXAMPLE 4 Use a Calculator

Enter the following in your calculator. Does the calculator display 6 or 1?

10 [−] 6 [÷] 2 [−] 1 [ENTER]

Solution

a. If your calculator uses the order of operations, it will display 6.

$$10 - 6 \div 2 - 1 = 10 - (6 \div 2) - 1$$
$$= (10 - 3) - 1$$
$$= 6$$

b. If your calculator does *not* use the order of operations and performs the operations as they are entered, it will display 1.

$$[(10 - 6) \div 2] - 1 = (4 \div 2) - 1$$
$$= 2 - 1$$
$$= 1$$

Link to
Sports

BASKETBALL SCORES
A field goal is worth 2 points.
A free throw is worth 1 point.

EXAMPLE 5 Evaluate a Real-Life Expression

BASKETBALL SCORES You are playing basketball. You make 8 field goals and 2 free throws. Your friend makes half as many field goals as you and no free throws. How many points ahead of your friend are you?

Solution

$$8 \cdot 2 + 2 \cdot 1 - \frac{8 \cdot 2}{2} = 16 + 2 - \frac{16}{2} \qquad \text{Multiply from left to right.}$$
$$= 16 + 2 - 8 \qquad \text{Divide.}$$
$$= 18 - 8 \qquad \text{Add.}$$
$$= 10 \qquad \text{Subtract.}$$

ANSWER ▶ You are 10 points ahead of your friend.

Checkpoint ✓ Evaluate a Real-Life Expression

8. Your friend makes 4 field goals. You make three times as many field goals as your friend plus one field goal. How many points do you have? Explain the order of operations you followed.

9. Your friend makes 6 field goals and 2 free throws. You make twice as many field goals as your friend and half the number of free throws. How many points do you have? Explain the order of operations you followed.

Guided Practice

Vocabulary Check

1. Place the operations in the order in which you should do them.

   a. Multiply and divide from left to right.

   b. Do operations within grouping symbols.

   c. Add and subtract from left to right.

   d. Evaluate powers.

2. What rule must be applied when evaluating an expression in which the operations have the same priority?

Skill Check

Evaluate the variable expression.

3. $5 \cdot 6 \cdot 2$ **4.** $16 \div 4 - 2$ **5.** $4 + 9 - 1$ **6.** $2 \cdot 8^2$

7. $15 + 6 \div 3$ **8.** $9 \div 3 \cdot 2$ **9.** $2 \cdot 3^2 + 5$ **10.** $2^3 \cdot 3^2$

Evaluate the variable expression when $x = 3$.

11. $x^2 - 5$ **12.** $x^3 + 5x$ **13.** $x + 3x^4$

14. $\dfrac{27}{x} - 2 + 16$ **15.** $\dfrac{15}{x} + 2^3 - 10$ **16.** $\dfrac{24}{x} \cdot 5$

Practice and Applications

NUMERICAL EXPRESSIONS **Evaluate the expression.**

17. $13 + 3 \cdot 7$ **18.** $7 + 8 \div 2$ **19.** $2^4 - 5 \cdot 3$

20. $6^2 + 4$ **21.** $4^3 + 9 \cdot 2$ **22.** $3 \cdot 2 + \dfrac{5}{9}$

VARIABLE EXPRESSIONS **Evaluate the expression for the given value of the variable.**

23. $6 \cdot 2p^2$ when $p = 5$ **24.** $2g \cdot 5$ when $g = 4$

25. $14 (n + 1)$ when $n = 2$ **26.** $\dfrac{x}{7} + 16$ when $x = 14$

Student Help

▶**HOMEWORK HELP**
Example 1: Exs. 17–26
Example 2: Exs. 27–35
Example 3: Exs. 36–41
Example 4: Exs. 42–45
Example 5: Exs. 46–52

NUMERICAL EXPRESSIONS **Evaluate the expression.**

27. $2^3 + 5 - 2$ **28.** $4 \cdot 2 + 15 \div 3$ **29.** $6 \div 3 + 2 \cdot 7$

30. $5 + 8 \cdot 2 - 4$ **31.** $16 + 8 \cdot 2^2$ **32.** $2 \cdot 3^2 - 7$

33. $10 - 3 + (2 + 5)$ **34.** $7 + 18 - (6 - 3)$ **35.** $[(7 \cdot 4) + 3] + 15$

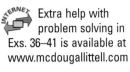
EXPRESSIONS WITH FRACTION BARS Evaluate the expression. Then simplify the answer.

36. $\dfrac{6 \cdot 4}{4 + 3^2 - 1}$

37. $\dfrac{13 - 4}{18 - 4^2 + 1}$

38. $\dfrac{5^2 \cdot 2}{1 + 6^2 - 12}$

39. $\dfrac{21 + 9}{5^2 + 40 - 5}$

40. $\dfrac{3^3 + 8 - 7}{2 \cdot 7}$

41. $\dfrac{4 \cdot 2^5}{16 - 4^2 + 1}$

42. LOGICAL REASONING Which is correct?

A. $\dfrac{9^2 + 3}{5} = 9^2 + 3 \div 5$

B. $\dfrac{9^2 + 3}{5} = [9^2 + 3] \div 5$

CRITICAL THINKING In Exercises 43–46, two calculators were used to evaluate the expression. Determine which calculator performed the correct order of operations.

43. 15 − 6 ÷ 3 × 4 ENTER

Calculator A: 12   Calculator B: 7

44. 15 − 9 ÷ 3 + 7 ENTER

Calculator A: 19   Calculator B: 9

45. 15 + 10 ÷ 5 + 4 ENTER

Calculator A: 21   Calculator B: 9

46. 4 × 3 ÷ 6 ÷ 2 ENTER

Calculator A: 9   Calculator B: 15

FOOTBALL UNIFORMS
In Exercises 47 and 48, use the table showing the costs of parts of a football player's uniform.

47. A sporting goods company offers a $2000 discount for orders of 30 or more complete uniforms. Your school orders 35 complete uniforms. Write an expression for the total cost.

48. Evaluate the expression you wrote in Exercise 47.

Part of uniform	Jersey and pants	Shoulder pads	Lower body pads	Knee pads	Cleats	Helmet
Cost	$230	$300	$40	$15	$100	$200

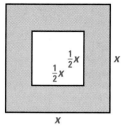

Geometry Link In Exercises 49 and 50, refer to the squares shown at the right.

49. Write an expression that represents the area of the shaded region. *HINT:* Subtract the area of the inner square from the area of the outer square.

50. If $x = 8$, what is the area of the shaded region?

Link to
State Fairs

ADMISSION PRICES Every year nearly 1,000,000 people attend the California State Fair.

ADMISSION PRICES In Exercises 51 and 52, use the table below. It shows the admission prices for the California State Fair.

California State Fair Admission Prices	
Age	**Admission price**
General Admission (13–61 years of age)	$7.00
Seniors (62 years and above)	$5.00
Children (5–12 years)	$4.00
Children (4 years and under)	Free

▶ Source: *Sacramento Bee*

51. Write an expression that represents the admission price for a group consisting of 2 adults, 1 senior, and 3 children. The children's ages are 12 years, 10 years, and 18 months.

52. Evaluate the expression you wrote in Exercise 51. Then find the total cost of admission for the group.

53. CHALLENGE At a concert you buy a hat for $10.00, a hot dog for $2.75, and nachos for $3.50. There is a 6% sales tax on the hat. Your calculator follows the established order of operations. Write a keystroke sequence for the amount you owe. Then find the amount you owe. *HINT:* 6% = 0.06

Standardized Test Practice

54. MULTIPLE CHOICE Evaluate the expression $4^2 - 10 \div 2$.

    A 3   **B** 11   **C** 13   **D** 21

55. MULTIPLE CHOICE Evaluate the expression $32 - x^2 + 9$ when $x = 2$.

    F 19   **G** 21   **H** 37   **J** 39

56. MULTIPLE CHOICE Which expression has a value of 12?

    A $3 + 3 \times 5 - 2$

    B $18 \div 6 \times 3 + 3$

    C $7 + 14 \div 7 \times 4$

    D $2^2 \cdot 3 - 6 \cdot 2$

57. MULTIPLE CHOICE Evaluate the expression $\dfrac{3^2 + 6 - 5}{2 \cdot 5}$.

    F 1   **G** 5   **H** 7   **J** 10

EVALUATING EXPRESSIONS Evaluate the expression for the given value of the variable. *(Lesson 1.1)*

58. $(8)(a)$ when $a = 4$ **59.** $\dfrac{24}{x}$ when $x = 3$ **60.** $c + 15$ when $c = 12$

61. $\dfrac{x}{2} \cdot x$ when $x = 18$ **62.** $9t$ when $t = 7$ **63.** $25 - y$ when $y = 14$

WRITING POWERS Write the expression in exponential form. *(Lesson 1.2)*

64. twelve squared   **65.** z to the sixth power   **66.** $2b \cdot 2b \cdot 2b$

EXPONENTIAL EXPRESSIONS Evaluate the expression for the given value of the variable. *(Lesson 1.2)*

67. $9t^2$ when $t = 3$ **68.** $(7h)^3$ when $h = 1$ **69.** $(6w)^2$ when $w = 5$

FACTORS Determine whether the number is prime or composite. If it is composite, list all of its factors. *(Skills Review p. 761)*

70. 15   **71.** 9   **72.** 13   **73.** 38

74. 46   **75.** 50   **76.** 64   **77.** 29

Quiz 1

Evaluate the variable expression when **x = 3**. *(Lessons 1.1, 1.2)*

1. $6x$ **2.** $42 \div x$ **3.** $x + 29$

4. $12 - x$ **5.** $5x - 10$ **6.** $10 + 2x$

7. $x^2 - 3$ **8.** $2x^3$ **9.** $(2x)^3$

Find the distance traveled using **d = rt**. *(Lesson 1.1)*

10. A car travels at an average speed of 50 miles per hour for 4 hours.

11. A plane flies at 500 miles per hour for 4 hours.

12. A marathon runner keeps a steady pace of 10 miles per hour for 2 hours.

Write the expression in exponential form. *(Lesson 1.2)*

13. six cubed   **14.** $4 \cdot 4 \cdot 4 \cdot 4 \cdot 4$ **15.** $5y \cdot 5y \cdot 5y$

16. $3 \cdot 3 \cdot 3$ **17.** $2x \cdot 2x \cdot 2x \cdot 2x$ **18.** eight squared

19. PACKING BOXES A cubic packing box has dimensions of 4 feet on each edge. What is the volume of the box? *(Lesson 1.2)*

Evaluate the expression. Then simplify the answer. *(Lesson 1.3)*

20. $\dfrac{7 \cdot 2^2}{7 + (2^3 - 1)}$ **21.** $\dfrac{(3^2 - 3)}{2 \cdot 9}$ **22.** $\dfrac{6^2 - 11}{2(17 + 2 \cdot 4)}$

DEVELOPING CONCEPTS
Finding Patterns

1.4

GOAL

Use algebraic expressions to describe patterns.

MATERIALS

• graph paper
• toothpicks

Question How can you use algebra to describe a pattern?

Explore

1 Copy the first four figures on graph paper. Then draw the fifth and sixth figures of the sequence.

Figure 1   Figure 2   Figure 3   Figure 4

2 The table shows the mathematical pattern for the perimeters of the first four figures. Copy and complete the table.

Figure	1	2	3	4	5	6
Perimeter	4	8	12	16	?	?
Pattern	4 • 1	4 • 2	4 • 3	4 • 4	4 • ?	4 • ?

3 Observe that $4(1) = 4$, $4(2), = 8$, $4(3) = 12$, and so on. This suggests that the perimeter of the nth figure is $4n$, where $n = 1, 2, 3, 4, \ldots$.

Think About It

1. Copy the four figures below. Then draw the fifth and sixth figures.

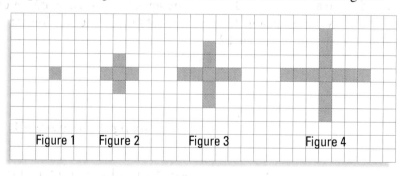

Figure 1   Figure 2   Figure 3   Figure 4

2. Calculate the perimeters of all six figures. Organize your results in a table.

3. What is the perimeter of the 10th figure? Can you guess a formula for the nth figure?

Explore

1 Use toothpicks to model the perimeter of all six figures in Explore on page 22. Notice that the perimeter of each figure is equal to the number of toothpicks used to form the figure.

2 Change the shape of Figures 2–6 by moving toothpicks until the figures consist of *n* unit squares. Figures 2 and 3 in the sequence are shown below. Complete Figures 4, 5, and 6 on a separate sheet of paper.

Figure 2

Figure 3

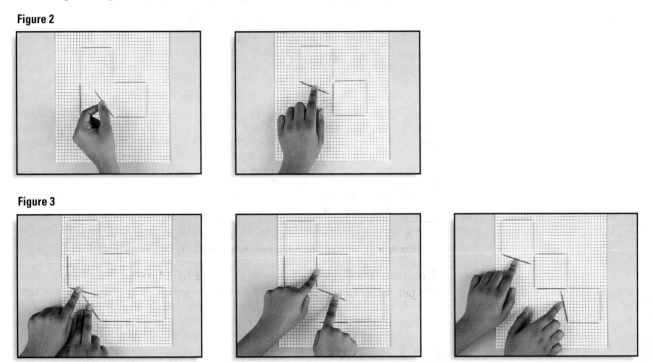

3 You should be able to conclude that if one square unit has a perimeter of 4 • 1, then *n* squares must have a perimeter of 4*n*. This conclusion verifies the pattern you found on page 22.

Think About It

1. Use toothpicks to model the perimeter of all six figures in Exercise 1 on page 22.

2. Change the shape of the figures modeled above in Exercise 1 until they consist of *n* unit squares.

3. Do the number of unit squares verify the pattern found in Exercise 3 on page 22? Explain your reasoning.

Equations and Inequalities

Goal
Check solutions of equations and inequalities.

Key Words
- equation
- solution
- inequality

How much do the ingredients cost?

You can use an *equation* to solve a real-life problem. In Example 3 you will use an equation to estimate the cost of ingredients for nachos.

An **equation** is a statement formed by placing an equal sign (=) between two expressions. An equation has a left side and a right side.

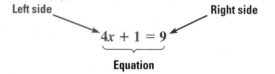

Left side   Right side

$$4x + 1 = 9$$

Equation

When the variable in an equation is replaced by a number, the resulting statement is either true or false. If the statement is true, the number is a **solution** of the equation.

EXAMPLE 1 Check Possible Solutions

Check to see if 2 and 3 are solutions of the equation $4x + 1 = 9$.

Solution

Substitute the x values 2 and 3 into the equation. If both sides of the equation are equal in value, then the number is a solution.

X VALUE	SUBSTITUTE	SIMPLIFY	CONCLUSION
2	$4(2) + 1 \stackrel{?}{=} 9$	$9 = 9$	True, 2 is a solution.
3	$4(3) + 1 \stackrel{?}{=} 9$	$13 \neq 9$	False, 3 is *not* a solution.

is not equal to

ANSWER ▶ The number 2 is a solution of the equation $4x + 1 = 9$, because the statement is true. The number 3 is not a solution, because the statement is false.

SOLVING EQUATIONS Finding all the solutions of an equation is called *solving* the equation. Some equations are simple enough to be solved with mental math. Later in the book you will learn how to systematically solve more complex equations.

EXAMPLE 2 Solve Equations with Mental Math

To solve equations with mental math, think of the equation as a question.

EQUATION	QUESTION	SOLUTION
$2x = 10$	2 times what number gives 10?	$2 \cdot 5 = 10$, so $x = 5$
$4 = x - 3$	4 is equal to what number minus 3?	$4 = 7 - 3$, so $x = 7$
$2 + x = 6$	2 plus what number gives 6?	$2 + 4 = 6$, so $x = 4$
$\frac{x}{3} = 1$	What number divided by 3 gives 1?	$\frac{3}{3} = 1$, so $x = 3$

Then check each solution by substituting the number in the original equation. If the statement is true, the number is a solution.

Checkpoint✓ **Solve Equations and Check Solutions**

Use mental math to solve the equation. Then check your solution.

1. $2 = 6 - x$ **2.** $x + 3 = 11$ **3.** $\frac{x}{4} = 5$ **4.** $14 = 2x$

EXAMPLE 3 Use Mental Math to Solve a Real-Life Equation

You are buying ingredients for nachos. At the market you find that tortilla chips cost $2.99, beans cost $.99, cheese costs $3.99, two tomatoes cost $1.00, and olives cost $1.49. There is no tax. You have $10. About how much more money do you need?

Nachos

20 tortilla chips

1 1/2 cups beans

1 cup diced tomatoes

1/2 cup grated cheese

1/2 cup sliced olives

Spread beans on chips. Add tomatoes, then cheese and olives. Bake at 400°F for 5 minutes.

Solution

Ask: The total cost equals 10 plus what number of dollars? Let x represent the extra money you need. Use rounding to estimate the total cost.

$$3 + 1 + 4 + 1 + 1.5 = 10 + x$$
$$10.5 = 10 + x$$

ANSWER▶ The total cost is about 10.5 or $10.50, so you need about $.50 more to purchase all the ingredients.

Checkpoint✓ **Use Mental Math to Solve a Real-Life Equation**

5. Solve the equation in Example 3 if a large bag of chips costs $3.99. About how much more money would you need to buy the nacho ingredients?

Student Help

▶ STUDY TIP
The "wide end" of the inequality symbol faces the greater number. For help with comparing numbers, see p. 770.

An **inequality** is a statement formed by placing an inequality symbol, such as <, between two expressions.

INEQUALITY SYMBOL	MEANING	EXAMPLE
<	is less than	$1 + 3 < 5$
≤	is less than or equal to	$6 - 1 \leq 5$
>	is greater than	$10 > 2(4)$
≥	is greater than or equal to	$10 \geq 9 - 1$

For inequalities involving a single variable, a solution is a number that produces a true statement when it is substituted for the variable in the inequality.

EXAMPLE 4 Check Solutions of Inequalities

Check to see if $x = 4$ is or is not a solution of the inequality.

INEQUALITY	SUBSTITUTE	SIMPLIFY	CONCLUSION
$x + 3 \geq 9$	$4 + 3 \overset{?}{\geq} 9$	$7 \not\geq 9$	False, 4 is *not* a solution.
$2x - 1 < 8$	$2(4) - 1 \overset{?}{<} 8$	$7 < 8$	True, 4 is a solution.

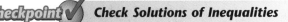

Checkpoint ✓ **Check Solutions of Inequalities**

Check to see if the value of n is or is not a solution of $3n - 4 \leq 8$.

6. $n = 2$ **7.** $n = 3$ **8.** $n = 4$ **9.** $n = 5$

VETERINARIANS specialize in the health care of either small animals, such as cats, or large animals, such as horses.

EXAMPLE 5 Check Solutions in Real Life

VETERINARIANS Your vet tells you to restrict your cat's caloric intake to less than or equal to 500 calories a day. Two times a day, you give your cat a serving of food that has x calories. Does 250 calories for each serving meet the vet's restriction?

Solution

❶ **Write** the inequality. $2x \leq 500$

❷ **Substitute** 250 for x. $2(250) \overset{?}{\leq} 500$

❸ **Simplify** by multiplying. $500 \leq 500$

ANSWER ▶ Yes, 250 calories per serving meets the vet's restriction.

Checkpoint ✓ **Check Solutions in Real Life**

10. Check to see if 300 calories per serving meets the vet's restriction in Example 5.

Guided Practice

Vocabulary Check

Explain if the following is an expression, an equation, or an inequality.

1. $3x + 1 = 14$

2. $7y - 6$

3. $5(y^2 + 4) - 7$

4. $5x - 1 = 3 + x$

5. $3x + 2 \leq 8$

6. $5x > 20$

7. Complete: An x value of 4 is a __?__ of the equation $x + 1 = 5$, because $4 + 1 = 5$.

Skill Check

Check to see if $a = 5$ is or is not a solution of the equation.

8. $a + 8 = 13$

9. $27 = 36 - 2a$

10. $a - 0 = 5$

11. $2a + 1 = 11$

12. $6a - 5 = 15$

13. $5a + 4 = 26$

14. $45 \div a = 9$

15. $a^2 + 2 = 27$

16. $\dfrac{40}{a} = 8$

Check to see if $b = 8$ is or is not a solution of the inequality.

17. $b + 10 > 19$

18. $14 - b \leq 3$

19. $5b > 35$

20. $8 \geq 64 \div b$

21. $3b - 24 > 0$

22. $16 \leq b^2$

23. $60 > 7b + 3$

24. $18 - b < 10$

25. $37 \geq 4b$

Practice and Applications

CHECKING SOLUTIONS OF EQUATIONS Check to see if the given value of the variable is or is not a solution of the equation.

26. $3b + 1 = 13; b = 4$

27. $5r - 10 = 11; r = 5$

28. $4c + 2 = 10; c = 2$

29. $6d - 5 = 31; d = 6$

30. $5 + x^2 = 17; x = 3$

31. $2y^3 + 3 = 5; y = 1$

32. $9 + 2t = 15; t = 12$

33. $n^2 - 5 = 20; n = 5$

SOLVING WITH MENTAL MATH Use mental math to solve the equation.

34. $x + 3 = 8$

35. $n + 6 = 11$

36. $p - 13 = 20$

37. $r - 1 = 7$

38. $3y = 12$

39. $4p = 36$

40. $z \div 4 = 5$

41. $\dfrac{x}{7} = 3$

42. $2b = 28$

43. $11t = 22$

44. $29 - d = 10$

45. $3 + y = 8$

46. $r + 30 = 70$

47. $\dfrac{42}{x} = 7$

48. $7m = 49$

Student Help

▶**HOMEWORK HELP**
   Example 1: Exs. 26–33
   Example 2: Exs. 34–48
   Example 3: Exs. 49, 50
   Example 4: Exs. 51–56
   Example 5: Exs. 57, 58

49. TIME MANAGEMENT You have a hair appointment in 60 minutes. It takes 20 minutes to get to the gas station and fill your tank. It takes 15 minutes to go from the gas station to the hair stylist. You wait x minutes before leaving your house and arrive on time for your appointment. Use the diagram to help decide which equation best models the situation.

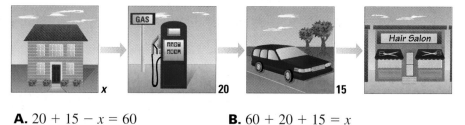

A. $20 + 15 - x = 60$

B. $60 + 20 + 15 = x$

C. $60 - 20 + 15 + x = 60$

D. $x + 20 + 15 = 60$

50. MENTAL MATH Solve the equation you chose in Exercise 49.

CHECKING SOLUTIONS OF INEQUALITIES Check to see if the given value of the variable is or is not a solution of the inequality.

51. $n - 2 < 6$; $n = 3$

52. $a - 7 \geq 15$; $a = 22$

53. $6 + y \leq 8$; $y = 3$

54. $s + 5 > 8$; $s = 4$

55. $7g \geq 47$; $g = 7$

56. $72 \div t > 6$; $t = 12$

57. SELLING CARDS Your community center is selling cards. Your goal is to sell $100 worth of cards. Each box sells for $3. Using mental math, solve the inequality $3b \geq 100$ to determine at least how many boxes you must sell to meet your goal.

58. BUYING A GUITAR You are budgeting money to buy a guitar that costs $150 including tax. If you save $20 per month, will you have enough money in 6 months? Use the inequality $20n \geq 150$ to model the situation, where n represents the number of months.

59. Science Link *Mach number* is the maximum speed at which a plane can fly divided by the speed of sound. Copy and complete the table. Use the equation $m = \dfrac{v}{660}$, where m is the Mach number and v is the speed (in miles per hour) of the aircraft, to find the Mach number for each type of aircraft.

Airplane type	Test aircraft	Supersonic	Jet
Speed v	4620	1320	660
Mach number m	?	?	?

Test aircraft

Supersonic aircraft

Jet aircraft

60. Puzzler Use mental math to fill in the missing number so that all the equations have the number 6 as a solution.

  a. ? $+ x = 18$ **b.** ? $x = 30$ **c.** $\dfrac{?}{x} = 6$

Standardized Test Practice

61. MULTIPLE CHOICE Which is a solution of the equation $5(8 - x) = 25$?

  Ⓐ 2   Ⓑ 3   Ⓒ 4   Ⓓ 5

62. MULTIPLE CHOICE For which inequality is $x = 238$ a solution?

  Ⓕ $250 \geq x + 12$ Ⓖ $250 < x + 12$

  Ⓗ $250 > x + 12$ Ⓙ $250 \leq x + 1$

63. MULTIPLE CHOICE The width of a soccer field cannot be greater than 100 yards. The area cannot be greater than 13,000 square yards. Which of the following would you use to find the possible length x of a soccer field?

  Ⓐ $100x \geq 13{,}000$ Ⓑ $100x \leq 13{,}000$

  Ⓒ $100 + x \leq 13{,}000$ Ⓓ $100x = 13{,}000$

Mixed Review

EVALUATING EXPRESSIONS Evaluate the expression for the given value of the variable. *(Lesson 1.1)*

64. $b - 12$ when $b = 43$ **65.** $12 + x$ when $x = 4$

66. $12n$ when $n = 4$ **67.** $\dfrac{y}{15}$ when $y = 30$

WRITING POWERS Write the expression in exponential form. *(Lesson 1.2)*

68. $3 \cdot 3 \cdot 3 \cdot 3 \cdot 3$ **69.** seven squared   **70.** $y \cdot y \cdot y \cdot y$

71. $9 \cdot 9 \cdot 9 \cdot 9 \cdot 9 \cdot 9$ **72.** twelve cubed   **73.** $8d \cdot 8d \cdot 8d$

NUMERICAL EXPRESSIONS Evaluate the expression. Then simplify the answer. *(Lesson 1.3)*

74. $9 + 12 - 4$ **75.** $7 + 56 \div 8 - 2$ **76.** $63 \div 3 \cdot 3$

77. $4 \cdot 2 - 5$ **78.** $3 + 13 - 6$ **79.** $49 \div 7 + 2$

80. $(28 \div 4) + 3^2$ **81.** $\dfrac{4^2 + 2}{2}$ **82.** $2[(2 + 3)^2 - 10]$

Maintaining Skills

ROUNDING Round the number to the underlined place value. *(Skills Review p. 774)*

83. 5.6̲4   **84.** 0.26̲25   **85.** 0.456̲95

86. 15.2̲95   **87.** 758.94̲9   **88.** 32.658̲2

89. 0.3̲25   **90.** 26.9̲6   **91.** 4.096̲5

Translating Words into Mathematical Symbols

Goal
Translate words into mathematical symbols.

Key Words
- translate
- phrase
- sentence

How long were you on the phone?

Account Summary
New Charges
Basic Service..........$36.00
Long Distance ....$ 6.00
Total Charges $42.00
Total Amount Due $42.00

In Example 6 you will translate words into an algebraic equation to find the length of a long distance phone call.

To solve real-life problems, you often need to translate words into mathematical symbols. To do this, look for words, such as *sum* or *difference*, that indicate mathematical operations.

EXAMPLE 1 Translate Addition Phrases

Write the phrase as a variable expression. Let x represent the number.

PHRASE	TRANSLATION
The *sum* of 6 and a number	$6 + x$
8 *more than* a number	$x + 8$
A number *plus* 5	$x + 5$
A number *increased* by 7	$x + 7$

EXAMPLE 2 Translate Subtraction Phrases

Write the phrase as a variable expression. Let y represent the number.

PHRASE	TRANSLATION
The *difference* between 5 and a number	$5 - y$
7 *minus* a number	$7 - y$
A number *decreased* by 9	$y - 9$
4 *less than* a number	$y - 4$

Student Help

▶ READING ALGEBRA
Order is important for subtraction. "4 less than a number" means $y - 4$, *not* $4 - y$.

Checkpoint ✓ *Translate Addition and Subtraction Phrases*

Write the phrase as a variable expression. Let x represent the number.

1. 11 more than a number

2. A number decreased by 10

Student Help

▶ **VOCABULARY TIP**
Quotient comes from a word meaning "how many times." When you divide you are finding how many times one quantity goes into another.

Notice that order does not matter for addition and multiplication. "The sum of 6 and a number" can be written as either $6 + x$ or $x + 6$. Order *is important* for subtraction and division. "The quotient of a number and 4" means $\frac{n}{4}$, *not* $\frac{4}{n}$.

EXAMPLE 3 Translate Multiplication and Division Phrases

Write the phrase as a variable expression. Let *n* represent the number.

PHRASE	TRANSLATION
The *product* of 9 and a number	$9n$
10 *times* a number	$10n$
A number *multiplied* by 3	$3n$
One fourth *of* a number	$\frac{1}{4}n$
The *quotient* of a number and 6	$\frac{n}{6}$
7 *divided* by a number	$\frac{7}{n}$

Checkpoint ✓ *Translate Multiplication and Division Phrases*

Write each phrase as a variable expression. Let *x* represent the number.

3. The quotient of 8 and a number

4. The product of 2 and a number

TRANSLATING SENTENCES In English there is a difference between a phrase and a sentence. Phrases are translated into variable expressions. Sentences are translated into equations or inequalities.

PHRASE ⟶ EXPRESSION

SENTENCE ⟶ EQUATION OR INEQUALITY

EXAMPLE 4 Translate Sentences

Write the sentence as an equation or an inequality.

SENTENCE	TRANSLATION
The sum of a number x and 12 *is* 16.	$x + 12 = 16$
The quotient of 15 and a number x *is less than* 3.	$\frac{15}{x} < 3$

Checkpoint ✓ *Translate Sentences*

Write the sentence as an equation or an inequality.

5. The product of 5 and a number x is 25.

6. 10 times a number x is greater than or equal to 50.

Student Help

▶ **READING ALGEBRA**
In mathematics, the
word *difference* means
"subtraction."

EXAMPLE 5 **Write and Solve an Equation**

a. Translate into mathematical symbols: "The difference between 13 and a number is 7." Let x represent the number.

b. Use mental math to solve the equation.

c. Check your solution.

Solution

a. The equation is $13 - x = 7$.

b. Using mental math, you can find that the solution is $x = 6$.

c. CHECK ✓

$13 - x = 7$	Write original equation.
$13 - 6 \stackrel{?}{=} 7$	Substitute 6 for x.
$7 = 7$ ✓	Solution checks.

Translating sentences into mathematical symbols is an important skill for solving real-life problems. Try your skills in Example 6.

EXAMPLE 6 **Translate and Solve a Real-Life Problem**

You make a long distance telephone call. The rate is $.20 for each minute. The total cost of the call is $6.00. How long was the call?

Student Help

▶ **SKILLS REVIEW**
For help with decimal
operations, see p. 759.

Solution

Let x represent the length of the call in minutes.

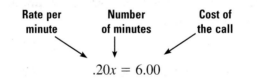

Rate per minute	Number of minutes	Cost of the call

$$.20x = 6.00$$

Ask what number times 0.2 equals 6. Use mental math to find $x = 30$.

ANSWER ▶ Your call was 30 minutes long.

Checkpoint ✓ **Translate and Solve a Real-Life Problem**

7. You make a long distance telephone call. The rate is $.10 for each minute. The total cost of the call is $5.00. How long was the call? Check to see if your solution is reasonable.

8. You make a long distance telephone call. The rate is $.20 for each minute. The total cost of the call is $4.00. How long was the call? Check to see if your solution is reasonable.

Guided Practice

Vocabulary Check   **Consider the phrase *seven decreased by a number n*.**

1. What operation does *decreased by* indicate?

2. Translate the phrase into a variable expression.

Skill Check   **Match the phrase with its variable expression. Let *x* represent the number.**

3. A number increased by 11   **A.** $x - 11$

4. The product of 11 and a number   **B.** $x + 11$

5. The difference of a number and 11   **C.** $\frac{x}{11}$

6. The quotient of a number and 11   **D.** $11x$

Write the sentence as an equation or an inequality.

7. A number x increased by 10 is 24.

8. The product of 7 and a number y is 42.

9. 20 divided by a number n is less than or equal to 2.

Practice and Applications

TRANSLATING PHRASES   **Write the phrase as a variable expression. Let *x* represent the number.**

10. A number decreased by 3   **11.** Difference of 10 and a number

12. The sum of 5 and a number   **13.** 9 more than a number

14. Product of 4 and a number   **15.** Quotient of a number and 50

16. 15 increased by a number   **17.** A number plus 18

18. 6 less than a number   **19.** A number minus 7

Student Help

▶ **HOMEWORK HELP**
Example 1: Exs. 10–19
Example 2: Exs. 10–19
Example 3: Exs. 10–19
Example 4: Exs. 20–31
Example 5: Exs. 32–35
Example 6: Exs. 36–39

TRANSLATING SENTENCES   **Match the sentence with its equation. Let *x* represent the number.**

20. A number increased by 2 is 4.   **A.** $x - 4 = 2$

21. The product of 2 and a number is 4.   **B.** $x + 2 = 4$

22. A number decreased by 4 is 2.   **C.** $\frac{x}{4} = 2$

23. A number divided by 4 is 2.   **D.** $2x = 4$

TRANSLATING SENTENCES Write the sentence as an equation or an inequality. Let *x* represent the number.

24. The sum of 20 and a number is 30.

25. A number increased by 10 is greater than or equal to 44.

26. 18 decreased by a number is 6.

27. 35 is less than the difference of 21 and a number.

28. The product of 13 and a number is greater than 60.

29. 7 times a number is 56.

30. A number divided by 22 is less than 3.

31. The quotient of 35 and a number is 7.

WRITING AND SOLVING EQUATIONS Write the sentence as an equation. Let *x* represent the number. Use mental math to solve the equation. Then check your solution.

32. The sum of a number and 10 is 15.

33. 28 decreased by a number is 18.

34. The product of a number and 25 is 100.

35. The quotient of 49 and a number is 7.

36. **Puzzler** The area of the rectangle is less than or equal to 50 square meters. Write an inequality for the area using the dimensions in the diagram.

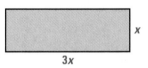

37. PLANNING A TRIP You want to go to an amusement park. The distance between your house and the amusement park is 110 miles. Your rate of travel is 55 miles per hour. Use the formula $d = rt$ to write an equation. Use mental math to solve the equation for the time you spend traveling.

38. **History Link** The Land Ordinance of 1785 divided the Northwest Territory into squares of land called townships. Every township was divided into 36 square sections, 1 mile on each side. How many square miles were in each township? How many acres?
HINT: 1 mi^2 = 640 acres

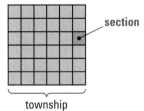

CHALLENGE You want to hire a live band for a school dance. You have $175 in your budget. The live band charges $75 per hour and each student pays $2 admission.

39. If the band is to play for 3 hours, how much extra money do you need to raise?

40. MULTIPLE CHOICE Translate into mathematical symbols "the difference of
a number and 4 is 10." Let n represent the number.

    (A) $n - 4 = 10$ (B) $4 - n = 10$ (C) $10 - 4 = n$ (D) $10 - 4$

41. MULTIPLE CHOICE Which is the correct algebraic translation of "Howard's
hourly wage h is \$2 greater than Marla's hourly wage m?"

    (F) $h < m + 2$ (G) $h = m + 2$ (H) $m = h + 2$ (J) $h > m + 2$

Mixed Review

42. **Geometry Link** Find the volume of a cube when each side x is 10 feet.
(Lesson 1.2)

CHECKING SOLUTIONS OF EQUATIONS **Check to see if the given value
of the variable is or is not a solution of the equation.** *(Lesson 1.4)*

43. $8k - 2 = 30; k = 4$ **44.** $15 + 2c = 5c; c = 5$

45. $\dfrac{r^2}{2} = 40; r = 9$ **46.** $50 = 3w; w = 15$

Maintaining Skills

PERCENTS AND DECIMALS **Write the percent as a decimal.**
(Skills Review p. 768)

47. 28%   **48.** 25%   **49.** 40%   **50.** 22%

51. 45%   **52.** 90%   **53.** 17.4%   **54.** 6.51%

Quiz 2

Check to see if $x = 4$ is or is not a solution of the equation. *(Lesson 1.4)*

1. $10x - 5 = 35$ **2.** $\dfrac{x}{4} = 0$ **3.** $x^2 + 5 = 21$

Check to see if $a = 20$ is or is not a solution of the inequality. *(Lesson 1.4)*

4. $3a > 50$ **5.** $10 + a < 30$ **6.** $40 + 3a \geq 50$

7. $\dfrac{a}{5} \leq 5$ **8.** $\dfrac{80}{a} \geq 5$ **9.** $\dfrac{a}{5} - 2 \leq 5$

10. **Geometry Link** The rectangle shown at the
right has an area of 32 square units. Write an
equation to find the width x. Use mental math to
solve the equation. *HINT:* The area of a rectangle
equals length times width. *(Lesson 1.4)*

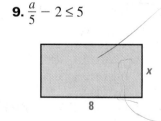

Write the sentence as an equation or an inequality. *(Lesson 1.5)*

11. A number x divided by 9 is less than 17.

12. The product of 10 and a number x is 50.

13. A number y plus 10 is greater than or equal to 57.

14. A number y minus 6 is 15.

1.6 A Problem Solving Plan Using Models

Goal
Model and solve real-life problems.

Key Words
- modeling
- verbal model
- algebraic model

How much food did you order?

In Chinese restaurants the bill is sometimes totaled by counting the number of plates ordered. In Example 1 you will use an *algebraic model* to find out how many plates of food you ordered.

Writing algebraic expressions, equations, or inequalities that represent real-life situations is called **modeling**. First you write a **verbal model** using words. Then you translate the verbal model into an **algebraic model**.

| Write a verbal model. | → | Assign labels. | → | Write an algebraic model. |

EXAMPLE 1 Write an Algebraic Model

You and some friends are at a Chinese restaurant. You order several $2 plates of wontons, egg rolls, and dumplings. Your bill is $25.20, which includes tax of $1.20. Use modeling to find how many plates you ordered.

Student Help

▶ **STUDY TIP**
Be sure you understand the problem before you write a model. For example, notice that the tax is added *after* the cost of the plates is figured.

Solution

VERBAL MODEL

$$\boxed{\text{Cost per plate}} \cdot \boxed{\text{Number of plates}} = \boxed{\text{Amount of bill}} - \boxed{\text{Tax}}$$

LABELS

Cost per plate $= 2$ (dollars)

Number of plates $= p$ (plates)

Amount of bill $= 25.20$ (dollars)

Tax $= 1.20$ (dollars)

ALGEBRAIC MODEL

$2p = 25.20 - 1.20$ Write algebraic model.

$2p = 24$ Subtract.

$p = 12$ Solve using mental math.

ANSWER ▶ Your group ordered 12 plates of food costing $24.

A PROBLEM SOLVING PLAN USING MODELS

VERBAL MODEL	Ask yourself what you need to know to solve the problem. Then write a verbal model that will give you what you need to know.
LABELS	Assign labels to each part of your verbal model.
ALGEBRAIC MODEL	Use the labels to write an algebraic model based on your verbal model.
SOLVE	Solve the algebraic model and answer the original question.
CHECK	Check that your answer is reasonable.

EXAMPLE 2 Write an Algebraic Model

A football field is about 53 yards wide and 120 yards long. A soccer field has the same area, but is 60 yards wide. How long is the soccer field?

Solution

Write a verbal model showing that the area (width × length) of the soccer field equals the area (width × length) of the football field.

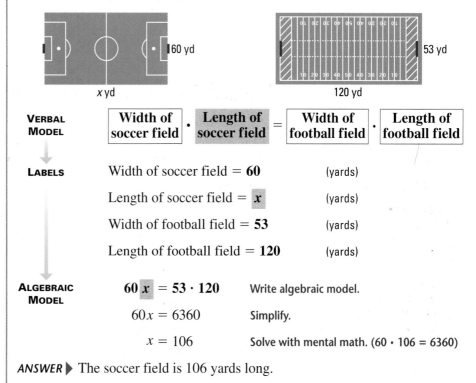

VERBAL MODEL

$$\boxed{\textbf{Width of soccer field}} \cdot \boxed{\textbf{Length of soccer field}} = \boxed{\textbf{Width of football field}} \cdot \boxed{\textbf{Length of football field}}$$

LABELS

Width of soccer field = **60**   (yards)

Length of soccer field = x (yards)

Width of football field = **53**   (yards)

Length of football field = **120**   (yards)

ALGEBRAIC MODEL

$60\,x = 53 \cdot 120$ Write algebraic model.

$60x = 6360$ Simplify.

$x = 106$ Solve with mental math. (60 · 106 = 6360)

ANSWER ▶ The soccer field is 106 yards long.

Student Help

▶ **STUDY TIP**
Sometimes a diagram can help you see what you know and what you need to find to solve the problem.

Checkpoint ✓ Write an Algebraic Model

1. You want two rectangular gardens to have equal areas. The first garden is 5 meters by 16 meters. The second garden is 8 meters wide. How long should the second garden be? Apply the problem solving plan to find the answer.

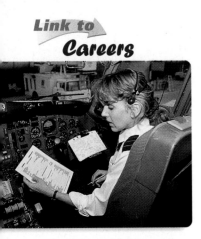

JET PILOTS select a route, an altitude, and a speed that will provide the fastest and safest flight.

More about jet pilots available at
www.mcdougallittell.com

EXAMPLE **3** **Write an Algebraic Model**

JET PILOTS A jet pilot is flying from Los Angeles to Chicago at a speed of 500 miles per hour. When the plane is 600 miles from Chicago, an air traffic controller tells the pilot that it will be 2 hours before the plane can get clearance to land.

a. At what speed would the jet have to fly to arrive in Chicago in 2 hours?

b. The pilot knows that at her present altitude, the speed of the jet must be greater than 322 miles per hour or the plane could stall. Is it reasonable for the pilot to fly directly to Chicago at the reduced speed from part (a) or should the pilot take some other action?

Solution

a. You can use the formula (rate)(time) = (distance) to write a verbal model.

VERBAL MODEL

$$\boxed{\text{Speed of jet}} \cdot \boxed{\text{Time}} = \boxed{\text{Distance to travel}}$$

LABELS

Speed of jet = x (miles per hour)

Time = **2**   (hours)

Distance to travel = **600**   (miles)

ALGEBRAIC MODEL

$2x = 600$ Write algebraic model.

$x = 300$ Solve using mental math.

ANSWER ▶ To arrive in 2 hours, the pilot would have to slow the jet down to a speed of 300 miles per hour.

b. It is not reasonable for the pilot to fly at 300 miles per hour, because the plane could stall. The pilot should take some other action, such as circling in a holding pattern, to use some of the time.

You can ignore information that is not needed to solve a problem. To solve Example 3, you do not need to know that the plane is traveling at 500 miles per hour.

Checkpoint ✓ **Write an Algebraic Model**

Use the following information to write and solve an algebraic model.

You are running in a marathon. During the first 20 miles, your average speed is 8 miles per hour. During the last 6.2 miles, you increase your average speed by 2 miles per hour.

2. How long will it take you to run the last 6.2 miles of the marathon? Use the problem solving plan with models to answer the question.

3. A friend of yours completed the marathon in 3.2 hours. Did you finish ahead of your friend or behind your friend? Explain.

1.6 Exercises

Guided Practice

Vocabulary Check

In Exercises 1 and 2, complete the sentence.

1. Writing expressions, equations, or inequalities to represent real-life situations is called __?__ .

2. A __?__ model with labels is used to form an algebraic model.

3. Write the steps of the problem solving plan.

Skill Check

4. ADMISSION PRICES Your family and friends are going to an amusement park. Adults pay $25 per ticket and children pay $15 per ticket. Your group has 13 children and your total bill for tickets is $370. How many adults are in your group? Choose the verbal model that represents this situation.

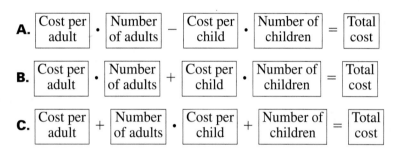

Practice and Applications

WALK OR TAKE THE SUBWAY? **In Exercises 5–10, use the following information.**
You are one mile from your home. You can walk at a speed of 4 miles per hour. The subway comes by every 15 minutes, and you heard one come by 3 minutes ago. The subway ride takes 8 minutes.

5. How many minutes will it take to get home by subway if you take the next train?

6. Write a verbal model that relates the time it would take to walk home, your walking speed, and the distance to your home.

$$\underline{\quad ? \quad} \times \underline{\quad ? \quad} = \underline{\quad ? \quad}$$

7. Assign labels to your verbal model. Use t to represent the unknown value.

8. Use the labels to translate your verbal model into an equation.

9. Use mental math to solve the equation.

10. Which will get you home faster, walking or taking the subway? Explain.

Student Help

▶ **HOMEWORK HELP**
Example 1: Exs. 5–20
Example 2: Exs. 5–20
Example 3: Exs. 5–20

Link to
Science

PLANT GROWTH Kudzu was introduced to the United States in 1876. Today kudzu covers over 7 million acres of the southeastern United States.

Student Help

▶ **HOMEWORK HELP**

Extra help with problem solving in Exs. 16–20 is available at www.mcdougallittell.com

---

Science Link In Exercises 11–15, use the following information.
Kudzu is a type of Japanese vine that grows at a rate of 1 foot per day during the summer. On August 1, the length of one vine was 50 feet. What was the length on July 1? *HINT:* July has 31 days.

11. Use the verbal phrases to complete the verbal model.

Total length

Original length

Number of days   _?_ + _?_ × _?_ = _?_

Growth rate

12. Assign labels to the verbal model. Use x to represent the unknown value.

13. Choose the algebraic model that best represents the verbal model.

   A. $(x + 1) \cdot 31 = 50$ **B.** $x + (1 \cdot 31) = 50$

   C. $x = 50 \div 1$ **D.** $x + (1 + 31) = 50$

14. Use mental math to solve the algebraic model you chose in Exercise 13.

15. Check that your answer is reasonable.

BUYING A STEREO In Exercises 16–20, use the following information.
An appliance store sells two stereo models. The model without a CD player is $350. The model with a CD player is $480. Your summer job allows you to save $50 a week for 8 weeks. At the end of the summer, you have enough to buy the stereo without the CD player. How much would you have needed to save each week to buy the other model?

16. Write a verbal model that relates the number of weeks worked, the amount you would have needed to save each week, and the price of the stereo with the CD player.

_?_ × _?_ = _?_

17. Assign labels to your verbal model. Use m to represent the unknown value.

18. Use the labels to translate your verbal model into an equation.

19. Use mental math to solve the equation.

20. Check that your answer is reasonable.

21. CHALLENGE You are running for class president. By two o'clock on election day you have 95 votes and your opponent has 120 votes. Forty-five more students will be voting. Let x represent the number of students (of the 45) who vote for you.

   a. Write an inequality that shows the values of x that will allow you to win the election.

   b. What is the smallest value of x that is a solution of the inequality?

22. MULTIPLE CHOICE A jet is flying from Baltimore to Orlando at a speed r of 500 miles per hour. The distance d between the two cities is about 793 miles. Which equation can be used to find the time t it takes to make the trip?

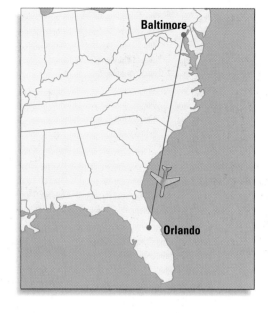

Baltimore

Orlando

Ⓐ $793 = 500t$

Ⓑ $t = \dfrac{500}{793}$

Ⓒ $793t = 500$

Ⓓ $t = 793(500)$

Student Help

▸**TEST TIP**
In Exercise 22, you can use unit analysis (p. 8) to see which answer choice is correct.

23. MULTIPLE CHOICE Jim lives in a state in which speeders are fined $25 for a speeding ticket plus $10 for each mile per hour over the speed limit. Jim was given a ticket for $175 for speeding in a 45 mile per hour zone. Which equation can be used to find how fast Jim was driving?

Ⓕ $45 + (x - 45) \cdot 10 = 175 - 25$ Ⓖ $x - 45 \cdot 10 = 175 - 25$

Ⓗ $(x + 45) \cdot 10 = 175 - 25$ Ⓙ $(x - 45) \cdot 10 = 175 - 25$

Mixed Review

EVALUATING EXPRESSIONS **Evaluate the expression for the given value of the variable.** *(Lesson 1.2)*

24. $x^2 - 2$ when $x = 7$ **25.** $(2x)^3$ when $x = 5$ **26.** $(10 - x)^2$ when $x = 6$

NUMERICAL EXPRESSIONS **Evaluate the expression.** *(Lesson 1.3)*

27. $22 - 4^2 \div 2$ **28.** $4 + 8 \cdot 4 - 1$ **29.** $2 \cdot 4 + (7 - 3)$

CHECKING SOLUTIONS **Check to see if the given value of the variable is or is not a solution of the equation or the inequality.** *(Lesson 1.4)*

30. $2x - 3 < 15; x = 9$ **31.** $3x + 4 \le 16; x = 4$ **32.** $16 + x^2 \div 4 = 17; x = 2$

33. FUNDRAISING Your fundraising group earns 25¢ for each lemonade and 50¢ for each taco sold. One hundred tacos are sold. Your total profit is $100. How many lemonades are sold? Write an equation that models this situation. Solve the equation using mental math. *(Lesson 1.5)*

Maintaining Skills

FRACTIONS AND MIXED NUMBERS **Write the improper fraction as a mixed number.** *(Skills Review p. 763)*

34. $\dfrac{3}{2}$ **35.** $\dfrac{7}{4}$ **36.** $\dfrac{11}{3}$ **37.** $\dfrac{13}{6}$

38. $\dfrac{16}{5}$ **39.** $\dfrac{21}{9}$ **40.** $\dfrac{18}{4}$ **41.** $\dfrac{15}{7}$

42. $\dfrac{30}{8}$ **43.** $\dfrac{54}{12}$ **44.** $\dfrac{84}{36}$ **45.** $\dfrac{20}{3}$

1.7 Tables and Graphs

Goal

Organize data using a table or graph.

Key Words

- data
- bar graph
- line graph

How much does it cost to make a movie?

Almost every day you have the chance to interpret *data* that describe real-life situations. In Example 3 you will interpret data about the average cost of making a movie.

Data are information, facts, or numbers that describe something. It is easier to see patterns when you organize data in a table.

EXAMPLE 1 Organize Data in a Table

The table shows the top three categories of food eaten by Americans.

Student Help

▶ **STUDY TIP**
To find how much dairy was consumed in 1980, you go across the row labeled **Dairy** and stop at the column for **1980**.

Top Categories of Food Consumed by Americans (lb per person per year)							
Year	1970	1975	1980	1985	1990	1995	2000
Dairy	563.8	539.1	543.2	593.7	568.4	584.4	590.0
Vegetables	335.4	337.0	336.4	358.1	382.8	405.0	410.0
Fruit	237.7	252.1	262.4	269.4	273.5	285.4	290.0

DATA UPDATE of U.S. Department of Agriculture at www.mcdougallittell.com; 2000 data are estimated by authors.

Make a table showing total dairy and vegetables consumed (pounds per person) per year. In which year did Americans consume the least dairy and vegetables? In which year did Americans consume the most dairy and vegetables?

Solution

To make the table, add the data for dairy and vegetables for the given year.

Year	1970	1975	1980	1985	1990	1995	2000
Total	899.2	876.1	879.6	951.8	951.2	989.4	1000.0

ANSWER ▶ The least consumption was in 1975 and the greatest in 2000.

Checkpoint ✓ **Organize Data in a Table**

1. Make a table showing the total dairy products, vegetables, and fruit consumed (pounds per person) per year. Which year had the least consumption? Which had the greatest consumption?

BAR GRAPHS One way to represent the data in a table is with a **bar graph**. The bars can be either vertical or horizontal. Example 2 shows a vertical bar graph of the data from Example 1.

EXAMPLE **2** Interpret a Bar Graph

The bar graph shows the total amount of dairy products, vegetables, and fruit consumed by the average American in a given year. It appears that Americans ate about five times the amount of dairy products, vegetables, and fruit in 1995 as compared with 1970.

If you study the data in Example 1, you can see that the bar graph could be misinterpreted. Explain why the graph could be misinterpreted.

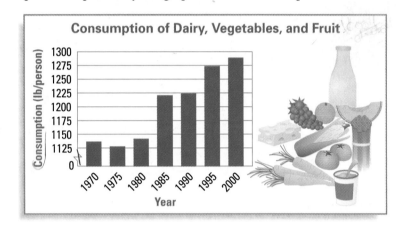

Consumption of Dairy, Vegetables, and Fruit

Solution

The bar graph could be misinterpreted because the vertical scale is not consistent. The zigzag line shows a break where part of the scale is not shown. Because of the break, the first tick mark on the vertical scale represents 1125 pounds of food consumed per person. The other tick marks on the vertical scale represent 25 pounds of food consumed per person.

To make a bar graph that could *not* be misinterpreted, you must evenly space the tick marks and make sure that each tick mark represents the same amount.

Checkpoint ✓ *Make and Interpret a Bar Graph*

2. The bar graph at the right is set up so that it is not misleading. The first two bars are drawn for you.

Copy and complete the bar graph using the data from Example 2. Describe the pattern from 1970 through 2000.

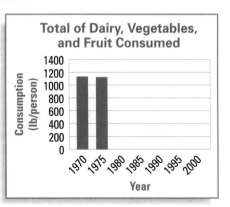

Total of Dairy, Vegetables, and Fruit Consumed

▶ **SKILLS REVIEW**
For help with drawing bar graphs, see p. 777.

Student Help

LINE GRAPHS As an alternative to a vertical bar graph, data is sometimes represented by a **line graph**. Here the vertical bars are replaced by a single point located at the top of the bar. These points are then connected by line segments. Line graphs are especially useful for showing changes in data over time.

EXAMPLE 3 Make and Interpret a Line Graph

MOVIE MAKING From 1983 to 1996, the average cost (in millions of dollars) of making a movie is given in the table. Draw a line graph of the data. Then determine in which three years did the cost decrease from the prior year.

Average Cost of Making a Movie							
Year	1983	1984	1985	1986	1987	1988	1989
Cost (millions)	$11.8	$14.0	$16.7	$17.5	$20.0	$18.1	$23.3

Year	1990	1991	1992	1993	1994	1995	1996
Cost (millions)	$26.8	$26.1	$28.9	$29.9	$34.3	$36.4	$33.6

▶ Source: *International Motion Picture Almanac*

Solution

Draw the vertical scale from 0 to 40 million dollars. Mark the number of years on the horizontal axis starting with 1983. For each average cost in the table, draw a point on the graph. Then draw a line from each point to the next point.

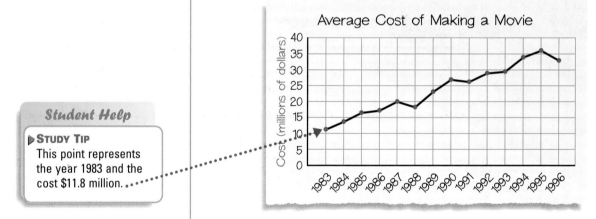

In 1988, 1991, and 1996 the average cost of making a movie decreased from the prior year.

Checkpoint Make and Interpret a Line Graph

3. Make a line graph of the data above changing the tick marks on the vertical scale to 0, 10, 20, 30, and 40. Which graph is easier to interpret? Why?

Guided Practice

Vocabulary Check

1. Explain what data are. Give an example.

2. Name two ways to display organized data.

Skill Check

WEATHER **Use the graph to classify the statement as true or false.**

3. Rainfall increases each month over the previous month.

4. The amount of rainfall is the same in May and July.

5. The greatest amount of rainfall occurs in August.

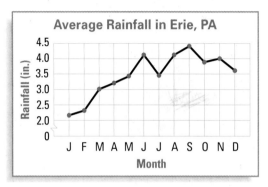

Average Rainfall in Erie, PA

▶ Source: National Oceanic and Atmospheric Administration

Practice and Applications

GOLF **In Exercises 6 and 7, use the table showing scores for two rounds of golf.**

	Player 1	Player 2	Player 3	Player 4
Round 1	90	88	79	78
Round 2	94	84	83	80

6. Make a table showing the average score of each player. *HINT:* Find each average by adding the two scores and dividing by the number of rounds.

7. Which player has the lowest average? Which one has the highest average?

8. SCHOOL ENROLLMENT The table shows the number of students (in millions) enrolled in school in the United States by age. Make a table showing the total number of students enrolled for each given year.

Age	1980	1985	1990	1995	2000
14–15 years old	7282	7362	6555	7651	8100
16–17 years old	7129	6654	6098	6997	7600
18–19 years old	3788	3716	4044	4274	4800

▶ Source: U.S. Bureau of the Census; 2000 data are estimated by authors.

9. Which year had the least number of students enrolled? Which had the greatest number of students enrolled?

10. Did the total enrollment increase for each 5 year period? Explain.

Student Help

▶**HOMEWORK HELP**
Example 1: Exs. 6–10
Example 2: Exs. 11–14
Example 3: Exs. 15–18

BRAKING DISTANCE is the distance it takes for a vehicle to come to a complete stop after the brakes have been activated. The length of a skid mark indicates the speed at which a vehicle was traveling.

BRAKING DISTANCE In Exercises 11–13, use the bar graph showing average braking distances for medium sized cars.

11. Estimate the braking distance for a car traveling 50 miles per hour.

12. Does it take twice as far to stop a car that is going twice as fast? Explain.

13. Explain why it would be dangerous to follow another car too closely when driving at 70 miles per hour.

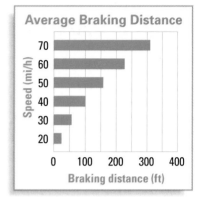

14. **Science Link** The table shows the number of gallons of water needed to produce one pound of some foods. Make a bar graph of the data.

Food (1 lb)	Lettuce	Tomatoes	Melons	Broccoli	Corn
Water (gallons)	21	29	40	42	119

▶ Source: Water Education Foundation

MINIMUM WAGE

In Exercises 15–17, use the line graph showing the minimum wage for 1991–1999.

15. For how many years did the minimum wage remain the same as it was in 1991?

16. Estimate the minimum wage during 1992.

17. In which year did the minimum wage first increase to over $5?

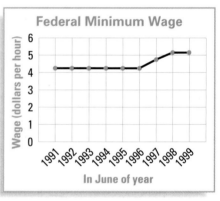

▶ Source: U.S. Bureau of Labor Statistics

▶HOMEWORK HELP
Extra help with problem solving in Ex. 18 is available at www.mcdougallittell.com

Student Help

18. **History Link** The table shows the population (in thousands) of California following the Gold Rush of 1849. Make a line graph of the data.

Year	1850	1860	1870	1880	1890
Population	93	380	560	865	1213

19. **CRITICAL THINKING** The table shows the average fuel efficiency for passenger cars for different years. Organize the data into a graph. Explain why you chose the type of graph you used.

Year	1980	1985	1990	1995	2000
Fuel efficiency (miles per gallon)	24.3	27.6	28.0	28.6	29.2

DATA UPDATE of National Highway Traffic Safety Administration at www.mcdougallittell.com; 2000 data are estimated by authors.

20. MULTIPLE CHOICE Which way of organizing data is useful for showing changes in data over time?

    A Table   **B** Line graph   **C** Circle graph   **D** None of these

MULTIPLE CHOICE In Exercises 21 and 22, use the bar graph showing one household's monthly electricity usage in kilowatt-hours (kWh).

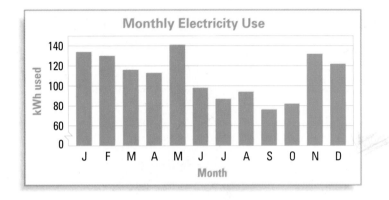

21. Which month shows the greatest decrease in use from the prior month?

    F May   **G** October

    H June   **J** November

22. About how many total kilowatt-hours were used for the months of January through April?

    A 480   **B** 400   **C** 550   **D** 600

Mixed Review

Geometry Link **Find the perimeter and area of the geometric figure.** *(Lesson 1.1)*

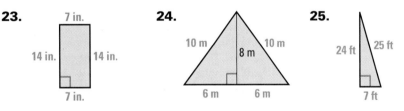

23.   **24.**   **25.**

CHECKING SOLUTIONS **Check to see if $x = 5$ is or is not a solution of the equation or the inequality.** *(Lesson 1.4)*

26. $17 - x < 12$ **27.** $x + 3x \geq 18$ **28.** $5x \div 2 = 12.5$

29. $2.5 > 1.2x - 3$ **30.** $x^2 = 25$ **31.** $(3x)^2 \leq 255$

32. $3x + 2x = 25$ **33.** $19 - 2x > 10$ **34.** $16 \leq 3x + 1$

Maintaining Skills

COMPARING DECIMALS **Compare using <, > or =.** *(Skills Review p. 770)*

35. 71.717 ? 77.117 **36.** 2.6 ? 2.65 **37.** 0.01 ? 0.0001

38. 1.666 ? 1.67 **39.** 15.7 ? 15.700 **40.** 0.4321 ? 0.434

41. 0.48 ? 0.479 **42.** 3.11 ? 3.09 **43.** 9.54 ? 9.540

1.8 An Introduction to Functions

Goal
Use four different ways to represent functions.

Key Words
- function
- input
- output
- input-output table
- domain
- range

What is the altitude of the balloon?

You are in a hot-air balloon. You rise at a steady rate of 20 feet per minute. In Example 2 you will use the relationship between time and height to find the altitude of the balloon after a given number of minutes.

A **function** is a rule that establishes a relationship between two quantities, called the **input** and the **output**. For each input, there is exactly one output—even though two different inputs may give the same output.

One way to describe a function is to make an **input-output table**.

EXAMPLE 1 Make an Input-Output Table

GEOMETRY LINK The diagram shows the first six triangular numbers.

1	3	6	10	15	21
Figure 1	Figure 2	Figure 3	Figure 4	Figure 5	Figure 6

a. Using the first six figures, make an input-output table in which the input is the figure number n and the output is the triangular number T.

b. Does the table represent a function? Justify your answer.

Solution

a. Use the diagram to make an input-output table, as shown below.

Input n	1	2	3	4	5	6
Output T	1	3	6	10	15	21

b. This is a function, because for each input there is exactly one output.

DOMAIN AND RANGE The collection of all input values is the **domain** of the function and the collection of all output values is the **range** of the function. The domain of the function in Example 1 is 1, 2, 3, 4, 5, 6; the range of the function is 1, 3, 6, 10, 15, 21.

When you are given the rule for a function, you can prepare to graph the function by making a table showing numbers in the domain and their corresponding output values.

EXAMPLE 2 *Use a Table to Graph a Function*

BALLOONING You are at an altitude of 250 feet in a hot-air balloon. You turn on the burner and rise at a rate of 20 feet per minute for 5 minutes. Your altitude h in feet after you have risen for t minutes is given by

$$h = 250 + 20t, \text{ where } t \geq 0 \text{ and } t \leq 5.$$

a. Use the function to find the output h in feet for several inputs. Then organize the data into an input-output table.

b. Use the data in the table to draw a graph that represents the function.

Solution

a. Find the outputs for $t = 0, 1, 2, 3, 4,$ and 5. Then make a table.

INPUT (MINUTES)	FUNCTION	OUTPUT (FEET)
$t = 0$	$h = 250 + 20(0)$	$h = 250$
$t = 1$	$h = 250 + 20(1)$	$h = 270$
$t = 2$	$h = 250 + 20(2)$	$h = 290$
$t = 3$	$h = 250 + 20(3)$	$h = 310$
$t = 4$	$h = 250 + 20(4)$	$h = 330$
$t = 5$	$h = 250 + 20(5)$	$h = 350$

Input t	0	1	2	3	4	5
Output h	250	270	290	310	330	350

Student Help

▶**STUDY TIP**
To plot the first point (t, h) find $t = 0$ on the horizontal axis. Then find $h = 250$ on the vertical axis. Mark the point (0, 250). ·····

b.

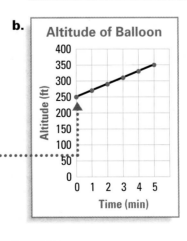

Altitude of Balloon

Let the horizontal axis represent the input t (in minutes). Label the axis from 0 to 5. Let the vertical axis represent the output h (in feet). Label the axis from 0 to 400.

Plot the data points given in the table. Finally, connect the points.

The graph shows that as the time increases, the height of the balloon increases.

The graph represents the function $h = 250 + 20t$, where $t \geq 0$ and $t \leq 5$.

EXAMPLE 3 **Write an Equation to Represent a Function**

SCUBA DIVING As you dive deeper and deeper into the ocean, the pressure of the water on your body steadily increases. The pressure at the surface of the water is 14.7 pounds per square inch (psi). The pressure increases at a rate of 0.445 psi for each foot you descend. Write an equation to represent the pressure P as a function of the depth d for every 20 feet you descend until you reach a depth of 60 feet.

Solution

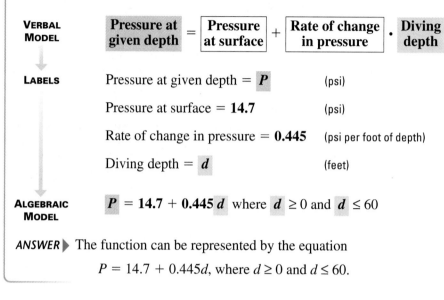

| VERBAL MODEL | Pressure at given depth = Pressure at surface + Rate of change in pressure · Diving depth |

LABELS

Pressure at given depth = P (psi)

Pressure at surface = **14.7**   (psi)

Rate of change in pressure = **0.445**   (psi per foot of depth)

Diving depth = d (feet)

ALGEBRAIC MODEL

$P = 14.7 + 0.445\,d$ where $d \geq 0$ and $d \leq 60$

ANSWER ▶ The function can be represented by the equation
$P = 14.7 + 0.445d$, where $d \geq 0$ and $d \leq 60$.

Checkpoint✓ **Represent a Function**

Use the algebraic model from Example 3.

1. Make an input-output table for the function. Use $d = 0$, 20, 40, and 60.

2. Draw a graph that represents the function.

SUMMARY

Four Ways to Represent Functions

INPUT-OUTPUT TABLE	WORDS	EQUATION	GRAPH

INPUT-OUTPUT TABLE

Input n	Output P
1	1
2	3
3	6
4	10
5	15
6	21

WORDS

You are in a hot-air balloon at a height of 250 feet. You begin to rise higher at a rate of 20 feet per minute for a period of 5 minutes.

EQUATION

$h = 250 + 20t$, where $t \geq 0$ and $t \leq 5$

GRAPH

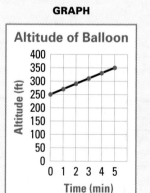

Guided Practice

Vocabulary Check   **Complete the sentence.**

1. A function is a relationship between two quantities, called the __?__ and the __?__.

2. The collection of all input values is the __?__ of the function.

3. The collection of all output values is the __?__ of the function.

Skill Check   **CAMPING In Exercises 4–6, use the following information.**
You are going camping. The cost for renting a cabin at Shady Knoll Campground is $65.00 plus $12.00 per person. The cost in dollars is

$$C = 65 + 12n, \text{ where } n \text{ is the number of people.}$$

4. Copy and complete the input-output table.

Input n	1	2	3	4	5	6
Output C	?	?	?	?	?	?

5. Draw a graph that is made up of isolated points representing the cost of renting a cabin.

6. Determine the range of the function from the given input values in the input-output table.

Practice and Applications

INPUT-OUTPUT TABLES Make an input-output table for the function. Use 0, 1, 2, 3, 4, and 5 as values for x.

7. $y = 6x + 5$ 8. $y = 26 - 2x$ 9. $y = (x + 3) \cdot 7$

10. $y = 85 - 15x$ 11. $y = 5(15 - x)$ 12. $y = 2(6x + 10)$

LINE GRAPHS Draw a line graph to represent the function given by the input-output table.

13.

Input x	1	2	3	4	5	6
Output y	14	12	10	8	6	4

14.

Input x	1	2	3	4	5	6
Output y	8	11	14	17	20	23

15. **Science Link** The distance d (in miles) that sound travels in air in time t (in seconds) is represented by the function $d = 0.2t$. Make a table of the input t and the output d. Use t values of 0, 5, 10, 15, 20, 25, and 30. Use your table to help you draw the graph of the function.

Student Help

▶ HOMEWORK HELP

INTERNET Extra help with problem solving in Exs. 16–19 is available at www.mcdougallittell.com

CRITICAL THINKING **Determine whether the table represents a function.**

16.

Input	Output
1	3
2	4
3	5

17.

Input	Output
1	2
3	3
3	4

18.

Input	Output
2	2
3	4
4	6

19.

Input	Output
1	3
1	4
2	5

CAR RACING **In Exercises 20–22, use the following information.**
The fastest winning speed in the Daytona 500 is about 178 miles per hour. In the table below, calculate the distance traveled d (in miles) after time t (in hours) using the equation $d = 178t$.

20. Copy and complete the input-output table.

Time (hours)	0.25	0.50	0.75	1.00	1.25	1.50
Distance traveled (miles)	?	?	?	?	?	?

21. Use the data to draw a graph.

22. For what values of t does the formula $d = 178t$ correspond to the situation being modeled?

23. **History Link** In 1866 Texas cowhands used the Chisholm Trail to drive cattle north to the railroads in Kansas. The average rate r that the cattle could be moved along the trail was 11 miles per day.

a. Write an equation, where d is distance and t is time in days.

b. Make a table of input t and output d for $t = 7$, 14, and 28. Then graph the data.

c. The distance d from San Antonio to Abilene was about 1100 miles. How long did it take to drive cattle the entire length of the trail?

JESSE CHISHOLM, the person for whom the Chisholm Trail is named, was a trader who was part Cherokee.

SCUBA DIVERS must take an instructional class in order to become certified.

Standardized Test Practice

24. SCUBA DIVERS While you are on vacation, you want to rent scuba equipment. It costs about $90 a day to rent the equipment. Find the cost of renting equipment for 1, 2, 3, and 4 days.

   a. Write an equation where R is the total rental cost and n is the number of days. Make an input-output table.

   b. Draw a graph that represents the function.

25. WATER TEMPERATURE The table below gives the temperature of water as it cools. Using this table, draw a graph that estimates the temperature of the water for $t \geq 0$ and $t \leq 25$.

Time (minutes)	0	5	10	15	20	25
Temperature (°C)	100	90	81	73	66	60

26. CHALLENGE The function $y = x^2$ has a U-shaped graph called a *parabola*. If the domain of this function is given as $x \geq 0$ and $x \leq 4$, find the range.

27. MULTIPLE CHOICE Which table does *not* represent a function?

Ⓐ

Input	Output
1	3
2	3
3	3
4	3

Ⓑ

Input	Output
1	2
2	4
3	6
4	8

Ⓒ

Input	Output
5	4
6	4
7	5
8	5

Ⓓ

Input	Output
5	1
5	3
6	1
6	3

28. MULTIPLE CHOICE Which function has an output of $j = 27$ for an input of $a = 3$?

   Ⓕ $j = 4a + 15$ **Ⓖ** $j = 15a + 4$ **Ⓗ** $j = 15 \cdot 4a$ **Ⓙ** $j = 27a$

29. MULTIPLE CHOICE Which function is best represented by the graph?

   Ⓐ $F = 50 + 25t$

   Ⓑ $F = 25 + t$

   Ⓒ $F = 25 + 50t$

   Ⓓ $F = 25t$

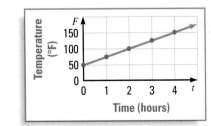

1.8 *An Introduction to Functions*   **53**

Mixed Review

EVALUATING EXPRESSIONS Evaluate the variable expression when $a = 3$ and $c = 5$. *(Lessons 1.1 and 1.2)*

30. $a + c$ **31.** $(a + c)^2$ **32.** $a^2 + c^2$

33. ac **34.** $a \cdot (c^2)$ **35.** $(a^2) \cdot c$

36. TRANSLATING PHRASES Write a variable expression for the phrase *9 decreased by a number n.* *(Lesson 1.5)*

37. TRANSLATING SENTENCES Write the inequality for the sentence: *The quotient of 72 and a number x is greater than 7.* *(Lesson 1.5)*

Maintaining Skills

ADDING FRACTIONS Add. Write the answer as a fraction or a mixed number in lowest terms. *(Skills Review p. 764)*

38. $\dfrac{2}{9} + \dfrac{8}{9}$ **39.** $\dfrac{5}{12} + \dfrac{1}{12}$ **40.** $\dfrac{12}{15} + \dfrac{7}{15}$

41. $\dfrac{11}{3} + \dfrac{2}{3}$ **42.** $\dfrac{5}{6} + \dfrac{7}{6}$ **43.** $\dfrac{2}{8} + \dfrac{1}{8}$

44. $\dfrac{3}{5} + \dfrac{1}{5}$ **45.** $\dfrac{3}{4} + \dfrac{9}{4}$ **46.** $\dfrac{9}{14} + \dfrac{3}{14}$

Quiz 3

1. RECYCLING A recycling center pays 5¢ apiece for aluminum cans and certain glass bottles. Jean has four cans and the total amount paid for her collection of cans and bottles is 50¢. Use a verbal model to find how many glass bottles are in Jean's collection. *(Lesson 1.6)*

ARTS ACTIVITIES In Exercises 2 and 3, use the table showing the percent of 18-to-24-year-olds that attended various arts activities at least once a year. *(Lesson 1.7)*

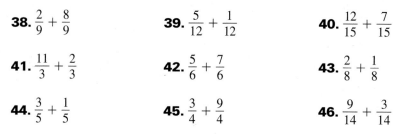

Arts Activities Attended by 18-to-24-year-olds				
Jazz	Musical play	Non-musical play	Art museum	Historic park
15%	26%	20%	38%	46%

2. Make a bar graph of the data.

3. What conclusions can you draw from the bar graph?

HOT-AIR BALLOONS You are at an altitude of 200 feet in a hot-air balloon. You rise at a rate of 25 feet per minute for 4 minutes. Your altitude h (in feet) after you have risen for t minutes is given by

$$h = 200 + 25t, \text{ where } t \geq 0 \text{ and } t \leq 4. \text{ (Lesson 1.8)}$$

4. Make an input-output table using 0, 1, 2, 3, and 4 as values for x.

5. Use your table to draw a graph that represents the function.

6. Determine the range of the function.

- **variable**, *p. 3*
- **variable expression**, *p. 3*
- **value**, *p. 3*
- **numerical expression**, *p. 3*
- **evaluate**, *p. 4*
- **power**, *p. 9*
- **exponent**, *p. 9*
- **base**, *p. 9*
- **grouping symbols**, *p. 10*

- **order of operations**, *p. 15*
- **left-to-right rule**, *p. 16*
- **equation**, *p. 24*
- **solution**, *p. 24*
- **inequality**, *p. 26*
- **modeling**, *p. 36*
- **verbal model**, *p. 36*
- **algebraic model**, *p. 36*
- **data**, *p. 42*

- **bar graph**, *p. 43*
- **line graph**, *p. 44*
- **function**, *p. 48*
- **input**, *p. 48*
- **output**, *p. 48*
- **input-output table**, *p. 48*
- **domain**, *p. 49*
- **range**, *p. 49*

1.1 VARIABLES IN ALGEBRA

Examples on pp. 3–5

EXAMPLES Evaluate the variable expression when $y = 4$.

a. $10 - y = 10 - 4$
$= 6$

b. $11y = 11(4)$
$= 44$

c. $\dfrac{16}{y} = \dfrac{16}{4}$
$= 4$

d. $y + 9 = 4 + 9$
$= 13$

Evaluate the expression for the given value of the variable.

1. $a + 14$ when $a = 6$

2. $18x$ when $x = 2$

3. $\dfrac{m}{3}$ when $m = 18$

4. $\dfrac{15}{y}$ when $y = 3$

5. $p - 12$ when $p = 22$

6. $5b$ when $b = 6$

7. You are walking at a rate of 3 miles per hour. Find the distance you travel in 2 hours.

8. You hike at a rate of 2 miles per hour. Find the distance you travel in 6 hours.

9. A race car driver maintains an average speed of 175 miles per hour. How far has she traveled in 3 hours?

Geometry Link **Find the perimeter of the geometric figure.**

10.

11.

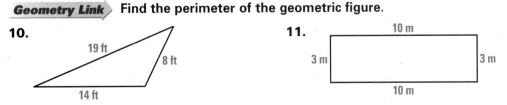

1.2 EXPONENTS AND POWERS

Examples on pp. 9–11

EXAMPLES Evaluate the variable expression when $b = 3$.

a. $b^2 = 3^2$

$= 3 \cdot 3$

$= 9$

b. $(10 - b)^3 = (10 - 3)^3$

$= 7^3$

$= 7 \cdot 7 \cdot 7$

$= 343$

c. $10(5^b) = 10(5^3)$

$= 10(5 \cdot 5 \cdot 5)$

$= 10(125)$

$= 1250$

Write the expression in exponential form.

12. eight to the fourth power

13. six cubed

14. $5 \cdot 5 \cdot 5 \cdot 5 \cdot 5$

Evaluate the expression for the given value of the variable.

15. x^4 when $x = 2$

16. $(5x)^3$ when $x = 5$

17. $6 + (b^3)$ when $b = 3$

1.3 ORDER OF OPERATIONS

Examples on pp. 15–17

EXAMPLE Evaluate $550 - 4(3 + 5)^2$.

$550 - 4(3 + 5)^2 = 550 - 4(8)^2$ — Add numbers within grouping symbols.

$= 550 - 4 \cdot 64$ — Evaluate the power.

$= 550 - 256$ — Multiply.

$= 294$ — Subtract.

Evaluate the numerical expression.

18. $9 + (3 - 2) - 3^2$

19. $(14 - 7)^2 + 5$

20. $6 + 2^2 - (7 - 5)$

21. $\dfrac{15 - 6}{6 + 3^2 - 12}$

22. $\dfrac{28 + 4}{4^2}$

23. $\dfrac{3^3 + 7}{4 \cdot 2}$

1.4 EQUATIONS AND INEQUALITIES

Examples on pp. 24–26

EXAMPLES Check to see if $x = 4$ is a solution of the equation $5x + 3 = 18$ or the inequality $7x - 5 > 20$.

Substitute: $5(4) + 3 \stackrel{?}{=} 18$ **Simplify:** $23 \neq 18$ **Conclusion:** False, 4 is *not* a solution.

Substitute: $7(4) - 5 \stackrel{?}{>} 20$ **Simplify:** $23 > 20$ **Conclusion:** True, 4 is a solution.

Check to see if the given value of the variable is or is not a solution of the equation or the inequality.

24. $2a - 3 = 2; a = 4$

25. $x^2 - x = 2; x = 2$

26. $9y - 3 > 24; y = 3$

27. $5x + 2 \leq 27; x = 5$

Use mental math to solve the equation.

28. $w + 7 = 15$

29. $10 - r = 7$

30. $4h = 32$

31. $\frac{c}{4} = 4$

32. $16 + k = 20$

33. $10g = 100$

1.5   **TRANSLATING WORDS INTO MATHEMATICAL SYMBOLS**

Examples on pp. 30–32

> **EXAMPLES**   Write the phrase or sentence as a variable expression, an equation, or an inequality. Let x represent the number.
>
> | | |
> |---|---|
> | A number increased by 10 | $x + 10$ |
> | The difference of 15 and a number is 8. | $15 - x = 8$ |
> | The quotient of a number and 7 | $\dfrac{x}{7}$ |
> | The product of 5 and a number is less than or equal to 10. | $5x \leq 10$ |

Write the phrase or sentence as a variable expression, an equation, or an inequality. Let x represent the number.

34. 27 divided by a number is 3.

35. A number plus 30

36. A number times 8 is greater than 5.

37. A number decreased by 9

1.6   **A PROBLEM SOLVING PLAN USING MODELS**

Examples on pp. 36–38

> **EXAMPLE**   You can model problems like the following: If you can save $5.00 a week, how many weeks must you save to buy a CD that costs $15.00?
>
> **VERBAL MODEL**
>
> | Amount saved per week | · | Number of weeks | = | Cost of CD |
> |---|---|---|---|---|
>
> **LABELS**
>
> Amount saved per week = **5**   (dollars per week)
>
> Number of weeks = **w**   (weeks)
>
> Cost of CD = **15**   (dollars)
>
> **ALGEBRAIC MODEL**
>
> $5 w = 15$ Write algebraic model.
>
> $w = 3$ Solve with mental math.
>
> **ANSWER** ▶ You must save for 3 weeks.

38. You are given $75 to buy juice for the school dance. Each bottle of juice costs
$.75. Write a verbal and an algebraic model to find how many bottles of juice
you can buy. Then use mental math to solve the equation.

1.7 TABLES AND GRAPHS

Examples on pp. 42–44

EXAMPLE The table shows the number of tennis titles won by United States
women. Write an inequality to determine if the number of Wimbledon titles won
by United States women is greater than the number of Australian Open titles plus
the number of French Open titles.

Event	Number of Titles
Australian Open	14
French Open	25
Wimbledon	43

▶ Source: *USA Today as of July 1999*

Inequality $43 \overset{?}{>} 14 + 25$

$43 > 39$

ANSWER ▶ The number of Wimbledon titles won
is greater.

39. Make a bar graph of the data showing the percent of the voting-age population
that voted. Write an inequality to determine if the percent in 1996 plus the
percent in 1992 is less than the percent in 1976 plus the percent in 1984.

Percent of Voting-Age Population That Voted for President, 1976–1996						
Year	1976	1980	1984	1988	1992	1996
Percent	53.5	52.8	53.3	50.3	55.1	48.9

▶ Source: *US Bureau of the Census*

1.8 AN INTRODUCTION TO FUNCTIONS

Examples on pp. 48–50

EXAMPLE Make an input-output table for the equation

$$C = 5n + 10$$

where $n = 1, 2, 3$, and 4. Then determine the range of the
function from the given input values in the table.

ANSWER ▶ The range for the input values in the table is 15, 20, 25, 30.

n	C
1	15
2	20
3	25
4	30

40. The perimeter P for rectangular picture frames with side lengths of $2w$ and
$3w$ is given by the function $P = 4w + 6w$. Make an input-output table that
shows the perimeter when $w = 1, 2, 3, 4$, and 5. Then determine the range of
the function from the values in the table.

Evaluate the variable expression when $y = 3$ and $x = 5$.

1. $5y + x^2$ **2.** $\dfrac{24}{y} - x$ **3.** $2y + 9x - 7$ **4.** $(5y + x) \div 4$

In Exercises 5–7, write the expression in exponential form.

5. $5y \cdot 5y \cdot 5y \cdot 5y$ **6.** nine cubed **7.** six to the nth power

8. Insert grouping symbols in $5 \cdot 4 + 6$ so that the value of the expression is 50.

9. TRAVEL If you can travel only 35 miles per hour, is 3 hours enough time to get to a concert that is 100 miles away? Give the expression you used to find the answer.

Write the phrase or sentence as a variable expression, an equation, or an inequality.

10. 7 times a number n **11.** x is at least 90. **12.** quotient of m and 2

13. y decreased by 3 **14.** 8 minus s is 4. **15.** 9 is less than t.

In Exercises 16–21, decide whether the statement is *true* or *false*.

16. $(2 \cdot 3)^2 = 2 \cdot 3^2$ **17.** $8 - 6 = 6 - 8$ **18.** The sum of 1 and 3 is 4.

19. $x^3 = 8$ when $x = 2$ **20.** $9x > x^3$ when $x = 3$ **21.** $8 \leq y^2$ when $y = 3$

22. The senior class is planning a trip that will cost \$35 per student. If \$3920 has been collected, how many seniors have paid for the trip?

MARCHING BAND **In Exercises 23 and 24, use the following information.** Members of the marching band are making their own color-guard flags. Each rectangular flag requires 0.6 square yards of material. The material costs \$2 per square yard.

23. Write a verbal model that relates the number of flags and the total cost of the material.

24. How much will it cost to make 20 flags?

PET OWNERS **In Exercises 25 and 26, use the table showing the number of pet owners in your eighth-grade class.**

25. Draw a bar graph of the data.

26. From the bar graph, what is the most popular household pet?

Kind of pet	Number of pet owners
Hamster	7
Dog	12
Cat	15
Bird	4
Fish	5

Chapter Standardized Test

1. Which of the following numbers is a solution of the inequality $9 - x \geq 2$?

  (A) 7   **(B)** 8   **(C)** 9   **(D)** 10

2. What is the value of the expression $[(5 \cdot 9) \div x] + 6$ when $x = 3$?

  (A) 5   **(B)** 15   **(C)** 18   **(D)** 21

3. Which variable expression is a translation of "5 times the difference of 8 and a number x"?

  (A) $5(8 - x)$ **(B)** $x - 5 \cdot 8$ **(C)** $5 \cdot 8 - x$ **(D)** $5 - 8x$

4. The number of students on the football team is 2 more than 3 times the number of students on the basketball team. If the basketball team has y students, write a variable expression for the number of students on the football team.

  (A) $3y$ **(B)** $3y - 2$ **(C)** $2 + 3y$ **(D)** $2y + 3$

5. Which of the following represent a function?

I.

Input	Output
1	4
2	4
3	6
4	6

II.

Input	Output
1	3
2	3
3	4
4	4

III.

Input	Output
1	3
1	3
2	4
3	5

  (A) All   **(B)** I and II   **(C)** I and III   **(D)** II and III   **(E)** None of these

Use the graph to compare the amount of chocolate eaten in different countries.

6. About how many more pounds of chocolate per person is consumed in Switzerland than in the United States?

  (A) 7   **(B)** 6   **(C)** 9   **(D)** 3

7. About how many more pounds of chocolate per person is consumed in Norway than in the United States?

  (A) 1.1   **(B)** 5.7   **(C)** 6.8   **(D)** 7.8

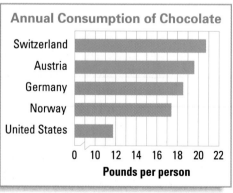

Annual Consumption of Chocolate

▶ Source: Chocolate Manufacturers Association

Maintaining Skills

EXAMPLE 1 Add and Subtract Decimals

Add 3.52 and 12.698.

Solution

```
    1     1       Line up decimals.
    3 . 5 2 0  ← Write a zero in the
 +1 2 . 6 9 8     thousandths place.
  1 6 . 2 1 8     Add columns from
                  right to left.
```

Subtract 8.28 and 4.095.

Solution

```
       1 17 10      Line up decimals.
   8 . 2 8 0  ← Write a zero in the
  -4 . 0 9 5     thousandths place.
   4 . 1 8 5     Borrow from the
                 left and subtract
                 from right to left.
```

Try These

Add or Subtract.

1. $2.3 + 0.4$ **2.** $3.5 - 2.1$ **3.** $8.75 + 3.35$ **4.** $10.6 - 2.6$

5. $3.006 + 2.8$ **6.** $4.25 - 0.08$ **7.** $3.99 + 0.254$ **8.** $6.2 - 0.17$

9. $123.5 + 32.3$ **10.** $32.8 - 12.21$ **11.** $0.09 + 0.9$ **12.** $17.0 - 16.5$

EXAMPLE 2 Use a Number Line

Plot 0.3 and $\frac{3}{2}$ on a number line.

Solution Begin by writing the fraction as a decimal, $\frac{3}{2} = 1.5$. Draw a number line. Mark equally spaced tick marks to represent a distance of 0.1 on the number line. Label several numbers as shown.

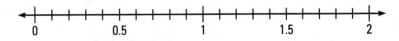

Plot 0.3 and $\frac{3}{2}$ by marking a solid dot on the number line.

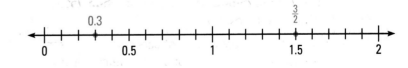

Try These

Draw a number line and plot the numbers.

13. $\frac{9}{10}$ **14.** $\frac{1}{2}$ **15.** $\frac{11}{10}$ **16.** $\frac{4}{5}$

17. 0.2 **18.** 1.7 **19.** 0.4 **20.** 1.9

Student Help

▶ **EXTRA EXAMPLES**

More examples and practice exercises are available at www.mcdougallittell.com

Properties of Real Numbers

▶ Why are helicopters able to take off and land without runways?

APPLICATION: Helicopters

▶ **Helicopters are capable of vertical flight—** flying straight up and straight down. Rotor blades generate an upward force (lift) as they whirl through the air.

Mathematics provides a useful way of distinguishing between upward and downward motion. In this chapter you will use positive numbers to measure the velocity of upward motion and negative numbers to measure the velocity of downward motion.

Think & Discuss

1. Describe some real-life situations that you might represent with negative numbers. What do positive and negative numbers represent in each situation?

2. Describe the average speed and direction of each helicopter's movement if it travels the given distance in 15 seconds.

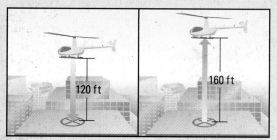

Not drawn to scale

Learn More About It

You will calculate the speed and velocity of different objects in Exercises 47–50 on page 75.

 APPLICATION LINK More about helicopters is available at www.mcdougallittell.com

PREVIEW

What's the chapter about?

- Adding, subtracting, multiplying, and dividing real numbers

> **KEY WORDS**
>
> - **real number**, *p. 65*
> - **integer**, *p. 65*
> - **opposite**, *p. 71*
> - **absolute value**, *p. 71*
> - **closure property**, *p. 78*
> - **term**, *p. 87*
> - **distributive property**, *p. 100*
> - **coefficient**, *p. 107*
> - **like terms**, *p. 107*
> - **reciprocal**, *p. 113*

PREPARE

Chapter Readiness Quiz

Take this quick quiz. If you are unsure of an answer, look back at the reference pages for help.

VOCABULARY CHECK *(refer to pp. 3, 24)*

1. Identify the variable in the expression $-2r^3 - 8$.

 (A) -2 **(B)** r **(C)** 3 **(D)** -8

2. Complete: A(n) __?__ is a statement formed by placing an equal sign between two expressions.

 (A) equation   **(B)** solution   **(C)** inequality   **(D)** function

SKILL CHECK *(refer to pp. 763, 765, 770)*

3. Write the numbers $2\frac{5}{6}$, $2\frac{2}{3}$, $\frac{11}{4}$, $2\frac{5}{8}$, and $\frac{25}{11}$ in order from least to greatest.

 (A) $\frac{11}{4}, \frac{25}{11}, 2\frac{2}{3}, 2\frac{5}{6}, 2\frac{5}{8}$ **(B)** $2\frac{2}{3}, \frac{11}{4}, 2\frac{5}{6}, 2\frac{5}{8}, \frac{25}{11}$

 (C) $2\frac{2}{3}, 2\frac{5}{6}, 2\frac{5}{8}, \frac{11}{4}, \frac{25}{11}$ **(D)** $\frac{25}{11}, 2\frac{5}{8}, 2\frac{2}{3}, \frac{11}{4}, 2\frac{5}{6}$

4. Write the quotient $9\frac{1}{6} \div 1\frac{3}{8}$ as a mixed number.

 (A) $\frac{48}{605}$ **(B)** $\frac{3}{20}$ **(C)** $6\frac{2}{3}$ **(D)** $12\frac{29}{48}$

STUDY TIP

Study a Lesson

Take notes. Add to your list of vocabulary words, rules, and properties in your notebook.

Lesson 2.3

Commutative Property of Addition
$a + b = b + a$ $-4 + 6 = 6 + (-4)$

Associative Property of Addition
$(a + b) + c = a + (b + c)$
$(-8 + 5) + 3 = -8 + (5 + 3)$

2.1 The Real Number Line

What was the coldest temperature in Nome, Alaska?

Goal

Graph, compare, and order real numbers.

Key Words

- real number
- real number line
- positive number
- negative number
- integer
- whole number
- graph of a number

In meteorology, temperatures that are above zero are represented by *positive* numbers and temperatures that are below zero are represented by *negative* numbers. In Example 5 you will compare low temperatures for Nome, Alaska.

The numbers used in this book are **real numbers**. Real numbers can be pictured as points on a line called a **real number line**, or simply a number line.

Every real number is either **positive**, **negative**, or zero. Points to the left of zero represent the negative real numbers. Points to the right of zero represent the positive real numbers. Zero is neither positive nor negative.

REAL NUMBER LINE

Negative numbers   Positive numbers

-6 -5 -4 -3 -2 -1 0 1 2 3 4 5 6

The scale marks on the real number line are equally spaced and represent **integers**. An integer is either negative, zero, or positive. Zero and the positive integers are also called **whole numbers**.

$$\ldots, -3, -2, -1, \qquad 0, \qquad 1, 2, 3, \ldots$$

Negative integers   Zero   Positive integers

The point on a number line that corresponds to a number is the **graph** of the number. Drawing the point is called graphing the number or plotting the point.

Student Help

▶ READING ALGEBRA
In Example 1, -2 is read as "negative two," 0 is read as "zero," and 3 is read as "three" or as "positive three."

EXAMPLE 1 Graph Integers

Graph -2, 0, and 3 on a number line.

Solution

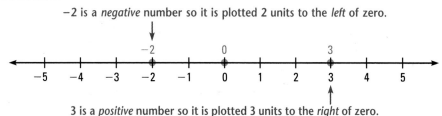

-2 is a *negative* number so it is plotted 2 units to the *left* of zero.

-5 -4 -3 -2 -1 0 1 2 3 4 5

3 is a *positive* number so it is plotted 3 units to the *right* of zero.

On a number line, numbers that are to the left are less than numbers to the right and numbers that are to the right are greater than numbers to the left.

Student Help

▶ SKILLS REVIEW
For help with comparing and ordering numbers, see pp. 770–771.

EXAMPLE 2 Compare Integers

Graph -4 and -5 on a number line. Then write two inequalities that compare the numbers.

Solution

On the graph, -5 is to the left of -4, so -5 **is less than** -4. You can write this using symbols:

$$-5 < -4$$

On the graph, -4 is to the right of -5, so -4 **is greater than** -5. You can write this using symbols:

$$-4 > -5$$

Checkpoint ✓ Compare Integers

Graph the numbers on a number line. Then write two inequalities that compare the numbers.

1. -6 and -2 **2.** 2 and -3 **3.** 5 and 7

You can graph decimals and fractions, as well as integers, on a real number line. The scale marks on a number line do not have to be integers. They can be in units of 0.1, 0.5, 2, 5, or any other amount.

Student Help

▶ STUDY TIP
When you work with fractions, sometimes it is easier to first convert the fraction to a decimal. For example:
$$\frac{4}{7} = 4 \div 7 \approx 0.57$$

EXAMPLE 3 Graph Real Numbers

Graph -0.8 and $\frac{4}{7}$ on a number line.

Solution

Because -0.8 and $\frac{4}{7}$ are not integers, use a number line that has scale marks in smaller units.

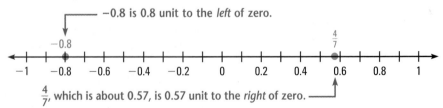

$\frac{4}{7}$, which is about 0.57, is 0.57 unit to the *right* of zero.

Student Help

▶ MORE EXAMPLES

More examples
are available at
www.mcdougallittell.com

EXAMPLE 4 **Order Real Numbers**

Write the numbers $-2, 4, 0, 1.5, \frac{1}{2}$, and $-\frac{3}{2}$ in increasing order.

Solution Graph the numbers on a number line. Remember that $\frac{1}{2} = 0.5$ and that $-\frac{3}{2} = -1.5$.

ANSWER ▶ From the graph, you can see that the order is: $-2, -\frac{3}{2}, 0, \frac{1}{2}, 1.5, 4$.

Checkpoint ✓ **Order Real Numbers**

Link to
Science

NOME, ALASKA The coldest low temperature on record for Nome, Alaska, is $-54°F$.

🔗 DATA UPDATE of National Oceanic and Atmospheric Administration data at www.mcdougallittell.com

Write the numbers in increasing order.

4. $-3, 0, 4, -\frac{5}{4}, \frac{3}{2}, -1$

5. $-3, 3, 3.2, -\frac{1}{2}, -8, 4.5$

EXAMPLE 5 **Compare Real Numbers**

NOME, ALASKA The table shows the low temperatures in Nome, Alaska, for five days in December. Which low temperature was the coldest?

Date	Dec. 18	Dec. 19	Dec. 20	Dec. 21	Dec. 22
Low Temp.	$-10°F$	$-11°F$	$16°F$	$3°F$	$2°F$

Solution First graph the temperatures on a number line.

ANSWER ▶ The coldest low temperature was $-11°F$.

Checkpoint ✓ **Compare Real Numbers**

6. The table shows the low temperatures in Nome, Alaska, for five days in February. Which dates had low temperatures above $10°F$?

Date	Feb. 22	Feb. 23	Feb. 24	Feb. 25	Feb. 26
Low Temp.	$-20°F$	$-11°F$	$20°F$	$17°F$	$-15°F$

Exercises

Guided Practice

Vocabulary Check

Complete the statement.

1. On a number line, the numbers to the left of zero are __?__ numbers, and the numbers to the right of zero are __?__ numbers.

2. Zero and the positive integers are also called __?__ numbers.

Skill Check

Graph the numbers on a number line.

3. $-5, -1, 4$ **4.** $-3, 0, 3$ **5.** $6, -2, 0.5$ **6.** $-1, -2, -\frac{2}{3}$

Complete the statement using < or >. Use the number line shown.

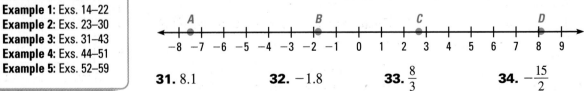

7. -4 **?** -5 **8.** 0 **?** -8 **9.** 6.7 **?** -6.7 **10.** $\frac{3}{2}$ **?** $\frac{2}{3}$

Write the numbers in increasing order.

11. $2, -3, -8, 1, -2$ **12.** $1.2, -4, 5, 7, -6.1$ **13.** $-7, -9, 2, \frac{5}{4}, -\frac{1}{5}$

Practice and Applications

GRAPHING INTEGERS Graph the numbers on a number line.

14. $0, 2, 6$ **15.** $10, 9, 3$ **16.** $5, 2, 8$

17. $-7, -4, -8$ **18.** $-1, -6, -7$ **19.** $-2, -4, -6$

20. $1, -2, 3$ **21.** $-3, 1, 5$ **22.** $-4, 4, -5$

COMPARING INTEGERS Graph the numbers on a number line. Then write two inequalities that compare the numbers.

23. $-2, 3$ **24.** $4, -6$ **25.** $-1, -6$ **26.** $-7, -5$

27. $0, -4$ **28.** $8, -8$ **29.** $10, 11$ **30.** $9, -12$

Student Help

▶**HOMEWORK HELP**
 Example 1: Exs. 14–22
 Example 2: Exs. 23–30
 Example 3: Exs. 31–43
 Example 4: Exs. 44–51
 Example 5: Exs. 52–59

REAL NUMBERS Match the number with its position on the number line.

31. 8.1 **32.** -1.8 **33.** $\frac{8}{3}$ **34.** $-\frac{15}{2}$

GRAPHING REAL NUMBERS **Graph the numbers on a number line.**

35. $0.5, -1.5, 2.5$ **36.** $-5.6, -0.3, 2$ **37.** $4.2, 4.4, 4.6$

38. $-\frac{7}{8}, 0, -0.5$ **39.** $4.3, -\frac{9}{2}, -2.8$ **40.** $\frac{3}{4}, -\frac{7}{3}, -3$

41. $\frac{1}{2}, -\frac{2}{3}, -\frac{1}{2}$ **42.** $\frac{1}{3}, \frac{3}{2}, \frac{11}{4}$ **43.** $\frac{9}{10}, -\frac{2}{5}, -\frac{8}{3}$

Student Help

▶ **HOMEWORK HELP**

INTERNET   Extra help with problem solving in Exs. 44–49 is available at www.mcdougallittell.com

ORDERING REAL NUMBERS **Write the numbers in increasing order.**

44. $4.6, 0.7, -4, -1.8, 3, -0.6$ **45.** $-0.3, 0.2, 0, 2.0, -0.2, -3.0$

46. $6.3, -6.8, -6.1, 6.1, -6.2, 6.7$ **47.** $\frac{9}{2}, 3.4, 4.1, -5.2, -5.1, -\frac{10}{4}$

48. $7, -\frac{1}{2}, 2, -\frac{3}{4}, -5, \frac{1}{6}$ **49.** $4.8, -2.6, 0, -\frac{7}{2}, \frac{1}{2}, -\frac{1}{2}$

LOGICAL REASONING **Complete the statement using < or >.**

50. If $x > -4$, then -4 **?** x.   **51.** If $3 < y$, then y **?** 3.

ELEVATION **In Exercises 52–54, write a positive number, a negative number, or zero to represent the elevation of the location.**

Elevation is represented by comparing a location to sea level, which is given a value of zero. A location above sea level has a positive elevation, and a location below sea level has a negative elevation.

52. Granite Peak, Montana, 12,799 feet above sea level

53. New Orleans, Louisiana, 8 feet below sea level

54. Long Island Sound, Connecticut, sea level

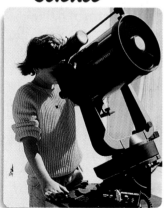

Link to Science

ASTRONOMY A star may appear dim because it is far from Earth. It may actually be brighter than a star that looks very bright only because it is closer to Earth.

Science Link **In Exercises 55–59, use the table shown which gives the apparent magnitude of several stars.**

A star's brightness as it appears to a person on Earth is measured by its *apparent magnitude*. The lesser the apparent magnitude, the brighter the star.

55. Graph the apparent magnitudes on a number line. Label each point with the name of the star.

56. Which stars have an apparent magnitude that is less than the apparent magnitude of Altair?

57. Which stars have an apparent magnitude that is greater than the apparent magnitude of Procyon?

58. Which star has the least apparent magnitude and so looks the brightest?

59. Which star has the greatest apparent magnitude and so looks the dimmest?

Star	Apparent magnitude
Canopus	-0.7
Procyon	0.4
Pollux	1.1
Altair	0.8
Spica	1.0
Regulus	1.4
Sirius	-1.5
Deneb	1.3

60. MULTIPLE CHOICE Which inequality is true?

     (A) $-9 > -5$ (B) $9 < 5$ (C) $9 < -5$ (D) $-9 < 5$

61. MULTIPLE CHOICE Which number is less than -0.1?

     (F) -10 (G) 0 (H) 0.001 (J) 10

62. MULTIPLE CHOICE Which set of numbers is in increasing order?

     (A) $-1.9, 1.8, -0.5, 0, 0.5$ (B) $-1.9, -0.5, 0, 0.5, 1.8$

     (C) $0, -0.5, 0.5, 1.8, -1.9$ (D) $-0.5, 0, 0.5, 1.8, -1.9$

Mixed Review

Geometry Link **Find the area of the object.** *(Lesson 1.2)*

63. The top of a computer desk measures 2 feet by 2 feet.

64. The cover of a children's book is 4 inches long and 4 inches wide.

65. A square piece of construction paper has a side length of 9 centimeters.

MENTAL MATH **Use mental math to solve the equation.** *(Lesson 1.4)*

66. $9 - y = 1$ **67.** $t + 6 = 10$ **68.** $2a = 8$

69. $15 \div r = 3$ **70.** $\dfrac{k}{2} = 8$ **71.** $\dfrac{27}{n} = 9$

72. BIRTHS The table shows the number of births (in thousands) in the United States by month for 1997. Make a bar graph of the data. *(Lesson 1.7)*

Jan.	Feb.	Mar.	Apr.	May	June	July	Aug.	Sep.	Oct.	Nov.	Dec.
305	289	313	342	311	324	345	341	353	329	304	324

Science Link **When it is 70°F, the function $T = 0.08H + 64.3$ gives the** *apparent* **temperature T (in degrees Fahrenheit) based on the relative humidity H (as a percent).** *(Lesson 1.8)*

73. Copy and complete the input-output table.

Input H	20%	40%	60%	70%	100%
Output T	?	?	?	?	?

74. Use the table to draw a graph that represents the function.

75. Determine the range of the function.

Maintaining Skills

FACTORS **Write the prime factorization of the number if it is not a prime. If the number is a prime, write** *prime.* *(Skills Review p. 761)*

76. 18   **77.** 35   **78.** 47   **79.** 64

80. 100   **81.** 101   **82.** 110   **83.** 144

Absolute Value

Goal
Find the opposite and the absolute value of a number.

Key Words
• opposite
• absolute value
• counterexample

What is a launch pad elevator's velocity and speed?

Velocity and speed are different concepts. Velocity tells you how fast an object is moving and in what direction. It can be positive or negative. Speed tells you only how fast an object is moving. It can only be positive. In Example 4 you will find the velocity and speed of a launch pad elevator for a space shuttle.

Two numbers that are the same distance from 0 on a number line but on opposite sides of 0 are **opposites**. The numbers -3 and 3 are opposites because each is 3 units from 0.

EXAMPLE 1 Find the Opposite of a Number

Use a number line to find the opposite of -4.

Solution

You can see that -4 is 4 units to the *left* of 0. The opposite of -4 is 4 units to the *right* of 0. So the opposite of -4 is 4.

ABSOLUTE VALUE The **absolute value** of a number is its distance from zero on a number line. The symbol $|a|$ represents the absolute value of a.

Student Help

▶ READING ALGEBRA
The expression $-a$ can be read as "negative a" or as "the opposite of a."

THE ABSOLUTE VALUE OF A NUMBER

• If a is a positive number, then $|a| = a$.   **Example:** $|3| = 3$
• If a is zero, then $|a| = 0$.   **Example:** $|0| = 0$
• If a is a negative number, then $|a| = -a$.   **Example:** $|-3| = -(-3) = 3$

EXAMPLE 2 Find Absolute Value

Evaluate the expression.

a. $|5|$ **b.** $|-2.3|$ **c.** $-\left|\dfrac{1}{2}\right|$ **d.** $-|-8|$

Solution

a. $|5| = 5$ If a is positive, then $|a| = a$.

b. $|-2.3| = -(-2.3)$ If a is negative, then $|a| = -a$.
$\qquad\qquad = 2.3$ Use definition of opposites.

c. $-\left|\dfrac{1}{2}\right| = -\left(\dfrac{1}{2}\right)$ The absolute value of $\dfrac{1}{2}$ is $\dfrac{1}{2}$.

$\qquad\quad = -\dfrac{1}{2}$ Use definition of opposites.

d. $-|-8| = -(8)$ The absolute value of -8 is 8.
$\qquad\qquad = -8$ Use definition of opposites.

Checkpoint ✓ *Find Absolute Value*

Evaluate the expression.

1. $|-4|$ **2.** $|0|$ **3.** $\left|\dfrac{3}{2}\right|$ **4.** $-|1.7|$

Student Help

▶**LOOK BACK**
For help with the solution of an equation, see p. 24.

EXAMPLE 3 Solve an Absolute Value Equation

Use mental math to solve the equation.

a. $|x| = 7$ **b.** $|x| = 5.1$ **c.** $|x| = -\dfrac{2}{9}$

Solution

a. Ask, "What numbers are 7 units from 0?" Both 7 and -7 are 7 units from 0, so there are two solutions: 7 and -7.

b. Ask, "What numbers are 5.1 units from 0?" Both 5.1 and -5.1 are 5.1 units from 0, so there are two solutions: 5.1 and -5.1.

c. The absolute value of a number is never negative, so there is no solution.

Checkpoint ✓ *Solve an Absolute Value Equation*

Use mental math to solve the equation. If there is no solution, write *no solution*.

5. $|x| = -4$ **6.** $|x| = 1.5$ **7.** $|x| = \dfrac{1}{6}$

VELOCITY AND SPEED *Velocity* indicates both speed and direction (up is positive and down is negative). The *speed* of an object is the absolute value of its velocity.

EXAMPLE 4 Find Velocity and Speed

SCIENCE LINK A launch pad elevator for a space shuttle drops at a rate of about 12 feet per second. What are its velocity and speed?

Solution

Velocity $= -12$ feet per second	Motion is downward.
Speed $= \lvert -12 \rvert = 12$ feet per second	Speed is never negative.

Checkpoint ✓ **Find Velocity and Speed**

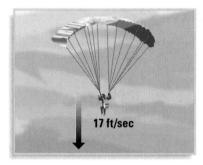

17 ft/sec

A parachutist descends at a rate of about 17 feet per second.

8. What is the parachutist's velocity?

9. What is the parachutist's speed?

COUNTEREXAMPLE To prove that a statement is true, you need to show that it is true for *all* examples. To prove that a statement is false, it is enough to show that it is *not* true for a single example, called a **counterexample**.

Student Help

▶ **MORE EXAMPLES**

More examples are available at www.mcdougallittell.com

EXAMPLE 5 Use a Counterexample

Determine whether the statement is *true* or *false*. If it is false, give a counterexample.

   a. The opposite of a number is always negative.

   b. The absolute value of a number is never negative.

Solution

   a. False. Counterexample: The opposite of -5 is 5, which is positive.

   b. True, by definition.

Checkpoint ✓ **Use a Counterexample**

Determine whether the statement is *true* or *false*. If it is false, give a counterexample.

10. The expression $-a$ is never positive.

11. The expression $\lvert a \rvert$ is always greater than or equal to a.

12. The absolute value of a negative number is always negative.

Guided Practice

Vocabulary Check

1. What is the opposite of 2?

2. Complete: The absolute value of a number is its distance from ___?___ on a number line.

Skill Check

Find the opposite of the number.

3. 1   **4.** −3   **5.** −2.4   **6.** $\frac{1}{2}$

Evaluate the expression.

7. $|-12|$ **8.** $|6|$ **9.** $-|5.1|$ **10.** $\left|-\frac{1}{5}\right|$

Use mental math to solve the equation. If there is no solution, write *no solution*.

11. $|x| = 8$ **12.** $|x| = -9$ **13.** $|x| = 5.5$ **14.** $|x| = \frac{2}{3}$

Determine whether the statement is *true* or *false*. If it is false, give a counterexample.

15. The opposite of a number is always less than the number.

16. The absolute value of a number is always positive or zero.

Practice and Applications

FINDING OPPOSITES **Find the opposite of the number.**

17. 8   **18.** −3   **19.** −10   **20.** 0

21. −3.8   **22.** 2.5   **23.** $-\frac{1}{9}$ **24.** $\frac{5}{6}$

FINDING ABSOLUTE VALUE **Evaluate the expression.**

25. $|7|$ **26.** $|-4|$ **27.** $-|3|$ **28.** $-|-2|$

29. $|-0.8|$ **30.** $|-4.5|$ **31.** $\left|\frac{2}{3}\right|$ **32.** $-\left|-\frac{8}{9}\right|$

Student Help

▶ HOMEWORK HELP
Example 1: Exs. 17–24
Example 2: Exs. 25–32,
   41, 42
Example 3: Exs. 33–40
Example 4: Exs. 43–50
Example 5: Exs. 51–53

SOLVING AN EQUATION **Use mental math to solve the equation. If there is no solution, write *no solution*.**

33. $|x| = 4$ **34.** $|x| = 0$ **35.** $|x| = -2$ **36.** $|x| = 1$

37. $|x| = 3.7$ **38.** $|x| = -9.6$ **39.** $|x| = \frac{11}{2}$ **40.** $|x| = \frac{5}{6}$

Science Link In Exercises 41 and 42,
use the table at the right which shows
the average high and low surface
temperatures for the planets in our
solar system.

Planet	High (°F)	Low (°F)
Mercury	800	−280
Venus	847	847
Earth	98	8
Mars	98	−190
Jupiter	−244	−244
Saturn	−301	−301
Uranus	−353	−353
Neptune	−373	−373
Pluto	−393	−393

41. The range of temperatures for
Mercury and Mars is the sum of the
absolute values of the high and low
temperatures. Find the range of
temperatures for these planets.

42. The range of temperatures for the
other planets is the difference of
the absolute values of the high and
low temperatures. Find the range of
temperatures for these planets.

VELOCITY Determine whether to use a *positive* or a *negative* number to
represent the velocity.

43. The velocity of a descending hot-air balloon

44. The velocity of a rising rocket

45. The velocity of a kite as is lifts into the air

46. The velocity of a falling meteorite

VELOCITY AND SPEED A helicopter is descending at a rate of 6 feet
per second.

47. What is the helicopter's velocity? **48.** What is the helicopter's speed?

VELOCITY AND SPEED The elevator in the Washington Monument
in Washington, D.C., climbs at a rate of about 400 feet per minute.

49. What is the elevator's velocity? **50.** What is the elevator's speed?

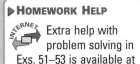
USING COUNTEREXAMPLES Determine whether the statement is *true* or
false. If it is false, give a counterexample.

51. The opposite of $-a$ is always positive.

52. The opposite of $|a|$ is never positive.

53. The expression $|-a|$ is never negative.

CHALLENGE Determine whether the statement is *always*, *sometimes*, or
never true. Explain.

54. The absolute value of a number is the same as the absolute value of the
opposite number. In other words, $|x| = |-x|$.

55. The opposite of the absolute value of a number is the same as the absolute
value of the opposite of the number. In other words, $-|x| = |-x|$.

56. MULTIPLE CHOICE What is the opposite of 5?

$\textcircled{A}$ $\frac{1}{5}$ $\qquad$ $\textcircled{B}$ $-\frac{1}{5}$ $\qquad$ $\textcircled{C}$ 5 $\qquad$ $\textcircled{D}$ -5

57. MULTIPLE CHOICE What is the value of $-|-2|$?

$\textcircled{F}$ 2 $\qquad$ $\textcircled{G}$ -2 $\qquad$ $\textcircled{H}$ $|2|$ $\qquad$ $\textcircled{J}$ $|-2|$

58. MULTIPLE CHOICE What is the solution of $|x| = 18$?

$\textcircled{A}$ 18 $\qquad\qquad\qquad$ $\textcircled{B}$ -18

$\textcircled{C}$ 18 and -18 $\qquad\qquad$ $\textcircled{D}$ none of these

59. MULTIPLE CHOICE What is the velocity of a diver who descends to the ocean floor at a rate of 3 meters per second?

$\textcircled{F}$ $|-3|$ m/sec $\qquad\qquad$ $\textcircled{G}$ $|3|$ m/sec

$\textcircled{H}$ -3 m/sec $\qquad\qquad$ $\textcircled{J}$ 3 m/sec

Mixed Review

EVALUATING EXPRESSIONS **Evaluate the expression for the given value of the variable.** *(Lesson 1.1)*

60. $x + 3$ when $x = 2$ $\qquad\qquad$ **61.** $a - 7$ when $a = 10$

62. $3y$ when $y = 0$ $\qquad\qquad$ **63.** $(t)(5)$ when $t = 15$

64. $\frac{z}{2}$ when $z = 8$ $\qquad\qquad$ **65.** $\frac{9}{p}$ when $p = 3$

TRANSLATING SENTENCES **Write the sentence as an equation or an inequality. Let *x* represent the number.** *(Lesson 1.5)*

66. 5 less than a number is 8.

67. 8 more than a number is 17.

68. The quotient of 15 and a number is greater than or equal to 3.

69. 9 times a number is less than 6.

COMPARING NUMBERS **Graph the numbers on a number line. Then write two inequalities that compare the numbers.** *(Lesson 2.1)*

70. 7, -7 $\qquad\qquad$ **71.** $-2, -6$ $\qquad\qquad$ **72.** $-10, -1$

73. 0.4, -3 $\qquad\qquad$ **74.** 2.2, -3.3 $\qquad\qquad$ **75.** $-10, -\frac{1}{10}$

Maintaining Skills

SUBTRACTING FRACTIONS **Subtract. Write the answer in lowest terms.** *(Skills Review p. 764)*

76. $\frac{3}{4} - \frac{1}{4}$ $\qquad\qquad$ **77.** $\frac{7}{9} - \frac{2}{9}$ $\qquad\qquad$ **78.** $\frac{7}{10} - \frac{3}{10}$

79. $\frac{14}{15} - \frac{4}{15}$ $\qquad\qquad$ **80.** $\frac{25}{27} - \frac{16}{27}$ $\qquad\qquad$ **81.** $\frac{41}{44} - \frac{19}{44}$

DEVELOPING CONCEPTS
Addition of Integers

GOAL

Use reasoning to find a pattern for adding integers.

MATERIALS

• algebra tiles

Question

How can you model the addition of integers with algebra tiles?

Each ➕ represents positive 1 and each ➖ represents negative 1. Combining a ➕ tile and a ➖ tile equals zero.

Explore

Use algebra tiles to find the sum of −8 and 3.

① Model negative 8 and positive 3 using algebra tiles.

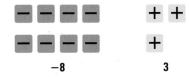

−8   3

② Group pairs of positive and negative tiles. Count the remaining tiles.

Each pair has a sum of 0. ⟶
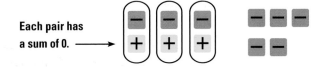

③ The remaining tiles show the sum of −8 and 3. Complete: −8 + 3 = __?__.

Think About It

Use algebra tiles to find the sum of the numbers given.

1.

2   4

2. −1   −5

3. 3   −3

Use algebra tiles to find the sum. Sketch your solution.

4. 3 + 3   **5.** −4 + (−2)   **6.** −3 + 2   **7.** 5 + (−2)

LOGICAL REASONING Based on your results from Exercises 1–7, complete the statement with *always*, *sometimes*, or *never*.

8. The sum of two positive integers is __?__ a positive integer.

9. The sum of two negative integers is __?__ a positive integer.

10. The sum of a positive integer and a negative integer is __?__ a negative integer.

2.3 Adding Real Numbers

Goal

Add real numbers using a number line or the rules of addition.

Key Words

- closure property
- commutative property
- associative property
- identity property
- inverse property

What is the profit or loss of a company?

In business a profit can be represented by a positive number and a loss can be represented by a negative number. In Example 4 you will add several profits and losses to find the overall profit of a summer excursion company.

The sum of any two real numbers is itself a unique real number. We say that the real numbers are *closed* under addition. This fact is called the **closure property of real number addition**. Addition can be modeled with movements on a number line.

- You add a **positive** number by moving to the **right** on the number line.

- You add a **negative** number by moving to the **left** on the number line.

EXAMPLE 1 Add Using a Number Line

Use a number line to find the sum.

a. $-2 + 5$ **b.** $2 + (-6)$

Solution

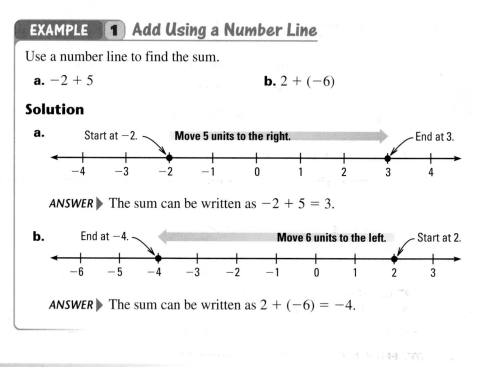

a. Start at −2. Move 5 units to the right. End at 3.

ANSWER ▶ The sum can be written as $-2 + 5 = 3$.

b. End at −4. Move 6 units to the left. Start at 2.

ANSWER ▶ The sum can be written as $2 + (-6) = -4$.

Checkpoint ✓ Add Using a Number Line

Use a number line to find the sum.

1. $-4 + 5$ **2.** $-1 + (-2)$ **3.** $4 + (-5)$ **4.** $0 + (-4)$

RULES OF ADDITION

To add two numbers with the *same sign*:

STEP ❶   **Add** their absolute values.

STEP ❷   **Attach** the common sign.

To add two numbers with *opposite signs*:

STEP ❶   **Subtract** the smaller absolute value from the larger one.

STEP ❷   **Attach** the sign of the number with larger absolute value.

Student Help

▶**LOOK BACK**
For help with absolute value, see p. 71.

EXAMPLE 2   Add Using Rules of Addition

a. Add -4 and -5, which have the same sign.

  ❶ **Add** their absolute values. $4 + 5 = 9$

  ❷ **Attach** the common (negative) sign. $-(9) = -9$

  ANSWER▶ $-4 + (-5) = -9$

b. Add 3 and -9, which have opposite signs.

  ❶ **Subtract** their absolute values. $9 - 3 = 6$

  ❷ **Attach** the sign of the number with larger absolute value. $-(6) = -6$

  ANSWER▶ $3 + (-9) = -6$

Checkpoint✓   Add Using Rules of Addition

Use the rules of addition to find the sum.

5. $-3 + (-7)$ **6.** $-1 + 3$ **7.** $8 + (-3)$ **8.** $2 + 3$

The rules of addition are a consequence of the following properties of addition.

PROPERTIES OF ADDITION

CLOSURE PROPERTY The sum of any two real numbers is a unique real number.

  $a + b$ is a unique real number   **Example:** $4 + 2 = 6$

COMMUTATIVE PROPERTY The order in which two numbers are added does not change the sum.

  $a + b = b + a$ **Example:** $3 + (-2) = -2 + 3$

ASSOCIATIVE PROPERTY The way three numbers are grouped when adding does not change the sum.

  $(a + b) + c = a + (b + c)$ **Example:** $(-5 + 6) + 2 = -5 + (6 + 2)$

IDENTITY PROPERTY The sum of a number and 0 is the number.

  $a + 0 = a$ **Example:** $-4 + 0 = -4$

INVERSE PROPERTY The sum of a number and its opposite is 0.

  $a + (-a) = 0$ **Example:** $5 + (-5) = 0$

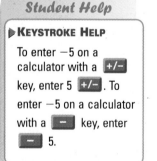
EXAMPLE 3 Add Using Properties of Addition

a. $4 + (-6) + 9 = 4 + (-6 + 9)$ Use associative property.

$$= 4 + 3$$ Add −6 and 9.

$$= 7$$ Add 4 and 3.

b. $-0.5 + 3 + 0.5 = -0.5 + 0.5 + 3$ Use commutative property.

$$= (-0.5 + 0.5) + 3$$ Use associative property.

$$= 0 + 3$$ Use inverse property.

$$= 3$$ Use identity property.

Checkpoint ✓ Add Using Properties of Addition

Use the properties of addition to find the sum.

9. $-7 + 11 + 7$ **10.** $-5 + 1 + 2$ **11.** $3 + \left(-\dfrac{1}{3}\right) + \left(-\dfrac{2}{3}\right)$

PROFIT AND LOSS A company has a *profit* if its income is greater than its expenses. It has a *loss* if its income is less than its expenses. Income and expenses are always positive, but business losses can be indicated by negative numbers.

EXAMPLE 4 Use Addition in Real Life

🖩 **BUSINESS** A summer excursion company had the monthly profits and losses shown. Add them to find the overall profit or loss of the company.

JANUARY	FEBRUARY	MARCH
-$13,143	-$6,783	-$4,735
APRIL	MAY	JUNE
$3,825	$7,613	$12,933

Solution With this many large numbers, you may want to use a calculator.

13143 [+/−] [+] 6783 [+/−] [+] 4735 [+/−] [+] 3825 [+] 7613 [+] 12933 [=] ⎧ −290 ⎫

ANSWER ▶ The company had an overall loss of $290.

Checkpoint ✓ Use Addition in Real Life

12. Find the total profit or loss of the company in Example 4 during the first quarter (January through March).

13. Find the total profit or loss of the company in Example 4 during the spring months (March through May).

Guided Practice

Vocabulary Check   **Match the property with the statement that illustrates it.**

1. Commutative property   **A.** $-8 + 0 = -8$

2. Associative property   **B.** $5 + (-9) = -9 + 5$

3. Identity property   **C.** $-8 + 8 = 0$

4. Inverse property   **D.** $5 + (4 + 9) = (5 + 4) + 9$

Skill Check   **5.** Write an addition equation for the sum modeled on the number line.

Use a number line to find the sum.

6. $7 + (-3)$ **7.** $0 + (-10)$ **8.** $-7 + 3$

Use the rules of addition to find the sum.

9. $12 + (-5)$ **10.** $-4 + 5$ **11.** $-7 + (-3)$

Use the properties of addition to find the sum.

12. $-4 + 3 + (-2)$ **13.** $5 + (-5) + 7$ **14.** $-3 + 0 + 7$

Practice and Applications

ADDING REAL NUMBERS   **Match the exercise with its answer.**

15. $-1 + (-2)$ **16.** $3 + (-5)$ **17.** $-2 + 2$

A. -2 **B.** 0 **C.** -3

NUMBER LINES   **Use a number line to find the sum.**

18. $-6 + 2$ **19.** $2 + (-8)$ **20.** $-3 + (-3)$

21. $-4 + (-7)$ **22.** $-4 + 5$ **23.** $3 + (-7)$

24. $-10 + 1$ **25.** $15 + (-9)$ **26.** $-12 + (-5)$

RULES OF ADDITION   **Find the sum.**

27. $9 + (-2)$ **28.** $-6 + (-11)$ **29.** $-7 + (-4)$

30. $-5 + 2$ **31.** $8 + (-5)$ **32.** $-6 + (-3)$

33. $-10 + (-21)$ **34.** $49 + (-58)$ **35.** $-62 + 27$

Student Help

▶ **HOMEWORK HELP**
Example 1: Exs. 15–26
Example 2: Exs. 27–35
Example 3: Exs. 36–49
Example 4: Exs. 50–55

GOLF If you complete a round of golf in 68 strokes at a course with a par of 71 strokes, you have shot "3 under par," or −3.

NAMING PROPERTIES Name the property shown by the statement.

36. $-16 + 0 = -16$

37. $-3 + (-5) = -5 + (-3)$

38. $(-4 + 3) + 5 = -4 + (3 + 5)$

39. $16 + (-16) = 0$

40. There is only one real number that is the sum of 4 and 6.

PROPERTIES OF ADDITION Find the sum.

41. $6 + 10 + (-6)$

42. $7 + (-2) + (-9)$

43. $8 + (-4) + (-4)$

44. $-24.5 + 6 + 8$

45. $5.4 + 2.6 + (-3)$

46. $2.2 + (-2.2) + (2.2)$

47. $4 + \frac{1}{10} + \left(-\frac{1}{10}\right)$

48. $9 + (-4) + \left(-\frac{1}{2}\right)$

49. $\frac{1}{7} + (-2) + \left(-\frac{5}{7}\right)$

FINDING SUMS Find the sum. Use a calculator if you wish.

50. $-2.95 + 5.76 + (-88.6)$

51. $10.97 + (-51.14) + (-40.97)$

52. $20.37 + 190.8 + (-85.13)$

53. $300.3 + (-22.24) + 78.713$

54. PROFIT AND LOSS A company had the following profits and losses over a 4-month period: April, $3,515; May, $5,674; June, −$8,993; July, −$907. Did the company make an overall profit or loss? Explain.

55. GOLF In golf *par* is the number of strokes estimated to finish a hole. A *bogey* is a score of one stroke over par. A *birdie* is a score of one stroke under par. An *eagle* is a score of two strokes under par. Using the table find the number of strokes you are off from par at the end of a round of golf.

Hole	1	2	3	4	5	6	7	8	9
Score	Birdie	Par	Birdie	Par	Eagle	Bogey	Bogey	Bogey	Birdie

56. CHALLENGE Determine whether the following statement is *true* or *false*. If it is true, give two examples. If it is false, give a counterexample.

The opposite of the sum of two numbers is equal to the sum of the opposites of the numbers.

Standardized Test Practice

In Exercises 57 and 58, use the financial data in the table.

57. MULTIPLE CHOICE In which month was the most money saved?

    (A) January   (B) March

    (C) May   (D) June

58. MULTIPLE CHOICE In which month did the money spent most exceed the money earned?

    (F) January   (G) February

    (H) April   (J) June

Month	$ Earned	$ Spent	$ Saved
Jan.	1676	1427	?
Feb.	1554	1771	?
Mar.	1851	1556	?
Apr.	1567	1874	?
May	1921	1602	?
June	1667	1989	?

WRITING POWERS Write the expression in exponential form. *(Lesson 1.2)*

59. four squared   **60.** k to the ninth power   **61.** x cubed

NUMERICAL EXPRESSIONS Evaluate the expression. *(Lesson 1.3)*

62. $15 - 5 + 5^2$ **63.** $18 \cdot 2 - 1 \cdot 3$ **64.** $1 + 3 \cdot 5 - 8$

65. $2(9 - 6 - 1)$ **66.** $10 - (3 + 2) + 4$ **67.** $2 \cdot (6 + 10) - 8$

CHECKING SOLUTIONS OF EQUATIONS Check to see if the given value of the variable is or is not a solution of the equation. *(Lesson 1.4)*

68. $x + 5 = 10; x = 7$ **69.** $7y - 15 = 6; y = 3$ **70.** $17 - 3w = 2; w = 5$

71. $a^2 - 3 = 5; a = 4$ **72.** $1 + p^3 = 9; p = 2$ **73.** $2n^2 + 10 = 14; n = 1$

ESTIMATING Round the values to the nearest hundred and estimate the answer. *(Skills Review p. 774)*

74. $422 + 451$ **75.** $8362 + 941$ **76.** $27 + 159$

77. $675 - 589$ **78.** $1084 - 179$ **79.** $3615 - 663$

Quiz 1

Graph the numbers on a number line. Then write two inequalities that compare the numbers. *(Lesson 2.1)*

1. $7, -2$ **2.** $-2, -3$ **3.** $1, -6$

Write the numbers in increasing order. *(Lesson 2.1)*

4. $-8, 2, -10, -3, 9$ **5.** $-5.2, 5, -7, 7.1, 3.3$ **6.** $-1, -\frac{2}{5}, 2, 0, \frac{1}{10}$

Evaluate the expression. *(Lesson 2.2)*

7. $|5|$ **8.** $|-13|$ **9.** $-|0.56|$

Use mental math to solve the equation. If there is no solution, write *no solution*. *(Lesson 2.2)*

10. $|x| = -10$ **11.** $|x| = 2.7$ **12.** $|x| = \frac{3}{5}$

Find the sum. *(Lesson 2.3)*

13. $-6 + (-7)$ **14.** $4 + (-10)$ **15.** $-5 + 9$

16. $-5 + 1 + (-3)$ **17.** $-6 + 2.9 + 1.1$ **18.** $\frac{1}{5} + 0 + \left(-\frac{1}{5}\right)$

19. FOOTBALL Your high school football team needs 9 yards to score a touchdown. The last four plays result in a 5 yard gain, a 2 yard gain, a 12 yard loss, and a 15 yard gain. Does your team score a touchdown? If not, how many yards do they still need? *(Lesson 2.3)*

DEVELOPING CONCEPTS
Subtraction of Integers

For use with Lesson 2.4

GOAL

Use reasoning to find a pattern for subtracting integers.

MATERIALS

• algebra tiles

Student Help

▶ **LOOK BACK**
For help with using algebra tiles, see p. 77.

Question How can you model the subtraction of positive integers with algebra tiles?

Explore

Use algebra tiles to model $3 - 6$.

1 Use 3 yellow tiles to model $+3$.

$+$ $+$ $+$

2 Before you can remove 6 yellow tiles you need to add three "zero pairs."

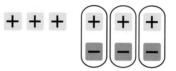

3 To subtract 6 from 3, remove six of the yellow tiles.

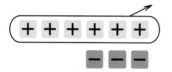

4 The remaining tiles show the difference of 3 and 6.

Complete: $3 - 6 = $ __?__

Think About It

Use algebra tiles to find the difference. Sketch your solution.

1. $7 - 2$ **2.** $2 - 3$ **3.** $4 - 7$

4. $-3 - 5$ **5.** $-5 - 8$ **6.** $-1 - 2$

Use algebra tiles to find the sum. Sketch your solution.

7. $7 + (-2)$ **8.** $2 + (-3)$ **9.** $4 + (-7)$

10. $-3 + (-5)$ **11.** $-5 + (-8)$ **12.** $-1 + (-2)$

LOGICAL REASONING Based on your results from Exercise 1–12, determine whether the statement is *true* or *false*. Explain.

13. To subtract a positive integer, add the opposite of the positive integer.

14. When you subtract a positive integer, the difference is always negative.

Question How can you model subtraction of negative integers with algebra tiles?

Explore

Use algebra tiles to model $-6 - (-2)$.

1 Use 6 red tiles to model -6.

2 To subtract -2 from -6, remove 2 red tiles.

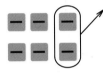

3 The remaining tiles show the difference of -6 and -2.

Complete: $-6 - (-2) =$ ___?___

Think About It

Use algebra tiles to find the difference. Sketch your solution.

1. $4 - (-2)$ **2.** $8 - (-1)$ **3.** $3 - (-4)$

4. $-7 - (-3)$ **5.** $-5 - (-1)$ **6.** $-6 - (-6)$

Use algebra tiles to find the sum. Sketch your solution.

7. $4 + 2$ **8** $8 + 1$ **9.** $3 + 4$

10. $-7 + 3$ **11.** $-5 + 1$ **12.** $-6 + 6$

LOGICAL REASONING Based on your results from Exercises 1–12, determine whether the statement is *true* or *false*. Explain.

13. To subtract a negative integer, add the opposite of the negative integer.

14. When you subtract a negative integer, the difference is always negative.

2.4 Subtracting Real Numbers

Goal

Subtract real numbers using the subtraction rule.

Key Words

• term

What is the change in a stock's value?

The daily change in the price of a company's stock can be calculated by subtracting one day's closing price from the previous day's closing price. In Example 5 you will see that this change can be positive or negative.

Some addition expressions can be evaluated using subtraction.

ADDITION PROBLEM	EQUIVALENT SUBTRACTION PROBLEM
$5 + (-3) = 2$	$5 - 3 = 2$
$-2 + (-6) = -8$	$-2 - 6 = -8$

Adding the opposite of a number is equivalent to subtracting the number.

SUBTRACTION RULE

To subtract b from a, add the opposite of b to a.

$$a - b = a + (-b)$$ Example: $3 - 5 = 3 + (-5)$

The result is the difference of a and b.

EXAMPLE 1 Use the Subtraction Rule

Find the difference.

a. $10 - 11$ **b.** $11 - 10$ **c.** $-4 - (-9)$

Solution

a. $10 - 11 = 10 + (-11)$ Add the opposite of 11.
$= -1$ Use rules of addition.

b. $11 - 10 = 11 + (-10)$ Add the opposite of 10.
$= 1$ Use rules of addition.

c. $-4 - (-9) = -4 + 9$ Add the opposite of -9.
$= 5$ Use rules of addition.

You can change subtractions to additions by "adding the opposite" as a first step in evaluating an expression.

EXAMPLE 2 Expressions with More than One Subtraction

Evaluate the expression $3 - (-4) - \frac{1}{2}$.

Solution

$$3 - (-4) - \frac{1}{2} = 3 + 4 + \left(-\frac{1}{2}\right) \qquad \text{Add the opposites of } -4 \text{ and } \frac{1}{2}.$$

$$= 7 + \left(-\frac{1}{2}\right) \qquad \text{Add 3 and 4.}$$

$$= 6\frac{1}{2} \qquad \text{Add 7 and } -\frac{1}{2}.$$

Checkpoint ✓ Use the Subtraction Rule

Use the subtraction rule to find the difference.

1. $-3 - 5$ **2.** $12.7 - 10$ **3.** $1 - (-2) - 6$ **4.** $7 - \frac{2}{3} - \frac{5}{3}$

EXAMPLE 3 Evaluate a Function

Student Help

▶**LOOK BACK**

For help with functions, see p. 48.

Evaluate the function $y = -5 - x$ when $x = -2, -1, 0,$ and 1. Organize your results in a table.

Solution

Input	Function	Output
$x = -2$	$y = -5 - (-2)$	$y = -3$
$x = -1$	$y = -5 - (-1)$	$y = -4$
$x = 0$	$y = -5 - 0$	$y = -5$
$x = 1$	$y = -5 - 1$	$y = -6$

Checkpoint ✓ Evaluate a Function

5. Evaluate the function $y = 4 - x$ when $x = -3, -1, 1,$ and 3. Organize your results in a table.

TERMS OF AN EXPRESSION When an expression is written as a sum, the parts that are added are the **terms** of the expression. For instance, you can write $-5 - x$ as the sum $-5 + (-x)$. The terms are -5 and $-x$. You can use the subtraction rule to write an expression as a sum of terms.

EXAMPLE 4 **Find the Terms of an Expression**

Find the terms of $-9 - 2x$.

Solution Use the subtraction rule to rewrite the difference as a sum.

$$-9 - 2x = -9 + (-2x)$$

ANSWER ▶ The terms of the expression are -9 and $-2x$.

Checkpoint ✓ **Find the Terms of an Expression**

Find the terms of the expression.

6. $x - 3$　　　**7.** $-2 - 5x$　　　**8.** $-4 + 6x$　　　**9.** $7x + 2$

Link to
History

STOCK MARKET When the New York Stock Exchange opened in 1792, it reported stock prices as fractions. Stock prices were not reported as decimals until 2000.

EXAMPLE 5 **Subtract Real Numbers**

STOCK MARKET The daily closing prices for a company's stock are given in the table. Find the change in the closing price since the previous day.

Date	Aug. 23	Aug. 24	Aug. 25	Aug. 26	Aug. 27
Closing Price	21.38	21.25	21.38	20.69	20.06
Change	——	?	?	?	?

Solution Subtract each day's closing price from the closing price for the previous day.

DATE	CLOSING PRICE	CHANGE
Aug. 23	21.38	——
Aug. 24	21.25	$21.25 - 21.38 = -0.13$
Aug. 25	21.38	$21.38 - 21.25 = 0.13$
Aug. 26	20.69	$20.69 - 21.38 = -0.69$
Aug. 27	20.06	$20.06 - 20.69 = -0.63$

Checkpoint ✓ **Subtract Real Numbers**

10. The daily closing prices for a company's stock are given in the table. Find the change in the closing price since the previous day.

Date	Nov. 10	Nov. 11	Nov. 12	Nov. 13	Nov. 14
Closing Price	46.75	47.44	47.31	47.75	48.75
Change	——	?	?	?	?

2.4 Exercises

Guided Practice

Vocabulary Check

1. Complete: In an expression that is written as a sum, the parts that are added are called the __?__ of the expression.

2. Is $7x$ a term of the expression $4y - 7x - 9$? Explain.

Skill Check

3. Use the number line to complete this statement: $-2 - 5 = $ **?**

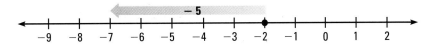

Find the difference.

4. $4 - 5$ **5.** $0 - (-7)$ **6.** $-2 - 8.7$

Evaluate the expression.

7. $2 - (-3) - 6$ **8.** $-3 - 2 - (-5)$ **9.** $6 - 2 - \frac{1}{2}$

10. Evaluate the function $y = 10 - x$, when $x = -5, -1, 1$ and 5. Organize your results in a table.

Find the terms of the expression.

11. $12 - 5x$ **12.** $5w - 8$ **13.** $-12y + 6$

Practice and Applications

SUBTRACTION RULE Find the difference.

14. $4 - 9$ **15.** $6 - (-3)$ **16.** $-8 - (-5)$ **17.** $-2 - 9$

18. $-10 - 5$ **19.** $25 - (-14)$ **20.** $-10 - (-42)$ **21.** $95 - 59$

22. $-3 - 1.7$ **23.** $5.4 - (-3.8)$ **24.** $9.6 - 6.5$ **25.** $-2.2 - (-1)$

26. $\frac{4}{3} - \frac{7}{3}$ **27.** $\frac{3}{4} - \left(-\frac{9}{4}\right)$ **28.** $-\frac{5}{8} - \left(-\frac{3}{8}\right)$ **29.** $-4 - \frac{1}{2}$

EVALUATING EXPRESSIONS Evaluate the expression.

Student Help

▶ **HOMEWORK HELP**
  Example 1: Exs. 14–29
  Example 2: Exs. 30–41
  Example 3: Exs. 42–47
  Example 4: Exs. 48–53
  Example 5: Exs. 54–57

30. $-1 - 5 - 8$ **31.** $2 - (-4) - 7$ **32.** $4 - (-3) - (-5)$

33. $46 - 17 - (-2)$ **34.** $-15 - 16 - 81$ **35.** $11 - (-23) - 77$

36. $-8 - 3.1 - 6.2$ **37.** $2.3 - (-9.5) - 1.6$ **38.** $8.4 - 5.2 - (-4.7)$

39. $\frac{5}{7} - \frac{4}{7} - \left(-\frac{6}{7}\right)$ **40.** $-\frac{4}{9} - \frac{2}{9} - \frac{5}{9}$ **41.** $\frac{7}{10} - \left(-\frac{3}{10}\right) - \left(-\frac{1}{10}\right)$

EVALUATING FUNCTIONS Evaluate the function when $x = -2, -1, 0,$ and 1. Organize your results in a table.

42. $y = x - 8$ **43.** $y = 12 - x$ **44.** $y = -x - (-5)$

45. $y = -8.5 - x$ **46.** $y = -x - 12.1$ **47.** $y = x - \dfrac{1}{2}$

FINDING TERMS Find the terms of the expression.

48. $-4 - y$ **49.** $-x - 7$ **50.** $-3x + 6$

51. $9 - 28x$ **52.** $-10 + 4b$ **53.** $a - 5$

54. STOCK MARKET The daily closing prices for a company's stock are given in the table. Find the change in the closing price since the previous day.

Date	Sept. 11	Sept. 12	Sept. 13	Sept. 14	Sept. 15
Closing Price	101.31	103.19	105.75	104.44	102.19
Change	————	?	?	?	?

55. SUBMARINE DEPTH A submarine is at a depth of 725 feet below sea level. Five minutes later it is at a depth of 450 feet below sea level. What is the change in depth of the submarine? Did it go up or down?

Student Help

▶**HOMEWORK HELP**

Extra help with problem solving in Exs. 56–57 is available at www.mcdougallittell.com

Science Link In Exercises 56 and 57, use the diagram below which shows the journey of a water molecule from A to B.

56. Find the change in elevation from each point to the next point.

57. Using your answers from Exercise 56, write an expression using addition and subtraction that models the change in elevation of the water molecule during its journey. Then evaluate the expression.

CHALLENGE Determine whether the statement is *true* or *false*. Use the subtraction rule or a number line to support your answer.

58. If you subtract a negative number from a positive number, the result is always a positive number.

59. If you subtract a positive number from a negative number, the result is always a negative number.

60. MULTIPLE CHOICE What does $5 - \left(-\frac{1}{3}\right) + \frac{2}{3}$ equal?

(A) 4   (B) $4\frac{2}{3}$ (C) $5\frac{1}{3}$ (D) 6

61. MULTIPLE CHOICE What does $-x - 7$ equal when $x = -1$?

(F) -8 (G) -6 (H) 6   (J) 8

62. MULTIPLE CHOICE Which of the following is *not* a term of the expression $-12x - 2y + 1$?

(A) $-12x$ (B) $2y$ (C) $-2y$ (D) 1

63. MULTIPLE CHOICE For a correct answer on a game show, a positive amount is added to a player's score. For an incorrect answer, a negative amount is added. If a player has a score of -100 and incorrectly answers a 300 point question, what is the player's new score?

(F) -400 (G) -200 (H) 200   (J) 400

Mixed Review

NUMERICAL EXPRESSIONS Evaluate the expression. *(Lesson 1.3)*

64. $9 - 2 \cdot 2 - 3$ **65.** $1 \cdot 10 + 5 \cdot 5$ **66.** $8^2 + 6 - 7$

67. $4 \cdot 2^3 + 9$ **68.** $4 \cdot (12 \div 6) - 5$ **69.** $(10 - 2) \cdot 7 + 8$

SPORTS The table below gives the number of male and female participants in high school sports for three school years. Based on the table, explain whether the statement is *true* or *false*. *(Lesson 1.7)*

High School Sports Participants (millions)			
Year	1994–95	1995–96	1996–97
Male	3.54	3.63	3.71
Female	2.24	2.37	2.24

DATA UPDATE of Statistical Abstract of the United States data at www.mcdougallittell.com

70. There were more than six million total participants during 1994–1995.

71. There were about six million participants in the 1996–1997 school year.

GRAPHING Graph the numbers on a number line. *(Lesson 2.1)*

72. $-1, 9, 3$ **73.** $-8, 4, -2$ **74.** $6, -5, 0$

75. $6.5, 2, -4.3$ **76.** $7, 0.5, -9.1$ **77.** $\frac{3}{4}, -\frac{3}{4}, 1$

Maintaining Skills

MULTIPLYING DECIMALS Multiply. *(Skills Review p. 759)*

78. 5×0.25 **79.** 0.1×0.4 **80.** 0.004×4.2

81. 1.69×0.02 **82.** 3.6×0.3 **83.** 9.4×2.04

GOAL

Use reasoning to find a pattern for multiplying integers.

MATERIALS

• paper
• pencil

Question

How can you use addition to find the product of integers?

Explore

1 Copy and complete the table. Use repeated addition to find the product.

Product	Equivalent sum	Solution
$3(-3)$	$-3 + (-3) + (-3)$	-9
$2(-5)$	$-5 + (-5)$	?
$4(-2)$	?	?

2 Copy and complete the table. Use the definition of opposites and your results from Step 1 to find the product.

Product	Use definition of opposites	Use result from Step 1	Solution
$-3(-3)$	$-(3)(-3)$	$-(-9)$	9
$-2(-5)$	$-(2)(-5)$	$-(?)$	?
$-4(-2)$	?	?	?

Think About It

Use repeated addition to find the product.

1. $3(2)$ **2.** $4(5)$ **3.** $2(-6)$ **4.** $5(-3)$

Use the definition of opposites and repeated addition to find the product.

5. $-2(6)$ **6.** $-3(4)$ **7.** $-5(-5)$ **8.** $-4(-3)$

LOGICAL REASONING Based on your results from Exercises 1–8, complete the statement with *always*, *sometimes*, or *never*.

9. The product of two positive integers is __?__ positive.

10. The product of a positive and a negative integer is __?__ positive.

11. The product of two negative integers is __?__ negative.

2.5 Multiplying Real Numbers

Goal
Multiply real numbers using the rule for the sign of a product.

Key Words
- closure property
- commutative property
- associative property
- identity property
- property of zero
- property of negative one

How far did a flying squirrel drop?

An object's change in position when it drops can be found by multiplying its velocity by the time it drops. In Example 4 you will find the change in position of a squirrel.

The product of any two real numbers is itself a unique real number. We say that the real numbers are *closed* under multiplication. This fact is called the **closure property of real number multiplication**. Multiplication by a positive integer can be modeled as repeated addition. For example:

$$3(-2) = (-2) + (-2) + (-2) = -6$$

This suggests that the product of a positive number and a negative number is negative. Using the definition of opposites you can see that:

$$-3(-2) = -(3)(-2) = -(-6) = 6$$

This suggests that the product of two negative numbers is positive. The general rules for the sign of a product are given below.

RULES FOR THE SIGN OF A PRODUCT OF NONZERO NUMBERS

- A product is negative if it has an *odd* number of negative factors.
- A product is positive if it has an *even* number of negative factors.

Student Help

▶ **STUDY TIP**
In Example 1 note that:
$(-2)^4 = (-2)(-2)(-2)(-2)$
$= 16$
is not the same as:
$-2^4 = -(2^4)$
$= (-1)(2)(2)(2)(2)$
$= -16$

EXAMPLE 1 Multiply Real Numbers

a. $-4(5) = -20$ — One negative factor, so product is negative.

b. $-2(5)(-3) = 30$ — Two negative factors, so product is positive.

c. $-10(-0.2)(-4) = -8$ — Three negative factors, so product is negative.

d. $(-2)^4 = 16$ — Four negative factors, so product is positive.

Checkpoint ✓ Multiply Real Numbers

Find the product.

1. $3(-5)$ **2.** $-2(4)(5)$ **3.** $-\dfrac{1}{3}(-3)(-2)$ **4.** $(-2)^3$

The rules for the sign of a product are a consequence of the following properties of multiplication.

PROPERTIES OF MULTIPLICATION

CLOSURE PROPERTY The product of any two real numbers is a unique real number.

ab is a unique real number   Example: $4 \cdot 2 = 8$

COMMUTATIVE PROPERTY The order in which two numbers are multiplied does not change the product.

$ab = ba$ Example: $3(-2) = (-2)3$

ASSOCIATIVE PROPERTY The way you group three numbers when multiplying does not change the product.

$(ab)c = a(bc)$ Example: $(-6 \cdot 2)3 = -6(2 \cdot 3)$

IDENTITY PROPERTY The product of a number and 1 is the number.

$1 \cdot a = a$ Example: $1 \cdot (-4) = -4$

PROPERTY OF ZERO The product of a number and 0 is 0.

$0 \cdot a = 0$ Example: $0 \cdot (-2) = 0$

PROPERTY OF NEGATIVE ONE The product of a number and -1 is the opposite of the number.

$-1 \cdot a = -a$ Example: $-1 \cdot (-3) = 3$

EXAMPLE 2 Products with Variable Factors

Simplify the expression.

a. $-2(-x)$ b. $3(-n)(-n)(-n)$ c. $-1(-a)^2$

Solution

a. $-2(-x) = 2x$ Two negative factors, so product is positive.

b. $3(-n)(-n)(-n) = 3(-n^3)$ Three negative factors, so product is negative.

$= -3n^3$ One negative factor, so product is negative.

c. $-1(-a)^2 = (-1)(-a)(-a)$ Write the power as a product.

$= (-1)(a^2)$ Two negative factors, so product is positive.

$= -a^2$ Property of negative one

Checkpoint ✓ Products with Variable Factors

Simplify the expression.

5. $8(-t)$ **6.** $-x(-x)(-x)(-x)$ **7.** $-7(-b)^3$

EXAMPLE ③ **Evaluate a Variable Expression**

Evaluate $-4(-1)(-x)$ when $x = -5$.

Solution   You can simplify the expression first, or substitute for x first.

$$-4(-1)(-x) = -4x$$ Simplify expression first.

$$= -4(-5)$$ Substitute −5 for x.

$$= 20$$ Two negative factors, so product is positive.

$$-4(-1)(-x) = -4(-1)[-(-5)]$$ Substitute −5 for x first.

$$= -4(-1)(5)$$ Use definition of opposites.

$$= 20$$ Two negative factors, so product is positive.

Checkpoint ✓ *Evaluate a Variable Expression*

Evaluate the expression when $x = -2$.

8. $-9(x)(-2)$ **9.** $3(4)(-x)$ **10.** $3(-x)^3$ **11.** $7(x^2)(-5)$

Link to
Science

FLYING SQUIRRELS glide through the air using "gliding membranes," which are flaps of skin that extend from their wrists to their ankles.

EXAMPLE ④ **Use Products in Real Life**

FLYING SQUIRRELS   A flying squirrel drops from a tree with a velocity of -6 feet per second. Find the *displacement*, which is the change in position, of the squirrel after 3.5 seconds.

Solution

VERBAL MODEL ┃ Displacement ┃ = ┃ Velocity ┃ · ┃ Time ┃

LABELS

Displacement = d (feet)

Velocity = -6 (feet per second)

Time = 3.5 (seconds)

ALGEBRAIC MODEL

$$d = -6 \cdot 3.5$$

$$d = -21$$

ANSWER ▶ The squirrel's change in position is -21 feet. The negative sign indicates downward motion.

Checkpoint ✓ *Use Products in Real Life*

12. A helicopter is descending at a velocity of -15 feet per second. Find the displacement of the helicopter after 4.5 seconds.

2.5 *Multiplying Real Numbers*   **95**

Guided Practice

Vocabulary Check   Match the property with the statement that illustrates it.

1. Commutative property   **A.** $-1 \cdot 9 = -9$

2. Associative property   **B.** $4(-2) = (-2)4$

3. Identity property   **C.** $0 \cdot 8 = 0$

4. Property of zero   **D.** $1 \cdot (-15) = -15$

5. Property of negative one   **E.** $-7(5 \cdot 2) = (-7 \cdot 5)2$

Skill Check   Find the product.

6. $9(-1)$ **7.** $-5(7)$ **8.** $-4(-6)$ **9.** $(-1)^5$

Simplify the expression.

10. $-3(-6)(a)$ **11.** $5(-t)(-t)(-t)(-t)$ **12.** $6(-x)^3$

Evaluate the expression for the given value of the variable.

13. $2(-5)(-x)$ when $x = 4$ **14.** $6(-2)(x)$ when $x = -3$

Practice and Applications

CLOSURE PROPERTY   Tell whether the set is closed under the operation by deciding if the combination of any two numbers in the set of numbers is itself in the set.

15. even integers under multiplication   **16.** odd integers under addition

MULTIPLYING REAL NUMBERS   Find the product.

17. $-7(4)$ **18.** $5(-5)$ **19.** $-6.3(2)$

20. $-7(-1.2)$ **21.** $-\dfrac{1}{2}\left(\dfrac{8}{3}\right)$ **22.** $-12\left(-\dfrac{1}{4}\right)$

23. $(-6)^3$ **24.** $(-4)^4$ **25.** $-(7)^2$

26. $-2(-5)(7)$ **27.** $6(9)(-1)$ **28.** $-5(-4)(-8)$

29. $2.7(-6)(-6)$ **30.** $-3.3(-1)(-1.5)$ **31.** $15\left(-\dfrac{2}{15}\right)\left(\dfrac{3}{4}\right)$

PRODUCTS WITH VARIABLE FACTORS   Simplify the expression.

32. $-3(-y)$ **33.** $7(-x)$ **34.** $-2(k)$

35. $5(-a)(-a)(-a)$ **36.** $-8(z)(z)$ **37.** $-2(5)(-r)(-r)$

38. $(-b)^3$ **39.** $-2(-x)^2$ **40.** $-(-y)^4$

Student Help

▶ **HOMEWORK HELP**
Example 1: Exs. 15–31
Example 2: Exs. 32–40
Example 3: Exs. 41–49
Example 4: Exs. 50–55

EVALUATING EXPRESSIONS **Evaluate the expression for the given value of the variable.**

41. $-8(d)$ when $d = 6$

42. $3(-4)(n)$ when $n = -2$

43. $-3(-a)(-a)$ when $a = -7$

44. $9(-2)(-r)^3$ when $r = 2$

45. $-4.1(-5)(h)$ when $h = 2$

46. $-2\left(\dfrac{11}{2}\right)(t)$ when $t = -3$

Student Help

▶**LOOK BACK**
For help with counterexamples, see p. 73

COUNTEREXAMPLES **Determine whether the statement is _true_ or _false_. If it is false, give a counterexample.**

47. $(-a) \cdot (-b) = (-b) \cdot (-a)$

48. The product $(-a) \cdot (-1)$ is always positive.

49. If $a > b$, then $a \cdot 0$ is greater than $b \cdot 0$.

Link to
Careers

MOUNTAIN GUIDES plan climbing expeditions. The guides also instruct students on basic climbing techniques, such as rappelling.

More about mountain guides is available at www.mcdougallittell.com

MOUNTAIN RAPPELLING **You rappel down the side of a mountain at a rate of 2 feet per second.**

50. Write an algebraic model for your displacement d (in feet) after t seconds.

51. What is your change in position after rappelling for 10 seconds?

52. If the mountain is 40 feet high, how much farther must you rappel before you reach the ground?

Science Link **Scientists estimate that a peregrine falcon can dive for its prey at a rate of about 300 feet per second.**

53. Write an algebraic model for the displacement d (in feet) of a peregrine falcon after t seconds.

54. What is a peregrine falcon's change in position after diving for 2 seconds?

55. If the peregrine falcon spotted its prey 750 feet below, how much farther must it dive to reach its prey?

Puzzler **A multiplication magic square is a square in which the product of the numbers in every horizontal, vertical, and main diagonal line is constant.**

56. Find the constant of the magic square shown by multiplying the numbers in the first row of the square.

57. Copy and complete the magic square by finding the missing number in each column.

58. Check your answer by finding the product of each main diagonal.

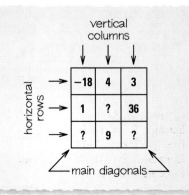

59. MULTIPLE CHOICE What does $-3(6)\left(-\dfrac{1}{3}\right)$ equal?

(A) -6 (B) -2 (C) 2 (D) 6

60. MULTIPLE CHOICE Which of the following statements is *not* true?

(F) The product of any number and zero is zero.

(G) The order in which two numbers are multiplied does not matter.

(H) The product of any number and -1 is a negative number.

(J) The product of any number and -1 is the opposite of the number.

61. MULTIPLE CHOICE Simplify the expression $2(-4)(-x)(-x)(-x)$.

(A) $-24x$ (B) $-8x^3$ (C) $8x^3$ (D) $24x$

62. MULTIPLE CHOICE Evaluate $9(-x)^2(-2)$ when $x = 3$.

(F) -162 (G) -108 (H) 108 (J) 162

Mixed Review

MENTAL MATH Use mental math to solve the equation. *(Lesson 1.4)*

63. $6 + c = 8$ **64.** $x - 7 = 4$ **65.** $8 - a = 4$

66. $3z = 15$ **67.** $(m)(2) = 24$ **68.** $r \div 6 = 2$

LINE GRAPHS Draw a line graph to represent the function given by the input-output table. *(Lesson 1.8)*

69.

Input x	1	2	3	4	5	6
Output y	22	20	18	16	14	12

70.

Input x	1	2	3	4	5	6
Output y	0	5	10	15	20	25

FINDING ABSOLUTE VALUE Evaluate the expression. *(Lesson 2.2)*

71. $|2|$ **72.** $|-6|$ **73.** $-|9|$ **74.** $-|-7|$

75. $|-7.2|$ **76.** $-|6.8|$ **77.** $|10.43|$ **78.** $-|-0.05|$

FINDING TERMS Identify the terms of the expression. *(Lesson 2.4)*

79. $12 - z$ **80.** $-t + 5$ **81.** $4w - 11$

82. $31 - 15n$ **83.** $-7x + 4x$ **84.** $-3c - 4$

Maintaining Skills

LEAST COMMON MULTIPLE Find the least common multiple of the numbers. *(Skills Review p. 761)*

85. 4 and 5   **86.** 24 and 36   **87.** 30 and 25

88. 111 and 55   **89.** 312 and 210   **90.** 176 and 264

DEVELOPING CONCEPTS
The Distributive Property

GOAL

Use reasoning to discover how to use the distributive property to write equivalent expressions.

MATERIALS

• algebra tiles

Student Help

▶ **LOOK BACK**
For help with using algebra tiles, see p. 77.

Question

How can you model equivalent expressions using algebra tiles?

Each ▢ represents 1 and each ▬ represents x.

Explore

① Model $3(2 + 4)$.

Make 3 groups each consisting of two plus four, or six, 1-tiles.

② Model $6 + 12$.

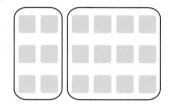

Make a group of six 1-tiles and a group of twelve 1-tiles.

Complete: The models show that $3(2 + 4) = \underline{\ ?\ }$.
This is an example of the *distributive property*.

③ Model $3(x + 4)$.

Make 3 groups each consisting of one x-tile and four 1-tiles.

④ Model $3x + 12$.

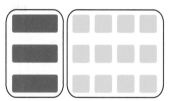

Make a group of three x-tiles and a group of twelve 1-tiles.

Complete: The models show that $3(x + 4) = \underline{\ ?\ }$.
This is another example of the distributive property.

Think About It

Each equation illustrates the distributive property. Use algebra tiles to model the equation. Draw a sketch of your models.

1. $5(1 + 2) = 5 + 10$ **2.** $2(4 + 3) = 8 + 6$ **3.** $7(1 + 1) = 7 + 7$

4. $6(x + 2) = 6x + 12$ **5.** $4(x + 4) = 4x + 16$ **6.** $3(x + 5) = 3x + 15$

7. $2(x + 3) = 2x + 6$ **8.** $5(x + 1) = 5x + 5$ **9.** $9(x + 2) = 9x + 18$

10. **LOGICAL REASONING** Use your own words to explain the distributive property. Then use a, b, and c to represent the distributive property algebraically.

The Distributive Property

Goal
Use the distributive property.

Key Words
• distributive property

How much will you pay for six CDs?

When you go shopping, you can use estimation or mental math to determine the total cost. In Example 5 you will learn how to use the *distributive property* to calculate the total cost of six CDs—*without* using a calculator.

The **distributive property** is an important algebraic property. Example 1 uses geometry to illustrate why the property is true for a single case. On the following page the property is formally defined.

Student Help

▶ **VOCABULARY TIP**
To *distribute* means to give something to each member of a group. In Example 1 you can think of the 3 as being distributed to each term in $(x + 2)$.

EXAMPLE 1 Use an Area Model

Find the area of a rectangle whose width is 3 and whose length is $x + 2$.

Solution You can find the area in two ways. Remember that the area of a rectangle is the product of the length times the width.

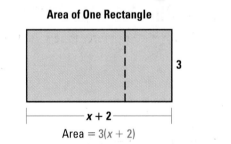

Area of One Rectangle

3

$x + 2$
Area $= 3(x + 2)$

Area of Two Rectangles

3

x 2
Area $= 3(x) + 3(2)$

ANSWER ▶ Because both expressions represent the same area, the following statement is true.

$$\text{Area} = 3(x + 2) = 3(x) + 3(2) = 3x + 6$$

Checkpoint ✓ Use an Area Model

1. Write two expressions for the area of the rectangle.

2. Write an algebraic statement that shows that the two expressions from Exercise 1 are equal.

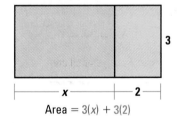

7

3   x

▶ STUDY TIP
Although four versions
of the distributive
property are listed, the
last three versions can
be derived from the first:
$a(b + c) = ab + ac$

THE DISTRIBUTIVE PROPERTY

The product of a and $(b + c)$:

$a(b + c) = ab + ac$ **Example:** $5(x + 2) = 5x + 10$

$(b + c)a = ba + ca$ **Example:** $(x + 4)8 = 8x + 32$

The product of a and $(b - c)$:

$a(b - c) = ab - ac$ **Example:** $4(x - 7) = 4x - 28$

$(b - c)a = ba - ca$ **Example:** $(x - 5)9 = 9x - 45$

EXAMPLE 2   **Use the Distributive Property with Addition**

Use the distributive property to rewrite the expression without parentheses.

a. $2(x + 5)$ **b.** $(1 + 2n)8$

Solution

a. $2(x + 5) = 2(x) + 2(5)$ Distribute 2 to each term of $(x + 5)$.

          $= 2x + 10$ Multiply.

b. $(1 + 2n)8 = (1)8 + (2n)8$ Distribute 8 to each term of $(1 + 2n)$.

          $= 8 + 16n$ Multiply.

Student Help

▶ MORE EXAMPLES

More examples
are available at
www.mcdougallittell.com

EXAMPLE 3   **Use the Distributive Property with Subtraction**

Use the distributive property to rewrite the expression without parentheses.

a. $3(1 - y)$ **b.** $(2x - 4)\frac{1}{2}$

Solution

a. $3(1 - y) = 3(1) - 3(y)$ Distribute 3 to each term of $(1 - y)$.

          $= 3 - 3y$ Multiply.

b. $(2x - 4)\frac{1}{2} = (2x)\frac{1}{2} - (4)\frac{1}{2}$ Distribute $\frac{1}{2}$ to each term of $(2x - 4)$.

          $= x - 2$ Multiply.

 **Use the Distributive Property**

**Use the distributive property to rewrite the expression without
parentheses.**

3. $5(n + 3)$ **4.** $(2p + 6)3$ **5.** $2(x - 5)$ **6.** $(3y - 9)\frac{2}{3}$

EXAMPLE **4** **Use the Distributive Property**

Use the distributive property to rewrite the expression without parentheses.

a. $-3(x + 4)$ **b.** $(y + 5)(-4)$ **c.** $-(6 - 3x)$ **d.** $(1 - t)(-9)$

Solution

a. $-3(x + 4) = -3(x) + (-3)(4)$ Use distributive property.

$= -3x - 12$ Multiply.

b. $(y + 5)(-4) = (y)(-4) + (5)(-4)$ Use distributive property.

$= -4y - 20$ Multiply.

c. $-(6 - 3x) = -1(6) - (-1)(3x)$ Use distributive property.

$= -6 + 3x$ Multiply.

d. $(1 - t)(-9) = (1)(-9) - (t)(-9)$ Use distributive property.

$= -9 + 9t$ Multiply.

Checkpoint✔ **Use the Distributive Property**

Use the distributive property to rewrite the expression without parentheses.

7. $-5(a + 2)$ **8.** $(x + 7)(-3)$ **9.** $-(4 - 2x)$ **10.** $(4 - m)(-2)$

Link to
History

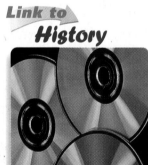

COMPACT DISCS CDs were released in the United States in 1984. That year the average cost of a CD was $17.81.

EXAMPLE **5** **Mental Math Calculations**

COMPACT DISCS You are shopping for compact discs. You want to buy 6 compact discs for $11.95 each including tax. Use the distributive property to mentally calculate the total cost of the compact discs.

Solution If you think of $11.95 as $12.00 − $.05, the mental math is easier.

$6(11.95) = 6(12 - 0.05)$ Write 11.95 as a difference.

$= 6(12) - 6(0.05)$ Use distributive property.

$= 72 - 0.30$ Find products mentally.

$= 71.70$ Find difference mentally.

ANSWER ▶ The total cost of 6 compact discs at $11.95 each is $71.70.

Checkpoint✔ **Mental Math Calculations**

Use the distributive property to mentally calculate the total cost.

11. You are buying birthday cards for 3 of your friends. Each card costs $1.25. What is the total cost of the cards?

Guided Practice

Vocabulary Check

Explain how you would use the distributive property to simplify the expression.

1. $2(x + 3)$ **2.** $(x + 4)5$ **3.** $7(x - 3)$ **4.** $(x - 6)4$

Skill Check

Use the area model shown.

5. Write two expressions for the area of the rectangle.

6. Write an algebraic statement that shows that the two expressions from Exercise 5 are equal.

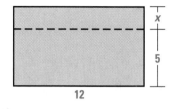

Match the expression with its simplified form.

7. $3(x + 2)$ **8.** $(x + 3)(-2)$ **9.** $-3(x - 2)$ **10.** $(3 - x)2$

A. $6 - 2x$ **B.** $-3x + 6$ **C.** $-2x - 6$ **D.** $3x + 6$

Use the distributive property and mental math to simplify the expression.

11. $4(1.15) = 4(1 + 0.15)$
$= \boxed{?}(\boxed{?}) + \boxed{?}(\boxed{?})$
$= \boxed{?} + \boxed{?}$
$= \boxed{?}$

12. $9(1.95) = 9(\boxed{?} - \boxed{?})$
$= \boxed{?}(\boxed{?}) - \boxed{?}(\boxed{?})$
$= \boxed{?} - \boxed{?}$
$= \boxed{?}$

Practice and Applications

AREA MODEL Use the area model to find two expressions for the area of the rectangle. Then write an algebraic statement that shows the two expressions are equal.

13.

14.

15.

16.

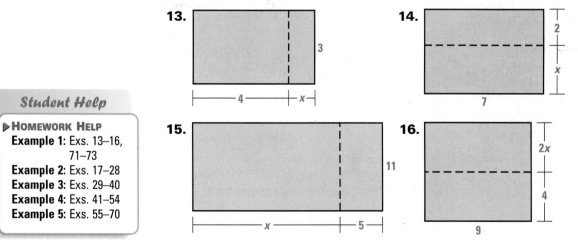

Student Help

▶ **HOMEWORK HELP**
Example 1: Exs. 13–16, 71–73
Example 2: Exs. 17–28
Example 3: Exs. 29–40
Example 4: Exs. 41–54
Example 5: Exs. 55–70

DISTRIBUTIVE PROPERTY WITH ADDITION Use the distributive property to rewrite the expression without parentheses.

17. $3(x + 4)$

18. $5(w + 6)$

19. $7(1 + t)$

20. $(y + 4)5$

21. $(2 + u)6$

22. $(x + 8)7$

23. $2(2y + 1)$

24. $(3x + 7)4$

25. $3(4 + 6a)$

26. $(9 + 3n)2$

27. $(x + 2)1.3$

28. $\frac{1}{5}(10 + 15r)$

DISTRIBUTIVE PROPERTY WITH SUBTRACTION Use the distributive property to rewrite the expression without parentheses.

29. $5(y - 2)$

30. $2(x - 3)$

31. $9(7 - a)$

32. $(x - 2)2$

33. $(7 - m)4$

34. $(n - 7)2$

35. $10(1 - 3t)$

36. $7(6w - 1)$

37. $(3x - 3)6$

38. $(9 - 5a)4$

39. $(-3.1u - 0.8)3$

40. $5\left(\frac{1}{10}x - \frac{2}{15}\right)$

DISTRIBUTIVE PROPERTY Use the distributive property to rewrite the expression without parentheses.

41. $-3(r + 8)$

42. $-2(x - 6)$

43. $-(1 + s)$

44. $(2 + t)(-2)$

45. $(y + 9)(-1)$

46. $(x - 4)(-3)$

47. $-6(4a + 3)$

48. $(9x + 1)(-7)$

49. $-(6y - 5)$

50. $(3d - 8)(-5)$

51. $(2.3 - 7w)(-6)$

52. $-\frac{3}{8}\left(x + 24\right)$

ERROR ANALYSIS In Exercises 53 and 54, find and correct the error.

53.

$9(3 - 5) = 9(3) - 5$
$\qquad = 27 - 5$
$\qquad = 22$

54.

$-2(7 - 8) = -2(7) - 2(8)$
$\qquad = -14 - 6$
$\qquad = -30$

Student Help

▶**HOMEWORK HELP**

Extra help with problem solving in Exs. 55–66 is available at www.mcdougallittell.com

MENTAL MATH Use the distributive property and mental math to simplify the expression.

55. $4(6.11)$

56. $10(7.25)$

57. $3(9.20)$

58. $7(5.98)$

59. $2(2.90)$

60. $6(8.75)$

61. $-3(4.10)$

62. $-9(1.02)$

63. $-2(11.05)$

64. $-8(2.80)$

65. $-5(10.99)$

66. $-4(5.95)$

67. CONTACT LENS SUPPLIES The saline solution that you use to clean your contact lenses is on sale for $4.99 a bottle. You decide to stock up and buy 4 bottles. Use the distributive property to mentally calculate the total cost of the bottles of saline.

68. SCHOOL SUPPLIES You are shopping for school supplies. You want to buy 7 notebooks for $1.05 each. Use the distributive property to mentally calculate the total cost of the notebooks.

69. DECORATIONS You are volunteering for a charity that is operating a haunted house. You are sent to the store to buy 5 bags of cotton balls that will be used to make spider web decorations. Each bag costs $2.09. Use the distributive property to mentally calculate the total cost of the cotton balls.

70. GROCERIES You see a sign at the grocery store that reads, "Buy 2 half-gallons of frozen yogurt and get one free." Each half-gallon of frozen yogurt costs $4.95. You decide to get three half-gallons. Use the distributive property to mentally calculate the total cost of the frozen yogurt.

FARMING You are trying to determine the size of a cornfield, so you will know how many rows of corn to plant. Let x be the width of the cornfield. Use the diagram of the farming field shown.

71. Use the diagram to find two expressions for the area of the entire field.

72. Write an algebraic statement that shows the two expressions from Exercise 71 are equal.

73. You decide to plant the cornfield so that $x = 75$ yards. What is the area of the entire field? Use one expression from Exercise 71 to find the solution and the other to check your solution.

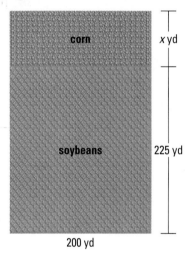

74. MULTIPLE CHOICE Which expression is equivalent to $(x + 7)3$?

   Ⓐ $x + 21$ Ⓑ $3x + 7$

   Ⓒ $3x + 10$ Ⓓ $3x + 21$

75. MULTIPLE CHOICE Which expression is equivalent to $6(x - 2)$?

   Ⓕ $6x - 2$ Ⓖ $6x - 12$

   Ⓗ $6x + 2$ Ⓙ $6x + 12$

76. MULTIPLE CHOICE Which expression is equivalent to $(5 - x)(-17)$?

   Ⓐ $5 - 17x$ Ⓑ $5 + 17x$

   Ⓒ $-85 - 17x$ Ⓓ $-85 + 17x$

77. MULTIPLE CHOICE You are buying 5 new shirts to wear to school. All of the shirts are on sale for $19.99. What expression would you use to mentally calculate the total cost of the shirts?

   Ⓕ $5(20) - 0.01$ Ⓖ $5(20 - 0.01)$ Ⓗ $5(20) + 0.01$ Ⓙ $5(20 + 0.01)$

EXPRESSIONS WITH FRACTION BARS Evaluate the expression. Then simplify the answer. *(Lesson 1.3)*

78. $\dfrac{10 \cdot 8}{4^2 \cdot 4}$ **79.** $\dfrac{6^2 - 12}{3^2 + 1}$ **80.** $\dfrac{75 - 5^2}{13 + 3 \cdot 4}$

81. $\dfrac{3 \cdot 7 + 9}{2^4 + 5 - 11}$ **82.** $\dfrac{4 \cdot 2 + 5^3}{3^2 - 2}$ **83.** $\dfrac{6 + 7^2}{3^3 - 9 - 7}$

NAMING PROPERTIES Name the property shown by the statement. *(Lesson 2.3)*

84. $-10 + (-25) = -25 + (-10)$ **85.** $-19 + 0 = -19$

86. $32 + (-32) = 0$ **87.** $(-13 + 8) + 7 = -13 + (8 + 7)$

EVALUATING EXPRESSIONS Evaluate the expression. *(Lesson 2.4)*

88. $6 - 7$ **89.** $9 - (-3)$ **90.** $4 - 8 - 3$

91. $6 - (-8) - 11$ **92.** $7.2 - 9 - 8.5$ **93.** $\dfrac{1}{3} - \dfrac{2}{3} - 1$

DECIMALS AND FRACTIONS Write the decimal as a fraction in simplest form. *(Skills Review p. 767)*

94. 0.14 **95.** 0.25 **96.** 0.34 **97.** 0.50

98. 0.75 **99.** 0.82 **100.** 0.90 **101.** 0.96

Quiz 2

Evaluate the function when $x = -3, -1, 1,$ and 3. Organize your results in a table. *(Lesson 2.4)*

1. $y = x - 12$ **2.** $y = 27 - x$ **3.** $y = x - \dfrac{1}{4}$

Find the terms of the expression. *(Lesson 2.4)*

4. $2x - 9$ **5.** $8 - x$ **6.** $-10x + 4$

7. STOCK MARKET The daily closing prices for a company's stock are $19.63, $19.88, $20.00, $19.88, and $19.75. Find the day-to-day change in the closing price. *(Lesson 2.4)*

Find the product. *(Lesson 2.5)*

8. $-7(9)$ **9.** $-5(-6)$ **10.** $35(-80)$

11. $-1.8(-6)$ **12.** $-15\left(\dfrac{1}{5}\right)$ **13.** $-10(-3)(9)$

Rewrite the expression without parentheses. *(Lesson 2.6)*

14. $(x + 2)11$ **15.** $5(12 - y)$ **16.** $-4(3a - 4)$

17. SHOPPING You want to buy 2 pairs of jeans for $24.95 each. Use the distributive property to mentally calculate the total cost of the jeans. *(Lesson 2.6)*

2.7 Combining Like Terms

Goal
Simplify an expression by combining like terms.

Key Words
- coefficient
- like terms
- simplified expression

How far is it to the National Air and Space Museum?

An algebraic expression is easier to evaluate when it is *simplified*. In Example 4 you will use the distributive property to simplify an algebraic expression that represents the distance to the National Air and Space Museum.

In a term that is the product of a number and a variable, the number is called the **coefficient** of the variable.

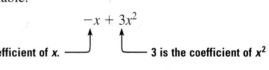

$$-x + 3x^2$$

−1 is the coefficient of *x*. 3 is the coefficient of x^2

Like terms are terms in an expression that have the same variable raised to the same power. For example, $8x$ and $3x$ are like terms. Numbers are considered to be like terms. The terms x^2 and x, however, are *not* like terms. They have the same variable, but it is not to the same power.

EXAMPLE 1 Identify Like Terms

Identify the like terms in the expression $-x^2 + 5x - 4 - 3x + 2$.

Solution

Begin by writing the expression as a sum:

$-x^2 + 5x + (-4) + (-3x) + 2$

ANSWER ▶ The terms $5x$ and $-3x$ are like terms. The terms -4 and 2 are also like terms.

Checkpoint ✓ *Identify Like Terms*

Identify the like terms in the expression.

1. $-5x^2 - x + 8 + 6x - 10$ 　　　　**2.** $-3x^2 + 2x + x^2 - 4 + 7x$

SIMPLIFIED EXPRESSIONS The distributive property allows you to *combine like terms* by adding their coefficients. An expression is **simplified** if it has no grouping symbols and if all the like terms have been combined.

EXAMPLE **2** **Combine Like Terms**

Simplify the expression.

a. $8x + 3x$

b. $2y^2 + 7y^2 - y^2 + 2$

Solution

a. $8x + 3x = (8 + 3)x$ Use distributive property.

$ = 11x$ Add coefficients.

b. $2y^2 + 7y^2 - y^2 + 2 = 2y^2 + 7y^2 - 1y^2 + 2$ Coefficient of $-y^2$ is -1.

$ = (2 + 7 - 1)y^2 + 2$ Use distributive property.

$ = 8y^2 + 2$ Add coefficients.

EXAMPLE **3** **Simplify Expressions with Grouping Symbols**

Simplify the expression.

a. $8 - 2(x + 4)$

b. $2(x + 3) + 3(5 - x)$

Solution

a. $8 - 2(x + 4)$

$ = 8 - 2(x) + (-2)(4)$ Use distributive property.

$ = 8 - 2x - 8$ Multiply.

$ = -2x + 8 - 8$ Group like terms.

$ = -2x$ Combine like terms.

b. $2(x + 3) + 3(5 - x)$

$ = 2(x) + 2(3) + 3(5) + 3(-x)$ Use distributive property.

$ = 2x + 6 + 15 - 3x$ Multiply.

$ = 2x - 3x + 6 + 15$ Group like terms.

$ = -x + 21$ Combine like terms.

Checkpoint ✓ **Simplify Expressions**

Simplify the expression.

3. $5x - 2x$

4. $8m - m - 3m + 5$

5. $-x^2 + 5x + x^2$

6. $3(y + 2) - 4y$

7. $9x - 4(2x - 1)$

8. $-(z + 2) - 2(1 - z)$

SUBWAY The Metrorail, in Washington, D.C., has over 90 miles of rail line and serves an area of about 1500 square miles.

EXAMPLE **4** **Simplify a Function**

SUBWAY It takes you 50 minutes to get to the National Air and Space Museum. You spend t minutes riding the subway at an average speed of 0.5 mile per minute. The rest of the time is spent walking at 0.05 mile per minute.

   a. Write and simplify a function that gives the total distance you travel.

   b. If you spend 40 minutes on the subway, how far is it to the museum?

Solution

a. **VERBAL MODEL**

$$\boxed{\text{Distance}} = \boxed{\begin{array}{c}\text{Subway}\\\text{speed}\end{array}} \cdot \boxed{\begin{array}{c}\text{Time}\\\text{riding}\end{array}} + \boxed{\begin{array}{c}\text{Walking}\\\text{speed}\end{array}} \cdot \boxed{\begin{array}{c}\text{Time}\\\text{walking}\end{array}}$$

LABELS

Distance = d (miles)

Subway speed = **0.5**   (mile per minute)

Time riding = t (minutes)

Walking speed = **0.05**   (mile per minute)

Time walking = **50 − t**   (minutes)

ALGEBRAIC MODEL

$$d = 0.5\,t + 0.05\,(50 - t)$$

You can use the distributive property to simplify the function.

$d = 0.5t + 0.05(50 - t)$	Write original function.
$\quad = 0.5t + 0.05(50) - 0.05(t)$	Use distributive property.
$\quad = 0.5t + 2.5 - 0.05t$	Multiply.
$\quad = 0.45t + 2.5$	Combine like terms.

ANSWER ▶ The total distance you travel is given by $d = 0.45t + 2.5$, where t represents 0 to 50 minutes.

b. To find the total distance, evaluate the function for a time of $t = 40$.

$d = 0.45t + 2.5$	Write simplified function.
$\quad = 0.45(40) + 2.5$	Substitute 40 for t.
$\quad = 20.5$	Multiply and add.

ANSWER ▶ It is about 21 miles to the museum.

 **Simplify a Function**

It takes you 45 minutes to get to school. You spend t minutes riding the bus at an average speed of 0.4 mile per minute. The rest of the time is spent walking at 0.06 mile per minute.

9. Write and simplify a function that gives the total distance you travel.

10. If you ride the bus for 30 minutes, how far away is your school?

Guided Practice

Vocabulary Check

1. In the expression $7x^2 - 5x + 10$, what is the coefficient of the x^2-term? What is the coefficient of the x-term?

2. Identify the like terms in the expression $-6 - 3x^2 + 3x - 4x + 9x^2$.

Skill Check

Simplify the expression by combining like terms if possible. If not possible, write *already simplified*.

3. $5r + r$ **4.** $w - 3w$ **5.** $-4k - 8 + 4k$

6. $12 - 10m + m - 3$ **7.** $2a^2 + 3a + 2a^2 - 5$ **8.** $8 - 4t + 6t^2$

Simplify the expression.

9. $14f + 4(f + 1)$ **10.** $21g - 2(g - 4)$ **11.** $-5(2m + 4) - m$

12. $7(3a + 2) + 5$ **13.** $5(x - 7) + 4(x + 2)$ **14.** $2(4t - 1) - 4(1 - t)$

Practice and Applications

IDENTIFY LIKE TERMS Identify the like terms in the expression.

15. $3a + 5a$ **16.** $5s^2 - 10s^2$

17. $m + 8 + 6m$ **18.** $2p + 1 + 2p + 5$

19. $-6w - 12 - 3w + 2w^2$ **20.** $3x^2 + 4x + 8x - 7x^2$

COMBINING LIKE TERMS Simplify the expression by combining like terms if possible. If not possible, write *already simplified*.

21. $-12m + 5m$ **22.** $4y - 3y$ **23.** $3c - 5 - c$

24. $5 - h + 2$ **25.** $r + 2r + 3r - 7$ **26.** $8 + 2z + 4 + 3z$

27. $2n - 3 - n^2$ **28.** $6a - 2a^2 + 4a - a^2$ **29.** $p^2 + 4p + 5p^2 - 2$

SIMPLIFYING EXPRESSIONS Simplify the expression.

30. $-10(b - 1) + 4b$ **31.** $9 - 4(9 + y)$ **32.** $6(4 + f) - 8f$

33. $1 - 2(6 + 3r)$ **34.** $-5(2 + 7x) - 3x$ **35.** $5(2m + 5) - 6$

36. $3(4p + 3) + 4(p - 1)$ **37.** $9(c + 3) - 7(c - 3)$ **38.** $4(x + 2) - (x + 2)$

ERROR ANALYSIS In Exercises 39 and 40, find and correct the error.

39.

$$3x + 7 - 2x = 16$$
$$8x = 16$$

40.

$$3(x - 2) + 5x = 3(6x - 2)$$
$$= 18x - 6$$

Student Help

▶ **HOMEWORK HELP**
Example 1: Exs. 15–20
Example 2: Exs. 21–29, 39, 41, 42
Example 3: Exs. 30–38, 40, 43, 44
Example 4: Exs. 45–52

2.8 Dividing Real Numbers

Goal
Divide real numbers and use division to simplify algebraic expressions.

Key Words
• reciprocal

How fast does a hot-air balloon descend?

In Lesson 2.5 you learned that a downward displacement is measured by a negative number. In the example on page 117 you will divide a negative displacement by time to find the velocity of a hot-air balloon that is descending.

Two numbers whose product is 1 are called **reciprocals**. For instance, $-\frac{2}{5}$ and $-\frac{5}{2}$ are reciprocals because $\left(-\frac{2}{5}\right)\left(-\frac{5}{2}\right) = 1$.

INVERSE PROPERTY OF MULTIPLICATION

For every nonzero number a, there is a unique number $\frac{1}{a}$ such that:

$$a \cdot \frac{1}{a} = 1 \text{ and } \frac{1}{a} \cdot a = 1$$

You can use a reciprocal to write a division expression as a product.

DIVISION RULE

To divide a number a by a nonzero number b, multiply a by the reciprocal of b. The result is the quotient of a and b.

$$a \div b = a \cdot \frac{1}{b}$$

Example: $-1 \div 3 = -1 \cdot \frac{1}{3} = -\frac{1}{3}$

EXAMPLE 1 Divide Real Numbers

a. $10 \div (-2) = 10 \cdot \left(-\frac{1}{2}\right) = -5$

b. $0 \div \frac{5}{7} = 0 \cdot \frac{7}{5} = 0$

c. $-39 \div \left(-4\frac{1}{3}\right) = -39 \div \left(-\frac{13}{3}\right) = -39 \cdot \left(-\frac{3}{13}\right) = 9$

Student Help

▶ **STUDY TIP**
When you divide by a mixed number, it is usually easiest to first rewrite the mixed number as an improper fraction.

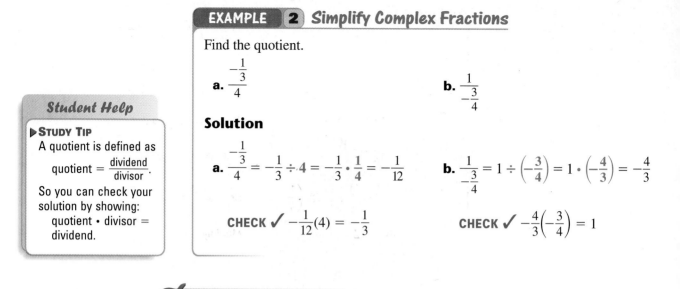

EXAMPLE 2 Simplify Complex Fractions

Find the quotient.

a. $\dfrac{-\frac{1}{3}}{4}$

b. $\dfrac{1}{-\frac{3}{4}}$

Solution

a. $\dfrac{-\frac{1}{3}}{4} = -\dfrac{1}{3} \div 4 = -\dfrac{1}{3} \cdot \dfrac{1}{4} = -\dfrac{1}{12}$

b. $\dfrac{1}{-\frac{3}{4}} = 1 \div \left(-\dfrac{3}{4}\right) = 1 \cdot \left(-\dfrac{4}{3}\right) = -\dfrac{4}{3}$

CHECK ✓ $-\dfrac{1}{12}(4) = -\dfrac{1}{3}$

CHECK ✓ $-\dfrac{4}{3}\left(-\dfrac{3}{4}\right) = 1$

Checkpoint ✓ **Divide Real Numbers**

Find the quotient.

1. $8 \div (-4)$　　**2.** $-5 \div \left(-2\frac{1}{2}\right)$　　**3.** $\dfrac{-\frac{3}{4}}{3}$　　　**4.** $\dfrac{3}{-\frac{3}{4}}$

In Examples 1 and 2 notice that applying the division rule suggests the following rule for finding the sign of a quotient.

THE SIGN OF A QUOTIENT RULE

• The quotient of two numbers with the same sign is positive.
$$-a \div (-b) = a \div b = \frac{a}{b}$$
Examples:　$-20 \div (-5) = 4$
$20 \div 5 = 4$

• The quotient of two numbers with opposite signs is negative.
$$-a \div b = a \div (-b) = -\frac{a}{b}$$
Examples:　$-20 \div 5 = -4$
$20 \div (-5) = -4$

EXAMPLE 3 Evaluate an Expression

Evaluate $\dfrac{-2a}{a+b}$ when $a = -2$ and $b = -3$.

Solution

$\dfrac{-2a}{a+b} = \dfrac{-2(-2)}{-2+(-3)}$　　　Substitute -2 for a and -3 for b.

$= \dfrac{4}{-5}$　　　Simplify numerator and denominator.

$= -\dfrac{4}{5}$　　　Quotient of two numbers with opposite signs is negative.

EXAMPLE 4 Simplify an Expression

Simplify $\dfrac{32x - 8}{4}$.

Solution

$$\dfrac{32x - 8}{4} = (32x - 8) \div 4 \qquad \text{Rewrite fraction as division expression.}$$

$$= (32x - 8) \cdot \dfrac{1}{4} \qquad \text{Multiply by reciprocal.}$$

$$= (32x)\left(\dfrac{1}{4}\right) - (8)\left(\dfrac{1}{4}\right) \qquad \text{Use distributive property.}$$

$$= 8x - 2 \qquad \text{Multiply.}$$

Checkpoint ✓ Evaluate and Simplify Expressions

5. Evaluate $\dfrac{-y}{2x + 1}$ when $x = 2$ and $y = -5$.   **6.** Simplify $\dfrac{24 - 8x}{-4}$.

When a function is defined by an equation and its domain is not specified otherwise, its domain consists of input values for which the function can be evaluated.

EXAMPLE 5 Find the Domain of a Function

Student Help

▶ **MORE EXAMPLES**

More examples are available at www.mcdougallittell.com

To find the domain of the function $y = \dfrac{-x}{1 - x}$, input some sample values of x.

INPUT	SUBSTITUTE	OUTPUT
$x = -1$	$y = \dfrac{-(-1)}{1 - (-1)}$	$y = \dfrac{1}{2}$
$x = 0$	$y = \dfrac{-0}{1 - 0}$	$y = 0$
$x = 1$	$y = \dfrac{-1}{1 - 1}$	Undefined
$x = 2$	$y = \dfrac{-2}{1 - 2}$	$y = 2$

ANSWER ▶ From the list you can see that $x = 1$ is not in the domain of the function because you cannot divide by zero. All other real numbers are in the domain. The domain is all real numbers *except* $x = 1$.

Checkpoint ✓ Find the Domain of a Function

Find the domain of the function.

7. $y = \dfrac{2x}{x - 2}$ **8.** $y = \dfrac{7}{8 - x}$ **9.** $y = \dfrac{5x}{2}$ **10.** $y = \dfrac{10}{x}$

Guided Practice

Vocabulary Check **Complete the statement.**

1. The product of a number and its ___?___ is 1.

2. The result of $a \div b$ is the ___?___ of a and b.

Skill Check **Find the reciprocal of the number.**

3. 32 **4.** -7 **5.** $-\dfrac{1}{5}$ **6.** $4\dfrac{2}{3}$

Find the quotient.

7. $-12 \div 3$ **8.** $-7 \div -\dfrac{1}{2}$ **9.** $\dfrac{1}{5} \div \left(-\dfrac{1}{10}\right)$ **10.** $-8 \div 2\dfrac{2}{3}$

11. Evaluate $\dfrac{a-4}{b}$ when $a = -2$ and $b = -3$. **12.** Simplify $\dfrac{36 - 12x}{-6}$.

Find the domain of the function.

13. $y = \dfrac{1}{x-4}$ **14.** $y = \dfrac{x}{5}$ **15.** $y = \dfrac{1}{7x}$ **16.** $\dfrac{x+1}{x+2}$

Practice and Applications

ERROR ANALYSIS **In Exercises 17 and 18, find and correct the error.**

17. $-9 \div \dfrac{1}{3} = -9 \cdot \dfrac{1}{3}$

18. $\dfrac{2}{5} \div \left(-\dfrac{8}{15}\right) = \dfrac{5}{2} \cdot \left(-\dfrac{8}{15}\right)$

DIVIDING REAL NUMBERS **Find the quotient.**

19. $9 \div (-3)$ **20.** $-10 \div (-5)$ **21.** $-4 \div 4$ **22.** $8 \div (-2)$

23. $-45 \div 9$ **24.** $-24 \div 4$ **25.** $-50 \div (-25)$ **26.** $-51 \div 17$

27. $6 \div \left(-\dfrac{1}{2}\right)$ **28.** $-9 \div \left(-\dfrac{3}{4}\right)$ **29.** $-7 \div 8\dfrac{2}{5}$ **30.** $54 \div \left(-2\dfrac{4}{7}\right)$

Student Help

▶**HOMEWORK HELP**
Example 1: Exs. 17–30
Example 2: Exs. 31–38
Example 3: Exs. 39–42
Example 4: Exs. 43–48
Example 5: Exs. 49–52

SIMPLIFYING COMPLEX FRACTIONS **Find the quotient.**

31. $\dfrac{-6}{-\frac{1}{2}}$ **32.** $\dfrac{3}{-\frac{5}{6}}$ **33.** $\dfrac{-18}{\frac{3}{8}}$ **34.** $\dfrac{-20}{-\frac{3}{5}}$

35. $\dfrac{\frac{1}{3}}{-3}$ **36.** $\dfrac{-\frac{8}{9}}{-2}$ **37.** $\dfrac{-\frac{21}{2}}{7}$ **38.** $\dfrac{-\frac{12}{5}}{-8}$

Student Help

▶HOMEWORK HELP

Extra help with problem solving in Exs. 39–42 is available at www.mcdougallittell.com

EVALUATING EXPRESSIONS Evaluate the expression for the given value(s) of the variable(s).

39. $\dfrac{x - 5}{6}$ when $x = 3$

40. $\dfrac{3r - 3}{11}$ when $r = -10$

41. $\dfrac{3a - b}{a}$ when $a = -3$ and $b = 3$

42. $\dfrac{2 - 4x}{y}$ when $x = 2$ and $y = \dfrac{1}{2}$

SIMPLIFYING EXPRESSIONS Simplify the expression.

43. $\dfrac{18x - 9}{3}$

44. $\dfrac{22r + 10}{-2}$

45. $\dfrac{-56 + h}{-8}$

46. $\dfrac{45 - 5n}{5}$

47. $\dfrac{-44 - 8t}{-4}$

48. $\dfrac{60y - 108}{12}$

FINDING THE DOMAIN Find the domain of the function.

49. $y = \dfrac{1}{x + 2}$

50. $y = \dfrac{1}{3x}$

51. $y = \dfrac{x + 6}{4}$

52. $y = \dfrac{10 - x}{7 - x}$

EXAMPLE Find a Velocity

HOT-AIR BALLOONING You are descending in a hot-air balloon at the rate of 500 feet every 40 seconds. What is your velocity?

Solution

VERBAL MODEL		
	$\textbf{Velocity} = \dfrac{\boxed{\textbf{Displacement}}}{\boxed{\textbf{Time}}}$	

LABELS

Velocity = $\boxed{v}$ (feet per second)

Displacement = $\boxed{-500}$ (feet)

Time = $\boxed{40}$ (seconds)

ALGEBRAIC MODEL

$v = \dfrac{-500}{40} = -12.5$

ANSWER ▶ Your velocity is -12.5 feet per second.

Find the velocity of the object.

53. A submarine descends 21 meters in 2 seconds.

54. An airplane descends 20,000 feet in 25 minutes.

Standardized Test Practice

55. MULTIPLE CHOICE Which of the following statements is *false*?

(A) The reciprocal of any negative number is a negative number.

(B) The reciprocal of any positive number is a positive number.

(C) Dividing by a nonzero number is the same as multiplying by its reciprocal.

(D) The reciprocal of any number is greater than zero and less than 1.

MENTAL MATH Use mental math to solve the equation. *(Lesson 1.4)*

56. $x + 17 = 25$ **57.** $a - 5 = 19$ **58.** $34 - n = 17$

59. $2b = 10$ **60.** $y \div 4 = 6$ **61.** $\dfrac{60}{x} = 6$

TRANSLATING SENTENCES Write the sentence as an equation or an inequality. Let *x* represent the number. *(Lesson 1.5)*

62. 9 is equal to a number decreased by 21.

63. The product of 2 and a number is greater than or equal to 7.

64. 3 is the quotient of a number and -6.

EVALUATING EXPRESSIONS Evaluate the expression. *(Lesson 2.4)*

65. $-8 - 4 - 9$ **66.** $12 - (-8) - 5$ **67.** $-6.3 - 4.1 - 9.5$

68. $1.4 - 6.2 - 9.1$ **69.** $5 - \dfrac{1}{2} - \dfrac{1}{4}$ **70.** $-\dfrac{2}{3} - \dfrac{1}{6} - \left(-\dfrac{5}{9}\right)$

Maintaining Skills

COMPARING NUMBERS Complete the statement using <, >, or =. *(Skills Review p. 770)*

71. -3 ? 3 **72.** 5 ? -6 **73.** -8 ? 9 **74.** -7 ? -4

75. 0 ? -2 **76.** -1 ? -1 **77.** -6 ? 2 **78.** -4 ? -5

Quiz 3

Identify the like terms in the expression. *(Lesson 2.7)*

1. $3x - 7x + 4$ **2.** $6a - 5 + 9a + 10$ **3.** $-5p + 7p^2 - p$

Simplify the expression. *(Lesson 2.7)*

4. $-17t - 9t$ **5.** $5 + 3d - d + 2$ **6.** $6g^2 - 8g - 5g^2$

7. $3(a + 1) - 7$ **8.** $-2(4 - p) + p - 1$ **9.** $-(w - 7) - 2(1 + w)$

Find the quotient. *(Lesson 2.8)*

10. $15 \div (-3)$ **11.** $-144 \div (-9)$ **12.** $-12 \div \dfrac{3}{8}$

13. $-28 \div \left(-2\dfrac{4}{7}\right)$ **14.** $\dfrac{-36}{\frac{2}{3}}$ **15.** $\dfrac{-\frac{1}{4}}{-2}$

Simplify the expression. *(Lesson 2.8)*

16. $\dfrac{20 - 8x}{4}$ **17.** $\dfrac{9x + 1}{-3}$ **18.** $\dfrac{-15x + 10}{-5}$

Find the domain of the function. *(Lesson 2.8)*

19. $y = \dfrac{2}{2 + x}$ **20.** $y = \dfrac{x}{8}$ **21.** $y = \dfrac{3x + 1}{x}$

Extension

Inductive and Deductive Reasoning

Goal

Identify and use inductive and deductive reasoning.

Key Words

- inductive reasoning
- deductive reasoning
- if-then statement
- hypothesis
- conclusion

INDUCTIVE REASONING Reasoning is used in mathematics, science, and everyday life. When you make a general statement based on several observations, you are using **inductive reasoning**. Such a statement is *not* always true. If you can find just one counterexample, then you have proved the statement to be false.

EXAMPLE **1** Inductive Reasoning in Everyday Life

Your math teacher has given your class a homework assignment every Monday for the last three weeks.

a. Using inductive reasoning, what could you conclude?

b. What counterexample would show that your conclusion is false?

Solution

a. From your observations, you conclude that your math teacher will give your class a homework assignment every Monday.

b. A counterexample would be for your teacher *not* to give a homework assignment one Monday.

Student Help

▶ LOOK BACK
For help with counterexamples, see p. 73.

For help with counterexamples, see p. 73.

EXAMPLE **2** Inductive Reasoning and Sequences

Observe the following sequence of numbers. Find the pattern. Then predict the next three numbers.

$$1, 5, 9, 13, 17, 21, \boxed{?}, \boxed{?}, ?$$

Solution

Notice that each number is 4 more than the previous number.

$$1, \quad 5, \quad 9, \quad 13, \quad 17, \quad 21$$

$$+4 \quad +4 \quad +4 \quad +4 \quad +4$$

You can conclude that the next three numbers would be $21 + 4 = \mathbf{25}$, $25 + 4 = \mathbf{29}$, and $29 + 4 = \mathbf{33}$.

Checkpoint ✓ *Use Inductive Reasoning*

Use inductive reasoning to predict the next three numbers in the sequence.

1. $0, 3, 6, 9, 12, 15, \boxed{?}, \boxed{?}, \boxed{?}$

2. $1, 4, 9, 16, 25, 36, \boxed{?}, \boxed{?}, \boxed{?}$

DEDUCTIVE REASONING When you use facts, definitions, rules, or properties to reach a conclusion, you are using **deductive reasoning**. A conclusion reached in this way is *always* true.

Student Help

▶ **LOOK BACK**
For help with the properties of addition, see p. 79.

EXAMPLE 3 Deductive Reasoning in Mathematics

Prove that $(a + b) + c = (c + b) + a$ is true when a, b, and c are real numbers. Justify each step using the properties of addition.

$$(a + b) + c = c + (a + b) \qquad \text{Commutative property of addition}$$
$$= c + (b + a) \qquad \text{Commutative property of addition}$$
$$= (c + b) + a \qquad \text{Associative property of addition}$$

IF-THEN STATEMENTS Deductive reasoning often uses **if-then statements**. The *if* part is called the **hypothesis** and the *then* part is called the **conclusion**. When deductive reasoning has been used to *prove* an if-then statement, then the fact that the hypothesis is true implies that the conclusion is true.

EXAMPLE 4 Use of If-Then Statements

Your teacher tells you the fact that if you receive an A on the final exam, then you will earn a final grade of A in the course. You receive an A on the final exam. Draw a conclusion about your final grade.

Solution The hypothesis of the if-then statement is "you receive an A on the final exam." The conclusion is "you will earn a final grade of A in the course." The hypothesis is true, so you can conclude that your final grade will be an A.

Exercises

In Exercises 1–3, tell whether the conclusion is based on inductive reasoning, deductive reasoning, or an if-then statement. Explain.

1. You have observed that in your neighborhood the mail is not delivered on Sunday. It is Sunday, so you conclude that the mail will not be delivered.

2. If the last digit of a number is 2, then the number is divisible by 2. You conclude that 765,432 is divisible by 2.

3. You notice that for several values of x, the value of x^2 is greater than x. You conclude that the square of a number is greater than the number itself.

4. Find a counterexample to show that the conclusion in Exercise 3 is false.

5. Use inductive reasoning to predict the next three numbers in the sequence: 1, 2, 4, 8, 16, 32, ? , ? , ? .

6. Use deductive reasoning to prove that $(x + 2) + (-2) = x$ is true when x is a real number. Write each step and justify it using the properties of addition.

7. Give an example of inductive reasoning and an example of deductive reasoning.

KEY WORDS

- **real number**, *p. 65*
- **real number line**, *p. 65*
- **positive number**, *p. 65*
- **negative number**, *p. 65*
- **integer**, *p. 65*
- **whole number**, *p. 65*
- **graph of a number**, *p. 65*
- **opposite**, *p. 71*
- **absolute value**, *p. 71*
- **counterexample**, *p. 73*
- **closure property of real number addition**, *p. 78*

- **commutative property of addition**, *p. 79*
- **associative property of addition**, *p. 79*
- **identity property of addition**, *p. 79*
- **inverse property of addition**, *p. 79*
- **term**, *p. 87*
- **closure property of real number multiplication**, *p. 93*
- **commutative property of multiplication**, *p. 94*

- **associative property of multiplication**, *p. 94*
- **identity property of multiplication**, *p. 94*
- **multiplicative property of zero**, *p. 94*
- **multiplicative property of negative one**, *p. 94*
- **distributive property**, *p. 100*
- **coefficient**, *p. 107*
- **like terms**, *p. 107*
- **simplified expression**, *p. 108*
- **reciprocal**, *p. 113*

2.1   THE REAL NUMBER LINE

Examples on pp. 65–67

EXAMPLE   Write the numbers 2, $-\frac{1}{2}$, 0.8, $-1\frac{1}{4}$, -2, and -0.8 in increasing order.

From the graph, you can see that the order is: -2, $-1\frac{1}{4}$, -0.8, $-\frac{1}{2}$, 0.8, and 2.

Write the numbers in increasing order.

1. $-3, 5, -4, -6, 2, 1$ **2.** $3.1, -1.9, 5, 4.6, 5.3, -2$ **3.** $4, -\frac{1}{2}, 6, -2, \frac{2}{3}, -1, 1$

2.2   ABSOLUTE VALUE

Examples on pp. 71–73

EXAMPLES   You can find the absolute value of any number.

a. $|6.7| = 6.7$ If a is positive, then $|a| = a$

b. $\left|-\frac{7}{9}\right| = -\left(-\frac{7}{9}\right) = \frac{7}{9}$ If a is negative, then $|a| = -a$; use definition of opposites.

Evaluate the expression.

4. $|3|$ **5.** $|-5|$ **6.** $-|100|$ **7.** $-|-45|$

8. $|-3.2|$ **9.** $-|-9.1|$ **10.** $-\left|\dfrac{1}{9}\right|$ **11.** $\left|3\dfrac{1}{2}\right|$

2.3   ADDING REAL NUMBERS

Examples on pp. 78–80

> **EXAMPLES** To add real numbers, use the rules and properties of addition.
>
> **a.** $4 + (-8) + (-6) = 4 + [-8 + (-6)]$ Use associative property of addition.
>
> $\qquad\qquad\qquad\quad = 4 + (-14)$ Add -8 and -6.
>
> $\qquad\qquad\qquad\quad = -10$ Add 4 and -14.
>
> **b.** $4.3 + (-7) + 5.7 = 4.3 + 5.7 + (-7)$ Use commutative property of addition.
>
> $\qquad\qquad\qquad\quad\ \ = 10 + (-7)$ Add 4.3 and 5.7.
>
> $\qquad\qquad\qquad\quad\ \ = 3$ Add 10 and -7.

Find the sum.

12. $9 + (-10) + (-3)$ **13.** $-35 + 41 + (-18)$ **14.** $-2.5 + 6 + (-3)$

15. $2.4 + (-3.4) + 6$ **16.** $9 + (-3) + \dfrac{1}{4}$ **17.** $\dfrac{1}{3} + (-8) + \left(-\dfrac{1}{3}\right)$

2.4   SUBTRACTING REAL NUMBERS

Examples on pp. 86–88

> **EXAMPLES** To subtract real numbers, add their opposites.
>
> **a.** $10 - (-8) - 16 = 10 + 8 + (-16)$ Add opposites of -8 and 16.
>
> $\qquad\qquad\qquad\ = 18 + (-16)$ Add 10 and 8.
>
> $\qquad\qquad\qquad\ = 2$ Add 18 and -16.
>
> **b.** $9.6 - 6 - 3.5 = 9.6 + (-6) + (-3.5)$ Add opposites of 6 and 3.5.
>
> $\qquad\qquad\qquad\ = 3.6 + (-3.5)$ Add 9.6 and -6.
>
> $\qquad\qquad\qquad\ = 0.1$ Add 3.6 and -3.5.

Evaluate the expression.

18. $-2 - 7 - (-8)$ **19.** $18 - 14 - (-15)$ **20.** $2 - 1.5 - 4$

21. $-5.7 - (-3.1) - 8.6$ **22.** $-7 - \dfrac{3}{8} - 13$ **23.** $-3 - \left(-\dfrac{1}{4}\right) - \dfrac{1}{2}$

2.5 MULTIPLYING REAL NUMBERS

Examples on pp. 93–95

EXAMPLES Use the rules for the sign of a product to find products and simplify expressions.

a. $-3(6) = -18$ One negative factor, so product is negative.

b. $-6(-2) = 12$ Two negative factors, so product is positive.

c. $-9(-4)(-x) = -36x$ Three negative factors, so product is negative.

d. $(-x)^4 = x^4$ Four negative factors, so product is positive.

Find the product.

24. $-3(12)$

25. $-40(-15)$

26. $-7(-6)(-2)$

27. $-14(-0.3)$

28. $-3.2(10)(-2)$

29. $24\left(-\dfrac{7}{12}\right)$

Simplify the expression.

30. $-5(-x)$

31. $3(-f)$

32. $10(-a)(-a)(-a)$

33. $-6(2)(t)(t)$

34. $(-y)^3$

35. $-81(-b)^2$

2.6 THE DISTRIBUTIVE PROPERTY

Examples on pp. 100–102

EXAMPLES Use the distributive property to rewrite expressions without parentheses.

a. $8(x + 3) = 8(x) + 8(3)$ Use distributive property.

      $= 8x + 24$ Multiply.

b. $(a - 6)4 = (a)(4) - (6)(4)$ Use distributive property.

      $= 4a - 24$ Multiply.

c. $-7(y - 5) = -7(y) - (-7)(5)$ Use distributive property.

      $= -7y + 35$ Multiply.

d. $(2 + x)(-2) = (2)(-2) + (x)(-2)$ Use distributive property.

      $= -4 - 2x$ Multiply.

Use the distributive property to rewrite the expression without parentheses.

36. $5(x + 12)$

37. $(y + 6)9$

38. $10(z - 1)$

39. $(3 - w)2$

40. $-2(x + 13)$

41. $(t + 11)(-3)$

42. $-8(m - 7)$

43. $(x - 10)(-6)$

44. $-2.5(s - 5)$

2.7 COMBINING LIKE TERMS

Examples on pp. 107–109

EXAMPLES To combine like terms, add their coefficients.

a. $7x - 6x + x = (7 - 6 + 1)x$ Use distributive property.

$= 2x$ Add coefficients.

b. $3 - 4(y + 4) = 3 - 4(y) + (-4)(4)$ Use distributive property.

$= 3 - 4y - 16$ Multiply.

$= -4y + 3 - 16$ Group like terms.

$= -4y - 13$ Combine like terms.

Simplify the expression.

45. $3a + 6a$ **46.** $2x^2 + 9x^2 + 4$ **47.** $4 + f - 1$

48. $3(d + 1) - 2$ **49.** $6t - 2(t - 1)$ **50.** $2(x + 3) + 3(2x - 5)$

2.8 DIVIDING REAL NUMBERS

Examples on pp. 113–115

EXAMPLES To divide real numbers, multiply by their reciprocals.

a. $9 \div (-3) = 9 \cdot \left(-\dfrac{1}{3}\right)$ Multiply by reciprocal of -3.

$= -3$ Simplify.

b. $-7 \div \dfrac{7}{6} = -7 \cdot \dfrac{6}{7}$ Multiply by reciprocal of $\dfrac{7}{6}$.

$= -6$ Simplify.

c. $-4 \div \left(-1\dfrac{2}{5}\right) = -4 \div \left(-\dfrac{7}{5}\right)$ Rewrite mixed number as improper fraction.

$= -4 \cdot \left(-\dfrac{5}{7}\right)$ Multiply by reciprocal of $-\dfrac{7}{5}$.

$= \dfrac{20}{7}$ Simplify.

Find the quotient.

51. $8 \div (-2)$ **52.** $-7 \div 7$ **53.** $-5 \div \left(-\dfrac{1}{2}\right)$ **54.** $-10 \div \left(-\dfrac{3}{7}\right)$

55. $\dfrac{1}{2} \div \left(-\dfrac{3}{4}\right)$ **56.** $\left(-\dfrac{3}{7}\right) \div \left(-\dfrac{9}{14}\right)$ **57.** $12 \div \left(-1\dfrac{1}{3}\right)$ **58.** $-63 \div 4\dfrac{1}{5}$

Write the numbers in increasing order.

1. $4, -9, -5, 9, -2, 3$ **2.** $8, -2.7, -6.4, 3.1, -4, 5$ **3.** $3, -5, -\frac{5}{4}, -\frac{5}{2}, \frac{3}{4}, 2$

Find the opposite of the number.

4. 5 **5.** -4 **6.** 9.2 **7.** $-\frac{5}{6}$

Evaluate the expression.

8. $|8|$ **9.** $|-17|$ **10.** $-|4.5|$ **11.** $-\left|-\frac{1}{4}\right|$

Find the sum.

12. $4 + (-9)$ **13.** $-25 + 31$ **14.** $9 + (-10) + 2$ **15.** $7 + 6.5 + (-3.5)$

16. PROFIT AND LOSS A company had the following profits and losses:
first quarter, $2,190; second quarter, $1,527; third quarter, $-$2,502;
fourth quarter, $-$267. What was the company's profit or loss for the year?

Find the difference.

17. $-6 - 8$ **18.** $15 - (-15)$ **19.** $6 - (-4) - (-3)$ **20.** $-2.47 - (-3.97) - 2$

Find the product.

21. $-6(4)$ **22.** $-8(-100)$ **23.** $-9(8)(-5)$ **24.** $-3(15)\left(-\frac{7}{15}\right)$

Simplify the expression.

25. $-8(-x)$ **26.** $5(-w)(-w)$ **27.** $8(-4)(a)(a)(a)$ **28.** $-15(-z)^2$

29. EAGLES An eagle dives down from its nest with a velocity of -44 feet per
second. Find the displacement of the eagle after 4.5 seconds.

Use the distributive property to rewrite the expression without parentheses.

30. $(a + 11)9$ **31.** $8(4 - x)$ **32.** $(6 + y)(-12)$ **33.** $(-5)(3 - z)$

Simplify the expression.

34. $t^2 - 9 + t^2$ **35.** $14p + 2(5 - p)$ **36.** $-9(y + 11) + 6$ **37.** $2(a + 3) - 5(a - 4)$

38. MOVIE THEATER It takes you 17 minutes to get to the movie theater. You
spend t minutes riding the bus at an average speed of 0.5 mile per minute.
The rest of the time is spent walking at 0.06 mile per minute. If you spend
10 minutes on the bus, how far is it to the movie theater?

Find the quotient.

39. $-36 \div (-4)$ **40.** $-56 \div \left(-\frac{7}{8}\right)$ **41.** $-\frac{3}{8} \div \frac{1}{2}$ **42.** $39 \div \left(-1\frac{3}{10}\right)$

Chapter Standardized Test

 **Test Tip** If you can, check your answer using a method that is different from the one you used originally to avoid making the same mistake twice.

1. Which inequality is true?

  (A) $-\dfrac{1}{4} > \dfrac{1}{3}$ (B) $\dfrac{1}{4} < -\dfrac{1}{3}$

  (C) $\dfrac{1}{4} < \dfrac{1}{3}$ (D) $\dfrac{1}{4} > \dfrac{1}{3}$

2. What is the opposite of 3?

  (A) -3 (B) 3

  (C) $-\dfrac{1}{3}$ (D) $\dfrac{1}{3}$

3. What is the solution of $|x| = 10$?

  (A) -10 (B) 10

  (C) $|10|$ (D) -10 and 10

4. What is the value of $-9 + 3 + (-4)$?

  (A) -16 (B) -10

  (C) -8 (D) -2

5. What is the value of $-4 - 6 - (-10)$?

  (A) -20 (B) 0

  (C) 8 (D) 12

6. Evaluate $-x - 13$ when $x = 9$.

  (A) -22 (B) -4

  (C) 4 (D) 22

7. On Monday the closing price for a company's stock was \$26.81. On Tuesday it was \$26.75. What was the change in the closing price?

  (A) -26.78 (B) -0.06

  (C) 0.06 (D) 26.78

8. What is the value of the expression $\left(-\dfrac{1}{2}\right)\left(-\dfrac{2}{3}\right)$?

  (A) $-\dfrac{3}{5}$ (B) $-\dfrac{1}{3}$

  (C) $\dfrac{1}{3}$ (D) $\dfrac{3}{5}$

9. Evaluate $(-2)(4)(-n)^3$ when $n = 3$.

  (A) -216 (B) -90

  (C) 90 (D) 216

10. Rewrite the expression $(4 - a)(-3)$ without using parentheses.

  (A) $4 - 3a$ (B) $4 + 3a$

  (C) $-12 - 3a$ (D) $12 - 3a$

11. You are buying 3 new pairs of slacks. All of the slacks are on sale for \$24.99. What expression would you use to mentally find the total cost of the slacks?

  (A) $3(25) + 0.01$ (B) $3(25 + 0.01)$

  (C) $3(25) - 0.01$ (D) $3(25 - 0.01)$

12. Simplify the expression $6(x + 3) - 2(4 - x)$.

  (A) $4x + 10$ (B) $5x - 5$

  (C) $5x + 11$ (D) $8x + 10$

  (E) none of these

13. Evaluate $\dfrac{4p + q}{p}$ when $p = -2$ and $q = -3$.

  (A) $-\dfrac{11}{2}$ (B) $-\dfrac{9}{2}$

  (C) $\dfrac{9}{2}$ (D) $\dfrac{11}{2}$

Maintaining Skills

EXAMPLE 1 Find the Area of a Figure

Find the area of the geometric figure.

a. square   **b.** rectangle   **c.** triangle

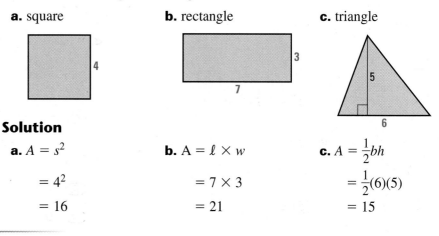

Solution

a. $A = s^2$

$= 4^2$

$= 16$

b. $A = \ell \times w$

$= 7 \times 3$

$= 21$

c. $A = \frac{1}{2}bh$

$= \frac{1}{2}(6)(5)$

$= 15$

Try These

Find the area of the geometric figure.

1. A square with side length 5   **2.** A rectangle with length 8 and width 4

3. A square with side length 10   **4.** A triangle with base 4 and height 4

EXAMPLE 2 Draw a Circle Graph

The table shows the number of pets a local pet store sold in one year. Draw a circle graph to display the data.

Pet	Dog	Cat	Bird
Number	312	270	46

Solution

First find the total number of pets:

$312 + 270 + 46 = 628$

To find the degree measure of each sector, write a fraction comparing the number of pets to the total. Then multiply by 360°. For example:

Dog: $\frac{312}{628} \cdot 360° \approx 179°$

Try These

5. The table shows the number of books a local bookstore sold in one year. Draw a circle graph to display the data.

Book type	Fiction	Nonfiction	Other
Number	549	103	348

Solving Linear Equations

How fast can an eagle fly?

APPLICATION: Bald Eagles

The bald eagle can fly at speeds up to 30 miles per hour and dive at speeds up to 100 miles per hour.

Think & Discuss

1. Use the formula $d = rt$ to find the distance a bald eagle can fly for the given flying rate and time.

Flying rate (miles per hour)	Time (hours)	Distance (miles)
30	1	?
30	$\frac{1}{2}$	?
30	$\frac{1}{6}$	?

Convert the flying time from hours to minutes.

2. 1 hour = ? minutes

3. $\frac{1}{2}$ hour = ? minutes

4. $\frac{1}{6}$ hour = ? minutes

5. How many minutes will it take an eagle flying at a rate of 30 miles per hour to fly 1 mile?

Learn More About It

You will solve equations to find flying rates of bald eagles in Exercises 40 and 41 on p. 181.

 APPLICATION LINK More about bald eagles is available at www.mcdougallittell.com

129

PREVIEW
What's the chapter about?

- Solving a **linear equation** systematically
- Using **ratios**, **rates**, and **percents**

> **KEY WORDS**
>
> - **equivalent equations,** *p. 132*
> - **inverse operations,** *p. 133*
> - **linear equation,** *p. 134*
> - **properties of equality,** *p. 140*
> - **identity,** *p. 153*
> - **rounding error,** *p. 164*
> - **formula,** *p. 171*
> - **ratio,** *p. 177*
> - **rate,** *p. 177*
> - **unit rate,** *p. 177*
> - **unit analysis,** *p. 178*
> - **percent,** *p. 183*
> - **base number,** *p. 183*

PREPARE
Chapter Readiness Quiz

Take this quick quiz. If you are unsure of an answer, look back at the reference pages for help.

VOCABULARY CHECK *(refer to pp. 71, 113)*

1. What is the opposite of -3?

    (A) -3 (B) $-\frac{1}{3}$ (C) $\frac{1}{3}$ (D) 3

2. Which number is the reciprocal of $\frac{3}{5}$?

    (A) $-\frac{5}{3}$ (B) $-\frac{3}{5}$ (C) 1   (D) $\frac{5}{3}$

SKILL CHECK *(refer to pp. 24, 102, 108)*

3. Which of the following is a solution of the equation $-11 = -4y + 1$?

    (A) -3 (B) 2   (C) 3   (D) 4

4. Which expression is equivalent to $-3(x - 4)$?

    (A) $3x - 12$ (B) $-3x + 12$ (C) $-3x - 4$ (D) $-3x - 12$

5. Simplify the expression $4x^2 - 5x - x^2 + 3x$.

    (A) $5x^2 - 2x$ (B) $3x^2 + 8x$ (C) $3x^2 - 2x$ (D) x^2

STUDY TIP
Make Formula Cards

Write a formula and a sample problem on each card. Make sure you know what each algebraic symbol represents in a formula.

Area of a Triangle

$A = \frac{1}{2}bh$

A = area
b = base
h = height

DEVELOPING CONCEPTS
One-Step Equations

For use with Lesson 3.1

GOAL

Use algebra tiles to solve one-step equations.

MATERIALS

• algebra tiles

Student Help

▶**LOOK BACK**
For help with algebra tiles, see pp. 77, 84, and 99.

Question

How can you use algebra tiles to solve a one-step equation?

Explore

① Model the equation $x + 5 = -2$.

② To find the value of x, get the x-tile by itself on one side of the equation. Take away five 1-tiles from the left side. Be sure to take away five 1-tiles from the right side to keep the two sides equal.

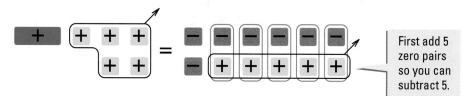

First add 5 zero pairs so you can subtract 5.

③ The remaining tiles show the value of x. So, $x = $ __?__ .

What operation did you use to solve this addition equation?

Think About It

Use algebra tiles to model and solve the equation. Sketch each step.

1. $x + 4 = 6$ **2.** $x + 3 = 8$ **3.** $x + 7 = -1$ **4.** $x + 2 = -7$

5. Use algebra tiles to model and solve $x - 3 = 2$. Start with the model below.

Use algebra tiles to model and solve the equation. Sketch each step.

6. $x - 1 = 5$ **7.** $x - 7 = 1$ **8.** $x - 2 = -6$ **9.** $x - 4 = -3$

10. A student solved the equation $x + 3 = -4$ by subtracting 3 on the left side of the equation and got $x = -4$. Is this the correct solution? Explain.

3.1 Solving Equations Using Addition and Subtraction

Goal
Solve linear equations using addition and subtraction.

Key Words
• equivalent equations
• transforming equations
• inverse operations
• linear equation

What size is a city park?

Griffith Park in Los Angeles is one of the largest city parks in the United States. It has miles of hiking trails, a theater, and an observatory. In Exercises 58 and 59 you will solve equations to find the sizes of some city parks.

You can solve an equation by writing an *equivalent equation* that has the variable isolated on one side. Linear equations are **equivalent equations** if they have the same solution(s). To change, or *transform*, an equation into an equivalent equation, think of an equation as having two sides that need to be "in balance."

Student Help

▶ **STUDY TIP**
When you subtract 3 from *each* side of the equation, the equation stays in balance.

Original equation:
$x + 3 = 5$

Subtract 3 from each side to isolate x on the left.

Simplify both sides.
Equivalent equation: $x = 2$

TRANSFORMING EQUATIONS

OPERATION	ORIGINAL EQUATION		EQUIVALENT EQUATION
• Add the same number to *each* side.	$x - 3 = 5$	Add 3.	$x = 8$
• Subtract the same number from *each* side.	$x + 6 = 10$	Subtract 6.	$x = 4$
• Simplify one or both sides.	$x = 8 - 3$	Simplify.	$x = 5$

INVERSE OPERATIONS Two operations that undo each other, such as addition and subtraction, are called **inverse operations**. Inverse operations can help you to isolate the variable on one side of an equation.

Student Help

▶ **MORE EXAMPLES**

More examples are available at www.mcdougallittell.com

EXAMPLE 1 Add to Each Side of an Equation

Solve $x - 5 = -13$.

Solution

This is a subtraction equation. Use the inverse operation of addition to undo the subtraction.

$x - 5 = -13$	Write original equation.
$x - 5 + 5 = -13 + 5$	Add 5 to each side to undo the subtraction.
$x = -8$	Simplify both sides.

CHECK ✓

$x - 5 = -13$	Write original equation.
$-8 - 5 \stackrel{?}{=} -13$	Substitute -8 for x.
$-13 = -13$ ✓	Solution is correct.

Student Help

▶ **STUDY TIP**
To subtract -4 from n, add the opposite of -4 to n. To review the subtraction rule, see p. 86.

EXAMPLE 2 Simplify First

Solve $-8 = n - (-4)$.

Solution

$-8 = n - (-4)$	Write original equation.
$-8 = n + 4$	Use subtraction rule to simplify.
$-8 - 4 = n + 4 - 4$	Subtract 4 from each side to undo the addition.
$-12 = n$	Simplify both sides.

CHECK ✓

To check the solution, substitute -12 for n in the *original* equation $-8 = n - (-4)$, not in the simplified equation $-8 = n + 4$.

$-8 = \mathbf{n} - (-4)$	Write original equation.
$-8 \stackrel{?}{=} \mathbf{-12} - (-4)$	Substitute -12 for n.
$-8 \stackrel{?}{=} -12 + 4$	Use subtraction rule to simplify.
$-8 = -8$ ✓	Solution is correct.

Checkpoint ✓ Solve an Equation

Solve the equation. Check your solution in the original equation.

1. $-2 = x - 4$ **2.** $x - (-9) = 6$ **3.** $y + 5 = -1$

4. $t - 7 = 30$ **5.** $-8 = x + 14$ **6.** $3 = x - (-11)$

LINEAR EQUATIONS The equations in this chapter are called *linear equations*. In a **linear equation** the exponent of the variable(s) is one.

LINEAR EQUATION	NOT A LINEAR EQUATION
$x + 5 = 9$	$x^2 + 5 = 9$
$y = 3x - 8$	$3x^2 - 8 = 0$

In Chapter 4 you will see how linear equations get their names from graphs.

PROBLEM SOLVING PLAN You can write linear equations to model many real-life situations. Example 3 shows how to model temperature change using the problem solving plan that you learned in Lesson 1.6.

Link to *Geography*

SPEARFISH is located in the Black Hills of South Dakota. Freezing and thawing can loosen the rock walls of Spearfish Canyon, causing landslides.

EXAMPLE 3 *Model Temperature Change*

SPEARFISH, SOUTH DAKOTA On January 22, 1943, the temperature in Spearfish fell from 54°F at 9:00 A.M. to −4°F at 9:27 A.M. Write and solve a linear equation to find how many degrees the temperature fell.

Solution

VERBAL MODEL	$\boxed{\text{Temperature at 9:27 A.M.}} = \boxed{\text{Temperature at 9:00 A.M.}} - \boxed{\text{Degrees fallen}}$

LABELS

Temperature at 9:27 A.M. = **−4**   (degrees Fahrenheit)

Temperature at 9:00 A.M. = **54**   (degrees Fahrenheit)

Degrees Fallen = T (degrees Fahrenheit)

ALGEBRAIC MODEL

$-4 = 54 - T$	Write linear equation.
$-4 - 54 = 54 - T - 54$	Subtract 54 from each side.
$-58 = -T$	Simplify both sides.
$58 = T$	T is the opposite of -58.

ANSWER▸ The temperature fell by 58°.

Checkpoint✓ *Model Temperature Change*

A record 24-hour temperature change occurred in Browning, Montana, on January 23–24, 1916. The temperature fell from 44°F to −56°F.

7. Write a verbal model that can be solved to find how many degrees the temperature fell.

8. Rewrite the verbal model as a linear equation.

9. Solve the linear equation to find the record temperature fall in degrees.

Guided Practice

Vocabulary Check   **Complete the sentence.**

1. Linear equations with the same solution(s) are called __?__ equations.

2. You can use __?__ operations, such as addition and subtraction, to help you isolate a variable on one side of an equation.

Tell whether each equation is *linear* or *not linear*. Explain your answer.

3. $a^2 + 1 = 9$ **4.** $y + 16 = 5$ **5.** $4 + 2r = -10$ **6.** $3x^2 = 8$

Skill Check   **Solve the equation.**

7. $r + 3 = 2$ **8.** $9 = x - 4$ **9.** $7 + c = -10$

10. $-1 = t - 6$ **11.** $4 + x = 8$ **12.** $x + 4 - 3 = 9$

13. $r - (-2) = 5$ **14.** $-1 = d - (-12)$ **15.** $6 - (-y) = 3$

SPENDING MONEY You put some money in your pocket. You spend $4.50 on lunch. You have $7.50 in your pocket after buying lunch.

16. Write an equation to find how much money you had before lunch.

17. Which inverse operation will you use to solve the equation?

18. Solve the equation. What does the solution mean?

Practice and Applications

STATING THE INVERSE **State the inverse operation.**

19. Add 28.   **20.** Add 17.   **21.** Subtract 3.

22. Subtract 15.   **23.** Add -12.   **24.** Subtract -2.

SOLVING EQUATIONS **Solve the equation.**

25. $x + 9 = 18$ **26.** $m - 20 = 45$ **27.** $x - 8 = -13$

28. $4 + x = 7$ **29.** $x + 5 = 15$ **30.** $11 = r - 4$

31. $t - 2 = 6$ **32.** $-9 = 2 + y$ **33.** $n - 5 = -9$

34. $y + 12 = -12$ **35.** $y - 12 = 12$ **36.** $a - 3 = -2$

37. $t - 5 = -20$ **38.** $x + 7 = -14$ **39.** $34 + x = 10$

40. $\frac{1}{3} + x = \frac{2}{3}$ **41.** $\frac{2}{5} = a - \frac{1}{5}$ **42.** $r + \frac{3}{4} = \frac{1}{4}$

Student Help

▶ **HOMEWORK HELP**
Example 1: Exs. 25–42
Example 2: Exs. 43–51
Example 3: Exs. 54–60

SOLVING EQUATIONS Solve the equation by simplifying first.

43. $t - (-4) = 4$　　**44.** $6 = y - (-11)$　　**45.** $x - (-8) = 13$

46. $r - (-7) = -16$　　**47.** $19 - (-y) = 25$　　**48.** $2 - (-b) = -6$

49. $x + 5 - 2 = 6$　　**50.** $12 - 5 = n + 7$　　**51.** $-3 = a + (-4)$

Geometry Link Find the length of the side marked *x*.

52. The perimeter is 12 feet.

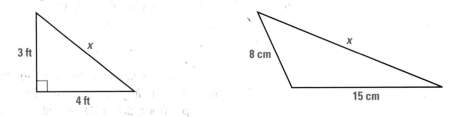

3 ft
x
4 ft

53. The perimeter is 43 centimeters.

8 cm
x
15 cm

MATCHING AN EQUATION In Exercises 54–56, match the real-life problem with an equation. Then solve the problem.

A. $x + 15 = 7$　　**B.** $15 - x = 7$　　**C.** $15 + 7 = x$　　**D.** $x + 15 = -7$

54. You own 15 CDs. You buy 7 more. How many CDs do you own now?

55. There are 15 members of a high school band brass section. After graduation there are only 7 members. How many members graduated?

56. The temperature rose 15 degrees to 7°F. What was the original temperature?

57. BASEBALL STADIUMS Turner Field in Atlanta, Georgia, has 49,831 seats. Jacobs Field in Cleveland, Ohio, has 43,368 seats. How many seats need to be added to Jacobs Field for it to have as many seats as Turner Field?

CITY PARKS In Exercises 58 and 59, use the table that shows the sizes (in acres) of the largest city parks in the United States.

Park (location)	Size (acres)
Cullen Park (Houston, TX)	?
Fairmount Park (Philadelphia, PA)	8700
Griffith Park (Los Angeles, CA)	4218
Eagle Creek Park (Indianapolis, IN)	?
Pelham Bay Park (Bronx, NY)	2764

▶ Source: The Trust for Public Land

Link to Careers

PARK RANGERS guide tours, provide information, manage resources, and maintain safety.

More about park rangers is available at www.mcdougallittell.com

58. Griffith Park is 418 acres larger than Eagle Creek Park. Write an equation that models the size of Eagle Creek Park. Solve the equation to find the size of Eagle Creek Park.

59. Cullen Park is 248 acres smaller than the sum of the sizes of Griffith Park, Eagle Creek Park, and Pelham Bay Park. Write and solve an equation to find the size of Cullen Park. *HINT:* Use your answer from Exercise 58.

60. CHECKBOOK BALANCE You thought the balance in your checkbook was $53, but when your bank statement arrived, you realized that you forgot to record a check. The bank statement lists your balance as $47. Let x represent the value of the check that you forgot to record. Which equation is a correct model for the situation? Solve the correct equation.

A. $53 - x = 47$ **B.** $x - 47 = 53$

61. LOGICAL REASONING Copy the solution steps shown. Then write an explanation for each step in the right-hand column.

Solution Step	Explanation
$-7 = x - (-2)$	Original Equation
$-7 = x + 2$	?
$-9 = x$	?

62. CHALLENGE You decide to try to ride the elevator to street level (Floor 0) without pushing any buttons. The elevator takes you up 4 floors, down 6 floors, up 1 floor, down 8 floors, down 3 floors, up 1 floor, and then down 6 floors to street level. Write and solve an equation to find your starting floor.

Standardized Test Practice

63. MULTIPLE CHOICE The selling price of a certain video is $7 more than the price the store paid. If the selling price is $24, find the equation that determines the price the store paid.

Ⓐ $x + 7 = 24$ Ⓑ $x = 7 + 24$ Ⓒ $7 - 24 = x$ Ⓓ $x = 24$

64. MULTIPLE CHOICE Which equation is *not* linear?

Ⓕ $7 + x = 15$ Ⓖ $x^2 = 10$ Ⓗ $3x - x = 1$ Ⓙ $x = 6^2$

Mixed Review

TRANSLATING SENTENCES Write the sentence as an equation. *(Lesson 1.5)*

65. The product of 5 and a number x is 160.

66. A number t divided by 6 is 48.

67. 36 decreased by a number k is 15.

68. The quotient of a number y and 3 is 12.

DISTRIBUTIVE PROPERTY Use the distributive property to rewrite the expression without parentheses. *(Lesson 2.6)*

69. $4(x + 2)$ **70.** $7(3 - 2y)$ **71.** $-5(y + 4)$

72. $(3x + 8)(-2)$ **73.** $-2(x - 6)$ **74.** $3(8 - 7x)$

Maintaining Skills

MULTIPLYING FRACTIONS Multiply. Write the answer as a fraction or as a mixed number in lowest terms. *(Skills Review p. 765)*

75. $\frac{2}{3} \cdot \frac{6}{7}$ **76.** $\frac{3}{8} \cdot \frac{4}{9}$ **77.** $\frac{1}{10} \cdot \frac{15}{16}$ **78.** $\frac{7}{8} \cdot \frac{1}{2}$

79. $\frac{3}{4} \cdot \frac{16}{21}$ **80.** $\frac{6}{7} \cdot \frac{3}{5}$ **81.** $\frac{7}{22} \cdot \frac{22}{7}$ **82.** $\frac{3}{16} \cdot \frac{4}{4}$

Solving Equations Using Multiplication and Division

Goal

Solve linear equations using multiplication and division.

Key Words

- inverse operations
- transforming equations
- reciprocal
- properties of equality

How heavy is a pile of newspapers?

Paper is the most recycled product in the United States. In Exercise 50 you will solve an equation to find the total weight of a pile of newspapers after it has been divided into smaller bundles.

Multiplication and division are *inverse operations* that can help you to isolate the variable on one side of an equation. You can use multiplication to undo division and use division to undo multiplication.

TRANSFORMING EQUATIONS

OPERATION	ORIGINAL EQUATION		EQUIVALENT EQUATION
• Multiply *each* side of the equation by the same nonzero number.	$\frac{x}{2} = 3$	Multiply by 2.	$x = 6$
• Divide *each* side of the equation by the same nonzero number.	$4x = 12$	Divide by 4.	$x = 3$

EXAMPLE 1 Divide Each Side of an Equation

Solve $-4x = 1$.

Solution

The operation is multiplication. Use the inverse operation of division to isolate the variable x.

$$-4x = 1$$ Write original equation.

$$\frac{-4x}{-4} = \frac{1}{-4}$$ Divide each side by -4 to undo the multiplication.

$$x = -\frac{1}{4}$$ Simplify.

ANSWER ▶ The solution is $-\frac{1}{4}$. Check this in the original equation.

EXAMPLE 2 **Multiply Each Side of an Equation**

Solve $\frac{x}{5} = -30$.

Solution

The operation is division. Use the inverse operation of multiplication to isolate the variable x.

$$\frac{x}{5} = -30 \qquad \text{Write original equation.}$$

$$5\left(\frac{x}{5}\right) = 5(-30) \qquad \text{Multiply each side by 5 to undo the division.}$$

$$x = -150 \qquad \text{Simplify.}$$

ANSWER ▶ The solution is -150.

Checkpoint ✓ *Solve an Equation*

Solve the equation. Check your solution in the original equation.

1. $60 = 5x$ **2.** $\frac{r}{3} = 11$ **3.** $\frac{n}{4} = -2$ **4.** $-3x = -9$

RECIPROCAL To solve an equation with a fractional coefficient, such as $10 = -\frac{2}{3}m$, multiply each side of the equation by the reciprocal of the fraction. This will isolate the variable because the product of a nonzero number and its reciprocal is 1.

Student Help

▶**MORE EXAMPLES**

More examples are available at www.mcdougallittell.com

EXAMPLE 3 **Multiply Each Side by a Reciprocal**

Solve $10 = -\frac{2}{3}m$.

Solution

The fractional coefficient is $-\frac{2}{3}$. The reciprocal of $-\frac{2}{3}$ is $-\frac{3}{2}$.

$$10 = -\frac{2}{3}m \qquad \text{Write original equation.}$$

$$-\frac{3}{2}(10) = -\frac{3}{2}\left(-\frac{2}{3}m\right) \qquad \text{Multiply each side by the reciprocal, } -\frac{3}{2}.$$

$$-15 = m \qquad \text{Simplify.}$$

ANSWER ▶ The solution is -15.

Checkpoint ✓ *Multiply Each Side by a Reciprocal*

Solve the equation. Check your solution in the original equation.

5. $6 = \frac{3}{4}x$ **6.** $12 = -\frac{4}{5}y$ **7.** $\frac{3}{5}x = 24$ **8.** $-6 = \frac{2}{7}m$

PROPERTIES OF EQUALITY The ways you have learned to transform an equation into an equivalent equation are based on rules of algebra called **properties of equality**.

SUMMARY

Properties of Equality

ADDITION PROPERTY OF EQUALITY	If $a = b$, then $a + c = b + c$.
SUBTRACTION PROPERTY OF EQUALITY	If $a = b$, then $a - c = b - c$.
MULTIPLICATION PROPERTY OF EQUALITY	If $a = b$, then $ca = cb$.
DIVISION PROPERTY OF EQUALITY	If $a = b$ and $c \neq 0$, then $\dfrac{a}{c} = \dfrac{b}{c}$.

Link to
Film

MOVIE FRAMES A motion picture camera takes separate pictures as frames. These are projected rapidly when the movie is shown.

EXAMPLE 4 Model a Real-Life Problem

MOVIE FRAMES A single picture on a roll of movie film is called a frame. The usual rate for taking and projecting professional movies is 24 frames per second. Find the total number of frames in a movie that is 90 minutes long.

Solution

Let $x =$ the total number of frames in the movie. To find the total number of seconds in the movie, multiply $90 \cdot 60$ because each minute is 60 seconds.

$$\frac{\text{Total number of frames in the movie}}{\text{Total number of seconds in the movie}} = \textbf{Number of frames per second}$$

$\dfrac{x}{5400} = 24$	Write equation.
$5400\left(\dfrac{x}{5400}\right) = 5400(24)$	Use multiplication property of equality.
$x = 129{,}600$	Simplify.

ANSWER ▶ A 90-minute movie has a total of 129,600 frames.

Checkpoint ✓ *Model a Real-Life Problem*

Motion picture studios try to save older films from decay by restoring the film frame by frame. Suppose that a worker can restore 8 frames per hour. Let $y =$ the number of hours of work needed to restore all the frames in a 90-minute movie.

9. Use the information from Example 4 and the verbal model shown below to write a linear equation.

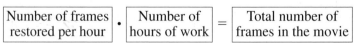

| Number of frames restored per hour | • | Number of hours of work | = | Total number of frames in the movie |

10. Use the division property of equality to solve the linear equation. How many hours of work are needed to restore all of the frames in the movie?

Guided Practice

Vocabulary Check

1. Name two pairs of inverse operations.

Match the property of equality with its description.

2. Addition Property of Equality   **A.** If $a = b$, then $ca = cb$.

3. Multiplication Property of Equality   **B.** If $a = b$, then $a - c = b - c$.

4. Division Property of Equality   **C.** If $a = b$, then $a + c = b + c$.

5. Subtraction Property of Equality   **D.** If $a = b$ and $c \neq 0$, then $\dfrac{a}{c} = \dfrac{b}{c}$.

Skill Check   **Solve the equation. Check your solution in the original equation.**

6. $3x = 18$ **7.** $19m = -19$ **8.** $-5x = 3$

9. $\dfrac{y}{4} = 8$ **10.** $\dfrac{r}{-5} = 20$ **11.** $\dfrac{b}{-7} = -4$

12. $\dfrac{3}{8}t = 6$ **13.** $4 = -\dfrac{2}{3}x$ **14.** $\dfrac{4}{5}t = 0$

15. CAR TRIP Suppose you drive 630 miles from St. Louis, Missouri, to Dallas, Texas, in 10.5 hours. Solve the equation $630 = r(10.5)$ for r to find your average speed.

Practice and Applications

STATING INVERSES   **State the inverse operation.**

16. Divide by 6.   **17.** Multiply by 5.   **18.** Multiply by $\dfrac{2}{3}$.

19. Multiply by -4.   **20.** Divide by -3.   **21.** Divide by 7.

SOLVING EQUATIONS   **Use division to solve the equation.**

22. $3r = 21$ **23.** $7y = -56$ **24.** $18 = -2a$

25. $-4n = 24$ **26.** $8x = 3$ **27.** $10x = 110$

28. $30b = 5$ **29.** $-10x = -9$ **30.** $288 = 16u$

Student Help

▶ **HOMEWORK HELP**
   Example 1: Exs. 22–30
   Example 2: Exs. 31–36
   Example 3: Exs. 37–45
   Example 4: Exs. 48–52

SOLVING EQUATIONS   **Use multiplication to solve the equation.**

31. $\dfrac{x}{2} = -5$ **32.** $\dfrac{t}{4} = -4$ **33.** $6 = \dfrac{d}{5}$

34. $\dfrac{m}{-4} = -\dfrac{3}{4}$ **35.** $\dfrac{y}{7} = 12$ **36.** $-\dfrac{h}{3} = -16$

SOLVING EQUATIONS Multiply by a reciprocal to solve the equation.

37. $\frac{3}{4}k = 1$

38. $-\frac{2}{5}y = 4$

39. $0 = \frac{7}{8}x$

40. $-\frac{1}{3}y = 6$

41. $10 = \frac{5}{6}x$

42. $\frac{5}{8}m = -20$

43. $12 = \frac{2}{3}x$

44. $\frac{3}{7}x = 6$

45. $-\frac{4}{5}x = 36$

ERROR ANALYSIS In Exercises 46 and 47, find and correct the error.

46.
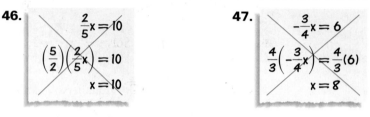
$$\frac{2}{5}x = 10$$
$$\left(\frac{5}{2}\right)\left(\frac{2}{5}x\right) = 10$$
$$x = 10$$

47.
$$-\frac{3}{4}x = 6$$
$$\frac{4}{3}\left(-\frac{3}{4}x\right) = \frac{4}{3}(6)$$
$$x = 8$$

MODELING REAL-LIFE PROBLEMS In Exercises 48 and 49, use the verbal model to write a linear equation. Then use the multiplication property of equality to solve the equation.

48. It takes 45 peanuts to make one ounce of peanut butter. How many peanuts will be needed to make a 12-ounce jar of peanut butter?

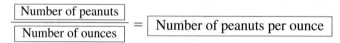
$$\frac{\boxed{\text{Number of peanuts}}}{\boxed{\text{Number of ounces}}} = \boxed{\text{Number of peanuts per ounce}}$$

49. You ate 3 of the 8 slices of a pizza. You paid \$3.30 as your share of the total cost of the pizza. How much did the whole pizza cost?

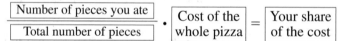
$$\frac{\boxed{\text{Number of pieces you ate}}}{\boxed{\text{Total number of pieces}}} \cdot \boxed{\substack{\text{Cost of the}\\\text{whole pizza}}} = \boxed{\substack{\text{Your share}\\\text{of the cost}}}$$

50. BUNDLING NEWSPAPERS You are loading a large pile of newspapers onto a truck. You divide the pile into four equal-size bundles. One bundle weighs 37 pounds. You want to know the weight x of the original pile. Which equation represents this situation? Solve the correct equation.

A. $\frac{x}{4} = 37$

B. $4x = 37$

C. $37x = 4$

51. MAIL DELIVERY Each household in the United States receives about 676 pieces of junk mail per year. If there are 52 weeks in a year, then about how many pieces of junk mail does a household receive per week? *HINT:* Let x = the number of pieces of junk mail received per week. Solve the equation $52x = 676$.

52. **Science Link** You can tell about how many miles you are from a thunderstorm by counting the seconds between seeing the lightning and hearing the thunder, and then dividing by five. How many seconds would you count for a thunderstorm that is nine miles away?

53. CHALLENGE A homeowner is installing a fence around the garden at the right. The garden has a perimeter of 220 feet. Write and solve an equation to find the garden's dimensions.

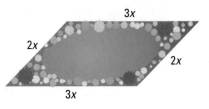

54. MULTIPLE CHOICE Which operation would you use to solve $\frac{1}{4} = -8x$?

  (A) Divide by 4.   **(B)** Divide by -8.

  (C) Multiply by -8.   **(D)** Multiply by 4.

55. MULTIPLE CHOICE Solve $-\frac{5}{7}x = -2$.

  (F) $\frac{14}{5}$ **(G)** $-\frac{14}{5}$ **(H)** $\frac{10}{7}$ **(J)** $\frac{7}{5}$

56. MULTIPLE CHOICE Which equations are equivalent?

  (A) I and II   **I.** $\frac{3}{5}x = 3$

  (B) II and IV   **II.** $\frac{x}{5} = 2$

  (C) I, II, and III   **III.** $2x = 10$

  (D) I, III, and IV   **IV.** $-x = -5$

▶ **TEST TIP**
Use mental math to solve each equation to help you answer Exercise 56.

SIMPLIFYING EXPRESSIONS Simplify the expression. *(Lesson 2.7)*

57. $15 - 8x + 12$ **58.** $4y - 9 + 3y$ **59.** $5x + 6 - 7x$

60. $-2(x + 8) + 36$ **61.** $5(y + 3) + 7y$ **62.** $3(y - 10) - 5y$

SOLVING EQUATIONS Solve the equation. *(Lesson 3.1)*

63. $4 + y = 12$ **64.** $t - 2 = 1$ **65.** $-14 = r + 5$

66. $-6 + x = -15$ **67.** $x - (-6) = 8$ **68.** $a - (-9) = -2$

69. PHOTOGRAPHY You take 24 pictures. Six of the pictures cannot be developed because of bad lighting. Let x represent the number of pictures that can be developed successfully. Which of the following is a correct model for the situation? Solve the correct equation. *(Lesson 3.1)*

  A. $x + 6 = 24$ **B.** $6x = 24$ **C.** $x - 6 = 24$ **D.** $x + 24 = 6$

GREATEST COMMON FACTOR Find the greatest common factor of the pair of numbers. *(Skills Review p. 761)*

70. 5, 35   **71.** 30, 40   **72.** 12, 22

73. 10, 25   **74.** 17, 51   **75.** 27, 36

76. 14, 42   **77.** 9, 24   **78.** 21, 49

3.3 Solving Multi-Step Equations

Goal
Use two or more steps to solve a linear equation.

Key Words
- like terms
- distributive property

How hot is Earth's crust?

Temperatures within Earth's crust can get hot enough to melt rocks. In Example 2 you will see how a multi-step equation can be used to predict the depth at which the temperature of Earth's crust is 114°C.

Solving a linear equation may require more than one step. Use the steps you already know for transforming an equation. Simplify one or both sides of the equation first, if needed. Then use inverse operations to isolate the variable.

Student Help

▶ **VOCABULARY TIP**
The prefix *multi-* means "more than one". A multi-step equation is solved by transforming the equation more than one time.

EXAMPLE 1 Solve a Linear Equation

Solve $3x + 7 = -8$.

Solution

To isolate the variable, undo the addition and then the multiplication.

$3x + 7 = -8$	Write original equation.
$3x + 7 - 7 = -8 - 7$	Subtract 7 from each side to undo the addition. (Subtraction Property of Equality)
$3x = -15$	Simplify both sides.
$\dfrac{3x}{3} = \dfrac{-15}{3}$	Divide each side by 3 to undo the multiplication. (Division Property of Equality)
$x = -5$	Simplify.

CHECK ✓ Check by substituting -5 for x in the *original* equation.

$3x + 7 = -8$	Write original equation.
$3(-5) + 7 \stackrel{?}{=} -8$	Substitute -5 for x.
$-15 + 7 \stackrel{?}{=} -8$	Multiply.
$-8 = -8$ ✓	Solution is correct.

Checkpoint ✓ **Solve a Linear Equation**

Solve the equation. Check your solution in the original equation.

1. $6x - 15 = 9$ **2.** $7x - 4 = -11$ **3.** $2y + 5 = 1$

EXAMPLE **2** **Use a Verbal Model**

SCIENCE LINK The temperature
within Earth's crust increases about
30°C for each kilometer beneath the
surface. If the temperature at Earth's
surface is 24°C, at what depth would
you expect the temperature to be 114°C?

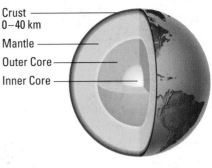

Crust
0–40 km

Mantle

Outer Core

Inner Core

Solution

VERBAL MODEL	Temperature inside Earth	=	Temperature at Earth's surface	+	Rate of temperature increase	·	Depth below surface

LABELS Temperature inside Earth = **114** (degrees Celsius)

Temperature at Earth's surface = **24** (degrees Celsius)

Rate of temperature increase = **30** (degrees Celsius per kilometer)

Depth below surface = *d* (kilometers)

ALGEBRAIC MODEL

$114 = 24 + 30d$ Write equation.

$90 = 30d$ Subtract 24 from each side.

$3 = d$ Divide each side by 30.

ANSWER ▶ The temperature will be 114°C at a depth of 3 kilometers.

Checkpoint ✓ **Use a Verbal Model**

4. If the temperature at Earth's surface is 24°C, at what depth would you expect
the temperature to be 174°C? Use the verbal model in Example 2 to solve.

EXAMPLE **3** **Combine Like Terms First**

Solve $7x - 3x - 8 = 24$.

Solution $7x - 3x - 8 = 24$ Write original equation.

$4x - 8 = 24$ Combine like terms $7x$ and $-3x$.

$4x - 8 + 8 = 24 + 8$ Add 8 to each side to undo the subtraction.

$4x = 32$ Simplify.

$\dfrac{4x}{4} = \dfrac{32}{4}$ Divide each side by 4 to undo the multiplication.

$x = 8$ Simplify.

EXAMPLE 4 Use the Distributive Property

Solve the equation.

a. $8x - 2(x + 7) = 16$ **b.** $5x + 3(x + 4) = 28$

Solution

Student Help

▶ **STUDY TIP**
Remember to distribute the negative sign to *each* term inside the parentheses, not to just the first term.••••••••••••▶

a. Distribute a negative number.

$$8x - 2(x + 7) = 16$$
$$8x - 2x - 14 = 16$$
$$6x - 14 = 16$$
$$6x - 14 + 14 = 16 + 14$$
$$6x = 30$$
$$\frac{6x}{6} = \frac{30}{6}$$
$$x = 5$$

b. Distribute a positive number.

$$5x + 3(x + 4) = 28$$
$$5x + 3x + 12 = 28$$
$$8x + 12 = 28$$
$$8x + 12 - 12 = 28 - 12$$
$$8x = 16$$
$$\frac{8x}{8} = \frac{16}{8}$$
$$x = 2$$

✓Checkpoint Use the Distributive Property and Combine Like Terms

Solve the equation. Check your solution in the original equation.

5. $6(x + 2) = 15$ **6.** $8 - 4(x + 1) = 8$ **7.** $3m + 2(m - 5) = 10$

EXAMPLE 5 Multiply by a Reciprocal First

Solve $4 = \frac{2}{3}(x + 3)$.

Student Help

▶ **STUDY TIP**
In Example 5 you can clear the equation of fractions by multiplying by the reciprocal of $\frac{2}{3}$.

Solution

$$4 = \frac{2}{3}(x + 3)$$ Write original equation.

$$\frac{3}{2}(4) = \frac{3}{2}\left(\frac{2}{3}\right)(x + 3)$$ Multiply each side by $\frac{3}{2}$, the reciprocal of $\frac{2}{3}$.

$$6 = x + 3$$ Simplify.

$$6 - 3 = x + 3 - 3$$ Subtract 3 from each side.

$$3 = x$$ Simplify both sides.

✓Checkpoint Multiply by a Reciprocal First

Solve the equation. Check your solution in the original equation.

8. $6 = \frac{3}{4}(x + 7)$ **9.** $\frac{4}{5}(x - 2) = 8$ **10.** $-\frac{3}{5}(x + 1) = 9$

Guided Practice

Vocabulary Check   Identify the like terms in the expression.

1. $3x^2 + 5x + 3 + x$ **2.** $8x - 4 + 5x^2 - 4x$ **3.** $2t + t^2 + 6t^2 - 6t$

4. $4x + 2(x + 1)$ **5.** $3 - m + 2(m - 2)$ **6.** $8 - 3(x + 4) + 3x$

Skill Check   Solve the equation.

7. $4x + 3 = 11$ **8.** $7y - 3 = 25$ **9.** $2x - 9 = -11$

10. $3r - r + 15 = 41$ **11.** $13 = 12t - 5 - 3t$ **12.** $-8 + 5a - 2 = 20$

13. $5(d - 7) = 90$ **14.** $3(8 + b) = 27$ **15.** $-4(x + 6) = 12$

16. $\frac{3}{4}(x + 6) = 12$ **17.** $\frac{1}{3}(x - 1) = 6$ **18.** $\frac{2}{3}(x + 8) = 8$

Practice and Applications

SOLVING EQUATIONS   Solve the equation.

19. $48 = 11n + 26$ **20.** $2x + 7 = 15$ **21.** $5p - 16 = 54$

22. $3g - 1 = 8$ **23.** $3y + 5 = 11$ **24.** $7t - 9 = 19$

25. $4a + 9a = 39$ **26.** $5w + 2w = 77$ **27.** $8n - 3n - 4 = 21$

28. $22x - 12x = 60$ **29.** $4c + (-7c) = 9$ **30.** $9t - 15t = -18$

SOLVING EQUATIONS WITH PARENTHESES   Solve the equation.

31. $5(6 + j) = 45$ **32.** $3(k - 2) = 18$ **33.** $-2(4 - m) = 10$

34. $x + 4(x + 3) = 17$ **35.** $8y - (8 + 6y) = 20$ **36.** $x - 2(3x - 2) = -6$

37. $\frac{3}{4}(x + 9) = 15$ **38.** $\frac{1}{4}(t + 10) = 5$ **39.** $\frac{2}{3}(x + 3) = 6$

ERROR ANALYSIS   In Exercises 40–42, find and correct the error.

Student Help

▶ **HOMEWORK HELP**
Example 1: Exs. 19–24
Example 2: Exs. 44, 45
Example 3: Exs. 25–30
Example 4: Exs. 31–36, 47–52
Example 5: Exs. 37–39

40.
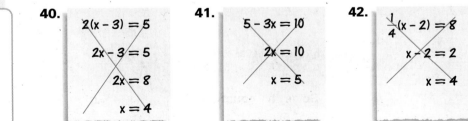

$2(x - 3) = 5$
$2x - 3 = 5$
$2x = 8$
$x = 4$

41.

$5 - 3x = 10$
$2x = 10$
$x = 5$

42.

$\frac{1}{4}(x - 2) = 8$
$x - 2 = 2$
$x = 4$

43. LOGICAL REASONING Copy the solution steps shown. Then write an explanation for each step in the right-hand column.

Solution Step	Explanation
$\dfrac{5x}{2} + 3 = 6$	Original Equation
$\dfrac{5x}{2} = 3$	?
$5x = 6$	?
$x = \dfrac{6}{5}$	?

Student Help

▶ **HOMEWORK HELP**

Extra help with problem solving in Exs. 44–46 is available at www.mcdougallittell.com

44. STUDENT THEATER Your school's drama club charges $4 per person for admission to the play *Our Town*. The club borrowed $400 from parents to pay for costumes and props. After paying back the parents, the drama club has $100. How many people attended the play? Choose the equation that represents this situation and solve it.

A. $4x + 400 = 100$ **B.** $4x + 100 = 400$ **C.** $4x - 400 = 100$

45. FARMING PROJECT You have a 90-pound calf you are raising for a 4-H project. You expect the calf to gain 65 pounds per month. In how many months will the animal weigh 1000 pounds?

46. FIREFIGHTING The formula $d = \dfrac{n}{2} + 26$ relates nozzle pressure n (in pounds per square inch) and the maximum distance the water reaches d (in feet) for a fire hose with a certain size nozzle. Solve for n to find how much pressure is needed to reach a fire 50 feet away. ▶ Source: Fire Department Hydraulics

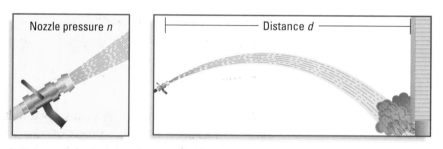

CHALLENGE Solve the equation.

47. $4(2y + 1) - 6y = 18$ **48.** $22x + 2(3x + 5) = 66$ **49.** $6x + 3(x + 4) = 15$

50. $7 - (2 - g) = -4$ **51.** $-x + (5x - 7) = -5$ **52.** $5a - (2a - 1) = -2$

Standardized Test Practice

53. MULTIPLE CHOICE Which is a solution to the equation $9x - 5x - 19 = 21$?

   Ⓐ -10 Ⓑ $-\dfrac{1}{2}$ Ⓒ $\dfrac{1}{2}$ Ⓓ 10

54. MULTIPLE CHOICE The bill (parts and labor) for the repair of a car is $458. The cost of parts is $339. The cost of labor is $34 per hour. Which equation could you use to find the number of hours of labor?

   Ⓕ $34(x + 339) = 458$ Ⓖ $34 + 339x = 458$

   Ⓗ $34x + 339 = 458$ Ⓙ $34 + x + 339 = 458$

WRITING POWERS Write the expression in exponential form.
(Lesson 1.2)

55. $a \cdot a \cdot a \cdot a \cdot a \cdot a$ **56.** x to the fifth power   **57.** $4 \cdot 4 \cdot 4$

58. five squared   **59.** t cubed   **60.** $3x \cdot 3x \cdot 3x \cdot 3x \cdot 3x$

EVALUATING EXPRESSIONS Evaluate the expression.
(Lessons 1.3, 2.4, 2.8)

61. $5 + 8 - 3$ **62.** $32 \cdot 4 + 8$ **63.** $5 \cdot (12 - 4) + 7$

64. $-6 \div 3 - 4 \cdot 5$ **65.** $2 - 8 \div \dfrac{-2}{3}$ **66.** $\dfrac{(3-6)^2 + 6}{-5}$

COMPARING FRACTIONS AND DECIMALS Complete the statement using
<, >, or =. *(Skills Review pp. 767, 770)*

67. $\dfrac{1}{4}$ **?** 0.35 **68.** 1.5 **?** $\dfrac{5}{5}$ **69.** 0.30 **?** $\dfrac{2}{3}$ **70.** $\dfrac{8}{5}$ **?** 1.6

71. $\dfrac{17}{2}$ **?** 9.5 **72.** 0 **?** $\dfrac{0}{7}$ **73.** 2.7 **?** $\dfrac{14}{5}$ **74.** $\dfrac{6}{8}$ **?** 0.75

Quiz 1

Solve the equation. *(Lessons 3.1, 3.2)*

1. $x - 14 = 7$ **2.** $y + 8 = -9$ **3.** $5 = m - (-12)$

4. $10x = -10$ **5.** $47 = \dfrac{x}{6}$ **6.** $3 = \dfrac{3}{5}x$

7. HISTORY TEST You take a history test that has 100 regular points and
8 bonus points. You get a score of 91, which includes 4 bonus points. Let x
represent the score you would have had without the bonus points. Which
equation represents this situation? Solve the equation. *(Lesson 3.1)*

   A. $x + 91 = 100$ **B.** $x + 4 = 91$ **C.** $x + 4 = 108$

8. TICKET PRICE You buy six tickets for a concert that you and your friends
want to attend. The total charge for all of the tickets is $72. Write and solve
an equation to find the price of one concert ticket. *(Lesson 3.2)*

Solve the equation. *(Lesson 3.3)*

9. $2x - 5 = 13$ **10.** $12 + 9x = 30$ **11.** $8n - 10 - 12n = -18$

12. $6(5y - 3) + 2 = 14$ **13.** $7x - 8(x + 3) = 1$ **14.** $\dfrac{2}{3}(x + 1) = 10$

15. FOOD PREPARATION You are helping to make potato salad for a family
picnic. You can peel 2 potatoes per minute. You need 30 peeled potatoes.
How long will it take you to finish if you have already peeled 12 potatoes?
(Lesson 3.3)

DEVELOPING CONCEPTS
Variables on Both Sides

For use with
Lesson 3.4

GOAL

Use algebra tiles to solve equations with variables on both sides.

MATERIALS

• algebra tiles

Question

How can you use algebra tiles to solve an equation with a variable on both the left and the right side of the equation?

Explore

1 Use algebra tiles to model the equation $4x + 5 = 2x + 9$.

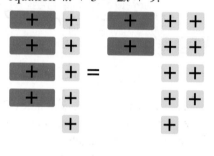

2 You want to have x-tiles on only one side of the equation. Subtract two x-tiles from each side. Write the new equation. ___?___ $+ 5 =$ ___?___

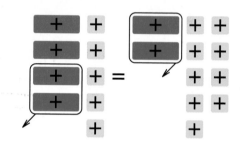

3 To isolate the x-tiles, subtract five 1-tiles from each side. Write the new equation. $2x =$ ___?___

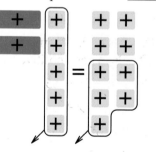

4 You know the value of $2x$. To find the value of x, split the tiles on each side of the equation in half to get $x =$ ___?___ .

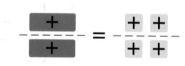

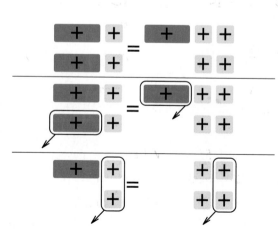

Think About It

Use algebra tiles to solve the equation.

1. $4x + 4 = 3x + 7$ **2.** $2x + 3 = 6 + x$

3. $6x + 5 = 3x + 14$ **4.** $5x + 2 = 10 + x$

5. $8x + 3 = 7x + 3$ **6.** $x + 9 = 1 + 3x$

7. The model at the left shows the solution of an equation. Copy the model. Write the solution step and an explanation of the step beside each part of the model.

3.4 Solving Equations with Variables on Both Sides

Goal
Solve equations that have variables on both sides.

Key Words
- identity
- variable term
- coefficient

Can a cheetah keep up the pace?

The cheetah is the fastest animal on land for running short distances. In Exercises 48 and 49 you will solve an equation to find out if a cheetah can catch up to a running gazelle.

Some equations have variables on both sides. To solve these equations, you can first collect the variable terms on one side of the equation. The examples will show you that collecting the variable terms on the side with the *greater* variable coefficient will result in a positive coefficient.

EXAMPLE 1 Collect Variables on Left Side

Solve $7x + 19 = -2x + 55$.

Solution

Look at the coefficients of the x-terms. Since 7 is greater than -2, collect the x-terms on the left side to get a positive coefficient.

$7x + 19 = -2x + 55$	Write original equation.
▶ $7x + 19 + 2x = -2x + 55 + 2x$	Add $2x$ to each side.
$9x + 19 = 55$	Combine like terms.
$9x + 19 - 19 = 55 - 19$	Subtract 19 from each side.
$9x = 36$	Simplify both sides.
$\dfrac{9x}{9} = \dfrac{36}{9}$	Divide each side by 9.
$x = 4$	Simplify.

ANSWER ▶ The solution is 4.

CHECK ✓

$7x + 19 = -2x + 55$	Write original equation.
$7(4) + 19 \stackrel{?}{=} -2(4) + 55$	Substitute 4 for each x.
$47 = 47$ ✓	Solution is correct.

Student Help

▶ LOOK BACK
For help with
identifying terms of an
expression, see p. 87.

EXAMPLE 2 Collect Variables on Right Side

Solve $80 - 9y = 6y$.

Solution Remember that $80 - 9y$ is the same as $80 + (-9y)$. Since 6 is greater than -9, collect the y-terms on the right side to get a positive coefficient.

$80 - 9y = 6y$	Write original equation.
$80 - 9y + 9y = 6y + 9y$	Add $9y$ to each side.
$80 = 15y$	Combine like terms.
$\dfrac{80}{15} = \dfrac{15y}{15}$	Divide each side by 15.
$\dfrac{16}{3} = y$	Simplify.

ANSWER ▶ The solution is $\dfrac{16}{3}$ or $5\dfrac{1}{3}$. Check this in the original equation.

Checkpoint ✓ **Collect Variables on One Side**

Solve the equation. Check your solution in the original equation.

1. $34 - 3x = 14x$ **2.** $5y - 2 = y + 10$ **3.** $-6x + 4 = -8x$

EXAMPLE 3 Combine Like Terms First

Solve $3x - 10 + 4x = 5x - 7$.

Solution $3x - 10 + 4x = 5x - 7$	Write original equation.
$7x - 10 = 5x - 7$	Combine like terms.
$7x - 10 - 5x = 5x - 7 - 5x$	Subtract $5x$ from each side.
$2x - 10 = -7$	Combine like terms.
$2x - 10 + 10 = -7 + 10$	Add 10 to each side.
$2x = 3$	Simplify both sides.
$\dfrac{2x}{2} = \dfrac{3}{2}$	Divide each side by 2.
$x = \dfrac{3}{2}$	Simplify.

ANSWER ▶ The solution is $\dfrac{3}{2}$ or $1\dfrac{1}{2}$. Check this in the original equation.

Checkpoint ✓ **Combine Like Terms First**

Solve the equation. Check your solution in the original equation.

4. $5x - 3x + 4 = 3x + 8$ **5.** $6x + 3 = 8 + 7x + 2x$

NUMBER OF SOLUTIONS So far you have seen linear equations that have only *one solution*. Some linear equations have *no solution*. An **identity** is an equation that is true for all values of the variable, so an identity has *many solutions*.

Student Help

▶**MORE EXAMPLES**

More examples are available at www.mcdougallittell.com

EXAMPLE 4 Identify Number of Solutions

Solve the equation if possible. Determine whether it has *one solution*, *no solution*, or is an *identity*.

a. $3(x + 2) = 3x + 6$ **b.** $3(x + 2) = 3x + 4$ **c.** $3(x + 2) = 2x + 4$

Solution

a.

$3(x + 2) = 3x + 6$	Write original equation.
$3x + 6 = 3x + 6$	Use distributive property.
$3x + 6 - 3x = 3x + 6 - 3x$	Subtract 3x from each side.
$6 = 6$	Combine like terms.

ANSWER ▶ The equation $6 = 6$ is always true, so all values of x are solutions. The original equation is an *identity*.

b.

$3(x + 2) = 3x + 4$	Write original equation.
$3x + 6 = 3x + 4$	Use distributive property.
$3x + 6 - 3x = 3x + 4 - 3x$	Subtract 3x from each side.
$6 \neq 4$	Combine like terms.

ANSWER ▶ The equation $6 = 4$ is never true no matter what the value of x. The original equation has *no solution*.

c.

$3(x + 2) = 2x + 4$	Write original equation.
$3x + 6 = 2x + 4$	Use distributive property.
$3x + 6 - 2x = 2x + 4 - 2x$	Subtract 2x from each side.
$x + 6 = 4$	Combine like terms.
$x + 6 - 6 = 4 - 6$	Subtract 6 from each side.
$x = -2$	Simplify both sides.

ANSWER ▶ The solution is -2. The original equation has *one solution*.

Checkpoint ✓ Identify Number of Solutions

Solve the equation if possible. Determine whether the equation has *one solution*, *no solution*, or is an *identity*.

6. $2(x + 4) = 2x + 8$ **7.** $2(x + 4) = x - 8$

8. $2(x + 4) = 2x - 8$ **9.** $2(x + 4) = x + 8$

Guided Practice

Vocabulary Check

1. Complete: An equation that is true for all values of the variable is called a(n) __?__ .

2. Is the equation $-2(4 - x) = 2x - 8$ an identity? Explain why or why not.

Identify the coefficient of each variable term.

3. $16 + 3y = 22$ **4.** $3x + 12 = 8x - 8$ **5.** $4x - 2x = 6$

6. $5x - 4x + 3 = 9 - x$ **7.** $5m + 4 = 8 - 7m$ **8.** $2(x + 1) = 14$

Skill Check

Solve the equation if possible. Determine whether the equation has *one solution*, *no solution*, or is an *identity*.

9. $7x + 3 = 2x - 2$ **10.** $5(x - 5) = 5x + 24$ **11.** $12 - 5a = -2a - 9$

12. $3(4c + 7) = 12c$ **13.** $x - 2x + 3 = 3 - x$ **14.** $6y - 3y + 6 = 5y - 4$

15. FUNDRAISING You are making pies to sell at a fundraiser. It costs $3 to make each pie, plus a one-time cost of $20 for a pastry blender and a rolling pin. You plan to sell the pies for $5 each. Which equation could you use to find the number of pies you need to sell to break even, or recover your costs?

A. $3x = 20 + 5x$ **B.** $3x + 20 = 5x$

C. $3x - 20 = 5x$ **D.** $20 - 5x = 3x$

16. Solve the correct equation in Exercise 15 to find the number of pies you need to sell to break even.

Practice and Applications

WRITING Describe the first step you would use to solve the equation.

17. $x + 2 = 3x - 4$ **18.** $5t + 12 = 2t$

19. $2x - 7 = -8x + 13$ **20.** $-4x = -9 + 5x$

SOLVING EQUATIONS Solve the equation.

21. $15 - 2y = 3y$ **22.** $2p - 9 = 5p + 12$

23. $5x - 16 = 14 - 5x$ **24.** $-3g + 9 = 15g - 9$

25. $11x - 21 = 17 - 8x$ **26.** $4x + 27 = 3x + 34$

27. $5x - 4x = -6x + 3$ **28.** $10y = 2y - 6y + 7$

29. $r - 2 + 3r = 6 + 5r$ **30.** $4 + 6x - 9x = 3x$

31. $2t - 3t + 8 = 3t - 8$ **32.** $13x + 8 + 8x = -9x - 22$

33. $-x + 6 - 5x = 14 - 2x$ **34.** $5x - 3x + 4 = 3x + 8$

ERROR ANALYSIS In Exercises 35 and 36, find and correct the error.

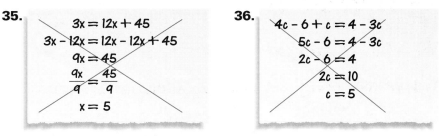

35.
$$3x = 12x + 45$$
$$3x - 12x = 12x - 12x + 45$$
$$9x = 45$$
$$\frac{9x}{9} = \frac{45}{9}$$
$$x = 5$$

36.
$$4c - 6 + c = 4 - 3c$$
$$5c - 6 = 4 - 3c$$
$$2c - 6 = 4$$
$$2c = 10$$
$$c = 5$$

Student Help

▶**HOMEWORK HELP**

Extra help with problem solving in Exs. 37–42 is available at www.mcdougallittell.com

IDENTIFYING NUMBER OF SOLUTIONS Solve the equation if possible. Determine whether the equation has *one solution*, *no solution*, or is an *identity*.

37. $8c - 4 = 20 - 4c$

38. $24 - 6r = 6(4 - r)$

39. $-7 + 4m = 6m - 5$

40. $6m - 5 = 7m + 7 - m$

41. $3x - 7 = 2x + 8 + 4x$

42. $6 + 3c = -c - 6$

MENTAL MATH Without writing the steps of a solution, determine whether the equation has *one solution*, *no solution*, or is an *identity*.

43. $8 + 6a = 6a - 1$

44. $6a + 8 = 2a$

45. $8 + 6a = 2a + 8$

46. $8 + 6a = 6a + 8$

47. **History Link** Steamboats carried cotton and passengers up and down the Mississippi River in the mid-1800s. A steamboat could travel 8 miles per hour downstream from Natchez, Mississippi, to New Orleans, Louisiana, and only 3 miles per hour upstream from New Orleans to Natchez. It was about 265 miles each way.

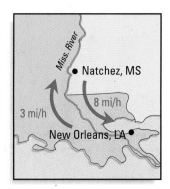

If it took a steamboat 55 more hours to go upstream than it did to go downstream, how long did it take to complete the roundtrip?

Solve $8t = 3(t + 55)$, where t is the time (in hours) it takes the steamboat to travel downstream and $(t + 55)$ is the time it takes to travel upstream.

48. **CHEETAH AND GAZELLE** A cheetah running 90 feet per second is 100 feet behind a gazelle running 70 feet per second. How long will it take the cheetah to catch up to the gazelle? Use the verbal model to write and solve a linear equation.

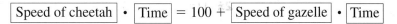

$$\boxed{\text{Speed of cheetah}} \cdot \boxed{\text{Time}} = 100 + \boxed{\text{Speed of gazelle}} \cdot \boxed{\text{Time}}$$

49. **WRITING** A cheetah can run faster than a gazelle, but a cheetah can only run at top speed for about 20 seconds. If a gazelle is too far away for a cheetah to catch it within 20 seconds, the gazelle is probably safe. Would the gazelle in Exercise 48 be safe if the cheetah starts running 500 feet behind it? Explain your answer. *HINT:* Use 500 feet instead of 100 feet in the verbal model.

CHALLENGE Solve the equation.

50. $2(2x + 3) = -6(x + 9)$

51. $7 - (-4t) = 4t - 14 - 21t$

52. $-\frac{3}{4}x + 5 = \frac{1}{4}x - 3$

53. $7 - \frac{1}{3}x = \frac{2}{3}x + 4$

Standardized Test Practice

54. MULTIPLE CHOICE Which equations are equivalent?

I. $3x - 4x + 18 = 5x$ **II.** $4 + 6x = 8x - 2$ **III.** $2x - 8 = 7 - x$

(A) I and II   (B) II and III   (C) All   (D) None

55. MULTIPLE CHOICE For which equation is $j = 4$ a solution?

(F) $-10 + 5j = -2 + 2j$ (G) $7j - 3j + 2 = 4j - 2$

(H) $6j - 4 = 4j + 4$ (J) $3j + 7 = 2j - 2$

56. MULTIPLE CHOICE Solve $15x + 6 - x = 16x + 6 - 2x$.

(A) $x = 0$ (B) $x = 6$ (C) No solution   (D) Identity

Mixed Review

57. DRIVING DISTANCE It takes you 3 hours to drive to your friend's house at an average speed of 48 miles per hour. How far did you travel? *(Lesson 1.1)*

EVALUATING EXPRESSIONS Evaluate the expression for the given value of the variable. *(Lessons 1.1, 1.2)*

58. $7 \cdot y$ when $y = 8$ **59.** $x - 5$ when $x = 13$ **60.** $\frac{x}{4}$ when $x = 56$

61. x^3 when $x = 6$ **62.** $4t^2$ when $t = 3$ **63.** $(3x)^2$ when $x = 4$

NUMERICAL EXPRESSIONS Evaluate the expression. *(Lesson 1.3)*

64. $(10 + 6) \div 2 - 3$ **65.** $8 + 4 \div (3 - 1)$ **66.** $14 - 2 \cdot 5 - 3$

67. MENTAL MATH You want to buy a pair of sneakers that costs $49.99. The state sales tax adds $2.99 to the total cost. If you have $53, do you have enough money to buy the sneakers? *(Lesson 1.4)*

RULES OF ADDITION Find the sum. *(Lesson 2.3)*

68. $3 + (-4)$ **69.** $-6 + 2$ **70.** $-11 + (-8)$

71. $5 + 16 + (-9)$ **72.** $8 + (-7) + (-10)$ **73.** $-22 + (-5) + 4$

SOLVING EQUATIONS Solve the equation. *(Lesson 3.2)*

74. $15x = 255$ **75.** $236x = 0$ **76.** $\frac{1}{5}x = 9$ **77.** $\frac{2}{3}x = 60$

Maintaining Skills

DIVIDING DECIMALS Divide. *(Skills Review p. 760)*

78. $15 \div 0.05$ **79.** $4 \div 0.002$ **80.** $20 \div 0.4$

81. $8.1 \div 0.9$ **82.** $0.72 \div 0.3$ **83.** $6.4 \div 0.8$

84. $46.2 \div 0.02$ **85.** $39.1 \div 0.01$ **86.** $23.4 \div 0.04$

More on Linear Equations

Goal

Solve more complicated equations that have variables on both sides.

Key Words

- inverse operations
- distributive property

Will it save money to join a health club?

In this lesson you will solve more linear equations that have variables on both sides. You will solve an equation to compare the costs of different payment plans at a health club in Example 4.

You have learned several ways to transform an equation into an equivalent equation. As you solve more complicated equations, you will continue to use these same steps to isolate the variable.

STEPS FOR SOLVING LINEAR EQUATIONS

❶ **Simplify** each side by distributing and/or combining like terms.

❷ **Collect** variable terms on the side where the coefficient is greater.

❸ **Use** inverse operations to isolate the variable.

❹ **Check** your solution in the *original* equation.

EXAMPLE 1 Solve a More Complicated Equation

Solve $4(1 - x) + 3x = -2(x + 1)$.

Solution

$4(1 - x) + 3x = -2(x + 1)$	Write original equation.
$4 - 4x + 3x = -2x - 2$	Use distributive property.
$4 - x = -2x - 2$	Combine like terms.
$4 - x + 2x = -2x - 2 + 2x$	Add 2x to each side.
$4 + x = -2$	Combine like terms.
$4 + x - 4 = -2 - 4$	Subtract 4 from each side.
$x = -6$	Simplify.

ANSWER ▸ The solution is -6.

Check by substituting -6 for each x in the original equation.

SOLUTION STEPS Simplify an equation before you decide whether to collect the variable terms on the right side or the left side. In Examples 2 and 3, use the distributive property and combine like terms to make it easier to see which coefficient is larger.

EXAMPLE **2** **Solve a More Complicated Equation**

Solve $-3(4x + 1) + 6x = 4(2x - 6)$.

Solution

$-3(4x + 1) + 6x = 4(2x - 6)$	Write original equation.
$-12x - 3 + 6x = 8x - 24$	Use distributive property.
$-6x - 3 = 8x - 24$	Combine like terms.
$-3 = 14x - 24$	Add $6x$ to each side.
$21 = 14x$	Add 24 to each side.
$\dfrac{21}{14} = x$	Divide each side by 14.
$\dfrac{3}{2} = x$	Simplify.

Student Help

▶**STUDY TIP**
You can use mental math to add $6x$ to each side of the equation. ⋯⋯⋯⋯⋯▶

ANSWER ▶ The solution is $\dfrac{3}{2}$ or $1\dfrac{1}{2}$. Check this in the original equation.

EXAMPLE **3** **Solve a More Complicated Equation**

Solve $\dfrac{1}{4}(12x + 16) = 10 - 3(x - 2)$.

Solution

$\dfrac{1}{4}(12x + 16) = 10 - 3(x - 2)$	Write original equation.
$\dfrac{12x}{4} + \dfrac{16}{4} = 10 - 3x + 6$	Use distributive property.
$3x + 4 = 16 - 3x$	Simplify.
$6x + 4 = 16$	Add $3x$ to each side.
$6x = 12$	Subtract 4 from each side.
$x = 2$	Divide each side by 6.

ANSWER ▶ The solution is 2. Check this in the original equation.

Checkpoint ✓ **Solve a More Complicated Equation**

Solve the equation.

1. $6(x + 3) + 3x = 3(x - 2)$

2. $4x + (2 - x) = -3(x + 2)$

3. $-2(4x + 2) = -2(x + 3) + 9$

4. $\dfrac{1}{3}(3y - 12) = 6 - 2(y - 1)$

Student Help

▶ **MORE EXAMPLES**

More examples
are available at
www.mcdougallittell.com

EXAMPLE **4** *Compare Payment Plans*

HEALTH CLUB COSTS A health club has two payment plans. You can become a member by paying a $10 new member fee and use the gym for $5 a visit. Or, you can use the gym as a nonmember for $7 a visit. Compare the costs of the two payment plans.

Solution Find the number of visits for which the plans would cost the same.

VERBAL MODEL

$$\underbrace{\boxed{\text{New member fee}} + \boxed{\text{Member's fee per visit}} \cdot \boxed{\text{Number of visits}}}_{\text{Member's cost}} =$$

$$\underbrace{\boxed{\text{Nonmember's fee per visit}} \cdot \boxed{\text{Number of visits}}}_{\text{Nonmember's cost}}$$

LABELS

New member fee = **10**   (dollars)

Member's fee per visit = **5**   (dollars)

Nonmember's fee per visit = **7**   (dollars)

Number of visits = x

ALGEBRAIC MODEL

$$10 + 5 \cdot x = 7 \cdot x$$ Write linear equation.

$$10 = 2x$$ Subtract 5x from each side.

$$x = 5$$ Divide each side by 2.

A table can help you interpret the result.

Number of visits	1	2	3	4	5	6	7
Member's cost	$15	$20	$25	$30	$35	$40	$45
Nonmember's cost	$7	$14	$21	$28	$35	$42	$49

Nonmember's cost is less   Member's cost is less

ANSWER ▶ If you visit the health club 5 times, the cost would be the same as a member or a nonmember. If you visit more than 5 times, it would cost less as a member. If you visit fewer than 5 times, it would cost less as a nonmember.

Checkpoint ✓ *Compare Payment Plans*

5. A video store charges $8 to rent a video game for five days. Membership to the video store is free. A video game club charges only $3 to rent a game for five days, but membership in the club is $50 per year. Compare the costs of the two rental plans.

Guided Practice

Vocabulary Check

State the inverse operation needed to solve the equation.

1. $x + 5 = 13$ **2.** $x - 4 = -9$ **3.** $7x = 28$ **4.** $36 = \dfrac{x}{6}$

Decide whether the equation is *true* or *false*. Use the distributive property to explain your answer.

5. $3(2 + 5) = 3(2) + 5$

6. $(2 + 5)3 = 2(3) + 5(3)$

7. $8(6 - 4) = 8(6) - 8(4)$

8. $(6 - 4)8 = 6 - 4(8)$

9. $-2(4 + 3) = -8 + 6$

10. $-2(4 - 3) = -8 + 6$

Skill Check

Solve the equation. Check your solution in the original equation.

11. $2(x - 1) = 3(x + 1)$

12. $3(x + 2) = 4(5 + x)$

13. $6(8 + 3a) = -2(a - 4)$

14. $8(4 - r) + r = -6(3 + r)$

15. $-4(m + 6) + 2m = 3(m + 2)$

16. $7(c - 7) + 4c = -2(c + 5)$

17. $\dfrac{3}{8}(16x - 8) = 9 - 5(x - 2)$

18. $\dfrac{1}{5}(25 - 5k) = 21 - 3(k - 4)$

Practice and Applications

SOLVING EQUATIONS Solve the equation.

19. $3(x + 6) = 5(x - 4)$

20. $7(6 - y) = -3(y - 2)$

21. $5(x + 2) = x + 6(x - 3)$

22. $8(x + 5) = 7(x + 8)$

23. $24y - 2(6 - y) = 6(3y + 2)$

24. $7(b + 2) - 4b = 2(b + 10)$

25. $4(m + 3) - 2m = 3(m - 3)$

26. $2(a + 4) = 2(a - 4) + 4a$

27. $4 + 5(3 - x) = 4(8 + 2x)$

28. $5(-x + 2) = -3(7x + 2) + 8x$

29. $10(2x + 4) = -(-8 - 9x) + 3x$

30. $9(t - 4) - 2t = 5(t - 2)$

SOLVING EQUATIONS Solve the equation by distributing the fraction first.

31. $3(x + 2) = \dfrac{1}{4}(12x + 4) - 5x$

32. $\dfrac{2}{5}(10x + 25) = -10 - 4(x + 3)$

33. $\dfrac{1}{2}(8n - 2) = -(-8 + 9n) - 5n$

34. $2(8 - 4x) = \dfrac{1}{3}(33 - 18x) + 3$

35. $\dfrac{3}{4}(24 - 20t) + 9t = 2(5t + 1)$

36. $\dfrac{2}{3}(9n - 6) = 4(n + 1)$

Student Help

▶ **HOMEWORK HELP**
Example 1: Exs. 19–30
Example 2: Exs. 19–30
Example 3: Exs. 31–36
Example 4: Exs. 40–43

37. LOGICAL REASONING Write the steps you would use to solve the equation $3(x - 4) + 2x = 6 - x$. Beside each step, write an explanation of the step. Then show how to check your answer.

ERROR ANALYSIS In Exercises 38 and 39, find and correct the error.

38.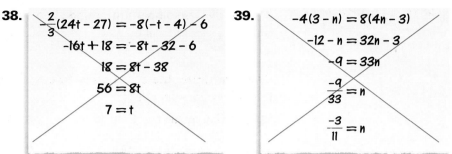

$$-\frac{2}{3}(24t - 27) = -8(-t - 4) - 6$$
$$-16t + 18 = -8t - 32 - 6$$
$$18 = 8t - 38$$
$$56 = 8t$$
$$7 = t$$

39.

$$-4(3 - n) = 8(4n - 3)$$
$$-12 - n = 32n - 3$$
$$-9 = 33n$$
$$\frac{-9}{33} = n$$
$$\frac{-3}{11} = n$$

40. COMPUTER TIME A local computer center charges nonmembers $5 per session to use the media center. Members are charged a one-time fee of $20 and $3 per session. Use the verbal model to write an equation that can help you decide whether to become a member. Solve the equation and explain your solution.

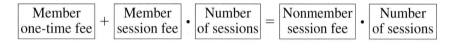

| Member one-time fee | + | Member session fee | $\cdot$ | Number of sessions | = | Nonmember session fee | $\cdot$ | Number of sessions |

41. PAINT YOUR OWN POTTERY You want to paint a piece of pottery. The total price is the cost of the piece plus an hourly painting rate. Studio A sells a vase for $12 and lets you paint for $7 an hour. Studio B sells a similar vase for $15 and lets you paint for $4 an hour. Which equation would you use to compare the total price at each studio?

A. $7x - 12 = 4x - 15$ **B.** $12 + 7x = 15 + 4x$

42. COMPARE COSTS Use the information in Exercise 41. If it takes you 2 hours to paint a vase, would Studio A or Studio B charge less to paint a vase?

43. ROCK CLIMBING A rock-climbing gym charges nonmembers $16 per day to use the gym and $8 per day for equipment rental. Members pay a yearly fee of $450 for unlimited climbing and $6 per day for equipment rental. Which equation represents this situation? Solve the equation to find how many times you must use the gym to justify becoming a member.

A. $(16 + 8)x = 450 - 6x$ **B.** $24x = 450 - 6x$

C. $(16 + 8)x = 450 + 6x$ **D.** $16x + 8 = 450 + 6x$

CHALLENGE Solve the equation.

44. $-3(7 - 3n) + 2n = 5(2n - 4)$ **45.** $4x + 3(x - 2) = -5(x - 4) - x$

46. $-7 + 8(5 - 3q) = 3(7 - 9q)$ **47.** $y + 2(y - 6) = -(2y - 14) + 49$

48. $\frac{1}{3}(3x - 12) = 6 - 2(x - 1)$ **49.** $2(6 - 2x) = -9x - \frac{1}{2}(-4x + 6)$

Science Link Use the following information for Exercises 50 and 51.

The diagram shows the orbits of Jupiter's four largest moons: Io, Europa, Ganymede, and Callisto. The orbits are circular.

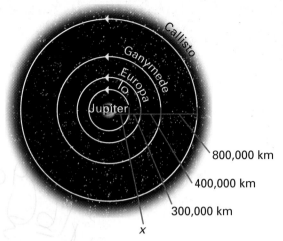

Io's orbit is x kilometers (km) from Jupiter. The distance between Io and Europa is 300,000 km. The distance between Europa and Ganymede is 400,000 km. The distance between Ganymede and Callisto is 800,000 km. The distance from Jupiter to Callisto is $4\frac{3}{4}x$, or $4\frac{3}{4}$ times the distance from Jupiter to Io.

800,000 km

400,000 km

300,000 km

x

50. Find the distance x between Jupiter and Io, using the equation

$$x + 300{,}000 + 400{,}000 + 800{,}000 = 4\frac{3}{4}x.$$

51. Use the solution to Exercise 50 to find the distance of each moon's orbit from Jupiter.

Moon's Orbit	Io	Europa	Ganymede	Callisto
Distance from Jupiter (km)	?	?	?	?

Standardized Test Practice

52. MULTIPLE CHOICE Which inverse operation can be used to solve the equation $6 + x = 15$?

  (A) Add 6 to each side.   **(B)** Subtract 6 from each side.

  (C) Multiply each side by 6.   **(D)** Divide each side by 6.

53. MULTIPLE CHOICE Solve $\frac{1}{3}(7x + 5) = 3x - 5$.

  (F) -5 **(G)** $-\frac{5}{2}$ **(H)** 10   **(J)** 15

Mixed Review

MULTIPLYING REAL NUMBERS Find the product. *(Lesson 2.5)*

54. $6(-6)$ **55.** $-3(-12)$ **56.** $-8(-5)$ **57.** $11(-7)$

COMBINING LIKE TERMS Simplify the expression by combining like terms if possible. If not possible, write *already simplified*. *(Lesson 2.7)*

58. $h + 7 - 6h$ **59.** $3w^2 + 2w - 3w$ **60.** $ab + 4a - b$

61. $3s + 5t - 2s + 6t$ **62.** $x - y + 2xy$ **63.** $-8m - m^2 + 2m$

Maintaining Skills

SUBTRACTING DECIMALS Subtract. *(Skills Review p. 759)*

64. $11.9 - 1.2$ **65.** $15.75 - 4.25$ **66.** $3.6 - 0.5$

67. $12.44 - 6.02$ **68.** $22.87 - 2.99$ **69.** $56.32 - 33.83$

Solving Decimal Equations

Goal

Find exact and approximate solutions of equations that contain decimals.

Key Words

• rounding error

What's the price of a slice?

Exact answers are not always practical. Sometimes rounded answers make more sense. In Example 3 you will round for a practical answer for each person's share in the cost of a pizza.

The giant pizza slice shown here was made in San Francisco, California, in 1989. Its shape was very close to a triangle with a base of 4 meters and a height of 6.5 meters.

EXAMPLE 1 Round for the Final Answer

Solve $-38x - 39 = 118$. Round to the nearest hundredth.

Solution

$-38x - 39 = 118$	Write original equation.
$-38x = 157$	Add 39 to each side.
$x = \dfrac{157}{-38}$	Divide each side by -38.
$x \approx -4.131578947$	Use a calculator to get an approximate solution.
$x \approx -4.13$	Round to nearest hundredth.

ANSWER ▶ The solution is approximately -4.13.

CHECK ✓

$-38x - 39 = 118$	Write original equation.
$-38(-4.13) - 39 \overset{?}{=} 118$	Substitute -4.13 for x.
$117.94 \approx 118$ ✓	Rounded answer is reasonable.

When you substitute a rounded answer into the original equation, the two sides of the equation may not be exactly equal, but they should be approximately equal. Use the symbol $\approx$ to show that quantities are approximately equal.

Checkpoint ✓ *Round for the Final Answer*

Solve the equation. Round to the nearest hundredth.

1. $24x + 43 = 66$ **2.** $-42x + 28 = 87$ **3.** $22x - 39x = 19$

Student Help

▶ **MORE EXAMPLES**

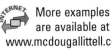 More examples are available at www.mcdougallittell.com

EXAMPLE 2 **Solve an Equation that Contains Decimals**

Solve $3.5x - 37.9 = 0.2x$. Round to the nearest tenth.

Solution

$3.5x - 37.9 = 0.2x$	Write original equation.
$3.3x - 37.9 = 0$	Subtract 0.2x from each side.
$3.3x = 37.9$	Add 37.9 to each side.
$\dfrac{3.3x}{3.3} = \dfrac{37.9}{3.3}$	Divide each side by 3.3.
$x \approx 11.48484848$	Use a calculator to get an approximate solution.
$x \approx 11.5$	Round to nearest tenth.

ANSWER ▶ The solution is approximately 11.5.

CHECK ✓

$3.5x - 37.9 = 0.2x$	Write original equation.
$3.5(\mathbf{11.5}) - 37.9 \stackrel{?}{=} 0.2(\mathbf{11.5})$	Substitute 11.5 for each x.
$2.35 \approx 2.3$ ✓	Rounded answer is reasonable.

 **Solve an Equation that Contains Decimals**

Solve the equation. Round to the nearest tenth.

4. $2.4x - 0.9 = 12.4$ **5.** $1.13y - 25.34 = 0.26y$

6. $14.7 + 2.3x = 4.06$ **7.** $3.25n - 4.71 = 0.52n$

ROUNDING ERROR Using a rounded solution in a real-life situation can lead to a **rounding error**, as in Example 3.

EXAMPLE 3 **Round for a Practical Answer**

Three people want to share equally in the cost of a pizza. The pizza costs $12.89. What is each person's share?

Solution

Find each person's share by solving $3x = 12.89$.

$3x = 12.89$	Write original equation.
$x = 4.29666\ldots$	Use a calculator to divide each side by 3. Exact answer is a repeating decimal.
$x \approx 4.30$	Round to nearest cent.

ANSWER ▶ Each person's share is $4.30.

Three times the rounded answer is one cent too much due to rounding error.

Student Help

▶**SKILLS REVIEW**
To review writing a
percent as a decimal,
see p. 768.

PERCENTS When you solve a problem involving percents, remember to write
the percent in decimal form.

5% of \$23.45 = 0.05(23.45)	Rewrite 5% as 0.05.
= 1.1725	Multiply.
≈ \$1.17	Round to nearest cent.

EXAMPLE 4 Use a Verbal Model

You buy a sweatshirt for a total cost of \$20. The total cost includes the price of
the sweatshirt and a 5% sales tax. What is the price of the sweatshirt?

Solution

**VERBAL
MODEL**

Price + Sales tax · Price = Total cost

LABELS

Price = x (dollars)

Sales tax = **0.05**   (no units)

Total cost = **20**   (dollars)

**ALGEBRAIC
MODEL**

$x + 0.05 \cdot x = 20$	Write linear equation.
$1.05x = 20$	Combine like terms.
$x = \dfrac{20}{1.05}$	Divide each side by 1.05.
$x \approx 19.04761905$	Use a calculator to get an approximate solution.
$x \approx 19.05$	Round to nearest cent.

ANSWER ▶ The price of the sweatshirt is \$19.05.

CHECK ✓

$x + 0.05 \cdot x = 20$	Write linear equation.
$19.05 + (0.05)(19.05) \stackrel{?}{=} 20$	Substitute 19.05 for each x.
$19.05 + 0.95 \stackrel{?}{=} 20$	Multiply and round to nearest cent.
$20 = 20$ ✓	Solution is correct.

The total cost of \$20 includes the \$19.05 price of the sweatshirt and the 5%
sales tax of \$.95.

Checkpoint ✓ Use a Verbal Model

8. You spend a total of \$25 on a gift. The total cost includes the price of the gift
and a 7% sales tax. What is the price of the gift without the tax? Use the
verbal model to solve the problem.

Price + Sales tax · Price = Total cost

Guided Practice

Vocabulary Check

1. Give an example of rounding error.

2. The solution of $13x = 6$ rounded to the nearest hundredth is 0.46. Which of the following is a better way to list the solution? Explain.

　　A. $x = 0.46$　　　　　　　　　　**B.** $x \approx 0.46$

Tell what each symbol means.

3. $=$　　　　　　**4.** $\approx$　　　　　　**5.** $\overset{?}{=}$　　　　　　**6.** $\neq$

Skill Check

Round to the nearest tenth.

7. 23.4459　　　**8.** 108.2135　　　**9.** -13.8953　　　**10.** 62.9788

11. 56.068　　　**12.** 0.555　　　**13.** 8.839　　　**14.** -75.1234

Solve the equation. Round the result to the nearest hundredth. Check the rounded solution.

15. $2.2x = 15$　　　　　　　　　　**16.** $14 - 9x = 37$

17. $3(3t - 14) = -4$　　　　　　　**18.** $2.69 - 3.64x = 23.78x$

19. BUYING DINNER You spend a total of $13.80 at a restaurant. This includes the price of dinner and a 15% tip. What is the price of dinner without the tip? Use a verbal model to solve the problem.

Practice and Applications

SOLVING AND CHECKING Solve the equation. Round the result to the nearest hundredth. Check the rounded solution.

20. $13x - 7 = 27$　　　　　　　　**21.** $38 = -14 + 9a$

22. $17x - 33 = 114$　　　　　　　**23.** $-7x + 32 = -21$

24. $-7x + 17 = -6$　　　　　　　**25.** $18 - 3y = 5$

26. $99 = 21t + 56$　　　　　　　**27.** $-35m + 75 = 48$

28. $-16x - 18 = 3$　　　　　　　**29.** $42 = 23x - 9$

Student Help

▶**HOMEWORK HELP**
Example 1: Exs. 20–29
Example 2: Exs. 30–35
Example 3: Ex. 36
Example 4: Exs. 37, 38

SOLVING EQUATIONS Solve the equation. Round the result to the nearest hundredth.

30. $9.47x = 7.45x - 8.81$　　　　　**31.** $39.21x + 2.65 = 42.03x$

32. $12.67 + 42.35x = 5.34x$　　　　**33.** $4.65x - 4.79 = -6.84x$

34. $7.87 - 9.65x = 8.52x - 3.21$　　**35.** $8.79x - 6.54 = 6.48 + 13.75x$

36. COCOA CONSUMPTION The 267.9 million people in the United States consumed 639.4 million kilograms of cocoa produced in the 1996–1997 growing year. Which choice better represents the amount of cocoa consumed per person that year? Explain your reasoning.

▶ Source: International Cocoa Organization

A. 2.38671146 kilograms **B.** about 2.4 kilograms

FUNDRAISING **To raise money, your student council is selling magazine subscriptions. The student council will receive a one-time bonus of $150 from the magazine publisher plus 38% of the subscription money. The following verbal model represents the situation.**

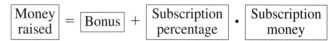

$$\boxed{\begin{array}{c}\text{Money}\\\text{raised}\end{array}} = \boxed{\text{Bonus}} + \boxed{\begin{array}{c}\text{Subscription}\\\text{percentage}\end{array}} \cdot \boxed{\begin{array}{c}\text{Subscription}\\\text{money}\end{array}}$$

37. Write a linear equation from the verbal model.
    HINT: Remember to write the percent in decimal form: 38% = 0.38.

38. How much subscription money is needed for the council to raise a total of $300? Round your answer to the nearest dollar.

EXAMPLE *Changing Decimals to Integers*

Solve $4.5 - 7.2x = 3.4x - 49.5$. Round to the nearest tenth.

Solution

You can multiply an equation with decimal coefficients by a power of ten to get an equivalent equation with integer coefficients. Multiply each side of this equation by 10 to rewrite the equation without decimals.

$4.5 - 7.2x = 3.4x - 49.5$	Write original equation.
$10(4.5 - 7.2x) = 10(3.4x - 49.5)$	Multiply each side by 10.
$45 - 72x = 34x - 495$	Use distributive property.
$45 = 106x - 495$	Add 72x to each side.
$540 = 106x$	Add 495 to each side.
$\dfrac{540}{106} = x$	Divide each side by 106.
$5.094339623 \approx x$	Use a calculator to get an approximate solution.
$5.1 \approx x$	Round to the nearest tenth.

ANSWER ▶ The solution is approximately 5.1. Check this in the original equation.

Solve the equation. Round to the nearest tenth.

39. $2.5x + 0.7 = 4.6 - 1.3x$ **40.** $1.1x + 3.2 = 0.2x - 1.4$

41. $3.35x + 2.29 = 8.61$ **42.** $0.625y - 0.184 = 2.506y$

FIELD TRIP In Exercises 43–45, use the following information.
School buses that have 71 seats will be used to transport
162 students and 30 adults.

43. Write an equation to find the number of buses needed.

44. Solve the equation in Exercise 43. Is the exact answer practical? Explain
your reasoning.

45. Would you round the answer to Exercise 44 up or down? Why?

**Standardized Test
Practice**

46. MULTIPLE CHOICE What power of ten would you multiply the equation
$5.692x - 1.346 = 8.451x$ by to change it to an equivalent equation with
integer coefficients?

(A) 10^1 **(B)** 10^2 **(C)** 10^3 **(D)** 10^4

47. MULTIPLE CHOICE What is the solution of the equation
$7.2x + 5.6 = -8.4 - 3.7x$ rounded to the nearest hundredth?

(F) -1.28 **(G)** -1.284 **(H)** -1.29 **(J)** 1.29

48. MULTIPLE CHOICE The cross-country track team ran 8.7 kilometers in
42.5 minutes during their workout. Which equation could you use to find r,
the team's average running speed (in kilometers per minute)?

(A) $8.7r = 42.5$ **(B)** $42.5r = 8.7$

(C) $42.5 + r = 8.7$ **(D)** $8.7 + r = 42.5$

49. MULTIPLE CHOICE Solve the equation you chose in Exercise 48 to find the
team's average running speed (in kilometers per minute).

(F) 0.2 **(G)** 4.1 **(H)** 32.0 **(J)** 32.2

Mixed Review

ACCOUNT ACTIVITY In Exercises
50–52, use the table. It shows all
the activity in a checking account
during June. Deposits are positive
and withdrawals are negative.
(*Lesson 1.7*)

Day	Activity
June 6	−$225.00
June 10	+$310.25
June 17	+$152.33
June 25	−$72.45
June 30	−$400.00

50. How did the amount of money in the account change from the beginning of
June through June 10?

51. Find the total amount withdrawn in June.

52. What was the total change in the account balance over the course of the
month?

53. INPUT-OUTPUT TABLES Make an input-output table for the function
$A = 8 + 5t$. Use 2, 3, 4, 5, and 6 as values for t. (*Lesson 1.8*)

54. 8   **55.** -3 **56.** 0.2   **57.** $\dfrac{4}{5}$

58. 7.5   **59.** 5.6   **60.** -4.9 **61.** -16

Maintaining Skills

ADDING FRACTIONS **Add. Write the answer as a fraction or as a mixed number in lowest terms.** (Skills Review p. 764)

62. $1\dfrac{2}{7} + 2\dfrac{3}{7}$ **63.** $4\dfrac{7}{8} + 9\dfrac{1}{8}$ **64.** $3\dfrac{5}{12} + 2\dfrac{5}{12}$

65. $5\dfrac{3}{14} + 8\dfrac{9}{14}$ **66.** $6\dfrac{21}{40} + 10\dfrac{9}{40}$ **67.** $9\dfrac{12}{16} + 15\dfrac{13}{16}$

68. $3\dfrac{8}{11} + 5\dfrac{3}{11}$ **69.** $8\dfrac{1}{3} + 2\dfrac{2}{3}$ **70.** $6\dfrac{7}{10} + 7\dfrac{5}{10}$

Quiz 2

Solve the equation. Tell whether it has *one solution*, *no solution*, or is an *identity*. (Lesson 3.4)

1. $27 - y = 7 - y$ **2.** $18 + 5n = 8n$

3. $-4(x + 4) = -2(2x + 8)$ **4.** $\dfrac{1}{8}(64r + 32) = \dfrac{1}{2}(16r - 8)$

Solve the equation. (Lessons 3.4, 3.5)

5. $2y + 5 = -y - 4$ **6.** $13m = 15m + 14$

7. $8x - 3 - 5x = 2x + 7$ **8.** $9 - 4x = 6x + 2 - 3x$

9. $5 + 4(x - 1) = 3(2 + x)$ **10.** $-3(4 - r) + 4r = 2(4 + r)$

11. $8n + 4(-5 - 7n) = -2(n + 1)$ **12.** $x - 5(x + 2) = x + 3(3 - 2x)$

13. $\dfrac{1}{2}(2k - 4) = 3(k + 2) - 3k$ **14.** $\dfrac{1}{3}(6x - 3) = 6(2 + x) - 5x$

15. BIKE SAFETY You live near a mountain bike trail. You can rent a mountain bike and a safety helmet for $10 an hour. If you have your own helmet, the bike rental is $7 an hour. You can buy a helmet for $28. How many hours do you need to use the trail to justify buying your own helmet? *(Lesson 3.5)*

Solve the equation. Round to the nearest hundredth. (Lesson 3.6)

16. $7x + 19 = 11$ **17.** $-13c + 51c = -26$

18. $3.6y + 7.5 = 8.2y$ **19.** $18y - 8 = 4y - 3$

20. $2.24x - 33.52 = 8.91x$ **21.** $3.2x - 4.9 = 8.4x + 6.7$

22. BASEBALL CARDS You have 39 baseball cards that you want to give to 5 of your friends. You want each friend to get the same number of cards. How many baseball cards should you give to each friend? *(Lesson 3.6)*

USING A GRAPHING CALCULATOR
Solving Multi-Step Equations

For use with Lesson 3.6

One way to solve multi-step equations is to use a graphing calculator to generate a table of values. The table can show a value of the unknown variable for which the two sides of the equation are approximately equal.

Sample

Use a table on a graphing calculator to solve $4.29x + 3.89(8 - x) = 2.65x$. Round your answer to the nearest tenth.

Solution

1 Use the *Table Setup* function on your graphing calculator to set up a table. Choose values of x beginning at 0 and increasing by 1.

```
TABLE SETUP
 TblStart=0
 △Tbl=1
Indpnt: Auto  Ask
Depend: Auto  Ask
```

2 Press Y= . Enter the left-hand side of the equation as Y_1 and the right-hand side of the equation as Y_2. Enter x for each multiplication. It prints as *.

```
Y1=4.29*X+3.89*(8-
X)
Y2=2.65*X
Y3=
Y4=
Y5=
Y6=
```

3 View your table. The first column of the table should show values of x. Scroll down until you find values in the Y_1 and Y_2 columns that are approximately equal. The values are closest to being equal when $x = 14$, so the solution must be greater than 13 and less than 15.

```
X    Y1     Y2
12   35.92  31.8
13   36.32  34.45
14   36.72  37.1
15   37.12  39.75
16   37.52  42.4
```

4 To find the solution to the nearest tenth, change the *Table Setup* so that x starts at 13.1 and increases by 0.1. You can see that the values in the Y_1 and Y_2 columns are closest to being equal when $x = 13.8$. The solution to the nearest tenth is 13.8.

```
X     Y1     Y2
13.6  36.56  36.04
13.7  36.6   36.305
13.8  36.64  36.57
13.9  36.68  36.835
14    36.72  37.1
```

Try These

Use a graphing calculator to solve the equation to the nearest tenth.

1. $19.65x + 2.2(x - 6.05) = 255.65$ **2.** $16.2(3.1 - x) - 31.55x = -19.5$

3. $3.56x + 2.43 = 6.17x - 11.40$ **4.** $3.5(x - 5.6) + 0.03x = 4.2x - 25.5$

3.7 Formulas

Goal
Solve a formula for one of its variables.

Key Words
• formula

How fast did Pathfinder travel to Mars?

The Mars *Pathfinder* Mission used a solar-powered spacecraft to carry a robotic explorer, Sojourner rover, to Mars. Sojourner, shown in the photograph, was the first wheeled vehicle operated on Mars.

In Example 5 you will solve a formula for one of its variables to estimate *Pathfinder's* average speed on its flight to Mars.

A **formula** is an algebraic equation that relates two or more quantities. You can solve a formula to describe one quantity in terms of the others as shown in the examples that follow.

EXAMPLE **1** **Solve a Temperature Conversion Formula**

The Celsius and Fahrenheit temperature scales are related by the formula $C = \frac{5}{9}(F - 32)$, where C represents degrees Celsius and F represents degrees Fahrenheit. Solve the temperature formula for degrees Fahrenheit F.

Solution

To solve for the variable F, transform the original formula to isolate F. Use the steps you already know for solving a linear equation.

$$C = \frac{5}{9}(F - 32)$$ Write original formula.

$$\frac{9}{5} \cdot C = \frac{9}{5} \cdot \frac{5}{9}(F - 32)$$ Multiply each side by $\frac{9}{5}$, the reciprocal of $\frac{5}{9}$.

$$\frac{9}{5}C = F - 32$$ Simplify.

$$\frac{9}{5}C + 32 = F - 32 + 32$$ Add 32 to each side.

$$\frac{9}{5}C + 32 = F$$ Simplify.

ANSWER ▶ The new formula is $F = \frac{9}{5}C + 32$.

Student Help

▶**LOOK BACK**
To review steps for solving linear equations, see p. 157.

EXAMPLE 2 Solve an Area Formula

The formula for the area of a triangle is $A = \frac{1}{2}bh$.

Find a formula for the base b in terms of area A and height h.

Solution

$$A = \frac{1}{2}bh \qquad \text{Write original formula.}$$

$$2A = bh \qquad \text{Multiply each side by 2.}$$

$$\frac{2A}{h} = b \qquad \text{Divide each side by } h.$$

EXAMPLE 3 Solve and Use an Area Formula

The formula for the area of a rectangle is $A = \ell w$.

a. Find a formula for length ℓ in terms of area A and width w.

b. Use the new formula to find the length of a rectangle that has an area of 35 square feet and a width of 5 feet.

Solution

a. Solve for length ℓ.

$$A = \ell w \qquad \text{Write original formula.}$$

$$\frac{A}{w} = \ell \qquad \text{Divide each side by } w.$$

b. Substitute the given values into the new formula.

$$\ell = \frac{A}{w} = \frac{35}{5} = 7$$

ANSWER ▶ The length of the rectangle is 7 feet.

Checkpoint ✓ Solve and Use an Area Formula

1. In the formula for the area of a triangle, solve for height h.

2. Use the new formula to find the height of a triangle that has an area of 25 square inches and a base of 10 inches.

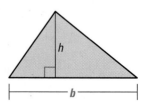

EXAMPLE 4 Solve and Use a Density Formula

The density of a substance is found by dividing its mass by its volume.

a. Solve the density formula $d = \dfrac{m}{v}$ for mass m.

b. Use the new formula to find the mass of a lead sample that has a density of 11.3 grams per cubic centimeter and a volume of 0.9 cubic centimeters. Round to the nearest tenth.

Solution

a. $d = \dfrac{m}{v}$ Write original formula.

     $dv = m$ Multiply each side by v.

b. Substitute the given values into the new formula.

     $m = dv = 11.3 \cdot 0.9 = 10.17 \approx 10.2$

     ANSWER ▶ The mass of the lead sample is approximately 10.2 grams.

Link to Careers

AEROSPACE ENGINEER
Donna Shirley was the manager of the Mars Exploration Program from 1994–1998 and the original leader of the team that built the Sojourner rover.

More about *Pathfinder* is at www.mcdougallittell.com

EXAMPLE 5 Solve and Use a Distance Formula

SPACE TRAVEL Mars *Pathfinder* was launched on December 4, 1996. During its 212-day flight to Mars, it traveled about 310 million miles.

a. Solve the distance formula $d = rt$ for rate r.

b. Estimate *Pathfinder's* average speed in miles per hour. Round your answer to the nearest whole number.

Solution

a. $d = rt$ Write original formula.

     $\dfrac{d}{t} = r$ Divide each side by t.

b. You are given the flight time in *days*, but you want to find the average speed in miles per *hour*. Because there are 24 hours in each day, there are 212(24) hours in 212 days. Time in hours, $t = 212(24) = 5088$ hours.

Substitute the given values into the new formula.

$$r = \frac{d}{t} = \frac{310{,}000{,}000}{5088} \approx 60{,}928$$

ANSWER ▶ *Pathfinder's* average speed was about 60,928 miles per hour.

Checkpoint ✓ **Solve and Use a Distance Formula**

3. Solve the distance formula $d = rt$ for t.

4. Use the result to find the time (in days) that it takes to travel 40 million miles at an average speed of 50,000 miles per day.

Guided Practice

Vocabulary Check · **Complete the sentence.**

1. A formula is an algebraic __?__ that relates two or more real-life quantities.

2. You can __?__ a formula to express one quantity in terms of the others.

Skill Check · **Solve the equation for the indicated variable.**

3. $r - s = t$; r
4. $ax + b = c$; b
5. $3y = x$; y

6. $2j + 5 = k$; j
7. $x = \frac{1}{2}(y + 4)$; y
8. $6(s - 1) = t$; s

In Exercises 9 and 10, use the formula for the area of a rectangle, $A = \ell w$.

9. Find a formula for w in terms of A and ℓ.

10. Use the new formula in Exercise 9 to find the width of a rectangle that has an area of 104 square inches and a length of 13 inches.

Practice and Applications

CONVERTING TEMPERATURE In Exercises 11 and 12, use the temperature conversion formula $F = \frac{9}{5}C + 32$.

11. Solve the formula for degrees Celsius C. Show all your steps.

12. Normal body temperature is given as 98.6°F. Use the formula you wrote in Exercise 11 to find this temperature in degrees Celsius.

SOLVING AN AREA FORMULA Solve the formula for the indicated variable. Show all your steps. Then evaluate the new formula by substituting the given values.

13. Area of a rectangle: $A = \ell w$
Solve for w.

Find the value of w when $A = 36$ and $\ell = 9$.

14. Area of a triangle: $A = \frac{1}{2}bh$
Solve for h.

Find the value of h when $A = 24$ and $b = 8$.

Student Help

▶ **HOMEWORK HELP**
Example 1: Exs. 11, 12
Example 2: Exs. 13–17
Example 3: Exs. 13–17
Example 4: Exs. 18, 19
Example 5: Exs. 20, 21

SOLVING AN AREA FORMULA Solve the formula for the indicated variable. Show all your steps. Then evaluate the new formula by substituting the given values.

15. Solve $A = \ell w$ for ℓ.

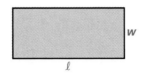

Find the value of ℓ
when $A = 112$ and $w = 7$.

16. Solve $A = \frac{1}{2}bh$ for b.

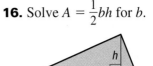

Find the value of b
when $A = 22$ and $h = 4$.

17. **Puzzler** The formula for the perimeter of a rectangle is $P = 2\ell + 2w$. Find the area of a rectangle that has perimeter P of 18 centimeters and length ℓ of 6 centimeters. *HINT:* You can begin by solving the perimeter formula for w.

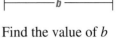
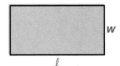

Science Link In Exercises 18 and 19, use the formula for density, $d = \frac{m}{v}$, where m = mass and v = volume.

18. Find a formula for v in terms of d and m.

19. Use the formula you wrote in Exercise 18 to find the volume of a piece of cork that has a density of 0.24 grams per cubic centimeter and a mass of 4.0 grams. Round to the nearest hundredth.

20. BOTTLE-NOSED WHALES A bottle-nosed whale can dive at a rate of 440 feet per minute. You want to find how long it will take for a bottle-nosed whale to dive 2475 feet at this rate. Which equation represents this situation?

A. $t = 2475 - 440$ **B.** $t = \frac{2475}{440}$

21. Solve the correct equation in Exercise 20. Round your answer to the nearest whole minute.

SCUBA DIVING In Exercises 22 and 23, use the following information.
A scuba diver starts at sea level. The pressure on the diver at a depth of d feet is given by the formula below, where P represents the total pressure in pounds per square foot.

$P = 64d + 2112.$

22. Find a formula for depth d in terms of pressure P.

23. If the current pressure on a diver is 4032 pounds per square foot, what is the diver's current depth?

24. LOGICAL REASONING Given a triangle whose sides have lengths a, b, and c, the formula for its perimeter P is $P = a + b + c$.

The steps at the right show a formula for finding a side length of a triangle given the perimeter and the lengths of the two other sides. Write an explanation for each step.

Solution Step	Explanation
$P = a + b + c$	Original Equation
$P - b = a + c$	___?___
$P - b - c = a$	___?___

Standardized Test Practice

25. MULTIPLE CHOICE You plan to drive to the mountains to go hiking. You estimate that you will travel on a highway for 205 miles at an average speed of 55 miles per hour. How much time will you need for this part of the trip? Round your answer to the nearest whole hour.

(A) 1 hour   (B) 2 hours   (C) 3 hours   (D) 4 hours

26. MULTIPLE CHOICE What is the equivalent of 25°C in degrees Fahrenheit? Use the formula $C = \frac{5}{9}(F - 32)$.

(F) −4°F   (G) 13°F   (H) 46°F   (J) 77°F

Mixed Review

CHECKING SOLUTIONS OF INEQUALITIES Check to see if the given value of the variable is or is not a solution of the inequality. *(Lesson 1.4)*

27. $x - 8 < 5$; $x = 12$ **28.** $4 + k \geq 32$; $k = 30$ **29.** $9a > 54$; $a = 5$

30. $t + 17 < 46$; $t = 21$ **31.** $12x \leq 70$; $x = 6$ **32.** $y - 33 \geq 51$; $y = 84$

33. $6x < 35$; $x = 6$ **34.** $14 - y > 12$; $y = 4$ **35.** $42 + x \leq 65$; $x = 23$

EVENT ATTENDANCE Use the bar graph for Exercises 36–38. Each bar shows the percent of teenagers that attended a selected event during a 12-month period. *(Lesson 1.7)*

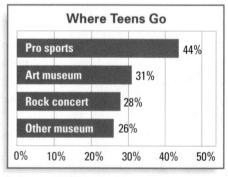

Where Teens Go

Pro sports	44%
Art museum	31%
Rock concert	28%
Other museum	26%

0%   10%   20%   30%   40%   50%

▶ Source: *YOUTH*views

36. Which event was attended by the most teens?

37. What percent of teens attended rock concerts?

38. On average, how many teens out of 100 attended art museums?

Maintaining Skills

SIMPLIFYING FRACTIONS Write the fraction in lowest terms.

39. $\frac{21}{49}$ **40.** $\frac{50}{85}$ **41.** $\frac{16}{72}$ **42.** $\frac{48}{64}$

43. $\frac{16}{32}$ **44.** $\frac{36}{48}$ **45.** $\frac{28}{32}$ **46.** $\frac{9}{27}$

3.8 Ratios and Rates

Goal
Use ratios and rates to solve real-life problems.

Key Words
- ratio
- rate
- unit rate
- unit analysis

How far can you drive on a full tank of gas?

Rates are useful for estimating the distance a truck can travel on a tank of gasoline. In Example 5 you will use a truck's average mileage to estimate how many miles it can travel on 18 gallons of gasoline.

The **ratio of *a* to *b*** is $\frac{a}{b}$. If *a* and *b* are measured in different units, then $\frac{a}{b}$ is called the **rate of *a* per *b*.** Rates are often expressed as *unit rates*. A **unit rate** is a rate per one given unit, such as 60 miles per 1 gallon.

Student Help

▶ **WRITING ALGEBRA**
A ratio, such as $\frac{5}{3}$, can be written as 5 to 3 or 5:3.

EXAMPLE 1 Find a Ratio

The tennis team won 10 of its 16 matches. Find the ratio of wins to losses.

Solution   Ratio $= \dfrac{\text{matches won}}{\text{matches lost}} = \dfrac{10 \text{ matches}}{6 \text{ matches}} = \dfrac{5}{3}$

ANSWER ▶ The win-loss ratio is $\frac{5}{3}$, which is read as "five to three."

EXAMPLE 2 Find a Unit Rate

You run a 10 kilometer race in 50 minutes. What is your average speed in kilometers per minute?

Solution   Rate $= \dfrac{10 \text{ km}}{50 \text{ min}} = \dfrac{1 \text{ km}}{5 \text{ min}} = 0.2 \text{ km/min}$

ANSWER ▶ Your average speed is 0.2 kilometers per minute.

Checkpoint ✓ Find a Ratio and a Unit Rate

1. Your school football team won 8 out of 15 games, with no tie games. What was the team's ratio of wins to losses?

Find the unit rate.

2. A plane flies 1200 miles in 4 hours.

3. You earn $45 for mowing 3 lawns.

▶STUDY TIP
A ratio compares two
quantities measured in
the *same* unit. The
ratio itself has no
units. A rate compares
two quantities that
have *different* units.

EXAMPLE 3 Find a Rate

You kept a record of the number of miles you drove in your truck and the
amount of gasoline used for 2 months.

Number of miles	290	242	196	237	184
Number of gallons	12.1	9.8	8.2	9.5	7.8

What was the average mileage for a gallon of gasoline? Round your result in
miles per gallon (mi/gal) to the nearest tenth.

Solution Average mileage is a rate that compares miles driven to the
amount of gasoline used. To find the average mileage, divide the number of
miles driven by the number of gallons of gasoline used.

$$\text{Rate} = \frac{290 + 242 + 196 + 237 + 184}{12.1 + 9.8 + 8.2 + 9.5 + 7.8} = \frac{1149 \text{ mi}}{47.4 \text{ gal}} \approx 24.2 \text{ mi/gal}$$

ANSWER ▶ The average mileage was about 24.2 miles per gallon.

UNIT ANALYSIS Writing the units when comparing each quantity of a rate is
called **unit analysis**. You can multiply and divide units just like you multiply and
divide numbers. When solving a rate problem, you can use unit analysis to help
determine the units for the rate.

EXAMPLE 4 Use Unit Analysis

Use unit analysis to convert the units.

   a. 3 hours to minutes   **b.** 72 inches to feet

Solution

   a. Use the fact that 60 minutes = 1 hour.   So, $\dfrac{60 \text{ minutes}}{1 \text{ hour}}$ equals 1.

$$3 \text{ hours} \cdot \frac{60 \text{ minutes}}{1 \text{ hour}} = 180 \text{ minutes}$$

    ANSWER ▶ 3 hours equals 180 minutes.

   b. Use the fact that 1 foot = 12 inches.   So, $\dfrac{1 \text{ foot}}{12 \text{ inches}}$ equals 1.

$$72 \text{ inches} \cdot \frac{1 \text{ foot}}{12 \text{ inches}} = 6 \text{ feet}$$

    ANSWER ▶ 72 inches equals 6 feet.

Checkpoint ✓ **Use Unit Analysis**

   4. Use unit analysis to convert 8 pounds to ounces. (1 pound = 16 ounces.)

   5. Use unit analysis to convert 84 days to weeks.

Student Help

▶MORE EXAMPLES

More examples
are available at
www.mcdougallittell.com

EXAMPLE 5 Use a Rate

Use the average mileage you found in Example 3 to estimate the number of miles you can drive on a full 18 gallon tank of gasoline. Round your answer to the nearest mile.

Solution

In Example 3 you found the average mileage to be about 24.2 miles per gallon. Multiply this rate by 18 gallons to estimate the distance you can drive.

$$\text{distance} = \left(24.2\ \frac{\text{mi}}{\text{gal}}\right)(18\ \text{gal}) \qquad \text{Substitute rate and gallons.}$$

$$= (24.2\ \text{mi})(18) \qquad \text{Use unit analysis.}$$

$$= 435.6\ \text{mi} \qquad \text{Multiply.}$$

ANSWER ▶ You can drive about 436 miles on an 18 gallon tank.

Checkpoint ✓ **Use a Rate**

6. A car uses fuel at a rate of 19 miles per gallon. Estimate how many miles the car can travel on 13 gallons of fuel.

Link to
Currency

EXAMPLE 6 Apply Unit Analysis

PESOS You are visiting Mexico and want to exchange $150 for pesos. The rate of currency exchange is 9.242 Mexican pesos per United States dollar on the day you exchange the money. How many pesos will you receive? Round to the nearest whole number.

Solution

You can use unit analysis to write an equation to convert dollars into pesos.

Use the fact that 9.242 pesos = 1 dollar.   So, $\dfrac{9.242\ \text{pesos}}{1\ \text{dollar}} = 1$.

$$P = 150\ \text{dollars}\left(\frac{9.242\ \text{pesos}}{1\ \text{dollar}}\right) \qquad \text{Write equation.}$$

$$P = 150\ (9.242\ \text{pesos}) \qquad \text{Use unit analysis.}$$

$$P = 1386.3\ \text{pesos} \qquad \text{Multiply.}$$

ANSWER ▶ You will receive 1386 pesos.

PESOS The peso is the basic unit of money in Mexico. Currency exchange rates vary according to economic conditions.

Checkpoint ✓ **Apply Unit Analysis**

7. You are visiting Canada and you want to exchange $140 in United States dollars for Canadian dollars. The rate of currency exchange is 1.466 Canadian dollars per United States dollar. How many Canadian dollars will you get? Round to the nearest whole number.

Guided Practice

Vocabulary Check   **Complete the sentence.**

1. If a and b are two quantities measured in the same unit, then the __?__ of a to b is $\frac{a}{b}$.

2. A rate compares two quantities measured in __?__ units.

3. A unit rate is a rate per __?__ given unit.

4. You can use __?__ to change from one unit of measure to another.

Skill Check   **Write the ratio in simplest form.**

5. $\frac{36}{45}$ 6. $\frac{12}{10}$ 7. 14 to 21   8. 77 to 55

Find the unit rate. Round your answer to the nearest hundredth.

9. Swim 2 miles in 40 minutes   10. Pay $1.50 for 24 tea bags

11. **MILEAGE** The average mileage for your old truck is 10.5 miles per gallon. Estimate the number of miles you can travel on a full 22 gallon tank of diesel fuel.

Practice and Applications

SIMPLIFYING RATIOS Write the ratio in simplest form.

12. 5 to 10   13. 30 to 120   14. 8 to 136   15. 60 to 100

16. $\frac{6}{8}$ 17. $\frac{66}{18}$ 18. $\frac{15}{20}$ 19. $\frac{28}{35}$

20. **FOOTBALL** During a football game, a quarterback throws 30 passes and completes 15 of them. What is the ratio of passes completed to passes thrown?

21. **DENTISTRY** Humans produce a set of 20 teeth during early jaw development. A second set of 32 permanent teeth replaces the first set of teeth as the jaw matures. What is the ratio of first teeth to permanent teeth?

UNIT RATE Find the unit rate.

22. Earn $126 for working 18 hours   23. Hike 45 miles in 3 days

24. $3 for 5 containers of yogurt   25. $2 for 5 cans of dog food

26. 440 grams of cereal in 8 servings   27. 20 ounces in 2.5 servings

Student Help

▶ **HOMEWORK HELP**
Example 1: Exs. 20, 21
Example 2: Exs. 22–27
Example 3: Exs. 28, 38
Example 4: Exs. 29–37, 39, 40
Example 5: Ex. 41
· **Example 6:** Exs. 42, 43

28. BOOK CLUB You belong to a book club at the library. You keep a list of how many books you read each month. Find the average number of books you read per month from September through December.

Month	Books
Sept.	2
Oct.	3
Nov.	4
Dec.	3

DETERMINING UNITS   **Write the appropriate unit.**

29. $\dfrac{50 \text{ miles}}{1 \text{ hour}} \cdot 2 \text{ hours} = 100 \underline{\quad ? \quad}$

30. $108 \text{ inches} \cdot \dfrac{1 \text{ foot}}{12 \text{ inches}} = 9 \underline{\quad ? \quad}$

31. UNIT ANALYSIS Choose the expression that completes the following equation: $720 \text{ seconds} \cdot \underline{\quad ? \quad} = 12 \text{ minutes}$.

A. $\dfrac{1 \text{ minute}}{60 \text{ seconds}}$

B. $\dfrac{60 \text{ seconds}}{1 \text{ minute}}$

CONVERTING UNITS   **In Exercises 32–37, convert the units. Round the result to the nearest tenth.**

32. 60 eggs to dozens of eggs

33. 2 years to months

34. 168 days to weeks

35. 1270 minutes to hours

36. 100 yards to feet
(1 yard = 3 feet)

37. 2000 meters to kilometers
(1 kilometer = 1000 meters)

38. AVERAGE SPEED You ride a stationary bike at the gym. After your last five visits you wrote down how long you rode the bike and how many miles you pedaled. What was your average speed in miles per minute?

Number of miles	9	10	12	15	18
Number of minutes	30	30	35	45	45

39. UNIT ANALYSIS Use unit analysis to write your answer to Exercise 38 in miles per hour.

BALD EAGLES   **In Exercises 40 and 41, use the following information from page 129. A bald eagle can fly at a rate of 30 miles per hour.**

40. Use unit analysis to find a bald eagle's flying rate in miles per minute.

41. Use the result of Exercise 40 to find how many minutes it would take a bald eagle to fly 6 miles.

EXCHANGE RATE   **In Exercises 42 and 43, use 9.242 pesos per dollar as the rate of currency exchange. You are visiting Mexico and have taken $325 United States dollars to spend on your trip. Round to the nearest whole number.**

42. If you exchange the entire amount, how many pesos will you receive?

43. You have 840 pesos left after your trip. How many dollars will you get back?

44. MULTIPLE CHOICE There are a total of 28 marbles in a bag. Six of the marbles are red and the rest are blue. What is the ratio of red marbles to blue marbles?

(A) $\frac{2}{11}$ (B) $\frac{6}{28}$ (C) $\frac{3}{14}$ (D) $\frac{3}{11}$

45. MULTIPLE CHOICE If you drive a car m miles in 2 hours, which expression will give the average speed of the car?

(F) $m + 2$ (G) $2m$ (H) $\frac{m - 2}{2}$ (J) $\frac{m}{2}$

46. MULTIPLE CHOICE You travel 154 miles on half a tank of fuel. Your car gets 22 miles per gallon. How many gallons of fuel can your tank hold?

(A) 7   (B) 14   (C) 22   (D) 132

47. MULTIPLE CHOICE You want to exchange $90 Canadian dollars into United States dollars. The exchange rate is 1.466 Canadian dollars per United States dollar on the day you exchange the money. How many United States dollars will you get?

(F) $41   (G) $46   (H) $131   (J) $221

48. POPULATION PROJECTIONS The table shows the projected number (in millions) of people 85 years and older in the United States for different years. Make a line graph of the data. *(Lesson 1.7)*

Year	2000	2010	2020	2030	2040	2050
Number of people 85 years and older (in millions)	4.1	5.0	5.0	5.8	8.3	9.6

DATA UPDATE of U.S. Bureau of the Census data at www.mcdougallittell.com

COMPARING INTEGERS Graph the numbers on a number line. Then write two inequalities that compare the numbers. *(Lesson 2.1)*

49. 4, −3   **50.** −5, −2   **51.** −6, 3

SOLVING AND CHECKING Solve the equation. Round the result to the nearest hundredth. Check the rounded solution. *(Lesson 3.6)*

52. $-7a - 9 = 6$ **53.** $10 - 3x = 4x$ **54.** $5x + 14 = -x$

55. SOCCER FIELD What is the width of a rectangular soccer field that has an area of 9000 square feet and a length of 120 feet? *(Lesson 3.7)*

LEAST COMMON DENOMINATOR Find the least common denominator of the pair of fractions. *(Skills Review p. 762)*

56. $\frac{3}{4}, \frac{2}{5}$ **57.** $\frac{2}{9}, \frac{3}{18}$ **58.** $\frac{5}{6}, \frac{8}{30}$ **59.** $\frac{2}{3}, \frac{4}{7}$

60. $\frac{1}{16}, \frac{9}{20}$ **61.** $\frac{14}{54}, \frac{31}{81}$ **62.** $\frac{3}{64}, \frac{17}{24}$ **63.** $\frac{8}{49}, \frac{59}{70}$

Percents

Goal

Solve percent problems.

Key Words

• percent
• base number

What is the discount percent?

There are three basic types of percent problems. In Example 4 you will solve one type to find the discount percent on a sale item.

A **percent** is a ratio that compares a number to 100. You can write a percent as a fraction, as a decimal, or as a number followed by a percent symbol %.

For example, you can write forty percent as $\frac{40}{100}$, 0.40, or 40%.

You can use a verbal model to help you write a percent equation.

VERBAL MODEL	$\boxed{\textbf{Number being compared to base}} = \boxed{\textbf{percent}} \cdot \boxed{\textbf{base number}}$

LABELS	Number compared to base = a	(same units as b)
	Percent = $p\% = \frac{p}{100}$	(no units)
	Base number = b	(assigned units)

ALGEBRAIC MODEL

$$a = \frac{p}{100} \cdot b$$

The **base number** is the number that is being compared *to* in any percent equation.

EXAMPLE 1 Number Compared to Base is Unknown

What is 30% of 70 feet?

VERBAL MODEL

$\boxed{a} = \boxed{p \text{ percent}} \cdot \boxed{b}$

LABELS

Number compared to base = a (feet)

Percent = $30\% = \frac{30}{100} = \mathbf{0.30}$ (no units)

Base number = **70**   (feet)

ALGEBRAIC MODEL

$a = (\mathbf{0.30})(\mathbf{70}) = 21$

ANSWER▶ 21 feet is 30% of 70 feet.

Student Help

▶ **STUDY TIP**
When you solve a
percent equation, first
convert the percent to
a decimal or a fraction.

EXAMPLE 2 Base Number is Unknown

Fourteen dollars is 25% of what amount of money?

VERBAL MODEL $\boxed{a} = \boxed{p \text{ percent}} \cdot b$

LABELS   Number compared to base = **14**   (dollars)

Percent = $25\% = \dfrac{25}{100} = \dfrac{1}{4}$ (no units)

Base number = b (dollars)

ALGEBRAIC MODEL

$$14 = \frac{1}{4} \cdot b$$

$$4(14) = 4\left(\frac{b}{4}\right)$$

$$56 = b$$

ANSWER ▶ $14 is 25% of $56.

EXAMPLE 3 Percent is Unknown

One hundred thirty-five is what percent of 27?

VERBAL MODEL $\boxed{a} = \boxed{p \text{ percent}} \cdot \boxed{b}$

LABELS   Number compared to base = **135**   (no units)

Percent = $\boxed{p\%} = \dfrac{p}{100}$ (no units)

Base number = **27**   (no units)

ALGEBRAIC MODEL

$$135 = \frac{p}{100}(27)$$

$$\frac{135}{27} = \frac{p}{100}$$

$$5 = \frac{p}{100}$$

$$500 = p$$

ANSWER ▶ 135 is 500% of 27.

Checkpoint ✓ **Solve a Percent Equation**

1. What is 15% of 100 meters?   **2.** 12 is 60% of what number?

3. 8 is what percent of 20?   **4.** 20 is what percent of 8?

DISCOUNT When an item is on sale, the difference between the regular price and the sale price is called the *discount*. To find the discount percent, use the regular price as the base number in the percent equation.

Student Help

▶ **MORE EXAMPLES**

More examples are available at www.mcdougallittell.com

EXAMPLE **4** Model and Use Percents

DISCOUNT PERCENT You are shopping for a portable CD player. You find one that has a regular price of $90. The store is selling the CD player at a sale price of $72. What is the discount percent?

VERBAL MODEL

$$\boxed{\text{Discount}} = \boxed{p \text{ percent}} \cdot \boxed{\text{Regular price}}$$

LABELS

Discount = Regular price − Sale price
= 90 − 72 = **18**   (dollars)

Percent = $p\%$ = $\dfrac{p}{100}$ (no units)

Regular price = **90**   (dollars)

ALGEBRAIC MODEL

$$18 = \frac{p}{100}(90)$$

$$\frac{18}{90} = \frac{p}{100}$$

$$0.20 = \frac{p}{100}$$

$$20 = p$$

ANSWER ▶ The discount percent is 20%.

Checkpoint ✓ Model and Use Percents

5. A radio has a regular price of $80. You receive a 10% discount when you purchase it. Find the amount of the discount. Then find the sale price of the radio with the 10% discount.

SUMMARY

Three Types of Percent Problems

QUESTION	GIVEN	NEED TO FIND	EXAMPLE
What is p percent of b?	b and p	Number compared to base, **a**	Example 1
a is p percent of **what**?	a and p	Base number, **b**	Example 2
a is **what percent** of b?	a and b	Percent, **p**	Example 3

Guided Practice

Vocabulary Check

In Exercises 1 and 2, consider the statement "10% of 160 is 16."

1. Write an equation that represents the statement.

2. What is the base number in the equation you wrote in Exercise 1?

Write an equation for each question. Do *not* solve the equation.

3. 15% of what number is 12? **4.** 99 is what percent of 212?

5. What is 6% of 27? **6.** 13 is 45% of what number?

Skill Check

Solve the percent problem.

7. 35 is what percent of 20? **8.** 12% of 5 is what number?

9. 18 is 25% of what number? **10.** 24 is 120% of what number?

SALES TAX **The price of a book without tax is $10. The sales tax rate on the price of the book is 6%.**

11. Model the situation with an equation of the form $a = \dfrac{p}{100}b$.

12. Solve the equation to find the amount of the tax.

Practice and Applications

UNDERSTANDING PERCENT EQUATIONS **Match the percent problem with the equation that represents it.**

13. $a = (0.39)(50)$ **A.** 39 is 50% of what number?

14. $39 = p(50)$ **B.** 39% of 50 is what number?

15. $39 = 0.50b$ **C.** $39 is what percent of $50?

SOLVE FOR a **Solve the percent problem.**

16. How much money is 35% of $750? **17.** What number is 25% of 80?

18. What distance is 24% of 710 miles? **19.** 14% of 220 feet is what length?

20. How much is 8% of 800 tons? **21.** What number is 200% of 5?

Student Help

▶**HOMEWORK HELP**
Example 1: Exs. 16–21
Example 2: Exs. 22–27
Example 3: Exs. 28–33
Example 4: Ex. 35

SOLVE FOR b **Solve the percent problem.**

22. 52 is 12.5% of what number? **23.** 42 feet is 50% of what length?

24. 45% of what distance is 135 miles? **25.** 2% of what amount is $20?

26. 30 grams is 20% of what weight? **27.** 90 is 45% of what number?

SOLVE FOR p Solve the percent problem.

28. 3 inches is what percent of 40 inches? **29.** $240 is what percent of $50?

30. 55 years is what percent of 20 years? **31.** 18 is what percent of 60?

32. 9 people is what percent of 60 people? **33.** 80 is what percent of 400?

34. **Puzzler** What percent of the region is shaded blue? What percent is shaded yellow?

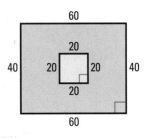

35. **THE BETTER BUY** Store A has a coat on sale for 30% off the regular price of $60. The same coat is on sale at Store B for 20% off the regular price of $60. You also have a Store B coupon for 10% off the sale price. Will you save money by going to Store B? Explain why or why not.

36. **History Link** The table below shows the number of electoral votes each candidate in the Election of 1860 received. What percent of the total number of electoral votes did each candidate receive?

Party	Candidate	Electoral votes
Republican	Abraham Lincoln	180
Southern Democratic	J.C. Breckinridge	72
Constitutional Union	John Bell	39
Northern Democratic	Stephen Douglas	12

CHOOSING A COLLEGE In Exercises 37–39, use the graph. It shows the responses of 3500 seniors from high schools around the United States.

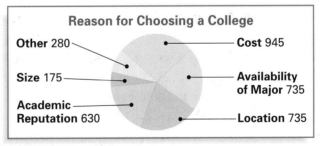

Reason for Choosing a College

Other 280 — Cost 945
Size 175 — Availability of Major 735
Academic Reputation 630 — Location 735

▶ Source: Careers and Colleges

37. What percent of the seniors said location was the reason for their choice?

38. What percent of the seniors said academic reputation was the reason for their choice?

39. What percent of the seniors said cost most influences their choice?

LOGICAL REASONING In Exercises 40 and 41, use $a = \dfrac{p}{100}b$.

40. Complete the sentence: When the percent p is a number greater than 100, the value of a is ___?___ than the value of the base number b.

41. Write a percent equation for the statement "a is 300 percent of b." Then choose one set of values for a, b, and p that make the equation true.

Standardized Test Practice

42. MULTIPLE CHOICE Choose the equation you would use to find 25% of 120.

Ⓐ $0.25x = 20$ Ⓑ $x = \dfrac{120}{0.25}$ Ⓒ $x = \dfrac{0.25}{120}$ Ⓓ $x = (0.25)(120)$

43. MULTIPLE CHOICE What amount would you leave for a 20% tip on a $35 restaurant bill?

Ⓕ $.70 Ⓖ $2.80 Ⓗ $7 Ⓙ $28

Mixed Review

WRITING AND SOLVING EQUATIONS Write the sentence as an equation. Let x represent the number. Use mental math to solve the equation. Then check your solution. *(Lesson 1.5)*

44. The sum of a number and 18 is 45.

45. The product of a number and 21 is 105.

FINDING ABSOLUTE VALUE Evaluate the expression. *(Lesson 2.2)*

46. $|9|$ **47.** $|-32|$ **48.** $-|5|$ **49.** $-|-16|$

Maintaining Skills

ORDERING NUMBERS Write the numbers in order from least to greatest. *(Skills Review p. 770)*

50. 1301, 1103, 1031, 1013, 1130   **51.** 217, 2017, 270, 2170, 2701

52. 23.5, 23.45, 23.4, 23.53, 23.25   **53.** 5.09, 5.9, 5.1, 5.19, 5.91

Quiz 3

Solve the formula for the indicated variable. *(Lesson 3.7)*

1. Solve $d = rt$ for t.   **2.** Solve $A = \dfrac{1}{2}bh$ for h.   **3.** Solve $d = \dfrac{m}{v}$ for v.

Use unit analysis to complete the equation. *(Lesson 3.8)*

4. 7 weeks • ___?___ = 49 days   **5.** 108 inches • ___?___ = 9 feet

6. $\dfrac{20 \text{ students}}{1 \text{ classroom}} \cdot \dfrac{15 \text{ classrooms}}{1 \text{ school}} = $ ___?___   **7.** $\dfrac{24 \text{ hours}}{1 \text{ day}} \cdot 10 \text{ days} = $ ___?___

DISCOUNT PERCENT In Exercises 8 and 9, the regular price of a shirt is $23. You buy it on sale for $17.25. *(Lesson 3.9)*

8. What is the amount of the discount?

9. Write and solve a percent equation to find the discount percent.

VOCABULARY

- **equivalent equations,** *p. 132*
- **inverse operations,** *p. 133*
- **linear equation,** *p. 134*
- **properties of equality,** *p. 140*
- **identity,** *p. 153*

- **rounding error,** *p. 164*
- **formula,** *p. 171*
- **ratio,** *p. 177*
- **rate,** *p. 177*

- **unit rate,** *p. 177*
- **unit analysis,** *p. 178*
- **percent,** *p. 183*
- **base number,** *p. 183*

3.1 SOLVING LINEAR EQUATIONS USING ONE OPERATION

Examples on pp. 132–134

EXAMPLES Use inverse operations of addition and subtraction to isolate the variable. Simplify first if necessary.

USE ADDITION

$y - 4 = -6$	Write original equation.
$y - 4 + 4 = -6 + 4$	Add 4 to each side.
$y = -2$	Simplify both sides.

USE SUBTRACTION

$x - (-2) = 12$	Write original equation.
$x + 2 = 12$	Simplify.
$x + 2 - 2 = 12 - 2$	Subtract 2 from each side.
$x = 10$	Simplify both sides.

Solve the equation. Check your solution in the original equation.

1. $y - 15 = -4$ **2.** $7 + x = -3$ **3.** $t - (-10) = 2$

3.2 SOLVING LINEAR EQUATIONS USING ONE OPERATION

Examples on pp. 138–140

EXAMPLES Use inverse operations of multiplication and division to isolate the variable.

USE MULTIPLICATION

$\frac{1}{8}m = -5$	Write original equation.
$8\left(\frac{1}{8}m\right) = 8(-5)$	Multiply each side by the reciprocal, 8.
$m = -40$	Simplify.

USE DIVISION

$-7n = 28$	Write original equation.
$\dfrac{-7n}{-7} = \dfrac{28}{-7}$	Divide each side by -7.
$n = -4$	Simplify.

Solve the equation. Check your solution in the original equation.

4. $81 = 3t$ **5.** $-6x = 54$ **6.** $\frac{x}{4} = -16$

3.3 **SOLVING MULTI-STEP EQUATIONS**

Examples on
pp. 144–146

EXAMPLE You may need more than one step to solve an equation.

$-2p - (-5) - 2p = 13$	Write original equation.
$-2p + 5 - 2p = 13$	Use subtraction rule to simplify.
$-4p + 5 = 13$	Combine like terms $-2p$ and $-2p$.
$-4p + 5 - 5 = 13 - 5$	Subtract 5 from each side to undo the addition.
$-4p = 8$	Simplify both sides.
$\dfrac{-4p}{-4} = \dfrac{8}{-4}$	Divide each side by -4 to undo the multiplication.
$p = -2$	Simplify.

Solve the equation.

7. $26 + 9x = -1$

8. $-32 = 4c - 12$

9. $9r - 2 - 6r = 1$

10. $-2(4 - x) - 7 = 5$

11. $n + 3(1 + 2n) = 17$

12. $\dfrac{3}{4}(x + 8) = 9$

3.4 **SOLVING EQUATIONS WITH VARIABLES ON BOTH SIDES**

Examples on
pp. 151–153

EXAMPLES Linear equations can have *one solution*, *no solution*, or *many solutions*. To solve, collect the variable terms on one side of the equation.

Equation with one solution:	Equation with no solution:	Equation with many solutions:
$15d + 20 = 7d - 4$	$-6x - 5 = -15 - 6x$	$2n - 5n + 11 = 2 - 3n + 9$
$8d = -24$	$-6x - 5 + 6x = -15 - 6x + 6x$	$-3n + 11 = 11 - 3n$
$d = -3$	$-5 \neq -15$	$11 = 11$
The solution is -3. The original equation has *one solution*.	$-5 = -15$ is never true no matter what the value of x. The original equation has *no solution*.	$11 = 11$ is always true, so all values of n are solutions. The original equation is an *identity*.

Solve the equation if possible. Determine whether the equation has *one solution*, *no solution*, or is an *identity*.

13. $24 - 3x = 9x$

14. $15x - 23 = 15x$

15. $2m - 9 = 6 - m$

16. $36 - 4d = 4(9 - d)$

17. $12 + 11h = -18 - 4h$

18. $2x + 18 + 4x = -2x + 10$

3.5 MORE ON LINEAR EQUATIONS

Examples on pp. 157–159

EXAMPLE You can use a verbal model to write and solve linear equations.

FUNDRAISER You are making sandwiches to sell at a fundraiser. It costs $.90 to make each sandwich plus a one-time cost of $24 for packaging. You plan to sell each sandwich for $2.50. Write and solve an equation to find how many sandwiches you need to sell to break even.

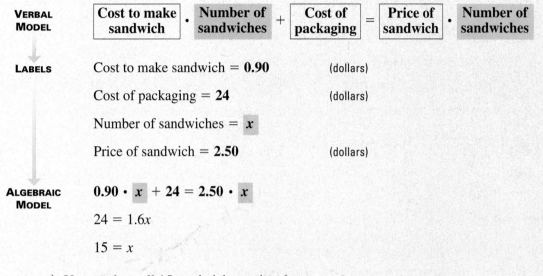

VERBAL MODEL

Cost to make sandwich	·	Number of sandwiches	+	Cost of packaging	=	Price of sandwich	·	Number of sandwiches

LABELS

Cost to make sandwich = **0.90**   (dollars)

Cost of packaging = **24**   (dollars)

Number of sandwiches = x

Price of sandwich = **2.50**   (dollars)

ALGEBRAIC MODEL

$0.90 \cdot x + 24 = 2.50 \cdot x$

$24 = 1.6x$

$15 = x$

ANSWER ▶ You need to sell 15 sandwiches to break even, or recover your costs.

19. TOMATOES One tomato plant is 12 inches tall and grows 1 inch per week. Another tomato plant is 6 inches tall and grows 2 inches per week. Write and solve an equation to find when the plants will be the same height.

3.6 SOLVING DECIMAL EQUATIONS

Examples on pp. 163–165

EXAMPLE For some equations, only an approximate solution is required.

$3.45m = -2.93m - 2.95$	Write original equation.
$6.38m = -2.95$	Add $2.93m$ to each side.
$m \approx -0.462382445$	Divide each side by 6.38. Use a calculator to get an approximate solution.
$m \approx -0.46$	Round to nearest hundredth.

Solve the equation. Round the result to the nearest hundredth.

20. $3x - 4 = 3$ **21.** $5x - 9 = 18x - 23$ **22.** $13.7t - 4.7 = 9.9 + 8.1t$

3.7 FORMULAS

Examples on pp. 171–173

EXAMPLE You can solve a formula for any one of its variables.

The formula for the area of a rectangle is $A = \ell w$. Find a formula for width w in terms of area A and length ℓ.

$A = \ell w$ Write original formula.

$\dfrac{A}{\ell} = w$ To isolate w, divide each side by ℓ.

Solve the formula for the indicated variable.

23. Solve for ℓ: $V = \ell wh$.
24. Solve for m: $d = \dfrac{m}{v}$.
25. Solve for b: $P = a + b + c$.

3.8–3.9 RATIOS, RATES, AND PERCENTS

Examples on pp. 177–179, 183–185

EXAMPLES Ratios, rates, and percents can be used to compare real-life quantities.

a. A football team has a record of 7 wins and 3 losses. What percent of the games did the team win?

The team won 7 out of 10 games. Use $a = p$ percent $\cdot\ b$.

$7 = \dfrac{p}{100}(10)$

$7 = \dfrac{p}{10}$

$70 = p$

ANSWER The team won 70% of its games.

b. The football team has a total of 900 rushing yards this season. Find the team's average rushing yards per game.

$$\text{Rate} = \frac{900 \text{ rushing yards}}{10 \text{ games}} = \frac{90 \text{ rushing yards}}{1 \text{ game}}$$

ANSWER The team's average is 90 rushing yards per game.

CAR MILEAGE At 60 miles per hour, a car travels 340 miles on 20 gallons of gasoline.

26. What is the average mileage per gallon of gasoline?

27. How many miles could this car travel on 5 gallons of gasoline at the same speed?

28. What percent of the 20 gallons is 5 gallons?

Solve the equation. Check your solution in the original equation.

1. $x + 3 = 8$ **2.** $19 = a - 4$ **3.** $-2y = -18$ **4.** $22 = 3p - 5$

5. $r - (-7) = 14$ **6.** $\frac{x}{2} = -6$ **7.** $\frac{5}{3}(9 + w) = -10$ **8.** $-\frac{3}{4}x - 2 = -8$

Solve the equation if possible. Determine whether the equation has *one solution, no solution,* or is an *identity*.

9. $14 - 5t = 3t$ **10.** $6x - 9 = 10x + 7$ **11.** $-3(x - 2) = 6 - 3x$

12. $\frac{3}{4}(9x + 2) = 15x$ **13.** $24y - (5y + 6) = 27y + 3$ **14.** $-5r - 6 + 4r = -r + 2$

Solve the equation. Round the result to the nearest hundredth.

15. $26 + 9p = 58p$ **16.** $-34 = 8x - 15$ **17.** $15x - 18 = 37$

18. $13.2k + 4.3 = 2.7k$ **19.** $42.6x - 29.4 = -3.5x$ **20.** $3.82 + 1.25x = 5.91$

Solve the formula for the indicated variable.

21. $A = \ell w$
Solve for ℓ.

22. $\frac{9}{5}C + 32 = F$
Solve for C.

23. $A = \frac{1}{2}bh$
Solve for h.

Convert the units.

24. 98 days to weeks   **25.** 37 hours to minutes   **26.** 15 yards to feet

Solve the percent problem.

27. What number is 30% of 650?   **28.** 15% of what amount is $36?

29. 4 is what percent of 20?   **30.** How much is 45% of 200 pounds?

31. SHOVELING SNOW You shovel snow to earn extra money and charge $12 per driveway. You earn $72 in one day. Let x represent the number of driveways you shoveled. Which of the following equations is an algebraic model for the situation?

   A. $72x = 12$ **B.** $\frac{1}{12}x = 72$ **C.** $12x = 72$ **D.** $\frac{1}{72}x = 12$

32. SUMMER JOB At your summer job you earn $8 per day, plus $3 for each errand you run. Write and solve an equation to find how many errands you need to run to earn $26 in one day.

33. EXCHANGE RATE You are visiting Canada and want to exchange $175 in United States dollars for Canadian dollars. The rate of currency exchange is 1.466 Canadian dollars per United States dollar. How many Canadian dollars will you get? Round to the nearest whole number.

Chapter Standardized Test

1. Which number is a solution of
$4 - x = -5$?

  (A) -9 (B) -1

  (C) $\dfrac{5}{4}$ (D) 9

2. Which step can you use to solve the
equation $\dfrac{3}{5}x = 12$?

  (A) Divide each side by $-\dfrac{3}{5}$.

  (B) Divide each side by $\dfrac{5}{3}$.

  (C) Multiply each side by $\dfrac{3}{5}$.

  (D) Multiply each side by $\dfrac{5}{3}$.

3. The perimeter of the rectangle is
40 centimeters. Find the value of x.

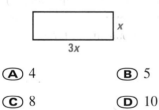

  (A) 4 (B) 5

  (C) 8 (D) 10

4. If $9x - 4(3x - 2) = 4$, then $x = $? .

  (A) -4 (B) $-\dfrac{4}{3}$

  (C) $\dfrac{4}{3}$ (D) 2

5. Solve the equation $\dfrac{1}{3}(27x + 18) = 12$.

  (A) $-\dfrac{2}{9}$ (B) $\dfrac{2}{3}$

  (C) 2 (D) $\dfrac{10}{3}$

6. How many solutions does the equation
$-2y + 3(4 - y) = 12 - 5y$ have?

  (A) none   (B) one

  (C) two   (D) more than two

7. If $0.75t = 12$, then $t = $? .

  (A) 3 (B) 9

  (C) 16 (D) 36

8. What is the value of y if
$13.6y - 14.8 = 4.1y - 6.3$?

  (A) -2.2 (B) -1.2

  (C) 0.5 (D) 0.9

9. Use the temperature conversion formula
$C = \dfrac{5}{9}(F - 32)$ to convert $10°$ Celsius to
degrees Fahrenheit.

  (A) $-12°F$ (B) $38°F$

  (C) $42°F$ (D) $50°F$

  (E) None of these

10. You can stuff 108 envelopes in 45 minutes.
At this rate, how many envelopes can you
stuff in 2 hours?

  (A) 50 (B) 144

  (C) 216 (D) 288

11. What is 26% of 250 meters?

  (A) 9.6 meters   (B) 65 meters

  (C) 185 meters   (D) 961.5 meters

Maintaining Skills

EXAMPLE 1 Make a Line Graph

Make a line graph of the following average monthly temperatures: January, 27°F; February, 34°F; March, 41°F; and April, 53°F.

Solution Draw the vertical scale from 0°F to 60°F. Mark the months on the horizontal axis. Label the axes. Draw a point on the grid for each data point. Connect the points with lines as shown at the right.

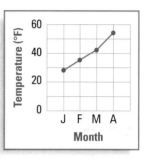

Try These

1. The table gives the wind speed and the wind chill temperature when the outside temperature is 40°F. Make a line graph of the data.

Wind speed (mi/h)	25	30	35	40	45
Wind chill temperature (°F)	15	13	11	10	9

EXAMPLE 2 Evaluate a Function

A campsite charges $85 for two people to rent a cabin and $10 for each additional person. The total cost is given by $C = 85 + 10n$, where n is the number of additional people. Make an input-output table for the cost when there is a total of 2, 4, or 6 people.

Solution

	INPUT	FUNCTION	OUTPUT
2 people	$n = 0$	$C = 85 + 10(0)$	$C = \$85$
4 people	$n = 2$	$C = 85 + 10(2)$	$C = \$105$
6 people	$n = 4$	$C = 85 + 10(4)$	$C = \$125$

Input n	0	2	4
Output C	$85	$105	$125

Student Help

▶ EXTRA EXAMPLES

More examples and practice exercises are available at www.mcdougallittell.com

Try These

2. The green fee for four people to golf 18 holes is $100. The cost of renting clubs is $9 per person. The total cost is given by $C = 100 + 9r$, where r is the number of people who rent clubs. Make an input-output table for 0, 2, and 4 people renting clubs.

Evaluate the expression for the given value of the variable.
(Lessons 1.1, 1.2, 1.3)

1. $20 - 4y$ when $y = 3$ **2.** $\frac{x}{4} + 12$ when $x = 8$ **3.** $x^2 - 8$ when $x = 7$

4. $(6 + x) + 3x$ when $x = 6$ **5.** $(3t)^3$ when $t = 2$ **6.** $8x^2$ when $x = 4$

Evaluate the expression. (Lessons 1.3, 2.3, 2.4)

7. $9 \div 3 + 2$ **8.** $-5 + 3 \cdot 8 - 6$ **9.** $\frac{4 \cdot 9}{3} - 5$

10. $20 - (-3) - 8$ **11.** $2 \cdot 35 + (-13)$ **12.** $[(6 \cdot 4) + 5] - 7$

Check to see if the given value of the variable is or is not a solution of the equation or inequality. (Lesson 1.4)

13. $4 + 2x = 12$; $x = 2$ **14.** $6x - 5 = 13$; $x = 3$ **15.** $3y + 7 = 31$; $y = 8$

16. $x - 4 < 6$; $x = 9$ **17.** $5m + 3 > 8$; $m = 1$ **18.** $9 \le 22 - 4x$; $x = 3$

In Exercises 19–22, write the phrase or sentence as a variable expression, equation, or inequality. (Lesson 1.5)

19. A number x cubed minus eight

20. Four less than twice a number x is equal to ten.

21. The product of negative three and a number x is less than twelve.

22. A number x plus fifteen is greater than or equal to thirty.

23. Draw a line graph to represent the data given by the input-output table.
(Lesson 1.8)

Input x	2	4	6	8	10	12
Output y	1	5	9	13	17	21

Complete the statement using < or >. (Lesson 2.1)

24. $0 \ ?\ 6$ **25.** $-9 \ ?\ -8$ **26.** $-1.5 \ ?\ -1$ **27.** $\frac{5}{4} \ ?\ \frac{4}{5}$

28. $-2.1 \ ?\ 1.2$ **29.** $-109 \ ?\ -101$ **30.** $2 \ ?\ -3$ **31.** $-6 \ ?\ 9$

Simplify the expression. (Lessons 2.5, 2.6, 2.7)

32. $-4(x)(6)$ **33.** $5(-y)^3$ **34.** $8(-3)(-x)(-x)$ **35.** $-(4 - 2t)$

36. $-2(x + 3) - 1$ **37.** $(6x - 9)\frac{2}{3}$ **38.** $3 + 6(x - 4)$ **39.** $5(9x + 5) - 2x$

FLYING SQUIRRELS In Exercises 40 and 41, use the following information. A flying squirrel drops from a tree with a downward velocity of −6 feet per second. (Lesson 2.5)

40. Write an algebraic model for the displacement of the squirrel (in feet) after t seconds.

41. Find the squirrel's change in position after 5 seconds. Is your answer a positive or negative number? Explain.

In Exercises 42 and 43, use the area model shown below. (Lesson 2.6)

42. Find two expressions for the area of the large rectangle.

43. Write an algebraic statement that shows that the two expressions are equal.

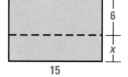

Solve the equation. (Lessons 3.1–3.5)

44. $x + 11 = 19$

45. $x - (-7) = -2$

46. $9b = 135$

47. $35 = 3c - 19$

48. $\frac{p}{2} - 9 = -1$

49. $4(2x - 9) = 6(10x - 6)$

50. $3(q - 12) = 5q + 2$

51. $\frac{3}{4}(2x + 5) = 6$

52. $9(2p + 1) - 3p = 4p - 6$

53. FUNDRAISER Your school band is planning to attend a competition. The total cost for the fifty band members to attend is $750. Each band member will pay $3 toward this cost and the rest of the money will be raised by selling wrapping paper. For each roll of wrapping paper sold, the band makes $2. Write and solve an equation to find how many rolls the band members need to sell to cover the cost. (Lesson 3.3)

Solve the equation. Round the result to the nearest hundredth. (Lesson 3.6)

54. $8x - 5 = 24$

55. $70 = 9 - 3x$

56. $-3.46y = -5.78$

57. $4.17n + 3.29 = 2.74n$

58. $2.4(0.3 + x) = 8.7$

59. $23.5a + 12.5 = 9.3a - 4.8$

In Exercises 60 and 61, use the formula for the area of a triangle, $A = \frac{1}{2}bh$. (Lesson 3.7)

60. Find a formula for h in terms of A and b.

61. Use the new formula to find the height of a triangle that has an area of 120 square centimeters and a base of 24 centimeters.

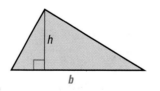

62. CAR TRIP You start a trip at 9:00 A.M. and the car's odometer reading is 66,300 miles. When you stop driving at 3:00 P.M., the odometer reading is 66,660 miles. What was your average speed? (Lesson 3.8)

63. SALE PRICE You buy a sweater that is on sale for 30% off the regular price of $65. How much did you pay for the sweater? (Lesson 3.9)

Planning a Car Wash

Materials
• graphing calculator or computer

OBJECTIVE Compare the income and expenses of a car wash to determine profit.

INVESTIGATING THE DATA

The booster club is planning a car wash to raise funds for the football team. Use the information below to answer Exercises 1–8.

Booster Club Car Wash

Income
• Wash only $4 per car
• Wash and vacuum $6 per car

Expenses
• 20 sponges $1.47 each
• 8 bottles of detergent $2.99 for a 24-ounce bottle
• 8 bottles of window cleaner $1.99 for a 32-ounce bottle
• 20 rolls of paper towels $.99 for an 80-sheet roll
• 6 poster boards $.79 each

---

1. The club members plan to bring buckets, hoses, and towels from home. Name another important item the group will need to bring from home.

2. Find the total car wash expenses.

3. Copy and complete the table. You may want to use a spreadsheet.

Number of cars washed	20	40	60	80	100
Income earned	?	?	?	?	?

4. Copy and complete the table. You may want to use a spreadsheet.

Number of cars washed and vacuumed	20	40	60	80	100
Income earned	?	?	?	?	?

5. How much income will be earned if 60 cars are washed and 40 cars are washed and vacuumed?

6. The *profit* earned from the car wash is the income minus the expenses. The profit earned is a function of the number of customers. How much profit will the club make if 60 cars are washed and 40 cars are washed and vacuumed?

7. Complete the equation for the total income I earned when x cars are washed and y cars are washed and vacuumed. $I = \boxed{?}\, x + \boxed{?}\, y$

8. Complete the equation for the total profit P earned when x cars are washed and y cars are washed and vacuumed. $P = \boxed{?}\, x + \boxed{?}\, y - \boxed{?}$

PRESENTING YOUR RESULTS

Write a report about the car wash fundraiser.

- Include a discussion of income, expenses, and profit.

- Include your answers to Exercises 1–8.

- Find how many cars the group would need to wash to break even (when income equals expenses).

- Find how many cars the group would need to wash and vacuum to break even.

- Suppose the booster club wants to earn at least $200 profit. Find three different combinations of car washes x, and car washes and vacuums y, so that the club would meet its goal.

- Find what local car washes charge for similar services.

EXTENDING THE PROJECT

Think of a different fundraising event that a club could use to earn money.

1. Describe the fundraiser.

2. Do some research to find out what kind of supplies or equipment you would need to get started and the cost of these items.

3. Survey some of your friends and neighbors to find what price they would be willing to pay for the product or service.

4. Decide what you would charge customers for your merchandise or service.

5. Write an equation for the total income I earned as a function of the number of customers n.

6. Write an equation for the total profit P earned as a function of the number of customers n.

7. Determine the number of customers n needed to break even.

8. Choose a profit goal. How many customers do you need to reach that goal?

CHAPTER 4

Graphing Linear Equations and Functions

▶ How steep are the hills of San Francisco?

APPLICATION: Cable Cars

In the 1870s, Andrew Hallidie designed the first cable car system in the United States to make it easier to climb the steep hills of San Francisco.

To design a transportation system, he needed a mathematical way to describe and measure the steepness of a hill.

Think & Discuss

1. Name another real-life situation where steepness is important. When is steepness helpful? When is steepness a problem?

2. How would you describe the steepness of the sections of the street below?

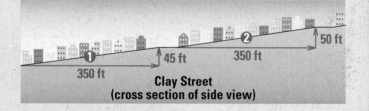

Clay Street
(cross section of side view)

Learn More About It

You will calculate the steepness of the sections of this street in Exercise 55 on p. 247.

 APPLICATION LINK More about cable cars is available at www.mcdougallittell.com

Study Guide

PREVIEW

What's the chapter about?

- Graphing **linear equations**
- Finding the **slope** of a line
- Determining if a graph represents a **function**

> **KEY WORDS**
>
> - **ordered pair,** *p. 203*
> - **linear equation,** *p. 210*
> - **x-intercept,** *p. 222*
> - **y-intercept,** *p. 222*
> - **slope,** *p. 229*
> - **direct variation,** *p. 236*
> - **slope-intercept form,** *p. 243*
> - **function notation,** *p. 254*

PREPARE

Chapter Readiness Quiz

Take this quick quiz. If you are unsure of an answer, look back at the reference pages for help.

VOCABULARY CHECK *(refer to p. 49)*

1. What is the domain of the following input-output table?

Input	-2	0	2	4
Output	3	5	7	9

    A 3, 5, 7, 9   **B** $-2, 0, 2, 4$

    C 3, 5, 7, 9, -2, 0, 2, 4   **D** all real numbers

SKILL CHECK *(refer to pp. 4, 10, 86)*

2. Evaluate $\dfrac{x - y}{2}$ when $x = -3$ and $y = -1$.

    A -2 **B** -1 **C** 1   **D** 2

3. Evaluate $(2x)^2$ when $x = 5$.

    A 10   **B** 20   **C** 25   **D** 100

STUDY TIP

Make Vocabulary Cards

Including a sketch will help you remember a definition.

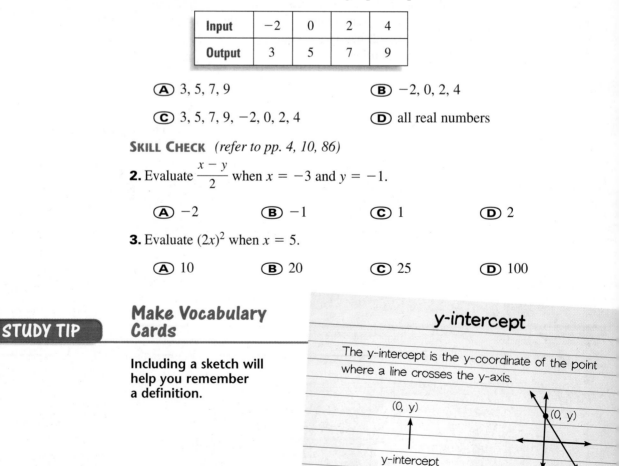

y-intercept

The y-intercept is the y-coordinate of the point where a line crosses the y-axis.

(0, y)

(0, y)

y-intercept

4.1 The Coordinate Plane

How are wing length and wing beat related?

wing length

In Exercises 33–35 you will use a coordinate plane to picture the relationship between the length of a bird's wing and the bird's wing-beat rate.

Goal

Plot points in a coordinate plane.

Key Words

- coordinate plane
- origin
- x-axis, y-axis
- ordered pair
- x-coordinate
- y-coordinate
- quadrant
- scatter plot

A **coordinate plane** is formed by two real number lines that intersect at a right angle at the **origin**. The horizontal axis is the **x-axis** and the vertical axis is the **y-axis**.

Each point in a coordinate plane corresponds to an **ordered pair** of real numbers. The first number in an ordered pair is the **x-coordinate** and the second number is the **y-coordinate**. In the graph at the right, the ordered pair (3, −2) has an x-coordinate of 3 and a y-coordinate of −2.

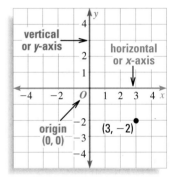

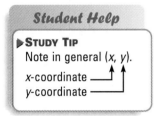

Student Help

▶ STUDY TIP
Note in general (x, y).

x-coordinate ⟶
y-coordinate ⟶

EXAMPLE 1 Identify Coordinates

Write the ordered pairs that correspond to points A, B, C, and D.

Solution

In the coordinate plane at the right, Point A is **3 units** to the right and **2 units** down from the origin. So, its x-coordinate is 3 and its y-coordinate is −2. The ordered pair is (3, −2).

Point B has coordinates (−2, −1).

Point C has coordinates (0, 2).

Point D has coordinates (−3, 4).

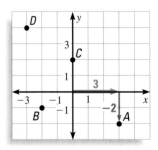

Checkpoint ✓ **Identify Coordinates**

1. Write the ordered pairs that correspond to points A, B, C, and D.

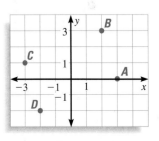

Student Help

▶ MORE EXAMPLES

More examples
are available at
www.mcdougallittell.com

EXAMPLE 2 Plot Points in a Coordinate Plane

Plot the point in a coordinate plane.

a. $(3, 4)$ **b.** $(-2, -3)$

Solution

a. To plot the point $(3, 4)$, start at the origin. Move 3 units to the right and 4 units up.

b. To plot the point $(-2, -3)$, start at the origin. Move 2 units to the left and 3 units down.

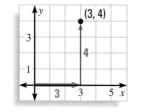

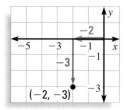

The *x*-axis and the *y*-axis divide the coordinate plane into four regions called **quadrants**. Each point in a coordinate plane is located in one of the four quadrants or on one of the axes.

You can tell which quadrant a point is in by looking at the signs of its coordinates. In the graph at the right, the point $(4, 3)$ is in Quadrant I. The point $(0, -4)$ is on the *y*-axis and is not inside any of the four quadrants.

EXAMPLE 3 Identify Quadrants

Name the quadrant the point is in.

a. $(-2, 3)$ **b.** $(4, -2)$

Solution

a. $(-2, 3)$ is in Quadrant II because its *x*-coordinate is negative and its *y*-coordinate is positive.

b. $(4, -2)$ is in Quadrant IV because its *x*-coordinate is positive and its *y*-coordinate is negative.

Checkpoint ✓ Plot Points and Identify Quadrants

Plot the point in a coordinate plane.

   2. $(-2, 5)$ **3.** $(3, 7)$ **4.** $(-1, -3)$ **5.** $(-2, 0)$

Name the quadrant the point is in.

   6. $(-5, -3)$ **7.** $(2, 0)$ **8.** $(4, -1)$ **9.** $(-3, 6)$

USING A SCATTER PLOT Many real-life situations can be described in terms of pairs of numbers. Medical charts record both the height and weight of a patient, while weather reports may include both temperature and windspeed. One way to analyze the relationships between two quantities is to graph the pairs of data on a coordinate plane. Such a graph is called a **scatter plot**.

EXAMPLE 4 Make a Scatter Plot

SNOWMOBILE SALES The amount (in millions of dollars) spent in the United States on snowmobiles is shown in the table. Make a scatter plot and explain what it indicates. ▶Source: National Sporting Goods Association

Year	1990	1991	1992	1993	1994	1995	1996
Spending	322	362	391	515	715	924	970

Solution

Because you want to see how spending changes over time, put time t on the horizontal axis and spending s on the vertical axis. Let t be the number of years since 1990. The scatter plot is shown below.

ANSWER ▶ From the scatter plot, you can see that the amount spent on snowmobiles tends to increase as time increases.

Checkpoint✓ Make a Scatter Plot

10. The age a (in years) of seven cars and the price p (in hundreds of dollars) paid for the cars are recorded in the following table. Make a scatter plot and explain what it indicates.

Age	4	5	3	5	6	4	7
Price	69	61	75	52	42	71	30

Guided Practice

Vocabulary Check

In Exercises 1–3, complete the sentence.

1. Each point in a coordinate plane corresponds to an __?__ of real numbers.

2. In the ordered pair (2, 5), the *y*-coordinate is __?__.

3. The *x*-axis and the *y*-axis divide the coordinate plane into four __?__.

Skill Check

Plot and label the ordered pairs in a coordinate plane.

4. $A(4, -1)$, $B(5, 0)$ 　　　　　　　　**5.** $A(-2, -3)$, $B(-3, -2)$

IDENTIFYING QUADRANTS Complete the statement with *always*, *sometimes*, or *never*.

6. A point plotted in Quadrant IV __?__ has a positive *y*-value.

7. A point plotted in Quadrant IV __?__ has a positive *x*-value.

8. A point plotted on the *x*-axis __?__ has *y*-coordinate 0.

9. A point with a positive *x*-coordinate is __?__ in Quadrant I, Quadrant IV, or on the *x*-axis.

Practice and Applications

IDENTIFYING ORDERED PAIRS Write the ordered pairs that correspond to the points labeled *A*, *B*, *C*, and *D* in the coordinate plane.

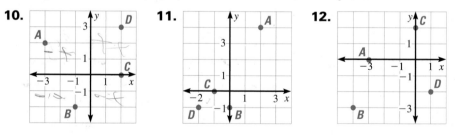

PLOTTING POINTS Plot and label the ordered pairs in a coordinate plane.

13. $A(0, 3)$, $B(-2, -1)$, $C(2, 0)$ 　　　　**14.** $A(5, 2)$, $B(4, 3)$, $C(-2, -4)$

15. $A(4, 1)$, $B(0, -3)$, $C(3, 3)$ 　　　　**16.** $A(0, 0)$, $B(2, -2)$, $C(-2, 0)$

17. $A(-4, 1)$, $B(-1, 5)$, $C(0, -4)$ 　　**18.** $A(3, -5)$, $B(5, 3)$, $C(-3, -1)$

Student Help

▶ **HOMEWORK HELP**
Example 1: Exs. 10–12
Example 2: Exs. 13–18
Example 3: Exs. 19–26
Example 4: Exs. 27–35

IDENTIFYING QUADRANTS Without plotting the point, tell whether it is in *Quadrant I*, *Quadrant II*, *Quadrant III*, or *Quadrant IV*.

19. $(5, -3)$ 　　　**20.** $(-2, 7)$ 　　　**21.** $(6, 17)$ 　　　**22.** $(14, -5)$

23. $(-4, -2)$ 　　**24.** $(3, 9)$ 　　　　**25.** $(-5, -2)$ 　　**26.** $(-5, 6)$

CAR COMPARISONS In Exercises 27–32, use the scatter plots below to compare the weight of a car to its length and to its gas mileage.

27. In the Weight *vs.* Length graph, what are the units on the horizontal axis? What are the units on the vertical axis?

28. In the Weight *vs.* Length graph, estimate the coordinates of the point for a car that weighs about 4000 pounds.

29. Which of the following is true?

    A. Length tends to decrease as weight increases.

    B. Length is constant as weight increases.

    C. Length tends to increase as weight increases.

    D. Length is not related to weight.

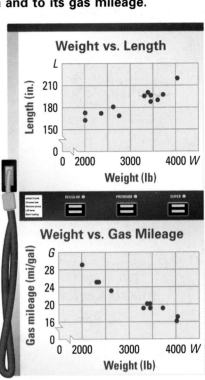

30. In the Weight *vs.* Gas Mileage graph, in the ordered pair (2010, 29), what is the value of W? What is the value of G?

31. **INTERPRETING DATA** In the Weight *vs.* Gas Mileage graph, how does a car's gas mileage tend to change as the weight of the car increases?

32. **CRITICAL THINKING** How would you expect the length of a car to affect its gas mileage? Explain your reasoning.

Biology Link In Exercises 33–35, the table shows the wing length (in millimeters) and the wing-beat rate (in beats per second) for five birds.

Bird	Flamingo	Shellduck	Velvet Scoter	Fulmar	Great Egret
Wing length	400	375	281	321	437
Wing-beat rate	2.4	3.0	4.3	3.6	2.1

BIOLOGISTS study animals in natural or controlled surroundings. Biologists who study birds are called *ornithologists*.

More about biologists is available at www.mcdougallittell.com

33. Make a scatter plot that shows the wing-beat rates and wing lengths for the five birds. Use the horizontal axis to represent the wing-beat rate.

34. What is the slowest wing-beat rate shown on the scatter plot? What is the fastest? Where are these located on your scatter plot?

35. **INTERPRETING DATA** Describe the relationship between the wing length and the wing-beat rate for the five birds.

36. MULTIPLE CHOICE Which ordered pair has an x-coordinate of -7?

(A) $(3, -7)$ **(B)** $(-7, 3)$ **(C)** $(7, 3)$ **(D)** $(3, 7)$

37. MULTIPLE CHOICE The point $(-9, -8)$ is in which quadrant?

(F) Quadrant I **(G)** Quadrant II

(H) Quadrant III **(J)** Quadrant IV

38. MULTIPLE CHOICE Which ordered pair is in Quadrant IV?

(A) $(7, 12)$ **(B)** $(-4, 3)$ **(C)** $(-5, -2)$ **(D)** $(8, -7)$

39. MULTIPLE CHOICE The vertical axis is also called the ___?___.

(F) x-axis **(G)** y-axis

(H) coordinate plane **(J)** origin

Mixed Review

EVALUATING EXPRESSIONS Evaluate the expression for the given value of the variable. *(Lessons 1.1, 2.4, and 2.5)*

40. $3x + 9$ when $x = 2$

41. $13 - (y + 2)$ when $y = 4$

42. $4.2t + 17.9$ when $t = 3$

43. $-x - y$ when $x = -2$ and $y = -1$

USING EXPONENTS Evaluate the expression. *(Lessons 1.2, 1.3)*

44. $x^2 - 3$ when $x = 4$

45. $12 + y^3$ when $y = 3$

46. $x^5 + 10$ when $x = 1.5$

47. $\dfrac{a^2 + b^2}{a - b}$ when $a = 2$ and $b = 3$

ABSOLUTE VALUE Evaluate the expression. *(Lesson 2.2)*

48. $\left| -2.6 \right|$ **49.** $\left| 1.07 \right|$ **50.** $\left| \dfrac{9}{10} \right|$ **51.** $\left| \dfrac{-2}{3} \right|$

SOLVING EQUATIONS Solve the equation. *(Lesson 3.3)*

52. $3x - 6 = 0$ **53.** $6x + 5 = 35$ **54.** $x + 1 = -3$

55. $a - 3 = -2$ **56.** $\dfrac{1}{2}x - 1 = -1$ **57.** $\dfrac{1}{5}r + 3 = 4$

Maintaining Skills

SUBTRACTING FRACTIONS Subtract. Write the answer as a fraction or as a mixed number in lowest terms. *(Skills Review p. 764)*

58. $7\dfrac{4}{9} - 4\dfrac{1}{9}$ **59.** $3\dfrac{2}{3} - 1\dfrac{1}{3}$ **60.** $8\dfrac{3}{4} - 7\dfrac{3}{4}$

61. $9\dfrac{8}{15} - 2\dfrac{4}{15}$ **62.** $8\dfrac{9}{13} - 5\dfrac{2}{13}$ **63.** $6\dfrac{7}{11} - 6\dfrac{2}{11}$

64. $17\dfrac{5}{8} - 10\dfrac{3}{8}$ **65.** $12\dfrac{17}{21} - 7\dfrac{2}{21}$ **66.** $18\dfrac{9}{14} - 3\dfrac{3}{14}$

Linear Equations

GOAL

Discover the relationship between ordered pairs that are solutions to a linear equation.

MATERIALS

• ruler
• graph paper
• pencil

Question What can you observe about the graph of the ordered pairs that are solutions to a linear equation?

A *linear equation* in x and y is an equation that can be written in the form $Ax + By = C$ where A and B are not both zero. A *solution* of a linear equation is an ordered pair (x, y) that makes the equation true. For example, $(0, 3)$ is a solution of the equation $x + 4y = 12$ because $0 + 4(3) = 12$.

Explore

1 Show that $(8, 1)$ is also a solution to the equation $x + 4y = 12$. Plot the two solutions, $(0, 3)$ and $(8, 1)$, on a coordinate graph. Draw a line through them.

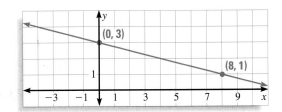

2 Determine whether the following ordered pairs are also solutions of the equation $x + 4y = 12$.

$\quad D(-4, 4) \qquad E(-1, 2) \qquad F(2, 1) \qquad G(4, 2)$

3 Plot the points in Step 2.

4 Make a conjecture about the graph of the ordered pairs that are solutions to the equation $x + 4y = 12$.

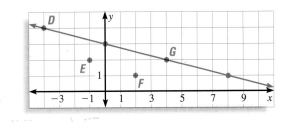

Think About It

In each exercise you are given a linear equation and two solutions. Plot the solutions and draw the line that connects them. Plot the points represented by the ordered pairs given and use the graph to guess whether the other ordered pairs are solutions to the equation. Test your results by substituting in the equation.

1. $2x + y = 3$; solutions: $I(0, 2)$ and $J(4, -5)$
ordered pairs: $K(2, 4)$, $L(1, 4)$, and $M(1, 0)$

2. $3x - 2y = 12$; solutions: $P(4, 0)$ and $Q(2, -3)$
ordered pairs: $R(6, 3)$, $S(2, -1)$, and $T(2, 4)$

3. Write a generalization about the solutions of a linear equation.

4.2 Graphing Linear Equations

Goal

Graph a linear equation using a table of values.

Key Words

• linear equation
• solution of an equation
• function form
• graph of an equation

How long will it take an athlete to burn 800 calories?

Many relationships between two real-life quantities are linear. In Exercise 49 you will see that the time an athlete exercises has a linear relationship to the number of calories burned.

As you saw in Developing Concepts 4.2, page 209, a **linear equation** in x and y is an equation that can be written in the form

$$Ax + By = C$$

where A and B are not both zero. A **solution of an equation** in two variables is an ordered pair (x, y) that makes the equation true.

EXAMPLE **1** **Check Solutions of Linear Equations**

Determine whether the ordered pair is a solution of $x + 2y = 5$.

a. $(1, 2)$ **b.** $(7, -3)$

Solution

a. $x + 2y = 5$ Write original equation.

$1 + 2(2) \stackrel{?}{=} 5$ Substitute 1 for x and 2 for y.

$5 = 5$ Simplify. True statement.

ANSWER ▶ $(1, 2)$ is a solution of the equation $x + 2y = 5$.

b. $x + 2y = 5$ Write original equation.

$7 + 2(-3) \stackrel{?}{=} 5$ Substitute 7 for x and -3 for y.

$1 \neq 5$ Simplify. Not a true statement.

ANSWER ▶ $(7, -3)$ is *not* a solution of the equation $x + 2y = 5$.

Checkpoint ✓ **Check Solutions of Linear Equations**

1. Determine whether the ordered pair is a solution of $2x + y = 1$.

a. $(-3, 7)$ **b.** $(3, -7)$ **c.** $\left(\frac{1}{2}, 0\right)$ **d.** $\left(\frac{5}{2}, -6\right)$

FUNCTION FORM A two-variable equation is written in **function form** if one of its variables is isolated on one side of the equation. For example, $y = 3x + 4$ is in function form while $2x + 3y = 6$ is *not* in function form.

EXAMPLE 2 Find Solutions of Linear Equations

Find three ordered pairs that are solutions of $-2x + y = -3$.

❶ **Rewrite** the equation in function form to make it easier to substitute values into the equation.

$-2x + y = -3$	Write original equation.
$y = 2x - 3$	Add $2x$ to each side.

❷ **Choose** any value for x and substitute it into the equation to find the corresponding y-value. The easiest x-value is 0.

$y = 2(0) - 3$	Substitute 0 for x.
$y = -3$	Simplify. The solution is $(0, -3)$.

❸ **Select** a few more values of x and make a table to record the solutions.

x	0	1	2	3	-1	-2
y	-3	-1	1	3	-5	-7

ANSWER ▶ $(0, -3), (1, -1),$ and $(2, 1)$ are three solutions of $-2x + y = -3$.

GRAPHS OF LINEAR EQUATIONS The **graph of an equation** in x and y is the set of *all* points (x, y) that are solutions of the equation. The graph of a linear equation can be shown to be a straight line.

EXAMPLE 3 Graph a Linear Equation

Use a table of values to graph $y = 3x - 2$.

❶ **Rewrite** the equation in function form. This equation is already written in function form: $y = 3x - 2$.

❷ **Choose** a few values of x and make a table of values.

x	-2	-1	0	1	2
y	-8	-5	-2	1	4

With this table of values you have found five solutions.

$(-2, -8), (-1, -5), (0, -2), (1, 1), (2, 4)$

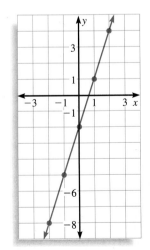

❸ **Plot** the points and draw a line through them.

ANSWER ▶ The graph of $y = 3x - 2$ is shown at the right.

► **STUDY TIP**
When choosing values
of x, try to choose
values that will
produce an integer.

EXAMPLE ④ **Graph a Linear Equation**

Use a table of values to graph $4y - 2x = 8$.

Solution

❶ *Rewrite* the equation in function form by solving for y.

$4y - 2x = 8$	Write original equation.
$4y = 2x + 8$	Add $2x$ to each side.
$y = \dfrac{2}{4}x + \dfrac{8}{4}$	Divide each side by 4.
$y = \dfrac{1}{2}x + 2$	Simplify.

❷ *Choose* a few values of x and make a table of values.

x	−4	−2	0	2	4
y	0	1	2	3	4

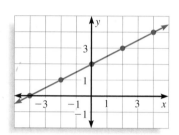

❸ *Plot* the points and draw a line
through them.

ANSWER ► The graph of $4y - 2x = 8$ is
shown at the right.

SUMMARY

Graphing a Linear Equation

STEP ❶ *Rewrite* the equation in function form, if necessary.

STEP ❷ *Choose* a few values of x and make a table of values.

STEP ❸ *Plot* the points from the table of values. A line through
these points is the graph of the equation.

Because the graph of a linear equation is a straight line, the graph can be drawn
using any two of the points on the line.

Checkpoint ✓ *Graph Linear Equations*

Rewrite the equation in function form.

    2. $2x - y = 7$ **3.** $6x + 3y = 18$ **4.** $4y - 3x = -28$

**Find three ordered pairs that are solutions of the equation. Then graph
the equation.**

    5. $y = -2x + 1$ **6.** $x - y = 7$ **7.** $4x + y = -3$

4.2 Exercises

Guided Practice

Vocabulary Check

1. Complete: An ordered pair that makes an equation in two variables true is called a __?__.

2. Complete: A linear equation in x and y can be written in __?__ form.

Skill Check

Determine whether the ordered pair is a solution of the equation.

3. $x - y = -7, (-3, 4)$

4. $x + y = 10, (2, -12)$

5. $4x - y = 23, (5, -3)$

6. $5x + 3y = -8, (2, -4)$

Rewrite the equation in function form.

7. $x + y = -2$

8. $x + 3y = 9$

9. $4x + 2 + 2y = 10$

Find three ordered pairs that are solutions of the equation.

10. $y = 4x - 1$

11. $y = 5x + 7$

12 $y = \frac{1}{2}x + 3$

Use a table of values to graph the equation.

13. $y = x - 4$

14. $y = x + 5$

15. $x + y = 6$

Practice and Applications

CHECKING SOLUTIONS Determine whether the ordered pair is a solution of the equation.

16. $y = 2x + 1, (5, 11)$

17. $y = 5 - 3x, (2, 0)$

18. $2y - 4x = 8, (-2, 8)$

19. $5x - 8y = 15, (3, 0)$

20. $6y - 3x = -9, (1, -1)$

21. $-2x - 9y = 7, (-1, -1)$

FUNCTION FORM Rewrite the equation in function form.

22. $-3x + y = 12$

23. $2x + 3y = 6$

24. $x + 4y = 4$

25. $5x + 5y = 19$

26. $5y - 2x = 15$

27. $-x - y = 5$

28. $2x + 5y = -15$

29. $3x + 2y = -3$

30. $4x - y = 18$

Student Help

▶ **HOMEWORK HELP**
Example 1: Exs. 16–21
Example 2: Exs. 22–39
Example 3: Exs. 40–48
Example 4: Exs. 40–48

FINDING SOLUTIONS Find three ordered pairs that are solutions of the equation.

31. $y = 3x - 5$

32. $y = 7 - 4x$

33. $y = -2x - 6$

34. $x + 2y = 8$

35. $2x + 3y = 9$

36. $3x - 5y = 15$

37. $5x + 2y = 10$

38. $y - 3x = 9$

39. $-5x - 3y = 12$

GRAPHING EQUATIONS Use a table of values to graph the equation.

40. $y = 3x + 3$ **41.** $y = 4x + 2$ **42.** $y = 3x - 4$

43. $y - 5x = -2$ **44.** $x + y = 1$ **45.** $2x + y = 3$

46. $y - 4x = -1$ **47.** $x + 4y = 48$ **48.** $5x + 5y = 25$

TRAINING FOR A TRIATHLON In Exercises 49–51, Mary Gordon is training for a triathlon. Like most triathletes she regularly trains in two of the three events every day. On Saturday she expects to burn about 800 calories during her workout by running and swimming.

Running: 7.1 calories per minute

Swimming: 10.1 calories per minute

Bicycling: 6.2 calories per minute

49. Copy and complete the model below. Let x represent the number of minutes she spends running, and let y represent the number of minutes she spends swimming.

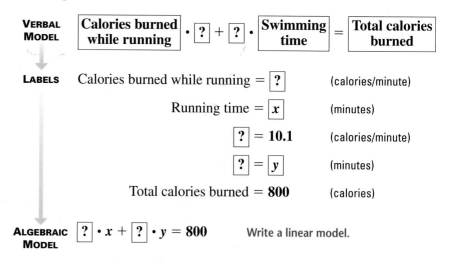

50. Make a table of values and sketch the graph of the equation from Exercise 49.

51. If Mary Gordon spends 45 minutes running, about how many minutes will she have to spend swimming to burn 800 calories?

Science Link In Exercises 52 and 53, use the table showing the boiling point of water (in degrees Fahrenheit) for various altitudes (in feet).

Altitude	0	500	1000	1500	2000	2500
Boiling Point	212.0	211.1	210.2	209.3	208.5	207.6

52. Make a graph that shows the boiling point of water and the altitude. Use the horizontal axis to represent the altitude.

53. **INTERPRETING DATA** Describe the relationship between the altitude and the boiling point of water.

INTERNET ACCESS In Exercises 54–56, use the following information. An internet service provider estimates that the number of households h (in millions) with internet access can be modeled by the equation $h = 6.76t + 14.9$ where t represents the number of years since 1996.

54. Make a table of values. Use $0 \le t \le 6$ for 1996–2002.

55. Graph the equation using the table of values from Exercise 54.

56. CRITICAL THINKING What does the graph mean in the context of the real-life situation?

Standardized Test Practice

57. MULTIPLE CHOICE Which ordered pair is a solution of $-3x + y = -5$?

Ⓐ $(8, -16)$ Ⓑ $(8, -29)$ Ⓒ $(8, -64)$ Ⓓ $(8, 19)$

58. MULTIPLE CHOICE Rewrite the equation $-2x + 5y = 10$ in function form.

Ⓕ $y = 2x + 2$ 　　　　　Ⓖ $y = 2x + 5$

Ⓗ $y = \frac{2}{5}x + 2$ 　　　　　Ⓙ $y = \frac{2}{5}x + 5$

59. MULTIPLE CHOICE Which equation does the graph represent?

Ⓐ $x + y = -2$

Ⓑ $6x + 3y = 0$

Ⓒ $2x - y = 3$

Ⓓ $-x + 2y = 6$

Mixed Review

EVALUATING EXPRESSIONS Find the sum. *(Lesson 2.3)*

60. $5 + 2 + (-3)$ 　　　　　**61.** $-6 + (-14) + 8$

62. $-18 + (-10) + (-1)$ 　　　　　**63.** $-\frac{1}{3} + 6 + \frac{1}{3}$

SIMPLIFYING EXPRESSIONS Simplify the expression. *(Lesson 2.7)*

64. $3a - 5b - 7a + 2b$ 　　　　　**65.** $-6x + 2y - 8x + 4y$

66. $n^2 + 3m - 9m - 3n^2$ 　　　　　**67.** $-4r - 5t^3 + 2r - 7r$

68. $2c^2 - 4c + 8c^2 - 4c^3$ 　　　　　**69.** $-3k^3 - 5k + h + 5k$

SOLVING EQUATIONS Solve the equation. *(Lesson 3.2)*

70. $-2z = -26$ 　　**71.** $\frac{2}{3}t = -10$ 　　**72.** $6c = -96$ 　　**73.** $-\frac{p}{7} = -9$

Maintaining Skills

DECIMALS AND PERCENTS Write the decimal as a percent.
(Skills Review p. 767)

74. 0.15 　　　**75.** 0.63 　　　**76.** 0.5 　　　**77.** 0.02

78. 0.005 　　　**79.** 1.27 　　　**80.** 3 　　　**81.** 8.6

4.3 Graphing Horizontal and Vertical Lines

Goal

Graph horizontal and vertical lines.

Key Words

- horizontal line
- vertical line
- coordinate plane
- *x*-coordinate
- *y*-coordinate
- constant function
- domain
- range

Is a volcano's height a function of time?

In Example 4 you will explore how the height of Mount St. Helens has changed.

Before the eruption

After the eruption

All linear equations in *x* and *y* can be written in the form $Ax + By = C$. When $A = 0$, the equation reduces to $By = C$ and the graph of the equation is a horizontal line. When $B = 0$, the equation reduces to $Ax = C$ and the graph of the equation is a vertical line.

Student Help

▶ **STUDY TIP**
The equations $y = 2$ and $0x + 1y = 2$ are equivalent. For any value of *x*, the ordered pair (*x*, 2) is a solution of $y = 2$.

EXAMPLE 1 Graph the Equation $y = b$

Graph the equation $y = 2$.

Solution

The equation does not have *x* as a variable. The *y*-coordinate is always 2, regardless of the value of *x*. For instance, here are some points that are solutions of the equation:

$(-3, 2), (0, 2),$ and $(3, 2)$

ANSWER ▶ The graph of the equation $y = 2$ is a horizontal line 2 units *above* the *x*-axis.

Checkpoint ✓ Graph the Equation y = b

Graph the equation.

1. $y = -3$ **2.** $y = 4$ **3.** $y = \frac{1}{2}$

EXAMPLE 2 **Graph the Equation** $x = a$

Graph the equation $x = -3$.

Solution

The x-coordinate is always -3, regardless
of the value of y. For instance, here are some
points that are solutions of the equation:

$$(-3, -2), (-3, 0), \text{ and } (-3, 3)$$

ANSWER ▶ The graph of the equation
$x = -3$ is a vertical line **3** units
to the left of the y-axis.

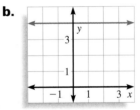

Checkpoint ✓ **Graph the Equation** x = a

Graph the equation.

4. $x = 2$ **5.** $x = -1$ **6.** $x = 3\frac{1}{2}$

EXAMPLE 3 **Write an Equation of a Line**

Write the equation of the line in the graph.

a.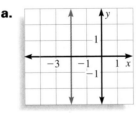

b.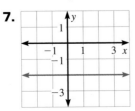

Solution

a. The graph is a vertical line. The x-coordinate is always -2.

ANSWER ▶ The equation of the line is $x = -2$.

b. The graph is a horizontal line. The y-coordinate is always 4.

ANSWER ▶ The equation of the line is $y = 4$.

Checkpoint ✓ **Write an Equation of a Line**

Write the equation of the line in the graph.

7. 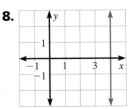 **8.**

CONSTANT FUNCTION A function of the form $y = b$, where b is a number, is called a **constant function**. Its range is the single number b and its graph is a *horizontal line*.

Student Help

▶ **LOOK BACK**
For help with domain and range, see p. 49.

EXAMPLE **4** **Write a Constant Function**

The graph below shows the height of Mount St. Helens from 1860 to May 1980. Write an equation to represent the height of Mount St. Helens for this period. What is the domain of the function? What is the range?

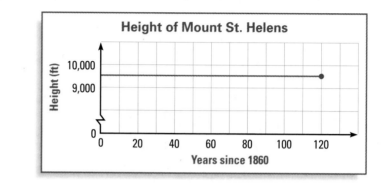

Height of Mount St. Helens

Solution

From the graph, you can see that between 1860 and 1980, the height H was about 9700 feet. Therefore, the equation for the height during this time is $H = 9700$. The domain is all values of t between 0 and 120. The range is the single number 9700.

Checkpoint ✓ **Write a Constant Function**

9. On May 18, 1980, Mount St. Helens erupted. The eruption blasted away most of the peak. The height of Mount St. Helens after the 1980 eruption was 8,364 feet. Write an equation that represents the height of Mount St. Helens after 1980. What is the domain of the function? What is the range?

SUMMARY

Equations of Horizontal and Vertical Lines

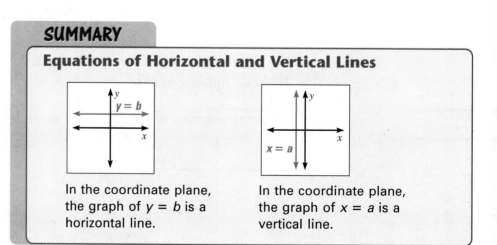

In the coordinate plane, the graph of $y = b$ is a horizontal line.

In the coordinate plane, the graph of $x = a$ is a vertical line.

Guided Practice

Vocabulary Check

1. Is the *x*-axis a *horizontal* or a *vertical* line?

2. Is the *y*-axis a *horizontal* or a *vertical* line?

3. Complete: A function of the form $y = b$ is called a __?__ function.

Skill Check

Graph the equation.

4. $y = 1$ **5.** $x = -10$ **6.** $y = -5$ **7.** $x = 7$

Write the equation of the line in the graph.

LOGICAL REASONING Complete the statement with *always, sometimes,* or *never*.

10. The graph of an equation of the form $y = b$ is __?__ a horizontal line.

11. A line that passes through the point $(2, -3)$ is __?__ a vertical line.

12. The graph of an equation of the form $x = a$ is __?__ a horizontal line.

13. The range of the function $x = 4$ is __?__ equal to 4.

Practice and Applications

CHECKING SOLUTIONS Determine whether the given ordered pair is a solution of the equation.

14. $y = -2, (-2, -2)$ **15.** $y = 3, (3, -3)$

16. $y = 0, (0, 1)$ **17.** $x = 5, (-5, -5)$

FINDING SOLUTIONS Find three ordered pairs that are solutions of the equation.

18. $x = 9$ **19.** $x = \frac{1}{2}$ **20.** $y = 10$

21. $y = -5$ **22.** $x = -10$ **23.** $y = 7$

Student Help

▶**HOMEWORK HELP**
 Example 1: Exs. 18–29
 Example 2: Exs. 18–29
 Example 3: Exs. 30–32
 Example 4: Exs. 33, 34

GRAPHING EQUATIONS Graph the equation.

24. $y = -7$ **25.** $y = 8$ **26.** $x = 4$

27. $x = -9$ **28.** $x = \frac{3}{4}$ **29.** $x = -\frac{1}{4}$

30.

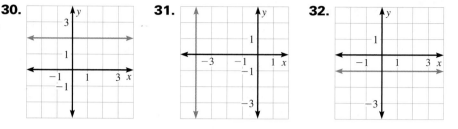

31.

32.

33. HEART RATE You decide to exercise using a treadmill. You warm-up with a 5 minute walk then do a 10 minute fast run. The graphs below show your heart rate during your warm-up and during the fast run.

a. Write an equation that gives your heart rate during your warm-up. What is the domain of the function? What is the range?

b. Write an equation that gives your heart rate during the fast run. What is the domain of the function? What is the range?

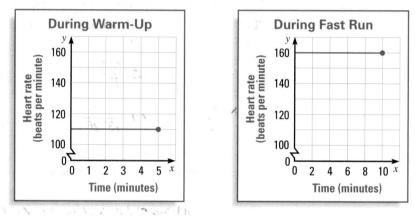

34. *Science Link* You are visiting Kentucky on your summer vacation. You go to Mammoth Cave National Park, the second oldest tourist attraction in the United States. One interesting fact about Mammoth Cave is that it has a constant temperature of 54° year round. The temperature outside the cave on the day you visited was 80°. The graphs below show the temperatures outside Mammoth Cave and inside Mammoth Cave.

a. Write an equation to represent the temperature outside the cave. What is the domain of the function? What is the range of the function?

b. Write an equation to represent the temperature inside Mammoth Cave What is the domain of the function? What is the range of the function?

MAMMOTH CAVE is the longest recorded cave system in the world, with more than 348 miles explored and mapped. About 130 forms of life can be found in the Mammoth Cave system.

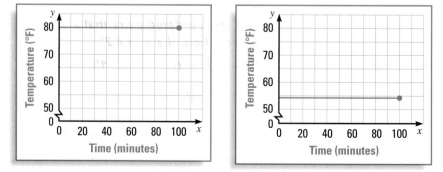

35. MULTIPLE CHOICE Which point does *not* lie on the graph of $y = 3$?

(A) $(0, 3)$ (B) $(-3, 3)$ (C) $(3, -3)$ (D) $\left(\frac{1}{3}, 3\right)$

36. MULTIPLE CHOICE The ordered pair $(3, 5)$ is a solution of __?__.

(F) $y = 5$ (G) $x = 5$ (H) $y = -3$ (J) $x = -5$

Mixed Review

EVALUATING EXPRESSIONS Evaluate the expression. *(Lesson 1.3)*

37. $17 - 6 + 4 - 8$ **38.** $6 + 9 \div 3 + 3$ **39.** $4 \cdot 5 - 2 \cdot 6$

40. $9 \cdot 6 \div 3 \cdot 18$ **41.** $22 - 8 \div 2 \cdot 3$ **42.** $0.75 \div 2.5 \cdot 2 + 1$

SOLVING EQUATIONS Solve the equation. *(Lesson 3.1)*

43. $r - (-4) = 9$ **44.** $-8 - (-c) = 10$ **45.** $15 - (-b) = 30$

Maintaining Skills

LEAST COMMON DENOMINATOR Find the least common denominator (LCD) of each pair of fractions. Then rewrite each pair with their LCD. *(Skills Review p. 762)*

46. $\frac{2}{3}, \frac{7}{8}$ **47.** $\frac{5}{7}, \frac{2}{3}$ **48.** $\frac{1}{2}, \frac{3}{7}$ **49.** $\frac{5}{7}, \frac{4}{21}$

50. $\frac{8}{9}, \frac{7}{12}$ **51.** $\frac{12}{13}, \frac{5}{26}$ **52.** $\frac{7}{18}, \frac{2}{15}$ **53.** $\frac{3}{20}, \frac{7}{15}$

Quiz 1

Plot and label the ordered pairs in a coordinate plane. *(Lesson 4.1)*

1. $A(-4, 1), B(0, 2), C(-3, 0)$ **2.** $A(-1, -5), B(0, -7), C(1, 6)$

3. $A(-1, -6), B(1, 3), C(-1, 1)$ **4.** $A(2, -6), B(5, 0), C(0, -4)$

Without plotting the point, name the quadrant the point is in. *(Lesson 4.1)*

5. $(6, 8)$ **6.** $(-4, -15)$ **7.** $(5, -9)$ **8.** $(-3, 3)$

Rewrite the equation in function form. *(Lesson 4.2)*

9. $2x + y = 0$ **10.** $5x - 2y = 20$ **11.** $-4x - 8y = 32$

Find three ordered pairs that are solutions of the equation. Then graph the equation. *(Lesson 4.2)*

12. $y = 2x - 6$ **13.** $y = 4x + 1$ **14.** $y = 2(-3x + 1)$

15. $y = -3(x - 4)$ **16.** $10x + y = 5$ **17.** $6 = 8x - 3y$

Graph the equation. *(Lesson 4.3)*

18. $x = -5$ **19.** $y = 2$ **20.** $x = 4$

4.4 Graphing Lines Using Intercepts

Goal

Find the intercepts of the graph of a linear equation and then use them to make a quick graph of the equation.

Key Words

- *x*-intercept
- *y*-intercept
- *x*-axis
- *y*-axis

How much should you charge for tickets?

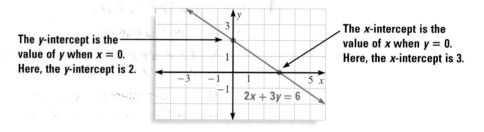

In Exercises 48–51 you will use the graph of a linear equation to determine how much you should charge for tickets to raise money for animal care in a zoo.

An **x-intercept** is the *x*-coordinate of a point where a graph crosses the *x*-axis. A **y-intercept** is the *y*-coordinate of a point where a graph crosses the *y*-axis.

The y-intercept is the value of y when x = 0. Here, the y-intercept is 2.

The x-intercept is the value of x when y = 0. Here, the x-intercept is 3.

$$2x + 3y = 6$$

Because two lines that are not parallel intersect in exactly one point:

- The *vertical line* given by $x = a$, $a \neq 0$ has one *x*-intercept and no *y*-intercept.
- The *horizontal line* given by $y = b$, $b \neq 0$ has one *y*-intercept and no *x*-intercept.
- A line that is neither *horizontal* nor *vertical* has exactly one *x*-intercept and one *y*-intercept.

EXAMPLE 1 Find an x-Intercept

Find the *x*-intercept of the graph of the equation $2x + 3y = 6$.

Solution

To find an *x*-intercept, substitute 0 for *y* and solve for *x*.

$2x + 3y = 6$	Write original equation.
$2x + 3(0) = 6$	Substitute 0 for *y*.
$x = 3$	Solve for *x*.

ANSWER ▸ The *x*-intercept is 3. The line crosses the *x*-axis at the point (3, 0).

EXAMPLE 2 **Find a *y*-Intercept**

Find the *y*-intercept of the graph of the equation $2x + 3y = 6$.

Solution

To find a *y*-intercept, substitute 0 for *x* and solve for *y*.

$2x + 3y = 6$ Write original equation.

$2(0) + 3y = 6$ Substitute 0 for *x*.

$y = 2$ Solve for *y*.

ANSWER ▶ The *y*-intercept is 2. The line crosses the *y*-axis at the point (0, 2).

Checkpoint ✓ Find Intercepts

1. Find the *x*-intercept of the graph of the equation $3x - 4y = 12$.

2. Find the *y*-intercept of the graph of the equation $3x - 4y = 12$.

Student Help

▶**STUDY TIP**
The Quick Graph process works because only two points are needed to determine a line.

SUMMARY

Making a Quick Graph

STEP ❶ **Find** the intercepts.

STEP ❷ **Draw** a coordinate plane that includes the intercepts.

STEP ❸ **Plot** the intercepts and draw a line through them.

EXAMPLE 3 **Make a Quick Graph**

Graph the equation $3x + 2y = 12$.

Solution

❶ **Find** the intercepts.

$3x + 2y = 12$ Write original equation.

$3x + 2(0) = 12$ Substitute 0 for *y*.

$x = 4$ The *x*-intercept is 4.

$3x + 2y = 12$ Write original equation.

$3(0) + 2y = 12$ Substitute 0 for *x*.

$y = 6$ The *y*-intercept is 6.

❷ **Draw** a coordinate plane that includes the points (4, 0) and (0, 6).

❸ **Plot** the points (4, 0) and (0, 6) and draw a line through them.

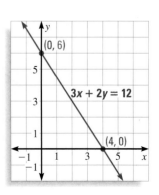

When you make a quick graph, find the intercepts *before* you draw the coordinate plane. This will help you find an appropriate scale on each axis.

EXAMPLE **4** *Choose Appropriate Scales*

Graph the equation $y = 4x + 40$.

Solution

❶ *Find* the intercepts.

$y = 4x + 40$	Write original equation.
$0 = 4x + 40$	Substitute 0 for *y*.
$-40 = 4x$	Subtract 40 from each side.
$-10 = x$	Divide each side by 4.

ANSWER ▶ The *x*-intercept is -10. The line crosses the *x*-axis at the point $(-10, 0)$.

$y = 4x + 40$	Write original equation.
$y = 4(0) + 40$	Substitute 0 for *x*.
$y = 40$	Simplify.

ANSWER ▶ The *y*-intercept is 40. The line crosses the *y*-axis at the point $(0, 40)$.

❷ *Draw* a coordinate plane that includes the points $(-10, 0)$ and $(0, 40)$. With these values, it is reasonable to use tick marks at 10-unit intervals.

You may want to draw axes with at least two tick marks to the left of -10 and to the right of 0 on the *x*-axis and two tick marks below 0 and above 40 on the *y*-axis.

❸ *Plot* the points $(-10, 0)$ and $(0, 40)$ and draw a line through them.

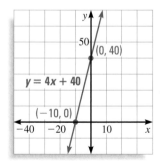

Checkpoint ✓ *Make a Quick Graph*

Find the intercepts of the graph of the equation.

3. $3x - 4y = 12$ **4.** $4x - 5y = 20$ **5.** $y = -2x + 50$

Graph the equation using intercepts.

6. $2x + 5y = 10$ **7.** $x - 6y = 6$ **8.** $12x - 4y = 96$

Guided Practice

Vocabulary Check

1. Complete: In the ordered pair (3, 0) the __?__ is the *x*-intercept.

2. Complete: In the ordered pair (0, 5) the __?__ is the *y*-intercept.

Skill Check

Find the *x*-intercept of the graph of the equation.

3. $5x + 4y = 30$ **4.** $y = 2x + 20$ **5.** $-7x - 3y = 21$

Find the *y*-intercept of the graph of the equation.

6. $6x + 3y = 51$ **7.** $-2x - 8y = 16$ **8.** $10x - y = -5$

Find the *x*-intercept and the *y*-intercept of the graph of the equation. Graph the equation.

9. $y = x + 2$ **10.** $y - 2x = 3$ **11.** $2x - y = 4$

12. $3y = -6x + 3$ **13.** $5y = 5x + 15$ **14.** $x - y = 1$

Practice and Applications

USING GRAPHS TO FIND INTERCEPTS Use the graph to find the *x*-intercept and the *y*-intercept of the line.

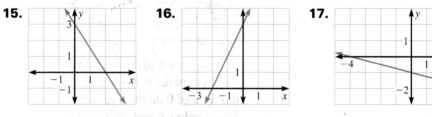

15.   **16.**   **17.**

FINDING X-INTERCEPTS Find the *x*-intercept of the line.

18. $x - 2y = 4$ **19.** $x + 4y = -2$ **20.** $2x - 3y = 6$

21. $5x + 6y = 95$ **22.** $-6x - 4y = 42$ **23.** $9x - 4y = 54$

24. $-x - 5y = 12$ **25.** $2x + 6y = -24$ **26.** $-13x - y = 39$

FINDING Y-INTERCEPTS Find the *y*-intercept of the line.

27. $y = 4x - 2$ **28.** $y = -3x + 7$ **29.** $y = 13x + 26$

30. $y = 6x - 24$ **31.** $3x - 4y = 16$ **32.** $2x - 17y = -51$

USING INTERCEPTS Graph the line that has the given intercepts.

33. *x*-intercept: -2 **34.** *x*-intercept: 4   **35.** *x*-intercept: -7
    y-intercept: 5   *y*-intercept: 6   *y*-intercept: -3

36. $y = 4x - 2$ **37.** $y = 4x + 2$ **38.** $y = 4x + 3$

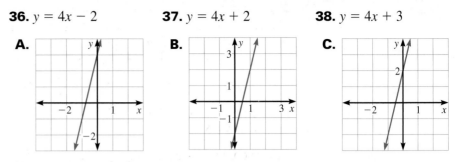

A.   **B.**   **C.**

GRAPHING LINES Find the *x*-intercepts and the *y*-intercepts of the line. Graph the equation. Label the points where the line crosses the axes.

39. $y = x + 3$ **40.** $y = x + 9$ **41.** $y = -4 + 2x$

42. $y = 2 - x$ **43.** $y = -3x + 9$ **44.** $y = 4x - 6$

45. $36x + 4y = 44$ **46.** $y = 10x + 50$ **47.** $-9x + y = 36$

EXAMPLE *Zoo Fundraising*

ZOO FUNDRAISING You are organizing a breakfast tour to raise funds for animal care. Your goal this quarter is to sell $1500 worth of tickets. Assuming 200 adults and 100 students will attend, how much should you charge for an adult ticket and a student ticket? Write a verbal model and an algebraic model to represent the situation.

Solution

VERBAL MODEL	Number of adults	·	Adult ticket price	+	Number of students	·	Student ticket price	=	Total sales

LABELS

     Number of adults = **200**   (people)

     Adult ticket price = **x**   (dollars per person)

     Number of students = **100**   (people)

     Student ticket price = **y**   (dollars per person)

     Total sales = **1500**   (dollars)

ALGEBRAIC MODEL

     $200x + 100y = 1500$ Write a linear model.

     $2x + y = 15$ Divide each side by 100 to simplify.

48. Graph the linear function $2x + y = 15$.

49. What is the *x*-intercept? What does it represent in this situation?

50. What is the *y*-intercept? What does it represent in this situation?

51. CRITICAL THINKING If students cannot afford to pay more than $3 for a ticket, what can you say about the price of an adult ticket?

Link to
Business

ZOO EXPENSES
The American Zoo and Aquarium Institute estimates that it costs a zoo about $22,000 per year to house, feed, and care for a lion and about $18,500 for a polar bear.

INTERNET More about zoo expenses available at www.mcdougallittell.com

RAILROAD EMPLOYEES In Exercises 52–54, use the following information. The number of people who worked for the railroads in the United States each year from 1989 to 1995 can be modeled by the equation $y = -6.6x + 229$, where x represents the number of years since 1989 and y represents the number of railroad employees (in thousands).

DATA UPDATE of the U.S. Bureau of the Census at www.mcdougallittell.com

52. Find the y-intercept of the line. What does it represent?

53. About how many people worked for the railroads in 1995?

54. CRITICAL THINKING Do you think the line in the graph will continue to be a good model for the next 50 years? Explain.

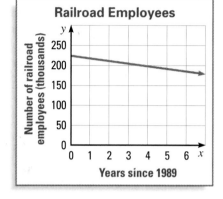

Railroad Employees

Standardized Test Practice

55. MULTIPLE CHOICE Find the x-intercept of the graph of the equation $3x + y = -9$.

(A) -3 (B) 3 (C) 9 (D) -9

56. MULTIPLE CHOICE Find the y-intercept of the graph of the equation $2x - 3y = 12$.

(F) -4 (G) -1 (H) 4 (J) 3

Mixed Review

EVALUATING DIFFERENCES Find the difference. *(Lesson 2.4)*

57. $5 - 9$ **58.** $17 - (-6)$ **59.** $|8| - 13$ **60.** $7 - |-8|$

61. $-\dfrac{2}{3} - \left(-\dfrac{7}{3}\right)$ **62.** $-4 - (-5)$ **63.** $-8 - 9$ **64.** $13.8 - 6.9$

EVALUATING QUOTIENTS Find the quotient. *(Lesson 2.8)*

65. $54 \div 9$ **66.** $-72 \div 8$ **67.** $26 \div (-13)$ **68.** $-1 \div 8$

69. $12 \div \left(-\dfrac{1}{5}\right)$ **70.** $3 \div \dfrac{1}{4}$ **71.** $\dfrac{1}{8} \div \dfrac{1}{2}$ **72.** $-20 \div \left(\dfrac{25}{2}\right)$

73. SCHOOL BAKE SALE You have one hour to make cookies for your school bake sale. You spend 24 minutes mixing the dough. It then takes 12 minutes to bake each tray of cookies. If you bake one tray at a time, which model can you use to find how many trays you can bake during the hour? *(Lesson 3.5)*

A. $x(24 + 12) = 60$ **B.** $12x + 24 = 60$

Maintaining Skills

ROUNDING Round to the nearest cent. *(Skills Review p. 774)*

74. $.298   **75.** $1.649   **76.** $.484   **77.** $8.357

78. $7.134   **79.** $3.152   **80.** $.005   **81.** $5.109

DEVELOPING CONCEPTS
Investigating Slope

For use with Lesson 4.5

GOAL

Use slope to describe the steepness of a ramp.

MATERIALS

• 5 books
• 2 rulers
• paper

Question

How can you use numbers to describe the steepness of a ramp?

You can use the ratio of the vertical rise to the horizontal run to describe the steepness, or *slope*, of a ramp.

$$\text{slope} = \frac{\text{vertical rise}}{\text{horizontal run}} = \frac{2}{5}$$

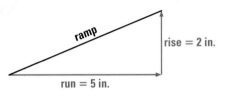

ramp
rise = 2 in.
run = 5 in.

Explore

1 Stack three books. Use a ruler as a ramp. Measure the rise and the run as shown in the *top photo*. Record the rise, the run, and the slope in a table like the one below.

Vertical rise (inches)	Horizontal run (inches)	Slope

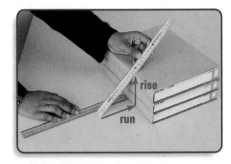

rise
run

2 Keeping the rise the same, move the position of the ruler to change the length of the run three times. Each time, measure and record the results.

3 Place a piece of paper under the edge of the stack of books. Mark the point that is 6 inches from the base of the stack. Place the end of the ramp on the mark as shown in the *middle photo*. Record the results.

4 Change the rise by adding or removing books as shown in the *bottom photo*. Using a run of 6 inches each time, create three more ramps with different rises. Each time, measure and record the results.

Think About It

1. What happens to the slope when the rise stays the same and the run changes?

2. What happens to the slope when the rise changes and the run stays the same?

3. Describe the relationship between the rise and the run when the slope is 1.

4.5 The Slope of a Line

Goal

Find the slope of a line.

Key Words

• rise
• run
• slope

How steep is a roller coaster?

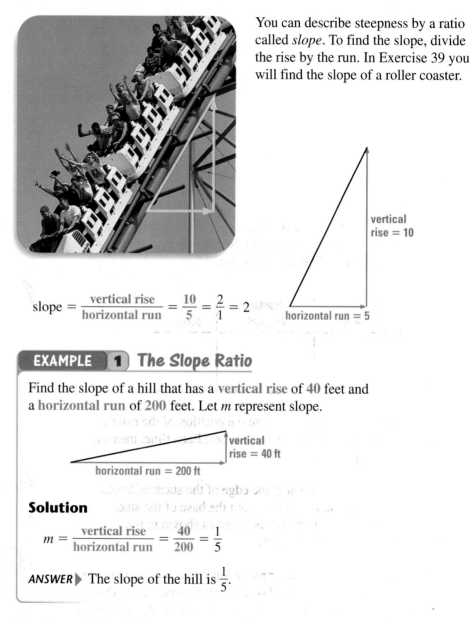

You can describe steepness by a ratio called *slope*. To find the slope, divide the rise by the run. In Exercise 39 you will find the slope of a roller coaster.

$$\text{slope} = \frac{\text{vertical rise}}{\text{horizontal run}} = \frac{10}{5} = \frac{2}{1} = 2$$

vertical rise = 10

horizontal run = 5

EXAMPLE **1** **The Slope Ratio**

Find the slope of a hill that has a **vertical rise** of **40** feet and a **horizontal run** of **200** feet. Let *m* represent slope.

vertical rise = 40 ft

horizontal run = 200 ft

Solution

$$m = \frac{\text{vertical rise}}{\text{horizontal run}} = \frac{40}{200} = \frac{1}{5}$$

ANSWER ▶ The slope of the hill is $\frac{1}{5}$.

The **slope** of a line is the ratio of the vertical rise to the horizontal run between any two points on the line. In the diagram, notice how you can subtract coordinates to find the rise and the run.

$$\text{slope} = \frac{\text{rise}}{\text{run}} = \frac{4-2}{8-3} = \frac{2}{5}$$

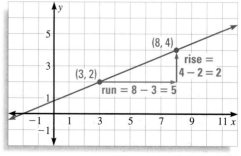

(8, 4)

rise = 4 − 2 = 2

(3, 2)

run = 8 − 3 = 5

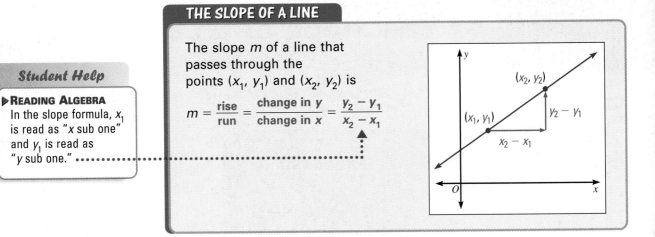

THE SLOPE OF A LINE

The slope m of a line that passes through the points (x_1, y_1) and (x_2, y_2) is

$$m = \frac{\text{rise}}{\text{run}} = \frac{\text{change in } y}{\text{change in } x} = \frac{y_2 - y_1}{x_2 - x_1}$$

SLOPE When you use the formula for slope, you can label either point as (x_1, y_1) and the other as (x_2, y_2). After labeling the points, you must subtract the coordinates in the same order in both the numerator and the denominator.

EXAMPLE 2 Positive Slope

Find the slope of the line that passes through the points $(1, 0)$ and $(3, 4)$.

Solution

Let $(x_1, y_1) = (1, 0)$ and $(x_2, y_2) = (3, 4)$.

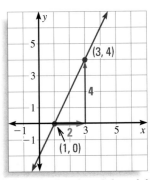

$$m = \frac{y_2 - y_1}{x_2 - x_1}$$ ⟵ Subtract y-values.
⟵ Use the same order to subtract x-values.

$$= \frac{4 - 0}{3 - 1}$$ Substitute values.

$$= \frac{4}{2}$$ Simplify.

$$= 2$$ Slope is positive.

The line rises from left to right.
The slope is positive.

ANSWER ▶ The slope of the line is 2.

Checkpoint ✓ Find a Positive Slope

Find the slope of the line that passes through the two points. Draw a sketch of the line to help you.

1. $(x_1, y_1) = (3, 5)$ and $(x_2, y_2) = (1, 4)$

2. $(x_1, y_1) = (2, 0)$ and $(x_2, y_2) = (4, 3)$

3. $(x_1, y_1) = (2, 7)$ and $(x_2, y_2) = (1, 3)$

Student Help

STUDY TIP
You can choose any two points on a line to find the slope. For example, you can use the points (0, 3) and (3, 2) in Example 3 and get the same slope. You will see this proof in Geometry.

EXAMPLE 3 Negative Slope

Find the slope of the line that passes through the points (0, 3) and (6, 1).

Solution

Let $(x_1, y_1) = (0, 3)$ and $(x_2, y_2) = (6, 1)$.

$m = \dfrac{y_2 - y_1}{x_2 - x_1}$ ← Subtract *y*-values.
← Use the same order to subtract *x*-values.

$= \dfrac{1 - 3}{6 - 0}$ Substitute values.

$= \dfrac{1 + (-3)}{6 - 0}$ To subtract, add the opposite.

$= \dfrac{-2}{6} = -\dfrac{1}{3}$ Simplify to find the negative slope.

ANSWER The slope of the line is $-\dfrac{1}{3}$.

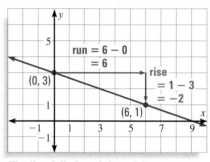

The line falls from left to right. The slope is negative.

Checkpoint ✓ **Find a Negative Slope**

Find the slope of the line that passes through the two points. Draw a sketch of the line to help you.

4. $(x_1, y_1) = (2, 4)$ and $(x_2, y_2) = (-1, 5)$

5. $(x_1, y_1) = (0, 9)$ and $(x_2, y_2) = (4, 7)$

6. $(x_1, y_1) = (-2, 1)$ and $(x_2, y_2) = (1, -3)$

EXAMPLE 4 Zero Slope

Find the slope of the line that passes through the points (1, 2) and (5, 2).

Solution

Let $(x_1, y_1) = (1, 2)$ and $(x_2, y_2) = (5, 2)$.

$m = \dfrac{y_2 - y_1}{x_2 - x_1}$ ← Subtract *y*-values.
← Use the same order to subtract *x*-values.

$= \dfrac{2 - 2}{5 - 1}$ Substitute values.

$= \dfrac{0}{4} = 0$ Simplify to find the slope is zero.

ANSWER The slope of the line is zero.

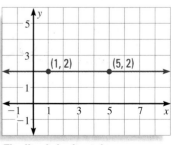

The line is horizontal. The slope is zero.

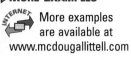
EXAMPLE 5 Undefined Slope

Find the slope of the line that passes through the points $(5, -1)$ and $(5, 3)$.

Solution

Let $(x_1, y_1) = (5, -1)$ and $(x_2, y_2) = (5, 3)$.

$$m = \frac{y_2 - y_1}{x_2 - x_1}$$ ⟵ Subtract y-values.
⟵ Use the same order to subtract x-values.

$$= \frac{3 - (-1)}{5 - 5}$$ Substitute values.

$$= \frac{3 + 1}{5 - 5}$$ Subtracting a negative is the same as adding a positive.

$$= \frac{4}{0}$$ Division by zero is undefined.

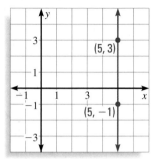

The line is vertical.
The slope is undefined.

ANSWER ▶ Because division by zero is undefined, the expression $\frac{4}{0}$ has no meaning. The slope of the line is undefined.

Checkpoint ✓ Find the Slope of a Line

For each line, determine whether the slope is *positive, negative, zero,* or *undefined*. If the slope is defined, find the slope.

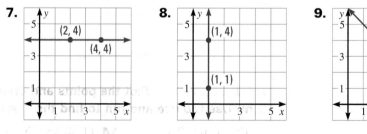

7.

8.

9.

SUMMARY

Slopes of Lines

A line with positive slope *rises* from left to right.

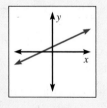

A line with negative slope *falls* from left to right.

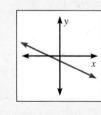

A line with zero slope is *horizontal.*

A line with undefined slope is *vertical.*

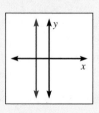

4.5 Exercises

Guided Practice

Vocabulary Check

Use the photo of a ramp.

1. What is the rise of the ramp?

2. What is the run of the ramp?

3. What is the slope of the ramp?

Skill Check

Plot the points and draw the line that passes through them. Without finding the slope, determine whether the slope is *positive, negative, zero,* or *undefined.*

4. $(1, 5)$ and $(5, 5)$ 5. $(-2, -2)$ and $(0, 1)$ 6. $(4, 2)$ and $(4, -1)$

7. $(-3, 1)$ and $(1, -3)$ 8. $(2, 1)$ and $(5, 3)$ 9. $(-4, -3)$ and $(0, -3)$

Find the slope of the line.

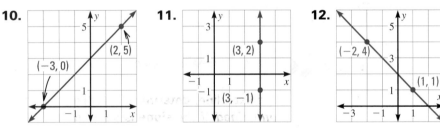

Practice and Applications

THE SLOPE RATIO Plot the points and draw a line that passes through them. Use the rise and run to find the slope.

13. $(2, 3)$ and $(0, 6)$ 14. $(1, 4)$ and $(3, 2)$ 15. $(3, 1)$ and $(-3, -2)$

16. $(2, 2)$ and $(6, -1)$ 17. $(-2, 1)$ and $(2, 4)$ 18. $(1, -3)$ and $(4, 0)$

GRAPHICAL REASONING Find the slope of the line.

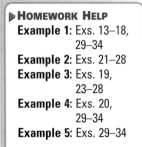

Student Help

▶**HOMEWORK HELP**
Example 1: Exs. 13–18, 29–34
Example 2: Exs. 21–28
Example 3: Exs. 19, 23–28
Example 4: Exs. 20, 29–34
Example 5: Exs. 29–34

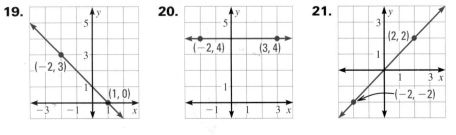

22. **CRITICAL THINKING** Is the slope *always* positive if the coordinates of two points on the line are positive? Justify your answer.

FINDING SLOPE Find the slope of the line that passes through the points.

23. (4, 3) and (8, 5)   **24.** (−2, 4) and (1, 6)   **25.** (3, 8) and (7, 7)

26. (3, −4) and (9, 4)   **27.** (−3, 5) and (−5, 8)   **28.** (−6, −7) and (−4, −4)

ZERO OR UNDEFINED SLOPE Determine whether the slope is *zero*, *undefined*, or *neither*.

29. (0, 4) and (−5, 7)   **30.** (1, 2) and (1, 6)   **31.** (6, 2) and (9, 2)

32. (5, −8) and (3, −8)   **33.** (8, 7) and (14, 1)   **34.** (3, 10) and (3, 5)

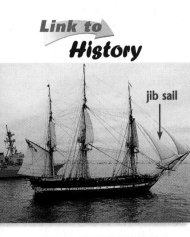
35. **History Link** The photo shows the U.S.S. *Constitution*. Built in the late 1700s, it is the oldest warship afloat. Find the slope of the edge of the *Constitution*'s jib sail.

72 ft

48 ft

36. **LADDER** The top of a ladder is 12 feet from the ground. The base of the ladder is 5 feet to the left of the wall. What is the slope of the ladder? Make a sketch to help you.

37. **INDUCTIVE REASONING** Choose three different pairs of points on the line. Find the slope of the line using each pair. What do you notice? What conclusion can you draw?

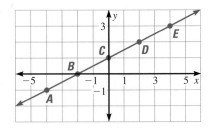

38. **INDUCTIVE REASONING** Based on your conclusion from Exercise 37, complete the following sentence: No matter what pair of points you choose on a line, the __?__ is constant.

ROLLER COASTER In Exercises 39 and 40, use the following information. You are supervising the construction of a roller coaster for young children. For the first 20 feet of horizontal distance, the track must rise off the ground at a constant rate. After your crew has constructed 5 feet of horizontal distance, the track is 1 foot off the ground.

1 ft

5 ft

20 ft

39. Plot points for the heights of the track in 5-foot intervals. Draw a line through the points. Find the slope of the line. What does it represent?

40. After 20 feet of horizontal distance is constructed, you are at the highest point of your roller coaster. How high off the ground is the track?

EXAMPLE **Road Grade**

Road signs sometimes describe the slope of a road in terms of its *grade*. The grade of a road is given as a positive percent. Find the grade of the road shown in the sketch.

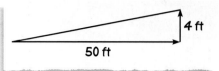

4 ft

50 ft

Solution

Find the slope: $\dfrac{\text{vertical rise}}{\text{horizontal run}} = \dfrac{4}{50}$.

Write $\dfrac{4}{50}$ as a fraction whose denominator is 100: $\dfrac{4}{50} = \dfrac{8}{100}$.

Write $\dfrac{8}{100}$ as a percent: 8%.

ANSWER ▶ The grade of the road is 8%.

41. Find the grade of a road that rises $1\frac{1}{2}$ feet for every horizontal distance of 25 feet.

42. Find the grade of a road that rises 70 feet for every horizontal distance of 1000 feet.

Standardized Test Practice

43. MULTIPLE CHOICE What is the slope of the line through the points (4, 3) and (11, 5)?

Ⓐ $\dfrac{7}{2}$ Ⓑ $-\dfrac{2}{7}$ Ⓒ $\dfrac{2}{7}$ Ⓓ $-\dfrac{7}{2}$

44. MULTIPLE CHOICE Which word describes the slope of a vertical line?

Ⓕ zero   Ⓖ positive   Ⓗ undefined   Ⓙ negative

Mixed Review

SOLVING EQUATIONS Solve the equation. *(Lesson 3.1)*

45. $x + 7 = 12$ **46.** $x - 3 = 11$ **47.** $x - (-2) = 6$

REWRITING EQUATIONS Rewrite the equation so that *y* is a function of *x*. *(Lesson 3.7)*

48. $5y = 10x - 5$ **49.** $\dfrac{1}{3}y = \dfrac{2}{3}x + 3$ **50.** $-4x + y = 11$

51. $-8x + 2y = 10$ **52.** $-3x + 6y = 12$ **53.** $x + \dfrac{2}{5}y = -1$

Maintaining Skills

OPERATIONS WITH DECIMALS Determine whether the equation is *true* or *false*. *(Skills Review p. 759)*

54. $1.3 - 2.7 = 1.4$ **55.** $\dfrac{1.8}{1.8} - 1 = 0$ **56.** $\left(\dfrac{2.7}{0.3} + 1\right) \div 10 = 0$

57. $14.4 + 0.14 = 2.88$ **58.** $(7.8)(1.5) + 4.6 = 16.3$ **59.** $12 + 0 \cdot 7.18 = 12$

4.6 Direct Variation

Goal
Write and graph equations that represent direct variation.

Key Words
- direct variation
- constant of variation
- origin

How much do 36 gold bars weigh?

If you know the weight of one standard mint gold bar, then you can determine the weight of 2, 3, or more gold bars. In Example 3 you will see that total weight is *directly proportional* to the number of bars.

When two quantities y and x have a constant ratio k, they are said to have **direct variation**. The constant k is called the **constant of variation**.

If $\dfrac{y}{x} = k$, then $y = kx$.

Model for Direct Variation: $y = kx$ or $\dfrac{y}{x} = k$, where $k \neq 0$.

Student Help

▶ **READING ALGEBRA**
The model for direct variation $y = kx$ is read as "y varies directly with x."

EXAMPLE 1 Write a Direct Variation Model

The variables x and y vary directly. One pair of values is $x = 5$ and $y = 20$.

a. Write an equation that relates x and y.

b. Find the value of y when $x = 12$.

Solution

a. Because x and y vary directly, the equation is in the form of $y = kx$.

$y = kx$ Write model for direct variation.

$20 = k(5)$ Substitute 5 for *x* and 20 for *y*.

$4 = k$ Divide each side by 5.

ANSWER ▶ An equation that relates x and y is $y = 4x$.

b. $y = 4(12)$ Substitute 12 for *x*.

$y = 48$ Simplify.

ANSWER ▶ When $x = 12$, $y = 48$.

Checkpoint ✓ Write a Direct Variation Model

The variables *x* and *y* vary directly. Use the given values to write a direct variation model that relates *x* and *y*.

    1. $x = 2, y = 6$ **2.** $x = 3, y = 21$ **3.** $x = 8, y = 96$

GRAPHING DIRECT VARIATION MODELS Because $x = 0$ and $y = 0$ is a solution of $y = kx$, the graph of a direct variation equation is always a line through the origin.

Student Help

▶ MORE EXAMPLES

More examples are available at www.mcdougallittell.com

EXAMPLE 2 Graph a Direct Variation Model

Graph the equation $y = 2x$.

Solution

❶ *Plot* a point at the origin.

❷ *Find* a second point by choosing any value for x and substituting it into the equation to find the corresponding y-value. Use the value 1 for x.

$y = 2x$	Write original equation.
$y = 2(1)$	Substitute 1 for x.
$y = 2$	Simplify. The y-value is 2.

ANSWER ▶ The second point is $(1, 2)$.

❸ *Plot* the second point and draw a line through the origin and the second point.

ANSWER ▶ The graph of $y = 2x$ is shown at the right.

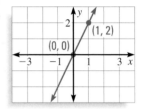

Checkpoint ✓ *Graph a Direct Variation Model*

Graph the equation.

4. $y = x$ **5.** $y = -2x$ **6.** $y = 3x$

Link to
History

FORT KNOX, the United States Bullion Depository, has stored many valuable items. During World War II, the English crown jewels and the Magna Carta were stored there.

More about Fort Knox is available at www.mcdougallittell.com

EXAMPLE 3 Use a Direct Variation Model

FORT KNOX The gold stored in Fort Knox is in the form of standard mint bars called *bullion*, of almost pure gold. Given that 5 gold bars weigh 137.5 pounds, find the weight of 36 gold bars.

Solution

Begin by writing a model that relates the weight W to the number n of gold bars.

$W = kn$	Write model for direct variation.
$137.5 = k(5)$	Substitute 137.5 for W and 5 for n.
$27.5 = k$	Divide each side by 5.

A direct variation model for the weight of a gold bar is $W = 27.5n$.

Use the model to find the weight of 36 gold bars.

$W = 27.5(36)$	Substitute 36 for n.
$W = 990$	Simplify.

ANSWER ▶ Thirty six gold bars weigh 990 pounds.

▶STUDY TIP
Sometimes real-life
data can be
approximated by a
direct variation model,
even though the data
do not fit this model
exactly.

EXAMPLE ④ Use a Direct Variation Model

ANIMAL STUDIES The tail length and body length (in feet) of 8 alligators are shown in the table below. The ages range from 2 years to over 50 years. Write a direct variation model that relates the tail length T to the body length B.

▶ Source: St. Augustine Alligator Farm

Body length B ──── Tail length T

Tail T	1.41	2.04	2.77	2.77	3.99	4.67	4.69	5.68
Body B	1.50	2.41	3.08	3.23	4.28	5.04	5.02	6.38

Solution

Begin by finding the ratio of tail length to body length for each alligator.

Tail T	1.41	2.04	2.77	2.77	3.99	4.67	4.69	5.68
Body B	1.50	2.41	3.08	3.23	4.28	5.04	5.02	6.38
Ratio	0.94	0.85	0.90	0.86	0.93	0.93	0.93	0.89

ANSWER▶ Since the values for the ratio are all close to 0.90 it is reasonable to choose $k = 0.90$. A direct variation model is $T = 0.90B$.

Checkpoint ✓ Use a Direct Variation Model

7. Use the direct variation model you found in Example 4 above to estimate the body length of an alligator whose tail length is 4.5 feet.

SUMMARY

Properties of Graphs of Direct Variation Models

- The graph of $y = kx$ is a line through the origin.

- The slope of the graph of $y = kx$ is k.

k is negative. k is positive.

4.6 Exercises

Guided Practice

Vocabulary Check

1. Explain what it means for x and y to *vary directly*.

2. What point is on the graph of every direct variation equation?

Skill Check

Find the constant of variation.

3. y varies directly with x, and $y = 3$ when $x = 27$.

4. y varies directly with x, and $y = 8$ when $x = 32$.

5. r varies directly with s, and $r = 5$ when $s = 35$.

The variables x and y vary directly. Use the given values to write an equation that relates x and y.

6. $x = 1, y = 2$ **7.** $x = 5, y = 25$ **8.** $x = 3, y = 36$

Graph the equation.

9. $y = x$ **10.** $y = -3x$ **11.** $y = 5x$

Practice and Applications

DIRECT VARIATION MODEL Find the constant of variation.

12. y varies directly with x, and $y = 54$ when $x = 6$.

13. y varies directly with x, and $y = 72$ when $x = 6$.

14. h varies directly with m, and $h = 112$ when $m = 12$.

15. W varies directly with m, and $W = 150$ when $m = 6$.

FINDING EQUATIONS In Exercises 16–24, the variables x and y vary directly. Use the given values to write an equation that relates x and y.

16. $x = 4, y = 12$ **17.** $x = 7, y = 35$ **18.** $x = 12, y = 48$

19. $x = 15, y = 90$ **20.** $x = 22, y = 11$ **21.** $x = 9, y = -3$

22. $x = -1, y = -1$ **23.** $x = -4, y = 40$ **24.** $x = 8, y = -56$

Student Help

▶ **HOMEWORK HELP**
Example 1: Exs. 12–26
Example 2: Exs. 27–30
Example 3: Exs. 34, 35
Example 4: Exs. 36, 37

RECOGNIZING DIRECT VARIATION In Exercises 25 and 26, state whether the two quantities model direct variation.

25. BICYCLING You ride your bike at an average speed of 14 miles per hour. The number of miles m you ride during h hours is modeled by $m = 14h$.

26. *Geometry Link* The circumference C of a circle and its diameter d are related by the equation $C = \pi d$.

GRAPHING EQUATIONS Graph the equation.

27. $y = 4x$ **28.** $y = -3x$ **29.** $y = -x$ **30.** $y = \frac{1}{2}x$

RECOGNIZING DIRECT VARIATION GRAPHS In Exercises 31–33, state whether the graph is a direct variation graph. Explain.

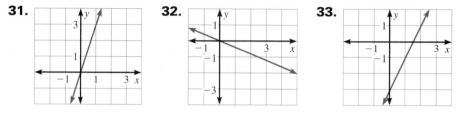

31. **32.** **33.**

34. **Science Link** Weight varies directly with gravity. With his equipment, Buzz Aldrin weighed 360 pounds on Earth but only 60 pounds on the moon. If Valentina V. Tereshkova had landed on the moon with her equipment and weighed 54 pounds, how much would she have weighed on Earth with her equipment?

35. TYPING SPEED The number of words typed varies directly with the time spent typing. If a typist can type 275 words in 5 minutes, how long will it take the typist to type a 935-word essay?

VIOLIN FAMILY In Exercises 36 and 37, use the following information.
The violin family includes the bass, the cello, the viola, and the violin. The size of each instrument determines its range. The shortest produces the highest notes, while the longest produces the deepest (lowest) notes.

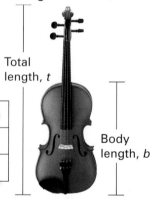

Total length, t

Body length, b

Violin family	Bass	Cello	Viola	Violin
Total length, t (inches)	72	47	26	23
Body length, b (inches)	44	30	?	14

36. Write a direct variation model that relates the body length of a member of the violin family to its total length. *HINT:* Round each ratio to the nearest tenth. Then write a direct variation model.

37. Use your direct variation model from Exercise 36 to estimate the body length of a viola.

Standardized Test Practice

38. MULTIPLE CHOICE Find the constant of variation of the direct variation model $3x = y$.

(A) 3 (B) $\frac{1}{3}$ (C) 1 (D) -3

39. MULTIPLE CHOICE The variables x and y vary directly. When $x = 4$, $y = 24$. Which equation correctly relates x and y?

(F) $x = 4y$ (G) $y = 4x$ (H) $x = 6y$ (J) $y = 6x$

SOLVING EQUATIONS Solve the equation. *(Lesson 3.3)*

40. $7x + 30 = -5$ **41.** $4y = 26 - 9y$ **42.** $2(w - 2) = 2$

43. $9x + 65 = -4x$ **44.** $55 - 5y = 9y + 27$ **45.** $7a - 3 = 4(a - 3)$

FUNCTIONS In Exercises 46 and 47, solve the equation for **y**. *(Lesson 3.7)*

46. $15 = 7(x - y) + 3x$ **47.** $3x + 12 = 5(x + y)$

48. HOURLY WAGE You get paid $152.25 for working 21 hours. Find your hourly rate of pay. *(Lesson 3.8)*

CHECKING SOLUTIONS Determine whether the ordered pair is a solution of the equation. *(Lesson 4.2)*

49. $x - y = 10, (5, -5)$ **50.** $3x - 6y = -2, (-4, -2)$

51. $5x + 6y = -1, (1, -1)$ **52.** $-4x - 3y = -8, (-4, 2)$

53. $3x + 4y = 36, (4, 6)$ **54.** $5x - 3y = 47, (2, 9)$

EVALUATING EXPRESSIONS Find the number with the given prime factorization. *(Skills Review p. 761)*

55. $2 \cdot 3 \cdot 11$ **56.** $3 \cdot 5 \cdot 7$ **57.** $2^3 \cdot 7$

58. $5^3 \cdot 7 \cdot 11$ **59.** $2 \cdot 3 \cdot 5 \cdot 7 \cdot 17$ **60.** $2^6 \cdot 3 \cdot 5^6$

Quiz 2

Find the **x-intercept** and the **y-intercept** of the line. Graph the equation. Label the points where the line crosses the axes. *(Lesson 4.4)*

1. $y = 3x + 6$ **2.** $y - 8x = -16$ **3.** $x - y = 10$

4. $2x - y = 5$ **5.** $4x + 2y = 20$ **6.** $x - 2y = 8$

Find the slope of the line passing through the points. *(Lesson 4.5)*

7. $(0, 0), (5, 2)$ **8.** $(1, -3), (-4, -5)$ **9.** $(3, 3), (-6, -4)$

10. $(-3, 2), (-5, -2)$ **11.** $(0, -4), (5, -4)$ **12.** $(1, -2), (-7, 6)$

The variables **x** and **y** vary directly. Use the given values to write an equation that relates **x** and **y**. *(Lesson 4.6)*

13. $x = 3, y = 9$ **14.** $x = 5, y = 40$ **15.** $x = 15, y = 60$

In Exercises 16–18, graph the equation. *(Lesson 4.6)*

16. $y = 5x$ **17.** $y = -6x$ **18.** $y = 10x$

19. The number of bolts b a machine can make varies directly with the time t it operates. The machine can make 4200 bolts in 2 hours. How many bolts can it make in 5 hours?

REASONING 4.7
Slope-Intercept Form

GOAL

Determine the effect that the slope and *y*-intercept have on the graph of $y = mx + b$.

MATERIALS

• graph paper
• pencil

Question

How do the slope and *y*-intercept affect the graph of $y = mx + b$?

Explore

1 Graph each equation on the same coordinate plane. Describe any patterns you see.

   a. $y = 2x$

   b. $y = 2x + 2$

   c. $y = 2x - 2$

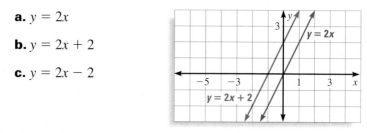

2 For each equation in Step 1, give the slope of the line and write the coordinates of the point where the graph crosses the *y*-axis.

3 Graph each equation on the same coordinate plane. Describe any patterns you see.

   a. $y = x$

   b. $y = 2x$

   c. $y = 3x$

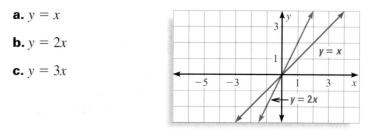

4 For each equation in Step 3, give the slope of the line and write the coordinates of the point where the graph crosses the *y*-axis.

Think About It

1. Based on your results in Steps 1 and 2, predict what the graph of $y = 2x + 5$ will look like. Predict the *y*-intercept. Explain your prediction.

2. Test your prediction by graphing the equation $y = 2x + 5$.

3. Based on your results in Steps 3 and 4, predict what the graph of $y = 5x$ will look like. Predict the slope. Explain your prediction.

4. Test your prediction by graphing the equation $y = 5x$.

5. Based on your observations, what information do you think the numbers *m* and *b* give you about a graph? Use graphs to support your answer.

4.7 Graphing Lines Using Slope-Intercept Form

Goal

Graph a linear equation in slope-intercept form.

Key Words

- slope
- *y*-intercept
- slope-intercept form
- parallel lines

How can you estimate production costs?

In Example 3 you will use the graph of a linear model to estimate the production costs for a small hat-making business.

In Lesson 4.5 you learned to find the slope of a line given two points on the line. There is also a method for finding the slope given an equation of a line.

SLOPE-INTERCEPT FORM OF THE EQUATION OF A LINE

The linear equation $y = mx + b$ is written in **slope-intercept form,** where m is the slope and b is the y-intercept.

slope $\cdots\cdots$ $\cdots\cdots$ y-intercept

$$y = mx + b$$

If $y = 2x + 3$, then $(0, 3)$ and $(1, 5)$ are on the line and the slope is 2. More generally, if $y = mx + b$, then $(0, b)$ and $(1, m + b)$ are on the line and the slope is $\dfrac{(m + b) - b}{1 - 0} = m$.

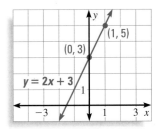

EXAMPLE 1 Find the Slope and y-Intercept

Find the slope and y-intercept of $2x - y = -3$.

Solution Rewrite the equation in slope-intercept form.

$2x - y = -3$	Write original equation.
$-y = -2x - 3$	Subtract $2x$ from each side.
$y = 2x + 3$	Divide each side by -1. $m = 2$ and $b = 3$.

ANSWER ▶ The slope is 2. The y-intercept is 3.

EXAMPLE 2 Graph an Equation in Slope-Intercept Form

Graph the equation $y = -3x + 2$.

❶ **Find** the slope, -3, and the y-intercept, 2.

❷ **Plot** the point $(0, b)$ when b is 2.

❸ **Use** the slope to locate a second point on the line.

$$m = \frac{-3}{1} = \frac{\text{rise}}{\text{run}} \longrightarrow \frac{\text{move 3 units down}}{\text{move 1 unit right}}$$

❹ **Draw** a line through the two points.

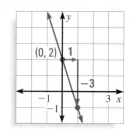

Checkpoint ✓ Graph an Equation in Slope-Intercept Form

1. $y = -2x + 3$ **2.** $y = 4x - 5$ **3.** $y = -\frac{2}{3}x + 2$

EXAMPLE 3 Use a Linear Model

PRODUCTION COSTS Chai has a small business making decorated hats. Based on data for the last eight months, she calculates her monthly cost y of producing x hats using the function $y = 1.9x + 350$.

a. Explain what the y-intercept and slope mean in this model.

b. Graph the model. Then use the graph to estimate the cost of 35 hats.

Solution

a. The y-intercept is 350. This means that her initial cost was $350. The slope is 1.9. This means that her cost will increase at a rate of $1.90 for each hat she makes.

b. Graph the line by using the slope to find a second point.

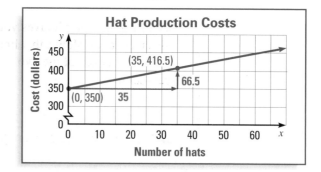

ANSWER ▶ From the graph, the cost of making 35 hats will be about $416.50.

Checkpoint ✓ Use a Linear Model

4. Use the graph in Example 3 above to find the cost of making 60 hats.

PARALLEL LINES Parallel lines are different lines in the same plane that never intersect. Two nonvertical lines are **parallel** if they have the same slope and different y-intercepts. Any two vertical lines are parallel.

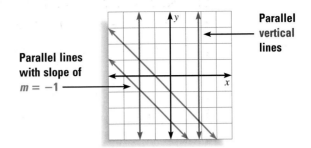

Parallel vertical lines

Parallel lines with slope of $m = -1$

Student Help

▶ **MORE EXAMPLES**

More examples are available at www.mcdougallittell.com

EXAMPLE 4 Identify Parallel Lines

Which of the following lines are parallel?

line *a*: $-x + 2y = 6$ line *b*: $-x + 2y = -2$ line *c*: $x + 2y = 4$

Solution

❶ *Rewrite* each equation in slope-intercept form.

line *a*: $y = \frac{1}{2}x + 3$ line *b*: $y = \frac{1}{2}x - 1$ line *c*: $y = -\frac{1}{2}x + 2$

❷ *Identify* the slope of each equation.

The slope of line a is $\frac{1}{2}$. The slope of line b is $\frac{1}{2}$. The slope of line c is $-\frac{1}{2}$.

❸ *Compare* the slopes.

Lines *a* and *b* are parallel because each has a slope of $\frac{1}{2}$.

Line *c* is *not* parallel to either of the other two lines because it has a slope of $-\frac{1}{2}$.

CHECK ✓ The graph gives you a visual check. It shows that line *c* intersects each of the two parallel lines.

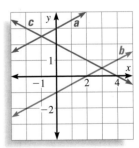

ANSWER ▶ Line *a* and line *b* are parallel.

Checkpoint ✓ Identify Parallel Lines

5. Which of the following lines are parallel?

line *a*: $3x + 2y = 6$ line *b*: $3x - 2y = 6$ line *c*: $6x + 4y = 6$

Guided Practice

Vocabulary Check

1. Complete: In the equation $y = 5x - 7$, __?__ is the y-intercept.

2. Complete: Two nonvertical lines are parallel if they have the same __?__ and different __?__ .

Skill Check

In Exercises 3–8, find the slope and y-intercept of the equation.

3. $y = 2x + 1$ **4.** $y = 8.5x$ **5.** $5x - y = 3$

6. $y - x = 3$ **7.** $y + x = 15$ **8.** $y = \frac{1}{2}x + 6$

9. Which equation best represents the graph at the right?

    A. $y = \frac{1}{2}x - 2$

    B. $y = 2x - 2$

    C. $y = 2x$

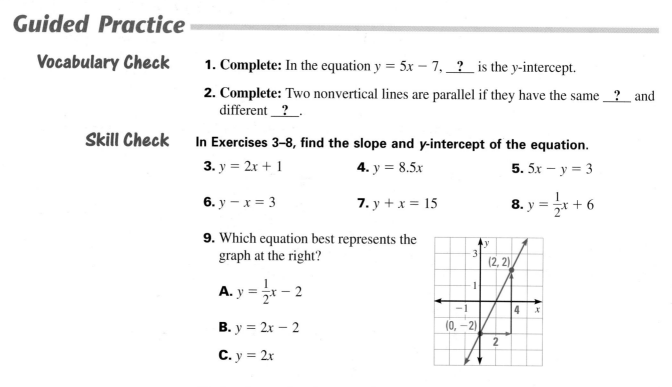

10. Are the graphs of $y = x + 2$ and $y = x - 4$ parallel lines?

Practice and Applications

SLOPE-INTERCEPT FORM   Rewrite the equation in slope-intercept form.

11. $-x + y = 9$ **12.** $3x + y = -11$ **13.** $10x - 5y = 50$

14. $y - 4x = 9$ **15.** $2y + 12 = x$ **16.** $3x - 6y = 18$

SLOPE AND Y-INTERCEPT   Find the slope and y-intercept of the graph of the equation.

17. $y = 6x + 4$ **18.** $y = 3x - 7$ **19.** $y = 2x - 9$

20. $y = \frac{1}{4}x - 3$ **21.** $y - 9x = 0$ **22.** $y = -2$

23. $12x + 4y = 24$ **24.** $3x + 4y = 16$ **25.** $7y - 14x = 28$

Student Help

▶ **HOMEWORK HELP**
Example 1: Exs. 11–25
Example 2: Exs. 26–48
Example 3: Exs. 56–62
Example 4: Exs. 49–54, 63, 64

GRAPHING LINES   Graph the equation.

26. $y = x + 3$ **27.** $y = 2x - 1$ **28.** $y = x + 5$

29. $y = -x + 4$ **30.** $y = 6 - x$ **31.** $y = 3x + 7$

32. $y = 4x + 4$ **33.** $y = x + 9$ **34.** $y = \frac{2}{3}x$

GRAPHING LINES Write the equation in slope-intercept form. Then graph the equation.

35. $x + y = 0$

36. $3x - 6y = 9$

37. $4x + 5y = 15$

38. $4x - y - 3 = 0$

39. $x - y + 4 = 0$

40. $2x - 3y - 6 = 0$

41. $5x + 15 + 5y = 10x$

42. $2x + 2y - 4 = x + 5$

MATCHING EQUATIONS AND GRAPHS Match the equation with its graph.

43. $y = \frac{1}{2}x + 1$

44. $y = \frac{1}{2}x - 1$

45. $y = x + 2$

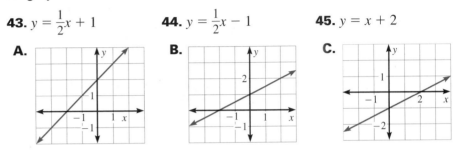

INTERPRETING A GRAPH Identify the slope and y-intercept of the graph.

46.

47.

48.

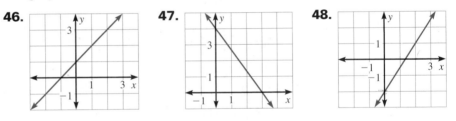

PARALLEL LINES Determine whether the graphs of the two equations are parallel lines. Explain your answer.

49. line *a*: $y = -3x + 2$
line *b*: $y + 3x = -4$

50. line *a*: $2x - 12 = y$
line *b*: $y = 10 + 2x$

51. line *a*: $y = x + 8$
line *b*: $x - y = -1$

52. line *a*: $2x - 5y = -3$
line *b*: $5x + 2y = 6$

53. line *a*: $y + 6x - 8 = 0$
line *b*: $2y = 12x - 4$

54. line *a*: $3y - 4x = 3$
line *b*: $3y = -4x + 9$

55. CABLE CARS In the 1870s, a cable car system was built in San Francisco to climb the steep streets. Find the steepness of the street sections shown below by calculating each labeled slope from left to right in the diagram.

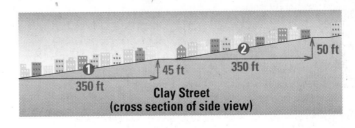

Clay Street
(cross section of side view)

SNOW In Exercises 56–58, use the following information.

Snow fell for 9 hours at a rate of $\frac{1}{2}$ inch per hour. Before the snowstorm began, there were already 6 inches of snow on the ground. The equation $y = \frac{1}{2}x + 6$ models the depth y (in inches) of snow on the ground after x hours.

56. What is the slope of $y = \frac{1}{2}x + 6$? What is the y-intercept?

57. CRITICAL THINKING Explain what the slope and y-intercept represent in the snowstorm model.

58. Graph the amount of snow on the ground during the storm.

SAVINGS ACCOUNT In Exercises 59 and 60, use the following information. You have $50 in your savings account at the beginning of the year. Each month you save $30. Assuming no interest is paid, the equation $s = 30m + 50$ models the amount of money s (in dollars) in your savings account after m months.

59. Explain what the y-intercept and slope represent in this model.

60. Graph the model. Then use the graph to predict your total savings after 18 months.

PHONE CALL In Exercises 61 and 62, the cost of a long-distance telephone call is $.87 for the first minute and $.15 for each additional minute.

61. Let c represent the total cost of a call that lasts t minutes. Plot points for the costs of calls that last 1, 2, 3, 4, 5, and 6 minutes.

62. CRITICAL THINKING Draw a line through the points you plotted in Exercise 61. Find the slope. What does the slope represent?

63. PARALLEL LINES Which of the following lines are parallel?

   line **a**: $-2x + y = 10$ line **b**: $-6x + 3y = 13$ line **c**: $-2x - y = 6$

64. PARALLEL LINES Write an equation of a line that is parallel to $y = 4x - 5$ but has a y-intercept of 3.

CHALLENGE A parallelogram is a quadrilateral with opposite sides parallel. Determine whether the figure is a parallelogram by using slopes. Explain your reasoning.

65.   **66.**

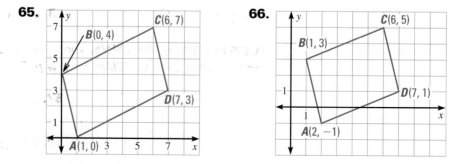

67. MULTIPLE CHOICE What is the slope of the graph of the equation $y + 8 = 0$?

Ⓐ Undefined   Ⓑ 1   Ⓒ 0   Ⓓ -1

68. MULTIPLE CHOICE Write the equation $6x - 9y + 45 = 0$ in slope-intercept form.

Ⓕ $y = \frac{2}{3}x - 5$ Ⓖ $y = \frac{3}{2}x + 5$ Ⓗ $y = \frac{2}{3}x + 5$ Ⓙ $y = \frac{3}{2}x - 5$

69. MULTIPLE CHOICE What is the slope of a line parallel to the graph of the equation $16x - 32y = 160$?

Ⓐ 2   Ⓑ $\frac{1}{2}$ Ⓒ 5   Ⓓ -5

Mixed Review

SOLVING EQUATIONS In Exercises 70–78, solve the equation. *(Lessons 3.1, 3.2, and 3.3)*

70. $x + 6 = 14$ **71.** $9 - y = 4$ **72.** $7b = 21$

73. $\frac{a}{4} = 3$ **74.** $\frac{1}{3}h - 2 = 1$ **75.** $3x - 12 = 6$

76. $2(v + 1) = 4$ **77.** $3(x - 1) = -18$ **78.** $5(w - 5) = 25$

79. Science Link You are studying the atomic numbers and weights of elements. You record several pairs in a table. Make a scatter plot. Then describe the relationship between the atomic numbers and the atomic weights. *(Lesson 4.1)*

Element	H	He	Li	Be	B	C	N	O
Atomic Number	1	2	3	4	5	6	7	8
Atomic Weight	1.0	4.0	6.9	9.0	10.8	12.0	14.0	16.0

Note: The abbreviations above are for the following elements: Hydrogen, Helium, Lithium, Beryllium, Boron, Carbon, Nitrogen, and Oxygen.

80. COIN COLLECTION You have 32 coins in a jar. Each coin is either copper or silver. You have 8 more copper coins than silver coins. Let c be the number of copper coins. Which equation correctly models the situation? *(Lesson 3.5)*

A. $(c - 8) + c = 32$ **B.** $c + (c + 8) = 32$

Maintaining Skills

ADDING FRACTIONS Add. Write the answer as a fraction or as a mixed number in lowest terms. *(Skills Review p. 764)*

81. $\frac{1}{8} + \frac{1}{5}$ **82.** $\frac{2}{3} + \frac{4}{5}$ **83.** $\frac{3}{4} + \frac{8}{9}$ **84.** $\frac{9}{11} + \frac{10}{33}$

85. $\frac{6}{7} + \frac{3}{8}$ **86.** $\frac{1}{4} + \frac{5}{6}$ **87.** $\frac{2}{3} + \frac{8}{21}$ **88.** $\frac{19}{24} + \frac{11}{12}$

USING A GRAPHING CALCULATOR
Graphing a Linear Equation

For use with Lesson 4.7

In Lesson 4.7, you learned how to graph a linear equation using the slope and y-intercept. With a graphing calculator or a computer, you can graph a linear equation and find solutions.

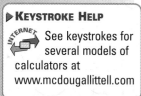

Student Help

▶ **KEYSTROKE HELP**

See keystrokes for several models of calculators at www.mcdougallittell.com

---

Sample

Use a graphing calculator to graph the equation $2x - 3y = 33$.

Solution

1 Rewrite the equation in function form.

$$2x - 3y = 33$$

$$-3y = -2x + 33$$

$$y = \frac{2}{3}x - 11$$

2 Press [Y=] [( ] 2 [÷] 3 [ )] x [−] 11 [ENTER] .

```
Y1=(2/3)X-11
Y2=
Y3=
Y4=
Y5=
Y6=
Y7=
```

Student Help

▶ **STUDY TIP**
Xmin means the minimum x-value, Xmax means the maximum x-value, and Xscl is the number of units between the tick marks.

3 Press [WINDOW] to set the size of the graph.

```
WINDOW
 Xmin=-10
 Xmax=10
 Xscl=1
 Ymin=-10
 Ymax=10
 Yscl=1
```

4 Press [GRAPH] to graph the equation. A standard viewing window is shown.

---

5 To see the point where the graph crosses the x-axis, you can adjust the viewing window. Press [WINDOW] and use the [▲] arrow to enter new values. Then press [GRAPH] to graph the equation.

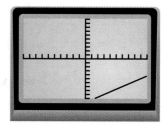

```
WINDOW
 Xmin=0
 Xmax=20
 Xscl=1
 Ymin=-15
 Ymax=5
 Yscl=1
```

Sample

Estimate the value of y when $x = -7$ in the equation $y = \frac{2}{3}x - \frac{45}{8}$.

Solution

1 Graph the equation $y = \frac{2}{3}x - \frac{45}{8}$ using a viewing window that will show the graph when $x \approx -7$.

2 Press **TRACE** and a flashing cursor appears. The x-coordinate and y-coordinate of the cursor's location are displayed at the bottom of the screen. Press the right and left arrows to move the cursor. Move the trace cursor until the x-coordinate of the point is approximately -7.

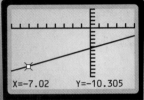

Student Help

▶**STUDY TIP**
You can continue to use zoom until the y-coordinate is to the nearest tenth, hundredth, or any other decimal place you need.

3 Use the **ZOOM** feature to get a more accurate estimate. A common way to zoom is to press **ZOOM** and select *Zoom In*. You now have a closer look at the graph at that point. Repeat **Step 2**.

ANSWER ▶ When $x = -7$, $y \approx -10.3$.

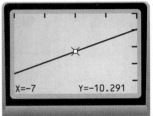

Try These

Use the standard viewing window to graph the equation.

1. $y = -2x - 3$ **2.** $y = 2x + 2$ **3.** $x + 2y = -1$ **4.** $x - 3y = 3$

Use the indicated viewing window to graph the equation.

5. $y = x + 25$
  Xmin = 10
  Xmax = 10
  Xscl = 1
  Ymin = 25
  Ymax = 35
  Yscl = 5

6. $y = 0.1x$
  Xmin = 10
  Xmax = 10
  Xscl = 1
  Ymin = 25
  Ymax = 1
  Yscl = 0.1

7. $y = 100x + 2500$
  Xmin = 0
  Xmax = 100
  Xscl = 10
  Ymin = 0
  Ymax = 15000
  Yscl = 1000

Determine a viewing window appropriate for viewing both intercepts of the equation.

8. $y = x - 330$ **9.** $y = 120x$ **10.** $y = 40,000 - 1500x$

Functions and Relations

Goal

Decide whether a relation is a function and use function notation.

Key Words

- relation
- function
- vertical line test
- function notation
- linear function

How far does a Monarch Butterfly fly during its migration?

Some real-life situations can be modeled by functions. In Exercises 56–58 you will see that the distance traveled by a monarch butterfly during its migration is a function of the traveling time.

Recall that a function is a rule that establishes a relationship between two quantities, called the *input* and the *output*, where for each input, there is exactly one output. There are other algebraic rules that associate *more than one* output with an input. For example, an input-output table corresponding to $x = y^2$ might include the following entries.

Input x	0	1	4	4
Output y	0	1	2	−2

Notice that the input $x = 4$ corresponds to two different outputs, $y = 2$ and $y = -2$. In this case the ordered pairs $(0, 0)$, $(1, 1)$, $(4, 2)$, $(4, -2)$ represent a *relation*, one that does not satisfy the requirements for a function. A **relation** is *any* set of ordered pairs. A relation is a *function* if for every input there is *exactly* one output.

EXAMPLE 1 Identify Functions

Decide whether the relation is a function. If it is a function, give the domain and the range.

Student Help

▶ **LOOK BACK**
For help with domain and range, see p. 49.

a. Input Output

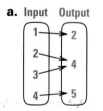

b. Input Output

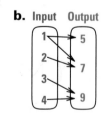

Solution

a. The relation is a function. For each input there is exactly one output. The domain is 1, 2, 3, and 4. The range is 2, 4, and 5.

b. The relation is *not* a function because the input 1 has two outputs: 5 and 7.

When you graph a function or relation, the input is given by the horizontal axis and the output is given by the vertical axis.

Student Help

▶ **STUDY TIP**
You can use your pencil to check. Keep your pencil straight to represent a vertical line and pass it across the graph. If it touches the graph at more than one point, the graph is not a function.

SUMMARY

Vertical Line Test for Functions

A graph is a function if any vertical line intersects the graph at no more than one point.

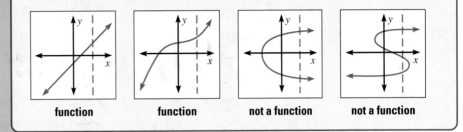

| function | function | not a function | not a function |

EXAMPLE 2 Use the Vertical Line Test

Use the vertical line test to determine whether the graph represents a function.

a.

b.

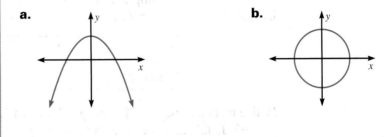

Solution

a. No vertical line can intersect the graph more than once. So, this graph does represent y as a function of x.

b. It is possible to draw a vertical line that intersects the graph twice. So, this graph does *not* represent a function.

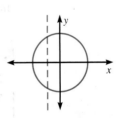

Checkpoint ✓ Use the Vertical Line Test

Use the vertical line test to determine whether the graph represents a function.

1.

2.

FUNCTION NOTATION When a function is defined by an equation, it is often convenient to name the function. Just as x is commonly used as a variable, the letter f is commonly used to name a function. To write a function using **function notation**, you use $f(x)$ in place of y.

x-y notation: $y = 3x + 2$ **function notation:** $f(x) = 3x + 2$

EXAMPLE 3 Evaluate a Function

Evaluate $f(x) = 2x - 3$ when $x = -2$.

Solution

You can evaluate a function for a given value by substituting the given value for the variable and simplifying.

$$f(x) = 2x - 3$$ Write original function.

$$f(-2) = 2(-2) - 3$$ Substitute -2 for x.

$$= -7$$ Simplify.

ANSWER ▶ When $x = -2$, $f(x) = -7$.

Checkpoint ✓ Evaluate a Function

3. Evaluate $f(x) = 4x + 5$ when $x = 2$. **4.** Evaluate $g(x) = x^2$ when $x = -3$.

A function is called a **linear function** if it is of the form $f(x) = mx + b$. For instance, the function in Checkpoint 3 is linear. But, the function in Checkpoint 4 is not linear. To graph a linear function, rewrite the function using x-y notation.

EXAMPLE 4 Graph a Linear Function

Graph $f(x) = -\dfrac{1}{2}x + 3$.

Solution

❶ **Rewrite** the function as $y = -\dfrac{1}{2}x + 3$.

❷ **Find** the slope and the y-intercept.

$$m = -\dfrac{1}{2} \text{ and } b = 3$$

❸ **Use** the slope to locate a second point.

❹ **Draw** a line through the two points.

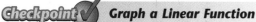

Checkpoint ✓ Graph a Linear Function

Graph the linear function.

5. $f(x) = 4x - 3$ **6.** $h(x) = -3x + 1$ **7.** $g(x) = -\dfrac{1}{4}x + 2$

4.8 Exercises

Guided Practice

Vocabulary Check

1. Complete: A relation is any set of __?__.

2. Complete: The function $f(x) = 6x$ is a __?__ function.

Skill Check

Evaluate the function $f(x) = -5x - 2$ for the given value of x.

3. $x = 4$ **4.** $x = 0$ **5.** $x = -2$ **6.** $x = -\dfrac{1}{5}$

Determine whether the relation is a function. If it is a function, give the domain and the range.

7. Input Output

10	→	100
20	→	200
30	→	300
40	→	400
50	→	500

8. Input Output

3 → 5, 4
6 → 3, 2

9. (graph)

Determine whether the graph represents a function. Explain your reasoning.

10. (graph)   **11.** (graph)   **12.** (graph)

Practice and Applications

RELATIONS AND FUNCTIONS Determine whether the relation is a function. If it is a function, give the domain and the range.

13. Input Output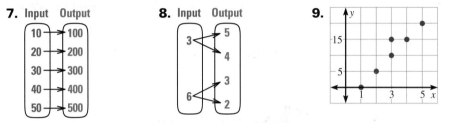

1 → 5
2 → 4
3 → 3
4 → 2

14. Input Output

1, 2, 3, 4 → 0

15. Input Output

7 → 7
9 → 9
10 → 8, 10

16.

Input	Output
0	2
1	4
2	6
3	8

17.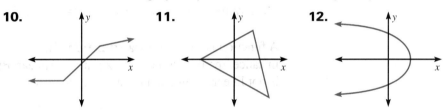

Input	Output
0	1
2	2
4	3
3	4

18.

Input	Output
1	1
3	2
5	3
7	1

Student Help

▶**HOMEWORK HELP**
Example 1: Exs. 13–18
Example 2: Exs. 19–24
Example 3: Exs. 25–33
Example 4: Exs. 37–45

GRAPHICAL REASONING Determine whether the graph represents a function. Explain your reasoning.

19.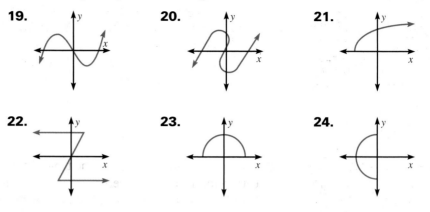

20.

21.

22.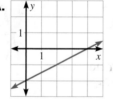

23.

24.

EVALUATING FUNCTIONS Evaluate the function when $x = 2$, $x = 0$, and $x = -2$.

25. $f(x) = 3x$

26. $g(x) = x + 4$

27. $h(x) = 3x - 5$

28. $g(x) = -x - 6$

29. $f(x) = 5x + 1$

30. $f(x) = -x - 3$

31. $h(x) = 8x + 7$

32. $f(x) = -4x + 15$

33. $g(x) = 5x - 6$

GRAPHICAL REASONING Match the function with its graph.

34. $f(x) = 3x - 2$

35. $f(x) = 2x + 2$

36. $f(x) = \frac{1}{2}x - 2$

A.

B.

C.

GRAPHING FUNCTIONS Graph the function.

37. $g(x) = 2x - 3$

38. $h(x) = 5x - 6$

39. $f(x) = 4x + 1$

40. $h(x) = 9x + 2$

41. $h(x) = -x + 4$

42. $g(x) = -2x + 5$

43. $f(x) = -3x - 2$

44. $g(x) = -4x - 5$

45. $h(x) = -\frac{1}{2}x + 1$

Student Help

HOMEWORK HELP
Extra help with problem solving in Exs. 46–53 is available at www.mcdougallittell.com

FINDING SLOPE Find the slope of the graph of the linear function f.

46. $f(2) = -3, f(-2) = 5$

47. $f(0) = 4, f(4) = 0$

48. $f(-3) = -9, f(3) = 9$

49. $f(6) = -1, f(3) = 8$

FINDING DOMAIN AND RANGE Determine whether the relation is a function. If it is a function, give the domain and range.

50. $(1, 3), (2, 6), (3, 9), (4, 12)$

51. $(-4, 4), (-2, 2), (0, 0), (-2, -2)$

52. $(3, 0), (3, 1), (3, 2), (3, -1)$

53. $(-2, -2), (0, 0), (1, 1), (2, 2)$

Link to
Music

54. ZYDECO MUSIC The graph shows the number of people who attended the Southwest Louisiana Zydeco Music Festival for different years, where *t* is the number of years since 1980. Is the number of people who attended the festival a function of the year? Explain.

▶ Source: Louisiana Zydeco Music Festival.

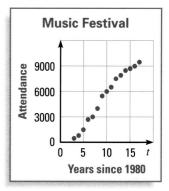

Music Festival

55. MASTERS TOURNAMENT The table shows the scores and prize money earned for the top 7 winners of the 1997 Masters Tournament at Augusta National Golf Club. Graph the relation. Is the money earned a function of the score? Explain. If it is a function, give the domain and range. ▶ Source: Golfweb

Score	270	282	283	284	285	285	286
Prize ($)	486,000	291,600	183,600	129,600	102,600	102,600	78,570

BUTTERFLIES In Exercises 56–58, use the diagram and caption about monarch butterfly migration at the right.

56. Write a linear function that models the distance traveled by a migrating monarch butterfly.

57. Use the model to estimate the distance traveled after 30 days of migration.

58. Graph your model and label the point that represents the distance traveled after 30 days.

narch butterflies migrate from the northern United ...es to Mexico. The 2000 mile trip takes about 40 days.

59. *Science Link* It takes 4.25 years for starlight to travel 25 trillion miles. Let *t* be the number of years and let $f(t)$ be trillions of miles traveled. Write a linear function $f(t)$ that expresses the distance traveled as a function of time.

Standardized Test Practice

60. MULTIPLE CHOICE Write the equation $3x + y = 5$ in function notation.

  Ⓐ $f(x) = y + 5$ Ⓑ $f(x) = -3x + 5$

  Ⓒ $f(x) = 3x - 5$ Ⓓ $f(x) = -y - 5$

61. MULTIPLE CHOICE Evaluate the function $f(x) = -x + 8$ when $x = -2$.

  Ⓕ 6   Ⓖ 10   Ⓗ 16   Ⓙ −16

SOLVING EQUATIONS Solve the equation if possible. Check your solution. *(Lesson 3.4)*

62. $4x + 8 = 24$ **63.** $3n = 5n - 12$ **64.** $9 - 5z = -8z$

65. $-5y + 6 = 4y + 3$ **66.** $3b + 8 = 9b - 7$ **67.** $-7q - 13 = 4 - 7q$

FINDING SLOPE Find the slope of the line that passes through the points. *(Lesson 4.5)*

68. $(0, 3)$ and $(2, 1)$ **69.** $(2, -3)$ and $(-2, 1)$ **70.** $(-1, -3)$ and $(-3, 3)$

71. $(2, 4)$ and $(4, -4)$ **72.** $(0, 6)$ and $(8, 0)$ **73.** $(4, 1)$ and $(6, 1)$

74. $(0, -6)$ and $(8, 0)$ **75.** $(2, 2)$ and $(-3, 5)$ **76.** $(0, 0)$ and $(4, 5)$

Maintaining Skills

MODELING FRACTIONS Write the fraction that represents the shaded portion of the figure. *(Skills Review p. 768)*

77.    **78.** 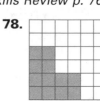   **79.**

Quiz 3

Rewrite the equation in slope-intercept form. Identify the slope and the y-intercept. *(Lesson 4.7)*

1. $y - 4 = 3x$ **2.** $x = -y + 2$ **3.** $2x + y = 6$

4. $5x + 8y = 32$ **5.** $4x - 3y = 24$ **6.** $-27 + 9y + 18 = 0$

Graph the equation. *(Lesson 4.7)*

7. $2x + 4y =$ **8.** $-6x - 3y = 21$ **9.** $-5x + y = 0$

Determine whether the two lines are parallel. *(Lesson 4.7)*

10. line a: $y = -7x + 3$ **11.** line a: $4x - 8y + 6 = 0$
      line b: $y - 7x = 10$ line b: $-12x + 6y = 2$

Evaluate the function when $x = 3$, $x = 0$, and $x = -4$. *(Lesson 4.8)*

12. $h(x) = -8x$ **13.** $g(x) = 5x - 9$ **14.** $f(x) = -4x + 3$

15. $g(x) = -3x - 12$ **16.** $h(x) = 1.4x$ **17.** $f(x) = \frac{1}{4}x$

Graph the function. *(Lesson 4.8)*

18. $f(x) = -5x$ **19.** $h(x) = 4x - 7$ **20.** $g(x) = -6x + 5$

VOCABULARY

- **coordinate plane,** *p. 203*
- **origin,** *p. 203*
- **x-axis,** *p. 203*
- **y-axis,** *p. 203*
- **ordered pair,** *p. 203*
- **x-coordinate,** *p. 203*
- **y-coordinate,** *p. 203*
- **quadrant,** *p. 204*

- **scatter plot,** *p. 205*
- **linear equation,** *p. 210*
- **solution of an equation,** *p. 210*
- **function form,** *p. 211*
- **graph of an equation,** *p. 211*
- **constant function,** *p. 218*
- **x-intercept,** *p. 222*
- **y-intercept,** *p. 222*

- **slope,** *p. 229*
- **direct variation,** *p. 236*
- **constant of variation,** *p. 236*
- **slope-intercept form,** *p. 243*
- **parallel lines,** *p. 245*
- **relation,** *p. 252*
- **function notation,** *p. 254*
- **linear function,** *p. 254*

4.1   THE COORDINATE PLANE

Examples on pp. 203–205

EXAMPLE

a. What are the coordinates of the point $(4, -2)$?

b. Plot the point $(4, -2)$ in the coordinate plane.

c. Name the quadrant the point $(4, -2)$ is in.

Solution

a. The point $(4, -2)$ has an x-coordinate of 4 and a y-coordinate of -2.

b. To plot the point $(4, -2)$, start at the origin. Move **4** units to the right and **2** units d....

c. $(4, -2)$ is in Quadrant IV.

In Exercises 1–4, plot the ordered pair in a coordinate plane. Then name the quadrant the point is in.

1. $(4, 6)$ **2.** $(0, -3)$ **3.** $(-3.5, 5)$ **4.** $(-2, -2)$

5. Make a scatter plot of the data in the table.

Time t (hours)	1	1.5	3	4.5
Distance d (miles)	20	24	32.5	41

4.2   GRAPHING LINEAR EQUATIONS

Examples on pp. 210–212

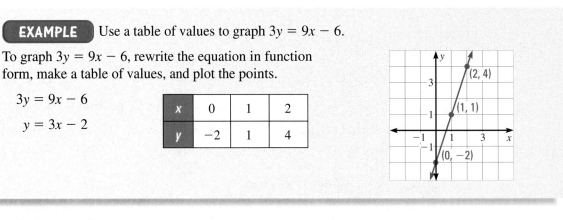

EXAMPLE   Use a table of values to graph $3y = 9x - 6$.

To graph $3y = 9x - 6$, rewrite the equation in function form, make a table of values, and plot the points.

$3y = 9x - 6$

$y = 3x - 2$

x	0	1	2
y	−2	1	4

Graph the equation.

6. $y = 2x + 2$ **7.** $y = 7 - x$ **8.** $y = -4(x + 1)$ **9.** $x - 10 = 2y$

4.3   GRAPHING HORIZONTAL AND VERTICAL LINES

Examples on pp. 216–218

EXAMPLE   Graph the equation $y = -3$.

The y-value is always -3, regardless of the value of x. Here are three solutions of the equation: $(-2, -3)$, $(0, -3)$, and $(2, -3)$. So, the graph of $y = -3$ is a horizontal line 3 units *below* the x-axis.

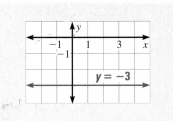

Graph the equation.

10. $y = 5$ **11.** $x = -6$ **12.** $y = 1\frac{1}{2}$ **13.** $x = 0$

4.4   GRAPHING LINES USING INTERCEPTS

Examples on pp. 222–224

EXAMPLE   Graph the equation $y + 2x = 10$.

To graph $y + 2x = 10$, first find the intercepts.

$y + 2x = 10$ $y + 2x = 10$

$0 + 2x = 10$ $y + 2(0) = 10$

$x = 5$ $y = 10$

The x-intercept is $(5, 0)$.
The y-intercept is $(0, 10)$.

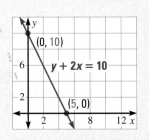

Graph the equation. Label the intercepts.

14. $-x + 4y = 8$ **15.** $3x + 5y = 15$ **16.** $4x - 5y = -20$ **17.** $2x + 3y = 10$

4.5   THE SLOPE OF A LINE

Examples on pp. 229–232

EXAMPLE   Find the slope of the line that passes through the points $(-2, 5)$ and $(4, -7)$.

To find the slope of the line passing through the points $(-2, 5)$ and $(4, -7)$, let $(x_1, y_1) = (-2, 5)$ and $(x_2, y_2) = (4, -7)$.

$m = \dfrac{y_2 - y_1}{x_2 - x_1}$ **Write formula for slope.**

$m = \dfrac{-7 - 5}{4 - (-2)}$ **Substitute values.**

$m = \dfrac{-12}{6}$ **Simplify.**

$m = -2$ **Divide. Slope is negative.**

Find the slope of the line that passes through the points.

18. $(2, -1), (3, 4)$ **19.** $(0, 8), (-1, 8)$ **20.** $(2, 4), (5, 0)$ **21.** $(3, 4), (3, -2)$

4.6   DIRECT VARIATION

Examples on pp. 236–238

EXAMPLE   If x and y vary directly and $x = 3$ when $y = 18$, write an equation that relates x and y.

If x and y vary directly, the equation that relates x and y is of the form $y = kx$.

$y = kx$ **Write model for direct variation.**

$18 = k(3)$ **Substitute 3 for x and 18 for y.**

$6 = k$ **Divide each side by 3.**

An equation that relates x and y is $y = 6x$.

In Exercises 22–25, the variables x and y vary directly. Use the given values of the variables to write an equation that relates x and y.

22. $x = 7, y = 35$ **23.** $x = 12, y = -4$ **24.** $x = 4, y = -16$ **25.** $x = 3, y = 10.5$

26. The distance traveled by a truck at a constant speed varies directly with the length of time it travels. If the truck travels 168 miles in 4 hours, how far will it travel in 7 hours?

4.7   GRAPHING LINES USING SLOPE-INTERCEPT FORM

Examples on pp. 243–245

> **EXAMPLE**   Graph the equation $4x + y = 0$.
>
> **1** **Write** the equation in slope-intercept form: $y = -4x$.
>
> **2** **Find** the slope and the y-intercept: $m = -4$, $b = 0$.
>
> **3** **Plot** the point $(0, 0)$. Draw a slope triangle to locate a second point on the line. Draw a line through the two points.

Rewrite the equation in slope-intercept form.

27. $2x + y = 6$ **28.** $y - 4x = -1$ **29.** $2x - 3y = 12$ **30.** $5y - 2x = -10$

Graph the equation.

31. $y = -x - 2$ **32.** $y - 5x = 0$ **33.** $x - 4y = 12$ **34.** $-x + 6y = -24$

4.8   FUNCTIONS AND RELATIONS

Examples on pp. 252–254

> **EXAMPLE**   Evaluate the function $f(x) = -\dfrac{1}{5}x + 1$ when $x = 5$.
>
> $f(x) = -\dfrac{1}{5}x + 1$ Write original function.
>
> $f(5) = -\dfrac{1}{5}(5) + 1$ Substitute 5 for x.
>
> $f(5) = 0$ Simpl

Evaluate the function for the given value of x. Then graph the function.

35. $f(x) = x - 7$ when $x = -2$ **36.** $f(x) = -x + 4$ when $x = 4$

37. $f(x) = 2x - 5$ when $x = 8$ **38.** $f(x) = \dfrac{1}{4}x + 3$ when $x = -24$

In Exercises 39–42, determine whether the relation is a function. If it is a function, give the domain and range.

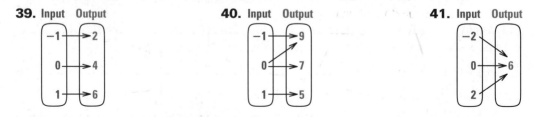

39. Input   Output

40. Input   Output

41. Input   Output

42. $(-2, -3)$, $(-1, -2)$, $(0, -1)$, $(1, 0)$, $(2, 1)$, $(3, 2)$, $(4, 3)$

Plot and label the points in a coordinate plane.

1. $A(2, 6)$, $B(-4, -1)$, $C(-1, 4)$, $D(3, -5)$ **2.** $A(-5, 1)$, $B(0, 3)$, $C(-1, -5)$, $D(4, 6)$

3. $A(7, 3)$, $B(-2, -2)$ $C(0, 4)$, $D(6, -2)$ **4.** $A(0, -1)$, $B(0, 3)$, $C(7, -2)$, $D(2,4)$

Without plotting the point, name the quadrant the point is in.

5. $(5, -2)$ **6.** $(-1, 4)$ **7.** $(-3, -4)$ **8.** $(6, 0)$

Use a table of values to graph the equation.

9. $y = -x + 3$ **10.** $y = 4$ **11.** $y = -(5 - x)$ **12.** $x = 6$

Graph the equation. Tell which method you used.

13. $y = 3x$ **14.** $y = 2x - 3$ **15.** $2x + y - 11 = 0$ **16.** $y - 4x = 1$

Find the slope of the line that passes through the points.

17. $(0, 1)$, $(-2, -6)$ **18.** $(-4, -1)$, $(5, -7)$ **19.** $(-3, 5)$, $(2, -2)$ **20.** $(-3, 1)$, $(2, 1)$

The variables *x* and *y* vary directly. Use the given values of the variables to write an equation that relates *x* and *y*.

21. $x = -2$, $y = -2$ **22.** $x = 2$, $y = 28$ **23.** $x = -3$, $y = 15$ **24.** $x = 13$, $y = 39$

Rewrite the equation in slope-intercept form.

25. $-7x - y = -49$ **26.** $18 - y - 4x = 0$ **27.** $\frac{2}{3}x + y - 9 = 0$ **28.** $x - 2y = 10$

Determine whether the graphs of the two equations are parallel lines. Explain your answer.

29. $y = 4x + 3$ and $y = -4x - 5$ **30.** $10y + 20 = 6x$ and $5y = 3x + 35$

In Exercises 31–33, evaluate the function when *x* = 3, *x* = 0, and *x* = −4.

31. $f(x) = 6x$ **32.** $g(x) = 3x + 8$ **33.** $f(x) = -(x - 2)$

34. SHOE SIZES The table below shows how foot length relates to women's shoe sizes. Is shoe size a function of foot length? Why or why not? If it is a function, give the domain and range.

Foot length x (in inches)	$9\frac{1}{4}$	$9\frac{1}{2}$	$9\frac{5}{8}$	$9\frac{3}{4}$	$9\frac{15}{16}$	$10\frac{1}{4}$	$10\frac{1}{2}$
Shoe size y	$6\frac{1}{2}$	7	7	8	8	$9\frac{1}{2}$	$9\frac{1}{2}$

Chapter Standardized Test

 Test Tip Read all of the answer choices before deciding which is the correct one.

1. What is the equation of the line shown?

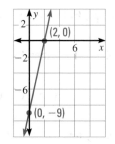

- **(A)** $9x - 2y = -18$
- **(B)** $-9x - 2y = 18$
- **(C)** $9x + 2y = 18$
- **(D)** $-9x + 2y = -18$

2. What is the y-intercept of the line
$$-4x - \frac{1}{2}y = 10?$$

- **(A)** -20
- **(B)** -4
- **(C)** 20
- **(D)** 5

3. Write the equation $3x - 4y = 20$ in slope-intercept form.

- **(A)** $y = \frac{3}{4}x + 5$
- **(B)** $y = -\frac{3}{4}x + 5$
- **(C)** $y = \frac{3}{4}x - 5$
- **(D)** $y = -\frac{3}{4}x - 5$

4. Find the slope of the line passing through the points $(1, 2)$ and $(2, 1)$.

- **(A)** 1
- **(B)** -2
- **(C)** 2
- **(D)** -1

5. What is the slope of the line shown?

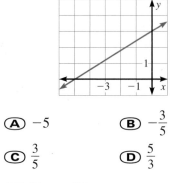

- **(A)** -5
- **(B)** $-\frac{3}{5}$
- **(C)** $\frac{3}{5}$
- **(D)** $\frac{5}{3}$
- **(E)** None of these

6. What is the slope of the graph of the equation $5x - y = -2$?

- **(A)** -5
- **(B)** 5
- **(C)** 1
- **(D)** -2

7. Which point does *not* lie on the graph of $x = -12$?

- **(A)** $(-12, 0)$
- **(B)** $(-12, -12)$
- **(C)** $(-12, 1)$
- **(D)** $(-1, -12)$

8. What is the x-intercept of $-13x - y = -65$?

- **(A)** 5
- **(B)** -5
- **(C)** 65
- **(D)** -65

9. Which point is in Quadrant III?

- **(A)** $(2, -3)$
- **(B)** $(-4, -5)$
- **(C)** $(-6, 4)$
- **(D)** $(3, 2)$

EXAMPLE 1 Dividing Fractions

Find the quotient of $\frac{7}{8} \div \frac{21}{16}$.

Solution

$\frac{7}{8} \div \frac{21}{16} = \frac{7}{8} \cdot \frac{16}{21}$ Multiply by the reciprocal of the second fraction.

$= \frac{112}{168}$ Multiply the numerators and the denominators.

$= \frac{2 \cdot 2 \cdot 2 \cdot 2 \cdot 7}{2 \cdot 2 \cdot 2 \cdot 3 \cdot 7}$ Factor numerator and denominator.

$= \frac{2}{3}$ Simplify fraction to lowest terms.

Try These

Find each quotient. Write each answer in lowest terms.

1. $\frac{1}{4} \div \frac{1}{2}$ **2.** $\frac{1}{15} \div \frac{2}{5}$ **3.** $\frac{1}{12} \div \frac{3}{4}$ **4.** $\frac{5}{12} \div \frac{15}{16}$

5. $\frac{3}{10} \div \frac{6}{25}$ **6.** $\frac{4}{9} \div \frac{8}{27}$ **7.** $\frac{3}{10} \div 3$ **8.** $\frac{16}{21} \div 4$

EXAMPLE 2 Order of Operations

Evaluate the expression $36 \div (8 - 5)^2 - (-3)(2)$.

Solution

$36 \div (8 - 5)^2 - (-3)(2)$

$= 36 \div (3)^2 - (-3)(2)$ Do operations within parentheses first.

$= 36 \div 9 - (-3)(2)$ Evaluate power.

$= 4 - (-6)$ Do multiplication and division.

$= 10$ Add.

Try These

Evaluate the expression.

9. $4 - 8 \div 2$ **10.** $2^2 \cdot 3 - 3$

11. $2(3 - 4) - (-3)^2$ **12.** $2^2 + 4[16 \div (3 - 5)]$

13. $3 - 2[8 - (3 - 2)]$ **14.** $6 + \frac{16 - 4}{2^2 + 2} - 2$

CHAPTER 5

Writing Linear Equations

▶ How can you figure out how old an object is?

APPLICATION: Archaeology

Archaeologists study how people lived in past times by studying the objects those people left behind. They often use a method called radiocarbon dating to estimate the age of certain objects.

Think & Discuss

In Exercises 1 and 2, use the graph below.

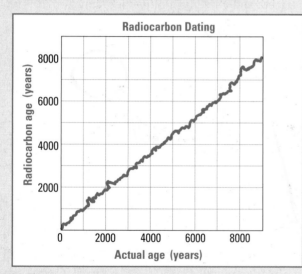

Radiocarbon Dating

1. What is the radiocarbon age of an object whose actual age is about 1000 years?

2. What is the actual age of an object whose radiocarbon age is about 5000 years?

Learn More About It

You will learn more about radiocarbon dating in Exercises 33 and 34 on p. 303.

APPLICATION LINK More about archaeology is available at www.mcdougallittell.com

What's the chapter about?

- Writing linear equations in **slope-intercept form**, **point-slope form**, and **standard form**
- Using a **linear model** to solve problems
- Writing an equation of a line **perpendicular** to another line

KEY WORDS

- **point-slope form,** *p. 278*
- **standard form,** *p. 291*
- **linear model,** *p. 298*
- **rate of change,** *p. 298*
- **perpendicular,** *p. 306*

Chapter Readiness Quiz

Take this quick quiz. If you are unsure of an answer, look back at the reference pages for help.

VOCABULARY CHECK *(refer to p. 222)*

1. What are the *x*-intercept and *y*-intercept of the line shown in the graph?

(A) *x*-intercept: -6
  y-intercept: -2

(B) *x*-intercept: 2
  y-intercept: 6

(C) *x*-intercept: -2
  y-intercept: -6

(D) *x*-intercept: 6
  y-intercept: 2

$6x + 2y = -12$

SKILL CHECK *(refer to pp. 155–157, 201)*

2. Solve the equation $4(x + 8) = 20x$.

(A) $x = -2$ (B) $x = \dfrac{1}{2}$ (C) $x = 2$ (D) $x = 3$

3. What are the coordinates of point *R*?

(A) $(-3, -1)$ (B) $(-4, -1)$

(C) $(-4, 1)$ (D) $(-1, -4)$

Create a Practice Test

Exchange practice tests with a classmate. After taking the tests, correct and discuss the answers.

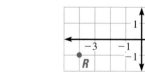

Practice Test for Chapter 5

1. Write in slope-intercept form the equation of the line whose *y*-intercept is -3 and whose slope is 9.

2. Write in slope-intercept form the equation of the line shown.

5.1 Slope-Intercept Form

Goal

Use slope-intercept form to write an equation of a line.

Key Words

- slope
- *y*-intercept
- slope-intercept form

How have Olympic hurdling times decreased?

A graph can describe a trend, such as the decrease in Olympic men's winning hurdling times. In Exercise 40 you will write the equation of the line that models this trend.

You can write an equation of a line if you know the slope and the *y*-intercept.

SLOPE-INTERCEPT FORM

The slope-intercept form of the equation of a line with slope *m* and *y*-intercept *b* is

$$y = mx + b$$

EXAMPLE 1 Equation of a Line

Write the equation of the line whose slope is **3** and whose *y*-intercept is **−4**.

Solution

❶ **Write** the slope-intercept form. $y = mx + b$

❷ **Substitute** slope 3 for *m* and −4 for *b*. $y = 3x + (-4)$

❸ **Simplify** the equation. $y = 3x - 4$

ANSWER ▶ The equation of the line is $y = 3x - 4$.

Checkpoint ✓ *Equation of a Line*

Write the equation of the line described below.

1. The slope is −2 and the *y*-intercept is 7.

2. The slope is $\frac{2}{5}$ and the *y*-intercept is −6.

EQUATIONS FROM GRAPHS When a graph clearly indicates the y-intercept and another point on the line, you can use the graph to write an equation of the line.

EXAMPLE **2** **Use a Graph to Write an Equation**

Write the equation of the line shown in the graph using slope-intercept form.

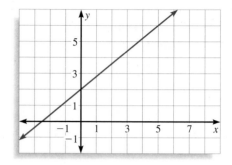

Student Help

▶**STUDY TIP**
Recall that the y-intercept is the y-coordinate of the point where the line crosses the y-axis.

Solution

❶ **Write** the slope-intercept form $y = mx + b$.

❷ **Find** the slope m of the line. Use any two points on the graph. Let $(0, 2)$ be (x_1, y_1) and let $(5, 6)$ be (x_2, y_2).

$$m = \frac{\text{rise}}{\text{run}} = \frac{y_2 - y_1}{x_2 - x_1}$$

$$= \frac{6 - 2}{5 - 0}$$

$$= \frac{4}{5}$$

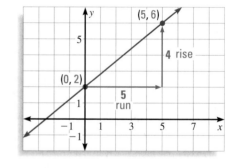

❸ **Use** the graph to find the y-intercept b. The graph of the line crosses the y-axis at $(0, 2)$. The y-intercept is 2.

❹ **Substitute** slope $\frac{4}{5}$ for m and 2 for b in the equation $y = mx + b$.

$$y = \frac{4}{5}x + 2$$

ANSWER ▶ The equation of the line is $y = \frac{4}{5}x + 2$.

Checkpoint ✓ **Use a Graph to Write an Equation**

Write the equation of the line in slope-intercept form.

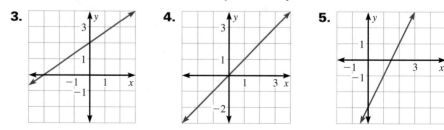

3. **4.** **5.**

Link to
Science

SPACE SHUTTLE LANDING The space shuttle lands as a glider with no power. The shuttle begins its approach at an altitude of 12,000 feet.

More about space shuttles is available at www.mcdougallittell.com

---

Student Help

▶ **STUDY TIP**
Notice that the scales on the axes are different. In this case you cannot calculate slope by counting squares. Instead you must use the formula.

| EXAMPLE | 3 | Model Negative Slope |

SPACE SHUTTLE LANDING
The graph at the right models the negative slope of the space shuttle as it descends from 12,000 to 2000 feet. Write the equation of the line in slope-intercept form.

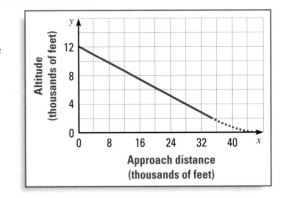

Solution

❶ **Write** the slope-intercept form $y = mx + b$.

❷ **Find** the slope m of the line. Use any two points on the graph.

Let $(0, 12)$ be (x_1, y_1) and let $(28, 4)$ be (x_2, y_2).

$$m = \frac{y_2 - y_1}{x_2 - x_1}$$

$$= \frac{4 - 12}{28 - 0}$$

$$= \frac{-8}{28}$$

$$= -\frac{2}{7}$$

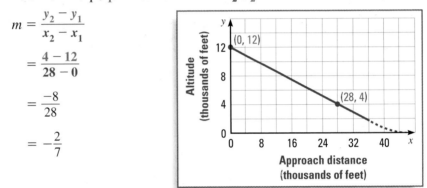

❸ **Use** the graph to find the y-intercept b. The graph of the line crosses the y-axis at $(0, 12)$. The y-intercept is 12.

❹ **Substitute** slope $-\frac{2}{7}$ for m and 12 for b in the equation $y = mx + b$.

$$y = -\frac{2}{7}x + 12$$

ANSWER ▶ The equation of the line is $y = -\frac{2}{7}x + 12$.

Checkpoint ✓ **Model Negative Slope**

Write the equation of the line in slope-intercept form.

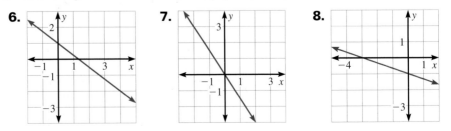

Guided Practice

Vocabulary Check

1. What is the name used to describe an equation in the form $y = mx + b$?

2. Identify the slope of the line that has the equation $y = -4x + 15$.

3. Name the y-intercept of the line that has the equation $y = 10x - 3$.

Skill Check

Determine whether the equation is in slope-intercept form.

4. $y = -8x - 11$ **5.** $y - 4 = 5(x + 3)$ **6.** $x + 23y = -15$

Write in slope-intercept form the equation of the line described below.

7. Slope $= 1$, y-intercept $= 0$ **8.** Slope $= -7$, y-intercept $= -2$

9. Slope $= -1$, y-intercept $= 3$ **10.** Slope $= 0$, y-intercept $= 4$

11. Slope $= 5$, y-intercept $= 5$ **12.** Slope $= 14$, y-intercept $= -6$

Practice and Applications

WRITING EQUATIONS Write in slope-intercept form the equation of the line described below.

13. $m = 3, b = 2$ **14.** $m = 1, b = -1$ **15.** $m = 0, b = 6$

16. $m = 10, b = 0$ **17.** $m = \dfrac{2}{5}, b = 7$ **18.** $m = -4, b = -\dfrac{3}{7}$

19. $m = -1, b = -\dfrac{2}{5}$ **20.** $m = 0, b = 0$ **21.** $m = -\dfrac{1}{5}, b = \dfrac{2}{3}$

SLOPE AND INTERCEPT Identify the slope and y-intercept of the line.

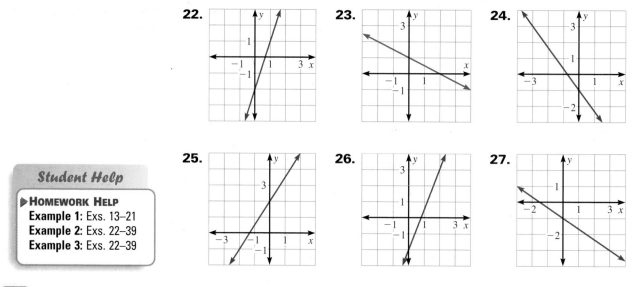

22.   **23.**   **24.**

25.   **26.**   **27.**

Student Help

▶ **HOMEWORK HELP**
Example 1: Exs. 13–21
Example 2: Exs. 22–39
Example 3: Exs. 22–39

Student Help

► **HOMEWORK HELP**

Extra help with problem solving in Exs. 28–33 is available at www.mcdougallittell.com

GRAPHICAL REASONING Write in slope-intercept form the equation of the line shown in the graph.

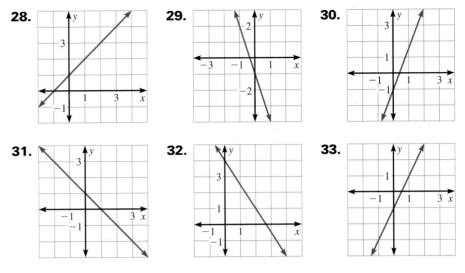

28.

29.

30.

31.

32.

33.

MATCHING Give the letter of the equation that matches the graph.

A. $y = x + 2$ **B.** $y = -x + 2$ **C.** $y = x - 2$

D. $y = x + 1$ **E.** $y = 1$ **F.** $y = x$

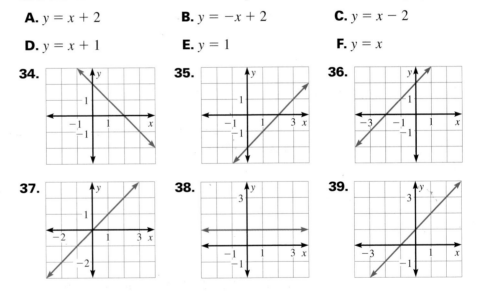

34.

35.

36.

37.

38.

39.

HURDLING The graph approximates winning times in the Olympic men's 110 meter hurdles. The *y*-intercept is 13.64 seconds.

DATA UPDATE of Olympic men's 110 meter hurdling times at www.mcdougallittell.com

Student Help

► **STUDY TIP**
When calculating the slope in Exercise 40, notice that the scale on the *y*-axis represents 0.2 seconds and the scale on the *x*-axis represents 4 years.

40. Write the equation of the line shown in the graph.

41. Use the equation from Exercise 40 to estimate the winning time in 1984.

42. Use the graph to predict the winning time in 2004.

43. How realistic do you think your prediction is? Explain.

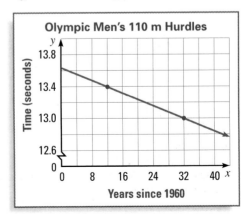

Olympic Men's 110 m Hurdles

Time (seconds)

Years since 1960

Geometry Link The graph at the right shows three parallel lines.

44. Write the equation of each line in slope-intercept form.

45. Compare the equations. What do you notice?

46. Write the equation for a line with y-intercept −1 that is parallel to the three lines shown.

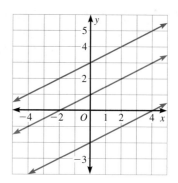

Puzzler The graph shows a regulation-sized baseball diamond. The units are in feet.

47. Write the equation of each solid line in slope-intercept form.

48. Compare the equations. What do you notice?

49. Write the equation for the dashed line.

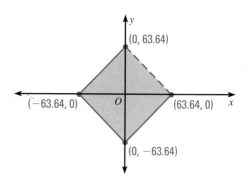

Link to
Science

OLD FAITHFUL geyser in Yellowstone National Park has erupted every day at intervals of less than two hours for over 100 years.

More about Old Faithful is available at www.mcdougallittell.com

CHALLENGE In Exercises 50 and 51, use the following information.
You walk home from school at a rate of 4 miles per hour. The graph shows your distance from home. Notice the units on the axes.

50. Write the equation of the line.

51. Use your equation to find how far from home you are after $\frac{3}{8}$ hour.

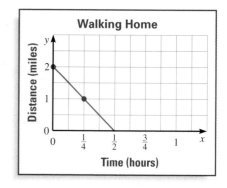

Science Link In Exercises 52 and 53, use the following information.
The time y until the next eruption of Old Faithful depends on the length x of each eruption. The y-intercept is 32.

52. Write the equation of the line shown in the graph.

53. The eruption that just ended had length 5 minutes. Estimate the time until the next eruption.

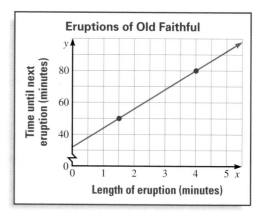

The United States Bureau of the Census predicts that the population of Florida will be about 17.4 million in 2010 and then will increase by about 0.22 million per year until 2025.

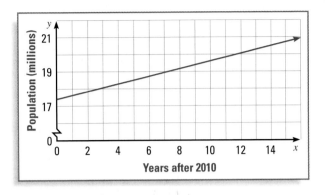

54. MULTIPLE CHOICE Choose the equation that predicts the population y of Florida (in millions) in terms of x, the number of years after 2010.

   (A) $y = 17.4x + 0.22$ **(B)** $y = -0.22x + 17.4$

   (C) $y = 0.22x + 17.4$ **(D)** $y = -17.4x + 0.22$

55. MULTIPLE CHOICE According to the prediction, about how many millions of people will live in Florida in 2011?

   (F) 17.18   **(G)** 17.5   **(H)** 17.62   **(J)** 19.91

Mixed Review

EVALUATING EXPRESSIONS Evaluate the expression when $x = -3$ and $y = 6$. *(Lesson 2.8)*

56. $\dfrac{3x}{x + y}$ **57.** $\dfrac{x}{x + 2}$ **58.** $x \cdot y$

59. $\dfrac{2x}{y}$ **60.** $x^2 y$ **61.** $\dfrac{-8x}{-4y}$

FINDING SOLUTIONS Find three solutions of the equation. *(Lesson 4.2)*

62. $y = 6x + 3$ **63.** $y = -x - 4$ **64.** $y = \dfrac{1}{2}x$

65. $y = -5x + 7$ **66.** $x + y = 1$ **67.** $x + 3y = 9$

GRAPHING LINEAR EQUATIONS Find the slope and the y-intercept of the graph of the equation. Then graph the equation. *(Lesson 4.7)*

68. $y + 2x = 2$ **69.** $3x - y = -5$ **70.** $9x + 3y = 15$

71. $4x + 2y = 6$ **72.** $4y + 12x = 16$ **73.** $25x - 5y = 30$

Maintaining Skills

PERCENTS AND FRACTIONS Write the percent as a fraction or as a mixed number in lowest terms. *(Skills Review p. 768)*

74. 50%   **75.** 75%   **76.** 1%   **77.** 62%   **78.** 100%

79. 0.5%   **80.** 5%   **81.** 128%   **82.** 501%   **83.** 6%

DEVELOPING CONCEPTS
5.2 Point-Slope Form

**For use with
Lesson 5.2**

GOAL

Develop the point-slope form of the equation of a line.

MATERIALS

• pencil
• ruler
• graph paper

Question How can you write an equation of a line given the slope and a point on the line?

Given a point on a line and the slope of the line, you have enough information to write the equation of the line. The steps below show how to find the equation of the line that passes through the point (2, 1) with slope $\frac{1}{3}$.

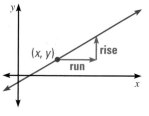

Explore

① On a coordinate grid, draw the line that passes through the point (2, 1) with slope $\frac{1}{3}$. Use a slope triangle and label the second point you find.

② Draw the slope triangle that shows the rise and run of the line through (2, 1) and (x, y).

③ Explain why the rise is given by $y - 1$. Explain why the run is given by $x - 2$.

④ Use these values of rise and run to express the slope of the line.

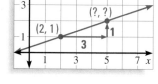

$$\frac{1}{3} = \frac{y - 1}{x - 2}$$

⑤ Clear the denominator on the right-hand side of the equation by multiplying both sides by $(x - 2)$. Then $y - 1 = \frac{1}{3}(x - 2)$ is the *point-slope form* of the equation of the line passing through (2, 1) with slope $\frac{1}{3}$.

Think About It

Follow Steps 1–5 above for the line described below.

1. Passes through (2, 3) with slope $-\frac{5}{2}$.

2. Passes through (−4, −2) with slope $\frac{4}{3}$.

GENERAL FORMULA The following steps lead you to a general formula for writing the equation of a line given a point on the line and the slope of the line. The formula is called the *point-slope form* of the equation of a line. We use (x_1, y_1) as the given point and m as the given slope.

Explore

① Sketch the line passing through (x_1, y_1) and (x, y), where (x, y) represents any other point on the line.

② Draw the slope triangle that shows the rise and run of the line through (x_1, y_1) and (x, y).

③ Explain why the rise is given by $y - y_1$. Explain why the run is given by $x - x_1$

④ Use the values of rise and run to express the slope of the line.

$$m = \frac{y - y_1}{x - x_1}$$

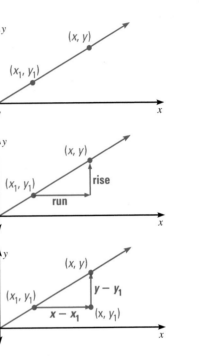

⑤ Clear the denominator on the right-hand side of the equation by multiplying each side of the equation by $(x - x_1)$. You get $y - y_1 = m(x - x_1)$, the general formula for the *point-slope form* of the equation of a line.

Think About It

Use the general formula from Step 5 above to write the equation in point-slope form of the line that passes through the given point and has the given slope.

1.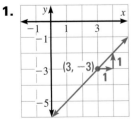

2.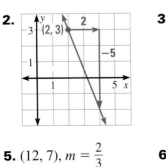

3.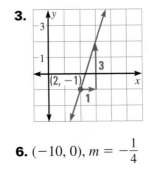

4. $(3, 2)$, $m = 5$

5. $(12, 7)$, $m = \dfrac{2}{3}$

6. $(-10, 0)$, $m = -\dfrac{1}{4}$

5.2 Point-Slope Form

Goal

Use point-slope form to write the equation of a line.

Key Words

• slope
• point-slope form

How much pressure is on a diver?

As you saw in Developing Concepts 5.2, page 276, you can write an equation of a line given the slope and a point on the line. In Exercise 44 you will write an equation that models the pressure on a diver.

POINT-SLOPE FORM

The **point-slope form** of the equation of the line through (x_1, y_1) with slope m is $y - y_1 = m(x - x_1)$.

EXAMPLE 1 Point-Slope Form from a Graph

Write the equation of the line in the graph in point-slope form.

Solution

Use the given point $(1, 2)$. From the graph, find $m = \dfrac{2}{3}$.

$$y - y_1 = m(x - x_1) \qquad \text{Write point-slope form.}$$

$$y - 2 = \frac{2}{3}(x - 1) \qquad \text{Substitute } \frac{2}{3} \text{ for } m, 1 \text{ for } x_1, \text{ and } 2 \text{ for } y_1.$$

ANSWER ▶ The equation $y - 2 = \dfrac{2}{3}(x - 1)$ is written in point-slope form.

Student Help

▶ **STUDY TIP**
Remember that you can calculate slope as $m = \dfrac{\text{rise}}{\text{run}}$.

Checkpoint ✓ *Point-Slope Form from a Graph*

Write the equation of the line in point-slope form.

1.   **2.**

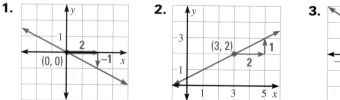

3.

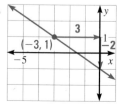

EXAMPLE ② **Write an Equation in Point-Slope Form**

Write in point-slope form the equation of the line that passes through the point $(1, -5)$ with slope 3.

❶ **Write** the point-slope form. $\qquad\qquad$ $y - y_1 = m(x - x_1)$

❷ **Substitute** 1 for x_1, -5 for y_1, and 3 for m. $\quad$ $y - (-5) = 3(x - 1)$

❸ **Simplify** the equation. $\qquad\qquad\qquad$ $y + 5 = 3(x - 1)$

ANSWER ▶ The equation in point-slope form of the line is $y + 5 = 3(x - 1)$.

Checkpoint ✓ **Write an Equation in Point-Slope Form**

4. Write in point-slope form the equation of the line that passes through the point $(2, 2)$ with slope $\frac{1}{2}$.

EXAMPLE ③ **Use Point-Slope Form**

Write in slope-intercept form the equation of the line that passes through the point $(-3, 7)$ with slope -2.

Solution

❶ **Write** the point-slope form. $\qquad\qquad$ $y - y_1 = m(x - x_1)$

❷ **Substitute** -2 for m, -3 for x_1, and 7 for y_1. $\quad$ $y - 7 = -2[x - (-3)]$

❸ **Simplify** the equation. $\qquad\qquad\qquad$ $y - 7 = -2(x + 3)$

❹ **Distribute** the -2. $\qquad\qquad\qquad$ $y - 7 = -2x - 6$

❺ **Add** 7 to each side. $\qquad\qquad\qquad\qquad$ $y = -2x + 1$

ANSWER ▶ The equation of the line in slope-intercept form is $y = -2x + 1$.

CHECK ✓ In general, you can use a graph to check whether your answer is reasonable.

In the graph at the right, notice that the line $y = -2x + 1$ has a slope of -2 and passes through the point $(-3, 7)$.

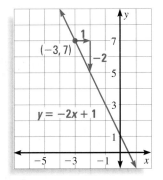

Checkpoint ✓ **Use Point-Slope Form**

5. Write in slope-intercept form the equation of the line that passes through the point $(2, 4)$ with slope 3. Check your answer by graphing.

EXAMPLE ④ Write an Equation of a Parallel Line

Write in slope-intercept form the equation of the line that is parallel to the line $y = 2x - 3$ and passes through the point $(3, -1)$.

Solution

The slope of the original line is $m = 2$. So, the slope of the parallel line is also $m = 2$. The line passes through the point $(x_1, y_1) = (3, -1)$.

$y - y_1 = m(x - x_1)$	Write point-slope form.
$y - (-1) = 2(x - 3)$	Substitute 2 for m, 3 for x_1, and −1 for y_1.
$y + 1 = 2(x - 3)$	Simplify.
$y + 1 = 2x - 6$	Use distributive property.
$y = 2x - 7$	Subtract 1 from each side.

ANSWER ▶ The equation of the line is $y = 2x - 7$.

CHECK ✓ You can check your answer graphically.

The line $y = 2x - 7$ is parallel to the line $y = 2x - 3$ and passes through the point $(3, -1)$.

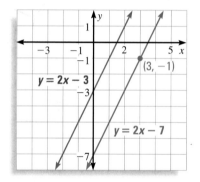

Checkpoint ✓ **Write an Equation of a Parallel Line**

6. Write in slope-intercept form the equation of the line that is parallel to the line $y = -2x + 1$ and passes through the point $(3, -2)$. Check your answer graphically.

CHOOSING A FORM Now you know two ways to write linear equations – in slope-intercept form or in point-slope form. Depending on the information you are given, sometimes it is easier to write a linear equation in one form rather than the other. The following summarizes when to use each form.

SUMMARY

Writing Equations of Lines

1. *Use slope-intercept form*
    $y = mx + b$
    if you are given the slope m and the y-intercept b.

2. *Use point-slope form*
    $y - y_1 = m(x - x_1)$
    if you are given the slope m and a point (x_1, y_1).

Exercises

Guided Practice

Vocabulary Check   **1.** Write the point-slope form of an equation of a line.

Skill Check   **Write in point-slope form the equation of the line that passes through the given point and has the given slope.**

2. $(2, -1)$, $m = 3$ **3.** $(3, 4)$, $m = 4$ **4.** $(-5, -7)$, $m = -2$

Write the equation of the line in point-slope form.

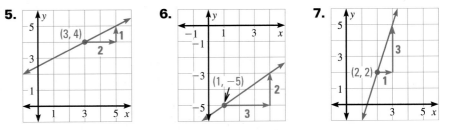

5.   **6.**   **7.**

Write in slope-intercept form the equation of the line that passes through the given point and has the given slope.

8. $(-4, 2)$, $m = 2$ **9.** $(-1, -3)$, $m = \frac{1}{2}$ **10.** $(2, -3)$, $m = 0$

Write in point-slope form the equation of the line that is parallel to the given line and passes through the given point.

11. $y = x + 5$, $(-1, -1)$ **12.** $y = -3x + 1$, $(2, 4)$ **13.** $y = \frac{1}{4}x - 6$, $(3, 3)$

Practice and Applications

USING A GRAPH **Write the equation of the line in point-slope form.**

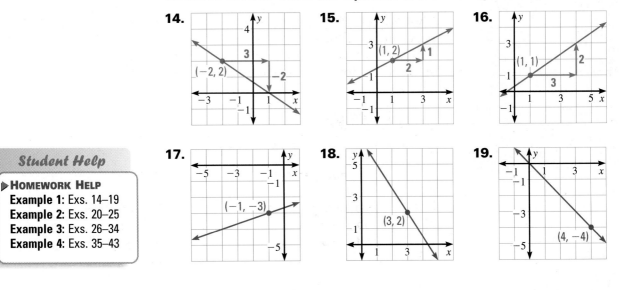

14.   **15.**   **16.**

17.   **18.**   **19.**

Student Help

▶**HOMEWORK HELP**
Example 1: Exs. 14–19
Example 2: Exs. 20–25
Example 3: Exs. 26–34
Example 4: Exs. 35–43

WRITING EQUATIONS Write in point-slope form the equation of the line that passes through the given point and has the given slope.

20. $(-1, -3), m = 4$ **21.** $(-6, 2), m = -5$ **22.** $(-10, 0), m = 2$

23. $(-8, -2), m = 2$ **24.** $(-4, 3), m = -6$ **25.** $(-3, 4), m = 6$

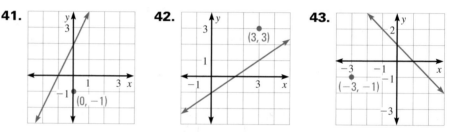

COMPARING FORMS Write in point-slope form the equation of the line. Then rewrite the equation in slope-intercept form.

26. $(12, 2), m = -7$ **27.** $(8, -1), m = 0$ **28.** $(5, -12), m = -11$

29. $(1, 4), m = 2$ **30.** $(-2, 4), m = 3$ **31.** $(-5, -5), m = -2$

32. $(6, 2), m = \frac{1}{2}$ **33.** $(-1, 1), m = -\frac{1}{3}$ **34.** $(4, -2), m = \frac{1}{4}$

Student Help

▶ **HOMEWORK HELP**

Extra help with problem solving in Exs. 26–34 is available at www.mcdougallittell.com

WRITING EQUATIONS OF PARALLEL LINES Write in slope-intercept form the equation of the line that is parallel to the given line and passes through the given point.

35. $y = 2x - 11, (3, 4)$ **36.** $y = -\frac{3}{5}x + 6, (-2, 7)$ **37.** $y = \frac{1}{3}x + 4, (-4, -4)$

38. $y = 7x - 1, (8, 0)$ **39.** $y = -9x - 3, (0, -5)$ **40.** $y = \frac{1}{2}x, (8, -10)$

EQUATIONS FROM GRAPHS Write in slope-intercept form the equation of the line that is parallel to the line in the graph and passes through the given point.

41.

42.

43.

Link to
Science

PYROTEUTHIDS are also known as fire squids because of their brilliant bioluminescent flashes. They live in ocean depths ranging from 0 to 500 meters.

Science Link As a diver descends, the pressure in the water increases by 0.455 pound per square inch (psi) for each foot of descent. At a depth of 40 feet, the pressure of the water on the diver is 32.5 pounds per square inch.

44. Using the point (40, 32.5) and the slope .455, write the equation in point-slope form that models this situation. Then rewrite the equation in slope-intercept form.

45. Use the equation you wrote in Exercise 44 to determine the pressure at a depth of 90 feet.

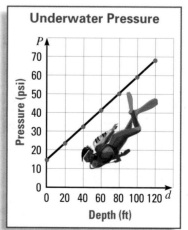

Underwater Pressure

CHALLENGE As shown in the graph below, between 1988 and 1998, the number of non-business trips taken by Americans increased by about 11 million per year. In 1993, Americans took about 413 million such trips.

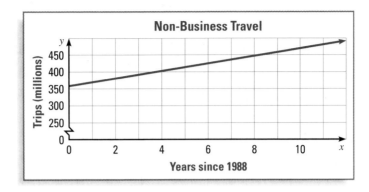

Non-Business Travel

▶ Source: Travel Industry Association of America

46. Write the equation in slope-intercept form that gives the number of non-business trips y (in millions) in terms of the year x. Let x represent the number of years after 1988.

47. According to the equation you wrote in Exercise 46, about how many non-business trips did Americans take in 1996?

48. Assuming the trend continues, estimate the number of non-business trips Americans will take in 2005.

Standardized Test Practice

49. MULTIPLE CHOICE Which equation is in point-slope form?

Ⓐ $y = 5x - 9$

Ⓑ $y + 4 = 3(-2x + 2)$

Ⓒ $x = 8(y - 1)$

Ⓓ $y + 4 = 3\left(x - \dfrac{3}{2}\right)$

50. MULTIPLE CHOICE What is the point-slope form of the equation of the line in the graph?

Ⓕ $y - 3 = 3(x - 0)$

Ⓖ $y = 3x + 3$

Ⓗ $y - (-1) = 3(x + 3)$

Ⓙ $y - 3 = 3[x - (-1)]$

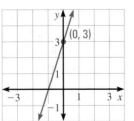

51. MULTIPLE CHOICE What is the slope-intercept form of the equation of the line parallel to the line in the graph that passes through the point $(-1, 1)$?

Ⓐ $y = 2x - 3$

Ⓑ $y - 3 = 2(x - 1)$

Ⓒ $y = -2x + 3$

Ⓓ $y = 2x + 3$

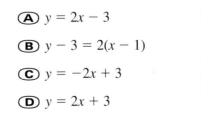
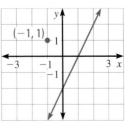

CHECKING SOLUTIONS OF INEQUALITIES Check whether the given value of the variable is a solution of the inequality. *(Lesson 1.4)*

52. $2x < 24;\ x = 8$ **53.** $7y + 6 > 10;\ y = 3$ **54.** $16p - 9 \geq 71;\ p = 5$

55. $12a \leq a - 9;\ a = -2$ **56.** $4x \leq 28;\ x = 7$ **57.** $6c - 4 > 14;\ c = 3$

GRAPHING FUNCTIONS Graph the function. *(Lesson 4.8)*

58. $g(x) = 3x + 1$ **59.** $h(x) = 4x - 4$ **60.** $f(x) = 2x + 10$

61. $f(x) = -3x + 4$ **62.** $g(x) = -x - 7$ **63.** $g(x) = \frac{6}{5}x + 5$

SUBTRACTING FRACTIONS Subtract. Write the answer as a fraction or as a mixed number in lowest terms. *(Skills Review p. 764)*

64. $\frac{5}{6} - \frac{1}{2}$ **65.** $\frac{1}{3} - \frac{1}{18}$ **66.** $\frac{7}{8} - \frac{2}{3}$ **67.** $\frac{1}{2} - \frac{1}{5}$

68. $\frac{8}{9} - \frac{1}{3}$ **69.** $\frac{5}{7} - \frac{2}{3}$ **70.** $\frac{3}{5} - \frac{1}{2}$ **71.** $\frac{3}{4} - \frac{1}{3}$

Quiz 1

Write the equation of the line in slope-intercept form. *(Lesson 5.1)*

1. Slope $= -2$, y-intercept $= 1$ **2.** Slope $= 5$, y-intercept $= 0$

Write the equation of the line in slope-intercept form. *(Lesson 5.1)*

3. **4.** **5.**

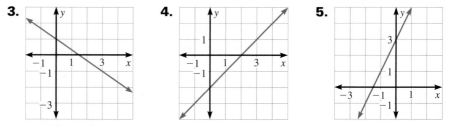

Write in point-slope form the equation of the line that passes through the given point and has the given slope. *(Lesson 5.2)*

6. $(7, 7),\ m = -2$ **7.** $(-8, -2),\ m = 3$ **8.** $(0, 0),\ m = -\frac{1}{2}$

Write in slope-intercept form the equation of the line that passes through the given point and has the given slope. *(Lesson 5.2)*

9. $(2, 3),\ m = 1$ **10.** $(-6, 4),\ m = 0$ **11.** $(1, -4),\ m = -4$

Write in slope-intercept form the equation of the line that is parallel to the given line and passes through the given point. *(Lesson 5.2)*

12. $y = 4x + 1,\ (1, 0)$ **13.** $y = -\frac{1}{3}x - 2,\ (-3, -3)$

14. $y = -2x + 3,\ (0, 5)$ **15.** $y = \frac{3}{7}x,\ (2, -1)$

5.3 Writing Linear Equations Given Two Points

Goal

Write an equation of a line given two points on the line.

Key Words

- slope
- slope-intercept form
- point-slope form

How steep is the mountain?

In this lesson you will learn to write an equation of a line given any two points on the line. In Example 1 you will write a linear equation that models a snowboarder's descent down a mountain.

EXAMPLE 1 Use a Graph

The line at the right models a snowboarder's descent down a mountain. Write the equation of the line in slope-intercept form.

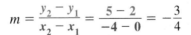

Solution

❶ **Find** the slope.

$$m = \frac{y_2 - y_1}{x_2 - x_1} = \frac{5 - 2}{-4 - 0} = -\frac{3}{4}$$

❷ **Write** the equation of the line. From the graph, you can see the y-intercept is $b = 2$. Use slope-intercept form.

$y = mx + b$	Write slope-intercept form.
$y = -\dfrac{3}{4}x + 2$	Substitute $-\dfrac{3}{4}$ for m and 2 for b.

ANSWER ▶ The equation of the line is $y = -\dfrac{3}{4}x + 2$.

Student Help

▶**STUDY TIP**
In Example 1, notice that the graph shows the y-intercept. Because you know the y-intercept, use the slope-intercept form to write the equation.

Checkpoint ✓ Use a Graph

1. The graph at the right models a car's ascent up a hill. Write the equation of the line in slope-intercept form.

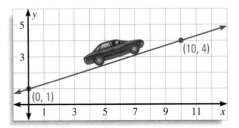

POINT-SLOPE FORM When you are given two points, but do not know the *y*-intercept, you should first use the point-slope form to write the equation of the line that passes through the points, as in Example 2.

EXAMPLE 2 **Write an Equation of a Line Given Two Points**

Write in slope-intercept form the equation of the line that passes through the points $(3, -2)$ and $(6, 0)$.

Solution

❶ Find the slope. Use $(x_1, y_1) = (3, -2)$ and $(x_2, y_2) = (6, 0)$.

$$m = \frac{y_2 - y_1}{x_2 - x_1} \qquad \text{Write formula for slope.}$$

$$= \frac{0 - (-2)}{6 - 3} \qquad \text{Substitute.}$$

$$= \frac{2}{3} \qquad \text{Simplify.}$$

❷ Write the equation of the line. Use point-slope form, because you do not know the *y*-intercept.

$$y - y_1 = m(x - x_1) \qquad \text{Write point-slope form.}$$

$$y - (-2) = \frac{2}{3}(x - 3) \qquad \text{Substitute } \tfrac{2}{3} \text{ for } m, 3 \text{ for } x_1, -2 \text{ for } y_1.$$

$$y + 2 = \frac{2}{3}x - 2 \qquad \text{Simplify and use distributive property.}$$

$$y = \frac{2}{3}x - 4 \qquad \text{Subtract 2 from each side.}$$

ANSWER ▶ The equation of the line is $y = \frac{2}{3}x - 4$.

CHECK ✓

You can check your answer by graphing.

Notice that the graph of $y = \frac{2}{3}x - 4$ passes through $(3, -2)$ and $(6, 0)$. You can also check your answer using substitution.

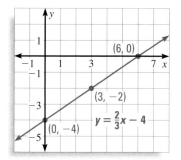

Checkpoint ✓ **Write an Equation of a Line Given Two Points**

Write in slope-intercept form the equation of the line that passes through the given points. Check your answer.

2. $(2, 3)$ and $(4, 7)$ **3.** $(-4, 5)$ and $(2, 2)$ **4.** $(1, -1)$ and $(4, -4)$

EXAMPLE 3 **Decide Which Form to Use**

Write the equation of the line in slope-intercept form.

a.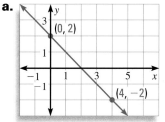

b.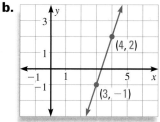

Solution

a. Find the slope.

$$m = \frac{y_2 - y_1}{x_2 - x_1} = \frac{2 - (-2)}{0 - 4} = -1$$

Since you know the y-intercept, use slope-intercept form.

The y-intercept is $b = 2$.

$$y = mx + b$$

$$y = (-1)x + 2$$

$$y = -x + 2$$

b. Find the slope.

$$m = \frac{y_2 - y_1}{x_2 - x_1} = \frac{2 - (-1)}{4 - 3} = 3$$

Since you do *not* know the y-intercept, use point-slope form.

$$y - y_1 = m(x - x_1)$$

$$y - (-1) = 3(x - 3)$$

$$y + 1 = 3x - 9$$

$$y = 3x - 10$$

Checkpoint **Decide Which Form to Use**

Write the equation of the line in slope-intercept form.

5.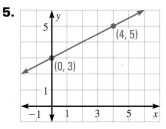

6.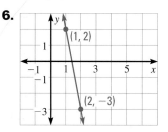

SUMMARY

Writing Linear Equations Given Two Points

❶ *Find* the slope $m = \frac{y_2 - y_1}{x_2 - x_1}$.

❷ *Write* the equation of the line.

• Use the **slope-intercept form** if you know the y-intercept.

$$y = mx + b$$

• Use the **point-slope form** if you do *not* know the y-intercept.

$$y - y_1 = m(x - x_1)$$

5.3 Exercises

Guided Practice

Vocabulary Check

1. When writing an equation of a line given two points, which form should you use if you do not know the *y*-intercept?

2. Write the slope-intercept form of an equation of a line.

Skill Check

Write the equation of the line in slope-intercept form.

3.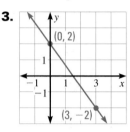

4.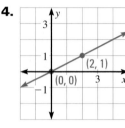

5.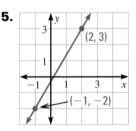

Write in slope-intercept form the equation of the line that passes through the given points.

6. $(-1, 1)$ and $(2, 5)$ **7.** $(3, -2)$ and $(-6, 4)$ **8.** $(4, 3)$ and $(1, 6)$

Practice and Applications

POINT-SLOPE FORM **Write in point-slope form the equation of the line that passes through the given points.**

9. $(2, 3)$ and $(0, 4)$ **10.** $(0, 0)$ and $(-6, -5)$ **11.** $(0, -10)$ and $(12, 4)$

12. $(0, 9)$ and $(8, 7)$ **13.** $(1, 1)$ and $(0, 2)$ **14.** $(-7, 2)$ and $(0, 1)$

15. $(-8, 6)$ and $(-13, 1)$ **16.** $(11, -2)$ and $(17, 6)$ **17.** $(-4, 5)$ and $(4, 5)$

USING A GRAPH **Write the equation of the line in slope-intercept form.**

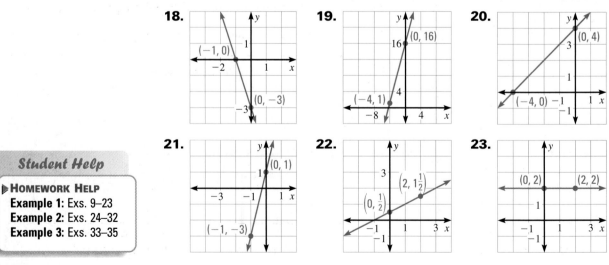

SLOPE-INTERCEPT FORM Write in slope-intercept form the equation of the line that passes through the given points.

24. $(-5, 7)$ and $(2, -7)$ **25.** $(2, 0)$ and $(-2, 6)$ **26.** $(1, -5)$ and $(3, 4)$

27. $(-1, -2)$ and $(2, 6)$ **28.** $(1, 4)$ and $(-1, -4)$ **29.** $(2, -3)$ and $(-3, 7)$

30. $(2, 2)$ and $(-7, -7)$ **31.** $(6, -4)$ and $(2, 8)$ **32.** $(1, 1)$ and $(7, 4)$

DECIDING WHICH FORM Decide which form of a linear equation to use. Then write the equation of the line in slope-intercept form.

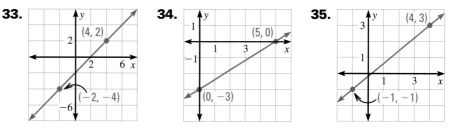

33.   **34.**   **35.**

36. AIRPLANE DESCENT The graph below models an airplane's descent from 12,500 to 2500 feet. Write in slope-intercept form the equation of the line shown.

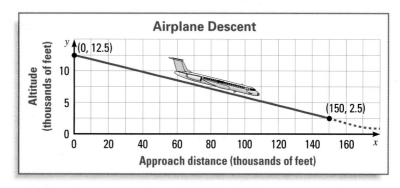

Airplane Descent

CHALLENGE In Exercises 37–39, use the diagram of the Chunnel below.

37. Write the equation of the line from point A to point B. What is the slope?

38. Write the equation of the line from point C to point D. What is the slope?

39. Is the Chunnel steeper on the English side or on the French side?

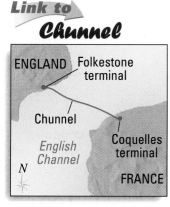
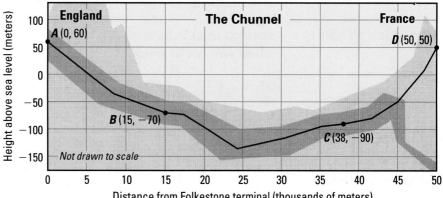

40. _Science Link_ At sea level, the speed of sound in air is linearly related to the air temperature. If the temperature is 35°C, sound will travel at a rate of 352 meters per second. If the temperature is 15°C, sound will travel at a rate of 340 meters per second. Given the points (35, 352) and (15, 340), write in slope-intercept form the equation of the line that models this relationship.

Standardized Test Practice

41. MULTIPLE CHOICE What is the equation of the line that passes through the points $(7, 4)$ and $(-5, -2)$?

(A) $y = \frac{1}{2}x - \frac{1}{2}$ (B) $y = -\frac{1}{2}x + \frac{1}{2}$

(C) $y = -\frac{1}{2}x - \frac{1}{2}$ (D) $y = \frac{1}{2}x + \frac{1}{2}$

42. MULTIPLE CHOICE What is the equation of the line shown in the graph?

(F) $y = 5x + \frac{1}{5}$

(G) $y = 5x - \frac{11}{5}$

(H) $y = \frac{11}{5}x + \frac{1}{2}$

(J) $y = \frac{1}{5}x + \frac{11}{5}$

Mixed Review

SOLVING EQUATIONS Solve the equation. _(Lesson 3.3)_

43. $4x - 11 = -31$ **44.** $5x - 7 + x = 19$ **45.** $7y = 9y - 8$

46. $20x = 3x + 17$ **47.** $3p + 10 = 5p - 7$ **48.** $12x + 10 = 2x + 5$

49. ROOF PITCH The center post of a roof is 8 feet high. The horizontal distance from the center post to the outer edge of the roof is 24 feet. Find the slope, or _pitch_, of the roof. _(Lesson 4.5)_

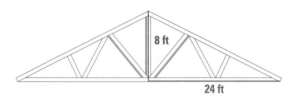

Maintaining Skills

ADDING MIXED NUMBERS Add. Write the answer as a fraction or as a mixed number in simplest form. _(Skills Review p. 765)_

50. $2\frac{5}{12} + 1\frac{1}{6}$ **51.** $5\frac{2}{3} + 2\frac{1}{8}$ **52.** $3 + \frac{2}{7}$

53. $3\frac{1}{8} + 5\frac{5}{6}$ **54.** $1\frac{1}{4} + 2\frac{5}{8}$ **55.** $17\frac{1}{3} + 9\frac{1}{2}$

56. $7\frac{3}{16} + 3\frac{19}{20}$ **57.** $1\frac{2}{9} + 5\frac{13}{18}$ **58.** $2\frac{3}{4} + 20\frac{1}{5}$

5.4 Standard Form

Goal
Write an equation of a line in standard form.

Key Words
- standard form
- slope-intercept form
- point-slope form
- integer
- coefficient

How much birdseed can you buy?

In this lesson you will learn about another form of linear equation. In Exercises 57 and 58 you will use this form to model different amounts of birdseed that you can buy.

STANDARD FORM

The **standard form** of an equation of a line is

$Ax + By = C$, where A and B are not both zero.

Student Help

▶ **VOCABULARY TIP**
Recall that a coefficient can be thought of as "the number in front of a variable." For example, $\frac{2}{5}$ is the coefficient in the variable expression $\frac{2}{5}x$.

In standard form, the variable terms are on the left side and the constant term is on the right side of the equation.

EXAMPLE 1 Convert to Standard Form

Write $y = \frac{2}{5}x - 3$ in standard form with integer coefficients.

Solution

❶ **Write** the original equation. $y = \frac{2}{5}x - 3$

❷ **Multiply** each side by 5 to clear the equation of fractions. $5y = 5\left(\frac{2}{5}x - 3\right)$

❸ **Use** the distributive property. $5y = 2x - 15$

❹ **Subtract** $2x$ from each side. $-2x + 5y = -15$

ANSWER ▶ In standard form, an equation is $-2x + 5y = -15$.

Checkpoint ✓ **Convert to Standard Form**

Write the equation in standard form with integer coefficients.

1. $y = -x + 5$ **2.** $y = -\frac{1}{2}x + 7$ **3.** $y = \frac{2}{3}x + 4$

EXAMPLE 2 Write an Equation in Standard Form

Write in standard form an equation of the line passing through $(-4, 3)$ with a slope of -2. Use integer coefficients.

Solution

❶ **Write** the point-slope form.　　　　　　　　　$y - y_1 = m(x - x_1)$

❷ **Substitute** -2 for m, -4 for x_1, and 3 for y_1.　$y - 3 = -2[x - (-4)]$

❸ **Simplify** the equation.　　　　　　　　　　　$y - 3 = -2(x + 4)$

❹ **Use** the distributive property.　　　　　　　　$y - 3 = -2x - 8$

❺ **Add** 3 to each side. (Slope-intercept form)　　　$y = -2x - 5$

❻ **Add** $2x$ to each side. (Standard form)　　　　$2x + y = -5$

Checkpoint ✓ Write an Equation in Standard Form

4. Write in standard form an equation of the line passing through $(3, -5)$ with a slope of -3. Use integer coefficients.

EXAMPLE 3 Write an Equation in Standard Form

A line intersects the axes at $(4, 0)$ and $(0, 3)$. Write an equation of the line in standard form. Use integer coefficients.

Solution

❶ **Find** the slope. Use $(x_1, y_1) = (4, 0)$ and $(x_2, y_2) = (0, 3)$.

$$m = \frac{y_2 - y_1}{x_2 - x_1} = \frac{3 - 0}{0 - 4} = -\frac{3}{4}$$

❷ **Write** an equation of the line, using slope-intercept form.

$$y = mx + b \qquad \text{Write slope-intercept form.}$$

$$y = -\frac{3}{4}x + 3 \qquad \text{Substitute } -\frac{3}{4} \text{ for } m \text{ and } 3 \text{ for } b.$$

$$4y = 4\left(-\frac{3}{4}x + 3\right) \qquad \text{Multiply each side by 4.}$$

$$4y = -3x + 12 \qquad \text{Use distributive property.}$$

$$3x + 4y = 12 \qquad \text{Add } 3x \text{ to each side.}$$

ANSWER ▶ The equation $3x + 4y = 12$ is in standard form.

Checkpoint ✓ Write an Equation in Standard Form

5. Write in standard form an equation of the line that intersects the axes at $(2, 0)$ and $(0, 5)$. Use integer coefficients.

HORIZONTAL AND VERTICAL LINES Recall from Chapter 4 that the slope of a horizontal line is zero and the slope of a vertical line is undefined. In Example 4 you will learn how to write equations of horizontal and vertical lines in standard form.

Student Help

▶ **STUDY TIP**
Notice that there is no *x*-term in the standard form of a horizontal line and no *y*-term in the standard form of a vertical line.

EXAMPLE 4 **Equations for Horizontal and Vertical Lines**

Write an equation of the blue line in standard form.

a.
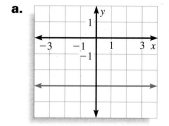

b.
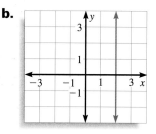

Solution

a. Each point on this horizontal line has a *y*-coordinate of -3. So, the equation of the line is $y = -3$.

b. Each point on this vertical line has an *x*-coordinate of 2. So, the equation of the line is $x = 2$.

Both equations are in standard form.

Checkpoint ✓ **Equations of Horizontal and Vertical Lines**

Write an equation of the line in standard form.

6.
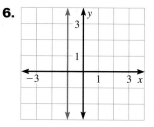

7.
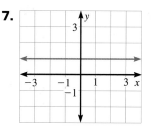

LINEAR EQUATIONS You have now studied all of the commonly used forms of linear equations. They are summarized in the following list.

SUMMARY

Equations of Lines

SLOPE-INTERCEPT FORM: $y = mx + b$

POINT-SLOPE FORM: $y - y_1 = m(x - x_1)$

VERTICAL LINE (Undefined Slope): $x = a$

HORIZONTAL LINE (Zero Slope): $y = b$

STANDARD FORM: $Ax + By = C$, where A and B are not both zero.

Exercises

Guided Practice

Vocabulary Check

1. Name the following form of an equation of a line: $y = mx + b$. What does m represent? What does b represent?

2. Name the following form of an equation of a line: $Ax + By = C$. Give an example of an equation in this form.

Skill Check

Write the equation in standard form with integer coefficients.

3. $y = 2x - 9$
4. $y = \frac{1}{2}x + 8$
5. $y = \frac{3}{4}x$

Write in standard form an equation of the line that passes through the given point and has the given slope. Use integer coefficients.

6. $(3, 4), m = -4$
7. $(1, -2), m = 5$
8. $(-2, -5), m = 3$

Write in standard form an equation of the line that passes through the two points. Use integer coefficients.

9. $(3, 1), (4, -2)$
10. $(1, 6), (1, -5)$
11. $(5, 0), (0, 3)$

Write an equation of the line in standard form.

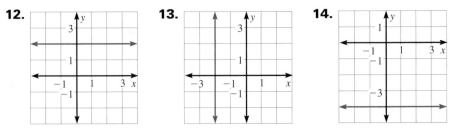

12.
13.
14.

Practice and Applications

CONVERTING TO STANDARD FORM Write the equation in standard form with integer coefficients.

15. $y = -5x + 2$
16. $y = 3x - 8$
17. $y = -9 + 4x$

18. $y = \frac{2}{3}x$
19. $y = -\frac{3}{8}x$
20. $y = 9x + \frac{1}{2}$

WRITING EQUATIONS Write in standard form an equation of the line that passes through the given point and has the given slope.

21. $(-8, 3), m = 2$
22. $(-2, 7), m = -4$
23. $(-1, 4), m = -3$

24. $(-6, -7), m = -1$
25. $(3, -2), m = 5$
26. $(10, 6), m = 0$

27. $(2, 9), m = \frac{2}{5}$
28. $(5, -8), m = \frac{1}{2}$
29. $(7, 3), m = -\frac{1}{3}$

Student Help

▶ HOMEWORK HELP
  Example 1: Exs. 15–20
  Example 2: Exs. 21–29
  Example 3: Exs. 30–38
  Example 4: Exs. 39–44

Student Help

▶STUDY TIP
In Exercises 30–38, find the slope first, use point-slope form, then convert to standard form.

WRITING EQUATIONS Write in standard form an equation of the line that passes through the two points. Use integer coefficients.

30. $(4, 0)$, $(0, 5)$ **31.** $(-3, 0)$, $(0, 2)$ **32.** $(0, 0)$, $(2, 0)$

33. $(0, 1)$, $(1, -1)$ **34.** $(-4, 0)$, $(0, -5)$ **35.** $(-4, 1)$, $(2, -5)$

36. $(9, -2)$, $(-3, 2)$ **37.** $(-3, 3)$, $(7, 2)$ **38.** $(4, -7)$, $(5, -1)$

HORIZONTAL AND VERTICAL LINES Write an equation of the line in standard form.

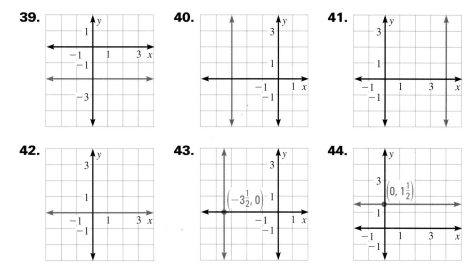

39.   **40.**   **41.**

42.   **43.** $\left(-3\tfrac{1}{2}, 0\right)$ **44.** $\left(0, 1\tfrac{1}{2}\right)$

Puzzler The names of different sports are hidden in the first quadrant of a coordinate plane, as shown on the grid below. Write an equation in standard form of each line containing the given sport. For example, an equation for "softball" is $-x + y = 2$.

45. Basketball

46. Lacrosse

47. Skiing

48. Football

49. Golf

50. Rugby

51. Hockey

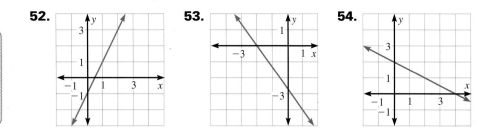

WRITING EQUATIONS FROM GRAPHS Write in standard form an equation of the line. Use integer coefficients.

Student Help

▶HOMEWORK HELP
INTERNET Extra help with problem solving in Exs. 52–54 is available at www.mcdougallittell.com

52.   **53.**   **54.**

BIRDSEED Thistle seed attracts goldfinches. Before a storm, goldfinches greatly increase the amount they eat in order to gain weight.
▶ Source: Canadian Wildlife Service

ERROR ANALYSIS In Exercises 55 and 56, find and correct the error.

55.

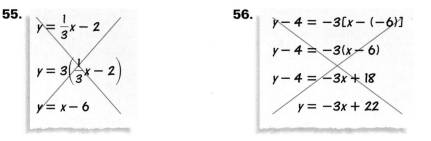

$$y = \frac{1}{3}x - 2$$
$$y = 3\left(\frac{1}{3}x - 2\right)$$
$$y = x - 6$$

56.

$$y - 4 = -3[x - (-6)]$$
$$y - 4 = -3(x - 6)$$
$$y - 4 = -3x + 18$$
$$y = -3x + 22$$

BIRDSEED MIXTURE In Exercises 57 and 58, use the following information.
You are buying $24 worth of birdseed that consists of two types of seed. Thistle seed costs $2 per pound. Dark oil sunflower seed costs $1.50 per pound. The equation $2x + 1.5y = 24$ models the number of pounds of thistle seed x and the number of pounds of dark oil sunflower seed y that you can buy.

57. Graph the line representing the possible seed mixtures.

58. Copy and complete the table. Label the points from the table on the graph created in Exercise 57.

Pounds of thistle seed, x	0	3	6	9	12
Pounds of dark oil sunflower seed, y	?	?	?	?	?

CHALLENGE The equation below represents the intercept form of the equation of a line. In the equation, the *x*-intercept is *a* and the *y*-intercept is *b*.

$$\frac{x}{a} + \frac{y}{b} = 1$$

59. Write the intercept form of the equation of the line whose *x*-intercept is 2 and *y*-intercept is 3.

60. Write the equation from Exercise 59 in standard form.

Standardized Test Practice

61. MULTIPLE CHOICE Which is an equation of the line in standard form?

(A) $-3x + 2y = 2$

(B) $y = \frac{3}{2}x + 1$

(C) $3x + 2y = 1$

(D) $y - 1 = \frac{3}{2}x$

62. MULTIPLE CHOICE Choose an equation in standard form of the line that passes through the point $(-1, -4)$ and has a slope of 2.

(F) $-2x + y = -2$

(G) $-3y = x - 9$

(H) $-x - y = 9$

(J) $x - 3y = -9$

SOLVING EQUATIONS Solve the equation. *(Lesson 3.3)*

63. $8 + y = 3$ **64.** $y - 9 = 2$ **65.** $6(q + 22) = -120$

66. $2(x + 5) = 18$ **67.** $7 - 2a = -14$ **68.** $-2 + 4c = 19$

GRAPHING EQUATIONS Use a table of values to graph the equation. Label the *x*-intercept and the *y*-intercept. *(Lesson 4.2)*

69. $y = x + 5$ **70.** $y = 4x - 4$ **71.** $y = -x + 8$

Maintaining Skills   **ROUNDING** Round to the nearest whole dollar. *(Skills Review p. 774)*

72. $14.76   **73.** $908.23   **74.** $4,573.70   **75.** $14,098.15

76. $99.99   **77.** $0.05   **78.** $0.51   **79.** $12,345.67

Quiz 2

Write in slope-intercept form the equation of the line that passes through the points. *(Lesson 5.3)*

   1. $(10, -3)$ and $(5, -2)$ **2.** $(6, 2)$ and $(7, 5)$ **3.** $(4, 4)$ and $(-7, 4)$

Write in slope-intercept form the equation of the line that passes through the two points. *(Lesson 5.3)*

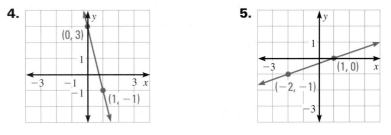

4.

5.

Write the equation in standard form with integer coefficients. *(Lesson 5.4)*

   6. $y = -3x + 9$ **7.** $y = \frac{1}{2}x + 4$ **8.** $y = \frac{2}{5}x - 1$

Write in standard form an equation of the line that passes through the point and has the given slope. *(Lesson 5.4)*

   9. $(6, 8)$, $m = 2$ **10.** $(4, 1)$, $m = -\frac{1}{2}$ **11.** $(1, 5)$, $m = \frac{2}{5}$

Write an equation of the line in standard form. *(Lesson 5.4)*

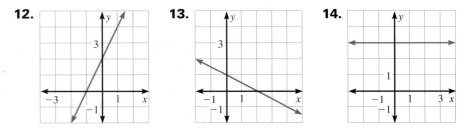

12.

13.

14.

5.5 # Modeling with Linear Equations

Goal
Write and use a linear equation to solve a real-life problem.

Key Words
• linear model
• rate of change

How many movie theaters will there be in 2005?

In Example 1 you will see that the number of movie theaters in the United States increased at a constant rate from 1985 through 1997. In Example 2 you will use this linear pattern to predict the number of movie theaters in the year 2005.

A **linear model** is a linear function that is used to model a real-life situation. A **rate of change** compares two quantities that are changing. Slope is often used to describe a real-life rate of change.

EXAMPLE 1 Write a Linear Model

From 1985 through 1997, the number of movie theaters in the United States increased by about 750 per year. In 1993, there were about 26,000 theaters. Write a linear model for the number of theaters y. Let $t = 0$ represent 1985.

DATA UPDATE of the number of movie theaters is available at www.mcdougallittell.com

Solution

The rate of increase is 750 per year, so the slope is $m = 750$. The year 1993 is represented by $t = 8$. Therefore, $(t_1, y_1) = (8, 26{,}000)$ is a point on the line.

❶ **Write** the point-slope form. $y - y_1 = m(t - t_1)$

❷ **Substitute** 750 for m, 8 for t_1, $y - 26{,}000 = (750)(t - 8)$
and 26,000 for y_1.

❸ **Use** the distributive property. $y - 26{,}000 = 750t - 6000$

❹ **Add** 26,000 to each side. $y = 750t + 20{,}000$

ANSWER ▶ The linear model for the number of theaters in the United States is $y = 750t + 20{,}000$, where $t = 0$ represents 1985.

Student Help

▶ **STUDY TIP**
Because you are given the slope and a point on the line, use point-slope form.

 **Checkpoint** ✓ **Write a Linear Model**

1. From 1985 through 1997, movie attendance in the United States increased by about 25 million per year. In 1994, movie attendance was about 1300 million. Write a linear model for movie attendance y (in millions). Let $t = 0$ represent 1985.

PREDICTING WITH LINEAR MODELS Once you have written a linear model, you can use it to predict unknown values. When you do this, you are assuming that the pattern established in the past will continue into the future.

EXAMPLE 2 Use a Linear Model to Predict

Use the linear model in Example 1

$$y = 750t + 20{,}000$$

to predict the number of theaters in the year 2005.
Recall that $t = 0$ represents the year 1985.

Solution

Method 1 Use an algebraic approach.

Because $t = 0$ represents the year 1985, 2005 is represented by $t = 20$.

❶ *Write* the linear model. $y = 750t + 20{,}000$

❷ *Substitute* 20 for t. $y = 750(20) + 20{,}000$

❸ *Simplify.* $y = 15{,}000 + 20{,}000 = 35{,}000$

ANSWER ▶ You can predict that there will be about 35,000 theaters in 2005.

Student Help

▶**STUDY TIP**
Graphs describing past behavior can be used to estimate future trends.

Method 2 Use a graphical approach.

A graph of the equation $y = 750t + 20{,}000$ is shown below.

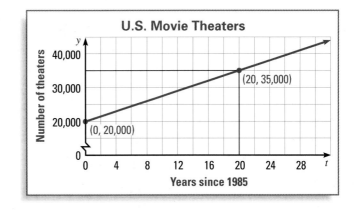

ANSWER ▶ From the graph, you can see that when $t = 20$ (which represents the year 2005), $y = 35{,}000$. Therefore, you can predict that there will be about 35,000 theaters in the year 2005.

Checkpoint ✓ Use a Linear Model to Predict

Use the linear model you wrote for Checkpoint 1 on page 298 to predict the movie attendance in the year 2005. Let $t = 0$ represent the year 1985.

2. Use an algebraic approach.

3. Use a graphical approach.

EXAMPLE **3** **Write and Use a Linear Model**

You are buying hamburger and chicken for a barbecue. The hamburger costs $3 per pound and the chicken costs $4 per pound. You have $60 to spend.

a. Write an equation that models the different amounts (in pounds) of hamburger and chicken you can buy.

b. Use the model to complete the table that illustrates several different amounts of hamburger and chicken you can buy.

Hamburger (lb), x	0	4	8	12	16	20
Chicken (lb), y	?	?	?	?	?	?

Solution

a. Model the possible combinations of hamburger and chicken.

VERBAL MODEL $\boxed{\dfrac{\text{Price of}}{\text{hamburger}}} \cdot \boxed{\dfrac{\text{Weight of}}{\text{hamburger}}} + \boxed{\dfrac{\text{Price of}}{\text{chicken}}} \cdot \boxed{\dfrac{\text{Weight of}}{\text{chicken}}} = \boxed{\dfrac{\text{Total}}{\text{cost}}}$

LABELS Price of hamburger = **3**   (dollars per pound)

Weight of hamburger = x (pounds)

Price of chicken = **4**   (dollars per pound)

Weight of chicken = y (pounds)

Total cost = **60**   (dollars)

ALGEBRAIC MODEL $3\,x + 4\,y = 60$ Linear model

b. Complete the table by substituting the given values of x into the equation $3x + 4y = 60$ to find y.

Hamburger (lb), x	0	4	8	12	16	20
Chicken (lb), y	15	12	9	6	3	0

Note that as the number of pounds of hamburger increases, the number of pounds of chicken decreases and as the number of pounds of hamburger decreases, the number of pounds of chicken increases.

Checkpoint ✓ **Write and Use a Linear Model**

You are buying pasta salad and potato salad for the barbecue. The pasta salad costs $4 per pound and the potato salad costs $5 per pound. You have $60 to spend.

4. Write an equation that models the different amounts (in pounds) of potato salad and pasta salad you can buy.

Student Help

▶**LOOK BACK**
For help with algebraic modeling, refer to pp. 36–38.

5.5 Exercises

Guided Practice

Vocabulary Check

Complete the sentence.

1. A __?__ is a linear function that is used to model a real-life situation.

2. Slope is often used to describe a real-life __?__.

Skill Check

Match the description with its graph. In each case, tell what the slope of the line represents.

3. An employee is paid $12.50 per hour plus $1.50 for each unit produced per hour.

4. A person is paying $10 per week to a friend to repay a $100 loan.

5. A sales representative receives $20 per day for food, plus $.32 for each mile driven.

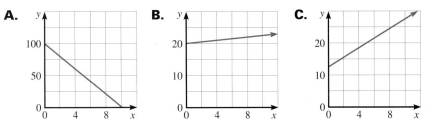

Practice and Applications

6. **COMPANY PROFITS** Between the years of 1990 and 2000, the annual profit for the Alpha Company increased by about $70,000 per year. In 1998, the company had an annual profit of $2,000,000. Write the equation in slope-intercept form that gives the annual profit P for the Alpha Company in terms of t. Let $t = 0$ represent the year 1990.

MOUNTAIN CLIMBING In Exercises 7–11, a mountain climber is scaling a 400-foot cliff. The climber starts at the bottom at $t = 0$ and climbs at a constant rate of 124 feet per hour.

7. What is the slope in the linear model for the situation?

8. The y-intercept represents the height at which the climber begins scaling the cliff. What is the y-intercept in the linear model?

9. Use the slope and y-intercept to write the linear model for the distance y (in feet) that the climber climbs in terms of time t (in hours). Use slope-intercept form.

10. After 3 hours, has the climber reached the top of the cliff?

11. Use the equation from Exercise 9 to determine the time that the climber will reach the top of the cliff.

Student Help

▶**HOMEWORK HELP**
  Example 1: Exs. 6–9,
            12–14, 18–20
  Example 2: Exs. 10, 11,
            15–17, 21–23
  Example 3: Exs. 24–32

CANOE RENTAL **In Exercises 12–17, use the following information.**
Renting a canoe costs $10 plus $28 per day. The linear model for this situation relates the total cost of renting a canoe, *y*, with the number of days rented, *x*.

12. What number corresponds to the slope in the linear model?

13. What number corresponds to the *y*-intercept in the linear model?

14. Use the slope and *y*-intercept form to write the linear model.

15. Graph the linear model from Exercise 14.

16. Use the linear model to find the cost of renting a canoe for 3 days.

17. If you had $66 to spend, for how many days could you rent a canoe?

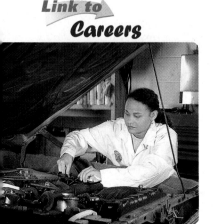

Link to
Careers

AUTO MECHANICS, often called automotive service technicians, inspect, maintain, or repair automobiles and light trucks.

CAR COSTS **In Exercises 18–23, use the following information.**
From 1994 through 1997, the cost of owning and operating a car per mile, which includes car maintenance and repair, increased by about 2.2 cents per year. In 1995, it cost about 48.9 cents per mile to own and operate a car. Let $t = 0$ represent the year 1994.
▶ Source: American Automobile Manufacturers Association, Inc.

18. Find the slope of the linear equation that models this situation.

19. Name one point on the line.

20. Use the slope from Exercise 18 and the point from Exercise 19 to write a linear model for the cost *C* of owning and operating an automobile in terms of time *t*.

21. Use an algebraic approach to predict the cost of owning and operating a car in 2003.

22. Graph the linear model from Exercise 20.

23. Use your graph to estimate the cost of owning and operating a car in 1996.

TICKET PURCHASE **In Exercises 24–26, use the following information.**
A school club visits a science museum. Student tickets cost $5 each. Non-student tickets cost $7 each. The club paid $315 for the tickets. Use the verbal model below.

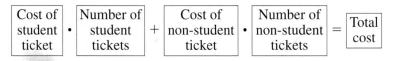

$$\boxed{\begin{array}{c}\text{Cost of}\\\text{student}\\\text{ticket}\end{array}} \cdot \boxed{\begin{array}{c}\text{Number of}\\\text{student}\\\text{tickets}\end{array}} + \boxed{\begin{array}{c}\text{Cost of}\\\text{non-student}\\\text{ticket}\end{array}} \cdot \boxed{\begin{array}{c}\text{Number of}\\\text{non-student}\\\text{tickets}\end{array}} = \boxed{\begin{array}{c}\text{Total}\\\text{cost}\end{array}}$$

24. Let *x* represent the number of student tickets. Let *y* represent the number of non-student tickets. Finish assigning labels.

25. Write the algebraic model from the verbal model.

26. Copy the table. Then use the algebraic model to complete the table.

Number of student tickets, *x*	7	14	28	35	56	63
Number of non-student tickets, *y*	?	?	?	?	?	?

BASKETBALL GAME In Exercises 27–30, use the following information. A basketball team scored 102 points in a playoff game. Each field goal is 2 points and each free throw is 1 point.

27. Write a linear model for the number of points the team scored in terms of field goals x and free throws y.

28. Write the equation from Exercise 27 in slope-intercept form.

29. Copy the table. Then use the linear equation to complete the table.

Number of field goals, x	20	25	30	35	40
Number of free throws, y	?	?	?	?	?

30. Plot the points from the table and sketch the line.

BUYING VEGETABLES In Exercises 31 and 32, use the following information. You are buying vegetables to make a vegetable tray for a party. You buy $10 worth of cauliflower and broccoli. The cauliflower costs $2 per pound and the broccoli costs $1.25 per pound.

31. Write an equation in standard form that represents the different amounts (in pounds) of cauliflower C and broccoli B that you could buy.

32. Copy the table. Then use the linear equation to complete the table.

Pounds of cauliflower, C	0	1	2	3	4	5
Pounds of broccoli, B	?	?	?	?	?	?

ARCHAEOLOGY In Exercises 33 and 34, use the graph and the following information. Radiocarbon dating is a method of estimating the age of ancient objects. The radiocarbon age and the actual age of an object are nearly the same for objects that are less than 2000 years old. As you can see in the graph, the radiocarbon age of objects that are more than 2000 years old does not agree with the actual age determined by other methods.

33. Use the graph to estimate the radiocarbon age of an object that is actually 5000 years old.

34. Now use the equation $y = \frac{6}{7}x + 285.7$, where $2000 < x < 9000$ to estimate the radiocarbon age of the same 5000-year-old object.

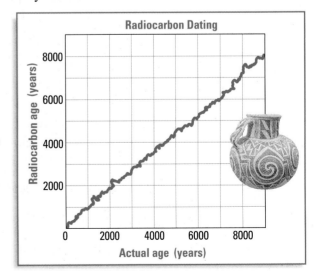

Radiocarbon Dating

35. MULTIPLE CHOICE You and a friend have $30 to spend at a health center. It costs $10 an hour to use the racquetball court and $5 an hour to use the tennis court. Which equation represents the number of hours you can spend on each court? Let x represent the number of hours on the racquetball court and y represent the number of hours on the tennis court.

   (A) $5x + 10y = 30$ (B) $10x + 5y = 30$

   (C) $5y = 10x - 30$ (D) $y = 5x + 6$

36. MULTIPLE CHOICE Your basketball team scores 84 points. Each free throw x is worth 1 point. Each field goal y is worth 2 points. Which equation relates the number of free throws with the number of field goals?

   (F) $y = 2x + 1$ (G) $x + y = 84$

   (H) $2x + y = 84$ (J) $x + 2y = 84$

Mixed Review

ORDER OF OPERATIONS Evaluate the numerical expression. *(Lesson 1.3)*

37. $6 - 3 \cdot 2$ **38.** $12 \div 3 - 3 \cdot 1$ **39.** $4^2 - 6 \cdot (4 + 7)$

RATIOS Convert the units. *(Lesson 3.8)*

40. 5 days to hours   **41.** 36 inches to feet   **42.** 12 years to months

43. SLOPE What is the slope of the ramp in the photo at the right? Explain how you arrived at your answer. *(Lesson 4.5)*

SLOPE-INTERCEPT FORM Write in slope-intercept form the equation of the line described below. *(Lesson 5.1)*

44. $m = 0, b = 7$ **45.** $m = -2, b = 3$ **46.** $m = \frac{1}{2}, b = 0$

WRITING EQUATIONS Write in slope-intercept form the equation of the line that passes through the given points. *(Lesson 5.3)*

47. $(0, -3)$ and $(6, 5)$ **48.** $(7, 4)$ and $(-3, 0)$ **49.** $(5, 2)$ and $(8, 2)$

Maintaining Skills

COMPARING PERCENTS AND DECIMALS Compare using <, >, or =. *(Skills Review pp. 768, 770)*

50. 25% ? 0.25   **51.** 0.3 ? 3%   **52.** 0.01 ? 1%

53. 0.065 ? 65%   **54.** 12% ? 1.2   **55.** 160% ? 1.6

56. 0.017 ? 17%   **57.** 5% ? 0.05   **58.** 0.889 ? 89%

DEVELOPING CONCEPTS
Perpendicular Lines

For use with Lesson 5.6

GOAL

Describe the relationship between the slopes of perpendicular lines.

MATERIALS

• pencil
• ruler
• graph paper
• protractor

Question

What is the relationship between the slopes of perpendicular lines?

Lines that intersect at a right, or 90°, angle are called *perpendicular* lines.

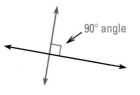

90° angle

Explore

1 The line at the right has a slope of $\frac{2}{3}$. Copy the line onto a piece of graph paper.

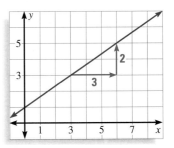

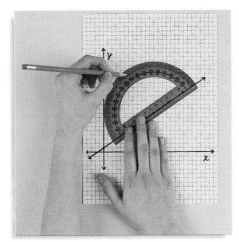

2 Use a protractor to draw a line on the graph paper that is perpendicular to the given line. Center the protractor on a point on the line with integer coordinates.

3 Find the slope of the perpendicular line using $m = \frac{\text{rise}}{\text{run}}$.

4 Find the product of the slopes of the two lines.

Think About It

Follow the steps above for the following lines. What do you notice about the relationship between the slopes of perpendicular lines?

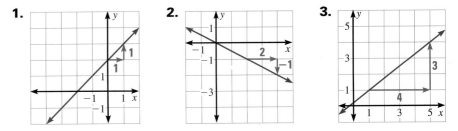

1.   **2.**   **3.**

4. Based on your observations, make a general statement about the product of the slopes of perpendicular lines.

5.6 Perpendicular Lines

Goal
Write equations of perpendicular lines.

Key Words
• perpendicular

What is the shortest flight path?

As you saw in Developing Concepts 5.6, page 305, the product of the slopes of perpendicular lines is -1. When you take geometry you will see a proof of this relationship. In Example 3 you will use perpendicular lines to plan the path of a helicopter flight.

Two lines in a plane are **perpendicular** if they intersect at a right, or 90°, angle.

PERPENDICULAR LINES

In a coordinate plane, two nonvertical lines are perpendicular if and only if the product of their slopes is -1.

Horizontal and vertical lines are perpendicular to each other.

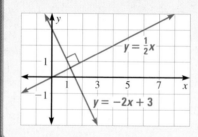

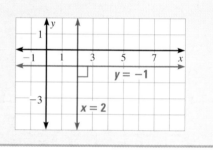

Student Help

▶ MORE EXAMPLES

More examples are available at www.mcdougallittell.com

EXAMPLE 1 Identify Perpendicular Lines

Determine whether the lines are perpendicular.

Solution

The lines have slopes of $\frac{3}{4}$ and $-\frac{4}{3}$. Because $\left(\frac{3}{4}\right) \cdot \left(-\frac{4}{3}\right) = -1$, the lines are perpendicular.

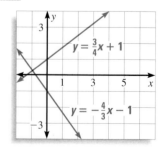

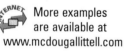 **Identify Perpendicular Lines**

Determine whether the lines are perpendicular.

1. $y = 3x + 2$, $y = -3x - 1$

2. $y = \frac{3}{2}x + 1$, $y = -\frac{2}{3}x + 1$

Graphing can be used to check whether your answer is reasonable. Graphing cannot be used to show that two lines are perpendicular.

EXAMPLE 2 Show that Lines are Perpendicular

a. Write in slope-intercept form the equation of the line passing through (2, 5) and (4, 4).

b. Show that the line is perpendicular to the line $y = 2x + 1$.

Solution

a. ❶ *Find* the slope. Let $(x_1, y_1) = (2, 5)$ and $(x_2, y_2) = (4, 4)$.

$$m = \frac{y_2 - y_1}{x_2 - x_1} = \frac{4 - 5}{4 - 2} = -\frac{1}{2}$$

❷ *Write* the equation of the line using point-slope form.

$y - y_1 = m(x - x_1)$	Write point-slope form.
$y - 5 = -\frac{1}{2}(x - 2)$	Substitute $-\frac{1}{2}$ for m, 2 for x_1, and 5 for y_1.
$y - 5 = -\frac{1}{2}x + 1$	Use distributive property.
$y = -\frac{1}{2}x + 6$	Add 5 to each side.

ANSWER ▶ The equation of the line is $y = -\frac{1}{2}x + 6$.

b. The lines have slopes of $-\frac{1}{2}$ and 2. Because $\left(-\frac{1}{2}\right) \cdot (2) = -1$, the lines are perpendicular.

CHECK ✓

You can check that your answer is reasonable by graphing both lines. From the graph, you can see that the lines appear to be perpendicular.

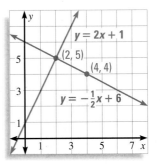

Checkpoint ✓ **Show that Lines are Perpendicular**

3. Write in slope-intercept form the equation of the line passing through (1, 3) and (3, 6). Show that this line is perpendicular to the line $y = -\frac{2}{3}x - 5$.

4. Write in slope-intercept form the equation of the line passing through (0, 0) and (1, 2). Show that this line is perpendicular to the line $y = -\frac{1}{2}x + 7$.

**HELICOPTER SEARCH
AND RESCUE CREWS** can
save people from sinking
ships, burning buildings,
floods, car and plane
crashes, and other dangers.

EXAMPLE **3** **Write an Equation of a Perpendicular Line**

HELICOPTER PATH You are in a helicopter as shown in the graph below. The shortest flight path to the shoreline is one that is perpendicular to the shoreline. Write the equation for this path.

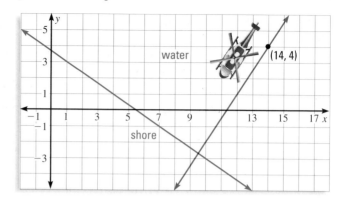

Solution

The slope of the shoreline is $-\frac{2}{3}$. To be perpendicular, the path of the

helicopter should have a slope of $m = \frac{3}{2}$. The helicopter's current location is

$(x_1, y_1) = (14, 4)$.

❶ Write the point-slope form. $y - y_1 = m(x - x_1)$

❷ Substitute $\frac{3}{2}$ for m, 14 for x_1, and 4 for y_1. $y - 4 = \frac{3}{2}(x - 14)$

❸ Use the distributive property. $y - 4 = \frac{3}{2}x - 21$

❹ Add 4 to each side. $y = \frac{3}{2}x - 17$

ANSWER ▶ The equation for the path of the helicopter is $y = \frac{3}{2}x - 17$.

Checkpoint ✓ **Write an Equation of a Perpendicular Line**

5. You are in a ship as shown in the graph below. The shortest path to the shore is one that is perpendicular to the shoreline. Write the equation for this path.

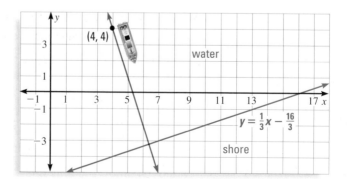

Exercises

Guided Practice

Vocabulary Check

1. Complete: Perpendicular lines intersect at a __?__ angle.

2. Two lines are perpendicular. If the slope of one of the lines is $-\frac{5}{7}$, then what is the slope of the other line?

Skill Check

Determine whether the lines are perpendicular.

3. $y = \frac{1}{5}x - 3$, $y = -5x + 3$

4. $y = -4x + 8$, $y = \frac{1}{4}x + 7$

5. $y = \frac{3}{8}x + 1$, $y = \frac{8}{3}x - 2$

6. $y = 3$, $x = 4$

Write the equation of the line passing through the two points. Show that this line is perpendicular to the given line.

7. $(-3, 0)$, $(3, 6)$; $y = -x - 2$

8. $(-4, -4)$, $(-2, 2)$; $y = -\frac{1}{3}x - 1$

Write the equation of the line passing through the point and perpendicular to the given line.

9. $(5, 2)$, $y = -\frac{1}{2}x + 4$

10. $(6, 0)$, $y = -2x + 7$

Practice and Applications

IDENTIFYING PERPENDICULAR LINES **Determine whether the lines are perpendicular.**

11. $y = x + 4$, $y = x - 4$

12. $y = -\frac{1}{3}x + 1$, $y = -3x + 3$

13. $y = \frac{1}{2}x - 7$, $y = -2x$

14. $y = \frac{3}{5}x + 2$, $y = -\frac{5}{3}x - 2$

15. $y = \frac{4}{7}x + 2$, $4y = -7x - 16$

16. $y = -5$, $x = 5$

GRAPHICAL REASONING **Write the equation of each line in the graph. Determine whether the lines are perpendicular.**

17.

18.

19.

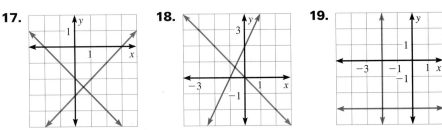

Student Help

▶**HOMEWORK HELP**
Example 1: Exs. 11–19
Example 2: Exs. 20–25
Example 3: Exs. 26–39

PERPENDICULAR LINES Write in slope-intercept form the equation of the line passing through the two points. Show that the line is perpendicular to the given line. Check your answer by graphing both lines.

20. $(8, 5), (5, -1); y = -\frac{1}{2}x + 4$ **21.** $(-2, -2), (1, -3); y = 3x - 1$

22. $(-3, 6), (3, 0); y = x + 2$ **23.** $(4, -7), (7, 5); y = -\frac{1}{4}x$

24. $(1, 9), (9, 9); x = 1$ **25.** $(-6, -4), (0, 0); y = -\frac{3}{2}x - 3$

USING GRAPHS Write in slope-intercept form the equation of the line passing through the given point and perpendicular to the given line.

Student Help

▶ **HOMEWORK HELP**

Extra help with problem solving in Exs. 26–31 is available at www.mcdougallittell.com

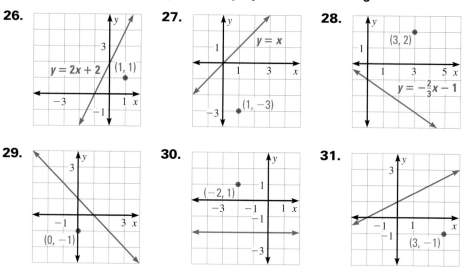

26.   **27.**   **28.**

29.   **30.**   **31.**

WRITING EQUATIONS Write in slope-intercept form the equation of the line passing through the given point and perpendicular to the given line.

32. $(2, 6), y = -\frac{1}{2}x + 4$ **33.** $(0, 3), y = \frac{7}{8}x$

34. $(0, 0), y = -\frac{1}{4}x - 7$ **35.** $(-2, 2), y = 7$

36. $(-3, -1), y = -2x + 8$ **37.** $(2, -1), y = \frac{2}{3}x - 1$

38. $(5, 0), y = x - 2$ **39.** $(-4, -7), y = -4x - 7$

LOGICAL REASONING Complete the statement with *always, sometimes,* or *never*.

40. A horizontal line is __?__ perpendicular to a vertical line.

41. The product of the slopes of two nonvertical perpendicular lines is __?__ -1.

42. The line $y = 2x + 3$ is __?__ perpendicular to a line with slope -2.

43. The line $y = -\frac{1}{3}x + 5$ is __?__ perpendicular to a line with slope 3.

44. **History Link** At the end of the eighteenth century Benjamin Banneker was recommended by Thomas Jefferson to help lay out the new capital, Washington, D.C. As you can see in the map below, the city is laid out in a grid system of perpendicular streets. Assuming the x-axis is F Street and the y-axis is 16th Street, what is the equation of the line that passes through the point $(-4, 1)$ and is perpendicular to 13th Street ($x = 3$)?

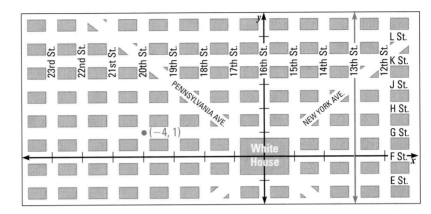

45. **CONSTRUCTION** The city water department is proposing the construction of a new water pipe. The new water pipe should be perpendicular to the old pipe. Use the graph below to write the equation for each water pipe.

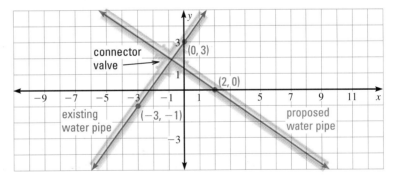

46. **CHALLENGE** Do the three points $(12, 0)$, $(0, 16)$, and $(12, 25)$ form the vertices of a right triangle? Explain your answer.

47. **MULTIPLE CHOICE** Choose which lines are perpendicular.

Line p passes through $(4, 0)$ and $(6, 4)$.

Line q passes through $(0, 4)$ and $(6, 4)$.

Line r passes through $(0, 4)$ and $(0, 0)$.

Ⓐ line p and line q　　　　　Ⓑ line p and line r

Ⓒ line q and line r　　　　　Ⓓ None of these

48. **MULTIPLE CHOICE** Which are *not* slopes of perpendicular lines?

Ⓕ 1 and -1　　　　　　　Ⓖ $-\dfrac{11}{16}$ and $\dfrac{16}{11}$

Ⓗ $\dfrac{1}{31}$ and -31　　　　　　Ⓙ $\dfrac{3}{2}$ and $\dfrac{2}{3}$

Mixed Review

SIMPLIFYING EXPRESSIONS Simplify the expression. *(Lesson 2.7)*

49. $2k - 8 - 8k$ 　　**50.** $-5c + 10 + 8c - 3$ 　**51.** $12x + 12y - 6x + 2$

SOLVING EQUATIONS Solve the equation. *(Lesson 3.3)*

52. $4x - 11 = -31$ 　　**53.** $5x - 7 + x = 19$ 　　**54.** $2x - 6 = 20$

HORIZONTAL AND VERTICAL LINES Determine whether the line is horizontal or vertical. Then graph the line. *(Lesson 4.3)*

55. $y = -2$ 　　**56.** $x = 7$ 　　**57.** $x = 4$ 　　**58.** $y = 3$

Maintaining Skills

DIVIDING FRACTIONS Divide. Write the answer as a fraction or as a mixed number in lowest terms. *(Skills Review p. 765)*

59. $\frac{3}{5} \div \frac{6}{7}$ 　　**60.** $\frac{4}{5} \div \frac{3}{10}$ 　　**61.** $\frac{4}{9} \div \frac{2}{3}$ 　　**62.** $\frac{5}{8} \div \frac{7}{3}$

63. $\frac{4}{9} \div \frac{9}{6}$ 　　**64.** $1\frac{4}{5} \div 2\frac{1}{2}$ 　　**65.** $2\frac{1}{3} \div \frac{1}{3}$ 　　**66.** $1\frac{1}{8} \div \frac{5}{6}$

67. $\frac{7}{8} \div \frac{13}{8}$ 　　**68.** $3\frac{3}{4} \div \frac{5}{4}$ 　　**69.** $\frac{2}{7} \div 3$ 　　**70.** $5\frac{7}{10} \div 5$

Quiz 3

FOOTBALL SCORE You are playing football. Each touchdown is worth 7 points (assuming the extra point is scored) and each field goal is worth 3 points. Your team scored 42 points. *(Lesson 5.5)*

1. Write a linear model for the number of points that your team scored in terms of touchdowns x and field goals y.

2. Write the equation in slope-intercept form. Then copy and complete the table.

Number of touchdowns, x	0	3	6
Number of field goals, y	?	?	?

3. Plot the points from the table and sketch the line.

Determine whether the lines are perpendicular. *(Lesson 5.6)*

4. $y = \frac{1}{2}x + 6, y = -2x + 6$ 　　**5.** $y = x - 5, y = -x$

Write the equation of the line passing through the two points. Show that the line is perpendicular to the given line. *(Lesson 5.6)*

6. $(5, 6), (0, 1); y = -x + 2$ 　　**7.** $(-3, 0), (0, -4); y = \frac{3}{4}x - 7$

8. Write the equation of the line passing through $(2, 7)$ and perpendicular to the line $y = \frac{1}{2}x + 3$.

5.1 Slope-Intercept Form

Examples on pp. 269–271

EXAMPLE Write in slope-intercept form the equation of the line shown in the graph.

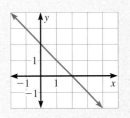

① **Write** the slope-intercept form.
$$y = mx + b$$

② **Find** the slope of the line. Use any two points on the graph. Let $(2, 0)$ be (x_1, y_1) and let $(0, 2)$ be (x_2, y_2).

$$m = \frac{y_2 - y_1}{x_2 - x_1} = \frac{2 - 0}{0 - 2} = \frac{2}{-2} = -1$$

③ **Use** the graph to find the y-intercept b. The line passes through the point $(0, 2)$ so the y-intercept is $b = 2$.

④ **Substitute** slope -1 for m and 2 for b into the equation $y = mx + b$.
$$y = -1x + 2$$

ANSWER ▶ The equation of the line is $y = -x + 2$.

Write the equation of the line in slope-intercept form.

1. $m = 6, b = -4$

2. $m = 1, b = \frac{1}{2}$

3. $m = -8, b = 8$

4. $m = 12, b = \frac{5}{6}$

5. $m = \frac{3}{2}, b = 0$

6. $m = 0, b = 10$

Write in slope-intercept form the equation of the line shown in the graph.

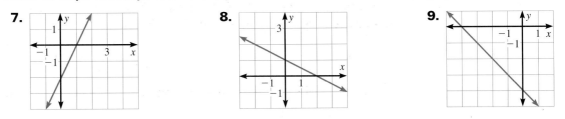

7.

8.

9.

5.2   Point-Slope Form

Examples on
pp. 278–280

> **EXAMPLE** Write in slope-intercept form the equation of the line that passes through
> $(5, -2)$ and that has slope -3.
>
> ❶ **Write** the point-slope form. $y - y_1 = m(x - x_1)$
>
> ❷ **Substitute** -3 for m, 5 for x_1 and -2 for y_1. $y - (-2) = -3(x - 5)$
>
> ❸ **Use** the distributive property and simplify. $y + 2 = -3x + 15$
>
> ❹ **Subtract** 2 from each side. $y = -3x + 13$

**Write the equation of the line in point-slope form. Then write the
equation in slope-intercept form.**

10.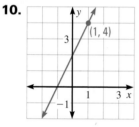

11.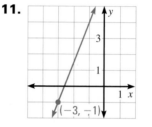

12.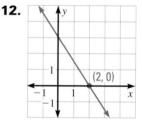

13. Write the equation of the line that is parallel to the line $y = 5x - 2$ and
passes through the point $(-2, 3)$.

5.3   Writing Linear Equations Given Two Points

Examples on
pp. 285–287

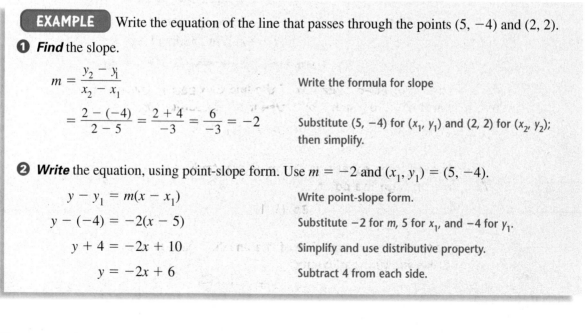

> **EXAMPLE** Write the equation of the line that passes through the points $(5, -4)$ and $(2, 2)$.
>
> ❶ **Find** the slope.
>
> $$m = \frac{y_2 - y_1}{x_2 - x_1}$$ Write the formula for slope
>
> $$= \frac{2 - (-4)}{2 - 5} = \frac{2 + 4}{-3} = \frac{6}{-3} = -2$$ Substitute $(5, -4)$ for (x_1, y_1) and $(2, 2)$ for (x_2, y_2); then simplify.
>
> ❷ **Write** the equation, using point-slope form. Use $m = -2$ and $(x_1, y_1) = (5, -4)$.
>
> $y - y_1 = m(x - x_1)$ Write point-slope form.
>
> $y - (-4) = -2(x - 5)$ Substitute -2 for m, 5 for x_1, and -4 for y_1.
>
> $y + 4 = -2x + 10$ Simplify and use distributive property.
>
> $y = -2x + 6$ Subtract 4 from each side.

Write in slope-intercept the equation of the line form that passes through the given points.

14. $(4, -9)$ and $(-3, 2)$ **15.** $(1, 8)$ and $(-2, -1)$ **16.** $(2, 5)$ and $(-8, 2)$

17. $(1, 4)$ and $(2, -4)$ **18.** $(0, 8)$ and $(2, 8)$ **19.** $(9, 16)$ and $(-9, -16)$

5.4   Standard Form

Examples on pp. 291–293

EXAMPLES

a. Write in standard form an equation of the line passing through $(3, 4)$ with slope $-\frac{2}{3}$. Use integer coefficients.

b. Write in standard form an equation of the line shown.

a. $y - y_1 = m(x - x_1)$ Write point-slope form.

$y - 4 = -\frac{2}{3}(x - 3)$ Substitute $-\frac{2}{3}$ for m, 3 for x_1 and 4 for y_1.

$y - 4 = -\frac{2}{3}x + 2$ Use distributive property.

$\frac{2}{3}x + y = 6$ Add 4 to each side. Then add $\frac{2}{3}x$ to each side.

$2x + 3y = 18$ Multiply each side by 3 to clear equation of fractions.

b. Each point on this vertical line has an x-coordinate of 3. Therefore, the equation of the line is $x = 3$. This equation is in standard form.

Write in standard form an equation of the line that passes through the given point and has the given slope. Use integer coefficients.

20. $(-2, -1)$, $m = 3$ **21.** $(6, -1)$, $m = 0$ **22.** $(2, 3)$, $m = -4$

Write in standard form equations of the horizontal line and the vertical line that pass through the point.

23. $(-1, 7)$ **24.** $(9, 11)$ **25.** $(-8, -6)$

Write in standard form an equation of the line that passes through the two points. Use integer coefficients.

26. $(-1, 0)$ and $(3, 10)$ **27.** $(0, 7)$ and $(1, 5)$ **28.** $(4, 9)$ and $(-2, -6)$

5.5 Modeling With Linear Equations

Examples on pp. 298–300

EXAMPLE Between 1995 and 2001, a company's profits decreased by about $1200 per year. In 1997, the company had an annual profit of $1,500,000. Write an equation that gives the annual profit P in terms of the year t. Let $t = 0$ represent 1995.

Because the profit *decreased* by 1200 per year, the slope is $m = -1200$. Because 1997 is represented by $t = 2$, you know $(t_1, P_1) = (2, 1,500,000)$ is a point on the line.

❶ *Write* the point-slope formula. $P - P_1 = m(t - t_1)$

❷ *Substitute* -1200 for m, 2 for t_1, and $P - 1,500,000 = -1200(t - 2)$
1,500,000 for P_1.

❸ *Use* the distributive property. $P - 1,500,000 = -1200t + 2400$

❹ *Add* 1,500,000 to each side and simplify. $P = 1,502,400 - 1200t$

29. Use the linear model in the example, $P = 1,502,400 - 1200t$, to predict the total profit for the company in 2006.

30. You have $36 to spend on posters for your bedroom. You can buy a large poster ℓ for $6.00 and a small poster s for $4.00. Write an equation that models the different amounts of small and large posters you can buy.

31. Use the equation from Exercise 30 to fill in the table.

Number of small posters, s	0	3	6	9
Number of large posters, ℓ	?	?	?	?

5.6 Perpendicular Lines

Examples on pp. 306–308

EXAMPLE Determine whether the line $y = 3x - 6$ is perpendicular to $y = -\frac{1}{3}x + 2$.

Recall that two lines are perpendicular if the product of their slopes is -1.

The lines have slopes 3 and $-\frac{1}{3}$. Because $3 \cdot \left(-\frac{1}{3}\right) = -1$, the lines are perpendicular.

Determine whether the lines are perpendicular.

32. $y = -\frac{7}{8}x, \; y = -\frac{8}{7}x - 6$ 　　　　**33.** $5x + 10y = 3, \; y = 2x - 9$

Write in slope-intercept form the equation of the line that passes through the given point and is perpendicular to the given line.

34. $(4, -6), \; y = \frac{5}{7}x + 17$ 　　**35.** $(0, 0), \; y = \frac{1}{2}x - 1$ 　　**36.** $(-2, 1), \; y = 3x + \frac{3}{4}$

Write in slope-intercept form the equation of the line with the given slope and *y*-intercept.

1. $m = 2, b = -1$

2. $m = -\dfrac{1}{4}, b = 3$

3. $m = 61, b = 9$

4. $m = \dfrac{1}{4}, b = -3$

5. $m = -3, b = 3$

6. $m = 0, b = 4$

Write in slope-intercept form the equation of the line that passes through the given point and has the given slope.

7. $(2, 6), m = 2$

8. $(3, -9), m = -5$

9. $(-5, -6), m = -3$

10. $(1, 8), m = -4$

11. $(4, -2), m = \dfrac{1}{2}$

12. $\left(\dfrac{1}{3}, -5\right), m = 8$

Write in slope-intercept form the equation of the line that passes through the given points.

13. $(-3, 2), (4, -1)$

14. $(6, 2), (8, -4)$

15. $(-2, 5), (2, 4)$

16. $(-2, -8), (-1, 0)$

17. $(-5, 2), (2, 4)$

18. $(9, -1), (1, -9)$

Write the equation in standard form with integer coefficients.

19. $-8y = 20 + \dfrac{2}{5}x$

20. $5y = 25x$

21. $-2y + \dfrac{1}{2}x = 4$

Write in slope-intercept form the equation of the line that passes through the given point and is perpendicular to the given line.

22. $(3, 5), y = -5x + 4$

23. $(-2, -2), y = x + 1$

24. $(9, -4), y = -3x - 2$

25. $(0, 0), y = \dfrac{1}{2}x + 6$

26. $(-7, 3), y = -\dfrac{2}{3}x$

27. $(4, 4), y = -2 + \dfrac{1}{4}x$

TICKET PURCHASE **In Exercises 28–30, use the following information.**
The math club goes to an amusement park. Student tickets cost $15 each. Non-student tickets cost $25 each. The club paid $315 for the tickets.

28. Write in standard form an equation that relates the number of student tickets x with the number of non-student tickets y.

29. Write the equation in slope-intercept form and complete the table.

Number of student tickets, *x*	1	6	11	16	21
Number of non-student tickets, *y*	?	?	?	?	?

30. Plot the points from the table and sketch the line.

Chapter Standardized Test

Test Tip  Spend no more than a few minutes on each question. Return to time-consuming questions once you've completed the others.

1. What is the slope-intercept form of the equation of the line that has slope 2 and y-intercept $\frac{2}{7}$?

   (A) $y = -\frac{2}{7}x + 2$ (B) $y = 2x + \frac{2}{7}$

   (C) $y = \frac{2}{7}x + 2$ (D) $-14x + y = 7$

2. What is the equation of the line that passes through the point $(4, -5)$ and has slope $\frac{1}{2}$?

   (A) $y = 4x - 5$ (B) $y = -\frac{1}{2}x + 7$

   (C) $y = \frac{1}{2}x + 7$ (D) $y = \frac{1}{2}x - 7$

3. An equation of the line parallel to the line $y = -2x - 3$ with a y-intercept of $-\frac{3}{4}$ is $\underline{\quad?\quad}$.

   (A) $y = -2x + \frac{3}{4}$ (B) $y = -2x - \frac{3}{4}$

   (C) $y = 2x - \frac{3}{4}$ (D) $y = \frac{1}{2}x - \frac{3}{4}$

4. What is the equation of the line that passes through the points $(8, -4)$ and $(6, 4)$?

   (A) $y = -\frac{1}{4}x + 28$

   (B) $y = -4x + 28$

   (C) $y = -\frac{1}{4}x + 7$

   (D) $y = -4x - 7$

5. What is the slope-intercept form of the equation of the line whose x-intercept is 3 and whose y-intercept is 5?

   (A) $y = \frac{5}{3}x + 5$ (B) $y = -\frac{3}{5}x + 5$

   (C) $y = -\frac{5}{3}x + 5$ (D) $y = \frac{3}{5}x + 5$

6. Which equation is in standard form with integer coefficients?

   (A) $x - \frac{1}{2}y = \frac{5}{2}$ (B) $y = 2x - 5$

   (C) $y = -5 + 2x$ (D) $-2x + y = -5$

7. What is the standard form of an equation of a line that passes through the point $(-6, 1)$ and has a slope of -2?

   (A) $2x + y = 13$

   (B) $2x - y = 11$

   (C) $2x + y = -11$

   (D) $\frac{1}{2}x + y = -13$

   (E) None of these

8. Which is the slope-intercept form of the equation of a line that is perpendicular to the line $y = 2x - 7$ and passes through the point $(-5, 6)$?

   (A) $x + 2y = -7$ (B) $y = -\frac{1}{2}x - \frac{7}{2}$

   (C) $y = -\frac{1}{2}x + \frac{1}{2}$ (D) $y = -\frac{1}{2}x + \frac{7}{2}$

Maintaining Skills

EXAMPLE 1 Numbers Lines

Draw the number line with a low number of negative ten and a high number of twenty-five using intervals of five.

Solution

❶ *Subtract* the low number from the high number. $25 - (-10) = 35$

❷ *Divide* the difference by the interval distance. $35 \div 5 = 7$

❸ *Create* a number line with seven equal parts, plus two sections at the ends.

❹ *Label* the number line.

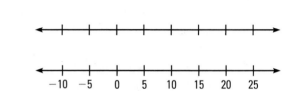

$$-10 \quad -5 \quad 0 \quad 5 \quad 10 \quad 15 \quad 20 \quad 25$$

Try These

Draw the number line described below.

1. A low number of negative twenty-one and a high number of twenty-eight with intervals of seven.

2. A low number of zero and a high number of sixteen with intervals of four.

3. A low number of zero and a high number of one hundred fifty with intervals of six.

4. A low number of ten and a high number of forty-six with intervals of nine.

EXAMPLE 2 Compare Decimals

Compare 0.045 and 0.0449.

Solution

0.045 is changed to 0.0450   Add zeros to make the two numbers end in the same place value.

0.0450 is larger than 0.0449   Compare the numbers.

$0.045 > 0.0449$ Use a greater than sign.

Try These

Compare the two numbers.

5. 0.033 and 0.0332   **6.** 0.005 and 0.0045   **7.** 0.0292 and 0.029

8. 0.006 and 0.00576   **9.** 0.01278 and 0.01   **10.** 0.007 and 0.065

11. 0.01 and 0.001   **12.** 0.0005 and 0.003   **13.** 0.0548 and 0.00549

CHAPTER 6

Solving and Graphing Linear Inequalities

▶ How can you describe sound?

APPLICATION: Music

Musical instruments produce vibrations in the air that we hear as sound. The *frequency* of a sound determines its pitch, that is, how high or low it sounds. When frequencies are measured as "cycles per second," we are using a unit called a *hertz*. The table below shows the frequency ranges of three different musical instruments.

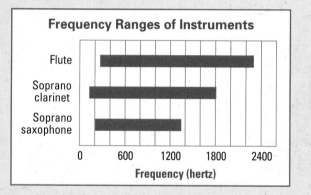

Frequency Ranges of Instruments

Think & Discuss

1. Estimate the frequency range of each instrument.

2. Which of these instruments has the greatest frequency range?

Learn More About It

You will write inequalities to describe frequency ranges in Exercises 23–26 on page 346.

APPLICATION LINK More information about music is available at www.mcdougallittell.com

PREVIEW **What's the chapter about?**

- Solving and graphing **inequalities**
- Solving and graphing **absolute-value equations** and **absolute-value inequalities**

KEY WORDS

- **graph of an inequality,** *p. 323*
- **addition property of inequality,** *p. 324*
- **subtraction property of inequality,** *p. 324*
- **multiplication property of inequality,** *pp. 330, 331*
- **division property of inequality,** *pp. 330, 331*
- **compound inequality** *p. 342*
- **absolute-value equation,** *p. 355*
- **absolute-value inequality,** *p. 361*
- **linear inequality in two variables,** *p. 367*

PREPARE **Chapter Readiness Quiz**

Take this quick quiz. If you are unsure of an answer, look back at the reference pages for help.

VOCABULARY CHECK *(refer to p. 26)*

1. Which of the following is *not* an inequality?

    (A) $x - 2 < 1$ **(B)** $6n - 4 \geq 26$ **(C)** $5a + 1 = 11$ **(D)** $y \leq -5$

SKILL CHECK *(refer to pp. 26, 151, 215)*

2. Which inequality has 5 as one solution?

    (A) $1 + 2x \geq 12$ **(B)** $3x - 2 \leq 13$ **(C)** $8 + x < 12$ **(D)** $4x > 28$

3. Which number is a solution of the equation $6x + 8 = 36 + 2x$?

    (A) 3   **(B)** 6   **(C)** 7   **(D)** 12

4. Which is the equation that represents the graph shown at the right?

    (A) $y = x + 1$ **(B)** $y = x - 1$

    (C) $y = -x + 1$ **(D)** $y = -x - 1$

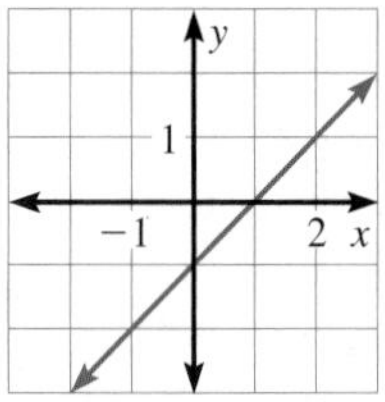

STUDY TIP **Check Your Work**

Showing all your steps when you do your homework helps you to find errors.

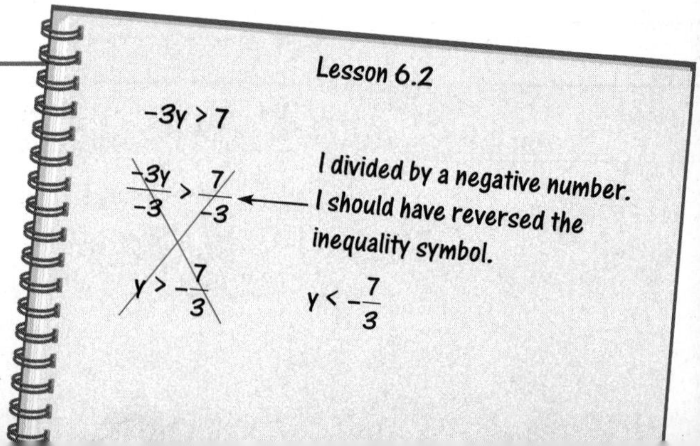

Lesson 6.2

$-3y > 7$

$\dfrac{-3y}{-3} > \dfrac{7}{-3}$ ← I divided by a negative number. I should have reversed the inequality symbol.

$y > -\dfrac{7}{3}$ $y < -\dfrac{7}{3}$

Solving Inequalities Using Addition or Subtraction

Goal

Solve and graph one-step inequalities in one variable using addition or subtraction.

Key Words

- graph of an inequality
- equivalent inequalities
- addition property of inequality
- subtraction property of inequality

How far away are the stars?

The star that appears brightest in the night sky is Sirius. Sirius is very far from Earth. It takes nearly 9 years for its light to reach us. In Example 4 you will write an inequality to describe even greater distances.

The **graph of an inequality** in one variable is the set of points on a number line that represent all solutions of the inequality. If the endpoint on the graph is a solution, draw a solid dot. If it is not a solution, draw an open dot. Draw an arrowhead to show that the graph continues on indefinitely.

Student Help

▶READING ALGEBRA
An open dot in a graph represents < or > inequalities. A solid dot represents ≤ or ≥ inequalities.

EXAMPLE 1 Graph an Inequality in One Variable

Write a verbal phrase to describe the inequality. Then graph the inequality.

a. $x < 2$ **b.** $a > -2$ **c.** $z \leq 1$ **d.** $d \geq 0$

Solution

INEQUALITY	VERBAL PHRASE	GRAPH
a. $x < 2$	All real numbers less than 2	$-3\ -2\ -1\ \ 0\ \ 1\ \ 2\ \ 3$
b. $a > -2$	All real numbers greater than -2	$-3\ -2\ -1\ \ 0\ \ 1\ \ 2\ \ 3$
c. $z \leq 1$	All real numbers less than or equal to 1	$-3\ -2\ -1\ \ 0\ \ 1\ \ 2\ \ 3$
d. $d \geq 0$	All real numbers greater than or equal to 0	$-3\ -2\ -1\ \ 0\ \ 1\ \ 2\ \ 3$

Checkpoint ✓ Graph an Inequality in One Variable

Write a verbal phrase to describe the inequality. Then graph the inequality.

1. $t > 1$ **2.** $x \geq -1$ **3.** $n < 0$ **4.** $y \leq 4$

A *solution* of an inequality in one variable is a value of the variable that makes the inequality true. To solve such an inequality, you may have to rewrite it as a simpler *equivalent inequality*. **Equivalent inequalities** have the same solutions. Adding the same number to, or subtracting the same number from, each side of an inequality in one variable produces an equivalent inequality.

$$3 < 7$$
$$3 + 2 < 7 + 2$$
$$5 < 9$$

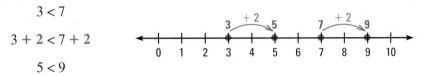

Student Help

▶**STUDY TIP**
The properties are stated for > and < inequalities. They are also true for ≥ and ≤ inequalities.

PROPERTIES OF INEQUALITY

Addition Property of Inequality

For all real numbers a, b, and c: If $a > b$, then $a + c > b + c$.
                                              If $a < b$, then $a + c < b + c$.

Subtraction Property of Inequality

For all real numbers a, b, and c: If $a > b$, then $a - c > b - c$.
                                              If $a < b$, then $a - c < b - c$.

EXAMPLE 2 Use Subtraction to Solve an Inequality

Solve $x + 5 \geq 3$. Then graph the solution.

Solution

$x + 5 \geq 3$	Write original inequality.
$x + 5 - 5 \geq 3 - 5$	Subtract 5 from each side.
	(Subtraction Property of Inequality)
▶ $x \geq -2$	Simplify.

Student Help

▶**STUDY TIP**
To check solutions, choose numbers that make the arithmetic easy. For Example 2 you could check zero as a value of x.
$$0 + 5 \overset{?}{\geq} 3$$
$$5 \geq 3 \checkmark$$

ANSWER ▶ The solution is all real numbers greater than or equal to -2. Check several numbers that are greater than or equal to -2 in the original inequality. The graph of the solution is shown below.

You cannot check all the solutions of an inequality. Instead, choose several solutions. Substitute them in the original inequality. Be sure they make it true. Then choose several numbers that are *not* solutions. Be sure they do *not* make the original inequality true.

Checkpoint ✓ *Use Subtraction to Solve an Inequality*

Solve the inequality. Then graph the solution.

5. $x + 4 < 7$ **6.** $n + 6 \geq 2$ **7.** $5 > a + 5$

EXAMPLE **3** Use Addition to Solve an Inequality

Solve $-2 > n - 4$. Then graph the solution.

Solution

$$-2 > n - 4 \qquad \text{Write original inequality.}$$

$$-2 + 4 > n - 4 + 4 \qquad \text{Add 4 to each side.}$$
$$\text{(Addition Property of Inequality)}$$

▶ $2 > n \qquad \text{Simplify.}$

ANSWER ▶ The solution is all real numbers less than 2. Check the solution. The graph of the solution is shown below.

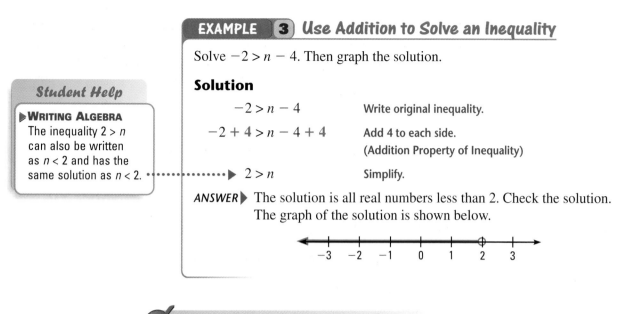

Checkpoint ✓ **Use Addition to Solve an Inequality**

Solve the inequality. Then graph the solution.

8. $x - 5 \geq 2$ **9.** $p - 1 \leq -4$ **10.** $-3 < y - 2$

Link to
Science

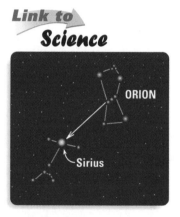

ORION

Sirius

ASTRONOMY You can use the constellation Orion to locate Sirius. Orion's belt points southwest to Sirius.

EXAMPLE **4** Write and Graph an Inequality in One Variable

ASTRONOMY A *light year* is the distance light travels in a year. One light year is about 6,000,000,000,000 miles. The star Sirius is about 8.8 light years from Earth. Write an inequality that describes distances to points in space that are farther from Earth than Sirius is. Then graph the inequality.

Solution Let d be the distance in light years of any point in space that is farther from Earth than Sirius is.

Write the inequality in words:	The distance is greater than 8.8.
Translate into mathematical symbols:	$d > 8.8$

ANSWER ▶ The inequality is $d > 8.8$. The graph of the inequality is shown below.

Checkpoint ✓ **Write and Graph an Inequality in One Variable**

11. In Example 4, suppose that d represented distances to points in space whose distance from Earth is greater than or equal to the distance from Earth to Sirius. How would the inequality change? How would the graph change?

12. Deneb is about 1600 light years from Earth. Write an inequality that describes the distances to points in space that are farther from Earth than Deneb is. Then graph the inequality.

Exercises

Guided Practice

Vocabulary Check

1. Describe the graph of an inequality of the form $x \geq a$.

2. Explain why $x - 6 > 10$ and $x > 16$ are equivalent inequalities.

Skill Check

Decide whether you would use an open dot or a solid dot to graph the inequality.

3. $a < 3$ **4.** $10 < k$ **5.** $j \geq -1$

6. $m + 5 < 4$ **7.** $x - 3 \geq 12$ **8.** $-1 \leq 3 + t$

Tell whether the arrow on the graph of the inequality points to the right or to the left.

9. $x < 8$ **10.** $y \geq 20$ **11.** $7 + a < 28$

12. $t + 8 \leq 12$ **13.** $-6 > r - 5$ **14.** $k - 8 \geq -1$

Practice and Applications

DESCRIBING INEQUALITIES Write a verbal phrase to describe the inequality.

15. $z < 8$ **16.** $t \leq -3$ **17.** $p \geq 21$ **18.** $m > 0$

CHECKING SOLUTIONS Check to see if the given number is or is not a solution of the inequality graphed below.

19. 3   **20.** -3 **21.** 0   **22.** -1

GRAPHING Match the inequality with its graph.

23. $n > -2$ **24.** $y < -2$ **25.** $x \geq 2$

26. $w \leq -2$ **27.** $2 \geq z$ **28.** $2 < c$

A.   **B.**   **C.**

D.   **E.**   **F.**

Student Help

▶**HOMEWORK HELP**
Example 1: Exs. 15–28
Examples 2 and 3:
        Exs. 29–52
Example 4: Exs. 53–57

USING INVERSE OPERATIONS Tell which number you would add to or subtract from each side of the inequality to solve it.

29. $k + 11 < -3$ **30.** $h - 2 > 14$ **31.** $r + 6 \leq -6$

32. $31 \leq -4 + y$ **33.** $-7 > -3 + x$ **34.** $17 + z \leq -6$

SOLVING AND MATCHING Solve the inequality. Then match the solution with its graph.

35. $d + 4 \leq 6$

36. $x - 3 > 2$

37. $q + 12 \geq 4$

38. $h + 6 \leq -2$

39. $s - 5 \geq -5$

40. $v - 3 < 2$

A. ⟨—+—●—+—+—+—→
       −1 0 1 2 3

B. ⟨—+—+—+—●—+—→
       −10 −9 −8 −7 −6

C. ⟨—+—+—○—+—+—→
       3 4 5 6 7

D. ⟨—+—+—+—●—+—→
       −1 0 1 2 3

E. ⟨—+—+—○—+—+—→
       3 4 5 6 7

F. ⟨—+—+—●—+—+—→
       −10 −9 −8 −7 −6

Student Help

▶ **HOMEWORK HELP**

Extra help with problem solving in Exs. 41–55 is available at www.mcdougallittell.com

SOLVING AND GRAPHING Solve the inequality. Then graph the solution.

41. $x + 6 < 8$

42. $-5 < 4 + f$

43. $-4 + f < 20$

44. $8 + w \leq -9$

45. $p - 12 \geq -1$

46. $-2 > b - 5$

47. $-8 \leq x - 14$

48. $m + 7 \geq -10$

49. $-6 > c - 4$

50. $-2 + z < 0$

51. $-10 > a - 6$

52. $5 + r \geq -5$

53. $x - 5 \geq 7$

54. $14 \leq 8 + n$

55. $c + 11 < 25$

56. CRITICAL THINKING Jesse finished a 200 meter dash in 35 seconds. Let r represent any rate of speed in meters per second faster than Jesse's.

a. Write an inequality that describes r. Then graph the inequality.

b. Every point on the graph represents a rate faster than Jesse's. Do you think every point could represent the rate of a runner?

Link to
Science

MERCURY The melting point of mercury is the temperature at which mercury becomes a liquid. Mercury is the only metal that is a liquid at room temperature.

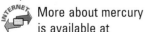
More about mercury is available at www.mcdougallittell.com

57. WALKING RACE A racer finished a 5 kilometer walking race in 45 minutes. Let r represent any faster rate in kilometers per minute. Write an inequality that describes r.

58. Science Link Mercury has the lowest melting point of any metallic element, $-38.87°C$. Let p represent the melting point in degrees Celsius of any other metallic element. Write an inequality that describes p.

59. ASTRONOMICAL DISTANCES The star Altair is about 5 parsecs from Earth. (A parsec is about 3.26 light years.) Let d represent the distance from Earth of any point in space that is more distant than Altair. Write an inequality that describes d in light years. Then graph the inequality.

60. SHARKS On July 27, 1999, a mako shark weighing 1324 pounds was caught off the coast of Massachusetts by a fisherman named Kevin Scola. It was the biggest mako shark ever caught using a rod and reel. Let w represent the possible weight in pounds of any mako shark caught before that time using a rod and reel. Write and graph an inequality that shows all possible values of w.

Photo by Kevin Scola of the fishing vessel *Survival*

61.

$x + 4 < 1$
$x < 1 + 4$
$x < 5$

62.

$-9 \geq -10 + b$
$-9 \geq -10 + 10 + b$
$-9 \geq b$

Standardized Test Practice

63. MULTIPLE CHOICE Which statement about the inequality $x - 3 \geq 2$ is true?

(A) The arrow on its graph points to the left.

(B) -1 is a solution.

(C) The dot on its graph is solid.

(D) 5 is not a solution.

64. MULTIPLE CHOICE Which number is *not* a solution of the inequality $-5 + t < 7$?

(F) 12   (G) -12 (H) 0   (J) 5

Mixed Review

SOLVING EQUATIONS Solve the equation. *(Lesson 3.3)*

65. $4x - 3 = 21$ **66.** $-5x + 10 = 30$ **67.** $-3s - 2 = -44$

68. $\frac{1}{3}x + 5 = -4$ **69.** $\frac{1}{2}(a + 4) = 18$ **70.** $\frac{3}{5}(x - 5) = 6$

71. $n + 2n + 5 = 14$ **72.** $3(x - 6) = 12$ **73.** $9 = -3(x - 2)$

74. BIKE RIDING You ride an exercise bike each day. The table below shows the time t in minutes and the distance d in miles that you rode on each of four days. Write a model that relates the variables d and t. *(Lesson 4.5)*

Time t	5	10	12	15
Distance d	0.60	1.20	1.44	1.80

WRITING EQUATIONS Write in slope-intercept form the equation of the line that passes through the given points. *(Lesson 5.3)*

75. $(1, 2), (4, -1)$ **76.** $(2, 0), (-4, -3)$ **77.** $(1, 1), (-3, 5)$

78. $(-1, 4), (2, 4)$ **79.** $(-1, -3), (2, 3)$ **80.** $(8, 1), (5, -2)$

81. $(-2, 4), (4, 2)$ **82.** $(1, -5), (6, 5)$ **83.** $(-3, 6), (2, 8)$

Maintaining Skills

RECIPROCALS Find the reciprocal. *(Skills Review p. 763)*

84. $\frac{4}{5}$ **85.** $-\frac{1}{3}$ **86.** $\frac{24}{25}$ **87.** $-\frac{7}{32}$

88. $\frac{2}{5}$ **89.** $-\frac{8}{15}$ **90.** 3   **91.** -1

92. 4   **93.** 9   **94.** $-\frac{8}{11}$ **95.** $\frac{5}{8}$

GOAL

Use reasoning to determine whether operations change an inequality.

MATERIALS

• paper
• pencil

Question How do operations affect an inequality?

Explore

1 Write a true inequality by choosing two different numbers and placing the appropriate symbol < or > between them.

2 Copy and complete the table. Apply the given rule to each side of your inequality. Write the correct inequality symbol between the resulting numbers.

Original inequality	Rule	Resulting inequality	Did you have to reverse the inequality?
?	Add 4.	?	?
?	Add −4.	?	?
?	Subtract 4.	?	?
?	Subtract −4.	?	?
?	Multiply by 4.	?	?
?	Multiply by −4.	?	?
?	Divide by 4.	?	?
?	Divide by −4.	?	?

3 Repeat Step 2 using different positive and negative integers.

Think About It

Using your results from Steps 2 and 3, predict whether the inequality symbol will change when you apply the given rule. Check your prediction.

1. $4 < 9$; add 7.　　　**2.** $15 > 12$; subtract −5.　**3.** $4 > -3$; multiply by 5.

4. $1 < 8$; multiply by −10.　**5.** $-6 < 2$; divide by −3.　**6.** $0 < 8$; divide by 2.

7. LOGICAL REASONING Copy and complete the table.

Must you reverse the inequality?		
	a positive number	a negative number
Add	?	?
Subtract	?	?
Multiply by	?	?
Divide by	?	?

Solving Inequalities Using Multiplication or Division

Goal

Solve and graph one-step inequalities in one variable using multiplication or division.

Key Words

- multiplication property of inequality
- division property of inequality

Should you rent or buy ice skates?

Aisha wants to learn to figure skate. Should she rent skates or buy them? In Exercise 56 you will solve an inequality to help her decide.

The results of Developing Concepts 6.2, page 329, suggest that you can solve an inequality by multiplying or dividing each side by the same *positive* number, *c*.

Developing Concepts 6.2, page 329

Student Help

▶ **STUDY TIP**
The properties are stated for > and < inequalities. They are also true for ≥ and ≤ inequalities.

PROPERTIES OF INEQUALITY

Multiplication Property of Inequality ($c > 0$)

For all real numbers a, b, and for $c > 0$:   If $a > b$, then $ac > bc$.
If $a < b$, then $ac < bc$.

Division Property of Inequality ($c > 0$)

For all real numbers a, b, and for $c > 0$:   If $a > b$, then $\dfrac{a}{c} > \dfrac{b}{c}$.

If $a < b$, then $\dfrac{a}{c} < \dfrac{b}{c}$.

EXAMPLE 1   Multiply by a Positive Number

$\dfrac{a}{4} \le 10$ Original inequality.

$4 \cdot \dfrac{a}{4} \le 4 \cdot 10$ Multiply each side by 4.
(Multiplication Property of Inequality)

$a \le 40$ Simplify.

ANSWER ▶ The solution is all real numbers less than or equal to 40. The graph of the solution is shown below.

```
<------+----+----+----+----+----●--->
      -10   0   10   20   30   40
```

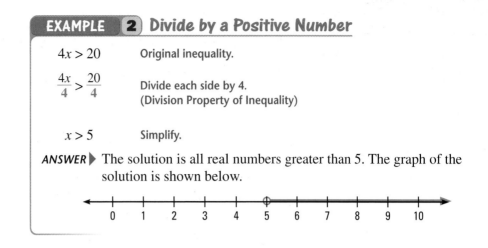

EXAMPLE **2** **Divide by a Positive Number**

$4x > 20$	Original inequality.
$\dfrac{4x}{4} > \dfrac{20}{4}$	Divide each side by 4. (Division Property of Inequality)
$x > 5$	Simplify.

ANSWER ▶ The solution is all real numbers greater than 5. The graph of the solution is shown below.

← | | | | | ⊕ | | | | →
0   1   2   3   4   5   6   7   8   9   10

Checkpoint ✓   *Multiply or Divide by a Positive Number*

Solve the inequality. Then graph the solution.

1. $\dfrac{k}{4} < \dfrac{1}{2}$ **2.** $18 \le 2k$ **3.** $6 < \dfrac{t}{5}$ **4.** $-21 < 3y$

The results of Developing Concepts 6.2, page 329, suggest that you must *reverse*, or change the direction of, the inequality when you multiply or divide each side by the same *negative* number, c.

Student Help

▶**WRITING ALGEBRA**
To reverse an inequality:
    < becomes >
    ≤ becomes ≥
    > becomes <
    ≥ becomes ≤

PROPERTIES OF INEQUALITY

Multiplication Property of Inequality ($c < 0$)

For all real numbers a, b, and for $c < 0$:   If $a > b$, then $ac < bc$.
                                             If $a < b$, then $ac > bc$.

Division Property of Inequality ($c < 0$)

For all real numbers a, b, and for $c < 0$:   If $a > b$, then $\dfrac{a}{c} < \dfrac{b}{c}$.

                                             If $a < b$, then $\dfrac{a}{c} > \dfrac{b}{c}$.

EXAMPLE **3** **Multiply by a Negative Number**

$-\dfrac{1}{2}y \le 5$	Original inequality.
$-2\left(-\dfrac{1}{2}y\right) \ge -2(5)$	Multiply each side by -2 and reverse the inequality.
$y \ge -10$	Simplify.

ANSWER ▶ The solution is all real numbers greater than or equal to -10. The graph of the solution is shown below.

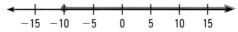

Student Help

▶**MORE EXAMPLES**

More examples are available at www.mcdougallittell.com

EXAMPLE 4 **Divide by a Negative Number**

Solve the inequality. Then graph the solution.

a. $-12m > 18$ **b.** $-8x \le 20$

Solution

a. $-12m > 18$ Write original inequality.

$\dfrac{-12m}{-12} < \dfrac{18}{-12}$ Divide each side by -12 and reverse the inequality.

$m < -1.5$ Simplify.

ANSWER▶ The solution is all real numbers less than -1.5. The graph of the solution is shown below.

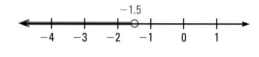

b. $-8x \le 20$ Write original inequality.

$\dfrac{-8x}{-8} \ge \dfrac{20}{-8}$ Divide each side by -8 and reverse the inequality.

$x \ge -2.5$ Simplify.

ANSWER▶ The solution is all real numbers greater than or equal to -2.5. The graph of the solution is shown below.

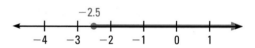

Checkpoint ✓ **Multiply or Divide by a Negative Number**

Solve the inequality. Then graph the solution.

5. $-\dfrac{1}{5}p > 1$ **6.** $-\dfrac{2}{3}x < -5$ **7.** $-\dfrac{1}{4}k \le -4$

8. $-14z \ge -70$ **9.** $-24 \le 6t$ **10.** $12 > -5n$

SUMMARY

Properties of Inequality

For all real numbers a, b, and c:

• If $a > b$, then $a + c > b + c$ and $a - c > b - c$.

• If $a < b$, then $a + c < b + c$ and $a - c < b - c$.

• If $a > b$ and $c > 0$, then $ac > bc$ and $\dfrac{a}{c} > \dfrac{b}{c}$.

• If $a > b$ and $c < 0$, then $ac < bc$ and $\dfrac{a}{c} < \dfrac{b}{c}$.

Guided Practice

Vocabulary Check

1. Explain what "reverse the inequality" means.

2. Are the inequalities $-x < 2$ and $2 < -x$ equivalent? Explain.

Skill Check

Describe the first step you would use to solve the inequality. Then tell whether you would reverse the inequality.

3. $\frac{c}{5} > 3$ **4.** $-9 \le \frac{y}{2}$ **5.** $4w > 48$

6. $-56 \ge 8d$ **7.** $-\frac{1}{6}b < 3$ **8.** $-4 \ge -d$

Tell whether the inequalities are equivalent. Explain your reasoning.

9. $-k \ge 42,\ k \ge -42$ **10.** $-\frac{2}{3} \le -g,\ g \le \frac{2}{3}$

11. $4 > -\frac{1}{7}c,\ c > -28$ **12.** $5z < -75,\ z > -15$

13. $-11x \ge 33,\ x \ge -3$ **14.** $-\frac{w}{3} \le -5,\ w \ge 15$

Practice and Applications

SOLVING INEQUALITIES **Describe the first step you would use to solve the inequality. Then tell whether you would reverse the inequality.**

15. $\frac{n}{3} \ge 6$ **16.** $81 < 9t$ **17.** $\frac{v}{2} \ge -26$ **18.** $2r \le -2$

19. $-7k > -56$ **20.** $4 > -\frac{1}{3}y$ **21.** $48 < -3b$ **22.** $-\frac{d}{6} < -6$

GRAPHING INEQUALITIES **Tell whether the graph below is the graph of the solution of the inequality.**

23. $-\frac{z}{6} \le -1$ **24.** $-\frac{1}{3}z \le 2$ **25.** $5z \ge 30$ **26.** $2z \ge 12$

LOGICAL REASONING **Tell whether the inequalities are equivalent. Explain your reasoning.**

27. $12y > -24;\ y < -2$ **28.** $-\frac{1}{8}m \ge -3;\ m \ge 24$

29. $15 < -b;\ -15 > b$ **30.** $\frac{1}{3}n < -2;\ n > -6$

31. $8 \le -\frac{1}{2}m;\ -16 \ge m$ **32.** $20b \ge -2;\ b \le -\frac{1}{10}$

Student Help

▶ **HOMEWORK HELP**
Examples 1 and 2:
   Exs. 15–18, 23–55
Examples 3 and 4:
   Exs. 19–22, 23–52

ERROR ANALYSIS In Exercises 33 and 34, find and correct the error.

33.

$$-3x \geq 15$$
$$\frac{-3x}{-3} \geq \frac{15}{-3}$$
$$x \geq -5$$

34.
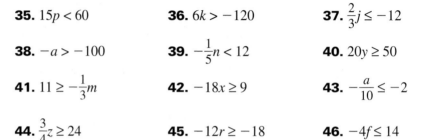
$$-\frac{1}{2}x \leq 0$$
$$-2\left(-\frac{1}{2}x\right) \geq -2(0)$$
$$x \geq -2$$

SOLVING INEQUALITIES Solve the inequality. Then graph the solution.

35. $15p < 60$

36. $6k > -120$

37. $\frac{2}{3}j \leq -12$

38. $-a > -100$

39. $-\frac{1}{5}n < 12$

40. $20y \geq 50$

41. $11 \geq -\frac{1}{3}m$

42. $-18x \geq 9$

43. $-\frac{a}{10} \leq -2$

44. $\frac{3}{4}z \geq 24$

45. $-12r \geq -18$

46. $-4f \leq 14$

ESTIMATION Estimate the solution and explain your method.

47. $10 > 1.999d$

48. $\frac{1}{2}r \leq -50.1155$

49. $-\frac{1}{3}a \geq 5.91$

LOGICAL REASONING Complete the statement with *always*, *sometimes*, or *never*.

50. If k is greater than 0, then kx is __?__ greater than 0.

51. If k is greater than 0 and x is greater than zero, then kx is __?__ greater than 0.

52. If k is less than 0, then kx is __?__ greater than 0.

53. If k is less than 0 and x is greater than zero, then kx is __?__ greater than 0.

54. POSTERS You want to buy some posters to decorate your dorm room. Posters are on sale for $5 each. Write and solve an inequality to determine how many posters you can buy and spend no more than $25.

55. FUNDRAISING Musicians are planning a fundraiser for local farmers. The admission fee will be $20. Write and solve an inequality to determine how many tickets must be sold to raise at least $25,000.

56. FIGURE SKATING Aisha plans to take figure skating lessons. She can rent skates for $5 per lesson. She can buy skates for $75. For what number of lessons is it cheaper for Aisha to buy rather than rent skates?

57. SUBWAY You can ride the subway one-way for $.85. A monthly pass costs $27.00. For what number of rides is it cheaper to pay the one-way fare than to buy the monthly pass?

58. CHALLENGE Solve the inequality $\frac{4}{x} \geq 2$ by multiplying each side by x.

HINT: Consider the cases $x > 0$ and $x < 0$ separately.

59. MULTIPLE CHOICE Which inequality is represented by the graph?

$$\xleftarrow{\hspace{0.3cm}} \overset{-2}{\mid} \quad \overset{-1}{\mid} \quad \overset{0}{\mid} \quad \overset{1}{\mid} \quad \overset{2}{\mid} \quad \overset{3}{\bullet} \quad \overset{4}{\mid} \quad \overset{5}{\mid} \xrightarrow{\hspace{0.3cm}}$$

Ⓐ $3x \geq 9$ Ⓑ $24 \geq 8y$ Ⓒ $\frac{r}{3} \geq 0$ Ⓓ $-6 \leq -\frac{a}{2}$

60. MULTIPLE CHOICE Which inequality is *not* equivalent to $k \leq -3$?

Ⓕ $3 \geq -k$ Ⓖ $-3k \geq 9$ Ⓗ $k + 4 \leq 1$ Ⓙ $\frac{2}{3}k \leq -2$

61. MULTIPLE CHOICE Solve $-5x \leq -10$.

Ⓐ $x \leq -2$ Ⓑ $x \leq 2$ Ⓒ $x \geq -2$ Ⓓ $x \geq 2$

FINDING DIFFERENCES Find the difference. *(Lesson 2.4)*

62. $12 - 19$ **63.** $-6 - 8$ **64.** $3 - (-1)$

65. $-7 - (-7)$ **66.** $-9 - 9$ **67.** $0 - (-2)$

FINDING QUOTIENTS Find the quotient. *(Lesson 2.8)*

68. $52 \div (-26)$ **69.** $-8 \div 2$ **70.** $-10 \div (-2)$

71. $-3 \div \frac{1}{9}$ **72.** $23 \div \left(-\frac{1}{2}\right)$ **73.** $-15 \div \left(-1\frac{2}{3}\right)$

SOLVING EQUATIONS Solve the equation. Check your solution in the original equation. *(Lesson 3.5)*

74. $2(x + 5) = 5(x - 1)$ **75.** $-4(y + 3) = -(6 - 2y)$

76. $8 - (c + 7) = 6(11 - c)$ **77.** $3(-x - 2) = 2x + 2(4 + x)$

SOLVING FORMULAS Solve the formula for the indicated variable. *(Lesson 3.7)*

78. $d = \dfrac{m}{v}$ **79.** $A = \dfrac{1}{2}bh$ **80.** $P = a + b + c$

Solve for m.   Solve for b.   Solve for c.

81. IDENTIFYING ORDERED PAIRS
Write the ordered pairs that correspond to the points labeled A, B, C, and D in the coordinate plane at the right. *(Lesson 4.1)*

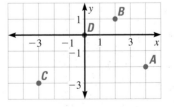

FACTORS List all the factors of the number. *(Skills Review p. 761)*

82. 98 **83.** 140 **84.** 114

85. 144 **86.** 289 **87.** 425

88. 1064 **89.** 2223 **90.** 5480

6.3 Solving Multi-Step Inequalities

Goal
Solve and graph multi-step inequalities in one variable.

Key Words
• multi-step inequality

Can you make a profit selling fishing flies?

In fishing, a fly is a lure that is made to look like a real insect. In Example 5 you will use an inequality to figure out how you can make a profit selling fishing flies.

The inequalities in Lessons 6.1 and 6.2 could be solved in one step using one operation. A multi-step inequality requires more than one operation.

EXAMPLE 1 Solve a Multi-Step Inequality

Solve $2y - 5 < 7$.

Solution

$2y - 5 < 7$	Write original inequality.
$2y < 12$	Add 5 to each side.
$y < 6$	Divide each side by 2.

ANSWER ▶ The solution is all real numbers less than 6.

EXAMPLE 2 Solve a Multi-Step Inequality

Solve $5 - x > 4$.

Solution

$5 - x > 4$	Write original inequality.
$-x > -1$	Subtract 5 from each side.
$x < 1$	Multiply each side by -1 and reverse the inequality.

ANSWER ▶ The solution is all real numbers less than 1.

Checkpoint ✓ Solve a Multi-Step Inequality

Solve the inequality.

1. $3x - 5 > 4$ **2.** $10 - n \leq 5$

Student Help

▶**MORE EXAMPLES**

INTERNET More examples are available at www.mcdougallittell.com

EXAMPLE **3** **Use the Distributive Property**

Solve $3(x + 2) < 7$.

Solution

$3(x + 2) < 7$	Write original inequality.
$3x + 6 < 7$	Use distributive property.
$3x < 1$	Subtract 6 from each side.
$x < \dfrac{1}{3}$	Divide each side by 3.

ANSWER ▶ The solution is all real numbers less than $\dfrac{1}{3}$.

Checkpoint ✓ **Use the Distributive Property**

Use the distributive property as the first step in solving the inequality. Then tell what the next step is and solve the inequality.

3. $3(n - 4) \geq 6$ **4.** $-2(x + 1) < 2$

EXAMPLE **4** **Collect Variable Terms**

Solve $2x - 3 \geq 4x - 1$.

Solution

Method 1

$2x - 3 \geq 4x - 1$	Write original inequality.
$2x \geq 4x + 2$	Add 3 to each side.
$-2x \geq 2$	Subtract 4x from each side.
$x \leq -1$	Divide each side by -2 and reverse the inequality.

Method 2

$2x - 3 \geq 4x - 1$	Write original inequality.
$-3 \geq 2x - 1$	Subtract 2x from each side.
$-2 \geq 2x$	Add 1 to each side.
$-1 \geq x$	Divide each side by 2.

ANSWER ▶ The solution is all real numbers less than or equal to -1.

Student Help

▶**STUDY TIP**
To avoid concerns about reversing the inequality, first collect variable terms on the side whose variable term has the greater coefficient.

Checkpoint ✓ **Collect Variable Terms**

Solve the inequality and describe the steps you used.

5. $5n - 21 < 8n$ **6.** $-3z + 15 > 2z$

7. $x + 3 \geq 2x - 4$ **8.** $4y - 3 < -y + 12$

FLY-FISHING A fishing fly is made by attaching feathers, pieces of shiny metal, or colored thread to a fishhook. The process is known as "tying flies."

EXAMPLE 5 **Write and Use a Linear Model**

FLY-FISHING You want to start tying and selling fishing flies. You purchase the book shown in the advertisement. The materials for each fly cost $.20. You plan to sell each fly for $.60. How many fishing flies must you sell to make a profit of at least $200?

Learn to tie flies at home for profit

Illustrated step-by-step book shows you how!

Send **$13.95** plus **$1.05** for shipping and handling to:

Solution

Profit is equal to income minus expenses. To find your income, multiply the price per fly by the number sold. Your total expenses include the cost of materials, $.20 per fly, and the cost of the book, $15.

VERBAL MODEL

$$\boxed{\frac{\text{Price}}{\text{per fly}}} \cdot \boxed{\frac{\text{Number of}}{\text{flies sold}}} - \boxed{\frac{\text{Total}}{\text{expenses}}} \geq \boxed{\frac{\text{Desired}}{\text{profit}}}$$

LABELS

Price per fly $= \mathbf{0.60}$ (dollars per fly)

Number of flies sold $= \boxed{x}$ (flies)

Total expenses $= \mathbf{0.20}\,\boxed{x} + \mathbf{15}$ (dollars)

Desired profit $\geq \mathbf{200}$ (dollars)

ALGEBRAIC MODEL

$0.60\,\boxed{x} - (0.20\,\boxed{x} + 15) \geq 200$ Write algebraic model.

$0.60x - 0.20x - 15 \geq 200$ Use distributive property.

$0.4x - 15 \geq 200$ Combine like terms.

$0.4x \geq 215$ Add 15 to each side.

$x \geq 537.5$ Divide each side by 0.4.

ANSWER ▶ You cannot sell half a fishing fly. So you must sell at least 538 flies to make a profit of at least $200.

Student Help

▶ **STUDY TIP**
Be sure to interpret the solution to reflect the real-life situation.

Checkpoint ✓ **Write and Use a Linear Model**

You plan to make and sell candles. You pay $12 for instructions. The materials for each candle cost $0.50. You plan to sell each candle for $2. Let x be the number of candles you sell.

9. Write an algebraic expression for each quantity.

     a. your income   **b.** cost of materials

     c. total expenses   **d.** your profit

10. Write and solve an inequality to determine how many candles you must sell to make a profit of at least $300.

Guided Practice

Vocabulary Check

1. Explain why $3a + 6 \geq 0$ is a multi-step inequality.

2. Describe the steps you could use to solve the inequality $-3y + 2 > 11$.

Skill Check

Determine whether the inequality is a multi-step inequality. Then explain how you would solve the inequality.

3. $d + 2 > -1$
4. $\frac{3}{4}a < 0$
5. $-4x \geq -12$

6. $4y - 3 < 13$
7. $5x + 12 \leq 62$
8. $10 - c \geq 6$

9. $\frac{1}{2}b + 2 > 6$
10. $3m + 2 \leq 7m$
11. $2w - 1 > 6w + 2$

Practice and Applications

COMPLETING THE SOLUTIONS Copy and complete the exercise to solve the inequality.

12.
$$4x - 3 \geq 21$$
$$4x - 3 + \boxed{?} \geq 21 + \boxed{?}$$
$$\frac{4x}{4} \geq \frac{\boxed{?}}{4}$$
$$x \geq \boxed{?}$$

13.
$$7 < 14 - k$$
$$7 - \boxed{?} < 14 - k - \boxed{?}$$
$$\boxed{?} < -k$$
$$-1(\boxed{?}) > -1(-k)$$
$$\boxed{?} > k$$

JUSTIFYING SOLUTIONS Describe the steps you would use to solve the inequality.

14. $7a - 4 < 17$
15. $11 - 2n > -5$
16. $\frac{3}{4}x + 5 > -15$

17. $22 + 3b \leq -2$
18. $\frac{4}{3}t + 5 > \frac{1}{3}t$
19. $6(z - 2) < 15$

SOLVING INEQUALITIES Solve the inequality.

20. $x + 5 > -13$
21. $-6 + 5x < 19$
22. $4x - 1 \leq -17$

23. $-5 \leq 6x - 12$
24. $-17 > 5x - 2$
25. $15 + x \geq 7$

26. $-x + 9 \geq 14$
27. $7 - 3x \leq 16$
28. $12 > -2x - 6$

Student Help

▶ **HOMEWORK HELP**
Examples 1 and 2:
      Exs. 12–30
Example 3: Exs. 31–43
Example 4: Exs. 36–43
Example 5: Exs. 44–52

MATCHING Match the inequality with its graph.

29. $3x + 9 > 6$
30. $-3x - 9 > 6$
31. $-3(x - 3) > 6$

A.
$$-1 \quad 0 \quad 1 \quad 2$$

B.
$$-10 \quad -5 \quad 0$$

C.
$$-2 \quad -1 \quad 0 \quad 1$$

SOLVING INEQUALITIES Solve the inequality.

32. $2(x - 4) \geq 3$

33. $\frac{1}{2}(x - 8) < 2$

34. $-(2x + 4) > 6$

35. $15 \leq \frac{3}{2}(x + 4)$

36. $-x - 4 > 3x - 2$

37. $6 + x \leq -4x + 1$

38. $2x + 10 \geq 7x + 7$

39. $9 - 3x > 5(-x + 2)$

40. $-3(x + 3) < 4x - 7$

41. $6(x + 2) > 3x - 2$

ERROR ANALYSIS In Exercises 42 and 43, find and correct the error.

42.
$$6x - 4 \geq 2x - 8$$
$$6x \geq 2x - 12$$
$$4x \geq -12$$
$$x \geq -3$$

43.
$$4(f - 1) < 3(2f + 1)$$
$$4f - 1 < 6f + 1$$
$$-2 < 2f$$
$$-1 < f$$

AMUSEMENT RIDE DESIGNERS use math and science to ensure rides are safe. An amusement ride designer usually has a degree in mechanical engineering.

More about amusement ride designers is available at www.mcdougallittell.com

AMUSEMENT RIDES In Exercises 44 and 45, use the following information.
An amusement park charges $5 for admission and $1.25 for each ride ticket. You have $25. How many ride tickets can you buy?

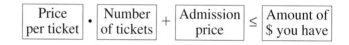

$$\boxed{\begin{array}{c}\text{Price} \\ \text{per ticket}\end{array}} \cdot \boxed{\begin{array}{c}\text{Number} \\ \text{of tickets}\end{array}} + \boxed{\begin{array}{c}\text{Admission} \\ \text{price}\end{array}} \leq \boxed{\begin{array}{c}\text{Amount of} \\ \$ \text{ you have}\end{array}}$$

44. Assign labels to the verbal model above and write the algebraic model.

45. Solve the inequality and interpret the result.

PIZZA TOPPINGS In Exercises 46–48, use the following information.
You have $18.50 to spend on pizza. A cheese pizza costs $14. Each extra topping costs $.75. How many extra toppings can you buy?

46. Write a verbal model to represent the problem.

47. Assign labels to your model and write the algebraic model.

48. Solve the inequality and interpret the result.

Student Help

▶ **SKILLS REVIEW**
For help with perimeter and area, see p. 772.

Geometry Link Write and solve an inequality for the values of *x*.

49. Perimeter > 26 meters

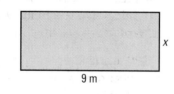

9 m

x

50. Perimeter ≤ 25 meters

x

x

51. Area < 12 square feet

x

8 ft

52. Area > 144 square inches

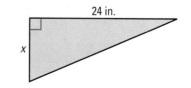

24 in.

x

53. MULTIPLE CHOICE Solve the inequality $2x - 10 > 3(-x + 5)$.

  (A) $x < 5$ **(B)** $x > -5$ **(C)** $x > 5$ **(D)** $x < -5$

54. MULTIPLE CHOICE Which number is *not* a solution of $4(x + 2) > 3x - 1$?

  (F) -10 **(G)** -8 **(H)** 0 **(J)** 10

Mixed Review

EVALUATING EXPRESSIONS Evaluate the expression. *(Lessons 1.1 and 1.2)*

55. $(a + 4) - 8$ when $a = 7$ **56.** $3x + 2$ when $x = -4$

57. $b^3 - 5$ when $b = 2$ **58.** $2(r + s)$ when $r = 2$ and $s = 4$

TRANSLATING SENTENCES Write the verbal sentence as an equation or an inequality. *(Lesson 1.5)*

59. Sarah's height h is 4 inches more than your height a.

60. The number c of cows is more than twice the number s of sheep.

61. SHOPPING You bought a pair of shoes for \$42.99, a shirt for \$14.50, and a pair of jeans for \$29.99. You used a coupon to save \$10 on your purchase. How much did you spend? *(Lesson 2.3)*

Maintaining Skills

MIXED NUMBERS AND IMPROPER FRACTIONS Write the mixed number as an improper fraction. *(Skills Review p. 763)*

62. $2\frac{1}{10}$ **63.** $1\frac{2}{7}$ **64.** $20\frac{6}{7}$ **65.** $3\frac{3}{4}$

Quiz 1

Graph the inequality. *(Lesson 6.1)*

1. $b > 12$ **2.** $j \geq -9$ **3.** $-8 > y$

Solve the inequality. Then graph the solution. *(Lessons 6.1 and 6.2)*

4. $a + 2 < 7$ **5.** $-3 + m \leq -11$ **6.** $-13 > b - 1$

7. $\frac{1}{3}z \geq -7$ **8.** $-\frac{3}{4}x \leq -27$ **9.** $105 > -15k$

10. RIDES A person must be at least 52 inches tall to ride the *Power Tower* ride at Cedar Point in Ohio. Let h represent the height of any person who meets the requirement. Write an inequality that describes h. *(Lesson 6.1)*

11. PLAYS It costs \$20 to attend a play at the playhouse. A season's pass costs \$180. For what number of plays is it cheaper to pay the \$20 price than to buy the season's pass? *(Lesson 6.2)*

Solve the inequality. *(Lesson 6.3)*

12. $5 \leq -\frac{x}{2} + 4$ **13.** $-4x + 2 \geq 14$ **14.** $-x - 4 > 3x - 12$

15. $-(-x + 8) > -10$ **16.** $-10 \leq -2(2x - 9)$ **17.** $x + 3 \leq 2(x - 7)$

6.4 Solving Compound Inequalities Involving "And"

Goal
Solve and graph compound inequalities involving *and*.

Key Words
• compound inequality

Where can plants grow on a mountain?

The types of plant life on a mountain depend on the elevation. At lower elevations, trees can grow. At higher elevations, there are flowering plants, but no trees. At very high elevations, there are no trees or flowering plants. In Example 2 you will use inequalities to describe such plant-life regions.

A **compound inequality** consists of two inequalities connected by the word *and* or the word *or*. You will study the first type of compound inequality in this lesson. You will study the second type in Lesson 6.5.

EXAMPLE 1 Write Compound Inequalities with *And*

Write a compound inequality that represents the set of all real numbers greater than or equal to 0 and less than 4. Then graph the inequality.

Solution

The set can be represented by two inequalities.

$$0 \le x \text{ and } x < 4$$

The two inequalities can then be combined in a single inequality.

$$0 \le x < 4$$

The compound inequality may be read in these two ways:

• x is greater than or equal to 0 and x is less than 4.

• x is greater than or equal to 0 and less than 4.

The graph of this compound inequality is shown below.

$$\xleftarrow{\hspace{1cm}} \overset{\bullet}{\underset{0}{\mid}} \quad \underset{1}{\mid} \quad \underset{2}{\mid} \quad \underset{3}{\mid} \quad \overset{\circ}{\underset{4}{\mid}} \quad \underset{5}{\mid} \xrightarrow{\hspace{1cm}}$$

$-1 \quad 0 \quad 1 \quad 2 \quad 3 \quad 4 \quad 5$

Student Help

▶ **STUDY TIP**
A number is a solution of a compound inequality with *and* if the number is a solution of *both* inequalities.

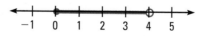 **Write Compound Inequalities with And**

Write a verbal sentence that describes the inequality.

1. $-2 < y < 0$ **2.** $7 \le t < 8$ **3.** $4 \le n \le 11$

Link to
Science

MOUNTAIN PLANT LIFE
The timberline on a mountain is the line above which no trees grow. Alpine flowers are flowers that grow above the timberline.

EXAMPLE 2 Compound Inequalities in Real Life

MOUNTAIN PLANT LIFE
Write a compound inequality that describes the approximate elevation range for the type of plant life on Mount Rainier, a mountain peak in Washington.

a. Trees below 6000 feet

b. Alpine flowers below 7500 feet

c. No trees or alpine flowers at or below 14,410 feet

Solution Let y represent the elevation in feet.

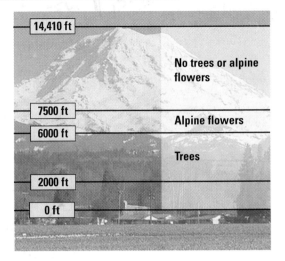

a. $2000 \le y < 6000$ **b.** $6000 \le y < 7500$ **c.** $7500 \le y \le 14{,}410$

EXAMPLE 3 Solve Compound Inequalities with *And*

Solve $-2 < x + 2 \le 4$. Then graph the solution.

Solution

Method 1 Separate the inequality. Solve the two parts separately.

$x + 2 > -2$	*and*	$x + 2 \le 4$	Separate inequality.
$x + 2 - 2 > -2 - 2$	*and*	$x + 2 - 2 \le 4 - 2$	Subtract 2 from each side.
$x > -4$	*and*	$x \le 2$	Simplify.
	$-4 < x \le 2$		Write compound inequality.

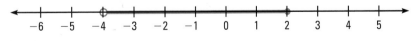

Student Help

▶ **STUDY TIP**
To perform any operation on a compound inequality with *and*, you must perform the operation on all *three* expressions. ········▶

Method 2 Isolate the variable between the inequality symbols.

$-2 < x + 2 \le 4$	Write original inequality.
$-2 - 2 < x + 2 - 2 \le 4 - 2$	Subtract 2 from each expression.
$-4 < x \le 2$	Simplify.

ANSWER ▶ The solution is all real numbers greater than -4 and less than or equal to 2. The graph of the solution is shown below.

$$\xleftarrow{\hspace{3cm}} \overset{-6\quad -5\quad -4\quad -3\quad -2\quad -1\quad\; 0\quad\; 1\quad\; 2\quad\; 3\quad\; 4\quad\; 5}{\rule{10cm}{0.4pt}} \xrightarrow{\hspace{1cm}}$$

Checkpoint ✓ *Solve Compound Inequalities with **And***

Choose a method from Example 3 to solve the inequality. Then graph the solution.

4. $-1 < x + 3 < 7$ **5.** $-6 \le 3x \le 12$ **6.** $0 < x - 4 \le 12$

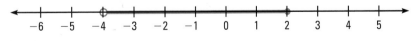

6.4 *Solving Compound Inequalities Involving "And"*   **343**

EXAMPLE 4 Solve Multi-Step Compound Inequalities

Solve $-3 \leq 2x + 1 \leq 5$. Then graph the solution.

Solution

Isolate the variable between the inequality symbols.

$-3 \leq 2x + 1 \leq 5$	Write original inequality.
$-3 - 1 \leq 2x + 1 - 1 \leq 5 - 1$	Subtract 1 from each expression.
$-4 \leq 2x \leq 4$	Simplify.
$\dfrac{-4}{2} \leq \dfrac{2x}{2} \leq \dfrac{4}{2}$	Divide each expression by 2.
$-2 \leq x \leq 2$	Simplify.

ANSWER ▶ The solution is all real numbers greater than or equal to -2 and less than or equal to 2. The graph of the solution is shown below.

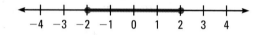

EXAMPLE 5 Reverse Both Inequalities

Solve $-2 < -2 - x < 1$. Then graph the solution.

Solution

Student Help

▶**STUDY TIP**
When you multiply or divide each expression of a compound inequality by a negative number, remember to reverse *both* inequalities. ⋯⋯⋯⋯

Isolate the variable x between the two inequality symbols.

$-2 < -2 - x < 1$	Write original inequality.
$-2 + 2 < -2 - x + 2 < 1 + 2$	Add 2 to each expression.
$0 < -x < 3$	Simplify.
$-1(0) > -1(-x) > -1(3)$	Multiply each expression by -1 and reverse *both* inequalities.
$0 > x > -3$	Simplify.

ANSWER ▶ The solution is all real numbers greater than -3 and less than 0. The graph of the solution is shown below.

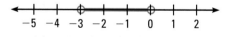

A compound inequality is usually written in a way that reflects the order of numbers on a number line. In Example 5 above, the solution would usually be written $-3 < x < 0$.

Checkpoint✓ Solve Compound Inequalities with And

Solve the inequality. Then graph the solution.

7. $3 \leq 2x + 3 \leq 7$ **8.** $-6 \leq -3x \leq 12$ **9.** $-3 \leq -4 - x \leq 2$

Guided Practice

Vocabulary Check

1. Name the two connecting words used in compound inequalities.

2. The word *compound* comes from a Latin word meaning "to put together." Explain why $3 \leq x < 9$ is called a compound inequality.

Skill Check

Match the compound inequality with its graph.

3. $-1 \leq x < 3$

4. $-1 < x$ and $x \leq 3$

A.

 −1 0 1 2 3

B.
 −1 0 1 2 3

Write a verbal sentence that describes the inequality.

5. $7 < 4 + x < 8$

6. $-1 < 2x + 3 \leq 13$

7. $4 \leq -8 - x < 7$

Write an inequality that represents the statement.

8. x is less than 5 and greater than 2.

9. x is greater than or equal to -4 and less than or equal to 4.

10. x is less than 7 and is greater than or equal to -1.

Practice and Applications

READING INEQUALITIES **Write a verbal sentence that describes the inequality.**

11. $-23 \leq x \leq -7$

12. $0 < x < 18$

13. $-4 \leq x < 19$

WRITING INEQUALITIES **Write an inequality that describes the graph.**

14.
 −4 −3 −2 −1 0

15.
 0 1 2 3 4

16.
 −7 −6 −5 −4 −3

17.
 −2 −1 0 1 2

WRITING AND GRAPHING INEQUALITIES **Write an inequality that represents the statement. Then graph the inequality.**

18. x is greater than -6 and less than -1.

19. x is greater than or equal to 0 and less than 5.

20. x is greater than 1 and less than or equal to 8.

21. x is less than or equal to -2 and greater than -4.

Student Help

▶ **HOMEWORK HELP**
Example 1: Exs. 11–21
Example 2: Exs. 22–28
Example 3: Exs. 29–34
Example 4: Exs. 35–38
Example 5: Exs. 39–46

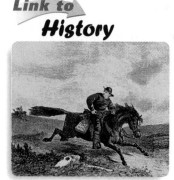
22. **History Link** In summer it took a Pony Express rider about 10 days to ride from St. Joseph, Missouri, to Sacramento, California. In winter it took as many as 16 days. Write an inequality to describe the number of days d that the trip might have taken.

FREQUENCY RANGES **In Exercises 23–26, use the following information.** Frequency is used to describe the pitch of a sound, which is how high or low it sounds. Frequencies are measured in *hertz*. Write an inequality to describe the frequency range f of the following sounds.

23. Sound of a human voice: 85 hertz to 1100 hertz

24. Sound of a bat's signals: 10,000 hertz to 120,000 hertz

25. Sound heard by a dog: 15 hertz to 50,000 hertz

26. Sound heard by a dolphin: 150 hertz to 150,000 hertz

27. TELEVISION ADVERTISING In 1967 a 60-second television commercial during the first Super Bowl cost $85,000. In 1998 advertisers paid $2.6 million for two 30-second spots. Assuming those were the least and greatest costs during that period, write an inequality that describes the cost c of 60 seconds of commercial time from 1967 to 1998.

28. STEEL ARCH BRIDGE The longest steel arch bridge in the world is the New River Gorge Bridge near Fayetteville, West Virginia. The bridge is 1700 feet long. Write an inequality that describes the length l (in feet) of any other steel arch bridge. Then graph the inequality.

SOLVING COMPOUND INEQUALITIES **Solve the inequality. Then graph the solution.**

29. $6 < x - 6 \leq 8$

30. $-5 < x - 3 < 6$

31. $0 \leq x + 9 < 17$

32. $-14 < 7x < 21$

33. $-4 \leq 2x < 18$

34. $4 < x - 7 < 15$

35. $-3 \leq 2x + 5 \leq 11$

36. $7 \leq 3x - 8 < 19$

37. $10 < 3x - 2 < 19$

38. $0 < 12x + 6 \leq 18$

SOLVING AND GRAPHING INEQUALITIES **Solve the inequality. Then graph the solution.**

39. $-7 \leq 3 - x < 5$

40. $-25 < -5x < 0$

41. $42 < -3x \leq 48$

42. $-5 < -6 - x < 3$

43. $-3 \leq 5 - 2x < 1$

44. $-7 \leq -1 - 6x \leq 11$

45. $-13 \leq 2 - 5x < -3$

46. $-44 \leq 1 - 9x < 55$

47. CHALLENGE Explain why the inequality $3 < x < 1$ has no solution.

48. MULTIPLE CHOICE Which of the following is the graph of $-2 \le x \le 3$?

(A) [number line from -3 to 2]

(B) [number line from -1 to 4]

(C) [number line from -2 to 3]

(D) [number line from -2 to 3]

49. MULTIPLE CHOICE Which inequality can be solved by reversing both inequality signs?

(F) $-1 < x < 1$

(G) $15 > 2x + 4 > 1$

(H) $-24 \le 3x - 4 \le -4$

(J) $-5 > -x > -2$

EVALUATING EXPRESSIONS Evaluate the expression for the given value of the variable. *(Lesson 1.1)*

50. $k + 5$ when $k = 2$ **51.** $6a$ when $a = 4$ **52.** $m - 20$ when $m = 30$

53. $\frac{x}{15}$ when $x = 30$ **54.** $5z$ when $z = 3.3$ **55.** $5p$ when $p = 4$

56. $4 - n$ when $n = 3$ **57.** $\frac{t}{3}$ when $t = -18$ **58.** $2x$ when $x = 3$

SOLVING EQUATIONS Solve the equation. *(Lessons 3.1, 3.2)*

59. $x + 17 = 9$ **60.** $-8 = x + 2$ **61.** $x - 4 = 12$ **62.** $x - (-9) = 15$

63. $\frac{x}{2} = -6$ **64.** $-3x = -27$ **65.** $4x = -28$ **66.** $-\frac{3}{4}x = 21$

67. ROLLER SKATING A roller skating rink charges $7 for admission and skate rental. If you bring your own skates, the admission is $4. You can buy a pair of roller skates for $75. How many times must you go skating to justify buying your own skates? *(Lesson 3.5)*

POPULATION In Exercises 68 and 69, use the following information.
In 1990 the population of the United States was about 249 million. Between 1990 and 1998 the population increased about 2.6 million per year. *(Lesson 5.5)*

 **DATA UPDATE** of U.S. Bureau of the Census data at www.mcdougallittell.com

68. Write an equation that models the population P (in millions) in terms of time t, where $t = 0$ represents the year 1990.

69. Use the model to estimate the population in 1995.

FRACTIONS AND PERCENTS Write the fraction as a percent. *(Skills Review p. 769)*

70. $\frac{1}{4}$ **71.** $\frac{3}{8}$ **72.** $\frac{4}{10}$ **73.** $\frac{1}{3}$

74. $\frac{37}{50}$ **75.** $\frac{3}{4}$ **76.** $\frac{3}{20}$ **77.** $\frac{21}{25}$

Solving Compound Inequalities Involving "Or"

Goal

Solve and graph compound inequalities involving *or*.

Key Words

• compound inequality

How fast is the baseball moving?

To practice catching pop flies, you might throw a baseball straight up into the air. As the ball rises, its velocity gradually decreases until it reaches its highest point. Then the ball begins to fall. As it falls, its velocity increases. In Example 5 you will solve a compound inequality dealing with the velocity of a baseball.

In Lesson 6.4 you studied compound inequalities that involve the word *and*. In this lesson you will study compound inequalities that involve the word *or*.

Student Help

▶ **STUDY TIP**
Recall from Lesson 6.4 that graphs of compound inequalities with *and* have only one part.

EXAMPLE **1** **Write a Compound Inequality with *Or***

Write a compound inequality that represents the set of all real numbers less than −1 or greater than 2. Then graph the inequality.

Solution

You can write this statement using the word *or*.

$$x < -1 \ or \ x > 2$$

The graph of this compound inequality is shown below. Notice that the graph has two parts. One part lies to the left of −1. The other part lies to the right of 2.

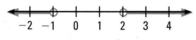

Checkpoint ✓ **Write a Compound Inequality with Or**

Write a verbal sentence to describe the inequality.

1. $x < 0 \ or \ x > 5$ **2.** $x \le -10 \ or \ x \ge 10$ **3.** $x < 2 \ or \ x \ge 3$

Write an inequality that represents the set of numbers. Tell whether the graph of the inequality has one part or two.

4. All real numbers less than or equal to −3 or greater than 0.

5. All real numbers less than 3 or greater than 6.

6. All real numbers greater than −2 and less than 7.

▶STUDY TIP
A number is a solution
of a compound
inequality with *or* if the
number is a solution of
either inequality.

EXAMPLE 2 Solve a Compound Inequality with *Or*

Solve the compound inequality $x - 4 \le 3$ *or* $2x > 18$. Then graph the solution.

Solution

A solution of this compound inequality is a solution of either of its parts. You can solve each part separately using the methods of Lessons 6.1 and 6.2.

$$x - 4 \le 3 \qquad or \quad 2x > 18 \qquad \text{Write original inequality.}$$

$$x - 4 + 4 \le 3 + 4 \quad or \quad \frac{2x}{2} > \frac{18}{2} \qquad \text{Isolate } x.$$

$$x \le 7 \qquad or \quad x > 9 \qquad \text{Simplify.}$$

ANSWER ▶ The solution is all real numbers less than or equal to 7 or greater than 9. The graph of the solution is shown below.

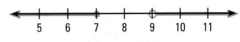

▶MORE EXAMPLES
More examples
are available at
www.mcdougallittell.com

EXAMPLE 3 Solve a Multi-Step Compound Inequality

Solve the compound inequality $3x + 1 < 4$ *or* $2x - 5 > 7$. Then graph the solution.

Solution

Solve each of the parts using the methods of Lesson 6.3.

$$3x + 1 < 4 \qquad or \qquad 2x - 5 > 7 \qquad \text{Write original inequality.}$$

$$3x + 1 - 1 < 4 - 1 \quad or \quad 2x - 5 + 5 > 7 + 5 \qquad \text{Isolate } x.$$

$$3x < 3 \qquad or \qquad 2x > 12 \qquad \text{Simplify.}$$

$$\frac{3x}{3} < \frac{3}{3} \qquad or \qquad \frac{2x}{2} > \frac{12}{2} \qquad \text{Solve for } x.$$

$$x < 1 \qquad or \qquad x > 6 \qquad \text{Simplify.}$$

ANSWER ▶ The solution is all real numbers less than 1 or greater than 6. The graph of the solution is shown below.

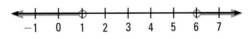

Checkpoint ✓ Solve a Compound Inequality with **Or**

Tell whether −5 is a solution of the inequality.

7. $x < -5 \ or \ x > -4$ **8.** $x \le -3 \ or \ x > 0$

Solve the inequality. Then graph the solution.

9. $x - 4 < -8 \ or \ x + 3 > 5$ **10.** $2x + 3 \le 1 \ or \ 3x - 5 > 1$

You can use compound inequalities to describe real-life situations. Examples 4 and 5 deal with velocity. Recall that positive numbers are used to measure velocity of upward motion and that negative numbers are used to measure velocity of downward motion.

EXAMPLE 4 Make a Table

A baseball is hit straight up in the air. Its initial velocity is 64 feet per second. Its velocity v (in feet per second) after t seconds is given by:

$$v = -32t + 64$$

Make a table that shows the velocity of the baseball for whole-number values of t from $t = 0$ to $t = 4$. Describe the results.

Solution

t (sec)	0	1	2	3	4
v (ft/sec)	64	32	0	-32	-64

The baseball starts with a velocity of 64 feet per second, moving upwards. It slows down and then stops rising at $t = 2$ seconds when the baseball is at its highest point. Then the baseball begins to fall downward. When $t = 4$, the velocity is -64 feet per second. The negative sign indicates the velocity has changed to a downward direction.

EXAMPLE 5 Solve a Compound Inequality with *Or*

Find the values of t for which the velocity of the baseball in Example 4 is greater than 32 feet per second *or* less than -32 feet per second.

Student Help

▶ **STUDY TIP**
When you multiply or divide by a negative number to solve a compound inequality with *or*, remember to reverse *both* inequalities. ·····

Solution The velocity is given by $-32t + 64$.

$$-32t + 64 > 32 \qquad or \qquad -32t + 64 < -32$$

$$-32t + 64 - 64 > 32 - 64 \quad or \quad -32t + 64 - 64 < -32 - 64$$

$$-32t > -32 \qquad or \qquad -32t < -96$$

$$\frac{-32t}{-32} < \frac{-32}{-32} \qquad or \qquad \frac{-32t}{-32} > \frac{-96}{-32}$$

$$t < 1 \qquad or \qquad t > 3$$

ANSWER ▶ The velocity is greater than 32 feet per second when t is less than 1 second and less than -32 feet per second when t is greater than 3 seconds.

Checkpoint ✓ **Solve a Compound Inequality with Or**

11. Refer to Example 5. Find the values of t for which the velocity of the baseball is less than 64 feet per second or greater than -64 feet per second.

6.5 Exercises

Guided Practice

Vocabulary Check

1. Describe how the solution of a compound inequality involving *or* differs from the solution of a compound inequality involving *and*.

Skill Check

Match the inequality with its graph.

2. $x \le -2$ *or* $x \ge 1$

3. $1 < x$ *or* $x \le -2$

4. $x < -2$ *or* $1 \le x$

5. $x < 1$ *or* $x > 2$

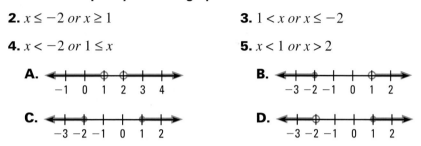

Write a verbal sentence that describes the inequality.

6. $x \le -25$ *or* $x > 7$

7. $x < 10$ *or* $x > 13$

8. $x < -9$ *or* $x > 3$

Write an inequality that represents the set of numbers. Then graph the inequality.

9. All real numbers less than -6 or greater than -1.

10. All real numbers less than 0 or greater than or equal to 5.

Practice and Applications

READING INEQUALITIES **Write a verbal sentence that describes the inequality.**

11. $x \le 15$ *or* $x \ge 31$

12. $x < 0$ *or* $x > 16$

13. $x > 11$ *or* $x \le -7$

WRITING INEQUALITIES **Write an inequality that describes the graph.**

14.

15.

16.

17.

Student Help

▶ HOMEWORK HELP
Example 1: Exs. 11–20
Example 2: Exs. 21–30
Example 3: Exs. 31–40
Example 4: Ex. 41
Example 5: Exs. 42–45

WRITING AND GRAPHING INEQUALITIES **Write an inequality that represents the set of numbers. Then graph the inequality.**

18. All real numbers less than -6 or greater than 2.

19. All real numbers greater than 7 or less than 0.

20. All real numbers less than 3 or greater than 10.

SOLVING INEQUALITIES Solve the inequality. Then graph the solution.

21. $x - 1 \le -3 \; or \; x + 3 > 8$

22. $-12 > 8x \; or \; 4x \ge 6$

23. $x + 3 \ge 2 \; or \; 12x \le -48$

24. $-22 > 11x \; or \; 4 + x > 4$

25. $7x < -42 \; or \; x + 5 \ge 3$

26. $5 + x \ge 20 \; or \; 3x \le -9$

27. $x - 4 < -12 \; or \; 2x \ge 12$

28. $-3x \le 15 \; or \; 5 + x < -11$

CHECKING SOLUTIONS Solve the inequality. Then determine whether the given value of *x* is a solution of the inequality.

29. $x - 7 < 3 \; or \; 2x > 24; \; x = 8$

30. $5x \ge -15 \; or \; x + 4 < -1; \; x = -4$

31. $-2x \ge 6 \; or \; 2x + 1 > 5; \; x = 0$

32. $3x < -21 \; or \; 4x - 8 \ge 0; \; x = 3$

SOLVING INEQUALITIES Solve the inequality. Then graph the solution.

33. $x + 10 < 8 \; or \; 3x - 7 \ge 5$

34. $-8x > 24 \; or \; 2x - 5 > 17$

35. $2x + 1 > 13 \; or \; -18 > 7x + 3$

36. $6 + 2x > 20 \; or \; 8 + x \le 0$

37. $2x + 7 < 3 \; or \; 5x + 5 \ge 10$

38. $3x + 8 > 17 \; or \; 2x + 5 \le 7$

39. $3x + 5 < -19 \; or \; 4x + 7 \ge -1$

40. $1 - 5x \le -14 \; or \; -3x - 2 \ge 7$

YO-YO In Exercises 41 and 42, use the following information.
A yo-yo is thrown toward the ground with an initial velocity of -4 feet per second. Its velocity *v* in feet per second *t* seconds after being thrown is given by $v = 4t - 4$, where *t* runs from 0 to 2 seconds.

41. Make a table that shows the yo-yo's velocity for $t = 0, 0.5, 1, 1.5,$ and 2 seconds. Describe the results.

42. Find the times for which the yo-yo's velocity is greater than 2 feet per second or less than -2 feet per second.

43. *Science Link* Water may be in the form of a solid, a liquid, or a gas. Under ordinary conditions at sea level, water is a solid (ice) at temperatures of 32°F or lower and a gas (water vapor) at temperatures of 212°F or higher. Write a compound inequality describing when water is *not* a liquid.

BUS FARES In Exercises 44 and 45, use the following information.
A public transit system charges fares based on age. Children under 5 ride free. Children who are 5 or older but less than 11 pay half fare. People who are at least 11 but younger than 65 pay full fare. Those 65 or over pay reduced fares.

44. Write a compound inequality to describe *a*, the ages in years of children who pay half fare.

45. Write a compound inequality to describe *y*, the ages in years of those eligible for reduced rates based on age.

46. CHALLENGE Describe the solutions of the inequality $x < 2 \; or \; x > 1$.

Link to
Transportation

BUS FARES Reduced bus fares are often available for the very young, the disabled, senior citizens, or students who ride the bus to get to and from school.

47. MULTIPLE CHOICE Which of the following is the graph of the compound inequality $x \leq -4$ *or* $x > 0$?

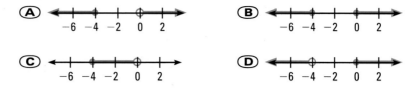

48. MULTIPLE CHOICE Which number is *not* a solution of the compound inequality $-2x \geq 18$ *or* $3x + 8 > 26$?

(F) -12 (G) -9 (H) 6 (J) 9

Mixed Review

INPUT-OUTPUT TABLE Make an input-output table for the function. Use $x = 0, 1, 2, 3,$ and 4 as values for *x*. *(Lesson 1.8)*

49. $y = 3x + 2$ **50.** $y = -2x + 1$ **51.** $y = 5 - x$

52. $y = 2x - 3$ **53.** $y = 2x - 4$ **54.** $y = 3x - 1$

GRAPHING Graph the numbers on a number line. *(Lesson 2.1)*

55. $-4, 6, -5$ **56.** $3.2, -6.4, 3.5$ **57.** $\frac{1}{2}, \frac{2}{3}, \frac{1}{4}$

SOLVING EQUATIONS Solve the equation. Round the result to the nearest hundredth. *(Lesson 3.6)*

58. $1.2x - 1.7 = 4.5$ **59.** $1.3 + 4.4x = 6.6$

60. $3.6x - 8.5 = 12.4$ **61.** $2.3x + 3.2 = 18.5$

62. $2.56 - 6.54x = -5.21 - 3.25x$ **63.** $2.32x + 6.56 = 3.74 - 7.43x$

SOLVING INEQUALITIES Solve the inequality. Then graph the solution. *(Lessons 6.1 and 6.2)*

64. $x + 6 > -6$ **65.** $16 < x + 7$ **66.** $9 \geq -15 + x$

67. $x - 10 \geq 15$ **68.** $2 \leq x - 7$ **69.** $-3x \leq -15$

70. $6x > -54$ **71.** $-\frac{1}{4}x > 2$ **72.** $\frac{3}{4}x \leq 6$

Maintaining Skills

MULTIPLYING Multiply the fraction by the whole number. *(Skills Review p. 765)*

73. $\frac{1}{3}(84)$ **74.** $\frac{1}{5}(375)$ **75.** $\frac{1}{4}(884)$

76. $\frac{1}{7}(21,000)$ **77.** $\frac{1}{3}(84,000)$ **78.** $\frac{1}{20}(72,000)$

79. $\frac{1}{15}(81,000)$ **80.** $\frac{1}{9}(31,500)$ **81.** $\frac{1}{11}(121,000)$

Absolute-Value Equations

GOAL

Use a number line to solve absolute-value equations.

MATERIALS

• graph paper
• colored pencils

Question How can you use a number line to solve absolute-value equations?

You can solve an absolute-value equation of the form $|x| = c$ by finding all points on the number line whose distance from zero is c.

For example, the equation $|x| = 2$ means x is 2 units from zero. As shown below, both -2 and 2 are 2 units from zero. Therefore, if $|x| = 2$, then $x = -2$ or $x = 2$.

Explore

1 One way to solve the equation $|x - 3| = 2$ is to use a table. Copy and complete the table, circling those values of x for which $|x - 3| = 2$.

x	$x - 3$	$|x - 3|$
0	-3	3
1	-2	?
2	?	?
3	?	?
4	?	?
5	?	?

2 Another way to solve the equation $|x - 3| = 2$ is to use the number line. The equation $|x - 3| = 2$ can be read as "The distance between x and 3 is 2." On the number line below, find the points whose distance from 3 is 2.

Think About It

1. LOGICAL REASONING Explain why the answers to **Steps 1** and **2** are the same.

Solve the absolute-value equation.

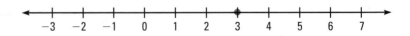

    2. $|x| = 5$ **3.** $|x - 2| = 4$ **4.** $|x + 2| = |x - (-2)| = 3$

6.6 Solving Absolute-Value Equations

Goal

Solve absolute-value equations in one variable.

Key Words

- absolute-value equation

How tall are miniature poodles?

Breeds of dogs are often classified based on physical traits. Poodles are divided into classes according to height. In Example 5 you will write an equation to describe the heights of miniature poodles.

An **absolute-value equation** is an equation of the form $|ax + b| = c$. You can solve this type of equation by solving two related linear equations.

SOLVING AN ABSOLUTE-VALUE EQUATION

For $c \geq 0$, x is a solution of $|ax + b| = c$ if x is a solution of:

$$ax + b = c \text{ or } ax + b = -c$$

For $c < 0$, the absolute-value equation $|ax + b| = c$ has no solution, since absolute value always indicates a number that is not negative.

EXAMPLE 1 Solve an Absolute-Value Equation

Solve the equation.

   a. $|x| = 8$ **b.** $|x| = -10$

Solution

a. There are two values of x that have an absolute value of 8.

$$|x| = 8$$
$$x = 8 \quad or \quad x = -8$$

ANSWER ▶ The equation has two solutions: 8 and -8.

b. The absolute value of a number is never negative.

ANSWER ▶ The equation $|x| = -10$ has no solution.

Checkpoint ✓ **Solve an Absolute-Value Equation**

Solve the absolute-value equation.

   1. $|x| = 6$ **2.** $|x| = 0$ **3.** $|x| = -6$

EXAMPLE **2** Solve an Absolute-Value Equation

Solve $|x - 2| = 5$.

Solution

Because $|x - 2| = 5$, the expression $x - 2$ is equal to 5 *or* -5.

Check the solutions to an absolute-value equation by substituting each solution in the original equation.········

x − 2 IS POSITIVE	*or*	**x − 2 IS NEGATIVE**
$x - 2 = 5$		$x - 2 = -5$
$x - 2 + 2 = 5 + 2$		$x - 2 + 2 = -5 + 2$
$x = 7$	*or*	$x = -3$

ANSWER ▶ The equation has two solutions: 7 and −3.

CHECK ✓ $|7 - 2| = |5| = 5$ $|-3 - 2| = |-5| = 5$

EXAMPLE **3** Solve an Absolute-Value Equation

Solve $|2x - 7| - 5 = 4$.

Solution

First isolate the absolute-value expression on one side of the equation.

$$|2x - 7| - 5 = 4$$
$$|2x - 7| - 5 + 5 = 4 + 5$$
$$|2x - 7| = 9$$

Because $|2x - 7| = 9$, the expression $2x - 7$ is equal to 9 *or* -9.

2x − 7 IS POSITIVE	*or*	**2x − 7 IS NEGATIVE**
$2x - 7 = 9$		$2x - 7 = -9$
$2x - 7 + 7 = 9 + 7$		$2x - 7 + 7 = -9 + 7$
$2x = 16$		$2x = -2$
$\dfrac{2x}{2} = \dfrac{16}{2}$		$\dfrac{2x}{2} = \dfrac{-2}{2}$
$x = 8$	*or*	$x = -1$

ANSWER ▶ The equation has two solutions: 8 and −1.

CHECK ✓ $|2(8) - 7| - 5 = |9| - 5 = 9 - 5 = 4$
$|2(-1) - 7| - 5 = |-9| - 5 = 9 - 5 = 4$

Checkpoint ✓ *Solve an Absolute-Value Equation*

Solve the absolute-value equation and check your solutions.

4. $|x + 3| = 5$ **5.** $|x - 3| = 5$ **6.** $|4x - 2| = 6$

7. $|3x - 2| = 0$ **8.** $|x + 1| + 2 = 4$ **9.** $|2x - 8| - 3 = 5$

You can use a number line to write an absolute-value equation that has two given numbers as its solutions.

EXAMPLE **4** **Write an Absolute-Value Equation**

Write an absolute-value equation that has 7 and 15 as its solutions.

Solution

Graph the numbers on a number line and locate the midpoint of the graphs.

The graph of each solution is 4 units from the midpoint, 11. You can use the midpoint and the distance to write an absolute-value equation.

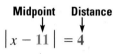

$$|x - 11| = 4$$

ANSWER ▶ The equation is $|x - 11| = 4$. Check that 7 and 15 are solutions of this equation.

Link to
Animals

Shoulder height

POODLES A poodle is labeled a toy, a miniature, or a standard based on its shoulder height. The smallest poodle is the toy. The largest is the standard.

EXAMPLE **5** **Write an Absolute-Value Equation**

POODLES The shoulder height of the shortest miniature poodle is 10 inches. The shoulder height of the tallest is 15 inches. Write an absolute-value equation that has these two heights as its solutions.

Solution

Graph the numbers on a number line and locate the midpoint of the graphs. Then use the method of Example 4 to write the equation.

The midpoint is 12.5. Each solution is 2.5 units from 12.5.

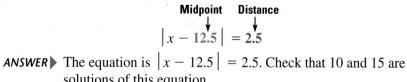

$$|x - 12.5| = 2.5$$

ANSWER ▶ The equation is $|x - 12.5| = 2.5$. Check that 10 and 15 are solutions of this equation.

Checkpoint ✓ **Write an Absolute-Value Equation**

10. Write an absolute-value equation that has 4 and 12 as its solutions.

Guided Practice

Vocabulary Check

1. Explain why the equation $x + \left|-2\right| = 5$ is *not* an absolute-value equation.

Skill Check

2. Choose the two equations you would use to solve the absolute-value equation $\left|x - 7\right| = 13$. Then solve the two equations.

    A. $x - 7 = 13$ **B.** $x + 7 = 13$ **C.** $x - 7 = -13$ **D.** $x + 7 = -13$

Tell how many solutions the equation has.

    3. $\left|x\right| = 17$ **4.** $\left|x\right| = -2$ **5.** $\left|x - 1\right| = -3$ **6.** $\left|x\right| + 1 = 1$

Write the two linear equations you would use to solve the absolute-value equation.

    7. $\left|x - 4\right| = 10$ **8.** $\left|2x - 3\right| = 8$ **9.** $\left|3x + 2\right| - 1 = 5$

Practice and Applications

SOLVING ABSOLUTE-VALUE EQUATIONS Solve the absolute-value equation. If the equation has no solution, write *no solution.*

    10. $\left|x\right| = 36$ **11.** $\left|x\right| = 9$ **12.** $\left|x\right| = -25$

    13. $\left|x\right| = -15$ **14.** $\left|x\right| = 10$ **15.** $\left|x\right| = 100$

SOLVING ABSOLUTE-VALUE EQUATIONS Solve the equation and check your solutions. If the equation has no solution, write *no solution.*

    16. $\left|x + 1\right| = 3$ **17.** $\left|x - 2\right| = 5$ **18.** $\left|4x\right| = 16$

    19. $\left|3x\right| = 36$ **20.** $\left|x + 8\right| = 9$ **21.** $\left|x - 4\right| = 6$

    22. $\left|x + 6\right| = -7$ **23.** $\left|8x\right| = 28$ **24.** $\left|x + 5\right| = 65$

    25. $\left|x - 3\right| = 7$ **26.** $\left|15 + x\right| = 3$ **27.** $\left|\frac{1}{2}x\right| = 9$

LOGICAL REASONING Complete the statement with *always, sometimes,* or *never.*

28. If $x^2 = a^2$, then $\left|x\right|$ is __?__ equal to $\left|a\right|$.

29. If a and b are real numbers, then $\left|a - b\right|$ is __?__ equal to $\left|b - a\right|$.

30. For any real number p, the equation $\left|x - 4\right| = p$ will __?__ have two solutions.

31. For any real number p, the equation $\left|x - p\right| = 4$ will __?__ have two solutions.

Student Help

▶ **HOMEWORK HELP**
Example 1: Exs. 10–15
Example 2: Exs. 16–27
Example 3: Exs. 32–40
Example 4: Exs. 41–46
Example 5: Exs. 47, 48

HOMEWORK HELP

Extra help with problem solving in Exs. 32–40 is available at www.mcdougallittell.com

SOLVING ABSOLUTE-VALUE EQUATIONS Solve the equation and check your solutions. If the equation has no solution, write *no solution*.

32. $|6x - 4| = 2$ **33.** $|4x - 2| = 22$ **34.** $|3x + 5| = 22$

35. $|2x + 5| = 3$ **36.** $|6x - 3| = 39$ **37.** $|2x - 7| = 9$

38. $|5 - 4x| - 3 = 4$ **39.** $|2x - 4| - 8 = 10$ **40.** $|5x - 4| + 3 = 19$

ABSOLUTE-VALUE EQUATIONS Match the absolute-value equation with its graph.

41. $|x + 2| = 6$ **42.** $|x - 6| = 2$ **43.** $|x - 2| = 6$

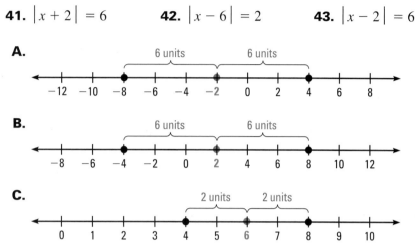

A.

B.

C.

WRITING ABSOLUTE-VALUE EQUATIONS Write an absolute-value equation that has the given solutions.

44. 8 and 18 **45.** −6 and 10 **46.** 2 and 9

ASTRONOMY In Exercises 47 and 48, use the following information.
The distance between Earth and the sun is not constant, because Earth's orbit around the sun is an ellipse. The maximum distance from Earth to the sun is 94.5 million miles. The minimum distance is about 91.4 million miles.

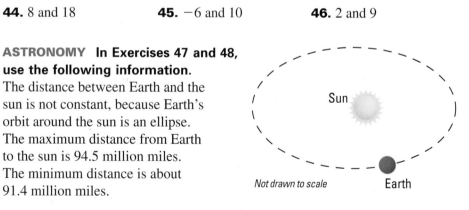

Not drawn to scale

47. Graph the maximum and minimum distances on a number line and locate the midpoint. Determine the distance from the midpoint to the minimum and from the midpoint to the maximum.

48. Use your answers from Exercises 47 to write an absolute-value equation that has the minimum and maximum distances between Earth and the sun (in millions of miles) as its solutions.

49. CHALLENGE The highest elevation in North America is 20,320 feet *above* sea level at Mount McKinley. The lowest elevation is 282 feet *below* sea level in Death Valley. Find an absolute-value equation that has the highest and lowest elevations in North America as its solutions.

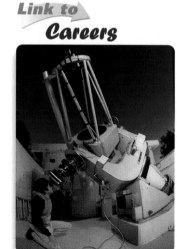

ASTRONOMERS study energy, matter, and natural processes throughout the universe. Professional astronomers need a doctoral degree. Nevertheless, amateur astronomers make important discoveries as well.

More about astronomers at www.mcdougallittell.com

50. MULTIPLE CHOICE Which number is a solution of $|x| - 5 = 6$?

(A) 6   (B) -6 (C) -1 (D) -11

51. MULTIPLE CHOICE Which numbers are solutions of $|2x - 4| + 7 = 23$?

(F) -6 and 10   (G) -13 and 17

(H) -12 and 20   (J) -10 and 6

Mixed Review

GRAPHING EQUATIONS **Graph the equation on a coordinate plane.**
(Lesson 4.3)

52. $x = -1$ **53.** $3y = 15$ **54.** $x + 6 = 7$

SLOPE-INTERCEPT FORM **Write the equation in slope-intercept form.**
(Lesson 5.1)

55. $5x + y = 20$ **56.** $3x - y = 21$ **57.** $12x = 3y + 36$

WRITING EQUATIONS **Write the slope-intercept form of the equation of the line that passes through the given point and has the given slope.**
(Lesson 5.2)

58. $(0, 4)$, $m = 3$ **59.** $(2, -5)$, $m = -2$ **60.** $(-3, 1)$, $m = 2$

Maintaining Skills

ROUNDING **Round 47,509.1258 to the indicated place value.**
(Skills Review p. 774)

61. thousands   **62.** tenths   **63.** hundreds

64. thousandths   **65.** hundredths   **66.** ones

Quiz 2

Solve the inequality. Then graph the solution. *(Lessons 6.4 and 6.5)*

1. $-5 < x - 8 < 4$ **2.** $-10 < 2x + 8 \leq 22$

3. $-10 \leq -4x - 18 \leq -2$ **4.** $5x > 25$ *or* $2x + 9 < -1$

5. $-3 > x + 6$ *or* $-x < 4$ **6.** $2 - x < -3$ *or* $2x + 14 < 12$

7. TEMPERATURES The lowest temperature recorded on Earth was $-128.6°F$ in Antarctica. The highest temperature recorded on Earth was $136°F$ in Libya. Write an inequality that describes any other record temperatures T.
(Lesson 6.4) ▶Source: National Climatic Data Center

Solve the equation. If the equation has no solution, write *no solution*.
(Lesson 6.6)

8. $|x| = 14$ **9.** $|x| = -43$ **10.** $|x - 9| = 24$

11. $|x + 15| = 6$ **12.** $|3x - 18| = 36$ **13.** $|5x + 10| + 15 = 60$

14. Write an absolute-value equation that has -3 and 18 as its solutions.
(Lesson 6.6)

6.7 Solving Absolute-Value Inequalities

Goal

Solve absolute-value inequalities in one variable.

Key Words

• absolute-value inequality

How fast does water from a fountain rise and fall?

When water is shot upward from a fountain, it gradually slows down. Then it stops and begins to fall with increasing speed. In Exercise 42 you will use an inequality to analyze the speed of water rising and falling in a fountain.

An **absolute-value inequality** is an inequality that has one of these forms:

$$|ax + b| < c \qquad |ax + b| \le c \qquad |ax + b| > c \qquad |ax + b| \ge c$$

To solve an absolute-value inequality, you solve two related inequalities. The inequalities for < and > inequalities are shown. Similar rules apply for $\le$ and $\ge$.

$|ax + b| < c$	$|ax + b| > c$
means	means
$ax + b < c \quad and \quad ax + b > -c$	$ax + b > c \quad or \quad ax + b < -c$

EXAMPLE 1 **Solve an Absolute-Value Inequality**

Solve $|x| > 5$. Then graph the solution.

Solution

The solution consists of all numbers x whose distance from 0 is greater than 5. In other words $|x| > 5$ means $x > 5$ or $x < -5$. The inequality involves > so the related inequalities are connected by *or*.

ANSWER ▶ The solution is all real numbers greater than 5 *or* less than -5. This can be written $x < -5$ *or* $x > 5$. The graph of the solution is shown below.

```
◄——+——⊕——+——+——+——+——+——+——+——+——+——⊕——+——►
   -6  -5  -4  -3  -2  -1   0   1   2   3   4   5   6
```

CHECK ✓ Test one value from each region of the graph.

$$|-6| = 6, 6 > 5 \qquad |0| = 0, 0 \text{ is } not \text{ greater than 5} \qquad |6| = 6, 6 > 5$$

EXAMPLE 2 Solve an Absolute-Value Inequality

Solve $|x - 4| < 3$. Then graph the solution.

Solution The solution consists of all numbers x whose distance from 4 is less than 3. The inequality involves < so the related inequalities are connected by *and*.

$|x - 4| < 3$			Write original inequality.
$x - 4 < 3$	*and*	$x - 4 > -3$	Write related inequalities.
$x - 4 + 4 < 3 + 4$	*and*	$x - 4 + 4 > -3 + 4$	Add 4 to each side.
$x < 7$	*and*	$x > 1$	Simplify.

ANSWER ▶ The solution is all real numbers greater than 1 *and* less than 7. This can be written $1 < x < 7$. The graph of the solution is shown below.

Check the solution.

EXAMPLE 3 Solve an Absolute-Value Inequality

Solve $|x + 5| \geq 2$. Then graph the solution.

Solution The solution consists of all numbers x whose distance from −5 is greater than or equal to 2. The inequality involves ≥ so the related inequalities are connected by *or*.

$|x + 5| \geq 2$			Write original inequality.
$x + 5 \geq 2$	*or*	$x + 5 \leq -2$	Write related inequalities.
$x + 5 - 5 \geq 2 - 5$	*or*	$x + 5 - 5 \leq -2 - 5$	Subtract 5 from each side.
$x \geq -3$	*or*	$x \leq -7$	Simplify.

ANSWER ▶ The solution is all real numbers greater than or equal to −3 *or* less than or equal to −7. This can be written $x \leq -7$ or $x \geq -3$. The graph of the solution is shown below.

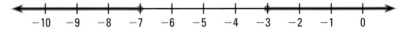

Check the solution.

Checkpoint ✓ *Solve an Absolute-Value Inequality*

Solve the absolute-value inequality.

1. $|x| \leq 6$ **2.** $|x - 2| < 5$ **3.** $|x + 1| \leq 4$

4. $|3x| > 9$ **5.** $|x - 2| \geq 7$ **6.** $|x - 3| > 12$

EXAMPLE **4** **Solve a Multi-Step Inequality**

Solve $|x + 1| - 3 \geq 2$.

Solution

First isolate the absolute-value expression on one side of the inequality.

$|x + 1| - 3 \geq 2$	Write original inequality.
$|x + 1| - 3 + 3 \geq 2 + 3$	Add 3 to each side.
$|x + 1| \geq 5$	Simplify.

The inequality involves $\geq$ so the related inequalities are connected by *or*.

$|x + 1| \geq 5$		Write simplified inequality.
$x + 1 \geq 5$ *or* $x + 1 \leq -5$		Write related inequalities.
$x + 1 - 1 \geq 5 - 1$ *or* $x + 1 - 1 \leq -5 - 1$		Subtract 1 from each side.
$x \geq 4$ *or* $x \leq -6$		Simplify.

ANSWER ▶ The solution is all real numbers greater than or equal to 4 *or* less than or equal to -6. This can be written $x \leq -6$ *or* $x \geq 4$.

Checkpoint ✓ **Solve a Multi-Step Inequality**

7. Solve the inequality $|3x - 2| > 4$.

Student Help

▶**STUDY TIP**
Compare Example 5 to Example 5 on page 350. Together the examples show the connection between absolute-value inequalities and compound inequalities.

EXAMPLE **5** **Use an Absolute-Value Inequality**

BASEBALL A baseball is hit straight up with an initial velocity of 64 feet per second. Its speed s (in ft/sec) after t seconds is given by $s = |-32t + 64|$. Find the values of t for which s is greater than 32 feet per second.

Solution Solve $|-32t + 64| > 32$.

The inequality involves $>$ so the related inequalities are connected by *or*.

$|-32t + 64| > 32$	Write original inequality.
$-32t + 64 > 32$ *or* $-32t + 64 < -32$	Write related inequalities.
$-32t > -32$ *or* $-32t < -96$	Subtract 64 from each side.
$t < 1$ *or* $t > 3$	Divide by -32 and reverse the inequalities.

ANSWER ▶ The speed is greater than 32 ft/sec when t is less than 1 second or greater than 3 seconds. This can be written $t < 1$ *or* $t > 3$.

Checkpoint ✓ **Use an Absolute-Value Inequality**

8. In Example 5 find the values of t for which s is greater than 48 ft/sec.

Guided Practice

Vocabulary Check   **Match the phrase with the example it describes.**

1. An absolute-value inequality   **A.** $\left| 2x - 9 \right| = 7$

2. An absolute-value equation   **B.** $\left| -15 \right|$

3. An absolute-value   **C.** $\left| -x + 4 \right| \geq 18$

4. Choose the two inequalities you would use to solve the inequality $\left| x - 8 \right| > 5$. Tell whether they are connected by *and* or by *or*.

    A. $x - 8 > -5$ **B.** $x - 8 < -5$ **C.** $x - 8 < 5$ **D.** $x - 8 > 5$

Tell whether the given number is a solution of the inequality.

5. $\left| x + 6 \right| < 4;\ -10$ 6. $\left| x - 2 \right| > 9;\ 7$ 7. $\left| 5x - 2 \right| \geq 8;\ 3$

Practice and Applications

RELATED INEQUALITIES   **Write the two inequalities you would use to solve the absolute-value inequality. Tell whether they are connected by *and* or by *or*.**

8. $\left| x \right| \geq 7$ 9. $\left| x \right| > 1$ 10. $\left| x - 16 \right| < 10$

11. $\left| x - 1 \right| \leq 9$ 12. $\left| 7x - 3 \right| < 2$ 13. $\left| 10 + 7x \right| \geq 11$

SOLVING ABSOLUTE-VALUE INEQUALITIES   **Solve the inequality. Then graph and check the solution.**

14. $\left| x \right| \geq 3$ 15. $\left| x \right| < 15$ 16. $\left| x \right| \geq 5$

17. $\left| x + 5 \right| > 1$ 18. $\left| 8x \right| > 20$ 19. $\left| x - 10 \right| \geq 20$

20. $\left| 7x \right| \leq 49$ 21. $\left| x - 4 \right| > 8$ 22. $\left| x + 3 \right| < 8$

23. $\left| -3 + x \right| < 18$ 24. $\left| 10 + x \right| \leq 13$ 25. $\left| 9 + x \right| \leq 7$

Student Help

▶**HOMEWORK HELP**
Example 1: Exs. 8, 9,
     14–16
Examples 2 and 3:
     Exs. 10, 11,
     17–25
Example 4: Exs. 12, 13,
     30–41
Example 5: Exs. 42–46

LOGICAL REASONING   **Complete the statement with *always*, *sometimes*, or *never*.**

26. If $a < 0$, then $\left| x \right| > a$ is __?__ true.

27. A solution to the inequality $\left| x - 5 \right| < 4$ will __?__ be negative.

28. A solution to the inequality $\left| x - 7 \right| > 9$ will __?__ be negative.

29. A solution to the inequality $\left| x + 7 \right| < 6$ will __?__ be negative.

Student Help

▶ HOMEWORK HELP

Extra help with problem solving in Exs. 30–41 is available at www.mcdougallittell.com

SOLVING MULTI-STEP INEQUALITIES Solve the inequality. Then graph and check the solution.

30. $|2x - 9| \le 11$ **31.** $|4x + 2| < 6$ **32.** $|32x - 16| > 32$

33. $|2x + 7| > 23$ **34.** $|8x - 10| \ge 6$ **35.** $|4x - 3| < 7$

36. $|x + 2| - 5 \ge 8$ **37.** $|10 + 8x| - 2 > 16$ **38.** $|-4 + 2x| + 5 \le 23$

39. $|5x - 15| - 4 \ge 21$ **40.** $|3x + 2| - 5 < 0$ **41.** $|3x - 9| - 2 \le 7$

WRITING AND SOLVING INEQUALITIES In Exercises 42 and 43, write and solve an absolute-value inequality to find the indicated values.

42. WATER FOUNTAIN A stream of water rises from a fountain straight up with an initial velocity of 96 feet per second. Because the speed is the absolute value of the velocity, its speed s (in feet per second) after t seconds is given by $s = |-32t + 96|$. Find the times t for which the speed of the water is greater than 32 feet per second.

43. CANNON BALLS A cannon ball is fired straight up in the air with an initial velocity of 160 feet per second. Its speed s (in feet per second) after t seconds is given by $s = |-32t + 160|$. Find the times t for which the speed of the cannon ball is greater than 64 feet per second.

Link to Science

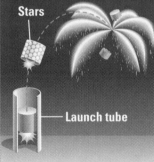

Stars

Launch tube

FIREWORKS The diagram above shows what happens when fireworks are launched.

More about fireworks is available at www.mcdougallittell.com

Science Link In Exercise 44–46, use the following information.
The color of light is determined by a property of light called its wavelength. When a firework star bursts, the chemicals in the firework burn. The color is determined by the wavelength of the light given off in the fire.

44. A firework star contains a copper compound. The absolute-value inequality $|w - 455| < 23$ describes the wavelengths w of the light given off by the compound when it burns. What color is the star?

45. A firework star contains a sodium compound. The absolute-value inequality $|w - 600| < 5$ describes the wavelengths w of the light given off by the compound when it burns. What color is the star?

Color	Wavelength, w
Ultraviolet	$w < 400$
Violet	$400 \le w < 424$
Blue	$424 \le w < 491$
Green	$491 \le w < 575$
Yellow	$575 \le w < 585$
Orange	$585 \le w < 647$
Red	$647 \le w < 700$
Infrared	$700 \le w$

46. A firework star contains a strontium compound. The absolute-value equation $|w - 643| < 38$ describes the wavelengths w of the light given off by the compound when it burns. What color is the star?

47. CHALLENGE Graph the solutions of $|x - 2| > x + 4$.

48. MULTIPLE CHOICE Which number is a solution of $|2x + 3| > 17$?

    Ⓐ −5   Ⓑ 0   Ⓒ 7   Ⓓ 10.5

49. MULTIPLE CHOICE Which is the graph of $|2x + 1| < 3$?

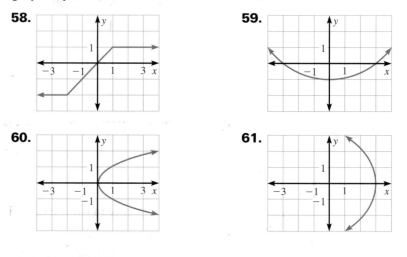

Mixed Review

FINDING THE DOMAIN Find the domain of the function. *(Lesson 2.8)*

50. $y = \dfrac{x}{8}$ **51.** $y = \dfrac{1}{x - 4}$ **52.** $y = \dfrac{7}{x + 1}$

EXCHANGE RATE Convert the currency using the given exchange rate. Round to the nearest whole number. *(Lesson 3.8)*

53. Convert 55 Canadian dollars to United States dollars.
(1 United States dollar = 1.466 Canadian dollars)

54. Convert 195 United States dollars to Mexican pesos.
(1 United States dollar = 9.242 pesos)

FINDING SOLUTIONS Find three different ordered pairs that are solutions of the equation. *(Lesson 4.3)*

55. $x = -12$ **56.** $y = 4$ **57.** $x = \dfrac{2}{3}$

VERTICAL LINE TEST Use the vertical line test to determine whether the graph represents a function. *(Lesson 4.8)*

58.

59.

60.

61.

Maintaining Skills

SUBTRACTING MIXED NUMBERS Subtract. Write the answer as a fraction or as a mixed number in lowest terms. *(Skills Review p. 765)*

62. $6\dfrac{2}{3} - 5\dfrac{2}{9}$ **63.** $8\dfrac{5}{6} - 3\dfrac{2}{9}$ **64.** $2\dfrac{2}{5} - 1\dfrac{3}{10}$

65. $15\dfrac{17}{18} - 4\dfrac{2}{3}$ **66.** $7\dfrac{7}{9} - 3\dfrac{5}{7}$ **67.** $19\dfrac{9}{12} - \dfrac{3}{8}$

6.8 Graphing Linear Inequalities in Two Variables

Goal

Graph linear inequalities in two variables.

Key Words

- linear inequality in two variables

How can you plan a healthy meal?

Nutritionists advise that you eat a variety of foods. Your diet should supply all the nutrients you need with neither too few nor too many calories. In Exercises 51 and 52 you will use inequalities to plan a meal.

A **linear inequality** in x and y is an inequality that can be written as follows,

$$ax + by < c \qquad ax + by \leq c \qquad ax + by > c \qquad ax + by \geq c$$

where a, b and c are given numbers. An ordered pair (x, y) is a solution of a linear inequality if the inequality is true when the values of x and y are substituted into the inequality.

EXAMPLE 1 Check Solutions of a Linear Inequality

Check whether the ordered pair is a solution of $2x - 3y \geq -2$.

  a. $(0, 0)$ **b.** $(0, 1)$ **c.** $(2, -1)$

Solution

(x, y)	$2x - 3y$	$2x - 3y \overset{?}{\geq} -2$	CONCLUSION
a. $(0, 0)$	$2(0) - 3(0) = 0$	$0 \geq -2$	$(0, 0)$ is a solution.
b. $(0, 1)$	$2(0) - 3(1) = -3$	$-3 \not\geq -2$	$(0, 1)$ is *not* a solution.
c. $(2, -1)$	$2(2) - 3(-1) = 7$	$7 \geq -2$	$(2, -1)$ is a solution.

The graph of a linear inequality in two variables is the graph of the solutions of the inequality.

The graph of $2x - 3y \geq -2$ is shown at the right. The graph includes the line $2x - 3y = -2$ and the shaded region *below* the line.

Every point that is on the line or in the shaded half-plane is a solution of the inequality. Every other point in the plane is *not* a solution.

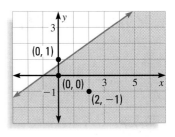

Student Help

▶ **STUDY TIP**
A dashed line indicates
that the points on the
line are *not* solutions.
A solid line indicates
that the points on the
line *are* solutions.

GRAPHING A LINEAR INEQUALITY

STEP ① **Graph** the corresponding equation. Use a *dashed line* for
> or <. Use a *solid line* for ≤ or ≥.

STEP ② **Test** the coordinates of a point in one of the half-planes.

STEP ③ **Shade** the half-plane containing the point if it is a solution
of the inequality. If it is not a solution, shade the other
half-plane.

EXAMPLE 2 Vertical Lines

Graph the inequality $x < -2$.

Solution

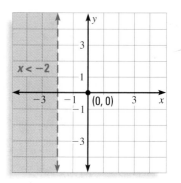

① **Graph** the corresponding equation $x = -2$.
The graph of $x = -2$ is a vertical line. The
inequality is <, so use a dashed line.

② **Test** a point. The origin $(0, 0)$ is *not* a
solution and it lies to the right of the line.
So the graph of $x < -2$ is all points to the
left of the line $x = -2$.

③ **Shade** the half-plane to the left of the line.

Student Help

▶ **STUDY TIP**
You can use any point
that is not on the line
as a test point. It is
convenient to use the
origin because 0 is
substituted for each
variable.

ANSWER ▶ The graph of $x < -2$ is the half-plane to the left of the graph
of $x = -2$. Check by testing any point to the left of the line.

EXAMPLE 3 Horizontal Lines

Graph the inequality $y \leq 1$.

Solution

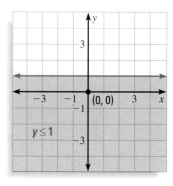

① **Graph** the corresponding equation $y = 1$.
The graph of $y = 1$ is a horizontal line. The
inequality is ≤, so use a solid line.

② **Test** a point. The origin $(0, 0)$ *is* a solution
and it lies below the line. So the graph of
$y \leq 1$ is all points on or *below* the line $y = 1$.

③ **Shade** the half-plane below the line.

ANSWER ▶ The graph of $y \leq 1$ is the graph of $y = 1$ and the half-plane below
the graph of $y = 1$. Check by testing any point below the line.

Checkpoint ✓ **Horizontal and Vertical Lines**

Graph the inequality.

1. $x \geq -1$ **2.** $x < 4$ **3.** $y > -3$ **4.** $y \leq 2$

DASHED VS. SOLID Tell whether you would use a dashed line or a solid line to graph the inequality.

23. $y \le -7$ **24.** $x > 10$ **25.** $x < 9$

SLOPE-INTERCEPT FORM Write the equation corresponding to the inequality in slope-intercept form. Tell whether you would use a dashed line or a solid line to graph the inequality.

26. $x + y > -15$ **27.** $x - y \le 0$ **28.** $4x + y < 9$

29. $x - 2y \ge 16$ **30.** $6x + 3y > 9$ **31.** $-4x - 2y < 6$

GRAPHING In Exercises 32–35, consider the inequality $2x - y \le 1$.

32. Write the equation corresponding to the inequality in slope-intercept form.

33. Tell whether you would use a solid or a dashed line to graph the corresponding equation. Then graph the equation.

34. Test the point $(0, 0)$ in the inequality.

35. Is the test point a solution? If so, shade the half-plane containing the point. If not, shade the other half-plane.

GRAPHING LINEAR INEQUALITIES Graph the inequality.

36. $x \ge -4$ **37.** $x \le 5$ **38.** $y > -1$

39. $x - 3 > -2$ **40.** $y + 6 \le 5$ **41.** $6y < 24$

42. $3x + y \ge 9$ **43.** $y + 4x \ge -1$ **44.** $x + y > -8$

45. $x + 2y < -10$ **46.** $x + 6y \le 12$ **47.** $4x + 3y < 24$

48. $2x - y > 6$ **49.** $-y + x \le 11$ **50.** $-x - y < 3$

Link to
Careers

NUTRITIONISTS plan nutrition programs and supervise preparation and serving of meals. Most nutritionists have a degree in food and nutrition or a related field.

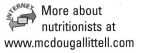

More about nutritionists at www.mcdougallittell.com

NUTRITION In Exercises 51 and 52, use the following information and the calorie counts of the breakfast foods that are in the table below.
You want to plan a nutritious breakfast. It should supply at least 500 calories or more. Be sure your choices would provide a reasonable breakfast.

51. You want to have apple juice, eggs, and one bagel. Let a be the number of glasses of apple juice and e the number of eggs. The inequality $123a + 75e + 195 > 500$ models the situation. Determine three ordered pairs (a, e) that are solutions of the inequality where $0 \le a \le 5$ and $0 \le e < 8$.

52. You decide on cereal, milk, and one glass of tomato juice. Let c be the number of cups of cereal and m the number of cups of milk. The inequality $102c + 150m + 41 > 500$ models the situation. Determine three ordered pairs (c, m) that are solutions of the inequality where $0 \le c < 8$ and $0 \le m < 4$.

Breakfast food	Calories
Plain bagel	195
Cereal, 1 cup	102
Apple juice, 1 glass	123
Tomato juice, 1 glass	41
Egg	75
Milk, 1 cup	150

GOLD AND SILVER Divers searching for gold and silver coins collect the coins in a wire basket that contains 50 pounds of material or less. Each gold coin weighs about 0.5 ounce. Each silver coin weighs about 0.25 ounce. What are the different numbers of coins that could be in the basket? Write an algebraic model that models this situation.

Solution

Find the weight in ounces of the contents of the basket. There are 16 ounces in a pound, so there are 50 • 16 or 800 ounces in 50 pounds.

Write an algebraic model.

VERBAL MODEL	Weight per gold coin	•	Number of gold coins	+	Weight per silver coin	•	Number of silver coins	≤	Weight in basket

LABELS

Weight per gold coin = **0.5**   (ounces per coin)

Number of gold coins = **x**   (coins)

Weight per silver coin = **0.25**   (ounces per coin)

Number of silver coins = **y**   (coins)

Maximum weight in basket = **800**   (ounces)

ALGEBRAIC MODEL

$$0.5\,x + 0.25\,y \le 800$$

GOLD Most metals deteriorate quickly in salt water. Gold, however, is not harmed by salt water, by air, or even by acid. Gold does not easily interact with other chemicals.

More about gold is available at www.mcdougallittell.com

---

53. Graph the algebraic model in the example above.

54. Name and interpret two solutions of your inequality from Exercise 53.

Standardized Test Practice

55. MULTIPLE CHOICE Choose the ordered pair that is a solution of the inequality whose graph is shown.

Ⓐ (0, 0)

Ⓑ (−2, 0)

Ⓒ (−2, −1)

Ⓓ (2, −1)

56. MULTIPLE CHOICE Choose the inequality whose graph is shown.

Ⓕ $2y − 6x < −4$

Ⓖ $2y − 6x \le −4$

Ⓗ $2y − 6x \ge −4$

Ⓙ $2y − 6x > −4$

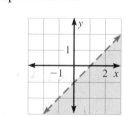

EVALUATING EXPRESSIONS **Evaluate the expression. Then simplify your answer.** *(Lesson 1.3)*

57. $\dfrac{16 + 11 + 18}{3}$
58. $\dfrac{20 + 15 + 22 + 19}{4}$
59. $\dfrac{37 + 65 + 89 + 72 + 82}{5}$

CONVERTING TEMPERATURES **In Exercises 60 and 61, use the temperature conversion formula $F = \dfrac{9}{5}C + 32$, where F represents degrees Fahrenheit and C represents degrees Celsius.** *(Lesson 3.7)*

60. Solve the temperature formula for C.

61. Use the formula you wrote in Exercise 60 to convert 86 degrees Fahrenheit to degrees Celsius.

FINDING SLOPES AND Y-INTERCEPTS **Find the slope and *y*-intercept of the graph of the equation.** *(Lesson 4.7)*

62. $y = -5x + 2$
63. $y = \dfrac{1}{2}x - 2$
64. $5x - 5y = 1$

65. $6x + 2y = 14$
66. $y = -2$
67. $y = 5$

Maintaining Skills

PERCENTS **Determine the percent of the graph that is shaded.** *(Skills Review p. 768)*

68.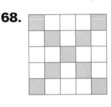

69.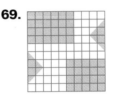

70.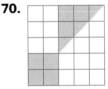

Quiz 3

Solve the inequality. Then graph and check the solution. *(Lesson 6.7)*

1. $|x| \geq 18$
2. $|x - 4| > 1$
3. $|x + 7| < 2$

4. $|3x - 12| \leq 9$
5. $|2x + 7| \leq 25$
6. $|4x + 2| - 5 > 17$

7. BASEBALL A baseball is thrown straight up with an initial velocity of 48 feet per second. Its speed s (in feet per second) after t seconds is given by $s = |-32t + 48|$. Find the times t for which the speed of the baseball is greater than 24 feet per second. *(Lesson 6.7)*

Check whether each ordered pair is a solution of the inequality. *(Lesson 6.8)*

8. $x + y \leq 4$; $(0, -1)$, $(2, 2)$
9. $y - 3x > 0$; $(0, 0)$, $(-4, 1)$

10. $-2x + 5y \geq 5$; $(2, 1)$, $(-1, 2)$
11. $-x - 2y < 4$; $(1, -1)$, $(2, -3)$

Graph the inequality. *(Lesson 6.8)*

12. $x \leq -4$
13. $y \geq 3$
14. $y - 5x > 0$

15. $y < -2x$
16. $3x + y > 1$
17. $2x - y \geq 5$

USING A GRAPHING CALCULATOR
Graphing Inequalities

The *Shade* feature of a graphing calculator can be used to graph an inequality.

Sample

Graph the inequality $x - 2y \leq -6$.

Solution

1 Rewrite the inequality to isolate y on the left side of the equation.

$$x - 2y \leq -6 \qquad \text{Write original inequality.}$$

$$-2y \leq -x - 6 \qquad \text{Subtract } x \text{ from each side.}$$

$$y \geq \frac{x}{2} + 3 \qquad \text{Divide each side by } -2 \text{ and reverse the inequality.}$$

2 Use your calculator's procedure for graphing and shading an inequality to graph $y \geq \frac{x}{2} + 3$. It may not be clear on the screen whether the graph of the corresponding equation is part of the graph. In that case, you must decide.

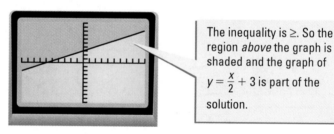

The inequality is $\geq$. So the region *above* the graph is shaded and the graph of $y = \frac{x}{2} + 3$ is part of the solution.

3 In the revised inequality, the inequality is $\geq$. So the graph of the corresponding equation should be indicated by a solid line.

Student Help

▶**KEYSTROKE HELP**

See keystrokes for several models of calculators at www.mcdougallittell.com

Try These

Use a graphing calculator to graph the inequality. Use an appropriate viewing window.

1. $y < -2x - 3$ **2.** $y > 2x + 2$ **3.** $x + 2y \leq -1$ **4.** $x - 3y \geq 3$

5. $y > 0.5x + 2$ **6.** $y < 3x - 3.2$ **7.** $\frac{3}{4}x + y \geq 1$ **8.** $\frac{x}{2} - 2y \leq 2$

9. $y < x + 25$ **10.** $y > -x + 25$ **11.** $y \leq 0.1x$ **12.** $y \geq 100x$

13. Write an inequality that represents all points that lie above the line $y = x$. Use a graphing calculator to check your answer.

14. Write an inequality that represents all points that lie below the line $y = x + 2$. Use a graphing calculator to check your answer.

VOCABULARY

- **graph of an inequality,** *p. 323*
- **equivalent inequalities,** *p. 324*
- **addition property of inequality,** *p. 324*
- **subtraction property of inequality,** *p. 324*

- **multiplication property of inequality,** *pp. 330, 331*
- **division property of inequality,** *pp. 330, 331*
- **compound inequality,** *p. 342*

- **absolute-value equation,** *p. 355*
- **absolute-value inequality,** *p. 361*
- **linear inequality in two variables,** *p. 367*

6.1 SOLVING INEQUALITIES USING ADDITION OR SUBTRACTION

Examples on pp. 323–325

> **EXAMPLE** Solve $n - 5 < -10$. Then graph the solution.
>
> $n - 5 < -10$ — Write original inequality.
>
> $n - 5 + 5 < -10 + 5$ — Add 5 to each side.
>
> $n < -5$ — Simplify.
>
> **ANSWER** ▶ The solution is all real numbers less than -5.
>
> (number line: -7 -6 -5 -4, open circle at -5)

Solve the inequality. Then graph the solution.

1. $x - 5 \le -3$ **2.** $a + 6 > 28$ **3.** $-8 < -10 + x$ **4.** $7 + z \ge 20$

6.2 SOLVING INEQUALITIES USING MULTIPLICATION OR DIVISION

Examples on pp. 330–332

> **EXAMPLE** Solve $-14x < 56$. Then graph the solution.
>
> $-14x < 56$ — Write original inequality.
>
> $\dfrac{-14x}{-14} > \dfrac{56}{-14}$ — Divide each side by -14 and reverse the inequality.
>
> $x > -4$ — Simplify.
>
> **ANSWER** ▶ The solution is all real numbers greater than -4.
>
> (number line: -5 -4 -3 -2, open circle at -4)

Solve the inequality. Then graph the solution.

5. $64 < 8x$ **6.** $-6k > -30$ **7.** $-81 \ge -3p$ **8.** $-81 > 9r$

9. $-\dfrac{3}{2}n \ge 9$ **10.** $3 < \dfrac{x}{5}$ **11.** $\dfrac{t}{14} \le 4$ **12.** $-\dfrac{1}{6}y \ge 3$

6.3   SOLVING MULTI-STEP INEQUALITIES

Examples on pp. 336–338

> **EXAMPLE** Solve $7 + 2x \geq -3$.
>
> $$7 + 2x \geq -3 \qquad \text{Write original inequality.}$$
> $$7 - 7 + 2x \geq -3 - 7 \qquad \text{Subtract 7 from each side.}$$
> $$2x \geq -10 \qquad \text{Simplify.}$$
> $$\frac{2x}{2} \geq -\frac{10}{2} \qquad \text{Divide each side by 2.}$$
> $$x \geq -5 \qquad \text{Simplify.}$$
>
> **ANSWER** ▶ The solution is all real numbers greater than or equal to -5.

Solve the inequality.

13. $6x - 8 \geq 4$

14. $10 - 3x < -5$

15. $4x - 9 \geq 11$

16. $5(x - 2) \leq 10$

17. $-3(x - 1) > 4$

18. $\frac{1}{4}(x + 8) < 1$

19. $5 - 8x \leq -3x$

20. $5x > 12 + x$

21. $3x - 9 \leq 2x + 4$

6.4   SOLVING COMPOUND INEQUALITIES INVOLVING "AND"

Examples on pp. 342–344

> **EXAMPLE** Solve $-1 < 3x + 2 \leq 11$. Then graph the solution.
>
> $$-1 < 3x + 2 \leq 11 \qquad \text{Write original inequality.}$$
> $$-1 - 2 < 3x + 2 - 2 \leq 11 - 2 \qquad \text{Subtract 2 from each expression.}$$
> $$-3 < 3x \leq 9 \qquad \text{Simplify.}$$
> $$-\frac{3}{3} < \frac{3x}{3} \leq \frac{9}{3} \qquad \text{Divide each expression by 3.}$$
> $$-1 < x \leq 3 \qquad \text{Simplify.}$$
>
> **ANSWER** ▶ The solution is all real numbers greater than -1 and less than or equal to 3. The graph of the solution is shown below.
>

Solve the inequality. Then graph the solution.

22. $9 < x + 1 < 13$

23. $-3 \leq 3x \leq 15$

24. $-1 \leq x - 2 < 3$

25. $1 < 2x - 3 < 5$

26. $0 < 4 - x \leq 5$

27. $-7 < 3 - \frac{1}{4}x \leq 1$

6.5   SOLVING COMPOUND INEQUALITIES INVOLVING "OR"

Examples on pp. 348–350

EXAMPLE   Solve the compound inequality $x + 3 \leq 7$ or $4x > 20$. Then graph the solution.

Solve each of the parts separately.

$$x + 3 \leq 7 \qquad or \qquad 4x > 20 \qquad \text{Write original inequality.}$$

$$x + 3 - 3 \leq 7 - 3 \quad or \quad \frac{4x}{4} > \frac{20}{4} \qquad \text{Isolate } x.$$

$$x \leq 4 \qquad or \qquad x > 5 \qquad \text{Simplify.}$$

ANSWER ▶ The solution is all real numbers less than or equal to 4 or greater than 5. The graph of the solution is shown below.

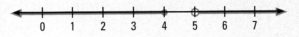

Solve the inequality. Then graph the solution.

28. $x > 4$ or $3x \leq -9$

29. $2x \leq -10$ or $x + 3 > 1$

30. $x - 7 \geq 0$ or $3 + x < -2$

31. $6x - 2 \leq 4$ or $3x > 21$

32. $3x + 2 \leq -7$ or $2x + 1 \geq 9$

33. $\frac{1}{4}x < \frac{1}{2}$ or $3x - 6 > 24$

6.6   SOLVING ABSOLUTE-VALUE EQUATIONS

Examples on pp. 355–357

EXAMPLE   Solve $|x - 4| = 6$.

Because $|x - 4| = 6$, the expression $x - 4$ is equal to 6 or -6.

x − 4 IS POSITIVE	*or*	**x − 4 IS NEGATIVE**
$x - 4 = 6$		$x - 4 = -6$
$x - 4 + 4 = 6 + 4$		$x - 4 + 4 = -6 + 4$
$x = 10$	*or*	$x = -2$

ANSWER ▶ The equation has two solutions: 10 and -2.

CHECK ✓ $|10 - 4| = |6| = 6$ $\qquad |-2 - 4| = |-6| = 6$

Solve the equation and check your solutions. If the equation has no solution, write *no solution*.

34. $|x| = 13$

35. $|x| = -7$

36. $|x - 1| = 6$

37. $|3x| = 27$

38. $|2x - 3| = 1$

39. $|6x - 1| + 5 = 2$

40. Write an absolute-value equation that has 9 and 21 as its solutions.

6.7 SOLVING ABSOLUTE-VALUE INEQUALITIES

Examples on pp. 361–363

EXAMPLE Solve $|x + 1| < 2$. Then graph the solution.

The inequality involves <, so the related inequalities are connected by *and*.

$|x + 1| < 2$			Write original inequality.
$x + 1 < 2$	*and*	$x + 1 > -2$	Write related inequalities.
$x + 1 - 1 < 2 - 1$	*and*	$x + 1 - 1 > -2 - 1$	Subtract 1 from each side.
$x < 1$	*and*	$x > -3$	Simplify.

ANSWER The solution is all real numbers greater than -3 and less than 1. This can be written $-3 < x < 1$. The graph of the solution is shown below. Check the solution.

Solve the inequality. Then graph and check the solution.

41. $|x| \leq 2$ **42.** $|6x| > 24$ **43.** $|x - 10| \leq 8$

44. $|4x + 8| \geq 20$ **45.** $|2x - 2| < 8$ **46.** $|5x + 3| > 2$

47. $|x - 4| - 5 < 1$ **48.** $|3x| + 2 \leq 11$ **49.** $|2x + 1| - 5 > 7$

6.8 GRAPHING LINEAR INEQUALITIES IN TWO VARIABLES

Examples on pp. 367–369

EXAMPLE Graph $y - x > 4$.

Write the corresponding equation in slope-intercept form.

$y - x = 4$	Write corresponding equation.
$y = x + 4$	Add x to each side.

The graph of the line has a slope of 1 and a y-intercept of 4. The inequality is >, so use a dashed line.

Test the origin. $(0, 0)$ is *not* a solution. Since it lies below the line, shade above the line.

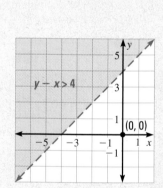

ANSWER The graph of $y - x > 4$ is all points above the line.

Check by testing any point above the line.

Graph the inequality.

50. $y > -5$ **51.** $x < 2$ **52.** $-2x + y \geq 4$

53. $x - 3y \geq 3$ **54.** $2y - 6x \geq -2$ **55.** $3x + 6y < 12$

Solve the inequality. Then graph the solution.

1. $x - 3 < 10$

2. $-6 > x + 5$

3. $-5 + x \geq 1$

4. $\frac{1}{4}x \leq 2$

5. $-3x < 21$

6. $-\frac{1}{2}x < 3$

7. $6 - x > 15$

8. $3x + 2 \leq 35$

9. $\frac{2}{3}x + 1 > 7$

10. $2(x + 1) \geq 6$

11. $3x + 5 \leq 2x - 1$

12. $-2(x + 4) > 3x + 17$

Solve the compound inequality. Then graph the solution.

13. $-15 \leq 5x < 20$

14. $-3 \leq x + 5 \leq 7$

15. $-5 < 3x - 4 < 17$

16. $-17 \leq 3x + 1 < 25$

17. $x - 2 > 8 \ or \ x + 1 \geq 7$

18. $-\frac{1}{2}x < -3 \ or \ 2x < -12$

19. $x < -2 \ or \ 3x - 5 > 1$

20. $8x - 11 < 5 \ or \ 4x - 7 > 13$

21. $6x + 9 \geq 21 \ or \ 9x - 5 \leq 4$

22. PAPER MAKING A machine makes rolls of paper. The rolls can be as wide as 33 feet or as narrow as 12 feet. Write a compound inequality that describes the possible widths w of a roll of paper produced by this machine.

Solve the equation and check your solution. If the equation has no solution, write *no solution*.

23. $|x + 7| = 11$

24. $|3x + 4| = 16$

25. $|x - 8| - 3 = 10$

Write an absolute-value equation that has the given solutions.

26. 1 and 5

27. -8 and -4

28. -1 and 9

Solve the inequality. Then graph and check the solution.

29. $|2x| > 14$

30. $|4x + 5| \leq 1$

31. $|3x - 9| + 6 < 18$

Graph the inequality in a coordinate plane.

32. $x > -1$

33. $y > 5$

34. $y \geq 3x - 3$

35. $x + y \leq 1$

36. $x + 2y > 6$

37. $3x + 4y \geq 12$

ALGEBRAIC MODELING In Exercises 38 and 39, use the following information. Your club plans to buy sandwiches and juice drinks for a club picnic. Each sandwich costs about $2 and each drink about $1. You want to find out how many of each you can buy if you have to spend less than $100.

38. Write and graph an algebraic model that models the situation.

39. Name two solutions of the inequality you graphed in Exercise 38. Interpret the solutions.

Chapter Standardized Test

Test Tip   Work as fast as you can through the easier
problems, but not so fast that you are careless.

1. Which graph represents the solution of the
inequality $x + 5 < 12$?

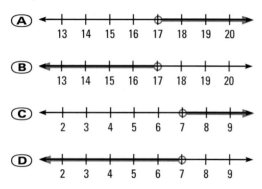

2. Which phrase describes the solution of the
inequality $5x < 10$?

Ⓐ All real numbers greater than 5

Ⓑ All real numbers less than 5

Ⓒ All real numbers greater than 2

Ⓓ All real numbers less than 2

3. Which inequality is equivalent to
$2 - 3x \geq -4$?

Ⓐ $x \geq 2$ Ⓑ $x \leq 2$

Ⓒ $x \geq -2$ Ⓓ $x \leq -2$

4. For which values of x is the inequality
$-3x + 4 \leq x - 2$ true?

Ⓐ $x \leq -3$ Ⓑ $x \geq -3$

Ⓒ $x \leq 1$ Ⓓ $x \geq \dfrac{3}{2}$

5. Which number is *not* a solution of the
inequality $-4 \leq x - 1 \leq 5$?

Ⓐ -4 Ⓑ -3

Ⓒ 5 Ⓓ 6

6. What is the solution of the compound
inequality $-3x + 2 > 11$ *or* $5x + 1 > 6$?

Ⓐ $x < -3$ *or* $x > 1$

Ⓑ $x < 3$ *or* $x > 1$

Ⓒ $x > -3$ *or* $x < 1$

Ⓓ $x > 3$ *or* $x < 1$

Ⓔ None of these

7. Which numbers are solutions of the
equation $|x - 7| + 5 = 17$?

Ⓐ -19 and 15 Ⓑ -15 and 19

Ⓒ -15 and 29 Ⓓ -5 and 19

8. Which graph represents the solution of the
inequality $|2x - 10| \geq 6$?

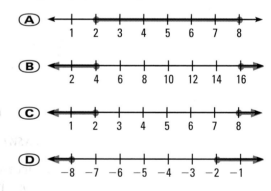

9. Choose the inequality whose solution is
shown in the graph.

Ⓐ $2x + y < 4$

Ⓑ $2x + y > 4$

Ⓒ $2x - y < 4$

Ⓓ $2x - y > 4$

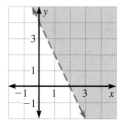

Maintaining Skills

EXAMPLE 1 Evaluate an Expression

Evaluate $2x + 4y$ when $x = 3$ and $y = 10$.

Solution

$2x + 4y$	Write original expression.
$2(3) + 4(10)$	Substitute 3 for x and 10 for y.
$6 + 40$	Simplify using the order of operations. First multiply.
46	Then add.

ANSWER ▶ When $x = 3$ and $y = 10$, $2x + 4y = 46$.

Try These

Evaluate the expression when $x = 5$ and $y = 9$.

1. $5x + 5y$ **2.** $9y + x$ **3.** $2x + 3y$ **4.** $7y + 3x$

5. $12x + y$ **6.** $4y + 4x$ **7.** $3x + 4y$ **8.** $6y + 2x$

EXAMPLE 2 Add Integers

Find the sum.

a. $-4 + (-7)$ **b.** $4 + (-7)$

Solution

a. Since -4 and -7 have the same sign, add the absolute values. Give the sum the same sign as the integers being added.

$$-4 + (-7) = -(|-4| + |-7|) = -(4 + 7) = -11$$

ANSWER ▶ $-4 + (-7) = -11$

b. Since 4 and -7 have opposite signs, subtract the smaller absolute value (4) from the larger absolute value (7). Give the difference the same sign as the integer with the larger absolute value.

$$4 + (-7) = -(|-7| - |4|) = -(7 - 4) = -3$$

ANSWER ▶ $4 + (-7) = -3$

Try These

Find the sum.

9. $-6 + (-11)$ **10.** $-4 + (-10)$ **11.** $8 + (-1)$ **12.** $-9 + (-9)$

13. $-21 + 24$ **14.** $-11 + 9$ **15.** $15 + (-8)$ **16.** $30 + (-16)$

Evaluate the expression for the given value of the variable. (1.1, 1.2, 1.3)

1. $x + 8$ when $x = -1$ **2.** $3x - 2$ when $x = 7$ **3.** $x(4 + x)$ when $x = 5$

4. $3(x - 5)$ when $x = 1$ **5.** $\dfrac{x + 8}{x}$ when $x = 4$ **6.** $x^3 - 3x + 1$ when $x = 2$

7. PHOTO COSTS A photography studio charges \$65 for a basic package of graduation photos. Each additional wallet-sized photo costs \$1. Use the equation $C = 65 + n$, where C is the total cost and n is the number of additional wallet-sized photos. Make an input-output table that shows the cost of ordering 0 through 6 additional wallet-sized photos. (1.8)

Evaluate the expression. (2.2, 2.3, 2.4)

8. $-|3|$ **9.** $|-2.5|$ **10.** $-15 + 7$

11. $2 + (-6) + (-14)$ **12.** $-8 - 12$ **13.** $3.1 - (-3.3) - 1.8$

14. VELOCITY AND SPEED A hot-air balloon descends at a rate of 800 feet per minute. What are the hot-air balloon's velocity and speed? (2.2)

15. TEMPERATURES On February 21, 1918, the temperature in Granville, North Dakota, rose from $-33°F$ to $50°F$ in 12 hours. By how many degrees did the temperature rise? (2.4)

Simplify the expression. (2.6, 2.7)

16. $4(a - 4)$ **17.** $3(6 + x)$ **18.** $(5 + n)2$ **19.** $(3 - t)(-5)$

20. $20x - 17x$ **21.** $4b + 7 + 7b$ **22.** $5x - 3(x - 9)$ **23.** $4(y + 1) + 2(y + 1)$

Solve the equation. (3.1–3.4)

24. $x + 4 = -1$ **25.** $-3 = n - (-15)$ **26.** $6b = -36$

27. $\dfrac{x}{4} = 6$ **28.** $3x + 4 = 13$ **29.** $5x + 2 = -18$

30. $6 + \dfrac{2}{3}x = 14$ **31.** $2x + 7x - 15 = 75$ **32.** $5(x - 2) = 15$

33. $\dfrac{1}{3}(x - 15) = 20$ **34.** $x - 8 = 3(x - 4)$ **35.** $-(x - 6) = 4x + 1$

In Exercises 36 and 37, use the formula for density, $d = \dfrac{m}{v}$, where m represents mass and v represents volume. (3.7)

36. Find a formula for v in terms of d and m.

37. Use the formula you wrote in Exercise 36 to find the volume (in cubic centimeters) of a piece of cork that has a density of 0.24 gram per cubic centimeter and a mass of 3 grams.

Find the unit rate. (3.8)

38. $1 for two cans of dog food

39. 156 miles traveled in 3 hours

40. $480 for working 40 hours

41. 125 feet in 5 seconds

Plot and label the ordered pairs in a coordinate plane. (4.1)

42. $A(2, 3)$, $B(2, -3)$, $C(-1, 1)$

43. $A(0, -2)$, $B(-3, -3)$, $C(2, 0)$

44. $A(2, 4)$, $B(3, 0)$, $C(-1, -4)$

45. $A(1, -4)$, $B(-2, 4)$, $C(0, -1)$

CATFISH SALES **In Exercises 46 and 47, use the following information.**
The table below shows the number of catfish (in millions) sold in the United States from 1990 through 1997. The numbers are rounded to the nearest million. (4.1)

Year	1990	1991	1992	1993	1994	1995	1996	1997
Number of catfish (millions)	273	333	374	379	348	322	375	387

▶ Source: U.S. Bureau of the Census

46. Draw a scatter plot of the data. Use the horizontal axis to represent the time.

47. Describe the relationship between the number of catfish sold and time.

Use a table of values to graph the equation. (4.2)

48. $x + y = 0$

49. $2x + y = 12$

50. $x - y = 8$

51. $x - y = 4$

52. $2x - y = -1$

53. $x + 2y = 4$

Write the equation of the line in slope-intercept form. (5.1)

54. Slope = 1; y-intercept = -3.

55. Slope = -2; y-intercept = 5.

56. Slope = 0; y-intercept = 0.

57. Slope = 4; y-intercept = 1.

Write in slope-intercept form the equation of the line that passes through the given point and has the given slope. (5.2)

58. $(-1, 1)$, $m = 2$

59. $(0, 1)$, $m = 1$

60. $(3, 3)$, $m = 0$

61. $(3, -1)$, $m = \dfrac{1}{4}$

62. $(-3, 6)$, $m = -5$

63. $(-2, 2)$, $m = -3$

Write in point-slope form the equation of the line that passes through the given points. (5.3)

64. $(2, 0)$ and $(0, -2)$

65. $(1, 4)$ and $(3, 6)$

66. $(1, 10)$ and $(3, 2)$

67. $(-1, -7)$ and $(-2, 1)$

68. $(0, 3)$ and $(2, 4)$

69. $(4, 7)$ and $(8, 10)$

Solve the inequality. (6.1–6.5, 6.7)

70. $-6 \leq x + 12$

71. $6 > 3x$

72. $-\dfrac{x}{6} \geq 8$

73. $-4 - 5x \leq 31$

74. $-4x + 3 > -21$

75. $-x + 2 < 2(x - 5)$

76. $-3 \leq x + 1 < 7$

77. $-4 \leq -2x \leq 10$

78. $2x > 10$ or $x + 1 < 3$

79. $x + 3 > 7$ or $2x + 3 \leq -1$

80. $|x - 8| > 10$

81. $|2x + 5| \leq 7$

Investigating Springs

Materials
- hole punch
- paper cup
- string
- scissors
- rubber band
- masking tape
- paper clip
- metric ruler
- 100 pennies

OBJECTIVE Model the movement of a spring.

When a weight is attached to a spring, the spring stretches as shown.

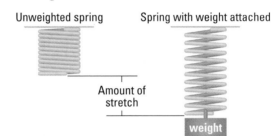

Unweighted spring   Spring with weight attached

Amount of stretch

weight

Let y be the weight attached to a spring and let x be the amount of stretch. The variables x and y vary directly, that is $y = kx$. The constant of variation k is called the *spring constant* for that particular spring.

In this project you will make a model of this direct variation using a rubber band to represent the spring. The weights attached to the spring will be groups of 10 pennies. You will estimate the "spring constant" k for your "spring" by finding the ratio of the number of pennies to the amount of stretch for each group of pennies.

COLLECTING THE DATA

❶ Punch two holes on opposite sides of the cup, about one half inch down from the rim. Thread the string through both holes and knot the ends. Trim any excess string. Attach the rubber band to the string.

❷ Tape the paper clip to the edge of a table or desk so that one end hangs over the edge. Attach the rubber band to the paper clip. The cup should be hanging over the side of the table as shown in the photo above.

❸ Tape the ruler to the table as shown. The "0" on the ruler should line up with the top of the rubber band. Record the distance from the top of the rubber band to the bottom of the cup. This is the initial distance d.

④ Add pennies to the cup in groups of 10. Each time, measure the distance D from the top of the rubber band to the bottom of the cup. The amount of stretch x is given by $x = D - d$. Copy and complete the table below.

Number of pennies y	0	10	20	30	40	50
Distance D (mm)	d	?	?	?	?	?
Amount of stretch x (mm)	0	?	?	?	?	?
$\dfrac{y}{x}$	—	?	?	?	?	?

INVESTIGATING THE DATA

1. Use the values of $\dfrac{y}{x}$ in the last row of your table to estimate the value of k, the spring constant for your spring. (The values may not all be the same because of minor variations in the weights of individual pennies or measuring errors.)

2. Use your answer to Exercise 1 to write a direct variation model that relates the number of pennies to the amount of stretch.

3. What do you the think the amount of stretch would be if you added a total of 100 pennies to the cup? Test your conjecture.

PRESENTING YOUR RESULTS

Write a report or make a poster to present your results.

• Include a table with your data and include your answers to Exercises 1–3.

• Describe any patterns you found when you discussed the results with others.

• Tell what advice you would give to someone who is going to do this project.

EXTENDING THE PROJECT

• How does the length of the rubber band affect the total distance it stretches? Tie a knot in the rubber band to shorten it and repeat the experiment.

• How does the thickness of the rubber band affect the distance it stretches? Repeat the experiment with a thicker rubber band of the same length.

• A grocery store scale operates in a similar way. When you put fruits or vegetables on the scale, the spring inside the scale stretches. The heavier the item, the larger the stretch. Can you think of other items that work in a similar way?

Systems of Linear Equations and Inequalities

▶ How can you analyze the need for low-income housing?

APPLICATION: Housing

▶ **To see how the need** for low-income rental housing changes over time, you can construct a model. The graph below shows the number of households with annual earnings of $12,000 or less that need to rent housing and the number of rental units available that they can afford.

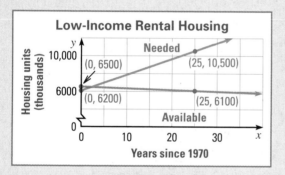

In this chapter you will learn how to use pairs of linear equations, as well as inequalities, to analyze problems.

Think & Discuss

Use the graph to answer the following questions.

1. How many low-cost housing units were available in 1995?

2. In 1995 how much greater was the need for low-income housing than the availability of low-cost units?

Learn More About It

You will use a linear system to analyze the need for low-income housing in Exercises 32 and 33 on page 413.

 APPLICATION LINK More about housing is available at www.mcdougallittell.com

PREVIEW

What's the chapter about?

- Graphing and solving **systems of linear equations**
- Determining the number of **solutions of a linear system**
- Graphing and solving **systems of linear inequalities**

> **KEY WORDS**
>
> - **system of linear equations,** *p. 389*
> - **solution of a linear system,** *p. 389*
> - **point of intersection,** *p. 389*
> - **linear combination,** *p. 402*
> - **system of linear inequalities,** *p. 424*
> - **solution of a system of linear inequalities,** *p. 424*

PREPARE

Chapter Readiness Quiz

Take this quick quiz. If you are unsure of an answer, look back at the reference pages for help.

VOCABULARY CHECK *(refer to pp. 134, 153)*

1. Which of the following is *not* a linear equation?

    Ⓐ $2x + y = 5$ Ⓑ $x = 3$

    Ⓒ $y = 2x^2 - 1$ Ⓓ $y = 3x$

2. Which equation is an identity?

    Ⓐ $7x + 6 = 5(2x + 1)$ Ⓑ $5(2x + 4) = 2(10 + 5x)$

    Ⓒ $-8x + 4 = -2(4x + 4)$ Ⓓ $-4(2 - 3x) = -8 - 12x$

SKILL CHECK *(refer to pp. 146, 367)*

3. What is the solution of the equation $2x + 6(x + 1) = -2$?

    Ⓐ -1 Ⓑ $-\dfrac{3}{8}$ Ⓒ $\dfrac{1}{2}$ Ⓓ 1

4. Which ordered pair is a solution of the inequality $7y - 8x > 56$?

    Ⓐ $(0, 8)$ Ⓑ $(0, 0)$ Ⓒ $(-6, 1)$ Ⓓ $(-7, 2)$

STUDY TIP

List Kinds of Problems

In your notebook keep a list of different types of problems and how to solve them.

> **Mixture Problems (p. 410)**
>
> $$x + y = 90 \longleftarrow \text{volume of mixture}$$
>
> $$0.2x + 0.5y = 36 \longleftarrow \text{acid in mixture}$$
>
> Since at least one of the variables has a coefficient of 1, use the substitution method to solve.

Graphing Linear Systems

Goal

Estimate the solution of a system of linear equations by graphing.

Key Words

- system of linear equations
- solution of a linear system
- point of intersection

How many hits are you getting at your Web site?

In this chapter you will study *systems of linear equations.* In Example 3 you will use two equations to predict when two Web sites will have the same number of daily visits.

Two or more linear equations in the same variable form a **system of linear equations**, or simply a *linear system.* Here is an example of a linear system.

$$x + 2y = 5 \qquad \text{Equation 1}$$
$$2x - 3y = 3 \qquad \text{Equation 2}$$

A **solution of a linear system** in two variables is a pair of numbers a and b for which $x = a$ and $y = b$ make each equation a true statement.

Such a solution can be written as an ordered pair (a, b) in which a and b are the values of x and y that solve the linear system. The point (a, b) that lies on the graph of each equation is called the **point of intersection** of the graphs.

Student Help

▶ **MORE EXAMPLES**

More examples are available at www.mcdougallittell.com

EXAMPLE 1 Find the Point of Intersection

Use the graph at the right to estimate the solution of the linear system. Then check your solution algebraically.

$$3x + 2y = 4 \qquad \text{Equation 1}$$
$$-x + 3y = -5 \qquad \text{Equation 2}$$

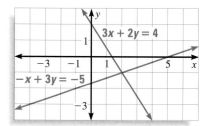

Solution

The lines appear to intersect at the point $(2, -1)$.

CHECK ✓ Substitute 2 for x and -1 for y in each equation.

EQUATION 1	EQUATION 2
$3x + 2y = 4$	$-x + 3y = -5$
$3(2) + 2(-1) \stackrel{?}{=} 4$	$-(2) + 3(-1) \stackrel{?}{=} -5$
$6 - 2 \stackrel{?}{=} 4$	$-2 - 3 \stackrel{?}{=} -5$
$4 = 4$ ✓	$-5 = -5$ ✓

ANSWER ▶ Because the ordered pair $(2, -1)$ makes each equation true, $(2, -1)$ is the solution of the system of linear equations.

SOLVING A LINEAR SYSTEM USING GRAPH-AND-CHECK

STEP 1 *Write* each equation in a form that is easy to graph.

STEP 2 *Graph* both equations in the same coordinate plane.

STEP 3 *Estimate* the coordinates of the point of intersection.

STEP 4 *Check* whether the coordinates give a solution by substituting them into each equation of the original linear system.

EXAMPLE 2 **Graph and Check a Linear System**

Use the graph-and-check method to solve the linear system.

$$x + y = -2 \qquad \text{Equation 1}$$
$$2x - 3y = -9 \qquad \text{Equation 2}$$

Solution

Student Help

▶ **LOOK BACK**
For help with writing equations in slope-intercept form, see p. 243.

1 *Write* each equation in slope-intercept form.

EQUATION 1	**EQUATION 2**
$x + y = -2$	$2x - 3y = -9$
$y = -x - 2$	$-3y = -2x - 9$
	$y = \frac{2}{3}x + 3$

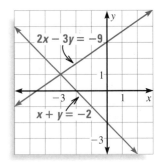

2 *Graph* both equations.

3 *Estimate* from the graph that the point of intersection is $(-3, 1)$.

4 *Check* whether $(-3, 1)$ is a solution by substituting -3 for x and 1 for y in each of the original equations.

EQUATION 1

$$x + y = -2$$
$$-3 + 1 \overset{?}{=} -2$$
$$-2 = -2 \ \checkmark$$

EQUATION 2

$$2x - 3y = -9$$
$$2(-3) - 3(1) \overset{?}{=} -9$$
$$-6 - 3 \overset{?}{=} -9$$
$$-9 = -9 \ \checkmark$$

ANSWER ▶ Because the ordered pair $(-3, 1)$ makes each equation true, $(-3, 1)$ is the solution of the linear system.

Checkpoint ✓ **Graph and Check a Linear System**

Use the graph-and-check method to solve the linear system.

1. $x + y = 4$
$2x + y = 5$

2. $x - y = 5$
$2x + 3y = 0$

3. $x - y = -2$
$x + y = -4$

Link to
Careers

WEBMASTERS build Web sites for clients. They design Web pages and update content.

More about Webmasters at www.mcdougallittell.com

EXAMPLE **3** **Write and Solve a Real-Life Linear System**

WEBMASTER You are the Webmaster of the Web sites for the science club and for the math club. Assuming that the number of visits at each site can be represented by a linear function, use the information in the table to predict when the number of daily visits to the two sites will be the same.

Club	Current daily visits	Increase (daily visits per month)
Science	400	25
Math	200	50

Solution

VERBAL MODEL

| Daily visits | = | Current visits to science site | + | Increase for science site | · | Number of months |

| Daily visits | = | Current visits to math site | + | Increase for math site | · | Number of months |

LABELS

Daily visits = V (daily visits)

Current visits (science) = **400** (daily visits)

Increase (science) = **25** (daily visits per month)

Number of months = t (months)

Current visits (math) = **200** (daily visits)

Increase (math) = **50** (daily visits per month)

ALGEBRAIC MODEL

$V = 400 + 25t$ **Equation 1 (science)**

$V = 200 + 50t$ **Equation 2 (math)**

Graph both equations. The point of intersection appears to be (8, 600).

CHECK ✓ Check this solution in each of the original equations.

Equation 1 $600 \stackrel{?}{=} 400 + 25(8)$

$600 = 400 + 200$ ✓

Equation 2 $600 \stackrel{?}{=} 200 + 50(8)$

$600 = 200 + 400$ ✓

ANSWER ▶ According to the model, the sites will have the same number of visits in 8 months.

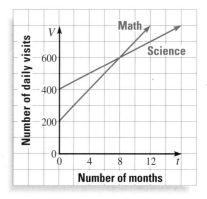

Student Help

▶**READING ALGEBRA**
The graph at the right tells you that in 8 months both sites should have the same number of daily visits, 600.

Checkpoint ✓ **Write and Solve a Real-Life Linear System**

4. The Spanish club Web site currently receives 500 daily visits. If the number of daily visits increases by 20 each month, when will the Spanish club site have the same number of daily visits as the science club site?

Guided Practice

Vocabulary Check

1. Explain what it means to solve a linear system using the graph-and-check method.

2. Use the graph at the right to find the point of intersection for the system of linear equations.
$$y = -x + 2$$
$$y = x + 2$$

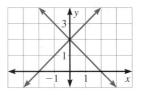

Skill Check

In Exercises 3–6, use the linear system below.

$$-x + y = -2$$
$$2x + y = 10$$

3. Write each equation in slope-intercept form.

4. Graph both equations in the same coordinate plane.

5. Estimate the coordinates of the point of intersection.

6. Check the coordinates algebraically by substituting them into each equation of the original linear system.

Practice and Applications

CHECKING SOLUTIONS Check whether the ordered pair is a solution of the system of linear equations.

7. $3x - 2y = 11$
$-x + 6y = 7$ $(5, 2)$

8. $6x - 3y = -15$
$2x + y = -3$ $(-2, 1)$

9. $x + 3y = 15$
$4x + y = 6$ $(3, -6)$

10. $-5x + y = 19$
$x - 7y = 3$ $(-4, -1)$

11. $-15x + 7y = 1$
$3x - y = 1$ $(3, 5)$

12. $-2x + y = 11$
$-x - 9y = -15$ $(6, 1)$

FINDING POINTS OF INTERSECTION Use the graph given to estimate the solution of the linear system. Then check your solution algebraically.

13. $-x + 2y = 6$
$x + 4y = 24$

14. $2x - y = -2$
$4x - y = -6$

15. $x + y = 3$
$-2x + y = -6$

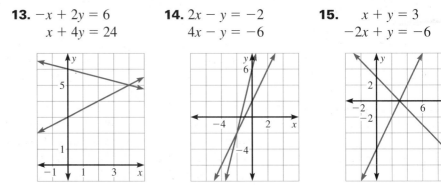

16. $y = -x + 3$
$y = x + 1$

17. $y = -6$
$x = 6$

18. $y = 2x - 4$
$2y = -x$

19. $2x - 3y = 9$
$x = -3$

20. $5x + 4y = 16$
$y = -16$

21. $x - y = 1$
$5x - 4y = 0$

22. $3x + 6y = 15$
$-2x + 3y = -3$

23. $y = -2x + 6$
$y = 2x + 2$

24. $5x + 6y = 54$
$-x + y = 9$

25. CARS Car model A costs $22,000 to purchase and $.12 per mile to maintain. Car model B costs $24,500 to purchase and $.10 per mile to maintain.

Use the graph to determine how many miles each car must be driven for the total costs of the two models to be the same.

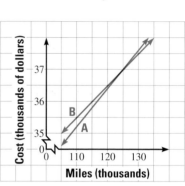

26. AEROBICS CLASSES A fitness club offers an aerobics class in the morning and in the evening. Assuming that the number of people in each class can be represented by a linear function, use the information in the table below to predict when the number of people in each class will be the same.

Class	Current attendance	Increase (people per month)
Morning	40	2
Evening	22	8

27. History Link The fast-changing world of the 1920s produced new roles for women in the workplace. From 1910 to 1930 the percent of women working in agriculture decreased, while the percent of women in professional jobs increased, as shown in the table.

Job type	Percent holding that job type in 1910	Average percent increase per year from 1910 to 1930
Agriculture	22.4%	−0.7%
Professional	9.1%	0.25%

Assuming that both percentages can be represented by a linear function, use the information in the table above to estimate when the percent of women working in agriculture equaled the percent of women working in professional jobs between 1910 and 1930.

28. PERSONAL FINANCE You and your sister are saving money from your allowances. You have $25 and save $3 each week. Your sister has $40 and saves $2 each week. After how many weeks will you and your sister have the same amount of money?

29. CHALLENGE You know how to solve the equation $x + 2 = 3x - 4$ algebraically. This equation can also be solved by graphing the following system of linear equations.

$$y = x + 2$$
$$y = 3x - 4$$

a. Explain how the system of linear equations is related to the original equation given.

b. Estimate the solution of the linear system graphically.

c. Check that the x-coordinate from part (b) satisfies the original equation by substituting the x-coordinate for x in $x + 2 = 3x - 4$.

Standardized Test Practice

30. MULTIPLE CHOICE Which ordered pair is a solution of the following system of linear equations?

$$x + y = 3$$
$$2x + y = 6$$

(A) $(0, 3)$ **(B)** $(1, 2)$ **(C)** $(2, 1)$ **(D)** $(3, 0)$

31. MULTIPLE CHOICE Which system of linear equations is graphed?

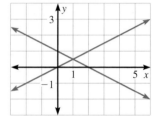

(F) $-x + 2y = 2$ **(G)** $x + 2y = 2$
       $-3x + 4y = 2$ $3x - 4y = 2$

(H) $-2x + y = 1$ **(J)** $2x + y = 1$
       $-4x + 3y = 2$ $4x + 3y = 2$

Mixed Review

SOLVING EQUATIONS **Solve the equation.** *(Lesson 3.3)*

32. $3x + 7 = -2$ **33.** $15 - 2a = 7$ **34.** $2y + 3y = 5$

35. $21 = 7(w - 2)$ **36.** $-2(t - 5) = 26$ **37.** $4(2x + 3) = -4$

WRITING EQUATIONS **Write in slope-intercept form the equation of the line that passes through the given point and has the given slope.** *(Lesson 5.2)*

38. $(3, 0)$, $m = -4$ **39.** $(-4, 3)$, $m = 1$ **40.** $(1, -5)$, $m = 4$

41. $(-4, -1)$, $m = -2$ **42.** $(2, 3)$, $m = 2$ **43.** $(-1, 5)$, $m = -3$

44. SUSPENSION BRIDGES The Verrazano-Narrows Bridge in New York is the longest suspension bridge in North America, with a main span of 4260 feet. Let x represent the length (in feet) of every other suspension bridge in North America. Write an inequality that describes x. Then graph the inequality. *(Lesson 6.1)*

Maintaining Skills

DECIMAL OPERATIONS **Perform the indicated operation.** *(Skills Review pp. 759, 760)*

45. $3.71 + 1.054$ **46.** $10.35 + 5.301$ **47.** $2.5 - 0.5$

48. $(2.1)(0.2)$ **49.** $\dfrac{0.3}{0.03}$ **50.** $\dfrac{5.175}{1.15}$

You can use a graphing calculator to graph linear systems and to estimate their solution.

Sample

Use a graphing calculator to estimate the solution of the linear system.

$$y = -0.3x + 1.8 \qquad \text{Equation 1}$$
$$y = 0.6x - 1.5 \qquad \text{Equation 2}$$

Solution

1 Enter the equations.

2 Set an appropriate viewing window to graph both equations.

3 Graph both equations. You can use the direction keys to move the cursor to the approximate intersection point.

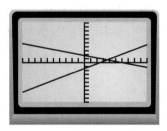

4 Use the *Intersect* feature to estimate a point where the graphs intersect. Follow your calculator's procedure to display the coordinate values.

ANSWER ▶ The solution of the linear system is approximately $(3.7, 0.7)$.

Try These

Use a graphing calculator to estimate the solution of the linear system. Check the result in each of the original equations.

1. $y = x + 6$
$y = -x - 1$

2. $y = -3x - 2$
$y = x + 8$

3. $y = -0.25x - 2.25$
$y = x - 1.25$

4. $y = 1.33x - 20$
$y = 0.83x - 8.5$

7.2 Solving Linear Systems by Substitution

Goal
Solve a linear system by substitution.

Key Words
• substitution method

How many softballs were ordered?

In Exercise 29 you will solve a linear system to analyze a problem about ordering softballs. You will use a method called the *substitution method*.

There are several ways to solve a linear system without using graphs. In this lesson you will study an algebraic method known as the *substitution method*.

EXAMPLE **1** **Substitution Method: Solve for y First**

Solve the linear system.

$$-x + y = 1 \qquad \textbf{Equation 1}$$
$$2x + y = -2 \qquad \textbf{Equation 2}$$

Solution

❶ **Solve** for y in Equation 1.

$$-x + y = 1 \qquad \text{Original Equation 1}$$
$$y = x + 1 \qquad \text{Revised Equation 1}$$

❷ **Substitute** $x + 1$ for y in Equation 2 and find the value of x.

$$2x + y = -2 \qquad \text{Write Equation 2.}$$
$$2x + (x + 1) = -2 \qquad \text{Substitute } x + 1 \text{ for } y.$$
$$3x + 1 = -2 \qquad \text{Combine like terms.}$$
$$3x = -3 \qquad \text{Subtract 1 from each side.}$$
$$x = -1 \qquad \text{Divide each side by 3.}$$

❸ **Substitute** -1 for x in the revised Equation 1 to find the value of y.

$$y = x + 1 = -1 + 1 = 0$$

❹ **Check** that $(-1, 0)$ is a solution by substituting -1 for x and 0 for y in each of the original equations.

ANSWER ▶ The solution is $(-1, 0)$.

EXAMPLE 2 **Substitution Method: Solve for *x* First**

Solve the linear system.

$$2x + 2y = 3 \qquad \text{Equation 1}$$
$$x - 4y = -1 \qquad \text{Equation 2}$$

Solution

❶ **Solve** for *x* in Equation 2 because it is easy to isolate *x*.

$x - 4y = -1$	Original Equation 2
$x = 4y - 1$	Revised Equation 2

❷ **Substitute** $4y - 1$ for *x* in Equation 1 and find the value of *y*.

$2x + 2y = 3$	Write Equation 1.
$2(4y - 1) + 2y = 3$	Substitute $4y - 1$ for *x*.
$8y - 2 + 2y = 3$	Use the distributive property.
$10y - 2 = 3$	Combine like terms.
$10y = 5$	Add 2 to each side.
$y = \dfrac{1}{2}$	Divide each side by 10.

❸ **Substitute** $\dfrac{1}{2}$ for *y* in the revised Equation 2 to find the value of *x*.

$$x = 4y - 1 = 4\left(\dfrac{1}{2}\right) - 1 = 2 - 1 = 1$$

❹ **Check** by substituting 1 for *x* and $\dfrac{1}{2}$ for *y* in the original equations.

ANSWER ▶ The solution is $\left(1, \dfrac{1}{2}\right)$.

Checkpoint ✓ **Substitution Method**

Name the variable you would solve for first. Explain.

1. $3x - y = -9$
$2x + 4y = 8$

2. $x + 3y = -11$
$2x - 5y = 33$

3. $x - 3y = 0$
$x - 2y = 10$

SUMMARY

Solving a Linear System by Substitution

STEP ❶ **Solve** one of the equations for one of its variables.

STEP ❷ **Substitute** the expression from Step 1 into the other equation and solve for the other variable.

STEP ❸ **Substitute** the value from Step 2 into the revised equation from Step 1 and solve.

STEP ❹ **Check** the solution in each of the original equations.

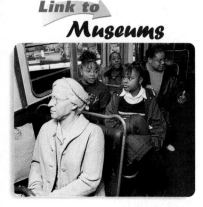

NATIONAL CIVIL RIGHTS MUSEUM The National Civil Rights Museum educates people about the history of the civil rights movement through its unique collections and powerful exhibits.

More about museums at www.mcdougallittell.com

EXAMPLE 3 **Write and Use a Linear System**

MUSEUM ADMISSIONS In one day the National Civil Rights Museum in Memphis, Tennessee, admitted 321 adults and children and collected $1590. The price of admission is $6 for an adult and $4 for a child. How many adults and how many children were admitted to the museum that day?

Solution

VERBAL MODEL

Number of adults	+	Number of children	=	Total number admitted

Price of adult admission	·	Number of adults	+	Price of child admission	·	Number of children	=	Total amount collected

LABELS

Number of adults $= x$ (people)

Number of children $= y$ (people)

Total number admitted $= 321$ (people)

Price of adult admission $= 6$ (dollars per person)

Price of child admission $= 4$ (dollars per person)

Total amount collected $= 1590$ (dollars)

ALGEBRAIC MODEL

$x + y = 321$ **Equation 1 (Number admitted)**

$6x + 4y = 1590$ **Equation 2 (Amount collected)**

Use the substitution method to solve the linear system.

$x = -y + 321$ Solve Equation 1 for x. (Revised Equation 1)

$6(-y + 321) + 4y = 1590$ Substitute $-y + 321$ for x in Equation 2.

$-6y + 1926 + 4y = 1590$ Use the distributive property.

$-2y + 1926 = 1590$ Combine like terms.

$-2y = -336$ Subtract 1926 from each side.

$y = 168$ Divide each side by -2.

$x = -(168) + 321 = 153$ Substitute 168 for y in revised Equation 1.

ANSWER ▸ 153 adults and 168 children were admitted to the National Civil Rights Museum that day.

Checkpoint ✓ **Write and Use a Linear System**

4. In one day a movie theater collected $4275 from 675 people. The price of admission is $7 for an adult and $5 for a child. How many adults and how many children were admitted to the movie theater that day?

7.2 Exercises

Guided Practice

Vocabulary Check

1. What four steps do you use to solve a system of linear equations by the substitution method?

2. When solving a system of linear equations, how do you decide which variable to isolate in Step 1 of the substitution method?

Skill Check

In Exercises 3–6, use the following system of equations.

$$3x + 2y = 7 \qquad \text{Equation 1}$$
$$5x - y = 3 \qquad \text{Equation 2}$$

3. Which equation would you use to solve for y? Explain why.

4. Solve for y in the equation you chose in Exercise 3.

5. Substitute the expression for y into the other equation and solve for x.

6. Substitute the value of x into your equation from Exercise 4. What is the solution of the linear system? Check your solution.

Use substitution to solve the linear system. Justify each step.

7. $3x + y = 3$
$7x + 2y = 1$

8. $2x + y = 4$
$-x + y = 1$

9. $3x - y = 0$
$5y = 15$

Practice and Applications

CRITICAL THINKING **Tell which equation you would use to isolate a variable. Explain.**

10. $2x + y = -10$
$3x - y = 0$

11. $m + 4n = 30$
$m - 2n = 0$

12. $5c + 3d = 11$
$5c - d = 5$

13. $3x - 2y = 19$
$x + y = 8$

14. $4a + 3b = -5$
$a - b = -3$

15. $3x + 5y = 25$
$x - 2y = -10$

SOLVING LINEAR SYSTEMS **Use the substitution method to solve the linear system.**

16. $y = x - 4$
$4x + y = 26$

17. $s = t + 4$
$2t + s = 19$

18. $2c - d = -2$
$4c + d = 20$

19. $2a = 8$
$a + b = 2$

20. $2x + 3y = 31$
$y = x + 7$

21. $p + q = 4$
$4p + q = 1$

22. $x - 2y = -25$
$3x - y = 0$

23. $u - v = 0$
$7u + v = 0$

24. $x - y = 0$
$12x - 5y = -21$

25. $m + 2n = 1$
$5m + 3n = -23$

26. $x - y = -5$
$x + 4 = 16$

27. $-3w + z = 4$
$-9w + 5z = -1$

28. TICKET SALES You are selling tickets for a high school play. Student tickets cost $4 and general admission tickets cost $6. You sell 525 tickets and collect $2876. Use the following verbal model to find how many of each type of ticket you sold.

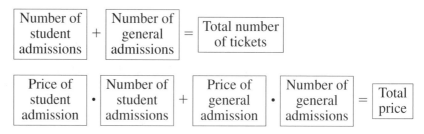

| Number of student admissions | + | Number of general admissions | = | Total number of tickets |

| Price of student admission | • | Number of student admissions | + | Price of general admission | • | Number of general admissions | = | Total price |

Student Help

▶HOMEWORK HELP

Extra help with problem solving in Exs. 29–31 is available at www.mcdougallittell.com

29. SOFTBALL You are ordering softballs for two softball leagues. The size of a softball is measured by its circumference. The Pony League uses an 11 inch softball priced at $3.50. The Junior League uses a 12 inch softball priced at $4.00. The bill smeared in the rain, but you know the total was 80 softballs for $305. How many of each size did you order?

30. *Geometry Link* The rectangle at the right has a perimeter of 40 centimeters. The length of the rectangle is 4 times as long as the width. Find the dimensions of the rectangle.

w

$\ell = 4w$

31. INVESTING One share of ABC stock is worth three times as much as XYZ stock. An investor has 100 shares of each. If the total value of the stocks is $4500, how much money is invested in each stock?

Link to Sports

RUNNING In Exercises 32 and 33, use the following information.
You can run 200 meters per minute uphill and 250 meters per minute downhill. One day you run a total of 2200 meters in 10 minutes.

32. Assign labels to the verbal model below. Then write an algebraic model.

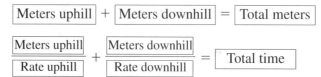

| Meters uphill | + | Meters downhill | = | Total meters |

$$\frac{\text{Meters uphill}}{\text{Rate uphill}} + \frac{\text{Meters downhill}}{\text{Rate downhill}} = \boxed{\text{Total time}}$$

33. Find the number of meters you ran uphill and the number of meters you ran downhill.

34. ERROR ANALYSIS Find and correct the error shown below.

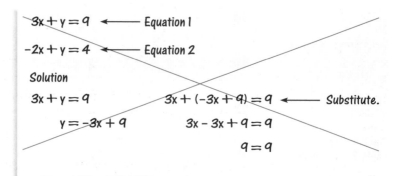

$3x + y = 9$ ⟵ Equation 1

$-2x + y = 4$ ⟵ Equation 2

Solution

$3x + y = 9$ $3x + (-3x + 9) = 9$ ⟵ Substitute.

$y = -3x + 9$ $3x - 3x + 9 = 9$

$9 = 9$

RUNNING at a rate of 200 meters per minute for one hour, a 140 pound person will burn 795 Calories. At a rate of 250 meters per minute, the same person will burn 953 Calories.

35. MULTIPLE CHOICE Which linear system has the solution $(6, 6)$?

(A) $4x - 3y = -1$
$-2x + y = -3$

(B) $x + y = 12$
$3x - 2y = 6$

(C) $3x + y = 4$
$4x - 3y = 1$

(D) $4x + 3y = 0$
$2x - y = 0$

36. MULTIPLE CHOICE Which linear system has been correctly solved for one of the variables from the following system?

$2x - y = -1$
$2x + y = -7$

(F) $2x - y = -1$
$y = 2x - 7$

(G) $2x - y = -1$
$y = -2x + 7$

(H) $y = 2x + 1$
$2x + y = -7$

(J) $y = -2x - 1$
$2x + y = -7$

37. MULTIPLE CHOICE Your math test is worth 100 points and has 38 problems. Each problem is worth either 5 points or 2 points. How many problems of each point value are on the test?

(A) 5 points: 54
2 points: 46

(B) 5 points: 46
2 points: 54

(C) 5 points: 30
2 points: 8

(D) 5 points: 8
2 points: 30

Mixed Review

SIMPLIFYING EXPRESSIONS Simplify the expression. *(Lesson 2.7)*

38. $4g + 3 + 2g - 3$

39. $3x + 2 - (5x + 2)$

40. $6(2 - m) - 3m - 12$

41. $4(3a + 5) + 3(-4a + 2)$

GRAPHING LINES Write the equation in slope-intercept form. Then graph the equation. *(Lesson 4.7)*

42. $6x + y = 0$

43. $8x - 4y = 16$

44. $3x + y = -5$

45. $5x + 3y = 3$

46. $x + y = 0$

47. $y = -4$

SOLVING AND GRAPHING Solve the inequality. Then graph the solution. *(Lessons 6.4, 6.5)*

48. $-5 < -x \le 1$

49. $-14 \le x + 5 \le 14$

50. $-2 < -3x + 1 < 10$

51. $x + 6 < 7 \text{ or } 4x > 12$

52. $3x - 2 \ge 4 \text{ or } 5 - x > 9$

Maintaining Skills

COMMON FACTORS List all the common factors of the pair of numbers. *(Skills Review p. 761)*

53. 3, 21

54. 4, 28

55. 21, 27

56. 10, 50

57. 12, 30

58. 18, 96

59. 78, 105

60. 84, 154

7.3 Solving Linear Systems by Linear Combinations

Goal
Solve a system of linear equations by linear combinations.

Key Words
• linear combination

How can a farmer find the location of a beehive?

In Exercise 44 you will solve a linear system to find the location of a beehive. You will use a method called *linear combinations*.

Sometimes it is not easy to isolate one of the variables in a linear system. In that case it may be easier to solve the system by *linear combinations*. A **linear combination** of two equations is an equation obtained by (1) multiplying one or both equations by a constant if necessary and (2) adding the resulting equations.

EXAMPLE 1 Add the Equations

Solve the linear system.

$4x + 3y = 16$ Equation 1
$2x - 3y = 8$ Equation 2

Solution

❶ **Add** the equations to get an equation in one variable.

$4x + 3y = 16$ Write Equation 1.
$2x - 3y = 8$ Write Equation 2.
$6x = 24$ Add equations.
$x = 4$ Solve for x.

❷ **Substitute** 4 for x into either equation and solve for y.

$4(4) + 3y = 16$ Substitute 4 for x.
$y = 0$ Solve for y.

❸ **Check** by substituting 4 for x and 0 for y in each of the original equations.

ANSWER ▶ The solution is (4, 0).

Checkpoint ✓ Add the Equations

Solve the linear system. Then check your solution.

1. $3x + 2y = 7$
$-3x + 4y = 5$

2. $4x - 2y = 2$
$3x + 2y = 12$

3. $5x + 2y = -4$
$-5x + 3y = 19$

Sometimes you can solve by adding the original equations because the coefficients of a variable are already opposites, as in Example 1. In Example 2 you need to multiply both equations by an appropriate number first.

EXAMPLE 2 Multiply Then Add

Solve the linear system.

$$3x + 5y = 6 \qquad \text{Equation 1}$$
$$-4x + 2y = 5 \qquad \text{Equation 2}$$

Solution

❶ Multiply Equation 1 by 4 and Equation 2 by 3 to get coefficients of x that are opposites.

$$3x + 5y = 6 \qquad \text{Multiply by 4.} \qquad 12x + 20y = 24$$
$$-4x + 2y = 5 \qquad \text{Multiply by 3.} \qquad \underline{-12x + 6y = 15}$$

❷ Add the equations and solve for y. $\qquad\qquad 26y = 39 \qquad$ Add equations.

$$y = 1.5 \qquad \text{Solve for } y.$$

❸ Substitute 1.5 for y into either equation and solve for x.

$$-4x + 2(\mathbf{1.5}) = 5 \qquad \text{Substitute 1.5 for } y.$$
$$-4x + 3 = 5 \qquad \text{Multiply.}$$
$$-4x = 2 \qquad \text{Subtract 3 from each side.}$$
$$x = -0.5 \qquad \text{Solve for } x.$$

❹ Check by substituting -0.5 for x and 1.5 for y in the original equations.

ANSWER ▶ The solution is $(-0.5, 1.5)$.

Checkpoint ✓ *Multiply Then Add*

Solve the linear system. Then check your solution.

4. $2x - 3y = 4$
$-4x + 5y = -8$

5. $3x + 4y = 6$
$2x - 5y = -19$

6. $6x + 2y = 2$
$-3x + 3y = -9$

SUMMARY

Solving a Linear System by Linear Combinations

STEP ❶ *Arrange* the equations with like terms in columns.

STEP ❷ *Multiply*, if necessary, the equations by numbers to obtain coefficients that are opposites for one of the variables.

STEP ❸ *Add* the equations from Step 2. Combining like terms with opposite coefficients will eliminate one variable. Solve for the remaining variable.

STEP ❹ *Substitute* the value obtained in Step 3 into either of the original equations and solve for the other variable.

STEP ❺ *Check* the solution in each of the original equations.

EXAMPLE **3** **Solve by Linear Combinations**

Solve the linear system. $\quad 3x + 2y = 8 \quad$ **Equation 1**
$\qquad\qquad\qquad\qquad\qquad 2y = 12 - 5x \quad$ **Equation 2**

Solution

❶ **Arrange** the equations with like terms in columns.

$3x + 2y = 8 \qquad$ Write Equation 1.

$5x + 2y = 12 \qquad$ Rearrange Equation 2.

❷ **Multiply** Equation 2 by -1 to get the coefficients of y to be opposites.

$$3x + 2y = 8 \qquad\qquad\qquad\qquad 3x + 2y = \;\;\;\; 8$$

$$5x + 2y = 12 \quad \text{Multiply by } -1. \Rightarrow \quad \underline{-5x - 2y = -12}$$

❸ **Add** the equations. $\qquad\qquad\qquad -2x \quad\quad\; = -4 \qquad$ Add equations.

$$x = 2 \qquad\qquad \text{Solve for } x.$$

❹ **Substitute** 2 for x into either equation and solve for y.

$3x + 2y = 8 \qquad$ Write equation 1.

$3(2) + 2y = 8 \qquad$ Substitute 2 for x.

$6 + 2y = 8 \qquad$ Multiply.

$2y = 2 \qquad$ Subtract 6 from each side.

$y = 1 \qquad$ Solve for y.

ANSWER ▶ The solution is $(2, 1)$.

❺ **Check** the solution in each of the original equations.

First check the solution in Equation 1.

$3x + 2y = 8 \qquad$ Write Equation 1.

$3(2) + 2(1) \stackrel{?}{=} 8 \qquad$ Substitute 2 for x and 1 for y.

$6 + 2 \stackrel{?}{=} 8 \qquad$ Multiply.

$8 = 8 \checkmark \qquad$ Add.

Then check the solution in Equation 2.

$2y = 12 - 5x \qquad$ Write Equation 2.

$2(1) \stackrel{?}{=} 12 - 5(2) \qquad$ Substitute 2 for x and 1 for y.

$2 \stackrel{?}{=} 12 - 10 \qquad$ Multiply.

$2 = 2 \checkmark \qquad$ Subtract.

Checkpoint ✓ **Solve by Linear Combinations**

Solve the linear system. Then check your solution.

7. $2x + 5y = -11$
$\quad\;\; 5y = 3x - 21$

8. $-13 = 4x - 3y$
$\quad\;\; 5x + 2y = 1$

9. $4x + 7y = -9$
$\quad\;\; 3x = 3y + 18$

Guided Practice

Vocabulary Check

1. When you use linear combinations to solve a linear system, what is the purpose of using multiplication as a first step?

Skill Check

ERROR ANALYSIS In Exercises 2 and 3, find and correct the error.

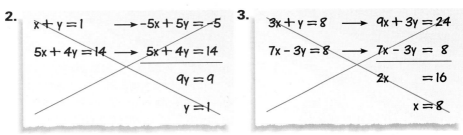

2.

$x + y = 1 \longrightarrow -5x + 5y = -5$

$5x + 4y = 14 \longrightarrow 5x + 4y = 14$

$\overline{\qquad\qquad}$

$9y = 9$

$y = 1$

3.

$3x + y = 8 \longrightarrow 9x + 3y = 24$

$7x - 3y = 8 \longrightarrow 7x - 3y = 8$

$\overline{\qquad\qquad}$

$2x \qquad = 16$

$x = 8$

Describe the steps you would use to solve the system of equations using linear combinations. Then solve the system. Justify each step.

4. $x + 3y = 6$
$x - 3y = 12$

5. $3x - 4y = 7$
$2x - y = 3$

6. $2y = 2x - 2$
$2x + 3y = 12$

Practice and Applications

USING ADDITION Use linear combinations to solve the linear system. Then check your solution.

7. $x + y = 4$
$x - y = -10$

8. $a - b = 8$
$a + b = 20$

9. $2x + y = 4$
$x - y = 2$

10. $m + 3n = 2$
$-m + 2n = 3$

11. $p + 4q = 23$
$-p + q = 2$

12. $3v - 2w = 1$
$2v + 2w = 4$

13. $g + 2h = 4$
$-g - h = 2$

14. $13x - 5y = 8$
$3x + 5y = 8$

USING MULTIPLICATION AND ADDITION Use linear combinations to solve the linear system. Then check your solution.

15. $x + 3y = 3$
$x + 6y = 3$

16. $v - w = -5$
$v + 2w = 4$

17. $2g - 3h = 0$
$3g - 2h = 5$

18. $x - y = 0$
$-3x - y = 2$

19. $2a + 6z = 4$
$3a - 7z = 6$

20. $5e + 4f = 9$
$4e + 5f = 9$

21. $2p - q = 2$
$2p + 3q = 22$

22. $9m - 3n = 20$
$3m + 6n = 2$

Student Help

▶ **HOMEWORK HELP**
Example 1: Exs. 7–14,
31–42
Example 2: Exs. 15–22,
31–42
Example 3: Exs. 23–42

ARRANGING LIKE TERMS Use linear combinations to solve the linear system. Then check your solution.

23. $x - 3y = 30$
$3y + x = 12$

24. $3b + 2c = 46$
$5c + b = 11$

25. $y = x - 9$
$x + 8y = 0$

26. $m = 3n$
$m + 10n = 13$

27. $2q = 7 - 5p$
$4p - 16 = q$

28. $2v = 150 - u$
$2u = 150 - v$

29. $g - 10h = 43$
$18 = -g + 5h$

30. $5s + 8t = 70$
$60 = 5s - 8t$

LINEAR COMBINATIONS Use linear combinations to solve the linear system. Then check your solution.

31. $x + 2y = 5$
$5x - y = 3$

32. $-3p + 2 = q$
$-q + 2p = 3$

33. $t + r = 1$
$2r - t = 2$

34. $3g - 24 = -4h$
$-2 + 2h = g$

35. $x + 1 = 3y$
$2x = 7 - 3y$

36. $4a = -b$
$a - b = 5$

37. $2m - 4 = 4n$
$m - 2 = n$

38. $3y = -5x + 15$
$-y = -3x + 9$

39. $3j + 5k = 19$
$j - 2k = -1$

40. $6x + 2y = 5$
$8x + 2y = 3$

41. $3x + 7y = 6$
$2x + 9y = 4$

42. $5y - 20 = -4x$
$4y = -20x + 16$

Link to
Science

VOLUME AND MASS
Legend has it that
Archimedes (above) was
asked to prove that a
crown was not pure gold.
Archimedes compared the
volume of water displaced by
the crown with the volume
displaced by an equal mass
of gold. The volume of water
displaced was *not* the same,
proving that the crown was
not pure gold.

EXAMPLE *Write and Use a Linear System*

VOLUME AND MASS A gold crown, suspected of containing some silver, was found to have a mass of 714 grams and a volume of 46 cubic centimeters. The density of gold is about 19 grams per cubic centimeter. The density of silver is about 10.5 grams per cubic centimeter. What percent of the crown is silver?

Solution

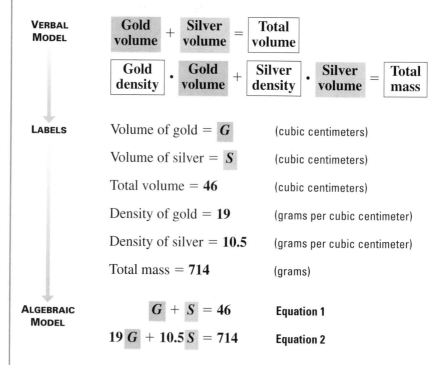

VERBAL MODEL

| Gold volume | + | Silver volume | = | Total volume |

| Gold density | · | Gold volume | + | Silver density | · | Silver volume | = | Total mass |

LABELS

Volume of gold = G (cubic centimeters)

Volume of silver = S (cubic centimeters)

Total volume = 46 (cubic centimeters)

Density of gold = 19 (grams per cubic centimeter)

Density of silver = 10.5 (grams per cubic centimeter)

Total mass = 714 (grams)

ALGEBRAIC MODEL

$$G + S = 46 \qquad \text{Equation 1}$$

$$19G + 10.5S = 714 \qquad \text{Equation 2}$$

Use linear combinations to solve for S.

$$\begin{aligned} -19G - 19S &= -874 \qquad &\text{Multiply Equation 1 by } -19. \\ 19G + 10.5S &= 714 \qquad &\text{Write Equation 2.} \\ \hline -8.5S &= -160 \qquad &\text{Add equations.} \\ S &\approx 18.8 \qquad &\text{Solve for } S. \end{aligned}$$

ANSWER ▶ The volume of silver is about 19 cm³. The crown has a volume of 46 cm³, so the crown is $\frac{19}{46} \approx 41\%$ silver by volume.

MODELING Use the example on the previous page as a model for Exercise 43.

43. VOLUME AND MASS A bracelet made of gold and copper has a mass of 46 grams. The volume of the bracelet is 4 cubic centimeters. Gold has a density of about 19 grams per cubic centimeter. Copper has a density of about 9 grams per cubic centimeter. How many cubic centimeters of copper are mixed with the gold?

44. BEEHIVE A farmer is tracking two wild honey bees in his field. He maps the first bee's path to the hive on the line $7y = 9x$. The second bee's path follows the line $y = -3x + 12$. Their paths cross at the hive. At what coordinates will the farmer find the hive?

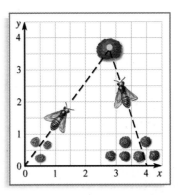

45. History Link The first known system of linear equations appeared in Chinese literature about 2000 years ago. Solve this problem from the book *Shu-shu Chiu-chang* which appeared in 1247.

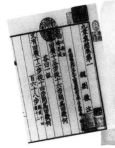

A storehouse has three kinds of stuff: cotton, floss silk, and raw silk. They take inventory of the materials and wish to cut out and make garments for the army. As for the cotton, if we use 8 rolls for 6 men, we have a shortage of 160 rolls; if we use 9 rolls for 7 men, there is a surplus of 560 rolls.... We wish to know the number of men [we can clothe] and the amount of cotton [we will use]...

$$x = \frac{8y}{6} - 160$$
$$-x = -\frac{9y}{7} - 560$$
$$\overline{}$$
$$0 = \frac{8y}{6} - \frac{9y}{7} - 720$$

46. CHALLENGE Solve for x, y, and z in the system of equations. Explain each step of your solution.

$$3x + 2y + z = 42$$
$$2y + z + 12 = 3x$$
$$x - 3y = 0$$

47. MULTIPLE CHOICE Solve the system and choose the true statement.

$$x + y = 4$$
$$x - 2y = 10$$

(A) The value of x is greater than y.   (B) The value of y is greater than x.

(C) The values of x and y are equal.   (D) None of these

48. MULTIPLE CHOICE Solve the system and choose the true statement.

$$3x + 5y = -8$$
$$x - 2y = 1$$

(F) The value of x is greater than y.   (G) The value of y is greater than x.

(H) The values of x and y are equal.   (J) None of these

Mixed Review

WRITING EQUATIONS Write in slope-intercept form the equation of the line that passes through the given point and has the given slope, or that passes through the given points. *(Lessons 5.2, 5.3)*

49. $(-2, 4)$, $m = 3$ **50.** $(5, 1)$, $m = 5$ **51.** $(9, 3)$, $m = -3$

52. $(-2, -1)$ and $(4, 2)$ **53.** $(6, 5)$ and $(2, 1)$ **54.** $(4, -5)$ and $(-1, -3)$

CHECKING SOLUTIONS Check whether each ordered pair is a solution of the inequality. *(Lesson 6.8)*

55. $3x - 2y < 2$; $(1, 3)$, $(2, 0)$ **56.** $5x + 4y \geq 6$; $(-2, 4)$, $(5, 5)$

SOLVING LINEAR SYSTEMS Use the substitution method to solve the linear system. *(Lesson 7.2)*

57. $-6x - 5y = 28$
$\quad\;\; x - 2y = 1$

58. $m + 2n = 1$
$\quad\; 5m - 4n = -23$

59. $g - 5h = 20$
$\quad\; 4g + 3h = 34$

Maintaining Skills

SIMPLIFYING FRACTIONS Decide whether the statement is *true* or *false*. Explain. *(Skills Review p. 763)*

60. $\dfrac{1}{4} \overset{\cdot}{=} \dfrac{3}{12}$ **61.** $\dfrac{5}{7} = \dfrac{25}{35}$ **62.** $\dfrac{6}{16} = \dfrac{3}{7}$

63. $\dfrac{2}{11} = \dfrac{10}{55}$ **64.** $\dfrac{9}{7} = \dfrac{18}{15}$ **65.** $\dfrac{250}{350} = \dfrac{2}{3}$

Quiz 1

Estimate the solution of the linear system graphically. Then check the solution algebraically. *(Lesson 7.1)*

1. $3x + y = 5$
$\quad\; -x + y = -7$

2. $x - 2y = 0$
$\quad\; 3x - y = 0$

3. $2x + 3y = 36$
$\quad\; -2x + y = -4$

Use substitution to solve the linear system. *(Lesson 7.2)*

4. $4x + 3y = 31$
$\quad\; y = 2x + 7$

5. $-12x + y = 15$
$\quad\; 3x + 2y = 3$

6. $x + 2y = 14$
$\quad\; 2x + 3y = 18$

Use linear combinations to solve the linear system. *(Lesson 7.3)*

7. $2x + 3y = 36$
$\quad\; 2x - y = 4$

8. $x + 7y = 12$
$\quad\; 3x - 5y = 10$

9. $3x - 5y = -4$
$\quad\; -9x + 7y = 8$

Choose a method to solve the linear system. *(Lessons 7.1–7.3)*

10. $2x + 3y = 1$
$\quad\;\; 4x - 2y = 10$

11. $x + 18y = 18$
$\quad\; x - 3y = -3$

12. $5x - 3y = 7$
$\quad\; x + 3y = 5$

13. COMPACT DISCS A store is selling compact discs for $10.50 and $8.50. You buy 10 discs for $93. Write and solve a linear system to find how many compact discs you bought at each price. *(Lessons 7.1–7.3)*

7.4 Linear Systems and Problem Solving

Goal
Use linear systems to solve real-life problems.

Key Words
- substitution method
- linear combinations method

How many violins were sold?

In Example 1 you will use a system of linear equations to find the number of violins a store sold. Once you have written a linear system that models a real-life problem, you need to decide which solution method is most efficient.

EXAMPLE 1   Choosing a Solution Method

VIOLINS In one week a music store sold 7 violins for a total of $1600. Two different types of violins were sold. One type cost $200 and the other type cost $300. How many of each type of violin did the store sell?

Solution

VERBAL MODEL

$$\boxed{\text{Number of type A}} + \boxed{\text{Number of type B}} = \boxed{\text{Total number sold}}$$

$$\boxed{\text{Price of type A}} \cdot \boxed{\text{Number of type A}} + \boxed{\text{Price of type B}} \cdot \boxed{\text{Number of type B}} = \boxed{\text{Total sales}}$$

LABELS

Number of type A = x	(violins)
Number of type B = y	(violins)
Total number sold = 7	(violins)
Price of type A = 200	(dollars per violin)
Price of type B = 300	(dollars per violin)
Total sales = 1600	(dollars)

ALGEBRAIC MODEL

$$x + y = 7 \qquad \text{Equation 1}$$
$$200x + 300y = 1600 \qquad \text{Equation 2}$$

The coefficients of x and y are 1 in Equation 1, so use the substitution method. You can solve Equation 1 for x and substitute the result into Equation 2. After simplifying, you will obtain $y = 2$. Then substitute this y-value into the revised Equation 1 and simplify to obtain $x = 5$.

ANSWER ▶ The store sold 5 type A violins and 2 type B violins.

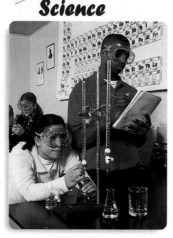

Link to
Science

CHEMISTRY To test the acidity of a substance, scientists use litmus paper. When the paper comes in contact with acid, it turns red.

EXAMPLE 2 Solve a Mixture Problem

CHEMISTRY You combine 2 solutions to form a mixture that is 40% acid. One solution is 20% acid and the other is 50% acid. If you have 90 milliliters of the mixture, how much of each solution was used to create the mixture?

Solution

VERBAL MODEL

$$\boxed{\text{Volume of solution A}} + \boxed{\text{Volume of solution B}} = \boxed{\text{Volume of mixture}}$$

$$\boxed{\text{Acid in solution A}} + \boxed{\text{Acid in solution B}} = \boxed{\text{Acid in Mixture}}$$

LABELS

Volume of solution A = x	(milliliters)
Volume of solution B = y	(milliliters)
Volume of mixture = **90**	(milliliters)
Acid in solution A = **0.2** x	(milliliters)
Acid in solution B = **0.5** y	(milliliters)
Acid in mixture = 0.4(90) = **36**	(milliliters)

ALGEBRAIC MODEL

$$x + y = 90 \qquad \text{Equation 1}$$
$$0.2\,x + 0.5\,y = 36 \qquad \text{Equation 2}$$

Solve Equation 1 for x and multiply each side of Equation 2 by 10 so that it contains only integers. Then use substitution to solve the system.

$x = 90 - y$	Revised Equation 1
$2x + 5y = 360$	Revised Equation 2
$2(90 - y) + 5y = 360$	Substitute $90 - y$ for x in Revised Equation 2.
$180 - 2y + 5y = 360$	Use the distributive property.
$3y = 180$	Combine like terms.
$y = 60$	Solve for y.
$x = 90 - 60 = 30$	Substitute 60 for y in Revised Equation 1.

ANSWER ▶ 30 mL of solution A and 60 mL of solution B were used.

Checkpoint ✓ Solve Mixture Problems

1. A store sold 32 pairs of jeans for a total of $1050. Brand A sold for $30 per pair and Brand B sold for $35 per pair. How many of each brand were sold?

2. A 10-pound mixture of peanuts and cashews sells for $5.32 per pound. The price of peanuts is $3.60 per pound and the price of cashews is $7.90 per pound. How many pounds of each type are in the mixture?

EXAMPLE 3 Compare Two Salary Plans

SALES JOBS Job A offers an annual salary of $30,000 plus a bonus of 1% of sales. Job B offers an annual salary of $24,000 plus a bonus of 2% of sales. How much would you have to sell to earn the same amount in each job?

Solution

VERBAL MODEL

Total earnings = $\boxed{\text{Job A salary}}$ + 1% · Total sales

Total earnings = $\boxed{\text{Job B salary}}$ + 2% · Total sales

LABELS

Total earnings = y (dollars)

Total sales = x (dollars)

Job A salary = 30,000   (dollars)

Job B salary = 24,000   (dollars)

ALGEBRAIC MODEL

$y = 30{,}000 + 0.01x$ Equation 1 (Job A)

$y = 24{,}000 + 0.02x$ Equation 2 (Job B)

It is convenient to use the linear combinations method.

$-y = -30{,}000 - 0.01x$	Multiply Equation 1 by −1.
$\underline{y = 24{,}000 + 0.02x}$	Write Equation 2.
$0 = -6000 + 0.01x$	Add Equations.
$x = 600{,}000$	Solve for x.

Substitute $x = 600{,}000$ into Equation 1 and simplify to obtain $y = 36{,}000$.

ANSWER ▶ You would have to sell $600,000 of merchandise to earn $36,000 in each job.

When a linear system has a solution (a, b), this solution can be found by substitution or by linear combinations.

SUMMARY

Ways to Solve a System of Linear Equations

SUBSTITUTION requires that one of the variables be isolated on one side of the equation. It is especially convenient when one of the variables has a coefficient of 1 or −1.
(Examples 1–3, pp. 396–398)

LINEAR COMBINATIONS can be applied to any system, but it is especially convenient when a variable appears in different equations with coefficients that are opposites.
(Examples 1–3, pp. 402–404)

GRAPHING can provide a useful method for estimating a solution.
(Examples 1–3, pp. 389–391)

Guided Practice

Vocabulary Check

1. Describe a system that you would use linear combinations to solve.

Skill Check

Choose a method to solve the linear system. Explain your choice.

2. $x + y = 300$
$x + 3y = 18$

3. $3x + 5y = 25$
$2x - 6y = 12$

4. $2x + y = 0$
$x + y = 5$

5. Solve Example 3 on page 411 using the substitution method.

POCKET CHANGE **In Exercises 6–8, use the following information.**
You have $2.65 in your pocket. You have a total of 16 coins, with only quarters and dimes. Let q equal the number of quarters and d equal the number of dimes.

6. Complete: __?__ + __?__ = 16

7. Complete: $25q + $ __?__ $= 265$

8. Use the equations you wrote in Exercises 6 and 7 to find how many of each coin you have.

Practice and Applications

COMPARING METHODS **Solve the linear system using both methods described on page 411. Then represent the solution graphically.**

9. $x + y = 2$
$6x + y = 2$

10. $x - y = 1$
$x + y = 5$

11. $3x - y = 3$
$-x + y = 3$

CHOOSING A SOLUTION METHOD **Choose a solution method to solve the linear system. Explain your choice, but do not solve the system.**

12. $6x + y = 2$
$9x - y = 5$

13. $2x + 3y = 3$
$5x + 5y = 10$

14. $\quad -3x = 36$
$-6x + y = 1$

15. $2x - 5y = 0$
$x - y = 3$

16. $3x + 2y = 10$
$2x + 5y = 3$

17. $x + 2y = 2$
$x + 4y = -2$

SOLVING LINEAR SYSTEMS **Choose a solution method to solve the linear system. Explain your choice, and then solve the system.**

18. $2x + y = 5$
$x - y = 1$

19. $\quad 2x - y = 3$
$4x + 3y = 21$

20. $\quad x - 2y = 4$
$6x + 2y = 10$

21. $\quad 3x + 6y = 8$
$-6x + 3y = 2$

22. $\quad x + y = 0$
$3x + 2y = 1$

23. $2x - 3y = -7$
$3x + y = -5$

24. $\quad 8x + 4y = 8$
$-2x + 3y = 12$

25. $x + 2y = 1$
$5x - 4y = -23$

26. $6x - y = 18$
$8x + y = 24$

Student Help

▶ **HOMEWORK HELP**
Example 1: Exs. 9–26
Example 2: Exs. 27–31
Example 3: Exs. 32–34

CRITICAL THINKING In Exercises 27–29, match the situation with the corresponding linear system.

27. You have 7 packages of paper towels. Some packages have 3 rolls, but some have only 1 roll. There are 19 rolls altogether.

28. You buy 5 pairs of socks for $19. The wool socks cost $5 per pair and the cotton socks cost $3 per pair.

29. You have only $1 bills and $5 bills in your wallet. There are 7 bills worth a total of $19.

A. $x + y = 7$	**B.** $x + y = 7$	**C.** $x + y = 5$
$x + 3y = 19$	$x + 5y = 19$	$3x + 5y = 19$

30. TREADMILLS You exercised on a treadmill for 1.5 hours. You jogged at 4 miles per hour and then sprinted at 6 miles per hour. The treadmill monitor says that you ran for a total of 7 miles. Using the verbal model below, calculate how long you ran at each speed.

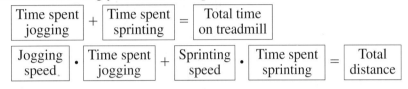

$$\boxed{\text{Time spent jogging}} + \boxed{\text{Time spent sprinting}} = \boxed{\text{Total time on treadmill}}$$

$$\boxed{\text{Jogging speed}} \cdot \boxed{\text{Time spent jogging}} + \boxed{\text{Sprinting speed}} \cdot \boxed{\text{Time spent sprinting}} = \boxed{\text{Total distance}}$$

31. COMMUNITY GARDENS You designate one row in your garden to broccoli and pea plants. Each broccoli plant needs 12 inches of space and each pea plant needs 6 inches of space. The row is 10 feet (120 inches) long. If you want a total of 13 plants, how many of each plant can you have?

HOUSING In Exercises 32 and 33, use the following information.
The graph below represents the need for low-income rental housing in the United States and the number of affordable rental units available.

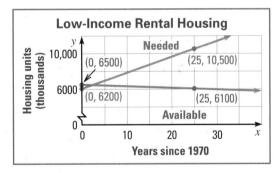

Low-Income Rental Housing

DATA UPDATE of Center on Budget and Policy Priorities data at www.mcdougallittell.com

32. Use the points (0, 6200) and (25, 10,500) to write an equation for the number of housing units needed. Then use the points (0, 6500) and (25, 6100) to write an equation for the number of affordable units available.

33. Solve the system you wrote in Exercise 32. Use the graph to check the reasonableness of your solution.

34. TREE GROWTH You plant a 14-inch spruce tree that grows 4 inches per year and an 8-inch hemlock tree that grows 6 inches per year. After how many years will the trees be the same height? How tall will each be?

Link to
Gardening

COMMUNITY GARDENS allow people without yards to plant their own gardens. A 25 foot by 35 foot garden can produce enough vegetables for a family of four.

More about community gardens at www.mcdougallittell.com

35. CHALLENGE It takes you 3 hours to drive to a concert 135 miles away. You drive 55 miles per hour on highways and 40 miles per hour the rest of the time. How much time did you spend driving at each speed?

36. *Puzzler* Let the variables a, b, g, and p represent the weights of an apple, a banana, a bunch of grapes, and a pineapple, respectively. Use these variables to write three equations that model the first three diagrams below. Then use substitution to determine how many apples will balance the pineapple and two bananas in the fourth diagram.

Standardized Test Practice

37. MULTIPLE CHOICE You and your friend go to a Mexican restaurant. You order 2 tacos and 2 enchiladas and your friend orders 3 tacos and 1 enchilada. Your bill was $4.80 and your friend's bill was $4.00. Which system of linear equations represents the situation?

(A) $2t + 2e = 4.00$
   $3t + e = 4.80$

(B) $2t + 2e = 4.00$
   $t + 3e = 4.80$

(C) $2t + 2e = 4.80$
   $3t + e = 4.00$

(D) $2t + 2e = 4.80$
   $t + 3e = 4.00$

38. MULTIPLE CHOICE Solve the system of equations you chose in Exercise 37.

(F) $t = \$1.60$
   $e = \$.80$

(G) $t = \$.80$
   $e = \$1.60$

(H) $t = \$1.40$
   $e = \$.60$

(J) $t = \$.60$
   $e = \$1.40$

Mixed Review

PARALLEL LINES Determine whether the graphs of the two equations are parallel lines. Explain. *(Lesson 4.7)*

39. line *a*: $y = 4x + 3$
line *b*: $2y - 8x = -3$

40. line *a*: $4y + 5x = 1$
line *b*: $10x + 2y = 2$

41. line *a*: $3x + 9y + 2 = 0$
line *b*: $2y = -6x + 3$

42. line *a*: $4y - 1 = 5$
line *b*: $6y + 2 = 8$

GRAPHING FUNCTIONS Graph the function. *(Lesson 4.8)*

43. $f(x) = 2x + 3$

44. $h(x) = x + 5$

45. $g(x) = 5x - 4$

46. $g(x) = -x + 2$

47. $f(x) = -4x + 1$

48. $h(x) = -3x - 1$

Maintaining Skills

ADDING FRACTIONS Add. Write the answer as a fraction or a mixed number in lowest terms. *(Skills Review p. 764)*

49. $\dfrac{9}{15} + \dfrac{3}{5}$

50. $\dfrac{1}{12} + \dfrac{1}{2}$

51. $\dfrac{3}{8} + \dfrac{7}{9}$

52. $\dfrac{3}{7} + \dfrac{2}{5}$

53. $\dfrac{1}{10} + \dfrac{2}{3}$

54. $\dfrac{3}{4} + \dfrac{1}{6}$

55. $\dfrac{17}{32} + \dfrac{1}{4}$

56. $\dfrac{19}{20} + \dfrac{7}{8}$

GOAL

Use reasoning to discover graphical and algebraic rules for finding the number of solutions of a linear system.

MATERIALS

• graph paper

Question

How can you identify the number of solutions of a linear system by graphing or by using an algebraic method?

Explore

1 Graph each linear system.

    a. $x + y = 0$ **b.** $2x - 4y = 6$ **c.** $x - y = 1$
       $3x - 2y = 5$ $x - 2y = 3$ $-3x + 3y = 3$

2 How are the three graphs different?

3 Write both equations of each system in the form $y = mx + b$.

4 How are the equations within each system alike or how are they different?

Student Help

▶ **LOOK BACK**
For help with graphing linear systems, see p. 390.

Think About It

1. Repeat **Steps 1** through **4** for the following systems.

    a. $x - 3y = 9$ **b.** $4x - y = 20$ **c.** $x + 2y = 3$
       $2x + 6y = -18$ $20x + y = 28$ $x + 2y = 6$

Write a linear system for the graphical model. If only one line is shown, write two different equations for the line.

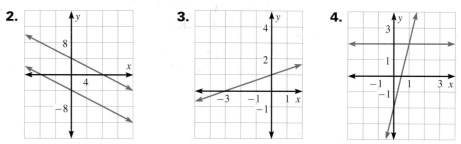

2.   **3.**   **4.**

LOGICAL REASONING The graph of a linear system is described. Determine whether the system has *no solution, exactly one solution,* or *infinitely many solutions*. **Explain.**

5. The lines have the same slope and the same y-intercept.

6. The lines have the same slope but different y-intercepts.

7. The lines have different slopes.

Question

How can you solve systems that have many solutions or recognize systems that have no solution?

Explore

1 Try to solve each linear system.

a. $x + y = 0$
$3x - 2y = 5$

b. $2x - 4y = 6$
$x - 2y = 3$

c. $x - y = 1$
$-3x + 3y = 3$

2 Refer to your graph of part (a) from **Step 1** on page 415. What does the algebra of part (a) tell you about the graphs of the equation?

3 Refer to your graph of part (b) from **Step 1** on page 415. What does the algebra of part (b) tell you about the graphs of the equation?

4 Refer to your graph of part (c) from **Step 1** on page 415. What does the algebra of part (c) tell you about the graphs of the equation?

Think About It

Describe the algebraic solution of the system. Then check your answer by solving the appropriate equation you wrote for Exercises 2–4 on page 415.

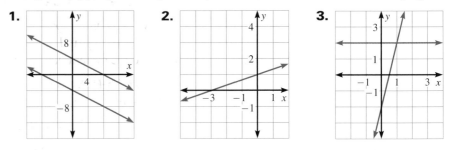

1. **2.** **3.**

Solve the linear system using linear combinations. Then describe the graphical solution of the system.

4. $2x - y = 3$
$-4x + 2y = 0$

5. $2x + y = 5$
$x - 3y = -1$

6. $x + 3y = 2$
$2x + 6y = 4$

7. LOGICAL REASONING Summarize your results from Exercises 1–6 by writing a rule for determining algebraically whether a system of linear equations has exactly one solution, no solution, or infinitely many solutions.

Special Types of Linear Systems

Goal
Identify how many solutions a linear system has.

Key Words
• linear system

What is the weight of a bead in a necklace?

Some linear systems have no solution or infinitely many solutions. In Exercise 31 you will see why this can be a problem as you try to find the weight of a jewelry bead.

EXAMPLE **1** **A Linear System with No Solution**

Show that the linear system has no solution.

$2x + y = 5$ **Equation 1**
$2x + y = 1$ **Equation 2**

Solution

Method 1 **GRAPHING** Rewrite each equation in slope-intercept form. Then graph the linear system.

$y = -2x + 5$ **Revised Equation 1**
$y = -2x + 1$ **Revised Equation 2**

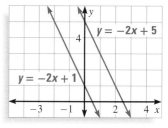

Because the lines have the same slope but different y-intercepts, they are parallel. Parallel lines never intersect, so the system has no solution.

Method 2 **SUBSTITUTION** Because revised Equation 2 is $y = -2x + 1$, you can substitute $-2x + 1$ for y in Equation 1.

$2x + y = 5$ Write Equation 1.

$2x + (-2x + 1) = 5$ Substitute $-2x + 1$ for y.

$1 \neq 5$ Combine like terms.

The variables are eliminated and you are left with a statement that is false. This tells you that the system has no solution.

Student Help

▶ **LOOK BACK**
For help with equations in one variable that have no solution, see p. 153.

Checkpoint ✓ **A Linear System with No Solution**

1. Show that the linear system has no solution.

$x + 3y = 4$ **Equation 1**
$2x + 6y = 4$ **Equation 2**

EXAMPLE **2** **A Linear System with Infinitely Many Solutions**

Show that the linear system has infinitely many solutions.

$$-2x + y = 3 \qquad \text{Equation 1}$$
$$-4x + 2y = 6 \qquad \text{Equation 2}$$

Solution

Method 1 **GRAPHING** Rewrite each
equation in slope-intercept form.
Then graph the linear system.

$$y = 2x + 3 \qquad \text{Revised Equation 1}$$
$$y = 2x + 3 \qquad \text{Revised Equation 2}$$

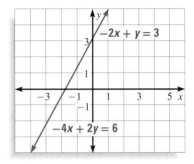

You can see that the equations represent
the same line. Every point on the line is
a solution of the system.

Method 2 **LINEAR COMBINATIONS** You can multiply Equation 1 by 2
to obtain an equation that is identical to Equation 2.

$$-4x + 2y = 6 \qquad \text{Revised Equation 1}$$

$$-4x + 2y = 6 \qquad \text{Equation 2}$$

The two equations are identical. Any solution of $-4x + 2y = 6$ is also a solution
of the system. This tells you that the linear system has infinitely many solutions.

Checkpoint ✓ **A Linear System with Infinitely Many Solutions**

2. Show that the linear system has infinitely many solutions.

$$x - 2y = 4 \qquad \text{Equation 1}$$
$$-x + 2y = -4 \qquad \text{Equation 2}$$

SUMMARY

Number of Solutions of a Linear System

If the two equations have different slopes, then the system has one solution.	If the two equations have the same slope but different y-intercepts, then the system has no solution.	If the two equations have the same slope and the same y-intercept, then the system has infinitely many solutions
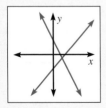	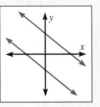	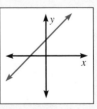
Lines intersect Exactly one solution	**Lines are parallel** No solution	**Lines coincide** Infinitely many solutions

EXAMPLE 3 **Identify the Number of Solutions**

a. $3x + y = -1$
$-9x - 3y = 3$

b. $x - 2y = 5$
$-2x + 4y = 2$

c. $2x + y = 4$
$4x - 2y = 0$

Solution

a. Use linear combinations.

You can multiply Equation 1 by -3 to obtain Equation 2.

$-9x - 3y = 3$ **Revised Equation 1**

$-9x - 3y = 3$ **Equation 2**

ANSWER ▶ The two equations are identical. Any solution of $-9x - 3y = 3$ is also a solution of the system. Therefore the linear system has infinitely many solutions.

b. Use linear combinations.

$x - 2y = 5$ **Multiply by 2.** ▶ $2x - 4y = 10$

$-2x + 4y = 2$ $\dfrac{-2x + 4y = \ \ 2}{0 \neq 12}$ **Add equations.**

ANSWER ▶ The resulting statement is false. The linear system has no solution.

c. Use the substitution method.

$2x + y = 4$	Write Equation 1.
$y = -2x + 4$	Solve Equation 1 for y. (Revised Equation 1)
$4x - 2y = 0$	Write Equation 2.
$4x - 2(-2x + 4) = 0$	Substitute $-2x + 4$ for y.
$4x + 4x - 8 = 0$	Use the distributive property.
$8x - 8 = 0$	Combine like terms.
$8x = 8$	Add 8 to each side.
$x = 1$	Solve for x.
$y = -2(1) + 4$	Substitute 1 for x in Revised Equation 1.
$y = -2 + 4$	Multiply.
$y = 2$	Solve for y.

ANSWER ▶ The linear system has exactly one solution, which is the ordered pair $(1, 2)$.

Checkpoint ✓ **Identify the Number of Solutions**

Solve the linear system and tell how many solutions the system has.

3. $x + y = 3$
$2x + 2y = 4$

4. $x + y = 3$
$2x + 2y = 6$

5. $x + y = 3$
$x + 2y = 4$

Guided Practice

Vocabulary Check   Describe the graph of a linear system that has the given number of solutions. Sketch an example.

1. No solution   **2.** Infinitely many solutions   **3.** Exactly one solution

Skill Check   Graph the system of linear equations. Does the system have *exactly one solution*, *no solution*, or *infinitely many solutions*? Explain.

4. $2x + y = 5$
$-6x - 3y = -15$

5. $-6x + 2y = 4$
$-9x + 3y = 12$

6. $2x + y = 7$
$3x - y = -2$

Use the substitution method or linear combinations to solve the linear system and tell how many solutions the system has.

7. $-x + y = 7$
$2x - 2y = -18$

8. $-4x + y = -8$
$-12x + 3y = -24$

9. $-4x + y = -8$
$2x - 2y = -14$

Practice and Applications

LINEAR SYSTEMS   Match the linear system with its graph and tell how many solutions the system has.

10. $-2x + 4y = 1$
$3x - 6y = 9$

11. $2x - 2y = 4$
$-x + y = -2$

12. $2x + y = 4$
$-4x - 2y = -8$

13. $-x + y = 1$
$x - y = 1$

14. $5x + 3y = 17$
$x - 3y = -2$

15. $x - y = 0$
$5x - 2y = 6$

A.

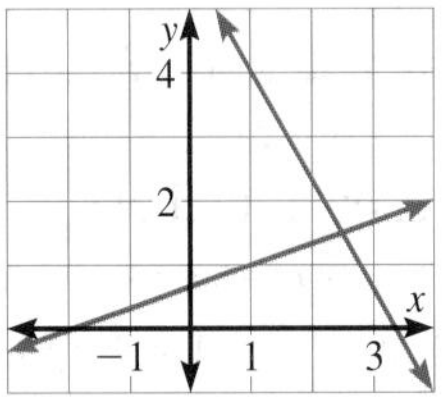

B.

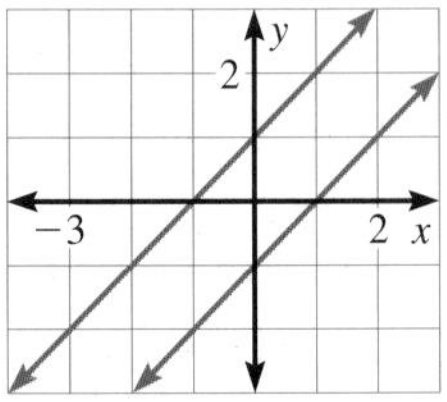

C.

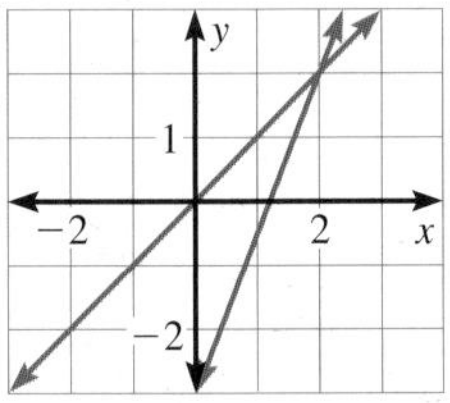

D.

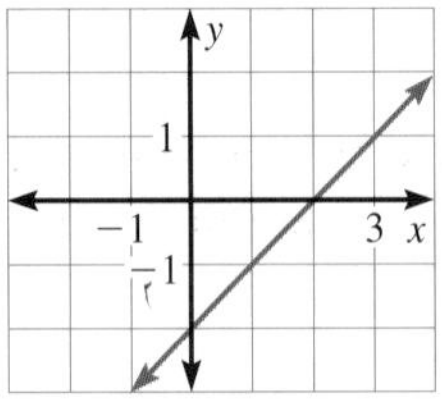

E.

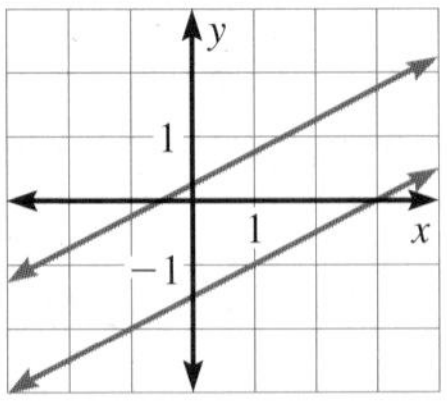

F.

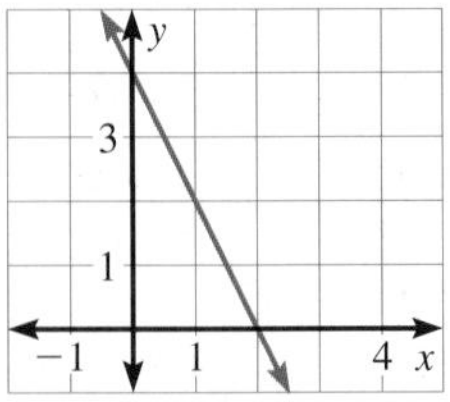

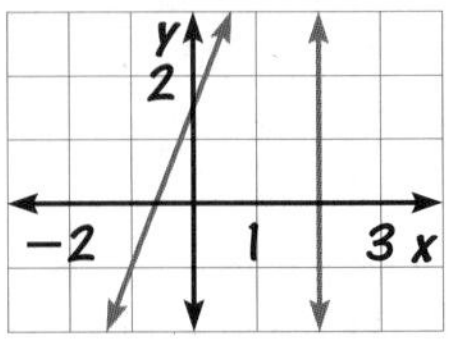

Student Help

▶ **HOMEWORK HELP**
Example 1: Exs. 10–33
Example 2: Exs. 10–33
Example 3: Exs. 10–33

16. ERROR ANALYSIS   Patrick says that the graph of the linear system shown at the right has no solution. Why is he wrong?

INTERPRETING GRAPHICAL RESULTS Use the graphing method to tell how many solutions the system has.

17. $x + y = 8$
$x + y = -1$

18. $3x - 2y = 3$
$-6x + 4y = -6$

19. $x - y = 2$
$-2x + 2y = 2$

20. $-x + 4y = -20$
$3x - 12y = 48$

21. $6x - 2y = 4$
$12x - 6y = 8$

22. $3x + 2y = 40$
$-3x - 2y = 8$

23. CRITICAL THINKING Explain how you can tell from the equations how many solutions the linear system has. Then solve the system.

$x - y = 2$ **Equation 1**
$4x - 4y = 8$ **Equation 2**

INTERPRETING ALGEBRAIC RESULTS Use the substitution method or linear combinations to solve the linear system and tell how many solutions the system has. Then describe the graph of the system.

24. $-7x + 7y = 7$
$2x - 2y = -18$

25. $4x + 4y = -8$
$2x + 2y = -4$

26. $2x + y = -4$
$4x - 2y = 8$

27. $15x - 5y = -20$
$-3x + y = 4$

28. $-6x + 2y = -2$
$-4x - y = 8$

29. $2x + y = -1$
$-6x - 3y = -15$

30. BUSINESS A contracting company rents a generator for 6 hours and a heavy-duty saw for 6 hours at a total cost of $48. For another job the company rents the generator for 4 hours and the saw for 8 hours for a total cost of $40. Find the hourly rates g (for the generator) and s (for the saw) by solving the system of equations $6g + 6s = 48$ and $4g + 8s = 40$.

31. JEWELRY You have a necklace and matching bracelet with 2 types of beads. There are 40 small beads and 6 large beads on the necklace. The bracelet has 20 small beads and 3 large beads. The necklace weighs 9.6 grams and the bracelet weighs 4.8 grams. If the threads holding the beads have no significant weight, can you find the weight of one large bead? Explain.

CARPENTRY In Exercises 32 and 33, use the following information.
A carpenter is buying supplies for the next job. The job requires 4 sheets of oak paneling and 2 sheets of shower tileboard. The carpenter pays $99.62 for these supplies. For the following job the carpenter buys 12 sheets of oak paneling and 6 sheets of shower tileboard and pays $298.86.

32. Can you find how much the carpenter is spending on 1 sheet of oak paneling? Explain.

33. If the carpenter later spends a total of $139.69 for 8 sheets of oak paneling and 1 sheet of shower tileboard, can you find how much 1 sheet of oak paneling costs? Explain.

CHALLENGE In Exercises 34 and 35, use the following system.

$6x - 9y = n$ **Equation 1**
$-2x + 3y = 3$ **Equation 2**

34. Find a value of n so that the linear system has infinitely many solutions.

35. Find a value of n so that the linear system has no solution.

36. MULTIPLE CHOICE
Which graph corresponds
to a linear system that has
no solution?

(A) I   (B) II

(C) III   (D) IV

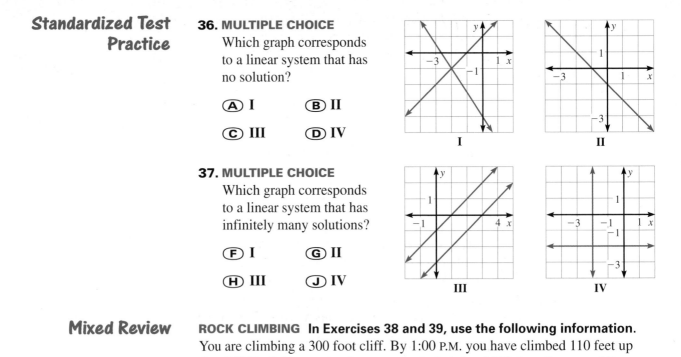

I

II

37. MULTIPLE CHOICE
Which graph corresponds
to a linear system that has
infinitely many solutions?

(F) I   (G) II

(H) III   (J) IV

III

IV

Mixed Review

ROCK CLIMBING In Exercises 38 and 39, use the following information.
You are climbing a 300 foot cliff. By 1:00 P.M. you have climbed 110 feet up
the cliff. By 3:00 P.M. you have reached a height of 220 feet. *(Lesson 4.5)*

38. Find the slope of the line that passes through the points (1, 110) and (3, 220).
What does it represent?

39. If you continue climbing the cliff at the same rate, at what time will you
reach the top of the cliff?

GRAPHING INEQUALITIES Graph the inequality. *(Lesson 6.8)*

40. $x < 2$

41. $y \geq 5$

42. $y \leq 3x + 1$

43. $y > x + 4$

44. $4x + y \leq 4$

45. $2x - 3y < 6$

Maintaining Skills

**ESTIMATING AREA Estimate the area of the figure to the nearest square
unit. Then find the exact area, if possible.** *(Skills Review p. 775)*

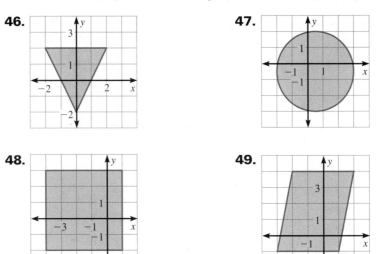

46.

47.

48.

49.

GOAL

Use graphing to describe the solution of a system of linear inequalities.

MATERIALS

• graph paper
• red and blue pencils

Question

How can you graph a system of linear inequalities?

Explore

Consider the following system of linear inequalities.

$$x + y \le 5 \qquad \text{Inequality 1}$$
$$x - y \ge 1 \qquad \text{Inequality 2}$$

1 Graph the boundary lines $x + y = 5$ and $x - y = 1$ in the same coordinate plane.

2 Test several points with integer coordinates in the first inequality. If a point is a solution, circle the point in blue.

3 Test several points with integer coordinates in the second inequality. If a point is a solution, circle the point in red.

4 Describe the points that are solutions of both inequalities (the points that are circled with both colors).

Think About It

Follow Steps 1 through 4 to graph the system of linear inequalities. Then describe the solution.

1. $x + y \ge 4$
  $x - 2y \le -2$

2. $x - y \le 0$
  $x + y \le 6$

3. $3x + 2y \ge 8$
  $-3x + y \le 1$

4. $x \ge 3$
  $x \le 5$

5. $y \le 4$
  $y \ge 1$

6. $4x + y \ge 2$
  $4x + y \le 8$

LOGICAL REASONING Use your results from Exercises 1–6 to answer the following questions.

7. When would the solution of a system of two linear inequalities be a horizontal strip? When would the solution of a system of two linear inequalities be a vertical strip?

8. When would a system of two linear inequalities have no solution?

9. When would a half-plane be the solution of a system of two linear inequalities?

10. What are the possible graphs of a general system of two linear inequalities?

Systems of Linear Inequalities

Goal
Graph a system of linear inequalities.

Key Words
- system of linear inequalities
- solution of a system of linear inequalities

How many spotlights can you afford?

In Exercises 34–36 you will graph a *system of linear inequalities* to analyze the number of spotlights that can be ordered for a theater.

From Lesson 6.8 remember that the graph of a linear inequality in two variables is a half-plane. The boundary line of the half-plane is dashed if the inequality is < or > and solid if the inequality is ≤ or ≥, as shown in the graphs below.

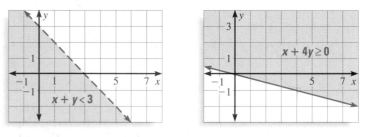

Two or more linear inequalities in the same variables form a **system of linear inequalities**, or a *system of inequalities*. A **solution of a system of linear inequalities** in two variables is an ordered pair that is a solution of each inequality in the system.

Student Help

▶ STUDY TIP
Notice how the two half-planes above can be used to find the solution in Example 1.

EXAMPLE 1 Graph a System of Two Linear Inequalities

Graph the system of linear inequalities.

$x + y < 3$ **Inequality 1**
$x + 4y \geq 0$ **Inequality 2**

Solution

Graph both inequalities in the same coordinate plane. The graph of the system is the overlap, or *intersection*, of the two half-planes shown at the right as the darker shade of blue.

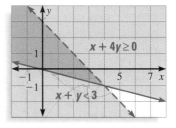

EXAMPLE **2** **Graph a System of Three Linear Inequalities**

Graph the system of linear inequalities.

$y < 2$	**Inequality 1**
$x \geq -1$	**Inequality 2**
$y > x - 2$	**Inequality 3**

Solution

The graph of $y < 2$ is the half-plane *below* the *dashed* line $y = 2$.

The graph of $x \geq -1$ is the half-plane *on and to the right* of the *solid* line $x = -1$.

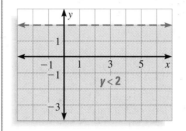

The graph of $y > x - 2$ is the half-plane *above* the *dashed* line $y = x - 2$.

Finally, the graph of the system is the intersection of the three half-planes shown.

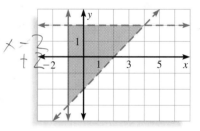

Checkpoint ✓ **Graph a System of Linear Inequalities**

Graph the system of linear inequalities.

1. $x + 2y \leq 6$
   $-x + y < 0$

2. $y < 3$
   $y > 1$

3. $x \geq 0$
   $y \geq 0$
   $2x + 3y \leq 12$

SUMMARY

Graphing a System of Linear Inequalities

STEP ① ***Graph*** the boundary lines of each inequality. Use a dashed line if the inequality is < or > and a solid line if the inequality is ≤ or ≥.

STEP ② ***Shade*** the appropriate half-plane for each inequality.

STEP ③ ***Identify*** the solution of the system of inequalities as the intersection of the half-planes from Step 2.

EXAMPLE 3 Write a System of Linear Inequalities

Write a system of linear inequalities that defines the shaded region shown.

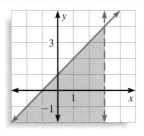

Solution

Since the shaded region is bounded by two lines, you know that the system must have two linear inequalities.

INEQUALITY 1 The first inequality is bounded by the line that passes through the points (0, 1) and (3, 4). The slope of this line can be found using the formula for slope.

$$m = \frac{y_2 - y_1}{x_2 - x_1}$$ Write formula for slope.

$$m = \frac{4 - 1}{3 - 0}$$ Substitute coordinates into formula.

$$m = 1$$ Simplify.

Since (0, 1) is the point where the line crosses the y-axis, an equation for this line can be found using the slope-intercept form.

$y = mx + b$ Write slope-intercept form.

$y = 1x + 1$ Substitute 1 for m and 1 for b.

$y = x + 1$ Simplify.

Since the shaded region is *below* this *solid* boundary line, the inequality is $y \le x + 1$.

INEQUALITY 2 The second inequality is bounded by the vertical line that passes through the point (3, 0). An equation of this line is $x = 3$.

Since the shaded region is *to the left* of this *dashed* boundary line, the inequality is $x < 3$.

ANSWER ▶ The system of inequalities that defines the shaded region is:

$$y \le x + 1 \qquad \textbf{Inequality 1}$$
$$x < 3 \qquad \textbf{Inequality 2}$$

Student Help

▶ LOOK BACK
For help with writing equations in slope-intercept form, see p. 269.

Checkpoint ✓ Write a System of Linear Inequalities

Write a system of linear inequalities that defines the shaded region shown.

4.
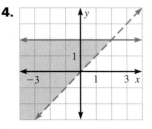

5.
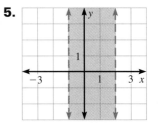

Guided Practice

Vocabulary Check

1. Determine whether the following statement is *true* or *false*. Explain.

> *A solution of a system of linear inequalities is an ordered pair that is a solution of any one of the inequalities in the system.*

Skill Check

Graph the system of linear inequalities.

2. $y \geq -2x + 2$
$y \leq -1$

3. $y > x$
$x < 1$

4. $x + 1 > y$
$y \geq 0$

ERROR ANALYSIS Use both the student graph shown at the right and the system of linear inequalities given below.

$y > -1$
$x \geq 2$
$y > x - 4$

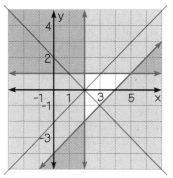

5. Find and correct the errors the student made while graphing the system.

6. Graph the system correctly.

Write a system of linear inequalities that defines the shaded region.

7.

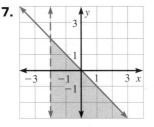

8.

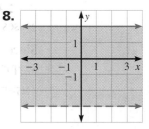

Practice and Applications

LINEAR INEQUALITIES Match the graph with the system of linear inequalities that defines it.

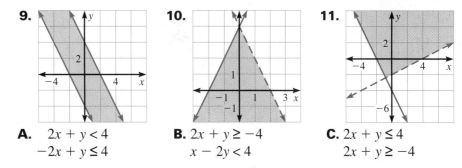

9.

10.

11.

A. $2x + y < 4$
$-2x + y \leq 4$

B. $2x + y \geq -4$
$x - 2y < 4$

C. $2x + y \leq 4$
$2x + y \geq -4$

GRAPHING SYSTEMS Graph the system of linear inequalities.

12. $y \geq 0$
$x \geq -2$

13. $y > -2$
$y \leq 4 - 2x$

14. $2x + 3y < 5$
$3x + 2y > 5$

15. $y < 2x - 1$
$y > -x + 2$

16. $2x - 2y \leq 6$
$x - y \leq 9$

17. $x - 3y \geq 12$
$x - 6y < 12$

18. $x + y \leq 6$
$x \geq 1$
$y \geq 0$

19. $x < 3$
$2y < 1$
$2x + y > 2$

20. $3x - 2y \geq -6$
$x + 4y > -2$
$4x + y < 2$

21. $x \geq 0$
$y \geq 0$
$x \leq 3$

22. $x > -2$
$y \geq -2$
$y < 4$

23. $x - 2y < 3$
$3x + 2y > 9$
$x + y < 6$

WRITING SYSTEMS Write a system of linear inequalities that defines the shaded region.

24.

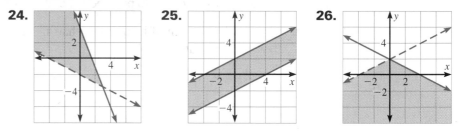

25.

26.

Geometry Link Plot the points and draw line segments connecting the points to create the polygon. Then write a system of linear inequalities that defines the polygonal region.

27. Triangle: $(-2, 0), (2, 0), (0, 2)$

28. Rectangle: $(1, 1), (7, 1), (7, 6), (1, 6)$

29. Triangle: $(0, 0), (-7, 0), (-3, 5)$

30. Trapezoid: $(-1, 1), (1, 3), (4, 3), (6, 1)$

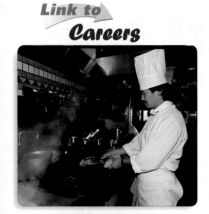
FOOD BUDGET In Exercises 31–33, use the following information.
You are planning the menu for your restaurant. For Saturday night you plan to serve roast beef and teriyaki chicken. You expect to serve at least 240 pounds of meat that evening and that less beef will be ordered than chicken. The roast beef costs $5 per pound and the chicken costs $3 per pound. You have a budget of at most $1200 for meat for Saturday night.

31. Copy and complete the following system of linear inequalities that shows the pounds b of roast beef meals and the pounds c of teriyaki chicken meals that you could prepare for Saturday night.

$$b + c \geq \boxed{?}$$
$$b \boxed{?} c$$
$$\boxed{?} \cdot b + \boxed{?} \cdot c \leq 1200$$

32. Graph the system of linear inequalities.

33. **CRITICAL THINKING** What quadrant should the graph in Exercise 32 be restricted to for the solutions of the system to make sense in the real-world situation described? Explain.

LIGHTING In Exercises 34–36, use the following information.

You have $10,000 to buy spotlights for your theater. A medium-throw spotlight costs $1000 and a long-throw spotlight costs $3500. The current play needs at least 3 medium-throw spotlights and at least 1 long-throw spotlight.

34. Write a system of linear inequalities for the number m of medium-throw spotlights and the number l of long-throw spotlights that models both your budget and the needs of the current play.

35. For $0 \leq m \leq 7$ and $0 \leq l \leq 7$, plot the pairs of integers (m, l) that satisfy the inequalities you wrote in Exercise 34.

36. Which of the options plotted in Exercise 35 correspond to a cost that is less than $8000?

EARNING MONEY In Exercises 37–39, use the following information.

You can work a total of no more than 20 hours per week at your two jobs. Baby-sitting pays $5 per hour, and your job as a cashier pays $6 per hour. You need to earn at least $90 per week to cover your expenses.

37. Write a system of inequalities that shows the various numbers of hours you can work at each job.

38. Graph the system of linear inequalities.

39. Give two possible ways you could divide your hours between the two jobs.

TREE FARMING In Exercises 40–42, use the tree farm graph shown.

40. Write a system of inequalities that defines the region containing maple trees.

41. Write a system of inequalities that defines the region containing sycamore trees.

42. CHALLENGE Find the area of the oak tree region. Explain the method you used.

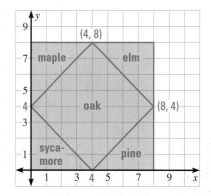

43. MULTIPLE CHOICE Which system of inequalities is graphed?

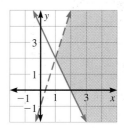

A $y < 3x - 1$
  $2x + y \geq 4$

B $y < 3x + 1$
  $2x + y \geq 4$

C $y < 3x - 1$
  $2x - y \geq -4$

D $y < 3x + 1$
  $2x - y \geq -4$

44. MULTIPLE CHOICE Which ordered pair is a solution of the following system of linear inequalities?

$y \leq x + 2$
$y + x > 4$

F $(1, 3)$ **G** $(2, 1)$ **H** $(2, 6)$ **J** $(4, 2)$

EVALUATING NUMERICAL EXPRESSIONS Evaluate the expression. *(Lessons 1.2, 1.3)*

45. 3^5

46. $8^2 - 17$

47. $5^3 + 12$

48. $2(3^3 - 20)$

49. $2^6 - 3 + 1$

50. $5 \cdot 2 + 4^2$

EVALUATING EXPONENTIAL EXPRESSIONS Evaluate the expression for the given values of the variables. *(Lesson 1.2)*

51. $(x + y)^2$ when $x = 5$ and $y = 2$

52. $(b - c)^2$ when $b = 2$ and $c = 1$

53. $g - h^2$ when $g = 4$ and $h = 8$

54. $x^2 + z$ when $x = 8$ and $z = 12$

55. TEST QUESTIONS Your teacher is giving a test worth 250 points. There are 68 questions. Some questions are worth 5 points and the rest are worth 2 points. How many of each question are on the test? *(Lesson 7.4)*

FRACTIONS, MIXED NUMBERS, AND DECIMALS Write the fraction or mixed number as a decimal. *(Skills Review pp. 763, 767)*

56. $\dfrac{22}{5}$

57. $\dfrac{37}{4}$

58. $\dfrac{51}{12}$

59. $\dfrac{56}{20}$

60. $1\dfrac{1}{2}$

61. $3\dfrac{4}{5}$

62. $4\dfrac{1}{4}$

63. $6\dfrac{7}{8}$

Quiz 2

1. **Geometry Link** The perimeter of the rectangle is 22 feet and the perimeter of the triangle is 12 feet. Find the dimensions of the rectangle. *(Lesson 7.4)*

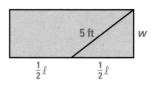

2. GASOLINE The cost of 12 gallons of regular gasoline and 18 gallons of premium gasoline is $44.46. Premium costs $.22 more per gallon than regular. What is the cost per gallon of each type of gasoline? *(Lesson 7.4)*

Use any method to solve the linear system and tell how many solutions the system has. *(Lesson 7.5)*

3. $3x + 2y = 12$
  $9x + 6y = 18$

4. $4x + 8y = 8$
  $x + y = 1$

5. $-4x + 11y = 44$
  $4x - 11y = -44$

Graph the system of linear inequalities. *(Lesson 7.6)*

6. $y < -x + 3$
  $y \geq 1$

7. $x - 2y < -6$
  $5x - 3y < -9$

8. $x + y \leq 1$
  $-x + y \leq 1$
  $y \geq 0$

9. Write a system of linear inequalities that defines the shaded region. *(Lesson 7.6)*

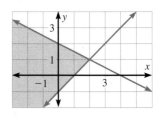

VOCABULARY

VOCABULARY

- **system of linear equations,** *p. 389*
- **solution of a linear system,** *p. 389*
- **point of intersection,** *p. 389*
- **linear combination,** *p. 402*
- **system of linear inequalities,** *p. 424*
- **solution of a system of linear inequalities,** *p. 424*

7.1 GRAPHING LINEAR SYSTEMS

Examples on pp. 389–391

EXAMPLE Estimate the solution of the linear system graphically. Then check the solution algebraically.

$$-x + y = 3 \qquad \text{Equation 1}$$
$$x + y = 7 \qquad \text{Equation 2}$$

First write each equation in slope-intercept form so that they are easy to graph.

EQUATION 1	**EQUATION 2**
$-x + y = 3$	$x + y = 7$
$y = x + 3$	$y = -x + 7$

Then graph both equations.

Estimate from the graph that the point of intersection is (2, 5).

Check whether (2, 5) is a solution by substituting 2 for x and 5 for y in each of the original equations.

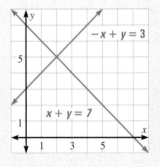

EQUATION 1	**EQUATION 2**
$-x + y = 3$	$x + y = 7$
$-(2) + 5 \stackrel{?}{=} 3$	$2 + 5 \stackrel{?}{=} 7$
$3 = 3 \checkmark$	$7 = 7 \checkmark$

ANSWER ▸ Because the ordered pair (2, 5) makes each equation true, (2, 5) is the solution of the linear system.

Estimate the solution of the linear system graphically. Then check the solution algebraically.

1. $x + y = 6$
$x - y = 12$

2. $4x - y = 3$
$3x + y = 4$

3. $x + 9y = 9$
$3x + 6y = 6$

4. $5x - y = -5$
$3x + 6y = -3$

5. $7x + 8y = 24$
$x - 8y = 8$

6. $2x - 3y = -3$
$x + 6y = -9$

7.2 SOLVING LINEAR SYSTEMS BY SUBSTITUTION

Examples on pp. 396–398

EXAMPLE Solve the linear system by substitution.

$2x - y = 0$ **Equation 1**
$4x - y = 8$ **Equation 2**

Solve for y in Equation 1 because it is easy to isolate y.

$2x - y = 0$	Original Equation 1
$y = 2x$	Revised Equation 1
$4x - y = 8$	Write Equation 2.
$4x - (2x) = 8$	Substitute $2x$ for y.
$x = 4$	Solve for x.
$y = 2x = 2(4) = 8$	Substitute 4 for x in Revised Equation 1 to solve for y.

ANSWER ▸ The solution is (4, 8). Check the solution in the original equations.

Use the substitution method to solve the linear system.

7. $x + 3y = 9$
$\quad 4x - 2y = -6$

8. $-2x - 5y = 7$
$\quad 7x + y = -8$

9. $4x - 3y = -2$
$\quad 4x + y = 4$

10. $-x + 3y = 24$
$\quad\, 5x + 8y = -5$

11. $4x + 9y = 2$
$\quad\,\, 2x + 6y = 1$

12. $9x + 6y = 3$
$\quad\,\, 3x - 7y = -26$

7.3 SOLVING SYSTEMS BY LINEAR COMBINATIONS

Examples on pp. 402–404

EXAMPLE Solve the linear system by linear combinations.

$2x - 15y = -10$ **Equation 1**
$-4x + 5y = -30$ **Equation 2**

You can get the coefficients of x to be opposites by multiplying Equation 1 by 2.

$2x - 15y = -10$ **Multiply by 2.** ⟶ $4x - 30y = -20$

$-4x + 5y = -30$ $\underline{-4x + 5y = -30}$

                                 $-25y = -50$ Add equations.

                                      $y = 2$ Solve for y.

Substitute 2 for y in Equation 2 and solve for x.

$-4x + 5y = -30$	Write Equation 2.
$-4x + 5(2) = -30$	Substitute 2 for y.
$x = 10$	Solve for x.

ANSWER ▸ The solution is (10, 2). Check the solution in the original equations.

Use linear combinations to solve the linear system.

13. $-4x - 6y = 7$
$\quad\ \ x + 5y = 8$

14. $2x + y = 0$
$\quad\ 5x - 4y = 26$

15. $\quad 3x + 5y = -16$
$\quad -2x + 6y = -36$

16. $9x + 6y = 3$
$\quad\ 3y + 6x = 18$

17. $2 - 7x = 9y$
$\quad 2y - 4x = 6$

18. $\quad 4x - 9y = 1$
$\quad 25x + 6y = 4$

7.4 **LINEAR SYSTEMS AND PROBLEM SOLVING**

Examples on pp. 409–411

EXAMPLE Your teacher is giving a test worth 150 points. There are 46 three-point and five-point questions. How many of each are on the test?

Write an algebraic model. Let x be the number of three-point questions and let y be the number of five-point questions.

$3x + 5y = 150$ **Equation 1**
$\ \ x + y = 46$ **Equation 2**

Since at least one variable has a coefficient of 1, use substitution to solve the system.

$y = -x + 46$	Solve Equation 2 for y. (Revised Equation 2)
$3x + 5(-x + 46) = 150$	Substitute $-x + 46$ for y in Equation 1.
$3x - 5x + 230 = 150$	Use the distributive property.
$-2x = -80$	Combine like terms.
$x = 40$	Divide each side by -2.
$y = -(40) + 46 = 6$	Substitute 40 for x in Revised Equation 2.

ANSWER ▶ There are 40 three-point questions and 6 five-point questions.

19. RENTING MOVIES You spend $13 to rent five movies for the weekend. New releases rent for $3 and regular movies rent for $2. How many regular movies did you rent? How many new releases did you rent?

7.5 **SPECIAL TYPES OF LINEAR SYSTEMS**

Examples on pp. 417–418

EXAMPLE Tell how many solutions the following linear system has.

$\quad 3x + 5y = 7$ **Equation 1**
$-3x - 5y = 8$ **Equation 2**

Use linear combinations.

$3x + 5y = 7$	Write Equation 1.
$-3x - 5y = 8$	Write Equation 2.
$0 \neq 15$	Add equations.

ANSWER ▶ There resulting statement is false. The linear system has no solution.

EXAMPLE Tell how many solutions the following linear system has.

$$-x - 3y = -5 \qquad \text{Equation 1}$$
$$2x + 6y = 10 \qquad \text{Equation 2}$$

You can multiply Equation 1 by -2 to obtain Equation 2.

$$2x + 6y = 10 \qquad \text{Revised Equation 1}$$
$$2x + 6y = 10 \qquad \text{Equation 2}$$

ANSWER ▶ The two equations are identical. Any solution of $2x + 6y = 10$ is also a solution of the system. This tells you that the linear system has infinitely many solutions.

Use the substitution method or linear combinations to solve the linear system and tell how many solutions the system has.

20. $-2x - 6y = -12$
$2x + 6y = 12$

21. $2x - 3y = 1$
$-2x + 3y = 1$

22. $-6x + 5y = 18$
$7x + 2y = 26$

7.6 SYSTEMS OF LINEAR INEQUALITIES

Examples on pp. 424–426

EXAMPLE Graph the system of linear inequalities.

$$x \geq 0 \qquad \text{Inequality 1}$$
$$y < -2x + 2 \qquad \text{Inequality 2}$$
$$y \geq 3x - 7 \qquad \text{Inequality 3}$$

Graph all three inequalities in the same coordinate plane. Use a dashed line if the inequality is $<$ or $>$ and a solid line if the inequality is $\leq$ or $\geq$.

The graph of $x \geq 0$ is the half-plane *on and to the right* of the line $x = 0$.

The graph of the $y < -2x + 2$ is the half-plane *below* the line $y = -2x + 2$.

The graph of $y \geq 3x - 7$ is the half-plane *on and above* the line $y = 3x - 7$.

The graph of the system is the intersection of the three half-planes shown.

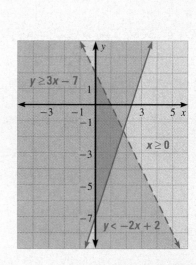

Graph the system of linear inequalities.

23. $x > -5$
$y < -2$

24. $2x - 10y > 8$
$x - 5y < 12$

25. $-x + 3y \leq 15$
$9x \geq 27$

26. $x < 5$
$y > -2$
$x + 2y > -4$

27. $x + y < 8$
$x - y < 0$
$y \geq 4$

28. $7y \geq -49$
$-7x + y \geq -14$
$x + y \leq 10$

Estimate the solution of the linear system graphically. Then check the solution algebraically.

1. $y = 2x - 3$
$-y = 2x - 1$

2. $6x + 2y = 16$
$-2x + y = -2$

3. $4x - y = 10$
$-2x + 4y = 16$

Use the substitution method to solve the linear system.

4. $-4x + 7y = -2$
$x = -y - 5$

5. $7x + 4y = 5$
$x - 6y = -19$

6. $-3x + 6y = 24$
$-2x - y = 1$

Use linear combinations to solve the linear system.

7. $6x + 7y = 5$
$4x - 2y = -10$

8. $-7x + 2y = -5$
$10x - 2y = 6$

9. $-3x + 3y = 12$
$4x + 2y = 20$

10. WILD BIRD FOOD You buy 6 bags of wild bird food to fill the feeders in your yard. Oyster shell grit, a natural calcium source, sells for $4.00 a bag. Sunflower seeds sell for $5.00 a bag. If you spend $28.00, how many bags of each type of bird food are you buying?

Use the substitution method or linear combinations to solve the linear system and tell how many solutions the system has.

11. $8x + 4y = -4$
$2x - y = -3$

12. $-6x + 3y = -6$
$2x + 6y = 30$

13. $-3x + y = -18$
$3x - y = -16$

14. $3x + y = 8$
$4x + 6y = 6$

15. $3x - 4y = 8$
$9x - 12y = 24$

16. $6x + y = 12$
$-4x - 2y = 0$

Graph the system of linear inequalities.

17. $x \le 4$
$y \ge 1$

18. $-3x + 2y > 3$
$x + 4y < -2$

19. $2x - 3y \le 12$
$-x - 3y \ge -6$

20. $x > -1$
$y < 3$
$y > -3$

21. $y \le 2$
$y \ge x - 2$
$y \ge -x - 2$

22. $x < 5$
$y \le 6$
$y > -2x + 3$

Write a system of linear inequalities that defines the shaded region.

23.
24.
25.

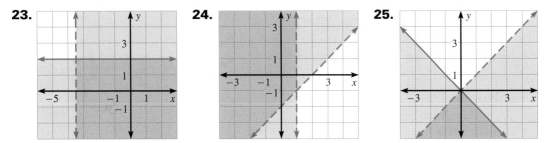

Chapter Standardized Test

1. Which point appears to be the solution of
the linear system graphed below?

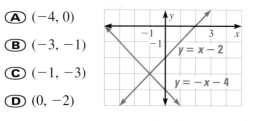

  (A) $(-4, 0)$

  (B) $(-3, -1)$

  (C) $(-1, -3)$

  (D) $(0, -2)$

2. The ordered pair $(3, 4)$ is a solution of
which linear system?

  (A) $x + y = 7$
     $x + 2y = 11$

  (B) $x - y = 1$
     $2x - y = 9$

  (C) $x - y = 1$
     $2x + y = 10$

  (D) $x + y = 7$
     $2x - 2y = 14$

3. What is the solution of the following
linear system?
$$-2x + 7y = -3$$
$$x - 7y = -2$$

  (A) 1

  (B) 5

  (C) $(1, 5)$

  (D) $(5, 1)$

4. What is the solution of the following
linear system?
$$5x - 6y = -10$$
$$-15x + 14y = 10$$

  (A) $(-5, -8)$

  (B) $(-2, 0)$

  (C) $(4, 5)$

  (D) $(10, 10)$

5. You have 50 ride tickets. You need 3 tickets
to ride the Ferris wheel and 5 tickets to ride
the roller coaster. You ride 12 times. How
many times did you ride the roller coaster?

  (A) 5

  (B) 7

  (C) 10

  (D) 18

6. How many solutions does the following
linear system have?
$$4x - 2y = 6$$
$$2x - y = 3$$

  (A) One

  (B) Two

  (C) Infinitely many

  (D) None

7. Which system of linear equations has
no solution?

  (A) $y = 2x + 4$
     $y = 2$

  (B) $3x + 4y = 10$
     $3x + 2y = 8$

  (C) $5x + 2y = 11$
     $10x + 4y = 11$

  (D) $2x - 4y = -5$
     $-3x + 6y = 15$

  (E) None of these

8. Which point is a solution of the following
system of linear inequalities?
$$y < -x$$
$$y < x$$

  (A) $(6, -2)$

  (B) $(-2, 6)$

  (C) $(-1, -6)$

  (D) $(-6, -1)$

9. Which system of inequalities is
represented by the graph below?

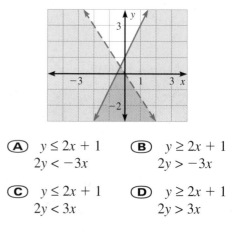

  (A) $y \le 2x + 1$
     $2y < -3x$

  (B) $y \ge 2x + 1$
     $2y > -3x$

  (C) $y \le 2x + 1$
     $2y < 3x$

  (D) $y \ge 2x + 1$
     $2y > 3x$

Maintaining Skills

EXAMPLE 1 Volume of a Solid

Find the volume of the figure shown.

Solution

$$\begin{aligned} \text{Volume} &= \text{Area of base} \times \text{Height} \\ &= \pi r^2 \times h \\ &= \pi (6)^2 5 \\ &= 180\pi \end{aligned}$$

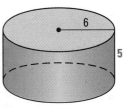

Try These

Find the volume of the geometric figure shown.

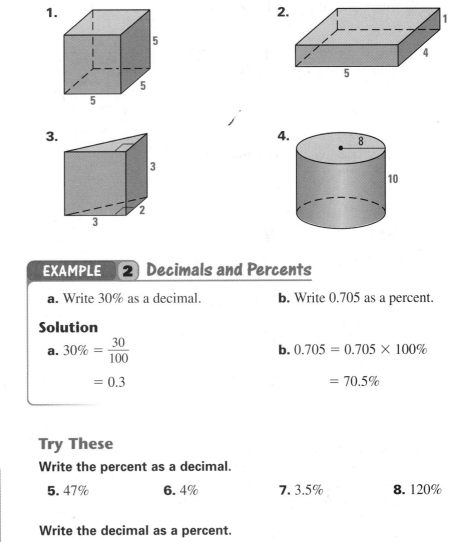

1. 5, 5, 5

2. 1, 4, 5

3. 3, 3, 2

4. 8, 10

EXAMPLE 2 Decimals and Percents

a. Write 30% as a decimal.   **b.** Write 0.705 as a percent.

Solution

a. $30\% = \dfrac{30}{100}$ **b.** $0.705 = 0.705 \times 100\%$

$= 0.3$ $= 70.5\%$

Try These

Write the percent as a decimal.

5. 47%   **6.** 4%   **7.** 3.5%   **8.** 120%

Write the decimal as a percent.

9. 0.61   **10.** 0.07   **11.** 2   **12.** 0.025

Exponents and Exponential Functions

▶ How are the speed of your bike and your air intake related?

APPLICATION: Bicycle Racing

Shifting into a higher gear helps racers increase speed but makes pedaling more difficult. When racers use more energy, their air intake increases.

The relationship between air intake and bicycle speed can be represented by a type of mathematical model that you will study in Chapter 8.

Think & Discuss

1. Construct a scatter plot of the data below. Draw a smooth curve through the points.

Bicycle speed, x (miles per hour)	Air intake, y (liters per minute)
0	6.4
5	10.7
10	18.1
15	30.5
20	51.4

2. Describe the change in the air intake after each increase of 5 miles per hour in bike speed. Does air intake increase by the same amount? Does it increase by the same percent?

Learn More About It

You will use an exponential model that relates air intake and bicycle speed in Exercises 35 and 36 on page 480.

 APPLICATION LINK More about bicycle racing is available at www.mcdougallittell.com

What's the chapter about?

- **Multiplying** and **dividing** expressions with exponents
- Using **scientific notation** to solve problems
- Using **exponential growth** and **decay models**

> **KEY WORDS**
>
> - **exponential functions,** p. 455
> - **scientific notation,** p. 469
> - **exponential growth,** p. 476
> - **growth factor,** p. 476
> - **exponential decay,** p. 482
> - **decay factor,** p. 482

Chapter Readiness Quiz

Take this quick quiz. If you are unsure of an answer, look back at the reference pages for help.

VOCABULARY CHECK *(refer to p. 9)*

1. Complete: In the expression 7^6, 7 is the __?__ .

   (A) base   (B) factor   (C) exponent   (D) power

2. Complete: In the expression 7^6, 6 is the __?__ .

   (A) base   (B) factor   (C) exponent   (D) power

SKILL CHECK *(refer to pp. 11, 16, 177)*

3. Evaluate $(3x)^2$ when $x = 2$.

   (A) 12   (B) 18   (C) 24   (D) 36

4. Evaluate $\dfrac{x^3}{y}$ when $x = 4$ and $y = 2$.

   (A) 6   (B) 8   (C) 21.5   (D) 32

5. How much do you earn per hour if you earn $123.75 for working 15 hours?

   (A) $8.25   (B) $12.12   (C) $108.75   (D) $1856.25

Plan Your Time

A schedule or weekly planner can be a useful tool that allows you to coordinate your study time with time for other activities.

FEBRUARY

MONDAY 5
Math homework–p. 446, #13–51 odd

TUESDAY 6
Swimming Practice 3–4 p.m.

WEDNESDAY 7
History report due

DEVELOPING CONCEPTS
Investigating Powers

For use with Lesson 8.1

GOAL
Find a pattern for multiplying exponential expressions.

MATERIALS
• paper
• pencil

Question

How do you multiply powers with the same base?

Explore

1 One way to multiply powers with the same base is to write the product in expanded form. Then count the number of factors and use this number as the exponent of the product of the powers.

			Number of factors	Product as a power
$7^3 \cdot 7^2 =$	$\underbrace{(7 \cdot 7 \cdot 7)}_{\text{3 factors}}\underbrace{(7 \cdot 7)}_{\text{2 factors}} =$	$\underbrace{(7)(7)(7)(7)(7)}_{\text{5 factors}}$	5	7^5

2 Notice that the exponent for the product of powers with the same base is the sum of the exponents of the powers: $3 + 2 = 5$. See if the same pattern applies to the following products.

$$7^3 \cdot 7^3 \qquad 2^3 \cdot 2^2 \qquad x^3 \cdot x^4$$

3 What can you conclude?

Think About It

Find the product. Write your answer as a single power.

1. $6^3 \cdot 6^2$ **2.** $2 \cdot 2^4$ **3.** $a^4 \cdot a^6$ **4.** $x^2 \cdot x^7$

5. Complete: For any nonzero number a and any positive integers m and n, $a^m \cdot a^n = \underline{\ ?\ }$.

Question

How do you find the power of a power?

Explore

1 To find the power of a power, you can write the product in expanded form. Then count the number of factors and use this number as the exponent of the product of the powers.

		Number of factors	Product as a power
$(7^3)^2 =$	$\overset{\text{2 times}}{\overbrace{(7^3)(7^3)}} = \underbrace{\overset{\text{3 factors 3 factors}}{\overbrace{(7)(7)(7)}\overbrace{(7)(7)(7)}}}_{\text{6 factors}}$	6	7^6

Student Help

▶**READING ALGEBRA**
When you read a power of a power, start with the power within the parentheses. For example, $(7^3)^2$ is read "seven cubed, squared."

Developing Concepts   **441**

2 Notice that the exponent for the power of a power is the product of the exponents: $2 \cdot 3 = 6$. See if the same pattern applies to the following powers of powers.

$$(5^2)^3 \qquad (3^2)^2 \qquad (x^5)^3$$

3 What can you conclude?

Think About It

Find the power of a power. Write your answer as a single power.

1. $(4^2)^3$ **2.** $(5^4)^2$ **3.** $(d^3)^3$ **4.** $(n^3)^4$

5. Complete: For any nonzero number a and any positive integers m and n, $(a^m)^n = \underline{\ ?\ }$.

Question

How do you find the power of a product?

Explore

1 One way to find the power of a product is to write the product in expanded form and group like factors. Then count the number of each factor and write the answer as a power of each factor.

		Number of each factor	Product as a power
$(5 \cdot 4)^2 = \underbrace{(5 \cdot 4)(5 \cdot 4)}_{2 \text{ times}} = \underbrace{(5 \cdot 5)}_{2 \text{ factors}}\underbrace{(4 \cdot 4)}_{2 \text{ factors}}$		2 and 2	$5^2 \cdot 4^2$

2 Notice that the exponent for a product of factors is distributed to each of the factors: $(5 \cdot 4)^2 = 5^2 \cdot 4^2$. See if the same pattern applies to the following powers of products.

$$(3 \cdot 2)^3 \qquad (3 \cdot 6)^4 \qquad (a \cdot b)^5$$

3 What can you conclude?

Think About It

Find the power of the product.

1. $(2 \cdot 6)^3$ **2.** $(3 \cdot 4)^5$ **3.** $(a \cdot b)^2$ **4.** $(x \cdot y)^4$

5. Complete: For any nonzero numbers a and b and any positive integer m, $(a \cdot b)^m = \underline{\ ?\ }$.

8.1 Multiplication Properties of Exponents

Goal
Use multiplication properties of exponents.

Key Words
- power
- base
- exponent

How do the areas of two irrigation circles compare?

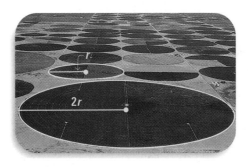

What does it mean to say that one circle is twice as big as another? Does it mean that the radius r is twice as big or that the area is twice as big? In Example 5 you will see that these two interpretations are not the same.

PRODUCT OF POWERS As you saw in Developing Concepts 8.1, page 441, to multiply powers that have the same base, you add the exponents. This property is called the *product of powers property*. Here is an example.

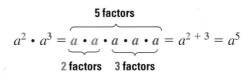

$$a^2 \cdot a^3 = \underbrace{a \cdot a}_{\text{2 factors}} \cdot \overbrace{\underbrace{a \cdot a \cdot a}_{\text{3 factors}}}^{\text{5 factors}} = a^{2+3} = a^5$$

Student Help

▶ **LOOK BACK**
For help with exponential expressions, see p. 9.

EXAMPLE ① Use the Product of Powers Property

Write the expression as a single power of the base.

a. $5^3 \cdot 5^6$ **b.** $-2(-2)^4$ **c.** $x^2 \cdot x^3 \cdot x^4$

Solution

a. $5^3 \cdot 5^6 = 5^{3+6}$ Use product of powers property.

$= 5^9$ Add the exponents.

b. $-2(-2)^4 = (-2)^1(-2)^4$ Rewrite -2 as $(-2)^1$.

$= (-2)^{1+4}$ Use product of powers property.

$= (-2)^5$ Add the exponents.

c. $x^2 \cdot x^3 \cdot x^4 = x^{2+3+4}$ Use product of powers property.

$= x^9$ Add the exponents.

Checkpoint✓ Use the Product of Powers Property

Write the expression as a single power of the base.

1. $4^2 \cdot 4^3$ **2.** $(-3)^2(-3)$ **3.** $a \cdot a^7$ **4.** $n^5 \cdot n^2 \cdot n^3$

POWER OF A POWER To find a power of a power, you multiply the exponents. This property is called the *power of a power property*. Here is an example.

$$(a^2)^3 = a^2 \cdot a^2 \cdot a^2 = a^{2+2+2} = a^6$$

Student Help

▶ **LOOK BACK**
For help with exponents and grouping symbols, see p. 11.

EXAMPLE **2** **Use the Power of a Power Property**

Write the expression as a single power of the base.

a. $(3^3)^2$ $\qquad\qquad\qquad\qquad$ **b.** $(p^4)^4$

Solution

a. $(3^3)^2 = 3^{3\,\cdot\,2}$ $\qquad$ Use power of a power property.

$ = 3^6$ $\qquad$ Multiply exponents.

b. $(p^4)^4 = p^{4\,\cdot\,4}$ $\qquad$ Use power of a power property.

$ = p^{16}$ $\qquad$ Multiply exponents.

Checkpoint ✔ **Use the Power of a Power Property**

Write the expression as a single power of the base.

5. $(4^4)^3$ $\qquad$ **6.** $[(-3)^5]^2$ $\qquad$ **7.** $(n^4)^5$ $\qquad$ **8.** $(x^3)^3$

POWER OF A PRODUCT To find a power of a product, find the power of each factor and multiply. This property is called the *power of a product property*. Here is an example.

$$(a \cdot b)^3 = (a \cdot b)(a \cdot b)(a \cdot b) = (a \cdot a \cdot a)(b \cdot b \cdot b) = a^3 b^3$$

EXAMPLE **3** **Use the Power of a Product Property**

Simplify the expression.

a. $(-6 \cdot 5)^2$ $\qquad\qquad\qquad\qquad$ **b.** $(4yz)^3$

Student Help

▶ **STUDY TIP**
Notice that $(-6)^2 \cdot 5^2$ is equivalent to:
$(-6 \cdot 5)^2 = (-30)^2$
$ = 900$

Solution

a. $(-6 \cdot 5)^2 = (-6)^2 \cdot 5^2$ $\qquad$ Use power of a product property.

$ = 36 \cdot 25$ $\qquad$ Evaluate each power.

$ = 900$ $\qquad$ Multiply.

b. $(4yz)^3 = 4^3 \cdot y^3 \cdot z^3$ $\qquad$ Use power of a product property.

$ = 64y^3 z^3$ $\qquad$ Evaluate power.

Checkpoint ✔ **Use the Power of a Product Property**

Simplify the expression.

9. $(2 \cdot 4)^3$ $\qquad$ **10.** $(-3 \cdot 5)^2$ $\qquad$ **11.** $(2w)^6$ $\qquad$ **12.** $(7a)^2$

EXAMPLE 4 Use All Three Properties

Simplify the expression $(4x^2)^3 \cdot x^5$.

Solution

$$(4x^2)^3 \cdot x^5 = 4^3 \cdot (x^2)^3 \cdot x^5 \qquad \text{Use power of a product property.}$$
$$= 64 \cdot x^6 \cdot x^5 \qquad \text{Use power of a power property.}$$
$$= 64x^{11} \qquad \text{Use product of powers property.}$$

Checkpoint ✓ **Use All Three Properties**

Simplify the expression.

13. $(4x^3)^4$ 　　　**14.** $(-3a^4)^2$ 　　　**15.** $9 \cdot (9z^5)^2$ 　　　**16.** $(n^2)^3 \cdot n^7$

Student Help

▶**STUDY TIP**
In the formula for the area of a circle, $A = \pi r^2$, r is the radius of the circle, and π is a constant, approximately 3.14.

EXAMPLE 5 Use Multiplication Properties of Exponents

FARMING Find the ratio of the area of the larger irrigation circle to the area of the smaller irrigation circle.

Solution

The area of a circle can be found using the formula $A = \pi r^2$.

$$\text{Ratio} = \frac{\pi(2r)^2}{\pi r^2} = \frac{\pi \cdot 2^2 \cdot r^2}{\pi \cdot r^2} = \frac{\pi \cdot 4 \cdot r^2}{\pi \cdot r^2} = \frac{4}{1}$$

ANSWER ▶ The ratio of the areas is 4 to 1.

Checkpoint ✓ **Use Multiplication Properties of Exponents**

17. Find the ratio of the area of the smaller irrigation circle in Example 5 to the area of an irrigation circle with radius $3r$.

SUMMARY

Multiplication Properties of Exponents

Let a and b be real numbers and let m and n be positive integers.

PRODUCT OF POWERS PROPERTY	POWER OF A POWER PROPERTY	POWER OF A PRODUCT PROPERTY
To multiply powers that have the same base, add the exponents.	To find a power of a power, multiply the exponents.	To find a power of a product, find the power of each factor and multiply.
$a^m \cdot a^n = a^{m+n}$	$(a^m)^n = a^{m \cdot n}$	$(a \cdot b)^m = a^m \cdot b^m$

Guided Practice

Vocabulary Check   **Match the multiplication property of exponents with the example that illustrates it.**

1. Product of powers property   **A.** $(3 \cdot 6)^2 = 3^2 \cdot 6^2$

2. Power of a power property   **B.** $4^3 \cdot 4^5 = 4^{3+5}$

3. Power of a product property   **C.** $(2^4)^4 = 2^{4 \cdot 4}$

Skill Check   **Use the product of powers property to write the expression as a single power of the base.**

4. $2^2 \cdot 2^3$ **5.** $(-5)^4 \cdot (-5)^2$ **6.** $a^4 \cdot a^6$

Use the power of a power property to write the expression as a single power of the base.

7. $(2^4)^3$ **8.** $(4^3)^3$ **9.** $(y^4)^5$

Use the power of a product property to simplify the expression.

10. $(3 \cdot 4)^3$ **11.** $(2n)^4$ **12.** $(3pq)^3$

Practice and Applications

COMPLETING EQUATIONS   **Copy and complete the statement.**

13. $3^2 \cdot 3^? = 3^7$ **14.** $5^? \cdot 5^8 = 5^9$ **15.** $4^{10} \cdot 4^8 = 4^?$

16. $x^3 \cdot x^2 = x^?$ **17.** $r^? \cdot r^7 = r^{14}$ **18.** $a^2 \cdot a^? = a^5$

PRODUCT OF POWERS   **Write the expression as a single power of the base.**

19. $4^3 \cdot 4^6$ **20.** $8^9 \cdot 8^5$ **21.** $(-2)^3 \cdot (-2)^3$

22. $b \cdot b^4$ **23.** $x^6 \cdot x^3$ **24.** $t^3 \cdot t^2$

COMPLETING EQUATIONS   **Copy and complete the statement.**

25. $(5^?)^3 = 5^9$ **26.** $(2^2)^? = 2^8$ **27.** $[(-9)^4]^3 = (-9)^?$

28. $(a^2)^? = a^{10}$ **29.** $(x^3)^3 = x^?$ **30.** $(p^?)^6 = p^{12}$

Student Help

▶ **HOMEWORK HELP**
Example 1: Exs. 13–24
Example 2: Exs. 25–36
Example 3: Exs. 37–51
Example 4: Exs. 52–60
Example 5: Exs. 61–68

POWER OF A POWER   **Write the expression as a single power of the base.**

31. $(2^3)^2$ **32.** $(7^4)^2$ **33.** $[(-4)^5]^3$

34. $(t^5)^6$ **35.** $(c^8)^{10}$ **36.** $(x^3)^2$

POWER OF A PRODUCT **Simplify the expression.**

37. $(3 \cdot 7)^2$ **38.** $(4 \cdot 9)^3$ **39.** $(-4 \cdot 6)^2$

40. $(5x)^3$ **41.** $(-2d)^6$ **42.** $(ab)^2$

43. $(2mn)^6$ **44.** $(10xy)^2$ **45.** $(-rst)^5$

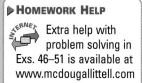

Student Help

▶ **HOMEWORK HELP**

Extra help with problem solving in Exs. 46–51 is available at www.mcdougallittell.com

WRITING INEQUALITIES **Copy and complete the statement using < or >.**

46. $(5 \cdot 6)^4$? $5 \cdot 6^4$ **47.** $5^2 \cdot 5^3$? $(5 \cdot 5)^6$ **48.** $(3 \cdot 2)^6$? $(3^2)^6$

49. $4^2 \cdot 4^8$? $(4 \cdot 4)^{10}$ **50.** $7^3 \cdot 7^4$? $(7 \cdot 7)^4$ **51.** $(6 \cdot 3)^3$? $6 \cdot 3 \cdot 3$

SIMPLIFYING EXPRESSIONS **Simplify the expression.**

52. $(3b)^3 \cdot b$ **53.** $-4x \cdot (x^3)^2$ **54.** $(5a^4)^2$

55. $(r^2 s^3)^4$ **56.** $(6z^4)^2 \cdot z^3$ **57.** $2x^3 \cdot (-3x)^2$

58. $4x \cdot (-x \cdot x^3)^2$ **59.** $(abc^2)^3 \cdot ab$ **60.** $(5y^2)^3 \cdot (y^3)^2$

61. *Geometry Link* The volume V of a sphere is given by the formula $V = \frac{4}{3}\pi r^3$, where r is the radius. What is the volume of the sphere in terms of a?

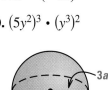

62. *Geometry Link* The volume V of a circular cone is given by the formula $V = \frac{1}{3}\pi r^2 h$, where r is the radius of the base and h is the height. What is the volume of the cone in terms of b?

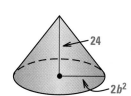

Link to
Careers

ALTERNATIVE ENERGY TECHNICIANS solve technical problems in the development, maintenance, and inspection of machinery, such as windmills.

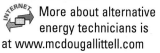

More about alternative energy technicians is at www.mcdougallittell.com

ALTERNATIVE ENERGY **The power generated by a windmill can be modeled by $w = 0.015s^3$, where w is the power measured in watts and s is the wind speed in miles per hour.**

63. Find the ratio of the power generated when the wind speed is 20 miles per hour to the power generated when the wind speed is 10 miles per hour.

64. Find the ratio of the power generated when the wind speed is 5 miles per hour to the power generated when the wind speed is 10 miles per hour.

PENNIES **Someone offers to double the amount of money you have every day for 1 month (30 days). You have 1 penny.**

65. At the end of the first day, you will have $2 \cdot 1 = 2$ pennies. On the second day, you will have $2 \cdot 2 = 4$ pennies. On the third day, you will have $2 \cdot 4 = 8$ pennies. Write each of these equations using only powers of 2.

66. Using the pattern you find in Exercise 65, write an expression for the number of pennies you will have on the nth day.

67. How many pennies will you have on the 30th day?

68. How much money (in dollars) will you have after 30 days?

69. CHALLENGE Fill in the blanks and give a reason for each step to complete a convincing argument that the power of a power property is true for this case.

$$(b^3)^2 = b^3 \cdot \underline{?}$$
$$= \underline{?} \cdot \underline{?} \cdot \underline{?} \cdot \underline{?} \cdot \underline{?} \cdot \underline{?}$$
$$= \underline{?}$$

Standardized Test Practice

70. MULTIPLE CHOICE Simplify the expression $5^2 \cdot 5^4$.

(A) 5^6 (B) 5^8 (C) 10^6 (D) 25^8

71. MULTIPLE CHOICE Evaluate the expression $(2^3)^2$.

(F) 18 (G) 32 (H) 36 (J) 64

72. MULTIPLE CHOICE Evaluate the expression $(4 \cdot 6)^2$.

(A) 48 (B) 96 (C) 144 (D) 576

73. MULTIPLE CHOICE Simplify the expression $(3x^2y)^3$.

(F) $3x^2y^3$ (G) $9x^5y^3$ (H) $9x^6y^3$ (J) $27x^6y^3$

Mixed Review

VARIABLE EXPRESSIONS Evaluate the expression for the given value of the variable. *(Lesson 1.3)*

74. b^2 when $b = 8$ **75.** $(5y)^4$ when $y = 2$ **76.** $\frac{1}{2}n^3$ when $n = -2$

77. $\frac{1}{y^2}$ when $y = 5$ **78.** $\frac{24}{x^3}$ when $x = 2$ **79.** $\frac{45}{a^2}$ when $a = 2$

GRAPHING EQUATIONS Use a table of values to graph the equation. *(Lessons 4.2, 4.3)*

80. $y = x + 2$ **81.** $y = -(x - 4)$ **82.** $y = \frac{1}{2}x - 5$

83. $y = \frac{3}{4}x + 2$ **84.** $y = 2$ **85.** $x = -3$

SOLVING INEQUALITIES Solve the inequality. *(Lesson 6.3)*

86. $-x - 2 < -5$ **87.** $3 - x > -4$ **88.** $7 + 3x \geq -2$

89. $6x - 10 \leq -4$ **90.** $2 < 2x + 7$ **91.** $9 - 4x \leq 2$

Maintaining Skills

LCM AND GCF Decide whether the statement is *true* or *false*. If it is false, correct the statement to make it true. *(Skills Review p. 761)*

92. The least common multiple of 6 and 10 is 60.

93. The greatest common factor of 6 and 10 is 2.

94. The least common multiple of 10 and 30 is 30.

95. The greatest common factor of 10 and 30 is 5.

96. The least common multiple of 45 and 82 is 105.

97. The greatest common factor of 45 and 82 is 3.

8.2 Zero and Negative Exponents

Goal

Evaluate powers that have zero or negative exponents.

Key Words

- zero exponent
- negative exponent
- reciprocal

What was the population of the U.S. in 1776?

Many real-life quantities can be modeled by functions that contain exponents. In Exercise 64 you will use such a model to estimate the population of the United States in 1776.

The definition of a^0 is determined by the product of powers property:

$$a^0 a^n = a^{0 + n} = a^n$$

In order to have $a^0 a^n = a^n$, a^0 must equal 1.

The definition of a^{-n} is similarly determined:

$$a^n a^{-n} = a^{n - n} = a^0 = 1$$

In order to have $a^n a^{-n} = 1$, a^{-n} must be the reciprocal of a^n.

Student Help

▶ WRITING ALGEBRA
The definition of a negative exponent can also be written as:

$$\frac{1}{a^{-n}} = a^n$$

ZERO AND NEGATIVE EXPONENTS

Let a be a nonzero number and let n be an integer.

- A nonzero number to the zero power is 1:

$$a^0 = 1, \ a \neq 0$$

- a^{-n} is the reciprocal of a^n:

$$a^{-n} = \frac{1}{a^n}, \ a \neq 0$$

EXAMPLE 1 Powers with Zero Exponents

Evaluate the expression.

a. $5^0 = 1$ a^0 is equal to 1.

b. 0^0 (Undefined) a^0 is defined only for a *nonzero* number a.

c. $(-2)^0 = 1$ a^0 is equal to 1.

d. $\left(\dfrac{1}{9}\right)^0 = 1$ a^0 is equal to 1.

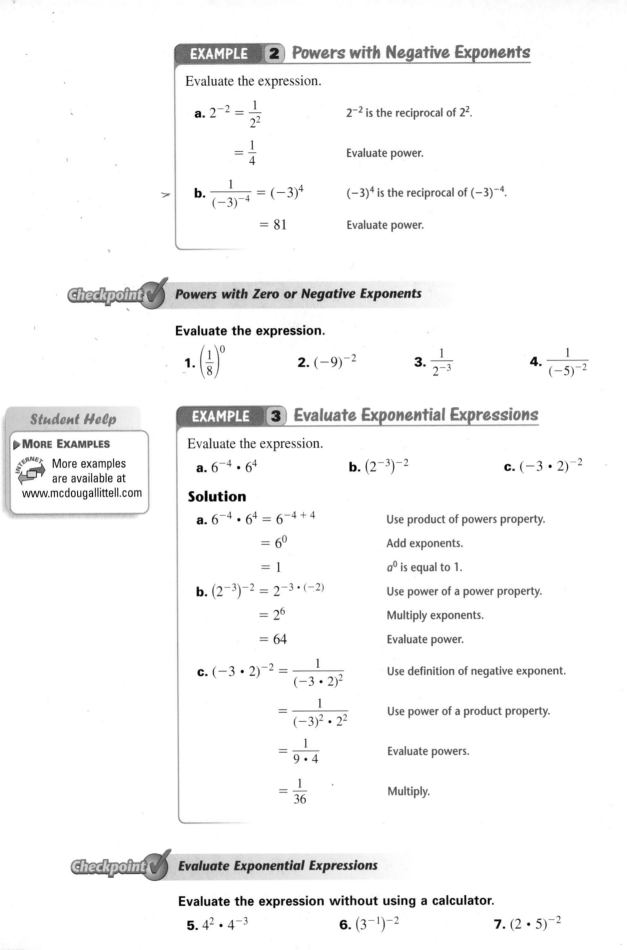

EXAMPLE 2 Powers with Negative Exponents

Evaluate the expression.

a. $2^{-2} = \dfrac{1}{2^2}$ 2^{-2} is the reciprocal of 2^2.

      $= \dfrac{1}{4}$ Evaluate power.

b. $\dfrac{1}{(-3)^{-4}} = (-3)^4$ $(-3)^4$ is the reciprocal of $(-3)^{-4}$.

      $= 81$ Evaluate power.

Checkpoint ✓ *Powers with Zero or Negative Exponents*

Evaluate the expression.

1. $\left(\dfrac{1}{8}\right)^0$ **2.** $(-9)^{-2}$ **3.** $\dfrac{1}{2^{-3}}$ **4.** $\dfrac{1}{(-5)^{-2}}$

Student Help

▶ **MORE EXAMPLES**

More examples are available at www.mcdougallittell.com

EXAMPLE 3 Evaluate Exponential Expressions

Evaluate the expression.

a. $6^{-4} \cdot 6^4$ **b.** $\left(2^{-3}\right)^{-2}$ **c.** $(-3 \cdot 2)^{-2}$

Solution

a. $6^{-4} \cdot 6^4 = 6^{-4+4}$ Use product of powers property.

      $= 6^0$ Add exponents.

      $= 1$ a^0 is equal to 1.

b. $\left(2^{-3}\right)^{-2} = 2^{-3 \cdot (-2)}$ Use power of a power property.

      $= 2^6$ Multiply exponents.

      $= 64$ Evaluate power.

c. $(-3 \cdot 2)^{-2} = \dfrac{1}{(-3 \cdot 2)^2}$ Use definition of negative exponent.

      $= \dfrac{1}{(-3)^2 \cdot 2^2}$ Use power of a product property.

      $= \dfrac{1}{9 \cdot 4}$ Evaluate powers.

      $= \dfrac{1}{36}$ Multiply.

Checkpoint ✓ *Evaluate Exponential Expressions*

Evaluate the expression without using a calculator.

5. $4^2 \cdot 4^{-3}$ **6.** $\left(3^{-1}\right)^{-2}$ **7.** $(2 \cdot 5)^{-2}$

EXAMPLE 4 Evaluate Expressions with a Calculator

Use a calculator to evaluate $(2^{-2})^4$.

Solution You can simplify the expression first.

$(2^{-2})^4 = 2^{-8}$ Use power of a power property.

KEYSTROKES   **DISPLAY**

2 y^x 8 +/−   =   0.00390625

ANSWER ▶ $(2^{-2})^4 \approx 0.0039$

Checkpoint✓ *Evaluate Expressions with a Calculator*

Use a calculator to evaluate the expression.

8. 7^{-3} **9.** $6^{-2} \cdot 6^{-1}$ **10.** $(3^3)^{-2}$

EXAMPLE 5 Simplify Exponential Expressions

Rewrite the expression with positive exponents.

a. $2x^{-2}y^{-3}$ **b.** $\dfrac{c^{-2}}{d^{-3}}$ **c.** $(5a)^{-2}$

Solution

a. $2x^{-2}y^{-3} = 2 \cdot \dfrac{1}{x^2} \cdot \dfrac{1}{y^3}$ Use definition of negative exponents.

$= \dfrac{2}{x^2y^3}$ Multiply.

b. $\dfrac{c^{-2}}{d^{-3}} = c^{-2} \cdot \dfrac{1}{d^{-3}}$ Multiply by reciprocal.

$= \dfrac{1}{c^2} \cdot d^3$ Use definition of negative exponents.

$= \dfrac{d^3}{c^2}$ Multiply.

c. $(5a)^{-2} = \dfrac{1}{(5a)^2}$ Use definition of negative exponents.

$= \dfrac{1}{5^2 \cdot a^2}$ Use power of a product property.

$= \dfrac{1}{25a^2}$ Evaluate power.

Checkpoint✓ *Simplify Exponential Expressions*

Rewrite the expression with positive exponents.

11. $2x^{-3}y^3$ **12.** $\dfrac{3}{x^{-2}}$ **13.** $(5b)^{-3}$

Exercises

Guided Practice

Vocabulary Check

Tell whether the statement is *true* or *false*. Explain your answer.

1. A nonzero number to the zero power is zero.

2. Let a be a nonzero number and let n be an integer. Then $a^{-n} = \dfrac{1}{a^n}$.

Skill Check

Evaluate the expression.

3. 6^0 **4.** 3^{-1} **5.** $\dfrac{1}{4^{-3}}$ **6.** $\dfrac{1}{(-2)^{-1}}$

Evaluate the expression without using a calculator.

7. $2^{-4} \cdot 2^5$ **8.** $(3^4)^{-1}$ **9.** $(4 \cdot 1)^{-2}$ **10.** $(9^{-1})^2$

Use a calculator to evaluate the expression. Round your answer to the nearest ten thousandth.

11. 5^{-4} **12.** $7^{-1} \cdot 7^{-3}$ **13.** $(8^2)^{-1}$ **14.** $(3 \cdot 4)^{-3}$

Rewrite the expression with positive exponents.

15. m^{-2} **16.** $a^5 b^{-8}$ **17.** $\dfrac{3}{c^{-5}}$ **18.** $(2x)^{-3}$

Practice and Applications

RECIPROCALS Copy and complete the table.

19.

x	2	5	6
x^{-1}	?	?	?

20.

x	?	?	?
x^{-1}	$\dfrac{1}{3}$	$\dfrac{1}{8}$	$\dfrac{1}{7}$

ZERO AND NEGATIVE EXPONENTS Evaluate the expression.

21. 3^0 **22.** $(-5)^0$ **23.** 4^{-2} **24.** 9^{-1}

25. $(-7)^{-3}$ **26.** $\dfrac{1}{10^{-1}}$ **27.** $\dfrac{1}{4^{-4}}$ **28.** $\dfrac{1}{(-8)^{-2}}$

EVALUATING EXPRESSIONS Evaluate the expression without using a calculator.

29. $2^{-3} \cdot 2^0$ **30.** $10^{-5} \cdot 10^7$ **31.** $6^2 \cdot 6^{-4}$ **32.** $4^{-1} \cdot 4^{-1}$

33. $(4^{-1})^{-3}$ **34.** $(5^{-2})^2$ **35.** $(3^2)^{-1}$ **36.** $[(-8)^{-2}]^{-1}$

37. $(10 \cdot 2)^{-2}$ **38.** $(1 \cdot 7)^{-3}$ **39.** $(-2 \cdot 2)^{-2}$ **40.** $[4 \cdot (-3)]^{-1}$

Student Help

▶ **HOMEWORK HELP**
Examples 1 and 2:
        Exs. 19–28
Example 3: Exs. 29–40
Example 4: Exs. 41–48
Example 5: Exs. 49–62

EVALUATING EXPRESSIONS Use a calculator to evaluate the expression. Round your answer to the nearest ten thousandth.

41. 2^{-5} **42.** 11^{-2} **43.** $5^{-1} \cdot 5^{-3}$ **44.** $9^{-4} \cdot 9^2$

45. $(4^2)^{-1}$ **46.** $(3^{-3})^2$ **47.** $(2 \cdot 7)^{-1}$ **48.** $(8 \cdot 3)^{-2}$

ERROR ANALYSIS In Exercises 49 and 50, find and correct the error.

49.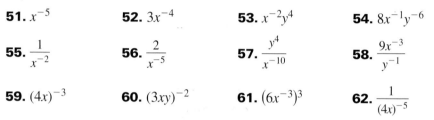
$$5x^{-3} = \frac{1}{5x^3}$$

50.
$$a^{-2}b^3 = \frac{b^3}{a^{-2}}$$

SIMPLIFYING EXPRESSIONS Rewrite the expression with positive exponents.

51. x^{-5} **52.** $3x^{-4}$ **53.** $x^{-2}y^4$ **54.** $8x^{-1}y^{-6}$

55. $\dfrac{1}{x^{-2}}$ **56.** $\dfrac{2}{x^{-5}}$ **57.** $\dfrac{y^4}{x^{-10}}$ **58.** $\dfrac{9x^{-3}}{y^{-1}}$

59. $(4x)^{-3}$ **60.** $(3xy)^{-2}$ **61.** $(6x^{-3})^3$ **62.** $\dfrac{1}{(4x)^{-5}}$

Link to
History

States in 1790

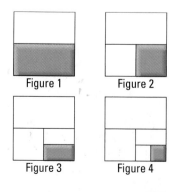

STATEHOOD After 1790, when the last of the original 13 colonies became a state, a population of at least 60,000 people was required for statehood.

EXAMPLE **Using Zero and Negative Exponents**

STATEHOOD The population P (in millions) of the United States from the late 1700s to the mid-1800s can be modeled by $P = 5.31(1.03)^y$, where y represents the number of years since 1800. Estimate the population of the United States in 1790 when the first census was taken.

Solution Since 1790 is 10 years before 1800, you want to know the value of P when $y = -10$.

$$P = 5.31(1.03)^y \qquad \text{Write model.}$$
$$= 5.31(1.03)^{-10} \qquad \text{Substitute } -10 \text{ for } y.$$
$$\approx 3.95 \qquad \text{Use a calculator to evaluate.}$$

ANSWER ▶ The population in 1790 was about 3.95 million people.

63. Estimate the population of the United States in 1800.

64. Estimate the population of the United States in 1776.

Puzzler Refer to the squares shown.

65. What fraction of each figure is shaded?

66. Rewrite each fraction from Exercise 65 in the form 2^x.

67. Look for a pattern in your answers to Exercise 66. If this pattern continues, what fraction of Figure 10 will be shaded?

Figure 1   Figure 2

Figure 3   Figure 4

68. MULTIPLE CHOICE Which expression equals $\frac{1}{8}$?

(A) -8 (B) 4^{-2} (C) 2^{-3} (D) 1^{-8}

69. MULTIPLE CHOICE Evaluate the expression $(4^{-1})^{-2}$.

(F) $\frac{1}{64}$ (G) $\frac{1}{16}$ (H) 16 (J) 64

70. MULTIPLE CHOICE Evaluate the expression $3 \cdot 3^{-5}$.

(A) $\frac{1}{81}$ (B) $\frac{1}{5}$ (C) 45 (D) 81

71. MULTIPLE CHOICE Rewrite the expression $\frac{3x^{-2}}{y^3 z^{-1}}$ with positive exponents.

(F) $\frac{z}{3x^2 y^3}$ (G) $\frac{3z}{x^2 y^3}$ (H) $\frac{3y^3 z}{x^2}$ (J) $3x^2 y^3 z$

Mixed Review

EVALUATING EXPRESSIONS Evaluate the expression. Then simplify the answer. *(Lesson 1.3)*

72. $\frac{6 \cdot 5}{1 + 7 \cdot 2}$ **73.** $\frac{8 \cdot 8}{10 + 3 \cdot 2}$ **74.** $\frac{2 \cdot 4^2}{1 + 3^2 - 2}$

75. $\frac{9 + 3^3 - 4}{8 \cdot 2}$ **76.** $\frac{(5 - 3)^2}{2 \cdot (6 - 2)}$ **77.** $\frac{2 \cdot 3^4}{20 - 4^2 + 8}$

SOLVING EQUATIONS Solve the equation. *(Lesson 3.1)*

78. $x + 1 = 6$ **79.** $-2 = 7 + x$ **80.** $15 = x - (-4)$

81. $10 = x - 5$ **82.** $-3 + x = -8$ **83.** $x - (-6) = -9$

SOLVING INEQUALITIES Solve the inequality. Then graph and check the solution. *(Lesson 6.7)*

84. $|x + 3| > 4$ **85.** $|x + 9| < 4$ **86.** $|3x + 2| \geq 10$

87. $|5 + 2x| \leq 7$ **88.** $|x + 2| + 6 < 15$ **89.** $|3x + 7| - 5 > 8$

SOLVING SYSTEMS Use substitution to solve the system. *(Lesson 7.2)*

90. $2x - y = -2$
$4x + y = 5$

91. $-3x + y = 4$
$-9x + 5y = 10$

92. $x + 4y = 30$
$x - 2y = 0$

93. $2x - 3y = 10$
$x + y = 5$

94. $x + 15y = 6$
$-x - 5y = 84$

95. $4x - y = 5$
$2x + 4y = 16$

Maintaining Skills

EQUIVALENT FRACTIONS Write three equivalent fractions for the given fraction. *(Skills Review p. 764)*

96. $\frac{1}{4}$ **97.** $\frac{3}{5}$ **98.** $\frac{5}{6}$ **99.** $\frac{1}{8}$

100. $\frac{2}{3}$ **101.** $\frac{15}{16}$ **102.** $\frac{5}{32}$ **103.** $\frac{25}{32}$

8.3 Graphs of Exponential Functions

Key Words
• exponential function

How many shipwrecks occurred from 1680 to 1980?

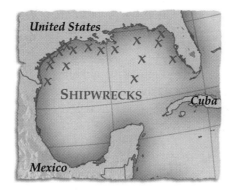

Many real-life relationships can be modeled by *exponential functions*. In Example 5 the number of shipwrecks that occurred in the northern part of the Gulf of Mexico from 1680 to 1980 is modeled by an *exponential function*.

In Lesson 8.2 the definition of b^n was extended to allow for zero and negative integer values of n. This lesson makes use of the expression b^x, where $b > 0$ and x is allowed to be any real number.

A function of the form $y = a \cdot b^x$ or simply $y = ab^x$, where $b > 0$ and $b \neq 1$ is an **exponential function**.

EXAMPLE 1 **Evaluate an Exponential Function**

Make a table of values for the exponential function $y = 2^x$. Use x-values of $-2, -1, 0, 1, 2,$ and 3.

Solution To evaluate an exponential function, use the definitions you learned in Lesson 8.2. For example, when $x = -2$ you find y as follows:

$$y = 2^{-2} = \frac{1}{2^2} = \frac{1}{4}$$

x	-2	-1	0	1	2	3
$y = 2^x$	$\frac{1}{4}$	$\frac{1}{2}$	1	2	4	8

Checkpoint **Evaluate an Exponential Function**

1. Make a table of values for the exponential function $y = 3^x$. Use x-values of $-2, -1, 0, 1, 2,$ and 3.

2. Make a table of values for the exponential function $y = 2\left(\frac{1}{3}\right)^x$. Use x-values of $-2, -1, 0, 1, 2,$ and 3.

Student Help

EXAMPLE **2** **Graph an Exponential Function when $b > 1$**

a. Use the table of values in Example 1 to graph the function $y = 2^x$.

b. Use a calculator to evaluate $y = 2^x$ when $x = 1.5$.

Solution Begin by writing the six points given by the table on page 455:

$$\left(-2, \frac{1}{4}\right), \left(-1, \frac{1}{2}\right), (0, 1), (1, 2), (2, 4), (3, 8)$$

a. Draw a coordinate plane and plot the six points listed above. Then draw a smooth curve through the points.

Notice that the graph has a y-intercept of 1, and that it gets closer to the negative side of the x-axis as the x-values decrease.

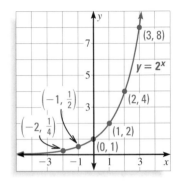

b. KEYSTROKES

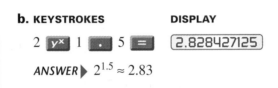

ANSWER ▶ $2^{1.5} \approx 2.83$

EXAMPLE **3** **Graph an Exponential Function when $0 < b < 1$**

Graph the function $y = 3\left(\frac{1}{2}\right)^x$.

Solution Make a table of values that includes both positive and negative x-values. Be sure to follow the order of operations when evaluating the function. For example, when $x = -2$ you find y as follows:

$$y = 3\left(\frac{1}{2}\right)^{-2} = 3(2)^2 = 3(4) = 12$$

x	−2	−1	0	1	2	3
$y = 3\left(\frac{1}{2}\right)^x$	12	6	3	$\frac{3}{2}$	$\frac{3}{4}$	$\frac{3}{8}$

Draw a coordinate plane and plot the six points given by the table. Then draw a smooth curve through the points.

Notice that the graph has a y-intercept of 3, and that it gets closer to the positive side of the x-axis as the x-values increase.

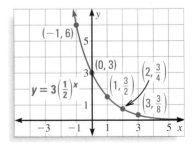

Student Help

▶ MORE EXAMPLES

More examples
are available at
www.mcdougallittell.com

EXAMPLE 4 Find Domain and Range

a. Describe the domain and range of the function $y = 2^x$, which is graphed in Example 2.

b. Describe the domain and range of the function $y = 3\left(\frac{1}{2}\right)^x$, which is graphed in Example 3.

Solution

a. You can see from the graph of the function that $y = 2^x$ is defined for all x-values, but only has y-values that are greater than 0. So the domain of $y = 2^x$ is all real numbers and the range is all positive real numbers.

b. You can see from the graph of the function that $y = 3\left(\frac{1}{2}\right)^x$ is defined for all x-values, but only has y-values that are greater than 0. So the domain of $y = 3\left(\frac{1}{2}\right)^x$ is all real numbers and the range is all positive real numbers.

Checkpoint ✓ Graph an Exponential Function and Find its Domain and Range

3. Graph the function $y = 3^x$. Then describe its domain and range.

4. Graph the function $y = 2\left(\frac{1}{3}\right)^x$. Then describe its domain and range.

EXAMPLE 5 Use an Exponential Model

SHIPWRECKS From 1680 to 1980 the number of shipwrecks per 10-year period t that occurred in the northern part of the Gulf of Mexico can be modeled by $S = 180(1.2)^t$, where S is the number of shipwrecks and $t = 0$ represents the 10-year period from 1900 to 1909. Graph the function.

Solution Make a table of values that includes positive and negative x-values.

t	-4	-2	0	2	4	6
$S = 180(1.2)^t$	87	125	180	259	373	537

Draw a coordinate plane and plot the six points given by the table. Then draw a smooth curve through the points.

Notice that the graph has a y-intercept of 180, and that it gets closer to the negative side of the x-axis as the x-values decrease.

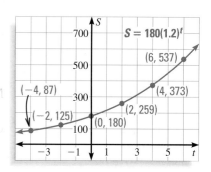

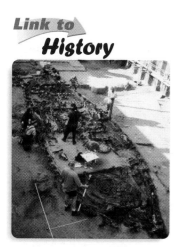

SHIPWRECKS In 1685 La Salle claimed part of the United States for France. In 1686 his ship the *Belle* sank near Texas. This shipwreck wasn't discovered until 1995.

More about
shipwrecks at
www.mcdougallittell.com

Guided Practice

Vocabulary Check
1. Define exponential function.

Skill Check
2. Copy and complete the table of values for the exponential function.

x	-2	-1	0	1	2	3
$y = 4^x$	?	?	?	?	?	?

3. Graph $y = 4^x$. Use the points found in Exercise 2.

4. Graph the function $y = 3\left(\dfrac{1}{4}\right)^x$.

Using the graph shown, describe the domain and range of the function.

5. $y = 2^x$

6. $y = -2^x$

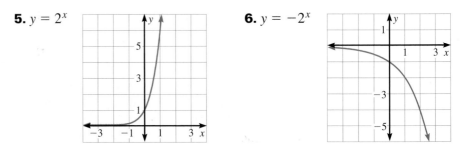

Practice and Applications

CHECKING POINTS Tell whether the graph of the function contains the point (0, 1). Explain your answer.

7. $y = 2^x$ **8.** $y = 5^x$ **9.** $y = 2(3)^x$ **10.** $y = 5(7)^x$

11. $y = \left(\dfrac{1}{8}\right)^x$ **12.** $y = \left(\dfrac{3}{4}\right)^x$ **13.** $y = 7\left(\dfrac{1}{5}\right)^x$ **14.** $y = 4\left(\dfrac{4}{9}\right)^x$

MAKING TABLES Make a table of values for the exponential function. Use x-values of -2, -1, 0, 1, 2, and 3.

15. $y = 3^x$ **16.** $y = 8^x$ **17.** $y = 5(4)^x$ **18.** $y = 3(5)^x$

19. $y = \left(\dfrac{1}{6}\right)^x$ **20.** $y = \left(\dfrac{2}{3}\right)^x$ **21.** $y = 2\left(\dfrac{1}{7}\right)^x$ **22.** $y = 5\left(\dfrac{4}{5}\right)^x$

Student Help

▶**HOMEWORK HELP**
  Example 1: Exs. 7–22
  Example 2: Exs. 23–41
  Example 3: Exs. 31–41
  Example 4: Exs. 42–49
  Example 5: Exs. 50, 51

EVALUATING FUNCTIONS Use a calculator to evaluate the exponential function when $x = 2.5$. Round your answer to the nearest hundredth.

23. $y = 5^x$ **24.** $y = 9^x$ **25.** $y = 8(2)^x$ **26.** $y = 3(4)^x$

27. $y = \left(\dfrac{1}{9}\right)^x$ **28.** $y = \left(\dfrac{5}{8}\right)^x$ **29.** $y = 6\left(\dfrac{1}{2}\right)^x$ **30.** $y = -\left(\dfrac{3}{5}\right)^x$

EXPONENTIAL FUNCTIONS Match the equation with its graph.

31. $y = 3^x$ **32.** $y = 2^x$ **33.** $y = 9^x$

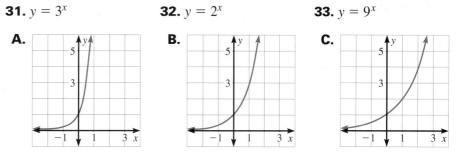

A.   **B.**   **C.**

GRAPHING FUNCTIONS Graph the exponential function.

34. $y = 4^x$ **35.** $y = -7^x$ **36.** $y = 4(2)^x$ **37.** $y = -3(8)^x$

38. $y = \left(\dfrac{1}{2}\right)^x$ **39.** $y = \left(\dfrac{2}{5}\right)^x$ **40.** $y = -5\left(\dfrac{1}{5}\right)^x$ **41.** $y = 2\left(\dfrac{2}{3}\right)^x$

DOMAIN AND RANGE Using your graphs from Exercises 34–41, describe
the domain and the range of the function.

42. $y = 4^x$ **43.** $y = -7^x$ **44.** $y = 4(2)^x$ **45.** $y = -3(8)^x$

46. $y = \left(\dfrac{1}{2}\right)^x$ **47.** $y = \left(\dfrac{2}{5}\right)^x$ **48.** $y = -5\left(\dfrac{1}{5}\right)^x$ **49.** $y = 2\left(\dfrac{2}{3}\right)^x$

50. SALARY INCREASE The company you work for has been giving a
5% increase in salary every year. Your salary S can be modeled by
$S = 38,000(1.05)^t$ where $t = 0$ represents the year 2000. Make a table
showing your salary in 1995, 2000, 2005, and 2010. Then graph the points
given by this table and draw a smooth curve through these points.

51. WORLD WIDE WEB The number of users U (in millions) of the World Wide
Web can be modeled by $U = 135(1.5)^t$ where $t = 0$ represents the year 2000.
Make a table showing the number of users (in millions) in 1995, 2000, 2005,
and 2010. Then graph the points given by this table and draw a smooth curve
through these points. ▶ Source: *WinOpportunity*

52. CHALLENGE If $a^0 = 1$ ($a \neq 0$), what point do all graphs of the form $y = a^x$
have in common? Is there a point that all graphs of the form $y = 2(a)^x$ have
in common? If so, name the point.

Standardized Test
Practice

53. MULTIPLE CHOICE What is the
equation of the graph?

   Ⓐ $y = 2^x$ **Ⓑ** $y = 2(2)^x$

   Ⓒ $y = \left(\dfrac{1}{2}\right)^x$ **Ⓓ** $y = 2\left(\dfrac{1}{2}\right)^x$

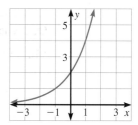

54. MULTIPLE CHOICE What is the
equation of the graph?

   Ⓕ $y = 2^x$ **Ⓖ** $y = 2(2)^x$

   Ⓗ $y = \left(\dfrac{1}{2}\right)^x$ **Ⓙ** $y = 2\left(\dfrac{1}{2}\right)^x$

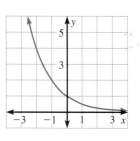

Mixed Review

SOLVING AND CHECKING Solve the equation. Round the result to the nearest hundredth. Check the rounded solution. *(Lesson 3.6)*

55. $8x + 9 = 12$ **56.** $3y - 5 = 11$ **57.** $13t + 8 = 2$

58. $14 - 6r = -17$ **59.** $11k + 12 = -9$ **60.** $-7x - 7 = -6$

STANDARD FORM Write the equation in standard form with integer coefficients. *(Lesson 5.4)*

61. $y = -8x + 4$ **62.** $y = 5x - 2$ **63.** $y = \dfrac{7}{8}x$

64. $y = -\dfrac{2}{5}x$ **65.** $y = -\dfrac{3}{16}x + \dfrac{9}{16}$ **66.** $y = \dfrac{1}{10}x - \dfrac{9}{10}$

GRAPHING SYSTEMS Use the graphing method to tell how many solutions the system has. *(Lesson 7.5)*

67. $2x - 2y = 4$ **68.** $-x + y = -1$ **69.** $6x + 2y = 3$
$x + 3y = 9$ $2x + 3y = 12$ $3x + y = -2$

70. $x + y = 0$ **71.** $4x - y = -2$ **72.** $-x + 3y = 3$
$x + 2y = 6$ $-12x + 3y = 6$ $2x - y = -8$

Maintaining Skills

ORDERING NUMBERS Write the numbers in increasing order. *(Skills Review pp. 770, 771)*

73. $-4, -5, 6$ **74.** $\dfrac{3}{5}, \dfrac{5}{7}, \dfrac{4}{8}$ **75.** $-2\dfrac{3}{4}, -3\dfrac{4}{5}, -2\dfrac{1}{5}$

76. $-6.57, -6.9, -6.56$ **77.** $3.001, 3.25, 3.01$ **78.** $7.99, 7.09, 7.9$

Quiz 1

Evaluate the expression. *(Lessons 8.1, 8.2)*

1. $3^4 \cdot 3^6$ **2.** $(2^3)^2$ **3.** $(8 \cdot 5)^2$

4. $6^{-7} \cdot 6^9$ **5.** $(5^2)^{-1}$ **6.** $(4 \cdot 9)^0$

Simplify the expression. Use only positive exponents. *(Lessons 8.1, 8.2)*

7. $r^5 \cdot r^8$ **8.** $(k^4)^2$ **9.** $(3d)^2$

10. $2x^{-3}y^{-9}$ **11.** $\dfrac{1}{5a^{-10}b^{-12}}$ **12.** $(mn)^{-7}$

13. SAVINGS ACCOUNT You started a savings account in 1994. The balance A is given by $A = 1600(1.08)^t$ where $t = 0$ represents the year 2000. What is the balance in the account in 1994? in 2004? *(Lesson 8.2)*

Graph the exponential function. *(Lesson 8.3)*

14. $y = 10^x$ **15.** $y = 3(2)^x$ **16.** $y = 4\left(\dfrac{2}{3}\right)^x$

USING A GRAPHING CALCULATOR
Exponential Functions

You can use a graphing calculator to graph exponential functions.

Sample

Graph $y = \left(\dfrac{1}{2}\right)^x$.

Solution

1 To enter the function in your graphing calculator, press [Y=].
Enter the function as
[( ] [1] [÷] [2] [ )] [^] [X, T, θ] .

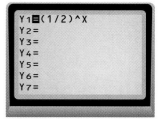

2 Adjust the *viewing window* to get the best scale for your graph.

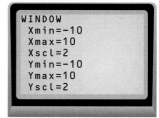

3 Now you are ready to graph the function. Press [GRAPH] to see the graph.

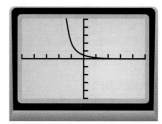

Try These

Use a graphing calculator to graph the exponential function.

1. $y = 2^x$

2. $y = 10^x$

3. $y = -3^x$

4. $y = \left(\dfrac{1}{5}\right)^x$

5. $y = \left(\dfrac{2}{7}\right)^x$

6. $y = -\left(\dfrac{2}{3}\right)^x$

LOGICAL REASONING **Use your results from Exercises 1–6 to answer the following questions.**

7. If $a > 1$, what does the graph of $y = a^x$ look like? the graph of $-a^x$?

8. If $0 < a < 1$, what does the graph of $y = a^x$ look like? the graph of $-a^x$?

Division Properties of Exponents

Goal
Use division properties of exponents.

Key Words
- power
- base
- exponent
- quotient

How much does a baseball player earn?

One way to compare numerical values is to look at their ratio. In Exercise 59 you will use division properties of exponents to compare the average salary of a baseball player in 1985 to the average salary of a baseball player in 1990.

QUOTIENT OF POWERS To divide powers that have the same base, you subtract the exponents. This is called the *quotient of powers property*. Here is an example.

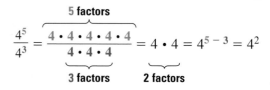

$$\frac{4^5}{4^3} = \frac{\overbrace{4 \cdot 4 \cdot 4 \cdot 4 \cdot 4}^{5 \text{ factors}}}{\underbrace{4 \cdot 4 \cdot 4}_{3 \text{ factors}}} = \underbrace{4 \cdot 4}_{2 \text{ factors}} = 4^{5-3} = 4^2$$

EXAMPLE 1 **Use the Quotient of Powers Property**

Simplify the quotient.

a. $\dfrac{6^5}{6^4} = 6^{5-4}$ Use quotient of powers property.

$\phantom{\dfrac{6^5}{6^4}} = 6^1$ Subtract exponents.

$\phantom{\dfrac{6^5}{6^4}} = 6$ Evaluate power.

b. $\dfrac{y^3}{y^5} = y^{3-5}$ Use quotient of powers property.

$\phantom{\dfrac{y^3}{y^5}} = y^{-2}$ Subtract exponents.

$\phantom{\dfrac{y^3}{y^5}} = \dfrac{1}{y^2}$ Use definition of negative exponent.

Student Help

▶ **STUDY TIP**
In Example 1(b) note that the same answer would have been reached by cancelling common factors:

$$\frac{y^3}{y^5} = \frac{\cancel{y} \cdot \cancel{y} \cdot \cancel{y}}{\cancel{y} \cdot \cancel{y} \cdot \cancel{y} \cdot y \cdot y}$$

$$= \frac{1}{y^2}$$

Checkpoint ✓ **Using the Quotient of Powers Property**

Simplify the quotient.

1. $\dfrac{8^4}{8^6}$ **2.** $\dfrac{(-3)^3}{(-3)^2}$ **3.** $\dfrac{x^4}{x^4}$ **4.** $\dfrac{a^9}{a^5}$

POWER OF A QUOTIENT Recall that $\dfrac{a}{b} \cdot \dfrac{a}{b} = \dfrac{a^2}{b^2}$. To find a power of a quotient, first find the power of the numerator and the power of the denominator, and then divide. This is called the *power of a quotient property*. Here is an example.

$$\left(\frac{2}{3}\right)^4 = \frac{2}{3} \cdot \frac{2}{3} \cdot \frac{2}{3} \cdot \frac{2}{3} = \frac{2 \cdot 2 \cdot 2 \cdot 2}{3 \cdot 3 \cdot 3 \cdot 3} = \frac{2^4}{3^4}$$

EXAMPLE 2 **Use the Power of a Quotient Property**

Simplify the quotient.

a. $\left(\dfrac{2}{3}\right)^2 = \dfrac{2^2}{3^2}$ Use power of a quotient property.

  $= \dfrac{4}{9}$ Evaluate powers.

b. $\left(\dfrac{-3}{y}\right)^3 = \dfrac{(-3)^3}{y^3}$ Use power of a quotient property.

  $= \dfrac{-27}{y^3}$ Evaluate power.

c. $\left(\dfrac{7}{4}\right)^{-3} = \dfrac{7^{-3}}{4^{-3}}$ Use power of a quotient property.

  ▶ $= \dfrac{4^3}{7^3}$ Use definition of negative exponents.

  $= \dfrac{64}{343}$ Evaluate powers.

Student Help

▶**STUDY TIP**
One step in simplifying a quotient is to make sure only positive exponents are used. ·············▶

Checkpoint✓ **Use the Power of a Quotient Property**

Simplify the quotient.

5. $\left(\dfrac{5}{4}\right)^3$ **6.** $\left(\dfrac{-x}{2}\right)^4$ **7.** $\left(\dfrac{3}{5}\right)^{-2}$ **8.** $\left(\dfrac{1}{x}\right)^{-5}$

SUMMARY

Division Properties of Exponents

Let a and b be real numbers and let m and n be integers.

QUOTIENT OF POWERS PROPERTY

To divide powers that have the same base, subtract the exponents.

$$\frac{a^m}{a^n} = a^{m-n},\ a \neq 0$$

POWER OF A QUOTIENT PROPERTY

To find a power of a quotient, find the power of the numerator and the power of the denominator and divide.

$$\left(\frac{a}{b}\right)^m = \frac{a^m}{b^m},\ b \neq 0$$

Student Help

▶ MORE EXAMPLES

INTERNET
More examples
are available at
www.mcdougallittell.com

EXAMPLE 3 Simplify Expressions using Multiple Properties

Simplify the expression. Use only positive exponents.

a. $\dfrac{2x^2y}{3x} \cdot \dfrac{9xy^2}{y^4}$

b. $\left(\dfrac{2x}{y^2}\right)^4$

Solution

a. $\dfrac{2x^2y}{3x} \cdot \dfrac{9xy^2}{y^4} = \dfrac{18x^3y^3}{3xy^4}$ Use product of powers property.

$\qquad\qquad = 6x^2y^{-1}$ Use quotient of powers property.

$\qquad\qquad = \dfrac{6x^2}{y}$ Use definition of negative exponents.

b. $\left(\dfrac{2x}{y^2}\right)^4 = \dfrac{(2x)^4}{(y^2)^4}$ Use power of a quotient property.

$\qquad\qquad = \dfrac{2^4 \cdot x^4}{y^{2\,\cdot\,4}}$ Use power of a product property.
Use power of a power property.

$\qquad\qquad = \dfrac{16x^4}{y^8}$ Evaluate power.
Multiply exponents.

EXAMPLE 4 Simplify Expressions with Negative Exponents

Simplify the expression $\dfrac{x}{y^{-1}} \cdot \left(\dfrac{x^2}{y}\right)^{-3}$. Use only positive exponents.

Solution

$\dfrac{x}{y^{-1}} \cdot \left(\dfrac{x^2}{y}\right)^{-3} = \dfrac{x}{y^{-1}} \cdot \dfrac{(x^2)^{-3}}{y^{-3}}$ Use power of a quotient property.

$\qquad\qquad = x \cdot y \cdot \dfrac{y^3}{(x^2)^3}$ Use definition of negative exponents.

$\qquad\qquad = \dfrac{xy^4}{x^6}$ Use product of powers property.
Use power of a power property.

$\qquad\qquad = x^{-5}y^4$ Use quotient of powers property.

$\qquad\qquad = \dfrac{y^4}{x^5}$ Use definition of negative exponents.

Checkpoint ✓ **Simplify Expressions**

Simplify the expression. Use only positive exponents.

9. $\dfrac{3xy^4}{x^3} \cdot \dfrac{y}{xy^3}$

10. $\left(\dfrac{5x}{y^3}\right)^3$

11. $\dfrac{y^{-2}}{x^2} \cdot \left(\dfrac{x^4}{y}\right)^{-1}$

Guided Practice

Vocabulary Check

Match the division property of exponents with the example that illustrates it.

1. Quotient of powers property

A. $\left(\dfrac{3}{6}\right)^2 = \dfrac{3^2}{6^2}$

2. Power of a quotient property

B. $\dfrac{4^3}{4^5} = 4^{3-5}$

Skill Check

Use the quotient of powers property to simplify the expression.

3. $\dfrac{5^4}{5^1}$

4. $\dfrac{7^6}{7^9}$

5. $\dfrac{(-2)^8}{(-2)^3}$

6. $\dfrac{5^3 \cdot 5^5}{5^9}$

7. $\dfrac{x^{12}}{x^9}$

8. $\dfrac{a^5}{a^2}$

9. $\dfrac{m^5}{m^{11}}$

10. $\dfrac{x^7 \cdot x}{x^2}$

Use the power of a quotient property to simplify the expression.

11. $\left(\dfrac{1}{2}\right)^5$

12. $\left(\dfrac{3}{5}\right)^3$

13. $\left(\dfrac{-4}{3}\right)^4$

14. $\left(\dfrac{5}{4}\right)^{-3}$

15. $\left(\dfrac{-5}{m}\right)^2$

16. $\left(\dfrac{x}{y}\right)^6$

17. $\left(\dfrac{m^3}{n^5}\right)^2$

18. $\left(\dfrac{a^6}{b^9}\right)^{-5}$

Practice and Applications

COMPLETING EQUATIONS Copy and complete the statement.

19. $\dfrac{3^9}{3^5} = 3^{?}$

20. $\dfrac{7^{?}}{7^2} = 7^4$

21. $\dfrac{9^5}{9^{?}} = 9^{-6}$

22. $\dfrac{x^5}{x^{?}} = x^2$

23. $\dfrac{a^{10}}{a^4} = a^{?}$

24. $\dfrac{w^{?}}{w} = w^3$

QUOTIENT OF POWERS Simplify the quotient.

25. $\dfrac{5^6}{5^3}$

26. $\dfrac{8^2}{8^3}$

27. $\dfrac{(-3)^6}{(-3)^6}$

28. $\dfrac{6^3 \cdot 6^2}{6^5}$

29. $\dfrac{x^4}{x^5}$

30. $x^3 \cdot \dfrac{1}{x^2}$

31. $\dfrac{1}{x^8} \cdot x^5$

32. $\dfrac{x^3 \cdot x^5}{x^2}$

Student Help

▶**HOMEWORK HELP**
Example 1: Exs. 19–32
Example 2: Exs. 33–46
Example 3: Exs. 47–54
Example 4: Exs. 55–57

COMPLETING EQUATIONS Copy and complete the statement.

33. $\left(\dfrac{1}{6}\right)^4 = \dfrac{1}{?}$

34. $\left(\dfrac{-3}{5}\right)^2 = \dfrac{?}{25}$

35. $\left(\dfrac{2}{7}\right)^{?} = \dfrac{8}{343}$

36. $\left(\dfrac{x}{y}\right)^{?} = \dfrac{y^2}{x^2}$

37. $\left(\dfrac{a^2}{b}\right)^5 = \dfrac{a^{?}}{b^5}$

38. $\left(\dfrac{m^3}{n^{?}}\right)^4 = \dfrac{m^{12}}{n^8}$

POWER OF A QUOTIENT Simplify the quotient.

39. $\left(\dfrac{1}{5}\right)^4$ **40.** $\left(\dfrac{3}{4}\right)^2$ **41.** $\left(\dfrac{-2}{3}\right)^3$ **42.** $\left(\dfrac{9}{6}\right)^{-1}$

43. $\left(\dfrac{3}{x}\right)^4$ **44.** $\left(\dfrac{-x}{2}\right)^3$ **45.** $\left(\dfrac{x}{y}\right)^5$ **46.** $\left(\dfrac{8}{x}\right)^{-2}$

ERROR ANALYSIS In Exercises 47 and 48, find and correct the error.

47.

48.

SIMPLIFYING EXPRESSIONS Simplify the expression. Use only positive exponents.

49. $\dfrac{4x^3y^3}{2xy} \cdot \dfrac{5xy^2}{2y}$ **50.** $\dfrac{16x^3y}{-4xy^3} \cdot \dfrac{-2xy}{x}$ **51.** $\dfrac{36a^8b^2}{ab} \cdot \dfrac{ab^2}{6}$

52. $\left(\dfrac{2m^3n^4}{3mn}\right)^3$ **53.** $\dfrac{6x^2y^2}{xy^3} \cdot \dfrac{(4x^2y)^2}{xy^2}$ **54.** $\dfrac{16x^5y^8}{x^7y^4} \cdot \left(\dfrac{x^3y^2}{8xy}\right)^4$

55. $\dfrac{x^2}{xy^{-4}} \cdot \dfrac{2x^{-3}y^4}{3xy^{-1}}$ **56.** $\dfrac{5x^{-3}y^2}{x^5y^{-1}} \cdot \dfrac{(2xy^3)^{-2}}{xy}$ **57.** $\dfrac{4xy}{2x^{-1}y^{-3}} \cdot \left(\dfrac{2xy^2}{3xy}\right)^{-2}$

STOCKBROKERS who work on the floor of a stock exchange use hand signals that date back to the 1880s to relay information about stock trades.

More about stockbrokers at www.mcdougallittell.com

EXAMPLE *Use Division Properties of Exponents*

STOCK EXCHANGE The number of shares n (in billions) listed on the New York Stock Exchange (NYSE) from 1977 through 1997 can be modeled by

$$n = 93.4 \cdot (1.11)^t$$

where $t = 0$ represents 1990. Find the ratio of shares listed in 1997 to the shares listed in 1977. ▶ Source: New York Stock Exchange

Solution

Since 1997 is 7 years after 1990, use $t = 7$ for 1997. Since 1977 is 13 years before 1990, use $t = -13$ for 1977. Because 93.4 is a common factor to the number of shares for both years, you may omit it from the ratio below.

$$\dfrac{\text{Number listed in 1997}}{\text{Number listed in 1977}} = \dfrac{(1.11)^7}{(1.11)^{-13}}$$
$$= (1.11)^{7-(-13)}$$
$$= (1.11)^{20}$$
$$\approx 8.06 \quad \longleftarrow \text{Use a calculator.}$$

ANSWER ▶ The ratio of shares listed in 1997 to the shares listed in 1977 is 8.06 to 1. There were about 8 times as many shares listed in 1997 as there were in 1977.

Use the example on the previous page as a model for Exercises 58–61.

58. RETAIL SALES From 1994 to 1998 the sales for a clothing store increased by about the same percent each year. The sales S (in millions of dollars) for year t can be modeled by $S = 3723\left(\dfrac{6}{5}\right)^t$, where $t = 0$ corresponds to 1994. Find the ratio of 1998 sales to 1995 sales.

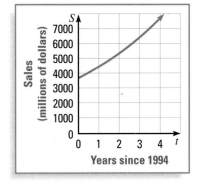

59. BASEBALL SALARIES The average salary s (in thousands) for a professional baseball player in the United States can be modeled by
$$s = 136(1.18)^t$$
where $t = 0$ represents the year 1980. Find the ratio of the average salary in 1985 to the average salary in 1990. ▶ Source: National Baseball Library and Archive

60. ATLANTIC COD The average weight w (in pounds) of an Atlantic cod can be modeled by
$$w = 1.21(1.42)^t$$
where t is the age of the fish (in years). Find the ratio of the weight of a 5-year-old cod to the weight of a 2-year-old cod.
▶ Source: National Marine Fisheries Service

61. LEARNING SPANISH You memorized a list of 200 Spanish vocabulary words. Unfortunately, each week you forget one fifth of the words you knew the previous week. The number of Spanish words S you remember after n weeks can be modeled by:

$$S = 200\left(\dfrac{4}{5}\right)^n$$

Copy and complete the table showing the number of words you remember after n weeks.

Weeks n	0	1	2	3	4	5	6
Words S	?	?	?	?	?	?	?

LOGICAL REASONING Give a reason for each step to show that the definitions of zero and negative exponents hold true for the properties of exponents.

62. $a^0 = a^{n-n}$

$\quad = \dfrac{a^n}{a^n}$

$\quad = 1$

63. $a^{-n} = a^{n-2n}$

$\quad = \dfrac{a^n}{a^{2n}}$

$\quad = \dfrac{a^n}{a^n \cdot a^n}$

$\quad = \dfrac{1}{a^n}$

64. CHALLENGE A piece of notebook paper is about 0.0032 inch thick. If you begin with a stack consisting of a single sheet and double the stack 25 times, how thick will the stack be? *HINT:* You will need to write and solve an exponential equation.

65. MULTIPLE CHOICE Simplify the expression $\dfrac{x^{-9}}{x^{-3}}$.

    Ⓐ $\dfrac{1}{x^{-6}}$ Ⓑ $\dfrac{1}{x^6}$ Ⓒ x^{-3} Ⓓ x^3

66. MULTIPLE CHOICE Simplify the expression $\left(\dfrac{2}{9}\right)^{-3}$.

    Ⓕ $-\dfrac{6}{27}$ Ⓖ $\dfrac{27}{6}$ Ⓗ $-\dfrac{8}{729}$ Ⓙ $\dfrac{729}{8}$

67. MULTIPLE CHOICE Simplify the expression $\dfrac{4x^3y}{18x^2} \cdot \dfrac{9}{16x^2y}$.

    Ⓐ $\dfrac{x}{16}$ Ⓑ $\dfrac{x}{8}$ Ⓒ $\dfrac{x^3}{8}$ Ⓓ $\dfrac{1}{8x}$

68. MULTIPLE CHOICE Simplify the expression $\dfrac{x^{-2}}{y^{-3}} \cdot \left(\dfrac{x}{y}\right)^{-1}$.

    Ⓕ $\dfrac{y^2}{x}$ Ⓖ $\dfrac{y^4}{x^3}$ Ⓗ $\dfrac{x^2}{y^3}$ Ⓙ $\dfrac{x^3}{y^4}$

Mixed Review

POWERS OF TEN **Evaluate the expression.** *(Lessons 1.2, 8.2)*

69. 10^5 **70.** 10^1 **71.** 10^0 **72.** 10^{-4}

SLOPE-INTERCEPT FORM **Write in slope-intercept form the equation of the line that passes through the given points.** *(Lesson 5.3)*

73. $(-4, 2)$ and $(4, 6)$ **74.** $(-4, -5)$ and $(0, 3)$ **75.** $(-1, -7)$ and $(3, -11)$

76. $(3, 9)$ and $(1, -3)$ **77.** $(5, -2)$ and $(-4, 7)$ **78.** $(1, 8)$ and $(-4, -2)$

CHECKING FOR SOLUTIONS **Decide whether the ordered pair is a solution of the system of linear equations.** *(Lesson 7.1)*

79. $2x + 4y = 2$
    $-x + 5y = 13$ $(-3, 2)$

80. $3x - 4y = 5$
    $x + 6y = 8$ $(3, 1)$

81. $8x + 4y = 6$
    $4x + y = 3$ $(1, -1)$

82. $x - 5y = 9$
    $3x + 5y = 11$ $(4, -1)$

SOLVING LINEAR SYSTEMS **Use linear combinations to solve the system. Then check your solution.** *(Lesson 7.3)*

83. $x - y = 4$
    $x + y = 12$

84. $-p + 2q = 12$
    $p + 6q = 20$

85. $2a + 3b = 17$
    $3a + 4b = 24$

86. $2m + 3n = 7$
    $m + n = 1$

87. $x + 10y = -1$
    $2x + 9y = 9$

88. $8r - 3t = 2$
    $2r - 2t = 3$

Maintaining Skills

ESTIMATION **Use front-end estimation to estimate the sum or difference.** *(Skills Review p. 774)*

89. $287 + 165$ **90.** $4672 + 1807$ **91.** $46.18 + 34.42$

92. $172 - 112$ **93.** $4882 - 3117$ **94.** $3.84 - 1.68$

8.5 Scientific Notation

Goal
Read and write numbers in scientific notation.

Key Words
• scientific notation

What was the price of Alaska per square mile?

In 1867 the United States purchased Alaska by writing a check for $7.2 million. In Example 5 you will use *scientific notation* to find the price per square mile of that purchase.

Numbers such as 100, 14.2, and 0.07 are written in *decimal form. Scientific notation* uses powers of ten to express decimal numbers. A number is written in **scientific notation** if it is of the form $c \times 10^n$ where $1 \le c < 10$ and n is an integer. Here are three examples.

$$1.2 \times 10^3 = 1.2 \times 1000 = 1200$$

$$5.6 \times 10^0 = 5.6 \times 1 = 5.6$$

$$3.5 \times 10^{-1} = 3.5 \times 0.1 = 0.35$$

Student Help

▶ **STUDY TIP**
When multiplying by 10^n and $n > 0$, move the decimal point n places to the **right**. When $n < 0$ move the decimal point n places to the **left**.

EXAMPLE 1 Write Numbers in Decimal Form

Write the number in decimal form.

a. 2.83×10^1 **b.** 4.9×10^5 **c.** 8×10^{-1} **d.** 1.23×10^{-3}

Solution

a. $2.83 \times 10^1 = 28.3$ Move decimal point 1 place to the right.

b. $4.9 \times 10^5 = 490\,000$ Move decimal point 5 places to the right.

c. $8 \times 10^{-1} = 0.8$ Move decimal point 1 place to the left.

d. $1.23 \times 10^{-3} = 0.00123$ Move decimal point 3 places to the left.

Checkpoint ✓ **Write Numbers in Decimal Form**

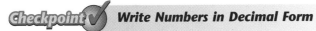

Write the number in decimal form.

1. 2.39×10^4 **2.** 1.045×10^7 **3.** 3.7×10^8

4. 8.4×10^{-6} **5.** 1.0×10^{-2} **6.** 9.2×10^{-8}

EXAMPLE 2 Write Numbers in Scientific Notation

Write the number in scientific notation.

a. 34,000   **b.** 1.78   **c.** 0.0007

Solution

a. $34,000 = 3.4 \times 10^4$ Move decimal point 4 places to the left.

b. $1.78 = 1.78 \times 10^0$ Move decimal place 0 places.

c. $0.0007 = 7 \times 10^{-4}$ Move decimal point 4 places to the right.

Checkpoint ✓ **Write Numbers in Scientific Notation**

Write the number in scientific notation.

7. 423   **8.** 2,000,000   **9.** 0.0001   **10.** 0.0098

Student Help

▶ **MORE EXAMPLES**

More examples are available at www.mcdougallittell.com

EXAMPLE 3 Operations with Scientific Notation

Perform the indicated operation. Write the result in scientific notation.

a. $(1.4 \times 10^4)(7.6 \times 10^3)$

$= (1.4 \cdot 7.6) \times (10^4 \cdot 10^3)$ Use properties of multiplication.

$= 10.64 \times 10^7$ Use product of powers property.

$= (1.064 \times 10^1) \times 10^7$ Write in scientific notation.

$= 1.064 \times 10^8$ Use product of powers property.

b. $\dfrac{1.2 \times 10^{-1}}{4.8 \times 10^{-4}} = \dfrac{1.2}{4.8} \times \dfrac{10^{-1}}{10^{-4}}$ Write as a product.

$= 0.25 \times 10^3$ Use quotient of powers property.

$= (2.5 \times 10^{-1}) \times 10^3$ Write in scientific notation.

$= 2.5 \times 10^2$ Use product of powers property.

c. $(4 \times 10^{-2})^3 = 4^3 \times (10^{-2})^3$ Use power of a product property.

$= 64 \times 10^{-6}$ Use power of a power property.

$= (6.4 \times 10^1) \times 10^{-6}$ Write in scientific notation.

$= 6.4 \times 10^{-5}$ Use product of powers property.

Checkpoint ✓ **Operations with Scientific Notation**

Perform the indicated operation. Write the result in scientific notation.

11. $(2.3 \times 10^3)(1.8 \times 10^{-5})$ **12.** $\dfrac{5.2 \times 10^3}{1.3 \times 10^1}$ **13.** $(5 \times 10^{-4})^2$

Many calculators automatically use scientific notation to display large or small numbers. Try multiplying 98,900,000 by 500 on a calculator. If the calculator follows standard procedures, it will display the product using scientific notation.

$$4.945^{\;10}$$ ◄——— Calculator display for 4.945×10^{10}

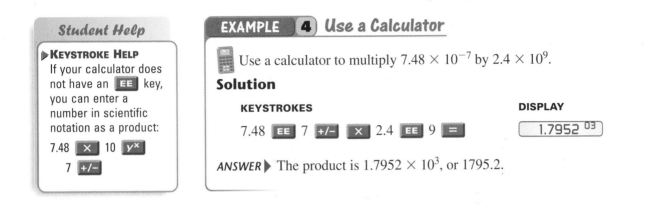

Student Help

▶ **KEYSTROKE HELP**
If your calculator does not have an **EE** key, you can enter a number in scientific notation as a product:

7.48 **×** 10 **yˣ**
7 **+/−**

EXAMPLE 4 *Use a Calculator*

Use a calculator to multiply 7.48×10^{-7} by 2.4×10^{9}.

Solution

KEYSTROKES

7.48 **EE** 7 **+/−** **×** 2.4 **EE** 9 **=**

DISPLAY

$$1.7952^{\;03}$$

ANSWER ▶ The product is 1.7952×10^{3}, or 1795.2.

Checkpoint✓ *Use a Calculator*

Use a calculator to perform the indicated operation.

14. $(5.1 \times 10^{2})(0.8 \times 10^{-4})$ **15.** $\dfrac{8.9 \times 10^{0}}{6.4 \times 10^{-5}}$ **16.** $(1.5 \times 10^{6})^{-1}$

EXAMPLE 5 *Scientific Notation in Real Life*

ALASKA PURCHASE In 1867 the United States purchased Alaska from Russia for \$7.2 million. The total area of Alaska is about 5.9×10^{5} square miles. What was the price per square mile?

Solution

The price per square mile is a unit rate.

Student Help

▶ **LOOK BACK**
For help with unit rates, see p. 177.

$$\text{Price per square mile} = \frac{\text{Total price}}{\text{Number of square miles}}$$

$$= \frac{7.2 \times 10^{6}}{5.9 \times 10^{5}} \quad \text{◄——— 7.2 million} = 7.2 \times 10^{6}$$

$$\approx 1.22 \times 10^{1}$$

$$= 12.2$$

ANSWER ▶ The price was about \$12.20 per square mile.

Checkpoint✓ *Scientific Notation in Real Life*

17. In 1994 the population of California was about 3.1×10^{7}. In that year about 5.6×10^{10} local calls were made in California. Estimate the number of local calls made per person in California in 1994.

Guided Practice

Vocabulary Check

1. Is the number 12.38×10^2 in scientific notation? Explain.

Skill Check

Write the number in decimal form.

2. 9×10^4 **3.** 4.3×10^2 **4.** 8.11×10^3

5. 5×10^{-2} **6.** 9.4×10^{-5} **7.** 2.45×10^{-1}

Write the number in scientific notation.

8. 15 **9.** $6,900,000$ **10.** 39.6

11. 0.99 **12.** 0.0003 **13.** 0.0205

Perform the indicated operation. Write the result in scientific notation.

14. $(5 \times 10^6)(6 \times 10^{-2})$ **15.** $\dfrac{1.4 \times 10^{-3}}{7 \times 10^7}$ **16.** $(9 \times 10^{-9})^2$

Practice and Applications

MOVING DECIMALS **Tell whether you would move the decimal *left* or *right* and how many places to write the number in decimal form.**

17. 1.5×10^2 **18.** 6.89×10^5 **19.** 9.04×10^{-7}

DECIMAL FORM **Write the number in decimal form.**

20. 5×10^5 **21.** 8×10^3 **22.** 1×10^6

23. 2.1×10^4 **24.** 7.75×10^0 **25.** 4.33×10^8

26. 3×10^{-4} **27.** 9×10^{-3} **28.** 4×10^{-5}

29. 9.8×10^{-2} **30.** 6.02×10^{-6} **31.** 1.1×10^{-10}

LOGICAL REASONING **Decide whether the number is in scientific notation. If not, write the number in scientific notation.**

32. 0.7×10^2 **33.** 2.9×10^5 **34.** 10×10^{-3}

Student Help

▶ **HOMEWORK HELP**
Example 1: Exs. 17–31
Example 2: Exs. 32–46
Example 3: Exs. 47–55
Example 4: Exs. 56–61
Example 5: Exs. 62–69

SCIENTIFIC NOTATION **Write the number in scientific notation.**

35. 900 **36.** $700,000,000$ **37.** $88,000,000$

38. 1012 **39.** 95.2 **40.** 370.2

41. 0.1 **42.** 0.05 **43.** 0.000006

44. 0.0422 **45.** 0.0085 **46.** 0.000459

EVALUATING EXPRESSIONS Perform the indicated operation without using a calculator. Write the result in scientific notation.

47. $(4.1 \times 10^2)(3 \times 10^6)$ **48.** $(9 \times 10^{-6})(2 \times 10^4)$ **49.** $(6 \times 10^5)(2.5 \times 10^{-1})$

50. $\dfrac{8 \times 10^{-3}}{4 \times 10^{-5}}$ **51.** $\dfrac{3.5 \times 10^{-4}}{5 \times 10^{-1}}$ **52.** $\dfrac{6.6 \times 10^{-1}}{1.1 \times 10^{-1}}$

53. $(3 \times 10^2)^3$ **54.** $(2 \times 10^{-3})^4$ **55.** $(1.5 \times 10)^{-2}$

CALCULATOR Use a calculator to perform the indicated operation. Write the result in scientific notation and in decimal form.

56. $6{,}000{,}000 \cdot 324{,}000$ **57.** $(2.79 \times 10^{-4})(3.94 \times 10^9)$

58. $\dfrac{3{,}940{,}000}{0.0002}$ **59.** $\dfrac{6.45 \times 10^{-6}}{4.3 \times 10^5}$ **60.** $(0.000094)^3$ **61.** $(2.4 \times 10^{-4})^5$

DECIMAL FORM Write the number in decimal form.

62. The distance that light travels in one year is 9.46×10^{12} kilometers.

63. The length of a dust mite is 9.8×10^{-4} foot.

SCIENTIFIC NOTATION Write the number in scientific notation.

64. At the end of 1999 the population of the world was estimated at 6,035,000,000. **DATA UPDATE** of U.S. Census Bureau data at www.mcdougallittell.com

65. The mass of a carbon atom is 0.00000000000000000000002 gram.

66. **Science Link** Light travels at a speed of about 3×10^5 kilometers per second. It takes about 1.5×10^4 seconds for light to travel from the sun to Neptune. What is the approximate distance (in kilometers) between Neptune and the sun?

History Link In Exercises 67 and 68, use the following information.

In 1803 the Louisiana Purchase added 8.28×10^5 square miles to the United States. The price of the land was \$15 million. In 1853 the Gadsden Purchase added 2.96×10^4 square miles. The price was \$10 million.

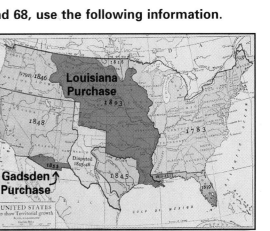

67. Find the price per square mile of the Louisiana Purchase.

68. Find the price per square mile of the Gadsden Purchase.

69. **Science Link** Jupiter, the largest planet in our solar system, has a radius of about 7.15×10^4 kilometers. Use the formula for the volume of a sphere, $V = \dfrac{4}{3}\pi r^3$, to estimate Jupiter's volume.

Link to History

70. MULTIPLE CHOICE Which number is *not* in scientific notation?

    Ⓐ 1×10^4 Ⓑ 3.4×10^{-3} Ⓒ 9.02×10^2 Ⓓ 12.25×10^{-5}

71. MULTIPLE CHOICE Evaluate $\dfrac{1.1 \times 10^{-1}}{5.5 \times 10^{-5}}$.

    Ⓕ 0.2×10^{-6} Ⓖ 0.2×10^{-4} Ⓗ 2×10^3 Ⓙ 2×10^4

Mixed Review

GRAPHING Use the graphing method to tell how many solutions the system has. *(Lesson 7.5)*

72. $4x + 2y = 12$
$-6x + 3y = 6$

73. $3x - 2y = 0$
$3x - 2y = -4$

74. $x - 5y = 8$
$-x + 5y = -8$

GRAPHING Graph the system of linear inequalities. *(Lesson 7.6)*

75. $2x + y \le 1$
$-2x + y \le 1$

76. $x + 2y < 3$
$x - 3y > 1$

77. $2x + y \ge 2$
$x < 2$

Maintaining Skills

FRACTIONS, DECIMALS, AND PERCENTS Write the given fraction, decimal, or percent in the indicated form. *(Skills Review pp. 767–769)*

78. Write $\dfrac{1}{3}$ as a decimal.

79. Write $\dfrac{53}{25}$ as a percent.

80. Write 1.45 as a fraction.

81. Write 0.674 as a percent.

82. Write 15% as a fraction.

83. Write 756.7% as a decimal.

Quiz 2

Simplify the quotient. *(Lesson 8.4)*

1. $\dfrac{6^7}{6^2}$ **2.** $\dfrac{x^9}{x^{11}}$ **3.** $\left(\dfrac{-7}{2}\right)^3$ **4.** $\left(\dfrac{a}{b}\right)^{-5}$

Simplify the expression. Use only positive exponents. *(Lesson 8.4)*

5. $\dfrac{3xy^5}{9x^4y^6} \cdot \dfrac{4x^4}{xy^8}$ **6.** $\dfrac{20x^3y}{4xy^2} \cdot \dfrac{-6xy}{-x}$ **7.** $\dfrac{5ab^3}{-2a^{-1}b^2} \cdot \dfrac{10a^{-3}b}{a^2b^{-4}}$

8. $\left(\dfrac{-2m^2n}{3mn^2}\right)^4$ **9.** $\dfrac{xy^{10}}{5x^3y^6} \cdot \dfrac{(2x^2y)^4}{4x^3y}$ **10.** $\dfrac{9wz^{-2}}{w^{-3}z^3} \cdot \left(\dfrac{w^2z}{3z^{-1}}\right)^{-3}$

Write the number in decimal form. *(Lesson 8.5)*

11. 5×10^9 **12.** 4.8×10^3 **13.** 3.35×10^4

14. 7×10^{-6} **15.** 1.1×10^{-2} **16.** 2.08×10^{-5}

Write the number in scientific notation. *(Lesson 8.5)*

17. 105   **18.** 99,000   **19.** 30,700,000

20. 0.25   **21.** 0.0004   **22.** 0.0000067

GOAL

Use reasoning to compare exponential and linear functions.

MATERIALS

• graph paper

Question

How are linear and exponential functions different?

Explore

1 The equation $y = 5^x$ is an *exponential function*. Copy and complete the table using this equation.

x	0	1	2	3	4	5
y	1	5	?	?	?	?

2 Use the table in Step 1 to graph $y = 5^x$.

3 The equation $y = 5x + 20$ is a *linear function*. Copy and complete the table using this equation.

x	0	1	2	3	4	5
y	20	25	?	?	?	?

4 Use the table in Step 3 to graph $y = 5x + 20$.

5 Which of the graphs below shows a *linear function*? Which shows an *exponential function*? Explain how you know.

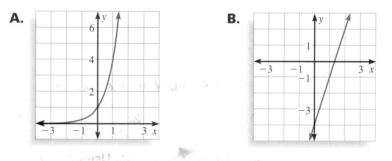

A.

B.

Think About It

Graph the function.

1. $y = x + 5$ **2.** $y = 3^x$ **3.** $y = 10 + 2x$

4. $y = -3(2)^x$ **5.** $y = 5(4x - 7)$ **6.** $y = 10(1.2)^x$

LOGICAL REASONING In Exercises 7–9, use the results from Exercises 1–6.

7. Complete: A linear function increases the __?__ amount for each unit on the *x*-axis.

8. Describe the rate of increase in an exponential growth model.

9. Explain one way that an equation for a linear function differs from an equation for an exponential function.

Exponential Growth Functions

Goal

Write and graph exponential growth functions.

Key Words

- exponential growth
- growth rate
- growth factor

How does a catfish's weight change as it grows?

In Lesson 8.3 you learned about exponential functions. One use of exponential functions is to model *exponential growth*. In Example 1 you will analyze the weight of a newly hatched catfish when that weight is increasing by 10% each day.

A quantity is *growing exponentially* if it increases by the same percent *r* in each unit of time *t*. This is called **exponential growth**. Exponential growth can be modeled by the equation

$$y = C(1 + r)^t$$

where *C* is the initial amount (the amount before any growth occurs), *r* is the **growth rate** (as a decimal), *t* represents time, and both *C* and *r* are positive. The expression $(1 + r)$ is called the **growth factor**.

Student Help

▶ **STUDY TIP**
To write a percent as a decimal, remove the percent sign from the number and divide the number by 100.

$$10\% = \frac{10}{100} = 0.10$$

EXAMPLE 1 Write an Exponential Growth Model

CATFISH GROWTH A newly hatched channel catfish typically weighs about 0.06 gram. During the first six weeks of life, its weight increases by about 10% each day. Write a model for the weight of the catfish during the first six weeks.

Solution

Let *y* be the weight of the catfish during the first six weeks and let *t* be the number of days. The initial weight of the catfish *C* is 0.06. The growth rate is *r* is 10%, or 0.10.

$y = C(1 + r)^t$	Write exponential growth model.
$= 0.06(1 + 0.10)^t$	Substitute 0.06 for *C* and 0.10 for *r*.
$= 0.06(1.1)^t$	Add.

Checkpoint✓ Write an Exponential Growth Model

1. A TV station's local news program has 50,000 viewers. The managers of the station hope to increase the number of viewers by 2% per month. Write an exponential growth model to represent the number of viewers in *t* months.

COMPOUND INTEREST *Compound interest* is interest paid on the *principal P*, the original amount deposited, and on the interest that has already been earned. Compound interest is a type of exponential growth, so you can use the exponential growth model to find the account balance A.

EXAMPLE 2 Find the Balance in an Account

COMPOUND INTEREST You deposit $500 in an account that pays 8% interest compounded yearly. What will the account balance be after 6 years?

Solution

The initial amount P is $500, the growth rate is 8%, and the time is 6 years.

$$A = P(1 + r)^t \qquad \text{Write yearly compound interest model.}$$

$$= 500(1 + 0.08)^6 \qquad \text{Substitute 500 for } P, 0.08 \text{ for } r, \text{ and 6 for } t.$$

$$= 500(1.08)^6 \qquad \text{Add.}$$

$$\approx 793 \qquad \text{Use a calculator.}$$

ANSWER ▶ The balance after 6 years will be about $793.

Checkpoint ✓ **Find the Balance in an Account**

2. You deposit $750 in an account that pays 6% interest compounded yearly. What is the balance in the account after 10 years?

EXAMPLE 3 Use an Exponential Growth Model

POPULATION GROWTH An initial population of 20 mice triples each year for 5 years. What is the mice population after 5 years?

Solution

You know that the population triples each year. This tells you the factor by which the population is growing, not the percent change in the population. Therefore the *growth factor* (not the growth rate) is 3. The initial population is 20 and the time is 5 years.

$$y = C(1 + r)^t \qquad \text{Write exponential growth model.}$$

$$= 20(3)^5 \qquad \text{Substitute for 20 for } C, 3 \text{ for } 1 + r, \text{ and 5 for } t.$$

$$= 4860 \qquad \text{Evaluate.}$$

ANSWER ▶ There will be 4860 mice after 5 years.

Checkpoint ✓ **Use an Exponential Growth Model**

3. An initial population of 30 rabbits doubles each year for 6 years. What is the rabbit population after 6 years?

EXAMPLE 4 — A Model with a Large Growth Rate

Graph the exponential growth model from Example 3.

Solution

Make a table of values, plot the points in a coordinate plane, and draw a smooth curve through the points.

t	0	1	2	3	4
y	20	60	180	540	1620

Student Help

▶ **STUDY TIP**
A large growth rate corresponds to a rapid increase in the y-values.

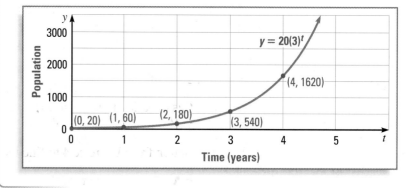

$y = 20(3)^t$

(0, 20) (1, 60) (2, 180) (3, 540) (4, 1620)

Population

Time (years)

EXAMPLE 5 — A Model with a Small Growth Rate

In 1980 there were only 73 peregrine falcons along the Colville River in Alaska. From 1980 to 1987 the population grew by about 9% per year. Therefore the population P of peregrine falcons can be modeled by $P = 73(1.09)^t$ where $t = 0$ represents 1980. Graph the function.

Solution

Make a table of values, plot the points in a coordinate plane, and draw a smooth curve through the points.

t	0	1	2	3	4
P	73	80	87	95	103

Student Help

▶ **STUDY TIP**
A small growth rate corresponds to a slow increase in the y-values.

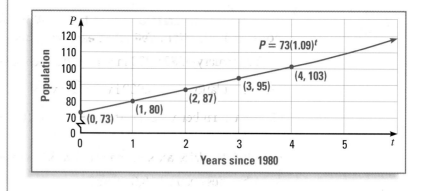

$P = 73(1.09)^t$

(0, 73) (1, 80) (2, 87) (3, 95) (4, 103)

Population

Years since 1980

Checkpoint ✓ **Graph an Exponential Growth Model**

4. Graph the exponential growth model you found in Checkpoint 3.

Guided Practice

Vocabulary Check

1. Complete: In the exponential growth model, $y = C(1 + r)^t$, C is the __?__ and $(1 + r)$ is the __?__.

Skill Check

COMPOUND INTEREST **You deposit $500 in an account that pays 4% interest compounded yearly.**

2. What is the initial amount P?

3. What is the growth rate r?

4. Complete this equation to write an exponential growth model for the balance after t years: $A = $ __?__ $(1 + $ __?__ $)^t$.

5. Use the equation from Exercise 4 to find the balance after 5 years.

6. CHOOSE A MODEL Which model best represents the growth curve shown in the graph at the right?

A. $y = 100(2)^t$ **B.** $y = 100(1.2)^t$

C. $y = 200(2)^t$ **D.** $y = 200(1.2)^t$

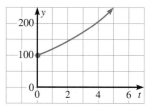

Practice and Applications

EXPONENTIAL GROWTH **Identify the initial amount and the growth rate in the exponential function.**

7. $y = 100(1 + 0.5)^t$ **8.** $y = 12(1 + 2)^t$ **9.** $y = 7.5(1.75)^t$

WRITING EXPONENTIAL FUNCTIONS **Write an exponential function to model the situation. Tell what each variable represents.**

10. Your salary of $25,000 increases 7% each year.

11. A population of 310,000 increases by 15% each year.

12. An annual benefit concert attendance of 10,000 increases by 5% each year.

BUSINESS **Write an exponential growth model for the profit.**

13. A business had a $10,000 profit in 1990. Then the profit increased by 25% per year for the next 10 years.

14. A business had a $20,000 profit in 1990. Then the profit increased by 20% per year for the next 10 years.

15. A business had a $15,000 profit in 1990. Then the profit increased by 30% per year for the next 15 years.

Student Help

▶ **HOMEWORK HELP**
Example 1: Exs. 7–15
Example 2: Exs. 16–27
Example 3: Exs. 28–35
Examples 4 and 5:
　　Exs. 36–40

COMPOUND INTEREST You deposit $1400 in an account that pays 6% interest compounded yearly. Find the balance at the end of the given time period.

16. 5 years   **17.** 8 years   **18.** 12 years   **19.** 20 years

Student Help

▶ **HOMEWORK HELP**

Extra help with problem solving in Exs. 33–34 is available at www.mcdougallittell.com

COMPOUND INTEREST You deposit money in an account that pays 5% interest compounded yearly. Find the balance after 5 years for the given initial amount.

20. $250   **21.** $300   **22.** $350   **23.** $400

COMPOUND INTEREST You deposit $900 in an account that compounds interest yearly. Find the balance after 10 years for the given interest rate.

24. 4%   **25.** 5%   **26.** 6%   **27.** 7%

GROWTH RATES AND FACTORS Identify the growth rate and the growth factor in the exponential function.

28. $y = 50(1 + 1)^t$ **29.** $y = 31(4)^t$ **30.** $y = 5.6(2.3)^t$

POPULATION GROWTH An initial population of 1000 starfish doubles each year for 4 years.

31. What is the growth factor for the population?

32. What is the starfish population after 4 years?

SUNFISH GROWTH An ocean sunfish, the mola mola, is about 0.006 foot long when it hatches. By the time it reaches adulthood, the largest of the mola mola will have tripled its length about 7 times.

33. What is the growth factor for the length of a mola mola?

34. What is the maximum length of an adult mola mola?

BICYCLE RACING In Exercises 35 and 36, use the following information. The air intake b (in liters per minute) of a cyclist on a racing bike can be modeled by $b = 6.37(1.11)^s$, where s is the speed of the bike (in miles per hour).

35. Use a calculator to find the cyclist's air intake if the racing bike is traveling 7 miles per hour, 19 miles per hour, or 25 miles per hour.

36. GRAPHING Graph the exponential growth model.

EXPONENTIAL GROWTH MODELS Match the description with its graph.

37. $C = \$300 \ r = 6\%$ **38.** $C = \$300 \ r = 12\%$ **39.** $C = \$300 \ r = 20\%$

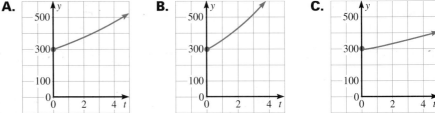

40. CRITICAL THINKING Graph the exponential growth models you found in Exercises 13–15. Which business would you rather own? Explain.

41. CHALLENGE What is the value of an $1000 investment after 5 years if it earns 6% annual interest compounded *quarterly* (four times a year).

HINT: Use the compound interest formula $A = P\left(1 + \dfrac{r}{n}\right)^{tn}$, where A is the value of the account, P is the initial investment, r is the interest rate, n is the number of times per year the interest is compounded, and t is the time period (in years).

42. MULTIPLE CHOICE The hourly rate of your new job is $5.00 per hour. You expect a raise of 9% at the end of each year. What will your hourly rate be at the end of your fifth year?

　Ⓐ $5.45　　　Ⓑ $7.25　　　Ⓒ $7.69　　　Ⓓ $9.50

43. MULTIPLE CHOICE What is the equation of the graph?

　Ⓕ $y = (2 \cdot 1.3)^x$　　　Ⓖ $y = 1.3(2)^x$

　Ⓗ $y = 2(1 - 0.3)^x$　　　Ⓙ $y = 2(1.3)^x$

VARIABLE EXPRESSIONS **Evaluate the expression for the given value of the variable.** *(Lesson 1.3)*

44. $24 + m^2$ when $m = 5$ 　　　　**45.** $6x - 1$ when $x = 1$

46. $3 \cdot 15y$ when $y = 2$ 　　　　**47.** $1 - \dfrac{a}{3}$ when $a = 9$

SOLVING EQUATIONS **Solve the equation.** *(Lesson 3.5)*

48. $-2(4 - 3x) = 6(2x + 1) + 4$ 　　**49.** $7x - (4x + 3) = 4(3x + 15)$

50. $\dfrac{2}{3}(6m - 3) + 10 = -8(m + 2)$ 　　**51.** $\dfrac{1}{4}(12y - 4) - 2y = -3(y - 5)$

52. BAGELS AND DONUTS You buy 6 bagels and 8 donuts for a total of $8.60. Then you decide to buy 3 extra bagels and 3 extra donuts for a total of $3.75. How much did each bagel and donut cost? *(Lesson 7.4)*

PRODUCT OF POWERS **Write the expression as a single power of the base.** *(Lesson 8.1)*

53. $2^2 \cdot 2^2$ 　　　　**54.** $7^6 \cdot 7^2$ 　　　　**55.** $3^5 \cdot 3^2$

56. $y^3 \cdot y$ 　　　　**57.** $r^2 \cdot r^4$ 　　　　**58.** $a^9 \cdot a^4$

SIMPLIFYING FRACTIONS **Write the fraction in lowest terms.** *(Skills Review p. 763)*

59. $\dfrac{25}{100}$ 　　**60.** $\dfrac{215}{645}$ 　　**61.** $\dfrac{53}{424}$ 　　**62.** $\dfrac{71}{355}$

8.7 Exponential Decay Functions

What will your car be worth after 8 years?

Goal

Write and graph exponential decay functions.

Key Words

• exponential decay
• decay rate
• decay factor

In Lesson 8.6 you used exponential functions to model values that were increasing. Exponential functions can also be used to model values that are decreasing. In Examples 1–3 you will analyze a car's value that is *decreasing exponentially* over time.

A quantity is *decreasing exponentially* if it decreases by the same percent r in each unit of time t. This is called **exponential decay**. Exponential decay can be modeled by the equation

$$y = C(1 - r)^t$$

where C is the initial amount (the amount before any decay occurs), r is the **decay rate** (as a decimal), t represents time, and where $0 < r < 1$. The expression $(1 - r)$ is called the **decay factor**.

EXAMPLE 1 Write an Exponential Decay Model

CARS You bought a car for $16,000. You expect the car to lose value, or depreciate, at a rate of 12% per year. Write an exponential decay model to represent this situation.

Solution

Let y be the value of the car and let t be the number of years of ownership. The initial value of the car C is $16,000. The decay rate r is 12%, or 0.12.

$y = C(1 - r)^t$ Write exponential decay model.

$= \mathbf{16,000}(1 - \mathbf{0.12})^t$ Substitute 16,000 for C and 0.12 for r.

$= 16,000(0.88)^t$ Subtract.

ANSWER ▶ The exponential decay model is $y = 16,000(0.88)^t$.

Checkpoint ✓ **Write an Exponential Decay Model**

1. Your friend bought a car for $24,000. The car depreciates at the rate of 10% per year. Write an exponential decay model to represent the car's value.

EXAMPLE 2 **Use an Exponential Decay Model**

Use the model in Example 1 to find the value of your car after 8 years.

Solution   To find the value after 8 years, substitute 8 for t.

$y = 16,000(0.88)^t$ Write exponential decay model.

$\quad = 16,000(0.88)^8$ Substitute 8 for t.

$\quad \approx 5754$ Use a calculator.

ANSWER ▶ Your car will be worth about $5754 after 8 years.

EXAMPLE 3   **Graph an Exponential Decay Model**

a. Graph the exponential decay model in Example 1.

b. Use the graph to estimate the value of your car after 5 years.

Solution

a. Make a table of values, plot the points in a coordinate plane, and draw a smooth curve through the points.

t	0	2	4	6	8
y	16,000	12,390	9595	7430	5754

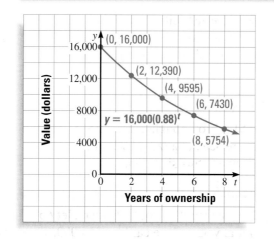

b. According to the graph, the value of your car after 5 years will be about $8400. You can check this answer by using the model in Example 1.

Checkpoint ✓   **Graph and Use an Exponential Decay Model**

Use the model in Checkpoint 1.

2. Find the value of your friend's car after 6 years.

3. Graph the exponential decay model.

4. Use the graph to estimate the value of your friend's car after 5 years.

In Lesson 8.3 you learned that for $b > 0$ a function of the form $y = ab^x$ is an exponential function. In the model for exponential growth, b is replaced by $1 + r$ where $r > 0$. In the model for exponential decay, b is replaced by $1 - r$ where $0 < r < 1$. Therefore you can conclude that an exponential model $y = Cb^t$ represents exponential growth if $b > 1$ and exponential decay if $0 < b < 1$.

EXAMPLE 4 Compare Growth and Decay Models

Classify the model as *exponential growth* or *exponential decay*. Then identify the growth or decay factor and graph the model.

a. $y = 30(1.2)^t$, where $t \geq 0$

b. $y = 30\left(\dfrac{3}{5}\right)^t$, where $t \geq 0$

Solution

a. Because $1.2 > 1$, the model $y = 30(1.2)^t$ is an exponential growth model. The growth factor $(1 + r)$ is 1.2. The graph is shown below.

b. Because $0 < \dfrac{3}{5} < 1$, the model $y = 30\left(\dfrac{3}{5}\right)^t$ is an exponential decay model. The decay factor $(1 - r)$ is $\dfrac{3}{5}$. The graph is shown below.

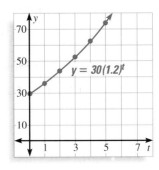

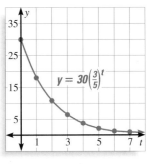

 **Compare Growth and Decay Models**

Classify the model as *exponential growth* or *exponential decay*. Then identify the growth or decay factor and graph the model.

5. $y = (2)^t$
6. $y = (0.5)^t$
7. $y = 5(0.2)^t$
8. $y = 0.7(1.1)^t$

SUMMARY

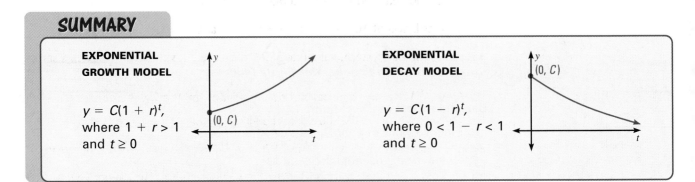

EXPONENTIAL GROWTH MODEL

$y = C(1 + r)^t$, where $1 + r > 1$ and $t \geq 0$

EXPONENTIAL DECAY MODEL

$y = C(1 - r)^t$, where $0 < 1 - r < 1$ and $t \geq 0$

8.7 Exercises

Guided Practice

Vocabulary Check

1. In the exponential decay model, $y = C(1 - r)^t$, what is the decay factor?

Skill Check

2. BUSINESS A business earned $85,000 in 1990. Then its earnings decreased by 2% each year for 10 years. Write an exponential decay model to represent the decreasing annual earnings of the business.

CARS **You buy a used car for $7000. The car depreciates at the rate of 6% per year. Find the value of the car after the given number of years.**

3. 2 years **4.** 5 years **5.** 8 years **6.** 10 years

7. CHOOSE A MODEL Which model best represents the decay curve shown in the graph at the right?

A. $y = 60(0.08)^t$ **B.** $y = 60(1.20)^t$

C. $y = 60(0.40)^t$ **D.** $y = 60(1.05)^t$

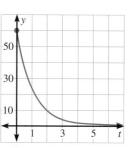

Classify the model as *exponential growth* or *exponential decay*.

8. $y = 0.55(3)^t$ **9.** $y = 3(0.55)^t$ **10.** $y = 55(3)^t$ **11.** $y = 55(0.3)^t$

Practice and Applications

EXPONENTIAL DECAY MODEL **Identify the initial amount and the decay factor in the exponential function.**

12. $y = 10(0.2)^t$ **13.** $y = 18(0.11)^t$ **14.** $y = 2\left(\dfrac{1}{4}\right)^t$ **15.** $y = 0.5\left(\dfrac{5}{8}\right)^t$

WRITING EXPONENTIAL MODELS **Write an exponential model to represent the situation. Tell what each variable represents.**

16. A $25,000 car depreciates at a rate of 9% each year.

17. A population of 100,000 decreases by 2% each year.

18. A new sound system, valued at $800, decreases in value by 10% each year.

Student Help

▶ **HOMEWORK HELP**
Example 1: Exs. 12–21
Example 2: Exs. 22–30
Example 3: Exs. 31–41
Example 4: Exs. 42–53

FINANCE **Write an exponential decay model for the investment.**

19. A stock is valued at $100. Then the value decreases by 9% per year.

20. $550 is placed in a mutual fund. Then the value decreases by 4% per year.

21. A bond is purchased for $70. Then the value decreases by 1% per year.

TRUCKS You buy a used truck for $20,000. The truck depreciates 7% per year. Find the value of the truck after the given number of years.

22. 3 years   **23.** 8 years   **24.** 10 years   **25.** 12 years

PHARMACEUTICALS In Exercises 26–28, use the following information. The amount of aspirin y (in milligrams) in a person's blood can be modeled by $y = A(0.8)^t$ where A represents the dose of aspirin taken (in milligrams) and t represents the number of hours since the aspirin was taken. Find the amount of aspirin remaining in a person's blood for the given dosage and time.

26. Dosage: 250 mg
Time: after 2 hours

27. Dosage: 500 mg
Time: after 3.5 hours

28. Dosage: 750 mg
Time: after 5 hours

BASKETBALL In Exercises 29 and 30, use the following information. At the start of a basketball tournament consisting of six rounds, there are 64 teams. After each round, one half of the remaining teams are eliminated.

29. Write an exponential decay model showing the number of teams left in the tournament after each round.

30. How many teams remain after 3 rounds? after 4 rounds?

GRAPHING Graph the exponential decay model.

31. $y = 15(0.9)^t$ **32.** $y = 72(0.85)^t$ **33.** $y = 10\left(\dfrac{1}{2}\right)^t$ **34.** $y = 55\left(\dfrac{3}{4}\right)^t$

GRAPHING AND ESTIMATING Write an exponential decay model for the situation. Then graph the model and use the graph to estimate the value at the end of the given time period.

35. A $22,000 investment decreases in value by 9% per year for 8 years.

36. A population of 2,000,000 decreases by 2% per year for 15 years.

37. You buy a new motorcycle for $10,500. It's value depreciates by 10% each year for the 10 years you own it.

CABLE CARS In Exercises 38–41, use the following information. From 1894 to 1903 the number of miles of cable car track in the United States decreased by about 11% per year. There were 302 miles of track in 1894.

38. Write an exponential decay model showing the number of miles of cable car track left each year.

39. Copy and complete the table. You may want to use a calculator.

Year	1894	1896	1898	1900	1902
Miles of track	?	?	?	?	?

40. Graph the results.

41. Use your graph to estimate the number of miles of cable car track in 1903.

MATCHING Match the equation with its graph.

42. $y = 4 - 3t$

43. $y = 4(0.6)^t$

A.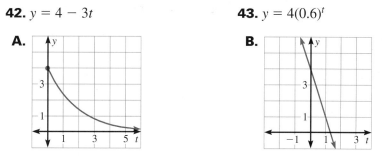

B.

COMPARING MODELS Classify the model as *exponential growth* or *exponential decay*. Then identify the growth or decay factor and graph the model.

44. $y = 24(1.18)^t$ **45.** $y = 14(0.98)^t$ **46.** $y = 97(1.01)^t$

47. $y = 112\left(\dfrac{2}{3}\right)^t$ **48.** $y = 9\left(\dfrac{2}{5}\right)^t$ **49.** $y = 35\left(\dfrac{5}{4}\right)^t$

Student Help

▶**HOMEWORK HELP**

Extra help with problem solving in Exs. 50-52 is available at www.mcdougallittell.com

EXPONENTIAL FUNCTIONS Use a calculator to investigate the effects of *a* and *b* on the graph of $y = ab^x$.

50. In the same viewing rectangle, graph $y = 2(2)^x$, $y = 4(2)^x$, and $y = 8(2)^x$. How does an increase in the value of *a* affect the graph of $y = ab^x$?

51. In the same viewing rectangle, graph $y = 2^x$, $y = 4^x$, and $y = 8^x$. How does an increase in the value of *b* affect the graph of $y = ab^x$ when $b > 1$?

52. In the same viewing rectangle, graph $y = \left(\dfrac{1}{2}\right)^x$, $y = \left(\dfrac{1}{4}\right)^x$, and $y = \left(\dfrac{1}{8}\right)^x$. How does a decrease in the value of *b* affect the graph of $y = ab^x$ when $0 < b < 1$?

53. LOGICAL REASONING Choose a positive value for *b* and graph $y = b^x$ and $y = \left(\dfrac{1}{b}\right)^x$. What do you notice about the graphs?

54. CHALLENGE A store is having a sale on sweaters. On the first day the price of the sweaters is reduced by 20%. The price will be reduced another 20% each day until the sweaters are sold. On the fifth day of the sale will the sweaters be free? Explain.

Standardized Test Practice

55. MULTIPLE CHOICE In 1995 you purchase a parcel of land for $8000. The value of the land depreciates by 4% every year. What will the approximate value of the land be in 2002?

Ⓐ $224   Ⓑ $5760   Ⓒ $6012   Ⓓ $7999

56. MULTIPLE CHOICE Which model best represents the decay curve shown in the graph at the right?

Ⓕ $y = 50(0.25)^t$ Ⓖ $y = 50(0.75)^t$

Ⓗ $y = 50(1.5)^t$ Ⓙ $y = 50(2)^t$

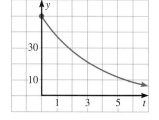

VARIABLE EXPRESSIONS Evaluate the expression for the given value of the variable(s). *(Lesson 1.3)*

57. $x^2 - 12$ when $x = 6$ **58.** $49 - 4w$ when $w = 2$

59. $100 - rs$ when $r = 4$, $s = 7$ **60.** $b^2 - 4ac$ when $a = 1$, $b = 5$, $c = 3$

SOLVING EQUATIONS Solve the equation. Round the result to the nearest hundredth. *(Lesson 3.6)*

61. $1.29x = 5.22x + 3.61$ **62.** $1.33x - 7.42 = 5.48x$

63. $10.52x + 1.15 = -1.12x - 6.35$ **64.** $8.75x + 2.16 = 18.28x - 6.59$

WRITING EQUATIONS Write in point-slope form the equation of the line that passes through the given point and has the given slope. *(Lesson 5.2)*

65. $(2, 5)$, $m = 3$ **66.** $(0, -3)$, $m = 5$ **67.** $(-1, -4)$, $m = 4$

68. $(6, 3)$, $m = -1$ **69.** $(-1, 7)$, $m = -6$ **70.** $(-4, -5)$, $m = -2$

Maintaining Skills

DIVIDING DECIMALS Divide. *(Skills Review p. 760)*

71. $0.5 \div 0.2$ **72.** $4.62 \div 0.4$ **73.** $0.074 \div 0.37$

74. $0.084 \div 0.007$ **75.** $0.451 \div 0.082$ **76.** $0.6064 \div 0.758$

Quiz 3

COMPOUND INTEREST You deposit $250 in an account that pays 8% interest compounded yearly. Find the balance at the end of the given time period. *(Lesson 8.6)*

1. 1 years   **2.** 3 years   **3.** 5 years   **4.** 8 years

5. POPULATION GROWTH An initial population of 50 raccoons doubles each year for 5 years. What is the raccoon population after 5 years? *(Lesson 8.6)*

CAR DEPRECIATION You buy a used car for $15,000. The car depreciates at a rate of 9% per year. Find the value of the car after the given number of years. *(Lesson 8.7)*

6. 2 years   **7.** 4 years   **8.** 5 years   **9.** 10 years

10. CAMPERS You buy a camper for $20,000. The camper depreciates at a rate of 8% per year. Write an exponential decay model to represent this situation. Then graph the model and use the graph to estimate the value of the camper after 5 years. *(Lesson 8.7)*

Classify the model as *exponential growth* or *exponential decay*. Then identify the growth or decay factor and graph the model. *(Lesson 8.7)*

11. $y = 6(0.1)^t$ **12.** $y = 10(1.2)^t$ **13.** $y = 3\left(\dfrac{9}{2}\right)^t$ **14.** $y = 2\left(\dfrac{1}{10}\right)^t$

VOCABULARY

- **exponential functions**, *p. 455*
- **scientific notation**, *p. 469*
- **exponential growth**, *p. 476*
- **growth rate**, *p. 476*
- **growth factor**, *p. 476*
- **exponential decay**, *p. 482*
- **decay rate**, *p. 482*
- **decay factor**, *p. 482*

8.1 MULTIPLICATION PROPERTIES OF EXPONENTS

Examples on pp. 443–445

EXAMPLES Use multiplication properties of exponents to simplify expressions.

a. $4^2 \cdot 4^7 = 4^{2+7} = 4^9$ Use product of powers property.

b. $(x^2)^4 = x^{2 \cdot 4} = x^8$ Use power of a power property.

c. $(6a)^3 = 6^3 \cdot a^3 = 216a^3$ Use power of a product property.

d. $w^3(v^2w)^4 = w^3 \cdot (v^2)^4 \cdot w^4$ Use power of a product property.

       $= w^3 \cdot v^8 \cdot w^4$ Use power of a power property.

       $= v^8w^7$ Use product of powers property.

Simplify the expression.

1. $2^2 \cdot 2^5$ **2.** $x^3 \cdot x^3$ **3.** $(4^3)^2$ **4.** $(n^4)^3$

5. $(3x)^4$ **6.** $(st^2)^2$ **7.** $p(2p)^3$ **8.** $(3a)^3(2a)^2$

8.2 ZERO AND NEGATIVE EXPONENTS

Examples on pp. 449–451

EXAMPLES Use the definition of zero and negative exponents to simplify expressions.

a. $9^0 = 1$ a^0 is equal to 1.

b. $10^{-2} = \dfrac{1}{10^2}$ 10^{-2} is the reciprocal of 10^2.

      $= \dfrac{1}{100}$ Evaluate power.

c. $7x^{-3}y = 7 \cdot \dfrac{1}{x^3} \cdot y$ Use definition of negative exponents.

      $= \dfrac{7y}{x^3}$ Multiply.

Evaluate the expression.

9. 2^0 **10.** 5^{-3} **11.** $(-7)^{-2}$ **12.** $\dfrac{1}{2^{-1}}$

Rewrite the expression with positive exponents.

13. $x^6 y^{-6}$ **14.** $\dfrac{5}{q^{-3}}$ **15.** $\dfrac{a^{-2}}{b^{-5}}$ **16.** $(2y)^{-4}$

8.3   **GRAPHS OF EXPONENTIAL FUNCTIONS**   *Examples on pp. 455–457*

> **EXAMPLE** Graph the function $y = 3^x$.
>
> **Solution** Make a table of values that includes both positive and negative x-values.
>
> | x | -2 | -1 | 0 | 1 | 2 | 3 |
> |---|---|---|---|---|---|---|
> | $y = 3^x$ | $\dfrac{1}{9}$ | $\dfrac{1}{3}$ | 1 | 3 | 9 | 27 |
>
> Draw a coordinate plane and plot the six points given by the table. Then draw a smooth curve through the points.
>
> Notice that the graph has a y-intercept of 1, and that it gets closer to the negative side of the x-axis as the x-values decrease.

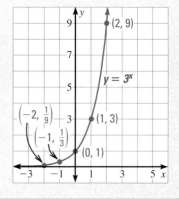

Graph the exponential function.

17. $y = 5^x$ **18.** $y = 2(3)^x$ **19.** $y = \left(\dfrac{1}{4}\right)^x$ **20.** $y = -\left(\dfrac{3}{2}\right)^x$

8.4   **DIVISION PROPERTIES OF EXPONENTS**   *Examples on pp. 462–464*

> **EXAMPLES** Use division properties of exponents to simplify expressions.
>
> **a.** $\dfrac{5^4}{5^2} = 5^{4-2} = 5^2 = 25$ Use quotient of powers property.
>
> **b.** $\left(\dfrac{x}{3}\right)^3 = \dfrac{x^3}{3^3} = \dfrac{x^3}{27}$ Use power of a quotient property.
>
> **c.** $\dfrac{2x^7 y}{x^2} \cdot \dfrac{y^3}{4xy^5} = \dfrac{2x^7 y^4}{4x^3 y^5} = \dfrac{x^4}{2y}$ Use multiplication and division properties of exponents.

Simplify the quotient.

21. $\dfrac{3^2}{3^3}$ **22.** $\dfrac{x^5}{x^2}$ **23.** $\left(\dfrac{4}{9}\right)^2$ **24.** $\left(\dfrac{r}{3}\right)^{-3}$

Simplify the expression. Use only positive exponents.

25. $\dfrac{9x^6}{y} \cdot \dfrac{y^2}{x^6}$ **26.** $\dfrac{m^7}{3n^4} \cdot \dfrac{3m^2n^2}{mn}$ **27.** $\left(\dfrac{2a^4b^5}{5a^2b}\right)^3$ **28.** $\dfrac{8s^4t^{-2}}{2s^3t^3} \cdot \dfrac{3s^2t^7}{2s^{-1}}$

8.5   SCIENTIFIC NOTATION

Examples on
pp. 469–471

EXAMPLES   You can write numbers in decimal form and in scientific notation. Use the properties of exponents to perform operations with numbers in scientific notation.

a. $1.24 \times 10^2 = 124$ Move decimal point 2 places to the right.

b. $1.5 \times 10^{-3} = 0.0015$ Move decimal point 3 places to the left.

c. $79\,000 = 7.9 \times 10^4$ Move decimal point 4 places to the left.

d. $0.0588 = 5.88 \times 10^{-2}$ Move decimal point 2 places to the right.

e. $(7.4 \times 10^2)(5 \times 10^3) = (7.4 \cdot 5) \times (10^2 \cdot 10^3)$ Use properties of multiplication.

$\qquad\qquad = 37 \times 10^5$ Use product of powers property.

$\qquad\qquad = (\mathbf{3.7 \times 10^1}) \times 10^5$ Write in scientific notation.

$\qquad\qquad = 3.7 \times 10^6$ Use product of powers property.

f. $\dfrac{4.25 \times 10^{-2}}{8.5 \times 10^5} = \dfrac{4.25}{8.5} \times \dfrac{10^{-2}}{10^5}$ Write as a product.

$\qquad\qquad = 0.5 \times 10^{-7}$ Use quotient of powers property.

$\qquad\qquad = (\mathbf{5 \times 10^{-1}}) \times 10^{-7}$ Write in scientific notation.

$\qquad\qquad = 5 \times 10^{-8}$ Use product of powers property.

Write the number in decimal form.

29. 7×10^1 **30.** 6.7×10^3 **31.** 2×10^{-4} **32.** 7.68×10^{-5}

Write the number in scientific notation.

33. $52{,}000{,}000$ **34.** 63.5 **35.** 0.009 **36.** 0.00000023

Perform the indicated operation. Write the result in scientific notation.

37. $(5 \times 10^4)(3 \times 10^2)$ **38.** $(4.1 \times 10^{-1})(6 \times 10^5)$ **39.** $(1.2 \times 10^7)(1.2 \times 10^0)$

40. $\dfrac{9 \times 10^6}{3 \times 10^3}$ **41.** $\dfrac{4.9 \times 10^1}{7 \times 10^{-8}}$ **42.** $\dfrac{3.4 \times 10^{-4}}{6.8 \times 10^{-3}}$

8.6 EXPONENTIAL GROWTH FUNCTIONS

Examples on pp. 476–478

EXAMPLE You deposit $1200 in an account that pays 9% interest compounded yearly. What is the account balance after 8 years?

Solution The initial amount P is $1200, the growth rate r is 0.09, and the time period t is 8 years. Let A be the account balance.

$A = P(1 + r)^t$ Write compound interest model.

$= 1200(1 + 0.09)^8$ Substitute 1200 for P, 0.09 for r, and 8 for t.

$= 1200(1.09)^8$ Add.

≈ 2391 Use a calculator.

ANSWER The balance after 8 years will be about $2391.

FITNESS PROGRAM **You start a walking program. The first week you walk 2 miles. Over the next 10 weeks you increase your distance 5% per week.**

43. Write an exponential growth function to model the situation.

44. How far will you walk in the tenth week?

8.7 EXPONENTIAL DECAY FUNCTIONS

Examples on pp. 482–484

EXAMPLE You bought a 32-inch television for $600. The television is depreciating (losing value) at the rate of 8% per year. What is the value of the television after 6 years?

Solution The initial value of the television C is $600, the decay rate r is 0.08, and the time t is 6 years. Let y be the value of the television.

$y = C(1 - r)^t$ Write exponential decay model.

$= 600(1 - 0.08)^6$ Substitute 600 for C, 0.08 for r, and 6 for t.

$= 600(0.92)^6$ Subtract.

≈ 364 Use a calculator.

ANSWER The value of the television after 6 years will be about $364.

TENNIS CLUB **A tennis club had a declining enrollment from 1993 to 2000. The enrollment in 1993 was 125 people. Each year for 7 years, the enrollment decreased by 3%.**

45. Write an exponential decay model to represent the enrollment in each year.

46. Estimate the enrollment in 2000.

Simplify the expression. Use only positive exponents.

1. $x^3 \cdot x^4$

2. $(a^3)^7$

3. $(2d)^3$

4. $(mn)^2 \cdot n^4$

5. 9^0

6. $\dfrac{1}{5^{-2}}$

7. $8x^2y^{-4}$

8. $\dfrac{9p^{-3}}{q^{-4}}$

Graph the exponential function.

9. $y = 2^x$

10. $y = -5(3)^x$

11. $y = \left(\dfrac{2}{3}\right)^x$

12. $y = 10\left(\dfrac{1}{4}\right)^x$

13. RADIOACTIVE DECAY The time it takes for a radioactive substance to decay to half of its original amount is called its *half-life*. If you start with 16 grams of carbon-14, the number of grams g remaining after h half-life periods is $g = 16(0.5)^h$. Copy and complete the table and graph the function.

Half-life periods, *h*	0	1	2	3	4
Grams of carbon-14, *g*	?	?	?	?	?

Simplify the expression. Use only positive exponents.

14. $\dfrac{5^4}{5}$

15. $\left(\dfrac{3}{4}\right)^3$

16. $\dfrac{x^3}{xy^4} \cdot \dfrac{y^5}{x^5}$

17. $\dfrac{a^{-1}b^2}{ab} \cdot \dfrac{a^2b^3}{a^{-2}}$

Write the number in decimal form.

18. 4×10^5

19. 8.56×10^3

20. 5×10^{-2}

21. 6.28×10^{-4}

Write the number in scientific notation.

22. 9,000,000

23. 6550

24. 0.012

25. 0.0000317

26. AMAZON RIVER Each second 4.2×10^6 cubic feet of water flow from the Amazon River into the Atlantic Ocean. How much water flows from the Amazon River into the Atlantic Ocean each year? *HINT:* There are about 3.2×10^7 seconds in one year.

SAVINGS **In Exercises 27 and 28, use the following information.**
You deposit $500 in an account that pays 7% interest compounded yearly.

27. Write an exponential growth model to represent this situation.

28. What is the account balance after 7 years?

SALES **In Exercises 29 and 30, use the following information.**
In 1996 you started your own business. In the first year your sales totaled $88,500. Each year for the next 5 years your sales decreased by 10%.

29. Write an exponential decay model to represent this situation.

30. Estimate your sales in 2001.

Chapter Standardized Test

1. Simplify the expression $7^4 \cdot 7^7$.

   (A) 7^{11} (B) 7^{28}

   (C) 49^{11} (D) 49^{28}

2. Simplify the expression $(a^3)^4$.

   (A) a^{-1} (B) a^7

   (C) a^{12} (D) a^{81}

3. Simplify the expression $(2x^2y^3)^2$.

   (A) $2x^4y^5$ (B) $2x^4y^6$

   (C) $4x^4y^6$ (D) $4x^4y^9$

4. Simplify the expression $\dfrac{2a^{-1}}{b^{-2}c^2}$.

   (A) $\dfrac{2b^2c^2}{a}$ (B) $\dfrac{b^2c^2}{2a}$

   (C) $\dfrac{2b^2}{ac^2}$ (D) $\dfrac{b^2}{2ac^2}$

5. What is the equation of the graph?

   (A) $y = 4^x$

   (B) $y = 5(4)^x$

   (C) $y = \left(\dfrac{1}{4}\right)^x$

   (D) $y = 5\left(\dfrac{1}{4}\right)^x$

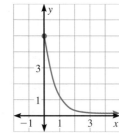

   (E) none of these

6. Which expression simplifies to x^3?

   (A) $\dfrac{x^{-2}}{x^5}$ (B) $\dfrac{x^2}{x^5}$

   (C) $\dfrac{x^5}{x^{-2}}$ (D) $\dfrac{x^5}{x^2}$

7. Simplify the expression $\left(\dfrac{3}{5}\right)^{-2}$.

   (A) $\dfrac{9}{25}$ (B) $\dfrac{25}{9}$

   (C) $\dfrac{6}{10}$ (D) $\dfrac{10}{6}$

8. Simplify the expression $\dfrac{4x^2y^2}{4xy} \cdot \dfrac{8xy^3}{4y}$.

   (A) $2xy^2$ (B) $2xy^3$

   (C) $2x^2y^3$ (D) $2x^2y^4$

9. Which of the following numbers is *not* written in scientific notation?

   (A) 8.62×10^4 (B) 2.12×10

   (C) 21.2×10^{-5} (C) 9.9132×10^{-1}

10. Evaluate the expression $\dfrac{1.55 \times 10^4}{2.5 \times 10^{-3}}$. Write the result in scientific notation.

   (A) 0.62×10^1 (B) 0.62×10^7

   (C) 6.2×10^0 (D) 6.2×10^6

11. You deposit $450 in an account that pays 6% interest compounded yearly. What is the account balance after 6 years?

   (A) $471.00   (B) $612.00

   (C) $638.33   (D) $2862.00

12. A business had a profit of $42,000 in 1994. Then its profit decreased by 8% each year for 6 years. How much did the business earn in 2000?

   (A) $11,010   (B) $20,160

   (C) $21,840   (D) $25,476

The basic skills you'll review on this page will help prepare you for the next chapter.

Maintaining Skills

EXAMPLE 1 Write the Prime Factorization of a Number

Write the prime factorization of 1078.

Solution

Use a tree diagram to factor the number until all factors are prime numbers. To determine the factors, test the prime numbers in order.

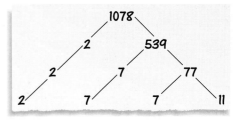

ANSWER ▶ The prime factorization of 1078 is $2 \cdot 7 \cdot 7 \cdot 11$. This may also be written as $2 \cdot 7^2 \cdot 11$.

Try These

Write the prime factorization of the number.

1. 8   **2.** 60   **3.** 105   **4.** 700

EXAMPLE 2 Rewrite Improper Fractions as Mixed Numbers

Rewrite the improper fraction as a mixed number.

a. $\dfrac{16}{3}$ **b.** $\dfrac{30}{4}$

Solution

a. $\dfrac{16}{3} = 16 \div 3$ Write fraction as a division problem.

$= 5$ remainder 1   Divide 16 by 3.

$= 5\dfrac{1}{3}$ Write remainder over divisor to form fraction.

b. $\dfrac{30}{4} = 30 \div 4$ Write fraction as a division problem.

$= 7$ remainder 2   Divide 30 by 4.

$= 7\dfrac{2}{4}$ Write remainder over divisor to form fraction.

$= 7\dfrac{1}{2}$ Reduce fraction.

Student Help

▶ **EXTRA EXAMPLES**

INTERNET More examples and practice exercises are available at www.mcdougallittell.com

Try These

Rewrite the improper fraction as a mixed number.

5. $\dfrac{21}{8}$ **6.** $\dfrac{42}{5}$ **7.** $\dfrac{27}{15}$ **8.** $\dfrac{75}{9}$

CHAPTER

9

Quadratic Equations and Functions

▶ What is the path of a home run ball?

APPLICATION: Baseball

▶ **A baseball player** usually scores a home run by hitting a ball over the outfield wall. If the ball stays in the air long enough, and drops in the outfield without being caught, a batter can score an inside-the-park home run.

The path of a baseball can be modeled with a quadratic equation. In Chapter 9 you will use mathematical models to solve different types of vertical motion problems.

Think & Discuss

1. Use the graph to approximate the maximum height the ball reaches.

2. Use the graph to approximate the maximum horizontal distance the ball travels.

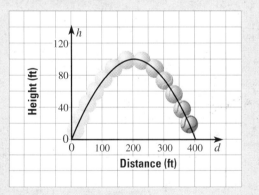

Learn More About It

You will use a vertical motion model to learn more about the path of a baseball in Exercise 79 on p. 538.

INTERNET **APPLICATION LINK** More about baseball is available at www.mcdougallittell.com

PREVIEW
What's the chapter about?

- Evaluating and approximating **square roots**
- Simplifying **radicals**
- Solving **quadratic equations**
- Sketching graphs of **quadratic functions** and **quadratic inequalities**

KEY WORDS

- **square root,** *p. 499*
- **radicand,** *p. 499*
- **perfect square,** *p. 500*
- **radical expression,** *p. 501*
- **quadratic equation,** *p. 505*
- **quadratic function,** *p. 520*
- **parabola,** *p. 520*

- **vertex,** *p. 521*
- **axis of symmetry,** *p. 521*
- **roots of a quadratic equation,** *p. 527*
- **quadratic formula,** *p. 533*
- **discriminant,** *p. 540*
- **quadratic inequalities,** *p. 547*

PREPARE
Chapter Readiness Quiz

Take this quick quiz. If you are unsure of an answer, look back at the reference pages for help.

VOCABULARY CHECK *(refer to p. 220)*

1. Complete: The __?__ of the line shown at the right is 1.

   (A) origin   **(B)** *x*-intercept

   (C) *y*-intercept   **(D)** slope

SKILL CHECK *(refer to pp. 15, 95, 367)*

2. Evaluate the expression $3x^2 - 108$ when $x = -4$.

   (A) -184 **(B)** -156 **(C)** -120 **(D)** -60

3. Which ordered pair is a solution of the inequality $3x + 4y < 5$?

   (A) $(0, 3)$ **(B)** $(-1, 2)$ **(C)** $(-2, 2)$ **(D)** $(1, 1)$

STUDY TIP
Explain Your Ideas

Talking about math and explaining your ideas to another person can help you understand a topic better.

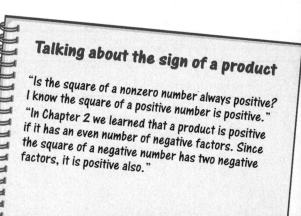

Talking about the sign of a product

"Is the square of a nonzero number always positive? I know the square of a positive number is positive."

"In Chapter 2 we learned that a product is positive if it has an even number of negative factors. Since the square of a negative number has two negative factors, it is positive also."

9.1 Square Roots

How many squares are on each side of a chessboard?

A chessboard is a large square made up of 64 small squares. In Exercises 84 and 85, you will use *square roots* to investigate whether game boards of other sizes can be constructed.

You know how to find the square of a number. For instance, the square of 3 is $3^2 = 9$. The square of -3 is also 9. In this lesson you will learn about the inverse operation: finding a *square root* of a number.

SQUARE ROOT OF A NUMBER If $b^2 = a$, then b is a **square root** of a.

> **Examples:** $3^2 = 9$, so 3 is a square root of 9.
>
> $(-3)^2 = 9$, so -3 is a square root of 9.

All *positive* real numbers have two square roots: a **positive square root** (or *principal* square root) and a **negative square root**. Square roots are written with a radical symbol $\sqrt{\ }$. The number or expression inside a radical symbol is the **radicand**. In the following example, 9 is the radicand. As shown in part (a), the radical symbol indicates the positive square root of a positive number.

EXAMPLE 1 Read Square Root Symbols

Write the equation in words.

a. $\sqrt{9} = 3$ **b.** $-\sqrt{9} = -3$ **c.** $\pm\sqrt{9} = \pm3$

Solution

Equation	Words
a. $\sqrt{9} = 3$	The positive square root of 9 is 3.
b. $-\sqrt{9} = -3$	The negative square root of 9 is -3.
c. $\pm\sqrt{9} = \pm3$	The positive and negative square roots of 9 are 3 and -3.

Checkpoint ✓ *Read Square Root Symbols*

Write the equation in words.

1. $\sqrt{4} = 2$ **2.** $\sqrt{25} = 5$ **3.** $-\sqrt{16} = -4$ **4.** $\pm\sqrt{36} = \pm6$

NUMBER OF SQUARE ROOTS Positive real numbers have two square roots. Zero has only one square root: zero. Negative numbers do not have real square roots because the square of every real number is either positive or zero.

Student Help

▶ **READING ALGEBRA**
Since negative numbers do not have real square roots, we say that $\sqrt{-64}$ is *undefined*.

EXAMPLE 2 Find Square Roots of Numbers

Evaluate the expression.

a. $\sqrt{64}$ **b.** $-\sqrt{64}$ **c.** $\pm\sqrt{64}$ **d.** $\sqrt{0}$

Solution

a. $\sqrt{64} = \sqrt{8^2} = 8$ Positive square root

b. $-\sqrt{64} = -\sqrt{8^2} = -8$ Negative square root

c. $\pm\sqrt{64} = \pm\sqrt{8^2} = \pm 8$ Two square roots

d. $\sqrt{0} = 0$ Square root of zero is zero.

Checkpoint ✓ *Find Square Roots of Numbers*

Evaluate the expression.

5. $\pm\sqrt{100}$ **6.** $-\sqrt{25}$ **7.** $\sqrt{36}$ **8.** $\sqrt{16}$

The square of an integer is called a **perfect square**. Of course a square root of a perfect square is an integer. On the other hand, if n is a positive integer that is *not* a perfect square, then it can be shown that $\sqrt{n}$ is an *irrational number*. An irrational number is a number that is not the quotient of integers. In Lesson 12.9 you will use an indirect proof to prove that $\sqrt{2}$ is an irrational number.

$\sqrt{4} = 2$ 4 is a perfect square. $\sqrt{4}$ is an integer.

$\sqrt{2} \approx 1.414$ 2 is not a perfect square. $\sqrt{2}$ is neither an integer nor a rational number.

Student Help

▶ **STUDY TIP**
You can use a calculator or the Table of Square Roots on p. 801 to approximate an irrational square root.

EXAMPLE 3 Evaluate Square Roots of Numbers

Evaluate the expression. Give the exact value if possible. Otherwise, approximate to the nearest hundredth.

a. $-\sqrt{49}$ **b.** $\sqrt{3}$

Solution

a. $-\sqrt{49} = -\sqrt{7^2} = -7$ 49 is a perfect square.

b. $\sqrt{3} \approx 1.73$ Round to nearest hundredth.

Checkpoint ✓ *Evaluate Square Roots of Numbers*

Evaluate the expression. Give the exact value if possible. Otherwise, approximate to the nearest hundredth.

9. $\sqrt{100}$ **10.** $-\sqrt{5}$ **11.** $\sqrt{23}$ **12.** $-\sqrt{81}$

RADICAL EXPRESSIONS An expression written with a radical symbol is called a **radical expression**, or sometimes just a *radical*.

EXAMPLE 4 **Evaluate a Radical Expression**

Evaluate $\sqrt{b^2 - 4ac}$ when $a = 1$, $b = -2$, and $c = -3$.

Solution

The radical symbol is a grouping symbol. You must evaluate the expression inside the radical symbol before you find the square root.

$$\sqrt{b^2 - 4ac} = \sqrt{(-2)^2 - 4(1)(-3)}$$ Substitute values for *a*, *b*, and *c*.

$$= \sqrt{4 + 12}$$ Simplify.

$$= \sqrt{16}$$ Add.

$$= 4$$ Find the positive square root.

Checkpoint ✓ *Evaluate a Radical Expression*

Evaluate $\sqrt{b^2 - 4ac}$ for the given values.

13. $a = 2$, $b = 3$, $c = -5$ **14.** $a = -1$, $b = 8$, $c = 20$

Student Help

▶**KEYSTROKE HELP**
To find the square root of 3 on your calculator you may need to press
[√] [3] or
[3] [√]. Test your calculator to find out which order it uses.

EXAMPLE 5 **Use a Calculator to Evaluate an Expression**

Use a calculator to evaluate $\dfrac{1 \pm 2\sqrt{3}}{4}$. Round the results to the nearest hundredth.

Solution

When the symbol $\pm$ precedes the radical, the expression represents two different numbers.

KEYSTROKES   **DISPLAY**

(1 [+] 2 [×] 3 [√]) [÷] 4 [ENTER]   `1.116025404`

(1 [−] 2 [×] 3 [√]) [÷] 4 [ENTER]   `−0.616025403`

ANSWER ▶ The expression represents 1.12 and −0.62.

Checkpoint ✓ *Use a Calculator to Evaluate an Expression*

Use a calculator to evaluate the expression. Round the results to the nearest hundredth.

15. $6 \pm \sqrt{5}$ **16.** $4 \pm \sqrt{8}$ **17.** $\dfrac{2 \pm \sqrt{3}}{3}$ **18.** $\dfrac{2 \pm 3\sqrt{6}}{4}$

Guided Practice

Vocabulary Check

1. Complete: Since $(-2)^2 = 4$, -2 is a __?__ of 4.

2. State the meaning of the symbols $\sqrt{}$, $-\sqrt{}$, and $\pm\sqrt{}$ when applied to a positive number n.

3. Identify the radicand in the equation $\sqrt{4} = 2$.

Skill Check

Evaluate the expression.

4. $\sqrt{81}$ **5.** $\pm\sqrt{121}$ **6.** $-\sqrt{36}$ **7.** $-\sqrt{4}$

Determine whether each expression is *rational* or *irrational*.

8. $\sqrt{25}$ **9.** $\sqrt{6}$ **10.** $\sqrt{100}$ **11.** $\sqrt{10}$

Use a calculator or a table of square roots to evaluate the expression. Round the results to the nearest hundredth.

12. $1 \pm \sqrt{2}$ **13.** $6 \pm 5\sqrt{3}$ **14.** $3 \pm \sqrt{7}$ **15.** $2 \pm 4\sqrt{8}$

Practice and Applications

READING SQUARE ROOT SYMBOLS   Write the equation in words.

16. $\sqrt{625} = 25$ **17.** $\pm\sqrt{16} = \pm 4$ **18.** $\pm\sqrt{4} = \pm 2$

19. $\sqrt{225} = 15$ **20.** $-\sqrt{121} = -11$ **21.** $-\sqrt{289} = -17$

22. $\sqrt{49} = 7$ **23.** $\sqrt{1} = 1$ **24.** $\sqrt{\dfrac{1}{9}} = \dfrac{1}{3}$

FINDING SQUARE ROOTS   Evaluate the expression. Check the results by squaring each root.

25. $\sqrt{144}$ **26.** $\pm\sqrt{25}$ **27.** $\sqrt{196}$ **28.** $\pm\sqrt{900}$

29. $\pm\sqrt{49}$ **30.** $\sqrt{0}$ **31.** $-\sqrt{256}$ **32.** $-\sqrt{100}$

33. $\sqrt{400}$ **34.** $-\sqrt{225}$ **35.** $\sqrt{121}$ **36.** $\sqrt{289}$

37. $-\sqrt{1}$ **38.** $\pm\sqrt{81}$ **39.** $\sqrt{169}$ **40.** $-\sqrt{625}$

Student Help

▶ **HOMEWORK HELP**
Example 1: Exs. 16–24
Example 2: Exs. 25–40
Example 3: Exs. 53–64
Example 4: Exs. 65–74
Example 5: Exs. 75–83

PERFECT SQUARES   Determine whether the number is a perfect square.

41. 10   **42.** 81   **43.** -5 **44.** 120

45. 16   **46.** 1   **47.** 111   **48.** 225

49. -4 **50.** 10,000   **51.** $\dfrac{9}{4}$ **52.** $\dfrac{1}{2}$

Student Help

▶ **HOMEWORK HELP**

Extra help with problem solving in Exs. 53–64 is available at www.mcdougallittell.com

EVALUATING SQUARE ROOTS Evaluate the expression. Give the exact value if possible. Otherwise, approximate to the nearest hundredth.

53. $\sqrt{5}$ **54.** $\sqrt{25}$ **55.** $\sqrt{13}$ **56.** $-\sqrt{125}$

57. $-\sqrt{49}$ **58.** $\pm\sqrt{70}$ **59.** $\pm\sqrt{1}$ **60.** $\sqrt{10}$

61. $\pm\sqrt{15}$ **62.** $-\sqrt{400}$ **63.** $-\sqrt{20}$ **64.** $\pm\sqrt{144}$

EVALUATING RADICAL EXPRESSIONS Evaluate $\sqrt{b^2 - 4ac}$ for the given values.

65. $a = 4, b = 5, c = 1$ **66.** $a = 2, b = 4, c = -6$

67. $a = -2, b = 8, c = -8$ **68.** $a = -5, b = 5, c = 10$

EVALUATING RADICAL EXPRESSIONS Evaluate the radical expression when $a = 2$ and $b = 4$.

69. $\sqrt{b^2 + 10a}$ **70.** $\sqrt{b^2 - 8a}$ **71.** $\sqrt{a^2 + 45}$

72. $\dfrac{\sqrt{b^2 + 42a}}{a}$ **73.** $\dfrac{10 + 2\sqrt{b}}{a}$ **74.** $\dfrac{36 - \sqrt{8a}}{b}$

EVALUATING RADICAL EXPRESSIONS Use a calculator to evaluate the expression. Round the results to the nearest hundredth.

75. $8 \pm \sqrt{5}$ **76.** $2 \pm 5\sqrt{3}$ **77.** $-6 \pm 4\sqrt{2}$

78. $\dfrac{1 \pm 6\sqrt{8}}{6}$ **79.** $\dfrac{7 \pm 3\sqrt{2}}{-1}$ **80.** $\dfrac{4 \pm 7\sqrt{3}}{2}$

81. $\dfrac{5 \pm 6\sqrt{3}}{3}$ **82.** $\dfrac{3 \pm 4\sqrt{5}}{4}$ **83.** $\dfrac{7 \pm 3\sqrt{12}}{-6}$

CHESSBOARD A chessboard has 8 small squares on a side and therefore has a total of 64 small squares.

84. Could a similar square game board be constructed that has a total of 81 small squares?

85. If a square game board has a total of m small squares of equal size, what can you say about m?

LOGICAL REASONING In Exercises 86–88, determine whether the statement is *true* or *false*. If it is true, give an example. If it is false, give a counterexample.

86. All positive numbers have two different square roots.

87. No number has only one square root.

88. Some numbers have no real square root.

89. CHALLENGE Evaluate $3 \pm \sqrt{(-3)^2 - 4(0.5)(-8)}$.

Link to
History

CHESS This illustration of Spanish women playing chess is from a thirteenth century manuscript written for the King of Spain. Historians believe the game of chess originated in India in the seventh century.

90. MULTIPLE CHOICE Evaluate $\dfrac{15 \pm 5\sqrt{225}}{3}$.

    Ⓐ -70 and 80 Ⓑ -20 and 30

    Ⓒ 20 and 30 Ⓓ 70 and 80

91. MULTIPLE CHOICE Which is an example of a perfect square?

    Ⓕ -100 Ⓖ 10 Ⓗ 121 Ⓙ 150

92. MULTIPLE CHOICE Which two consecutive integers does $\sqrt{200}$ fall between?

    Ⓐ 10 and 11 Ⓑ 13 and 14

    Ⓒ 14 and 15 Ⓓ 19 and 20

Student Help

▶ **TEST TIP**
Square each integer to find which perfect squares 200 falls between to help you estimate $\sqrt{200}$ in Exercise 92.

93. MULTIPLE CHOICE If $a^2 = 36$ and $b^2 = 49$, choose the greatest possible value for the expression $b - a$.

    Ⓕ -13 Ⓖ -1 Ⓗ 1 Ⓙ 13

Mixed Review

GRAPH AND CHECK Graph the linear system and estimate a solution. Then check your solution algebraically. *(Lesson 7.1)*

94. $y = -3$
    $x = 4$

95. $2x - 4y = 12$
        $y = -2$

96. $2x - y = 10$
        $x + y = 5$

97. BASKETBALL TICKETS The admission price for a high school basketball game is $2 for students and $3 for adults. At one game, 324 tickets were sold and $764 was collected. How many students and adults attended the game? *(Lesson 7.2)*

98. FLOWERS You are buying a combination of irises and lilies for a flower arrangement. The irises are $4 each and the lilies are $3 each. You spend $50 for an arrangement of 15 flowers. How many of each type of flower did you buy? *(Lesson 7.2)*

LINEAR COMBINATIONS Use linear combinations to solve the system of linear equations. *(Lesson 7.3)*

99. $10x - 3y = 17$
    $-7x + y = 9$

100. $12x - 4y = -32$
       $x + 3y = 4$

101. $8x - 5y = 70$
       $2x + y = 4$

Maintaining Skills

FRACTIONS AND DECIMALS Write the fraction as a terminating or repeating decimal. *(Skills Review p. 767)*

102. $\dfrac{3}{4}$ **103.** $\dfrac{8}{15}$ **104.** $\dfrac{6}{11}$ **105.** $\dfrac{7}{8}$

106. $\dfrac{2}{9}$ **107.** $\dfrac{5}{16}$ **108.** $\dfrac{5}{6}$ **109.** $\dfrac{2}{5}$

110. $\dfrac{5}{8}$ **111.** $\dfrac{8}{9}$ **112.** $\dfrac{3}{5}$ **113.** $\dfrac{9}{10}$

9.2 Solving Quadratic Equations by Finding Square Roots

Goal
Solve a quadratic equation by finding square roots.

Key Words
• quadratic equation
• leading coefficient

How long does it take for an egg to drop?

An egg is placed in a container and dropped from a height of 32 feet. Can you tell how long it will take the egg to reach the ground? In Example 5 you will use a *quadratic equation* to find the answer.

A **quadratic equation** is an equation that can be written in the standard form

$$ax^2 + bx + c = 0, \text{ where } a \neq 0; a \text{ is called the } leading\ coefficient.$$

When $b = 0$, this equation becomes $ax^2 + c = 0$. One way to solve a quadratic equation of the form $ax^2 + c = 0$ is to isolate x^2 on one side of the equation. Then find the square root(s) of each side. In Example 3 you will see how to use inverse operations to isolate x^2.

Student Help

▶ **STUDY TIP**
Remember that squaring a number and finding a square root of a number are inverse operations.

EXAMPLE 1 Solve Quadratic Equations

Solve the equation. Write the solutions as integers if possible. Otherwise, write them as radical expressions.

a. $x^2 = 4$ **b.** $n^2 = 5$

Solution **a.** $x^2 = 4$ Write original equation.

$\qquad\qquad\quad x = \pm\sqrt{4}$ Find square roots.

$\qquad\qquad\quad x = \pm2$ $2^2 = 4$ and $(-2)^2 = 4$

$\qquad\qquad$ **ANSWER** ▶ The solutions are 2 and -2.

$\qquad$ **b.** $n^2 = 5$ Write original equation.

$\qquad\qquad\quad n = \pm\sqrt{5}$ Find square roots.

$\qquad\qquad$ **ANSWER** ▶ The solutions are $\sqrt{5}$ and $-\sqrt{5}$.

Checkpoint ✓ Solve Quadratic Equations

Solve the equation. Write the solutions as integers if possible. Otherwise, write them as radical expressions. Check the results by squaring each root.

1. $x^2 = 81$ **2.** $y^2 = 11$ **3.** $n^2 = 25$ **4.** $x^2 = 10$

EXAMPLE 2 Solve Quadratic Equations

Solve the equation.

a. $x^2 = 0$ **b.** $y^2 = -1$

Solution **a.** $x^2 = 0$ Write original equation.

$\quad\quad\quad\quad x = 0$ Find square roots.

ANSWER ▶ The only solution is zero.

b. $y^2 = -1$ has no real solution because the square of a real number is never negative.

ANSWER ▶ There is no real solution.

Student Help

▶ **MORE EXAMPLES**

More examples are available at www.mcdougallittell.com

EXAMPLE 3 Rewrite Before Finding Square Roots

Solve $3x^2 - 48 = 0$.

Solution
$$3x^2 - 48 = 0 \quad\quad\quad \text{Write original equation.}$$
$$3x^2 = 48 \quad\quad\quad \text{Add 48 to each side.}$$
$$x^2 = 16 \quad\quad\quad \text{Divide each side by 3.}$$
$$x = \pm\sqrt{16} \quad\quad\quad \text{Find square roots.}$$
$$x = \pm 4 \quad\quad\quad 4^2 = 16 \text{ and } (-4)^2 = 16$$

ANSWER ▶ The solutions are 4 and −4. Check both solutions in the *original* equation.

CHECK ✓ $3(4)^2 - 48 \stackrel{?}{=} 0$ $3(16) - 48 = 0$ ✓

         $3(-4)^2 - 48 \stackrel{?}{=} 0$ $3(16) - 48 = 0$ ✓

Both 4 and −4 make the equation true, so $3x^2 - 48 = 0$ has two solutions.

Checkpoint ✓ *Rewrite Before Finding Square Roots*

Solve the equation.

5. $x^2 - 1 = 0$ **6.** $2x^2 - 72 = 0$ **7.** $27 - 3y^2 = 0$

As Examples 1, 2, and 3 suggest, a quadratic equation can have no real solution, one solution, or two solutions.

SUMMARY

Solving $x^2 = d$ by Finding Square Roots

- If $d > 0$, then $x^2 = d$ has two solutions: $x = \pm\sqrt{d}$. (Examples 1 and 3)
- If $d = 0$, then $x^2 = d$ has one solution: $x = 0$. (Example 2a)
- If $d < 0$, then $x^2 = d$ has no real solution. (Example 2b)

FALLING OBJECT MODEL When an object is dropped, the speed with which it falls continues to increase. Ignoring air resistance, its height h can be approximated by the falling object model.

Falling object model: $h = -16t^2 + s$

Here h is measured in feet, t is the number of seconds the object has fallen, and s is the initial height from which the object was dropped.

EXAMPLE 4 **Write a Falling Object Model**

An engineering student is a contestant in an egg dropping contest. The goal is to create a container for an egg so it can be dropped from a height of 32 feet without breaking. Write a model for the egg's height. Disregard air resistance.

Solution

The initial height is $s = 32$ feet.

$h = -16t^2 + s$	Write falling object model.
$h = -16t^2 + 32$	Substitute 32 for s.

ANSWER ▶ The falling object model for the egg is $h = -16t^2 + 32$.

EXAMPLE 5 **Use a Falling Object Model**

How long will it take the egg container in Example 4 to reach the ground? Round your solution to the nearest tenth.

Solution

Ground level is represented by $h = 0$ feet. To find the time it takes for the egg to reach the ground, substitute 0 for h in the model and solve for t.

$h = -16t^2 + 32$	Write falling egg model from Example 4.
$0 = -16t^2 + 32$	Substitute 0 for h.
$-32 = -16t^2$	Subtract 32 from each side.
$2 = t^2$	Divide each side by -16.
$\pm\sqrt{2} = t$	Find square roots.
$1.4 \approx t$	Use a calculator or table of square roots to approximate the positive square root of 2.

ANSWER ▶ The egg container will reach the ground in about 1.4 seconds.

Student Help

▶ **STUDY TIP**
The negative square root, $-\sqrt{2}$, does not make sense in this situation, so you can ignore that solution.

Checkpoint ✓ **Write and Use a Falling Object Model**

Suppose the egg dropping contest in Example 4 requires the egg to be dropped from a height of 64 feet.

8. Write a falling object model for the egg container when $s = 64$.

9. According to the model, how long will it take the egg container to reach the ground?

Guided Practice

Vocabulary Check

1. Is $2x - 7 = 15$ a quadratic equation? Explain why or why not.

2. Write $7x^2 = 12 + 3x$ in standard form. What is the leading coefficient?

Skill Check

Determine the number of real solutions for each equation.

3. $x^2 = 6$ **4.** $x^2 = 0$ **5.** $x^2 = -17$

6. $x^2 - 8 = -8$ **7.** $x^2 - 15 = 5$ **8.** $x^2 + 2 = -2$

Solve the equation or write *no real solution*.

9. $y^2 = 49$ **10.** $x^2 = -16$ **11.** $n^2 = 7$

12. $3x^2 - 20 = -2$ **13.** $5x^2 = -25$ **14.** $2x^2 - 8 = 0$

FALLING OBJECTS Use the falling object model, $h = -16t^2 + s$. Given the initial height s, find the time it would take for the object to reach the ground, disregarding air resistance. Round the result to the nearest tenth.

15. $s = 48$ feet   **16.** $s = 160$ feet   **17.** $s = 192$ feet

Practice and Applications

QUADRATIC EQUATIONS Solve the equation or write *no real solution*. Write the solutions as integers if possible. Otherwise, write them as radical expressions.

18. $x^2 = 9$ **19.** $m^2 = 1$ **20.** $x^2 = 17$ **21.** $k^2 = -44$

22. $y^2 = 15$ **23.** $x^2 = 225$ **24.** $r^2 = -81$ **25.** $x^2 = 121$

26. $t^2 = 39$ **27.** $x^2 = 256$ **28.** $y^2 = 0$ **29.** $n^2 = 49$

30. $y^2 = 400$ **31.** $x^2 = 64$ **32.** $m^2 = -9$ **33.** $x^2 = 16$

QUADRATIC EQUATIONS Solve the equation or write *no real solution*. Write the solutions as integers if possible. Otherwise, write them as radical expressions.

34. $5x^2 = 500$ **35.** $3x^2 = 6$ **36.** $5y^2 = 25$

37. $a^2 + 3 = 12$ **38.** $x^2 - 7 = 57$ **39.** $x^2 + 36 = 0$

40. $2s^2 - 5 = 27$ **41.** $3x^2 - 75 = 0$ **42.** $7x^2 + 30 = 9$

43. $5x^2 + 5 = 20$ **44.** $5t^2 + 10 = 135$ **45.** $3x^2 - 50 = 58$

46. $m^2 - 12 = 52$ **47.** $2y^2 + 13 = 41$ **48.** $20 - x^2 = 4$

Student Help

▶ **HOMEWORK HELP**
Example 1: Exs. 18–33
Example 2: Exs. 18–33
Example 3: Exs. 34–48,
        50–55
Example 4: Ex. 59
Example 5: Ex. 60

---

49. ERROR ANALYSIS Find and correct the error at the right.

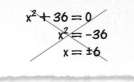

$x^2 + 36 = 0$
$x^2 = -36$
$x = \pm 6$

SOLVING EQUATIONS Use a calculator to solve the equation. Round the result to the nearest hundredth.

50. $4x^2 - 3 = 57$ **51.** $6y^2 + 22 = 34$ **52.** $2x^2 - 4 = 10$

53. $3x^2 + 7 = 31$ **54.** $7n^2 - 6 = 15$ **55.** $5x^2 - 12 = 5$

LOGICAL REASONING In Exercises 56–58, decide whether the statement is *true* or *false*. If it is true, give a reason. If it is false, give a counterexample.

56. $x^2 = c$ has no real solution when $c < 0$.

57. $x^2 = c$ has two solutions when $c > 0$.

58. $x^2 = c$ has no solution when $c = 0$.

FALLING ROCK In Exercises 59 and 60, a boulder falls off the top of an overhanging cliff during a storm. The cliff is 96 feet high. Find how long it will take for the boulder to hit the road below.

59. Write a falling object model when $s = 96$.

60. Solve the falling object model for $h = 0$. Round to the nearest tenth.

Science Link In Exercises 61–66, use the following information.
Mineralogists use the Vickers scale to measure the hardness of minerals. The hardness H of a mineral can be determined by hitting the mineral with a pyramid-shaped diamond and measuring the depth d of the indentation. The harder the mineral, the smaller the depth of the indentation. A model that relates mineral hardness with the indentation depth (in millimeters) is $Hd^2 = 1.89$.

Use a calculator to find the depth of the indentation for the mineral with the given value of H. Round to the nearest hundredth of a millimeter.

61. Graphite: $H = 12$ **62.** Gold: $H = 50$ **63.** Galena: $H = 80$

 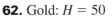  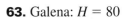

64. Platinum: $H = 125$ **65.** Copper: $H = 140$ **66.** Hematite: $H = 755$

 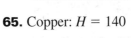  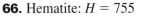 

History Link In Exercises 67 and 68, use the following information.
Population estimates for the 1800s lead a student to model the population of the United States by $P = 5,500,400 + 683,300t^2$, where $t = 0, 1, 2, 3, \ldots$ represents the years 1800, 1810, 1820, 1830, ...

67. Use this population model to estimate the United States population in 1800, 1850, and 1900.

68. Use this model to estimate the year in which the United States population reached 50 million.

Standardized Test Practice

69. MULTIPLE CHOICE Which quadratic equation is written in standard form?

Ⓐ $8x + 5x^2 - 9 = 0$ Ⓑ $5x^2 + 8x = 9$

Ⓒ $5x^2 + 8x - 9 = 0$ Ⓓ $9 - 8x - 5x^2 = 0$

70. MULTIPLE CHOICE Consider the equation $3x^2 - 44 = x^2 + 84$. Which statement is correct?

Ⓕ The equation has exactly one solution.

Ⓖ The equation has two solutions.

Ⓗ The equation has no real solution.

Ⓙ The number of solutions cannot be determined.

Mixed Review

EVALUATING EXPRESSIONS Evaluate the expression when $x = -2$. *(Lessons 1.3, 2.3, 2.5)*

71. $2x^3 + 2x + 2$ **72.** $4x^2 + 3x + 5$ **73.** $3x^2 + 4x + 8$ **74.** $x^2 + 7x + 9$

SLOPE AND Y-INTERCEPT Find the slope and *y*-intercept of the graph of the equation. *(Lesson 4.7)*

75. $y = 5x + 6$ **76.** $y = -4x + 5$ **77.** $y - 8x = 2$ **78.** $2x + 3y = 6$

SOLVING AND GRAPHING Solve the inequality. Then graph the solution. *(Lesson 6.1)*

79. $-9 \le x - 7$ **80.** $-15 > x - 8$ **81.** $2 + x < 4$ **82.** $6 \ge x + 1$

SCIENTIFIC NOTATION Write the number in scientific notation. *(Lesson 8.5)*

83. 0.0000008 **84.** 564 **85.** 8721 **86.** 23,000

Maintaining Skills

SIMPLIFYING FRACTIONS Write the fraction in lowest terms. *(Skills Review p. 763)*

87. $\frac{6}{9}$ **88.** $\frac{4}{8}$ **89.** $\frac{5}{15}$ **90.** $\frac{30}{48}$

91. $\frac{20}{24}$ **92.** $\frac{50}{100}$ **93.** $\frac{12}{16}$ **94.** $\frac{28}{35}$

9.3 Simplifying Radicals

Goal

Simplify radical expressions.

Key Words

- radical
- simplest form of a radical expression
- product property of radicals
- quotient property of radicals

What is the maximum speed of a sailboat?

The design of a sailboat affects its maximum speed. In Example 4 you will use a boat's water line length to estimate its maximum speed.

The **simplest form of a radical expression** is an expression that has no perfect square factors other than 1 in the radicand, no fractions in the radicand, and no radicals in the denominator of a fraction. Properties of radicals can be used to simplify expressions that contain radicals.

PRODUCT PROPERTY OF RADICALS

$\sqrt{ab} = \sqrt{a} \cdot \sqrt{b}$ where $a \geq 0$ and $b \geq 0$ **Example:** $\sqrt{4 \cdot 5} = \sqrt{4} \cdot \sqrt{5} = 2\sqrt{5}$

Student Help

▶ **STUDY TIP**
There can be more than one way to factor the radicand. An efficient method is to find the largest perfect square factor. For example, you can simplify $\sqrt{48}$ using $\sqrt{48} = \sqrt{16 \cdot 3} = \sqrt{16} \cdot \sqrt{3} = 4\sqrt{3}$.

EXAMPLE 1 Simplify with the Product Property

Simplify the expression.

a. $\sqrt{50}$ **b.** $\sqrt{48}$

Solution Look for perfect square factors to remove from the radicand.

a. $\sqrt{50} = \sqrt{25 \cdot 2}$ Factor using perfect square factor.

$\phantom{\sqrt{50}} = \sqrt{25} \cdot \sqrt{2}$ Use product property.

$\phantom{\sqrt{50}} = 5\sqrt{2}$ Simplify: $\sqrt{25} = 5$.

b. $\sqrt{48} = \sqrt{4 \cdot 12}$ Factor using perfect square factor.

$\phantom{\sqrt{48}} = \sqrt{4 \cdot 4 \cdot 3}$ Factor using perfect square factor.

$\phantom{\sqrt{48}} = \sqrt{4^2} \cdot \sqrt{3}$ Use product property.

$\phantom{\sqrt{48}} = 4\sqrt{3}$ Simplify: $\sqrt{4^2} = 4$.

Checkpoint ✓ **Simplify with the Product Property**

Simplify the expression.

1. $\sqrt{12}$ **2.** $\sqrt{32}$ **3.** $\sqrt{75}$ **4.** $\sqrt{180}$

QUOTIENT PROPERTY OF RADICALS

$$\sqrt{\frac{a}{b}} = \frac{\sqrt{a}}{\sqrt{b}} \text{ where } a \geq 0 \text{ and } b > 0 \qquad \textbf{Example: } \sqrt{\frac{9}{25}} = \frac{\sqrt{9}}{\sqrt{25}} = \frac{3}{5}$$

Student Help

▶ MORE EXAMPLES

More examples are available at www.mcdougallittell.com

EXAMPLE **2** Simplify with the Quotient Property

Simplify $\sqrt{\dfrac{32}{50}}$.

Solution $\quad \sqrt{\dfrac{32}{50}} = \sqrt{\dfrac{2 \cdot 16}{2 \cdot 25}} \qquad$ Factor using perfect square factors.

$$= \sqrt{\frac{16}{25}} \qquad \text{Divide out common factors.}$$

$$= \frac{\sqrt{16}}{\sqrt{25}} \qquad \text{Use quotient property.}$$

$$= \frac{4}{5} \qquad \text{Simplify.}$$

In Example 3 you will see how to eliminate a radical from the denominator by multiplying the radical expression by an appropriate value of 1. This process is called *rationalizing the denominator*.

Student Help

▶ STUDY TIP

$\dfrac{1}{\sqrt{2}}$ and $\dfrac{\sqrt{2}}{2}$ are equivalent radical expressions. The second expression is in simplest form with a rational denominator.

EXAMPLE **3** Rationalize the Denominator

Simplify $\sqrt{\dfrac{1}{18}}$.

Solution

$$\sqrt{\frac{1}{18}} = \frac{\sqrt{1}}{\sqrt{18}} \qquad \text{Use quotient property.}$$

$$= \frac{1}{\sqrt{9} \cdot \sqrt{2}} \qquad \text{Use product property.}$$

$$= \frac{1}{3\sqrt{2}} \qquad \text{Remove perfect square factor.}$$

$$= \frac{1}{3\sqrt{2}} \cdot \frac{\sqrt{2}}{\sqrt{2}} \qquad \text{Multiply by a value of 1: } \frac{\sqrt{2}}{\sqrt{2}} = 1.$$

$$= \frac{\sqrt{2}}{6} \qquad \text{Simplify: } 3\sqrt{2} \cdot \sqrt{2} = 3 \cdot 2 = 6.$$

Checkpoint ✓ *Simplify with the Quotient Property*

Simplify the expression.

5. $\sqrt{\dfrac{4}{9}}$ **6.** $5\sqrt{\dfrac{1}{25}}$ **7.** $\sqrt{\dfrac{1}{3}}$ **8.** $\sqrt{\dfrac{27}{15}}$

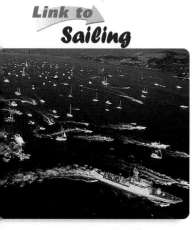

Link to Sailing

BOAT SPEED Mathematical formulas help designers choose dimensions for a boat's water line length, sail area, and displacement that will produce the greatest speed.

More about sailing is available at www.mcdougallittell.com

EXAMPLE 4 Simplify a Radical Expression

BOAT SPEED The maximum speed s (in knots, or nautical miles per hour) that certain kinds of boats can travel can be modeled by the quadratic equation $s^2 = \frac{16}{9}x$, where x is the boat's water line length (in feet).

The water line of a boat is the line on the main body of the boat that the surface of the water reaches.

32 ft water line

Use this model to express the maximum speed of a sailboat with a 32 foot water line in terms of radicals. Then find the speed to the nearest tenth.

Solution

$s^2 = \frac{16}{9}x$	Write quadratic model.
$s^2 = \frac{16}{9} \cdot 32$	Substitute 32 for x.
$\sqrt{s^2} = \sqrt{\frac{16}{9} \cdot 32}$	Find square root of each side.
$s = \frac{\sqrt{16}}{\sqrt{9}} \cdot \sqrt{32}$	Use quotient and product properties.
$= \frac{4}{3} \cdot 4\sqrt{2}$	Remove perfect square factors from radicands.
$= \frac{16\sqrt{2}}{3}$	Multiply.
≈ 7.5	Use a calculator or square root table.

ANSWER ▶ The sailboat's maximum speed is $\frac{16\sqrt{2}}{3}$ knots, or approximately 7.5 knots.

Checkpoint ✓ *Simplify a Radical Expression*

9. Use the model in Example 4 to express the maximum speed of a sailboat with a 50 foot water line in terms of radicals. Then find the speed to the nearest tenth.

SUMMARY

Simplest Form of a Radical Expression

- No perfect square factors other than 1 are in the radicand. $\sqrt{8}$ ⟹ $\sqrt{4 \cdot 2}$ ⟹ $2\sqrt{2}$

- No fractions are in the radicand. $\sqrt{\frac{5}{16}}$ ⟹ $\frac{\sqrt{5}}{\sqrt{16}}$ ⟹ $\frac{\sqrt{5}}{4}$

- No radicals are in the denominator of a fraction. $\frac{1}{\sqrt{7}}$ ⟹ $\frac{1}{\sqrt{7}} \cdot \frac{\sqrt{7}}{\sqrt{7}}$ ⟹ $\frac{\sqrt{7}}{7}$

Guided Practice

Vocabulary Check   Determine whether the radical expression is in simplest form. Explain.

1. $\frac{3}{5}\sqrt{2}$ **2.** $\sqrt{\frac{3}{16}}$ **3.** $5\sqrt{40}$ **4.** $\frac{1}{\sqrt{2}}$

Skill Check   Match the radical expression with its simplest form.

5. $\sqrt{45}$ **6.** $\sqrt{98}$ **7.** $\sqrt{75}$ **8.** $\sqrt{54}$

A. $3\sqrt{6}$ **B.** $5\sqrt{3}$ **C.** $7\sqrt{2}$ **D.** $3\sqrt{5}$

Simplify the expression.

9. $\sqrt{36}$ **10.** $\sqrt{24}$ **11.** $\sqrt{60}$ **12.** $\sqrt{\frac{64}{25}}$

13. $\sqrt{\frac{15}{16}}$ **14.** $\frac{1}{2}\sqrt{20}$ **15.** $\sqrt{\frac{2}{5}}$ **16.** $9\sqrt{\frac{1}{3}}$

Practice and Applications

SIMPLEST FORM   Determine whether the radical expression is in simplest form. Explain.

17. $\frac{19}{\sqrt{9}}$ **18.** $3\sqrt{20}$ **19.** $5\sqrt{31}$ **20.** $\sqrt{\frac{2}{8}}$

PRODUCT PROPERTY   Simplify the expression.

21. $\sqrt{44}$ **22.** $\sqrt{54}$ **23.** $\sqrt{18}$ **24.** $\sqrt{56}$

25. $\sqrt{27}$ **26.** $\sqrt{63}$ **27.** $\sqrt{200}$ **28.** $\sqrt{90}$

29. $\sqrt{125}$ **30.** $\sqrt{132}$ **31.** $\sqrt{144}$ **32.** $\sqrt{196}$

QUOTIENT PROPERTY   Simplify the expression.

33. $\sqrt{\frac{4}{16}}$ **34.** $\sqrt{\frac{9}{49}}$ **35.** $\sqrt{\frac{4}{25}}$ **36.** $\sqrt{\frac{81}{100}}$

37. $\sqrt{\frac{36}{25}}$ **38.** $\sqrt{\frac{7}{9}}$ **39.** $\sqrt{\frac{11}{81}}$ **40.** $\sqrt{\frac{5}{4}}$

41. $\sqrt{\frac{18}{32}}$ **42.** $\sqrt{\frac{27}{36}}$ **43.** $\sqrt{\frac{10}{162}}$ **44.** $\sqrt{\frac{12}{147}}$

ERROR ANALYSIS   In Exercises 45 and 46, find and correct the error.

45. $\sqrt{20} = \sqrt{2 \cdot 10} = 2\sqrt{10}$

46. $\frac{\sqrt{9}}{3} = 3$

Student Help

▶**HOMEWORK HELP**
Example 1: Exs. 21–32,
      59–74
Example 2: Exs. 33–44,
      59–74
Example 3: Exs. 47–58,
      59–74
Example 4: Exs. 75, 76

RATIONALIZING THE DENOMINATOR Simplify the expression.

47. $\sqrt{\dfrac{1}{5}}$ **48.** $\sqrt{\dfrac{5}{6}}$ **49.** $\sqrt{\dfrac{1}{2}}$ **50.** $\sqrt{\dfrac{3}{5}}$

51. $\sqrt{\dfrac{5}{15}}$ **52.** $\sqrt{\dfrac{3}{21}}$ **53.** $\sqrt{\dfrac{4}{10}}$ **54.** $\sqrt{\dfrac{4}{3}}$

55. $\sqrt{\dfrac{1}{11}}$ **56.** $\sqrt{\dfrac{3}{2}}$ **57.** $\sqrt{\dfrac{25}{3}}$ **58.** $\sqrt{\dfrac{16}{10}}$

SIMPLIFYING Write the radical expression in simplest form.

59. $4\sqrt{25}$ **60.** $9\sqrt{100}$ **61.** $-2\sqrt{27}$ **62.** $\dfrac{1}{3}\sqrt{63}$

63. $-6\sqrt{4}$ **64.** $3\sqrt{44}$ **65.** $-\dfrac{1}{7}\sqrt{49}$ **66.** $\dfrac{1}{2}\sqrt{32}$

67. $\dfrac{3}{2}\sqrt{24}$ **68.** $\dfrac{1}{8}\sqrt{56}$ **69.** $-\dfrac{1}{2}\sqrt{360}$ **70.** $\sqrt{\dfrac{48}{81}}$

71. $\sqrt{\dfrac{3}{5}}$ **72.** $-4\sqrt{\dfrac{1}{10}}$ **73.** $6\sqrt{\dfrac{5}{9}}$ **74.** $2\sqrt{\dfrac{6}{18}}$

TSUNAMI In Exercises 75–77, use the following information. A *tsunami* is a destructive, fast-moving ocean wave that is caused by an undersea earthquake, landslide, or volcano. Scientists can predict arrival times of tsunamis by using water depth to calculate the speed of a tsunami.

A model for the speed s (in meters per second) at which a tsunami moves is $s = \sqrt{gd}$ where d is the depth (in meters) and g is 9.8 meters per second per second.

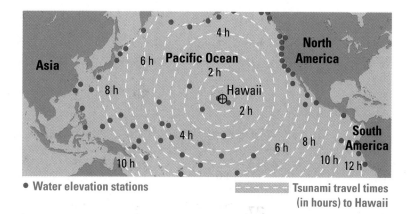

• Water elevation stations   ------ Tsunami travel times (in hours) to Hawaii

75. Find the speed of a tsunami in a region of the ocean that is 1000 meters deep. Write your solution in simplest form.

76. Find the speed of a tsunami in a region of the ocean that is 4000 meters deep. Write your solution in simplest form.

77. CRITICAL THINKING Is the speed of a tsunami in water that is 4000 meters deep four times the speed of a tsunami in water that is 1000 meters? Explain why or why not.

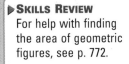

SKILLS REVIEW
For help with finding
the area of geometric
figures, see p. 772.

Geometry Link In Exercises 78 and 79, use the formula $A = \ell w$ to find the area of the figure. Write your solution in simplest form.

78.

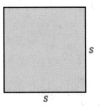

$\sqrt{10}$

$\sqrt{20}$

79.

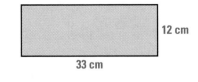

$7\sqrt{2}$

$7\sqrt{2}$

80. **Puzzler** Find the length of a side s of a square that has the same area as a rectangle that is 12 centimeters wide and 33 centimeters long. Write your solution in simplest form.

s

s

12 cm

33 cm

81. **LOGICAL REASONING** Copy and complete the *proof* of the following statement:

If $\dfrac{x^2}{4} = 9$, then $x = \pm 6$.

Solution Step	Explanation
$\dfrac{x^2}{4} = 9$	Original Equation
$x^2 = 36$	__?__ Property of Equality
$x = \pm 6$	Definition of __?__ root

CHALLENGE Write the radical expression in simplest form.

82. $3\sqrt{63} \cdot \sqrt{4}$

83. $-2\sqrt{27} \cdot \sqrt{3}$

84. $\sqrt{9} \cdot 4\sqrt{25}$

85. $\dfrac{1}{2}\sqrt{32} \cdot \sqrt{2}$

86. $-\sqrt{4} \cdot \dfrac{\sqrt{81}}{\sqrt{36}}$

87. $-5\sqrt{2} \cdot \sqrt{\dfrac{9}{50}}$

Standardized Test Practice

88. **MULTIPLE CHOICE** Which is the simplest form of $\sqrt{80}$?

(A) $2\sqrt{5}$ (B) $4\sqrt{5}$ (C) $2\sqrt{20}$ (D) 20

89. **MULTIPLE CHOICE** Which is the simplest form of $\dfrac{\sqrt{125}}{\sqrt{25}}$?

(F) $\sqrt{5}$ (G) $2\sqrt{5}$ (H) 5 (J) $5\sqrt{5}$

90. **MULTIPLE CHOICE** Which of the following does *not* equal $\sqrt{48}$?

(A) $\sqrt{2} \cdot \sqrt{24}$ (B) $2\sqrt{12}$ (C) $4\sqrt{3}$ (D) $12\sqrt{16}$

91. **MULTIPLE CHOICE** Which step would you use to rationalize the denominator of $\dfrac{\sqrt{3}}{\sqrt{10}}$?

(F) Multiply by $\dfrac{\sqrt{10}}{\sqrt{10}}$.

(G) Multiply by $\dfrac{\sqrt{10}}{\sqrt{3}}$.

(H) Multiply by $\sqrt{10}$.

(J) Multiply by 10.

GRAPHING EQUATIONS Use a table to graph the equation. *(Lesson 4.2)*

92. $y = x + 5$ **93.** $x + y = -4$ **94.** $y = 3x - 1$ **95.** $2x + y = 6$

POWER OF A PRODUCT Simplify the expression. *(Lesson 8.1)*

96. $(5 \cdot 2)^5$ **97.** $(3x)^4$ **98.** $(-5x)^3$ **99.** $(-3 \cdot 4)^2$

100. $(ab)^6$ **101.** $(8xy)^2$ **102.** $(-3mn)^4$ **103.** $(-abc)^3$

DOMAIN AND RANGE Use the graph to describe the domain and the range of the function. *(Lesson 8.3)*

104. $y = 4^x$ **105.** $y = -4^x$

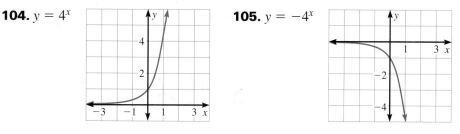

FRACTION OPERATIONS Divide. Write the answer as a fraction or as a mixed number in lowest terms. *(Skills Review p. 765)*

106. $\frac{1}{2} \div 4$ **107.** $\frac{3}{4} \div 3$ **108.** $\frac{7}{8} \div \frac{3}{4}$ **109.** $\frac{1}{5} \div \frac{8}{15}$

110. $\frac{4}{5} \div 10$ **111.** $\frac{2}{3} \div 63$ **112.** $\frac{5}{6} \div \frac{1}{5}$ **113.** $\frac{7}{10} \div 7$

Quiz 1

Evaluate the expression. *(Lesson 9.1)*

1. $\sqrt{81}$ **2.** $-\sqrt{25}$ **3.** $\sqrt{16}$ **4.** $-\sqrt{4}$

5. $\pm\sqrt{1}$ **6.** $\sqrt{100}$ **7.** $\pm\sqrt{49}$ **8.** $\sqrt{121}$

Solve the equation or write *no real solution*. Write the solutions as integers if possible. Otherwise, write them as radical expressions. *(Lesson 9.2)*

9. $x^2 = 64$ **10.** $x^2 = 63$ **11.** $-8x^2 = -48$

12. $12x^2 = -120$ **13.** $4x^2 = 64$ **14.** $5x^2 - 44 = 81$

Write the expression in simplest form. *(Lesson 9.3)*

15. $\sqrt{18}$ **16.** $\sqrt{60}$ **17.** $\frac{1}{5}\sqrt{75}$ **18.** $-3\sqrt{9}$

19. $2\sqrt{120}$ **20.** $\frac{1}{3}\sqrt{12}$ **21.** $\frac{\sqrt{45}}{9}$ **22.** $\sqrt{\frac{5}{20}}$

23. $\sqrt{\frac{5}{16}}$ **24.** $\sqrt{\frac{32}{4}}$ **25.** $\sqrt{\frac{2}{3}}$ **26.** $\sqrt{\frac{36}{5}}$

*For use with
Lesson 9.4*

GOAL

Use reasoning to discover how the value of *a* affects the graph of $y = ax^2$.

MATERIALS
• graph paper
• pencil

Question What is the shape of the graph of $y = ax^2$ and $y = -ax^2$?

In this Developing Concepts, you will explore the shape of a quadratic function and how the value of the leading coefficient *a* affects the shape of the graph.

Explore

1 Complete the table of values for $y = x^2$. The value of *a* is 1.

x	−3	−2	−1	0	1	2	3
y	?	?	?	?	?	?	?

2 Complete the table of values for $y = -x^2$. The value of *a* is −1.

x	−3	−2	−1	0	1	2	3
y	?	?	?	?	?	?	?

The graphs of $y = x^2$ and $y = -x^2$ are shown below on the same coordinate plane. Use them to help you answer the following questions.

Think About It

1. How would you describe the shape of each graph?

2. In what direction (*up or down*) does the graph of $y = x^2$ open?

3. Does the graph of $y = x^2$ have a highest point or a lowest point?

4. In what direction (*up or down*) does the graph of $y = -x^2$ open?

5. Does the graph of $y = -x^2$ have a highest point or a lowest point?

6. Use the tables to compare the values of *y* for $y = x^2$ and $y = -x^2$. What is the value of *y* for each function when $x = 2$? when $x = 0$? when $x = -1$?

7. Generalize your results and complete the statement: For every point (k, k^2) on the graph of $y = x^2$, there is a corresponding point $(k, \underline{\ ?\ })$ on the graph of $y = -x^2$.

8. The graph of $y = x^2$ is a *reflection*, or mirror image, of the graph of $y = -x^2$. The line of reflection is $y = \underline{\ ?\ }$.

Question What happens to the shape of the graph of $y = ax^2$ when $|a|$ increases?

Explore

1 Sketch the graphs of $y = \frac{1}{2}x^2$, $y = x^2$, and $y = 2x^2$ on the same coordinate plane by plotting points and connecting them with a smooth curve.

Think About It

1. Do the graphs open up or down?

2. Identify the lowest point on each graph.

3. Describe how changing the value of a from $\frac{1}{2}$ to 1 to 2 changes the shape of the graph of $y = ax^2$.

You have just explored how the graph of $y = ax^2$ changes when the value of a is positive and increases. On page 518 you explored how the graphs of $y = ax^2$ and $y = -ax^2$ are related. Use this information to help you in the next section.

Explore

2 Predict how changing the value of a from $-\frac{1}{2}$ to -1 to -2 changes the shape of the graph of $y = ax^2$. Check your prediction by sketching the graphs of $y = -\frac{1}{2}x^2$, $y = -x^2$, and $y = -2x^2$ in the same coordinate plane that you used for the Explore at the top of the page.

Think About It

1. Do the graphs open up or down?

2. Identify the highest point on each graph.

3. Describe how changing the value of a from $-\frac{1}{2}$ to -1 to -2 changes the shape of the graph of $y = ax^2$.

4. Generalize your results and complete the statement: As $|a|$ increases, the graph of $y = ax^2$ becomes __?__.

Determine whether the graph of the function opens *up* or *down* and whether the graph is *wider* or *narrower* than the graph of $y = x^2$.

5. $y = 5x^2$ **6.** $y = -4x^2$ **7.** $y = \frac{1}{4}x^2$

9.4 Graphing Quadratic Functions

Goal

Sketch the graph of a quadratic function.

Key Words

- quadratic function
- parabola
- vertex
- axis of symmetry

How high was the shot put?

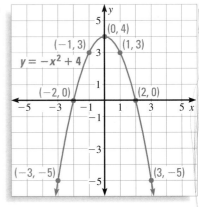

In Exercise 48 you will find the highest point of a parabola to estimate the highest point on the path of a record-breaking shot-put throw.

A **quadratic function** is a function that can be written in the standard form

$$y = ax^2 + bx + c, \text{ where } a \neq 0.$$

Every quadratic function has a U-shaped graph called a **parabola**. As you saw in Developing Concepts 9.4, pages 518-519, the parabola opens up if the value of a is positive. The parabola opens down if the value of a is negative.

EXAMPLE **1** **Describe the Graph of a Parabola**

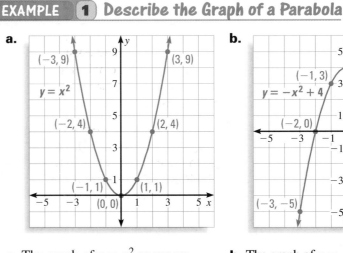

a. The graph of $y = x^2$ opens up. The lowest point is $(0, 0)$.

b. The graph of $y = -x^2 + 4$ opens down. The highest point is $(0, 4)$.

Checkpoint **Describe the Graph of a Parabola**

Decide whether the parabola opens *up* or *down*.

1. $y = -x^2$ **2.** $y = 2x^2 - 4$ **3.** $y = -3x^2 + 5x - 1$

The **vertex** is the highest or lowest point on a parabola. The vertical line passing through the vertex that divides the parabola into two symmetric parts is called the **axis of symmetry**. The two symmetric parts are mirror images of each other.

GRAPHING A QUADRATIC FUNCTION

The graph of $y = ax^2 + bx + c$, where $a \neq 0$, is a parabola.

STEP ❶ Find the x-coordinate of the vertex, which is $x = -\dfrac{b}{2a}$.

STEP ❷ Make a table of values, using x-values to the left and right of the vertex.

STEP ❸ Plot the points and connect them with a smooth curve to form a parabola.

EXAMPLE 2 **Graph Quadratic Function with Positive *a*-Value**

Sketch the graph of $y = x^2 - 2x - 3$.

Solution In this quadratic function, $a = 1$, $b = -2$, and $c = -3$.

❶ **Find** the x-coordinate of the vertex. $-\dfrac{b}{2a} = -\dfrac{-2}{2(1)} = 1$

❷ **Make** a table of values, using x-values to the left and right of $x = 1$.

x	−2	−1	0	1	2	3	4
y	5	0	−3	−4	−3	0	5

Student Help

▶**STUDY TIP**
If you fold the graph along the axis of symmetry, the two halves of the parabola will match up exactly.

❸ **Plot** the points. The vertex is $(1, -4)$. Connect the points to form a parabola that opens up since a is positive.

The axis of symmetry passes through the vertex $(1, -4)$. The x-coordinate of the vertex is 1, and the axis of symmetry is the vertical line $x = 1$.

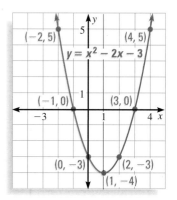

The axis of symmetry of $y = ax^2 + bx + c$ is the vertical line $x = -\dfrac{b}{2a}$.

Checkpoint ✓ **Graph a Quadratic Function with a Positive *a*-Value**

Sketch the graph of the function. Label the coordinates of the vertex.

4. $y = x^2 + 2$ **5.** $y = 2x^2 - 4x - 1$ **6.** $y = x^2 + 2x$

EXAMPLE 3 **Graph Quadratic Function with Negative *a*-Value**

Sketch the graph of $y = -x^2 - 3x + 1$.

Solution

In this quadratic function, $a = -1$, $b = -3$, and $c = 1$.

❶ **Find** the x-coordinate of the vertex: $-\dfrac{b}{2a} = -\dfrac{-3}{2(-1)} = -\dfrac{3}{2}$, or $-1\dfrac{1}{2}$.

This tells you that the axis of symmetry is the vertical line $x = -1\dfrac{1}{2}$.

❷ **Make** a table of values, using x-values to the left and right of $x = -1\dfrac{1}{2}$.

x	−4	−3	−2	$-1\frac{1}{2}$	−1	0	1
y	−3	1	3	$3\frac{1}{4}$	3	1	−3

Student Help

▶**STUDY TIP**
If the x-coordinate of the vertex is a fraction, you can still choose whole numbers when you make a table.

❸ **Plot** the points. The vertex is $\left(-1\dfrac{1}{2}, 3\dfrac{1}{4}\right)$. Connect the points to form a parabola that opens down since a is negative.

To find the y-intercept of $y = -x^2 - 3x + 1$, let $x = 0$. The y-intercept is 1.

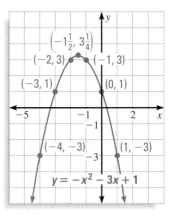

Since $y = c$ when $x = 0$ in $y = ax^2 + bx + c$, the y-intercept of the graph is c.

Checkpoint ✓ **Graph a Quadratic Function with a Negative *a*-Value**

Sketch the graph of the function. Label the coordinates of the vertex.

7. $y = -x^2 + 1$ **8.** $y = -x^2 + 3x$ **9.** $y = -2x^2 + 4x + 1$

SUMMARY

Graph of a Quadratic Function

The graph of $y = ax^2 + bx + c$ is a parabola.

• If a is positive, the parabola opens up.

• If a is negative, the parabola opens down.

• The vertex has an x-coordinate of $-\dfrac{b}{2a}$.

• The axis of symmetry is the vertical line $x = -\dfrac{b}{2a}$.

• The y-intercept is c.

Guided Practice

Vocabulary Check

1. Identify the values of a, b, and c for the quadratic function in standard form $y = -5x^2 + 7x - 4$.

2. What is the U-shaped graph of a quadratic function called?

Skill Check

Decide whether the graph of the quadratic function opens *up* or *down*.

3. $y = x^2 + 4x - 1$ **4.** $y = 3x^2 + 8x + 6$ **5.** $y = -x^2 + 7x - 3$

6. $y = -x^2 - 4x + 2$ **7.** $y = 5x^2 - 2x + 4$ **8.** $y = -8x^2 - 4$

Sketch the graph of the function. Label the coordinates of the vertex. Write an equation for the axis of symmetry.

9. $y = -3x^2$ **10.** $y = -5x^2 + 10$ **11.** $y = x^2 + 4$

12. $y = x^2 - 6x + 8$ **13.** $y = -3x^2 + 6x + 2$ **14.** $y = 2x^2 - 8x + 3$

Practice and Applications

DESCRIBING GRAPHS   **Decide whether the parabola opens *up* or *down*.**

15. $y = 2x^2$ **16.** $y = -5x^2$ **17.** $y = -7x^2 + 5$

18. $y = 5x + 6x^2 - 1$ **19.** $y = -8x^2 - 9$ **20.** $y = 3x^2 - 2x + 7$

21. $y = -3x^2 + 24x$ **22.** $y = -6x^2 - 15x$ **23.** $y = 8x - x^2$

PREPARING TO GRAPH   **Find the coordinates of the vertex. Make a table of values, using *x*-values to the left and to the right of the vertex.**

24. $y = 3x^2$ **25.** $y = 6x^2$ **26.** $y = -12x^2$

27. $y = 2x^2 - 10x$ **28.** $y = -7x^2 + 2x$ **29.** $y = 6x^2 + 2x + 4$

30. $y = 5x^2 + 10x + 7$ **31.** $y = -4x^2 - 4x + 8$ **32.** $y = -x^2 + 8x + 32$

GRAPHS OF FUNCTIONS   **Match the quadratic function with its graph.**

33. $y = -x^2 + 3$ **34.** $y = x^2 - 3$ **35.** $y = x^2 - 3x$

Student Help

▶**HOMEWORK HELP**
Example 1: Exs. 15–23
Example 2: Exs. 24–32,
         36–44
Example 3: Exs. 24–32,
         36–44

A.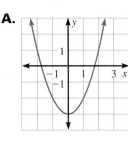

B.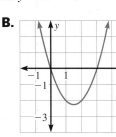

C.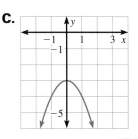

SKETCHING GRAPHS Sketch the graph of the function. Label the coordinates of the vertex.

36. $y = -2x^2$

37. $y = 4x^2$

38. $y = x^2 + 4x - 1$

39. $y = 4x^2 + 8x - 3$

40. $y = x^2 + x + 4$

41. $y = 3x^2 - 2x - 1$

42. $y = 2x^2 + 5x - 3$

43. $y = -4x^2 + 4 + 7$

44. $y = -3x^2 - 3x + 4$

EXAMPLE ▶ Use a Quadratic Model

TABLE TENNIS The path of a table-tennis ball that bounces over the net can be modeled by $h = -4.9x^2 + 2.07x$, where h is the height above the table (in meters) and x is the time (in seconds). Estimate the maximum height reached by the table-tennis ball. Round to the nearest tenth.

Solution The maximum height of the table-tennis ball occurs at the vertex of the parabolic path. Use $a = -4.9$ and $b = 2.07$ to find the x-coordinate of the vertex. Round your solution to the nearest tenth.

$$-\frac{b}{2a} = -\frac{2.07}{2(-4.9)} \approx 0.2$$

Substitute 0.2 for x in the model and use a calculator to find the maximum height.

$$h = -4.9(0.2)^2 + 2.07(0.2) = 0.218 \approx 0.2$$

ANSWER ▶ The maximum height of the table-tennis ball is about 0.2 meters.

45. **BASKETBALL** You throw a basketball. The height of the ball can be modeled by $h = -16t^2 + 15t + 6$, where h represents the height of the basketball (in feet) and t represents time (in seconds). Find the vertex of the graph of the function. Interpret the result to find the maximum height that the basketball reaches.

Link to
Nature

DOLPHINS follow the path of a parabola when they jump out of the water.

More about dolphins is available at
www.mcdougallittell.com

DOLPHINS In Exercises 46 and 47, use the following information.
A bottle-nosed dolphin jumps out of the water. The path the dolphin travels can be modeled by $h = -0.2d^2 + 2d$, where h represents the height of the dolphin and d represents horizontal distance.

46. What is the vertex of the parabola? Interpret the result.

47. What horizontal distance did the dolphin travel?

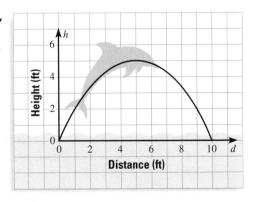

Student Help

HOMEWORK HELP

INTERNET Extra help with problem solving in Exercise 48 is available at www.mcdougallittell.com

48. **TRACK AND FIELD** Natalya Lisovskaya holds the world record for the women's shot put. The path of her record-breaking throw can be modeled by $h = -0.0137x^2 + 0.9325x + 5.5$, where h is the height (in feet) and x is the horizontal distance (in feet). Use a calculator to find the maximum height of the throw by Lisovskaya. Round to the nearest tenth.

CHALLENGE In Exercises 49–51, sketch the graphs of the three functions in the same coordinate plane. Then describe how the three parabolas are similar to each other and how they are different.

49. $y = -\frac{1}{2}x^2 + x + 1$
$y = -x^2 + x + 1$
$y = -2x^2 + x + 1$

50. $y = x^2 + x + 1$
$y = x^2 + 2x + 1$
$y = x^2 + 3x + 1$

51. $y = x^2 - x + 1$
$y = x^2 - x + 3$
$y = x^2 - x - 2$

Standardized Test Practice

52. **MULTIPLE CHOICE** Which equation is represented by the graph below?

(A) $y = x^2 - 2x + 1$

(B) $y = -x^2 - 2x + 1$

(C) $y = x^2 + 2x + 1$

(D) $y = -x^2 + 2x - 1$

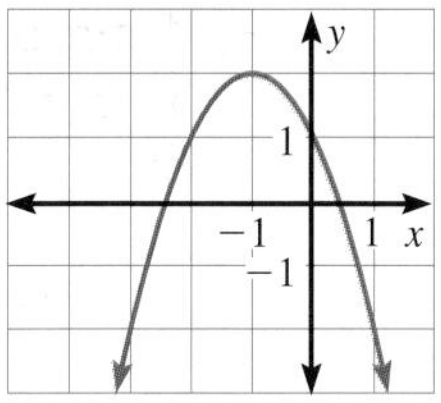

53. **MULTIPLE CHOICE** What are the coordinates of the vertex of the graph of $y = -2x^2 + 8x - 5$?

(F) $(-2, -29)$ (G) $(2, 3)$ (H) $(2, 7)$ (J) $(4, -5)$

54. **MULTIPLE CHOICE** What is the axis of symmetry of the graph of $y = x^2 + 3x - 2$?

(A) $x = -\frac{17}{4}$ (B) $x = -\frac{3}{2}$ (C) $x = \frac{3}{2}$ (D) $x = \frac{19}{4}$

Mixed Review

GRAPHING A SYSTEM Graph the system of linear inequalities. *(Lesson 7.6)*

55. $x - 3y \geq 3$
$x - 3y < 12$

56. $x + y \leq 5$
$x \geq 2$
$y \geq 0$

57. $x + y < 10$
$2x + y > 10$
$x - y < 2$

PRODUCT OF POWERS Write the expression as a single power of the base. *(Lesson 8.1)*

58. $4^2 \cdot 4^5$ **59.** $(-5) \cdot (-5)^8$ **60.** $x^2 \cdot x^4 \cdot x^6$ **61.** $x^3 \cdot x^5$

62. $t \cdot (t^3)$ **63.** $m \cdot m^4 \cdot m^3$ **64.** $5 \cdot 5^2 \cdot 5^3$ **65.** $2(2)^4$

Maintaining Skills

ORDERING FRACTIONS Write the numbers in order from least to greatest. *(Skills Review p. 770)*

66. $\frac{1}{2}, \frac{2}{3}, \frac{5}{12}$ **67.** $\frac{1}{3}, \frac{4}{15}, \frac{2}{5}$ **68.** $\frac{3}{5}, \frac{4}{10}, \frac{5}{15}$ **69.** $\frac{9}{10}, \frac{7}{8}, \frac{3}{4}$

9.5 # Solving Quadratic Equations by Graphing

Goal

Use a graph to find or check a solution of a quadratic equation.

Key Words

- *x*-intercept
- roots of a quadratic equation

How far apart are the Golden Gate Bridge towers?

The Golden Gate Bridge in California hangs from steel cables that are supported by two towers. In Example 3 you will use the graph of a parabola to estimate the distance between the towers.

The *x*-intercepts of the graph of $y = ax^2 + bx + c$ are the solutions of the related equation $ax^2 + bx + c = 0$. Recall that an *x*-intercept is the *x*-coordinate of a point where a graph crosses the *x*-axis. At this point, $y = 0$.

EXAMPLE 1 Use a Graph to Solve an Equation

The graph of $y = \frac{1}{2}x^2 - 8$ is shown at the right. Use the graph to estimate the solutions of $\frac{1}{2}x^2 - 8 = 0$.

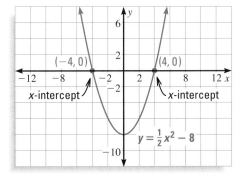

Solution

The graph appears to intersect the *x*-axis at $(-4, 0)$ and $(4, 0)$. By substituting $x = -4$ and $x = 4$ in $\frac{1}{2}x^2 - 8 = 0$, you can check that -4 and 4 are solutions of the given equation.

Checkpoint ✓ Use a Graph to Solve an Equation

1. The graph of $y = 2x^2 - 4x$ is shown at the right. Use the graph to estimate the solutions of $2x^2 - 4x = 0$. Check your solutions algebraically by substituting each one for *x* in the given equation.

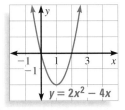

The solutions of a quadratic equation in one variable x can be estimated by graphing. Use the following steps:

STEP ❶ *Write* the equation in the standard form $ax^2 + bx + c = 0$.

STEP ❷ *Sketch* the graph of the related quadratic function $y = ax^2 + bx + c$.

STEP ❸ *Estimate* the values of the x-intercepts, if any.

The solutions, or **roots**, of $ax^2 + bx + c = 0$ are the x-intercepts of the graph.

Student Help

▶ MORE EXAMPLES

More examples are available at www.mcdougallittell.com

EXAMPLE 2 Solve an Equation by Graphing

Use a graph to estimate the solutions of $x^2 - x = 2$. Check your solutions algebraically.

Solution

❶ *Write* the equation in the standard form $ax^2 + bx + c = 0$.

$$x^2 - x = 2 \qquad \text{Write original equation.}$$

$$x^2 - x - 2 = 0 \qquad \text{Subtract 2 from each side.}$$

❷ *Sketch* the graph of the related quadratic function $y = x^2 - x - 2$.

❸ *Estimate* the values of the x-intercepts. From the graph, the x-intercepts appear to be -1 and 2.

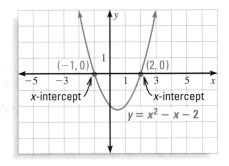

CHECK ✓

You can check your solutions algebraically using substitution.

CHECK x = −1:

$$x^2 - x = 2$$
$$(-1)^2 - (-1) \stackrel{?}{=} 2$$
$$1 + 1 = 2 \checkmark$$

CHECK x = 2:

$$x^2 - x = 2$$
$$2^2 - 2 \stackrel{?}{=} 2$$
$$4 - 2 = 2 \checkmark$$

ANSWER ▶ The solutions are -1 and 2.

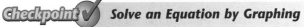

Checkpoint ✓ *Solve an Equation by Graphing*

2. Use a graph to estimate the solutions of $x^2 - x = 6$.

3. Check your solutions algebraically.

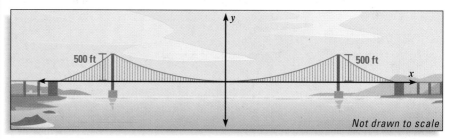

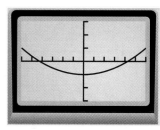

Student Help

EXAMPLE ③ **Points on a Parabola**

The main suspension cables of the Golden Gate Bridge form a parabola that can be modeled by the quadratic function

$$y = 0.000112x^2 + 8$$

where x is the horizontal distance from the middle of the bridge (in feet) and y is the vertical distance from the road (in feet).

The cables are connected to the towers at points that are 500 feet above the road. How far apart are the towers?

Solution

You can find the distance between the towers by finding the x-values for which $y = 500$, or $0.000112x^2 + 8 = 500$. Use a graphing calculator to find the solutions of the equation.

Write the equation in the standard form $ax^2 + bx + c = 0$.

$$0.000112x^2 + 8 = 500 \qquad \text{Write original equation.}$$

$$0.000112x^2 - 492 = 0 \qquad \text{Subtract 500 from each side.}$$

Sketch the graph of the related quadratic function $y = 0.000112x^2 - 492$ using a graphing calculator.

Estimate the values of the x-intercepts. From the graphing calculator screen, you can see that the x-intercepts are approximately -2100 and 2100.

Each tower is approximately 2100 feet from the midpoint. Because the towers are on opposite sides of the midpoint, the distance between the towers is $2100 + 2100 = 4200$.

ANSWER ▶ The towers are approximately 4200 feet apart.

Checkpoint ✓ **Points on a Parabola**

4. The main suspension cables of the Royal Gorge Bridge can be modeled by the quadratic function $y = 0.0007748x^2$. In the equation, x is the horizontal distance from the middle of the bridge (in feet) and y is the vertical distance from the road (in feet). The cables are connected to the towers at points that are 150 feet above the road. Approximately how far apart are the towers?

Guided Practice

Vocabulary Check

1. What are the roots of a quadratic equation?

2. Explain how you can use a graph to check the solutions of a quadratic equation.

Skill Check

Match the quadratic function with its graph.

3. $y = x^2 - 3$ **4.** $y = x^2 + x - 4$ **5.** $y = x^2 - 2x - 1$

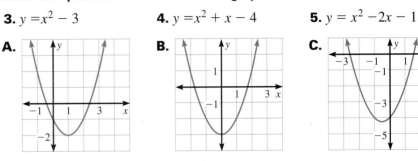

A.   **B.**   **C.**

Solve the equation algebraically. Check your solutions by graphing.

6. $3x^2 - 12 = 0$ **7.** $5x^2 - 5 = 0$ **8.** $-2x^2 = -18$

Estimate the solutions of the equation by graphing. Check your solutions algebraically.

9. $3x^2 = 48$ **10.** $x^2 - 4 = 5$ **11.** $-x^2 + 7x - 10 = 0$

Practice and Applications

WRITING IN STANDARD FORM Write the quadratic equation in standard form.

12. $4x^2 = 12$ **13.** $x^2 - 6x = -6$ **14.** $-x^2 = 15$

15. $5 + x = 3x^2$ **16.** $2x - x^2 = 1$ **17.** $6x^2 = 12x$

IDENTIFYING THE ROOTS Use the graph to identify the roots of the quadratic equation.

18. $-x^2 + 3x - 2 = 0$ **19.** $-x^2 - 2x + 3 = 0$ **20.** $x^2 - 2x - 8 = 0$

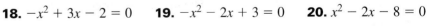

Student Help

▶**HOMEWORK HELP**
Example 1: Exs. 18–21
Example 2: Exs. 22–45
Example 3: Exs. 47–50, 52

21. CHECKING SOLUTIONS Use substitution to check the solutions of the quadratic equations in Exercises 18–20.

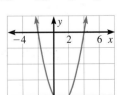

SOLVING GRAPHICALLY Use a graph to estimate the solutions of the equation. Check your solutions algebraically.

22. $x^2 + 2x = 3$

23. $-4x^2 - 8x = -12$

24. $-x^2 + 3x = -4$

25. $2x^2 + 4x = 6$

26. $3x^2 + 3x = 6$

27. $x^2 - 4x - 5 = 0$

28. $x^2 - x = 12$

29. $-x^2 - 4x = -5$

30. $x^2 + x = 2$

31. $-x^2 - x + 6 = 0$

32. $2x^2 - 8x = 10$

33. $-x^2 + x = -2$

CHECKING GRAPHICALLY Solve the equation algebraically. Check your solutions by graphing.

34. $2x^2 = 32$

35. $4x^2 = 100$

36. $4x^2 = 16$

37. $x^2 - 11 = 14$

38. $x^2 - 13 = 36$

39. $x^2 - 4 = 12$

40. $x^2 - 53 = 11$

41. $x^2 + 37 = 118$

42. $2x^2 - 89 = 9$

43. $2x^2 + 8 = 16$

44. $3x^2 + 5 = 32$

45. $2x^2 - 7 = 11$

46. SWISS CHEESE The consumption of Swiss cheese in the United States from 1970 to 1996 can be modeled by $P = -0.002t^2 + 0.056t + 0.889$. P is the number of pounds consumed per person and t is the number of years since 1970.

According to the graph of the model, in what year would the consumption of Swiss cheese drop to 0? Is this a realistic prediction?

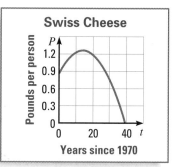

Swiss Cheese

▶ Source: U.S. Department of Agriculture

Link to
Science

MICROGRAVITY
Researchers can investigate the effects of microgravity aboard an airplane. A plane can attain low gravity conditions for 15-second periods by repeatedly flying in a parabolic path.

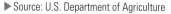 **APPROXIMATING SOLUTIONS** Use a graphing calculator to approximate the solutions of the equation.

47. $-x^2 - 3x + 4 = 0$

48. $x^2 + 6x - 7 = 0$

49. $-\frac{1}{2}x^2 + 2x + 16 = 0$

50. $\frac{5}{4}x^2 + 15x + 40 = 0$

Science Link In Exercises 51 and 52, use the following information.
Scientists use a state of free fall to simulate a gravity-free environment called *microgravity*. In microgravity conditions, the distance d (in meters) that an object that is dropped falls in t seconds can be modeled by the equation $d = 4.9t^2$.

In Japan a 490-meter-deep mine shaft has been converted into a free-fall facility. This creates the longest period of free fall currently available on Earth. How long is a period of free fall in this facility?

51. Solve the problem algebraically.

52.  Use a graphing calculator to check your answer by graphing the related function $y = 4.9x^2 - 490$.

53. MULTIPLE CHOICE What are the x-intercepts of $y = x^2 - 2x - 3$?

  Ⓐ 1 and -3 Ⓑ 2 and -3 Ⓒ 6 and -1 Ⓓ 3 and -1

54. MULTIPLE CHOICE Choose the equation whose roots are shown in the graph.

  Ⓕ $5x^2 - 1 = 0$

  Ⓖ $\frac{1}{5}x^2 - 5 = 0$

  Ⓗ $x^2 - 5 = 0$

  Ⓙ $\frac{1}{5}x^2 - 1 = 0$

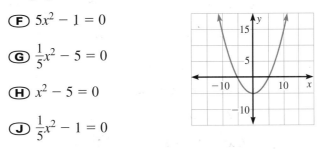

55. LUNCH TIME At lunch, you order 1 pasta dish and 1 type of salad. Your friend orders 1 pasta dish and 2 types of salads. The restaurant charges the same price for each pasta dish and the same price for each salad. Your bill is $7.90 and your friend's bill is $9.85. How much did each pasta dish and each salad cost? *(Lesson 7.4)*

SOLVING LINEAR SYSTEMS Use the substitution method or linear combinations to solve the linear system and tell how many solutions the system has. *(Lesson 7.5)*

56. $-2x + 8y = 11$
   $x + 6y = 2$

57. $-2x + 8y = 10$
   $x + 6y = 15$

58. $-2x + 2y = 4$
   $x - y = -2$

59. $8x + 4y = -4$
   $4x - y = -20$

60. $6x + 4y = -4$
   $2x - y = -6$

61. $5x + 4y = -3$
   $15x + 12y = 9$

EVALUATING RADICAL EXPRESSIONS Evaluate the radical expression when $a = -1$ and $b = 5$. *(Lesson 9.1)*

62. $\sqrt{b^2 - 11a}$ **63.** $\sqrt{b^2 + 9a}$ **64.** $\sqrt{a^2 + 8}$ **65.** $\sqrt{a^2 - 1}$

66. $\dfrac{\sqrt{b^2 + 24a}}{a}$ **67.** $\dfrac{\sqrt{b^2 - 75a}}{b}$ **68.** $\dfrac{\sqrt{65 - a^2}}{-a}$ **69.** $\dfrac{\sqrt{86 + ab}}{a}$

SIMPLIFYING RADICAL EXPRESSIONS Simplify the radical expression. *(Lesson 9.3)*

70. $\sqrt{40}$ **71.** $\sqrt{24}$ **72.** $\sqrt{60}$ **73.** $\sqrt{200}$

74. $\frac{1}{2}\sqrt{80}$ **75.** $\frac{1}{3}\sqrt{27}$ **76.** $\frac{1}{8}\sqrt{32}$ **77.** $\frac{2}{3}\sqrt{300}$

COMPARING FRACTIONS AND MIXED NUMBERS Complete the statement using <, >, or =. *(Skills Review pp. 763, 770, 771)*

78. $\frac{8}{7}$ ❓ $1\frac{1}{7}$ **79.** $\frac{8}{3}$ ❓ $2\frac{1}{3}$ **80.** $\frac{17}{5}$ ❓ $3\frac{4}{5}$ **81.** $\frac{13}{6}$ ❓ $1\frac{1}{6}$

82. $\frac{23}{10}$ ❓ $2\frac{3}{10}$ **83.** $\frac{100}{9}$ ❓ $11\frac{2}{9}$ **84.** $1\frac{7}{17}$ ❓ $1\frac{22}{17}$ **85.** $\frac{9}{4}$ ❓ $2\frac{3}{4}$

USING A GRAPHING CALCULATOR
Approximating Solutions

For use with Lesson 9.5

You can use the *root* or *zero* feature of a graphing calculator to approximate the solutions, or roots, of a quadratic equation.

Sample

Approximate the roots of $2x^2 + 3x - 4 = 0$.

Solution

Student Help

▶ **KEYSTROKE HELP**

See keystrokes for several models of graphing calculators at www.mcdougallittell.com

1 Enter the related function $y = 2x^2 + 3x - 4$ into the graphing calculator.

```
Y1=2X²+3X-4
Y2=
Y3=
Y4=
Y5=
Y6=
Y7=
```

2 Adjust the viewing window so you can see the graph cross the *x*-axis twice. Graph the function.

```
WINDOW
 Xmin=-10
 Xmax=10
 Xscl=1
 Ymin=-10
 Ymax=10
 Yscl=1
```

3 Choose the *Root* or *Zero* feature.

```
CALCULATE
1:value
2:zero
3:minimum
4:maximum
5:intersect
6:dy/dx
```

4 Follow your graphing calculator's procedure to find one root.

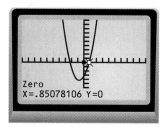

The positive root is approximately 0.85. Follow similar steps to find the negative root, -2.35.

Try These

APPROXIMATING ROOTS In Exercises 1–4, use a graphing calculator to approximate the roots of the quadratic equation to the nearest hundredth.

1. $x^2 - x - 2 = 0$

2. $6x^2 + 4x - 12 = 0$

3. $-4x^2 + 6x + 7 = 0$

4. $-2x^2 + 3x + 6 = 0$

5. Each equation in Exercises 1–4 has two solutions, or roots. How many *x*-intercepts does each related function have?

6. If a quadratic equation has one solution, how many times do you think the graph of its related function will cross the *x*-axis? No real solution?

9.6 Solving Quadratic Equations by the Quadratic Formula

Goal

Use the quadratic formula to solve a quadratic equation.

Key Words

• quadratic formula
• vertical motion model

When will a baseball hit the ground?

In Exercise 79 you will use the *quadratic formula* to find how long it takes a baseball to reach the ground after being hit by a batter.

The **quadratic formula** gives the solutions of $ax^2 + bx + c = 0$ in terms of the coefficients a, b, and c. In Lesson 12.5 you will see how the quadratic formula is developed from the standard form of a quadratic equation.

Student Help

▶ **READING ALGEBRA**
The quadratic formula is read as "x equals the opposite of b, plus or minus the square root of b squared minus $4ac$, all divided by $2a$."

THE QUADRATIC FORMULA

The solutions of the quadratic equation $ax^2 + bx + c = 0$ are

$$x = \frac{-b \pm \sqrt{b^2 - 4ac}}{2a}$$ when $a \neq 0$ and $b^2 - 4ac \geq 0$.

EXAMPLE 1 Use the Quadratic Formula

Solve $x^2 + 9x + 14 = 0$.

Solution $1x^2 + 9x + 14 = 0$ Identify $a = 1$, $b = 9$, and $c = 14$.

$$x = \frac{-9 \pm \sqrt{9^2 - 4(1)(14)}}{2(1)}$$ Substitute values in the quadratic formula: $a = 1$, $b = 9$, and $c = 14$.

$$x = \frac{-9 \pm \sqrt{25}}{2}$$ Simplify.

$$x = \frac{-9 \pm 5}{2}$$ Solutions.

ANSWER ▶ The two solutions are $x = \dfrac{-9 + 5}{2} = -2$ and $x = \dfrac{-9 - 5}{2} = -7$.

Checkpoint ✓ Use the Quadratic Formula

Use the quadratic formula to solve the equation.

1. $x^2 - 4x + 3 = 0$ **2.** $2x^2 + x - 10 = 0$ **3.** $-x^2 + 3x + 4 = 0$

EXAMPLE 2 **Write in Standard Form**

Solve $2x^2 - 3x = 8$. Round the results to the nearest hundredth.

Solution

$2x^2 - 3x = 8$	Write original equation.
$2x^2 - 3x - 8 = 0$	Rewrite equation in standard form.
$x = \dfrac{-(-3) \pm \sqrt{(-3)^2 - 4(2)(-8)}}{2(2)}$	Substitute values in the quadratic formula: $a = 2$, $b = -3$, $c = -8$.
$x = \dfrac{3 \pm \sqrt{9 + 64}}{4}$	Simplify.
$x = \dfrac{3 \pm \sqrt{73}}{4}$	Solutions.

ANSWER ▶ The two solutions are $x = \dfrac{3 + \sqrt{73}}{4} \approx 2.89$ and $x = \dfrac{3 - \sqrt{73}}{4} \approx -1.39$.

Checkpoint ✓ **Write in Standard Form**

Use the quadratic formula to solve the equation. If the solution involves radicals, round to the nearest hundredth.

4. $x^2 + x = 1$ **5.** $-x^2 = 2x - 3$ **6.** $7x^2 - 1 = -2x$

EXAMPLE 3 **Find the x-Intercepts of a Graph**

Find the x-intercepts, or roots, of the graph of $y = x^2 + 4x - 5$.

Solution The x-intercepts occur when $y = 0$.

$y = x^2 + 4x - 5$	Write original equation.
$0 = 1x^2 + 4x - 5$	Substitute 0 for y.
$x = \dfrac{-4 \pm \sqrt{(4)^2 - 4(1)(-5)}}{2(1)}$	Substitute values in the quadratic formula: $a = 1$, $b = 4$, $c = -5$.
$x = \dfrac{-4 \pm \sqrt{16 + 20}}{2}$	Simplify.
$x = \dfrac{-4 \pm 6}{2}$	Solutions

ANSWER ▶ The two solutions are $x = 1$ and $x = -5$.

CHECK ✓ Use a graph to check your solutions. You can see from the graph that the x-intercepts of $y = x^2 + 4x - 5$ are -5 and 1.

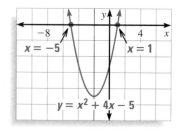

VERTICAL MOTION MODELS In Lesson 9.2 you studied the model for the height of a falling object that is *dropped*. For an object that is *thrown* up or down, the model has an extra term v. It is called the initial velocity.

VERTICAL MOTION MODELS

Object is dropped: $h = -16t^2 + s$ **Object is thrown:** $h = -16t^2 + vt + s$

h = height (feet) t = time in motion (seconds)

s = initial height (feet) v = initial velocity (feet per second)

EXAMPLE 4 Model Vertical Motion

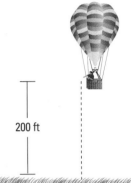

HOT-AIR BALLOONS You are competing in the field target event at a hot-air balloon festival. From a hot-air balloon directly over a target, you throw a marker with an initial downward velocity of -30 feet per second from a height of 200 feet. How long does it take the marker to reach the target?

200 ft

Not drawn to scale

Solution The marker is thrown *down*, so the initial velocity v is -30 feet per second. The initial height s is 200 feet. The marker will hit the target when its height is 0.

$h = -16t^2 + vt + s$ — Choose the vertical motion model for a thrown object.

$h = -16t^2 + (-30)t + 200$ — Substitute values for v and s in the vertical motion model.

$0 = -16t^2 - 30t + 200$ — Substitute 0 for h. Write in standard form.

$t = \dfrac{-(-30) \pm \sqrt{(-30)^2 - 4(-16)(200)}}{2(-16)}$ — Substitute values for a, b, and c in the quadratic formula.

$t = \dfrac{30 \pm \sqrt{13,700}}{-32}$ — Simplify.

$t \approx 2.72$ or -4.60 — Evaluate the radical expressions.

ANSWER ▶ The weighted marker will reach the ground about 2.72 seconds after it was thrown. The solution -4.60 doesn't make sense in this problem.

Checkpoint ✓ **Model Vertical Motion**

7. In Example 4, suppose you throw a marker with an initial downward velocity of -60 feet per second. Do you think it would hit the ground in half the time? Check your prediction using the quadratic formula.

Guided Practice

Vocabulary Check

1. Write the formula that you can use to solve any quadratic equation when $a \neq 0$ and $b^2 - 4ac \geq 0$.

2. Describe how you can check the solutions of a quadratic equation by looking at the graph of the related function.

3. What new feature was introduced in the vertical motion model used in Example 4?

Skill Check

Write the equation in standard form. Identify the values of *a*, *b*, and *c* that you would use to solve the equation using the quadratic formula.

4. $x^2 = 1$ **5.** $16x - 32 = 2x^2$ **6.** $x^2 - 7x + 42 = 6x$

Use the quadratic formula to solve the equation. Write your solutions in simplest form.

7. $x^2 + 6x - 7 = 0$ **8.** $x^2 - 2x - 15 = 0$ **9.** $x^2 + 12x + 36 = 0$

10. $4x^2 - 8x + 3 = 0$ **11.** $3x^2 + x - 1 = 0$ **12.** $x^2 + 6x - 3 = 0$

Write the equation in standard form. Then use the quadratic formula to solve the equation.

13. $2x^2 = -x + 6$ **14.** $-3x = 2x^2 + 1$ **15.** $2 = x^2 - x$

16. $-14x = -2x^2 + 36$ **17.** $-x^2 + 4x = 3$ **18.** $4x^2 + 4x = -1$

Practice and Applications

STANDARD FORM Write the equation in standard form. Identify the values of *a*, *b*, and *c*.

19. $3x^2 = 3x + 6$ **20.** $-2t^2 = -8$ **21.** $-x^2 = -5x + 6$

22. $3x^2 = 27x$ **23.** $-24x + 45 = -3x^2$ **24.** $32 - 4m^2 = 28m$

25. $k^2 = \frac{1}{4}$ **26.** $2x^2 - \frac{1}{5} = -\frac{2}{5}x$ **27.** $\frac{1}{3} - 2x = \frac{2}{3}x^2$

FINDING VALUES Find the value of $b^2 - 4ac$ for the equation.

28. $x^2 - 3x - 4 = 0$ **29.** $4x^2 + 5x + 1 = 0$ **30.** $-5w^2 - 3w + 2 = 0$

31. $r^2 - 11r + 30 = 0$ **32.** $s^2 - 13s + 42 = 0$ **33.** $3x^2 - 5x - 12 = 0$

34. $2x^2 + 4x - 1 = 0$ **35.** $3t^2 - 8t - 7 = 0$ **36.** $-8m^2 - 6m + 3 = 0$

37. $5x^2 + 5x + \frac{1}{5} = 0$ **38.** $\frac{1}{2}t^2 + 5t - 8 = 0$ **39.** $\frac{1}{4}v^2 - 6v - 3 = 0$

SOLVING EQUATIONS Use the quadratic formula to solve the equation.
If the solution involves radicals, round to the nearest hundredth.

40. $4x^2 - 13x + 3 = 0$ **41.** $y^2 + 11y + 10 = 0$ **42.** $7x^2 + 8x + 1 = 0$

43. $-3y^2 + 2y + 8 = 0$ **44.** $6n^2 - 10n + 3 = 0$ **45.** $9x^2 + 14x + 3 = 0$

46. $8m^2 + 6m - 1 = 0$ **47.** $-\frac{1}{2}x^2 + 6x + 13 = 0$ **48.** $2x^2 - 3x + 1 = 0$

STANDARD FORM Write the quadratic equation in standard form. Then
solve using the quadratic formula.

49. $2x^2 = 4x + 30$ **50.** $x^2 + 3x = -2$ **51.** $5 = x^2 + 6x$

52. $5x + 2 = 2x^2$ **53.** $5x - 2x^2 + 15 = 8$ **54.** $-2 + x^2 = -x$

55. $x^2 - 2x = 3$ **56.** $2x^2 + 4 = 6x$ **57.** $12 = 2x^2 - 2x$

FINDING INTERCEPTS Find the x-intercepts of the graph of the function.

58. $y = -x^2 + x + 6$ **59.** $y = x^2 + 5x + 6$ **60.** $y = x^2 - 11x + 24$

61. $y = x^2 + 10x + 16$ **62.** $y = -x^2 - 4x + 2$ **63.** $y = 2x^2 - 6x - 8$

64. $y = x^2 - 2x - 2$ **65.** $y = 2x^2 + 4x - 6$ **66.** $y = -3x^2 + 17x - 20$

Link to
Ecology

URBAN BIRDS Cities
provide a habitat for many
species of wildlife including
birds of prey such as
peregrine falcons and red-
tailed hawks.

FIELD TARGET EVENT In Exercises 67–72, six balloonists compete in a
field target event at a hot-air balloon festival. Calculate the amount of
time it takes for the marker to reach the target when thrown down from
the given initial height (in feet) with the given initial downward velocity
(in feet per second). Round to the nearest hundredth of a second.

67. $s = 200; v = -50$ **68.** $s = 150; v = -25$ **69.** $s = 100; v = -10$

70. $s = 150; v = -33$ **71.** $s = 50; v = -40$ **72.** $s = 50; v = -20$

73. PEREGRINE FALCON A falcon
dives toward a pigeon on the ground.
When the falcon is at a height of
100 feet, the pigeon sees the falcon,
which is diving at 220 feet per
second. Estimate the time the pigeon
has to escape. Round your solution to
the nearest tenth of a second.

74. RED-TAILED HAWK A hawk dives
toward a snake. When the hawk is at
a height of 200 feet, the snake sees
the hawk, which is diving at 105 feet
per second. Estimate the time the
snake has to escape. Round your
solution to the nearest tenth of
a second.

Student Help

▶HOMEWORK HELP

Extra help with
problem solving in
Exs. 75–78 is available at
www.mcdougallittell.com

VERTICAL MOTION In Exercises 75–78, use a vertical motion model to find how long it will take for the object to reach the ground. Round your solution to the nearest tenth.

75. You drop your keys from a window 30 feet above ground to your friend below. Your friend does not catch them.

76. An acorn falls 45 feet from the top of a tree.

77. A lacrosse player throws a ball upward from her playing stick from an initial height of 7 feet, with an initial velocity of 90 feet per second.

78. You throw a ball downward with an initial velocity of -10 feet per second out of a window to a friend 20 feet below. Your friend does not catch the ball.

79. BASEBALL A batter hits a pitched baseball when it is 3 feet off the ground. After it is hit, the height h (in feet) of the ball is modeled by $h = -16t^2 + 80t + 3$, where t is the time (in seconds). How long will it take for the ball to hit the ground? Round to the nearest hundredth.

80. *Science Link* An astronaut standing on the moon's surface throws a rock upward with an initial velocity of 50 feet per second. The height of the rock can be modeled by $m = -2.7t^2 + 50t + 6$, where m is the height of the rock (in feet) and t is the time (in seconds). If the astronaut throws the same rock upward with the same initial velocity on Earth, the height of the rock is modeled by $e = -16t^2 + 50t + 6$. Would the rock hit the ground in less time on the moon or on Earth? Explain your answer.

Standardized Test Practice

81. MULTIPLE CHOICE Which expression gives the solutions of $2x^2 - 10 = x$?

Ⓐ $\dfrac{1 \pm \sqrt{1 - (4)(2)(-10)}}{4}$

Ⓑ $\dfrac{-1 \pm \sqrt{1 - (4)(2)(10)}}{4}$

Ⓒ $\dfrac{10 \pm \sqrt{100 - (4)(2)(1)}}{4}$

Ⓓ $\dfrac{10 \pm \sqrt{100 - (4)(2)(-1)}}{4}$

82. MULTIPLE CHOICE What are the roots of the quadratic equation in Exercise 81?

Ⓕ $\dfrac{-5 \pm 3\sqrt{3}}{2}$ Ⓖ $\dfrac{1 \pm 9}{4}$ Ⓗ $\dfrac{5 \pm \sqrt{23}}{2}$ Ⓙ None of these

83. MULTIPLE CHOICE Which quadratic equation has the solutions $x = \dfrac{-9 \pm \sqrt{81 - 56}}{4}$?

Ⓐ $2x^2 + 9x - 7 = 0$

Ⓑ $2x^2 - 9x + 7 = 0$

Ⓒ $4x^2 + 9x + 14 = 0$

Ⓓ $2x^2 + 9x + 7 = 0$

84. MULTIPLE CHOICE Which equation would you use to model the height of an object that is thrown down with an initial velocity of -10 feet per second from a height of 100 feet?

Ⓕ $h = -16t^2 + 100$

Ⓖ $h = -16t^2 + 10t + 100$

Ⓗ $h = -16t^2 - 10t + 100$

Ⓙ $h = -16t^2 - 10t - 100$

EVALUATING EXPRESSIONS Evaluate the expression for the given value of the variable. *(Lesson 2.5)*

85. $-3(x)$ when $x = 9$

86. $-5(-n)(-n)$ when $n = 2$

87. $4(-6)(m)$ when $m = -2$

88. $2(-1)(-x)^3$ when $x = -3$

GRAPHING LINES Write the equation in slope-intercept form. Then graph the equation. *(Lesson 4.7)*

89. $-3x + y + 6 = 0$ **90.** $-x + y - 7 = 0$ **91.** $4x + 2y - 12 = 0$

SOLVING INEQUALITIES Solve the inequality. Then graph the solution. *(Lesson 6.2)*

92. $6x \le -2$ **93.** $-3x \ge 15$ **94.** $\frac{3}{4}x > 12$

95. RECREATION There were 1.4×10^7 people who visited Golden Gate Recreation Area in California in 1996. Find the average number of visitors per month. ▶Source: National Park Service *(Lesson 8.5)*

COMPARING FRACTIONS Complete the statement using <, >, or =. *(Skills Review pp. 770, 771)*

96. $\frac{8}{15}$ **?** $\frac{2}{15}$ **97.** $\frac{2}{3}$ **?** $\frac{5}{6}$ **98.** $\frac{1}{4}$ **?** $\frac{1}{5}$

99. $\frac{7}{8}$ **?** $\frac{11}{12}$ **100.** $4\frac{1}{8}$ **?** $4\frac{1}{5}$ **101.** $2\frac{2}{3}$ **?** $3\frac{1}{2}$

Quiz 2

Decide whether the graph of the function opens *up* or *down*. *(Lesson 9.4)*

1. $y = x^2 + 2x - 11$ **2.** $y = 2x^2 - 8x - 6$ **3.** $y = -3x^2 + 6x - 10$

4. $y = \frac{1}{2}x^2 + 5x - 3$ **5.** $y = -7x^2 - 7x + 7$ **6.** $y = -x^2 + 9x$

Sketch the graph of the function. Label the coordinates of the vertex. *(Lesson 9.4)*

7. $y = -x^2 + 2x - 3$ **8.** $y = -3x^2 + 12x - 10$ **9.** $y = 2x^2 - 6x + 7$

Use a graph to estimate the solutions of the equation. Check your solutions algebraically. *(Lesson 9.5)*

10. $x^2 - 3x = 10$ **11.** $x^2 - 12x = -36$ **12.** $3x^2 + 12x = -9$

Use the quadratic formula to solve the equation. If your solution involves radicals, round to the nearest hundredth. *(Lesson 9.6)*

13. $x^2 + 6x + 9 = 0$ **14.** $2x^2 + 13x + 6 = 0$ **15.** $-x^2 + 6x + 16 = 0$

16. $-2x^2 + 7x - 6 = 0$ **17.** $-3x^2 - 5x + 10 = 0$ **18.** $3x^2 - 4x - 1 = 0$

9.7 Using the Discriminant

Goal
Use the discriminant to determine the number of solutions of a quadratic equation.

Key Words
- discriminant

Can you throw a stick high enough?

One way that campers protect food from bears is to hang it from a high tree branch. In the example on page 545, you will determine whether a stick and a rope were thrown fast enough to go over a tree branch.

In the quadratic formula, the expression inside the radical is the **discriminant**.

$$x = \frac{-b \pm \sqrt{b^2 - 4ac}}{2a} \quad \longleftarrow \quad \text{Discriminant}$$

The discriminant $b^2 - 4ac$ of a quadratic equation can be used to find the number of solutions of the quadratic equation.

Student Help

▶ **STUDY TIP**
Recall that positive real numbers have two square roots, zero has only one square root, negative numbers have no real square roots.

THE NUMBER OF SOLUTIONS OF A QUADRATIC EQUATION

Consider the quadratic equation $ax^2 + bx + c = 0$.
- If the value of $b^2 - 4ac$ is positive, then the equation has two solutions.
- If the value of $b^2 - 4ac$ is zero, then the equation has one solution.
- If the value of $b^2 - 4ac$ is negative, then the equation has no real solution.

EXAMPLE 1 Find the Number of Solutions

Find the value of the discriminant. Then use the value to determine whether $x^2 - 3x - 4 = 0$ has *two solutions*, *one solution*, or *no real solution*.

Solution Use the standard form of a quadratic equation, $ax^2 + bx + c = 0$, to identify the coefficients.

$x^2 - 3x - 4 = 0$	Identify $a = 1$, $b = -3$, $c = -4$.
$b^2 - 4ac = (-3)^2 - 4(1)(-4)$	Substitute values for a, b, and c.
$= 9 + 16$	Simplify.
$= 25$	Discriminant is positive.

ANSWER ▶ The discriminant is positive, so the equation has two solutions.

EXAMPLE **2** **Find the Number of Solutions**

Find the value of the discriminant. Then use the value to determine whether the equation has *two solutions*, *one solution*, or *no real solution*.

a. $-x^2 + 2x - 1 = 0$ **b.** $2x^2 - 2x + 3 = 0$

Solution

a. $-x^2 + 2x - 1 = 0$ Identify $a = -1$, $b = 2$, $c = -1$.

$\quad b^2 - 4ac = (2)^2 - 4(-1)(-1)$ Substitute values for a, b, and c.

$\qquad\qquad = 4 - 4$ Simplify.

$\qquad\qquad = 0$ Discriminant is zero.

ANSWER ▶ The discriminant is zero, so the equation has one solution.

b. $2x^2 - 2x + 3 = 0$ Identify $a = 2$, $b = -2$, $c = 3$.

$\quad b^2 - 4ac = (-2)^2 - 4(2)(3)$ Substitute values for a, b, and c.

$\qquad\qquad = 4 - 24$ Simplify.

$\qquad\qquad = -20$ Discriminant is negative.

ANSWER ▶ The discriminant is negative, so the equation has no real solution.

Checkpoint ✓ **Find the Number of Solutions**

Find the value of the discriminant. Then use the value to determine whether the equation has *two solutions*, *one solution*, or *no real solution*.

1. $x^2 - 3x + 4 = 0$ **2.** $x^2 - 4x + 4 = 0$ **3.** $x^2 - 5x + 4 = 0$

Because each solution of $ax^2 + bx + c = 0$ represents an x-intercept of $y = ax^2 + bx + c$, you can use the discriminant to determine the number of times the graph of a quadratic function intersects the x-axis.

EXAMPLE **3** **Find the Number of x-Intercepts**

Determine whether the graph of $y = x^2 + 2x - 2$ will intersect the x-axis in *zero*, *one*, or *two* points.

Solution

Let $y = 0$. Then find the value of the discriminant of $x^2 + 2x - 2 = 0$.

$\quad x^2 + 2x - 2 = 0$ Identify $a = 1$, $b = 2$, $c = -2$.

$\quad b^2 - 4ac = (2)^2 - 4(1)(-2)$ Substitute values for a, b, and c.

$\qquad\qquad = 4 + 8$ Simplify.

$\qquad\qquad = 12$ Discriminant is positive.

ANSWER ▶ The discriminant is positive, so the equation has two solutions and the graph will intersect the x-axis in two points.

EXAMPLE 4 Find the Number of x-Intercepts

Determine whether the graph of the function will intersect the x-axis in *zero*, *one*, or *two* points.

a. $y = x^2 + 2x + 1$ **b.** $y = x^2 + 2x + 3$

Solution

a. Let $y = 0$. Then find the value of the discriminant of $x^2 + 2x + 1 = 0$.

$x^2 + 2x + 1 = 0$	Identify $a = 1$, $b = 2$, $c = 1$.
$b^2 - 4ac = (2)^2 - 4(1)(1)$	Substitute values for a, b, and c.
$= 4 - 4$	Simplify.
$= 0$	Discriminant is zero.

ANSWER ▶ The discriminant is zero, so the equation has one solution *and* the graph will intersect the x-axis in one point.

b. Let $y = 0$. Then find the value of the discriminant of $x^2 + 2x + 3 = 0$.

$x^2 + 2x + 3 = 0$	Identify $a = 1$, $b = 2$, $c = 3$.
$b^2 - 4ac = (2)^2 - 4(1)(3)$	Substitute values for a, b, and c.
$= 4 - 12$	Simplify.
$= -8$	Discriminant is negative.

ANSWER ▶ The discriminant is negative, so the equation has no real solution *and* the graph will intersect the x-axis in zero points.

EXAMPLE 5 Change the Value of c

Sketch the graphs of the functions in Examples 3 and 4 to check the number of x-intercepts of $y = x^2 + 2x + c$. What effect does changing the value of c have on the graph?

Solution By changing the value of c, you can move the graph of $y = x^2 + 2x + c$ up or down in the coordinate plane.

a. $y = x^2 + 2x - 2$

b. $y = x^2 + 2x + 1$

c. $y = x^2 + 2x + 3$

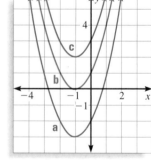

If the graph is moved high enough, it will not have an x-intercept and the equation $x^2 + 2x + c = 0$ will have no real solution.

Checkpoint ✓ Find the Number of x-Intercepts

Find the number of x-intercepts of the graph of the function.

4. $y = x^2 - 4x + 3$ **5.** $y = x^2 - 4x + 4$ **6.** $y = x^2 - 4x + 5$

Guided Practice

Vocabulary Check

1. Write the quadratic formula and circle the part that is the discriminant.

2. What can the discriminant tell you about a quadratic equation?

3. Describe how the graphs of $y = 4x^2$, $y = 4x^2 + 3$, and $y = 4x^2 - 6$ are alike and how they are different.

Skill Check

Use the discriminant to determine whether the quadratic equation has *two solutions*, *one solution*, or *no real solution*.

4. $3x^2 - 3x + 5 = 0$ **5.** $-3x^2 + 6x - 3 = 0$ **6.** $x^2 - 5x - 10 = 0$

Give the letter of the graph that matches the value of the discriminant.

7. $b^2 - 4ac = 2$ **8.** $b^2 - 4ac = 0$ **9.** $b^2 - 4ac = -3$

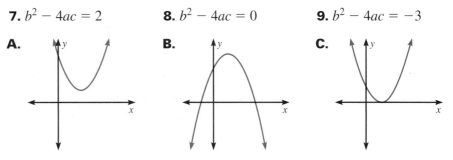

A.   **B.**   **C.**

Determine whether the graph of the function will intersect the *x*-axis in *zero*, *one*, or *two* points.

10. $y = x^2 + 2x + 4$ **11.** $y = -x^2 - 3x + 5$ **12.** $y = 6x - 3 - 3x^2$

Practice and Applications

WRITING THE DISCRIMINANT   Find the discriminant of the quadratic equation.

13. $-2x^2 - 5x + 3 = 0$ **14.** $3x^2 + 6x - 8 = 0$ **15.** $x^2 + 10 = 0$

16. $5x^2 + 3x = 12$ **17.** $2x^2 + 8x = -8$ **18.** $7 - 5x^2 + 9x = x$

19. $-x = 7x^2 + 4$ **20.** $2x = x^2 - x$ **21.** $-2 - x^2 = 4x^2$

USING THE DISCRIMINANT   Determine whether the equation has *two solutions*, *one solution*, or *no real solution*.

22. $x^2 - 3x + 2 = 0$ **23.** $2x^2 - 4x + 3 = 0$ **24.** $-3x^2 + 5x - 1 = 0$

25. $2x^2 + 3x - 2 = 0$ **26.** $x^2 - 2x + 4 = 0$ **27.** $6x^2 - 2x + 4 = 0$

28. $3x^2 - 6x + 3 = 0$ **29.** $4x^2 - 5x + 1 = 0$ **30.** $-5x^2 + 6x - 6 = 0$

31. $-\frac{1}{2}x^2 + x + 3 = 0$ **32.** $\frac{1}{4}x^2 - 2x + 4 = 0$ **33.** $5x^2 + 4x + \frac{4}{5} = 0$

Student Help

▶ **HOMEWORK HELP**
Example 1: Exs. 13–33
Example 2: Exs. 13–33
Example 3: Exs. 38–43
Example 4: Exs. 38–43
Example 5: Exs. 44–46

34. ERROR ANALYSIS For the equation $3x^2 + 4x - 2 = 0$, find and correct the error.

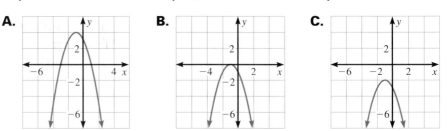

$$b^2 - 4ac$$
$$= (4)^2 - 4(3)(-2)$$
$$= 16 - 24$$
$$= -8$$

INTERPRETING THE DISCRIMINANT In Exercises 35–37, consider the quadratic equation $y = 2x^2 + 6x - 3$.

35. Evaluate the discriminant.

36. How many solutions does the equation have?

37. What does the discriminant tell you about the graph of $y = 2x^2 + 6x - 3$?

NUMBER OF X-INTERCEPTS Determine whether the graph of the function will intersect the x-axis in *zero*, *one*, or *two* points.

38. $y = 2x^2 + 3x - 2$ **39.** $y = x^2 - 2x + 4$ **40.** $y = -2x^2 + 4x - 2$

41. $y = 2x^2 + 2x + 6$ **42.** $y = 5x^2 + 2x - 3$ **43.** $y = 3x^2 - 6x + 3$

CHANGING THE VALUE OF C Match the function with its graph.

44. $y = -x^2 - 2x - 1$ **45.** $y = -x^2 - 2x - 3$ **46.** $y = -x^2 - 2x + 3$

A.

B.

C.

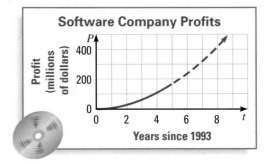
FINANCIAL ANALYSIS In Exercises 47–49, use a graphing calculator and the following information.

A software company's net profit for each year from 1993 to 1998 lead a financial analyst to model the company's net profit by
$P = 6.84t^2 - 3.76t + 9.29$,
where P is the profit in millions of dollars and t is the number of years since 1993. In 1993 the net profit was approximately 9.29 million dollars ($t = 0$).

Software Company Profits

Years since 1993

47. Give the domain and range of the function for 1993 through 1998.

48. Use the graph to predict whether the net profit will reach 650 million dollars.

49. Use a graphing calculator to estimate how many years it will take for the company's net profit to reach 475 million dollars according to the model.

EXAMPLE Using the Discriminant

CAMPING You and a friend want to get a rope over a tree branch that is 20 feet high. Your friend attaches a stick to the rope and throws the stick upward with an initial velocity of 29 feet per second. You then throw it with an initial velocity of 32 feet per second. Both throws have an initial height of 6 feet. Will the stick reach the branch each time it is thrown?

Solution

Use a vertical motion model for an object that is thrown: $h = -16t^2 + vt + s$, where h is the height you want to reach, t is the time in motion, v is the initial velocity, and s is the initial height.

$$h = -16t^2 + vt + s$$
$$20 = -16t^2 + 29t + 6$$
$$0 = -16t^2 + 29t - 14$$
$$b^2 - 4ac = (29)^2 - 4(-16)(-14)$$

The discriminant is -55.

ANSWER ▶ The discriminant is negative. The stick thrown by your friend *will not* reach the branch.

$$h = -16t^2 + vt + s$$
$$20 = -16t^2 + 32t + 6$$
$$0 = -16t^2 + 32t - 14$$
$$b^2 - 4ac = (32)^2 - 4(-16)(-14)$$

The discriminant is 128.

ANSWER ▶ The discriminant is positive. The stick thrown by you *will* reach the branch.

50. BASKETBALL You can jump with an initial velocity of 12 feet per second. You need to jump 2.2 feet to dunk a basketball. Use the vertical motion model $h = -16t^2 + vt + s$ to find if you can dunk the ball. Justify your answer.

Standardized Test Practice

51. MULTIPLE CHOICE For which value of c will $-3x^2 + 6x + c = 0$ *not* have a real solution?

(A) $c < -3$　　(B) $c = -3$　　(C) $c > -3$　　(D) $c = 3$

52. MULTIPLE CHOICE How many real solutions does $x^2 - 10x + 25 = 0$ have?

(F) No solutions　(G) One solution　(H) Two solutions　(J) Many solutions

Mixed Review

SOLVING AND GRAPHING INEQUALITIES Solve the inequality. Then graph the solution. *(Lesson 6.4)*

53. $2 \leq x + 1 < 5$　　　**54.** $8 > 2x > -4$　　　**55.** $-12 < 2x - 6 < 4$

GRAPHING LINEAR INEQUALITIES Graph the inequality. *(Lesson 6.8)*

56. $3x + y \leq 9$　　　**57.** $y - 4x < 0$　　　**58.** $-2x - y \geq 4$

Maintaining Skills

MULTIPLYING DECIMALS Find the product. *(Skills Review p. 759)*

59. 3×0.02　　　**60.** 0.7×0.8　　　**61.** 0.1×0.1

62. 0.05×0.003　　　**63.** 0.09×0.02　　　**64.** 0.06×0.0004

Graphing Quadratic Inequalities

For use with Lesson 9.8

GOAL

Use reasoning to discover a strategy for sketching the graph of a quadratic inequality.

MATERIALS

• graph paper
• pencil

Student Help

▶**LOOK BACK**
  To review strategies for graphing a linear inequality, see pp. 367–369.

Question How do you determine which portion of the graph of a quadratic inequality to shade?

In Lesson 6.8 you learned how to graph a *linear* inequality in two variables. You can use similar strategies to graph a *quadratic* inequality in two variables.

Explore

1 Consider the graphs of the following two quadratic inequalities.

a. $y < x^2 - 2x - 3$ **b.** $y \geq x^2 - 2x - 3$

Graph $y = x^2 - 2x - 3$. Use a *dashed line* for < and a *solid line* for ≥.

2 Use substitution to test points inside and outside the parabola. An ordered pair (x, y) is a solution of a quadratic inequality if the inequality is true when the values of x and y are substituted into the inequality. Try testing $(0, 0)$.

a.
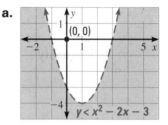

b.
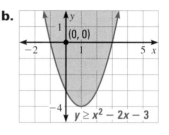

The point $(0, 0)$ __?__ a solution. The solutions appear to be the set of all points that lie *outside* the graph of $y = x^2 - 2x - 3$.

The point $(0, 0)$ __?__ a solution. The solutions appear to be the set of all points that lie *inside or on* the graph of $y = x^2 - 2x - 3$.

3 Can the inequality $y < x^2 - 2x - 3$ be interpreted as "all points (x, y) that lie below the parabola $y = x^2 - 2x - 3$"? Explain.

Think About It

Match the quadratic inequality with its graph. Explain your reasoning.

   1. $y \leq x^2 - 4$ **2.** $y > x^2 - 4x$ **3.** $y < (x - 4)^2$

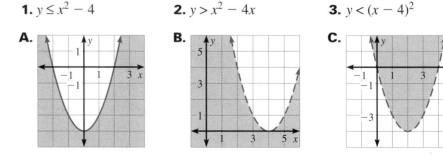

A.   **B.**   **C.**

9.8 Graphing Quadratic Inequalities

Goal

Sketch the graph of a quadratic inequality in two variables.

Key Words

• quadratic inequalities
• graph of a quadratic inequality

How does a flashlight work?

A flashlight has a *parabolic* reflector that helps to focus the light into a beam. In Exercise 34 you will use a *quadratic inequality* to learn more about how a flashlight works.

In this lesson you will study the following types of **quadratic inequalities**.

$$y < ax^2 + bx + c \qquad y \le ax^2 + bx + c$$

$$y > ax^2 + bx + c \qquad y \ge ax^2 + bx + c$$

The **graph of a quadratic inequality** consists of the graph of all ordered pairs (x, y) that are solutions of the inequality.

EXAMPLE 1 Check Points

Sketch the graph of $y = x^2 - 3x - 3$. Plot and label the points $A(3, 2)$, $B(1, 4)$, and $C(4, -3)$. Determine whether each point lies inside or outside the parabola.

Solution

❶ **Sketch** the graph of $y = x^2 - 3x - 3$.

❷ **Plot** and label the points $A(3, 2)$, $B(1, 4)$, and $C(4, -3)$.

ANSWER▶ Points A and B lie inside the parabola. Point C lies outside the parabola.

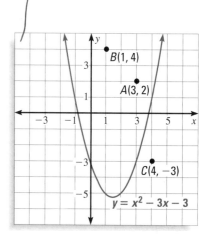

Checkpoint✓ **Check Points**

Sketch the graph of $y = x^2 - 4x + 3$. Plot the point and determine whether it lies *inside* or *outside* the parabola.

1. $A(-1, 2)$ **2.** $B(0, 0)$ **3.** $C(2, 1)$

The shaded part of the graph of a quadratic inequality contains all of the ordered pairs that are solutions of the inequality. Checking points tells you which region to shade. You can use the following steps to graph any quadratic inequality.

METHOD I: GRAPHING A QUADRATIC INEQUALITY

STEP ❶ Sketch the graph of $y = ax^2 + bx + c$ that corresponds to the inequality.

Sketch a dashed parabola for inequalities with < or > to show that the points on the parabola are *not* solutions.

Sketch a solid parabola for inequalities with ≤ or ≥ to show that the points on the parabola are solutions.

STEP ❷ The parabola separates the coordinate plane into two regions. Test a point that is *not* on the parabola to determine whether the point is a solution of the inequality.

STEP ❸ If the test point is a solution, shade its region. If not, shade the other region.

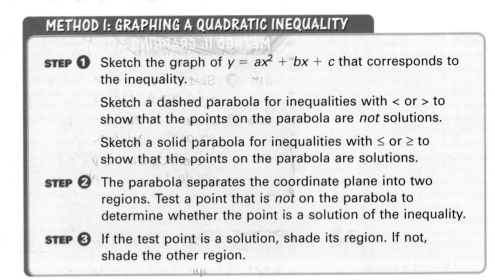

EXAMPLE 2 Graph a Quadratic Inequality

Sketch the graph of $y < 2x^2 - 3x$.

Solution

❶ **Sketch** the graph of the equation $y = 2x^2 - 3x$ that corresponds to the inequality $y < 2x^2 - 3x$. Use a dashed line since the inequality contains the symbol <.

The parabola opens up since a is positive.

The vertex is $\left(\dfrac{3}{4}, -1\dfrac{1}{4}\right)$.

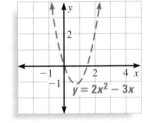

Student Help

▶ **STUDY TIP**
If the point (0, 0) is not on the parabola, then (0, 0) is usually good to use as a test point. For help with checking ordered pairs as solutions, see p. 367.

❷ **Test** a point, such as (1, 2), that is *not* on the parabola. The point (1, 2) lies inside the parabola.

$y < 2x^2 - 3x$	Write original inequality.
$2 \overset{?}{<} 2(1)^2 - 3(1)$	Substitute 1 for x and 2 for y.
$2 \not< -1$	2 is not less than −1.

Because 2 is *not* less than −1, the ordered pair (1, 2) is *not* a solution.

❸ **Shade** the region outside the parabola. The point (1, 2) is inside the parabola and it is not a solution, so the graph of $y < 2x^2 - 3x$ is all the points that are outside, but not on, the parabola.

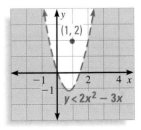

Until now you have used the fact that a parabola divides the plane into two regions, one of which is inside the parabola and one of which is outside. For parabolas given by $y = ax^2 + bx + c$, these regions can also be described as lying *above* and *below* the parabola and can be graphed using the following steps.

METHOD II: GRAPHING A QUADRATIC INEQUALITY

STEP ❶ Sketch the graph of $y = ax^2 + bx + c$, using a dashed or a solid curve as in Method I.

STEP ❷ If the inequality is $y > ax^2 + bx + c$ or $y \geq ax^2 + bx + c$, shade the region above the parabola.

If the inequality is $y < ax^2 + bx + c$ or $y \leq ax^2 + bx + c$, shade the region below the parabola.

Student Help

▶**MORE EXAMPLES**

More examples are available at www.mcdougallittell.com

EXAMPLE ❸ Graph a Quadratic Inequality

Sketch the graph of $y \leq -x^2 - 5x + 4$.

Solution

❶ *Sketch* the graph of the equation $y = -x^2 - 5x + 4$ that corresponds to the inequality $y \leq -x^2 - 5x + 4$. The x-coordinate of the vertex is $-\dfrac{b}{2a}$, or $-2\frac{1}{2}$. Make a table of values, using x-values to the left and right of $x = -2\frac{1}{2}$.

x	−5	−4	−3	$-2\frac{1}{2}$	−2	−1	0
y	4	8	10	$10\frac{1}{4}$	10	8	4

Plot the points and connect them with a smooth curve to form a parabola. Use a solid line since the inequality contains the symbol $\leq$.

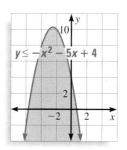

❷ *Shade* the region *below* the parabola because the inequality states that y is *less* than or equal to $-x^2 - 5x + 4$.

Checkpoint ✓ *Graph a Quadratic Inequality*

Sketch the graph of the inequality.

4. $y < x^2 + 2x + 2$ **5.** $y > -x^2 - 2x + 3$ **6.** $y \geq 2x^2 - 4x + 2$

9.8 Exercises

Guided Practice

Vocabulary Check

1. Give an example of each of the four types of quadratic inequalities.

2. *True* or *False*? For inequalities with < or >, you sketch a solid parabola to show that the points on the parabola are not solutions.

Skill Check

Sketch the graph of the equation $y = x^2 + 2x - 4$. Plot the point and determine whether it lies *inside* or *outside* the parabola.

3. $A(0, 0)$ **4.** $B(-1, 3)$ **5.** $C(2, -2)$

Decide whether each labeled ordered pair is a solution of the inequality.

6. $y < -x^2$ **7.** $y \geq x^2 - 2$ **8.** $y \leq 2x^2 + 5x$

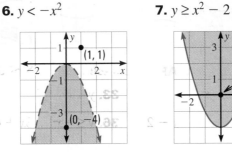
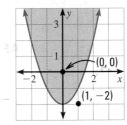
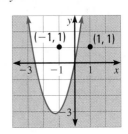

Sketch the graph of the inequality.

9. $y \leq x^2$ **10.** $y > -x^2 + 3$ **11.** $y < -x^2 + 2x$

12. $y \geq x^2 - 2x$ **13.** $y < -2x^2 + 6x$ **14.** $y \leq 2x^2 - 4x + 3$

Practice and Applications

SOLUTIONS Determine whether the ordered pair is a solution of the inequality.

15. $y \geq 2x^2 - x, (-2, 10)$ **16.** $y \leq 3x^2 + 7, (4, 31)$

17. $y < x^2 + 9x, (-3, 18)$ **18.** $y < 5x^2 + 8, (3, 45)$

19. $y > 4x^2 - 7x, (2, 0)$ **20.** $y \geq x^2 - 13x, (-1, 14)$

CHECKING POINTS Sketch the graph of the function. Plot the given point and determine whether the point lies *inside* or *outside* the parabola.

Student Help

▶ **HOMEWORK HELP**
  Example 1: Exs. 21–24
  Example 2: Exs. 29–38
  Example 3: Exs. 29–38

21. $y = x^2 - 2x + 5$
      $A(0, 4)$

22. $y = -x^2 + 4x - 2$
      $B(3, -2)$

23. $y = \frac{1}{2}x^2 + x - 4$
      $C(1, 0)$

24. $y = 4x^2 - x + 1$
      $D(-2, 5)$

LOGICAL REASONING Complete the statement with *always, sometimes,* or *never.*

25. If $a > b$, then a^2 __?__ greater than b^2.

26. If $a > b$ and $b > 0$, then a^2 __?__ greater than b^2.

27. If $a^2 = 4$, then a is __?__ equal to 2.

28. If a is a real number, then $\sqrt{a^2}$ is __?__ equal to $|a|$.

MATCHING INEQUALITIES Match the inequality with its graph.

29. $y \geq -2x^2 - 2x + 1$ **30.** $y > -2x^2 + 4x + 3$ **31.** $y \leq 2x^2 + x + 1$

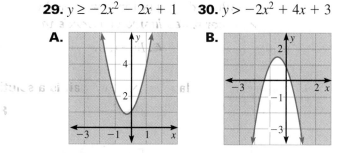

A.   **B.**   **C.**

SKETCHING GRAPHS Sketch the graph of the inequality.

32. $y < -x^2 + x$

33. $y < x^2 - 4$

34. $y \geq x^2 - 5x$

35. $y > -x^2 - 3x - 2$

36. $y \leq -x^2 + 3x + 4$

37. $y > -3x^2 - 5x - 1$

38. FLASHLIGHT Light rays from a flashlight bulb bounce off a parabolic reflector inside a flashlight. The reflected rays are parallel to the axis of the flashlight. In this way, flashlights produce narrow beams of light.

A cross section of a flashlight's parabolic reflector is shown in the graph at the right. An equation for the parabola is $y = \frac{1}{24}x^2 + 1$. Choose the region of the graph where the bulb is located.

A. $y < \frac{1}{24}x^2 + 1$ **B.** $y > \frac{1}{24}x^2 + 1$ **C.** $y \leq \frac{1}{24}x^2 + 1$

Standardized Test Practice

39. MULTIPLE CHOICE Which ordered pair is *not* a solution of the inequality $y \geq 2x^2 - 7x - 10$?

(A) $(0, -4)$ **(B)** $(-1, -1)$ **(C)** $(4, -13)$ **(D)** $(5, 15)$

40. MULTIPLE CHOICE Choose the statement that is *true* about the graph of the quadratic inequality $y < 5x^2 + 6x + 2$.

(A) Points on the parabola are solutions.

(B) The vertex is $\left(-\frac{3}{5}, \frac{1}{5}\right)$.

(C) The parabola opens down.

(D) $(0, 0)$ is not a solution.

FINDING EQUATIONS The variables x and y vary directly. Use the given values to write an equation that relates x and y. *(Lesson 4.6)*

41. $x = 6$, $y = 42$ **42.** $x = -9$, $y = 54$ **43.** $x = 14$, $y = 7$

44. $x = -13$, $y = -52$ **45.** $x = 3$, $y = -6$ **46.** $x = -5$, $y = 60$

GRAPHING FUNCTIONS Graph the exponential function. *(Lesson 8.3)*

47. $y = 3^x$ **48.** $y = 5^x$ **49.** $y = 3(2)^x$

50. $y = \left(\dfrac{1}{3}\right)^x$ **51.** $y = 2\left(\dfrac{1}{4}\right)^x$ **52.** $y = \left(\dfrac{2}{3}\right)^x$

PERCENTS AND FRACTIONS Write the percent as a fraction or as a mixed number in lowest terms. *(Skills Review p. 768)*

53. 4%   **54.** 392%   **55.** 45%   **56.** 500%

57. 3%   **58.** 6%   **59.** 24%   **60.** 10%

61. 390%   **62.** 225%   **63.** 175%   **64.** 8%

65. 91%   **66.** 2%   **67.** 25%   **68.** 16%

Quiz 3

Determine whether the equation has *two solutions*, *one solution*, or *no real solution*. *(Lesson 9.7)*

1. $x^2 - 15x + 56 = 0$ **2.** $x^2 + 8x + 16 = 0$ **3.** $x^2 - 3x + 4 = 0$

4. THROWING A BASEBALL Your friend is standing on a balcony that is 45 feet above the ground. You throw a baseball to her with an initial upward velocity of 50 feet per second. If you released the baseball 5 feet above the ground, did it reach your friend? Explain. *HINT:* Use a vertical motion model for an object that is thrown: $h = -16t^2 + vt + s$. *(Lesson 9.7)*

Match the inequality with its graph. *(Lesson 9.8)*

5. $y < -2x^2 + 4x - 2$ **6.** $y \le -2x^2 + 3x + 2$ **7.** $y \ge -2x^2 - 3x + 2$

A. 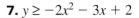   **B.**   **C.**

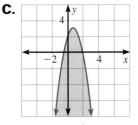

Sketch the graph of the inequality. *(Lesson 9.8)*

8. $y \ge 2x^2 + 5$ **9.** $y < x^2 + 3x$ **10.** $y > -x^2 - 2$

11. $y \le x^2 + 3x - 2$ **12.** $y > x^2 + 2x + 1$ **13.** $y \le -x^2 + 2x - 3$

Chapter Summary and Review

- **square root**, *p. 499*
- **positive square root**, *p. 499*
- **negative square root**, *p. 499*
- **radicand**, *p. 499*
- **perfect square**, *p. 500*
- **radical expression**, *p. 501*

- **quadratic equation**, *p. 505*
- **simplest form of a radical expression**, *p. 511*
- **quadratic function**, *p. 520*
- **parabola**, *p. 520*
- **vertex**, *p. 521*
- **axis of symmetry**, *p. 521*

- **roots of a quadratic equation**, *p. 527*
- **quadratic formula**, *p. 533*
- **discriminant**, *p. 540*
- **quadratic inequalities**, *p. 547*
- **graph of a quadratic inequality**, *p. 547*

9.1 SQUARE ROOTS

Examples on pp. 499–501

EXAMPLES Positive real numbers have a positive square root and a negative square root. The radical symbol $\sqrt{}$ indicates the positive square root of a positive number.

   a. $\sqrt{36} = 6$ 36 is a perfect square: $6^2 = 36$.

   b. $-\sqrt{81} = -9$ 81 is a perfect square: $9^2 = 81$, so $\sqrt{81} = 9$ and $-\sqrt{81} = -9$.

Evaluate the expression.

1. $-\sqrt{4}$ **2.** $\sqrt{144}$ **3.** $\sqrt{100}$ **4.** $-\sqrt{25}$

9.2 SOLVING QUADRATIC EQUATIONS BY FINDING SQUARE ROOTS

Examples on pp. 505–507

EXAMPLE To find the real solutions of a quadratic equation in the form $ax^2 + c = 0$, isolate x^2 on one side of the equation. Then find the square root(s) of each side.

$$2x^2 - 98 = 0 \qquad \text{Write original equation.}$$

$$2x^2 = 98 \qquad \text{Add 98 to each side.}$$

$$x^2 = 49 \qquad \text{Divide each side by 2.}$$

$$x = \pm\sqrt{49} \qquad \text{Find square roots.}$$

$$x = \pm 7 \qquad 7^2 = 49 \text{ and } (-7)^2 = 49$$

Solve the equation.

5. $x^2 = 144$ **6.** $8y^2 = 968$ **7.** $5y^2 - 80 = 0$ **8.** $3x^2 - 4 = 8$

9.3 SIMPLIFYING RADICALS

Examples on pp. 511–513

EXAMPLES You can use properties of radicals to simplify radical expressions.

a. $\sqrt{28} = \sqrt{4 \cdot 7}$ Factor using perfect square factor.

$\phantom{\sqrt{28}} = \sqrt{4} \cdot \sqrt{7}$ Use product property.

$\phantom{\sqrt{28}} = 2\sqrt{7}$ Remove perfect square factor from radicand.

b. $\sqrt{\dfrac{16}{3}} = \dfrac{\sqrt{16}}{\sqrt{3}}$ Use quotient property.

$\phantom{\sqrt{\dfrac{16}{3}}} = \dfrac{4}{\sqrt{3}}$ Remove perfect square factor from radicand.

$\phantom{\sqrt{\dfrac{16}{3}}} = \dfrac{4}{\sqrt{3}} \cdot \dfrac{\sqrt{3}}{\sqrt{3}}$ Multiply by a value of 1 : $\dfrac{\sqrt{3}}{\sqrt{3}} = 1$.

$\phantom{\sqrt{\dfrac{16}{3}}} = \dfrac{4\sqrt{3}}{3}$ Simplify.

Simplify the expression.

9. $\sqrt{45}$ **10.** $\sqrt{28}$ **11.** $\sqrt{\dfrac{36}{24}}$ **12.** $\sqrt{1\dfrac{1}{3}}$

9.4 GRAPHING QUADRATIC FUNCTIONS

Examples on pp. 520–522

EXAMPLE Sketch the graph of $y = x^2 - 4x - 3$. In this quadratic function, $a = 1$, $b = -4$, and $c = -3$.

❶ Find the x-coordinate of the vertex.

$$-\frac{b}{2a} = -\frac{-4}{2(1)} = 2$$

❷ Make a table of values, using x-values to the left and right of $x = 2$.

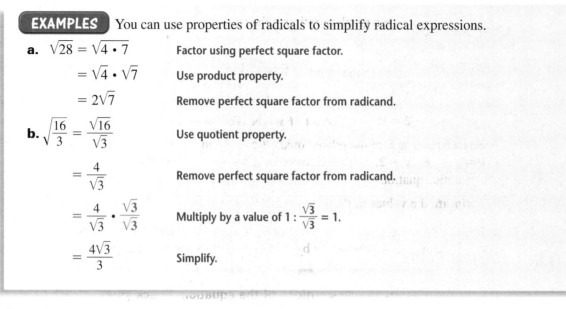

x	−1	0	1	2	3	4	5
y	2	−3	−6	−7	−6	−3	2

❸ Plot the points. The vertex is $(2, -7)$. Connect the points to form a parabola that opens up since a is positive. The axis of symmetry is the vertical line $x = 2$. The y-intercept is -3.

Sketch the graph of the function. Label the coordinates of the vertex.

13. $y = x^2 - 5x + 4$ **14.** $y = -x^2 + 2x - 1$ **15.** $y = 2x^2 - 3x - 2$

9.5 SOLVING QUADRATIC EQUATIONS BY GRAPHING

Examples on pp. 526–528

EXAMPLE Use a graph to estimate the solutions of $-x^2 + 3x = 2$.

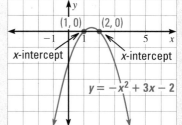

❶ **Write** the equation in the standard form $ax^2 + bx + c = 0$.

$-x^2 + 3x = 2$	Write original equation.
$-x^2 + 3x - 2 = 0$	Subtract 2 from each side.

❷ **Sketch** the graph of the related quadratic function $y = -x^2 + 3x - 2$. The x-intercepts of the graph are the solutions of the quadratic equation.

❸ **Estimate** the values of the x-intercepts.

ANSWER ▶ From the graph, the x-intercepts appear to be 1 and 2. Check your solutions algebraically by substituting each one in the original equation.

Use a graph to estimate the solutions of the equation. Check your solutions algebraically.

16. $x^2 - 3x = -2$ **17.** $-x^2 + 6x = 5$ **18.** $x^2 - 2x = 3$

9.6 SOLVING QUADRATIC EQUATIONS BY THE QUADRATIC FORMULA

Examples on pp. 533–535

EXAMPLE You can solve equations of the form $ax^2 + bx + c = 0$ by substituting the values of a, b, and c into the quadratic formula. Solve $x^2 + 6x - 16 = 0$.

Quadratic Formula: $x = \dfrac{-b \pm \sqrt{b^2 - 4ac}}{2a}$ when $a \neq 0$ and $b^2 - 4ac \geq 0$.

The equation $1x^2 + 6x - 16 = 0$ is in standard form. Identify $a = 1$, $b = 6$, and $c = -16$.

$$x = \frac{-6 \pm \sqrt{6^2 - 4(1)(-16)}}{2(1)}$$

$$x = \frac{-6 \pm \sqrt{36 + 64}}{2}$$

$$x = \frac{-6 \pm \sqrt{100}}{2}$$

$$x = \frac{-6 \pm 10}{2}$$

ANSWER ▶ The two solutions are $x = \dfrac{-6 + 10}{2} = 2$ and $x = \dfrac{-6 - 10}{2} = -8$.

Use the quadratic formula to solve the equation.

19. $3x^2 - 4x + 1 = 0$ **20.** $-2x^2 + x + 6 = 0$ **21.** $10x^2 - 11x + 3 = 0$

9.7 USING THE DISCRIMINANT

Examples on pp. 540–542

EXAMPLE You can use the discriminant, $b^2 - 4ac$, to find the number of solutions of a quadratic equation in the standard form $ax^2 + bx + c = 0$. A positive value indicates two solutions, zero indicates one solution, and a negative value indicates no real solution. The value of the discriminant can also be used to find the number of x-intercepts of the graph of $y = ax^2 + bx + c$.

EQUATION	DISCRIMINANT	NUMBER OF SOLUTIONS
$3x^2 - 6x + 2 = 0$	$(-6)^2 - 4(3)(2) = 12$	2
$2x^2 + 8x + 8 = 0$	$8^2 - 4(2)(8) = 0$	1
$x^2 + 7x + 15 = 0$	$7^2 - 4(1)(15) = -11$	0

Determine whether the equation has *two solutions, one solution,* or *no real solution.*

22. $3x^2 - 12x + 12 = 0$ **23.** $2x^2 + 10x + 6 = 0$ **24.** $-x^2 + 3x - 5 = 0$

Find the number of *x*-intercepts of the graph of the function.

25. $y = 2x^2 - 3x - 1$ **26.** $y = -x^2 - 3x + 3$ **27.** $y = x^2 + 2x + 1$

9.8 GRAPHING QUADRATIC INEQUALITIES

Examples on pp. 540–542

EXAMPLE Sketch the graph of $y < x^2 - 9$.

❶ ***Sketch*** the graph of $y = x^2 - 9$ that corresponds to $y < x^2 - 9$.

The x-coordinate of the vertex is $-\dfrac{b}{2a}$, or 0. Make a table of values, using x-values to the left and right of $x = 0$

x	-3	-2	-1	0	1	2	3
y	0	-5	-8	-9	-8	-5	0

❷ ***Plot*** the points and connect them with a smooth curve to form a parabola. Use a dashed line since the inequality contains the symbol $<$.

❸ ***Shade*** the region *below* the parabola because the inequality states that y is *less* than $x^2 - 9$.

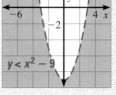

Sketch the graph of the inequality.

28. $y \le x^2 - 4$ **29.** $y \ge -x^2 - 2x + 3$ **30.** $y > 2x^2 - 4x - 6$

Evaluate the expression.

1. $\sqrt{64}$

2. $-\sqrt{25}$

3. $\pm\sqrt{169}$

4. $-\sqrt{100}$

Solve the equation or write *no real solution*.

5. $x^2 = 1$

6. $n^2 = 36$

7. $4y^2 = 16$

8. $8x^2 = 800$

9. $t^2 - 64 = 0$

10. $5x^2 + 125 = 0$

11. $2x^2 + 1 = 19$

12. $x^2 + 6 = -10$

Simplify the expression.

13. $\sqrt{150}$

14. $5\sqrt{\dfrac{4}{25}}$

15. $\sqrt{\dfrac{27}{45}}$

16. $\sqrt{\dfrac{9}{7}}$

Give the letter of the graph that matches the function.

17. $y = -x^2 - 2x + 3$

18. $y = -3x^2 - x + 2$

19. $y = 2x^2 + x - 3$

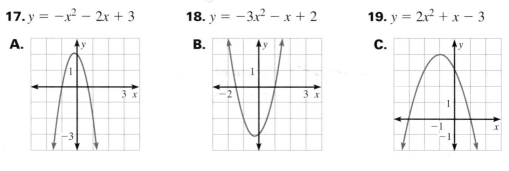

A.   **B.**   **C.**

Use a graph to estimate the solutions of the equation. Check your solutions algebraically.

20. $x^2 - 4 = 5$

21. $-x^2 + 7x - 10 = 0$

22. $-2x^2 + 4x + 6 = 0$

Use the quadratic formula to solve the equation.

23. $x^2 - 6x - 27 = 0$

24. $-x^2 + 3x + 10 = 0$

25. $3x^2 + 4x - 7 = 0$

Find the value of the discriminant. Then determine whether the equation has *two solutions*, *one solution*, or *no real solution*.

26. $-3x^2 + x - 2 = 0$

27. $x^2 - 4x + 4 = 0$

28. $5x^2 - 2x - 6 = 0$

Sketch the graph of the inequality.

29. $y < x^2 + 2x - 3$

30. $y \le -x^2 + 5x - 4$

31. $y \ge x^2 + 7x + 6$

VERTICAL MOTION In Exercises 32 and 33, suppose you are standing on a bridge over a creek, holding a stone 20 feet above the water.

32. You release the stone. How long will it take the stone to reach the water? Use a vertical motion model for an object that is dropped: $h = -16t^2 + s$.

33. You take another stone and toss it straight up with an initial velocity of 30 feet per second. How long will it take the stone to reach the water? Use a vertical motion model for an object that is thrown: $h = -16t^2 + vt + s$.

Chapter Standardized Test

 **Test Tip** If you are unsure of an answer, try to eliminate some of the choices so you can make an educated guess.

1. Which number is a perfect square?

  (A) -25 **(B)** $\sqrt{100}$

  (C) 55 **(D)** 100

2. Which one of the following is *not* a quadratic equation?

  (A) $x^2 - 4 = 0$ **(B)** $-9 + x^2 = 0$

  (C) $-7x + 12 = 0$ **(D)** $-2 + 9x + x^2 = 0$

3. Which value of t is a solution of $2t^2 - 21 = 51$?

  (A) -6 **(B)** -4

  (C) $\sqrt{15}$ **(D)** 4

4. What are the values of x when $3x^2 - 78 = 114$?

  (A) $\pm 2\sqrt{3}$ **(B)** ± 6

  (C) $\pm 4\sqrt{3}$ **(D)** ± 8

5. Which radical expression is in simplest form?

  (A) $\sqrt{\dfrac{8}{5}}$ **(B)** $\sqrt{\dfrac{5}{6}}$

  (C) $\dfrac{2}{\sqrt{3}}$ **(D)** $\sqrt{12}$

  (E) None of these

6. Find the area of the rectangle.

  (A) $4\sqrt{15}$

  (B) $12\sqrt{5}$

  (C) 60

  (D) 240

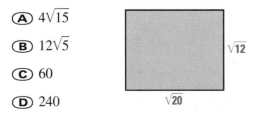

7. What is the x-coordinate of the vertex of the graph of $y = -2x^2 - x + 8$?

  (A) -1 **(B)** $-\dfrac{1}{4}$

  (C) $\dfrac{1}{4}$ **(D)** $\dfrac{1}{2}$

8. What are the x-intercepts of the graph of $y = -x^2 - 6x + 40$?

  (A) -10 and 4 **(B)** -4 and 10

  (C) 0 and 4 **(D)** 4 and 10

9. Which function has a y-intercept of 6?

  (A) $y = 6x^2 + 2$ **(B)** $y = 2x^2 + 6x$

  (C) $y = 2x^2 + 6$ **(D)** $y = 2x^2 - 6$

10. What is the value of the discriminant of the equation $5x^2 + 2x - 7 = 0$?

  (A) -136 **(B)** 2

  (C) 12 **(D)** 144

11. Which inequality is represented by the graph?

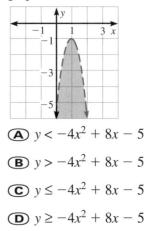

  (A) $y < -4x^2 + 8x - 5$

  (B) $y > -4x^2 + 8x - 5$

  (C) $y \le -4x^2 + 8x - 5$

  (D) $y \ge -4x^2 + 8x - 5$

Maintaining Skills

EXAMPLE 1 Use the Distributive Property

Use the distributive property to rewrite the expression without parentheses.

a. $6(14x + 9)$ **b.** $-3(5x - 2)$

Solution

a. $6(14x + 9) = 6(14x) + 6(9)$ Distribute 6 to each term of $(14x + 9)$.

$\qquad\qquad\quad\;\; = 84x + 54$ Multiply.

b. $-3(5x - 2) = -3(5x) - (-3)(2)$ Distribute -3 to each term of $(5x - 2)$.

$\qquad\qquad\quad\;\; = -15x + 6$ Multiply.

Try These

Use the distributive property to rewrite the expression without parentheses.

1. $8(2x - 12)$ **2.** $4(3x + 2)$ **3.** $-5(13 - m)$

4. $8(-5 + 6c)$ **5.** $10(8 + 3a)$ **6.** $-12(5 + 6t)$

EXAMPLE 2 Combine Like Terms

Simplify the expression.

a. $5x - 9y + 6x - 8y$ **b.** $6 + 3(x - 1)$

Solution

a. $5x - 9y + 6x - 8y = 5x + 6x - 9y - 8y$ Group like terms.

$\qquad\qquad\qquad\qquad\; = (5 + 6)x + (-9 - 8)y$ Use distributive property.

$\qquad\qquad\qquad\qquad\; = 11x - 17y$ Add coefficients.

b. $6 + 3(x - 1) = 6 + 3(x) - 3(1)$ Use distributive property.

$\qquad\qquad\qquad\; = 6 + 3x - 3$ Multiply.

$\qquad\qquad\qquad\; = 3x + 6 - 3$ Group like terms.

$\qquad\qquad\qquad\; = 3x + 3$ Combine like terms.

Student Help

▶ EXTRA EXAMPLES

More examples and practice exercises are available at www.mcdougallittell.com

Try These

Simplify the expression.

7. $8n - 2n + 18m + 3m$ **8.** $25c - 7d - 10d + 5c$

9. $4 + 2(x + 3)$ **10.** $2x + 4(2x - 5)$

Does the table represent a function? Explain. (Lesson 1.7)

1.

Input x	5	3	5	2
Output y	8	7	4	3

2.

Input x	3	6	9	12
Output y	5	8	5	8

Simplify the expression. (Lesson 2.8)

3. $\dfrac{27x - 54}{9}$
4. $\dfrac{66r + 39}{-3}$
5. $\dfrac{-72 + 16h}{-8}$
6. $\dfrac{-28 - 10t}{-2}$

7. PRETZELS You sell pretzels at a baseball game for $1.25 each. Write and solve an equation to find how many pretzels you need to sell to earn $60. (Lesson 3.2)

Solve the percent problem. (Lesson 3.9)

8. What number is 75% of 48?

9. 54 is 15% of what number?

10. 64 is what percent of 80?

11. 20 is what percent of 5?

Find the x-intercept and the y-intercept of the line. (Lesson 4.4)

12. $x + 2y = 8$
13. $x - 6y = -3$
14. $y = 12x - 2$

15. $y = -5x + 14$
16. $-2x - 7y = 20$
17. $-14x - y = 28$

Determine whether the graphs of the two equations are parallel lines. Explain your answer. (Lesson 4.7)

18. line a: $y = 2x + 3$
  line b: $y - 3x = 2$

19. line a: $y - 4x + 1 = 0$
  line b: $2y = 8x + 6$

20. line a: $2x - 5y = -30$
  line b: $-4x + 10y = -10$

Write in slope-intercept form the equation of the line that passes through the given points. (Lesson 5.3)

21. $(7, 3)$ and $(6, 4)$
22. $(2, 5)$ and $(11, 8)$
23. $(-4, 6)$ and $(3, -8)$

24. $(0, -12)$ and $(3, 3)$
25. $(5, 2)$ and $(-5, 7)$
26. $(5, -10)$ and $(8, 2)$

Write the equation in standard form with integer coefficients. (Lesson 5.4)

27. $3x - 5y + 6 = 0$
28. $6y = 2x + 4$
29. $-2x + 7y - 15 = 0$

30. $y = \dfrac{2}{3}x - 1$
31. $y = -\dfrac{1}{4}x + 6$
32. $y = \dfrac{4}{5}x + 5$

Solve the inequality. (Lessons 6.1–6.3)

33. $m + 5 \le -4$
34. $8 > c - 3$
35. $-5t \ge 40$

36. $\dfrac{2}{3}x < 9$
37. $-\dfrac{1}{2}y \le -7$
38. $-\dfrac{x}{5} \ge 2$

39. $5y + 6 > -14$
40. $4(a - 1) < 8$
41. $6 + 2k \le 3k - 1$

Solve the linear system. (Lessons 7.1–7.3)

42. $x + 4y = 0$
$ x = 12$

43. $x + y = 8$
$ 2x + y = 10$

44. $10x - 3y = -1$
$ -5x + 3y = 2$

45. $3x + y = -19$
$-32x + 4y = 144$

46. $-2x + 20y = 10$
$ x - 5y = -5$

47. $4x + 2y = 3$
$ 3x - 4y = 5$

48. VEGETABLES You buy 13 bell peppers to use in a vegetable platter. Green peppers cost $1.20 each and red peppers cost $1.50 each. If you spend a total of $18, how many of each kind are you buying? **(Lesson 7.4)**

Graph the system of linear inequalities. (Lesson 7.6)

49. $x \geq 0$
$ y \geq 0$
$ x < 5$
$ y < 2$

50. $ x > 2$
$ x - y \leq 2$
$ x + 2y \leq 6$

51. $3x + 5y \geq 15$
$ x - 2y < 10$
$ x > 1$

52. $-x + 4y \leq 8$
$ -4x + y \geq -4$
$ 2x + y \geq -4$

Simplify the expression. Use only positive exponents. (Lessons 8.1, 8.2, 8.4)

53. $x^3 \cdot x^6$

54. $(c^5)^4$

55. $(8t)^2$

56. $-3(-5)^2$

57. $3^2 \cdot 3^3$

58. $3x^5 y^{-3}$

59. $4^{-2} \cdot 4^0$

60. $\left(\dfrac{2}{3}\right)^{-4}$

61. $\dfrac{1}{4x^{-4} y^{-8}}$

62. $\dfrac{x^8}{x^3}$

63. $\dfrac{3x^2 y}{y^3} \cdot \dfrac{6xy^2}{2y}$

64. $\dfrac{2x^4}{y^{-3}} \cdot \left(\dfrac{x^3}{y^2}\right)^{-2}$

Perform the indicated operation without using a calculator. Write the result in scientific notation. (Lesson 8.5)

65. $(5 \times 10^{-2})(3 \times 10^4)$

66. $(6 \times 10^{-8})(7 \times 10^5)$

67. $(20 \times 10^6)(3 \times 10^3)$

68. $(7 \times 10^3)^{-3}$

69. $\dfrac{8.8 \times 10^{-1}}{1.1 \times 10^{-1}}$

70. $(2.8 \times 10^{-2})^3$

Simplify the radical expression. (Lesson 9.3)

71. $\sqrt{40}$

72. $\sqrt{52}$

73. $\sqrt{72}$

74. $\sqrt{96}$

75. $\dfrac{1}{4}\sqrt{84}$

76. $\sqrt{\dfrac{28}{36}}$

77. $3\sqrt{\dfrac{18}{9}}$

78. $\sqrt{\dfrac{12}{75}}$

79. $\dfrac{1}{\sqrt{10}}$

80. $-2\sqrt{\dfrac{1}{6}}$

81. $\sqrt{\dfrac{14}{21}}$

82. $\sqrt{\dfrac{1}{27}}$

Sketch the graph of the quadratic function or the quadratic inequality. (Lessons 9.4, 9.8)

83. $y = -3x^2 + 6x - 1$

84. $y \geq 5x^2 + 20x + 15$

85. $y < 2x^2 - 5x + 2$

SENDING UP FLARES In Exercises 86 and 87, a flare is fired straight up from ground level with an initial velocity of 100 feet per second. (Lesson 9.7)

86. How long will it take the flare to reach a height of 150 feet? Use the vertical motion model $h = -16t^2 + vt + s$.

87. Will the flare reach a height of 180 feet? Explain.

Designing a Stairway

Materials
• graph paper
• pencil
• ruler
• calculator

OBJECTIVE Compare step measurements to see how they affect stairway design.

INVESTIGATING THE DATA

The horizontal part of a step is the *tread*, and the vertical part is the *riser*. The table gives the tread and riser measurements of four different stairways.

Stairway	Tread (in.)	Riser (in.)
A	10	7
B	11	7
C	9	8
D	12	6

1. Use the measurements in the table to draw three steps for each Stairway A–D on a piece of graph paper.

2. Analyze your drawings. Which stairway is the steepest? Which stairway gives the most foot space on a step?

3. For each Stairway A–D, find the ratio of riser size to tread size $\left(\dfrac{\text{riser}}{\text{tread}}\right)$.

   Then write each ratio as a decimal rounded to the nearest tenth. What characteristic of a stairway do these ratios describe?

   > Two generally accepted rules for designing stairways are listed below.
   >
   > Rule 1: The sum of one tread and one riser is from 17 inches to 18 inches.
   >
   > Rule 2: The sum of one tread and two risers is from 24 inches to 25 inches.

4. You can use the following linear inequalities to represent Rule 1.

   $$t + r \geq 17 \text{ and } t + r \leq 18$$

   Write linear inequalities to represent Rule 2. Then use the inequalities to show that each Stairway A–D follows one of the rules.

5. Graph the system of four inequalities on the same coordinate plane. Use the horizontal axis for *t* and the vertical axis for *r*. Then use the values in the table to label the point (*t*, *r*) for each Stairway A–D. What does each solution of the system represent?

6. Name any other point *E* that is a solution of the system. Give tread and riser measurements for a Stairway E that the point represents.

PRESENTING YOUR RESULTS

Write a report about tread and riser measurements for stairways.

- Include a discussion of how various tread and riser measurements create stairways that are different.

- Compare Stairways A–E in terms of steepness and foot space. Use diagrams or numbers to support your comparison.

- Include your answers to Exercises 1–6.

- Explain how the two rules for designing stairways limit the possible measurements for treads and risers. Use the graph of the linear system to give the range of possible measurements for treads and the range of possible measurement for risers. *HINT:* You can use inequalities to represent these ranges.

- Give some examples of tread and riser measurements that do *not* follow one of the given rules for designing stairways. Explain how these measurements might create stairways that are hard to use or unsafe. Draw diagrams to support your explanation.

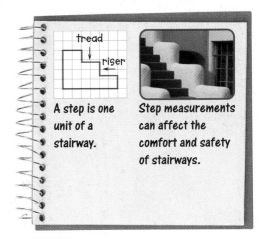

A step is one unit of a stairway.

Step measurements can affect the comfort and safety of stairways.

EXTENDING THE PROJECT

Design a stairway by determining its tread and riser measurements. Suppose the vertical distance from one floor to the next is 105 inches.

1. Decide on a riser measurement that will give you a whole number of steps on your stairway. *HINT:* You can choose fractional measurements for your treads and risers.

2. Decide on a tread measurement which, along with your riser measurement, follows one of the generally accepted rules for designing stairways.

3. Find the slope of your stairway.

4. On graph paper, make a scale drawing of your whole stairway. Number the steps.

CHAPTER 10

Polynomials and Factoring

▶ How wide and how deep are each of the dishes of the VLA radio telescope?

APPLICATION: Radio Telescopes

The Very Large Array (VLA) radio telescope in New Mexico is the most powerful radio telescope in the world. It consists of 27 mobile parabolic dishes that are combined electronically to provide images that would result from a single dish that is 22 miles (116,160 feet) across.

A cross section of one of the VLA dishes is shown below, where x and y are measured in feet. This cross section of a dish can be modeled by a polynomial equation.

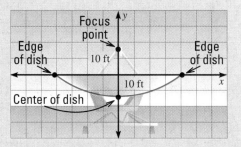

Think & Discuss

Use the graph above to answer the following questions.

1. Find the x-intercepts. How can you use this information to find the diameter of the dish?

2. Estimate the depth of the dish.

Learn More About It

You will use an algebraic model of the VLA radio telescope dishes in Exercises 46 and 47 on p. 592.

APPLICATION LINK More information about the VLA radio telescope is available at www.mcdougallittell.com

PREVIEW

What's the chapter about?

- Adding, subtracting, and multiplying **polynomials**
- **Factoring** polynomials
- Solving **quadratic** and **cubic equations** by factoring

KEY WORDS

- **monomial,** *p. 568*
- **degree of a monomial,** *p. 568*
- **polynomial,** *p. 569*
- **binomial,** *p. 569*
- **trinomial,** *p. 569*
- **standard form,** *p. 569*
- **degree of a polynomial,** *p. 569*

- **FOIL pattern,** *p. 576*
- **factored form,** *p. 588*
- **zero-product property,** *p. 588*
- **factor a trinomial,** *p. 595*
- **perfect square trinomial,** *p. 609*
- **prime polynomial,** *p. 617*
- **factor completely,** *p. 617*

PREPARE

Chapter Readiness Quiz

Take this quick quiz. If you are unsure of an answer, look back at the reference pages for help.

VOCABULARY CHECK *(refer to p. 100)*

1. Which equation uses the distributive property correctly?

   A $3x(x + 6) = 3x^2 + 6$ **B** $3x(x + 6) = 3x^2 + 18x$

   C $3x(x + 6) = x + 18x = 19x$ **D** $3x(x + 6) = 3x + 18x = 21x$

SKILL CHECK *(refer to pp. 444, 540)*

2. Simplify the expression $(x^6)^2$.

   A x^8 **B** x^4 **C** x^{12} **D** x^3

3. How many solutions does the equation $3x^2 - 4x + 6 = 0$ have?

   A Three solutions   **B** Two solutions

   C One solution   **D** No solution

STUDY TIP

Make Property Cards

Be sure to express the property in words and in symbols.

> Zero-product property
>
> If the product of two factors is zero, then at least one of the factors must be zero.
>
> If $ab = 0$, then $a = 0$ or $b = 0$.

Addition of Polynomials

For use with Lesson 10.1

GOAL
Use algebra tiles to model the addition of polynomials.

MATERIALS
• algebra tiles

Question

How can you model the addition of polynomials with algebra tiles?

Explore

Algebra tiles can be used to model polynomials.

1   −1

x $-x$

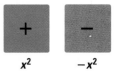

x^2 $-x^2$

Each of these 1-by-1 square tiles has an area of 1 square unit.

Each of these 1-by-x rectangular tiles has an area of x square units.

Each of these x-by-x square tiles has an area of x^2 square units.

1 You can use algebra tiles to add the polynomials $x^2 + 4x + 2$ and $2x^2 - 3x - 1$.

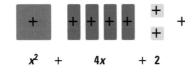

x^2 + $4x$ + 2 $2x^2$ − $3x$ − 1

2 To add the polynomials, combine like terms. Group the x^2-tiles, the x-tiles, and the 1-tiles.

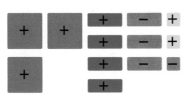

3 Rearrange the tiles to form zero pairs. Remove the zero pairs. The sum is $3x^2 + x + 1$.

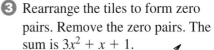
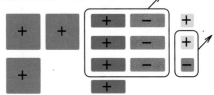

Student Help

▶ **LOOK BACK**
For help with zero pairs, see p. 77.

Think About It

In Exercises 1–6, use algebra tiles to find the sum. Sketch your solution.

1. $(-x^2 + x - 1) + (4x^2 + 2x - 3)$ **2.** $(3x^2 + 5x - 6) + (-2x^2 - 3x - 6)$

3. $(5x^2 - 3x + 4) + (-x^2 + 3x - 2)$ **4.** $(2x^2 - x - 1) + (-2x^2 + x + 1)$

5. $(2x^2 - x - 1) + (-2x^2 + x + 1)$ **6.** $(4x^2 + 5) + (4x^2 + 5x)$

7. Describe how to use algebra tiles to model *subtraction* of polynomials.

Use algebra tiles to find the difference. Sketch your solution.

8. $(x^2 + 3x + 4) - (x^2 + 3)$ **9.** $(x^2 - 2x + 5) - (3 - 2x)$

10.1 Adding and Subtracting Polynomials

Goal
Add and subtract polynomials.

Key Words
- monomial
- degree of a monomial in one variable
- polynomial
- binomial
- trinomial
- standard form
- degree of a polynomial in one variable

How large is the walkway around a pool?

In Example 5 you will use subtraction of polynomials to find the area of a walkway around a pool.

A **monomial in one variable** is a number, a variable, or a product of numbers and variables. The following expressions are monomials.

$$8 \qquad -2x \qquad 3x^2y \qquad \frac{1}{2}x^2$$

The expressions $\sqrt{x}$ and $\dfrac{1}{x}$ *are not* monomials.

The **degree of a monomial in one variable** is determined by the exponent of the variable. The degree of $3x^2$ is 2. The degree of $-6z^4$ is 4.

Student Help

▶ **READING ALGEBRA**
The monomial $-5x^4$ is read as "negative five times x to the fourth power." The coefficient is -5. • • • • • •

EXAMPLE 1 Find the Degree of a Monomial

State the degree of the monomial.

a. $-5x^4$ **b.** $\dfrac{1}{2}b^3$ **c.** 12

Solution

a. The exponent of x is 4.
ANSWER ▶ The degree of the monomial is 4.

b. The exponent of b is 3.
ANSWER ▶ The degree of the monomial is 3.

c. Recall $12 = 12x^0$, so the exponent is 0.
ANSWER ▶ The degree of the monomial is 0.

Checkpoint ✓ Find the Degree of a Monomial

State the degree of the monomial.

1. $6x^3$ **2.** $4p$ **3.** -10 **4.** $-3a^5$

Student Help

▶ MORE EXAMPLES

More examples are available at www.mcdougallittell.com

POLYNOMIALS A **polynomial** is a monomial or a sum of monomials. A polynomial such as $x^2 + (-4x) + (-5)$ is usually written as $x^2 - 4x - 5$. Each of the following expressions is a polynomial.

$$4x^3 \qquad x^3 - 8 \qquad 7x^2 - 4x + 6$$

A polynomial of *two* terms is a **binomial**. A polynomial of *three* terms is a **trinomial**. Polynomials are usually written in **standard form**, which means that the terms are arranged in decreasing order, from largest exponent to smallest exponent. The **degree of a polynomial in one variable** is the largest exponent of that variable.

EXAMPLE 2 Identify Polynomials

POLYNOMIAL	DEGREE	IDENTIFIED BY DEGREE	IDENTIFIED BY NUMBER OF TERMS
a. 6	0	constant	monomial
b. $3x + 1$	1	linear	binomial
c. $-x^2 + 2x - 5$	2	quadratic	trinomial
d. $4x^3 - 8x$	3	cubic	binomial

Checkpoint *Identify Polynomials*

Identify the polynomial by degree and by the number of terms.

5. $8x$ **6.** $10x - 5$ **7.** $x^2 - 4x + 4$ **8.** $-24 - x^3$

To add polynomials, you can use either a vertical format or a horizontal format, as shown in Example 3.

EXAMPLE 3 Add Polynomials

Find the sum. Write the answer in standard form.

a. $(5x^3 - 2x + x^2 + 7) + (3x^2 + 7 - 4x)$ **b.** $(2x^2 + x - 5) + (x + x^2 + 6)$

Solution

Student Help

▶ LOOK BACK
For help with combining like terms, see p. 108.

a. Vertical format: Write each expression in standard form. Line up like terms vertically.

$$\begin{array}{r} 5x^3 + x^2 - 2x + 7 \\ 3x^2 - 4x + 7 \\ \hline 5x^3 + 4x^2 - 6x + 14 \end{array}$$

b. Horizontal format: Group like terms.

$$(2x^2 + x - 5) + (x + x^2 + 6) = (2x^2 + x^2) + (x + x) + (-5 + 6)$$
$$= 3x^2 + 2x + 1$$

Checkpoint *Add Polynomials*

Find the sum. Write the answer in standard form.

9. $(x^2 + 3x + 2) + (2x^2 - 4x + 2)$ **10.** $(2x^2 - 4x + 3) + (x^2 - 4x - 4)$

EXAMPLE 4 Subtract Polynomials

Find the difference. Write the answer in standard form.

a. $(-2x^3 + 5x^2 - 4x + 8) - (-2x^3 + 3x - 4)$

b. $(3x^2 - 5x + 3) - (2x^2 - x - 4)$

Solution

a. Use a vertical format. To subtract one polynomial from another, you *add the opposite*. One way to do this is to multiply each term in the subtracted polynomial by -1 and line up like terms vertically. Then add.

$$(-2x^3 + 5x^2 - 4x + 8) \qquad\qquad -2x^3 + 5x^2 - 4x + 8$$
$$\underline{-(-2x^3 \qquad\quad + 3x - 4)} \text{ Add the opposite.} \quad + \underline{\quad 2x^3 \qquad\quad - 3x + 4}$$
$$\qquad\qquad\qquad\qquad\qquad\qquad\qquad\qquad\qquad\qquad\qquad\quad 5x^2 - 7x + 12$$

Student Help

▶ **STUDY TIP**
Remember to change signs correctly.

b. Use a horizontal format. Group like terms and simplify.

$$(3x^2 - 5x + 3) - (2x^2 - x - 4) = 3x^2 - 5x + 3 - 2x^2 + x + 4$$
$$= (3x^2 - 2x^2) + (-5x + x) + (3 + 4)$$
$$= x^2 - 4x + 7$$

EXAMPLE 5 Subtracting Polynomials

You are installing a swimming pool. Write a model for the area of the walkway.

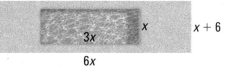

Solution

VERBAL MODEL			
$\boxed{\text{Area of walkway}}$	$=$	Total area	$-$ Area of pool

LABELS

Area of walkway $= A$ (square inches)

Total area $= (6x)(x + 6)$ (square inches)

Area of pool $= (3x)(x)$ (square inches)

ALGEBRAIC MODEL

$$A = (6x)(x + 6) - (3x)(x)$$
$$= 6x^2 + 36x - 3x^2$$
$$= 3x^2 + 36x$$

ANSWER ▶ A model for the area of the walkway is $A = 3x^2 + 36x$.

Checkpoint ✓ Subtract Polynomials

Find the difference. Write the answer in standard form.

11. $(2x^2 + 3x - 5) - (2x + 8 + x^2)$ **12.** $(4x^3 + 4x^2 - x - 2) - (3x^3 - 2x^2 + 1)$

Guided Practice

Vocabulary Check

1. Is $-4x^2 + 5x - 3x^3 + 6$ written in standard form? Explain.

2. Is $9x^2 + 8x - 4x^3 + 3$ a polynomial with a degree of 2? Explain.

Skill Check

Identify the polynomial by degree and by the number of terms.

3. $-9y + 5$

4. $6x^3$

5. $12x^2 + 7x$

6. $4w^3 - 8w + 9$

7. $7y + 2y^3 - y^2$

8. -15

ERROR ANALYSIS **In Exercises 9 and 10, find and correct the error.**

9.

$$7x^3 - 3x^2 + 5$$
$$+ 2x^3 - 5x - 7$$
$$\overline{9x^3 - 8x^2 - 2}$$

10.

$$(4x^2 - 9x) - (-8x^2 + 3x - 7)$$
$$= (4x^2 + 8x^2) + (-9x + 3x) - 7$$
$$= 12x^2 - 6x - 7$$

Find the sum or the difference of the polynomials.

11. $(2x - 9) + (x - 7)$

12. $(7x - 3) - (9x - 2)$

13. $(x^2 - 4x + 3) + (3x^2 - 3x - 5)$

14. $(3x^2 + 2x - 4) - (2x^2 + x - 1)$

Practice and Applications

LOGICAL REASONING **Complete the statement with *always*, *sometimes*, or *never*.**

15. The terms of a polynomial are __?__ monomials.

16. Like terms __?__ have the same coefficient and same variable part.

17. The sum of two trinomials is __?__ a trinomial.

18. A binomial is __?__ a polynomial of degree 2.

19. Subtraction is __?__ addition of the opposite.

FINDING THE DEGREE **State the degree of the monomial.**

20. $8n$

21. $12b^4$

22. $-c^3$

23. $-100w^4$

CLASSIFYING POLYNOMIALS **Write the polynomial in standard form. Then identify the polynomial by degree and by the number of terms.**

24. $2x$

25. $20m^3$

26. $7 - 3w$

27. -16

28. $8 + 5y^2 - 3y$

29. $-14 + 11y^3$

30. $-2x + 5x^3 - 6$

31. $-4b^2 + 7b^3$

32. $14w^2 + 9w^3$

33. $(12x^3 + x^2) - (18x^3 - 3x^2 + 6)$ **34.** $(a + 3a^2 + 2a^3) - (a^2 - a^3)$

35. $(2m - 8m^2 - 3) + (m^2 + 5m)$ **36.** $(8y^2 + 2) + (5 - 3y^2)$

37. $(3x^2 + 7x - 6) - (3x^2 + 7x)$ **38.** $(4x^2 - 7x + 2) + (-x^2 + x - 2)$

HORIZONTAL FORMAT Use a horizontal format to add or subtract.

39. $(x^2 - 7) + (2x^2 + 2)$ **40.** $(-3a^2 + 5) + (-a^2 + 4a - 6)$

41. $(z^3 + z^2 + 1) - z^2$ **42.** $12 - (y^3 + 10y + 16)$

43. $(3n^2 + 2n - 7) - (n^3 - n - 2)$ **44.** $(3a^3 - 4a^2 + 3) - (a^3 + 3a^2 - a - 4)$

POLYNOMIAL ADDITION AND SUBTRACTION Use a vertical format or a horizontal format to add or subtract.

45. $(9x^3 + 12x) + (16x^3 - 4x + 2)$ **46.** $(-2t^4 + 6t^2 + 5) - (-2t^4 + 5t^2 + 1)$

47. $(3x + 2x^2 - 4) - (x^2 + x - 6)$ **48.** $(u^3 - u) - (u^2 + 5)$

49. $(-7x^2 + 12) - (6 - 4x^2)$ **50.** $(10x^3 + 2x^2 - 11) + (9x^2 + 2x - 1)$

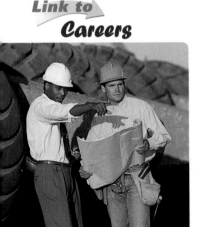

Link to
Careers

CONSTRUCTION
MANAGERS are responsible
for coordinating and
managing people, materials,
and equipment; budgets,
schedules, and contracts; and
the safety of employees and
the general public.

BUILDING A HOUSE In Exercises 51 and 52, use the following information.
You plan to build a house that is 1.5 times as long as it is wide. You want the land
around the house to be 20 feet wider than the width of the house, and twice as
long as the length of the house, as shown in the figure below.

51. Write an expression for the
area of the land surrounding
the house.

52. If $x = 30$ feet, what is the area
of the house? What is the area
of the entire property?

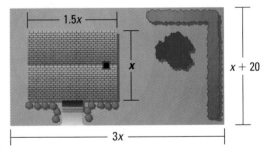

ENERGY USE In Exercises 53 and 54, use the following information. From
1989 through 1993, the amounts (in billions of dollars) spent on natural gas N
and electricity E by United States residents can be modeled by the following
equations, where t is the number of years since 1989.
▶ Source: U.S. Energy Information Administration

> **Gas spending model:** $N = 1.488t^2 - 3.403t + 65.590$
> **Electricity spending model:** $E = -0.107t^2 + 6.897t + 169.735$

53. Find a model for the total amount A (in billions of dollars) spent on natural
gas and electricity by United States residents from 1989 through 1993.

54. **CRITICAL THINKING** According to the models, will more money be spent
on natural gas or on electricity in 2020. *HINT:* It may be helpful to graph the
equations on a graphing calculator to answer this question.

55. MULTIPLE CHOICE Which of the following polynomials is *not* written in standard form?

(A) $8n^2 - 16n + 144$ (B) $3y^3 - y^2 - 15 + 4y$

(C) $3w^4 + 4w^2 - w - 9$ (D) $3p^4 - 6p^3 + 2p + 16$

56. MULTIPLE CHOICE What is the degree of $-6x^4$?

(F) 4   (G) -6 (H) -4 (J) 6

57. MULTIPLE CHOICE Which of the following is classified as a monomial?

(A) $x + 1$ (B) $5 - y^2$ (C) $a^3 - a - 1$ (D) $2y$

Mixed Review

DISTRIBUTIVE PROPERTY Simplify the expression. *(Lesson 2.6)*

58. $-3(x + 1) - 2$ **59.** $(2x - 1)(2) + x$

60. $11x + 3(8 - x)$ **61.** $(5x - 1)(-3) + 6$

62. $-4(1 - x) + 7$ **63.** $-12x - 5(11 - x)$

64. GAS MILEAGE The table below shows mileage and gasoline used for 6 months. For each of these months, find the mileage rate in miles per gallon. Round to the nearest tenth. *(Lesson 3.8)*

Mileage (miles)	295	320	340	280	310	355
Gas Used (gallons)	12.3	13.3	14.2	11.6	12.9	14.8

EXPONENTIAL EXPRESSIONS In Exercises 65–70, simplify. Then use a calculator to evaluate the expression. *(Lesson 8.1)*

65. $2^2 \cdot 2^3$ **66.** $(3^2 \cdot 1^3)^2$ **67.** $[(-1)^8 \cdot 2^4]^2$

68. $(-1 \cdot 3^2)^3$ **69.** $(2^2 \cdot 2^2)^2$ **70.** $(3^2 \cdot 2^3)^3$

71. ALABAMA The population P of Alabama (in thousands) for 1995 projected through 2025 can be modeled by $P = 4227(1.0104)^t$, where t is the number of years since 1995. Find the ratio of the population in 2025 to the population in 2000. Compare this ratio with the ratio of the population in 2000 to the population in 1995. *(Lesson 8.6)* ▶ Source: U.S. Bureau of the Census

Maintaining Skills

ADDING FRACTIONS Add. Write the answer as a mixed number in lowest terms. *(Skills Review p. 764)*

72. $\frac{12}{11} + 1\frac{3}{11}$ **73.** $\frac{2}{5} + 3\frac{3}{5}$ **74.** $1\frac{2}{3} + \frac{1}{6}$ **75.** $\frac{1}{8} + 1\frac{1}{2}$

76. $\frac{11}{3} + 5\frac{5}{6}$ **77.** $2\frac{3}{4} + \frac{19}{20}$ **78.** $5\frac{1}{2} + 4\frac{5}{16}$ **79.** $9\frac{2}{7} + 3\frac{11}{28}$

80. $2\frac{1}{2} + \frac{4}{3}$ **81.** $2\frac{1}{2} + \frac{5}{7}$ **82.** $12\frac{7}{12} + 8\frac{9}{32}$ **83.** $9\frac{7}{24} + 6\frac{5}{36}$

DEVELOPING CONCEPTS
Multiplying Polynomials

For use with Lesson 10.2

GOAL

Multiply two polynomials using the distributive property.

MATERIALS

• paper
• pencil

Question

How can you multiply two polynomials using the distributive property?

The arithmetic operations for polynomials are very much like the corresponding operations for integers. For example, you can multiply $(x + 3)(2x + 1)$ by using the distributive property.

$$
\begin{array}{r}
2x + 1 \\
\times \quad x + 3 \\
\hline
6x + 3 \\
2x^2 + \ x \\
\hline
2x^2 + 7x + 3
\end{array}
$$

← Multiply $2x + 1$ by 3.
← Multiply $2x + 1$ by x.

So $(x + 3)(2x + 1) = 2x^2 + 7x + 3$.

Explore

1 To multiply $(3x + 2)(x + 4)$, write the multiplication vertically.

$$
\begin{array}{r}
3x + 2 \\
\times \quad x + 4 \\
\hline
? + ? \\
? + ? \\
\hline
? + ? + ?
\end{array}
$$

2 Multiply $4 \times (3x + 2)$.

3 Multiply $x \times (3x + 2)$.

4 Add the terms by using a vertical format. Align like terms. Then add.

Try These

In Exercises 1–10, multiply the polynomials using the method shown above.

1. $(x + 3)(x + 7)$

2. $(2x + 5)(3x + 4)$

3. $(x - 5)(x + 7)$

4. $(4x + 1)(5x + 2)$

5. $(3x - 1)(5x - 2)$

6. $(3x + 7)(2x + 9)$

7. $(x + 4)(x^2 + 2x + 3)$

8. $(x - 2)(x^2 - 4x + 6)$

9. $(3x + 1)(x^2 + 3x + 5)$

10. $(4x - 1)(x^2 + 5x - 7)$

11. Explain how you can use the distributive property to multiply $(3x + 2)(x + 4)$ *horizontally*.
HINT: Use $(3x + 2)(x + 4) = (3x + 2)x + (3x + 2)4$ to do so.

Multiplying Polynomials

Goal
Multiply polynomials.

Key Words
• FOIL pattern

What is the total area of a window?

First degree polynomials are often used to represent length and width. In Example 5 you will multiply two polynomials to find the area of a window.

In Lesson 2.6 you learned how to multiply a polynomial by a monomial by using the distributive property.

$$3(2x - 3) = (3)(2x) - (3)(3) = 6x - 9$$

In this lesson you will learn how to multiply two binomials by using the distributive property twice to multiply $(x + 4)(x + 5)$.

First distribute the binomial $(x + 5)$ to each term of $(x + 4)$.

$$(x + 4)(x + 5) = x(x + 5) + 4(x + 5)$$

Then distribute the x and the 4 to each term of $(x + 5)$.

$$= x(x) + x(5) + 4(x) + 4(5)$$
$$= x^2 + 5x + 4x + 20 \qquad \text{Multiply.}$$
$$= x^2 + 9x + 20 \qquad \text{Combine like terms.}$$

EXAMPLE 1 Use the Distributive Property

Find the product $(x + 2)(x - 3)$.

Solution

$$(x + 2)(x - 3)$$
$$x(x - 3) + 2(x - 3) \qquad \text{Distribute } (x - 3) \text{ to each term of } (x + 2).$$
$$x(x) + x(-3) + 2(x) + 2(-3) \qquad \text{Distribute } x \text{ and 2 to each term of } (x - 3).$$
$$x^2 - 3x + 2x - 6 \qquad \text{Multiply.}$$
$$x^2 - x - 6 \qquad \text{Combine like terms.}$$

Student Help

▶ LOOK BACK
For help with the distributive property, see p. 101.

Checkpoint ✓ Use the Distributive Property

Use the distributive property to find the product.

1. $(x + 1)(x + 2)$ **2.** $(x - 2)(x + 4)$ **3.** $(2x + 1)(x + 2)$

FOIL PATTERN In using the distributive property for multiplying two binomials, you may have noticed the following pattern. Multiply the **F**irst, **O**uter, **I**nner, and **L**ast terms. Then combine like terms. This pattern is called the **FOIL pattern**.

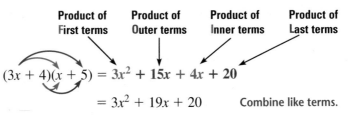

Product of First terms   Product of Outer terms   Product of Inner terms   Product of Last terms

$$(3x + 4)(x + 5) = 3x^2 + 15x + 4x + 20$$
$$= 3x^2 + 19x + 20 \qquad \text{Combine like terms.}$$

EXAMPLE 2 Multiply Binomials Using the FOIL Pattern

$$\begin{array}{cccc} F & O & I & L \\ \downarrow & \downarrow & \downarrow & \downarrow \end{array}$$

$$(2x + 3)(2x + 1) = 4x^2 + 2x + 6x + 3$$
$$= 4x^2 + 8x + 3 \qquad \text{Combine like terms.}$$

Checkpoint✓ Multiply Binomials Using the FOIL Pattern

Use the FOIL pattern to find the product.

4. $(x + 1)(x - 4)$ **5.** $(2x - 3)(x - 1)$ **6.** $(x - 2)(2x + 1)$

To multiply two polynomials that have three or more terms, remember that *each term of one polynomial must be multiplied by each term of the other polynomial.* Use a vertical or a horizontal format. Write each polynomial in standard form.

EXAMPLE 3 Multiply Polynomials Vertically

Find the product $(x - 2)(5 + 3x - x^2)$.

Solution

Line up like terms vertically. Then multiply as shown below.

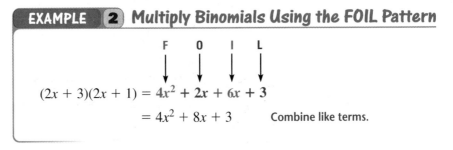

$$\begin{array}{r} -x^2 + 3x + 5 \qquad \text{Standard form} \\ \times \qquad\qquad x - 2 \qquad \text{Standard form} \\ \hline 2x^2 - 6x - 10 \quad \longleftarrow \quad -2(-x^2 + 3x + 5) \\ -x^3 + 3x^2 + 5x \qquad \longleftarrow \quad x(-x^2 + 3x + 5) \\ \hline -x^3 + 5x^2 - x - 10 \qquad \text{Combine like terms.} \end{array}$$

Checkpoint✓ Multiply Polynomials Vertically

Use a vertical format to find the product.

7. $(x + 1)(x^2 + 3x - 2)$ **8.** $(2x - 1)(2x^2 + x - 3)$ **9.** $(2x - 3)(3x^2 + x - 4)$

EXAMPLE 4 Multiply Polynomials Horizontally

Find the product $(4x^2 - 3x - 1)(2x - 5)$.

Solution Multiply $2x - 5$ by each term of $4x^2 - 3x - 1$.

$(4x^2 - 3x - 1)(2x - 5)$

$4x^2(2x - 5) - 3x(2x - 5) - 1(2x - 5)$	Use distributive property.
$8x^3 - 20x^2 - 6x^2 + 15x - 2x + 5$	Use distributive property.
$8x^3 + (-20x^2 - 6x^2) + (15x - 2x) + 5$	Group like terms.
$8x^3 - 26x^2 + 13x + 5$	Combine like terms.

EXAMPLE 5 Multiply Binomials to Find an Area

The glass has a height-to-width ratio of $3 : 2$. The frame adds 6 inches to the width and 10 inches to the height. Write a polynomial expression that represents the total area of the window, including the frame.

Solution

The window has a total height of $3x + 10$ and a total width of $2x + 6$. The area of the window is represented by the product of the height and width.

$A = \text{height} \cdot \text{width}$	Write area model for a rectangle.
$A = (3x + 10)(2x + 6)$	Substitute $(3x + 10)$ for height and $(2x + 6)$ for width.
$\quad = 6x^2 + 18x + 20x + 60$	Use FOIL pattern.
$\quad = 6x^2 + 38x + 60$	Combine like terms.

ANSWER The area of the window can be represented by the model $A = 6x^2 + 38x + 60$.

Checkpoint ✓ **Multiply Polynomials**

In Exercises 10–12, use a horizontal format to find the product.

10. $(x - 4)(x^2 + x + 1)$ **11.** $(x + 5)(x^2 - x - 3)$ **12.** $(2x + 1)(3x^2 + x - 1)$

13. Suppose the height-to-width ratio of the glass portion of the window in Example 5 above were $5 : 3$. Write a model to represent the total area.

Guided Practice

Vocabulary Check

1. How do the letters in "FOIL" help you remember how to multiply two binomials?

2. Give an example of a monomial, a binomial, and a trinomial.

Skill Check

Copy the equation and fill in the blanks.

3. $(x - 2)(x + 3) = x(\underline{?}) + (-2)(\underline{?})$ **4.** $(3x + 4)(2x - 1) = 3x(\underline{?}) + 4(\underline{?})$

5. $(x - 3)(x + 1) = x^2 - 2x - \underline{?}$ **6.** $(x + 2)(x + 6) = x^2 + \underline{?} + 12$

7. $(x - 4)(x - 5) = x^2 - 9x + \underline{?}$ **8.** $(x + 2)(2x + 1) = \underline{?} + 5x + 2$

Use the distributive property to find the product.

9. $(4x + 7)(-2x)$ **10.** $2x(x^2 + x - 5)$ **11.** $-4x^2(3x^2 + 2x - 6)$

12. $(a + 4)(a + 5)$ **13.** $(y - 2)(y + 8)$ **14.** $(2x + 3)(4x + 1)$

Use the FOIL pattern to find the product.

15. $(w - 3)(w + 5)$ **16.** $(x + 6)(x + 9)$ **17.** $(x - 4)(8x + 3)$

18. $(x - 3)(x + 4)$ **19.** $(x + 8)(x - 7)$ **20.** $(3x - 4)(2x - 1)$

Practice and Applications

MULTIPLYING EXPRESSIONS   **Find the product.**

21. $(2x - 5)(-4x)$ **22.** $3t^2(7t - t^3 - 3)$ **23.** $2x(x^2 - 8x + 1)$

24. $(-y)(6y^2 + 5y)$ **25.** $4w^2(3w^3 - 2w^2 - w)$ **26.** $-b^2(6b^3 - 16b + 11)$

DISTRIBUTIVE PROPERTY   **Use the distributive property to find the product.**

27. $(t + 8)(t + 5)$ **28.** $(x + 6)(x - 2)$ **29.** $(d - 5)(d + 3)$

30. $(a + 8)(a - 3)$ **31.** $(y + 2)(2y + 1)$ **32.** $(m - 2)(4m + 3)$

33. $(3s - 1)(s + 2)$ **34.** $(2d + 3)(3d + 1)$ **35.** $(4y - 7)(2y - 1)$

Student Help

▶**HOMEWORK HELP**
Example 1: Exs. 21–35
Example 2: Exs. 36–47
Example 3: Exs. 48–51
Example 4: Exs. 52–55
Example 5: Exs. 56–60

USING THE FOIL PATTERN   **Use the FOIL pattern to find the product.**

36. $(a + 6)(a + 7)$ **37.** $(y + 5)(y - 8)$ **38.** $(x + 6)(x - 6)$

39. $(2w - 5)(w + 5)$ **40.** $(4b - 1)(b - 6)$ **41.** $(x - 9)(2x + 15)$

42. $(3a - 1)(a - 9)$ **43.** $(2z + 7)(3z + 2)$ **44.** $(4q - 1)(3q + 8)$

45. $(5t - 3)(2t + 3)$ **46.** $(4x + 5)(4x - 3)$ **47.** $(9w - 5)(7w - 12)$

MULTIPLYING EXPRESSIONS Use a vertical format to find the product.

48. $(x + 2)(x^2 + 3x + 5)$

49. $(d - 5)(d^2 - 2d - 6)$

50. $(a - 3)(a^2 - 4a - 6)$

51. $(2x + 3)(3x^2 - 4x + 2)$

MULTIPLYING EXPRESSIONS Use a horizontal format to find the product.

52. $(x + 4)(x^2 - 2x + 3)$

53. $(a - 2)(a^2 + 6a - 7)$

54. $(m^2 + 2m - 9)(m - 4)$

55. $(4y^2 - 3y - 2)(y + 12)$

Link to
Careers

PICTURE FRAMERS use math when deciding on the dimensions of the frame, the matting, and the glass.

56. PICTURE FRAME The diagram at the right shows the dimensions of a picture frame. The glass has a height-to-width ratio of 2 : 3. The frame adds 4 inches to the width and 4 inches to the height. Write a polynomial expression that represents the total area of the picture, including the frame.

FOOTBALL In Exercises 57 and 58, a football field's dimensions are represented by a width of $(3x + 10)$ feet and a length of $(7x + 10)$ feet.

57. Find an expression for the area A of the football field. Give your answer as a quadratic trinomial.

58. An actual football field is 160 feet wide and 360 feet long. For what value of x do the expressions $3x + 10$ and $7x + 10$ give these dimensions?

VIDEOCASSETTES In Exercises 59 and 60, use the following information about videocassette sales from 1987 to 1996, where t is the number of years since 1987. The number of blank videocassettes B sold annually in the United States can be modeled by $B = 15t + 281$, where B is measured in millions. The wholesale price P for a videocassette can be modeled by $P = -0.21t + 3.52$, where P is measured in dollars.

▶ Source: EIA Market Research Department

Student Help

▶**HOMEWORK HELP**

Help with problem solving in Exs. 59 and 60 is available at www.mcdougallittell.com

59. Find a model for the revenue from sales of blank videocassettes. Give the model as a quadratic trinomial.

60. What conclusions can you make from your model about the revenue over time?

61. LOGICAL REASONING Find the product $(2x + 1)(x + 3)$ using the distributive property and explain how this leads to the FOIL pattern.

62. MULTIPLE CHOICE Find the product $2a^2(a^2 - 3a + 1)$.

  (A) $2a^2 - 6a + 2$ (B) $2a^4 - 6a^3 + 2a$

  (C) $2a^2 - 3a^3 + 2a^2$ (D) $2a^4 - 6a^3 + 2a^2$

63. MULTIPLE CHOICE Find the product $(x + 9)(x - 2)$.

  (F) $x^2 + 7x - 18$ (G) $x^2 - 11x - 18$

  (H) $x^2 - 18$ (J) $x^2 - 7x$

64. MULTIPLE CHOICE Find the product $(x - 1)(2x^2 + x + 1)$.

  (A) $2x^3 - 3x^2 - 1$ (B) $2x^3 - x^2 - 2x - 1$

  (C) $2x^3 - x^2 - 1$ (D) $2x^3 + 3x^2 + 2x + 1$

Mixed Review

SIMPLIFYING EXPRESSIONS **Simplify the expression. Write your answer as a power.** *(Lesson 8.1)*

65. $(7x)^2$ **66.** $\left(\frac{1}{3}m\right)^2$ **67.** $\left(\frac{2}{5}y\right)^2$ **68.** $(0.5w)^2$

69. $9^3 \cdot 9^5$ **70.** $(4^2)^4$ **71.** $b^2 \cdot b^5$ **72.** $(4c^2)^4$

73. $(2t)^4 \cdot 3^3$ **74.** $(-w^4)^3$ **75.** $(-3xy)^3(2y)^2$ **76.** $(8x^2y^8)^3$

USING THE DISCRIMINANT **Tell whether the equation has *two solutions*, *one solution*, or *no real solution*.** *(Lesson 9.7)*

77. $x^2 - 5x + 6 = 0$ **78** $x^2 + 7x + 12 = 0$ **79.** $x^2 - 2x - 24 = 0$

80. $2x^2 - 3x - 1 = 0$ **81.** $4x^2 + 4x + 1 = 0$ **82.** $3x^2 - 7x + 5 = 0$

83. $7x^2 - 8x - 6 = 0$ **84.** $10x^2 - 13x - 9 = 0$ **85.** $6x^2 - 12x - 6 = 0$

SKETCHING GRAPHS **In Exercises 86–88, sketch the graph of the inequality.** *(Lesson 9.8)*

86. $y \geq 4x^2 - 7x$ **87.** $y < x^2 - 3x - 10$ **88.** $y > -2x^2 + 4x + 16$

89. ASTRONOMY The distance from the sun to Earth is approximately 1.5×10^8 km. The distance from the sun to the planet Neptune is approximately 4.5×10^9 km. What is the ratio of Earth's distance from the sun to Neptune's distance from the sun? *(Lesson 8.4)*

Maintaining Skills

DIVIDING FRACTIONS **Divide. Write the answer in lowest terms.** *(Skills Review p. 765)*

90. $\frac{1}{6} \div \frac{2}{3}$ **91.** $\frac{3}{4} \div \frac{9}{24}$ **92.** $\frac{7}{8} \div \frac{5}{2}$

93. $\frac{3}{4} \div \frac{2}{9}$ **94.** $\frac{13}{15} \div \frac{7}{10}$ **95.** $\frac{29}{32} \div \frac{23}{24}$

96. $\frac{11}{16} \div \frac{11}{12}$ **97.** $1\frac{1}{2} \div \frac{3}{4}$ **98.** $2\frac{1}{3} \div \frac{7}{27}$

Special Products of Polynomials

Goal

Use special product patterns to multiply polynomials.

Key Words

- special product
- area model

What color will the offspring of two tigers be?

In Checkpoint Exercise 14 you will use the square of a binomial pattern to determine the possible coat colors of the offspring of two tigers.

Some pairs of binomials have *special products*. If you learn to recognize such pairs, finding the product of two binomials will sometimes be quicker and easier.

For example, to find the product of $(y + 3)(y - 3)$, you could multiply the two binomials using the FOIL pattern.

$$(y + 3)(y - 3) = y^2 + (-3y) + 3y - 9 \qquad \text{Use FOIL pattern.}$$
$$= y^2 - 9 \qquad \text{Combine like terms.}$$

Notice that the middle term is zero. This suggests a simple pattern for finding the product of the sum and difference of two terms:

$$(a + b)(a - b) = a^2 - b^2$$

Also, to find the product of $(x + 4)^2$, you could multiply $(x + 4)(x + 4)$.

$$(x + 4)(x + 4) = x^2 + 4x + 4x + 16 \qquad \text{Use FOIL pattern.}$$
$$= x^2 + 8x + 16 \qquad \text{Combine like terms.}$$

Notice that the middle term is twice the product of the terms of the binomial. This suggests a simple pattern for finding the product of the square of a binomial:

$$(a + b)^2 = a^2 + 2ab + b^2 \qquad or \qquad (a - b)^2 = a^2 - 2ab + b^2$$

SPECIAL PRODUCT PATTERNS

Sum and Difference Pattern

$(a + b)(a - b) = a^2 - b^2$ **Example:** $(3x - 4)(3x + 4) = 9x^2 - 16$

Square of a Binomial Pattern

$(a + b)^2 = a^2 + 2ab + b^2$ **Example:** $(x + 5)^2 = x^2 + 10x + 25$

$(a - b)^2 = a^2 - 2ab + b^2$ **Example:** $(2x - 3)^2 = 4x^2 - 12x + 9$

EXAMPLE 1 Use the Sum and Difference Pattern

Find the product $(5t - 2)(5t + 2)$.

Solution

$$(a - b)(a + b) = a^2 - b^2 \qquad \text{Write pattern.}$$

$$(5t - 2)(5t + 2) = (5t)^2 - 2^2 \qquad \text{Apply pattern.}$$

$$= 25t^2 - 4 \qquad \text{Simplify.}$$

CHECK ✓ You can use the FOIL pattern to check your answer.

$$(5t - 2)(5t + 2) = (5t)(5t) + (5t)(2) + (-2)(5t) + (-2)(2) \qquad \text{Use FOIL.}$$

$$= 25t^2 + 10t + (-10t) + (-4) \qquad \text{Simplify.}$$

$$= 25t^2 - 4 \qquad \text{Combine like terms.}$$

Checkpoint ✓ Use the Sum and Difference Pattern

Use the sum and difference pattern to find the product.

1. $(x + 2)(x - 2)$ **2.** $(n - 3)(n + 3)$ **3.** $(p + 8)(p - 8)$

4. $(2x - 1)(2x + 1)$ **5.** $(3x + 2)(3x - 2)$ **6.** $(2x + 5)(2x - 5)$

EXAMPLE 2 Use the Square of a Binomial Pattern

Find the product.

a. $(3n + 4)^2$ **b.** $(2x - 7y)^2$

Solution

a. $(a + b)^2 = a^2 + 2ab + b^2 \qquad \text{Write pattern.}$

$(3n + 4)^2 = (3n)^2 + 2(3n)(4) + 4^2 \qquad \text{Apply pattern.}$

$= 9n^2 + 24n + 16 \qquad \text{Simplify.}$

b. $(a - b)^2 = a^2 - 2ab + b^2 \qquad \text{Write pattern.}$

$(2x - 7y)^2 = (2x)^2 - 2(2x)(7y) + (7y)^2 \qquad \text{Apply pattern.}$

$= 4x^2 - 28xy + 49y^2 \qquad \text{Simplify.}$

Checkpoint ✓ Use the Square of a Binomial Pattern

Use the square of a binomial pattern to find the product.

7. $(x + 1)^2$ **8.** $(t - 3)^2$ **9.** $(a - 7)^2$

10. $(2x + 1)^2$ **11.** $(4x - 1)^2$ **12.** $(3a - 4)^2$

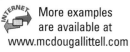
AREA MODELS Area models may be helpful when multiplying two binomials or using any of the special patterns.

The square of a binomial pattern $(a + b)^2 = a^2 + 2ab + b^2$ can be modeled as shown below.

The area of the large square is $(a + b)^2$, which is equal to the sum of the areas of the two small squares and two rectangles. Note that the two rectangles with area ab produce the middle term $2ab$.

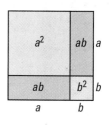

EXAMPLE 3 **Find the Area of a Figure**

GEOMETRY LINK Write an expression for the area of the blue region.

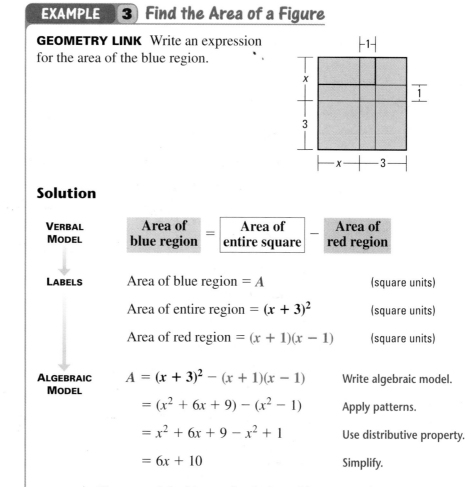

Solution

VERBAL MODEL	**Area of blue region**	=	**Area of entire square**	−	**Area of red region**

LABELS

Area of blue region = A (square units)

Area of entire region = $(x + 3)^2$ (square units)

Area of red region = $(x + 1)(x - 1)$ (square units)

ALGEBRAIC MODEL

$A = (x + 3)^2 - (x + 1)(x - 1)$ Write algebraic model.

$= (x^2 + 6x + 9) - (x^2 - 1)$ Apply patterns.

$= x^2 + 6x + 9 - x^2 + 1$ Use distributive property.

$= 6x + 10$ Simplify.

ANSWER ▶ The area of the blue region is $6x + 10$ square units.

Checkpoint ✓ **Find the Area of a Figure**

13. Write an expression for the area of the figure at the right. Name the special product pattern that is represented.

PUNNETT SQUARES are used in genetics to model the possible combinations of parents' genes in offspring.

EXAMPLE 4 **Use a Punnett Square**

PUNNETT SQUARES The Punnett square at the right shows the possible results of crossing two pink snapdragons, each with one red gene R and one white gene W. Each parent snapdragon passes along only one gene for color to its offspring. Show how the square of a binomial can be used to model the Punnett square.

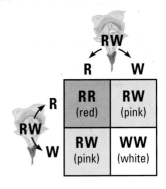

Solution

Each parent snapdragon has half red genes and half white genes. You can model the genetic makeup of each parent as follows:

$$0.5R + 0.5W$$

The genetic makeup of the offspring can be modeled by the product

$$(0.5R + 0.5W)^2$$

Expand the product to find the possible colors of the offspring.

$$(a + b)^2 = a^2 + 2ab + b^2$$ Write pattern.

$$(0.5R + 0.5W)^2 = (0.5R)^2 + 2(0.5R)(0.5W) + (0.5W)^2$$ Apply pattern.

$$= 0.25R^2 + 0.5RW + 0.25W^2$$ Simplify.

Red   Pink   White

ANSWER ▶ Given a sufficiently large number of offspring, 25% will be red, 50% will be pink, and 25% will be white.

Checkpoint ✓ *Use a Punnett Square*

14. SCIENCE LINK In tigers, the normal color gene *C* is dominant and the gene for white coat color *c* is recessive. This means that a tiger whose color genes are *CC* or *Cc* will have normal coloring. A tiger whose color genes are *cc* will be white. *Note:* The recessive gene *c* that results in a white tiger is extremely rare.

a. The Punnett square at the right shows the possible results of crossing two tigers, each with one dominant gene *C* and one recessive gene *c*. Find a model that can be used to represent the Punnett square. Write the model as a polynomial.

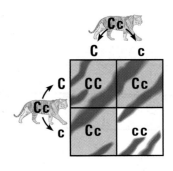

b. What percent of the offspring are likely to have normal coloring? What percent are likely to be white?

Guided Practice

Vocabulary Check

1. What is the sum and difference pattern for the product of two binomials?

2. Complete: $(x + 3)^2 = x^2 + 6x + 9$ is an example of the __?__ pattern.

Skill Check

Use a special product pattern to find the product.

3. $(x - 6)^2$ **4.** $(w + 11)(w - 11)$ **5.** $(6 + p)^2$

6. $(3y - 1)^2$ **7.** $(t - 6)(t + 6)$ **8.** $(a - 2)(a + 2)$

LOGICAL REASONING Complete the statement with *always*, *sometimes*, or *never*.

9. A trinomial is __?__ factorable.

10. If a binomial is multiplied times itself, the result is __?__ a perfect square trinomial.

11. In a perfect square trinomial, the first and last terms are __?__ perfect squares.

12. A polynomial containing four terms can __?__ be factored as a perfect square trinomial.

Practice and Applications

DIFFERENCE PATTERN Tell whether the expression is a difference of two squares.

13. $x^2 - 9$ **14.** $b^2 - 36$ **15.** $a^2 + 16$ **16.** $n^2 - 50$

SQUARE OF A BINOMIAL Tell whether the expression is the square of a binomial.

17. $a^2 + 8a + 16$ **18.** $m^2 - 12m - 36$ **19.** $y^2 - 10y + 25$

20. $x^2 - 3x + 9$ **21.** $n^2 - 18n + 81$ **22.** $b^2 + 22b + 121$

SUM AND DIFFERENCE PATTERN Write the product of the sum and difference.

23. $(x + 5)(x - 5)$ **24.** $(y - 1)(y + 1)$ **25.** $(2m + 2)(2m - 2)$

26. $(3b - 1)(3b + 1)$ **27.** $(3 + 2x)(3 - 2x)$ **28.** $(6 - 5n)(6 + 5n)$

SQUARE OF A BINOMIAL Write the square of the binomial as a trinomial.

29. $(x + 5)^2$ **30.** $(a + 8)^2$ **31.** $(3x + 1)^2$

32. $(2y - 4)^2$ **33.** $(4b - 3)^2$ **34.** $(x - 7)^2$

Student Help

▶ **HOMEWORK HELP**
Example 1: Exs. 13–16,
   23–28, 35–46
Example 2: Exs. 17–22,
   29–46
Example 3: Exs. 51–53
Example 4: Exs. 56, 57

SPECIAL PRODUCT PATTERNS Find the product.

35. $(x + 4)(x - 4)$ **36.** $(x - 3)(x + 3)$ **37.** $(3x - 1)^2$

38. $(4 - n)^2$ **39.** $(2y + 5)(2y - 5)$ **40.** $(4n - 3)^2$

41. $(a + 2b)(a - 2b)$ **42.** $(4x + 5)^2$ **43.** $(3x - 4y)(3x + 4y)$

44. $(3y + 8)^2$ **45.** $(9 - 4t)(9 + 4t)$ **46.** $(a - 2b)^2$

CHECKING PRODUCTS Tell whether the statement is *true* or *false*. If the statement is false, rewrite the right-hand side to make the statement true.

47. $(a + 2b)^2 = a^2 + 2ab + 4b^2$ **48.** $(3s + 2t)(3s - 2t) = 9s^2 + 4t^2$

49. $(9x + 8)(9x - 8) = 81x^2 - 64$ **50.** $(6y - 7w)^2 = 36y^2 - 49w^2$

AREA MODELS Write two expressions for the area of the figure. Describe the special product pattern that is represented.

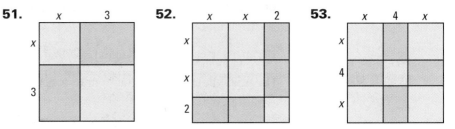

51. **52.** **53.**

54. **Geometry Link** The area of a square is given by $4x^2 - 20x + 25$. Express its perimeter as a function of x.

55. **Geometry Link** The side of a square is $(3x - 4)$ inches. What is its area?

Science Link In Exercises 56 and 57, use the following information. In chickens, neither the normal-feathered gene N nor the extremely rare frizzle-feathered gene F is dominant. So chickens whose feather genes are NN will have normal feathers. Chickens with NF will have mildly frizzled feathers. Chickens with FF will have extremely frizzled feathers.

56. The Punnett square at the right shows the possible results of crossing two chickens with mildly frizzled feathers. Find a model that can be used to represent the results shown in the Punnett square. Write the model as a polynomial.

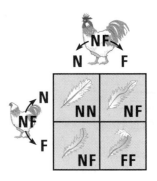

57. What percent of the offspring are likely to have normal feathers? What percent are likely to have mildly frizzled feathers? What percent are likely to have extremely frizzled feathers?

58. MULTIPLE CHOICE Find the product $(2x + 3)(2x - 3)$.

    (A) $2x^2 - 6x - 9$ (B) $4x^2 - 9$

    (C) $2x^2 - 9$ (D) $4x^2 + 12x + 9$

59. MULTIPLE CHOICE Find the product of $(3x + 5)^2$.

    (F) $3x^2 + 15x + 5$ (G) $9x^2 + 25$

    (H) $3x^2 + 25$ (J) $9x^2 + 30x + 25$

Mixed Review

SIMPLIFYING EXPRESSIONS **Simplify the expression. Use only positive exponents.** *(Lesson 8.4)*

60. $\left(\dfrac{6}{x}\right)^2$ **61.** $\dfrac{x^3}{x^2}$ **62.** $x^7 \cdot \dfrac{1}{x^4}$ **63.** $\dfrac{5x^4y}{3xy^2} \cdot \dfrac{9xy}{x^2y}$

SKETCHING GRAPHS **Sketch the graph of the function. Label the vertex.** *(Lesson 9.4)*

64. $y = 2x^2 + 3x + 6$ **65.** $y = 3x^2 - 9x - 12$ **66.** $y = -x^2 + 4x + 16$

Maintaining Skills

MULTIPLYING FRACTIONS **Multiply the fractions.** *(Skills Review p. 765)*

67. $\dfrac{1}{2} \cdot \dfrac{1}{2}$ **68.** $\dfrac{1}{4} \cdot \dfrac{1}{4}$ **69.** $\dfrac{2}{3} \cdot \dfrac{2}{3}$ **70.** $\dfrac{4}{9} \cdot \dfrac{4}{9}$

71. $\dfrac{1}{3} \cdot \dfrac{1}{3} \cdot \dfrac{1}{3}$ **72.** $\dfrac{2}{5} \cdot \dfrac{2}{5} \cdot \dfrac{2}{5}$ **73.** $\dfrac{3}{4} \cdot \dfrac{3}{4} \cdot \dfrac{3}{4}$ **74.** $\dfrac{5}{8} \cdot \dfrac{5}{8} \cdot \dfrac{5}{8}$

Quiz 1

State the degree of the monomial. *(Lesson 10.1)*

1. $6x^2$ **2.** -8 **3.** $-a^3$ **4.** $25m^5$

Use a vertical or a horizontal format to add or subtract. *(Lesson 10.1)*

5. $(2x^2 + 7x + 1) + (x^2 - 2x + 8)$

6. $(-4x^3 - 5x^2 + 2x) - (2x^3 + 9x^2 + 2)$

7. $(7t^2 - 3t + 5) - (4t^2 + 10t - 9)$

8. $(5x^3 - x^2 + 3x + 3) + (x^3 + 4x^2 + x)$

Find the product. *(Lesson 10.2)*

9. $(x + 8)(x - 1)$ **10.** $(y + 2)(y + 9)$ **11.** $-x^2(12x^3 - 11x^2 + 3)$

12. $(2x - 7y)(2x + 7y)$ **13.** $(4n + 7)(4n - 7)$ **14.** $(2x^2 + x - 4)(x - 2)$

Use a special product pattern to find the product. *(Lesson 10.3)*

15. $(x - 6)(x + 6)$ **16.** $(4x + 3)(4x - 3)$ **17.** $(5 + 3b)(5 - 3b)$

18. $(2x - 7y)(2x + 7y)$ **19.** $(3x + 6)^2$ **20.** $(-6 - 8x)^2$

10.4 Solving Quadratic Equations in Factored Form

Goal
Solve quadratic equations in factored form.

Key Words
- factored form
- zero-product property

How deep is a crater?

In Exercises 50 and 51 you will solve a quadratic equation to find the depth of the Barringer Meteor Crater.

A polynomial is in **factored form** if it is written as the product of two or more factors. The following equations are written in factored form.

$$x(x - 7) = 0 \qquad (x + 2)(x + 5) = 0 \qquad (x + 1)(x - 3)(x + 8) = 0$$

A value of x that makes any of the factors zero is a solution of the polynomial equation. That these are the *only* solutions follows from the **zero-product property**, stated below.

ZERO-PRODUCT PROPERTY

Let a and b be real numbers. If $ab = 0$, then $a = 0$ or $b = 0$.

If the product of two factors is zero, then at least one of the factors must be zero.

EXAMPLE 1 Solution by Factoring

Solve the equation $(x - 2)(x + 3) = 0$.

Solution

$(x - 2)(x + 3) = 0$	Write original equation.
$x - 2 = 0 \quad or \quad x + 3 = 0$	Set each factor equal to 0.
$x = 2 \quad \mid \quad x = -3$	Solve for x.

ANSWER ▶ The solutions are 2 and -3. Check these in the original equation.

Student Help

▶ STUDY TIP
The fact that the solutions 2 and -3 in Example 1 are the *only* solutions is a consequence of the zero-product property.

Checkpoint ✓ Solution by Factoring

Solve the equation and check the solutions.

1. $(x + 1)(x - 3) = 0$ **2.** $x(x - 2) = 0$ **3.** $(x - 5)(x + 7) = 0$

EXAMPLE 2 Solve a Repeated-Factor Equation

Solve $(x + 5)^2 = 0$.

Solution

This equation is a square of a binomial, so the factor $(x + 5)$ is a *repeated* factor. Repeated factors are used twice or more in an equation. To solve this equation you set $(x + 5)$ equal to zero.

$(x + 5)^2 = 0$	Write original equation.
$x + 5 = 0$	Set factor equal to 0.
$x = -5$	Solve for x.

ANSWER ▶ The solution is -5.

CHECK ✓ Substitute the solution into the original equation to check.

$(x + 5)^2 = 0$	Write original equation.
$(-5 + 5)^2 = 0$	Substitute -5 for x.
$0 = 0$ ✓	Simplify. Solution is correct.

Checkpoint ✓ *Solve a Repeated-Factor Equation*

Solve the equation and check the solutions.

4. $(x - 4)^2 = 0$ **5.** $(x + 6)^2 = 0$ **6.** $(2x - 5)^2 = 0$

EXAMPLE 3 Solve a Factored Cubic Equation

Solve $(2x + 1)(3x - 2)(x - 1) = 0$.

Solution

$(2x + 1)(3x - 2)(x - 1) = 0$ Write original equation.

$2x + 1 = 0$ *or* $3x - 2 = 0$ *or* $x - 1 = 0$ Set factors equal to 0.

$2x = -1$ $3x = 2$ $x = 1$ Solve for x.

$x = -\dfrac{1}{2}$ $x = \dfrac{2}{3}$

ANSWER ▶ The solutions are $-\dfrac{1}{2}, \dfrac{2}{3}$, and 1. Check these in the original equation.

Checkpoint ✓ *Solve a Factored Cubic Equation*

Solve the equation and check the solutions.

7. $(x - 4)(x + 6)(4x + 3) = 0$ **8.** $(x - 3)(x + 6)(3x + 2) = 0$

9. $(2x + 1)(x - 8)^2 = 0$ **10.** $(y - 3)^2(3y - 2) = 0$

EXAMPLE 4 Graph a Factored Equation

Sketch the graph of $y = (x - 3)(x + 2)$.

1 **Find** the x-intercepts. Solve $(x - 3)(x + 2) = 0$ to find the x-intercepts: 3 and -2.

2 **Use** the x-intercepts to find the coordinates of the vertex.

• The x-coordinate of the vertex is the average of the x-intercepts.

$$x = \frac{3 + (-2)}{2} = \frac{1}{2}$$

• Substitute the x-coordinate into the original equation to find the y-coordinate.

$$y = \left(\frac{1}{2} - 3\right)\left(\frac{1}{2} + 2\right) = -\frac{25}{4}$$

• The vertex is at $\left(\frac{1}{2}, -\frac{25}{4}\right)$.

3 **Sketch** the graph using the vertex and the x-intercepts.

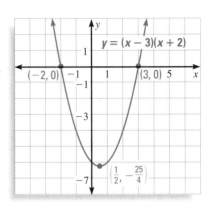

Checkpoint ✓ Graph a Factored Equation

Find the x-intercepts and the vertex of the graph of the function. Then sketch a graph of the function.

11. $y = x(x + 2)$ **12.** $y = (x + 4)(x - 5)$ **13.** $y = (x - 1)(x - 6)$

EXAMPLE 5 Use a Quadratic Model

An arch is modeled by $y = -0.15(x - 8)(x + 8)$, with x and y measured in feet. How wide is the arch at the base? How high is the arch?

1 **Find** the x-intercepts: 8 and -8.

• the width of the arch at the base is $8 + 8 = 16$

2 **Use** the x-intercepts to find the coordinates of the vertex.

• $x = \dfrac{8 + (-8)}{2} = 0$

• Substitute 0 into the original equation:
  $y = -0.15(0 - 8)(0 + 8) = 9.6$

• The vertex is at $(0, 9.6)$.

ANSWER ▶ The arch is 16 feet wide at the base and 9.6 feet high.

Student Help

▶ **SKILLS REVIEW**
For help with multiplying decimals, see p. 759.

10.4 Exercises

Guided Practice

Vocabulary Check

1. What is the zero-product property?

2. Is $(x - 2)(x^2 - 9) = 0$ in factored form? Explain.

Skill Check

3. Are -5, 2, and 3 the solutions of $3(x - 2)(x + 5) = 0$? Explain.

4. ERROR ANALYSIS Find and correct the error at the right.

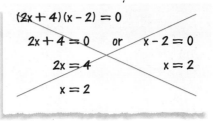

Does the graph of the function have *x*-intercepts of 4 and −5?

5. $y = 2(x + 4)(x - 5)$ 　　　　**6.** $y = 4(x - 4)(x - 5)$

7. $y = -(x - 4)(x + 5)$ 　　　　**8.** $y = 3(x + 5)(x - 4)$

Use the zero-product property to solve the equation.

9. $(b + 1)(b + 3) = 0$ 　　　　**10.** $(t - 3)(t - 5) = 0$

11. $(x - 7)^2 = 0$ 　　　　**12.** $(y + 9)(y - 2)(y - 5) = 0$

13. Sketch the graph of $y = (x + 2)(x - 2)$. Label the vertex and the *x*-intercepts.

Practice and Applications

ZERO-PRODUCT PROPERTY Use the zero-product property to solve the equation.

14. $(x + 4)(x + 1) = 0$ 　　**15.** $(t + 8)(t - 6) = 0$ 　　**16.** $x(x + 8) = 0$

17. $(y + 3)^2 = 0$ 　　**18.** $(b - 9)(b + 8) = 0$ 　　**19.** $(d + 7)^2 = 0$

20. $(y - 2)(y + 1) = 0$ 　　**21.** $(z + 2)(z + 3) = 0$ 　　**22.** $(v - 7)(v - 5) = 0$

23. $(w - 17)^2 = 0$ 　　**24.** $p(2p + 1) = 0$ 　　**25.** $4(c + 9)^2 = 0$

26. $(z + 9)(z - 11) = 0$ 　　**27.** $(a - 20)(a + 15) = 0$ 　**28.** $(d + 6)(3d - 4) = 0$

Student Help

▶**HOMEWORK HELP**
Example 1: Exs. 14–36
Example 2: Exs. 14–36
Example 3: Exs. 29–36
Example 4: Exs. 37–45
Example 5: Exs. 46–51

SOLVING FACTORED CUBIC EQUATIONS Solve the equation.

29. $(x + 1)(x + 2)(x - 4) = 0$ 　　　　**30.** $y(y - 4)(y - 8) = 0$

31. $(a + 5)(a - 6)^2 = 0$ 　　　　**32.** $r(r - 12)^2 = 0$

33. $5(d + 8)(d - 12)(d + 9) = 0$ 　　　　**34.** $8(n + 9)(n - 9)(n + 12) = 0$

35. $(b - 8)(2b + 1)(b + 2) = 0$ 　　　　**36.** $(y - 5)(y - 6)(3y - 2) = 0$

MATCHING FUNCTIONS AND GRAPHS Match the function with its graph.

37. $y = (x + 2)(x - 4)$ **38.** $y = (x - 2)(x + 4)$ **39.** $y = (x + 4)(x + 2)$

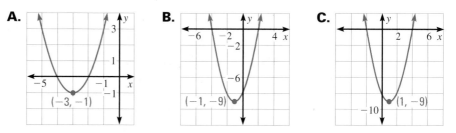

A. (graph with vertex $(-3, -1)$)

B. (graph with vertex $(-1, -9)$)

C. (graph with vertex $(1, -9)$)

SKETCHING GRAPHS Find the *x*-intercepts and the vertex of the graph of the function. Then sketch the graph of the function.

40. $y = (x - 4)(x + 2)$ **41.** $y = (x + 5)(x + 3)$ **42.** $y = (x - 3)(x + 3)$

43. $y = (x - 1)(x + 7)$ **44.** $y = (x - 2)(x - 6)$ **45.** $y = (x + 4)(x + 3)$

VLA TELESCOPE In Exercises 46 and 47, use the cross section of one of the Very Large Array's telescope dishes shown below.

The cross section of the telescope's dish can be modeled by the polynomial function

$$y = \frac{14}{41^2}(x + 41)(x - 41)$$

where *x* and *y* are measured in feet, and the center of the dish is at $x = 0$.

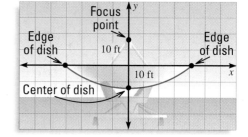

46. Find the width of the dish. Explain your reasoning.

47. Use the model to find the coordinates of the center of the dish.

GATEWAY ARCH In Exercises 48 and 49, use the following information.
The Gateway Arch in St. Louis, Missouri, has the shape of a catenary (a U-shaped curve similar to a parabola). It can be approximated by the following model, where *x* and *y* are measured in feet. ▶ Source: National Park Service

Gateway Arch model: $y = -\dfrac{7}{1000}(x + 300)(x - 300)$

48. How far apart are the legs of the arch at the base?

49. How high is the arch?

THE BARRINGER METEOR CRATER was formed about 49,000 years ago when a nickel and iron meteorite struck the desert at about 25,000 miles per hour.

BARRINGER METEOR CRATER In Exercises 50 and 51, use the following equation which models a cross section of the Barringer Meteor Crater, near Winslow, Arizona. Note that *x* and *y* are measured in meters and the center of the crater is at $x = 0$. ▶ Source: Jet Propulsion Laboratory

Barringer Meteor model: $y = \dfrac{1}{1800}(x - 600)(x + 600)$

50. Assuming the lip of the crater is at $y = 0$, how wide is the crater?

51. What is the depth of the crater?

52. MULTIPLE CHOICE Solve $6(x - 3)(x + 5)(x - 9) = 0$.

   Ⓐ 6, 3, 5, and 9   Ⓑ 3, −5, and 9

   Ⓒ 6, 3, −5, and 9   Ⓓ 6, 3, 5, and −9

53. MULTIPLE CHOICE Which function represents the graph at the right?

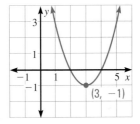

   Ⓕ $y = (x + 2)(x + 4)$

   Ⓖ $y = (x + 2)(x - 4)$

   Ⓗ $y = (x - 2)(x - 4)$

   Ⓙ $y = (x - 2)(x + 4)$

(3, −1)

DECIMAL FORM Write the number in decimal form. *(Lesson 8.5)*

54. 2.1×10^5 **55.** 4.443×10^{-2} **56.** 8.57×10^8 **57.** 1.25×10^6

58. 3.71×10^{-3} **59.** 9.96×10^6 **60.** 7.22×10^{-4} **61.** 8.17×10^7

MULTIPLYING EXPRESSIONS Find the product. *(Lesson 10.2)*

62. $(x - 2)(x - 7)$ **63.** $(x + 8)(x - 8)$ **64.** $(x - 4)(x + 5)$

65. $(2x + 7)(3x - 1)$ **66.** $(5x - 1)(5x + 2)$ **67.** $(3x + 1)(8x - 3)$

68. $(2x - 4)(4x - 2)$ **69.** $(x + 10)(x + 10)$ **70.** $(3x + 5)(2x - 3)$

EXPONENTIAL MODELS Tell whether the situation can be represented by a model of *exponential growth* or *exponential decay*. Then write a model that represents the situation. *(Lessons 8.6, 8.7)*

71. COMPUTER PRICES From 1996 to 2000, the average price of a computer company's least expensive home computer system decreased by 16% per year.

72. MUSIC SALES From 1995 to 1999, the number of CDs a band sold increased by 23% per year.

73. COOKING CLUB From 1996 to 2000, the number of members in the cooking club decreased by 3% per year.

74. INTERNET SERVICE From 1993 to 1998, the total revenues for a company that provides Internet service increased by about 137% per year.

FINDING FACTORS List all the factors of the number.
(Skills Review p. 761)

75. 12   **76.** 20   **77.** 18   **78.** 35

79. 51   **80.** 24   **81.** 36   **82.** 48

83. 64   **84.** 90   **85.** 84   **86.** 112

DEVELOPING CONCEPTS

Factoring $x^2 + bx + c$

GOAL

Use algebra tiles to model the factorization of a trinomial of the form $x^2 + bx + c$.

MATERIALS

• algebra tiles

Question

How can you use algebra tiles to factor $x^2 + 5x + 6$?

Explore

Factor the trinomial $x^2 + 5x + 6$.

1 Use algebra tiles to model $x^2 + 5x + 6$.

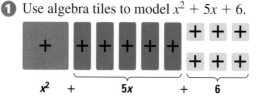

$$x^2 \quad + \qquad 5x \qquad + \quad 6$$

2 With the x^2-tile at the upper left, arrange the x-tiles and 1-tiles around the x^2-tile to form a rectangle.

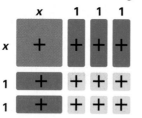

3 The width of the rectangle is (? + ?), and the length of the rectangle is (? + ?). Complete the statement: $x^2 + 5x + 6 = (? + ?) \cdot (? + ?)$.

Think About It

Write the factors of the trinomial represented by the algebra tiles.

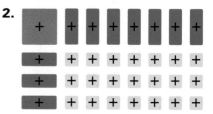

In Exercises 3–8, use algebra tiles to factor the trinomial. Sketch your model.

3. $x^2 + 7x + 6$ **4.** $x^2 + 6x + 8$ **5.** $x^2 + 8x + 15$

6. $x^2 + 6x + 9$ **7.** $x^2 + 4x + 4$ **8.** $x^2 + 7x + 10$

9. Use algebra tiles to show why the trinomial $x^2 + 3x + 4$ cannot be factored.

10.5 Factoring $x^2 + bx + c$

Goal

Factor trinomials of the form $x^2 + bx + c$.

Key Words

- factor a trinomial
- factored form

How wide should the border of a garden be?

In Example 7 you will factor a quadratic equation to find the width of a border around a garden.

A trinomial of the form $x^2 + bx + c$, where b and c are integers is shown below.

$$x^2 + 9x + 14, \qquad b = 9, \qquad c = 14$$

To **factor a trinomial** of this form means to write the trinomial as the product of two binomials (factored form).

Trinomial		Factored Form
$x^2 + 9x + 14$	$=$	$(x + 2)(x + 7)$
$x^2 - x - 12$	$=$	$(x + 3)(x - 4)$
$x^2 - 2x - 15$	$=$	$(x + 3)(x - 5)$

In order to write $x^2 + bx + c$ in the form $(x + p)(x + q)$, note that

$$(x + p)(x + q) = x^2 + (p + q)x + pq$$

This leads you to seek numbers p and q such that $p + q = b$ and $pq = c$.

EXAMPLE 1 Factor when *b* and *c* Are Positive

Factor $x^2 + 6x + 8$.

Solution

The first term of each binomial factor is x. For this trinomial, $b = 6$ and $c = 8$. You need to find numbers p and q whose product is 8 and whose sum is 6.

p and *q*	*p* + *q*	
1, 8	9	
2, 4	6	The numbers you need are 2 and 4.

ANSWER ▶ $x^2 + 6x + 8 = (x + 2)(x + 4)$. Check your answer by multiplying.

Checkpoint ✓ *Factor when b and c Are Positive*

Factor the trinomial.

1. $x^2 + 4x + 3$ **2.** $x^2 + 5x + 6$ **3.** $x^2 + 8x + 7$ **4.** $x^2 + 7x + 6$

EXAMPLE **2** **Factor when b Is Negative and c Is Positive**

Factor $x^2 - 5x + 6$.

Solution

The first term of each binomial factor is x.

$$(x \,\underline{\hspace{0.5cm}})(x \,\underline{\hspace{0.5cm}})$$

For this trinomial, $b = -5$ and $c = 6$. Because c is positive, you need to find numbers p and q with the same sign. Find numbers p and q whose sum is -5 and whose product is 6.

p and q	$p + q$	
$-1, -6$	-7	
$-2, -3$	-5	The numbers you need are -2 and -3.

ANSWER ▶ $x^2 - 5x + 6 = (x - 2)(x - 3)$. Check your answer by multiplying.

Checkpoint ✓ **Factor when b Is Negative and c Is Positive**

Factor the trinomial.

5. $x^2 - 5x + 4$ **6.** $x^2 - 4x + 4$ **7.** $x^2 - 8x + 7$ **8.** $x^2 - 7x + 12$

EXAMPLE **3** **Factor when b and c Are Negative**

Factor $x^2 - 11x - 12$.

Solution

The first term of each binomial factor is x.

$$(x \,\underline{\hspace{0.5cm}})(x \,\underline{\hspace{0.5cm}})$$

For this trinomial, $b = -11$ and $c = -12$. Because c is negative, you need to find numbers p and q with different signs. Find numbers p and q whose sum is -11 and whose product is -12.

p and q	$p + q$	
$-1, \quad 12$	11	
$1, -12$	-11	The numbers you need are 1 and -12.

ANSWER ▶ $x^2 - 11x - 12 = (x + 1)(x - 12)$. Check your answer by multiplying.

Checkpoint ✓ **Factor when b and c Are Negative**

Factor the trinomial.

9. $x^2 - 5x - 6$ **10.** $x^2 - 3x - 10$ **11.** $x^2 - 13x - 14$ **12.** $x^2 - 6x - 7$

Student Help

▶ **STUDY TIP**

As soon as you find the correct pair of numbers for a trinomial, you can stop listing all possible pairs. For example, in Example 4, you do not need the pairs -2 and 9, 2 and -9, -3 and 6, or 3 and -6.

EXAMPLE **4** **Factor when b Is Positive and c Is Negative**

Factor $x^2 + 17x - 18$.

Solution

The first term of each binomial factor is x.

$$(x \underline{})(x \underline{})$$

For this trinomial, $b = 17$ and $c = -18$. Because c is negative, you need to find numbers p and q with different signs. Find numbers p and q whose sum is 17 and whose product is -18.

p and q	$p + q$	
1, -18	-17	
-1, 18	17	The numbers you need are -1 and 18.

ANSWER ▶ $x^2 + 17x - 18 = (x - 1)(x + 18)$.

Checkpoint ✓ **Factor when b Is Positive and c Is Negative**

Factor the trinomial.

13. $x^2 + x - 6$ **14.** $x^2 + 2x - 8$ **15.** $x^2 + 8x - 20$ **16.** $x^2 + 3x - 10$

EXAMPLE **5** **Check Using a Graphing Calculator**

Factor $x^2 - 2x - 8$.

Solution

The first term of each binomial factor is x.

$$(x \underline{})(x \underline{})$$

For this trinomial, $b = -2$ and $c = -8$. Because c is negative, you need to find numbers p and q with different signs. Find numbers p and q whose sum is -2 and whose product is -8.

p and q	$p + q$	
-1, 8	7	
1, -8	-7	
-2, 4	2	
2, -4	-2	The numbers you need are 2 and -4.

ANSWER ▶ $x^2 - 2x - 8 = (x + 2)(x - 4)$.

CHECK ✓ Use a graphing calculator. Graph $y = x^2 - 2x - 8$ and $y = (x + 2)(x - 4)$ on the same screen. The graphs are the same, so your answer is correct.

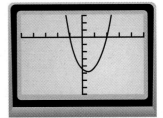

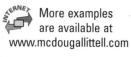
EXAMPLE **6** **Solve a Quadratic Equation**

Solve $x^2 - 3x = 10$ by factoring.

Solution

$x^2 - 3x = 10$	Write equation.
$x^2 - 3x - 10 = 0$	Write in standard form.
$(x - 5)(x + 2) = 0$	Factor left side.
$x - 5 = 0 \quad or \quad x + 2 = 0$	Use zero-product property.
$x = 5 \qquad\qquad x = -2$	Solve for x.

ANSWER ▶ The solutions are 5 and -2. Check these in the original equation.

EXAMPLE **7** **Write a Quadratic Model**

LANDSCAPE DESIGN You are putting a stone border along two sides of a rectangular Japanese garden that measures 6 yards by 15 yards. Your budget limits you to only enough stone to cover 46 square yards. How wide should the border be?

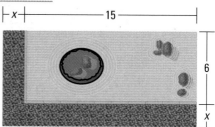

Solution

$$\boxed{\begin{array}{c}\text{Area of}\\\text{border}\end{array}} = \boxed{\begin{array}{c}\text{Total}\\\text{area}\end{array}} - \boxed{\begin{array}{c}\text{Garden}\\\text{area}\end{array}}$$

$46 = (x + 15)(x + 6) - (15)(6)$	Write quadratic model.
$46 = x^2 + 6x + 15x + 90 - 90$	Multiply.
$46 = x^2 + 21x$	Combine like terms.
$0 = x^2 + 21x - 46$	Write in standard form.
$0 = (x + 23)(x - 2)$	Factor.
$x + 23 = 0 \quad or \quad x - 2 = 0$	Use zero-product property.
$x = -23 \qquad\qquad x = 2$	Solve for x.

The solutions are -23 and 2. Only $x = 2$ is a reasonable solution, because negative values for dimension do not make sense.

ANSWER ▶ The border should be 2 yards wide.

Checkpoint ✓ *Solve a Quadratic Equation*

Solve the equation by factoring.

17. $0 = x^2 + 4x + 3$ **18.** $0 = x^2 - 5x + 4$ **19.** $0 = x^2 - 5x - 6$

20. Suppose the garden in Example 7 above measured 7 yards by 12 yards and the budget lets you cover 66 square yards. How wide should the border be?

10.5 Exercises

Guided Practice

Vocabulary Check

1. What does it mean to factor a trinomial of the form $x^2 + bx + c$?

Skill Check

Match the trinomial with a correct factorization.

2. $x^2 - x - 20$

3. $x^2 + x - 20$

4. $x^2 + 9x + 20$

5. $x^2 - 9x + 20$

A. $(x + 5)(x - 4)$

B. $(x + 4)(x + 5)$

C. $(x - 4)(x - 5)$

D. $(x + 4)(x - 5)$

Solve the equation by factoring.

6. $0 = x^2 - 4x + 4$ **7.** $0 = x^2 - 4x - 5$ **8.** $0 = x^2 + x - 6$

LOGICAL REASONING Complete the statement with *always, sometimes,* or *never.*

9. Factoring __?__ reverses the effects of multiplication.

10. In the factoring of a trinomial, if the constant term is positive, then the signs in both binomial factors will __?__ be the same.

11. In the factoring of a trinomial, if the constant term is negative, then the signs in both binomial factors will __?__ be negative.

Practice and Applications

FACTORED FORM   **Choose the correct factorization.**

12. $x^2 + 7x + 12$

13. $x^2 - 10x + 16$

14. $x^2 + 11x - 26$

A. $(x + 6)(x + 2)$

B. $(x + 4)(x + 3)$

A. $(x - 4)(x - 4)$

B. $(x - 8)(x - 2)$

A. $(x - 13)(x + 2)$

B. $(x + 13)(x - 2)$

FACTORING TRINOMIALS   **Factor the trinomial.**

15. $z^2 + 6z + 5$ **16.** $x^2 + 8x - 9$ **17.** $b^2 + 5b - 24$

18. $a^2 - a - 20$ **19.** $r^2 + 8r + 16$ **20.** $y^2 - 3y - 18$

21. $m^2 - 7m - 30$ **22.** $w^2 + 13w + 36$ **23.** $b^2 + 3b - 40$

Student Help

▶**HOMEWORK HELP**
Example 1: Exs. 12–23
Example 2: Exs. 12–23
Example 3: Exs. 12–23
Example 4: Exs. 12–23
Example 5: Exs. 39–41
Example 6: Exs. 24–35
Example 7: Exs. 42–45

SOLVING QUADRATIC EQUATIONS   **Solve the equation by factoring.**

24. $x^2 + 7x + 10 = 0$ **25.** $x^2 + 5x - 14 = 0$ **26.** $x^2 + 6x + 9 = 0$

27. $x^2 + 16x + 15 = 0$ **28.** $x^2 - 9x = -14$ **29.** $x^2 + 3x = 54$

30. $x^2 + 100 = 20x$ **31.** $x^2 - 15x + 44 = 0$ **32.** $x^2 - 20x = -51$

33. $x^2 + 8x = 65$ **34.** $x^2 + 42 = 13x$ **35.** $-x + x^2 = 56$

Solve $x^2 - 9x + 18 = 2x$.

Solution

$x^2 - 9x + 18 = 2x$	Write original equation.
$x^2 - 9x + 18 - 2x = 0$	Add $-2x$ to each side.
$x^2 - 11x + 18 = 0$	Combine like terms.
$(x - 2)(x - 9) = 0$	Factor.
$x - 2 = 0$ *or* $x - 9 = 0$	Use zero-product property.
$x = 2$	$x = 9$	Solve for x.

ANSWER ▶ The solutions are 2 and 9. Check your answers.

Solve the equation by factoring.

36. $x^2 - x - 8 = 82$ **37.** $n^2 + 8n + 32 = -4n$ **38.** $c^2 + 10c - 48 = 12c$

CHECKING GRAPHICALLY Solve the equation by factoring. Then use a graphing calculator to check your answer.

39. $x^2 - 17x + 30 = 0$ **40.** $x^2 - 20x + 19 = 0$ **41.** $x^2 + 3x - 18 = 0$

MAKING A SIGN In Exercises 42 and 43, a triangular sign has a base that is 2 feet less than twice its height. A local zoning ordinance restricts the surface area of street signs to be no more than 20 square feet.

42. Write an inequality involving the height that represents the largest triangular sign allowed.

43. Find the base and height of the largest triangular sign that meets the zoning ordinance.

THE TAJ MAHAL In Exercises 44 and 45, refer to the illustration of the Taj Mahal below.

44. The platform is about 38 meters wider than the main building. The total area of the platform is about 9025 square meters. Using the fact that the platform and the base of the building are squares, find their dimensions.

45. The entire complex of the Taj Mahal is about 245 meters longer than it is wide. The area of the entire complex is about 167,750 square meters. What are the dimensions of the entire complex? Explain your steps in finding the solution.

Link to
Architecture

TAJ MAHAL
It took more than 20,000 daily workers 22 years to complete the Taj Mahal around 1643 in India. Built mainly of white marble and red sandstone, the Taj Mahal is renowned for its beauty.

 More about the Taj Mahal is available at www.mcdougallittell.com

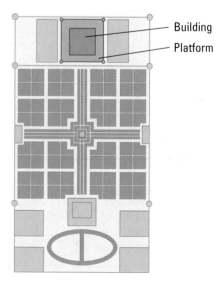

Building
Platform

46. MULTIPLE CHOICE Factor $x^2 - 10x - 24$.

    Ⓐ $(x - 4)(x - 6)$ **Ⓑ** $(x + 4)(x + 6)$

    Ⓒ $(x + 2)(x - 12)$ **Ⓓ** $(x - 2)(x + 12)$

47. MULTIPLE CHOICE Solve $x^2 - 9x = 36$ by factoring.

    Ⓕ 12 and -3 **Ⓖ** -12 and 3

    Ⓗ 4 and -9 **Ⓙ** 9 and -4

48. MULTIPLE CHOICE The length of a rectangular plot of land is 24 meters more than its width. A paved area measuring 8 meters by 12 meters is placed on the plot. The area of the unpaved part of the land is then 880 square meters. If w represents the width of the plot of land in meters, which of the following equations can be factored to find the possible values of w? *HINT:* Begin by drawing and labeling a diagram.

    Ⓐ $w^2 + 24w = 880$ **Ⓑ** $w^2 + 24w + 96 = 880$

    Ⓒ $w^2 + 24w - 96 = 880$ **Ⓓ** $w^2 + 24w = 96$

49. MULTIPLE CHOICE A triangle's base is 16 feet less than 2 times its height. If h represents the height in feet, and the total area of the triangle is 48 square feet, which of the following equations can be used to determine the height?

    Ⓕ $2h + 2(h + 4) = 48$ **Ⓖ** $h^2 - 8h = 48$

    Ⓗ $h^2 + 8h = 48$ **Ⓙ** $2h^2 - 16h = 48$

FINDING THE GCF Find the greatest common factor. *(Skills Review p. 761)*

50. 12, 36   **51.** 30, 45   **52.** 24, 72

53. 49, 64   **54.** 20, 32, 40   **55.** 36, 54, 90

MULTIPLYING EXPRESSIONS Find the product. *(Lessons 10.2 and 10.3)*

56. $3q(q^3 - 5q^2 + 6)$ **57.** $(y + 9)(y - 4)$ **58.** $(7x - 11)^2$

59. $(5 - w)(12 + 3w)$ **60.** $(3a - 2)(4a + 6)$ **61.** $(5t - 3)(4t - 10)$

SOLVING FACTORED EQUATIONS Solve the equation. *(Lesson 10.4)*

62. $(x + 12)(x + 7) = 0$ **63.** $(z + 2)(z + 3) = 0$

64. $(t - 19)^2 = 0$ **65.** $5(x - 9)(x - 6) = 0$

66. $(y + 47)(y - 27) = 0$ **67.** $(z - 1)(4z + 2) = 0$

68. $(a - 3)(a + 5)^2 = 0$ **69.** $(b + 4)(b - 3)(2b - 1) = 0$

ADDING DECIMALS Add. *(Skills Review p. 759)*

70. $3.7 + 1.04 + 5.2$ **71.** $6.7 + 0.356 + 4$

72. $7.421 + 5 + 8.09$ **73.** $8.1 + 0.2 + 3.56$

74. $6.012 + 2.9 + 5.6314$ **75.** $7.9 + 3.0204 + 10$

76. $3.2 + 5.013 + 0.0021$ **77.** $100 + 9.81 + 5.0006$

Factoring $ax^2 + bx + c$

For use with Lesson 10.6

GOAL

Use algebra tiles to model the factorization of a trinomial of the form $ax^2 + bx + c$.

MATERIALS

• algebra tiles

Question

How can you use algebra tiles to factor $2x^2 + 5x + 3$?

Explore

Factor the trinomial $2x^2 + 5x + 3$.

1 Use algebra tiles to model $2x^2 + 5x + 3$.

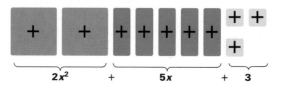

2 With the x^2-tiles at the upper left, arrange the x-tiles and the 1-tiles around the x^2-tiles to form a rectangle.

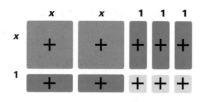

3 The width of the rectangle is (? + ?), and the length of the rectangle is (? + ?).
Complete the statement: $2x^2 + 5x + 3 = ($? $+$? $) \cdot ($? $+$? $)$.

Think About It

Use algebra tiles to factor the trinomial. Sketch your model.

1. $2x^2 + 9x + 9$ **2.** $2x^2 + 7x + 3$ **3.** $3x^2 + 4x + 1$

4. $3x^2 + 10x + 3$ **5.** $3x^2 + 10x + 8$ **6.** $4x^2 + 5x + 1$

ERROR ANALYSIS The algebra tile model shown below is incorrect. Sketch the correct model, and use the model to factor the trinomial.

7. $2x^2 + 3x + 1$ **8.** $2x^2 + 4x + 2$ **9.** $4x^2 + 4x + 1$

Factoring $ax^2 + bx + c$

Goal

Factor trinomials of the form $ax^2 + bx + c$.

Key Words

- factor a trinomial
- FOIL pattern
- quadratic

How long will it take a cliff diver to enter the water?

In Example 5 you will use a vertical motion model to find the time it takes a cliff diver to enter the water.

To factor a trinomial of the form $ax^2 + bx + c$, write the trinomial as the product of two binomials (factored form).

factors of 6

Example: $6x^2 + 22x + 20 = (3x + 5)(2x + 4)$ $b = 12 + 10 = 22$

factors of 20

One way to factor $ax^2 + bx + c$ is to find numbers m and n whose product is a and numbers p and q whose product is c so that the middle term is the sum of the **O**uter and **I**nner products of **FOIL**.

$m \times n = a$

$$ax^2 + bx + c = (mx + p)(nx + q) \qquad b = mq + np$$

$p \times q = c$

EXAMPLE 1 Factor when *a* and *c* Are Prime Numbers

Factor $2x^2 + 11x + 5$.

❶ **Write** the numbers m and n whose product is 2 and the numbers p and q whose product is 5.

m and *n*	*p* and *q*
1, 2	1, 5

❷ **Use** these numbers to write trial factors. Then use the **O**uter and **I**nner products of **FOIL** to check the middle term.

Trial Factors	Middle Term
$(x + 1)(2x + 5)$	$5x + 2x = 7x$
$(2x + 1)(x + 5)$	$10x + x = 11x$

ANSWER▶ $2x^2 + 11x + 5 = (2x + 1)(x + 5)$.

Checkpoint✔ **Factor when *a* and *c* Are Prime Numbers**

Factor the trinomial.

1. $2x^2 + 7x + 3$ **2.** $2x^2 + 5x + 3$ **3.** $3x^2 + 10x + 3$

EXAMPLE **2** Factor when *a* and *c* Are not Prime Numbers

Factor $6x^2 - 33x + 15$.

Solution

For this trinomial, $a = 6$, $b = -33$, and $c = 15$. Because c is positive, you need to find numbers p and q with the same sign. Because b is negative, only negative numbers p and q need to be tried.

Student Help

▶**STUDY TIP**
Once you find the correct binomial factors, it is not necessary to continue checking the remaining trial factors.

❶ **Write** the numbers m and n whose product is 6 and the numbers p and q whose product is 15.

m and *n*	*p* and *q*
1, 6	−1, −15
2, 3	−3, −5

❷ **Use** these numbers to write trial factors. Then use the **Outer** and **Inner** products of **FOIL** to check the middle term.

Trial Factors	Middle Term
$(x - 1)(6x - 15)$	$-15x - 6x = -21x$
$(x - 15)(6x - 1)$	$-x - 90x = -91x$
$(2x - 1)(3x - 15)$	$-30x - 3x = -33x$

ANSWER ▶ $6x^2 - 33x + 15 = (2x - 1)(3x - 15)$.

EXAMPLE **3** Factor with a Common Factor for *a*, *b*, and *c*

Factor $6x^2 + 2x - 4$.

Solution

The coefficients of this trinomial have a common factor 2.

$2(3x^2 + x - 2)$ Factor out the common factor.

It remains to factor a trinomial with $a = 3$, $b = 1$, and $c = -2$. Because c is negative, you need to find numbers p and q with different signs.

❶ **Write** the numbers m and n whose product is 3 and the numbers p and q whose product is −2.

m and *n*	*p* and *q*
1, 3	−1, 2
	1, −2

❷ **Use** these numbers to write trial factors. Then use the **Outer** and **Inner** products of **FOIL** to check the middle term.

Trial Factors	Middle Term
$(x - 1)(3x + 2)$	$2x - 3x = -x$
$(x + 2)(3x - 1)$	$-x + 6x = 5x$
$(x + 1)(3x - 2)$	$-2x + 3x = x$

Remember to include the common factor 2 in the complete factorization.

ANSWER ▶ $6x^2 + 2x - 4 = 2(x + 1)(3x - 2)$.

Checkpoint ✓ *Factor Trinomials*

Factor the trinomial.

4. $2x^2 + 5x + 2$ **5.** $5x^2 - 7x + 2$ **6.** $4x^2 + 8x + 3$

7. $8r^2 - 6r - 9$ **8.** $6x^2 - 14x + 4$ **9.** $20x^2 + 5x - 15$

Student Help

▶ MORE EXAMPLES

More examples are available at www.mcdougallittell.com

EXAMPLE 4 Solve a Quadratic Equation

$21n^2 + 14n + 7 = 6n + 11$	Write original equation.
$21n^2 + 8n - 4 = 0$	Write in standard form.
$(3n + 2)(7n - 2) = 0$	Factor left side.
$3n + 2 = 0$ or $7n - 2 = 0$	Use zero-product property.
$n = -\dfrac{2}{3}$ $\quad\quad$ $n = \dfrac{2}{7}$	Solve for n.

ANSWER ▶ The solutions are $-\dfrac{2}{3}$ and $\dfrac{2}{7}$. Check these in the original equation.

Checkpoint ✓ Solve a Quadratic Equation

Solve the equation.

10. $2x^2 + 7x + 3 = 0$　　**11.** $2x^2 - x - 3 = 0$　　**12.** $4x^2 - 16x + 15 = 0$

EXAMPLE 5 Write a Quadratic Model

Student Help

▶ LOOK BACK

For help with using a vertical motion model see p. 535.

When a diver jumps from a ledge, the vertical component of his motion can be modeled by the vertical motion model. Suppose the ledge is 48 feet above the ocean and the initial upward velocity is 8 feet per second. How long will it take until the diver enters the water?

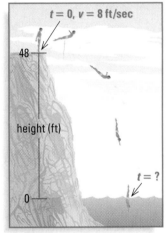

Not drawn to scale

Use a vertical motion model.
Let $v = 8$ and $s = 48$.

$h = -16t^2 + vt + s$	Vertical motion model
$= -16t^2 + 8t + \mathbf{48}$	Substitute values.

Solve the resulting equation for t to find the time when the diver enters the water.
Let $h = 0$.

$0 = -16t^2 + 8t + 48$	Write quadratic model.
$0 = (-8)(2t^2 - t - 6)$	Factor out common factor -8.
$0 = (-8)(t - 2)(2t + 3)$	Factor.
$t - 2 = 0$ or $2t + 3 = 0$	Use zero-product property.
$t = 2$ $\quad\quad$ $t = -\dfrac{3}{2}$	Solve for t.

The solutions are 2 and $-\dfrac{3}{2}$. Negative values of time do not make sense for this problem, so the only reasonable solution is $t = 2$.

ANSWER ▶ It will take 2 seconds until the diver enters the water.

Guided Practice

Vocabulary Check

1. What is the difference between factoring quadratic polynomials of the form $x^2 + bx + c$ and $ax^2 + bx + c$?

Skill Check

Copy and complete the statement.

2. $(2x + 1)(x + 1) = 2x^2$ __?__ $+ 1$ **3.** $(3x + 2)(x - 3) = 3x^2 - 7x$ __?__

4. $(3x - 4)(x - 5) = 3x^2$ __?__ $+ 20$ **5.** $(5x + 2)(2x + 1) =$ __?__ $+ 9x + 2$

Match the trinomial with a correct factorization.

6. $3x^2 - 17x - 6$ **A.** $(3x + 2)(x + 3)$

7. $3x^2 + 7x - 6$ **B.** $(3x + 1)(x - 6)$

8. $3x^2 + 11x + 6$ **C.** $(3x - 1)(x + 6)$

9. $3x^2 + 17x - 6$ **D.** $(3x - 2)(x + 3)$

Factor the trinomial.

10. $2x^2 + 17x + 21$ **11.** $2x^2 - 3x - 2$ **12.** $6t^2 - t - 5$

13. $12x^2 - 19x + 4$ **14.** $6x^2 + 7x - 20$ **15.** $3x^2 + 2x - 8$

Solve the equation.

16. $3b^2 + 26b + 35 = 0$ **17.** $2z^2 + 15z = 8$ **18.** $-7n^2 - 40n = -12$

Practice and Applications

FACTORIZATIONS Choose the correct factorization. If neither choice is correct, find the correct factorization.

19. $3x^2 + 2x - 8$ **20.** $6y^2 - 29y - 5$ **21.** $4w^2 - 14w - 30$

     A. $(3x - 4)(x + 2)$ **A.** $(2y + 1)(3y - 5)$ **A.** $(2w + 3)(2w - 10)$

     B. $(3x - 4)(x - 2)$ **B.** $(6y - 1)(y + 5)$ **B.** $(4w + 15)(w - 2)$

FACTORING TRINOMIALS Factor the trinomial.

22. $2x^2 - x - 3$ **23.** $3t^2 + 16t + 5$ **24.** $5x^2 + 2x - 3$

25. $6a^2 + 5a + 1$ **26.** $5w^2 - 9w - 2$ **27.** $6b^2 - 11b - 2$

28. $8b^2 + 2b - 3$ **29.** $6x^2 - 9x - 15$ **30.** $12y^2 - 20y + 8$

31. $2z^2 + 19z - 10$ **32.** $6y^2 - 11y - 10$ **33.** $4x^2 + 27x + 35$

34. $4n^2 - 22n - 42$ **35.** $3c^2 - 37c + 44$ **36.** $24r^2 - 6r - 45$

37. $6t^2 + t - 70$ **38.** $14y^2 - 15y + 4$ **39.** $8y^2 - 26y + 15$

Student Help

▶ **HOMEWORK HELP**
Example 1: Exs. 19–39
Example 2: Exs. 19–39
Example 3: Exs. 19–39
Example 4: Exs. 42–54
Example 5: Exs. 55–57

ERROR ANALYSIS Find and correct the error.

40.

$2x^2 - 3x + 1 = 10$

$2x^2 - 3x + 1 = (2x - 1)(x - 1)$

$2x - 1 = 0 \quad \text{or} \quad x - 1 = 0$

$x = \dfrac{1}{2} \qquad\qquad x = 1$

41.

$3y^2 - 16y - 35 = 0$

$3y^2 - 16y - 35 = (3y + 7)(y - 5)$

$3y + 7 = 0 \quad \text{or} \quad y - 5 = 0$

$y = -\dfrac{7}{3} \qquad\qquad y = 5$

SOLVING EQUATIONS Solve the equation by factoring.

42. $2x^2 - 9x - 35 = 0$ **43.** $7x^2 - 10x + 3 = 0$ **44.** $3x^2 + 34x + 11 = 0$

45. $4x^2 - 21x + 5 = 0$ **46.** $2x^2 - 17x - 19 = 0$ **47.** $5x^2 - 3x - 26 = 0$

48. $2x^2 + 19x = -24$ **49.** $4x^2 - 8x = -3$ **50.** $6x^2 - 23x = 18$

51. $8x^2 - 34x + 24 = -11$ **52.** $6x^2 + 19x - 10 = -20$

53. $28x^2 - 9x - 1 = -4x + 2$ **54.** $10x^2 + x - 10 = -2x + 8$

VERTICAL COMPONENT OF MOTION In Exercises 55–57, use the vertical motion model $h = -16t^2 + vt + s$ where h is the height (in feet), *t* is the time in motion (in seconds), *v* is the initial velocity (in feet per second), and *s* is the initial height (in feet). Solve by factoring.

55. GYMNASTICS A gymnast dismounts the uneven parallel bars at a height of 8 feet with an initial upward velocity of 8 feet per second.

  a. Write a quadratic equation that models her height above the ground.

  b. Use the model to find the time *t* (in seconds) it takes for the gymnast to reach the ground. Is your answer reasonable?

56. CIRCUS ACROBATS An acrobat is shot out of a cannon and lands in a safety net that is 10 feet above the ground. Before being shot out of the cannon, she was 4 feet above the ground. She left the cannon with an initial upward velocity of 50 feet per second.

  a. Write a quadratic model to represent this situation.

  b. Use the model to find the time *t* (in seconds) it takes for her to reach the net. Explain why only one of the two solutions is reasonable.

57. T-SHIRT CANNON At a basketball game, T-shirts are rolled-up into a ball and shot from a "T-shirt cannon" into the crowd. The T-shirts are released from a height of 6 feet with an initial upward velocity of 44 feet per second. If you catch a T-shirt at your seat 30 feet above the court, how long was it in the air before you caught it? Is your answer reasonable?

58. MULTIPLE CHOICE Factor $9x^2 - 6x - 35$.

    (A) $(9x - 5)(x + 7)$ (B) $(3x + 5)(3x - 7)$

    (C) $(9x + 5)(x - 7)$ (D) $(3x - 5)(3x + 7)$

59. MULTIPLE CHOICE Solve $2x^2 + 5x + 3 = 0$.

    (F) -1 and $-\dfrac{3}{2}$ (G) $-\dfrac{2}{3}$ and $\dfrac{5}{3}$ (H) $\dfrac{3}{2}$ and $-\dfrac{3}{2}$ (J) 1 and $\dfrac{3}{2}$

Mixed Review

SOLVING SYSTEMS Use linear combinations to solve the linear system. Then check your solution. *(Lesson 7.3)*

60. $4x + 5y = 7$
$6x - 2y = -18$

61. $6x - 5y = 3$
$-12x + 8y = 5$

62. $2x + y = 120$
$x + 2y = 120$

SPECIAL PRODUCT PATTERNS Find the product. *(Lesson 10.3)*

63. $(4t - 1)^2$ **64.** $(b + 9)(b - 9)$ **65.** $(3x + 5)(3x + 5)$

66. $(2a - 7)(2a + 7)$ **67.** $(11 - 6x)^2$ **68.** $(100 + 27x)^2$

Maintaining Skills

OPERATIONS WITH FRACTIONS Simplify. *(Skills Review p. 765)*

69. $\dfrac{2}{3} \cdot \dfrac{6}{9} \div \dfrac{11}{3}$ **70.** $\dfrac{1}{2} \div \dfrac{1}{9} \cdot \dfrac{2}{3}$ **71.** $\dfrac{1}{2} \cdot \dfrac{4}{9} \cdot \dfrac{5}{6}$ **72.** $\dfrac{8}{9} \div \dfrac{9}{8} \cdot \dfrac{8}{9}$

73. $\dfrac{2}{3} \cdot \dfrac{4}{5} \cdot \dfrac{6}{7}$ **74.** $\dfrac{12}{15} \cdot \dfrac{3}{4} \div \dfrac{1}{7}$ **75.** $\dfrac{5}{6} \cdot \dfrac{9}{4} \cdot \dfrac{1}{3} \div \dfrac{1}{2}$ **76.** $\dfrac{1}{2} \cdot \dfrac{1}{3} \div \dfrac{1}{4} \cdot \dfrac{1}{5}$

Quiz 2

Solve the equation. *(Lesson 10.4)*

1. $(x + 5)(2x + 10) = 0$ **2.** $(2x + 8)^2 = 0$ **3.** $(2x + 7)(3x - 12) = 0$

4. $x(5x - 2) = 0$ **5.** $3(x - 5)(2x + 1) = 0$ **6.** $x(x + 4)(x - 7)^2 = 0$

Find the *x*-intercepts and the vertex of the graph of the function. Then sketch the graph of the function. *(Lesson 10.4)*

7. $y = (x - 2)(x + 2)$ **8.** $y = (x + 3)(x + 5)$ **9.** $y = (x - 1)(x + 3)$

Factor the trinomial. *(Lesson 10.5)*

10. $y^2 + 3y - 4$ **11.** $w^2 + 13w + 22$ **12.** $n^2 + 16n - 57$

13. $x^2 + 7x + 24$ **14.** $b^2 - 6b - 16$ **15.** $r^2 - 3r - 28$

16. $m^2 - 4m - 45$ **17** $x^2 + 17x + 66$ **18.** $r^2 - 41r - 86$

Solve the equation by factoring. *(Lesson 10.6)*

19. $y^2 + 5y - 6 = 0$ **20.** $n^2 + 26n + 25 = 0$ **21.** $z^2 - 14z + 45 = 0$

22. $t^2 + 11t = -18$ **23.** $2a^2 + 11a + 5 = 0$ **24.** $3p^2 - 4p + 1 = 0$

25. $3b^2 - 10b - 8 = 0$ **26.** $4c^2 + 12c + 9 = 0$ **27.** $15b^2 + 41b = -14$

10.7 Factoring Special Products

Goal
Factor special products.

Key Words
• perfect square trinomial

What height can a pole-vaulter reach?

In Exercise 65 you will factor a quadratic polynomial to find the height a pole-vaulter can vault.

In Lesson 10.5 you learned to factor trinomials of the form $x^2 + bx + c$, where b and c are integers. For example, to factor $x^2 + 3x + 2$, you looked for two numbers whose product was 2 and whose sum was 3. The two numbers are 1 and 2, so you wrote $x^2 + 3x + 2 = (x + 1)(x + 2)$.

You can factor $x^2 - 9$ using the same reasoning. Since there is no middle term, its coefficient must be *zero*. So you will need two numbers whose product is -9 and whose sum is 0. The two numbers are 3 and -3. Thus, you can write

$$x^2 - 9 = (x + 3)(x - 3).$$

This suggests a simple pattern for factoring the difference of two squares.

$$a^2 - b^2 = (a + b)(a - b)$$

If we rewrite the square of a binomial pattern (from page 581) as shown below, two useful factoring patterns are created.

$$a^2 + 2ab + b^2 = (a + b)^2 \qquad \text{or} \qquad a^2 - 2ab + b^2 = (a - b)^2$$

Consider factoring $x^2 - 10x + 25$, for example. You can try the second pattern because the middle term is negative. Let $a = x$ and $b = 5$. The pattern requires that $-2ab$ be the constant term, which is true here because $-2(x)(5) = -10x$. Therefore, $x^2 - 10x + 25 = (x - 5)^2$.

Trinomials of the form $a^2 + 2ab + b^2$ and $a^2 - 2ab + b^2$ are called **perfect square trinomials** because they can be factored as the squares of binomials.

FACTORING SPECIAL PRODUCTS

Difference of Two Squares Patterns

$a^2 - b^2 = (a + b)(a - b)$ Example: $9x^2 - 25 = (3x + 5)(3x - 5)$

Perfect Square Trinomial Pattern

$a^2 + 2ab + b^2 = (a + b)^2$ Example: $x^2 + 14x + 49 = (x + 7)^2$

$a^2 - 2ab + b^2 = (a - b)^2$ Example: $x^2 - 12x + 36 = (x - 6)^2$

▶ STUDY TIP
You can check your
work by multiplying
the factors.

EXAMPLE 1 Factor the Difference of Two Squares

Factor the expression.

a. $m^2 - 4$ **b.** $4p^2 - 25$ **c.** $9q^2 - 64$ **d.** $a^2 - 8$

Solution

a. $m^2 - 4 = m^2 - 2^2$ Write as $a^2 - b^2$.

$= (m + 2)(m - 2)$ Factor using pattern.

b. $4p^2 - 25 = (2p)^2 - 5^2$ Write as $a^2 - b^2$.

$= (2p + 5)(2p - 5)$ Factor using pattern.

c. $9q^2 - 64 = (3q)^2 - 8^2$ Write as $a^2 - b^2$.

$= (3q + 8)(3q - 8)$ Factor using pattern.

d. $a^2 - 8$ cannot be factored using integers because it does not fit the difference of two squares pattern; 8 is not the square of an integer.

Checkpoint ✓ Factor the Difference of Two Squares

Factor the expression.

1. $x^2 - 16$ **2.** $n^2 - 36$ **3.** $r^2 - 20$ **4.** $m^2 - 100$

5. $8y^2 - 1$ **6.** $4y^2 - 49$ **7.** $9x^2 - 25$ **8.** $16q^2 - 45$

EXAMPLE 2 Factor Perfect Square Trinomials

Factor the expression.

a. $x^2 - 4x + 4$ **b.** $a^2 - 18a + 81$ **c.** $16y^2 + 24y + 9$

Solution

a. $x^2 - 4x + 4 = x^2 - 2(x)(2) + 2^2$ Write as $a^2 - 2ab + b^2$.

$= (x - 2)^2$ Factor using pattern.

b. $a^2 - 18a + 81 = a^2 - 2(a)(9) + 9^2$ Write as $a^2 - 2ab + b^2$.

$= (a - 9)^2$ Factor using pattern.

c. $16y^2 + 24y + 9 = (4y)^2 + 2(4y)(3) + 3^2$ Write as $a^2 + 2ab + b^2$.

$= (4y + 3)^2$ Factor using pattern.

Checkpoint ✓ Factor Perfect Square Trinomials

Factor the expression.

9. $x^2 + 6x + 9$ **10.** $n^2 - 8n + 16$ **11.** $a^2 + 18a + 81$

12. $4b^2 - 4b + 1$ **13.** $25m^2 + 10m + 1$ **14.** $9a^2 - 30a + 25$

EXAMPLE 3 **Factor Out a Constant First**

a. $50 - 98x^2 = 2(25 - 49x^2)$ Factor out common factor.

              $= 2[5^2 - (7x)^2]$ Write as $a^2 - b^2$.

              $= 2(5 + 7x)(5 - 7x)$ Factor using pattern.

b. $3x^2 - 30x + 75 = 3(x^2 - 10x + 25)$ Factor out common factor.

                     $= 3[x^2 - 2(x)(5) + 5^2]$ Write as $a^2 - 2ab + b^2$.

                     $= 3(x - 5)^2$ Factor using pattern.

c. $4x^2 + 24x + 44 = 4(x^2 + 6x + 11)$ Factor out common factor.

Since 11 is not the square of any integer, you cannot factor $4(x^2 + 6x + 11)$ with integers using the perfect square trinomial pattern.

Checkpoint ✓   **Factor Out a Constant First**

Factor the expression.

15. $2x^2 - 32$ **16.** $3p^2 + 36p + 108$ **17.** $3b^2 - 48$

18. $8n^2 - 24n + 18$ **19.** $1000 - 10m^2$ **20.** $2a^2 + 28a + 98$

EXAMPLE 4 **Graphical and Analytical Reasoning**

Solve the equation $-2x^2 + 12x - 18 = 0$.

     $-2x^2 + 12x - 18 = 0$ Write original equation.

     $-2(x^2 - 6x + 9) = 0$ Factor out common factor.

   $-2[x^2 - 2(x)(3) + 3^2] = 0$ Write as $a^2 - 2ab + b^2$.

         $-2(x - 3)^2 = 0$ Factor using pattern.

              $x - 3 = 0$ Set repeated factor equal to 0.

                 $x = 3$ Solve for x.

ANSWER ▶ The solution is 3.

CHECK ✓ You can check your answer by substitution or by graphing. Also, a graphing calculator will provide a graphical representation of the solution $x = 3$.

Graph $y = -2x^2 + 12x - 18$.

Graph the x-axis, $y = 0$.

Use your graphing calculator's *Intersect* feature to find the x-intercept, where $-2x^2 + 12x - 18 = 0$.

When $x = 3$, $-2x^2 + 12x - 18 = 0$, so your answer is correct.

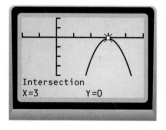

EXAMPLE 5 **Solve a Quadratic Equation**

Solve $4x^2 + 4x + 1 = 0$.

Solution

$4x^2 + 4x + 1 = 0$	Write original equation.
$(2x)^2 + 2(2x) + 1^2 = 0$	Write as $a^2 + 2ab + b^2$.
$(2x + 1)^2 = 0$	Factor using pattern.
$2x + 1 = 0$	Set repeated factor equal to 0.
$x = -\dfrac{1}{2}$	Solve for x.

ANSWER ▶ The solution is $-\dfrac{1}{2}$. Check this in the original equation.

Checkpoint ✓ **Solve a Quadratic Equation**

Solve the equation by factoring. Then use a graphing calculator to check your solutions.

21. $x^2 - 81 = 0$ **22.** $m^2 - 4m + 4 = 0$ **23.** $2n^2 - 288 = 0$

EXAMPLE 6 **Write and Use a Quadratic Model**

BLOCK AND TACKLE An object lifted with a rope or wire should not weigh more than the safe working load for the rope or wire. The safe working load S (in pounds) for a natural fiber rope is a function of C, the circumference of the rope in inches.

> **Safe working load model:** $150 \cdot C^2 = S$

You are setting up a block and tackle to lift a 1350-pound safe. What size natural fiber rope do you need to have a safe working load?

Solution

$150C^2 = S$	Write model.
$150C^2 = 1350$	Substitute 1350 for S.
$150C^2 - 1350 = 0$	Subtract 1350 from each side.
$150(C^2 - 9) = 0$	Factor out common factor.
$150(C + 3)(C - 3) = 0$	Factor.
$C + 3 = 0 \quad or \quad C - 3 = 0$	Use zero-product property.
$C = -3 \qquad\quad C = 3$	Solve for C.

ANSWER ▶ Negative values for circumference do not make sense, so you will need a rope with a circumference of at least 3 inches.

Link to
Science

BLOCK AND TACKLE A block and tackle makes it easier to lift a heavy object. For instance, using a block and tackle with 4 pulleys, you can lift 1000 pounds with only 250 pounds of applied force.

Guided Practice

Vocabulary Check
1. Write the three special product factoring patterns. Give an example of each pattern.

Skill Check
Factor the expression.

2. $x^2 - 9$ **3.** $b^2 + 10b + 25$ **4.** $p^2 + 25$

5. $w^2 - 16w + 64$ **6.** $16 - c^2$ **7.** $6y^2 - 24$

8. $18 - 2b^2$ **9.** $4x^2 - 4x + 1$ **10.** $4a^2 - b^2$

Solve the equation by factoring.

11. $x^2 + 6x + 9 = 0$ **12.** $144 - y^2 = 0$ **13.** $s^2 - 14s + 49 = 0$

14. $-25 + x^2 = 0$ **15.** $4y^2 - 24y + 36 = 0$ **16.** $7x^2 + 28x + 28 = 0$

17. VERTICAL COMPONENT OF MOTION You throw a ball upward from the ground with an initial velocity of 96 feet per second. How long will it take the ball to reach a height of 144 feet? *HINT:* Use the vertical motion model on page 607.

Practice and Applications

DIFFERENCE OF TWO SQUARES **Factor the expression.**

18. $n^2 - 16$ **19.** $q^2 - 64$ **20.** $b^2 - 48$

21. $9c^2 - 1$ **22.** $49 - a^2$ **23.** $81 - x^2$

24. $36x^2 + 25$ **25.** $w^2 - 9y^2$ **26.** $25s^2 - 16t^2$

PERFECT SQUARES **Factor the expression.**

27. $x^2 + 8x + 16$ **28.** $x^2 - 20x + 100$ **29.** $b^2 - 14b + 49$

30. $y^2 + 30y + 225$ **31.** $9x^2 + 6x + 1$ **32.** $4r^2 + 12r + 9$

33. $25n^2 - 20n + 4$ **34.** $18x^2 + 12x + 2$ **35.** $16w^2 - 80w + 100$

36. $36m^2 - 84m + 49$ **37.** $a^2 - 4ab + 4b^2$ **38.** $x^2 + 12xy + 36y^2$

Student Help

▶**HOMEWORK HELP**
Example 1: Exs. 18–26
Example 2: Exs. 27–38
Example 3: Exs. 39–50
Example 4: Exs. 51–58
Example 5: Exs. 51–58
Example 6: Exs. 60–65

COMMON FACTOR **Factor the expression.**

39. $4n^2 - 36$ **40.** $-32 + 18x^2$ **41.** $5c^2 + 20c + 20$

42. $6b^2 - 54$ **43.** $27t^2 + 18t + 9$ **44.** $28y^2 - 7$

45. $3k^2 - 39k + 90$ **46.** $24a^2 - 54$ **47.** $4b^2 - 40b + 100$

48. $32x^2 - 48x + 18$ **49.** $16w^2 + 80w + 100$ **50.** $2x^2 + 28xy + 98y^2$

SOLVING EQUATIONS Solve the equation by factoring. Use a graphing calculator to check your solution if you wish.

51. $4x^2 + 4x + 1 = 0$

52. $25x^2 - 4 = 0$

53. $3x^2 - 24x + 48 = 0$

54. $-27 + 3x^2 = 0$

55. $6b^2 - 72b + 216 = 0$

56. $90x^2 - 120x + 40 = 0$

57. $16x^2 - 56x + 49 = 0$

58. $50x^2 + 60x + 18 = 0$

59. VERTICAL COMPONENT OF MOTION A model rocket is fired upward with an initial velocity of 160 feet per second. How long will it take the rocket to reach a height of 400 feet? *Hint:* Use the vertical motion model on p. 607.

SAFE WORKING LOAD In Exercises 60 and 61, the safe working load S (in tons) for a wire rope is a function of D, the diameter of the rope (in inches).

Safe working load model for wire rope: $4 \cdot D^2 = S$

60. What diameter of wire rope do you need to lift a 9-ton load and have a safe working load?

61. When determining the safe working load S of a rope that is old or worn, decrease S by 50%. Write a model for S when using an old wire rope. What diameter of old wire rope do you need to safely lift a 9-ton load?

HANG TIME In Exercises 62 and 63, use the following information about a basketball player's hang time, the length of time spent in the air after jumping.

The maximum height h jumped (in feet) is a function of t, where t is the hang time (in seconds).

Hang time model: $h = 4t^2$

$h = 4t^2$

62. If you jump 1 foot into the air, what is your hang time?

63. If a professional player jumps 4 feet into the air, what is the hang time?

POLE-VAULTING In Exercises 64 and 65, use the following information. In the sport of pole-vaulting, the height h (in feet) reached by a pole-vaulter can be approximated by a function of v, the velocity of the pole-vaulter, as shown in the model below. The constant g is approximately 32 feet per second per second.

Pole-vaulter height model: $h = \dfrac{v^2}{2g}$

64. To reach a height of 9 feet, what is the pole-vaulter's velocity?

65. What height will a pole-vaulter reach if the pole-vaulter's velocity is 32 feet per second?

66. MULTIPLE CHOICE Which of the following is a correct factorization of $-12x^2 + 147$?

(A) $-3(2x + 7)^2$
(B) $3(2x - 7)(2x + 7)$
(C) $-2(2x - 7)(2x + 7)$
(D) $-3(2x - 7)(2x + 7)$

67. MULTIPLE CHOICE Which of the following is a correct factorization of $72x^2 - 24x + 2$?

(F) $-9(3x - 1)^2$
(G) $2(6x - 1)^2$
(H) $8(3x - 1)^2$
(J) $9(3x - 1)^2$

68. MULTIPLE CHOICE Solve $9x^2 - 12x + 4 = 0$.

(A) -3
(B) $-\frac{2}{3}$
(C) $\frac{2}{3}$
(D) 3

Mixed Review

CHECKING FOR SOLUTIONS Determine whether the ordered pair is a solution of the system of linear equations. *(Lesson 7.1)*

69. $x + 9y = -11$
$-4x + y = -30$ $\quad (7, -2)$

70. $2x + 6y = 22$
$-x - 4y = -13$ $\quad (-5, -2)$

71. $-2x + 7y = -41$
$3x + 5y = 15$ $\quad (-10, 3)$

72. $-5x - 8y = 28$
$9x - 2y = 48$ $\quad (4, -6)$

SOLVING LINEAR SYSTEMS Use the substitution method to solve the linear system. *(Lesson 7.2)*

73. $x - y = 2$
$2x + y = 1$

74. $x - 2y = 10$
$3x - y = 0$

75. $-x + y = 0$
$2x + y = 0$

76. $x - 2y = 4$
$2x + y = 3$

77. $x - y = 0$
$3x + 4y = 14$

78. $2x + 3y = -5$
$x - 2y = -6$

SIMPLIFYING RADICAL EXPRESSIONS Simplify the expression. *(Lesson 9.3)*

79. $\sqrt{216}$
80. $\sqrt{5} \cdot \sqrt{15}$
81. $\sqrt{10} \cdot \sqrt{20}$
82. $\sqrt{4} \cdot 3\sqrt{9}$

83. $\sqrt{\dfrac{28}{49}}$
84. $\dfrac{10\sqrt{8}}{\sqrt{25}}$
85. $\dfrac{12\sqrt{4}}{\sqrt{9}}$
86. $\dfrac{-6\sqrt{12}}{\sqrt{4}}$

SOLVING EQUATIONS Use the quadratic formula to solve the equation. *(Lesson 9.6)*

87. $9x^2 - 14x - 7 = 0$ **88.** $9d^2 - 58d + 24 = 0$ **89.** $7y^2 - 9y - 17 = 0$

Maintaining Skills

PRIME FACTORIZATION Write the prime factorization of the number if it is not a prime number. If a number is prime, write *prime*. *(Skills Review p. 761)*

90. 8
91. 20
92. 45
93. 57

94. 96
95. 80
96. 101
97. 120

98. 244
99. 345
100. 250
101. 600

Factoring Cubic Polynomials

Goal

Factor cubic polynomials.

Key Words

- prime polynomial
- factor a polynomial completely

What are the dimensions of a terrarium?

In Example 6 you will factor a cubic polynomial to determine the dimensions of a terrarium, which is an enclosed space for keeping small animals indoors.

You have already been using the distributive property to factor out constants that are common to the terms of a polynomial.

$$9x^2 - 15 = 3(3x^2 - 5)$$ Factor out common factor.

You can also use the distributive property to factor out *variable* factors that are common to the terms of a polynomial. When factoring a cubic polynomial, you should factor out the *greatest common factor* (GCF) first and then look for other patterns.

EXAMPLE 1 Find the Greatest Common Factor

Factor the greatest common factor out of $14x^3 - 21x^2$.

Solution

First find the greatest common factor of $14x^3$ and $21x^2$.

$$14x^3 = 2 \cdot 7 \cdot x \cdot x \cdot x$$

$$21x^2 = 3 \cdot 7 \cdot x \cdot x$$

$$\text{GCF} = 7 \cdot x \cdot x = 7x^2$$

Then use the distributive property to factor out the greatest common factor from each term.

ANSWER ▶ $14x^3 - 21x^2 = 7x^2(2x - 3)$.

Student Help

▶ **SKILLS REVIEW**
For help with finding the GCF, see p. 761.

Checkpoint ✓ Find the Greatest Common Factor

Factor out the greatest common factor.

1. $11x - 22$

2. $6x^2 + 12x + 18$

3. $8x^3 - 16x$

4. $3n^3 - 36n^2 + 12n$

5. $4y^3 - 10y^2$

6. $9x^3 + 6x^2 + 18x$

PRIME FACTORS A polynomial is **prime** if it cannot be factored using integer coefficients. To **factor a polynomial completely**, write it as the product of monomial and prime factors.

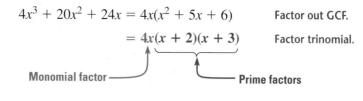

EXAMPLE 2 *Factor Completely*

Factor $4x^3 + 20x^2 + 24x$ completely.

Solution

$$4x^3 + 20x^2 + 24x = 4x(x^2 + 5x + 6) \qquad \text{Factor out GCF.}$$

$$= 4x(x + 2)(x + 3) \qquad \text{Factor trinomial.}$$

Monomial factor ⟶   ⟵ Prime factors

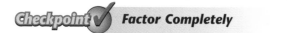

Checkpoint ✓ *Factor Completely*

Factor the expression completely.

7. $2n^3 + 4n^2 + 2n$ **8.** $3x^3 - 12x$ **9.** $5m^3 - 45m$

10. $x^3 + 4x^2 + 4x$ **11.** $2x^3 - 10x^2 + 8x$ **12.** $6p^3 + 21p^2 + 9p$

FACTORING BY GROUPING Another use of the distributive property is in factoring polynomials that have four terms. Sometimes you can factor the polynomial by grouping the terms into two groups and factoring the greatest common factor out of each term.

EXAMPLE 3 *Factor by Grouping*

Factor $x^3 - 2x^2 - 9x + 18$ completely.

Solution

$$x^3 - 2x^2 - 9x + 18 = (x^3 - 2x^2) + (-9x + 18) \qquad \text{Group terms.}$$

$$= x^2(x - 2) + (-9)(x - 2) \qquad \text{Factor each group.}$$

$$= (x - 2)(x^2 - 9) \qquad \text{Use distributive property.}$$

$$= (x - 2)(x - 3)(x + 3) \qquad \text{Factor difference of two squares.}$$

Checkpoint ✓ *Factor by Grouping*

Use grouping to factor the expression completely.

13. $2x^3 - 8x^2 + 3x - 12$ **14.** $x^3 + 5x^2 - 4x - 20$ **15.** $x^3 - 4x^2 - 9x + 36$

SUM OR DIFFERENCE OF TWO CUBES In Lessons 10.3 and 10.7, you used the difference property to study the special product pattern of the difference of two squares. You can also use the distributive property to confirm the following special product patterns for the sum or difference of two cubes.

FACTORING MORE SPECIAL PRODUCTS

Sum of Two Cubes Pattern

$a^3 + b^3 = (a + b)(a^2 - ab + b^2)$ **Example:** $(x^3 + 1) = (x + 1)(x^2 - x + 1)$

Difference of Two Cubes Pattern

$a^3 - b^3 = (a - b)(a^2 + ab + b^2)$ **Example:** $(x^3 - 8) = (x - 2)(x^2 + 2x + 4)$

EXAMPLE 4 Factor the Sum of Two Cubes

Factor $x^3 + 27$.

Solution

$x^3 + 27 = x^3 + 3^3$ Write as sum of cubes.

$\quad\quad\quad\quad = (x + 3)(x^2 - 3x + 9)$ Use special product pattern. Notice that $x^2 - 3x + 9$ is prime and does not factor.

Checkpoint ✓ **Factor the Sum of Two Cubes**

Factor the expression.

16. $x^3 + 125$ **17.** $n^3 + 8$ **18.** $2m^3 + 2$ **19.** $4x^3 + 32$

EXAMPLE 5 Factor the Difference of Two Cubes

Factor $n^3 - 64$.

Solution

$n^3 - 64 = n^3 - 4^3$ Write as difference of cubes.

$\quad\quad\quad\quad = (n - 4)(n^2 + 4n + 16)$ Use special product pattern. Notice that $n^2 + 4n + 16$ is prime and does not factor.

Checkpoint ✓ **Factor the Difference of Two Cubes**

Factor the expression.

20. $x^3 - 27$ **21.** $p^3 - 216$ **22.** $2n^3 - 250$ **23.** $4z^3 - 32$

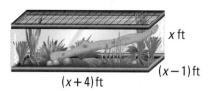

EXAMPLE 6 **Write and Use a Polynomial Model**

SPACE REQUIREMENTS A terrarium has a volume of 12 cubic feet. Find the dimensions of the terrarium. Do the dimensions meet the space requirements of an adult bearded dragon?

x ft
$(x-1)$ ft
$(x+4)$ ft

Solution

$V = \textbf{height} \cdot \textbf{width} \cdot \textbf{length}$	Write volume model for a prism.
$12 = x(x - 1)(x + 4)$	Substitute for height, width and length.
$12 = x^3 + 3x^2 - 4x$	Multiply.
$0 = (x^3 + 3x^2) + (-4x - 12)$	Write in standard form and group terms.
$0 = x^2(x + 3) + (-4)(x + 3)$	Factor each group of terms.
$0 = (x + 3)(x^2 - 4)$	Use distributive property.
$0 = (x + 3)(x - 2)(x + 2)$	Factor difference of two squares.

By setting each factor equal to zero, you can see that the solutions are -3, 2, and -2. The only positive solution is $x = 2$.

ANSWER▶ The dimensions of the terrarium are 2 feet by 1 foot by 6 feet. Because the height must be between 2 and 3.5 feet, the dimensions do *not* meet the space requirements of an adult bearded dragon lizard.

SUMMARY

Patterns Used to Solve Polynomial Equations

GRAPHING: Can be used to solve any equation, but gives only approximate solutions. Examples 2 and 3, pp. 527–528

THE QUADRATIC FORMULA: Can be used to solve any *quadratic* equation. Examples 1–3, pp. 533–534

FACTORING: Can be used with the zero-product property to solve an equation that is in standard form and whose polynomial is factorable.

- **Factoring** $x^2 + bx + c$: Examples 1–7, pp. 595–598

- **Factoring** $ax^2 + bx + c$: Examples 1–5, pp. 603–605

- **Special Products:** Examples 1–6, pp. 610–612 and Examples 4 and 5, p. 618

$$a^2 - b^2 = (a + b)(a - b)$$
$$a^2 + 2ab + b^2 = (a + b)^2$$
$$a^2 - 2ab + b^2 = (a - b)^2$$
$$a^3 + b^3 = (a + b)(a^2 - ab + b^2)$$
$$a^3 - b^3 = (a - b)(a^2 + ab + b^2)$$

- **Factoring Completely:** Examples 1–3, pp. 616–617

10.8 Exercises

Guided Practice

Vocabulary Check

1. What does it mean to say that a factor is prime?

Skill Check

ERROR ANALYSIS Find and correct the error.

2.
$$4x^3 + 36x$$
$$= 4x(x^2 + 9)$$
$$= -4x(x + 3)(x - 3)$$

3.
$$-2b^3 + 12b^2 - 14b$$
$$= -2b(b^2 + 6b - 7)$$
$$= -2b(b + 7)(b - 1)$$

Find the greatest common factor of the terms and factor it out of the expression.

4. $5n^3 - 20n$

5. $6x^2 + 3x^4$

6. $6y^4 + 14y^3 - 10y^2$

Factor the expression.

7. $x^3 - 1$

8. $x^3 + 64$

9. $27x^3 + 1$

10. $125x^3 - 1$

Factor the expression completely.

11. $2b^3 - 18b$

12. $7a^3 - 14a^2 - 21a$

13. $3t^3 + 18t^2 + 27t$

14. $y^3 - 6y^2 + 5y$

15. $x^3 - 16x$

16. $5b^3 - 25b^2 - 70b$

Practice and Applications

FACTORING THE GCF Find the greatest common factor of the terms and factor it out of the expression.

17. $6v^3 - 18v$

18. $4q^4 + 12q$

19. $3x - 9x^2$

20. $10x^2 + 15x^3$

21. $4a^2 - 8a^5$

22. $24t^5 + 6t^3$

23. $15x^3 - 5x^2 - 10x$

24. $4a^5 + 8a^3 - 2a^2$

25. $18d^6 - 6d^2 + 3d$

FACTOR BY GROUPING Factor the expression.

26. $x^2 + 2x + xy + 2y$

27. $a^2 + 3a + ab + 3b$

28. $2x^3 - 3x^2 - 4x + 6$

29. $10x^2 - 15x + 2x - 3$

30. $8x^2 - 3x - 8x + 3$

31. $10x^2 - 7x - 10x + 7$

Student Help

▶ **HOMEWORK HELP**
Example 1: Exs. 17–25
Example 2: Exs. 36–44
Example 3: Exs. 26–31
Example 4: Exs. 32–35
Example 5: Exs. 32–35
Example 6: Exs. 59–61

SUM AND DIFFERENCE OF TWO CUBES Factor the expression.

32. $m^3 + 1$

33. $c^3 - 8$

34. $r^3 + 64$

35. $m^3 - 125$

FACTORING COMPLETELY Factor the expression completely.

36. $24x^3 + 18x^2$ **37.** $2y^3 - 10y^2 - 12y$ **38.** $5s^3 + 30s^2 + 40s$

39. $4t^3 - 144t$ **40.** $-12z^3 + 3z^2$ **41.** $c^4 + c^3 - 12c - 12$

42. $x^3 - 3x^2 + x - 3$ **43.** $3x^3 + 3000$ **44.** $2x^3 - 6750$

SOLVING EQUATIONS Solve the equation. Tell which method you used.

45. $y^2 + 7y + 12 = 0$ **46.** $x^2 - 3x - 4 = 0$

47. $27 + 6w - w^2 = 0$ **48.** $5x^4 - 80x^2 = 0$

49. $-16x^3 + 4x = 0$ **50.** $10x^3 - 290x^2 - 620x = 0$

Student Help

▶ **LOOK BACK**
For help with finding roots, see. p. 534.

FINDING ROOTS OF POLYNOMIALS Use the quadratic formula or factoring to find the roots of the polynomial. Write your solutions in simplest form.

51. $4x^2 - 9x - 9$ **52.** $5x^2 + 2x - 3$ **53.** $2x^2 + 5x + 1$

54. $3x^2 - 4x + 1$ **55.** $6x^2 - 2x - 7$ **56.** $3x^2 + 8x - 2$

Science Link In Exercises 57 and 58, use the vertical motion models, where h is the height (in feet), v is the initial upward velocity (in feet per second), s is the initial height (in feet), and t is the time (in seconds) the object spends aloft.

Vertical motion model for Earth: $h = -16t^2 + vt + s$

Vertical motion model for the moon: $h = -\dfrac{16}{6}t^2 + vt + s$

Note: the two equations are different because the acceleration due to gravity on the moon's surface is about one-sixth that of Earth.

57. EARTH On Earth, you toss a tennis ball from a height of 96 feet with an initial upward velocity of 16 feet per second. How long will it take the tennis ball to reach the ground?

58. MOON On the moon, you toss a tennis ball from a height of 96 feet with an initial upward velocity of 16 feet per second. How long will it take the tennis ball to reach the surface of the moon?

Link to
Careers

PACKAGE DESIGNERS consider the function of a package to determine the appropriate size, shape, weight, color and materials to use.

PACKAGING In Exercises 59–61, use the following information. Refer to the diagram of the box.
The length ℓ of a box is 3 inches less than the height h. The width w is 9 inches less than the height. The box has a volume of 324 cubic inches.

59. Copy and complete the diagram by labeling the dimensions.

60. Write a model that you can solve to find the length, height, and width of the box.

61. What are the dimensions of the box?

62. MULTIPLE CHOICE Which of the following is the complete factorization of $x^3 - 5x^2 + 4x - 20$?

   Ⓐ $(x + 2)(x + 2)(x - 5)$ Ⓑ $(x + 2)(x - 2)(x - 5)$

   Ⓒ $(x^2 + 4)(x - 5)$ Ⓓ $(x - 4)(x - 1)(x - 20)$

63. MULTIPLE CHOICE Solve $x^3 - 4x = 0$.

   Ⓕ 0 and 2   Ⓖ 0, 2, and -2 Ⓗ 2 and -2 Ⓙ -2 and 0

SOLVING INEQUALITIES Solve the inequality. *(Lesson 6.3)*

64. $7 + x \leq -9$ **65.** $-3 > 2x - 5$ **66.** $-x + 6 \leq 12$

SOLVING ABSOLUTE-VALUE EQUATIONS Solve the equation. *(Lesson 6.6)*

67. $|x| = 3$ **68.** $|x - 5| = 7$ **69.** $|x + 6| = 13$ **70.** $|4x + 3| = 9$

GRAPHING INEQUALITIES Graph the inequality. *(Lesson 6.8)*

71. $x + y < 9$ **72.** $y - 3x \geq 2$ **73.** $y - 4x \leq 10$

RECIPROCALS Find the reciprocal. *(Skills Review p. 763)*

74. 18   **75.** -7 **76.** $\frac{2}{9}$ **77.** $1\frac{3}{4}$

78. $\frac{5}{6}$ **79.** $-2\frac{5}{8}$ **80.** $9\frac{7}{10}$ **81.** $-8\frac{3}{4}$

Quiz 3

Factor the expression. Tell which special product factoring pattern you used. *(Lesson 10.7)*

   1. $49x^2 - 64$ **2.** $121 - 9x^2$ **3.** $4t^2 + 20t + 25$

   4. $72 - 50y^2$ **5.** $9y^2 + 42y + 49$ **6.** $3n^2 - 36n + 108$

Solve the equation by factoring. *(Lesson 10.7)*

   7. $x^2 - 8x + 16 = 0$ **8.** $4x^2 + 32x + 64 = 0$ **9.** $x^3 + 9x^2 - 36x = 0$

Find the greatest common factor and factor it out of the expression. *(Lesson 10.8)*

   10. $3x^3 + 12x^2$ **11.** $6x^2 + 3x$ **12.** $18x^4 - 9x^3$ **13.** $8x^5 + 4x^2 - 2x$

Factor the expression completely. *(Lesson 10.8)*

   14. $2x^3 - 6x^2 + 4x$ **15.** $x^3 + 3x^2 + 4x + 12$ **16.** $4x^3 - 500$

Solve the equation by factoring. *(Lesson 10.8)*

   17. $108y^3 - 75y = 0$ **18.** $3x^3 - 6x^2 + 5x = 10$

Chapter Summary and Review

VOCABULARY

- **monomial**, *p. 568*
- **degree of a monomial in one variable**, *p. 568*
- **polynomial**, *p. 569*
- **binomial**, *p. 569*
- **trinomial**, *p. 569*

- **standard form**, *p. 569*
- **degree of a polynomial in one variable**, *p. 569*
- **FOIL pattern**, *p. 576*
- **factored form**, *p. 588*
- **zero-product property**, *p. 588*

- **factor a trinomial**, *p. 595*
- **perfect square trinomial**, *p. 609*
- **prime polynomial**, *p. 617*
- **factor a polynomial completely**, *p. 617*

10.1   ADDING AND SUBTRACTING POLYNOMIALS

Examples on pp. 568–570

EXAMPLES   To add or subtract polynomials, add or subtract like terms.

HORIZONTAL FORMAT

$(4x^3 + 6x - 8) - (-x^2 + 7x - 2)$

$= 4x^3 + 6x - 8 + x^2 - 7x + 2$

$= 4x^3 + x^2 - x - 6$

VERTICAL FORMAT

$$\begin{array}{r} -2x^3 - 4x^2 - x + 5 \\ 3x^3 + 2x^2 - 4x + 9 \\ +\ -x^3 + 5x^2 - x - 1 \\ \hline 3x^2 - 6x + 13 \end{array}$$

Use a vertical format or a horizontal format to add or subtract.

1. $(5x - 12) - (2x - 7)$

2. $(24m - 13) - (18m + 7) + (6m - 4)$

3. $(-x^2 + x + 2) + (3x^2 + 4x + 5)$

4. $(x^2 + 3x - 1) - (4x^2 - 5x + 6)$

5. $(x^3 + 5x^2 - 4x) - (3x^2 - 6x + 2)$

6. $(4x^3 + x^2 - 1) + (2 - x - x^2)$

10.2   MULTIPLYING POLYNOMIALS

Examples on pp. 575–577

EXAMPLES   To multiply polynomials, use the distributive property or FOIL pattern.

a. $(3x + 2)(5x^2 - 4x + 1) = 5x^2(3x + 2) + (-4x)(3x + 2) + 1(3x + 2)$

$$= 15x^3 + 10x^2 - 12x^2 - 8x + 3x + 2$$

$$= 15x^3 - 2x^2 - 5x + 2$$

              First   Outer   Inner   Last

b. $(4x + 5)(-3x - 6) = -12x^2 - 24x - 15x - 30$

$$= -12x^2 - 39x - 30 \qquad \text{Combine like terms.}$$

Find the product.

7. $3a(2a^2 - 5a + 1)$

8. $-4x^3(x^2 + 2x - 7)$

9. $(a - 5)(a + 8)$

10. $(4x - 1)(5x + 2)$

11. $(d + 2)(d^2 - 3d - 10)$

12. $(2b - 1)(3b^2 + 5b + 4)$

10.3   SPECIAL PRODUCTS OF POLYNOMIALS   *Examples on pp. 581–584*

> **EXAMPLES** Use special product patterns to multiply some polynomials.
>
> $$(a + b)(a + b) = a^2 + b^2 \qquad\qquad (a + b)^2 = a^2 + 2ab + b^2$$
>
> $$(3x + 7)(3x - 7) = (3x)^2 - 7^2 \qquad (5t + 4)^2 = (5t)^2 + 2(5t)(4) + 4^2$$
>
> $$= 9x^2 - 49 \qquad\qquad\qquad = 25t^2 + 40t + 16$$

In Exercises 13–16, find the product.

13. $(x + 15)(x - 15)$ **14.** $(5x - 2)(5x + 2)$ **15.** $(x + 2)^2$ **16.** $(7m - 6)^2$

17. Write two expressions for the area of the figure at the right. Describe the special product pattern that is represented.

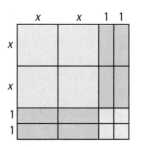

10.4   SOLVING QUADRATIC EQUATIONS IN FACTORED FORM   *Examples on pp. 588–590*

> **EXAMPLE** Solve the equation $(x + 1)(x - 5) = 0$.
>
> **Solution**
>
> $(x + 1)(x - 5) = 0$ Write original equation.
>
> $x + 1 = 0$ *or* $x - 5 = 0$ Use the zero product property.
>
> $x = -1$ | $x = 5$ Solve for x.
>
> *ANSWER*▶ The solutions are -1 and 5. Check these in the original equation.

Solve the equation.

18. $(x + 1)(x + 10) = 0$

19. $(x - 3)(x - 2) = 0$

20. $(y - 7)^2 = 0$

21. $b(5b - 3) = 1$

22. $6(5a - 1)(3a + 1) = 0$

23. $n(n + 9)(n - 12) = 0$

24. $(c + 5)(2c - 1)(3c + 2) = 0$ **25.** $(3x + 1)(x - 4)^2 = 0$

26. $2c(4c + 3)^2 = 0$

10.5 FACTORING $x^2 + bx + c$

Examples on pp. 595–598

EXAMPLE Factor $x^2 - 6x + 8$.

The first term of each binomial factor is x. For this trinomial, $b = -6$ and $c = 8$. Because c is positive, you need to find numbers p and q with the same sign. Find numbers p and q whose sum is -6 and whose product is 8.

p and q	$p + q$	
$-1, -8$	-9	
$-2, -4$	-6	The numbers you need are -2 and -4.

ANSWER ▶ $x^2 - 6x + 8 = (x - 2)(x - 4)$. Check your answer by multiplying.

Factor the trinomial.

27. $x^2 + 10x + 24$

28. $a^2 - 6a - 16$

29. $m^2 - 8m - 20$

Solve the equation by factoring.

30. $b^2 - 11b + 28 = 0$

31. $y^2 + 4y - 32 = 0$

32. $a^2 - 6a - 40 = 0$

10.6 FACTORING $ax^2 + bx + c$

Examples on pp. 603–605

EXAMPLE Factor $3x^2 + 5x - 2$.

For this trinomial, $a = 3$, $b = 5$ and $c = -2$. Because c is negative, you need to find numbers p and q with different signs.

❶ Write the numbers m and n whose product is 3 and the numbers p and q whose product is -2.

m and n	p and q
1, 3	$-1, 2$
	$1, -2$

❷ Use these numbers to write trial factors. Then use the **O**uter and **I**nner products of **FOIL** to check the middle term.

Trial Factors	Middle Term
$(x - 1)(3x + 2)$	$2x - 3x = -x$
$(x + 1)(3x - 2)$	$-2x + 3x = x$
$(x + 2)(3x - 1)$	$-x + 6x = \mathbf{5x}$

ANSWER ▶ $3x^2 + 5x - 2 = (x + 2)(3x - 1)$.

Factor the trinomial.

33. $12x^2 + 7x + 1$

34. $3x^2 - 8x + 4$

35. $4r^2 + 5r - 6$

36. $5c^2 - 33c - 14$

Solve the equation by factoring.

37. $2p^2 - p - 1 = 0$

38. $4x^2 - 3x - 1 = 0$

39. $2a^2 + 7a = 4$

10.7 FACTORING SPECIAL PRODUCTS

Examples on pp. 609–612

EXAMPLES Factor using the special product patterns to solve the equations.

$a^2 - b^2 = (a + b)(a - b)$

$x^2 - 64 = 0$

$x^2 - 8^2 = 0$

$(x + 8)(x - 8) = 0$

$x + 8 = 0 \quad or \quad x - 8 = 0$

$x = -8 \quad | \quad x = 8$

ANSWER ▶ The solutions are −8 and 8.

$a^2 - 2ab + b^2 = (a - b)^2$

$x^2 - 4x + 4 = 0$

$x^2 - 2(x)(2) + 2^2 = 0$

$(x - 2)^2 = 0$

$x - 2 = 0$

$x = 2$

ANSWER ▶ The solution is 2.

Use factoring to solve the equation.

40. $b^2 - 49 = 0$

41. $16a^2 - 1 = 0$

42. $9d^2 - 6d + 1 = 0$

43. $m^2 - 100 = 0$

44. $4b^2 - 12b + 9 = 0$

45. $25x^2 + 20x + 4 = 0$

10.8 FACTORING CUBIC POLYNOMIALS

Examples on pp. 616–619

EXAMPLES Factor using the distributive property or the special product patterns.

$a^3 + b^3 = (a + b)(a^2 - ab + a^2)$

$x^3 + 125 = x^3 + 5^3$

$= (x + 5)(x^2 - 5x + 25)$

$a^3 - b^3 = (a - b)(a^2 + ab + b^2)$

$c^3 - 216 = c^3 - 6^3$

$= (c - 6)(c^2 + 6c + 36)$

Factor by Grouping

$x^3 - 4x^2 - 4x + 16$

$= (x^3 - 4x^2) + (-4x + 16)$

$= x^2(x - 4) + (-4)(x - 4)$

$= (x - 4)(x^2 - 4)$

$= (x - 4)(x + 2)(x - 2)$

Factor the expression completely.

46. $-2x^3 + 6x^2 - 14x$

47. $5y^4 - 20y^3 + 10y^2$

48. $x^3 + 3x^2 - 4x - 12$

49. $3y^3 - 4y^2 - 6y + 8$

50. $x^3 - 64$

51. $27b^3 + 1$

Solve the equation.

52. $x^2 - 6x + 5 = 0$

53. $2x^2 - 50 = 0$

54. $8x^3 + 25x = 30x^2$

Use a vertical format or a horizontal format to add or subtract.

1. $(x^2 + 4x - 1) + (5x^2 + 2)$

2. $(5t^2 - 9t + 1) - (8t + 13)$

3. $(7n^3 + 2n^2 - n - 4) - (4n^3 - 3n^2 + 8)$ **4.** $(x^4 + 6x^2 + 7) + (2x^4 - 3x^2 + 1)$

Find the product.

5. $(x + 3)(2x + 3)$

6. $(3x - 1)(5x + 1)$

7. $(w - 6)(4w^2 + w - 7)$

8. $(5t + 2)(4t^2 + 8t - 7)$

9. $(3z^3 - 5z^2 + 8)(z + 2)$

10. $(4x + 1)(4x - 3)$

11. $(x - 12)^2$

12. $(7x + 2)^2$

13. $(8x + 3)(8x - 3)$

Use the zero-product property to solve the equation.

14. $(6x - 5)(x + 2) = 0$

15. $(x + 8)^2 = 0$

16. $(x + 3)(x - 1)(3x + 2) = 0$

Find the x-intercepts and the vertex of the graph of the function. Then sketch the graph.

17. $y = (x + 1)(x - 5)$

18. $y = (x - 4)(x + 4)$

19. $y = (x + 2)(x + 6)$

Solve the equation by factoring.

20. $x^2 + 13x + 30 = 0$

21. $x^2 - 19x + 84 = 0$

22. $x^2 - 34x - 240 = 0$

23. $2x^2 + 15x - 108 = 0$

24. $9x^2 - 9x = 28$

25. $18x^2 - 57x = -35$

Factor the expression.

26. $x^2 - 196$

27. $16x^2 - 36$

28. $128 - 50x^2$

29. $x^2 - 6x + 9$

30. $4x^2 + 44x + 121$

31. $-6x^3 - 3x^2 + 45x$

32. $9t^2 - 54$

33. $x^3 + 2x^2 - 16x - 32$

34. $2x^3 - 162x$

Solve the equation by a method of your choice.

35. $x^2 - 60 = -11$

36. $2x^2 + 15x - 8 = 0$

37. $x^2 - 13x = -40$

38. $x(x - 16) = 0$

39. $12x^2 + 3x = 0$

40. $x^4 + 7x^3 - 8x - 56 = 0$

41. $5x^3 - 605x = 0$

42. $4x^3 + 24x^2 + 36x = 0$

43. $16x^2 - 34x - 15 = 0$

44. ROOM DIMENSIONS A room's length is 3 feet less than twice its width. The area of the room is 135 square feet. What are the room's dimensions?

45. RUG SIZE A rug 4 meters by 5 meters covers $\frac{2}{3}$ of the floor area in a room.

The rug touches two walls, leaving a strip of uniform width around the other two walls. How wide is the strip?

Chapter Standardized Test

Test Tip  Some questions involve more than one step. Read each question carefully to avoid missing preliminary steps.

1. Classify $3x^2 - 7 + 4x^3 - 5x$ by degree and by the number of terms.

 Ⓐ quadratic trinomial

 Ⓑ cubic polynomial

 Ⓒ quartic polynomial

 Ⓓ quadratic polynomial

 Ⓔ None of these

2. Which of the following is equal to $(-x^2 - 5x + 7) + (-7x^2 + 5x - 2)$?

 Ⓐ $-8x^2 + 5$

 Ⓑ $-8x^2 + 10x + 5$

 Ⓒ $6x^2 + 5$

 Ⓓ $-8x^2 - 10x + 5$

3. Which of the following is equal to $(5x^3 + 3x^2 - x + 1) - (2x^3 + x - 5)$?

 Ⓐ $7x^3 + 3x^2 - 2x + 6$

 Ⓑ $3x^3 + 3x^2 - 2x - 4$

 Ⓒ $3x^3 + 3x^2 - 2x - 6$

 Ⓓ $3x^3 + 3x^2 - 2x + 6$

4. Which of the following is equal to $(4x - 1)(5x - 2)$?

 Ⓐ $20x^2 - 5x + 2$

 Ⓑ $20x^2 - 13x + 2$

 Ⓒ $20x^2 - 3x - 2$

 Ⓓ $20x^2 - 8x - 2$

5. Which of the following is equal to $(2x - 9)^2$?

 Ⓐ $4x^2 + 81$

 Ⓑ $4x^2 - 18x + 81$

 Ⓒ $4x^2 + 36x + 81$

 Ⓓ $4x^2 - 36x + 81$

6. Which of the following is one of the solutions of the equation $x^2 - 2x = 120$?

 Ⓐ -12 Ⓑ -10

 Ⓒ 20 Ⓓ 60

7. Which of the following is a correct factorization of $-45x^2 + 150x - 125$?

 Ⓐ $-5(3x + 5)^2$

 Ⓑ $-5(3x + 5)(3x - 5)$

 Ⓒ $-5(3x - 5)^2$

 Ⓓ $-5(9x + 25)$

8. Which of the following is equal to the expression $x^3 - 2x^2 - 11x + 22$?

 Ⓐ $(x - 2)(x - 11)$ Ⓑ $(x - 2)(x^2 + 11)$

 Ⓒ $(x - 2)(x + 11)$ Ⓓ $(x - 2)(x^2 - 11)$

9. Which of the following is equal to $x^3 + 64$?

 Ⓐ $x(x + 4)(x - 4)$

 Ⓑ $(x + 4)(x^2 - 4x + 16)$

 Ⓒ $(x - 4)(x^2 + 4x + 16)$

 Ⓓ $(x + 8)(x^2 - 8x + 16)$

Maintaining Skills

EXAMPLE 1 The Least Common Denominator

Write the numbers $\frac{3}{4}$, $\frac{2}{3}$, and $\frac{5}{8}$ in order from least to greatest.

Solution The LCD of the fractions is 24.

$$\frac{3}{4} = \frac{3 \cdot 6}{4 \cdot 6} = \frac{18}{24} \qquad \frac{2}{3} = \frac{2 \cdot 8}{3 \cdot 8} = \frac{16}{24} \qquad \frac{5}{8} = \frac{5 \cdot 3}{8 \cdot 3} = \frac{15}{24}$$

Compare the numerators: $15 < 16 < 18$, so $\frac{5}{8} < \frac{2}{3} < \frac{3}{4}$.

ANSWER ▶ In order from least to greatest, the fractions are $\frac{5}{8}$, $\frac{2}{3}$, and $\frac{3}{4}$.

Try These

Write the numbers in order from least to greatest.

1. $\frac{1}{4}, \frac{2}{5}$

2. $\frac{4}{7}, \frac{3}{8}$

3. $\frac{1}{3}, \frac{5}{6}, \frac{1}{2}$

4. $\frac{3}{4}, \frac{1}{6}, \frac{1}{2}$

5. $\frac{3}{10}, \frac{3}{4}, \frac{13}{20}$

6. $\frac{7}{8}, \frac{5}{4}, \frac{7}{24}$

7. $1\frac{1}{3}, \frac{5}{4}, \frac{5}{6}$

8. $2\frac{1}{4}, 1\frac{2}{3}, \frac{5}{6}$

EXAMPLE 2 Operations with Fractions

Add $\frac{5}{6} + \frac{3}{8}$.

Solution

$$\frac{5}{6} + \frac{3}{8} = \frac{20}{24} + \frac{9}{24} \qquad \text{Rewrite fractions using the LCD.}$$

$$= \frac{20 + 9}{24} \qquad \text{Add numerators.}$$

$$= \frac{29}{24}, \text{ or } 1\frac{5}{24} \qquad \text{Simplify.}$$

Student Help

▶ **EXTRA EXAMPLES**

 More examples and practice exercises are available at www.mcdougallittell.com

Try These

Add or subtract. Write the answer as a fraction or mixed number in lowest terms.

9. $\frac{2}{3} + \frac{5}{12}$

10. $\frac{1}{6} - \frac{3}{4}$

11. $\frac{2}{5} + \frac{3}{7}$

12. $\frac{7}{8} - \frac{5}{12}$

13. $\frac{7}{10} - \frac{1}{3}$

14. $\frac{5}{9} + \frac{11}{12}$

15. $1\frac{1}{2} + 3\frac{5}{6}$

16. $2\frac{3}{4} - \frac{17}{20}$

Rational Expressions and Equations

▶ How do scale models fit into the design process?

Application: Scale Models

A floor plan is a smaller diagram of a room or a building drawn as if seen from above. Two- and three-dimensional scale models are used by architects, builders, and city planners in the design process.

Think & Discuss

In the floor plan below, 1 inch represents 14 feet.

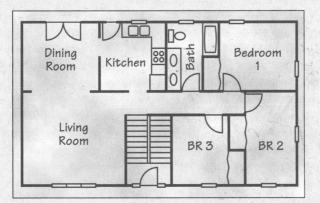

In the floor plan, Bedroom 2 is 1 inch by $\frac{1}{2}$ inch.

1. What is the actual length of Bedroom 2?

2. What is the actual width of Bedroom 2?

3. Solve the equation $\frac{3}{1} = \frac{x}{14}$ to find the actual length x of the whole floor of the house.

Learn More About It

You will write and use a proportion for a problem about a scale model in Exercise 37 on page 637.

 APPLICATION LINK More about scale models is available at www.mcdougallittell.com

What's the chapter about?

- Recognizing direct variation and **inverse variation** models
- Simplifying, adding, subtracting, multiplying, and dividing **rational expressions**
- Solving **proportions** and **rational equations**

> **KEY WORDS**
>
> - **proportion**, *p. 633*
> - **extremes**, *p. 633*
> - **means**, *p. 633*
> - **inverse variation**, *p. 639*
> - **rational number**, *p. 646*
> - **rational expression**, *p. 646*
> - **least common denominator (LCD)**, *p. 663*
> - **rational equation**, *p. 670*

Chapter Readiness Quiz

Take this quick quiz. If you are unsure of an answer, look back at the reference pages for help.

VOCABULARY CHECK *(refer to p. 132)*

1. Which of the following are equivalent equations?

   Ⓐ $y = x^2 + 3$
      $x^2 + y = 3$

   Ⓑ $y = (x - 5)(x + 1)$
      $y - x^2 = -4x - 5$

   Ⓒ $y = (2x + 1)(x + 4)$
      $y = 2x^2 + 8x + 4$

   Ⓓ $y = (x - 5)^2$
      $y = x^2 - 25$

SKILL CHECK *(refer to pp. 462, 605)*

2. Simplify the expression $49x^2 \div \dfrac{-7x}{3}$.

   Ⓐ $\dfrac{343x^3}{3}$ Ⓑ $-21x$ Ⓒ $-21x^2$ Ⓓ $21x$

3. Solve the equation $4x^2 - 10x + 6 = 0$ by factoring.

   Ⓐ $x = -\dfrac{3}{2}, -1$ Ⓑ $x = \dfrac{1}{2}, 3$ Ⓒ $x = -\dfrac{1}{2}, -3$ Ⓓ $x = \dfrac{3}{2}, 1$

Preview and Review

Before studying the chapter, list what you know about each topic. After studying the chapter, go back to each topic and list what you know about each topic. Compare the two sets of notes and see what you have learned.

Chapter 11 Preview

Proportions: deal with fractions, ratios

Direct and Inverse Variation:
  direct variation equation, $y = kx$
  graph of direct variation is linear

Proportions

Goal
Solve proportions.

Key Words
- ratio
- proportion
- extremes
- means
- reciprocal property
- cross product property
- cross multiplying

How many clay warriors were buried in the tomb?

Many real-life quantities are *proportional* to each other. In Example 5 you will use a proportion to estimate the number of clay warriors buried in Emperor Qin Shi Huang's tomb.

Student Help

▶ READING ALGEBRA
The proportion $\frac{a}{b} = \frac{c}{d}$ is read as "*a* is to *b* as *c* is to *d*."

An equation that states that two ratios are equal is a **proportion**,

$$\frac{a}{b} = \frac{c}{d}, \quad \text{where } a, b, c, d \neq 0.$$

When the ratios are written in this order, *a* and *d* are the **extremes** of the proportion and *b* and *c* are the **means** of the proportion. If two nonzero numbers are equal, then their reciprocals are equal. This property carries over to ratios.

RECIPROCAL PROPERTY OF PROPORTIONS

If two ratios are equal, then their reciprocals are also equal.

If $\frac{a}{b} = \frac{c}{d}$, then $\frac{b}{a} = \frac{d}{c}$.   **Example:** $\frac{2}{3} = \frac{4}{6}$ ➡ $\frac{3}{2} = \frac{6}{4}$

Student Help

▶ VOCABULARY TIP
Solving for a variable in a proportion is called *solving the proportion.*

EXAMPLE ① Use the Reciprocal Property

Solve the proportion $\frac{5}{2} = \frac{60}{x}$ using the reciprocal property.

❶ **Write** the original proportion. $\frac{5}{2} = \frac{60}{x}$

❷ **Use** the reciprocal property. $\frac{2}{5} = \frac{x}{60}$

❸ **Multiply** each side of the equation by 60 $24 = x$
to clear the equation of fractions.

ANSWER▶ The solution is $x = 24$. Check this in the original equation.

CROSS PRODUCT PROPERTY By writing both fractions in the proportion $\frac{a}{b} = \frac{c}{d}$ over a common denominator *bd,* the proportion becomes $\frac{ad}{bd} = \frac{bc}{bd}$. This observation is the basis for the cross product property, shown on the next page.

CROSS PRODUCT PROPERTY OF PROPORTIONS

The product of the extremes equals the product of the means.

If $\frac{a}{b} = \frac{c}{d}$, then $ad = bc$.   Example: $\frac{2}{3} = \frac{4}{6}$ ⟹ $2 \cdot 6 = 3 \cdot 4$

EXAMPLE 2 Use the Cross Product Property

Solve the proportion $\frac{3}{y} = \frac{5}{8}$ using the cross product property.

❶ **Write** the original proportion. $\frac{3}{y} = \frac{5}{8}$

❷ **Use** the cross product property. $3 \cdot 8 = y \cdot 5$

❸ **Simplify** the equation. $24 = 5y$

❹ **Solve** by dividing each side by 5. $\frac{24}{5} = y$

CHECK ✓ Substituting $\frac{24}{5}$ for y, $\frac{3}{\frac{24}{5}}$ becomes $3 \cdot \frac{5}{24}$, which simplifies to $\frac{5}{8}$.

Student Help

▶ **STUDY TIP**
Remember to check your solution in the *original* proportion. Since Example 3 has two solutions, you need to check both of them.

EXAMPLE 3 Use the Cross Product Property

Solve the proportion $\frac{3}{x} = \frac{x+1}{4}$.

❶ **Write** the original proportion. $\frac{3}{x} = \frac{x+1}{4}$

❷ **Use** the cross product property. $(3)(4) = (x)(x+1)$

❸ **Multiply.** $12 = x^2 + x$

❹ **Collect** terms on one side. $0 = x^2 + x - 12$

❺ **Factor** the right-hand side. $0 = (x-3)(x+4)$

❻ **Solve** the equation. $x = 3$ or -4

ANSWER ▶ The solutions are $x = 3$ and $x = -4$. Check both solutions.

Checkpoint ✓ Use the Cross Product Property

Solve the proportion. Check your solutions.

1. $\frac{2}{b} = \frac{5}{2}$ **2.** $\frac{25}{n} = \frac{n}{4}$ **3.** $\frac{-3}{x} = \frac{x+6}{3}$ **4.** $\frac{x}{4} = \frac{x-1}{x}$

Consider the equation $\frac{p}{q} = \frac{r}{s}$ where p, q, r and s are polynomials and q and s are restricted so that they do not equal zero. Writing both fractions with a common denominator leads to $\frac{ps}{qs} \stackrel{\bullet}{=} \frac{qr}{qs}$, and then to $ps = qr$. This reasoning is the basis for *cross multiplying*, a method of solving equations used in Example 4.

EXAMPLE 4 **Cross Multiply and Check Solutions**

Solve the equation $\dfrac{y^2 - 9}{y + 3} = \dfrac{y - 3}{2}$.

Solution

❶ *Write* the original equation.

$$\dfrac{y^2 - 9}{y + 3} = \dfrac{y - 3}{2}$$

❷ *Cross multiply.*

$$(y^2 - 9)2 = (y + 3)(y - 3)$$

❸ *Multiply.*

$$2y^2 - 18 = y^2 - 9$$

❹ *Isolate* the variable term.

$$y^2 = 9$$

❺ *Solve* by taking the square root of each side.

$$y = \pm 3$$

The solutions appear to be $y = 3$ and $y = -3$. However, you must discard $y = -3$, since the denominator of the left-hand side would become zero.

ANSWER ▶ The solution is $y = 3$. Check this in the original equation.

EXCLUDE ZERO DENOMINATORS Because division by zero is undefined, when dealing with proportions, you must check your answer to make sure that any values of a variable that result in a zero denominator are excluded from the final answer, as shown in Example 4.

Link to
Archaeology

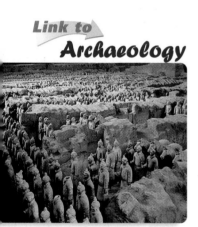

CLAY WARRIORS In 1974, archaeologists excavated the tomb of Emperor Qin Shi Huang (259–210 B.C.) in China. Buried close to the tomb was an entire army of life-sized clay warriors.

 More about this excavation at www.mcdougallittell.com

EXAMPLE 5 **Write and Use a Proportion**

CLAY WARRIORS Pit 1 of the tomb of Emperor Qin Shi Huang, shown below, consists of two end sites, containing a total of 450 warriors, and a central region. The site (shown in red) in the central region contains 282 warriors. This 10-meter-wide site is thought to be representative of the 200-meter central region. Estimate the total number of warriors in Pit 1.

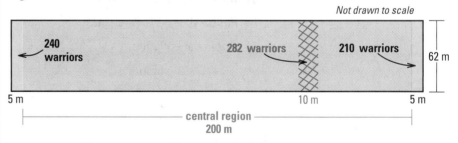

Not drawn to scale

240 warriors | 282 warriors | 210 warriors | 62 m
5 m | 10 m | 5 m
central region
200 m

Solution Let n represent the number of warriors in the 200-meter central region. You can find the value of n by solving a proportion.

$$\dfrac{\text{Number of warriors found}}{\text{Total number of warriors}} = \dfrac{\text{Number of meters excavated}}{\text{Total number of meters}}$$

$$\dfrac{282}{n} = \dfrac{10}{200}$$

ANSWER ▶ The solution is $n = 5640$, indicating that there are about 5640 warriors in the central region. With the 450 warriors at the ends, that makes a total of about 6090 warriors in Pit 1.

Guided Practice

Vocabulary Check

1. Identify the extremes and the means of the proportion.

a. $\dfrac{3}{4} = \dfrac{9}{12}$

b. $\dfrac{9}{12} = \dfrac{3}{4}$.

Skill Check

Solve the proportion. Check your solution.

2. $\dfrac{2}{x} = \dfrac{16}{40}$

3. $\dfrac{72}{96} = \dfrac{x}{4}$

4. $\dfrac{x}{3} = \dfrac{2}{7}$

5. $\dfrac{4}{x+1} = \dfrac{7}{2}$

6. $\dfrac{2}{2x+1} = \dfrac{1}{5}$

7. $\dfrac{x-2}{x} = \dfrac{2}{3}$

Determine whether the equation follows from $\dfrac{a}{b} = \dfrac{c}{d}$.

8. $ad = bc$

9. $ba = dc$

10. $\dfrac{a}{d} = \dfrac{b}{c}$

11. $\dfrac{b}{a} = \dfrac{d}{c}$

Practice and Applications

RECIPROCAL PROPERTY Solve the proportion using the reciprocal property. Check your solution.

12. $\dfrac{3}{x} = \dfrac{1}{2}$

13. $\dfrac{3}{4} = \dfrac{8}{3c}$

14. $\dfrac{13}{z} = \dfrac{1}{3}$

CROSS PRODUCT PROPERTY Solve the proportion using the cross product property. Check your solution.

15. $\dfrac{5}{8} = \dfrac{c}{56}$

16. $\dfrac{x}{3} = \dfrac{7}{3}$

17. $\dfrac{16}{4} = \dfrac{12}{z}$

18. $\dfrac{42}{28} = \dfrac{3}{x}$

19. $\dfrac{5}{y} = \dfrac{8}{9}$

20. $\dfrac{4}{2w} = \dfrac{7}{3}$

21. $\dfrac{5}{3d} = \dfrac{2}{3}$

22. $\dfrac{14}{3} = \dfrac{7b}{2}$

23. $\dfrac{3}{10} = \dfrac{1}{10a}$

CHECKING SOLUTIONS Solve the equation. Check your solutions.

24. $\dfrac{z}{9} = \dfrac{4}{z}$

25. $\dfrac{4}{p} = \dfrac{p}{16}$

26. $\dfrac{x+6}{3} = \dfrac{x-5}{2}$

27. $\dfrac{x-2}{4} = \dfrac{x+10}{10}$

28. $\dfrac{r+4}{3} = \dfrac{r}{5}$

29. $\dfrac{5}{2y} = \dfrac{7}{y-3}$

30. $\dfrac{2}{3t} = \dfrac{t-1}{t}$

31. $\dfrac{x}{2} = \dfrac{5}{x+3}$

32. $\dfrac{x-3}{18} = \dfrac{3}{x}$

33. $\dfrac{-2}{a-7} = \dfrac{a}{5}$

34. $\dfrac{x-3}{x} = \dfrac{x}{x+6}$

35. $\dfrac{9-x}{x+4} = \dfrac{5}{2x}$

Student Help

▶ **HOMEWORK HELP**
Example 1: Exs. 12–14
Example 2: Exs. 15–23
Example 3: Exs. 24–35
Example 4: Exs. 24–35
Example 5: Ex. 36

36. CLAY POTS Assume that a 15-meter-wide site is representative of a larger 60-meter-wide site. If an archaeologist excavates the 15-meter-wide site and finds 30 clay pots, estimate the number of clay pots in the larger 60-meter-wide site. Assume that both sites are the same length.

EXAMPLE *Scale Models*

You want to make a scale model of one of the clay horses found in Emperor Qin Shi Huang's tomb. The clay horse is 1.5 meters tall and 2 meters long. Your scale model will be 18 inches long. How tall should it be?

Solution Let h represent the height of the model.

$$\frac{\text{Height of actual statue}}{\text{Length of actual statue}} = \frac{\text{Height of model}}{\text{Length of model}} \qquad \text{Write verbal model.}$$

$$\frac{1.5}{2} = \frac{h}{18} \qquad \text{Write proportion.}$$

$$(1.5)(18) = 2h \qquad \text{Use cross product property.}$$

$$27 = 2h \qquad \text{Multiply.}$$

$$13.5 = h \qquad \text{Divide by 2.}$$

ANSWER ▶ Your scale model should be $13\frac{1}{2}$ inches tall.

37. **History Link** The ratio of the sculpture of John Wesley Dobbs' head to actual size is about 10 to 1. Suppose that his head was 9 inches high and $6\frac{1}{2}$ inches wide. Estimate the height and width of the sculpture. Write the answer in feet.

MURAL PROJECT In Exercises 38 and 39, use the following information. Refer to the example above if necessary.

Art is the Heart of the City is a fence mural project in Charlotte, North Carolina. Artists Cordelia Williams and Paul Rousso along with 22 high school students created drawings of the mural. Then slides of the drawings were made and projected to fit onto 4-foot-wide by 8-foot-long sheets of plywood used for the fence panels. Students traced and later painted the enlarged images.

38. If the paper used for the original drawings was 11 inches wide, how long did it need to be?

39. Suppose the height of a flower on the panel shown is $2\frac{1}{2}$ feet. Use Exercise 38 to find the height of the flower in the student's drawing.

40. CHALLENGE A scale model uses a scale of $\frac{1}{16}$ inch to represent 1 foot. Explain how you can use a proportion and the cross product property to show that a scale of $\frac{1}{16}$ in. to 1 ft is the same as a scale of 1 in. to 192 in.

Standardized Test Practice

41. MULTIPLE CHOICE What are the extremes of the proportion $\frac{1}{3} = \frac{x}{18}$? What are the extremes of $\frac{x}{18} = \frac{1}{3}$?

(A) 1, 3; x, 18 **(B)** x, 18; 1, 3 **(C)** x, 3; 1, 18 **(D)** 1, 18; x, 3

42. MULTIPLE CHOICE Solve $\frac{x-2}{x+5} = \frac{x-5}{x+2}$.

(F) 1 **(G)** -2 and -5 **(H)** 2 and 5 **(J)** No solution

43. MULTIPLE CHOICE Solve $\frac{c}{c-4} = \frac{8}{c-10}$.

(A) 0 **(B)** 2 and 16 **(C)** -18 and 32 **(D)** No solution

Mixed Review

POINT-SLOPE FORM Write in point-slope form the equation of the line that passes through the given point and has the given slope. *(Lesson 5.2)*

44. $(-1, -2)$, $m = 2$ **45.** $(5, -3)$, $m = -4$ **46.** $(-8, 8)$, $m = -1$

STANDARD FORM Write in standard form the equation of the line that passes through the given point and has the given slope. *(Lesson 5.4)*

47. $(10, 6)$, $m = -2$ **48.** $(-7, -7)$, $m = \frac{1}{2}$ **49.** $(1, 8)$, $m = \frac{3}{4}$

50. $(0, 5)$, $m = 3$ **51.** $(6, 12)$, $m = -12$ **52.** $(6, -1)$, $m = 0$

FINDING SQUARE ROOTS Evaluate the expression. Check the results by squaring the answer. *(Lesson 9.1)*

53. $\sqrt{64}$ **54.** $-\sqrt{9}$ **55.** $\sqrt{10,000}$ **56.** $\pm\sqrt{169}$

SIMPLIFYING RADICALS Simplify the radical expression. *(Lesson 9.3)*

57. $\sqrt{18}$ **58.** $\sqrt{20}$ **59.** $\sqrt{80}$ **60.** $\sqrt{162}$

61. $9\sqrt{36}$ **62.** $\sqrt{\frac{11}{9}}$ **63.** $\frac{1}{2}\sqrt{28}$ **64.** $\sqrt{\frac{5}{8}}$

Maintaining Skills

65. FRACTIONS, DECIMALS, AND PERCENTS Copy and complete the table. Write the fractions in simplest form. *(Skills Review pp. 767–769)*

Decimal	?	0.2	?	0.073	?	?
Percent	78%	?	?	?	3%	?
Fraction	?	?	$\frac{2}{3}$	?	?	$\frac{12}{25}$

11.2 Direct and Inverse Variation

Goal
Use direct and inverse variation.

Key Words
• direct variation
• inverse variation
• constant of variation

How are banking angle and turning radius related?

In Lesson 4.6 you studied direct variation. In Example 4 you will use a different kind of variation to relate the banking angle of a bicycle to its turning radius.

In this lesson you will review direct variation and learn about **inverse variation**, where the product of two variables is a constant.

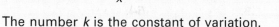

MODELS FOR DIRECT AND INVERSE VARIATION

Direct Variation

The variables x and y *vary directly* if for a constant k

$\dfrac{y}{x} = k$, or $y = kx$, where $k \neq 0$.

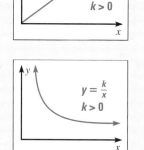

Inverse Variation

The variables x and y *vary inversely* if for a constant k

$xy = k$, or $y = \dfrac{k}{x}$, where $k \neq 0$

The number k is the constant of variation.

Student Help

▶ **STUDY TIP**
Direct and inverse variation are sometimes called *direct* and *inverse proportions*.

EXAMPLE 1 Use Direct Variation

Find an equation that relates x and y such that x and y vary directly, and $y = 4$ when $x = 2$.

Solution

❶ **Write** the direct variation model. $\dfrac{y}{x} = k$

❷ **Substitute** 2 for x and 4 for y. $\dfrac{4}{2} = k$

❸ **Simplify** the left-hand side. $2 = k$

ANSWER ▶ The direct variation that relates x and y is $\dfrac{y}{x} = 2$, or $y = 2x$.

EXAMPLE 2 Use Inverse Variation

Find an equation that relates x and y such that x and y vary inversely, and $y = 4$ when $x = 2$.

❶ **Write** the inverse variation model. $xy = k$

❷ **Substitute** 2 for x and 4 for y. $(2)(4) = k$

❸ **Simplify** the left-hand side. $8 = k$

ANSWER ▶ The inverse variation that relates x and y is $xy = 8$, or $y = \dfrac{8}{x}$.

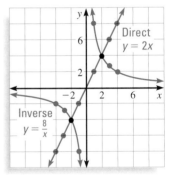

Student Help

▶ **STUDY TIP**
Direct and inverse variation models represent functions because for each value of x there is exactly one value of y. For inverse variation, the domain excludes 0.

EXAMPLE 3 Compare Direct and Inverse Variation

Compare the direct variation model and the inverse variation model you found in Examples 1 and 2 using $x = -4, -3, -2, -1, 1, 2, 3,$ and 4.

a. numerically   **b.** graphically

Solution

a. Use the models $y = 2x$ and $y = \dfrac{8}{x}$ to make a table.

x-value	−4	−3	−2	−1	1	2	3	4
Direct, $y = 2x$	−8	−6	−4	−2	2	4	6	8
Inverse, $y = \dfrac{8}{x}$	−2	$-\dfrac{8}{3}$	−4	−8	8	4	$\dfrac{8}{3}$	2

DIRECT VARIATION: Because k is positive, y increases as x increases. As x increases by 1, y increases by 2.

INVERSE VARIATION: Because k is positive, y decreases as x increases.

b. Use the table of values to graph each model.

DIRECT VARIATION: The graph for this model is a line passing through the origin.

Student Help

▶ **VOCABULARY TIP**
A *hyperbola* is a curve with two branches. You will learn more about hyperbolas in later math courses.

INVERSE VARIATION: The graph for this model is a *hyperbola*. Since neither x nor y can equal 0, the graph does not intersect either axis.

Checkpoint ✓ Compare Direct and Inverse Variation

1. Suppose $y = 6$ when $x = 2$. Find an equation that relates x and y such that:

a. x and y vary directly.   **b.** x and y vary inversely.

2. Compare the direct and inverse variation models in Checkpoint 1 numerically and graphically using $x = -4, -3, -2, -1, 1, 2, 3,$ and 4.

EXAMPLE **4** **Write and Use a Model**

BICYCLE BANKING ANGLE Assume that the graph below shows an inverse
relationship between the banking angle *B* and the turning radius *r* for a bicycle
traveling at a particular speed.

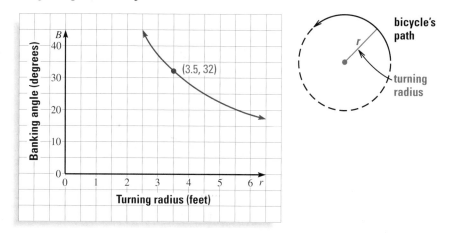

a. Find an inverse variation model that relates *B* and *r*.

b. Use the model to find the banking angle for a turning radius of 5 feet.

c. How does the banking angle change as the turning radius gets smaller?

Solution

  a. From the graph, you can see that $B = 32°$ when $r = 3.5$ feet.

    ❶ *Write* the inverse variation model. $B = \dfrac{k}{r}$

    ❷ *Substitute* **32** for *B* and **3.5** for *r*. $32 = \dfrac{k}{3.5}$

    ❸ *Multiply* each side by 3.5. $112 = k$

    ANSWER ▶ The model is $B = \dfrac{112}{r}$, where *B* is in degrees and *r* is in feet.

  b. Substitute 5 for *r* in the model found in part (a). $B = \dfrac{112}{5} = 22.4°$

  c. As the turning radius gets smaller, the banking angle becomes greater.
From the graph, you can see that the increase in the banking angle is about
10° for a 1-foot decrease in banking angle from 4 to 3 feet, but the increase
in banking angle is only about 4° for a 1-foot decrease from 6 feet to 5 feet.

Checkpoint ✓ **Write and Use a Model**

Use the inverse variation model $B = \dfrac{112}{r}$.

  3. What is the bicycle banking angle when the turning radius is 8 feet?

  4. Does this model apply when $r = 1$? Explain.

Guided Practice

Vocabulary Check

1. What does it mean for two quantities to vary directly?

2. What does it mean for two quantities to vary inversely?

Skill Check

Does the graph model *direct variation, inverse variation*, or *neither*? Explain.

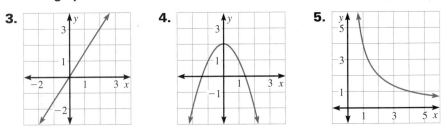

3.   **4.**   **5.**

Does the equation model *direct variation, inverse variation*, or *neither*?

6. $x = \dfrac{4}{y}$ **7.** $y = 7x - 2$ **8.** $x = 12y$ **9.** $xy = 9$

Suppose $y = 6$ when $x = 4$. For the given type of variation, find an equation that relates x and y.

10. x and y vary directly.   **11.** x and y vary inversely.

Practice and Applications

DIRECT VARIATION EQUATIONS The variables x and y vary directly. Use the given values to write an equation that relates x and y.

12. $x = 3, y = 9$ **13.** $x = 2, y = 8$ **14.** $x = 18, y = 6$

15. $x = 8, y = 24$ **16.** $x = 36, y = 12$ **17.** $x = 27, y = 3$

INVERSE VARIATION EQUATIONS The variables x and y vary inversely. Use the given values to write an equation that relates x and y.

18. $x = 2, y = 5$ **19.** $x = 3, y = 7$ **20.** $x = 16, y = 1$

21. $x = 11, y = 2$ **22.** $x = \dfrac{1}{2}, y = 8$ **23.** $x = 5, y = \dfrac{13}{5}$

24. $x = 1.5, y = 50$ **25.** $x = 45, y = 0.6$ **26.** $x = 10.5, y = 7$

Student Help

▶ **HOMEWORK HELP**
Example 1: Exs. 12–17
Example 2: Exs. 18–26
Example 3: Exs. 27–34
Example 4: Exs. 35–42

DIRECT OR INVERSE VARIATION Make a table of values for $x = -4, -3, -2, -1, 1, 2, 3,$ and 4. Use the table to sketch the graph. State whether x and y vary *directly* or *inversely*.

27. $y = \dfrac{4}{x}$ **28.** $y = \dfrac{3x}{2}$ **29.** $y = 3x$ **30.** $y = \dfrac{6}{x}$

VARIATION MODELS IN CONTEXT In Exercises 31–33, state whether the variables model *direct variation*, *inverse variation*, or *neither*.

31. BASE AND HEIGHT The area B of the base and the height h of a prism with a volume of 10 cubic units are related by the equation $Bh = 10$.

32. MASS AND VOLUME The mass m and the volume V of a substance are related by the equation $2V = m$, where 2 is the density of the substance.

33. HOURS AND PAY RATE The number of hours h that you must work to earn \$480 and your hourly rate of pay p are related by the equation $ph = 480$.

34. MODELING WITH GRAPHS Which graph models direct variation where the constant of variation is 3?

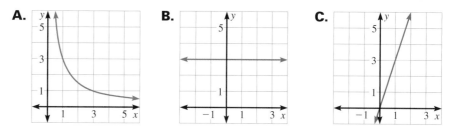

A. **B.** **C.**

SNOWSHOES In Exercises 35–37, use the following information.

When a person walks, the pressure on each boot sole varies inversely with the area of the sole. Denise is walking through deep snow, wearing boots that have a sole area of 29 square inches each. The pressure on the sole is 4 pounds per square inch when she stands on one foot.

35. Use unit analysis to explain why the constant of variation is Denise's weight. How much does she weigh?

36. Using the constant of variation from Exercise 35, write an equation that relates area of the sole A and pressure P.

37. If Denise wears snowshoes, each with an area of 319 square inches, what is the pressure on the snowshoe when she stands on one foot?

SNOWSHOES distribute a person's weight over a large area, allowing a person to walk over deep snow without sinking. Native Americans were among the first people to use snowshoes.

OCEAN TEMPERATURES In Exercises 38 and 39, use the graph and the following information.

The graph at the right shows water temperatures for part of the Pacific Ocean. At depths greater than 900 meters, the temperature of ocean water (in degrees Celsius) varies inversely with depth (in meters).

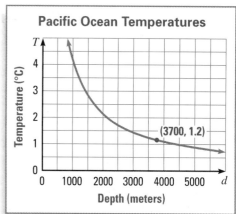

Pacific Ocean Temperatures

(3700, 1.2)

Temperature (°C)

Depth (meters)

38. Find a model that relates the temperature T and the depth d.

39. Find the temperature at a depth of 2000 meters. Round to the nearest tenth.

CHALLENGE You are taking a trip on a highway in a car that gets a gas mileage of 26 miles per gallon for highway driving. You start with a full tank of 12 gallons of gasoline.

40. Find your rate of gas consumption (gallons of gas used to drive 1 mile).

41. Use your results from Exercise 40 to write an equation relating the number of gallons of gas g in your tank and the number of miles m you have driven.

42. Do the variables g and m vary *directly*, *inversely*, or *neither*? Explain.

43. MULTIPLE CHOICE Assuming $y = 14$ when $x = 6$, find an equation that relates x and y such that x and y vary directly.

    (**A**) $xy = 84$ (**B**) $y = \frac{7}{3}x$ (**C**) $y = \frac{3}{7}x$ (**D**) $xy = \frac{7}{3}$

44. MULTIPLE CHOICE Assuming $y = 9$ when $x = 10$, find an equation that relates x and y such that x and y vary inversely.

    (**F**) $xy = 90$ (**G**) $y = \frac{9}{10}x$ (**H**) $y = \frac{10}{9}x$ (**J**) $xy = \frac{9}{10}$

Mixed Review

USING PERCENTS Evaluate. *(Lesson 3.9)*

45. 45% of 10   **46.** 30% of 42   **47.** $\frac{1}{2}$% of 200

48. 150% of 300   **49.** 11% of 50   **50.** 99% of 10,000

CHECKING SOLUTIONS Decide whether the ordered pair is a solution of the inequality. *(Lesson 9.8)*

51. $y < x^2 + 6x + 12$; $(-1, 4)$ **52.** $y \le x^2 - 7x + 9$; $(-1, 2)$

53. $y \ge x^2 - 25$; $(5, 5)$ **54.** $y > x^2 - 2x + 5$; $(1, -7)$

FACTORING EXPRESSIONS Completely factor the expression. *(Lesson 10.6)*

55. $x^2 + 5x - 14$ **56.** $7x^2 + 8x + 1$ **57.** $5x^2 - 51x + 54$

58. $36x^3 - 9x$ **59.** $15x^4 - 50x^3 - 40x^2$ **60.** $6x^2 + 16x$

61. POPULATION The population P of Texas (in thousands), as projected through 2025, is modeled by $P = 18{,}870(1.0124)^t$, where $t = 0$ represents 1995. Find the ratio of the population in 2025 to the population in 2000.
  ▶ Source: U.S. Bureau of the Census *(Lesson 8.3)*

Maintaining Skills

SUBTRACTING FRACTIONS Subtract. Write the answer as a whole number, fraction, or mixed number in lowest terms. *(Skills Review p. 765)*

62. $2\frac{7}{8} - \frac{7}{8}$ **63.** $\frac{16}{9} - 1\frac{1}{9}$ **64.** $4\frac{1}{2} - \frac{20}{8}$ **65.** $3\frac{1}{3} - \frac{4}{3}$

66. $\frac{10}{4} - \frac{1}{2}$ **67.** $\frac{41}{3} - 4\frac{1}{5}$ **68.** $12\frac{5}{6} - \frac{50}{7}$ **69.** $\frac{43}{11} - 2\frac{2}{5}$

For use with Lesson 11.2

Use a graphing calculator to develop an inverse or direct variation model.

Sample

During a chemistry experiment, the volume of a fixed mass of air was decreased and the pressure at different volumes was recorded. The data are shown at the left, where x is the volume (in cubic centimeters) and y is the pressure (in atmospheres). Use a graphing calculator to determine if a direct or an inverse variation model is appropriate. Then make a scatter plot to check your model.

x	y
20	1.06771
19	1.11276
18	1.17583
17	1.24341
16	1.32450
15	1.40559
14	1.51371
13	1.62183
12	1.74347
11	1.90566

Solution

Since y increases as x decreases, direct variation can be ruled out.

1. Let L_1 represent the volume x and L_2 represent the pressure y. Use the *Stat Edit* feature to enter the ordered pairs from the table. Then create lists L_3 and L_4 using $\boxed{L_2}$ $\boxed{\div}$ $\boxed{L_1}$ $\boxed{\text{STO} \blacktriangleright}$ $\boxed{L_3}$ and $\boxed{L_1}$ $\boxed{\times}$ $\boxed{L_2}$ $\boxed{\text{STO} \blacktriangleright}$ $\boxed{L_4}$.

2. Notice that the values in L_3 are all different. However, the values in L_4 are all about 21.1. Thus, x and y can be modeled using inverse variation.

```
L2       L3       L4
1.0677  .05339   21.354
1.1128  .05857   21.142
1.1758  .06532   21.165
1.2434  .07314   21.138
1.3245  .08278   21.192
L4=(21.3542,21. ...
```

3. Choose the constant of variation k using the *List Math* feature to calculate mean(L_4). Use the rounded value, 21.12, to write an inverse variation model in the form $y = \dfrac{k}{x}$.

4. Set the viewing rectangle so that $11 \le x \le 20$ and $1 \le y \le 2$. Use the *Stat Plot* feature to make a scatter plot of L_1 and L_2. Then graph $y = \dfrac{21.12}{x}$ on the same screen.

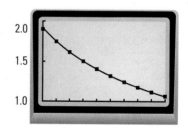

Try These

Decide whether the data might vary directly or inversely. Then choose the constant of variation and write a model for the data.

1. (10, 8.25), (9, 7.425), (8, 6.6), (7, 5.775), (6, 4.95), (5, 4.125), (4, 3.3)

2. (18, 1.389), (17, 1.471), (16, 1.563), (15, 1.667), (14, 1.786), (13, 1.923)

11.3 Simplifying Rational Expressions

Goal
Simplify rational expressions.

Key Words
- rational number
- rational expression
- simplest form of a rational expression

What is the air pressure at 36,000 feet?

In Exercise 47 you will simplify an expression that models the relationship between air pressure and altitude. Then you will use the simplified expression to determine the air pressure on *Breitling Orbiter 3*, the first manned balloon to circle Earth.

A **rational number** is a number that can be written as the quotient of two integers, such as $\frac{1}{2}$, $\frac{4}{3}$, and $\frac{7}{1}$. A fraction whose numerator and denominator are nonzero polynomials is a **rational expression**. Here are some examples.

$$\frac{3}{x+4} \qquad \frac{2x}{x^2-9} \qquad \frac{3x+1}{x^2+1} \qquad \frac{2x^2+x-2}{3x}$$

Simplifying rational expressions is similar to simplifying fractions because the variables in a rational expression represent real numbers. To simplify a rational expression, we factor the numerator and denominator and then divide out any common factors. (Exercise 48, page 650, shows the reasoning used.) A rational expression is in *simplest form* if its numerator and denominator have no factors in common other than ± 1.

SIMPLIFYING RATIONAL EXPRESSIONS

Let *a*, *b*, and *c* be nonzero polynomials.

$$\frac{ac}{bc} = \frac{a \cdot \cancel{c}}{b \cdot \cancel{c}} = \frac{a}{b}$$

EXAMPLE 1 Simplify Rational Expressions

Simplify the rational expression if possible.

a. $\frac{14x}{7} = \frac{2 \cdot \cancel{7} \cdot x}{\cancel{7}} = 2x$

b. $\frac{6x}{9x^2} = \frac{2 \cdot \cancel{3} \cdot \cancel{x}}{\cancel{3} \cdot 3 \cdot \cancel{x} \cdot x} = \frac{2}{3x}$

Student Help

▶ STUDY TIP
When you simplify rational expressions, you can divide out only *factors*, not *terms*.

For example,
$\frac{x \cdot 4}{x} = 4$, but $\frac{x + 4}{x}$ cannot be simplified.

EXAMPLE 2 Write in Simplest Form

Simplify the expression if possible.

a. $\frac{2x}{2(x + 5)}$ **b.** $\frac{x(x^2 + 6)}{x^2}$ **c.** $\frac{x + 4}{x}$

Solution

a. $\frac{2x}{2(x + 5)} = \frac{2 \cdot x}{2 \cdot (x + 5)}$ Divide out the common factor 2.

$= \frac{x}{x + 5}$ Simplify.

b. $\frac{x(x^2 + 6)}{x^2} = \frac{x \cdot (x^2 + 6)}{x \cdot x}$ Divide out the common factor x.

$= \frac{x^2 + 6}{x}$ Simplify.

c. $\frac{x + 4}{x}$ Already in simplest form.

Checkpoint ✓ Write in Simplest Form

Simplify the expression. If not possible, write *already in simplest form*.

1. $\frac{3x^3}{6x^2}$ **2.** $\frac{3m}{3(m - 4)}$ **3.** $\frac{x^2(x + 3)}{x}$ **4.** $\frac{5}{n + 5}$

Student Help

▶ MORE EXAMPLES
More examples are available at www.mcdougallittell.com

EXAMPLE 3 Factor Numerator and Denominator

Simplify $\frac{2x^2 - 6x}{6x^2}$.

Solution

❶ **Write** the original expression. $\frac{2x^2 - 6x}{6x^2}$

❷ **Factor** the numerator and denominator. $\frac{2x(x - 3)}{2 \cdot 3 \cdot x \cdot x}$

❸ **Divide** out the common factors 2 and x. $\frac{2x(x - 3)}{2 \cdot 3 \cdot x \cdot x}$

❹ **Simplify** the expression. $\frac{x - 3}{3x}$

Checkpoint ✓ Factor Numerator and Denominator

Simplify the expression.

5. $\frac{2x - 6}{4}$ **6.** $\frac{5x}{10x^2 - 5x}$ **7.** $\frac{4m^3}{2m^3 + 8m^2}$ **8.** $\frac{p^3 - p^2}{p^2}$

Rational expressions in

the form $\dfrac{a-b}{b-a}$ are

equal to -1 because
of the following.

$$\dfrac{a-b}{b-a} = \dfrac{-(-a+b)}{b-a} =$$

$$\dfrac{-(b-a)}{b-a} = -1$$

EXAMPLE ④ **Recognize Opposite Factors**

Simplify $\dfrac{4-x^2}{x^2-x-2}$.

Solution

❶ **Write** the original expression. $\qquad \dfrac{4-x^2}{x^2-x-2}$

❷ **Factor** the numerator and denominator. $\qquad \dfrac{(2-x)(2+x)}{(x-2)(x+1)}$

❸ **Factor** -1 from $(2-x)$. $\qquad \dfrac{-(x-2)(2+x)}{(x-2)(x+1)}$

❹ **Divide** out the common factor $(x-2)$. $\qquad \dfrac{-(x-2)(x+2)}{(x-2)(x+1)}$

❺ **Simplify** the expression. $\qquad -\dfrac{x+2}{x+1}$

Checkpoint ✓ *Recognize Opposite Factors*

Simplify the expression.

9. $\dfrac{3(4-m)}{3(m-4)}$ **10.** $\dfrac{3-x}{x^2-9}$ **11.** $\dfrac{4(1-m)}{m^2-2m+1}$

12. $\dfrac{2x-5}{20-8x}$ **13.** $\dfrac{y^2+3y-28}{16-y^2}$ **14.** $\dfrac{10x-5}{1-2x}$

EXAMPLE ⑤ **Divide a Polynomial by a Binomial**

Divide (x^2-2x-3) by $(x-3)$.

Solution

❶ **Rewrite** the problem as a rational expression. $\qquad \dfrac{x^2-2x-3}{x-3}$

❷ **Factor** the numerator. $\qquad \dfrac{(x-3)(x+1)}{x-3}$

❸ **Divide** out the common factor $(x-3)$. $\qquad \dfrac{(x-3)(x+1)}{x-3}$

❹ **Simplify** the expression. $\qquad x+1$

Checkpoint ✓ *Divide a Polynomial by a Binomial*

Find the quotient.

15. Divide (x^2-4) by $(x+2)$. **16.** Divide $(2n^2-8n+8)$ by $(n-2)$.

17. $(m^2-4m+3) \div (m-1)$ **18.** $(x^2-2x-8) \div (x-4)$

Guided Practice

Vocabulary Check

1. Define *rational number*. Which of the following are rational numbers?

$$5, \quad \frac{2}{3}, \quad \frac{-17}{2}, \quad \sqrt{3}, \quad 1.45, \quad 0, \quad \pi$$

2. Define *rational expression*. Give an example of a rational expression.

3. Define the *simplest form* of a rational expression. Give an example of a rational expression in simplest form.

Skill Check

Simplify the expression. If not possible, write *already in simplest form*.

4. $\dfrac{28y}{4}$

5. $\dfrac{16}{128c}$

6. $\dfrac{12x^2}{6x}$

7. $\dfrac{a - 8}{4}$

8. $\dfrac{t^4}{t^2(t + 2)}$

9. $\dfrac{8n^3}{12n^4 + 40n^2}$

10. $\dfrac{18}{2x + 4}$

11. $\dfrac{y^7 - y^3}{y^3}$

12. $\dfrac{7 - m}{m^2 - 49}$

Find the quotient.

13. Divide $(3y^2 + 22x + 7)$ by $(y + 7)$.

14. Divide $(x^2 + 5x + 6)$ by $(x + 3)$.

15. Divide $(2x^2 - 5x - 7)$ by $(2x - 7)$.

Practice and Applications

SIMPLIFYING EXPRESSIONS Simplify the expression. If not possible, write *already in simplest form*.

16. $\dfrac{4x}{20}$

17. $\dfrac{45x}{15}$

18. $\dfrac{-18x^2}{12x}$

19. $\dfrac{14x^2}{50x^4}$

20. $\dfrac{10x^5}{16x^3}$

21. $\dfrac{36x}{27x}$

22. $\dfrac{x - 14}{x}$

23. $\dfrac{t^4}{t^2(t + 2)}$

24. $\dfrac{10(r - 6)}{10r}$

FACTORING AND SIMPLIFYING Simplify the expression. If not possible, write *already in simplest form*.

Student Help

▶ **HOMEWORK HELP**
Example 1: Exs. 16–21
Example 2: Exs. 22–24
Example 3: Exs. 25–42
Example 4: Exs. 25–42
Example 5: Exs. 43–46

25. $\dfrac{7x}{12x + x^2}$

26. $\dfrac{3x^2 - 18x}{-9x^2}$

27. $\dfrac{42x - 6x^3}{36x}$

28. $\dfrac{x^2 + 25}{2x + 10}$

29. $\dfrac{2(5 - d)}{2(d - 5)}$

30. $\dfrac{x^2 + 8x + 16}{3x + 12}$

31. $\dfrac{x^2 + x - 20}{x^2 + 2x - 15}$

32. $\dfrac{x^3 + 9x^2 + 14x}{x^2 - 4}$

33. $\dfrac{x^3 - x}{x^3 + 5x^2 - 6x}$

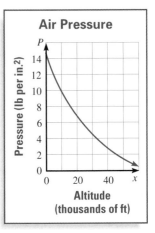

BALLOONING On March 20, 1999, Dr. Bertrand Piccard (pictured above) and Brian Jones became the first balloonists to circle the globe nonstop. The 29,000 mile trip at an altitude of 36,000 feet took them 19 days, 21 hours, and 55 minutes.

SIMPLIFYING EXPRESSIONS Simplify the expression if possible.

34. $\dfrac{x^2 - 9}{x^2 - 5x - 6}$ **35.** $\dfrac{2x^2 + 11x - 6}{x + 6}$ **36.** $\dfrac{121 - x^2}{x^2 + 15x + 44}$

37. $\dfrac{1 - x}{x^2 - x}$ **38.** $\dfrac{12 - 5x}{10x^2 - 24x}$ **39.** $\dfrac{8y^2 - 7y}{14y^2 - 16y^3}$

40. $\dfrac{5 - x}{x^2 - 8x + 15}$ **41.** $\dfrac{9 - 2y}{2y^2 - 3y - 27}$ **42.** $\dfrac{3x - 5}{25 - 30x + 9x^2}$

DIVIDING POLYNOMIALS Find the quotient.

43. Divide $(a^2 - 3a + 2)$ by $(a - 1)$. **44.** Divide $(5g^2 + 13g - 6)$ by $(g + 3)$.

45. Divide $(x^2 - 6x - 16)$ by $(x + 2)$. **46.** Divide $(-5m^2 + 25m)$ by $5m$.

47. Science Link The air pressure at sea level is about 14.7 pounds per square inch. As the altitude increases, the air pressure decreases. For altitudes between 0 and 6000 feet, a model that relates air pressure to altitude is

$$P = \dfrac{2952x - 44x^2}{200x + 5x^2},$$ where P is

measured in pounds per square inch and x is measured in thousands of feet. Simplify this rational expression. Suppose you are in *Breitling Orbiter 3* at 36,000 feet. What is the pressure at that altitude?

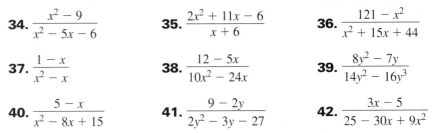

48. LOGICAL REASONING Copy and complete the *proof* to show why you can divide out common factors.

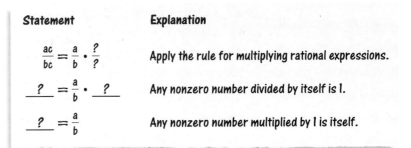

Statement	Explanation
$\dfrac{ac}{bc} = \dfrac{a}{b} \cdot \dfrac{?}{?}$	Apply the rule for multiplying rational expressions.
$\underline{\quad?\quad} = \dfrac{a}{b} \cdot \underline{\quad?\quad}$	Any nonzero number divided by itself is 1.
$\underline{\quad?\quad} = \dfrac{a}{b}$	Any nonzero number multiplied by 1 is itself.

Standardized Test Practice

49. MULTIPLE CHOICE Simplify the expression $\dfrac{6 + 2x}{x^2 + 5x + 6}$.

Ⓐ $\dfrac{2}{x + 2}$ Ⓑ $\dfrac{2}{x + 3}$ Ⓒ $\dfrac{2}{x + 5}$ Ⓓ $\dfrac{2x}{x^2 + 5x}$

50. MULTIPLE CHOICE Simplify the expression $\dfrac{3 - x}{x^2 - 5x + 6}$.

Ⓕ $\dfrac{1}{x + 2}$ Ⓖ $\dfrac{1}{x - 2}$ Ⓗ $\dfrac{-1}{x + 2}$ Ⓙ $\dfrac{-1}{x - 2}$

PRODUCTS AND QUOTIENTS **Simplify.** *(Lessons 2.5, 2.8)*

51. $\left(-\dfrac{1}{2}\right)\left(\dfrac{2}{3}\right)$ **52.** $(-15)\left(-\dfrac{5}{6}\right)$ **53.** $\dfrac{2}{7} \div \dfrac{14}{24}$

54. $\dfrac{4}{9} \div (-36)$ **55.** $\left(-\dfrac{3}{4}\right)\left(\dfrac{3y}{-5}\right)$ **56.** $-(-5)^2(2j)$

57. $\dfrac{2m}{3} \cdot 6m^2$ **58.** $\dfrac{36}{45a} \div \dfrac{-9a}{5}$ **59.** $18c^3 \div \dfrac{-27c}{-4}$

60. **Geometry Link** The area of the triangle is 192 square meters. What is the value of x? What is the perimeter? *(Lesson 9.2)*

SKETCHING GRAPHS **Sketch the graph of the function.** *(Lesson 9.4)*

61. $y = x^2$ **62.** $y = 4 - x^2$ **63.** $y = \dfrac{1}{2}x^2$

64. $y = 5x^2 + 4x - 5$ **65.** $y = 4x^2 - x + 6$ **66.** $y = -3x^2 - x + 7$

ADDING DECIMALS **Find the sum.** *(Skills Review p. 759)*

67. $0.987 + 1.4$ **68.** $0.009 + 9$ **69.** $75.6 + 35.8$

70. $1.23 + 0.45$ **71.** $0.01 + 0.01$ **72.** $100.02 + 10$

Quiz 1

Solve the proportion. Check your solutions. *(Lesson 11.1)*

1. $\dfrac{x}{10} = \dfrac{4}{5}$ **2.** $\dfrac{3}{x} = \dfrac{7}{9}$ **3.** $\dfrac{x}{4x - 8} = \dfrac{2}{x}$ **4.** $\dfrac{6x + 4}{5} = \dfrac{2}{x}$

The variables x and y vary directly. Use the given values to write an equation that relates x and y. *(Lesson 11.2)*

5. $x = 8, y = 32$ **6.** $x = 5, y = 3$ **7.** $x = 10, y = 15$

The variables x and y vary inversely. Use the given values to write an equation that relates x and y. *(Lesson 11.2)*

8. $x = 12, y = 2$ **9.** $x = 4, y = 4$ **10.** $x = 3, y = 2.5$

Simplify the expression if possible. *(Lesson 11.3)*

11. $\dfrac{15x^2}{10x}$ **12.** $\dfrac{x^2 - 7x + 12}{x^2 + 3x - 18}$ **13.** $\dfrac{3 - x}{x^2 + x - 12}$ **14.** $\dfrac{5x}{11x + x^2}$

Find the quotient. *(Lesson 11.3)*

15. Divide $(x^2 - 3x - 28)$ by $(x - 7)$.

16. Divide $(6x^2 + 11x + 3)$ by $(3x + 1)$.

11.4 Multiplying and Dividing Rational Expressions

Goal
Multiply and divide rational expressions.

Key Words
- rational expression
- reciprocal
- divisor

What is the ratio of two prairie dog populations?

In Exercise 47 you will use the rules for dividing rational expressions to compare the growth of two prairie dog populations.

Because the variables in a rational expression represent real numbers, the rules for multiplying and dividing rational expressions are the same as the rules for multiplying and dividing fractions that you learned in previous courses.

MULTIPLYING AND DIVIDING RATIONAL EXPRESSIONS

Let a, b, c, and d be nonzero polynomials.

TO MULTIPLY, multiply numerators and denominators. $\dfrac{a}{b} \cdot \dfrac{c}{d} = \dfrac{ac}{bd}$

TO DIVIDE, multiply by the reciprocal of the divisor. $\dfrac{a}{b} \div \dfrac{c}{d} = \dfrac{a}{b} \cdot \dfrac{d}{c}$

Student Help

▶ STUDY TIP
In Step 3, you do not need to write the prime factorizations of 24 and 60 if you recognize 12 as their greatest common factor.

EXAMPLE 1 Multiply Rational Expressions

Simplify $\dfrac{3x^3}{4x} \cdot \dfrac{8x}{15x^4}$.

❶ **Write** the original expression. $\dfrac{3x^3}{4x} \cdot \dfrac{8x}{15x^4}$

❷ **Multiply** the numerators and denominators. $\dfrac{24x^4}{60x^5}$

❸ **Factor** and divide out the common factors. $\dfrac{2 \cdot 2 \cdot 2 \cdot 3 \cdot x \cdot x \cdot x \cdot x}{2 \cdot 2 \cdot 3 \cdot 5 \cdot x \cdot x \cdot x \cdot x \cdot x}$

❹ **Simplify** the expression. $\dfrac{2}{5x}$

► STUDY TIP
In some cases it saves
work to simplify the
rational expressions
before multiplying.

EXAMPLE 2 **Multiply Rational Expressions**

Simplify $\dfrac{x}{3x^2 - 9x} \cdot \dfrac{x - 3}{2x^2 + x - 3}$.

❶ *Write* the original expression.

$$\dfrac{x}{3x^2 - 9x} \cdot \dfrac{x - 3}{2x^2 + x - 3}$$

❷ *Factor* the numerators and denominators.

$$\dfrac{x}{3x(x - 3)} \cdot \dfrac{x - 3}{(x - 1)(2x + 3)}$$

❸ *Multiply* the numerators and denominators.

$$\dfrac{x(x - 3)}{3x(x - 3)(x - 1)(2x + 3)}$$

❹ *Divide* out the common factors.

$$\dfrac{\cancel{x}\cancel{(x - 3)}}{3\cancel{x}\cancel{(x - 3)}(x - 1)(2x + 3)}$$

❺ *Simplify* the expression.

$$\dfrac{1}{3(x - 1)(2x + 3)}$$

Checkpoint ✓ **Multiply Rational Expressions**

Write the product in simplest form.

1. $\dfrac{y^3}{2y^2} \cdot \dfrac{4y^2}{6}$

2. $\dfrac{5x + 10}{x - 3} \cdot \dfrac{x^2 - 9}{5}$

3. $\dfrac{4x^2}{(x + 2)^2} \cdot \dfrac{x^2 + 3x + 2}{x^2 + 1}$

EXAMPLE 3 **Multiply by a Polynomial**

Simplify $\dfrac{7x}{x^2 + 5x + 4} \cdot (x + 4)$.

Solution

$$\dfrac{7x}{x^2 + 5x + 4} \cdot (x + 4) = \dfrac{7x}{x^2 + 5x + 4} \cdot \dfrac{x + 4}{1}$$

Write $x + 4$ as $\dfrac{x + 4}{1}$.

$$= \dfrac{7x}{(x + 1)(x + 4)} \cdot \dfrac{x + 4}{1}$$

Factor.

$$= \dfrac{7x(x + 4)}{(x + 1)(x + 4)}$$

Multiply numerators and
denominators.

$$= \dfrac{7x\cancel{(x + 4)}}{(x + 1)\cancel{(x + 4)}}$$

Divide out common factor.

$$= \dfrac{7x}{x + 1}$$

Write in simplest form.

Checkpoint ✓ **Multiply by a Polynomial**

Write the product in simplest form.

4. $\dfrac{3}{x + 1} \cdot (2x + 2)$

5. $\dfrac{x}{2x + 4} \cdot (x^2 + 2x)$

6. $(x - 3) \cdot \dfrac{x + 3}{x^2 - 9}$

EXAMPLE 4 Divide Rational Expressions

Simplify $\dfrac{4n}{n+5} \div \dfrac{n-9}{n+5}$.

❶ **Write** the original problem.

$$\dfrac{4n}{n+5} \div \dfrac{n-9}{n+5}$$

❷ **Multiply** by the reciprocal.

$$\dfrac{4n}{n+5} \cdot \dfrac{n+5}{n-9}$$

❸ **Multiply** the numerators and denominators.

$$\dfrac{4n(n+5)}{(n+5)(n-9)}$$

❹ **Divide** out the common factor $(n+5)$.

$$\dfrac{4n\cancel{(n+5)}}{\cancel{(n+5)}(n-9)}$$

❺ **Simplify** the expression.

$$\dfrac{4n}{n-9}$$

Checkpoint ✓ **Divide Rational Expressions**

Write the quotient in simplest form.

7. $\dfrac{4}{x+2} \div \dfrac{3}{x+2}$

8. $\dfrac{x+3}{4} \div \dfrac{2x+6}{3}$

9. $\dfrac{3x}{2x-4} \div \dfrac{6x^2}{x-2}$

EXAMPLE 5 Divide by a Polynomial

Simplify $\dfrac{x^2-9}{4x^2} \div (x-3)$.

Solution

$$\dfrac{x^2-9}{4x^2} \div (x-3) = \dfrac{x^2-9}{4x^2} \cdot \dfrac{1}{x-3} \qquad \text{Multiply by reciprocal.}$$

$$= \dfrac{(x+3)(x-3)}{4x^2} \cdot \dfrac{1}{x-3} \qquad \text{Factor.}$$

$$= \dfrac{(x+3)(x-3)}{4x^2(x-3)} \qquad \text{Multiply numerators and denominators.}$$

$$= \dfrac{(x+3)\cancel{(x-3)}}{4x^2\cancel{(x-3)}} \qquad \text{Divide out common factor.}$$

$$= \dfrac{x+3}{4x^2} \qquad \text{Write in simplest form.}$$

Checkpoint ✓ **Divide by a Polynomial**

Write the quotient in simplest form.

10. $\dfrac{x+1}{x+2} \div (2x+2)$

11. $\dfrac{x+2}{x-1} \div (x^2+2x)$

12. $\dfrac{x^2-4}{x+2} \div (4x-8)$

Guided Practice

Vocabulary Check

In Exercises 1 and 2, complete the sentence.

1. To multiply rational expressions, multiply the __?__ and __?__.

2. To divide rational expressions, multiply by the __?__ of the __?__.

Skill Check

Simplify the expression.

3. $\dfrac{3x}{8x^2} \cdot \dfrac{4x^3}{3x^4}$

4. $\dfrac{x^2 - 1}{x} \cdot \dfrac{2x}{3x - 3}$

5. $\dfrac{x}{x^2 - 25} \cdot \dfrac{x - 5}{x + 5}$

6. $\dfrac{3x}{x^2 - 2x - 15} \cdot (x + 3)$ **7.** $\dfrac{x}{8 - 2x} \div \dfrac{2x}{4 - x}$

8. $\dfrac{4x^2 - 25}{4x} \div (2x - 5)$

9. ERROR ANALYSIS Find and correct the error.

$$\dfrac{x+3}{x-3} \div \dfrac{4x}{x^2-9} = \dfrac{x+3}{x-3} \cdot \dfrac{4x}{(x+3)(x-3)} = \dfrac{4x}{(x-3)^2}$$

Practice and Applications

MULTIPLYING RATIONAL EXPRESSIONS **Write the product in simplest form.**

10. $\dfrac{4x}{3} \cdot \dfrac{1}{x}$

11. $\dfrac{9x^2}{4} \cdot \dfrac{8}{18x}$

12. $\dfrac{7d^2}{6d} \cdot \dfrac{12d^2}{2d}$

13. $\dfrac{6x}{14} \cdot \dfrac{2x^3}{5x^5}$

14. $\dfrac{y}{16} \cdot \dfrac{4y^4}{y^2}$

15. $\dfrac{-3}{x - 4} \cdot \dfrac{x - 4}{12(x - 7)}$

16. $\dfrac{3x}{x^2 - 2x - 24} \cdot \dfrac{x - 6}{6x^2}$ **17.** $\dfrac{z^2 + 8z + 7}{10z} \cdot \dfrac{z^2}{z^2 - 49}$ **18.** $\dfrac{5 - 2x}{6} \cdot \dfrac{24}{10 - 4x}$

19. $\dfrac{3a}{a + 4} \cdot \dfrac{a^2 + 5a + 4}{a^2 + a}$ **20.** $\dfrac{3x^2 - 6x}{2x + 1} \cdot \dfrac{4x + 2}{x - 2}$ **21.** $\dfrac{x}{x - 2} \cdot \dfrac{x^2 - 3x + 2}{x - 1}$

22. $\dfrac{45x^3 - 9x^2}{x} \cdot \dfrac{2}{6(x - 5)}$ **23.** $\dfrac{c^2 - 64}{4c^3} \cdot \dfrac{c}{c^2 + 9c + 8}$ **24.** $\dfrac{3}{x^2 - 5x + 6} \cdot \dfrac{x - 3}{x - 2}$

MULTIPLYING BY POLYNOMIALS **Write the product in simplest form.**

Student Help

▶**HOMEWORK HELP**
Example 1: Exs. 10–15
Example 2: Exs. 16–24
Example 3: Exs. 25–30
Example 4: Exs. 31–39
Example 5: Exs. 40–45

25. $\dfrac{3x}{x + 4} \cdot (3x + 12)$

26. $\dfrac{7x - 15}{11x + 121} \cdot (x + 11)$

27. $(y - 3)^2 \cdot \dfrac{2y - 2}{y^2 - 4y + 3}$

28. $(x^2 + 2x + 1) \cdot \dfrac{x + 2}{x^2 + 3x + 2}$

29. $\dfrac{2x + 3}{2x^2 - 3x - 9} \cdot (x^2 - 9)$

30. $3z^2 + 10z + 3 \cdot \dfrac{z + 3}{3z^2 + 4z + 1}$

DIVIDING RATIONAL EXPRESSIONS Write the quotient in simplest form.

31. $\dfrac{25x^2}{10x} \div \dfrac{5x}{10x}$

32. $\dfrac{16x^2}{8x} \div \dfrac{4x^2}{16x}$

33. $\dfrac{3x^2}{10} \div \dfrac{9x^3}{25}$

34. $\dfrac{x}{x+2} \div \dfrac{x+5}{x+2}$

35. $\dfrac{2(x+2)}{5(x-3)} \div \dfrac{4(x-2)}{5x-15}$

36. $\dfrac{x}{x-2} \div \dfrac{2x-2}{x^2-3x+2}$

37. $\dfrac{x}{x+6} \div \dfrac{x+3}{x^2-36}$

38. $\dfrac{3x+12}{4x} \div \dfrac{x+4}{2x}$

39. $\dfrac{2x^2+3x+1}{12x-12} \div \dfrac{x^2-1}{6x}$

DIVIDING BY POLYNOMIALS Write the quotient in simplest form.

40. $\dfrac{x+5}{2+3x} \div (x^2-25)$

41. $\dfrac{x^2-36}{-5x^2} \div (x-6)$

42. $\dfrac{x^2+19x-20}{x^2} \div (x^2-1)$

43. $\dfrac{y-12}{2y+3} \div (y^2-14y+24)$

44. $\dfrac{3x^2+2x-8}{3x} \div (3x-4)$

45. $\dfrac{4x+3}{x-1} \div (4x^2+x-3)$

PRAIRIE DOGS In Exercises 46–49, use the following information.
Scientists are monitoring two distinct prairie dog populations, P_1 and P_2, modeled as follows.

$$P_1 = \frac{100x^2}{x+1} \text{ and } P_2 = \frac{100x^2}{x+3} \text{ where } x \text{ is time in years.}$$

46. Copy and complete the table below. Round to the nearest whole number.

x	1	2	3	4	5	6	7	8	9	10
P_1	?	?	?	?	?	?	?	?	?	?
P_2	?	?	?	?	?	?	?	?	?	?

47. Find the ratio in simplest form of Population 1 to Population 2, that is $\dfrac{P_1}{P_2}$.

48. Add another row to your table labeled $\dfrac{P_1}{P_2}$ and evaluate for each value of x.

49. Describe the pattern in the ratios you found in Exercise 48. If the value of x gets very large, what value does $\dfrac{P_1}{P_2}$ approach? Explain.

50. *Geometry Link* Write the ratio in simplest form comparing the area of the smaller rectangle to the area of the larger rectangle.

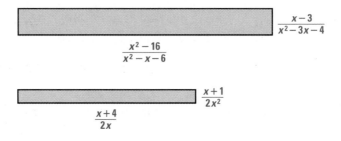

51. CHALLENGE Write the expression in simplest form.

$$\frac{x^2 + 11x + 18}{x^2 - 25} \div \frac{14x^3}{x^2 - x - 20} \cdot \frac{x}{x + 4} \div \frac{2x - 1}{6x} \cdot \frac{2x^2 + 9x - 5}{x^2 + 3x + 2}$$

52. MULTIPLE CHOICE Which of the following represents the expression $\frac{x^2 - 3x}{x^2 - 5x + 6} \cdot \frac{(x - 2)^2}{2x}$ in simplest form?

(A) $\frac{x(x - 3)}{2}$ (B) $\frac{x^2 - 4x + 4}{x - 2}$ (C) $\frac{x - 2}{2}$ (D) $\frac{x}{2}$

53. MULTIPLE CHOICE Which product represents $(2x + 2) \div \frac{x^2 + x}{4}$?

(F) $\frac{2x + 2}{2x + 2} \cdot \frac{4}{x^2 + x}$ (G) $\frac{2x + 2}{1} \cdot \frac{x^2 + x}{4}$

(H) $\frac{1}{2x + 2} \cdot \frac{4}{x^2 + x}$ (J) $\frac{2x + 2}{1} \cdot \frac{4}{x^2 + x}$

FUNCTIONS In Exercises 54–56, use the function $y = x + 9$, where $2 \le x \le 6$. *(Lesson 1.8)*

54. Calculate the output y for several inputs x.

55. Make an input-output table.

56. State the domain and range of the function.

ABSOLUTE-VALUE INEQUALITIES Solve the absolute-value inequality. *(Lesson 6.7)*

57. $|x + 7| < 12$ **58.** $|2x - 15| \le 15$ **59.** $|x + 13| \ge 33$

60. $|3x - 10| < 4$ **61.** $|x + 5| > 17$ **62.** $|5x - 1| \le 0$

QUADRATIC EQUATIONS Solve the quadratic equation. *(Lesson 9.6)*

63. $2x^2 + 12x - 6 = 0$ **64.** $x^2 - 6x + 7 = 0$ **65.** $3x^2 + 11x + 10 = 0$

66. $6x^2 = 130$ **67.** $5 = 6x^2 + 7x$ **68.** $2x^2 + 4x = 7$

POLYNOMIALS Add or subtract the polynomials. *(Lesson 10.1)*

69. $(-5x^2 + 2x - 12) - (6 - 9x - 7x^2)$ **70.** $(a^4 - 12a) + (4a^3 + 11a - 1)$

71. $(16p^3 - p^2 + 24) + (12p^2 - 8p - 16)$ **72.** $(4t^2 + 5t + 2) - (t^2 - 3t - 8)$

ADDING FRACTIONS AND DECIMALS Add. Write the answer as a decimal. *(Skills Review pp. 759, 767)*

73. $0.35 + \frac{1}{2}$ **74.** $0.58 + \frac{2}{5}$ **75.** $0.99 + \frac{3}{4}$ **76.** $0.06 + \frac{1}{8}$

77. $\frac{7}{8} + 0.25$ **78.** $\frac{3}{5} + 0.4$ **79.** $\frac{12}{12} + 0.12$ **80.** $\frac{3}{10} + 0.45$

11.5 Adding and Subtracting with Like Denominators

Goal

Add and subtract rational expressions with like denominators.

Key Words

- rational expression
- common denominator

What happens when you hit a tennis ball?

In Exercises 42–45 you will subtract rational expressions with like denominators to analyze the effects of hitting a tennis ball with a racket.

As with fractions, to add or subtract rational expressions with *like*, or the same, denominators, combine their numerators and write the result over the common denominator.

ADDING OR SUBTRACTING WITH LIKE DENOMINATORS

Let a, b, and c be polynomials, with $c \neq 0$.

TO ADD, add the numerators.
$$\frac{a}{c} + \frac{b}{c} = \frac{a+b}{c}$$

TO SUBTRACT, subtract the numerators.
$$\frac{a}{c} - \frac{b}{c} = \frac{a-b}{c}$$

EXAMPLE 1 Add Rational Expressions

Simplify $\dfrac{5}{2x} + \dfrac{x-5}{2x}$.

Solution

❶ **Write** the original expression. $\dfrac{5}{2x} + \dfrac{x-5}{2x}$

❷ **Add** the numerators. $\dfrac{5 + (x-5)}{2x}$

❸ **Combine** like terms. $\dfrac{x}{2x}$

❹ **Simplify** the expression. $\dfrac{1}{2}$

EXAMPLE 2 Subtract Rational Expressions

Simplify $\dfrac{4}{x+2} - \dfrac{x+4}{x+2}$.

Student Help

▶ STUDY TIP
When you are subtracting rational expressions, make sure the quantity that you are subtracting is in parentheses so that you remember to distribute the negative.

Solution

❶ **Write** the original expression. $\dfrac{4}{x+2} - \dfrac{x+4}{x+2}$

❷ **Subtract** the numerators. $\dfrac{4-(x+4)}{x+2}$

❸ **Distribute** the negative. $\dfrac{4-x-4}{x+2}$

❹ **Simplify** the numerator. $-\dfrac{x}{x+2}$

Checkpoint ✓ *Add and Subtract Rational Expressions*

Simplify the expression.

1. $\dfrac{x+2}{x} + \dfrac{3x-2}{x}$ 2. $\dfrac{x+2}{x^2+5} - \dfrac{3x+2}{x^2+5}$ 3. $\dfrac{3x-4}{x-4} - \dfrac{2x}{x-4}$

EXAMPLE 3 Simplify after Subtracting

Student Help

▶ MORE EXAMPLES
More examples are available at www.mcdougallittell.com

Simplify $\dfrac{4x}{3x^2-x-2} - \dfrac{x-2}{3x^2-x-2}$.

Solution

$$\dfrac{4x}{3x^2-x-2} - \dfrac{x-2}{3x^2-x-2} = \dfrac{4x-(x-2)}{3x^2-x-2}$$ Subtract numerators.

$$= \dfrac{3x+2}{3x^2-x-2}$$ Simplify.

$$= \dfrac{3x+2}{(3x+2)(x-1)}$$ Factor.

$$= \dfrac{3x+2}{(3x+2)(x-1)}$$ Divide out common factor.

$$= \dfrac{1}{x-1}$$ Write simplest form.

Checkpoint ✓ *Simplify after Adding or Subtracting*

Write the sum or difference in simplest form.

4. $\dfrac{2x}{x^2+2x+1} + \dfrac{2}{x^2+2x+1}$ 5. $\dfrac{2x-4}{x^2+3x} - \dfrac{x-7}{x^2+3x}$

11.5 *Adding and Subtracting with Like Denominators*   **659**

Guided Practice

Vocabulary Check

1. Complete: To add or subtract rational expressions with like denominators, add or subtract their numerators, and write the result over the ⎯?⎯.

Skill Check

Add. Simplify your answer.

2. $\dfrac{1}{3x} + \dfrac{5}{3x}$

3. $\dfrac{8y}{y+3} + \dfrac{10-3y}{y+3}$

4. $\dfrac{x}{x^2-9} + \dfrac{3x+1}{x^2-9}$

Subtract. Simplify your answer.

5. $\dfrac{8}{3r} - \dfrac{1}{3r}$

6. $\dfrac{12k}{k^2} - \dfrac{3k+7}{k^2}$

7. $\dfrac{c+1}{c^2-4} - \dfrac{c+6}{c^2-4}$

Add or subtract, then factor and simplify.

8. $\dfrac{5x}{x+4} + \dfrac{20}{4+x}$

9. $\dfrac{-12y}{y^2-9y+14} + \dfrac{84}{y^2-9y+14}$

10. $\dfrac{2y+3}{y^2-4y} - \dfrac{-y+15}{y^2-4y}$

11. $\dfrac{10}{r^2+9r+20} - \dfrac{-2r}{r^2+9r+20}$

Practice and Applications

ADDING RATIONAL EXPRESSIONS Simplify the expression.

12. $\dfrac{7}{2x} + \dfrac{x+2}{2x}$

13. $\dfrac{2}{x+7} + \dfrac{5}{x+7}$

14. $\dfrac{4t-1}{1-4t} + \dfrac{2t+3}{1-4t}$

15. $\dfrac{4}{x+1} + \dfrac{2x-2}{x+1}$

16. $\dfrac{a+1}{15a} + \dfrac{2a-1}{15a}$

17. $\dfrac{2x}{4x+6} + \dfrac{3}{4x+6}$

SUBTRACTING RATIONAL EXPRESSIONS Simplify the expression.

18. $\dfrac{7x}{x^3} - \dfrac{6x}{x^3}$

19. $\dfrac{8+6t}{3t} - \dfrac{5t-6}{3t}$

20. $\dfrac{2x}{x+2} - \dfrac{2x+1}{x+2}$

21. $\dfrac{2}{3x-1} - \dfrac{5x}{3x-1}$

22. $\dfrac{4x}{2x+6} - \dfrac{16}{2x+6}$

23. $\dfrac{4m}{m-2} - \dfrac{2m+4}{m-2}$

FACTORING AFTER ADDING OR SUBTRACTING Simplify the expression.

24. $\dfrac{x}{x^2+5x-24} + \dfrac{8}{x^2+5x-24}$

25. $\dfrac{a^2-2}{a^2-25} + \dfrac{4a-3}{a^2-25}$

26. $\dfrac{2x}{x^2+5x+4} + \dfrac{8}{x^2+5x+4}$

27. $\dfrac{x^2-10}{x^2-4} + \dfrac{3x}{x^2-4}$

28. $\dfrac{2x}{x^2+5x} - \dfrac{x}{x^2+5x}$

29. $\dfrac{2x(x+4)}{(x+1)^2} - \dfrac{3x-3}{(x+1)^2}$

30. $\dfrac{y^2-2y}{y^2-7y-18} - \dfrac{9(y-2)}{y^2-7y-18}$

31. $\dfrac{y^2}{y^2-3y-28} - \dfrac{12-y}{y^2-3y-28}$

Student Help

▶ **HOMEWORK HELP**
Example 1: Exs. 12–17
Example 2: Exs. 18–23
Example 3: Exs. 24–31

ERROR ANALYSIS In Exercises 32 and 33, find and correct the error.

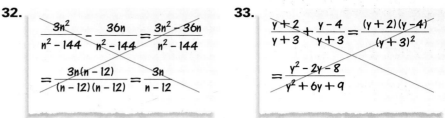

32.

$$\frac{3n^2}{n^2-144} - \frac{36n}{n^2-144} = \frac{3n^2-36n}{n^2-144}$$

$$= \frac{3n(n-12)}{(n-12)(n-12)} = \frac{3n}{n-12}$$

33.

$$\frac{y+2}{y+3} + \frac{y-4}{y+3} = \frac{(y+2)(y-4)}{(y+3)^2}$$

$$= \frac{y^2-2y-8}{y^2+6y+9}$$

Student Help

▶**HOMEWORK HELP**

Extra help with problem solving in Exs. 34–39 is available at www.mcdougallittell.com

COMBINING OPERATIONS In Exercises 34–39, simplify the expression.

34. $\dfrac{11x-5}{2x+5} + \dfrac{11x+12}{2x+5} + \dfrac{3x-100}{2x+5}$

35. $\dfrac{4+x}{x-9} + \dfrac{6+x}{x-9} - \dfrac{1-x}{x-9}$

36. $\dfrac{c-15}{2c+6} - \dfrac{2c}{2c+6} + \dfrac{12}{2c+6}$

37. $\dfrac{2x}{x^2-9} - \dfrac{4x+2}{x^2-9} - \dfrac{4}{x^2-9}$

38. $\left(\dfrac{3x^2}{56}\right)\left(\dfrac{3}{x} + \dfrac{5}{x}\right)$

39. $\left(\dfrac{3x-5}{x} + \dfrac{1}{x}\right) \div \left(\dfrac{x}{6x-8}\right)$

Geometry Link Find expressions for the perimeter of the rectangle and triangle. Simplify your answer.

40.

$$\frac{2x-5}{x-2}$$

$$\frac{x^2-3}{x-2}$$

41.

$$\frac{5x}{x+1}$$

$$\frac{4x}{x+1}$$

$$\frac{5x}{x+1}$$

Link to Science

KINETIC ENERGY Every moving object has kinetic energy. The tennis player and tennis racket have kinetic energy as he swings the racket at the ball. The ball has kinetic energy as it flies through the air.

Science Link In Exercises 42–45, use the following information.

When a tennis player hits a ball that is already moving, the work done by the racket is the change in the ball's kinetic energy. The total work done on an object is given by the formula

$$W = K_2 - K_1$$

where W represents work, K_1 represents the initial kinetic energy of an object, and K_2 represents the final kinetic energy of an object. Work and energy are measured in joules. (A joule is the amount of work done when a force of 1 newton acts on an object that moves 1 meter.)

Copy and complete the table, by computing the work done on the tennis ball.

	K_2	K_1	Work
42.	$\dfrac{9}{x}$	$\dfrac{7}{x}$	?
43.	$\dfrac{5}{a}$	$\dfrac{5-a}{a}$	?
44.	$\dfrac{2t}{t-1}$	$\dfrac{t+4}{t-1}$	?
45.	$\dfrac{x^2-7}{x^2-100}$	$\dfrac{-10x-7}{x^2-100}$	?

46. MULTIPLE CHOICE Which of the following expressions can be simplified to $x + 3$?

    Ⓐ $\dfrac{x^2}{x + 3} - \dfrac{9}{x + 3}$ Ⓑ $\dfrac{x^2}{x - 7} - \dfrac{4x + 21}{x - 7}$

    Ⓒ $\dfrac{x - 6}{x - 3} - \dfrac{x + 9}{x - 3}$ Ⓓ None of these

47. MULTIPLE CHOICE Simplify $\dfrac{x^2}{x + 5} - \dfrac{25}{x + 5}$.

    Ⓕ $\dfrac{1}{x - 5}$ Ⓖ $\dfrac{x^2 - 25}{x + 5}$ Ⓗ $x - 5$ Ⓙ $\dfrac{x - 5}{x + 5}$

48. MULTIPLE CHOICE Simplify $\dfrac{24y^2 + 24}{8y - 3} - \dfrac{73y}{8y - 3}$.

    Ⓐ $\dfrac{(8y + 3)(3y + 8)}{8y - 3}$ Ⓑ $\dfrac{3y - 8}{(8y - 3)^2}$

    Ⓒ $\dfrac{3y - 8}{8y - 3}$ Ⓓ $3y - 8$

Mixed Review

SIMPLIFYING EXPRESSIONS Rewrite the expression with positive exponents. *(Lesson 8.2)*

49. $x^5 y^{-6}$ **50.** $8x^{-1}y^{-3}$ **51.** $\dfrac{1}{2x^8 y^{-5}}$ **52.** $\dfrac{3}{10t^{-3}r^{-1}}$

53. $(-6c)^{-4}$ **54.** $(-y)^0 n$ **55.** $\dfrac{1}{c^{-2d}}$ **56.** $\dfrac{1}{(-7m)^{-3}}$

SIMPLIFYING EXPRESSIONS Simplify the expression. The simplified expression should have no negative exponents. *(Lesson 8.4)*

57. $\dfrac{p^6}{p^8}$ **58.** $x^5 \cdot \dfrac{1}{x^4}$ **59.** $\left(\dfrac{a^8}{a^3}\right)^{-1}$ **60.** $\left(\dfrac{y^5}{y^7}\right)^{-2}$

61. $\dfrac{m^8 \cdot m^{10}}{m^2}$ **62.** $\dfrac{(a^3)^4}{(a^3)^8}$ **63.** $\left(\dfrac{-2u^2 v}{uv^4}\right)^{-3}$ **64.** $\left(\dfrac{42a^3 b^{-4}}{6ab}\right)^3$

EVALUATING EXPRESSIONS Perform the indicated operation. Write the result in scientific notation. *(Lesson 8.5)*

65. $\dfrac{8 \times 10^{-3}}{5 \times 10^{-5}}$ **66.** $\dfrac{1.4 \times 10^{-1}}{3.5 \times 10^{-4}}$ **67.** $\left(3 \times 10^{-2}\right)^4$

68. $2 \times 10^3 + 3 \times 10^2$ **69.** $(2.5 \times 10)^{-2}$ **70.** $3.2 \times 10 + 5.8 \times 10$

Maintaining Skills

PATTERNS List the next three numbers suggested by the sequence. *(Skills Review pp. 781)*

71. $1, 3, 5, 7, \text{?}, \text{?}, \text{?}$ **72.** $1, 3, 6, 10, \text{?}, \text{?}, \text{?}$

73. $60, 57, 53, 48, \text{?}, \text{?}, \text{?}$ **74.** $\dfrac{1}{2}, \dfrac{2}{3}, \dfrac{3}{4}, \dfrac{4}{5}, \text{?}, \text{?}, \text{?}$

75. $2, \dfrac{7}{2}, 5, \dfrac{13}{2}, \text{?}, \text{?}, \text{?}$ **76.** $100, 81, 64, 49, \text{?}, \text{?}, \text{?}$

Adding and Subtracting with Unlike Denominators

Goal

Add and subtract rational expressions with unlike denominators.

Key Words

- least common denominator (LCD)

How should you plan a 300-mile car trip?

In Example 6 you will add rational expressions with *unlike* denominators to analyze the total time needed for a 300-mile car trip.

As with fractions, to add or subtract rational expressions with *unlike* denominators, you first rewrite the expressions so that they have *like* denominators. The like denominator that you usually use is the least common multiple of the original denominators, called the **least common denominator** or **LCD**.

Student Help

▶ **SKILLS REVIEW**
For practice on finding the LCD of numerical fractions, see p. 762.

EXAMPLE 1 Find the LCD of Rational Expressions

Find the least common denominator of $\dfrac{1}{12x}$ and $\dfrac{2+x}{40x^4}$.

Solution

❶ **Factor** the denominators.

$$12x = 2^2 \cdot 3 \cdot x$$
$$40x^4 = 2^3 \cdot 5 \cdot x^4$$

❷ **Find** the highest power of each factor that appears in either denominator.

$$2^3, 3, 5, x^4$$

❸ **Multiply** these to find the LCD.

$$2^3 \cdot 3 \cdot 5 \cdot x^4 = 120x^4$$

ANSWER ▶ The LCD is $120x^4$.

Checkpoint ✓ *Find the LCD of Rational Expressions*

Find the least common denominator.

1. $\dfrac{x+1}{5}, \dfrac{2x}{6}$

2. $\dfrac{1}{36x}, \dfrac{3x+1}{9x^5}$

3. $\dfrac{5x+9}{16x^3}, \dfrac{7}{24x^2}$

4. $\dfrac{x}{x-5}, \dfrac{2x^3}{x+7}$

5. $\dfrac{12}{x+1}, \dfrac{x}{x-1}$

6. $\dfrac{2x+3}{30x^5}, \dfrac{1}{8x}$

EXAMPLE 2 Rewrite Rational Expressions

Find the missing numerator.

a. $\dfrac{2}{3y} = \dfrac{?}{15y}$

b. $\dfrac{3x - 7}{4x^2} = \dfrac{?}{36x^5}$

Solution

a. $\dfrac{2}{3y} = \dfrac{?}{15y}$ Multiply $3y$ by 5 to get $15y$.

    $\dfrac{2}{3y} = \dfrac{10}{15y}$ Therefore, multiply 2 by 5 to get 10.

b. $\dfrac{3x - 7}{4x^2} = \dfrac{?}{36x^5}$ Multiply $4x^2$ by $9x^3$ to get $36x^5$.

    $\dfrac{3x - 7}{4x^2} = \dfrac{(3x - 7) \cdot 9x^3}{36x^5}$ Therefore, multiply $(3x - 7)$ by $9x^3$ to get $(3x - 7) \cdot 9x^3$.

    $\dfrac{3x - 7}{4x^2} = \dfrac{27x^4 - 63x^3}{36x^5}$ Simplify.

Checkpoint ✓ *Rewrite Rational Expressions*

Find the missing numerator.

7. $\dfrac{9}{5x} = \dfrac{?}{30x^5}$

8. $\dfrac{y - 1}{y} = \dfrac{?}{13y^2}$

9. $\dfrac{c}{c + 1} = \dfrac{?}{(c + 1)(c - 3)}$

EXAMPLE 3 Add with Unlike Denominators

Simplify $\dfrac{2}{x} + \dfrac{1 - 2x}{x^2}$.

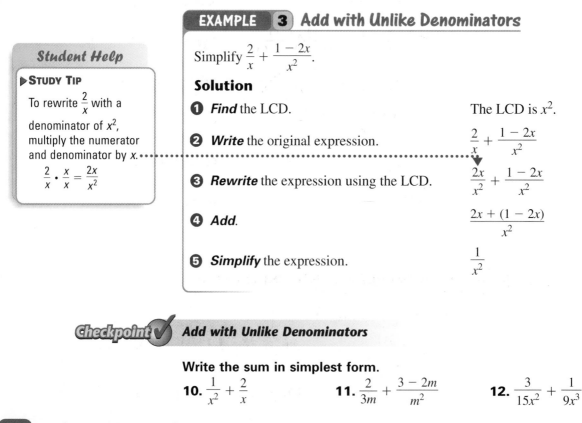

Solution

❶ Find the LCD.   The LCD is x^2.

❷ Write the original expression. $\dfrac{2}{x} + \dfrac{1 - 2x}{x^2}$

❸ Rewrite the expression using the LCD. $\dfrac{2x}{x^2} + \dfrac{1 - 2x}{x^2}$

❹ Add. $\dfrac{2x + (1 - 2x)}{x^2}$

❺ Simplify the expression. $\dfrac{1}{x^2}$

Student Help

▶ **STUDY TIP**

To rewrite $\dfrac{2}{x}$ with a denominator of x^2, multiply the numerator and denominator by x.

$\dfrac{2}{x} \cdot \dfrac{x}{x} = \dfrac{2x}{x^2}$

Checkpoint ✓ *Add with Unlike Denominators*

Write the sum in simplest form.

10. $\dfrac{1}{x^2} + \dfrac{2}{x}$

11. $\dfrac{2}{3m} + \dfrac{3 - 2m}{m^2}$

12. $\dfrac{3}{15x^2} + \dfrac{1}{9x^3}$

EXAMPLE 4 Subtract with Unlike Denominators

Simplify $\dfrac{7}{6x} - \dfrac{x+1}{8x^2}$.

Solution

The LCD is $24x^2$.

$$\dfrac{7}{6x} - \dfrac{x+1}{8x^2} = \dfrac{7}{6x} \cdot \dfrac{4x}{4x} - \dfrac{(x+1)}{8x^2} \cdot \dfrac{3}{3} \qquad \text{Rewrite using LCD.}$$

$$= \dfrac{28x}{24x^2} - \dfrac{3x+3}{24x^2} \qquad \text{Simplify numerators and denominators.}$$

$$= \dfrac{28x - (3x+3)}{24x^2} \qquad \text{Subtract.}$$

$$= \dfrac{25x - 3}{24x^2} \qquad \text{Simplify.}$$

EXAMPLE 5 Add with Unlike Binomial Denominators

Simplify $\dfrac{x+2}{x-1} + \dfrac{12}{x+6}$.

Solution

Neither denominator can be factored. The least common denominator is the product $(x-1)(x+6)$ because it must contain both of these factors.

$$\dfrac{x+2}{x-1} + \dfrac{12}{x+6} \qquad \text{Write original expression.}$$

$$\dfrac{(x+2)(x+6)}{(x-1)(x+6)} + \dfrac{12(x-1)}{(x-1)(x+6)} \qquad \text{Rewrite using LCD.}$$

$$\dfrac{x^2 + 8x + 12}{(x-1)(x+6)} + \dfrac{12x - 12}{(x-1)(x+6)} \qquad \text{Simplify numerators.}$$

$$\dfrac{x^2 + 8x + 12 + (12x - 12)}{(x-1)(x+6)} \qquad \text{Add.}$$

$$\dfrac{x^2 + 20x}{(x-1)(x+6)} \qquad \text{Combine like terms.}$$

$$\dfrac{x(x+20)}{(x-1)(x+6)} \qquad \text{Factor.}$$

Checkpoint ✓ Add or Subtract with Unlike Denominators

Simplify the expression.

13. $\dfrac{3}{x^2} - \dfrac{2}{3x}$

14. $\dfrac{2}{p} - \dfrac{3 - 10p}{5p^2}$

15. $\dfrac{3 + 4x}{4x^3} - \dfrac{1}{10x^2}$

16. $\dfrac{1}{x+1} + \dfrac{1}{x-1}$

17. $\dfrac{3}{x-6} + \dfrac{1}{x}$

18. $\dfrac{x-5}{x+5} - \dfrac{x+2}{x-2}$

EXAMPLE **6** *Write and Use a Model*

PLANNING A TRIP You are planning a 300-mile car trip. You can make the trip using a combination of two roads: a highway on which you can drive 60 mi/h and a country road on which you can drive 40 mi/h. Write an expression for the total time the trip will take driving on both roads.

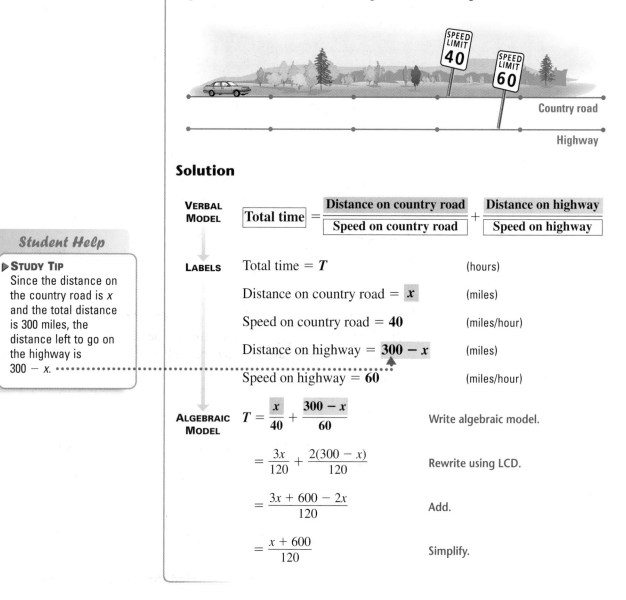

Country road

Highway

Solution

Student Help

▶ **STUDY TIP**
Since the distance on the country road is *x* and the total distance is 300 miles, the distance left to go on the highway is $300 - x$.

VERBAL MODEL

$$\boxed{\text{Total time}} = \frac{\boxed{\text{Distance on country road}}}{\boxed{\text{Speed on country road}}} + \frac{\boxed{\text{Distance on highway}}}{\boxed{\text{Speed on highway}}}$$

LABELS

Total time = T (hours)

Distance on country road = x (miles)

Speed on country road = **40**   (miles/hour)

Distance on highway = **300 − x**   (miles)

Speed on highway = **60**   (miles/hour)

ALGEBRAIC MODEL

$$T = \frac{x}{40} + \frac{300 - x}{60} \qquad \text{Write algebraic model.}$$

$$= \frac{3x}{120} + \frac{2(300 - x)}{120} \qquad \text{Rewrite using LCD.}$$

$$= \frac{3x + 600 - 2x}{120} \qquad \text{Add.}$$

$$= \frac{x + 600}{120} \qquad \text{Simplify.}$$

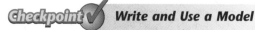 **Write and Use a Model**

19. Evaluate the expression for the total time at 60 mile intervals by completing the table. The table can help you decide how many miles to drive on each road.

Distance (country), *x*	0	60	120	180	240	300
Total time, *T*	?	?	?	?	?	?

11.6 Exercises

Guided Practice

Vocabulary Check

1. Explain what is meant by the *least common denominator* of two rational expressions.

Skill Check

2. ERROR ANALYSIS Find and correct the error.

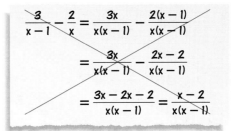

$$\frac{3}{x-1} - \frac{2}{x} = \frac{3x}{x(x-1)} - \frac{2(x-1)}{x(x-1)}$$

$$= \frac{3x}{x(x-1)} - \frac{2x-2}{x(x-1)}$$

$$= \frac{3x-2x-2}{x(x-1)} = \frac{x-2}{x(x-1)}$$

In Exercises 3–6, simplify the expression.

3. $\dfrac{x}{12} + \dfrac{x}{4}$

4. $\dfrac{3}{10x} - \dfrac{1}{4x^2}$

5. $\dfrac{x+6}{x+1} - \dfrac{4}{2x+3}$

6. $\dfrac{x-2}{2x-10} + \dfrac{x+3}{x-5}$

7. You can use $x - 3$ as the LCD when finding the sum $\dfrac{5}{x-3} + \dfrac{2}{3-x}$. What number can you multiply the numerator and the denominator of the second fraction by to get an equivalent fraction with $x - 3$ as the new denominator?

Practice and Applications

FINDING THE LCD Find the least common denominator of the pair of rational expressions.

8. $\dfrac{1}{3x}, \dfrac{1}{9x^3}$

9. $\dfrac{4x}{15}, \dfrac{3x^2}{5}$

10. $\dfrac{17y^4}{z^2}, \dfrac{8z}{3y}$

11. $\dfrac{3}{c^3}, \dfrac{-5}{7c^5}$

12. $\dfrac{10}{13v^7}, \dfrac{10}{3v^5}$

13. $\dfrac{6b}{5}, \dfrac{-5}{b}$

14. $\dfrac{x-1}{x-2}, \dfrac{x-3}{x-4}$

15. $\dfrac{x+1}{15x}, \dfrac{25}{18x^3}$

REWRITING RATIONAL EXPRESSIONS Find the missing numerator.

16. $\dfrac{11}{3x} = \dfrac{?}{12x^3}$

17. $\dfrac{8}{5} = \dfrac{?}{15y^2}$

18. $\dfrac{x-3}{2} = \dfrac{?}{28x}$

19. $\dfrac{3a+1}{9a^5} = \dfrac{?}{63a^{11}}$

20. $\dfrac{x-9}{2x+3} = \dfrac{?}{x(2x+3)}$

21. $\dfrac{2a-3}{35a^2} = \dfrac{?}{140a^5}$

Student Help

▶**HOMEWORK HELP**
Example 1: Exs. 8–15
Example 2: Exs. 16–21
Example 3: Exs. 22–27
Example 4: Exs. 28–33
Example 5: Exs. 34–42
Example 6: Exs. 43–48

ADDING Write the sum in simplest form.

22. $\dfrac{3}{2z} + \dfrac{1}{z}$

23. $\dfrac{11}{6x} + \dfrac{2}{13x}$

24. $\dfrac{9}{4x} + \dfrac{7}{-5x}$

25. $\dfrac{2x+3}{4} + \dfrac{x+1}{2}$

26. $\dfrac{3}{12m^3} + \dfrac{m+1}{4m^3}$

27. $\dfrac{3n}{15} + \dfrac{n^2+1}{30n}$

SUBTRACTING Write the difference in simplest form.

28. $\dfrac{2x}{5} - \dfrac{x+1}{4}$

29. $\dfrac{9}{2x} - \dfrac{2}{7x^2}$

30. $\dfrac{3}{6b^2} - \dfrac{1}{4b}$

31. $\dfrac{x-1}{6x^2} - \dfrac{2}{3x}$

32. $\dfrac{5c}{15} - \dfrac{2+c}{25c}$

33. $\dfrac{2x-1}{3x} - \dfrac{1}{11}$

ADDING OR SUBTRACTING Simplify the expression.

34. $\dfrac{2}{x+1} + \dfrac{3}{x-2}$

35. $\dfrac{x}{x-10} + \dfrac{x+4}{x+6}$

36. $\dfrac{x-3}{x+3} + \dfrac{x+9}{x-3}$

37. $\dfrac{x+8}{3x-1} + \dfrac{x+3}{x+1}$

38. $\dfrac{4}{x+4} - \dfrac{7}{5x}$

39. $\dfrac{2x+1}{3x-1} - \dfrac{x+4}{x-2}$

40. $\dfrac{4x}{5x-2} - \dfrac{2x}{5x+1}$

41. $\dfrac{2x}{x-1} - \dfrac{7x}{x+4}$

42. $\dfrac{3x+10}{7x-4} - \dfrac{x}{4x+3}$

TRAVEL BY BIKE In Exercises 43–45, use the following information.
You are riding your bike to a pond that is 8 miles away. You have a choice to ride in the woods, on the road, or both. In the woods, you can ride at a speed of 10 mi/h. On the road, you can ride at a speed of 20 mi/h.

43. Write an expression for your total time.

44. Write your answer to Exercise 43 in simplest form.

45. Evaluate the expression for total time at 2 mile intervals.

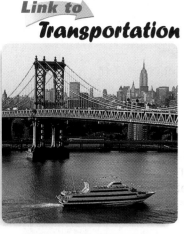
TRAVEL BY BOAT In Exercises 46–48, use the following information.
A boat moves through still water at x kilometers per hour (km/h). It travels 24 km upstream against a current of 2 km/h and then returns to the starting point with the current. The rate upstream is $x - 2$ because the boat moves against the current, and the rate downstream is $x + 2$ because the boat moves with the current.

46. Write an algebraic model for the total time for the round trip.

47. Write your answer to Exercise 46 as a single rational expression.

48. Use your answer to Exercise 47 to find how long the round trip will take if the boat travels 10 km/h through still water.

Geometry Link In Exercises 49–51, use the diagram of the rectangle.

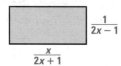

49. Find an expression for the perimeter of the rectangle.

50. What is the perimeter of the rectangle when $x = 3$?

51. What is the area of the rectangle when $x = 3$?

52. MULTIPLE CHOICE Find the LCD of $\dfrac{15}{3t^6}$ and $\dfrac{9}{2t^4}$.

(A) $\dfrac{1}{6t^6}$ (B) $6t^2$ (C) $6t^6$ (D) $6t^{10}$

53. MULTIPLE CHOICE Find the missing numerator $\dfrac{5x+6}{8x^2} = \dfrac{?}{48x^3}$.

(F) $6x$ (G) $41x$ (H) $30x^2 + 36x$ (J) $11x + 6$

54. MULTIPLE CHOICE What is the difference of $\dfrac{x}{x-1}$ and $\dfrac{1}{2x+1}$ in simplest form?

(A) $\dfrac{x-1}{(x-1)(2x+1)}$ (B) $-\dfrac{x}{x-1}$

(C) $\dfrac{2x^2+1}{(x-1)(2x+1)}$ (D) $\dfrac{2x^2-1}{(x-1)(2x+1)}$

Mixed Review

POINT-SLOPE FORM Write in point-slope form the equation of the line that passes through the given point and has the given slope. *(Lesson 5.2)*

55. $(-3, -2), m = 2$ **56.** $(0, 5), m = -1$ **57.** $(-3, 6), m = \dfrac{1}{2}$

58. $(5, 5), m = 5$ **59.** $(7, 0), m = \dfrac{3}{7}$ **60.** $(14, -3), m = \dfrac{1}{3}$

SIMPLIFYING EXPRESSIONS Simplify the expression. *(Lesson 8.4)*

61. $\dfrac{5}{10x}$ **62.** $\dfrac{4m^2}{6m}$ **63.** $\dfrac{16x^4}{32x^8}$ **64.** $\dfrac{42x^4y^3}{6x^3y^9}$

65. $\dfrac{12x}{144x^2}$ **66.** $\dfrac{2x^2y^3z^4}{5x^4y^3z^2}$ **67.** $\dfrac{33p^4}{44p^2q}$ **68.** $\dfrac{15w^2}{9w^5}$

STANDARD FORM Write the equation in standard form. *(Lesson 9.6)*

69. $6x^2 = 5x - 7$ **70.** $9 - 6x = 2x^2$ **71.** $-4 + 3y^2 = y$

72. $12x = x^2 + 25$ **73.** $7 - 12x^2 = 5x$ **74.** $8 = 5x^2 - 4x$

75. GAME SHOW A contestant on a television game show must guess the price of a trip within $1000 of the actual price in order to win. The actual price of the trip is $8500. Write an absolute-value inequality that shows the range of possible guesses that will win the trip. *(Lesson 6.7)*

Maintaining Skills

FRACTIONS AND DECIMALS Write the fraction as a decimal rounded to the nearest thousandth. *(Skills Review p. 767)*

76. $\dfrac{47}{99}$ **77.** $\dfrac{63}{200}$ **78.** $\dfrac{32}{155}$ **79.** $\dfrac{59}{199}$

80. $-\dfrac{115}{144}$ **81.** $-\dfrac{63}{89}$ **82.** $-\dfrac{12}{43}$ **83.** $-\dfrac{79}{145}$

84. $-\dfrac{23}{25}$ **85.** $\dfrac{8}{77}$ **86.** $\dfrac{12}{7}$ **87.** $-\dfrac{18}{35}$

11.7 Rational Equations

Goal
Solve rational equations.

Key Words
- rational equation
- cross product property
- least common denominator (LCD)

How long does it take to shovel a driveway?

If you can shovel a snowy driveway in 3 hours and your friend can do it in 2 hours, how long would it take to shovel it together? In Example 4 you will write and solve a rational equation to answer this question.

A **rational equation** is an equation that contains rational expressions. Example 1 and Example 2 show the two basic strategies for solving a rational equation.

Student Help

▶ **STUDY TIP**
When you solve rational equations, be sure to check your answers. Remember, values of the variable that make any denominator equal to 0 are excluded.

EXAMPLE 1 Cross Multiply

Solve $\dfrac{5}{y+2} = \dfrac{y}{3}$.

❶ **Write** the original equation. $\dfrac{5}{y+2} = \dfrac{y}{3}$

❷ **Cross multiply.** $5(3) = y(y+2)$

❸ **Simplify** each side of the equation. $15 = y^2 + 2y$

❹ **Write** the equation in standard form. $0 = y^2 + 2y - 15$

❺ **Factor** the right-hand side. $0 = (y+5)(y-3)$

ANSWER ▶ The solutions are $y = -5$ and $y = 3$.

CHECK ✓ Neither -5 nor 3 results in a zero denominator. Substitute $y = -5$ and $y = 3$ into the original equation.

y = −5: $\dfrac{5}{(-5)+2} \overset{?}{=} \dfrac{-5}{3}$ Since $\dfrac{5}{-3} = \dfrac{-5}{3}$, $y = -5$ is a solution. ✓

y = 3: $\dfrac{5}{3+2} \overset{?}{=} \dfrac{3}{3}$ Since $\dfrac{5}{5} = \dfrac{3}{3}$, $y = 3$ is a solution. ✓

Checkpoint ✓ Cross Multiply

Solve the equation. Check your solutions.

1. $\dfrac{x}{2} = \dfrac{x+2}{6}$ **2.** $\dfrac{3}{2m} = \dfrac{m+1}{4m}$ **3.** $\dfrac{y}{5} = \dfrac{6}{y+7}$

TWO METHODS Cross multiplying is appropriate for solving equations in which each side is a single rational expression. A second method, multiplying by the LCD, works for any rational equation.

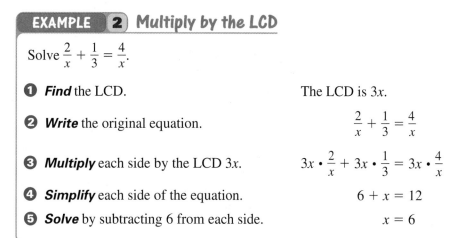

EXAMPLE 2 Multiply by the LCD

Solve $\dfrac{2}{x} + \dfrac{1}{3} = \dfrac{4}{x}$.

❶ **Find** the LCD.   The LCD is $3x$.

❷ **Write** the original equation. $\dfrac{2}{x} + \dfrac{1}{3} = \dfrac{4}{x}$

❸ **Multiply** each side by the LCD $3x$. $3x \cdot \dfrac{2}{x} + 3x \cdot \dfrac{1}{3} = 3x \cdot \dfrac{4}{x}$

❹ **Simplify** each side of the equation. $6 + x = 12$

❺ **Solve** by subtracting 6 from each side. $x = 6$

Student Help

▶ **STUDY TIP**
In Example 2, you must check that the solution $x = 6$ does not result in a zero denominator in the original equation.

EXAMPLE 3 Factor First, then Multiply by the LCD

Solve $\dfrac{3}{x + 3} + \dfrac{4}{x^2 + 6x + 9} = 1$.

Solution

$$\dfrac{3}{x + 3} + \dfrac{4}{x^2 + 6x + 9} = 1 \qquad \text{Write original equation.}$$

$$\dfrac{3}{x + 3} + \dfrac{4}{(x + 3)^2} = 1 \qquad \text{Factor denominator.}$$

$$\dfrac{3}{x + 3} \cdot (x + 3)^2 + \dfrac{4}{(x + 3)^2} \cdot (x + 3)^2 = 1 \cdot (x + 3)^2 \qquad \begin{array}{l}\text{Multiply by}\\ \text{LCD } (x + 3)^2.\end{array}$$

$$3(x + 3) + 4 = (x + 3)^2 \qquad \text{Simplify.}$$

$$3x + 13 = x^2 + 6x + 9 \qquad \text{Simplify each side.}$$

$$0 = x^2 + 3x - 4 \qquad \begin{array}{l}\text{Write in standard}\\ \text{form.}\end{array}$$

$$0 = (x + 4)(x - 1) \qquad \text{Factor.}$$

$$x = -4 \text{ and } x = 1 \qquad \text{Solve.}$$

ANSWER ▶ The solutions are $x = -4$ and $x = 1$. Check both values.

Student Help

▶ **STUDY TIP**
To find the LCD in Example 3, look at the equation in factored form. The product of the highest powers of the factors in either denominator is $(x + 3)^2$.

Checkpoint ✓ **Multiply by the LCD**

Solve the equation. Check your solutions.

4. $\dfrac{3}{x} + \dfrac{1}{4} = \dfrac{4}{x}$ **5.** $\dfrac{1}{n + 1} + \dfrac{1}{n} = \dfrac{11}{n^2 + n}$ **6.** $\dfrac{4}{x - 3} + \dfrac{x}{x + 3} = 1$

WORK PROBLEMS Writing and solving rational equations can help to solve problems such as finding out how long it would take you and a friend to clear snow off of a driveway.

Student Help

▶MORE EXAMPLES

More examples are available at www.mcdougallittell.com

EXAMPLE **4** **Solve a Work Problem**

SHOVELING SNOW Alone, you can shovel your driveway in 3 hours. Your friend Amy can shovel the driveway in 2 hours. How long will it take you and Amy to shovel your driveway, working together?

Solution

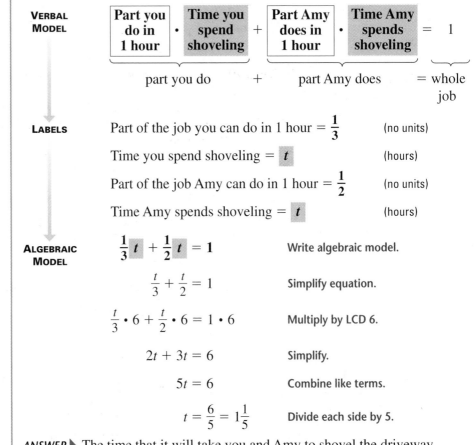

| VERBAL MODEL | | Part you do in 1 hour | · | Time you spend shoveling | + | Part Amy does in 1 hour | · | Time Amy spends shoveling | = | 1 |

part you do + part Amy does = whole job

LABELS

Part of the job you can do in 1 hour $= \frac{1}{3}$ (no units)

Time you spend shoveling $= t$ (hours)

Part of the job Amy can do in 1 hour $= \frac{1}{2}$ (no units)

Time Amy spends shoveling $= t$ (hours)

ALGEBRAIC MODEL

$$\frac{1}{3}t + \frac{1}{2}t = 1$$ Write algebraic model.

$$\frac{t}{3} + \frac{t}{2} = 1$$ Simplify equation.

$$\frac{t}{3} \cdot 6 + \frac{t}{2} \cdot 6 = 1 \cdot 6$$ Multiply by LCD 6.

$$2t + 3t = 6$$ Simplify.

$$5t = 6$$ Combine like terms.

$$t = \frac{6}{5} = 1\frac{1}{5}$$ Divide each side by 5.

ANSWER ▶ The time that it will take you and Amy to shovel the driveway is $1\frac{1}{5}$ hours, or 1 hour 12 minutes.

Student Help

▶STUDY TIP
To find how many minutes are in $\frac{1}{5}$ hour, do the following calculation.
$\frac{1}{5} \cdot 60$ minutes $=$ 12 minutes. Therefore $1\frac{1}{5}$ hours equals 1 hour 12 minutes.

Checkpoint ✓ **Solve a Work Problem**

7. You can clean your house in 4 hours. Your sister can clean it in 6 hours. How long will it take you to clean the house, working together?

8. A roofing contractor estimates that he can shingle a house in 20 hours and that his assistant can do it in 30 hours. How long will it take them to shingle the house, working together?

MIXTURE PROBLEMS *Mixture problems*—problems that involve combining two or more items—occur in many different settings. Example 5 discusses mixing roasted nuts and raisins. The exercise set presents mixture problems from other fields, such as chemistry.

EXAMPLE **5** **Solve a Mixture Problem**

RAISINS AND NUTS A store sells a mixture of raisins and roasted nuts. Raisins cost $3.50 per kilogram and nuts cost $4.75 per kilogram. How many kilograms of each should be mixed to make 20 kilograms of this snack worth $4.00 per kilogram?

Solution

When you solve a mixture problem, it is helpful to make a chart.

Let x = Number of kilograms of raisins.

Then $20 - x$ = Number of kilograms of nuts.

Student Help

▶**STUDY TIP**
Because the number of kilograms of the mixture is 20 and the number of kilograms of raisins is x, the number of kilograms of nuts is $20 - x$. • • • • • • •

Use the information from the problem to complete the chart below. Then write and solve an equation that relates the cost of the raisins, the cost of nuts, and the cost of mixture.

	Number of kg	× Price per kg	= Cost
Raisins	x	3.50	$3.5x$
Nuts	$20 - x$	4.75	$4.75(20 - x)$
Mixture	20	4.00	80

Cost of raisins + Cost of nuts = Cost of mixture	Write verbal model.
$3.5x + 4.75(20 - x) = 80$	Write algebraic model.
$350x + 475(20 - x) = 8000$	Multiply each side by 100 to clear equation of decimals.
$350x + 9500 - 475x = 8000$	Use distributive property.
$9500 - 125x = 8000$	Combine like terms.
$-125x = -1500$	Subtract 9500 from each side.
$x = 12$	Divide each side by -125.

Therefore, $20 - x = 8$

ANSWER ▶ 12 kilograms of raisins and 8 kilograms of nuts are needed.

Checkpoint ✓ **Solve a Mixture Problem**

9. You make a mixture of dried apples costing $6.00 per kilogram and dried apricots costing $8.00 per kilogram. How many kilograms of each do you need to make 10 kilograms of a mixture worth $7.20 per kilogram? Make a chart to help you solve the problem.

Guided Practice

Vocabulary Check

1. What are two methods of solving rational equations?

2. Which method is limited to solving equations in which each side is a single rational expression?

Skill Check

Find the least common denominator.

3. $\dfrac{1}{x}, \dfrac{x}{3}, \dfrac{2}{3x}$

4. $\dfrac{3}{4x}, \dfrac{1}{6x^2}, \dfrac{1}{8x^2}$

5. $\dfrac{5}{x}, \dfrac{2}{3x^2}, \dfrac{1}{x^3}$

Solve the equation using the cross product property. Remember to check your solutions.

6. $\dfrac{3}{x} = \dfrac{x}{12}$

7. $\dfrac{x}{x+2} = \dfrac{3}{x-2}$

8. $\dfrac{3}{u+2} = \dfrac{1}{u-2}$

Solve the equation by multiplying by the least common denominator. Check your solutions.

9. $\dfrac{1}{5} - \dfrac{2}{5x} = \dfrac{1}{x}$

10. $\dfrac{2}{x} + \dfrac{1}{4} = \dfrac{1}{x}$

11. $\dfrac{1}{x} + \dfrac{x}{x+2} = 1$

Practice and Applications

CROSS MULTIPLYING Solve the equation by cross multiplying. Check your solutions.

12. $\dfrac{x}{5} = \dfrac{7}{3}$

13. $\dfrac{x}{10} = \dfrac{14}{5}$

14. $\dfrac{4}{x} = \dfrac{12}{5(x+2)}$

15. $\dfrac{7}{x+1} = \dfrac{5}{x-3}$

16. $\dfrac{6}{x+2} = \dfrac{x}{4}$

17. $\dfrac{5}{x+4} = \dfrac{5}{3(x+1)}$

18. $\dfrac{1}{y} = \dfrac{2}{y-3}$

19. $\dfrac{3(t^2+1)}{6t^2-t-1} = \dfrac{1}{2}$

20. $\dfrac{(x+1)^2}{(x-3)^2} = 1$

MULTIPLYING BY THE LCD Solve the equation by multiplying each side by the least common denominator. Check your solutions.

21. $\dfrac{5}{x} + 2 = \dfrac{x}{4}$

22. $\dfrac{x}{x+9} = \dfrac{9}{x+9} + 4$

23. $\dfrac{3x}{x-1} = \dfrac{x}{5}$

24. $\dfrac{3}{t} - \dfrac{1}{3t} = \dfrac{2}{3}$

25. $\dfrac{4}{x(x+1)} = \dfrac{3}{x}$

26. $\dfrac{x}{x+3} + \dfrac{1}{x-3} = 1$

27. $\dfrac{1}{s} + \dfrac{s}{s+2} = 1$

28. $\dfrac{2}{3x+1} + 2 = \dfrac{2}{3}$

29. $\dfrac{5}{2r+1} - \dfrac{3}{2r-1} = 0$

30. $u = \dfrac{2}{5} - \dfrac{u}{2}$

31. $\dfrac{5}{x+1} - \dfrac{7}{x+1} = \dfrac{12}{x}$

32. $\dfrac{5}{3} + \dfrac{250}{9r} = \dfrac{r}{9}$

Student Help

▶ **HOMEWORK HELP**
Example 1: Exs. 12–20
Example 2: Exs. 21–32
Example 3: Exs. 33–38
Example 4: Exs. 48–50
Example 5: Exs. 51–53

Student Help

▶HOMEWORK HELP

Extra help with problem solving in Exs. 33–38 is available at www.mcdougallittell.com

FACTOR FIRST **Factor first, then solve the equation. Check your solutions.**

33. $\dfrac{2}{y - 2} + \dfrac{1}{y + 2} = \dfrac{4}{y^2 - 4}$

34. $\dfrac{3}{x + 1} - \dfrac{1}{x - 2} = \dfrac{1}{x^2 - x - 2}$

35. $\dfrac{3}{x - 1} + \dfrac{10}{x^2 - 2x + 1} = 4$

36. $\dfrac{x}{x + 3} + \dfrac{1}{x - 1} = \dfrac{4}{x^2 + 2x - 3}$

37. $\dfrac{2}{x - 1} - \dfrac{x}{x + 3} = \dfrac{6}{x^2 + 2x - 3}$

38. $\dfrac{1}{y^2 - 16} - \dfrac{2}{y + 4} = \dfrac{2}{y - 4}$

CHOOSING A METHOD **Solve the equation. Check your solutions.**

39. $\dfrac{1}{4} + \dfrac{4}{x} = \dfrac{1}{x}$

40. $\dfrac{-3x}{x + 1} = \dfrac{-2}{x - 1}$

41. $\dfrac{x}{6} - \dfrac{1}{x} = \dfrac{1}{6}$

42. $\dfrac{x}{9} - \dfrac{8}{x} = \dfrac{1}{9}$

43. $\dfrac{x + 42}{x} = x$

44. $\dfrac{2}{x} - \dfrac{x}{8} = \dfrac{3}{4}$

45. $\dfrac{-3}{x + 7} = \dfrac{2}{x + 2}$

46. $\dfrac{2}{x + 3} + \dfrac{1}{x} = \dfrac{4}{3x}$

47. $\dfrac{1}{x} - \dfrac{2}{x^2} = \dfrac{1}{9}$

48. MOWING THE LAWN With your new lawn mower, you can mow a lawn in 4 hours. With an older mower, your friend can mow the same lawn in 5 hours. How long will it take you to mow the lawn, working together?

49. HIGHWAY PAVING The county's new asphalt paving machine can surface one mile of highway in 10 hours. A much older machine can surface one mile in 18 hours. How long will it take them to surface 1 mile of highway, working together? How long will it take them to surface 20 miles?

50. CAR WASHING Arthur can wash a car in 30 minutes, Bonnie can wash a car in 40 minutes, and Claire can wash a car in 60 minutes. How will it take them to wash a car, working together?

51. NOODLE MIXTURE A grocer mixes 5 pounds of egg noodles costing $.80 per pound with 2 pounds of spinach noodles costing $1.50 per pound. What is the cost per pound of the mixture?

52. JUICE MIXTURE A farm stand owner mixes apple juice and cranberry juice. How much should he charge if he mixes 8 liters of apple juice selling for $0.45 per liter with 10 liters of cranberry juice selling for $1.08 per liter?

53. COINS You have 12 coins worth $1.95. If you only have dimes and quarters, how many of each do you have?

54. BATTING AVERAGE You have 35 hits in 140 times at bat. Your batting average is $\dfrac{35}{140} = 0.250$. How many consecutive hits must you get to increase your batting average to 0.300? Use the following verbal model to answer the question.

Desired Batting average $= \dfrac{\text{Past hits} + \text{Future hits}}{\text{Past times at bat} + \text{Future times at bat}}$

Link to

Careers

SPORTS REPORTER
Sports reporters gather statistics, such as a baseball player's batting average, and prepare stories that cover all aspects of sports from local sporting events to international competitions.

More about sports reporters is available at www.mcdougallittell.com

55. CHALLENGE How many liters of water must be added to 50 liters of a 30% acid solution in order to produce a 20% acid solution? Copy and complete the chart to help you solve the problem.

	Number of liters × % acid = Liters of acid		
Original Solution	?	?	?
Water Added	x	?	?
New Solution	?	?	?

56. MULTIPLE CHOICE What is the LCD of $\dfrac{1}{2x}$, $\dfrac{3x}{7x^2}$, and $\dfrac{3+x}{4x}$?

(A) $56x^4$ (B) $28x^2$ (C) $28x$ (D) $7x^2$

57. MULTIPLE CHOICE What is the solution of the equation
$$\dfrac{10r}{r+1} + \dfrac{1}{r+1} = 2?$$

(F) 8   (G) $\dfrac{1}{8}$ (H) 10   (J) $\dfrac{1}{2}$

58. MULTIPLE CHOICE What is the solution of the equation $\dfrac{x}{6} - \dfrac{6}{x} = 0$?

(A) 6, −6   (B) 6   (C) 36   (D) None of these

59. MULTIPLE CHOICE Solve the equation $\dfrac{5}{x+1} + \dfrac{x}{x^2-1} = \dfrac{1}{x-1}$.

(F) 1   (G) 0   (H) $\dfrac{5}{6}$ (J) $\dfrac{6}{5}$

FUNCTION VALUES Evaluate the function when $x = 0, 1, 2, 3,$ and 4. *(Lesson 4.8)*

60. $f(x) = 4x$ **61.** $f(x) = -x + 9$ **62.** $f(x) = 3x + 1$

63. $f(x) = -x^2$ **64.** $f(x) = x^2 - 1$ **65.** $f(x) = \dfrac{x^2}{2}$

EVALUATING EXPRESSIONS Evaluate the expression. *(Lessons 8.1, 8.2)*

66. $2^4 \cdot 2^3$ **67.** $6^3 \cdot 6^{-1}$ **68.** $\left(3^3\right)^2$

69. $\left(4^5\right)^0$ **70.** $12^{-5} \cdot 12^3$ **71.** $5^2 \cdot 5^1$

RADICAL EXPRESSIONS Simplify the radical expression. *(Lesson 9.3)*

72. $\sqrt{50}$ **73.** $\sqrt{72}$ **74.** $\dfrac{1}{4}\sqrt{112}$ **75.** $\dfrac{1}{2}\sqrt{52}$

76. $\sqrt{128}$ **77.** $\dfrac{1}{4}\sqrt{90}$ **78.** $3\sqrt{63}$ **79.** $\dfrac{7}{8}\sqrt{153}$

80. $\dfrac{2}{3}\sqrt{18}$ **81.** $\sqrt{27}$ **82.** $\dfrac{1}{5}\sqrt{500}$ **83.** $\dfrac{3}{7}\sqrt{147}$

OPERATIONS WITH FRACTIONS Evaluate the expression. Write the answer as a fraction or mixed number in lowest terms. *(Skills Review p. 764)*

84. $\frac{2}{3} + \frac{1}{6} - \frac{1}{3}$

85. $\frac{3}{4} + \frac{5}{8} - \frac{1}{2}$

86. $\frac{2}{5} + \frac{3}{8} - \frac{1}{4}$

87. $\frac{2}{9} - \frac{1}{3} + \frac{4}{5}$

88. $\frac{1}{10} + \frac{1}{5} - \frac{3}{10} + \frac{2}{5}$

89. $\frac{1}{4} + \frac{2}{4} - \frac{3}{4} + \frac{4}{4}$

90. $\frac{3}{17} - \frac{3}{34} + \frac{1}{2}$

91. $\frac{1}{2} - \frac{3}{4} + \frac{5}{6} - \frac{7}{8}$

92. $\frac{12}{13} + \frac{7}{26} - \frac{1}{2}$

93. $\frac{103}{202} + \frac{1}{2} - \frac{1}{101}$

94. $\frac{7}{3} + \frac{1}{5} - \frac{2}{15}$

95. $\frac{5}{11} - \frac{4}{5} + \frac{3}{4}$

Quiz 2

Multiply or divide. Simplify the expression. *(Lesson 11.4)*

1. $\frac{5x^2}{2x} \cdot \frac{14x^2}{10x}$

2. $\frac{5}{10 + 4x} \cdot (20 + 8x)$

3. $\frac{3x + 12}{4x} \div \frac{x + 4}{2x}$

4. $\frac{5x^2 - 30x + 45}{x + 2} \div (5x - 15)$

Add or subtract. Simplify the expression. *(Lessons 11.5, 11.6)*

5. $\frac{x}{x^2 - 2x - 35} + \frac{5}{x^2 - 2x - 35}$

6. $\frac{4x - 1}{3x^2 + 8x + 5} - \frac{x - 6}{3x^2 + 8x + 5}$

7. $\frac{6}{x^2 - 1} + \frac{7x}{x + 1}$

8. $\frac{3x^2}{3x - 9} - \frac{2x}{x^2 - x - 6}$

Solve the equation. Check your solution. *(Lesson 11.7)*

9. $\frac{3}{x} = \frac{9}{2(x + 2)}$

10. $\frac{1}{2} + \frac{2}{t} = \frac{1}{t}$

11. $\frac{1}{x - 5} + \frac{1}{x + 5} = \frac{x + 3}{x^2 - 25}$

12. $\frac{7}{8} - \frac{16}{x - 2} = \frac{3}{4}$

CANOEING In Exercises 13–15, use the following information.
You are on a canoe trip. You can paddle your canoe at a rate of $x + 2$ miles per hour downstream and $x - 2$ miles per hour upstream. You travel 15 miles downstream and 15 miles back upstream. *(Lesson 11.6)*

13. Write an expression for the travel time downstream and an expression for the travel time upstream.

14. Write and simplify an expression for the total travel time.

15. Find the total travel time if $x = 3$.

16. RAKING LEAVES You can rake your neighbor's yard in 3 hours. Your neighbor can rake his yard in 4 hours. How long will it take you if you rake the yard together? *(Lesson 11.7)*

Rational Functions

Goal

Perform operations on rational functions.

Key Words

• rational function

The inverse variation models you graphed in Lesson 11.2 are a type of *rational function*. A **rational function** is a function that can be written as a quotient of polynomials.

$$f(x) = \frac{\text{polynomial}}{\text{polynomial}}$$

In this lesson you will perform arithmetic operations on rational functions using properties to combine and simplify functions.

OPERATIONS ON FUNCTIONS

Let *f* and *g* be two functions. Each function listed below is defined for all values of *x* in the domain of both *f* and *g*.

Sum of functions *f* and *g*	$(f + g)(x) = f(x) + g(x)$
Difference of functions *f* and *g*	$(f - g)(x) = f(x) - g(x)$
Product of functions *f* and *g*	$(f \cdot g)(x) = f(x) \cdot g(x)$
Quotient of functions *f* and *g*, if *g*(x) = 0	$(f \div g)(x) = f(x) \div g(x)$

Student Help

▶ READING ALGEBRA
The function notation
$f(x)$ is read "*f* of *x*."

EXAMPLE 1 Add Rational Functions

Let $f(x) = \dfrac{1}{2x + 2}$ and $g(x) = \dfrac{x}{2x + 2}$. Find a rule for the function $(f + g)(x)$.

Solution

❶ **Write** the rule for the sum of functions. $(f + g)(x) = f(x) + g(x)$

❷ **Substitute** $\dfrac{1}{2x + 2}$ for $f(x)$ and $\dfrac{x}{2x + 2}$ for $g(x)$. $= \dfrac{1}{2x + 2} + \dfrac{x}{2x + 2}$

❸ **Add.** $= \dfrac{1 + x}{2x + 2}$

❹ **Factor** the denominator. $= \dfrac{(1 + x)}{2(x + 1)}$

❺ **Divide** out common factors and simplify. $= \dfrac{1(1 + x)}{2(1 + x)} = \dfrac{1}{2}$

ANSWER ▶ $(f + g)(x) = \dfrac{1}{2}$

Checkpoint ✓ Add Rational Functions

Find a rule for the function $(f + g)(x)$.

1. $f(x) = \dfrac{x + 1}{x}, g(x) = \dfrac{1}{x}$

2. $f(x) = \dfrac{1}{x - 3}, g(x) = \dfrac{1}{x + 3}$

EXAMPLE 2 **Subtract Rational Functions**

Let $f(x) = \dfrac{x}{x + 2}$ and $g(x) = \dfrac{1}{x}$. Find a rule for the function $(f - g)(x)$.

❶ **Write** the rule for the difference of functions.

$$(f - g)(x) = f(x) - g(x)$$

❷ **Substitute** $\dfrac{x}{x + 2}$ for $f(x)$ and $\dfrac{1}{x}$ for $g(x)$.

$$= \dfrac{x}{x + 2} - \dfrac{1}{x}$$

❸ **Rewrite** the expressions using the LCD $x(x + 2)$.

$$= \dfrac{x(x)}{x(x + 2)} - \dfrac{1(x + 2)}{x(x + 2)}$$

❹ **Simplify** the numerators.

$$= \dfrac{x^2}{x(x + 2)} - \dfrac{x + 2}{x(x + 2)}$$

❺ **Subtract.**

$$= \dfrac{x^2 - x - 2}{x(x + 2)}$$

❻ **Factor** the numerator.

$$= \dfrac{(x - 2)(x + 1)}{x(x + 2)}$$

ANSWER ▶ $(f - g)(x) = \dfrac{(x - 2)(x + 1)}{x(x + 2)}$

Student Help

▶ **STUDY TIP**
In Step 6, you must factor the numerator to determine whether the numerator and denominator have any common factors.

Checkpoint ✓ *Subtract Rational Functions*

Find a rule for the function $(f - g)(x)$.

3. $f(x) = \dfrac{x + 1}{x}$, $g(x) = \dfrac{1}{x}$

4. $f(x) = \dfrac{1}{x - 3}$, $g(x) = \dfrac{1}{x + 3}$

EXAMPLE 3 **Multiply and Divide Rational Functions**

Let $f(x) = \dfrac{x - 4}{x}$ and $g(x) = \dfrac{x + 4}{x - 4}$. Find a rule for the function.

a. $(f \cdot g)(x) = f(x) \cdot g(x)$

$$= \dfrac{x - 4}{x} \cdot \dfrac{x + 4}{x - 4}$$

$$= \dfrac{(x - 4)(x + 4)}{x(x - 4)}$$

$$= \dfrac{x + 4}{x}$$

b. $(f \div g)(x) = f(x) \div g(x)$

$$= \dfrac{x - 4}{x} \div \dfrac{x + 4}{x - 4}$$

$$= \dfrac{x - 4}{x} \cdot \dfrac{x - 4}{x + 4}$$

$$= \dfrac{(x - 4)^2}{x(x + 4)}$$

Checkpoint ✓ *Multiply and Divide Rational Functions*

5. Let $f(x) = \dfrac{x}{x + 7}$ and $g(x) = \dfrac{2x + 14}{8}$. Find a rule for the function $(f \cdot g)(x)$.

6. Let $f(x) = \dfrac{1 - x}{x}$ and $g(x) = \dfrac{x - 1}{x^2}$. Find a rule for the function $(f \div g)(x)$.

Exercises

SUMS Find a rule for the function $(f + g)(x)$.

1. $f(x) = \dfrac{1}{x - 9}$, $g(x) = \dfrac{9}{x - 9}$

2. $f(x) = \dfrac{x}{x^2 - 25}$, $g(x) = \dfrac{5}{x^2 - 25}$

3. $f(x) = \dfrac{x - 1}{x^2}$, $g(x) = \dfrac{1}{x}$

4. $f(x) = \dfrac{2}{x - 3}$, $g(x) = \dfrac{7}{3 - x}$

5. $f(x) = \dfrac{6x}{x - 7}$, $g(x) = \dfrac{5x}{x + 7}$

6. $f(x) = \dfrac{x - 3}{20x}$, $g(x) = \dfrac{x + 4}{15x}$

DIFFERENCES Find a rule for the function $(f - g)(x)$.

7. $f(x) = \dfrac{4x}{3x + 7}$, $g(x) = \dfrac{x - 5}{3x + 7}$

8. $f(x) = \dfrac{x}{x^2 - 36}$, $g(x) = \dfrac{6}{x^2 - 36}$

9. $f(x) = \dfrac{1}{x}$, $g(x) = \dfrac{2x + 3}{x^2}$

10. $f(x) = \dfrac{3}{x + 4}$, $g(x) = \dfrac{4}{x - 2}$

11. $f(x) = \dfrac{1}{x + 9}$, $g(x) = \dfrac{1}{x - 9}$

12. $f(x) = \dfrac{2x}{x - 3}$, $g(x) = \dfrac{3}{2x - 6}$

PRODUCTS Find a rule for the function $(f \cdot g)(x)$.

13. $f(x) = \dfrac{1}{2x}$, $g(x) = \dfrac{6}{x + 15}$

14. $f(x) = \dfrac{4}{3x + 6}$, $g(x) = \dfrac{x + 2}{x}$

15. $f(x) = \dfrac{x^2 - 5x + 6}{2x}$, $g(x) = \dfrac{3x - 6}{x - 3}$

16. $f(x) = \dfrac{x + 2}{x^2}$, $g(x) = \dfrac{8x}{4x^2 - 16}$

17. $f(x) = \dfrac{x^2 + 3x - 10}{x + 2}$, $g(x) = \dfrac{x^2 - 4}{x + 5}$

18. $f(x) = \dfrac{x^2 - 3x + 2}{x^2 + 3x + 2}$, $g(x) = \dfrac{8x + 8}{4x + 8}$

QUOTIENTS Find a rule for the function $(f \div g)(x)$.

19. $f(x) = \dfrac{x + 3}{x^2}$, $g(x) = \dfrac{x + 1}{x^3}$

20. $f(x) = \dfrac{2}{3x}$, $g(x) = \dfrac{1}{4x}$

21. $f(x) = \dfrac{x}{2x + 1}$, $g(x) = \dfrac{2x + 1}{x}$

22. $f(x) = \dfrac{2x}{x^3 - 5x^2}$, $g(x) = \dfrac{10}{x^2 - 5x}$

23. $f(x) = \dfrac{x^2 + 3x - 10}{x + 2}$, $g(x) = \dfrac{x^2 - 4}{x + 5}$

24. $f(x) = \dfrac{x^2 - x - 20}{5x - 25}$, $g(x) = \dfrac{x - 1}{x^2 - 25}$

GRAPHING Graph the function by making a table of values, plotting the points, and then connecting them with two smooth curves.

Student Help

▶ **HOMEWORK HELP**
 Example 1: Exs. 1–6
 Example 2: Exs. 7–12
 Example 3: Exs. 13–24

25. $f(x) = \dfrac{1}{x - 9}$

26. $f(x) = \dfrac{1}{2x} - 3$

27. $g(x) = \dfrac{x}{2x + 3}$

28. $g(x) = \dfrac{-1}{x + 2} + 1$

- **proportion**, *p. 633*
- **extremes**, *p. 633*
- **means**, *p. 633*
- **inverse variation**, *p. 639*
- **rational number**, *p. 646*
- **rational expression**, *p. 646*
- **least common denominator (LCD)**, *p. 663*
- **rational equation**, *p. 670*

11.1 PROPORTIONS

Examples on pp. 633–635

EXAMPLE Solve the proportion $\frac{12}{7} = \frac{5}{x}$ using the cross product property.

❶ **Write** the original proportion.

$$\frac{12}{7} = \frac{5}{x}$$

❷ **Use** the cross product property.

$$12 \cdot x = 7 \cdot 5$$

❸ **Divide** each side by 12.

$$x = \frac{35}{12}$$

Solve the proportion. Check your solutions.

1. $\frac{x}{2} = \frac{4}{7}$

2. $\frac{7}{10} = \frac{9 + x}{x}$

3. $\frac{x^2 - 16}{x + 4} = \frac{x - 4}{3}$

4. $\frac{5}{x + 6} = \frac{x - 6}{x}$

11.2 DIRECT AND INVERSE VARIATION

Examples on pp. 639–641

EXAMPLES Assuming $y = 4$ when $x = 8$, find an equation that relates x and y in each case.

a. x and y vary directly.

b. x and y vary inversely.

Solution

a. $\frac{y}{x} = k$ Write direct variation model.

$\frac{4}{8} = k$ Substitute 8 for *x* and 4 for *y*.

$\frac{1}{2} = k$ Simplify.

ANSWER ▶ $\frac{y}{x} = \frac{1}{2}$ or $y = \frac{1}{2}x$.

b. $xy = k$ Write inverse variation model.

$(8)(4) = k$ Substitute 8 for *x* and 4 for *y*.

$32 = k$ Simplify.

ANSWER ▶ $xy = 32$ or $y = \frac{32}{x}$.

Find an equation such that *x* and *y* vary directly.

5. $y = 50$ when $x = 10$ **6.** $y = 6$ when $x = 24$ **7.** $y = 36$ when $x = 45$

8. $y = 20$ when $x = 2$ **9.** $y = 7$ when $x = \dfrac{1}{2}$ **10.** $y = 132$ when $x = 66$

Find an equation such that *x* and *y* vary inversely.

11. $y = 3$ when $x = 12$ **12.** $y = 10$ when $x = 20$ **13.** $y = 5$ when $x = 90$

14. $y = 3$ when $x = \dfrac{2}{3}$ **15.** $y = \dfrac{11}{2}$ when $x = 4$ **16.** $y = \dfrac{1}{4}$ when $x = 24$

11.3 SIMPLIFYING RATIONAL EXPRESSIONS

Examples on pp. 646–648

> **EXAMPLE** Simplify $\dfrac{2x^2 + 3x - 2}{2x^2 + 5x + 2}$.
>
> To simplify a rational expression, look for common factors.
>
> **Solution**
>
> ❶ **Write** the original expression. $\dfrac{2x^2 + 3x - 2}{2x^2 + 5x + 2}$
>
> ❷ **Factor** the numerator and denominator. $\dfrac{(2x - 1)(x + 2)}{(2x + 1)(x + 2)}$
>
> ❸ **Divide** out the common factor $(x + 2)$. $\dfrac{(2x - 1)\cancel{(x + 2)}}{(2x + 1)\cancel{(x + 2)}}$
>
> ❹ **Simplify** the expression. $\dfrac{2x - 1}{2x + 1}$

In Exercises 17–25, simplify the expression.

17. $\dfrac{3x}{9x^2 + 3}$ **18.** $\dfrac{6x^2}{12x^4 + 18x^2}$ **19.** $\dfrac{7x^3 - 28x}{3x^2 + 8x + 4}$

20. $\dfrac{5x^2 + 21x + 4}{25x + 100}$ **21.** $\dfrac{x^2 + 4x + 4}{x^2 + 9x + 14}$ **22.** $\dfrac{6x^2 - 19x + 10}{2x^2 - 5x}$

23. $\dfrac{2x^2 + 17x + 21}{2x^2 + x - 3}$ **24.** $\dfrac{13x^2 - 39x}{3x^2 - 8x - 3}$ **25.** $\dfrac{y^2 - 2y - 48}{2y^2 + 9y - 18}$

26. Find the ratio of the area of the smaller rectangle to the area of the larger rectangle. Simplify the expression.

11.4 MULTIPLYING AND DIVIDING RATIONAL EXPRESSIONS

Examples on pp. 652–654

EXAMPLE Simplify $\dfrac{6x^2 + x - 1}{2x + 1} \div \dfrac{9x - 3}{x + 1}$.

To divide rational expressions, multiply by the reciprocal.

$$\dfrac{6x^2 + x - 1}{2x + 1} \div \dfrac{9x - 3}{x + 1} = \dfrac{6x^2 + x - 1}{2x + 1} \cdot \dfrac{x + 1}{9x - 3}$$ Multiply by reciprocal.

$$= \dfrac{(2x + 1)(3x - 1)}{2x + 1} \cdot \dfrac{x + 1}{3(3x - 1)}$$ Factor numerators and denominators.

$$= \dfrac{(2x + 1)(3x - 1)(x + 1)}{(2x + 1) \cdot 3(3x - 1)}$$ Multiply and divide out common factors.

$$= \dfrac{x + 1}{3}$$ Write in simplest form.

Simplify the expression.

27. $\dfrac{12x^2}{5x^3} \cdot \dfrac{25x^4}{3x}$

28. $\dfrac{a^2 - 7a - 18}{4a^2 + 8a} \cdot \dfrac{12}{a^2 - 81}$

29. $\dfrac{2x^2 + 9x + 7}{2x} \cdot \dfrac{16x^2}{x^3 - x}$

30. $\dfrac{6y^2}{y + 3} \div \dfrac{9y}{(y + 3)^2}$

31. $\dfrac{9x^3}{x^3 - x^2} \div \dfrac{x - 8}{x^2 - 9x + 8}$

32. $\dfrac{x^2 + 3x + 2}{x^2 + 7x + 12} \div \dfrac{x^2 + 5x + 4}{x^2 + 5x + 6}$

11.5 ADDING AND SUBTRACTING WITH LIKE DENOMINATORS

Examples on pp. 658–659

EXAMPLE Simplify $\dfrac{5x}{x^2 + 2x - 8} - \dfrac{2x + 6}{x^2 + 2x - 8}$.

$$\dfrac{5x}{x^2 + 2x - 8} - \dfrac{2x + 6}{x^2 + 2x - 8} = \dfrac{5x - (2x + 6)}{x^2 + 2x - 8}$$ Subtract numerators.

$$= \dfrac{3x - 6}{x^2 + 2x - 8}$$ Simplify numerator.

$$= \dfrac{3(x - 2)}{(x - 2)(x + 4)}$$ Factor and divide out common factor $(x - 2)$.

$$= \dfrac{3}{x + 4}$$ Write in simplest form.

In Exercises 33–36, simplify the expression.

33. $\dfrac{2x + 1}{3x} + \dfrac{x + 5}{3x}$

34. $\dfrac{-2b - 5}{b^2} + \dfrac{5}{b^2}$

35. $\dfrac{6x}{x + 4} - \dfrac{5x - 4}{x + 4}$

36. $\dfrac{x(x + 1)}{(x - 3)^2} - \dfrac{12}{(x - 3)^2}$

37. Find an expression in simplest form for the perimeter of a rectangle whose side lengths are $\dfrac{x + 1}{16}$ and $\dfrac{x + 3}{16}$.

Examples on pp. 663–666

11.6   ADDING AND SUBTRACTING WITH UNLIKE DENOMINATORS

EXAMPLE Simplify $\dfrac{x}{x-5} - \dfrac{2}{x+2}$.

The LCD is $(x-5)(x+2)$.

$$\dfrac{x}{x-5} - \dfrac{2}{x+2} = \dfrac{x(x+2)}{(x-5)(x+2)} - \dfrac{2(x-5)}{(x-5)(x+2)}$$ Rewrite fractions using LCD.

$$= \dfrac{x^2+2x}{(x-5)(x+2)} - \dfrac{2x-10}{(x-5)(x+2)}$$ Simplify numerators.

$$= \dfrac{(x^2+2x)-(2x-10)}{(x-5)(x+2)}$$ Subtract fractions.

$$= \dfrac{x^2+10}{(x-5)(x+2)}$$ Simplify.

In Exercises 38–41, simplify the expression.

38. $\dfrac{x+3}{3x-1} + \dfrac{4}{x-3}$ **39.** $\dfrac{-5x-10}{x^2-4} + \dfrac{4x}{x-2}$ **40.** $\dfrac{p}{p-1} - \dfrac{p}{p+1}$ **41.** $\dfrac{x-4}{2x} - \dfrac{x-6}{3x}$

42. Find an expression in simplest form for the perimeter of a rectangle whose side lengths are $\dfrac{x+3}{x-2}$ and $\dfrac{6}{x+4}$.

Examples on pp. 670–673

11.7   RATIONAL EQUATIONS

EXAMPLE Solve the equation $\dfrac{2x}{9} - \dfrac{1}{x} = \dfrac{1}{3}$.

The LCD is $9x$.

$$9x \cdot \dfrac{2x}{9} - 9x \cdot \dfrac{1}{x} = 9x \cdot \dfrac{1}{3}$$ Multiply each side of original equation by LCD 9x.

$$2x^2 - 9 = 3x$$ Simplify equation.

$$2x^2 - 3x - 9 = 0$$ Write equation in standard form.

$$(2x+3)(x-3) = 0$$ Factor left side of equation.

ANSWER ▶ When you set each factor equal to 0, you find that the solutions are $x = -\dfrac{3}{2}$ and 3. Check your solutions back into the original equation.

Solve the equation. Check your solutions.

43. $\dfrac{x+2}{2} = \dfrac{4}{x}$ **44.** $\dfrac{1}{s} + \dfrac{s}{s+2} = 1$ **45.** $\dfrac{1}{x-1} + \dfrac{1}{x+2} = \dfrac{3}{x^2+x-2}$

Solve the proportion. Check your solutions.

1. $\dfrac{6}{x} = \dfrac{17}{5}$

2. $\dfrac{x}{4} = \dfrac{x+8}{x}$

3. $\dfrac{x}{-3} = \dfrac{7}{x-10}$

4. $\dfrac{x}{x^2+4} = \dfrac{4}{5x}$

Make a table of values for $x = 1, 2, 3,$ and 4. Use the table to sketch the graph. State whether x and y vary *directly* or *inversely*.

5. $y = 4x$

6. $y = \dfrac{50}{x}$

7. $y = \dfrac{9}{2}x$

8. $y = \dfrac{15}{2x}$

Simplify the expression.

9. $\dfrac{56x^6}{4x^4}$

10. $\dfrac{5x^2 - 15x}{15x^4}$

11. $\dfrac{x^2 - x - 6}{x^2 - 4}$

12. $\dfrac{2x - 14}{3x^2 - 21x}$

13. $\dfrac{x^2 - 1}{2x^2 + x - 1}$

14. $\dfrac{2x^2 + 12x + 18}{x^2 - x - 12}$

Write the product or quotient in simplest form.

15. $\dfrac{6x^2}{8x} \cdot \dfrac{-4x^3}{2x^2}$

16. $\dfrac{x^3 + x^2}{x^2 - 16} \cdot \dfrac{x+4}{3x^4 + x^3 - 2x^2}$

17. $\dfrac{3x^2 - 6x}{x^2 - 6x + 9} \cdot \dfrac{x^2 - x - 6}{x^2 - 4}$

18. $\dfrac{3x^2 + 6x}{4x} \div \dfrac{15}{8x^2}$

19. $\dfrac{x+3}{x^3 - x^2 - 6x} \div \dfrac{x^2 - 9}{x}$

20. $\dfrac{x^2}{x-1} \div \dfrac{x}{x^2 + x - 2}$

Write the sum or difference in simplest form.

21. $\dfrac{12x - 4}{x - 1} + \dfrac{4x}{x - 1}$

22. $\dfrac{6(2y+1)}{y^2 - 100} - \dfrac{2(5y - 7)}{y^2 - 100}$

23. $\dfrac{5}{2x^2} + \dfrac{4}{3x}$

24. $\dfrac{4}{x+3} + \dfrac{3x}{x-2}$

25. $\dfrac{8}{5x} - \dfrac{4}{x^2}$

26. $\dfrac{5x+1}{x-3} - \dfrac{2x}{x-1}$

Solve the equation. Check your solutions.

27. $\dfrac{3}{4x - 9} = \dfrac{x}{3}$

28. $\dfrac{5}{9} + \dfrac{2}{9x} = \dfrac{3}{x}$

29. $\dfrac{x}{7} - \dfrac{6}{x} = \dfrac{1}{7}$

30. $\dfrac{3}{u+2} = \dfrac{1}{u-2}$

31. $\dfrac{1}{4} - \dfrac{6}{x} = \dfrac{3}{x}$

32. $\dfrac{x}{x+1} + \dfrac{x}{x-2} = 2$

33. LENGTH AND WIDTH The length ℓ and width w of a rectangle with an area of 60 square units are related by the equation $\ell w = 60$. Does this model represent *direct variation*, *inverse variation*, or *neither*?

34. STREET SWEEPERS A town's old street sweeper can clean the streets in 60 hours. The new street sweeper can clean the streets in 20 hours. How long would it take the old sweeper and the new sweeper to clean the streets together?

Chapter Standardized Test

1. Which of the following is the solution of the proportion $\dfrac{4}{y+9} = \dfrac{6}{y-7}$?

   (A) -82 **(B)** -41

   (C) 7 **(D)** 41

2. The variables x and y vary inversely. When x is 9, y is 36. If x is 3, what is y?

   (A) 12 **(B)** 36

   (C) 108 **(D)** 324

3. What is the simplest form of the expression $\dfrac{x^3 - 10x^2 + 9x}{x^2 + 5x - 6}$?

   (A) $\dfrac{x-9}{x+6}$ **(B)** $\dfrac{x}{x+6}$

   (C) $\dfrac{x}{(x-1)(x+6)}$ **(D)** $\dfrac{x(x-9)}{x+6}$

4. What is the simplest form of the product $\dfrac{9x^2}{4x} \cdot \dfrac{16x^3}{x^5}$?

   (A) $36x$ **(B)** $\dfrac{64}{9x^3}$

   (C) $\dfrac{36}{x}$ **(D)** $36x^3$

5. Divide $\dfrac{x^2 - 64}{3x^2}$ by $(x-8)$.

   (A) $\dfrac{x+8}{3x^2}$ **(B)** $\dfrac{x-8}{3x^2}$

   (C) $\dfrac{x+8}{3x^2(x-8)}$ **(D)** $\dfrac{x^3-512}{3x}$

6. What is the simplest form of the sum $\dfrac{x+2}{x^2-25} + \dfrac{3}{x^2-25}$?

   (A) $\dfrac{x+5}{x^2-25}$ **(B)** $\dfrac{x+5}{(x^2-25)^2}$

   (C) $\dfrac{3x+6}{x-5}$ **(D)** $\dfrac{1}{x-5}$

7. What is the simplest form of the difference $\dfrac{2x+9}{x+5} - \dfrac{x-4}{x-2}$?

   (A) $\dfrac{x^2+6x+2}{(x+5)(x-2)}$ **(B)** $\dfrac{x^2+6x-38}{(x+5)(x-2)}$

   (C) $\dfrac{x^2+4x-38}{(x+5)(x-2)}$ **(D)** $\dfrac{x^2+4x+2}{(x+5)(x-2)}$

8. Solve the equation $\dfrac{4}{x+2} + \dfrac{3}{x} = 1$.

   (A) -1 **(B)** -2

   (C) $1, -6$ **(D)** $-1, 6$

   (E) None of these

9. What is the ratio in simplest form of the area of the red rectangle to the area of the blue rectangle?

   (A) $\dfrac{1}{2}$ **(B)** $\dfrac{1}{6}$

   (C) $\dfrac{x+7}{3x+21}$ **(D)** $\dfrac{x(x+7)}{6x(x+7)}$

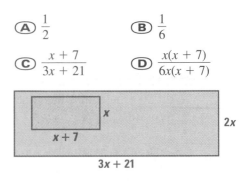

The basic skills you'll review on this page will help prepare you for the next chapter.

Maintaining Skills

EXAMPLE 1 Simplify Radicals

Simplify the expression $\sqrt{\dfrac{63}{100}}$ using the quotient property.

Solution

$\sqrt{\dfrac{63}{100}}$	Write original expression.
$\dfrac{\sqrt{63}}{\sqrt{100}}$	Use quotient property.
$\dfrac{\sqrt{9 \cdot 7}}{\sqrt{100}}$	Factor using perfect square factors.
$\dfrac{\sqrt{9} \cdot \sqrt{7}}{\sqrt{100}}$	Use product property.
$\dfrac{3\sqrt{7}}{10}$	Simplify.

Try These

Simplify the expression using the quotient property.

1. $\sqrt{\dfrac{32}{49}}$ **2.** $\sqrt{\dfrac{32}{64}}$ **3.** $\sqrt{\dfrac{125}{225}}$ **4.** $\sqrt{\dfrac{162}{4}}$

5. $\sqrt{\dfrac{363}{144}}$ **6.** $\sqrt{\dfrac{288}{400}}$ **7.** $\sqrt{\dfrac{72}{9}}$ **8.** $\sqrt{\dfrac{14}{200}}$

EXAMPLE 2 Factor Perfect Squares

Factor $x^2 + 16x + 64$.

Solution Recall from Chapter 10 the pattern for factoring a perfect square trinomial: $a^2 + 2ab + b^2 = (a + b)^2$ or $a^2 - 2ab - b^2 = (a - b)^2$.

$x^2 + 16x + 64 = x^2 + 2(x)(8) + 8^2$ Write as $a^2 + 2ab + b^2$.

$\quad\quad\quad\quad\quad = (x + 8)^2$ Factor using pattern.

Student Help

▶ **EXTRA EXAMPLES**

More examples and practice exercises are available at www.mcdougallittell.com

Try These

Factor the trinomial.

9. $a^2 - 18a + 81$ **10.** $x^2 + 6x + 9$ **11.** $y^2 - 22y + 121$

12. $169 + 26m + m^2$ **13.** $225 + 30r + r^2$ **14.** $100 - 20t + t^2$

15. $4x^2 + 20x + 25$ **16.** $9b^2 - 6a + 1$ **17.** $16 - 56x + 49x^2$

Maintaining Skills   **687**

CHAPTER 12

Radicals and More Connections to Geometry

▶ How are passengers kept in place on a spinning amusement ride?

APPLICATION: Spinning Rides

Some amusement park rides spin so fast that the riders "stick" to the walls of the ride. The force exerted by the wall on the rider is called *centripetal force*. You'll learn more about calculating centripetal force in Chapter 12.

Think & Discuss

When designing spinning rides, engineers must calculate the dimensions of the ride as well as how many times per minute it will spin. The table shows the height and revolutions per minute for four spinning rides.

Ride name	Height (feet)	Revolutions per minute
Football Ride	34.4	15
Chaos	36	12
Centrox	44.3	17.5
Galactica	44.3	17

1. Based on the numbers in the table, is revolutions per minute a function of height? Explain.

2. You are designing a spinning ride that is 40 feet high. Use the information in the table to decide on a reasonable range for how many revolutions per minute the ride would make.

Learn More About It

You will calculate the centripetal force exerted on a rider in Example 5 on p. 706.

 APPLICATION LINK More about amusement park rides is available at www.mcdougallittell.com

PREVIEW

What's the chapter about?

- Solving **radical equations** and graphing **radical functions**
- Applying the **Pythagorean theorem**
- **Proving theorems** by using algebraic properties and logical reasoning

> **KEY WORDS**
>
> - **square root function,** *p. 692*
> - **extraneous solution,** *p. 705*
> - **rational exponent,** *p. 711*
> - **completing the square,** *p. 716*
>
> - **theorem,** *p. 724*
> - **Pythagorean theorem,** *p. 724*
> - **hypotenuse,** *p. 724*
> - **legs of a right triangle,** *p. 724*
> - **converse,** *p. 726*
> - **distance formula,** *p. 730*
>
> - **midpoint,** *p. 736*
> - **midpoint formula,** *p. 736*
> - **postulate,** *p. 740*
> - **axiom,** *p. 740*
> - **conjecture,** *p. 741*
> - **indirect proof,** *p. 742*

PREPARE

Chapter Readiness Quiz

Take this quick quiz. If you are unsure of an answer, look back at the reference pages for help.

VOCABULARY CHECK *(refer to p. 512)*

1. Which is the simplest form of the radical expression $\dfrac{\sqrt{36}}{\sqrt{9}}$?

(A) $\dfrac{\sqrt{6}}{3}$ **(B)** $\sqrt{2}$ **(C)** $\dfrac{\sqrt{36}}{3}$ **(D)** 2

SKILL CHECK *(refer to pp. 511, 596)*

2. Which is the simplest form of $\sqrt{140}$?

(A) $2\sqrt{35}$ **(B)** $4\sqrt{35}$ **(C)** $10\sqrt{7}$ **(D)** $14\sqrt{5}$

3. Which of the following is the correct factorization of the trinomial $x^2 - 3x - 18$?

(A) $(x + 3)(x + 6)$ **(B)** $(x + 3)(x - 6)$
(C) $(x - 3)(x - 6)$ **(D)** $(x - 3)(x + 6)$

STUDY TIP

Draw Diagrams

Including a diagram or another visual aid when you take notes can be helpful.

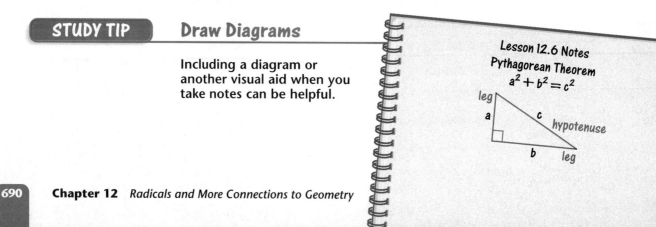

Lesson 12.6 Notes
Pythagorean Theorem
$a^2 + b^2 = c^2$

leg
a c hypotenuse

b leg

Functions with Radicals

GOAL

Use a function's graph to determine its domain and range.

MATERIALS

• graph paper
• pencil

Question How do you determine the domain and range of functions with radicals?

A function's graph can provide a representation of the domain and range. Recall that when a function is given by a formula, its domain is all possible input values. The range of a function is the set of output values.

Explore

① Copy and complete the table of values for the function $y = \sqrt{x}$. Round to the nearest tenth.

x	−2	−1	0	1	2	3	4	5
y	?	?	?	?	?	?	?	?

For what values of x is $\sqrt{x}$ *not* defined?

② For those values of x for which $\sqrt{x}$ *is* defined, plot the points from the table on a piece of graph paper and connect them with a smooth curve.

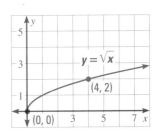

③ The table of values suggests that the domain of the function is the set of all nonnegative real numbers. You can verify this observation as follows: (1) The square root of a negative number is not defined. (2) The square root of any nonnegative real number is defined. The range is the set of all nonnegative real numbers because every nonnegative real number has a nonnegative square root.

Think About It

Use the formula for *y* to identify the domain and range of the function. Explain your reasoning.

1. $y = \sqrt{x + 1}$

2. $y = 2 + \sqrt{x}$

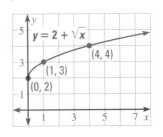

Functions Involving Square Roots

Goal

Evaluate and graph a function involving square roots.

Key Words

- square root function
- domain
- range

How fast can a dinosaur walk?

The maximum walking speed of a dinosaur is a function of the length of its leg. In Exercise 56 you will use a function involving a square root to compare the maximum walking speeds for two species of dinosaurs.

The **square root function** is defined by the equation

$$y = \sqrt{x}.$$

Its domain is all nonnegative numbers, and its range is all nonnegative numbers. Understanding the square root function will help you work with other functions involving square roots.

Student Help

▶ STUDY TIP
Recall that the square root of a negative number is undefined. $\sqrt{x}$ can be evaluated only when $x \geq 0$.

EXAMPLE 1 Evaluate Functions Involving Square Roots

Find the domain of $y = 2\sqrt{x}$. Use several values in the domain to make a table of values for the function.

Solution

A square root is defined only when the radicand is nonnegative. Therefore the domain of $y = 2\sqrt{x}$ consists of all nonnegative numbers. A table of values for $x = 0, 1, 2, 3, 4,$ and 5 is shown at the right.

x	y
0	$y = 2\sqrt{0} = 0$
1	$y = 2\sqrt{1} = 2$
2	$y = 2\sqrt{2} \approx 2.8$
3	$y = 2\sqrt{3} \approx 3.5$
4	$y = 2\sqrt{4} = 4$
5	$y = 2\sqrt{5} \approx 4.5$

Checkpoint ✓ **Evaluate Functions Involving Square Roots**

Find the domain of the function. Then use several values in the domain to make a table of values for the function.

1. $y = -\sqrt{x}$ **2.** $y = 3\sqrt{x}$ **3.** $y = \sqrt{2x}$ **4.** $y = \sqrt{x} - 1$

It is a good idea to find the domain of a function before you make a table of values. This will help you choose appropriate values of x for the table.

EXAMPLE 2 Graph $y = 2\sqrt{x}$

Sketch the graph of $y = 2\sqrt{x}$. Then find its range.

Solution

From Example 1, you know the domain is all nonnegative real numbers. Use the table of values from Example 1. Then plot the points and connect them with a smooth curve. The range is all nonnegative real numbers.

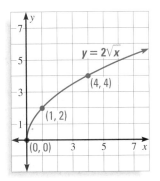

EXAMPLE 3 Graph $y = \sqrt{x} + 1$

Find the domain of $y = \sqrt{x} + 1$. Then sketch its graph and find the range.

Solution

The domain is the values of x for which the radicand is nonnegative, so the domain consists of all nonnegative real numbers. Make a table of values, plot the points, and connect them with a smooth curve.

x	y
0	$y = \sqrt{0} + 1 = 1$
1	$y = \sqrt{1} + 1 = 2$
2	$y = \sqrt{2} + 1 \approx 2.4$
3	$y = \sqrt{3} + 1 \approx 2.7$
4	$y = \sqrt{4} + 1 = 3$
5	$y = \sqrt{5} + 1 \approx 3.2$

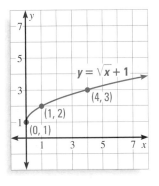

The range is all real numbers that are greater than or equal to 1.

Checkpoint ✓ **Graph Functions Involving Square Roots**

Find the domain of the function. Then sketch its graph and find the range.

5. $y = 3\sqrt{x}$ **6.** $y = -2\sqrt{x}$ **7.** $y = \sqrt{x} + 2$

8. $y = \sqrt{x} - 2$ **9.** $y = 3 - \sqrt{x}$ **10.** $y = 2\sqrt{x} + 1$

EXAMPLE 4 Graph $y = \sqrt{x - 3}$

Find the domain of $y = \sqrt{x - 3}$. Then sketch its graph.

Solution

To find the domain, find the values of x for which the radicand is nonnegative.

$x - 3 \geq 0$ Write an inequality for the domain.

$x \geq 3$ Add 3 to each side.

The domain is all numbers that are greater than or equal to 3. Make a table of values, plot the points, and connect them with a smooth curve.

x	y
3	$y = \sqrt{3 - 3} = 0$
4	$y = \sqrt{4 - 3} = 1$
5	$y = \sqrt{5 - 3} \approx 1.4$
6	$y = \sqrt{6 - 3} \approx 1.7$
7	$y = \sqrt{7 - 3} = 2$
8	$y = \sqrt{8 - 3} \approx 2.2$

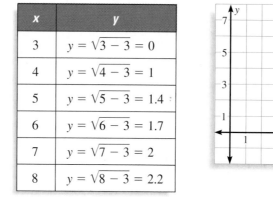

Link to Science

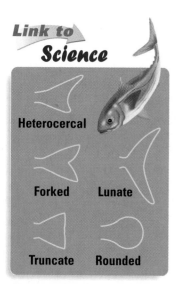

Heterocercal

Forked   Lunate

Truncate   Rounded

FISH TAILFINS, also called caudal fins, help fish swim and steer. The speed at which a fish moves through the water is affected by the size of the fish tailfin.

EXAMPLE 5 Use a Square Root Model

FISH TAILFINS The tailfin height h of a tuna can be modeled by $h = \sqrt{7.5A}$ where A is the surface area of the tailfin. Sketch the graph of the model.

Solution

The domain is all nonnegative numbers. Make a table of values, plot the points, and connect them with a smooth curve.

A	h
0	$h = \sqrt{7.5 \cdot 0} = 0$
1	$h = \sqrt{7.5 \cdot 1} \approx 2.7$
2	$h = \sqrt{7.5 \cdot 2} \approx 3.9$
3	$h = \sqrt{7.5 \cdot 3} \approx 4.7$
4	$h = \sqrt{7.5 \cdot 4} \approx 5.5$

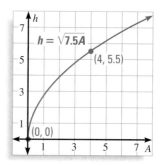

Checkpoint ✓ **Graph Functions Involving Square Roots**

11. The tailfin height h of a bottom-dwelling fish can be modeled by $h = \sqrt{0.6A}$, where A is the surface area of the tailfin. Sketch the graph of the model.

Guided Practice

Vocabulary Check

1. Describe the square root function.

2. Complete: Finding the __?__ of a square root function helps you choose appropriate input values of x for a table of values.

Skill Check

Evaluate the function for $x = 0$, 1, 2, 3, and 4. Round your answers to the nearest tenth.

3. $y = 4\sqrt{x}$ **4.** $y = -\sqrt{x}$ **5.** $y = 3\sqrt{x} + 4$

6. $y = 6\sqrt{x} - 3$ **7.** $y = \sqrt{x + 2}$ **8.** $y = \sqrt{4x - 1}$

Find the domain and the range of the function.

9. $y = 5\sqrt{x}$ **10.** $y = \sqrt{x}$ **11.** $y = \sqrt{x} - 10$

12. $y = \sqrt{x} + 6$ **13.** $y = \sqrt{x + 5}$ **14.** $y = \sqrt{x - 10}$

Find the domain of the function. Then sketch its graph.

15. $y = 4\sqrt{x}$ **16.** $y = \sqrt{x} + 5$ **17.** $y = 3\sqrt{x + 1}$

FIRE HOSES In Exercises 18 and 19, use the following information. For a particular fire hose, the flow rate f (in gallons per minute) can be modeled by $f = 120\sqrt{p}$, where p is the nozzle pressure in pounds per square inch.

18. Find the domain of the flow rate model. Then sketch its graph.

19. If the nozzle pressure is 100 pounds per square inch, what is the flow rate?

Practice and Applications

EVALUATING FUNCTIONS Evaluate the function for the given value of x.

20. $y = 2\sqrt{x}$; 9   **21.** $y = -2\sqrt{x}$; 25   **22.** $y = \sqrt{32x}$; 2

23. $y = \sqrt{3x}$; 12   **24.** $y = \sqrt{x} + 4$; 4   **25.** $y = 10 - \sqrt{x}$; 16

26. $y = \sqrt{x - 7}$; 56   **27.** $y = \sqrt{3x - 5}$; 7   **28.** $y = \sqrt{21 - 2x}$; -2

Student Help

▶ **HOMEWORK HELP**
Example 1: Exs. 20–39
Example 2: Exs. 40–55
Example 3: Exs. 40–55
Example 4: Exs. 40–55
Example 5: Exs. 56–59

FINDING THE DOMAIN Find the domain of the function. Then use several values in the domain to make a table of values for the function.

29. $y = 6\sqrt{x}$ **30.** $y = \sqrt{x - 17}$ **31.** $y = \sqrt{3x - 10}$

32. $y = \sqrt{x + 1}$ **33.** $y = 4 + \sqrt{x}$ **34.** $y = \sqrt{x} - 3$

35. $y = \sqrt{x + 9}$ **36.** $y = 2\sqrt{4x}$ **37.** $y = x\sqrt{x}$

INVESTIGATING ACCIDENTS In Exercises 38 and 39, use the following information. When a car skids to a stop, its speed S (in miles per hour) before the skid can be modeled by the equation $S = \sqrt{30df}$, where d is the length of the tires' skid marks (in feet) and f is the coefficient of friction for the road.

38. In an accident, a car makes skid marks that are 120 feet long. The coefficient of friction is 1.0. What can you say about the speed the car was traveling before the accident?

39. In an accident, a car makes skid marks that are 147 feet long. The coefficient of friction is 0.4. A witness says that the driver was traveling under the speed limit of 35 miles per hour. Can the witness's statement be correct? Explain your reasoning.

GRAPHING FUNCTIONS Find the domain of the function. Then sketch its graph and find the range.

40. $y = 7\sqrt{x}$ **41.** $y = 4\sqrt{x}$ **42.** $y = 5\sqrt{x}$ **43.** $y = 6\sqrt{x}$

44. $y = \sqrt{3x}$ **45.** $y = -\sqrt{2x}$ **46.** $y = \sqrt{x} + 4$ **47.** $y = \sqrt{x} - 3$

48. $y = 5 - \sqrt{x}$ **49.** $y = 6 - \sqrt{x}$ **50.** $y = 2\sqrt{x} + 3$ **51.** $y = 5\sqrt{x} - 2$

52. $y = \sqrt{x - 4}$ **53.** $y = \sqrt{x + 1}$ **54.** $y = \sqrt{3x + 1}$ **55.** $y = 2\sqrt{4x + 10}$

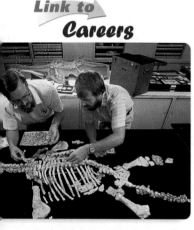

Link to
Careers

PALEONTOLOGISTS study fossils of animals and plants to better understand the history of life on Earth.

More about paleontologists at www.mcdougallittell.com

DINOSAURS In Exercises 56 and 57, use the following information. In a natural history museum you see leg bones for two species of dinosaurs and want to know how fast they walked. The maximum walking speed S (in feet per second) of a dinosaur can be modeled by the equation below, where L is the length (in feet) of the dinosaur's leg. ▶ Source: *Discover*

    Walking speed model: $S = \sqrt{32L}$

56. Find the domain of the walking speed model. Then sketch its graph.

57. For one dinosaur the length of the leg is 1 foot. For the other dinosaur the length of the leg is 4 feet. How much faster does the taller dinosaur walk than the shorter dinosaur?

CHALLENGE In Exercises 58 and 59, use the following information. The lateral surface area S of a cone whose base has radius r can be found using the formula

$$S = \pi \cdot r\sqrt{r^2 + h^2}$$

where h is the height of the cone.

58. For $r = 14$ and $h \geq 0$, sketch the graph of the function.

59. Find the lateral surface area of a cone that has a height of 30 centimeters and whose base has a radius of 14 centimeters.

60. CRITICAL THINKING Find the domain of $y = \dfrac{3}{\sqrt{x} - 2}$.

61. MULTIPLE CHOICE Which function best represents the graph?

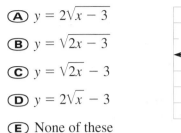

Ⓐ $y = 2\sqrt{x} - 3$

Ⓑ $y = \sqrt{2x - 3}$

Ⓒ $y = \sqrt{2x} - 3$

Ⓓ $y = 2\sqrt{x} - 3$

Ⓔ None of these

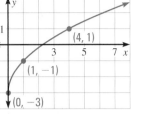

Mixed Review

SIMPLIFYING Simplify the radical expression. *(Lesson 9.3)*

62. $\sqrt{24}$

63. $\sqrt{60}$

64. $\sqrt{175}$

65. $\sqrt{360}$

66. $\sqrt{\dfrac{20}{25}}$

67. $\dfrac{1}{2}\sqrt{80}$

68. $\dfrac{3\sqrt{7}}{\sqrt{9}}$

69. $4\sqrt{\dfrac{11}{16}}$

SOLVING EQUATIONS Use the quadratic formula to solve the equation. If the solution involves radicals, round to the nearest hundredth. *(Lesson 9.6)*

70. $x^2 + 4x - 8 = 0$

71. $x^2 - 2x - 4 = 0$

72. $x^2 - 6x + 1 = 0$

73. $x^2 + 3x - 1 = 0$

74. $2x^2 + x - 3 = 0$

75. $4x^2 - 6x + 1 = 0$

MULTIPLYING EXPRESSIONS Find the product. *(Lesson 10.2)*

76. $(x - 2)(x + 11)$

77. $(x + 4)(3x - 7)$

78. $(x - 5)(x - 4)$

79. $(2x - 3)(5x - 9)$

80. $(6x + 2)(x^2 - x - 1)$

81. $(2x - 1)(x^2 + x + 1)$

82. MOUNT RUSHMORE Carved on Mount Rushmore are the faces of four Presidents of the United States: Washington, Jefferson, Roosevelt, and Lincoln. The ratio of each face on the cliff to a scale model is 12 to 1. How tall is Washington's face on Mount Rushmore if the scale model is 5 feet tall? *(Lesson 11.1)*

MULTIPLYING RATIONAL EXPRESSIONS Write the product in simplest form. *(Lesson 11.4)*

83. $\dfrac{8x}{3} \cdot \dfrac{1}{x}$

84. $\dfrac{8x^2}{3} \cdot \dfrac{9}{16x}$

85. $\dfrac{x}{x + 6} \cdot \dfrac{x + 6}{x + 1}$

Maintaining Skills

AREA Find the area of a triangle with the given base and height. *(Skills Review p. 774)*

86. $b = 4, h = 9$

87. $b = 1, h = 1$

88. $b = 12, h = 9$

89. $b = 6, h = 8$

90. $b = 8, h = 3$

91. $b = 10, h = 7$

92. $b = 0.75, h = 4$

93. $b = 0.85, h = 0.62$

94. $b = 0.25, h = 1.75$

12.2 Operations with Radical Expressions

Goal
Add, subtract, multiply, and divide radical expressions.

Key Words
- simplest form of a radical expression

How far can you see to the horizon?

The distance you can see to Earth's horizon depends on your eye-level height. In Example 4 you will compare the distance you can see to the distance a friend can see when you are at different heights on a schooner's mast.

You can use the distributive property to simplify sums and differences of radical expressions when the expressions have the same radicand.

SUM: $\sqrt{2} + 3\sqrt{2} = (1 + 3)\sqrt{2} = 4\sqrt{2}$

DIFFERENCE: $\sqrt{2} - 3\sqrt{2} = (1 - 3)\sqrt{2} = -2\sqrt{2}$

In part (b) of Example 1, the first step is to identify a perfect square factor in the radicand, as you learned on page 511.

Student Help

▶ **LOOK BACK**
For help simplifying radical expressions, see pp. 511–512.

EXAMPLE 1 Add and Subtract Radicals

Simplify the radical expression.

a. $2\sqrt{2} + \sqrt{5} - 6\sqrt{2} = (2\sqrt{2} - 6\sqrt{2}) + \sqrt{5}$ — Group radicals having the same radicand.

$\qquad\qquad\qquad\qquad = -4\sqrt{2} + \sqrt{5}$ — Subtract.

b. $4\sqrt{3} - \sqrt{27} = 4\sqrt{3} - \sqrt{9 \cdot 3}$ — Factor using perfect square factor.

$\qquad\qquad\quad = 4\sqrt{3} - \sqrt{9} \cdot \sqrt{3}$ — Use product property.

$\qquad\qquad\quad = 4\sqrt{3} - 3\sqrt{3}$ — Simplify.

$\qquad\qquad\quad = \sqrt{3}$ — Subtract.

Checkpoint ✓ Add and Subtract Radicals

Simplify the radical expression.

1. $\sqrt{3} + 2\sqrt{3}$
2. $3\sqrt{5} - 2\sqrt{5}$
3. $\sqrt{7} + \sqrt{2} + 3\sqrt{7}$

4. $\sqrt{8} - \sqrt{2}$
5. $\sqrt{18} + \sqrt{2}$
6. $5\sqrt{3} - \sqrt{12}$

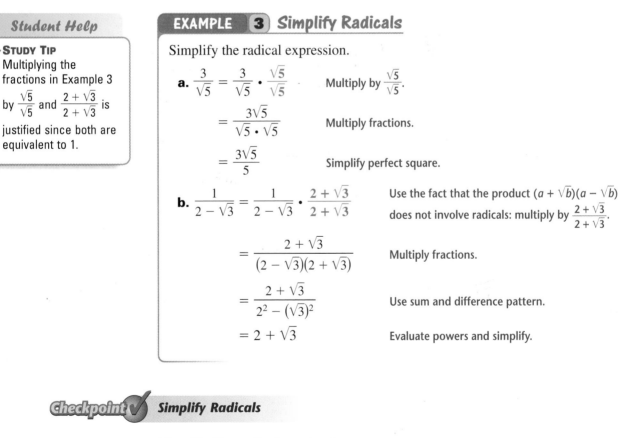

Student Help

▶ **STUDY TIP**
As you can see in part (c) of Example 2, the product of two radical expressions having the sum and difference pattern has no radical. In general,
$(a + \sqrt{b})(a - \sqrt{b}) = a^2 - b.$

EXAMPLE **2** **Multiply Radicals**

Simplify the radical expression.

a. $\sqrt{2} \cdot \sqrt{8} = \sqrt{16} = 4$ Use product property and simplify.

b. $\sqrt{2}(5 - \sqrt{3}) = \sqrt{2} \cdot 5 - \sqrt{2} \cdot \sqrt{3}$ Use distributive property.

            $= 5\sqrt{2} - \sqrt{6}$ Use product property.

c. $(2 + \sqrt{3})(2 - \sqrt{3}) = 2^2 - (\sqrt{3})^2$ Use sum and difference pattern.

            $= 4 - 3 = 1$ Evaluate powers and simplify.

Checkpoint ✓ *Multiply Radicals*

Simplify the radical expression.

7. $\sqrt{3} \cdot \sqrt{12}$ **8.** $\sqrt{5}(\sqrt{2} + 1)$ **9.** $(\sqrt{2} + 1)(\sqrt{2} - 1)$

To simplify expressions with radicals in the denominator, you may be able to rewrite the denominator as a rational number without changing the value of the expression, as you learned on page 512.

Student Help

▶ **STUDY TIP**
Multiplying the fractions in Example 3 by $\frac{\sqrt{5}}{\sqrt{5}}$ and $\frac{2 + \sqrt{3}}{2 + \sqrt{3}}$ is justified since both are equivalent to 1.

EXAMPLE **3** **Simplify Radicals**

Simplify the radical expression.

a. $\dfrac{3}{\sqrt{5}} = \dfrac{3}{\sqrt{5}} \cdot \dfrac{\sqrt{5}}{\sqrt{5}}$ Multiply by $\frac{\sqrt{5}}{\sqrt{5}}$.

     $= \dfrac{3\sqrt{5}}{\sqrt{5} \cdot \sqrt{5}}$ Multiply fractions.

     $= \dfrac{3\sqrt{5}}{5}$ Simplify perfect square.

b. $\dfrac{1}{2 - \sqrt{3}} = \dfrac{1}{2 - \sqrt{3}} \cdot \dfrac{2 + \sqrt{3}}{2 + \sqrt{3}}$ Use the fact that the product $(a + \sqrt{b})(a - \sqrt{b})$ does not involve radicals: multiply by $\frac{2 + \sqrt{3}}{2 + \sqrt{3}}$.

     $= \dfrac{2 + \sqrt{3}}{(2 - \sqrt{3})(2 + \sqrt{3})}$ Multiply fractions.

     $= \dfrac{2 + \sqrt{3}}{2^2 - (\sqrt{3})^2}$ Use sum and difference pattern.

     $= 2 + \sqrt{3}$ Evaluate powers and simplify.

Checkpoint ✓ *Simplify Radicals*

Simplify the radical expression.

10. $\dfrac{1}{\sqrt{2}}$ **11.** $\dfrac{\sqrt{18}}{\sqrt{2}}$ **12.** $\dfrac{7}{3 - \sqrt{2}}$ **13.** $\dfrac{11}{5 + \sqrt{3}}$

EXAMPLE **4** *Use a Radical Model*

SAILING You and a friend are working on a schooner. The distance d (in miles) you can see to the horizon can be modeled by the equation

$$d = \sqrt{\frac{3h}{2}}$$

where h is your eye-level height (in feet) above the water. Your eye-level height is 32 feet and your friend's eye-level height is 18 feet. Write an expression that shows how much farther you can see than your friend. Simplify the expression.

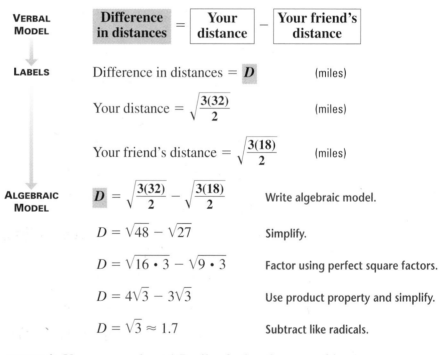

Not drawn to scale

Solution

VERBAL MODEL	Difference in distances	=	Your distance	−	Your friend's distance

LABELS   Difference in distances = D (miles)

Your distance = $\sqrt{\dfrac{3(32)}{2}}$ (miles)

Your friend's distance = $\sqrt{\dfrac{3(18)}{2}}$ (miles)

ALGEBRAIC MODEL

$D = \sqrt{\dfrac{3(32)}{2}} - \sqrt{\dfrac{3(18)}{2}}$ Write algebraic model.

$D = \sqrt{48} - \sqrt{27}$ Simplify.

$D = \sqrt{16 \cdot 3} - \sqrt{9 \cdot 3}$ Factor using perfect square factors.

$D = 4\sqrt{3} - 3\sqrt{3}$ Use product property and simplify.

$D = \sqrt{3} \approx 1.7$ Subtract like radicals.

ANSWER ▶ You can see about 1.7 miles farther than your friend.

Checkpoint ✓ *Use a Radical Model*

14. Your eye-level height is 16 feet and your friend's eye-level height is 20 feet. Write an expression showing how much farther your friend can see than you.

12.2 Exercises

Guided Practice

Vocabulary Check

1. Complete: In the expression "$3\sqrt{2}$", 2 is called the __?__ .

2. Which of the following is the simplest form of the radical expression $\dfrac{4}{\sqrt{3}}$?

A. $\dfrac{4\sqrt{3}}{9}$ **B.** $\dfrac{4\sqrt{3}}{3}$ **C.** $\dfrac{4}{\sqrt{3}}$ **D.** $\dfrac{\sqrt{12}}{3}$

Skill Check — Simplify the expression.

3. $4 + \sqrt{5} + 5\sqrt{5}$ **4.** $3\sqrt{7} - 2\sqrt{7}$ **5.** $3\sqrt{6} + \sqrt{24}$

6. $\sqrt{3} \cdot \sqrt{8}$ **7.** $\left(3 + \sqrt{7}\right)^2$ **8.** $\sqrt{3}(5\sqrt{3} - 2\sqrt{6})$

9. $\dfrac{4}{\sqrt{13}}$ **10.** $\dfrac{3}{8 - \sqrt{10}}$ **11.** $\dfrac{6}{\sqrt{10}}$

12. SAILING In Example 4 on page 700, suppose your eye-level height is 24 feet and your friend's is 12 feet. Write an expression that shows how much farther you can see than your friend. Simplify the expression.

Practice and Applications

ADDING AND SUBTRACTING RADICALS Simplify the expression.

13. $5\sqrt{7} + 2\sqrt{7}$ **14.** $\sqrt{3} + 5\sqrt{3}$ **15.** $11\sqrt{3} - 12\sqrt{3}$

16. $2\sqrt{6} - \sqrt{6}$ **17.** $4\sqrt{5} + \sqrt{3} + \sqrt{5}$ **18.** $3\sqrt{11} - \sqrt{5} + \sqrt{11}$

19. $\sqrt{32} + \sqrt{2}$ **20.** $\sqrt{75} + \sqrt{3}$ **21.** $\sqrt{80} - \sqrt{45}$

22. $\sqrt{72} - \sqrt{18}$ **23.** $4\sqrt{5} + \sqrt{125} + \sqrt{45}$ **24.** $\sqrt{24} - \sqrt{96} + \sqrt{6}$

MULTIPLYING RADICALS Simplify the expression.

25. $\sqrt{3} \cdot \sqrt{12}$ **26.** $\sqrt{16} \cdot \sqrt{4}$ **27.** $\sqrt{18} \cdot \sqrt{5}$

28. $\sqrt{5} \cdot \sqrt{8}$ **29.** $\sqrt{6}(\sqrt{6} - 1)$ **30.** $\sqrt{6}(7\sqrt{3} + 6)$

31. $\sqrt{5}(4 + \sqrt{5})$ **32.** $\sqrt{2}(\sqrt{8} - 4)$ **33.** $\sqrt{3}(5\sqrt{2} + \sqrt{3})$

MULTIPLYING RADICALS Simplify the expression using the sum and difference pattern.

34. $\left(\sqrt{2} + 6\right)\left(\sqrt{2} - 6\right)$ **35.** $\left(1 + \sqrt{13}\right)\left(1 - \sqrt{13}\right)$

36. $\left(\sqrt{2} + \sqrt{3}\right)\left(\sqrt{2} - \sqrt{3}\right)$ **37.** $\left(\sqrt{7} + \sqrt{2}\right)\left(\sqrt{7} - \sqrt{2}\right)$

Student Help

▶ **HOMEWORK HELP**
Example 1: Exs. 13–24, 53
Example 2: Exs. 25–40
Example 3: Exs. 41–52, 54
Example 4: Exs. 55, 56

Geometry Link Find the area. (See the Table of Formulas on page 798).

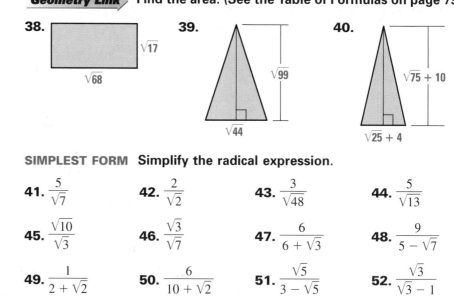

38. $\sqrt{17}$ $\sqrt{68}$

39. $\sqrt{99}$ $\sqrt{44}$

40. $\sqrt{75} + 10$ $\sqrt{25} + 4$

Student Help

▶ **HOMEWORK HELP**

Extra help with problem solving in Exs. 41–52 is available at www.mcdougallittell.com

SIMPLEST FORM Simplify the radical expression.

41. $\dfrac{5}{\sqrt{7}}$

42. $\dfrac{2}{\sqrt{2}}$

43. $\dfrac{3}{\sqrt{48}}$

44. $\dfrac{5}{\sqrt{13}}$

45. $\dfrac{\sqrt{10}}{\sqrt{3}}$

46. $\dfrac{\sqrt{3}}{\sqrt{7}}$

47. $\dfrac{6}{6 + \sqrt{3}}$

48. $\dfrac{9}{5 - \sqrt{7}}$

49. $\dfrac{1}{2 + \sqrt{2}}$

50. $\dfrac{6}{10 + \sqrt{2}}$

51. $\dfrac{\sqrt{5}}{3 - \sqrt{5}}$

52. $\dfrac{\sqrt{3}}{\sqrt{3} - 1}$

ERROR ANALYSIS In Exercises 53 and 54, find and correct the error.

53. $\sqrt{12} + \sqrt{13} = \sqrt{25} = 5$

54. $\dfrac{5}{1 + \sqrt{3}} = \dfrac{5(1 - \sqrt{3})}{(1 + \sqrt{3})(1 - \sqrt{3})} = \dfrac{5 - 5\sqrt{3}}{1 + 3} = \dfrac{5 - 5\sqrt{3}}{4}$

55. POLE-VAULTING A pole-vaulter's approach velocity v (in feet per second) and height reached h (in feet) are related by the following equation.

Pole-vaulter model: $v = 8\sqrt{h}$

Suppose you are a pole-vaulter and reach a height of 20 feet and your opponent reaches a height of 16 feet. Write an expression that shows how much faster you ran than your opponent. Simplify the expression and round your answer to the nearest hundredth.

56. Science Link Many birds drop clams or other shellfish in order to break the shell and get the food inside. The time t (in seconds) it takes such an object to fall a certain distance d (in feet) is given by the following equation.

$$t = \dfrac{\sqrt{d}}{4}$$

A gull drops a clam from a height of 50 feet. A second gull drops a clam from a height of 32 feet. Write an expression that shows the difference in the time that it takes for the two clams to reach the ground. Simplify the expression.

57. MULTIPLE CHOICE Simplify $\sqrt{5}(6 + \sqrt{5})$.

Ⓐ $\sqrt{30} + 5$ Ⓑ $5\sqrt{6} + 5$ Ⓒ $6\sqrt{5} + 5$ Ⓓ $11\sqrt{5}$

58. MULTIPLE CHOICE Which of the following is equal to the difference $\sqrt{3} - 5\sqrt{9}$?

Ⓕ $\sqrt{3} - 15$ Ⓖ $-4\sqrt{3}$ Ⓗ $\sqrt{3} - 3$ Ⓙ $3 + 2\sqrt{5}$

59. MULTIPLE CHOICE Simplify $\dfrac{3}{5 - \sqrt{2}}$.

Ⓐ $\dfrac{15 + 3\sqrt{2}}{23}$ Ⓑ $\dfrac{15 + 3\sqrt{2}}{25}$ Ⓒ $\dfrac{15 + \sqrt{6}}{23}$ Ⓓ $\dfrac{15 + \sqrt{6}}{25}$

Mixed Review

PERCENTS Solve the percent problem. *(Lesson 3.9)*

60. What is 30% of 160?　　　　**61.** 105 is what percent of 240?

62. 203 is what percent of 406?　　**63.** What is 70% of 210?

SOLVING QUADRATIC EQUATIONS Solve the equation by factoring.
(Lesson 10.5)

64. $x^2 - 25 = 0$ 　　**65.** $x^2 + 2x - 15 = 0$ 　　**66.** $x^2 - 13x = -42$

67. $x^2 - 26 = 11x$ 　　**68.** $-9x + 4 = -2x^2$ 　　**69.** $2 + 3x^2 = -5x$

CROSS PRODUCT PROPERTY Solve the equation using the cross product property. Check your solutions. *(Lesson 11.7)*

70. $\dfrac{2}{x + 3} = \dfrac{1}{x - 6}$ 　　**71.** $\dfrac{6}{x} = \dfrac{7}{x - 5}$ 　　**72.** $\dfrac{7}{x + 4} = \dfrac{2}{x - 6}$

FINDING THE DOMAIN Find the domain of the function. Then use several values in the domain to make a table of values for the function.
(Lesson 12.1)

73. $y = \sqrt{x} - 3$ 　　**74.** $y = \sqrt{x} + 4$ 　　**75.** $y = 6\sqrt{x}$

76. $y = 11\sqrt{x}$ 　　**77.** $y = \sqrt{x + 3}$ 　　**78.** $y = \sqrt{x - 8}$

Maintaining Skills

COMPARING PERCENTS AND DECIMALS Complete the statement using <, >, or =. *(Skills Review pp. 768, 770)*

79. 40% ? 0.35 　　**80.** 110% ? 110 　　**81.** 1.8 ? 180%

82. 0.22 ? 20% 　　**83.** 200% ? 1.0 　　**84.** 12% ? 1

85. 0.3 ? 33% 　　**86.** 0.75 ? 85% 　　**87.** 1% ? 0.1

88. 5% ? 0.5 　　**89.** 1.5 ? 150% 　　**90.** 0.9 ? 89%

91. 101% ? 1.1 　　**92.** 20% ? 0.25 　　**93.** 0.66 ? 60%

94. 2.25 ? 250% 　　**95.** 80% ? 1.8 　　**96.** 100% ? 1.0

12.3 Solving Radical Equations

Goal

Solve a radical equation.

Key Words

• radical
• extraneous solution

What is the nozzle pressure of a de-icing hose?

The nozzle pressure of a hose is a function of the flow rate of the hose and the diameter of the nozzle. In Exercises 37 and 38 you will use an equation involving radicals to find the nozzle pressure of a hose used to de-ice an airplane.

In solving an equation involving radicals, the following property can be useful.

SQUARING BOTH SIDES OF AN EQUATION

If $a = b$, then $a^2 = b^2$, where a and b are algebraic expressions.

Example: $\sqrt{x + 1} = 5$, so $x + 1 = 25$.

EXAMPLE 1 Solve a Radical Equation

a. Solve $\sqrt{x} - 7 = 0$. **b.** Solve $3\sqrt{x + 4} = 15$.

Solution

a.
$\sqrt{x} - 7 = 0$	Write original equation.
$\sqrt{x} = 7$	Isolate the radical expression on one side of the equation.
$(\sqrt{x})^2 = 7^2$	Square each side.
$x = 49$	Simplify.

ANSWER▸ The solution is 49. Check the solution in the original equation.

b.
$3\sqrt{x + 4} = 15$	Write original equation.
$\sqrt{x + 4} = 5$	Divide each side by 3.
$(\sqrt{x + 4})^2 = 5^2$	Square each side.
$x + 4 = 25$	Simplify.
$x = 21$	Subtract 4 from each side.

ANSWER▸ The solution is 21. Check the solution in the original equation.

EXAMPLE **2** Solve a Radical Equation

To solve the equation $\sqrt{2x - 3} + 4 = 5$, you need to isolate the radical expression first.

❶ Write the original equation. $\qquad\qquad\qquad$ $\sqrt{2x - 3} + 4 = 5$

❷ Subtract 4 from each side of the equation. $\qquad$ $\sqrt{2x - 3} = 1$

❸ Square each side of the equation. $\qquad\qquad\quad$ $(\sqrt{2x - 3})^2 = 1^2$

❹ Simplify the equation. $\qquad\qquad\qquad\qquad$ $2x - 3 = 1$

❺ Add 3 to each side of the equation. $\qquad\qquad\quad$ $2x = 4$

❻ Divide each side of the equation by 2. $\qquad\qquad$ $x = 2$

ANSWER ▶ The solution is 2. Check the solution in the original equation.

Checkpoint ✓ *Solve a Radical Equation*

Solve the equation.

1. $\sqrt{x} = 3$ $\qquad\qquad\qquad$ **2.** $\sqrt{m} - 4 = 0$ $\qquad\qquad$ **3.** $\sqrt{x - 6} = 4$

4. $\sqrt{n + 1} = 1$ $\qquad\qquad$ **5.** $\sqrt{x - 4} + 5 = 11$ $\qquad$ **6.** $\sqrt{3n + 1} - 3 = 1$

EXTRANEOUS SOLUTIONS Squaring both sides of an equation can introduce a solution to the squared equation that does *not* satisfy the original equation. Such a solution is called an **extraneous solution**. When you solve by squaring both sides of an equation, check each solution in the original equation.

Student Help

▶**MORE EXAMPLES**

INTERNET More examples are available at www.mcdougallittell.com

EXAMPLE 3 **Check for Extraneous Solutions**

Solve $\sqrt{x + 2} = x$ and check for extraneous solutions.

Solution

❶ Write the original equation. $\qquad\qquad\qquad\qquad$ $\sqrt{x + 2} = x$

❷ Square each side of the equation. $\qquad\qquad\quad$ $(\sqrt{x + 2})^2 = x^2$

❸ Simplify the equation. $\qquad\qquad\qquad\qquad\quad$ $x + 2 = x^2$

❹ Write the equation in standard form. $\qquad\quad$ $x^2 - x - 2 = 0$

❺ Factor the equation. $\qquad\qquad\qquad\qquad$ $(x - 2)(x + 1) = 0$

❻ Use the zero-product property to solve for *x*. $\quad$ $x = 2 \ or \ x = -1$

CHECK ✓ Substitute 2 and -1 in the *original* equation.

$$\sqrt{2 + 2} \stackrel{?}{=} 2 \qquad\qquad \sqrt{-1 + 2} \stackrel{?}{=} -1$$

$$2 = 2 ✓ \qquad\qquad\qquad 1 \neq -1$$

ANSWER ▶ The only solution is 2, because $x = -1$ does not satisfy the original equation.

EXAMPLE 4 Check for Extraneous Solutions

Solve $\sqrt{x} + 13 = 0$ and check for extraneous solutions.

Solution

$\sqrt{x} + 13 = 0$	Write original equation.
$\sqrt{x} = -13$	Subtract 13 from each side.
$(\sqrt{x})^2 = (-13)^2$	Square each side.
$x = 169$	Simplify.

ANSWER ▶ $\sqrt{169} + 13 \neq 0$, so $x = 169$ is not a solution. The equation has no solution because $\sqrt{x} \geq 0$ for all values of x.

Checkpoint ✓ *Check for Extraneous Solutions*

Solve the equation. Check for extraneous solutions.

7. $\sqrt{x + 6} = x$ **8.** $x = \sqrt{8 - 2x}$ **9.** $\sqrt{n} + 4 = 0$

Science

CENTRIPETAL FORCE
keeps you spinning in a circle
on an amusement park ride.
Forces can be measured
in newtons. A force of one
newton will accelerate a
mass of one kilogram at one
meter per second per second.

EXAMPLE 5 Use a Radical Model

CENTRIPETAL FORCE The centripetal force F exerted on a passenger by a spinning amusement park ride and the number of seconds t the ride takes to complete one revolution are related by the following equation.

$$t = \sqrt{\frac{1620\pi^2}{F}}$$

Find the centripetal force experienced by this person if $t = 10$.

Solution

$t = \sqrt{\dfrac{1620\pi^2}{F}}$	Write model for centripetal force.
$10^2 = \left(\sqrt{\dfrac{1620\pi^2}{F}}\right)^2$	Substitute 10 for t and square each side.
$100 = \dfrac{1620\pi^2}{F}$	Simplify.
$F = \dfrac{1620\pi^2}{100} \approx 160$	Solve for F.

ANSWER ▶ The person experiences a centripetal force of about 160 newtons.

Checkpoint ✓ *Use a Radical Model*

10. Find the centripetal force exerted on the passenger in Example 5 if the amusement park ride takes 11 seconds to complete one revolution.

12.3 Exercises

Guided Practice

Vocabulary Check

1. Explain what a *radical equation* is.

2. Explain what an *extraneous solution* is.

Skill Check

Solve the equation. Check for extraneous solutions.

3. $8 = \sqrt{x}$ **4.** $\sqrt{x} = 11$ **5.** $14 = \sqrt{x}$

6. $\sqrt{x} = -7$ **7.** $6 = \sqrt{x}$ **8.** $\sqrt{x} = 1$

9. $\sqrt{x} + 6 = 0$ **10.** $\sqrt{x} - 20 = 0$ **11.** $\sqrt{4x} - 1 = 3$

12. $x = \sqrt{x + 12}$ **13.** $-5 + \sqrt{x} = 0$ **14.** $x = \sqrt{5x + 24}$

15. $\sqrt{5x + 1} + 8 = 12$ **16.** $\sqrt{4x + 5} = x$ **17.** $\sqrt{x + 6} = x$

Practice and Applications

SOLVING RADICAL EQUATIONS Solve the equation.

18. $\sqrt{x} - 9 = 0$ **19.** $\sqrt{x} - 1 = 0$ **20.** $\sqrt{x} - 5 = 0$

21. $\sqrt{x} - 10 = 0$ **22.** $\sqrt{x} - 15 = 0$ **23.** $\sqrt{x} - 16 = 0$

24. $\sqrt{6x} - 13 = 23$ **25.** $\sqrt{4x + 1} + 5 = 10$ **26.** $\sqrt{9 - x} - 10 = 14$

27. $\sqrt{5x + 1} + 2 = 6$ **28.** $\sqrt{6x - 2} - 3 = 7$ **29.** $4 = 7 - \sqrt{33x - 2}$

30. $4\sqrt{3x + 3} = 24$ **31.** $\sqrt{2x + 4} + 1 = 11$ **32.** $8\sqrt{x + 3} = 64$

ERROR ANALYSIS In Exercises 33 and 34, find and correct the error.

33.

$\sqrt{x} = 7$
$(\sqrt{x})^2 = (\sqrt{7})^2$
$x^2 = 7$
$x = \sqrt{7}$

34.

$\sqrt{x} - 15 = 0$
$\sqrt{x} = 15$
$(\sqrt{x})^2 = (15)^2$
$x = 225$ and -225

Student Help

▶ **HOMEWORK HELP**
Example 1: Exs. 18–36
Example 2: Exs. 18–36
Example 3: Exs. 40–54
Example 4: Exs. 40–54
Example 5: Exs. 37, 38, 55, 56

Geometry Link Find the value of *x*.

35. Perimeter $= 30$

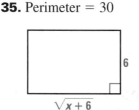

36. Area $= 88$

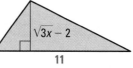

PLANE DE-ICING In Exercises 37 and 38, use the following information.
You work for a commercial airline and remove ice from planes. The relationship among the flow rate r (in gallons per minute) of the antifreeze for de-icing, the nozzle diameter d (in inches), and the nozzle pressure P (in pounds per square inch) is shown in the diagram. You want a flow rate of 250 gallons per minute.

37. Find the nozzle pressure
P for a nozzle whose
diameter is 1.25 inches.

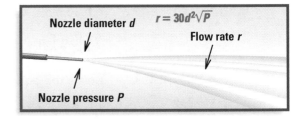

Nozzle diameter d $r = 30d^2\sqrt{P}$

Flow rate r

Nozzle pressure P

38. Find the nozzle pressure
P for a nozzle whose
diameter is 1.75 inches.

39. MATHEMATICAL REASONING Write a radical equation that has a solution of 18.

CHECKING SOLUTIONS Solve the equation. Check for extraneous solutions.

40. $\sqrt{x} - 3 = 4$ **41.** $\sqrt{x} + 6 = 0$ **42.** $\sqrt{x} + 5 = 1$

43. $6 + \sqrt{3x} = -3$ **44.** $\sqrt{x + 5} = 7$ **45.** $\sqrt{5x + 10} = -5$

46. $\sqrt{x + 11} = 1$ **47.** $x = \sqrt{x + 6}$ **48.** $\sqrt{x} - 5 = 20$

49. $\sqrt{x - 10} = -1$ **50.** $3\sqrt{x} = -21$ **51.** $x = \sqrt{2x + 3}$

52. $2\sqrt{x} = -18$ **53.** $x = \sqrt{x + 12}$ **54.** $2\sqrt{x} + 7 = 19$

SPORTS In Exercises 55 and 56, use the following information.
During the hammer throw event, a hammer is swung around in a circle several times until the thrower releases it. As the hammer travels in the path of the circle, it accelerates toward the center. This acceleration is known as *centripetal acceleration*. The speed s that the hammer is thrown can be modeled by the formula $s = \sqrt{1.2a}$, where a is the centripetal acceleration of the hammer prior to being released.

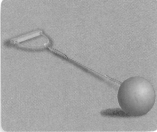
55. Find the approximate
centripetal acceleration
(in meters per second per
second) when the ball is
thrown with a speed of
18 meters per second.

56. Find the approximate
centripetal acceleration
(in meters per second per
second) when the ball is
thrown with a speed of
24 meters per second.

57. LOGICAL REASONING Determine whether the statement is *true* or *false*. Explain your reasoning.

36 is a solution of $\sqrt{x} = -6$.

58. MULTIPLE CHOICE Which of the following is a solution of $x = \sqrt{30 - x}$?

    Ⓐ -6 Ⓑ 0 Ⓒ 5 Ⓓ 30

59. MULTIPLE CHOICE Which of the following is a solution of $x = \sqrt{x + 20}$?

    Ⓕ -5 Ⓖ -4 Ⓗ 4 Ⓙ 5

Mixed Review

QUADRATIC EQUATIONS Solve the equation. Write the solutions as integers if possible. Otherwise, write them as radical expressions. *(Lesson 9.2)*

60. $x^2 = 36$ **61.** $x^2 = 11$ **62.** $7x^2 = 700$

63. $25x^2 - 9 = 91$ **64.** $x^2 - 16 = -7$ **65.** $-16x^2 + 48 = 0$

SPECIAL PRODUCT PATTERNS Find the product. *(Lesson 10.3)*

66. $(x + 5)^2$ **67.** $(2x - 3)^2$ **68.** $(6y - 4)(6y + 4)$

69. $(3x + 5y)(3x - 5y)$ **70.** $(x + 7y)^2$ **71.** $(2a - 9b)^2$

PERFECT SQUARES Factor the expression. *(Lesson 10.7)*

72. $x^2 + 18x + 81$ **73.** $x^2 - 12x + 36$ **74.** $4x^2 + 28x + 49$

Maintaining Skills

RECIPROCALS Find the reciprocal of the mixed number. Write your answer in lowest terms. *(Skills Review p. 763)*

75. $2\frac{1}{9}$ **76.** $4\frac{2}{5}$ **77.** $1\frac{3}{10}$ **78.** $6\frac{1}{2}$

79. $1\frac{7}{50}$ **80.** $8\frac{1}{6}$ **81.** $3\frac{7}{9}$ **82.** $5\frac{8}{25}$

Quiz 1

Find the domain of the function. Then sketch its graph and find the range. *(Lesson 12.1)*

  1. $y = 10\sqrt{x}$ **2.** $y = \sqrt{x - 9}$ **3.** $y = \sqrt{2x - 1}$ **4.** $y = \sqrt{x} - 2$

Simplify the expression. *(Lesson 12.2)*

  5. $7\sqrt{10} + 11\sqrt{10}$ **6.** $\sqrt{3}(3\sqrt{2} + \sqrt{3})$ **7.** $4\sqrt{7} + \sqrt{125} - \sqrt{80}$

Solve the equation. Check for extraneous solutions. *(Lesson 12.3)*

  8. $\sqrt{x} - 2 = 0$ **9.** $\sqrt{x} - 8 = 0$ **10.** $\sqrt{3x + 2} + 2 = 3$

11. $\sqrt{3x - 2} + 3 = 7$ **12.** $\sqrt{77 - 4x} = x$ **13.** $x = \sqrt{2x + 3}$

14. NOZZLE PRESSURE Using the flow rate equation $r = 30d^2\sqrt{P}$ given in Exercises 37 and 38 on page 708, find the nozzle pressure for a hose that has a flow rate of 250 gallons per minute and a diameter of 2.5 inches. *(Lesson 12.3)*

12.4 Rational Exponents

Goal
Evaluate expressions involving rational exponents.

Key Words
- cube root of *a*
- radical notation
- rational exponent
- rational exponent notation

How large is the sphere used in women's shot put?

The metal sphere used in women's shot put is called a shot. In Exercise 46 you will find the size of this shot.

CUBE ROOT OF A NUMBER In Chapter 1 you learned how to cube a number. Now we define a *cube root*.

If $b^3 = a$, then b is called a **cube root of *a***.

For instance, 2 is a cube root of 8 because $2^3 = 8$. In radical notation, a cube root of *a* is written as $\sqrt[3]{a}$. In general, for any integer *n* greater than 1,

if $b^n = a$, then *b* is an *n*th root of *a*.

In radical notation, the *n*th root of *a* is written as $\sqrt[n]{a}$.

RATIONAL EXPONENT NOTATION Because $\sqrt[3]{a} \cdot \sqrt[3]{a} \cdot \sqrt[3]{a} = a$, it is natural to define $\sqrt[3]{a} = a^{1/3}$. With this definition the product of powers property for exponents holds for fractional exponents:

$$\sqrt[3]{a} \cdot \sqrt[3]{a} \cdot \sqrt[3]{a} = a^{1/3} \cdot a^{1/3} \cdot a^{1/3} = a^{(1/3 + 1/3 + 1/3)} = a^1 = a$$

More generally, $\sqrt[n]{a} = a^{1/n}$ for any $a > 0$ and integer *n* greater than 1.

Student Help

▶ **READING ALGEBRA**
When the *cube root of a* is written in rational exponent notation, $a^{1/3}$, it is read "*a* raised to the one-third power."

EXAMPLE 1 Find Cube and Square Roots

Find the cube root or square root.

a. $27^{1/3}$ **b.** $\sqrt[3]{1000}$ **c.** $64^{1/2}$

Solution

a. Because $3^3 = 27$, you know that $27^{1/3} = 3$.

b. Because $10^3 = 1000$, you know that $\sqrt[3]{1000} = 10$.

c. Because $8^2 = 64$, you know that $64^{1/2} = 8$.

RATIONAL EXPONENTS A rational exponent does not have to be of the form $\frac{1}{n}$. Other rational numbers, such as $\frac{3}{2}$ and $\frac{4}{3}$, may also be used as exponents. For integers m and n we have the rule $(a^m)^n = a^{mn}$. This produces a basis for the following definition of **rational exponents**.

RATIONAL EXPONENTS

Let $a^{1/n}$ be an nth root of a, m and n be positive integers, and $a \geq 0$.
$$a^{m/n} = (a^{1/n})^m = (\sqrt[n]{a})^m$$

EXAMPLE 2 Evaluate Expressions with Rational Exponents

Rewrite the expressions using rational exponent notation *and* radical notation.

a. $16^{3/2}$ **b.** $8^{4/3}$

Solution

a. Use rational exponent notation. $16^{3/2} = (16^{1/2})^3 = 4^3 = 64$

Use radical notation. $16^{3/2} = (\sqrt{16})^3 = 4^3 = 64$

b. Use rational exponent notation. $8^{4/3} = (8^{1/3})^4 = 2^4 = 16$

Use radical notation. $8^{4/3} = (\sqrt[3]{8})^4 = 2^4 = 16$

Checkpoint ✔ *Evaluate Expressions with Rational Exponents*

Evaluate the expression without using a calculator.

1. $\sqrt[3]{64}$ **2.** $625^{1/2}$ **3.** $225^{1/2}$ **4.** $216^{1/3}$

5. $64^{3/2}$ **6.** $(\sqrt[3]{27})^2$ **7.** $(\sqrt{4})^5$ **8.** $1000^{2/3}$

The multiplication properties of exponents presented in Lesson 8.1 can also be applied to rational exponents.

SUMMARY

Properties of Rational Exponents

Let a and b be nonnegative real numbers and let m and n be rational numbers.

PROPERTY	EXAMPLE
$a^m \cdot a^n = a^{m+n}$	$3^{1/2} \cdot 3^{3/2} = 3^{(1/2 + 3/2)} = 3^2 = 9$
$(a^m)^n = a^{mn}$	$(4^{3/2})^2 = 4^{(3/2 \cdot 2)} = 4^3 = 64$
$(ab)^m = a^m b^m$	$(9 \cdot 4)^{1/2} = 9^{1/2} \cdot 4^{1/2} = 3 \cdot 2 = 6$

EXAMPLE 3 Use Properties of Rational Exponents

Evaluate the expression using the properties of rational exponents.

a. $5^{1/3} \cdot 5^{2/3}$ **b.** $\left(7^{1/3}\right)^6$ **c.** $(4 \cdot 25)^{1/2}$

Solution

a. Use the product of powers property.

$$5^{1/3} \cdot 5^{2/3} = 5^{(1/3 + 2/3)} = 5^{3/3} = 5^1 = 5$$

b. Use the power of a power property.

$$\left(7^{1/3}\right)^6 = 7^{(1/3 \cdot 6)} = 7^2 = 49$$

c. Use the power of a product property.

$$(4 \cdot 25)^{1/2} = 4^{1/2} \cdot 25^{1/2} = 2 \cdot 5 = 10$$

Checkpoint ✓ **Use Properties of Rational Exponents**

Evaluate the expression using the properties of rational exponents.

9. $\left(8^{1/3}\right)^2$ **10.** $(4 \cdot 16)^{1/2}$ **11.** $4^{1/2} \cdot 4^{3/2}$ **12.** $\left(3^{1/2}\right)^2$

13. $(27 \cdot 64)^{1/3}$ **14.** $2^{5/2} \cdot 2^{1/2}$ **15.** $\left(6^{2/3}\right)^{3/2}$ **16.** $(64 \cdot 81)^{1/2}$

EXAMPLE 4 Use Properties of Rational Exponents

Simplify the variable expression $(x \cdot y^{1/2})^2 \sqrt{x}$ using the properties of rational exponents.

Solution

❶ **Use** the power of a product property. $(x \cdot y^{1/2})^2\sqrt{x} = \left(x^2 \cdot y^{1/2 \cdot 2}\right)\sqrt{x}$

❷ **Write** $\sqrt{x}$ in rational exponent notation. $= x^2 \cdot y^1 \cdot x^{1/2}$

❸ **Use** the product of powers property. $= x^{2 + 1/2} \cdot y^1$

❹ **Add** the exponents. $= x^{5/2}y$

Checkpoint ✓ **Use Properties of Rational Exponents**

Simplify the expression.

17. $(x \cdot y^{1/2})^4 x$ **18.** $(x^{3/2} \cdot y)^2$ **19.** $\left(y^3\right)^{1/6}$

20. $\left(x^{1/3} \cdot x^{5/3}\right)^{1/2}$ **21.** $\left(x^{1/2} \cdot y^{1/3}\right)^6$ **22.** $\sqrt[3]{x}(x^3 \cdot y^2)^{1/3}$

Guided Practice

Vocabulary Check

1. Write "the cube root of 27" in both radical notation and rational exponent notation.

Skill Check

Evaluate the expression without using a calculator.

2. $\sqrt[3]{64}$ **3.** $49^{1/2}$ **4.** $\left(\sqrt[3]{8}\right)^5$ **5.** $25^{3/2}$

6. $121^{1/2}$ **7.** $9^{3/2}$ **8.** $\sqrt[3]{343}$ **9.** $\left(\sqrt{81}\right)^3$

Practice and Applications

RATIONAL EXPONENTS Rewrite the expression using rational exponent notation.

10. $\sqrt{14}$ **11.** $\sqrt[3]{11}$ **12.** $\left(\sqrt[3]{5}\right)^2$ **13.** $\left(\sqrt{16}\right)^5$

RADICALS Rewrite the expression using radical notation.

14. $6^{1/3}$ **15.** $7^{1/2}$ **16.** $10^{3/2}$ **17.** $8^{7/3}$

EVALUATING EXPRESSIONS Evaluate the expression without using a calculator.

18. $\sqrt[3]{8}$ **19.** $\sqrt{10,000}$ **20.** $216^{1/3}$ **21.** $4^{1/2}$

22. $1^{1/3}$ **23.** $256^{1/2}$ **24.** $\left(\sqrt{16}\right)^4$ **25.** $\left(\sqrt[3]{27}\right)^4$

26. $4^{3/2}$ **27.** $125^{2/3}$ **28.** $\left(\sqrt{100}\right)^3$ **29.** $\left(\sqrt[3]{64}\right)^4$

PROPERTIES OF RATIONAL EXPONENTS Evaluate the expression.

30. $3^{5/3} \cdot 3^{1/3}$ **31.** $4^{3/2} \cdot 4^{1/2}$ **32.** $\left(8^{2/3}\right)^{1/2}$

33. $\left(6^{1/3}\right)^6$ **34.** $(8 \cdot 27)^{1/3}$ **35.** $(16 \cdot 25)^{1/2}$

36. $\left(2^3 \cdot 3^3\right)^{1/3}$ **37.** $\left(2^{2/3} \cdot 2^{1/3}\right)^6$ **38.** $\left(4^2 \cdot 5^2\right)^{1/2}$

PROPERTIES OF RATIONAL EXPONENTS Simplify the variable expression.

39. $x^{1/3} \cdot x^{1/2}$ **40.** $x \cdot \sqrt[3]{y^6} + y^2 \cdot \sqrt[3]{x^3}$ **41.** $\left(y^{1/6}\right)^3 \cdot \sqrt{x}$

42. $\left(36x^3\right)^{1/2}$ **43.** $\left(y \cdot y^{1/3}\right)^{3/2}$ **44.** $\left(x^{1/3} \cdot y^{1/2}\right)^6 \cdot \sqrt{x}$

45. LOGICAL REASONING Complete the statement with *always*, *sometimes*, or *never*.

If a and b are whole numbers, then $\sqrt{a^2 + b^2}$ is __?__ equal to $a + b$.

Student Help

▶**HOMEWORK HELP**
 Example 1: Exs. 10–29
 Example 2: Exs. 18–29
 Example 3: Exs. 30–38
 Example 4: Exs. 39–44

EXAMPLE Volume of a Sphere

The formula for the volume of a sphere is $V = \frac{4}{3}\pi r^3$, where r is the radius of the sphere. Find the radius of a sphere that has a volume of 33.5 cubic centimeters.

Solution

To find the radius of the sphere, first solve the equation $V = \frac{4}{3}\pi r^3$ for r.

❶ **Write** the formula for the volume of a sphere. $V = \frac{4}{3}\pi r^3$

❷ **Multiply** each side by $\frac{3}{4}$ and divide each side by π. $\dfrac{\frac{3}{4}V}{\pi} = r^3$

❸ **Take** the cube root of each side. $r = \sqrt[3]{\dfrac{\frac{3}{4}V}{\pi}}$

❹ **Substitute** 33.5 for V. $r = \sqrt[3]{\dfrac{\frac{3}{4}(33.5)}{\pi}}$

❺ **Evaluate** the radicand. $r \approx \sqrt[3]{8.0}$

❻ **Solve** for r. $r \approx 2$

ANSWER ▶ The radius of the sphere is about 2 centimeters.

46. SHOT PUT The shot (a metal sphere) used in the women's shot put has a volume of about 524 cubic centimeters. Find the radius of the shot.

Standardized Test Practice

47. MULTIPLE CHOICE Evaluate the expression $100^{3/2}$.

Ⓐ 10   Ⓑ 100   Ⓒ 1000   Ⓓ 10,000

Mixed Review

QUADRATIC EQUATIONS Solve the equation. Write the solutions as integers if possible. Otherwise, write them as radical expressions. *(Lesson 9.2)*

48. $16 + x^2 = 64$ **49.** $x^2 + 25 = 81$ **50.** $x^2 + 81 = 144$

51. $4x^2 - 144 = 0$ **52.** $x^2 - 30 = -3$ **53.** $x^2 = \frac{20}{25}$

SOLVING EQUATIONS Solve the equation. *(Lesson 10.4)*

54. $(x + 4)^2 = 0$ **55.** $(x + 4)(x - 8) = 0$ **56.** $x(x - 14)^2 = 0$

Maintaining Skills

FACTORS Determine whether the number is prime or composite. If it is composite, give its prime factorization. *(Skills Review p. 761)*

57. 13   **58.** 28   **59.** 75   **60.** 99

61. 18   **62.** 33   **63.** 69   **64.** 80

Completing the Square

GOAL
Use algebra tiles to complete the square.

MATERIALS
- pencil
- algebra tiles

Student Help

▶**LOOK BACK**
For help with algebra tiles, see p. 567.

Question How can you use algebra tiles to complete the square?

Explore

1 You can use algebra tiles to model the expression $x^2 + 6x$.

> You will need one x^2-tile and six x-tiles.

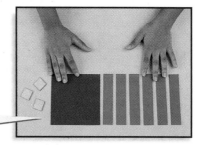

2 Arrange the x^2-tile and the x-tiles to form part of a square. Your arrangement will be incomplete in one corner.

> You want the length and width of your "square" to be equal.

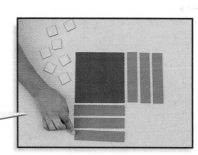

3 To complete the square, you need to add nine 1-tiles.

> By adding nine 1-tiles, you can see that $x^2 + 6x + 9 = (x + 3)^2$.

Think About It

1. Copy and complete the table by following the steps above.

Expression	Number of tiles to complete the square	Number of tiles as a perfect square
$x^2 + 6x$	9	3^2
$x^2 + 4x$	?	?
$x^2 + 2x$	?	?

2. How is the number in the third column related to the coefficient of x?

3. Use the pattern you found in Exercise 2 to predict how many tiles you would need to add to complete the square for the expression $x^2 + 8x$.

12.5 Completing the Square

Goal

Solve a quadratic equation by completing the square.

Key Words

• completing the square
• quadratic formula
• perfect square trinomial

How far does a penguin leap?

Penguins leap out of the water every few feet when swimming. The distance a penguin leaps can be modeled by a quadratic equation, as you will see in Example 4.

In Developing Concepts 12.5, page 715, you **completed the square** for expressions of the form $x^2 + bx$ when $b = 2, 4, 6,$ and 8. In each case, $x^2 + bx + \left(\dfrac{b}{2} \cdot \dfrac{b}{2}\right)$ was modeled by a square with sides of length $x + \dfrac{b}{2}$.

By using FOIL to expand $\left(x + \dfrac{b}{2}\right)\left(x + \dfrac{b}{2}\right)$, you can show that this pattern holds for any real number b.

COMPLETING THE SQUARE

To complete the square of the expression $x^2 + bx$, add the square of half the coefficient of x, that is, add $\left(\dfrac{b}{2}\right)^2$.

$$x^2 + bx + \left(\dfrac{b}{2}\right)^2 = \left(x + \dfrac{b}{2}\right)^2$$

EXAMPLE 1 Complete the Square

What term should you add to $x^2 - 8x$ to create a perfect square trinomial?

The coefficient of x is -8, so you should add $\left(\dfrac{-8}{2}\right)^2$, or 16, to the expression.

$$x^2 - 8x + \left(\dfrac{-8}{2}\right)^2 = x^2 - 8x + 16$$
$$= (x - 4)^2$$

Checkpoint ✓ **Complete the Square**

Find the term that should be added to the expression to create a perfect square trinomial.

1. $x^2 + 2x$ **2.** $x^2 - 4x$ **3.** $x^2 + 6x$ **4.** $x^2 - 10x$

EXAMPLE 2 Solve a Quadratic Equation

Solve $x^2 + 10x = 24$ by completing the square.

Solution

$x^2 + 10x = 24$	Write original equation.
$x^2 + 10x + 5^2 = 24 + 5^2$	Add $\left(\dfrac{10}{2}\right)^2$, or 5^2, to each side.
$(x + 5)^2 = 49$	Write left side as perfect square.
$x + 5 = \pm 7$	Find square root of each side.
$x = -5 \pm 7$	Subtract 5 from each side.
$x = 2 \quad or \quad x = -12$	Simplify.

ANSWER ▶ The solutions are 2 and -12. Check these in the original equation to confirm that both are solutions.

Checkpoint ✓ Solve a Quadratic Equation

Solve the equation by completing the square.

5. $x^2 - 2x - 3 = 0$ **6.** $x^2 - 12x + 4 = 0$ **7.** $x^2 + 16x + 4 = 0$

EXAMPLE 3 Develop the Quadratic Formula

The quadratic formula can be established by completing the square for the general quadratic equation $ax^2 + bx + c = 0$, where $a \neq 0$.

❶ Write the original equation.　　　　$ax^2 + bx + c = 0$

❷ Subtract c from each side.　　　　$ax^2 + bx = -c$

❸ Divide each side by a.　　　　$x^2 + \dfrac{b}{a}x = -\dfrac{c}{a}$

❹ Add $\left(\dfrac{b}{2a}\right)^2 = \dfrac{b^2}{4a^2}$ to each side.　　$x^2 + \dfrac{b}{a}x + \dfrac{b^2}{4a^2} = \dfrac{b^2}{4a^2} - \dfrac{c}{a}$

❺ Write the left side of the equation as a perfect square.　　$\left(x + \dfrac{b}{2a}\right)^2 = \dfrac{b^2 - 4ac}{4a^2}$

❻ Find the square root of each side.　　$x + \dfrac{b}{2a} = \pm\sqrt{\dfrac{b^2 - 4ac}{4a^2}}$

❼ Subtract $\dfrac{b}{2a}$ from each side.　　$x = -\dfrac{b}{2a} \pm \dfrac{\sqrt{b^2 - 4ac}}{2a}$

❽ Write the right side of the equation as a single fraction.　　$x = \dfrac{-b \pm \sqrt{b^2 - 4ac}}{2a}$

This result is the quadratic formula.

EXAMPLE 4 Choose a Solution Method

PENGUINS The path followed by a penguin leaping out of the water is given by $h = -0.05x^2 + 1.178x$, where h is the vertical height (in feet) of the penguin above the water and x is the horizontal distance (in feet) traveled over the water. Find the horizontal distance traveled by this penguin when it reaches a vertical height of 6 feet.

Solution

To find the horizontal distance when $h = 6$, solve the quadratic equation $6 = -0.05x^2 + 1.178x$. This equation cannot be factored easily and cannot be solved easily by completing the square. The quadratic formula is a good choice.

$$x = \frac{-b \pm \sqrt{b^2 - 4ac}}{2a}$$ 　　Write quadratic formula.

$$x = \frac{-1.178 \pm \sqrt{1.178^2 - 4(-0.05)(-6)}}{2(-0.05)}$$ 　　Substitute values for a, b, and c.

$$x \approx 7.4 \quad or \quad x \approx 16.1$$ 　　Use a calculator.

ANSWER ▶ The penguin reaches a vertical height of 6 feet at horizontal distances of about 7.4 feet and about 16.1 feet. Check these solutions in the original equation.

Checkpoint ✓ *Choose a Solution Method*

Choose a method and solve the quadratic equation. Explain your choice.

8. $x^2 - 3 = 0$ 　　　　**9.** $2x^2 = 8$ 　　　　**10.** $x^2 + 3x + 4 = 6$

You have learned the following five methods for solving quadratic equations.

SUMMARY

Methods for Solving Quadratic Equations

Method	Comments
FINDING SQUARE ROOTS (Lesson 9.2)	Efficient way to solve $ax^2 + c = 0$.
GRAPHING (Lesson 9.5)	Can be used for *any* quadratic equation. Enables you to approximate solutions.
USING THE QUADRATIC FORMULA (Lesson 9.6)	Can be used for *any* quadratic equation.
FACTORING (Lesson 10.5–10.8)	Efficient way to solve a quadratic equation if the quadratic expression can be factored easily.
COMPLETING THE SQUARE (Lesson 12.5)	Can be used for *any* quadratic equation, but is best suited for quadratic equations where $a = 1$ and b is an even number.

Guided Practice

Vocabulary Check

1. Explain how to complete the square of the expression $x^2 + bx$.

2. LOGICAL REASONING Determine whether the statement is *true* or *false*. Explain your reasoning.

To solve $x^2 + 6x = 12$ by completing the square, add 6 to both sides.

Skill Check

Find the term that should be added to the expression to create a perfect square trinomial.

3. $x^2 + 20x$ **4.** $x^2 + 30x$ **5.** $x^2 - 10x$

6. $x^2 - 14x$ **7.** $x^2 - 22x$ **8.** $x^2 + 24x$

9. Solve $x^2 - 3x = 8$ by completing the square. Solve the equation by using the quadratic formula. Which method did you find easier?

Solve the quadratic equation by completing the square.

10. $x^2 - 2x - 18 = 0$ **11.** $x^2 + 10x - 10 = 0$

12. $x^2 + 8x = -3$ **13.** $x^2 + 14x = -13$

Choose a method and solve the quadratic equation. Explain your choice.

14. $x^2 - x - 2 = 0$ **15.** $3x^2 + 17x + 10 = 0$ **16.** $x^2 - 9 = 0$

17. $-3x^2 + 5x + 5 = 0$ **18.** $x^2 + 2x - 14 = 0$ **19.** $3x^2 - 2 = 0$

Practice and Applications

PERFECT SQUARES Find the term that should be added to the expression to create a perfect square trinomial.

20. $x^2 - 12x$ **21.** $x^2 + 8x$ **22.** $x^2 + 10x$

23. $x^2 + 22x$ **24.** $x^2 + 14x$ **25.** $x^2 - 40x$

26. $x^2 + 4x$ **27.** $x^2 - 6x$ **28.** $x^2 + 16x$

COMPLETING THE SQUARE Solve by completing the square.

29. $x^2 - 8x + 12 = 0$ **30.** $x^2 - 2x = 3$ **31.** $x^2 + 6x - 16 = 0$

32. $x^2 + 4x = 12$ **33.** $x^2 + 10x = 12$ **34.** $x^2 + 8x = 15$

35. $x^2 + 10x = 39$ **36.** $x^2 + 16x = 17$ **37.** $x^2 - 24x = -44$

38. $x^2 - 6x - 11 = 0$ **39.** $x^2 - 2x = 5$ **40.** $x^2 + 30x - 7 = 0$

41. $x^2 - 4x - 1 = 0$ **42.** $x^2 + 20x + 3 = 0$ **43.** $x^2 + 14x - 2 = 0$

Student Help

▶**HOMEWORK HELP**
  Example 1: Exs. 20–28
  Example 2: Exs. 29–55
  Example 3: Exs. 29–56
  Example 4: Exs. 57–76

SOLVING EQUATIONS Solve the quadratic equation.

44. $x^2 + 4x + 5 = 0$ **45.** $x^2 + 10x - 3 = 0$ **46.** $x^2 + 16x + 9 = 0$

47. $x^2 + 22x + 1 = 0$ **48.** $x^2 + 2x - 11 = 0$ **49.** $x^2 + 8x - 6 = 0$

50. $x^2 + 14x - 7 = 0$ **51.** $x^2 + 20x + 2 = 0$ **52.** $x^2 - 6x - 10 = 0$

53. $x^2 - 12x - 3 = 0$ **54.** $x^2 - 18x + 5 = 0$ **55.** $x^2 - 2x - 4 = 0$

56. LOGICAL REASONING Explain why the quadratic formula gives real solutions only if $a \neq 0$ and $b^2 - 4ac \geq 0$.

Geometry Link In Exercises 57–59, make a sketch and write a quadratic equation to model the situation. Then solve the equation.

57. In art class you are designing the floor plan of a house. The kitchen is supposed to have 150 square feet of space. What should the dimensions of the kitchen floor be if you want it to be square?

58. A rectangle is $2x$ feet long and $x + 5$ feet wide. The area is 600 square feet. What are the dimensions of the rectangle?

59. The base of a triangle is x feet and the height is $(4 + 2x)$ feet. The area of the triangle is 60 square feet. What are the dimensions of the triangle?

CHOOSING A METHOD Choose a method and solve the quadratic equation. Explain your choice.

60. $x^2 - x - 12 = 0$ **61.** $x^2 - 9 = 0$ **62.** $x^2 - 4x = 8$

63. $x^2 + 5x - 14 = 0$ **64.** $x^2 - 2x = 2$ **65.** $3x^2 + 5x - 12 = 0$

66. $x^2 + 5x - 6 = 0$ **67.** $x^2 - 6x + 7 = 0$ **68.** $x^2 + 2 = 6$

69. $2x^2 + 7x + 3 = 0$ **70.** $2x^2 - 200 = 0$ **71.** $x^2 - 24x = 6$

72. $3x^2 - 48 = 0$ **73.** $x^2 + 3x + 4 = 1$ **74.** $3x^2 + 7x + 2 = 0$

75. DIVING The path of a diver diving from a 10-foot high diving board is

$$h = -0.44x^2 + 2.61x + 10$$

where h is the height (in feet) of the diver above water and x is the horizontal distance from the end of the board. How far from the end of the board will the diver enter the water?

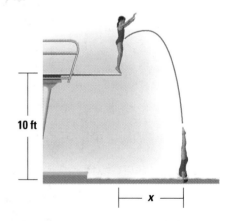

10 ft

x

76. VERTICAL MOTION Suppose you throw a ball upward from a height of 5 feet and with an initial velocity of 15 feet per second. The vertical motion model $h = -16t^2 + 15t + 5$ gives the height h (in feet) of the ball, where t is the number of seconds that the ball is in the air. Find the time that it takes for the ball to reach the ground ($h = 0$) after it has been thrown.

77. MULTIPLE CHOICE Which of the following is a solution of the equation
$2x^2 + 8x - 25 = 5$?

(A) $-\sqrt{19} - 2$ (B) $\sqrt{17} - 2$ (C) $\sqrt{21} - 2$ (D) $\sqrt{17} + 1$

78. MULTIPLE CHOICE What term should you add to $x^2 - \frac{1}{2}x$ to create a
perfect square trinomial?

(F) $\frac{1}{2}$ (G) $\frac{1}{4}$ (H) $\frac{1}{16}$ (J) $\frac{1}{32}$

79. MULTIPLE CHOICE Solve $x^2 + 8x - 2 = 0$.

(A) $-4 \pm 3\sqrt{2}$ (B) $-4 \pm 2\sqrt{2}$ (C) $4 \pm 3\sqrt{2}$ (D) $4 \pm \sqrt{16}$

Mixed Review

SOLVING LINEAR SYSTEMS Solve the linear system. *(Lessons 7.2, 7.3)*

80. $\begin{aligned} y &= 4x \\ x + y &= 10 \end{aligned}$
81. $\begin{aligned} 3x + y &= 12 \\ 9x - y &= 36 \end{aligned}$
82. $\begin{aligned} 2x - y &= 8 \\ 2x + 2y &= 2 \end{aligned}$

QUADRATIC EQUATIONS Solve the equation. Write the solutions as
integers if possible. Otherwise, write them as radical expressions.
(Lesson 9.2)

83. $3x^2 - 147 = 0$ **84.** $x^2 - 5 = 20$ **85.** $x^2 + 2 = 83$

86. $9 + x^2 = 49$ **87.** $x^2 - 16 = 144$ **88.** $x^2 + 64 = 169$

SOLVING GRAPHICALLY Use a graph to estimate the solutions of the
equation. Check your solutions algebraically. *(Lesson 9.5)*

89. $x^2 + x + 2 = 0$ **90.** $-3x^2 - x - 4 = 0$ **91.** $2x^2 - 3x + 4 = 0$

92. $x^2 - x - 12 = 0$ **93.** $x^2 - 2x - 3 = 0$ **94.** $2x^2 + 10x + 12 = 0$

ZERO-PRODUCT PROPERTY Use the zero-product property to solve the
equation. *(Lesson 10.4)*

95. $(x + 4)(x - 8) = 0$ **96.** $(x - 3)(x - 2) = 0$ **97.** $(x + 5)(x + 6) = 0$

98. $(x + 4)^2 = 0$ **99.** $(x - 3)^2 = 0$ **100.** $6(x - 14)^2 = 0$

FACTORING TRINOMIALS Factor the trinomial. *(Lessons 10.5, 10.6)*

101. $x^2 + x - 20$ **102.** $x^2 - 10x + 24$ **103.** $x^2 + 4x + 4$

104. $3x^2 - 15x + 18$ **105.** $2x^2 - x - 3$ **106.** $14x^2 - 19x - 3$

Maintaining Skills

PERCENTS AND FRACTIONS Subtract. Write the answer as a fraction in
lowest terms. *(Skills Review p. 768)*

107. $\frac{3}{4} - 15\%$ **108.** $\frac{7}{8} - 80\%$ **109.** $\frac{1}{2} - 39\%$

110. $\frac{4}{5} - 45\%$ **111.** $26\% - \frac{1}{4}$ **112.** $75\% - \frac{3}{4}$

113. $8\% - \frac{1}{20}$ **114.** $100\% - \frac{2}{5}$ **115.** $50\% - \frac{1}{8}$

DEVELOPING CONCEPTS
The Pythagorean Theorem

For use with Lesson 12.6

GOAL

Work in groups to investigate the Pythagorean theorem and its converse.

MATERIALS

• graph paper
• scissors
• glue or tape

Question If you are able to classify a triangle as acute, right, or obtuse, what conclusions can you draw about the lengths of its sides?

Explore

1 Cut graph paper into squares with the following side lengths: 3, 4, 5, 6, 7, 8, 10, 12, and 13.

2 Create a triangle with side lengths $a = 3$, $b = 4$, and $c = 6$, as shown. Label the vertices A, B, and C, placing C opposite the longest side.

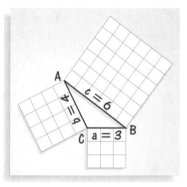

Student Help

▶ **VOCABULARY TIP**
An obtuse triangle has one angle measuring between 90° and 180°. An acute triangle has three angles that each measure between 0° and 90°.

---

3 Using a protractor, classify the triangle as acute, right, or obtuse.

4 Repeat Steps 2 and 3 using the remaining squares. Create one triangle with side lengths $a = 5$, $b = 12$, $c = 13$ and one triangle with side lengths $a = 7$, $b = 8$, $c = 10$.

5 Compare the values of $a^2 + b^2$ with the values of c^2 for each of the three triangles. Then copy and complete the table below.

Type of triangle	Side lengths	$a^2 + b^2$	<, >, or =	c^2
obtuse	3, 4, 6	25	?	36
?	5, 12, 13	?	?	?
?	7, 8, 10	?	?	?

Think About It

In Exercises 1 and 2, *a*, *b*, and *c* are the lengths of the sides of a triangle, and *c* is the length of the longest side.

1. Repeat Steps 1–4 above with a number of different triangles. Be sure to include acute triangles, right triangles, and obtuse triangles.

2. Complete the following statements using <, >, or = as conjectures based on your observations.

In an obtuse triangle, $a^2 + b^2$ **?** c^2.

In a right triangle, $a^2 + b^2$ **?** c^2. (Pythagorean theorem)

In an acute triangle, $a^2 + b^2$ **?** c^2.

Question Does the converse of the Pythagorean theorem hold true?

Explore

1 Select three of the graph paper squares and form a triangle. Label the vertices A, B, and C, placing C opposite the longest side. Two triangles are shown.

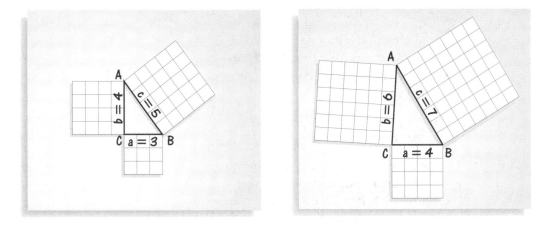

2 Compare the values of $a^2 + b^2$ with the values of c^2 for each triangle. Based on your answers in Exercise 2 on page 722, classify the triangle as acute, right, or obtuse. Then copy and complete the table below.

Side lengths	$a^2 + b^2$	<, >, or =	c^2	Type of triangle
3, 4, 5	25	=	25	?
4, 6, 7	130	>	121	?

Think About It

Let a, b, and c be the side lengths of a triangle with c the longest side.

1. Repeat Steps 1 and 2 above with a number of different triangles. Choose a variety of lengths so $a^2 + b^2 = c^2$ is sometimes true, and sometimes not.

2. Complete the following conjectures based on your observations.

If the sides of a triangle satisfy $a^2 + b^2 = c^2$, then the triangle is a __?__ triangle. (Converse of the Pythagorean theorem)

If the sides of a triangle satisfy $a^2 + b^2 < c^2$, then the triangle is a __?__ triangle.

If the sides of a triangle satisfy $a^2 + b^2 > c^2$, then the triangle is a __?__ triangle.

12.6 The Pythagorean Theorem and Its Converse

Goal

Use the Pythagorean theorem and its converse

Key Words

- theorem
- Pythagorean theorem
- hypotenuse
- legs of a right triangle
- converse

What is the distance from home plate to second base?

You will use the *Pythagorean theorem* in Exercise 31 to find the distance from home plate to second base of a standard baseball diamond.

A **theorem** is a statement that can be proven to be true. The **Pythagorean theorem** states a relationship among the sides of a right triangle. The **hypotenuse** is the side opposite the right angle. The other two sides are the **legs.**

THE PYTHAGOREAN THEOREM

If a triangle is a right triangle, then the sum of the squares of the lengths of the legs a and b equals the square of the length of the hypotenuse c.

$$a^2 + b^2 = c^2$$

In Exercise 23 in Lesson 12.9, you will outline a proof of the Pythagorean theorem.

In Exercise 23 in Lesson 12.9, you will outline a proof of the Pythagorean theorem.

Student Help

▶ **STUDY TIP**
When you use the Pythagorean theorem to find the length of a side of a right triangle, you need only the positive square root because the length of a side cannot be negative.

EXAMPLE 1 Use the Pythagorean Theorem

a. Given $a = 6$ and $b = 8$, find c. Use the Pythagorean theorem: $a^2 + b^2 = c^2$.

$$6^2 + 8^2 = c^2$$
$$100 = c^2$$
$$\sqrt{100} = \sqrt{c^2}$$
$$10 = c$$

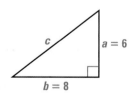

b. Given $a = 5$ and $c = 6$, find b. Use the Pythagorean theorem: $a^2 + b^2 = c^2$.

$$5^2 + b^2 = 6^2$$
$$b^2 = 6^2 - 5^2$$
$$b^2 = 11$$
$$b = \sqrt{11} \approx 3.32$$

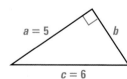

EXAMPLE 2 **Use the Pythagorean Theorem**

A right triangle has one leg that is 3 inches longer than the other leg. The hypotenuse is 15 inches. Find the unknown lengths.

Solution

Sketch a right triangle and label the sides. Let x be the length of the shorter leg. Use the Pythagorean theorem to solve for x.

$a^2 + b^2 = c^2$	Write Pythagorean theorem.
$x^2 + (x + 3)^2 = 15^2$	Substitute for a, b, and c.
$x^2 + x^2 + 6x + 9 = 225$	Simplify.
$2x^2 + 6x - 216 = 0$	Write in standard form.
$2(x - 9)(x + 12) = 0$	Factor.
$x = 9 \quad or \quad x = -12$	Zero-product property

ANSWER ▶ Length is positive, so the solution $x = -12$ is extraneous. The sides have lengths 9 inches and $9 + 3 = 12$ inches.

EXAMPLE 3 **Use the Pythagorean Theorem**

A board game is a square 2 feet by 2 feet. What is the length of the diagonal from one corner of the board game to the opposite corner?

Solution

The diagonal is the hypotenuse c of a right triangle. Each leg is 2 feet in length.

$c^2 = a^2 + b^2$	Write Pythagorean theorem.
$c^2 = 2^2 + 2^2$	Substitute 2 for a and 2 for b.
$c^2 = 8$	Simplify right side of the equation.
$c = \sqrt{8} \approx 2.8$	Find square root of each side.

ANSWER ▶ The length from one corner of the board game to the opposite corner is about 2.8 feet.

Checkpoint ✓ **Use the Pythagorean Theorem**

Find the hypotenuse of the right triangle with the given legs.

1. $a = 12$, $b = 5$ **2.** $a = 3$, $b = 4$ **3.** $a = 12$, $b = 16$

Solve for x to find the missing lengths of the right triangle.

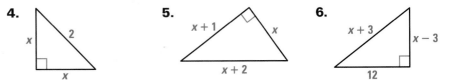

4.   **5.**   **6.**

Student Help

▶**LOOK BACK**
For help with if-then statements, see p. 120.

LOGICAL REASONING In mathematics an *if-then statement* is a statement of the form "If p, then q," where p is the *hypothesis* and q is the *conclusion*. The **converse** of the statement "If p, then q" is the related statement "If q, then p," in which the hypothesis and conclusion are interchanged.

In many cases, a theorem is true, but its converse is false. For example, the statement "If $a = b$, then $a^2 = b^2$" is true, while the converse "If $a^2 = b^2$, then $a = b$" is false. In the case of the Pythagorean theorem, however, both the theorem and its converse are true.

CONVERSE OF THE PYTHAGOREAN THEOREM

If a triangle has side lengths a, b, and c such that $a^2 + b^2 = c^2$, then the triangle is a right triangle.

Student Help

▶**STUDY TIP**
In a right triangle the hypotenuse is always the longest side.

EXAMPLE 4 Determine Right Triangles

Determine whether the given lengths are sides of a right triangle: 15, 20, 25.

Solution Use the converse of the Pythagorean theorem. The lengths are sides of a right triangle because

$$15^2 + 20^2 = 225 + 400 = 625 = 25^2.$$

EXAMPLE 5 Use the Pythagorean Converse

You can take a rope and tie 12 equally spaced knots in it. You can then use the rope to check that a corner is a right angle. Why does this method work?

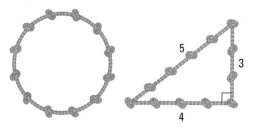

Solution

You can use the rope to form a triangle with longest side of length 5 and other sides of lengths 3 and 4. Check that

$$3^2 + 4^2 = 9 + 16 = 25 = 5^2.$$

Therefore, by the converse of the Pythagorean theorem, the triangle is a right triangle.

ANSWER ▶ Because you can use the knots to form the sides of a right triangle, one angle of the triangle must measure 90°. This is why you can check with a rope that a corner is a right angle.

Checkpoint ✓ **Use the Pythagorean Converse**

Determine whether the given lengths are sides of a right triangle.

7. 5, 11, 12   **8.** 5, 12, 13   **9.** 11.9, 12, 16.9

Guided Practice

Vocabulary Check

1. **Complete:** Sides of a right triangle that are not the hypotenuse are the __?__.

2. State the hypothesis and the conclusion of the statement "If x is an even number, then x^2 is an even number."

Skill Check

Find the missing length of the right triangle if a and b are the lengths of the legs and c is the length of the hypotenuse.

3. $a = 7, b = 24$ **4.** $a = 5, c = 13$ **5.** $b = 15, c = 17$

6. $a = 9, c = 41$ **7.** $b = 11, c = 61$ **8.** $a = 12, b = 35$

Find each unknown length of the right triangle.

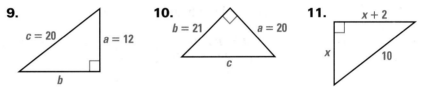

9. $c = 20$, $a = 12$, b

10. $b = 21$, $a = 20$, c

11. $x + 2$, x, 10

12. Explain how you can use the converse of the Pythagorean theorem to tell whether three given lengths can be sides of a right triangle.

Practice and Applications

USING THE PYTHAGOREAN THEOREM Find the missing length of the right triangle if a and b are the lengths of the legs and c is the length of the hypotenuse.

13. $a = 3, c = 4$ **14.** $a = 10, b = 24$ **15.** $b = 3, c = 7$

16. $b = 9, c = 16$ **17.** $a = 5, c = 10$ **18.** $a = 14, c = 21$

19. $a = 2, b = 8$ **20.** $a = 11, b = 15$ **21.** $b = 3, c = 10$

22. $b = 1, c = 3$ **23.** $a = 4, c = 7$ **24.** $a = 8, c = 10$

MISSING LENGTH Find the unknown lengths of the right triangle.

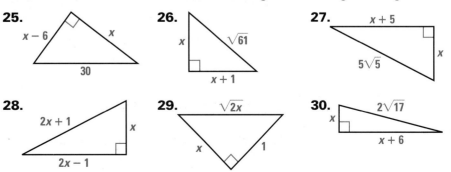

25. $x - 6$, x, 30

26. x, $\sqrt{61}$, $x + 1$

27. $x + 5$, $5\sqrt{5}$, x

28. $2x + 1$, x, $2x - 1$

29. $\sqrt{2x}$, x, 1

30. x, $2\sqrt{17}$, $x + 6$

Student Help

▶ **HOMEWORK HELP**
Example 1: Exs. 13–24
Example 2: Exs. 25–30
Example 3: Exs. 31–35
Example 4: Exs. 36–41
Example 5: Exs. 42–44

31. BASEBALL The length of each side of a baseball diamond is 90 feet. What is the diagonal distance c from home plate to second base?

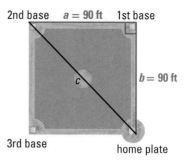

2nd base $a = 90$ ft   1st base

$b = 90$ ft

3rd base   home plate

32. DIAGONAL OF A FIELD A field hockey field is a rectangle 60 yards by 100 yards. What is the length of the diagonal from one corner of the field to the opposite corner?

Student Help

▶ HOMEWORK HELP

Extra help with problem solving in Exs. 33–34 is available at www.mcdougallittell.com

DESIGNING A STAIRCASE
You are building the staircase shown at the right.

33. Find the distance d between the edges of each step.

34. The staircase will also have a handrail that is as long as the distance between the edge of the first step and the edge of the top step. How long is the handrail?

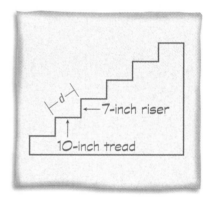

←7-inch riser

10-inch tread

35. PLANTING A NEW TREE. You have just planted a new tree. To support the tree, you attach four guy wires from the trunk of the tree to stakes in the ground. Each guy wire has a length of 7 feet.

Suppose you put the stakes in the ground 5 feet from the base of the trunk. Approximately how far up the trunk should you attach the guy wires?

guy wire 7 ft

5 ft

DETERMINING RIGHT TRIANGLES Determine whether the given lengths are sides of a right triangle. Explain your reasoning.

36. 2, 10, 11   **37.** 5, 12, 13   **38.** 12, 16, 20

39. 11, 60, 61   **40.** 7, 24, 26   **41.** 3, 9, 10

DETERMINING RIGHT TRIANGLES Determine whether the given lengths are sides of a right triangle. Explain your reasoning.

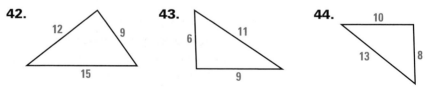

42. 12, 9, 15   **43.** 6, 11, 9   **44.** 10, 13, 8

45. CHALLENGE You have a rope with 24 equally spaced knots in it. Form a triangle with the rope and give the length of each side. How can you use this rope to check that a corner is a right angle?

46. MULTIPLE CHOICE Given the lengths of the three sides of a triangle, determine which triangle is *not* a right triangle.

(A) $a = 9, b = 40, c = 41$ (B) $a = 3, b = 4, c = 5$

(C) $a = 7, b = 24, c = 25$ (D) $a = 10, b = 49, c = 50$

PLOTTING POINTS **Plot and label the ordered pairs in a coordinate plane.** *(Lesson 4.1)*

47. $A(2, 5), B(0, -1), C(3, 1)$ **48.** $A(2, -5), B(2, 4), C(-3, 0)$

49. $A(-1, -2), B(-4, 5), C(0, 2)$ **50.** $A(1, 4), B(-2, -1), C(3, -1)$

NUMBER OF X-INTERCEPTS **Determine whether the graph of the function intersects the x-axis in** *zero, one,* **or** *two* **points.** *(Lesson 9.7)*

51. $y = x^2 + 2x + 15$ **52.** $y = x^2 + 8x + 12$ **53.** $y = x^2 + x - 10$

54. $y = x^2 + 8x + 16$ **55.** $y = x^2 + 3x + 1$ **56.** $y = x^2 - 8x - 11$

ESTIMATING AREA **Estimate the area of a rectangle whose sides are given. First round each side length to the nearest whole number. Then multiply to find the area.** *(Skills Review p. 775)*

57. 5.1 by 7.2 **58.** 10.6 by 17.3 **59.** 5.1 by 9.9

60. 100.4 by 7.0 **61.** 17.3 by 2.8 **62.** 20.5 by 1.5

Quiz 2

Evaluate the radical expression using the properties of rational exponents. *(Lesson 12.4)*

1. $2^{1/3} \cdot 2^{2/3}$ **2.** $(36 \cdot 49)^{1/2}$ **3.** $\left(3^{1/2}\right)^4$

Solve the quadratic equation by completing the square. *(Lesson 12.5)*

4. $x^2 - 6x + 7 = 0$ **5.** $x^2 + 4x - 1 = 0$ **6.** $x^2 + 2x = 2$

Determine whether the given lengths are sides of a right triangle. Explain your reasoning. *(Lesson 12.6)*

7. 6, 9, 11 **8.** 12, 35, 37 **9.** 1, 1, $\sqrt{2}$

10. DEPTH OF A SUBMARINE
The sonar of a Navy cruiser detects a submarine that is 2500 feet away. The point on the water directly above the submarine is 1500 feet away from the front of the cruiser. What is the depth of the submarine? *(Lesson 12.6)*

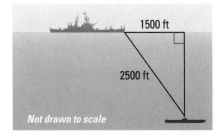

1500 ft

2500 ft

Not drawn to scale

The Distance Formula

Goal

Find the distance between two points in a coordinate plane.

Key Words

• distance formula

How far was the soccer ball kicked?

You can use the *distance formula* to find the distance between two points in a coordinate plane. In Example 3 you will find the distance that a soccer ball was kicked.

To find a general formula for the distance between two points $A(x_1, y_1)$ and $B(x_2, y_2)$, draw a right triangle as shown at the right. Using the Pythagorean theorem, you can write the equation

$$(x_2 - x_1)^2 + (y_2 - y_1)^2 = d^2.$$

Solving the equation for d leads to the following **distance formula**.

THE DISTANCE FORMULA

The distance d between the points (x_1, y_1) and (x_2, y_2) is

$$d = \sqrt{(x_2 - x_1)^2 + (y_2 - y_1)^2}.$$

EXAMPLE 1 Find the Distance Between Two Points

Use the distance formula to find the distance between $(1, 4)$ and $(-2, 3)$.

$$d = \sqrt{(x_2 - x_1)^2 + (y_2 - y_1)^2} \qquad \text{Write distance formula.}$$

$$= \sqrt{(-2 - 1)^2 + (3 - 4)^2} \qquad \text{Substitute.}$$

$$= \sqrt{(-3)^2 + (-1)^2} \qquad \text{Simplify.}$$

$$= \sqrt{9 + 1} \qquad \text{Evaluate powers.}$$

$$= \sqrt{10} \qquad \text{Add.}$$

$$\approx 3.16 \qquad \text{Use a calculator.}$$

Find the distance between the points. Round your solution to the nearest hundredth if necessary.

1. $(2, 5), (0, 4)$

2. $(-3, 2), (2, -2)$

3. $(8, 0), (0, 6)$

4. $(-4, 2), (-1, 3)$

EXAMPLE **2** **Check a Right Triangle**

Determine whether the points $(3, 2), (2, 0),$ and $(-1, 4)$ are vertices of a right triangle.

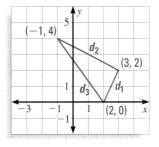

Solution

Use the distance formula to find the lengths of the three sides.

$$d_1 = \sqrt{(3 - 2)^2 + (2 - 0)^2} = \sqrt{1^2 + 2^2} = \sqrt{1 + 4} = \sqrt{5}$$

$$d_2 = \sqrt{[3 - (-1)]^2 + (2 - 4)^2} = \sqrt{4^2 + (-2)^2} = \sqrt{16 + 4} = \sqrt{20}$$

$$d_3 = \sqrt{[2 - (-1)]^2 + (0 - 4)^2} = \sqrt{3^2 + (-4)^2} = \sqrt{9 + 16} = \sqrt{25}$$

Next find the sum of the squares of the lengths of the two shorter sides.

$$d_1^2 + d_2^2 = (\sqrt{5})^2 + (\sqrt{20})^2 \qquad \text{Substitute for } d_1 \text{ and } d_2.$$
$$= 5 + 20 \qquad \text{Simplify.}$$
$$= 25 \qquad \text{Add.}$$

The sum of the squares of the lengths of the two shorter sides is 25, which is equal to the square of the length of the longest side, $(\sqrt{25})^2$.

ANSWER ▶ By the converse of the Pythagorean theorem, the given points are vertices of a right triangle.

Checkpoint ✓ *Check a Right Triangle*

Determine whether the points are the vertices of a right triangle.

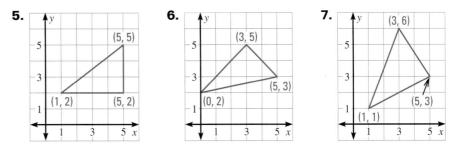

DRAW A DIAGRAM To use the distance formula to find a distance in a real-life problem, the first step is to draw a diagram with coordinate axes and assign coordinates to the points. This process is called *superimposing* a coordinate system on the diagram.

EXAMPLE ③ Apply the Distance Formula

SOCCER A player kicks a soccer ball from a position that is 10 yards from a sideline and 5 yards from a goal line. The ball lands 45 yards from the same goal line and 40 yards from the same sideline. How far was the ball kicked?

Solution

Begin by superimposing a coordinate system on the soccer field as below. Assuming the kicker is left of the goalie, the ball is kicked from the point (10, 5) and lands at the point (40, 45). Use the distance formula.

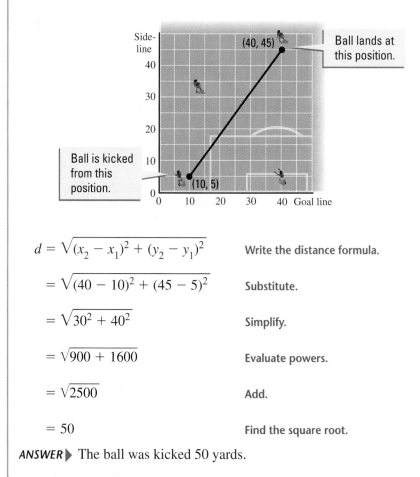

$$d = \sqrt{(x_2 - x_1)^2 + (y_2 - y_1)^2}$$ Write the distance formula.

$$= \sqrt{(40 - 10)^2 + (45 - 5)^2}$$ Substitute.

$$= \sqrt{30^2 + 40^2}$$ Simplify.

$$= \sqrt{900 + 1600}$$ Evaluate powers.

$$= \sqrt{2500}$$ Add.

$$= 50$$ Find the square root.

ANSWER ▶ The ball was kicked 50 yards.

Checkpoint ✓ *Apply the Distance Formula*

8. A player kicks a football from a position that is 15 yards from a sideline and 25 yards from a goal line. The ball lands at a position that is 30 yards from the same sideline and 65 yards from the same goal line. Find the distance that the ball was kicked.

Guided Practice

Vocabulary Check

1. The distance formula is related to which theorem?

Skill Check

Use the coordinate plane to estimate the distance between the two points. Then use the distance formula to find the distance between the points. Round your solution to the nearest hundredth.

2. $(1, 5), (-3, 1)$ **3.** $(-3, -2), (4, 1)$ **4.** $(5, -2), (-1, 1)$

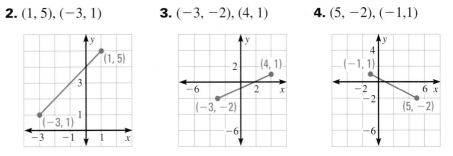

Determine whether the points are vertices of a right triangle.

5. $(0, 0), (20, 0), (20, 21)$ **6.** $(4, 0), (4, -4), (10, -4)$

7. $(-2, 0), (-1, 0), (1, 7)$ **8.** $(2, 0), (-2, 2), (-3, -5)$

9. SOCCER Suppose the soccer ball in Example 3 on page 732 lands in a position that is 25 yards from the same goal line and 25 yards from the same sideline. How far was the ball kicked?

Practice and Applications

FINDING DISTANCE **Find the distance between the two points. Round your solution to the nearest hundredth if necessary.**

10. $(2, 0), (8, -3)$ **11.** $(2, -8), (-3, 3)$ **12.** $(3, -2), (0, 3)$

13. $(5, 8), (-2, 3)$ **14.** $(-3, 1), (2, 6)$ **15.** $(-6, -2), (-3, -5)$

16. $(4, 5), (-1, 3)$ **17.** $(-6, 1), (3, 1)$ **18.** $(-2, -1), (3, -3)$

19. $(7, 12), (-7, -4)$ **20.** $(2, 1), (8, 4)$ **21.** $(2, 1), (-4, 16)$

22. $(-1, 9), (0, 7)$ **23.** $(4, 11), (-5, 2)$ **24.** $(-10, -2), (1, 7)$

Student Help

▶**HOMEWORK HELP**
Example 1: Exs. 10–24
Example 2: Exs. 25–30
Example 3: Exs. 31–37

RIGHT TRIANGLES **Graph the points. Determine whether they are vertices of a right triangle.**

25. $(4, 0), (2, 1), (-1, -5)$ **26.** $(5, 4), (2, 1), (-3, 2)$

27. $(1, -5), (2, 3), (-3, 4)$ **28.** $(-1, 1), (-3, 3), (-7, -1)$

29. $(-3, 2), (-3, 5), (0, 2)$ **30.** $(3, -1), (2, 4), (-3, 0)$

In Exercises 31 and 32, use the diagram at the right.

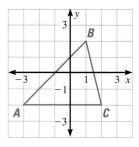

31. Copy the diagram of triangle *ABC* on graph paper. Find the length of each side of the triangle.

32. Find the perimeter of triangle *ABC* to the nearest hundredth.

Puzzler **In Exercises 33 and 34, use the following information.**

You are planning a family vacation. Each side of a square in the coordinate plane that is superimposed on the map represents 50 miles.

33. How far is it from your home to the amusement park?

34. You leave your home and go to the amusement park. After visiting the amusement park, you go to the beach. You return home. How far did you travel?

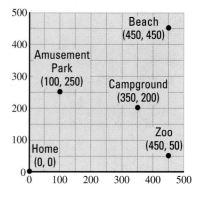

Link to
Careers

CARTOGRAPHERS prepare maps using information from surveys, aerial photographs, and satellite data.

More about cartographers at www.mcdougallittell.com

MAPS **In Exercises 35–37, use the map. Each side of a square in the coordinate plane that is superimposed on the map represents 95 miles. The points represent city locations.**

35. Use the distance formula to estimate the distance between Pierre, South Dakota, and Santa Fe, New Mexico.

36. Use the distance formula to estimate the distance between Wichita, Kansas, and Santa Fe, New Mexico.

37. Use the distance formula to estimate the distance between Pierre, South Dakota, and Wichita, Kansas.

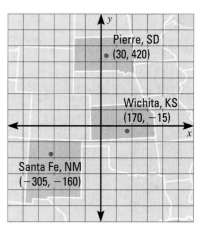

CHALLENGE **In Exercises 38 and 39, use the distance formula to find the perimeter of the geometric figure.**

38.

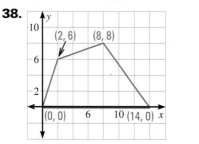

39.

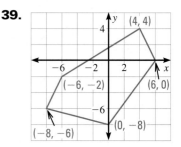

40. MULTIPLE CHOICE What is the distance between $(-6, -2)$ and $(2, 4)$?

    Ⓐ $2\sqrt{5}$ Ⓑ $2\sqrt{7}$ Ⓒ 10   Ⓓ 28

41. MULTIPLE CHOICE The vertices of a right triangle are $(0, 0)$, $(0, 6)$, and $(6, 0)$. What is the length of the hypotenuse?

    Ⓕ 6   Ⓖ $6\sqrt{2}$ Ⓗ 36   Ⓙ 72

Mixed Review

FACTORING Factor the expression. *(Lesson 10.7)*

42. $m^2 - 25$ **43.** $81x^2 - 144$ **44.** $16t^2 - 49$

45. $x^2 + 12x + 36$ **46.** $c^2 - 22c + 121$ **47.** $9s^2 + 6s + 1$

48. $4n^2 - 64$ **49.** $72 - 50p^2$ **50.** $60y^2 - 240$

FACTORING COMPLETELY Factor the expression completely. *(Lesson 10.8)*

51. $3y^3 + 15y^2 - 18y$ **52.** $2t^3 - 98t$

53. $2x^4 - 8x^2$ **54.** $c^3 + 2c^2 - 8c - 16$

SIMPLIFYING EXPRESSIONS Simplify the expression. *(Lesson 11.3)*

55. $\dfrac{4x}{28}$ **56.** $\dfrac{15x}{75}$ **57.** $\dfrac{-48x^3}{-12x^2}$

58. $\dfrac{18x^3}{56x^7}$ **59.** $\dfrac{-3x^2 + 21x}{12x^2}$ **60.** $\dfrac{35x - 7x^3}{49x}$

DIVIDING POLYNOMIALS Find the quotient. *(Lesson 11.3)*

61. Divide $(-4x^2 - 24x)$ by $-4x$.   **62.** Divide $(7p^5 + 18p^4)$ by p^4.

63. Divide $(9a^2 - 27a - 36)$ by $(a + 1)$.   **64.** Divide $(4n^2 - 41n + 45)$ by $(4n - 5)$.

ADDING RATIONAL EXPRESSIONS Simplify the expression. *(Lessons 11.5, 11.6)*

65. $\dfrac{3}{x} + \dfrac{x + 9}{x}$ **66.** $\dfrac{8}{4a + 1} + \dfrac{5}{4a + 1}$ **67.** $\dfrac{2}{2x} + \dfrac{12}{x}$

68. $\dfrac{2x}{x + 1} + \dfrac{5}{x + 3}$ **69.** $\dfrac{5}{4x} + \dfrac{7}{3x}$ **70.** $\dfrac{6x}{x + 1} + \dfrac{2x + 4}{x + 1}$

Maintaining Skills

FRACTIONS AND PERCENTS Write the fraction as a percent. *(Skills Review p. 769)*

71. $\dfrac{2}{5}$ **72.** $\dfrac{4}{5}$ **73.** $\dfrac{1}{3}$ **74.** $\dfrac{9}{10}$

75. $\dfrac{5}{8}$ **76.** $\dfrac{11}{20}$ **77.** $\dfrac{4}{100}$ **78.** $\dfrac{9}{25}$

The Midpoint Formula

Goal

Find the midpoint of a line segment in a coordinate plane.

Key Words

- midpoint
- midpoint formula

How are computer games designed?

You can use the *midpoint formula* to find the midpoint of a line segment in a coordinate plane. In Example 3 you will locate the midpoint as part of designing a computer game.

The **midpoint** of a line segment is the point on the segment that is equidistant from its endpoints.

Student Help

▶**STUDY TIP**
Midpoint can be thought of as an average.

THE MIDPOINT FORMULA

The midpoint between (x_1, y_1) and (x_2, y_2) is $\left(\dfrac{x_1 + x_2}{2}, \dfrac{y_1 + y_2}{2} \right)$.

EXAMPLE 1 Find the Midpoint

Find the midpoint of the line segment connecting the points $(-2, 3)$ and $(4, 2)$. Use a graph to explain the result.

Solution

Let $(-2, 3) = (x_1, y_1)$ and $(4, 2) = (x_2, y_2)$.

$$\left(\frac{x_1 + x_2}{2}, \frac{y_1 + y_2}{2} \right) = \left(\frac{-2 + 4}{2}, \frac{3 + 2}{2} \right) = \left(\frac{2}{2}, \frac{5}{2} \right) = \left(1, \frac{5}{2} \right)$$

ANSWER ▶ The midpoint is $\left(1, \dfrac{5}{2} \right)$.

From the graph, you can see that the point $\left(1, \dfrac{5}{2} \right)$ appears to be halfway between $(-2, 3)$ and $(4, 2)$. In Example 2 you will use the distance formula to check a midpoint.

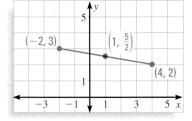

Checkpoint ✓ **Find the Midpoint**

Find the midpoint of the line segment connecting the given points.

1. $(-2, 3), (4, 1)$ **2.** $(2, 5), (2, -1)$ **3.** $(0, 0), (4, 6)$ **4.** $(1, 2), (2, -2)$

You can use the distance formula to check that the distances from the midpoint to each given point are equal.

EXAMPLE **2** **Check a Midpoint**

Use the distance formula to check the midpoint in Example 1.

Solution

The distance between $\left(1, \frac{5}{2}\right)$ and $(-2, 3)$ is

$$d_1 = \sqrt{(-2 - 1)^2 + \left(3 - \frac{5}{2}\right)^2} = \sqrt{(-3)^2 + \left(\frac{1}{2}\right)^2} = \sqrt{9 + \frac{1}{4}} = \sqrt{\frac{37}{4}} = \frac{\sqrt{37}}{2}.$$

The distance between $\left(1, \frac{5}{2}\right)$ and $(4, 2)$ is

$$d_2 = \sqrt{(4 - 1)^2 + \left(2 - \frac{5}{2}\right)^2} = \sqrt{(3)^2 + \left(-\frac{1}{2}\right)^2} = \sqrt{9 + \frac{1}{4}} = \sqrt{\frac{37}{4}} = \frac{\sqrt{37}}{2}.$$

ANSWER ▶ The distances from $\left(1, \frac{5}{2}\right)$ to the ends of the segment are equal.

Link to
Careers

SOFTWARE ENGINEERS design and develop computer programs that are used to perform desired tasks. These programs are referred to as computer software.

EXAMPLE **3** **Apply the Midpoint Formula**

COMPUTERS You are using software to design a computer game. You want to place a buried treasure chest halfway between the points corresponding to a palm tree and a boulder. Where should you place the treasure chest?

Solution

The palm tree is located at (200, 75). The boulder is at (25, 175). Use the midpoint formula to find the halfway point between the two landmarks.

$$\left(\frac{x_1 + x_2}{2}, \frac{y_1 + y_2}{2}\right) = \left(\frac{25 + 200}{2}, \frac{175 + 75}{2}\right)$$

$$= \left(\frac{225}{2}, \frac{250}{2}\right)$$

$$= (112.5, 125)$$

ANSWER ▶ You should place the treasure chest at (112.5, 125).

Checkpoint ✓ **Apply the Midpoint Formula**

5. In the computer video game in Example 3, you want to place another buried treasure halfway between the boulder and the treasure chest. What are the coordinates of the point?

12.8 Exercises

Guided Practice

Vocabulary Check

1. What is meant by the *midpoint* of a line segment?

2. Give two methods for checking the midpoint of a line segment.

Skill Check

Find the midpoint of the line segment with the given endpoints.

3. $(4, 4), (-1, 2)$ **4.** $(6, 2), (2, -3)$ **5.** $(-5, 3), (-3, -3)$

6. $(-4, 4), (2, 0)$ **7.** $(0, 0), (0, 10)$ **8.** $(2, 1), (14, 6)$

Find the midpoint of the line segment with the given endpoints. Then show that the midpoint is the same distance from each given point.

9. $(-2, 0), (6, 2)$ **10.** $(-2, 2) (2, -10)$ **11.** $(2, 6), (4, 2)$

12. $(-6, 0), (-10, -2)$ **13.** $(-3, 6), (1, 8)$ **14.** $(0, 0), (-8, 12)$

Practice and Applications

FINDING THE MIDPOINT Find the midpoint of the line segment connecting the given points.

15. $(1, 2), (5, 4)$ **16.** $(0, 0), (0, 8)$ **17.** $(-1, 2), (7, 4)$

18. $(0, -3), (-4, 2)$ **19.** $(-3, 3), (2, -2)$ **20.** $(5, -5), (-5, 1)$

21. $(-1, 1), (-4, -4)$ **22.** $(-4, 0), (-1, -5)$ **23.** $(-4, -3), (-1, -5)$

CHECKING A MIDPOINT Find the midpoint of the line segment connecting the given points. Then show that the midpoint is the same distance from each point.

24. $(7, -3), (-1, -9)$ **25.** $(1, 2), (0, 0)$ **26.** $(3, 0), (-5, 4)$

27. $(5, 1), (1, -5)$ **28.** $(2, 7), (4, 3)$ **29.** $(-3, -2), (1, 7)$

30. $(-3, -3), (6, 7)$ **31.** $(-9, 17), (5, -7)$ **32.** $(-4, -2), (10, -6)$

Geometry Link   **In Exercises 33 and 34, use the diagram below.**

33. Find the midpoint of each side of the triangle.

34. Join the midpoints to form a new triangle. Find the length of each of its sides.

Student Help

▶**HOMEWORK HELP**
Example 1: Exs. 15–23
Example 2: Exs. 24–32
Example 3: Exs. 33–37

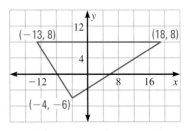

35. History Link Pony Express stations were 10 to 15 miles apart. The latitude-longitude coordinates of 2 former stations in Nevada are (40.0° N, 115.5° W) and (39.9° N, 115.2° W). These stations were about 22 miles apart. Find the coordinates of the station halfway between them.

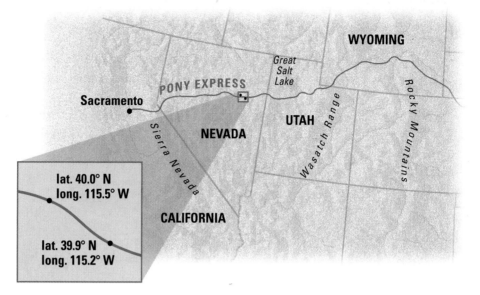

HIKING TRIP **In Exercises 36 and 37, use the following information.**
You and a friend go hiking. You hike 3 miles north and 2 miles west. Starting from the same point, your friend hikes 4 miles east and 1 mile south.

36. At the end of the hike how far apart are you and your friend? *HINT:* Draw a diagram on a grid.

37. If you and your friend want to meet for lunch, where could you meet so that both of you hike the same distance? How far do you have to hike?

Standardized Test Practice

38. MULTIPLE CHOICE What is the midpoint between $(-2, -3)$ and $(1, 7)$?

Ⓐ $\left(\frac{1}{2}, -2\right)$　　Ⓑ $\left(-\frac{1}{2}, 2\right)$　　Ⓒ $\left(\frac{1}{2}, 2\right)$　　Ⓓ $\left(-\frac{1}{2}, 5\right)$

Mixed Review

ARRANGING LIKE TERMS **Use linear combinations to solve the linear system. Then check your solution.** *(Lesson 7.3)*

39. $4x + 3y = 1$
$2x - 3y = 1$

40. $3x + 5y = 6$
$-4x + 2y = 5$

41. $2x + 3y = 1$
$5x - 4y = 14$

INTERPRETING ALGEBRAIC RESULTS **Use the substitution method or linear combinations to solve the linear system and tell how many solutions the system has.** *(Lesson 7.5)*

42. $2x + y = 3$
$4x + 2y = 8$

43. $2x + 2y = 3$
$4x + 2y = 6$

44. $2x + y = -4$
$y + 2x = 8$

Maintaining Skills

COMPARING FRACTIONS, DECIMALS, AND PERCENTS **Complete the statement using <, >, or =.** *(Skills Review pp. 768–771)*

45. 54% ? 0.54　**46.** $\frac{2}{3}$? $6\frac{2}{3}\%$　**47.** $\frac{3}{1000}$? 0.03　**48.** 0.23 ? $\frac{23}{100}$

12.9 Logical Reasoning: Proof

Goal

Use logical reasoning and proof to prove that a statement is true or false.

Key Words

- postulate
- axiom
- theorem
- indirect proof
- counterexample

How can a lawyer prove that a client is not guilty?

Often lawyers use logical reasoning to defend a client in court. In Example 4 you will use logical reasoning to prove your client's innocence.

LOGICAL REASONING Mathematics is believed to have begun with practical "rules of thumb" that were developed to deal with real-life problems. Then, about 2500 years ago, Greek geometers (specialists in geometry) developed a different approach to mathematics. Starting with a handful of properties that they believed to be true, they insisted on logical reasoning as the basis for developing more elaborate mathematical tools, or *theorems*.

AXIOMS The properties that mathematicians accept without proof are called **postulates** or **axioms**. Many of the rules discussed in Chapter 2 fall in this category. The following is a summary of the rules that underlie algebra.

THE BASIC AXIOMS OF ALGEBRA

Let a, b, and c be real numbers.

Axioms of Addition and Multiplication

CLOSURE:	$a + b$ is a real number	ab is a real number
COMMUTATIVE:	$a + b = b + a$	$ab = ba$
ASSOCIATIVE:	$(a + b) + c = a + (b + c)$	$(ab)c = a(bc)$
IDENTITY:	$a + 0 = a, 0 + a = a$	$a(1) = a, 1(a) = a$
INVERSE:	$a + (-a) = 0$	$a\left(\dfrac{1}{a}\right) = 1, a \neq 0$

Axiom Relating Addition and Multiplication

DISTRIBUTIVE:	$a(b + c) = ab + ac$	$(a + b)c = ac + bc$

Axioms of Equality

ADDITION:	If $a = b$, then $a + c = b + c$.
MULTIPLICATION:	If $a = b$, then $ac = bc$.
SUBSTITUTION:	If $a = b$, then a can be substituted for b.

DEFINITIONS In order to formulate the axioms and postulates of mathematics, one needs a vocabulary of terms such as *number*, *equal*, *addition*, *point*, and *line*. Aside from their role in formulating axioms, these terms can also be used to define other terms. For example, *whole number* and *addition* are used to define *integer* and *subtraction*. Definitions do not need to be proved.

THEOREMS Recall that a theorem is a statement that can be proven to be true. All proposed theorems have to be proved. For instance, you can use the basic axioms to prove the theorem that for all real numbers b and c, $c(-b) = -cb$. Once a theorem is proved, it can be used as a reason in proofs of other theorems.

Student Help

▶ STUDY TIP
When you are proving a theorem, every step must be justified by an axiom, a definition, given information, or a previously proved theorem.

EXAMPLE 1 Prove a Theorem

Use the subtraction property, $a - b = a + (-b)$, to prove the following theorem: $c(a - b) = ca - cb$.

Solution

$c(a - b)$	$= c[a + (-b)]$	Subtraction property
	$= ca + c(-b)$	Distributive property
	$= ca + (-cb)$	Theorem stated above
	$= ca - cb$	Subtraction property

Checkpoint ✓ *Prove a Theorem*

1. Use the associative and commutative properties to prove the following theorem.

If a, b, *and* c *are real numbers, then* (a + b) + c = (b + c) + a.

CONJECTURES A **conjecture** is a statement that is thought to be true but has not yet been proved. Conjectures are often based on observations.

EXAMPLE 2 Goldbach's Conjecture

Christian Goldbach (1690–1764) thought the following statement might be true. It is now referred to as *Goldbach's Conjecture*.

Every even integer, except 2, is equal to the sum of two prime numbers.

The following list shows that every even number between 4 and 26 is equal to the sum of two prime numbers. Does this list prove Goldbach's Conjecture?

$4 = 2 + 2$	$6 = 3 + 3$	$8 = 3 + 5$	$10 = 3 + 7$
$12 = 5 + 7$	$14 = 3 + 11$	$16 = 3 + 13$	$18 = 5 + 13$
$20 = 3 + 17$	$22 = 3 + 19$	$24 = 5 + 19$	$26 = 3 + 23$

Solution

This list of examples *does not* prove the conjecture. No number of examples can prove that the rule is true for *every* even integer greater than 2. (At the time this book was published, no one had been able to prove or disprove Goldbach's Conjecture.)

Student Help

▶ LOOK BACK
  For help with counter-
  examples, see p. 73.

COUNTEREXAMPLES Sometimes a person makes a general statement they suppose to be true. To show that a general statement is false, you need only one *counterexample*.

EXAMPLE 3 Find a Counterexample

Show that the statement below is false by finding a counterexample.

  For all numbers a *and* b, a + (−b) = (−a) + b.

Solution The statement claims that $a + (−b) = (−a) + b$ for all values of a and b. If we let $a = 1$ and $b = 2$, we find $a + (−b) = 1 + (−2) = −1$, but $(−a) + b = (−1) + 2 = 1$. Since $−1 \neq 1$, the counterexample $a = 1$ and $b = 2$ shows that the general statement proposed above is false.

INDIRECT PROOF In this lesson you have used direct proofs to prove that statements are true and counterexamples to prove that statements are false.

Another type of proof is **indirect proof**. To prove a statement indirectly, assume that the statement is false. If this assumption leads to an impossibility, then you have proved that the original statement is true. An indirect proof is also called a *proof by contradiction*.

Link to
Careers

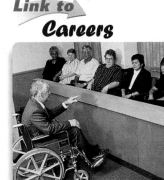

LAWYERS represent people in criminal and civil trials by presenting evidence supporting their client's case. They also give advice on legal matters.

More about lawyers is available at www.mcdougallittell.com

EXAMPLE 4 Use of Contradiction in Real Life

LAWYERS You are a lawyer defending a client accused of violating a law on the north side of town at 10:00 A.M. on March 22. You argue that if guilty, your client must have been there at that time. You have a video of your client being interviewed by a TV reporter on the south side of town at the same time.

You argue that it would be impossible for your client to be in two different places at the same time on March 22. Therefore your client cannot be guilty.

EXAMPLE 5 Use an Indirect Proof

Use an indirect proof to prove the following statement.

  If a *is a positive integer and* a^2 *is divisible by 2, then* a *is divisible by 2.*

Solution Suppose the statement is false. Then there exists a positive integer a such that a^2 is divisible by 2, but a is not divisible by 2. If so, a is odd and can be written as $a = 2n + 1$.

$a = 2n + 1$	Definition of odd integer
$a^2 = 4n^2 + 4n + 1$	Apply FOIL to $(2n + 1)(2n + 1)$.
$a^2 = 2(2n^2 + 2n) + 1$	Distributive property
a^2 is odd	Definition of odd integer

The proof contradicts the assumption, thereby showing a is divisible by 2.

►MORE EXAMPLES

More examples
are available at
www.mcdougallittell.com

EXAMPLE 6 Use an Indirect Proof

Use an indirect proof to prove that $\sqrt{2}$ is an irrational number.

Solution

If you assume that $\sqrt{2}$ is *not* an irrational number, then $\sqrt{2}$ is rational and can be written as the quotient of two integers a and b that have no common factors other than 1.

$$\sqrt{2} = \frac{a}{b} \qquad \text{Assume } \sqrt{2} \text{ is a rational number.}$$

$$2 = \frac{a^2}{b^2} \qquad \text{Square each side.}$$

$$2b^2 = a^2 \qquad \text{Multiply each side by } b^2.$$

This implies that 2 is a factor of a^2. Therefore 2 is also a factor of a. Thus a can be written as $2c$.

$$2b^2 = (2c)^2 \qquad \text{Substitute } 2c \text{ for } a.$$

$$2b^2 = 4c^2 \qquad \text{Simplify.}$$

$$b^2 = 2c^2 \qquad \text{Divide each side by 2.}$$

This implies that 2 is a factor of b^2 and also a factor of b. So 2 is a factor of both a and b. But this is impossible because a and b have no common factors other than 1. Therefore it is impossible that $\sqrt{2}$ is a rational number. So you can conclude that $\sqrt{2}$ must be an irrational number.

Checkpoint ✓ *Use of Contradiction in Real Life*

2. You are defending a client who is accused of violating a law near her home at 9:00 A.M. on June 5. Your client's boss and coworkers testify that she arrived at work at 9:15 A.M. on June 5. It takes your client 45 minutes to commute from her house to work. Construct an argument to prove that your client is *not* guilty.

12.9 Exercises

Guided Practice

Vocabulary Check

1. Explain the difference between an *axiom* and a *theorem*.

2. What is the first step in an indirect proof?

Skill Check

In Exercises 3–8, state the basic axiom of algebra that is represented.

3. $y(1) = y$

4. $2x + 3 = 3 + 2x$

5. $5(x + y) = 5x + 5y$

6. $(4x)y = 4(xy)$

7. $y + 0 = y$

8. $x + (-x) = 0$

Practice and Applications

9. STATING REASONS Copy and complete the proof of the statement:

For all real numbers a *and* b, $(a + b) - b = a$.

$$
\begin{aligned}
(a + b) - b &= (a + b) + (-b) &&\text{Definition of subtraction}\\
&= a + [b + (-b)] &&\text{Associative property of addition}\\
&= a + 0 &&\underline{\hspace{2cm}?\hspace{2cm}}\\
&= a &&\underline{\hspace{2cm}?\hspace{2cm}}
\end{aligned}
$$

PROVING THEOREMS In Exercises 10 and 11, prove the theorem. Use the basic axioms of algebra and the definition of subtraction given in Example 1.

10. If a and b are real numbers, then $a - b = -b + a$.

11. If a, b, and c are real numbers, then $(a - b)c = ac - bc$.

12. MAKING A CONJECTURE A student proposes the following conjecture:

The sum of the first n *odd integers is* n^2.

She gives four examples: $1 = 1^2$, $1 + 3 = 4 = 2^2$, $1 + 3 + 5 = 9 = 3^2$, and $1 + 3 + 5 + 7 = 16 = 4^2$. Do the examples prove her conjecture? Explain. Do you think the conjecture is true?

FINDING A COUNTEREXAMPLE In Exercises 13–16, find a counterexample to show that the statement is *not* true.

13. If a and b are real numbers, then $(a + b)^2 = a^2 + b^2$.

14. If a, b, and c are nonzero real numbers, then $(a \div b) \div c = a \div (b \div c)$. (*Note*: The counterexample shows that the associative property does not hold for division.)

15. If a and b are integers, then $a \div b$ is an integer.

16. If $a > 4$, then $\sqrt{a}$ is not rational.

17. THE FOUR-COLOR PROBLEM
A famous theorem states that any map can be colored with four different colors so that no two countries that share a border have the same color. No matter how the map shown at the right is colored with three different colors, at least two countries having a common border will have the same color. Does this map serve as a counterexample to the following statement? Explain.

Any map can be colored with three different colors so that no two countries that share a border have the same color.

Student Help

▶HOMEWORK HELP

Extra help with problem solving in Exs. 13–16 is available at www.mcdougallittell.com

Student Help

▶HOMEWORK HELP
Example 1: Exs. 9–11
Example 2: Exs. 12, 18
Example 3: Exs. 13–17
Example 4: Exs. 19–22
Example 5: Exs. 19–22

18. *Geometry Link* Explain how the diagrams below can be used to give a geometrical argument to support the conjecture in Exercise 12 on page 744.

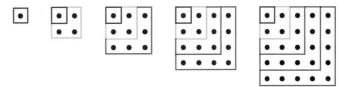

INDIRECT PROOF **In Exercises 19–21, use an indirect proof to prove that the conclusion is true**.

19. Your bus leaves a track meet at 4:30 P.M. and does not travel faster than 60 miles per hour. The meet is 45 miles from home. Your bus will not get you home in time for dinner at 5:00 P.M.

20. If $a < b$, then $a + c < b + c$.

21. If $ac > bc$ and $c > 0$, then $a > b$.

22. PROOF USING THE MIDPOINT Let D represent the midpoint between B and C, as shown at the right. Prove that for any right triangle, the midpoint of its hypotenuse is equidistant from the three vertices of the triangle. In order to prove this, you must first find the distance between B and C. Using the distance formula, you get $BC = \sqrt{x^2 + y^2}$, so BD and CD must be $\frac{1}{2}\sqrt{x^2 + y^2}$.

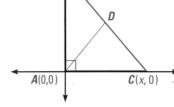

HINT: Use the distance formula to find the distance between A and D.

23. CHALLENGE Explain how the following diagrams could be used to give a geometrical proof of the Pythagorean theorem.

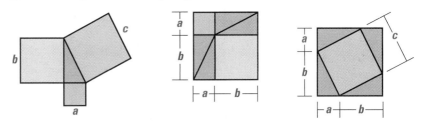

24. MULTIPLE CHOICE What is the first step to prove the following theorem: *If* a *and* b *are real numbers and* $(x + a) = b$, *then* $x = b - a$.

   (A) $x + (a - a) = b - a$ **(B)** $x = b - a$

   (C) $(x + a) - a = b - a$ **(D)** $x + 0 = b - a$

25. MULTIPLE CHOICE Which represents the distributive property?

   (F) $(4x)y = 4(xy)$ **(G)** $z(1) = z$

   (H) $4(x + 1) = 4x + 4$ **(J)** $y + 0 = y$

PERCENTS **Solve the percent problem.** (Lesson 3.9)

26. How much is 15% of $15?   **27.** 100 is 1% of what number?

28. 6 is what percent of 3?   **29.** 5 is 25% of what number?

USING THE DISCRIMINANT **Determine whether the equation has *two solutions, one solution,*** **or** ***no real solution.*** (Lesson 9.7)

30. $x^2 - 2x + 4 = 0$ **31.** $2x^2 + 4x - 2 = 0$ **32.** $8x^2 - 8x + 2 = 0$

33. $x^2 - 14x + 49 = 0$ **34.** $3x^2 - 5x + 1 = 0$ **35.** $6x^2 - x + 5 = 0$

SOLUTIONS **Determine whether the ordered pair is a solution of the inequality.** (Lesson 9.8)

36. $y > x^2 - 2x - 5$, $(1, 1)$ **37.** $y \geq 2x^2 - 8x + 8$, $(3, -2)$

38. $y \leq 2x^2 - 3x + 10$, $(-2, 20)$ **39.** $y \geq 4x^2 - 48x + 61$, $(1, 17)$

Maintaining Skills

OPERATIONS WITH FRACTIONS **Evaluate the expression. Write the answer as a fraction or as a mixed number in lowest terms.** (Skills Review pp. 764–765)

40. $\dfrac{2}{3} \cdot \dfrac{2}{5} + \dfrac{1}{5}$ **41.** $\dfrac{2}{7} \div \dfrac{1}{14} - \dfrac{5}{4}$ **42.** $\dfrac{11}{2}\left(\dfrac{1}{10} - \dfrac{1}{4}\right)$

43. $\dfrac{5}{3} - \left(\dfrac{2}{9} \cdot \dfrac{3}{4} + \dfrac{7}{12}\right)$ **44.** $\dfrac{1}{2} + \dfrac{2}{3} - \dfrac{3}{4} \cdot \dfrac{4}{5}$ **45.** $\left(\dfrac{3}{8} - \dfrac{2}{3}\right) \div \dfrac{1}{3}$

Quiz 3

Use the distance formula to determine whether the points are the vertices of a right triangle. (Lesson 12.7)

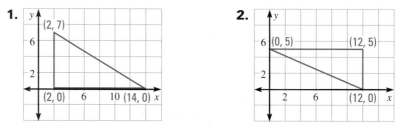

1. (2, 7), (2, 0), (14, 0)   **2.** (0, 5), (12, 5), (12, 0)

Find the distance between the two points. Round your solution to the nearest hundredth if necessary. Then find the midpoint of the line segment connecting the two given points. (Lessons 12.7, 12.8)

3. $(1, 3)$, $(7, -9)$ **4.** $(2, -5)$, $(6, -11)$ **5.** $(0, 0)$, $(8, -14)$

6. $(-8, -8)$, $(-8, 8)$ **7.** $(3, 4)$, $(-3, 4)$ **8.** $(1, 7)$, $(-4, -2)$

Find a counterexample to show that the statement is *not* true. (Lesson 12.9)

9. If a, b, and c are real numbers and $a < b$, then $ac < bc$.

10. If a and b are real numbers, then $-(a + b) = (-a) - (-b)$.

VOCABULARY

- **square root function,** *p. 692*
- **extraneous solution,** *p. 705*
- **cube root of *a*,** *p. 710*
- **rational exponent,** *p. 711*
- **completing the square,** *p. 716*
- **theorem,** *p. 724*

- **Pythagorean theorem,** *p. 724*
- **hypotenuse,** *p. 724*
- **legs of a right triangle,** *p. 724*
- **converse,** *p. 726*
- **distance formula,** *p. 730*
- **midpoint,** *p. 736*

- **midpoint formula,** *p. 736*
- **postulate,** *p. 740*
- **axiom,** *p. 740*
- **conjecture,** *p. 741*
- **indirect proof,** *p. 742*

12.1 FUNCTIONS INVOLVING SQUARE ROOTS

Examples on pp. 692–694

EXAMPLE To sketch the graph of $y = \sqrt{x} - 1$, note that the rule is defined for all nonnegative numbers. Make a table of values, plot the points, and connect them with a smooth curve. The range is all numbers greater than or equal to -1.

x	y
0	$y = \sqrt{0} - 1 = -1$
1	$y = \sqrt{1} - 1 = 0$
2	$y = \sqrt{2} - 1 \approx .41$
3	$y = \sqrt{3} - 1 \approx .73$
4	$y = \sqrt{4} - 1 = 1$

Find the domain of the function. Then sketch its graph and find the range.

1. $y = 11\sqrt{x}$

2. $y = 2\sqrt{x} - 5$

3. $y = \sqrt{x} + 3$

12.2 OPERATIONS WITH RADICAL EXPRESSIONS

Examples on pp. 698–700

EXAMPLE You can use radical operations and the distributive property to simplify radical expressions.

$$4\sqrt{20} - 3\sqrt{5} = 4\sqrt{\mathbf{4 \cdot 5}} - 3\sqrt{5} \qquad \text{Perfect square factor}$$

$$= 4\sqrt{\mathbf{2 \cdot 2}} \cdot \sqrt{5} - 3\sqrt{5} \qquad \text{Product property}$$

$$= 8\sqrt{5} - 3\sqrt{5} \qquad \text{Simplify.}$$

$$= 5\sqrt{5} \qquad \text{Subtract like radicals.}$$

Simplify the expression.

4. $6\sqrt{2} - \sqrt{2}$

5. $\sqrt{5} + \sqrt{20} - \sqrt{3}$

6. $(3 - \sqrt{10})(3 + \sqrt{10})$

7. $\sqrt{6}(2\sqrt{3} - 4\sqrt{2})$

8. $\dfrac{21}{\sqrt{3}}$

9. $\dfrac{8}{6 - \sqrt{7}}$

12.3   SOLVING RADICAL EQUATIONS

Examples on pp. 704–706

EXAMPLE   Solve $\sqrt{3x - 2} = x$.

❶ Square both sides of the equation. $(\sqrt{3x - 2})^2 = x^2$

❷ Simplify the left side of the equation. $3x - 2 = x^2$

❸ Write in standard form. $0 = x^2 - 3x + 2$

❹ Factor the quadratic equation. $0 = (x - 2)(x - 1)$

❺ Solve for x. $x = 2 \quad or \quad x = 1$

CHECK ✓ Substitute 2 and 1 in the original equation.

$$\sqrt{3(2) - 2} \stackrel{?}{=} 2 \qquad\qquad \sqrt{3(1) - 2} \stackrel{?}{=} 1$$

$$2 = 2 \checkmark \qquad\qquad\qquad 1 = 1 \checkmark$$

ANSWER ▶ The solutions are 2 *and* 1.

Solve the equation. Check for extraneous solutions.

10. $2\sqrt{x} - 4 = 0$

11. $\sqrt{-4x - 4} = x$

12. $\sqrt{x - 3} + 2 = 8$

13. $\sqrt{x - 1} = 5$

14. $8\sqrt{x} - 16 = 0$

15. $\sqrt{5x + 36} = x$

12.4   RATIONAL EXPONENTS

Examples on pp. 710–712

EXAMPLE   Simplify the expression $(x^2 \cdot x^{1/2} \cdot y)^2$.

❶ Use the product of powers property. $(x^2 \cdot x^{1/2} \cdot y)^2 = (x^{5/2} \cdot y)^2$

❷ Use the power of a product property. $= x^{(5/2 \cdot 2)} \cdot y^2$

❸ Simplify by multiplying exponents. $= x^5 y^2$

Evaluate the expression without using a calculator.

16. $27^{2/3}$

17. $(\sqrt[3]{64})^2$

18. $121^{3/2}$

19. $(\sqrt{4})^4$

Simplify the expression.

20. $5^{1/3} \cdot 5^{5/3}$

21. $(4 \cdot 121)^{1/2}$

22. $(125^{2/3})^{1/2}$

12.5 COMPLETING THE SQUARE

Examples on pp. 716–718

> **EXAMPLE** Solve $x^2 - 6x - 1 = 6$ by completing the square.
>
> $x^2 - 6x = 7$ Isolate x^2-term and x-term.
>
> $x^2 - 6x + \mathbf{9} = 7 + \mathbf{9}$ Add $\left(\dfrac{-6}{2}\right)^2 = 9$ to each side.
>
> $(x - 3)^2 = 16$ Write left side as perfect square.
>
> $x - 3 = \pm 4$ Find square root of each side.
>
> $x = 7$ *or* $x = -1$ Solve for x.

Solve the equation by completing the square.

23. $x^2 - 4x - 1 = 7$ **24.** $x^2 + 20x + 19 = 0$ **25.** $x^2 - 16x + 8 = 0$

Choose a method and solve the quadratic equation. Explain your choice.

26. $4x^2 + 8x + 8 = 0$ **27.** $x^2 - x - 3 = 0$ **28.** $3x^2 - x + 2 = 0$

12.6 PYTHAGOREAN THEOREM AND ITS CONVERSE

Examples on pp. 724–726

> **EXAMPLE** Given $a = 6$ and $c = 12$, find b.
>
> ❶ **Write** the Pythagorean theorem. $a^2 + b^2 = c^2$
>
> ❷ **Substitute** 6 for a and 12 for c. $6^2 + b^2 = 12^2$
>
> ❸ **Subtract** 6^2 from each side and simplify. $b^2 = 108$
>
> ❹ **Find** square root of each side. $b = 6\sqrt{3}$

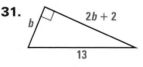

Find the missing length of the right triangle.

29.   **30.**   **31.**

Determine whether the given lengths are sides of a right triangle. Explain your reasoning.

32.   **33.**   **34.**

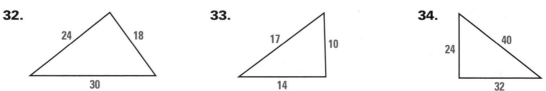

THE DISTANCE AND MIDPOINT FORMULAS

Examples on pp. 730–732, 736–737

EXAMPLE Find the distance d and the midpoint m between $(-6, -2)$ and $(4, 3)$.

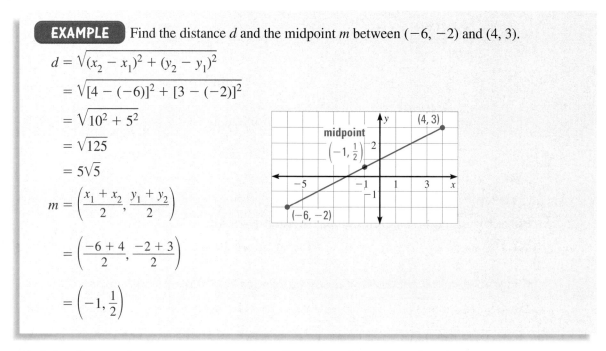

$$d = \sqrt{(x_2 - x_1)^2 + (y_2 - y_1)^2}$$

$$= \sqrt{[4 - (-6)]^2 + [3 - (-2)]^2}$$

$$= \sqrt{10^2 + 5^2}$$

$$= \sqrt{125}$$

$$= 5\sqrt{5}$$

$$m = \left(\frac{x_1 + x_2}{2}, \frac{y_1 + y_2}{2}\right)$$

$$= \left(\frac{-6 + 4}{2}, \frac{-2 + 3}{2}\right)$$

$$= \left(-1, \frac{1}{2}\right)$$

Find the distance between the two points. Round to the nearest hundredth.

35. $(8, 5)$ and $(11, -4)$ **36.** $(-3, 6)$ and $(1, 7)$ **37.** $(-2, -2)$ and $(2, 8)$

38. Use the distance formula to decide whether the points $(-4, 1)$, $(0, -2)$, and $(-4, -2)$ are the vertices of a right triangle.

Find the midpoint of the line segment connecting the given points. Use a graph to check the result.

39. $(-1, -3)$ and $(5, 1)$ **40.** $(0, 4)$ and $(-2, 4)$ **41.** $(9, -5)$ and $(-10, -8)$

12.9   **LOGICAL REASONING: PROOF**

Examples on pp. 740–743

EXAMPLE Prove that for all numbers a and b, $(a + b) - b = a$.

$(a + b) - b = (a + b) + (-b)$ Definition of subtraction

$\qquad\qquad = a + [b + (-b)]$ Associative property of addition

$\qquad\qquad = a + 0$ Inverse property of addition

$\qquad\qquad = a$ Identity property of addition

42. Which basic axiom of algebra is represented by $\left(\frac{2}{3}\right)\left(\frac{4}{5}\right) = \left(\frac{4}{5}\right)\left(\frac{2}{3}\right)$?

43. Prove that $(c)(-b) = -cb$ for all real numbers c and b.

Find the domain of the function. Then sketch its graph and find the range of the function.

1. $y = 12\sqrt{x}$ **2.** $y = \sqrt{2x + 7}$ **3.** $y = \sqrt{3x} - 3$ **4.** $y = \sqrt{x} - 5$

Simplify the expression.

5. $3\sqrt{2} - \sqrt{2}$ **6.** $(4 + \sqrt{7})(4 - \sqrt{7})$ **7.** $\dfrac{4}{\sqrt{10}}$ **8.** $\dfrac{8}{3 - \sqrt{5}}$

9. $\dfrac{1}{\sqrt{6}}$ **10.** $\dfrac{\sqrt{11}}{2 - \sqrt{11}}$ **11.** $(8 - \sqrt{5})(8 + \sqrt{5})$ **12.** $\sqrt{3}(\sqrt{12} + 4)$

Solve the equation. Check for extraneous solutions.

13. $\sqrt{y} + 6 = 10$ **14.** $\sqrt{2m + 3} - 6 = 4$ **15.** $n = \sqrt{9n - 18}$ **16.** $p = \sqrt{-3p + 18}$

Simplify the variable expression using the rules for rational exponents.

17. $x^{1/2} \cdot x^{3/2}$ **18.** $\sqrt{25x^3}$ **19.** $(x^{1/3})^2 \cdot \sqrt{y}$ **20.** $(x^2 \cdot x^{1/3})^{3/2}$

Solve the equation by completing the square.

21. $x^2 - 6x = -5$ **22.** $x^2 - 2x = 2$ **23.** $x^2 + 16x - 1 = 0$

Find the missing length of the right triangle if a and b are the lengths of the legs and c is the length of the hypotenuse.

24. $a = 7, b = 24$ **25.** $a = 5, c = 13$ **26.** $b = 15, c = 17$

27. $a = 30, b = 40$ **28.** $a = 6, c = 10$ **29.** $b = 12, c = 15$

Determine whether the given lengths are sides of a right triangle. Explain your reasoning.

30. 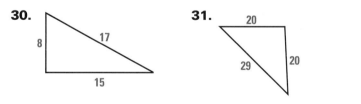 **31.**

32.

In Exercises 33–35, use the diagram shown at the right.

33. Use the distance formula to find the length of each side of the parallelogram.

34. Use your answers from Exercise 33 to find the perimeter of the parallelogram.

35. Find the coordinates of the midpoint of each side of the parallelogram.

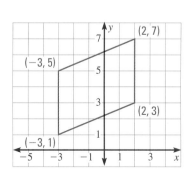

36. Prove that if a, b, and c are real numbers and $a + c = b + c$, then $a = b$.

Chapter Standardized Test

1. What is the value of $y = \dfrac{x\sqrt{x^2 - 1}}{x^2 + 8}$ when $x = 8$?

  (A) $\dfrac{3\sqrt{7}}{16}$ (B) $\dfrac{7}{8}$

  (C) $\dfrac{\sqrt{7}}{3}$ (D) $\dfrac{8}{9}$

2. What is the range of the function $y = \sqrt{x} + 7$?

  (A) All positive real numbers

  (B) All real numbers

  (C) All real numbers greater than 7

  (D) All real numbers less than 7

3. Which of the following is the value of the expression $5\sqrt{7} + \sqrt{448} + \sqrt{175} - \sqrt{63}$?

  (A) $15\sqrt{7}$ (B) $16\sqrt{7}$

  (C) $18\sqrt{7}$ (D) $20\sqrt{7}$

4. Which of the following is the simplest form of $\dfrac{2}{3 - \sqrt{6}}$?

  (A) $\dfrac{6 + \sqrt{12}}{3}$ (B) $\dfrac{6 + 2\sqrt{6}}{3}$

  (C) $\dfrac{6 + 2\sqrt{6}}{15}$ (D) $\dfrac{6 + \sqrt{12}}{15}$

5. Which of the following is a solution of the equation $x = \sqrt{880 - 18x}$?

  (A) -22 (B) 0

  (C) 22 (D) 40

6. Which of the following is the simplest form of $(xy^{1/3}x^{2/3})^3$?

  (A) x^6y (B) $x^6y^{1/9}$

  (C) x^5y (D) $x^5y^{10/3}$

7. What term should you add to $x^2 - 18x$ to create a perfect square trinomial?

  (A) -36 (B) -9

  (C) 9 (D) 81

8. What is the length of the missing side of the triangle?

  (A) 10 (B) 11

  (C) 12 (D) 13

9. What is the distance between points P and Q?

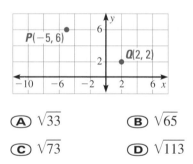

  (A) $\sqrt{33}$ (B) $\sqrt{65}$

  (C) $\sqrt{73}$ (D) $\sqrt{113}$

10. Use the graph in Exercise 9. Find the midpoint of the line segment connecting the points P and Q.

  (A) $\left(\dfrac{-3}{2}, 4\right)$ (B) $\left(\dfrac{-7}{2}, 2\right)$

  (C) $\left(\dfrac{-3}{2}, 2\right)$ (D) $\left(\dfrac{-7}{2}, 4\right)$

11. Choose the missing reason in the following proof that for all real numbers a and b, $-(a + b) = (-a) + (-b)$.

STATEMENTS	REASONS
1. a and b are real numbers	**1.** Given
2. $-(a + b) = (-1)(a + b)$	**2.** Multiplication property of -1
3. $\quad\quad = (-1)a + (-1)b$	**3.** _____?_____
4. $\quad\quad = (-a) + (-b)$	**4.** Multiplicative property of -1

⑰ **A** Definition of subtraction

⑰ **B** Associative property of addition

⑰ **C** Inverse property of addition

⑰ **D** Distributive property

⑰ **E** None of these

12. Which graph best represents the function $y = 3\sqrt{x} - 2$?

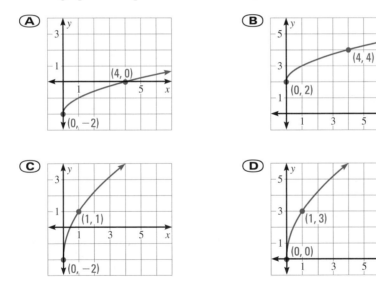

A graph with points $(4, 0)$ and $(0, -2)$

B graph with points $(4, 4)$ and $(0, 2)$

C graph with points $(1, 1)$ and $(0, -2)$

D graph with points $(1, 3)$ and $(0, 0)$

13. Which of the following triangles *is* a right triangle?

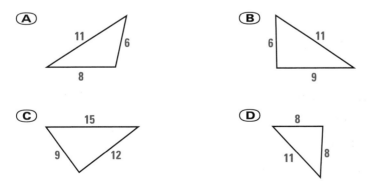

A triangle with sides 11, 6, 8

B triangle with sides 6, 11, 9

C triangle with sides 15, 9, 12

D triangle with sides 8, 11, 8

Write the sentence as an equation or an inequality. Then use mental math to solve the equation or the inequality. (1.4–1.5)

1. The quotient of m and 7 is greater than or equal to 16.

2. The sum of 4 and the second power of b is equal to 104.

3. The distance t you travel by train is 3 times the distance d you live from the train station. You drive 3 miles to get from your house to the train station.

Evaluate the expression for the given value of the variable. (2.2–2.6, 2.8)

4. $3 + x + (-4)$ when $x = 5$ **5.** $2x + 12 - 5$ when $x = 9$ **6.** $3.5 - (-x)$ when $x = 1.5$

7. $-(-3)^2(x)$ when $x = 7$ **8.** $6x(x + 2)$ when $x = 2$ **9.** $(8x + 1)(-3)$ when $x = 1$

10. $\frac{1}{4}|(x)(x)(-x)|$ when $x = 4$ **11.** $\frac{x^2 + 4}{6}$ when $x = 8$ **12.** $(-5)\left(-\frac{3}{4}x\right)$ when $x = 6$

Solve the equation. Round your solution to the nearest hundredth. (3.1–3.4, 3.6)

13. $-\frac{2}{9}(x - 5) = 12$ **14.** $7x - (3x - 2) = 38$ **15.** $\frac{1}{3}x + 7 = -7x - 5$

16. $8(x + 3) - 2x = 4(x - 8)$ **17.** $11 + 6.23x = 7 + 5.51x$ **18.** $-3(2.9 - 4.1x) = 9.2x + 6$

In Exercises 19 and 20, use the graph. (4.7, 5.3, 5.6)

19. Write an equation of a line passing through the point $(2, -2)$ and parallel to the line shown.

20. Write an equation of a line passing through the point $(-4, 2)$ and perpendicular to the line shown. Graph the equation in the same coordinate plane to check your answer.

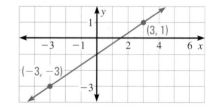

Determine whether the relation is a function. If it is a function, give the domain and the range. (4.8)

21.

Input	Output
-1	-1
1	-1
3	1
5	3

22. **23.** **24.**

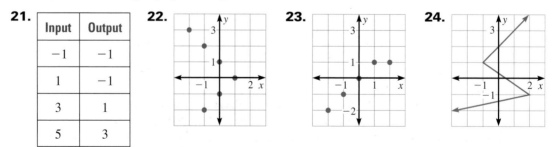

Write in standard form the equation of the line described below. (5.1–5.2)

25. Slope $= \frac{4}{5}$, y-intercept $= -3$ **26.** $(-1, 2)$, $m = \frac{1}{3}$

Solve the inequality. Then graph the solution. (6.3–6.5)

27. $-3 < -4x + 9 \leq 14$ **28.** $|3x + 16| + 2 < 10$ **29.** $3x - 4 > 5$ or $5x + 1 < 11$

Solve the linear system. (7.2–7.3)

30. $4y = 8x + 16$
     $2y = 11x - 7$

31. $-2x + 3y = 15$
     $10x - 11y = 9$

32. $y = 5x - 2$
     $3x + 7y = 5$

Simplify. Then evaluate the expression when $a = 1$ and $b = 2$. (8.1–8.2, 8.4)

33. $\dfrac{b^8}{b^2}$ **34.** $3a^4 \cdot a^{-3}$ **35.** $(-a^3)(2b^2)^3$

36. $4b^3 \cdot (2 + b)^2$ **37.** $\dfrac{4a^{-3}b^3}{ab^{-2}}$ **38.** $\dfrac{(5ab^2)^{-2}}{a^{-3}b}$

Determine whether the equation has *two solutions, one solution,* or *no real solution.* Then solve the equation. (9.2, 9.6–9.7, 10.5)

39. $6x^2 + 8 = 34$ **40.** $4x^2 - 9x + 5 = 0$ **41.** $3x^2 + 6x + 3 = 0$

Completely factor the expression. (10.5–10.7)

42. $x^2 + 6x + 8$ **43.** $x^2 - 24x - 112$ **44.** $3x^2 + 17x - 6$

45. $4x^2 + 12x + 9$ **46.** $x^2 + 10x + 25$ **47.** $x^2 - 14x + 49$

Solve the equation. (10.4–10.8)

48. $(3x + 1)(2x + 7) = 0$ **49.** $6x^2 - x - 7 = 8$ **50.** $x^2 - 4x + 4 = 0$

51. $4x^2 + 16x + 16 = 0$ **52.** $x^3 + 5x^2 - 4x - 20 = 0$ **53.** $x^4 + 9x^3 + 18x^2 = 0$

Simplify the expression. (11.3–11.7)

54. $\dfrac{4x}{12x^2}$ **55.** $\dfrac{2x + 6}{x^2 - 9}$ **56.** $\dfrac{3x}{x^2 - 2x - 24} \cdot \dfrac{x - 6}{6x^2 + 9x}$

57. $\dfrac{x^2 - 6x + 8}{x^2 - 2x} \div (3x - 12)$ **58.** $\dfrac{4}{x + 2} + \dfrac{15x}{3x + 6}$ **59.** $\dfrac{3x}{x + 4} - \dfrac{x}{x - 1}$

Simplify the expression. (12.2)

60. $4\sqrt{7} + 3\sqrt{7}$ **61.** $9\sqrt{2} - 12\sqrt{8}$ **62.** $\sqrt{6}(5\sqrt{3} + 6)$ **63.** $\dfrac{11}{7 - \sqrt{3}}$

Solve the equation by completing the square. (12.5)

64. $x^2 + 24x = -3$ **65.** $x^2 - 12x = 19$ **66.** $x^2 + 20x = -7$

67. $x^2 - 6x - 13 = 0$ **68.** $x^2 + 16x - 1 = 0$ **69.** $x^2 + 22x + 5 = 0$

Find the distance between the two points. Round your solution to the nearest hundredth if necessary. Then find the midpoint of the line segment connecting the two points. (12.7–12.8)

70. $(3, 0), (-5, 4)$ **71.** $(2, 7), (4, 3)$ **72.** $(5, 1), (1, -5)$ **73.** $(6, 2), (-2, -3)$

74. $(-1, 2), (6, 9)$ **75.** $(0, 4), (10, 11)$ **76.** $(-5, -7), (5, 7)$ **77.** $(1, -1), (3, 10)$

Investigating the Golden Ratio

Materials
- graph paper
- metric ruler
- graphing calculator (optional)

OBJECTIVE Explore what the golden ratio is and how it is used.

Over the centuries, the *golden rectangle* has fascinated artists, architects, and mathematicians. For example, the golden rectangle was used in the original design of the Parthenon in Athens, Greece. A **golden rectangle** has the special shape such that when a square is cut from one end, the ratio of length to width of the remaining rectangle is equal to the ratio of length to width of the original rectangle.

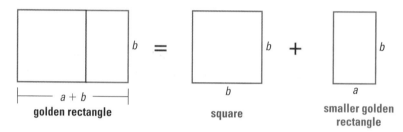

b = b + b

$a + b$
golden rectangle

b
square

a
smaller golden rectangle

Before the pediment on top of the Parthenon in Athens was destroyed, the front of the building fit almost exactly into a golden rectangle.

INVESTIGATING THE GOLDEN RATIO

From the picture, the large rectangle has a ratio of length to width $\frac{a + b}{b}$, while the small b-by-a rectangle that remains after cutting off the b-by-b square has a ratio of length to width $\frac{b}{a}$. For a golden rectangle, the ratio of length to width of the large rectangle is equal to the ratio of the small rectangle. In other words,

$$\frac{a + b}{b} = \frac{b}{a}.$$

Let $r = \frac{b}{a}$ represent the ratio of length to width of a golden rectangle. This ratio r is called the golden ratio. To derive the exact value of r, rewrite the equality above.

$\frac{a}{b} + 1 = \frac{b}{a}$ Rewrite $\frac{a + b}{b}$ as $\frac{a}{b} + 1$.

$\frac{1}{r} + 1 = r$ Substitute r for $\frac{b}{a}$.

$1 + r = r^2$ Multiply each side by r.

$r^2 - r - 1 = 0$ Write equation in standard form.

$r = \frac{1 + \sqrt{5}}{2}$ or $r = \frac{1 - \sqrt{5}}{2}$ Use quadratic equation to solve for r.

Since $r > 0$, the golden ratio r is given by $r = \frac{1 + \sqrt{5}}{2}$, or about 1.618034.

CONSTRUCTING GOLDEN RECTANGLES

1 On graph paper, draw a **1-by-1** square.

2 On one side of the square add another **1-by-1** square.

3 Build a **2-by-2** square on the longest side of the 1-by-2 rectangle.

4 Build a **3-by-3** square on the longest side of the 3-by-2 rectangle.

 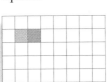 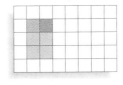 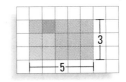

None of the rectangles in Steps 1–4 are golden rectangles. It is *not* possible to construct a golden rectangle with integer side lengths. However, it *is* possible to construct rectangles with integer side lengths whose ratios of length to width are very close to the golden ratio.

1. Continue the pattern from Steps 1–4 to draw the next four rectangles.

2. Copy and complete the table. If necessary, round to four decimal places.

length *b*	3	5	8	13	21	34
width *a*	2	3	5	8	13	21
$\frac{b}{a}$	1.5	1.6667	?	?	?	?

3. How do the ratios in your table compare to the golden ratio?

PRESENTING THE RESULTS

Write a report or make a poster to present your results. Include a sketch of a golden rectangle and include your answers to Exercises 1–3. Then describe what you learned about the golden ratio and the golden rectangle.

EXTENDING THE PROJECT

- The average chicken egg fits inside a golden rectangle. Measure the lengths and widths of six eggs and find the approximate ratio of length to width for each. Then find the average of these ratios.

- Find some rectangular objects that you think may have a length to width ratio close to the golden ratio. Measure them to see if they approximate golden rectangles. You might try a picture frame, a $1 bill, or a TV screen.

Contents of Student Resources

Skills Review Handbook

DECIMALS

To add and subtract decimals, you can use a vertical format. When you do this, line up the decimal places. Use zeros as placeholders as needed to help keep the decimal places aligned correctly. The steps are similar to those used for adding and subtracting whole numbers.

EXAMPLE Add 3.7 + 0.77 + 9.

SOLUTION Write the addition problem in vertical form. Line up the decimal points. Use zeros as placeholders.

```
   3.70
   0.77
 + 9.00
  13.47
```

ANSWER ▶ 3.7 + 0.77 + 9 = 13.47

EXAMPLE Subtract 21.32 − 18.78.

SOLUTION Write the subtraction problem in vertical form. Line up the decimal points.

```
   21.32
 − 18.78
    2.54
```

ANSWER ▶ 21.32 − 18.78 = 2.54

Decimal multiplication is similar to multiplication with whole numbers. When multiplying decimals, you need to know where to put the decimal point in the product. The number of decimal places in the product is equal to the sum of the number of decimal places in the factors.

EXAMPLE Multiply 6.84 × 5.3.

SOLUTION Write the multiplication problem in vertical form. When multiplying decimals, you do not need to line up the decimal points.

```
    6.84        two decimal places
  × 5.3         one decimal place
   2052
  34200
  36.252        three decimal places
```

ANSWER ▶ 6.84 × 5.3 = 36.252

You can divide decimals using long division. The steps for dividing decimals using long division are the same as the steps for dividing whole numbers using long division. When you use long division to divide decimals, line up the decimal place in the quotient with the decimal place in the the dividend. If there is a remainder, write zeros in the dividend as needed and continue to divide.

EXAMPLE Divide 0.085 ÷ 0.2.

SOLUTION Write the problem in long division form.

$$0.2\overline{)0.085}$$

Move the decimal points in the divisor and dividend the same number of places until the divisor is a whole number. Then divide.

$$0.2\overline{)0.085}$$

Move decimal points one place to the right.

Line up decimal place in quotient with decimal place in dividend.

Write a zero in dividend so you can continue to divide.

$$\begin{array}{r} 0.425 \\ 2\overline{)0.850} \\ \underline{0.8} \\ 5 \\ \underline{4} \\ 10 \\ \underline{10} \\ 0 \end{array}$$

ANSWER ▶ 0.085 ÷ 0.2 = 0.425

Practice

Find the sum.

1. 7.92 + 6.5

2. 12.36 + 9

3. 28.012 + 94.3

4. 19.9 + 93.8 + 5.992

5. 9.02 + 8 + 8.7

6. 2.25 + 7.789 + 4.32

Find the difference.

7. 3.42 − 2.4

8. 0.88 − 0.39

9. 2.91 − 0.452

10. 15 − 6.32 − 1.44

11. 10.24 − 3.1 − 0.07

12. 94.48 − 16.7 − 42.902

Find the product.

13. 6.25 × 6.5

14. 0.26 × 9.58

15. 0.15 × 24

16. 64 × 3.51

17. 183.62 × 2.834

18. 510.375 × 80.2

Find the quotient.

19. 133.6 ÷ 8

20. 57.3 ÷ 0.003

21. 231.84 ÷ 12.6

22. 100.38 ÷ 21

23. 84.4 ÷ 0.02

24. 2712.15 ÷ 35

25. You bought a shirt for $24, a pair of pants for $25.99, and a pair of shoes for $12.45. How much did you spend all together? If you give the cashier $70, how much change will you receive?

FACTORS AND MULTIPLES

The **natural numbers** are all the numbers in the sequence 1, 2, 3, 4, 5, ...
When two or more natural numbers are multiplied, each of the numbers is a
factor of the product. For example, **3** and **7** are factors of 21, because $3 \cdot 7 = 21$.
A **prime number** is a natural number that has exactly two factors, itself and 1.
To write the **prime factorization** of a number, write the number as a product of
prime numbers.

EXAMPLE   Write the prime factorization of 315.

SOLUTION   Use a tree diagram to factor
the number until all factors are prime
numbers. To determine the factors, test
the prime numbers in order.

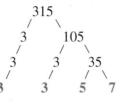

ANSWER ▶ The prime factorization of 315
is $3 \cdot 3 \cdot 5 \cdot 7$, or $3^2 \cdot 5 \cdot 7$.

A **common factor** of two natural numbers is a number that is a factor of both
numbers. For example, **7** is a common factor of 35 and 56, because $35 = 5 \cdot 7$
and $56 = 8 \cdot 7$. The **greatest common factor** (GCF) of two natural numbers is
the largest number that is a factor of both.

EXAMPLE   Find the greatest common factor of 180 and 84.

SOLUTION   First write the prime factorization of each number. Multiply the
common prime factors to find the greatest common factor.

$$180 = 2 \cdot 2 \cdot 3 \cdot 3 \cdot 5 \qquad 84 = 2 \cdot 2 \cdot 3 \cdot 7$$

ANSWER ▶ The greatest common factor of 180 and 84 is $2 \cdot 2 \cdot 3 = 12$.

A **common multiple** of two natural numbers is a number that is a multiple of
both numbers. For example, **42** is a common multiple of **6** and **14**, because
$42 = 6 \cdot 7$ and $42 = 14 \cdot 3$. The **least common multiple** (LCM) of two natural
numbers is the smallest number that is a multiple of both.

EXAMPLE   Find the least common multiple of 24 and 30.

SOLUTION   First write the prime factorization of each number. The least
common multiple is the product of the common prime factors and all the
prime factors that are not common.

$$24 = 2 \cdot 2 \cdot 2 \cdot 3 \qquad 30 = 2 \cdot 3 \cdot 5$$

ANSWER ▶ The least common multiple of 24 and 30 is $2 \cdot 3 \cdot 2 \cdot 2 \cdot 5 = 120$.

The **least common denominator** (LCD) of two fractions is the least common multiple of their denominators.

> **EXAMPLE** Find the least common denominator of the fractions $\frac{5}{8}$ and $\frac{1}{6}$.
>
> **SOLUTION**
>
> Begin by finding the least common multiple of the denominators 8 and 6.
>
> Multiples of 8: 8, 16, ⓐ24, 32, 40, 48, 56, 64, 72, . . .
>
> Multiples of 6: 6, 12, 18, ⓐ24, 30, 36, 42, 48, 54, . . .
>
> The least common multiple of 8 and 6 is 24.
>
> **ANSWER** ▶ The least common denominator of $\frac{5}{8}$ and $\frac{1}{6}$ is 24.

Practice

List all the factors of the number.

1. 18   **2.** 10   **3.** 77   **4.** 35

5. 27   **6.** 100   **7.** 42   **8.** 49

Write the prime factorization of the number if it is not a prime number. If a number is prime, write *prime*.

9. 27   **10.** 24   **11.** 32   **12.** 61

13. 55   **14.** 68   **15.** 148   **16.** 225

List all the common factors of the pair of numbers.

17. 15, 22   **18.** 36, 54   **19.** 5, 20   **20.** 14, 21

21. 9, 36   **22.** 24, 25   **23.** 20, 55   **24.** 12, 30

Find the greatest common factor of the pair of numbers.

25. 25, 30   **26.** 32, 40   **27.** 17, 24   **28.** 35, 150

29. 14, 28   **30.** 65, 39   **31.** 102, 51   **32.** 128, 104

Find the least common multiple of the pair of numbers.

33. 5, 7   **34.** 7, 12   **35.** 16, 26   **36.** 5, 10

37. 9, 15   **38.** 12, 35   **39.** 6, 14   **40.** 20, 25

Find the least common denominator of the pair of fractions.

41. $\frac{1}{3}, \frac{11}{12}$ **42.** $\frac{4}{9}, \frac{7}{12}$ **43.** $\frac{1}{6}, \frac{3}{10}$ **44.** $\frac{5}{8}, \frac{9}{14}$

45. $\frac{3}{4}, \frac{9}{70}$ **46.** $\frac{7}{10}, \frac{13}{24}$ **47.** $\frac{1}{3}, \frac{8}{17}$ **48.** $\frac{4}{15}, \frac{27}{40}$

FRACTIONS

A fraction is in **simplest form** if its numerator and denominator have a greatest common factor of 1. To simplify a fraction, divide the numerator and denominator by their greatest common factor.

EXAMPLE Simplify the fraction $\frac{28}{63}$.

SOLUTION The greatest common factor of 28 and 63 is 7. Divide both the numerator and denominator by 7.

$$\frac{28}{63} = \frac{28 \div 7}{63 \div 7} = \frac{4}{9}$$

EXAMPLE Rewrite the improper fraction $\frac{14}{3}$ as a mixed number.

SOLUTION Begin by dividing 14 by 3. The remainder will be the numerator of the mixed number's fraction.

$$\frac{14}{3} \longrightarrow 3\overline{)14}^{\,4R2} \longrightarrow 4\frac{2}{3}$$

EXAMPLE Rewrite the mixed number $5\frac{3}{7}$ as an improper fraction.

SOLUTION To find the numerator of the improper fraction, multiply the whole number by the denominator and add the numerator of the fraction. The denominator of the improper fraction will be the same as the denominator of the mixed number.

$$5\frac{3}{7} = \frac{5 \cdot 7 + 3}{7} = \frac{38}{7}$$

Two numbers are **reciprocals** of each other if their product is 1. Every number except 0 has a reciprocal.

$\frac{2}{3} \times \frac{3}{2} = 1$, so $\frac{2}{3}$ and $\frac{3}{2}$ are reciprocals.

To find the reciprocal of a number, write the number as a fraction. Then interchange the numerator and the denominator.

EXAMPLE Find the reciprocal of $3\frac{1}{4}$.

SOLUTION $3\frac{1}{4} = \frac{13}{4}$ Write $3\frac{1}{4}$ as a fraction.

$\frac{13}{4} \implies \frac{4}{13}$ Interchange numerator and denominator.

ANSWER ▶ The reciprocal of $3\frac{1}{4}$ is $\frac{4}{13}$.

CHECK ✓ $3\frac{1}{4} \times \frac{4}{13} = \frac{13}{4} \times \frac{4}{13} = \frac{13 \times 4}{4 \times 13} = 1$

To add or subtract two fractions with the same denominator, add or subtract the numerators.

EXAMPLES **a. Add** $\frac{3}{5} + \frac{4}{5}$. **b. Subtract** $\frac{7}{10} - \frac{2}{10}$.

a. $\frac{3}{5} + \frac{4}{5} = \frac{3+4}{5}$ Add numerators.

$= \frac{7}{5}$, or $1\frac{2}{5}$ Simplify.

b. $\frac{7}{10} - \frac{2}{10} = \frac{7-2}{10}$ Subtract numerators.

$= \frac{5}{10}$ Simplify.

$= \frac{5}{2 \cdot 5}$ Factor.

$= \frac{1}{2}$ Simplify.

EXAMPLE

Find the least common denominator of the fractions $\frac{3}{5}$ and $\frac{1}{2}$. Then rewrite the fractions with the least common denominator.

SOLUTION

Begin by finding the least common multiple of the denominators 5 and 2.

Multiples of 5: 5, ⑩, 15, 20, 25, 30, 35, 40, . . .

Multiples of 2: 2, 4, 6, 8, ⑩, 12, 14, 16, 18, . . .

The least common multiple of 5 and 2 is 10. Now rewrite each fraction with a common denominator of 10.

$\frac{3}{5} = \frac{3 \cdot 2}{5 \cdot 2} = \frac{6}{10}$ Multiply by $\frac{2}{2}$.

$\frac{1}{2} = \frac{1 \cdot 5}{2 \cdot 5} = \frac{5}{10}$ Multiply by $\frac{5}{5}$.

To add or subtract two fractions with different denominators, write equivalent fractions with a common denominator.

EXAMPLE **Add** $\frac{3}{5} + \frac{5}{6}$.

$\frac{3}{5} + \frac{5}{6} = \frac{18}{30} + \frac{25}{30}$ Use the LCD, 30.

$= \frac{18+25}{30}$ Add numerators.

$= \frac{43}{30}$, or $1\frac{13}{30}$ Simplify.

To add or subtract mixed numbers, you can first rewrite them as fractions.

EXAMPLE Subtract $3\frac{2}{3} - 2\frac{1}{4}$.

$$3\frac{2}{3} - 2\frac{1}{4} = \frac{11}{3} - \frac{9}{4} \qquad \text{Rewrite mixed numbers as fractions.}$$

$$= \frac{44}{12} - \frac{27}{12} \qquad \text{Use the LCD, 12.}$$

$$= \frac{44 - 27}{12} \qquad \text{Subtract numerators.}$$

$$= \frac{17}{12}, \text{ or } 1\frac{5}{12} \qquad \text{Simplify.}$$

To multiply two fractions, multiply the numerators and multiply the denominators.

EXAMPLE Multiply $\frac{3}{4} \times \frac{5}{6}$.

$$\frac{3}{4} \times \frac{5}{6} = \frac{3 \times 5}{4 \times 6} \qquad \text{Multiply numerators and multiply denominators.}$$

$$= \frac{15}{24} \qquad \text{Simplify.}$$

$$= \frac{3 \cdot 5}{3 \cdot 8} \qquad \text{Factor numerator and denominator.}$$

$$= \frac{5}{8} \qquad \text{Simplify fraction to lowest terms.}$$

To divide by a fraction, multiply by its reciprocal.

EXAMPLES a. Divide $\frac{3}{4} \div \frac{5}{6}$.   b. Divide $2\frac{1}{2} \div 4\frac{1}{6}$.

$$\textbf{a. } \frac{3}{4} \div \frac{5}{6} = \frac{3}{4} \times \frac{6}{5} \qquad \text{The reciprocal of } \frac{5}{6} \text{ is } \frac{6}{5}.$$

$$= \frac{3 \times 6}{4 \times 5} \qquad \text{Multiply numerators and denominators.}$$

$$= \frac{18}{20} = \frac{9}{10} \qquad \text{Simplify.}$$

$$\textbf{b. } 2\frac{1}{2} \div 4\frac{1}{6} = \frac{5}{2} \div \frac{25}{6} \qquad \text{Write mixed numbers as fractions.}$$

$$= \frac{5}{2} \times \frac{6}{25} \qquad \text{The reciprocal of } \frac{25}{6} \text{ is } \frac{6}{25}.$$

$$= \frac{5 \times 6}{2 \times 25} \qquad \text{Multiply numerators and denominators.}$$

$$= \frac{30}{50} = \frac{3}{5} \qquad \text{Simplify.}$$

Practice

Find the reciprocal of the number.

1. 7

2. $\dfrac{1}{14}$

3. $\dfrac{7}{12}$

4. $\dfrac{5}{8}$

5. $\dfrac{1}{20}$

6. 100

7. $\dfrac{5}{13}$

8. $\dfrac{6}{7}$

9. $1\dfrac{1}{5}$

10. $2\dfrac{3}{5}$

11. $\dfrac{3}{9}$

12. $\dfrac{12}{17}$

13. $6\dfrac{2}{5}$

14. $10\dfrac{1}{3}$

15. $\dfrac{2}{7}$

16. $4\dfrac{3}{4}$

Add or subtract. Write the answer as a fraction or a mixed number in simplest form.

17. $\dfrac{1}{6} + \dfrac{4}{6}$

18. $\dfrac{5}{8} - \dfrac{3}{8}$

19. $\dfrac{4}{9} - \dfrac{1}{9}$

20. $\dfrac{5}{12} + \dfrac{3}{12}$

21. $\dfrac{1}{2} + \dfrac{1}{8}$

22. $\dfrac{3}{5} - \dfrac{1}{10}$

23. $\dfrac{7}{10} + \dfrac{1}{3}$

24. $\dfrac{15}{24} - \dfrac{7}{12}$

25. $5\dfrac{1}{8} - 2\dfrac{3}{4}$

26. $1\dfrac{3}{7} + \dfrac{1}{2}$

27. $4\dfrac{3}{8} - 2\dfrac{5}{6}$

28. $\dfrac{3}{7} + \dfrac{3}{4}$

29. $7\dfrac{1}{2} + \dfrac{7}{10}$

30. $5\dfrac{5}{9} - 2\dfrac{1}{3}$

31. $4\dfrac{5}{8} - 1\dfrac{3}{16}$

32. $9\dfrac{2}{5} + 3\dfrac{1}{3}$

Multiply or divide. Write the answer as a fraction or a mixed number in simplest form.

33. $\dfrac{1}{2} \times \dfrac{1}{2}$

34. $\dfrac{2}{3} \times \dfrac{4}{5}$

35. $\dfrac{5}{8} \times \dfrac{4}{15}$

36. $\dfrac{3}{7} \times \dfrac{7}{9}$

37. $\dfrac{3}{4} \times \dfrac{8}{9}$

38. $1\dfrac{2}{3} \times \dfrac{3}{5}$

39. $3 \times 2\dfrac{5}{9}$

40. $5\dfrac{1}{4} \times 1\dfrac{1}{7}$

41. $\dfrac{7}{8} \div \dfrac{3}{4}$

42. $\dfrac{5}{12} \div \dfrac{1}{2}$

43. $\dfrac{4}{5} \div \dfrac{2}{3}$

44. $\dfrac{11}{16} \div 1\dfrac{1}{2}$

45. $4\dfrac{1}{2} \div \dfrac{3}{4}$

46. $2\dfrac{1}{4} \div 1\dfrac{1}{3}$

47. $3\dfrac{2}{5} \div 4$

48. $7\dfrac{1}{5} \div 2\dfrac{1}{4}$

Add, subtract, multiply, or divide. Write the answer as a fraction or a mixed number in simplest form.

49. $\dfrac{15}{16} - \dfrac{1}{8}$

50. $\dfrac{5}{9} \times 1\dfrac{1}{2}$

51. $\dfrac{12}{13} \div \dfrac{12}{13}$

52. $\dfrac{24}{25} + \dfrac{1}{5}$

53. $5\dfrac{1}{2} - \dfrac{1}{8}$

54. $\dfrac{3}{10} \div \dfrac{1}{5}$

55. $\dfrac{7}{8} \times \dfrac{4}{9}$

56. $\dfrac{1}{3} + \dfrac{1}{6}$

57. $4\dfrac{1}{4} \times \dfrac{2}{3}$

58. $9\dfrac{2}{5} + 3\dfrac{1}{2}$

59. $\dfrac{4}{5} \div \dfrac{1}{2}$

60. $6\dfrac{5}{7} - 2\dfrac{1}{5}$

61. $\dfrac{9}{10} + \dfrac{3}{8}$

62. $8\dfrac{1}{2} \times \dfrac{1}{4}$

63. $\dfrac{11}{15} \times \dfrac{3}{8}$

64. $\dfrac{4}{7} \div \dfrac{4}{5}$

WRITING FRACTIONS AND DECIMALS

A fraction can be written as a decimal by dividing the numerator by the denominator. If the division stops with an exact quotient, then the decimal form of the number is a **terminating decimal**. If the resulting quotient includes a decimal digit or group of digits that repeats over and over, then the decimal form of the number is a **repeating decimal**.

EXAMPLES **Write the fraction as a decimal.** **a.** $\frac{9}{20}$ **b.** $\frac{7}{11}$

SOLUTION

Divide the numerator by the denominator.

a. $20\overline{)9.00}$ → 0.45

ANSWER ▶ $\frac{9}{20} = 0.45$, a terminating decimal.

b. $11\overline{)7.000000...}$ → $0.636363...$

ANSWER ▶ $\frac{7}{11} = 0.636363...$, a repeating decimal. Write a repeating decimal with a bar over the digits that repeat: $\frac{7}{11} = 0.\overline{63}$.

EXAMPLES **Write the decimal as a fraction.** **a.** 0.12 **b.** $0.\overline{18}$

SOLUTION

a. To write a terminating decimal as a fraction, use the name for the last place to the right of the decimal as the denominator. The first place to the right is tenths, the second place is hundredths, and so on.

$0.12 = \frac{12}{100}$ Write as hundredths.

$= \frac{3}{25}$ Simplify.

ANSWER ▶ $0.12 = \frac{3}{25}$

b.
$x = 0.181818...$ Let x represent the repeating decimal.

$100x = 18.181818...$ Multiply x by 10^n where n is the number of digits that repeat. (Here, $n = 2$.)

$-\ x = 0.181818...$

$99x = 18$ Subtract x from $100x$ to eliminate repeating decimal.

$x = \frac{18}{99}$ Divide each side by 99.

$= \frac{2}{11}$ Simplify.

ANSWER ▶ $0.\overline{18} = \frac{2}{11}$

Practice

Write the fraction as a decimal.

1. $\frac{1}{4}$ **2.** $\frac{7}{10}$ **3.** $\frac{2}{25}$ **4.** $\frac{41}{50}$

5. $\frac{1}{3}$ **6.** $\frac{4}{9}$ **7.** $\frac{10}{11}$ **8.** $\frac{27}{37}$

Write the decimal as a fraction. Simplify if possible.

9. 0.5 **10.** 0.16 **11.** 0.289 **12.** 0.1234

13. $0.\overline{7}$ **14.** $0.\overline{15}$ **15.** $0.6\overline{13}$ **16.** $0.5\overline{840}$

FRACTIONS, DECIMALS, AND PERCENTS

To write a percent as a decimal, move the decimal point two places to the left and remove the percent symbol.

EXAMPLES **Write the percent as a decimal.**

a. $85\% = 85\% = 0.85$ **b.** $3\% = 03\% = 0.03$

c. $427\% = 427\% = 4.27$ **d.** $12.5\% = 12.5\% = 0.125$

To write a percent as a fraction in simplest form, first write the percent as a fraction with a denominator of 100. Then simplify if possible.

EXAMPLES **Write the percent as a fraction or a mixed number.**

a. $71\% = \frac{71}{100}$ **b.** $10\% = \frac{10}{100} = \frac{1}{10}$

c. $4\% = \frac{4}{100} = \frac{1}{25}$ **d.** $350\% = \frac{350}{100} = \frac{7}{2} = 3\frac{1}{2}$

To write a decimal as a percent, move the decimal point two places to the right and add a percent symbol.

EXAMPLES **Write the decimal as a percent.**

a. $0.93 = 0.93 = 93\%$ **b.** $1.47 = 1.47 = 147\%$

c. $0.025 = 0.025 = 2.5\%$ **d.** $0.005 = 0.005 = 0.5\%$

To write a fraction as a percent, first determine whether the denominator of the fraction is a factor of 100. If it is, rewrite the fraction with a denominator of 100. If not, divide the numerator by the denominator.

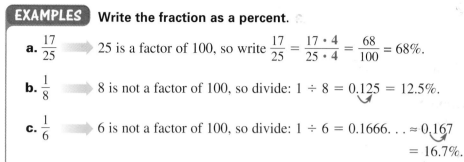

EXAMPLES **Write the fraction as a percent.**

a. $\dfrac{17}{25}$ ⟹ 25 is a factor of 100, so write $\dfrac{17}{25} = \dfrac{17 \cdot 4}{25 \cdot 4} = \dfrac{68}{100} = 68\%$.

b. $\dfrac{1}{8}$ ⟹ 8 is not a factor of 100, so divide: $1 \div 8 = 0.125 = 12.5\%$.

c. $\dfrac{1}{6}$ ⟹ 6 is not a factor of 100, so divide: $1 \div 6 = 0.1666\ldots \approx 0.167$
$= 16.7\%$.

You should memorize the relationships in this chart.

Equivalent percents, decimals, and fractions		
$1\% = 0.01 = \dfrac{1}{100}$	$33\frac{1}{3}\% = 0.\overline{3} = \dfrac{1}{3}$	$66\frac{2}{3}\% = 0.\overline{6} = \dfrac{2}{3}$
$10\% = 0.1 = \dfrac{1}{10}$	$40\% = 0.4 = \dfrac{2}{5}$	$75\% = 0.75 = \dfrac{3}{4}$
$20\% = 0.2 = \dfrac{1}{5}$	$50\% = 0.5 = \dfrac{1}{2}$	$80\% = 0.8 = \dfrac{4}{5}$
$25\% = 0.25 = \dfrac{1}{4}$	$60\% = 0.6 = \dfrac{3}{5}$	$100\% = 1$

Practice

Write the percent as a decimal and as a fraction or a mixed number in simplest form.

1. 63%
2. 7%
3. 24%
4. 35%
5. 17%

6. 125%
7. 45%
8. 250%
9. 33.3%
10. 96%

11. 62.5%
12. 725%
13. 5.2%
14. 0.8%
15. 0.12%

Write the decimal as a percent and as a fraction or a mixed number in simplest form.

16. 0.39
17. 0.08
18. 0.12
19. 1.5
20. 0.72

21. 0.05
22. 2.08
23. 4.8
24. 0.02
25. 3.75

26. 0.85
27. 0.52
28. 0.9
29. 0.005
30. 2.01

Write the fraction or mixed number as a decimal and as a percent.

31. $\dfrac{7}{10}$
32. $\dfrac{13}{20}$
33. $\dfrac{11}{25}$
34. $\dfrac{3}{10}$
35. $\dfrac{3}{8}$

36. $2\frac{3}{4}$
37. $5\frac{1}{8}$
38. $\dfrac{19}{20}$
39. $\dfrac{7}{8}$
40. $3\frac{7}{25}$

COMPARING AND ORDERING NUMBERS

When you compare two numbers *a* and *b*, *a* is either *less than*, *equal to*, or *greater than b*. To compare two whole numbers or decimals, compare the digits of the two numbers from left to right. Find the first place in which the digits are different.

a is less than *b*.	$a < b$
a is equal to *b*.	$a = b$
a is greater than *b*.	$a > b$

EXAMPLES

Compare the two numbers. Write the answer using <, >, or =.

a. 27.52 and 27.39

b. −4.5 and −4.25

SOLUTION

a. 27.52 and 27.39

ANSWER ▶ $5 > 3$, so $27.52 > 27.39$.

You can picture this on a number line. The numbers on a number line increase from left to right.

27.52 is *greater* than **27.39**.

27.52 is to the *right* of **27.39**.

b. Begin by graphing −4.5 and −4.25 on a number line.

−4.5 is *less* than **−4.25**.

−4.5 is to the *left* of **−4.25**.

ANSWER ▶ From the number line, −4.5 is to the left of −4.25, so $-4.5 < -4.25$.

To compare fractions that have the same denominator, compare the numerators. If the fractions have different denominators, first rewrite the fractions to produce equivalent fractions with a common denominator.

EXAMPLE   Write the numbers $\frac{3}{4}$, $\frac{7}{8}$, and $\frac{5}{12}$ in order from least to greatest.

SOLUTION

The LCD of the fractions is 24.

$$\frac{3}{4} = \frac{3 \cdot 6}{4 \cdot 6} = \frac{18}{24} \qquad \frac{7}{8} = \frac{7 \cdot 3}{8 \cdot 3} = \frac{21}{24} \qquad \frac{5}{12} = \frac{5 \cdot 2}{12 \cdot 2} = \frac{10}{24}$$

Compare the numerators: $10 < 18 < 21$, so $\frac{10}{24} < \frac{18}{24} < \frac{21}{24}$, or $\frac{5}{12} < \frac{3}{4} < \frac{7}{8}$.

ANSWER ▶ In order from least to greatest, the fractions are $\frac{5}{12}$, $\frac{3}{4}$, and $\frac{7}{8}$.

EXAMPLE Compare $4\frac{3}{4}$ and $4\frac{2}{3}$. Write the answer using <, >, or =.

SOLUTION The whole number parts of the mixed numbers are the same, so compare the fraction parts.

The LCD of $\frac{3}{4}$ and $\frac{2}{3}$ is 12.

$$\frac{3}{4} = \frac{3 \cdot 3}{4 \cdot 3} = \frac{9}{12} \qquad\qquad \frac{2}{3} = \frac{2 \cdot 4}{3 \cdot 4} = \frac{8}{12}$$

Compare the numerators: $9 > 8$, so $\frac{9}{12} > \frac{8}{12}$, or $\frac{3}{4} > \frac{2}{3}$.

ANSWER ▶ Since $\frac{3}{4} > \frac{2}{3}$, it follows that $4\frac{3}{4} > 4\frac{2}{3}$.

$4\frac{3}{4}$ is *greater* than $4\frac{2}{3}$.

$4\frac{3}{4}$ is to the *right* of $4\frac{2}{3}$.

Practice

Compare the two numbers. Write the answer using <, >, or =.

1. 12,428 and 15,116

2. 905 and 961

3. $-140{,}999$ and $-142{,}109$

4. -16.82 and -14.09

5. 0.40506 and 0.00456

6. 23.03 and 23.3

7. 1005.2 and 1050.7

8. 932,778 and 934,112

9. -0.058 and -0.102

10. $\frac{7}{13}$ and $\frac{3}{13}$

11. $17\frac{1}{4}$ and $17\frac{2}{8}$

12. $\frac{7}{10}$ and $\frac{3}{4}$

13. $-\frac{5}{9}$ and $-\frac{15}{27}$

14. $-\frac{1}{2}$ and $-\frac{3}{8}$

15. $\frac{1}{8}$ and $\frac{1}{9}$

16. $\frac{4}{5}$ and $\frac{2}{3}$

17. $42\frac{1}{5}$ and $41\frac{7}{8}$

18. 508.881 and 508.793

19. 32,227 and 32,226.5

20. $\frac{5}{8}$ and $\frac{2}{3}$

21. $-17\frac{5}{6}$ and $-17\frac{5}{7}$

Write the numbers in order from least to greatest.

22. 1207, 1702, 1220, 1772

23. $-45{,}617, -45{,}242, -40{,}099, -40{,}071$

24. $-23.12, -23.5, -24.0, -23.08, -24.01$

25. 9.027, 9.10, 9.003, 9.3, 9.27

26. 4.07, 4.5, 4.01, 4.22

27. $\frac{1}{3}, \frac{5}{6}, \frac{3}{8}, \frac{5}{4}$

28. $\frac{3}{5}, \frac{3}{2}, \frac{3}{4}, \frac{3}{10}, \frac{3}{7}$

29. $1\frac{2}{5}, \frac{7}{4}, \frac{5}{3}, 1\frac{1}{8}, \frac{15}{16}$

30. $-14\frac{7}{9}, -15\frac{1}{3}, -14\frac{5}{6}, -15\frac{1}{4}$

31. $-\frac{7}{8}, -\frac{5}{4}, -1\frac{1}{3}, -\frac{5}{12}$

32. You need a piece of trim that is $6\frac{5}{8}$ yards long for a craft project. You have a piece of trim that is $6\frac{3}{4}$ yards long. Is the trim you have long enough?

PERIMETER, AREA, AND VOLUME

The **perimeter** P of a figure is the distance around it.

EXAMPLES

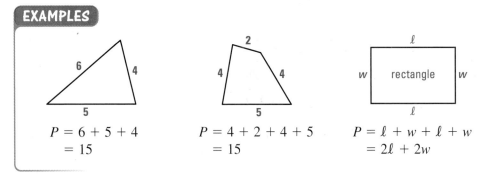

$P = 6 + 5 + 4$
$= 15$

$P = 4 + 2 + 4 + 5$
$= 15$

$P = \ell + w + \ell + w$
$= 2\ell + 2w$

EXAMPLE Find the perimeter of a rectangle with length 14 centimeters and width 6 centimeters.

SOLUTION $P = 2\ell + 2w = (2 \times 14) + (2 \times 6) = 28 + 12 = 40$

ANSWER ▶ The perimeter is 40 centimeters.

A **regular polygon** is a polygon in which all the angles have the same measure and all the sides have the same length. The perimeter of a regular polygon can be found by multiplying the length of a side by the number of sides.

EXAMPLES

regular (equilateral) triangle   square   regular pentagon

$P = 3s$ $P = 4s$ $P = 5s$

The **area** A of a figure is the number of square units enclosed by the figure.

EXAMPLES

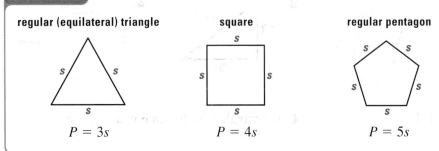

$A = \text{length} \times \text{width}$
$= \ell \times w$
$= \ell w$

$A = \text{side} \times \text{side}$
$= s \times s$
$= s^2$

$A = \dfrac{1}{2} \times \text{base} \times \text{height}$
$= \dfrac{1}{2} \times b \times h$
$= \dfrac{1}{2}bh$

Volume is a measure of how much space is occupied by a solid figure. Volume is measured in cubic units.

One such unit is the cubic centimeter (cm^3). It is the amount of space occupied by a cube whose length, width, and height are each 1 centimeter.

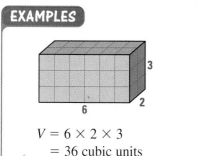

EXAMPLES

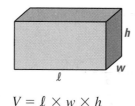

$V = 6 \times 2 \times 3$
    $= 36$ cubic units

$V = \ell \times w \times h$

EXAMPLE Find the volume of a rectangular prism with length 8 feet, width 5 feet, and height 9 feet.

SOLUTION $V = \ell \times w \times h = 8 \times 5 \times 9 = 360$

ANSWER ▶ The volume is 360 cubic feet (ft^3).

Practice

Find the perimeter.

1.
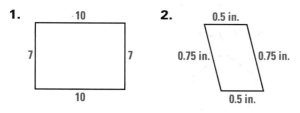

2.
3.
4.
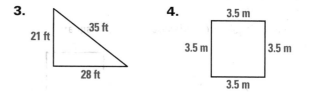

5. a square with sides of length 18 ft

6. a rectangle with length 6 m and width 7 m

Find the area.

7. a square with sides of length 29 yd

8. a rectangle with length 7 km and width 4 km

9. a square with sides of length 3.5 in.

10. a rectangle with length 24 ft and width 6 ft

11. a triangle with base 8 in. and height 5 in.

12. triangle with base 7.2 cm and height 5.3 cm

Find the volume.

13. a cube with sides of length 25 ft

14. a cube with sides of length 4.2 cm

15. a rectangular prism with length 15 yd, width 7 yd, and height 4 yd

16. a rectangular prism with length 7.3 cm, width 5 cm, and height 3.2 cm

17. a rectangular prism with length 5.3 in., width 4 in., and height 10 in.

ESTIMATION

You can use estimation to provide a quick answer when an exact answer is not needed. You also can use estimation to check if your answer is reasonable. Three methods of estimation are rounding, front-end estimation, and using compatible numbers.

To round, decide to which place you are rounding.

- If the digit to the right of that place is less than 5, round down.
- If the digit to the right of that place is greater than or equal to 5, round up.

EXAMPLE Estimate the difference of 688 and 52 by rounding to the nearest ten.

SOLUTION

$$
\begin{array}{rl}
688 \longrightarrow & 690 \qquad \text{Round 688 to the nearest ten.} \\
- 52 \longrightarrow & \underline{- 50} \qquad \text{Round 52 to the nearest ten.} \\
& 640 \qquad \text{Subtract.}
\end{array}
$$

ANSWER ▶ The difference of 688 and 52 is about 640.

EXAMPLE Estimate the quotient of 110.23 and 10.85 by rounding to the nearest whole number.

SOLUTION

$$110.23 \div 10.85 \longrightarrow 11\overline{)110} \;\;^{10} \qquad \text{Round 110.23 and 10.85 to the nearest whole numbers and divide.}$$

ANSWER ▶ The quotient of 110.23 and 10.85 is about 10.

To use **front-end estimation**, add the front digits. Then estimate the sum of the remaining digits, and add that sum to the front-end sum.

EXAMPLE Use front-end estimation to estimate the cost of 3 shirts marked $14.96, $11.78, and $8.25.

SOLUTION

Add the front digits.	Estimate what's left.
$14.96	$0.96 } about $1
$11.78	$0.78 ⎫
+ $8.25	$0.25 ⎬ about $1
$33	$2

ANSWER ▶ The cost of the shirts is about $33 + $2 = $35.

There are two methods to estimate products and quotients. You can use rounding or compatible numbers. **Compatible numbers** are numbers that are easy to compute mentally.

EXAMPLE Use compatible numbers to estimate the product of 116.11 and 41.09.

SOLUTION

$$
\begin{array}{ll}
116.11 \longrightarrow & 115 \\
\times\ 41.09 \longrightarrow & \times\ 40 \\
\hline
& 4600
\end{array}
$$

Use compatible numbers 115 and 40 since they are easy to multiply.

ANSWER ▶ The product of 116.11 and 41.09 is about 4600.

You can estimate the area of a figure by placing it on a grid. Count the number of squares that are completely covered by the figure. Then count the number of squares that are partially covered. You can assume that on average a partially covered square is about half covered. So you can estimate the total area of the figure by adding the number of squares that are totally covered to one-half the number of squares that are partially covered.

EXAMPLE Estimate the area of the figure shown to the nearest square unit.

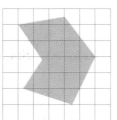

SOLUTION

First count the number of squares that are completely covered.

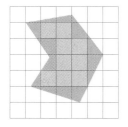

There are 9 squares that are completely covered.

Then count the number of squares that are partially covered.

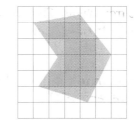

There are 18 squares that are partially covered.

So an estimate for the area of the figure can be calculated as follows:

$$\text{Area} = 9 + \frac{1}{2}(18) = 9 + 9 = 18$$

ANSWER ▶ The area of the figure is approximately 18 square units.

Practice

Round to the nearest ten or hundred to estimate the sum or difference.

1. 36 + 11

2. 249 + 782

3. 1585 + 791

4. 16 + 23 + 74

5. 108 + 92 + 345

6. 1023 + 5062 + 3873

7. 58 − 39

8. 1375 − 911

9. 2014 − 389

10. 65 − 42 − 12

11. 1059 − 238 − 111

12. 8375 − 3847 − 1224

Use front-end estimation to estimate the sum.

13. 15.98 + 6.46

14. 62.36 + 44.68

15. 156.22 + 324.72

16. 533.2 + 37.2

17. 912.14 + 428.13

18. 588.61 + 120.37

19. 24.22 + 4.53 + 12.31

20. 16.1 + 34.2 + 25.2

21. 59.31 + 71.21 + 78.47

22. 113.73 + 97.1 + 65.18

23. 88.9 + 86.19 + 92.14

24. 0.4 + 120.46 + 584.53

Use rounding to estimate the product or quotient.

25. 52 × 48

26. 27 × 414

27. 602 × 53

28. 42 × 6.1

29. 10.34 × 2.69

30. 108.8 × 435

31. 642 ÷ 219

32. 121 ÷ 57

33. 838 ÷ 22

34. 77 ÷ 3.84

35. 58.9 ÷ 14

36. 40.32 ÷ 1.25

Use compatible numbers to estimate the product or quotient.

37. 74.94 × 11.6

38. 397.25 × 41.37

39. 3997.63 × 18.87

40. 536.2 × 22.1

41. 498.75 × 13.55

42. 2465.83 × 68.52

43. 68.66 ÷ 2.96

44. 995.88 ÷ 102.34

45. 523.12 ÷ 51.87

46. 948.68 ÷ 47.96

47. 1487.81 ÷ 28.65

48. 148.64 ÷ 14.71

Estimate the area of the figure to the nearest square unit.

49.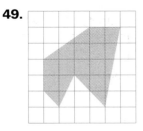

50.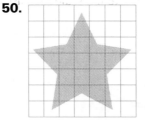

51.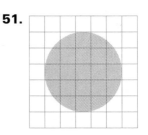

52.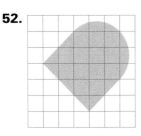

53.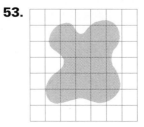

54.

DATA DISPLAYS

A **bar graph** can be used to display data that fall into distinct categories. The bars in a bar graph are the same width. The height or length of each bar is determined by the data it represents and by the scale you choose.

EXAMPLE

In 1998, baseball player Mark McGwire hit a record 70 home runs. The table shows the locations to which the home runs were hit. Draw a bar graph to display the data. ▶ Source: *Stats Inc.*

Field location	Number of runs
left	31
left-center	21
center	15
right-center	3
right	0

❶ Choose a scale. Since the data range from 0 to 31, make the scale increase from 0 to 35 by fives.

❷ Draw and label the axes. Mark intervals on the vertical axis according to the scale you chose.

❸ Draw a bar for each category.

❹ Give the bar graph a title.

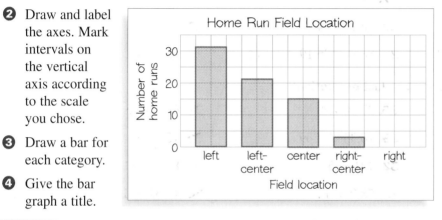

A **histogram** is a bar graph that shows how many data items occur within given intervals. The number of data items in an interval is the **frequency**.

EXAMPLE The table shows the distances of McGwire's home runs. Draw a histogram to display them.

Distance (ft)	Frequency
300–350	4
351–400	24
401–450	27
451–500	11
501–550	4

SOLUTION Use the same method you used for drawing the bar graph above. However, do not leave spaces between the bars.

❶ Since the frequencies range from 4 to 27, make the scale increase from 0 to 30 by fives.

❷ Draw and label the axes. Mark intervals on the vertical axis.

❸ Draw a bar for each category. Do not leave spaces between the bars.

❹ Give the histogram a title.

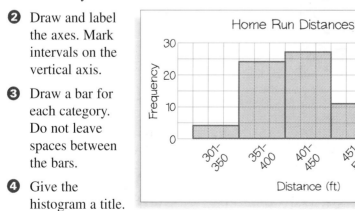

A **line graph** can be used to show how data change over time.

EXAMPLE

A science class recorded the highest temperature each day from December 1 to December 14. The temperatures are given in the table. Draw a line graph to display the data.

Date	1	2	3	4	5	6	7
Temperature (°F)	40	48	49	61	24	35	34

Date	8	9	10	11	12	13	14
Temperature (°F)	42	41	40	22	20	28	30

❶ Choose a scale.

❷ Draw and label the axes. Mark evenly spaced intervals on both axes.

❸ Graph each data item as a point. Connect the points.

❹ Give the line graph a title.

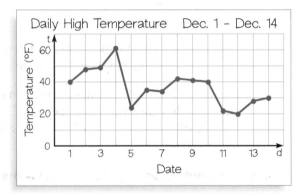

A **circle graph** can be used to show how parts relate to a whole and to each other.

EXAMPLE

The table shows the number of sports-related injuries treated in the hospital emergency room in one year. Draw a circle graph to display the data.

❶ Find the total number of injuries.

$$56 + 34 + 22 + 10 + 28 = 150$$

To find the degree measure for each sector of the circle, write a fraction comparing the number of injuries to the total. Then multiply the fraction by 360°. For example:

Football: $\frac{34}{150} \cdot 360° = 81.6°$

❷ Draw a circle. Use a protractor to draw the angle for each sector.

❸ Label each sector.

❹ Give the circle graph a title.

Related sport	Number of injuries
basketball	56
football	34
skating/hockey	22
track and field	10
other	28

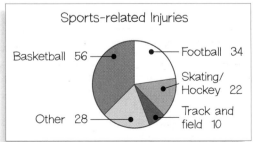

Practice

In 1998, baseball player Sammy Sosa hit 66 home runs. The tables show the field locations and distances of his home runs. ▶Source: *Stats Inc.*

1. The location data range from 10 to 22. The scale must start at 0. Choose a reasonable scale for a bar graph.

2. Draw a bar graph to display the field locations of Sosa's home runs.

3. The distance data range from 1 to 16. The scale must start at 0. Choose a reasonable scale for a histogram.

4. Draw a histogram to display the distances of Sosa's home runs.

Field location	Number of runs
left	12
left-center	22
center	10
right-center	11
right	11

For Exercises 1 and 2

Distance (ft)	Frequency
326–350	5
351–375	12
376–400	14
401–425	16
426–450	14
451–475	1
476–500	4

For Exercises 3 and 4

5. There are 150 runs at a ski resort: 51 expert runs, 60 intermediate runs, and 39 beginner runs. Draw a circle graph to display the data.

6. A patient's temperature (in degrees Fahrenheit) was taken every 3 hours from 9 A.M. until noon of the following day. The temperature readings were 102°F, 102°F, 101.5°F, 101.1°F, 100°F, 101°F, 101.5°F, 100°F, 99.8°F, and 99°F. Draw a line graph to display the data.

Choose an appropriate graph to display the data. Draw the graph.

7.

Value of One Share of Company stock						
Year	1994	1995	1996	1997	1998	1999
Value ($)	15	18	16	12	10	15

8.

Passenger Car Stopping Distance (dry road)				
Speed (mi/h)	35	45	55	65
Distance (ft)	160	225	310	410

9.

Fat in One Tablespoon of Canola Oil	
Type of fat	Number of grams
saturated	22
polyunsaturated	10
monounsaturated	11

▶Source: U.S. Department of Agriculture

10.

Enrollment in Capital City Schools by Age					
Age	4–6	7–9	10–12	13–15	16–18
Enrollment	912	2556	4812	2232	1502

MEASURES OF CENTRAL TENDENCY

A **measure of central tendency** for a set of numerical data is a single number that represents a "typical" value for the set. Three important measures of central tendency are the *mean*, the *median*, and the *mode*.

- The **mean**, or average, of a data set is the sum of the values in the set divided by the number of values in the set.

- The **median** of a data set with an odd number of values is the middle value when the values are written in numerical order. The median of a data set with an even number of values is the mean of the two middle values when the values are written in numerical order.

- The **mode** of a data set is the value or values in the set that occur most often. If no value occurs more often than any of the others, there is no mode.

EXAMPLE   Find the mean, median, and mode of the following data set.

$$10, 12, 7, 11, 20, 7, 8, 19, 9, 5$$

SOLUTION

To find the mean, divide the sum of the data values by the number of data values.

$$\text{Mean} = \frac{10 + 12 + 7 + 11 + 20 + 7 + 8 + 19 + 9 + 5}{10} = \frac{108}{10} = 10.8$$

Since there are an even number of values, find the median by writing the data values in numerical order and finding the mean of the two middle values.

$$5, 7, 7, 8, \mathbf{9}, \mathbf{10}, 11, 12, 19, 20 \qquad \text{Median} = \frac{9 + 10}{2} = \frac{19}{2} = 9.5$$

The mode is the number that occurs most often in the data set.

$$\text{Mode} = 7$$

Practice

Find the mean, median, and mode(s) of the data set.

1. 0, 0, 0, 0, 0, 1, 2, 2, 4, 4

2. 3, 1, 1, 8, 2, 1, 3, 5, 3

3. 10, 15, 20, 25, 30, 35, 40, 45, 50

4. 14, 10, 45, 38, 60, 14, 23, 35, 68, 50

5. 376, 376, 386, 393, 487, 598, 737, 745, 853

6. 101, 76, 52, 50, 26, 7, 13, 1000

PROBLEM SOLVING

One of your primary goals in mathematics should be to become a good problem solver. It will help to approach every problem with an organized plan.

STEP ❶ UNDERSTAND THE PROBLEM. Read the problem carefully. Organize the information you are given and decide what you need to find. Determine whether some of the information given is unnecessary, or whether enough information is given. Supply missing facts, if possible.

STEP ❷ MAKE A PLAN TO SOLVE THE PROBLEM. Choose a strategy. (Get ideas from the list given on page 782.) Choose the correct operations. Decide whether a graphing calculator or a computer is necessary.

STEP ❸ CARRY OUT THE PLAN TO SOLVE THE PROBLEM. Use the strategy and any technology you have chosen. Estimate before you calculate, if possible. Do any calculations that are needed. Answer the question that the problem asks.

STEP ❹ CHECK TO SEE IF YOUR ANSWER IS REASONABLE. Reread the problem and see if your answer agrees with the given information.

> **EXAMPLE** How many segments can be drawn between 7 points, no three of which lie on the same line?

❶ You are given a number of points, along with the information that no three points lie on the same line. You need to determine how many segments can be drawn between the points.

❷ Some strategies to consider are: draw a diagram, solve a simpler problem and look for a pattern.

❸ Consider the problem for fewer points.

| 2 points | 3 points | 4 points | 5 points |
| 1 segment | 3 segments | 6 segments | 10 segments |

Look for a pattern. Then continue the pattern to find the number of segments for 7 points.

Number of points	2	3	4	5	6	7
Number of segments	1	3	6	10	15	21

> *ANSWER* ▶ Given 7 points, no three of which lie on the same line, 21 segments can be drawn between the points.

❹ You can check your solution by making a sketch.

In **Step 2** of the problem solving plan, you may want to consider the following strategies.

PROBLEM SOLVING STRATEGIES

- **Guess, check, and revise.**   When you do not seem to have enough information.
- **Draw a diagram or a graph.**   When words describe a picture.
- **Make a table or an organized list.** When you have data or choices to organize.
- **Use an equation or a formula.**   When you know a relationship between quantities.
- **Use a proportion.**   When you know that two ratios are equal.
- **Look for a pattern.**   When you can examine several cases.
- **Break the problem into simpler parts.** When you have a multi-step problem.
- **Solve a simpler problem.**   When easier numbers help you understand a problem.
- **Work backward.**   When you are looking for a fact leading to a known result.

Practice

1. Tasha bought salads at $2.75 each and cartons of milk at $.80 each. The total cost was $16.15. How many of each did Tasha buy?

2. A rectangular garden is 45 feet long and has perimeter 150 feet. Rows of plants are planted 3 feet apart. Find the area of the garden.

3. If five turkey club sandwiches cost $18.75, how much would seven sandwiches cost?

4. How many diagonals can be drawn from one vertex of a 12-sided polygon?

5. Nguyen wants to arrive at school no later than 7:25 A.M. for his first class. It takes him 25 minutes to shower and dress, 15 minutes to eat breakfast, and at least 20 minutes to get to school. What time should he plan to get out of bed?

6. There are 32 players in a single-elimination chess tournament. That is, a player who loses once is eliminated. Assuming that no ties are allowed, how many games must be played to determine a champion?

7. Andrea, Betty, Joyce, Karen, and Paula are starters on their school basketball team. How many different groups of three can be chosen for a newspaper photo?

8. Carl has $135 in the bank and plans to save $5 per week. Jean has $90 in the bank and plans to save $10 per week. How many weeks will it be before Jean has at least as much in the bank as Carl?

9. The Peznolas are planning to use square tiles to tile a kitchen floor that is 18 feet long and 15 feet wide. Each tile covers one square foot. A carton of tiles costs $18. How much will it cost to cover the entire kitchen floor?

Extra Practice

Chapter 1

Evaluate the expression for the given value of the variable. *(Lesson 1.1)*

1. $15a$ when $a = 7$ **2.** $7 + x$ when $x = 15$ **3.** $\frac{c}{4}$ when $c = 32$

Evaluate the expression for the given value(s) of the variable(s). *(Lesson 1.2)*

4. $3y^2$ when $y = 5$ **5.** $(4x)^3$ when $x = 2$ **6.** $6x^4$ when $x = 4$

7. $a^4 - 5$ when $a = 3$ **8.** $(x + 2)^3$ when $x = 4$ **9.** $(c - d)^2$ when $c = 10$ and $d = 3$

Evaluate the expression. *(Lesson 1.3)*

10. $33 - 12 \div 4$ **11.** $10^2 \div 4 + 6$ **12.** $10^2 \div (4 + 6)$ **13.** $2 + 21 \div 3 - 6$

14. $3 + 7 \cdot 35 \div 5$ **15.** $15 \div (6 - 1) - 2$ **16.** $[(5 \cdot 8) + 8] \div 16$ **17.** $\dfrac{9 \cdot 7^2}{5 + 8^2 - 6}$

Use mental math to solve the equation. *(Lesson 1.4)*

18. $x + 7 = 13$ **19.** $n - 4 = 8$ **20.** $3y = 21$ **21.** $\frac{m}{4} = 6$

Check to see if the given value of the variable is or is not a solution of the inequality. *(Lesson 1.4)*

22. $y + 10 < 22;\ y = 12$ **23.** $6n \geq 25;\ n = 5$ **24.** $3t \leq 12;\ t = 4$

25. $4 + x \geq 11;\ x = 6$ **26.** $48 \div g < 4;\ g = 16$ **27.** $a - 5 > 3;\ a = 9$

Write the sentence as an equation or an inequality. Let *x* represent the number. *(Lesson 1.5)*

28. The product of a number and 4 is less than or equal to 36.

29. 16 is the difference of 20 and a number.

30. SPORTS Your friend's score in a game is 48. This is twice your score. Write a verbal model that relates your friend's score to your score. What is your score? *(Lesson 1.6)*

31. WIRELESS INDUSTRY The table shows the estimated number of cellular telephone subscribers (in millions) in the United States. Make a bar graph and a line graph of the data. *(Lesson 1.7)*

Year	1993	1994	1995	1996	1997	1998	1999
Subscribers (millions)	13	19	28	38	49	61	76

▶ Source: Cellular Telecommunications Industry Association

Make an input-output table for the function. Use 0, 1, 2, 3, 4, and 5 as values for *x*. *(Lesson 1.8)*

32. $y = 8 - 2x$ **33.** $y = 7x + 1$ **34.** $y = 3(x - 4)$

Chapter 2

Graph the numbers on a number line. Then write two inequalities that compare the numbers. *(Lesson 2.1)*

1. $-7, 8$ **2.** $3, -5$ **3.** $-4, -7$ **4.** $0, -3$

Evaluate the expression. *(Lesson 2.2)*

5. $|-3|$ **6.** $-|4|$ **7.** $|8.5|$ **8.** $\left|-\dfrac{3}{4}\right|$

Find the sum. *(Lesson 2.3)*

9. $-3 + 8$ **10.** $18 + 27$ **11.** $5 + (-7)$ **12.** $-4 + (-11)$

13. $-4 + 13 + (-6)$ **14.** $15 + (-12) + (-4)$ **15.** $-2 + (-9) + 8$ **16.** $17 + (-5) + 15$

Find the difference. *(Lesson 2.4)*

17. $-8 - 5$ **18.** $-3 - (-7)$ **19.** $4.1 - 6.3$ **20.** $-\dfrac{2}{5} - \dfrac{3}{5}$

21. $6 - 13$ **22.** $5 - (-2)$ **23.** $-10 - (-3.5)$ **24.** $-2 - 14$

Evaluate the expression. *(Lesson 2.4)*

25. $-6 - (-3) - 4$ **26.** $-15 - 4 - 12$ **27.** $2 - 5 - (-18)$

Find the product. *(Lesson 2.5)*

28. $-6(-7)$ **29.** $-5(90)$ **30.** $4(-1.5)$ **31.** $-14\left(-\dfrac{3}{7}\right)$

32. $(-4)^3$ **33.** $-(3)^4$ **34.** $-(-2)^5$ **35.** $3(-8)(-2)$

WHALES In Exercises 36 and 37, suppose a whale is diving at a rate of about 6 feet per second. *(Lesson 2.5)*

36. Write an algebraic model for the displacement d (in feet) of the whale after t seconds.

37. What is the whale's change in position after diving for 15 seconds?

Use the distributive property to rewrite the expression without parentheses. *(Lesson 2.6)*

38. $6(y + 5)$ **39.** $4(a - 6)$ **40.** $(3 + w)2$ **41.** $(4x + 3)2$

42. $-3(r - 5)$ **43.** $-(2 + t)$ **44.** $(x + 4)(-6)$ **45.** $(y - 3)1.5$

Simplify the expression by combining like terms if possible. If not possible, write *already simplified*. *(Lesson 2.7)*

46. $3x + 7x$ **47.** $8r - r^2$ **48.** $6 + 2y - 3$

49. $w + 2w + 4w - 4$ **50.** $7 + 5r - 6 + 4r$ **51.** $m^2 + 3m - 2m^2 - m$

Find the quotient. *(Lesson 2.8)*

52. $18 \div (-2)$ **53.** $-48 \div 12$ **54.** $16 \div \left(-\dfrac{4}{5}\right)$ **55.** $\dfrac{-22}{-\frac{1}{3}}$

Chapter 3

Solve the equation. *(Lesson 3.1)*

1. $y - 6 = 8$ **2.** $5 + n = -10$ **3.** $3 = r - 14$ **4.** $-4 = 5 + q$

5. $8 = x - (-1)$ **6.** $t - 4 = -7$ **7.** $m + 6 = 9$ **8.** $-2 = r - (-5)$

Use division to solve the equation. *(Lesson 3.2)*

9. $7x = 35$ **10.** $-15m = 150$ **11.** $6a = 3$ **12.** $-144 = -12t$

Use multiplication to solve the equation. *(Lesson 3.2)*

13. $\dfrac{x}{5} = -4$ **14.** $\dfrac{y}{10} = -\dfrac{2}{5}$ **15.** $-\dfrac{g}{6} = -14$ **16.** $\dfrac{t}{-8} = -\dfrac{3}{8}$

Solve the equation. *(Lesson 3.3)*

17. $6x + 8 = 32$ **18.** $2x - 1 = 11$ **19.** $4m + 8m - 2 = 22$

20. $2x - 3(x + 4) = -1$ **21.** $\dfrac{1}{3}(m - 1) = -5$ **22.** $\dfrac{2}{5}(n + 3) = 4$

Solve the equation. *(Lesson 3.4)*

23. $-6 + 5x = 8x - 9$ **24.** $8r + 1 = 23 - 3r$ **25.** $2w + 3 = 3w + 1$

26. $3a + 12 = 4a - 2a + 1$ **27.** $5x + 6 = 2x + x + 2$ **28.** $6d - 2d = 10d + 6$

Solve the equation. *(Lesson 3.5)*

29. $4(a + 3) = 3(a + 5)$ **30.** $8(r - 2) + 6 = 2(r + 1)$

31. $6(x - 1) = 5(2x + 3) - 15$ **32.** $\dfrac{1}{2}(4q + 12) = 2 + 3(6 - q)$

Solve the equation. Round the result to the nearest hundredth. Check the rounded solution. *(Lesson 3.6)*

33. $-26x - 59 = 135$ **34.** $18.25d - 4.15 = 2.75d$ **35.** $2.3 - 4.8w = 8.2w + 5.6$

In Exercises 36 and 37, use the distance formula $d = rt$. *(Lesson 3.7)*

36. Solve the formula for rate r.

37. You ride your bike for 3 hours and travel 36 miles. Use the formula you wrote in Exercise 36 to find your average speed.

Find the unit rate. *(Lesson 3.8)*

38. 33 ounces in 6 cans of juice   **39.** Earn $50.75 for working 7 hours

40. Hike 10.5 miles in 3 hours   **41.** 16 grams of protein in 8 granola bars

Solve the percent problem. *(Lesson 3.9)*

42. How much money is 40% of $800?   **43.** 15% of 320 meters is what length?

44. 24 is what percent of 60?   **45.** What number is 30% of 150?

Chapter 4

Plot and label the ordered pairs in a coordinate plane. *(Lesson 4.1)*

1. $A(2, 4)$, $B(-2, 0)$, $C(5, -2)$ **2.** $A(4, 4)$, $B(0, -2)$, $C(-3, -3)$ **3.** $A(4, -4)$, $B(2.5, 5)$, $C(-3, 2)$

4. $A(0, -1)$, $B(1, -3)$, $C(3, 1)$ **5.** $A(-4, -2)$, $B(-2, 4)$, $C(4, 0)$ **6.** $A(-3, -4)$, $B(1, -1)$, $C(-1, 1)$

Use a table of values to graph the equation. *(Lesson 4.2)*

7. $y = 5x + 1$ **8.** $y = -2x + 4$ **9.** $4x + y = -8$ **10.** $2y - x = -1$

11. $y - 2x = -5$ **12.** $y = 3x - 1$ **13.** $y = -2x + 1$ **14.** $5y - 10x = 20$

Graph the equation. *(Lesson 4.3)*

15. $y = -2$ **16.** $x = 3$ **17.** $x = -\dfrac{1}{2}$ **18.** $y = 5$

Find the *x*-intercept of the line. *(Lesson 4.4)*

19. $5x + y = -5$ **20.** $2x - y = 6$ **21.** $6y + 2x = 12$ **22.** $8x + 2y = -16$

Find the *y*-intercept of the line. *(Lesson 4.4)*

23. $y = 2x - 5$ **24.** $y = 2x + 14$ **25.** $y = 6 - 3x$ **26.** $10x - 15y = 30$

Find the slope of the line that passes through the points. *(Lesson 4.5)*

27. $(6, 1)$ and $(-4, 1)$ **28.** $(2, 2)$ and $(-1, 4)$ **29.** $(-4, 2)$ and $(-3, -5)$

30. $(4, 5)$ and $(2, 2)$ **31.** $(3, 6)$ and $(3, -1)$ **32.** $(0, 6)$ and $(3, 0)$

In Exercises 33–40, the variables *x* and *y* vary directly. Use the given values to write an equation that relates *x* and *y*. *(Lesson 4.6)*

33. $x = 6$, $y = 18$ **34.** $x = 4$, $y = 1$ **35.** $x = 8$, $y = -7$ **36.** $x = -1$, $y = -20$

37. $x = -2$, $y = -2$ **38.** $x = 8$, $y = -4$ **39.** $x = 2$, $y = -6$ **40.** $x = 5$, $y = 2$

Write the equation in slope-intercept form. Then graph the equation. *(Lesson 4.7)*

41. $x - y = 1$ **42.** $-3x + 2y = 6$ **43.** $x + y + 4 = 0$

44. $2x - 4y + 6 = 0$ **45.** $2x + 2y + 2 = 4y$ **46.** $5x - 3y + 2 = 14 - 4x$

Determine whether the relation is a function. If it is a function, give the domain and the range. *(Lesson 4.8)*

47.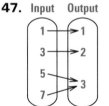

48.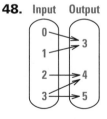

49.

Input	Output
4	-2
0	0
4	2
2	4

Chapter 5

Write in slope-intercept form the equation of the line described below.
(Lesson 5.1)

1. $m = 2, b = 1$ **2.** $m = -3, b = -2$ **3.** $m = \frac{1}{2}, b = -3$ **4.** $m = -4, b = 0$

Write in point-slope form the equation of the line that passes through the given point and has the given slope. *(Lesson 5.2)*

5. $(-1, 0), m = 3$ **6.** $(5, 2), m = -2$ **7.** $(3, 6), m = 0$ **8.** $(-2, 1), m = -5$

9. $(-3, -1), m = 4$ **10.** $(1, 5), m = 8$ **11.** $(2, -1), m = \frac{1}{2}$ **12.** $(-4, 3), m = -\frac{1}{3}$

Write in slope-intercept form the equation of the line that passes through the given points. *(Lesson 5.3)*

13. $(3, -2)$ and $(5, 4)$ **14.** $(5, 1)$ and $(0, -6)$ **15.** $(-2, -1)$ and $(4, -4)$

16. $(-1, 7)$ and $(5, 7)$ **17.** $(-3, 5)$ and $(-6, 8)$ **18.** $(5, 2)$ and $(1, 4)$

Write in standard form an equation of the line that passes through the given point and has the given slope. *(Lesson 5.4)*

19. $(5, -2), m = 3$ **20.** $(-2, 5), m = 5$ **21.** $(-4, 3), m = -\frac{5}{6}$ **22.** $(5, 7), m = \frac{3}{4}$

23. $(0, 8), m = -7$ **24.** $(-1, -7), m = 4$ **25.** $(3, 6), m = -2$ **26.** $(4, 5), m = -5$

In Exercises 27–29, use the following information. You buy $10.00 worth of apples and oranges. The apples cost $.80 a pound and the oranges cost $1.00 a pound. *(Lesson 5.5)*

27. Write an equation in standard form that represents the different amounts (in pounds) of apples A and oranges R that you could buy.

28. Copy the table. Then use the linear equation to complete the table.

Pounds of apples, A	0	1	2	3	4	5
Pounds of oranges, R	?	?	?	?	?	?

29. Plot the points from the table and sketch the line.

Determine whether the lines are perpendicular. *(Lesson 5.6)*

30. $y = x - 2, y = -x + 4$ **31.** $y = \frac{1}{4}x - 5, y = -\frac{1}{4}x + 5$

32. $y = \frac{1}{2}x - 1, y = -2x + 2$ **33.** $3y = -2x + 12, y = -\frac{3}{2}x - 12$

Write in slope-intercept form the equation of the line passing through the given point and perpendicular to the given line. *(Lesson 5.6)*

34. $(1, 2), y = x + 2$ **35.** $(-1, 4), y = \frac{3}{4}x - 1$ **36.** $(3, -2), y = 1$

Chapter 6

Solve the inequality. Then graph the solution. *(Lesson 6.1)*

1. $x + 1 < 2$ 　　　　**2.** $r + 5 > -4$ 　　　　**3.** $3 \geq y - 4$ 　　　　**4.** $8 + t \leq -2$

Solve the inequality. Then graph the solution. *(Lesson 6.2)*

5. $9x \geq 36$ 　　　　**6.** $5w < -15$ 　　　　**7.** $\dfrac{k}{9} \leq 2$ 　　　　**8.** $-\dfrac{2}{3}n > 4$

Solve the inequality. *(Lesson 6.3)*

9. $2x + 5 > 3$ 　　　　　　**10.** $-3x - 7 < 2$ 　　　　　　**11.** $4(x + 5) \geq 10$

12. $3x + 8 \geq -2x + 3$ 　　　**13.** $4(x - 2) \leq 3x + 1$ 　　　**14.** $-(x + 5) < -4x - 11$

Write an inequality that represents the statement. Then graph the inequality. *(Lesson 6.4)*

15. x is greater than -5 and less than 2.

16. x is greater than or equal to 4 and less than 6.

17. x is less than or equal to 5 and greater than -3.

18. x is less than 6 and greater than or equal to -1.

Solve the inequality. Then graph the solution. *(Lesson 6.4)*

19. $3 \leq x + 4 < 8$ 　　**20.** $-36 < 6x < 12$ 　　**21.** $-2 < 2x - 4 \leq 10$ 　　**22.** $0 \leq 5x - 6 < 9$

Solve the inequality. Then graph the solution. *(Lesson 6.5)*

23. $x - 3 \leq -2 \text{ or } x + 2 > 6$ 　　　　　**24.** $x + 1 > 4 \text{ or } 2x + 3 \leq 5$

25. $2x + 1 > 9 \text{ or } 3x - 5 < 4$ 　　　　　**26.** $-4x + 1 \geq 17 \text{ or } 5x - 4 > 6$

Solve the equation and check your solutions. If the equation has no solution, write *no solution*. *(Lesson 6.6)*

27. $|x| = 14$ 　　　　　**28.** $|x| = -10$ 　　　　　**29.** $|x| = 12$

30. $|5x| = 15$ 　　　　**31.** $|10 + x| = 4$ 　　　　**32.** $|x - 8| = 2$

33. $|5x - 3| = 2$ 　　　**34.** $|2x + 3| = 9$ 　　　　**35.** $|x - 4| + 4 = 7$

Solve the inequality. Then graph and check the solution. *(Lesson 6.7)*

36. $|x| \geq 2$ 　　　　　**37.** $|x| \leq 8$ 　　　　　**38.** $|x - 5| < 10$

39. $|6x| \leq 30$ 　　　　**40.** $|4 + x| > 8$ 　　　　**41.** $|4x + 5| \geq 3$

42. $|10 - 4x| \leq 2$ 　　　**43.** $|6x - 5| + 1 < 8$ 　　　**44.** $|3x + 4| - 6 \geq 14$

Graph the inequality in a coordinate plane. *(Lesson 6.8)*

45. $y \geq -2$ 　　　　**46.** $x - y \leq 0$ 　　　　**47.** $x + y \geq 5$ 　　　　**48.** $4y + x < 4$

49. $x - 3y \leq 0$ 　　　**50.** $3y - 2x < 6$ 　　　**51.** $5x - 3y > 9$ 　　　**52.** $2y - x > 10$

Chapter 7

Estimate the solution of the linear system graphically. Then check the solution algebraically. *(Lesson 7.1)*

1. $y = 5$
$x = -2$

2. $x = 0$
$y = 3x + 7$

3. $x + y = 10$
$x - y = -2$

4. $-2x + 4y = 12$
$5x - 2y = 10$

Use the substitution method to solve the linear system. *(Lesson 7.2)*

5. $x = 5y$
$2x + 3y = -13$

6. $y = -2x$
$x + y = 7$

7. $x + y = 9$
$x - y = 3$

8. $2a + 3b = 3$
$a - 6b = -6$

9. $-s - t = -5$
$3s + 4t = 16$

10. $5x - 8y = -17$
$3x - y = 5$

11. $2m + n = 7$
$4m + 3n = -1$

12. $5a + b = 4$
$7a + 5b = 11$

Use linear combinations to solve the linear system. Then check your solution. *(Lesson 7.3)*

13. $x + y = 6$
$x - y = 2$

14. $3x + 3y = 6$
$2x - 3y = 4$

15. $4x - 5y = 10$
$2x + 5y = -10$

16. $2x + 8y = 9$
$x - y = 0$

17. $-x + y = -15$
$x + 4y = 5$

18. $2x + 3y = 15$
$3y + 5x = 12$

19. $y = 2x - 3$
$3x - 5y = 1$

20. $-4x - 15 = 5y$
$2y = 11 - 5x$

Choose a solution method to solve the linear system. Explain your choice, and then solve the system. *(Lesson 7.4)*

21. $x - 2y = -10$
$3x + y = 5$

22. $5x + 3y = 15$
$4x - 3y = 12$

23. $y = -2x - 6$
$y = -4$

24. $x + y = 8$
$x - y = 4$

25. $2x - 3y = 6$
$x + y = 3$

26. $2x + y = -8$
$6x + y = -2$

27. $5x - y = 10$
$2x + y = 4$

28. $-4x + 3y = 1$
$-8x + 4y = -4$

29. STUDENT THEATER You sell 20 tickets for admission to your school play and collect a total of $104. Admission prices are $6 for adults and $4 for students. How many of each type of ticket did you sell? *(Lesson 7.4)*

Use the graphing method to tell how many solutions the system has. *(Lesson 7.5)*

30. $x + y = 4$
$2x + 3y = 9$

31. $x + y = 6$
$3x + 3y = 3$

32. $x + 2y = 5$
$3x - 15 = -6y$

33. $12x - y = 5$
$-8x + y = -5$

34. $y = -3x$
$6y - x = 38$

35. $2x - 3y = 3$
$6x - 9y = 9$

36. $3x + 6 = 7y$
$x + 2y = 11$

37. $3x - 8y = 4$
$6x - 42 = 16y$

Graph the system of linear inequalities. *(Lesson 7.6)*

38. $y \geq 0$
$x \leq 0$

39. $y > x + 1$
$y < x + 3$

40. $x \geq 1$
$y + x \leq 5$

41. $y + 2 < -x$
$2y - 4 > 3x$

42. $x < 5$
$x \geq 1$
$y \geq -2$
$y < 7$

43. $y > x - 4$
$y \geq -x - 1$
$y \leq 0$

44. $y > x - 3$
$y < x + 2$
$x \leq 3$

45. $3x - 1 < 5$
$-x + y \leq 10$
$-5x + 2 < 12$

Chapter 8

Simplify the expression. *(Lesson 8.1)*

1. $7^2 \cdot 7^3$

2. $(2^3)^4$

3. $(12x)^3$

4. $(-3cd)^4$

5. $(m^3)^2$

6. $(4r)^2 \cdot r$

7. $(7x^2)^2 \cdot 2x^3$

8. $(3x)^3(-5y)^2$

Rewrite as an expression with positive exponents. *(Lesson 8.2)*

9. x^{-4}

10. $2x^{-2}$

11. $x^{-3}y^{-2}$

12. $\dfrac{2}{x^{-2}}$

13. $\dfrac{4x}{y^{-5}}$

14. $\dfrac{3y^{-3}}{x^{-1}}$

15. $(4y^{-2})^2$

16. $\dfrac{2}{(5x)^{-2}}$

Graph the exponential function. *(Lesson 8.3)*

17. $y = 5^x$

18. $y = -3^x$

19. $y = \left(\dfrac{1}{4}\right)^x$

20. $y = 2\left(\dfrac{1}{3}\right)^x$

Simplify the quotient. *(Lesson 8.4)*

21. $\dfrac{2^{11}}{2^8}$

22. $x^5 \cdot \dfrac{1}{x^4}$

23. $\left(\dfrac{2}{3}\right)^4$

24. $\left(\dfrac{x}{4}\right)^{-2}$

25. $\dfrac{(-4)^2}{(-4)^5}$

26. $\dfrac{a^3}{a^4}$

27. $\left(\dfrac{3}{8}\right)^{-1}$

28. $\left(\dfrac{4}{x}\right)^3$

Simplify the expression. Use only positive exponents. *(Lesson 8.4)*

29. $\dfrac{2x^4y^2}{xy} \cdot \dfrac{3x^2y}{4x}$

30. $\dfrac{16r^5s^9}{-2rs^2} \cdot \dfrac{r^2s}{-8}$

31. $\left(\dfrac{3x^2z^4}{2xz}\right)^3$

32. $\dfrac{3x^2y}{2x} \cdot \dfrac{2y^2}{x^2y}$

33. $\dfrac{4a^{-1}b^3}{a^4b^{-2}} \cdot \left(\dfrac{3a}{ab}\right)^{-2}$

34. $\dfrac{(a^2)^4}{(a^5)^4}$

Write the number in decimal form. *(Lesson 8.5)*

35. 4.813×10^{-6}

36. 3.11×10^4

37. 8.4162×10^{-2}

38. 9.43×10^0

39. 5.0645×10^1

40. 1.2468×10^{-3}

41. 2.34×10^{-8}

42. 6.09013×10^{10}

Write the number in scientific notation. *(Lesson 8.5)*

43. 5280

44. 0.0378

45. 11.38

46. $33,000,000$

47. 827.66

48. 0.208054

49. 16.354

50. 0.000891

51. 3.95

52. 78.4

53. 0.008

54. $67,000$

INTEREST You deposit $1100 in an account that pays 5% interest compounded yearly. Find the balance at the end of the given time period. *(Lesson 8.6)*

55. 1 year

56. 10 years

57. 15 years

58. 25 years

59. DEPRECIATION A piece of equipment originally costs $120,000. Its value decreases at a rate of 10% per year. Write an exponential decay model to represent the decreasing value of the piece of equipment. *(Lesson 8.7)*

Chapter 9

Evaluate the expression. Give the exact value if possible. Otherwise, approximate to the nearest hundredth. *(Lesson 9.1)*

1. $\sqrt{3}$

2. $\sqrt{625}$

3. $-\sqrt{100}$

4. $\pm\sqrt{676}$

5. $\sqrt{15}$

6. $-\sqrt{125}$

7. $\sqrt{220}$

8. $\pm\sqrt{90}$

Solve the equation or write *no solution*. Write the solutions as integers if possible. Otherwise, write them as radical expressions. *(Lesson 9.2)*

9. $x^2 = 25$

10. $4x^2 - 8 = 0$

11. $x^2 = -16$

12. $x^2 + 1 = 1$

13. $3x^2 - 48 = 0$

14. $6x^2 + 6 = 4$

15. $2x^2 - 6 = 0$

16. $x^2 - 4 = -3$

17. FALLING OBJECT A ball is dropped from a bridge 80 feet above a river. How long will it take for the ball to hit the surface of the water? Round your solution to the nearest tenth. *(Lesson 9.2)*

Simplify the expression. *(Lesson 9.3)*

18. $\sqrt{60}$

19. $\sqrt{88}$

20. $\sqrt{250}$

21. $\sqrt{112}$

22. $\sqrt{\dfrac{11}{16}}$

23. $\dfrac{\sqrt{20}}{\sqrt{5}}$

24. $2\sqrt{\dfrac{9}{2}}$

25. $\dfrac{1}{3}\sqrt{27}$

Sketch the graph of the function. Label the coordinates of the vertex. *(Lesson 9.4)*

26. $y = 3x^2$

27. $y = x^2 - 4$

28. $y = -x^2 - 2x$

29. $y = x^2 - 6x + 8$

30. $y = 4x^2 + 4x - 5$

31. $y = x^2 - 2x + 3$

32. $y = -x^2 + 3x + 2$

33. $y = -3x^2 + 12x - 1$

Solve the equation algebraically. Check your solution by graphing. *(Lesson 9.5)*

34. $x^2 - 6x = -5x$

35. $x^2 + 5x = -6$

36. $x^2 - 3x = 4$

37. $x^2 + 3x = 10$

38. $x^2 - 9 = 0$

39. $-2x^2 + 4x + 6 = 0$

Write the quadratic equation in standard form. Then solve using the quadratic formula. *(Lesson 9.6)*

40. $x^2 + x = 12$

41. $x^2 - 12 = 4x$

42. $3x^2 + 11x = 4$

43. $-x^2 + 5x = 4$

44. $x^2 - 3x - 4 = -6$

45. $-x^2 - 5x = 6$

46. $x^2 - 8 = 7x$

47. $10 - 2x^2 = -x$

Determine whether the equation has *two solutions*, *one solution*, or *no real solution*. *(Lesson 9.7)*

48. $3x^2 + 14x - 5 = 0$

49. $4x^2 + 12x + 9 = 0$

50. $x^2 + 10x + 9 = 0$

51. $2x^2 + 8x + 8 = 0$

52. $5x^2 + 125 = 0$

53. $x^2 - 2x + 35 = 0$

54. $2x^2 - x - 3 = 0$

55. $-3x^2 + 5x - 6 = 0$

Sketch the graph of the inequality. *(Lesson 9.8)*

56. $y > -x^2 + 4$

57. $y \geq 4x^2$

58. $y < 5x^2 + 10x$

59. $y \leq -x^2 + 4x + 5$

Chapter 10

Use a vertical format or a horizontal format to add or subtract. *(Lesson 10.1)*

1. $(7x^2 - 4) + (x^2 + 5)$

2. $(3x^2 - 2) - (2x - 6x^2)$

3. $(8x^2 - 3x + 7) + (6x^2 - 4x + 1)$

4. $(-z^3 + 3z) + (-z^2 - 4z - 6)$ **5.** $(5x^2 + 7x - 4) - (4x^2 - 2x)$ **6.** $(3a + 2a^4 - 5) - (a^3 + 2a^4 + 5a)$

Find the product. *(Lesson 10.2)*

7. $x(4x^2 - 8x + 7)$

8. $-3x(x^2 + 5x - 5)$

9. $5b^2(3b^3 - 2b^2 + 1)$

10. $(t + 9)(2t + 1)$

11. $(d - 1)(d + 5)$

12. $(3z + 4)(5z - 8)$

13. $(x + 3)(x^2 - 2x + 6)$ **14.** $(3 + 2s - s^2)(s - 1)$

Find the product. *(Lesson 10.3)*

15. $(x + 9)^2$

16. $(-c - d)^2$

17. $(a - 2)(a + 2)$

18. $(-7 + m)(-7 - m)$

19. $(4x + 5)^2$

20. $(5p - 6q)^2$

21. $(2a + 3b)(2a - 3b)$ **22.** $(10x - 5y)(10x + 5y)$

Solve the equation. *(Lesson 10.4)*

23. $(x + 3)(x + 6) = 0$ **24.** $(x - 11)^2 = 0$

25. $(z - 1)(z + 5) = 0$ **26.** $w(w - 4) = 0$

27. $(6n - 9)(n - 7) = 0$ **28.** $3(x + 2)^2 = 0$

29. $(2d - 2)(4d - 8) = 0$ **30.** $x(3x + 1) = 0$

Find the *x*-intercepts and the vertex of the graph of the function. Then sketch the graph of the function. *(Lesson 10.4)*

31. $y = (x - 8)(x - 6)$ **32.** $y = (x + 4)(x - 4)$ **33.** $y = (x - 5)(x - 7)$ **34.** $y = (x + 1)(x + 6)$

35. $y = (-x + 5)(x - 9)$ **36.** $y = (-x + 1)(x + 5)$ **37.** $y = (x - 3)(x + 1)$ **38.** $y = (-x - 3)(x + 7)$

Solve the equation by factoring. *(Lesson 10.5)*

39. $x^2 + 6x + 9 = 0$ **40.** $x^2 + 2x - 35 = 0$ **41.** $x^2 - 12x = -36$ **42.** $-x^2 - 4x = 3$

43. $x^2 - 15x = -54$ **44.** $-x^2 + 14x = 48$ **45.** $x^2 - 2x = 24$ **46.** $x^2 - 5x + 4 = 0$

Solve the equation by factoring. *(Lesson 10.6)*

47. $2x^2 + x - 6 = 0$ **48.** $2x^2 + 7x = -3$ **49.** $9x^2 + 24x = -16$ **50.** $20x^2 + 23x + 6 = 0$

51. $4x^2 - 5x = 6$ **52.** $3x^2 - 5 = -14x$ **53.** $3x^2 - 17x = 56$ **54.** $12x^2 + 46x - 36 = 0$

Factor the expression. *(Lesson 10.7)*

55. $x^2 - 1$

56. $9b^2 - 81$

57. $121 - x^2$

58. $12 - 27x^2$

59. $t^2 + 2t + 1$

60. $x^2 + 20x + 100$

61. $64y^2 + 48y + 9$

62. $20x^2 - 100x + 125$

Factor the expression completely. *(Lesson 10.8)*

63. $x^4 - 9x^2$

64. $m^3 + 11m^2 + 28m$

65. $x^4 + 4x^3 - 45x^2$

66. $x^3 + 2x^2 - 4x - 8$

67. $-3y^3 - 15y^2 - 12y$ **68.** $x^3 - x^2 + 4x - 4$

69. $7x^6 - 21x^4$

70. $8t^3 - 3t^2 + 16t - 6$

71. GEOMETRY The width of a box is 2 feet less than the length. The height is 8 feet greater than the length. The box has a cubic volume of 96 cubic feet. What are the dimensions of the box? *(Lesson 10.8)*

Chapter 11

Solve the equation. Check your solutions. *(Lesson 11.1)*

1. $\dfrac{9}{m} = \dfrac{15}{10}$

2. $\dfrac{x}{2} = \dfrac{8}{x}$

3. $\dfrac{3}{5} = \dfrac{x+2}{6}$

4. $\dfrac{12}{8} = \dfrac{5+t}{t-3}$

5. $\dfrac{c^2 - 16}{c+4} = \dfrac{c-4}{3}$

6. $\dfrac{x+15}{16} = \dfrac{-9}{x-10}$

The variables *x* and *y* vary directly. Use the given values to write an equation that relates *x* and *y*. *(Lesson 11.2)*

7. $x = 4, y = 12$

8. $x = 5, y = 10$

9. $x = 16, y = 4$

10. $x = 21, y = 7$

The variables *x* and *y* vary inversely. Use the given values to write an equation that relates *x* and *y*. *(Lesson 11.2)*

11. $x = 3, y = 5$

12. $x = 7, y = 1$

13. $x = 4, y = \dfrac{1}{2}$

14. $x = 5.5, y = 6$

Simplify the expression. If not possible, write *already in simplest form*. *(Lesson 11.3)*

15. $\dfrac{12x^4}{42x}$

16. $\dfrac{5x^2 - 15x^3}{10x}$

17. $\dfrac{x+6}{x^2 + 7x + 6}$

18. $\dfrac{x^2 - 8x + 15}{x-3}$

19. $\dfrac{8x^2}{12x^3}$

20. $\dfrac{6}{x+2}$

21. $\dfrac{4-y}{y^2 - 16}$

22. $\dfrac{x^2 - 9x + 18}{x^2 - 4x - 12}$

Write the product in simplest form. *(Lesson 11.4)*

23. $\dfrac{3x}{5} \cdot \dfrac{15}{18x}$

24. $\dfrac{z^2 + 5z + 6}{z^2 + z} \cdot \dfrac{z}{z+3}$

25. $\dfrac{10x^2}{x^2 - 25} \cdot (x-5)$

Write the quotient in simplest form. *(Lesson 11.4)*

26. $\dfrac{1}{4x} \div \dfrac{6x}{16}$

27. $\dfrac{5x}{x^2 - 6x + 9} \div \dfrac{x}{x-3}$

28. $\dfrac{x^2 + 5x - 36}{x^2 - 81} \div (x^2 - 16)$

Simplify the expression. *(Lesson 11.5)*

29. $\dfrac{3}{5x} + \dfrac{2}{5x}$

30. $\dfrac{3x}{x+2} + \dfrac{4x-1}{x+2}$

31. $\dfrac{x}{x-1} - \dfrac{3x+2}{x-1}$

32. $\dfrac{6x}{2x-1} - \dfrac{3}{2x-1}$

Simplify the expression. *(Lesson 11.6)*

33. $\dfrac{5}{x^2} - \dfrac{3}{x}$

34. $\dfrac{8}{3x} - \dfrac{x+2}{9x^2}$

35. $\dfrac{x-1}{x+8} + \dfrac{4}{x-3}$

36. $\dfrac{x+1}{3x^2} + \dfrac{3}{4x}$

37. $\dfrac{5x+3}{x^2 - 25} + \dfrac{5}{x-5}$

38. $\dfrac{4x-1}{3x+2} - \dfrac{3x}{x-4}$

Solve the equation. Check your solutions. *(Lesson 11.7)*

39. $\dfrac{4}{x} = \dfrac{3}{25}$

40. $\dfrac{1}{x-3} = \dfrac{5}{x+9}$

41. $\dfrac{-2}{3x} = \dfrac{4+x}{6}$

42. $\dfrac{4}{x} + \dfrac{2}{3} = \dfrac{6}{x}$

43. $\dfrac{x}{x-5} - \dfrac{11}{x-5} = 7$

44. $\dfrac{5}{x-1} + 1 = \dfrac{4}{x^2 + 3x - 4}$

Chapter 12

Find the domain of the function. Then sketch its graph and find the range. *(Lesson 12.1)*

1. $y = 8\sqrt{x}$ **2.** $y = \sqrt{5x}$ **3.** $y = \sqrt{x} - 5$ **4.** $y = \sqrt{x} + 1$

5. $y = \sqrt{x - 2}$ **6.** $y = \sqrt{x + 3}$ **7.** $y = \sqrt{3x + 2}$ **8.** $y = \sqrt{4x - 3}$

Simplify the expression. *(Lesson 12.2)*

9. $3\sqrt{5} + 2\sqrt{5}$ **10.** $8\sqrt{7} - 15\sqrt{7}$ **11.** $2\sqrt{8} + 3\sqrt{32}$ **12.** $\sqrt{20} - \sqrt{45} + \sqrt{80}$

13. $\sqrt{3}(7 - \sqrt{6})$ **14.** $(4 + \sqrt{10})^2$ **15.** $\dfrac{4}{\sqrt{24}}$ **16.** $\dfrac{3}{5 - \sqrt{2}}$

Solve the equation. Check for extraneous solutions. *(Lesson 12.3)*

17. $\sqrt{x} - 11 = 0$ **18.** $\sqrt{2x - 1} + 4 = 7$ **19.** $\sqrt{x} + 10 = 2$

20. $12 = \sqrt{3x + 1} + 7$ **21.** $x = \sqrt{4x - 3}$ **22.** $4\sqrt{x} + 5 = 21$

Evaluate the expression. *(Lesson 12.4)*

23. $4^{2/3} \cdot 4^{4/3}$ **24.** $(27^{1/2})^{2/3}$ **25.** $(8^{1/4})^8$ **26.** $(2^2 \cdot 3^2)^{1/2}$

Simplify the variable expression. *(Lesson 12.4)*

27. $x^{1/4} \cdot x^{1/2}$ **28.** $(x^2)^{1/4}$ **29.** $(x \cdot y^{1/3})^6 \cdot \sqrt{y}$ **30.** $(x \cdot x^{1/3})^{3/4}$

Solve the quadratic equation by completing the square. *(Lesson 12.5)*

31. $x^2 + 10x = 56$ **32.** $x^2 + 2x = 3$ **33.** $x^2 + 6x + 8 = 0$

34. $x^2 - 12x = 13$ **35.** $x^2 - 6x = 16$ **36.** $x^2 - 10x - 39 = 0$

Find the missing length of the right triangle if *a* and *b* are the lengths of the legs and *c* is the length of the hypotenuse. *(Lesson 12.6)*

37. $a = 1, b = 1$ **38.** $a = 1, c = 2$ **39.** $b = 6, c = 10$

40. $a = 7, b = 10$ **41.** $b = 15, c = 25$ **42.** $a = 30, c = 50$

Find the distance between the two points. Round your solution to the nearest hundredth if necessary. *(Lesson 12.7)*

43. $(7, -6), (-1, -6)$ **44.** $(5, 2), (5, -4)$ **45.** $(12, -7), (-4, 2)$ **46.** $(-4, -5), (-8, 9)$

47. $(5, 8), (0, -3)$ **48.** $(10, -1), (4, 11)$ **49.** $(-3, -8), (-1, -4)$ **50.** $(12, 11), (9, 15)$

Find the midpoint of the line segment connecting the given points. Then show that the midpoint is the same distance from each point. *(Lesson 12.8)*

51. $(0, 4), (4, 5)$ **52.** $(-3, 3), (6, -1)$ **53.** $(1, 0), (4, -4)$ **54.** $(0, 0), (3, -2)$

55. $(-2, 0), (2, 8)$ **56.** $(3, 7), (-5, -9)$ **57.** $(6, 2), (4, 10)$ **58.** $(4, -6), (-8, 3)$

59. INDIRECT PROOF Use an indirect proof to prove that the following conclusion is true. If $xy = 0$, then either $x = 0$ or $y = 0$. *(Lesson 12.9)*

End-of-Course Test

VARIABLES, EXPRESSIONS, AND PROPERTIES

Evaluate the variable expression when $a = 7$, $b = 2$, $c = -4$, and $d = 1$.

1. $a^2 - 3b + bc$

2. $|c + d|$

3. $-d - (-c)$

4. $-6\left(\frac{2}{3}\right)(d)$

5. $\frac{b - c}{d}$

6. $a(b + 2d)$

7. $c^3 d$

8. $5(2^{-4})$

Simplify the expression. Name each property that you used.

9. $-ab + ba$

10. $0 + \sqrt{2}$

11. $5(x + 4)$

12. $-1 \cdot n + 0 \cdot n$

13. $7^{-3} \cdot 7^5 \cdot 7^3$

14. $(2y^2)^4$

15. $\frac{a^6}{a^9}$

16. $\left(\frac{3}{x}\right)^{-3}$

LINEAR EQUATIONS AND INEQUALITIES

Solve the equation or inequality.

17. $4s - 6 = 18$

18. $0.2b - 1.3 \geq 6.7$

19. $\frac{1}{3}p - 1 < 11$

20. $4m - 2(5 - m) = 14$

21. $9 + \frac{1}{2}k = 14$

22. $7(a + 5) = -(2a + 1)$

23. $0.15x + 5.01 = 1.44$

24. $-7 > 5 - 2y$

25. $0 \leq 1 - c \leq \frac{2}{3}$

26. $4t < -12$ or $-t < -4$

27. $|2 - x| = 1$

28. $|2n + 5| > 3$

LINEAR SYSTEMS

Solve the system of linear equations. Then check your solution.

29. $4x - y = 6$
$x + 3y = 8$

30. $5p + 3q = 4$
$7p + 2q = 21$

31. $6a - 9b = 18$
$b = \frac{2}{3}a + 2$

Graph the system of linear inequalities.

32. $2x + 3y > -6$
$y \geq 3x - 13$

33. $x + 4y > 0$
$y \geq 0$

34. $3x - y \geq 1$
$y \geq x$

QUADRATIC EQUATIONS AND INEQUALITIES

Solve the quadratic equation. Write the exact solution.

35. $a^2 + 5 = 37$ **36.** $x^2 + 2x = 35$ **37.** $2v^2 - 6v - 9 = 0$

38. Sketch the graph of $y < x^2 + 3x$.

POLYNOMIALS AND FACTORING

Add, subtract, or multiply.

39. $(t^2 + 3t - 2) - (t + 6)$ **40.** $(x + 2) + (x^2 - 6x - 1)$

41. $(x + 2)(x^2 - 6x - 1)$ **42.** $(9c - 5)(9c + 5)$

Factor the expression completely.

43. $y^2 + y - 30$ **44.** $z^3 - 3z^2 + 2z$ **45.** $8 + 27n^3$

RATIONAL EXPRESSIONS AND EQUATIONS

Write the expression in simplest form.

46. $\dfrac{x^2 - 6x + 9}{4x - 12}$ **47.** $\dfrac{x^2 - 7x + 6}{2x - 12} \cdot \dfrac{4x}{3x - 3}$ **48.** $\dfrac{6k^2}{4k + 8} \div \dfrac{4k^3}{k^2 - 4}$

49. $\dfrac{3x}{x^2 - 3x} - \dfrac{9}{x^2 - 3x}$ **50.** $\dfrac{4}{9z} - \dfrac{z + 1}{6z^2}$ **51.** $\dfrac{x}{x - 2} + \dfrac{x - 2}{x - 1}$

Solve the equation.

52. $\dfrac{d}{d + 4} = \dfrac{d - 5}{d + 1}$ **53.** $\dfrac{1}{2} + \dfrac{2}{s} = \dfrac{15}{4s}$ **54.** $\dfrac{n}{n - 1} + \dfrac{2}{n + 1} = 2$

RADICAL EXPRESSIONS AND EQUATIONS

Simplify the expression.

55. $\sqrt{18} \cdot \sqrt{2}$ **56.** $\sqrt{98} \cdot \sqrt{8}$ **57.** $2\sqrt{6}(5 - \sqrt{6})$

58. $\dfrac{8}{2 + \sqrt{3}}$ **59.** $4^{5/2} \cdot 4^{1/2}$ **60.** $(100^2)^{1/4}$

Solve the equation. Check for extraneous solutions.

61. $\sqrt{x} + 4 = 0$ **62.** $\sqrt{4x - 3} = 3$ **63.** $\sqrt{x + 2} = x$

Table of Symbols

Symbol		Page
$\cdot, (a)(b)$	multiplied by or times ($\times$)	3
a^n	nth power of a	9
$\ldots$	continues on	9
$(\ )$	parentheses	10
$[\ ]$	brackets	10
$=$	equal sign, is equal to	24
$\overset{?}{=}$	Is this statement true?	24
$\neq$	is not equal to	24
$<$	is less than	26
$\leq$	is less than or equal to	26
$>$	is greater than	26
$\geq$	is greater than or equal to	26
$\circ$	degree(s)	67
$-a$	the opposite of a	71
$|a|$	absolute value of a	71
$\dfrac{1}{a}$	reciprocal of a, $a \neq 0$	113

Symbol		Page
$\approx$	is approximately equal to	163
$\dfrac{a}{b}$	ratio of a to b, or $a{:}b$	177
$\dfrac{a}{b}$	rate of a per b, where a and b are measured in different units	177
$\%$	percent	183
(x, y)	ordered pair	203
m	slope	229
k	constant of variation	236
b	y-intercept	243
$f(x)$	the value of f at x	254
π	pi, an irrational number approximately equal to 3.14	445
a^{-n}	$\dfrac{1}{a^n}$, $a \neq 0$	449
$c \times 10^n$	scientific notation, where $1 \leq c < 10$ and n is an integer	469
$\sqrt{a}$	the positive square root of a when $a > 0$	499
$\pm$	plus or minus	499

Table of Formulas

Geometric Formulas

Perimeter of a polygon	$P = a + b + \ldots + z$ where $a, b, \ldots, z =$ side lengths
Area of a triangle	$A = \frac{1}{2}bh$ where $b =$ base and $h =$ height
Area of a square	$A = s^2$ where $s =$ side length
Area of a rectangle	$A = \ell w$ where $\ell =$ length and $w =$ width
Area of a trapezoid	$A = \frac{1}{2}h(b_1 + b_2)$ where $h =$ height and $b_1, b_2 =$ bases
Volume of a cube	$V = s^3$ where $s =$ edge length
Volume of a rectangular prism	$V = \ell wh$ where $\ell =$ length, $w =$ width, and $h =$ height
Circumference of a circle	$C = \pi d$ where $\pi \approx 3.14$ and $d =$ diameter $C = 2\pi r$ where $\pi \approx 3.14$ and $r =$ radius
Area of a circle	$A = \pi r^2$ where $\pi \approx 3.14$ and $r =$ radius
Surface area of a sphere	$S = 4\pi r^2$ where $\pi \approx 3.14$ and $r =$ radius
Volume of a sphere	$V = \frac{4}{3}\pi r^3$ where $\pi \approx 3.14$ and $r =$ radius

Other Formulas

Average speed	$r = \dfrac{d}{t}$ where $r =$ average rate or speed, $d =$ distance, and $t =$ time

Algebraic Formulas

Slope formula	$m = \dfrac{y_2 - y_1}{x_2 - x_1}$ where $m =$ slope and (x_1, y_1) and (x_2, y_2) are two points
Quadratic formula	The solutions of $ax^2 + bx + c = 0$ are $x = \dfrac{-b \pm \sqrt{b^2 - 4ac}}{2a}$ when $a \neq 0$ and $b^2 - 4ac \geq 0$.
Pythagorean theorem	$a^2 + b^2 = c^2$ where $a, b =$ length of the legs and $c =$ length of the hypotenuse of a right triangle
Distance formula	The distance between (x_1, y_1) and (x_2, y_2) is $\sqrt{(x_2 - x_1)^2 + (y_2 - y_1)^2}$.
Midpoint formula	The midpoint between (x_1, y_1) and (x_2, y_2) is $\left(\dfrac{x_1 + x_2}{2}, \dfrac{y_1 + y_2}{2}\right)$.

Table of Properties

Basic Properties

	Addition	**Multiplication**
Closure	$a + b$ is a unique real number.	ab is a unique real number.
Commutative	$a + b = b + a$	$ab = ba$
Associative	$(a + b) + c = a + (b + c)$	$(ab)c = a(bc)$
Identity	$a + 0 = a, 0 + a = a$	$a(1) = a, 1(a) = a$
Property of zero	$a + (-a) = 0$	$a(0) = 0$
Property of negative one		$(-1)a = -a$ or $a(-1) = -a$
Distributive	$a(b + c) = ab + ac$ or $(b + c)a = ba + ca$	

Properties of Equality

Addition	If $a = b$, then $a + c = b + c$.
Subtraction	If $a = b$, then $a - c = b - c$.
Multiplication	If $a = b$, then $ca = cb$.
Division	If $a = b$ and $c \neq 0$, then $\dfrac{a}{c} = \dfrac{b}{c}$.

Properties of Exponents

Product of Powers	$a^m \cdot a^n = a^{m + n}$
Power of a Power	$\left(a^m\right)^n = a^{m \cdot n}$
Power of a Product	$(a \cdot b)^m = a^m \cdot b^m$
Quotient of Powers	$\dfrac{a^m}{a^n} = a^{m - n}, a \neq 0$
Power of a Quotient	$\left(\dfrac{a}{b}\right)^m = \dfrac{a^m}{b^m}, b \neq 0$
Negative Exponent	$a^{-n} = \dfrac{1}{a^n}, a \neq 0$
Zero Exponent	$a^0 = 1, a \neq 0$

Properties of Radicals

Product Property	$\sqrt{ab} = \sqrt{a} \cdot \sqrt{b}$
Quotient Property	$\sqrt{\dfrac{a}{b}} = \dfrac{\sqrt{a}}{\sqrt{b}}, b \neq 0$

Properties of Proportions

Reciprocal	If $\dfrac{a}{b} = \dfrac{c}{d}$, then $\dfrac{b}{a} = \dfrac{d}{c}$.
Cross-multiplying	If $\dfrac{a}{b} = \dfrac{c}{d}$, then $ad = bc$.

Special Products and Their Factors

Sum and Difference Pattern	$(a + b)(a - b) = a^2 - b^2$
Square of a Binomial Pattern	$(a + b)^2 = a^2 + 2ab + b^2$
	$(a - b)^2 = a^2 - 2ab + b^2$

Properties of Rational Expressions

Multiplication	$\dfrac{a}{b} \cdot \dfrac{c}{d} = \dfrac{ac}{bd}$
Division	$\dfrac{a}{b} \div \dfrac{c}{d} = \dfrac{a}{b} \cdot \dfrac{d}{c}$
Addition	$\dfrac{a}{c} + \dfrac{b}{c} = \dfrac{a + b}{c}, \dfrac{a}{b} + \dfrac{c}{d} = \dfrac{ad + bc}{bd}$
Subtraction	$\dfrac{a}{c} - \dfrac{b}{c} = \dfrac{a - b}{c}, \dfrac{a}{b} - \dfrac{c}{d} = \dfrac{ad - bc}{bd}$

Using the Table

EXAMPLE 1

Find 54^2.

Solution

Find 54 in the numbers' column. Read across that line to the squares' column.
So, $54^2 = 2916$.

No.	Square	Sq. Root
51	2601	7.141
52	2704	7.211
53	2809	7.280
54	2916	7.348
55	3025	7.416

EXAMPLE 2

Find a decimal approximation of $\sqrt{54}$.

Solution

Find 54 in the numbers' column. Read across that line to the square roots' column.
This number is a three-decimal place approximation of $\sqrt{54}$, so $\sqrt{54} \approx 7.348$.

No.	Square	Sq. Root
51	2601	7.141
52	2704	7.211
53	2809	7.280
54	2916	7.348
55	3025	7.416

EXAMPLE 3

Estimate $\sqrt{3000}$.

Solution

Find the two numbers in the squares' column that 3000 is between. Read across
these two lines to the numbers' column; $\sqrt{3000}$ is between 54 and 55, but closer
to 55. So, $\sqrt{3000} \approx 55$. A more accurate approximation can be found using a
calculator: 54.772256.

No.	Square	Sq. Root
51	2601	7.141
52	2704	7.211
53	2809	7.280
54	2916	7.348
55	3025	7.416

Table of Squares and Square Roots

No.	Square	Sq. Root	No.	Square	Sq. Root	No.	Square	Sq. Root
1	1	1.000	51	2601	7.141	101	10,201	10.050
2	4	1.414	52	2704	7.211	102	10,404	10.100
3	9	1.732	53	2809	7.280	103	10,609	10.149
4	16	2.000	54	2916	7.348	104	10,816	10.198
5	25	2.236	55	3025	7.416	105	11,025	10.247
6	36	2.449	56	3136	7.483	106	11,236	10.296
7	49	2.646	57	3249	7.550	107	11,449	10.344
8	64	2.828	58	3364	7.616	108	11,664	10.392
9	81	3.000	59	3481	7.681	109	11,881	10.440
10	100	3.162	60	3600	7.746	110	12,100	10.488
11	121	3.317	61	3721	7.810	111	12,321	10.536
12	144	3.464	62	3844	7.874	112	12,544	10.583
13	169	3.606	63	3969	7.937	113	12,769	10.630
14	196	3.742	64	4096	8.000	114	12,996	10.677
15	225	3.873	65	4225	8.062	115	13,225	10.724
16	256	4.000	66	4356	8.124	116	13,456	10.770
17	289	4.123	67	4489	8.185	117	13,689	10.817
18	324	4.243	68	4624	8.246	118	13,924	10.863
19	361	4.359	69	4761	8.307	119	14,161	10.909
20	400	4.472	70	4900	8.367	120	14,400	10.954
21	441	4.583	71	5041	8.426	121	14,641	11.000
22	484	4.690	72	5184	8.485	122	14,884	11.045
23	529	4.796	73	5329	8.544	123	15,129	11.091
24	576	4.899	74	5476	8.602	124	15,376	11.136
25	625	5.000	75	5625	8.660	125	15,625	11.180
26	676	5.099	76	5776	8.718	126	15,876	11.225
27	729	5.196	77	5929	8.775	127	16,129	11.269
28	784	5.292	78	6084	8.832	128	16,384	11.314
29	841	5.385	79	6241	8.888	129	16,641	11.358
30	900	5.477	80	6400	8.944	130	16,900	11.402
31	961	5.568	81	6561	9.000	131	17,161	11.446
32	1024	5.657	82	6724	9.055	132	17,424	11.489
33	1089	5.745	83	6889	9.110	133	17,689	11.533
34	1156	5.831	84	7056	9.165	134	17,956	11.576
35	1225	5.916	85	7225	9.220	135	18,225	11.619
36	1296	6.000	86	7396	9.274	136	18,496	11.662
37	1369	6.083	87	7569	9.327	137	18,769	11.705
38	1444	6.164	88	7744	9.381	138	19,044	11.747
39	1521	6.245	89	7921	9.434	139	19,321	11.790
40	1600	6.325	90	8100	9.487	140	19,600	11.832
41	1681	6.403	91	8281	9.539	141	19,881	11.874
42	1764	6.481	92	8464	9.592	142	20,164	11.916
43	1849	6.557	93	8649	9.644	143	20,449	11.958
44	1936	6.633	94	8836	9.695	144	20,736	12.000
45	2025	6.708	95	9025	9.747	145	21,025	12.042
46	2116	6.782	96	9216	9.798	146	21,316	12.083
47	2209	6.856	97	9409	9.849	147	21,609	12.124
48	2304	6.928	98	9604	9.899	148	21,904	12.166
49	2401	7.000	99	9801	9.950	149	22,201	12.207
50	2500	7.071	100	10,000	10.000	150	22,500	12.247

Table of Measures

Time

60 seconds (sec) = 1 minute (min)	365 days $\Big]$
60 minutes = 1 hour (h)	52 weeks (approx.) $\Big]$ = 1 year
24 hours = 1 day	12 months
7 days = 1 week	10 years = 1 decade
4 weeks (approx.) = 1 month	100 years = 1 century

Metric

Length

10 millimeters (mm) = 1 centimeter (cm)

$\left.\begin{array}{l}100 \text{ cm} \\ 1000 \text{ mm}\end{array}\right]$ = 1 meter (m)

1000 m = 1 kilometer (km)

Area

100 square millimeters = 1 square centimeter
(mm^2)   (cm^2)

10,000 cm^2 = 1 square meter (m^2)

10,000 m^2 = 1 hectare (ha)

Volume

1000 cubic millimeters = 1 cubic centimeter
(mm^3)   (cm^3)

1,000,000 cm^3 = 1 cubic meter (m^3)

Liquid Capacity

1000 milliliters (mL) = 1 liter (L)

1000 L = 1 kiloliter (kL)

Mass

1000 milligrams (mg) = 1 gram (g)

1000 g = 1 kilogram (kg)

1000 kg = 1 metric ton (t)

Temperature — Degrees Celsius (°C)

0°C = freezing point of water

37°C = normal body temperature

100°C = boiling point of water

United States Customary

Length

12 inches (in.) = 1 foot (ft)

$\left.\begin{array}{l}36 \text{ in.} \\ 3 \text{ ft}\end{array}\right]$ = 1 yard (yd)

$\left.\begin{array}{l}5280 \text{ ft} \\ 1760 \text{ yd}\end{array}\right]$ = 1 mile (mi)

Area

144 square inches (in.^{2}) = 1 square foot (ft^2)

9 ft^2 = 1 square yard (yd^2)

$\left.\begin{array}{l}43,560 \text{ ft}^2 \\ 4840 \text{ yd}^2\end{array}\right]$ = 1 acre (A)

Volume

1728 cubic inches (in.^{3}) = 1 cubic foot (ft^3)

27 ft^3 = 1 cubic yard (yd^3)

Liquid Capacity

8 fluid ounces (fl oz) = 1 cup (c)

2 c = 1 pint (pt)

2 pt = 1 quart (qt)

4 qt = 1 gallon (gal)

Weight

16 ounces (oz) = 1 pound (lb)

2000 lb = 1 ton (t)

Temperature — Degrees Fahrenheit (°F)

32°F = freezing point of water

98.6°F = normal body temperature

212°F = boiling point of water

Glossary

absolute value (p. 71) The distance between zero and the point representing a real number on the number line. The symbol $|a|$ represents the absolute value of a number a.

absolute value equation (p. 355) An equation of the form $|ax + b| = c$.

absolute value inequality (p. 361) An inequality that has one of these forms: $|ax + b| < c$, $|ax + b| \leq c$, $|ax + b| > c$, or $|ax + b| \geq c$.

addition property of equality (p. 140) If $a = b$, then $a + c = b + c$.

addition property of inequality (p. 324) If $a > b$, then $a + c > b + c$ and if $a < b$, then $a + c < b + c$.

algebraic model (p. 36) An expression, equation, or inequality that uses variables to represent a real-life situation.

associative property of addition (p. 79) The way three numbers are grouped when adding does not change the sum. For any real numbers a, b, and c, $(a + b) + c = a + (b + c)$.

associative property of multiplication (p. 94) The way three numbers are grouped when multiplying does not change the product. For any real numbers a, b, and c, $(ab)c = a(bc)$.

axiom (p. 740) A rule that is accepted as true without proof. An axiom is also called a *postulate*.

axis of symmetry of a parabola (p. 521) The vertical line passing through the vertex of a parabola or the line dividing a parabola into two symmetrical parts that are mirror images of each other.

bar graph (p. 43) A graph that represents a collection of data by using horizontal or vertical bars whose lengths allow the data to be compared.

base (p. 9) In exponential notation, the number or variable that undergoes repeated multiplication. For example, 4 is the base in the expression 4^6.

base number of a percent equation (p. 183) The number that is the basis for comparison in a percent equation. The number b in the verbal model "a is p percent of b."

binomial (p. 569) A polynomial consisting of two terms.

closure property of real number addition (p. 78) The sum of any two real numbers is again a real number.

closure property of real number multiplication (p. 93) The product of any two real numbers is again a real number.

coefficient (p. 107) If a term of an expression consists of a number multiplied by one or more variables, the number is the coefficient of the term.

commutative property of addition (p. 79) The order in which two numbers are added does not change the sum. For any real numbers a and b, $a + b = b + a$.

commutative property of multiplication (p. 94) The order in which two numbers are multiplied does not change the product. For any real numbers a and b, $ab = ba$.

completing the square (p. 716) The process of rewriting a quadratic equation so that one side is a perfect square trinomial.

compound inequality (p. 342) Two inequalities connected by the word *and* or the word *or*.

conclusion (p. 120) The *then* part of an if-then statement is called the conclusion.

conjecture (p. 741) A statement that is thought to be true but has not been proved.

constant function (p. 218) A function of the form $y = b$, where b is some number.

constant of variation (pp. 236, 639) The constant in a variation model. It is equal to $\dfrac{y}{x}$ in the case of direct variation, and xy in the case of inverse variation.

converse of a statement (p. 726) A related statement in which the hypothesis and conclusion are interchanged. The converse of the statement "If p, then q" is "If q, then p."

converse of the Pythagorean theorem (p. 726) If a triangle has side lengths a, b, and c such that $a^2 + b^2 = c^2$, then the triangle is a right triangle.

coordinate plane (p. 203) The coordinate system formed by two real number lines that intersect at a right angle.

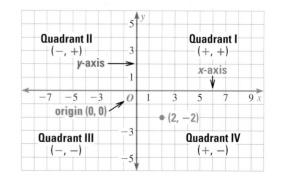

counterexample (p. 73) An example used to show that a given statement is false.

cross product property (p. 634) In a proportion, the product of the extremes equals the product of the means. If $\frac{a}{b} = \frac{c}{d}$, then $ad = bc$.

cube root (p. 710) If $b^3 = a$, then b is a cube root of a.

data (p. 42) Information, facts, or numbers used to describe something.

decay factor (p. 482) The expression $1 - r$ in the exponential decay model where r is the decay rate. *See also* exponential decay.

decay rate (p. 482) In an exponential decay model, the proportion by which the quantity decreases each time period. *See also* exponential decay.

decimal form (p. 469) A number written with place values corresponding to powers of ten. For example, 100, 14.2, and 0.007 are in decimal form.

deductive reasoning (p. 120) Using facts, definitions, rules, or properties to reach a conclusion.

degree of a monomial (p. 568) The sum of the exponents of each variable in the monomial. The degree of $5x^2y$ is $2 + 1 = 3$.

degree of a polynomial in one variable (p. 569) The largest exponent of that variable.

direct variation (p. 236) The relationship between two variables x and y for which there is a nonzero number k such that $y = kx$, or $\frac{y}{x} = k$. The variables x and y *vary directly*.

discriminant (p. 540) The expression $b^2 - 4ac$ where a, b, and c are coefficients of the quadratic equation $ax^2 + bx + c = 0$; the expression inside the radical in the quadratic formula.

distance formula (p. 730) The distance d between the points (x_1, y_1) and (x_2, y_2) is
$$d = \sqrt{(x_2 - x_1)^2 + (y_2 - y_1)^2}.$$

distributive property (pp. 100, 101) For any real numbers a, b, and c, $a(b + c) = ab + ac$, $(b + c)a = ba + ca$, $a(b - c) = ab - ac$, and $(b - c)a = ba - ca$.

division property of equality (p. 140) If $a = b$ and $c \neq 0$, then $\frac{a}{c} = \frac{b}{c}$.

division property of inequality (pp. 330, 331) If $a > b$ and $c > 0$, then $\frac{a}{c} > \frac{b}{c}$ and if $a < b$, then $\frac{a}{c} < \frac{b}{c}$. If $a > b$, and $c < 0$, then $\frac{a}{c} < \frac{b}{c}$ and if $a < b$, then $\frac{a}{c} > \frac{b}{c}$.

domain of a function (p. 49) The collection of all input values of a function.

E

equation (p. 24) A statement formed by placing an equal sign between two expressions.

equivalent equations (p. 132) Equations that have the same solution(s).

equivalent inequalities (p. 324) Inequalities that have the same solution(s).

evaluate an expression (p. 4) Find the value of an expression by substituting a specific numerical value for each variable, and simplifying the result.

exponent (p. 9) In exponential notation, the number of times the base is used as a factor. For example, 6 is the exponent in the expression 4^6.

exponential decay (p. 482) A quantity displays exponential decay if it decreases by the same proportion r in each time period t. If C is the initial amount, the amount at time t is given by $y = C(1 - r)^t$, where r is called the decay rate, $0 < r < 1$, and $(1 - r)$ is called the decay factor.

exponential function (p. 455) A function of the form $y = ab^x$, where $b > 0$ and $b \neq 1$.

exponential growth (p. 476) A quantity displays exponential growth if it increases by the same proportion r in each unit of time. If C is the initial amount, the amount after t units of time is given by $y = C(1 + r)^t$, where r is called the growth rate and $(1 + r)$ is called the growth factor.

extraneous solution (p. 705) A trial solution that does not satisfy the original equation.

extremes of a proportion (p. 633) In the proportion $\frac{a}{b} = \frac{c}{d}$, a and d are the extremes.

F

factor a polynomial completely (p. 617) To write a polynomial as the product of monomial and prime factors.

factor a trinomial (p. 595) Write the trinomial as the product of two binomials.

factored form of a polynomial (p. 588) A polynomial that is written as the product of two or more factors.

formula (p. 171) An algebraic equation that relates two or more variables.

function (p. 48) A rule that establishes a relationship between two quantities, the input and the output. There is exactly one output for each input.

function form (p. 211) A two-variable equation is written in function form if one of its variables is isolated on one side of the equation. The isolated variable is the output and is a function of the input.

function notation (p. 254) A way to describe a function by means of an equation. For the equation $y = f(x)$ the symbol $f(x)$ denotes the output and is read as "the value of f at x" or simply as "f of x."

G

graph of an equation in two variables (p. 211) The set of all points (x, y) that are solutions of the equation.

graph of an inequality in one variable (p. 323) The set of points on the number line that represent all the solutions of the inequality.

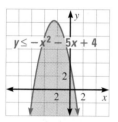

graph of a number (p. 65) The point on a number line that corresponds to a number.

graph of a quadratic inequality (p. 547) The graph of all ordered pairs (x, y) that are solutions of the inequality.

grouping symbols (p. 10) Symbols such as parentheses ( ) and brackets [ ] that indicate the order in which operations should be performed. Operations within the innermost set of grouping symbols are done first.

growth factor (p. 476) The expression $1 + r$ in the exponential growth model where r is the growth rate. *See also* exponential growth.

growth rate (p. 476) In an exponential growth model, the proportion by which the quantity increases each unit of time.

H

hypotenuse (p. 724) The side opposite the right angle in a right triangle.

hypothesis (p. 120) The *if* part of an if-then statement.

I

identity (p. 153) An equation that is true for all values of the variable.

identity property of addition (p. 79) The sum of a number and 0 is the number. For any real number a, $a + 0 = 0 + a = a$.

identity property of multiplication (p. 94) The product of a number and 1 is the number. For any real number a, $1 \cdot a = a$.

if-then statement (p. 120) A form of statement used in deductive reasoning where the *if* part is the hypothesis and the *then* part is the conclusion.

indirect proof (p. 742) A type of proof in which a statement is assumed false. If this assumption leads to an impossibility, then the original statement has been proved to be true.

inductive reasoning (p. 119) Making a general statement based on several observations.

inequality (p. 26) A statement formed by placing an inequality symbol, such as <, between two expressions.

input (p. 48) A value in the domain of a function.

input-output table (p. 48) A table used to describe a function by listing the outputs for several different inputs.

integers (p. 65) The numbers . . . $-3, -2, -1, 0, 1, 2, 3, \ldots$.

inverse operations (p. 133) Two operations that undo each other, such as addition and subtraction.

inverse property of addition (p. 79) The sum of a number and its opposite is 0: $a + (-a) = 0$.

inverse variation (p. 639) The relationship between two variables x and y for which there is a nonzero number k such that $xy = k$, or $y = \dfrac{k}{x}$. The variables x and y are said to *vary inversely*.

L

leading coefficient (p. 505) For a quadratic equation in standard form, $ax^2 + bx + c = 0$ where $a \neq 0$, a is the leading coefficient.

least common denominator, LCD (p. 663) The least common multiple of the denominators of two or more fractions.

left-to-right rule (p. 16) When operations have the same priority, you perform them in order from left to right.

legs of a right triangle (p. 724) The two sides of a right triangle that are not opposite the right angle.

like terms (p. 107) Terms that have the same variables with each variable of the same kind raised to the same power. For example, $3x^2y$ and $-7x^2y$ are like terms.

line graph (p. 44) A graph that uses line segments to connect data points. Line graphs are especially useful for showing changes in data over time.

linear combination of two equations (p. 402) An equation obtained by (1) multiplying one or both equations by a constant and (2) adding the resulting equations.

linear equation in one variable (p. 134) An equation in which the variable appears only to the first power.

linear equation in *x* and *y* (p. 210) An equation that can be written in the form $Ax + By = C$, where A and B are not both zero.

linear function of *x* (p. 254) A function of the form $f(x) = mx + b$.

linear inequality in *x* and *y* (p. 367) An inequality that can be written in one of these forms: $ax + by < c$, $ax + by \le c$, $ax + by > c$, or $ax + by \ge c$.

linear model (p. 298) A linear equation or function that is used to model a real-life situation.

linear system (p. 389) Two or more linear equations in the same variables. This is also called a system of linear equations.

means of a proportion (p. 633) In the proportion $\frac{a}{b} = \frac{c}{d}$, b and c are the means.

midpoint of a line segment (p. 736) The point on the segment that is equidistant from its endpoints.

midpoint formula (p. 736) The midpoint between (x_1, y_1) and (x_2, y_2) is $\left(\dfrac{x_1 + x_2}{2}, \dfrac{y_1 + y_2}{2} \right)$.

modeling (p. 36) Representing real-life situations by means of equations or inequalities.

monomial (pp. 568, 569) A number, a variable, or a product of numbers and variables; a polynomial with only one term.

multiplication property of equality (p. 140) If $a = b$, then $ca = cb$.

multiplication property of inequality (p. 324) If $a > b$ and $c > 0$, then $ac > bc$ and if $a < b$, then $ac < bc$. If $a > b$ and $c < 0$, then $ac < bc$ and if $a < b$, then $ac > bc$.

multiplicative property of negative one (p. 94) The product of a number and -1 is the opposite of the number: $-1 \cdot a = -a$.

multiplicative property of zero (p. 94) The product of a number and 0 is 0. That is, $0 \cdot a = 0$.

negative number (p. 65) A number less than zero. *See also* real number line.

negative square root (p. 499) The negative number that is a square root of a positive number. For example, the negative square root of 9 is -3.

numerical expression (p. 3) An expression that represents a particular number.

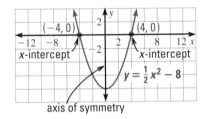

opposites (p. 71) Two numbers that are the same distance from zero on a number line but on opposite sides of zero.

order of operations (p. 15) The rules for evaluating an expression involving more than one operation.

ordered pair (p. 203) A pair of numbers used to identify a point in a coordinate plane. The first number is the *x*-coordinate and the second number is the *y*-coordinate. *See also* coordinate plane.

origin (p. 203) The point in a coordinate plane where the horizontal axis intersects the vertical axis. The point (0, 0). *See also* coordinate plane.

output (p. 48) A value in the range of a function.

parabola (p. 520) The U-shaped graph of a quadratic function, $y = ax^2 + bx + c$ where $a \ne 0$.

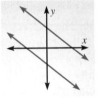

parallel lines (p. 245) Two different lines in the same plane that do not intersect. (Identical lines are sometimes considered to be parallel.)

percent (p. 183) A ratio that compares a number to 100.

perfect square trinomials (p. 609) Trinomials of the form $a^2 + 2ab + b^2$ and $a^2 - 2ab + b^2$; perfect square trinomials can be factored as the squares of binomials.

perpendicular lines (p. 306) Two lines in a plane are perpendicular if they intersect at a right, or 90°, angle. If two nonvertical lines are perpendicular, the product of their slopes is -1.

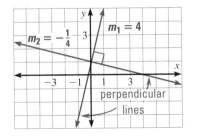

GLOSSARY

point of intersection (p. 389) A point (a, b) that lies on the graphs of two or more equations is a point of intersection for the graphs.

point-slope form (p. 278) An equation of a nonvertical line in the form $y - y_1 = m(x - x_1)$ where the line passes through a given point (x_1, y_1) and the line has a slope of m.

polynomial (p. 569) A monomial or a sum of monomials. *See* monomial.

positive number (p. 65) A number greater than zero.

positive square root, or principal square root (p. 499) The square root of a positive number that is itself positive. For example, the positive square root of 9 is 3.

postulate (p. 740) A rule that is accepted as true without proof. A postulate is also called an *axiom*.

power (p. 9) An expression of the form a^b or the value of such an expression. For example, 2^4 is a power, and since $2^4 = 16$, 16 is the fourth power of 2.

power of a power property (pp. 444, 445) To find a power of a power, multiply the exponents. For any real number a and integers m and n, $(a^m)^n = a^{mn}$.

power of a product property (p. 444) To find a power of a product, find the power of each factor and multiply. For any real numbers a and b and integer m, $(ab)^m = a^m \cdot b^m$.

power of a quotient property (pp. 462, 463) To find a power of a quotient, find the power of the numerator and the power of the denominator and divide. For any integer m and real numbers a and b, where $b \neq 0$,
$$\left(\frac{a}{b}\right)^m = \frac{a^m}{b^m}.$$

prime polynomial (p. 617) A polynomial that is not the product of factors with integer coefficients and of lower degree.

product of powers property (pp. 443, 445) To multiply powers having the same base, add the exponents. For any real number a and integers m and n, $a^m \cdot a^n = a^{m+n}$.

product property of radicals (p. 511) If a and b are real numbers such that $a \geq 0$ and $b \geq 0$, then $\sqrt{ab} = \sqrt{a} \cdot \sqrt{b}$.

properties of equality (p. 140) The rules of algebra used to transform equations into equivalent equations.

proportion (p. 633) An equation stating that two ratios are equal.

Pythagorean theorem (p. 724) If a right triangle has legs of lengths a and b and hypotenuse of length c, then $a^2 + b^2 = c^2$.

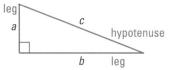

quadrant (p. 204) One of four regions into which the axes divide a coordinate plane.

quadratic equation (p. 505) An equation that can be written in the standard form $ax^2 + bx + c = 0$, where $a \neq 0$.

quadratic formula (p. 533) A formula used to find the solutions of a quadratic equation $ax^2 + bx + c = 0$ when $a \neq 0$ and $b^2 - 4ac \geq 0$:
$$x = \frac{-b \pm \sqrt{b^2 - 4ac}}{2a}.$$

quadratic function (p. 520) A function that can be written in the standard form $y = ax^2 + bx + c$, where $a \neq 0$.

quadratic inequality (p. 547) An inequality that can be written in one of the forms
$y < ax^2 + bx + c$, $y \leq ax^2 + bx + c$,
$y > ax^2 + bx + c$, or $y \geq ax^2 + bx + c$.

quotient of powers property (pp. 462, 463) To divide powers having the same base, subtract the exponents. For any real number $a \neq 0$ and integers m and n,
$\frac{a^m}{a^n} = a^{m-n}$.

quotient property of radicals (p. 512) If a and b are real numbers such that $a \geq 0$ and $b > 0$, then
$$\sqrt{\frac{a}{b}} = \frac{\sqrt{a}}{\sqrt{b}}.$$

R

radical expression, or radical (p. 501) An expression written with a radical symbol.

radicand (p. 499) The number or expression inside a radical symbol.

range of a function (p. 49) The collection of all output values of a function.

rate of a per b (p. 177) The relationship $\frac{a}{b}$ of two quantities a and b that are measured in different units.

rate of change (p. 298) The quotient of two different quantities that are changing. In a linear model, the slope gives the rate of change of one variable with respect to the other.

ratio of a to b (p. 177) The relationship $\frac{a}{b}$ of two quantities a and b.

rational equation (p. 670) An equation that contains rational expressions.

rational exponent (p. 711) For any integer n and real number $a \geq 0$, the nth root of a is denoted $a^{1/n}$ or $\sqrt[n]{a}$. Let $a^{1/n}$ be an nth root of a, m be a positive integer and $a \geq 0$. Then $a^{m/n} = (a^{1/n})^m = (\sqrt[n]{a})^m = \sqrt[n]{a^m}$.

rational expression (p. 646) A fraction whose numerator and denominator are nonzero polynomials.

rational function (p. 678) A rational function is a function that is a quotient of polynomials.

rational number (p. 646) A number that can be written as the quotient of two integers.

real number line (p. 65) A line whose points correspond to the real numbers.

Negative numbers   Positive numbers

$-4 \quad -3 \quad -2 \quad -1 \quad 0 \quad 1 \quad 2 \quad 3 \quad 4$

real numbers (p. 65) The set of numbers consisting of the positive numbers, the negative numbers, and zero. (The real numbers can also be thought of as the set of all decimals, finite or infinite in length.)

reciprocals (p. 113) Two numbers are reciprocals if their product is 1. If $\frac{a}{b}$ is a nonzero number, then its reciprocal is $\frac{b}{a}$.

relation (p. 252) Any set of ordered pairs.

roots of a quadratic equation (p. 527) The solutions of a quadratic equation.

rounding error (p. 164) The error produced when a decimal expansion is limited to a specified number of digits to the right of the decimal point.

S

scatter plot (p. 205) A coordinate graph containing points that represent a set of ordered points; used to analyze relationships between two real-life quantities.

scientific notation (p. 469) A number expressed in the form $c \times 10^n$, where $1 \leq c < 10$ and n is an integer.

simplified expression (p. 108) An expression is simplified if it has no grouping symbols and if all the like terms have been combined.

simplest form of a radical expression (p. 511) An expression that has no perfect square factors other than 1 in the radicand, no fractions in the radicand, and no radicals in the denominator of a fraction.

slope (p. 229, 230) The ratio of the vertical rise to the horizontal run between any two points on a line.

The slope is $m = \dfrac{(y_2 - y_1)}{(x_2 - x_1)}$.

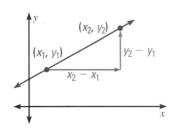

slope-intercept form (p. 243) A linear equation written in the form $y = mx + b$. The slope of the line is m. The y-intercept is b. *See also* slope *and* y-intercept.

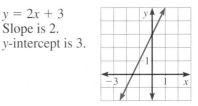

$y = 2x + 3$
Slope is 2.
y-intercept is 3.

solution of an equation or inequality (p. 24) A number that, when substituted for the variable in an equation or inequality, results in a true statement.

solution of an equation in two variables (p. 210) An ordered pair (x, y) that makes the equation true.

solution of a linear system in two variables (p. 389) An ordered pair (x, y) that makes each equation in the system a true statement.

solution of a system of linear inequalities in two variables (p. 424) An ordered pair that is a solution of each inequality in the system.

square root (p. 499) If $b^2 = a$, then b is a square root of a. Square roots can be written with a radical symbol, $\sqrt{\ }$.

square root function (p. 692) The function defined by the equation $y = \sqrt{x}$, for $x \geq 0$.

standard form of an equation of a line (p. 291) A linear equation of the form $Ax + By = C$, where A and B are not both zero.

standard form of a polynomial in one variable (p. 569) A polynomial whose terms are written in decreasing order, from largest exponent to smallest exponent.

standard form of a quadratic equation (p. 505) An equation in the form $ax^2 + bx + c = 0$, where $a \neq 0$.

subtraction property of equality (p. 140) If $a = b$, then $a - c = b - c$.

subtraction property of inequality (p. 324) If $a > b$, then $a - c > b - c$ and if $a < b$, then $a - c < b - c$.

system of linear equations (p. 389) Two or more linear equations in the same variables. This is also called a linear system.

system of linear inequalities (p. 424) Two or more linear inequalities in the same variables. This is also called a system of inequalities.

T

terms of an expression (p. 87) The parts that are added to form an expression. For example, in the expression $5 - x$, the terms are 5 and $-x$.

theorem (p. 724) A statement that has been proven to be true.

trinomial (p. 569) A polynomial of three terms.

unit analysis (p. 178) Using the units for each variable in a real-life problem to determine the units for the answer.

unit rate (p. 177) A rate expressing the amount of one given quantity per unit of another quantity, such as miles per gallon.

V

values (p. 3) The numbers a variable represents.

variable (p. 3) A letter used to represent a range of numbers.

variable expression (p. 3) A symbolic form made up of constants, variables, and operations.

verbal model (p. 36) An expression that uses words to describe a real-life situation.

vertex of a vertically oriented parabola (p. 521) The lowest point on the graph of a parabola opening up or the highest point on the graph of a parabola opening down. *See also* parabola.

vertical motion models (p. 535) Models that give the height of an object as a function of time. They include the case of a falling object.

W

whole numbers (p. 65) The positive integers together with zero.

X

x-axis (p. 203) The horizontal axis in a coordinate plane. *See also* coordinate plane.

x-coordinate (p. 203) The first number in an ordered pair. *See also* ordered pair.

x-intercept (p. 222) The x-coordinate of a point where a graph crosses the x-axis.

Y

y-axis (p. 203) The vertical axis in a coordinate plane. *See also* coordinate plane.

y-coordinate (p. 203) The second number in an ordered pair. *See also* ordered pair.

y-intercept (p. 222) The y-coordinate of a point where a graph crosses the y-axis.

Z

zero-product property (p. 588) If the product of two factors is zero, then at least one of the factors must be zero.

English-to-Spanish Glossary

A

absolute value (p. 71) valor absoluto Distancia existente entre el cero y el punto que representa en la recta numérica un número real. El símbolo $|a|$ representa el valor absoluto de un número a.

absolute value equation (p. 355) ecuación de valor absoluto La de la forma $|ax + b| = c$.

absolute value inequality (p. 361) desigualdad de valor absoluto Aquella que presenta una de estas formas: $|ax + b| < c$, $|ax + b| \le c$, $|ax + b| > c$, ó $|ax + b| \ge c$.

addition property of equality (p. 140) propiedad de igualdad en la suma Si $a = b$, entonces $a + c = b + c$.

addition property of inequality (p. 324) propiedad de desigualdad en la suma Si $a > b$, entonces $a + c > b + c$ y si $a < b$, entonces $a + c < b + c$.

algebraic model (p. 36) modelo algebraico Expresión, ecuación o desigualdad que usa variables para representar una situación de la vida real.

associative property of addition (p. 79) propiedad asociativa de la suma La agrupación que tengan tres números al sumarse no altera la suma. Para todos los números reales a, b, y c, $(a + b) + c = a + (b + c)$.

associative property of multiplication (p. 94) propiedad asociativa de la multiplicación La agrupación que tengan tres números al multiplicarse no altera el producto. Para todos los números reales a, b, y c, $(ab)c = a(bc)$.

axiom (p. 740) axioma Regla que se acepta como cierta sin demostración. Al axioma se le llama también *postulado*.

axis of symmetry of a parabola (p. 521) eje de simetría de una parábola Recta vertical que pasa por el vértice de una parábola o la recta que divide la parabola en dos partes simétricas, las cuales son reflejos exactos entre sí.

B

bar graph (p. 43) gráfica de barras La que representa un conjunto de datos mediante barras horizontales o verticales y cuya longitud permite la comparación de esos datos.

base (p. 9) base En notación exponencial, el número o variable que sostiene multiplicación repetida. Por ejemplo, 4 es la base en la expresión 4^6.

base number of a percent equation (p. 183) número base de una ecuación de porcentajes El número de una ecuación de porcentajes que es la base de una comparación. El número b en el modelo verbal "a es el p por ciento de b".

binomial (p. 569) binomio Polinomio que consiste de dos términos.

C

closure property of real number addition (p. 78) propiedad de cierre de la suma de números reales La suma de dos números reales cualesquiera es otra vez un número real.

closure property of real number multiplication (p. 93) propiedad de cierre de la multiplicación de números reales El producto de dos números reales cualesquiera es otra vez un número real.

coefficient (p. 107) coeficiente Si un término de una expresión consta de un número multiplicado por una o más variables, entonces ese número es el coeficiente del término.

commutative property of addition (p. 79) propiedad conmutativa de la suma El orden de dos números al sumarse no altera la suma. Para todos los números reales a y b, $a + b = b + a$.

commutative property of multiplication (p. 94) propiedad conmutativa de la multiplicación El orden de dos números al multiplicarse no altera el producto. Para todos los números reales a y b, $ab = ba$.

completing the square (p. 716) completar cuadrados Proceso de escribir una ecuación cuadrática de manera que uno de sus miembros sea un trinomio cuadrado perfecto.

compound inequality (p. 342) desigualdad compuesta Dos desigualdades unidas entre sí mediante la palabra *y* u *o*.

conclusion (p. 120) conclusión La parte del *entonces* en un enunciado de si-entonces.

conjecture (p. 741) conjetura Enunciado que se considera probable sin que haya sido demostrado.

constant function (p. 218) función constante La de la forma $y = b$, donde b es un número.

constant of variation (pp. 236, 639) constante de variación Constante de un modelo de variación. Es equivalente a $\dfrac{y}{x}$ en el caso de una variación directa y a xy en el caso de una variación inversa.

converse of a statement (p. 726) recíproco de un enunciado Afirmación relacionada en la que se intercambian la hipótesis y la conclusión. El recíproco del enunciado "Si p, entonces q" es "Si q, entonces p".

converse of the Pythagorean theorem (p. 726) recíproco del teorema de Pitágoras Si un triángulo tiene lados de longitudes a, b, y c tales que $a^2 + b^2 = c^2$, entonces es un triángulo rectángulo.

coordinate plane (p. 203) **plano de coordenadas** El sistema de coordenadas formado por dos rectas numéricas reales que al cortarse configuran un ángulo recto.

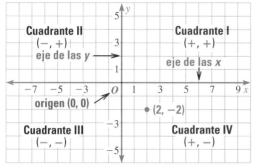

counterexample (p. 73) **contraejemplo** Ejemplo que sirve para mostrar la falsedad de un enunciado dado.

cross product property (p. 634) **propiedad de los productos cruzados** En una proporción, el producto de los extremos es igual al de los medios. Si $\frac{a}{b} = \frac{c}{d}$, entonces $ad = bc$.

cube root (p. 710) **raíz cúbica** Si $b^3 = a$, entonces b es una raíz cúbica de a.

D

data (p. 42) **datos** Informaciones, hechos o números que sirven para describir algo.

decay factor (p. 482) **factor de decrecimiento** La expresión $1 - r$, en el modelo de decrecimiento exponencial donde r es la tasa de decrecimiento. *Ver también* decrecimiento exponencial.

decay rate (p. 482) **tasa de decrecimiento** La proporción de un modelo de decrecimiento exponencial en la cual disminuye la cantidad durante cada período de tiempo. *Ver también* decrecimiento exponencial.

decimal form (p. 469) **forma decimal** Número escrito con valores relativos que corresponden a potencias de diez. Por ejemplo, 100, 14.2 y 0.007 están expresados en forma decimal.

deductive reasoning (p. 120) **razonamiento deductivo** Empleo de hechos, definiciones, reglas o propiedades para sacar una conclusión.

degree of a monomial (p. 568) **grado de un monomio** Suma de los exponentes de cada una de las variables del monomio. El grado de $5x^2y$ es $2 + 1 = 3$.

degree of a polynomial in one variable (p. 569) **grado de un polinomio de una variable** Mayor exponente de esa variable.

direct variation (p. 236) **variación directa** Relación entre dos variables x e y para la cual hay un número k distinto a cero tal que $y = kx$, ó $\frac{y}{x} = k$. Las variables x e y *varían directamente* entre sí.

discriminant (p. 540) **discriminante** La expresión $b^2 - 4ac$ donde a, b y c son coeficientes de la ecuación cuadrática $ax^2 + bx + c = 0$; la expresión del radical de la fórmula cuadrática.

distance formula (p. 730) **fórmula de la distancia** La distancia d que hay entre los puntos (x_1, y_1) y (x_2, y_2) es $d = \sqrt{(x_2 - x_1)^2 + (y_2 - y_1)^2}$.

distributive property (pp. 100, 101) **propiedad distributiva** Para todos los números reales a, b y c, $a(b + c) = ab + ac$, $(b + c)a = ba + ca$, $a(b - c) = ab - ac$ y $(b - c)a = ba - ca$.

division property of equality (p. 140) **propiedad de igualdad en la división** Si $a = b$ y $c \neq 0$, entonces $\frac{a}{c} = \frac{b}{c}$.

division property of inequality (pp. 330, 331) **propiedad de desigualdad en la división** Si $a > b$ y $c > 0$, entonces $\frac{a}{c} > \frac{b}{c}$ y si $a < b$, entonces $\frac{a}{c} < \frac{b}{c}$. Si $a > b$, y $c < 0$, entonces $\frac{a}{c} < \frac{b}{c}$ y si $a < b$, entonces $\frac{a}{c} > \frac{b}{c}$.

domain of a function (p. 49) **dominio de una función** Conjunto de todos los valores de entrada de una función.

E

equation (p. 24) **ecuación** Enunciado formado por dos expresiones unidas entre sí mediante el signo de igual.

equivalent equations (p. 132) **ecuaciones equivalentes** Las que tienen la misma solución o soluciones.

equivalent inequalities (p. 324) **desigualdades equivalentes** Aquellas que tienen la misma solución o soluciones.

evaluate an expression (p. 4) **evaluar una expresión** Hallar el valor de una expresión mediante la sustitución de cada variable por un valor numérico específico y la simplificación del resultado.

exponent (p. 9) **exponente** En notación exponencial, el número de veces que la base se usa como factor. Por ejemplo, 6 es el exponente en la expresión 4^6.

exponential decay (p. 482) **decrecimiento exponencial** Una cantidad presenta un decrecimiento exponencial cuando disminuye en una misma proporción r durante cada período de tiempo t. Si C es la cantidad inicial, la existente tras transcurrir el tiempo t viene dada por $y = C(1 - r)^t$, donde r es la tasa de decrecimiento, $0 < r < 1$, y $(1 - r)$ el factor de decrecimiento.

exponential function (p. 455) **función exponencial** La de la forma $y = ab^x$, donde $b > 0$ y $b \neq 1$.

exponential growth (p. 476) **crecimiento exponencial** Una cantidad presenta un crecimiento exponencial cuando aumenta en una misma proporción r durante cada unidad de tiempo. Si C es la cantidad inicial, la existente después de t unidades de tiempo viene dada por $y = C(1 + r)^t$, donde r es la tasa de crecimiento y $(1 + r)$ el factor de crecimiento.

extraneous solution (p. 705) **solución extraña** Solución de prueba que no satisface la ecuación original.

extremes of a proportion (p. 633) **extremos de una proporción** En la proporción $\frac{a}{b} = \frac{c}{d}$, a y d son los extremos.

factor a polynomial completely (p. 617) **descomponer un polinomio en todos sus factores** Escribir un polinomio como producto de factores monómicos y primos.

factor a trinomial (p. 595) **descomponer un trinomio en factores** Escribir el trinomio como producto de dos binomios.

factored form of a polynomial (p. 588) **forma factorial de un polinomio** Polinomio escrito como producto de dos o más factores.

formula (p. 171) **fórmula** Ecuación algebraica que relaciona dos o más variables.

function (p. 48) **función** Regla que establece una relación entre dos cantidades: la de entrada y la de salida. A cada entrada le corresponde una sola salida.

function form (p. 211) **forma de función** Una ecuación de dos variables está expresada en forma de función si una de sus variables está aislada en un miembro de la ecuación. La variable aislada es la salida que además está en función de la entrada.

function notation (p. 254) **notación de función** Forma de describir una función por medio de una ecuación. Para la ecuación $y = f(x)$, el símbolo $f(x)$ indica la salida y se lee "el valor de f en x" o simplemente "f de x".

graph of an equation in two variables (p. 211) **gráfica de una ecuación de dos variables** Conjunto de todos los puntos (x, y) que son soluciones de la ecuación.

graph of an inequality in one variable (p. 323) **representación gráfica de una desigualdad de una variable** Conjunto de puntos de la recta numérica que representan todas las soluciones de la desigualdad.

$x < 2$

$$-3 \quad -2 \quad -1 \quad 0 \quad 1 \quad 2 \quad 3$$

graph of a number (p. 65) **representación gráfica de un número** Punto situado en una recta numérica que corresponde a un número.

graph of a quadratic inequality (p. 547) **gráfica de una desigualdad cuadrática** Gráfica de todos los pares ordenados (x, y) que son soluciones de la desigualdad.

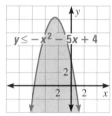

grouping symbols (p. 10) **signos de agrupación** Signos como los paréntesis ( ) o los corchetes [ ] que indican el orden en que deben realizarse las operaciones. Se efectúan primero las operaciones de los signos de agrupación situados más en el interior.

growth factor (p. 476) **factor de crecimiento** La expresión $1 + r$, en el modelo de crecimiento exponencial donde r es la tasa de crecimiento. *Ver también* crecimiento exponencial.

growth rate (p. 476) **tasa de crecimiento** La proporción de un modelo de crecimiento exponencial en la cual aumenta la cantidad durante cada unidad de tiempo.

hypotenuse (p. 724) **hipotenusa** El lado opuesto al ángulo recto de un triángulo rectángulo.

hypothesis (p. 120) **hipótesis** La parte del *si* en un enunciado de si-entonces.

identity (p. 153) **identidad** Ecuación que es cierta para todos los valores de la variable.

identity property of addition (p. 79) **propiedad de identidad de la suma** La suma de un número y 0 es igual a ese número. Para todo número real a, $a + 0 = 0 + a = a$.

identity property of multiplication (p. 94) propiedad de identidad de la multiplicación El producto de un número y 1 es igual a ese número. Para todo número real a, $1 \cdot a = a$.

if-then statement (p. 120) enunciado de si-entonces Tipo de enunciado que se emplea en el razonamiento deductivo y en el cual la parte del *si* es la hipótesis y la parte del *entonces* la conclusión.

indirect proof (p. 742) prueba indirecta Tipo de pruebas en que se supone que el enunciado es falso. Si mediante esa suposición se da una imposibilidad, entonces la certeza del enunciado original queda demostrada.

inductive reasoning (p. 119) razonamiento inductivo Formulación de un enunciado general basándose en varias observaciones.

inequality (p. 26) desigualdad Enunciado compuesto de dos expresiones unidas entre sí mediante un signo de desigual como <.

input (p. 48) entrada Un valor en el dominio de una función.

input-output table (p. 48) tabla de entradas y salidas La que describe una función mediante la presentación de las salidas correspondientes a varias entradas diferentes.

integers (p. 65) números enteros Los números . . . $-3, -2, -1, 0, 1, 2, 3, \ldots$.

inverse operations (p. 133) operaciones inversas Dos operaciones que se anulan mutuamente como son la suma y la resta.

inverse property of addition (p. 79) propiedad del elemento inverso de la suma La suma de un número y su opuesto es igual a 0: $a + (-a) = 0$.

inverse variation (p. 639) variación inversa La relación entre dos variables x e y para la cual hay un número k distinto a cero tal que $xy = k$ ó $y = \dfrac{k}{x}$.

Se dice que las variables x e y *varían inversamente* entre sí.

Ⓛ

leading coefficient (p. 505) coeficiente dominante En una ecuación cuadrática expresada en forma normal, $ax^2 + bx + c = 0$, donde $a \neq 0$, a es el coeficiente dominante.

least common denominator, LCD (p. 663) mínimo común denominador, mcd El menor de los múltiplos comunes a los denominadores de dos o más fracciones.

left-to-right rule (p. 16) regla de izquierda a derecha Las operaciones de igual prioridad se efectúan de izquierda a derecha.

legs of a right triangle (p. 724) catetos de un triángulo rectángulo Los dos lados de un triángulo rectángulo que no están opuestos al ángulo recto.

like terms (p. 107) términos semejantes Aquellos que tienen iguales variables y en los que cada una de éstas está elevada a igual potencia. Por ejemplo, $3x^2y$ y $-7x^2y$ son términos semejantes.

line graph (p. 44) gráfica lineal La que utiliza segmentos de recta para unir puntos de datos. Es de mucha utilidad para indicar los cambios producidos en los datos a lo largo del tiempo.

linear combination of two equations (p. 402) combinación lineal de dos ecuaciones Ecuación obtenida (1) al multiplicar una o ambas ecuaciones por una constante y (2) al sumar las ecuaciones resultantes.

linear equation in one variable (p. 134) ecuación lineal con una variable Una ecuación en que la variable viene elevada sólo a la primera potencia.

linear equation in x and y (p. 210) ecuación lineal con x e y La que puede escribirse en la forma $Ax + By = C$, donde A y B no son ambos cero.

linear function of x (p. 254) función lineal de x Función de la forma $f(x) = mx + b$.

linear inequality in x and y (p. 367) desigualdad lineal con x e y La que puede escribirse en una de estas formas: $ax + by < c$, $ax + by \leq c$, $ax + by > c$, ó $ax + by \geq c$.

linear model (p. 298) modelo lineal Una ecuación o función lineal que sirve para representar una situación de la vida real.

linear system (p. 389) sistema lineal Dos o más ecuaciones lineales con las mismas variables. Se le denomina también sistema de ecuaciones lineales.

Ⓜ

means of a proportion (p. 633) medios de una proporción En la proporción $\dfrac{a}{b} = \dfrac{c}{d}$, b y c son los medios.

midpoint of a line segment (p. 736) punto medio de un segmento de recta El punto del segmento que es equidistante de los extremos.

ENGLISH-TO-SPANISH GLOSSARY

midpoint formula (p. 736) **fórmula del punto medio** El punto medio entre (x_1, y_1) y (x_2, y_2) es $\left(\dfrac{x_1 + x_2}{2}, \dfrac{y_1 + y_2}{2} \right)$.

modeling (p. 36) **hacer un modelo** La representación de situaciones de la vida real por ecuaciones o desigualdades.

monomial (pp. 568, 569) **monomio** Número, variable o producto de números y variables; polinomio de un solo término.

multiplication property of equality (p. 140) **propiedad de igualdad en la multiplicación** Si $a = b$, entonces $ca = cb$.

multiplication property of inequality (p. 324) **propiedad de desigualdad en la multiplicación** Si $a > b$ y $c > 0$, entonces $ac > bc$ y si $a < b$, entonces $ac < bc$. Si $a > b$ y $c < 0$, entonces $ac < bc$ y si $a < b$, entonces $ac > bc$.

multiplicative property of negative one (p. 94) **propiedad multiplicativa del uno negativo** El producto de un número y -1 es igual al opuesto de ese número: $-1 \cdot a = -a$.

multiplicative property of zero (p. 94) **propiedad multiplicativa del cero** El producto de un número y 0 es igual a 0. Es decir, $0 \cdot a = 0$.

negative number (p. 65) **número negativo** Número menor que cero. *Ver también* recta numérica real.

negative square root (p. 499) **raíz cuadrada negativa** Número negativo que es una raíz cuadrada de un número positivo. Por ejemplo, la raíz cuadrada negativa de 9 es -3.

numerical expression (p. 3) **expresión numérica** La que representa un número determinado.

O

opposites (p. 71) **opuestos** Dos números situados a igual distancia del cero en una recta numérica pero en lados opuestos del mismo.

order of operations (p. 15) **orden de las operaciones** Reglas establecidas para evaluar una expresión relacionada con más de una operación.

ordered pair (p. 203) **par ordenado** Par de números empleados para identificar un punto situado en un plano de coordenadas. El primer número es la coordenada x y el segundo la coordenada y. *Ver también* plano de coordenadas.

origin (p. 203) **origen** Punto de un plano de coordenadas donde el eje horizontal corta al vertical. El punto $(0, 0)$. *Ver también* plano de coordenadas.

output (p. 48) **salida** Un valor en el recorrido de una función.

P

parabola (p. 520) **parábola** Gráfica en forma de U de una función cuadrática, $y = ax^2 + bx + c$ donde $a \neq 0$.

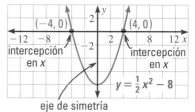

eje de simetría

parallel lines (p. 245) **rectas paralelas** Dos rectas diferentes del mismo plano que no se cortan.

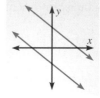

percent (p. 183) **porcentaje** Razón que relaciona un número con 100.

perfect square trinomials (p. 609) **trinomios cuadrados perfectos** Los de la forma $a^2 + 2ab + b^2$ y $a^2 - 2ab + b^2$; este tipo de trinomios pueden descomponerse en factores como cuadrados de binomios.

perpendicular lines (p. 306) **rectas perpendiculares** Dos rectas situadas en un plano son perpendiculares si al cortarse forman un ángulo recto, o sea de 90°. Si dos rectas no verticales son perpendiculares, el producto de sus pendientes es -1.

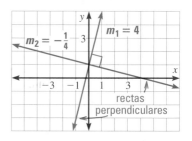

point of intersection (p. 389) **punto de intersección** Un punto (a, b) situado en las gráficas de dos o más ecuaciones es un punto de intersección de esas gráficas.

point-slope form (p. 278) **ecuación punto pendiente de una recta** Ecuación de una recta no vertical de la forma $y - y_1 = m(x - x_1)$, donde la recta pasa por un punto dado (x_1, y_1) y la recta tiene pendiente m.

positive number (p. 65) **número positivo** Número mayor que cero. *Ver también* recta numérica real.

positive square root, or principal square root (p. 499) **raíz cuadrada positiva, o raíz cuadrada principal** Raíz cuadrada de un número positivo que resulta también positiva. Por ejemplo, la raíz cuadrada positiva o principal de 9 es 3.

postulate (p. 740) **postulado** Regla que se acepta como cierta sin demostración. Al postulado se le llama también *axioma*.

power (p. 9) **potencia** Expresión de la forma a^b o valor de ese tipo de expresiones. Por ejemplo, 2^4 es una potencia, y como $2^4 = 16$, 16 es la cuarta potencia de 2.

power of a power property (pp. 444, 445) **propiedad de la potencia de una potencia** Para hallar una potencia de otra se multiplican los exponentes. Para todo número real a y para los números enteros m y n, $(a^m)^n = a^{mn}$.

power of a product property (p. 444) **propiedad de la potencia de un producto** Para hallar la potencia de un producto se halla la potencia de cada factor y se multiplica. Para todos los números reales a y b y para el número entero m, $(ab)^m = a^m \cdot b^m$.

power of a quotient property (pp. 462, 463) **propiedad de la potencia de un cociente** Para hallar la potencia de un cociente se halla la potencia del numerador y la del denominador y se divide. Para todo número entero m y todos los números reales a y b, donde $b \neq 0$, $\left(\dfrac{a}{b}\right)^m = \dfrac{a^m}{b^m}$.

prime polynomial (p. 617) **polinomio primo** El que no es el producto de factores con coeficientes de número entero y de grado menor.

product of powers property (pp. 443, 445) **propiedad del producto de potencias** Para multiplicar potencias de igual base se suman los exponentes. Para todo número real a y para los números enteros m y n, $a^m \cdot a^n = a^{m+n}$.

product property of radicals (p. 511) **propiedad del producto de radicales** Si a y b son números reales tales que $a \geq 0$ y $b \geq 0$, entonces $\sqrt{ab} = \sqrt{a} \cdot \sqrt{b}$.

properties of equality (p. 140) **propiedades de igualdad** Reglas de álgebra que sirven para transformar ecuaciones en otras equivalentes.

proportion (p. 633) **proporción** Ecuación estableciendo la igualdad de dos razones.

Pythagorean theorem (p. 724) **teorema de Pitágoras** Si un triángulo rectángulo tiene catetos de longitudes a y b y la hipotenusa de longitud c, entonces $a^2 + b^2 = c^2$.

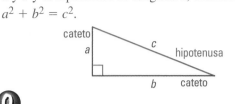

quadrant (p. 204) **cuadrante** Una de las cuatro regiones en que los ejes dividen al plano de coordenadas. *Ver también* plano de coordenadas.

quadratic equation (p. 505) **ecuación cuadrática** La que puede escribirse en la forma normal $ax^2 + bx + c = 0$, donde $a \neq 0$.

quadratic formula (p. 533) **fórmula cuadrática** Aquella que sirve para hallar las soluciones de una ecuación cuadrática $ax^2 + bx + c = 0$ cuando $a \neq 0$ y $b^2 - 4ac \geq 0$: $x = \dfrac{-b \pm \sqrt{b^2 - 4ac}}{2a}$.

quadratic function (p. 520) **función cuadrática** La que puede escribirse en la forma normal $y = ax^2 + bx + c$, donde $a \neq 0$.

quadratic inequality (p. 547) **desigualdad cuadrática** Aquella que puede escribirse de una de estas formas: $y < ax^2 + bx + c$, $y \leq ax^2 + bx + c$, $y > ax^2 + bx + c$, ó $y \geq ax^2 + bx + c$.

quotient of powers property (pp. 462, 463) **propiedad del cociente de potencias** Para dividir potencias de igual base se restan los exponentes. Para todo número real $a \neq 0$ y para los números enteros m y n, $\dfrac{a^m}{a^n} = a^{m-n}$.

quotient property of radicals (p. 512) **propiedad del cociente de radicales** Si a y b son números reales tales que $a \geq 0$ y $b > 0$, entonces $\sqrt{\dfrac{a}{b}} = \dfrac{\sqrt{a}}{\sqrt{b}}$.

radical expression, or radical (p. 501) **expresión radical, o radical** Expresión escrita con el signo radical.

radicand (p. 499) **radicando** Número o expresión que aparece debajo del signo radical.

range of a function (p. 49) **recorrido de una función** Conjunto de todos los valores de salida de una función.

rate of *a* per *b* (p. 177) **relación de *a* por *b*** Relación $\frac{a}{b}$ de dos cantidades *a* y *b* que se miden con unidades diferentes.

rate of change (p. 298) **tasa de variación** Cociente de dos cantidades diferentes que cambian. En un modelo lineal, la pendiente indica la tasa de variación de una variable con respecto a la otra.

ratio of *a* to *b* (p. 177) **razón de *a* a *b*** Relación $\frac{a}{b}$ de dos cantidades *a* y *b* que se miden con las mismas unidades.

rational equation (p. 670) **ecuación racional** Aquella que contiene expresiones racionales.

rational exponent (p. 711) **exponente racional** Para todo número entero *n* y para el número real $a \geq 0$, la raíz enésima de *a* es denotada por $a^{1/n}$ ó $\sqrt[n]{a}$. Sea $a^{1/n}$ una raíz enésima de *a*, *m* un número entero positivo y $a \geq 0$. Entonces
$$a^{m/n} = (a^{1/n})^m = (\sqrt[n]{a})^m = \sqrt[n]{a^m}.$$

rational expression (p. 646) **expresión racional** Fracción que tiene por numerador y denominador polinomios distintos a cero.

rational function (p. 678) **función racional** La que puede escribirse como cociente de polinomios.

rational number (p. 646) **número racional** El que puede escribirse como cociente de dos números enteros.

real number line (p. 65) **recta numérica real** Recta cuyos puntos corresponden a los números reales.

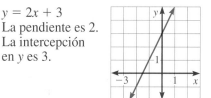

real numbers (p. 65) **números reales** Conjunto de números compuesto por los positivos, los negativos y cero. *Ver también* recta numérica real.

reciprocals (p. 113) **recíprocos** Dos números cuyo producto es 1. Si $\frac{a}{b}$ es un número distinto a cero, entonces su recíproco es $\frac{b}{a}$.

relation (p. 252) **relación** Conjunto cualquiera de pares ordenados.

roots of a quadratic equation (p. 527) **raíces de una ecuación cuadrática** Soluciones de una ecuación cuadrática.

rounding error (p. 164) **error de redondeo** El producido tras limitar la expansión de un decimal a un número específico de enteros a la derecha del punto decimal.

scatter plot (p. 205) **diagrama de dispersión** Gráfica de coordenadas cuyos puntos representan un conjunto de pares ordenados; es de utilidad para analizar las relaciones entre dos cantidades reales.

scientific notation (p. 469) **notación científica** Número expresado en la forma $c \times 10^n$, donde $1 \leq c < 10$ y *n* es un número entero.

simplified expression (p. 108) **expresión simplificada** Aquella que carece de signos de agrupación y tiene combinados todos los términos semejantes.

simplest form of a radical expression (p. 511) **expresión radical en su mínima expresión** La que no tiene en el radicando factores de raíz exacta distintos a 1 ni fracciones, además de no tener radicales en el denominador de una fracción.

slope (p. 229, 230) **pendiente** Razón de la distancia vertical a la distancia horizontal existente entre dos puntos cualesquiera de una recta. La pendiente es
$$m = \frac{(y_2 - y_1)}{(x_2 - x_1)}.$$

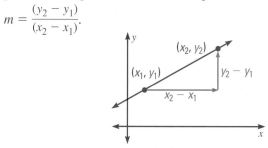

slope-intercept form (p. 243) **ecuación pendiente intercepción de una recta** Ecuación lineal escrita en la forma $y = mx + b$. La pendiente de la recta es *m* y la intercepción en *y* es *b*. *Ver también* pendiente e intercepción en *y*.

$y = 2x + 3$
La pendiente es 2.
La intercepción
en *y* es 3.

solution of an equation or inequality (p. 24) **solución de una ecuación o desigualdad** Número que cumple una ecuación o desigualdad al sustituir a la variable de la misma.

solution of an equation in two variables (p. 210) **solución de una ecuación de dos variables** Par ordenado (x, y) que cumple la ecuación.

solution of a linear system in two variables (p. 389) **solución de un sistema lineal de dos variables** Par ordenado (x, y) que satisface cada ecuación del sistema.

solution of a system of linear inequalities in two variables (p. 424) **solución de un sistema de desigualdades lineales de dos variables** Par ordenado que cumple cada desigualdad del sistema.

square root (p. 499) **raíz cuadrada** Si $b^2 = a$, entonces b es una raíz cuadrada de a. Las raíces cuadradas pueden escribirse con el signo radical, $\sqrt{}$.

square root function (p. 692) **función de raíz cuadrada** La definida por la ecuación $y = \sqrt{x}$, para $x \geq 0$.

standard form of an equation of a line (p. 291) **forma usual de la ecuación de una recta** Ecuación lineal de la forma $Ax + By = C$, donde A y B no son ambos cero.

standard form of a polynomial in one variable (p. 569) **forma usual de un polinomio de una variable** Polinomio cuyos términos están escritos en orden descendente, del exponente mayor al menor.

standard form of a quadratic equation (p. 505) **forma usual de una ecuación cuadrática** Ecuación de la forma $ax^2 + bx + c = 0$, donde $a \neq 0$.

subtraction property of equality (p. 140) **propiedad de igualdad en la resta** Si $a = b$, entonces $a - c = b - c$.

subtraction property of inequality (p. 324) **propiedad de desigualdad en la resta** Si $a > b$, entonces $a - c > b - c$, y si $a < b$, entonces $a - c < b - c$.

system of linear equations (p. 389) **sistema de ecuaciones lineales** Dos o más ecuaciones lineales que tienen las mismas variables. Se le llama también sistema lineal.

system of linear inequalities (p. 424) **sistema de desigualdades lineales** Dos o más desigualdades lineales que tienen las mismas variables. Se le llama también sistema de desigualdades.

terms of an expression (p. 87) **términos de una expresión** Partes que se unen para formar una expresión. Por ejemplo, en la expresión $5 - x$, los términos son 5 y $-x$.

theorem (p. 724) **teorema** Afirmación cuya certeza ha sido demostrada.

trinomial (p. 569) **trinomio** Polinomio de tres términos.

unit analysis (p. 178) **análisis por unidades** Usar las unidades de cada variable de un problema real para así determinar las unidades de la solución.

unit rate (p. 177) **tasa unitaria** Relación que expresa la magnitud de una cantidad dada por unidad de otra cantidad como, por ejemplo, millas por galón.

values (p. 3) **valores** Números que representa una variable.

variable (p. 3) **variable** Letra empleada para representar una gama de números.

variable expression (p. 3) **expresión algebraica** Forma simbólica compuesta por constantes, variables y operaciones.

verbal model (p. 36) **modelo verbal** Expresión que emplea palabras para describir una situación de la vida real.

vertex of a vertically oriented parabola (p. 521) **vértice de una parábola orientada verticalmente** Punto inferior de la gráfica de una parábola que abre hacia arriba o punto superior de la gráfica de una parábola que abre hacia abajo. *Ver también* parábola.

vertical motion models (p. 535) **modelos de movimiento vertical** Aquellos que dan la altura de un objeto como una función del tiempo. Incluyen el caso de un objeto que cae.

whole numbers (p. 65) **números naturales** Números enteros positivos y cero.

X

x-axis (p. 203) **eje de las x** Eje horizontal de un plano de coordenadas. *Ver también* plano de coordenadas.

x-coordinate (p. 203) **coordenada x** Primer número de un par ordenado. *Ver también* par ordenado.

x-intercept (p. 222) **intercepción en x** Coordenada x de un punto donde una gráfica cruza al eje de las x.

Y

y-axis (p. 203) **eje de las y** Eje vertical de un plano de coordenadas. *Ver también* plano de coordenadas.

y-coordinate (p. 203) **coordenada y** Segundo número de un par ordenado. *Ver también* par ordenado.

y-intercept (p. 222) **intercepción en y** Coordenada y de un punto donde una gráfica cruza al eje de las y.

Z

zero-product property (p. 588) **propiedad del producto cero** Si el producto de dos factores es cero, entonces al menos uno de ellos debe ser cero.

Index

INDEX

Division rule, 113

Dobbs, John Wesley, 637

Domain
    of a constant function, 218
    definition of, 49
    division by zero and, 115, 116, 117
    of an exponential function, 457
    of a radical function, 691, 692

E

End-of-Course Test, *See* Assessment

Enrichment, *See* Challenge
    exercises; Extension

Equality, properties of, 140

Equation(s), *See also* Formulas;
    Functions; Graphs; Linear
    equations; Modeling;
    Polynomials; Quadratic
    equations
    absolute value, 72–76, 354–360,
      377
    addition and subtraction of linear,
      132–137, 189, 402–407
    checking solutions of, 24–29,
      56–57
    compound interest, 477
    cubic, 619, 621–622
    decimal, 163–169, 191
    definition of, 24
    direct variation, 236–240, 261,
      639–640, 642–644, 681–682
    equivalent, 132
    exponential decay, 482
    exponential growth, 476
    of horizontal lines, 293, 295
    identity, 153, 154, 155
    for linear functions, 50–54, 58
    using mental math to solve, 25,
      27, 28
    quadratic, 505–510, 553
    radical, 704–709, 748
    rational, 670–676, 684
    repeated factor, 589–593
    solution of, 24
    systems of, 386–436
    transforming, 132, 138
    translating words into, 31–35, 57
    with variables on both sides,
      150–162, 190
    of vertical lines, 293, 295

Equivalent equations, 132

Error analysis, 104, 110, 116, 142,
    147, 155, 161, 296, 328, 334,
    340, 400, 405, 420, 427, 453,
    466, 509, 514, 544, 571, 591,
    602, 607, 620, 655, 661, 667,
    702, 707

Estimation, *See also* Prediction
    area, 5, 422, 775–776
    compatible numbers and, 775–776
    exercises, 83, 334, 468, 544
    using exponential models, 483,
      486, 493
    front-end, 774, 776
    using a graph, 46, 244, 321, 390,
      393, 395, 431, 497, 530
    using linear models, 298–304, 316
    of roots of a quadratic equation,
      532
    rounding and, 774, 776
    using slope-intercept form, 243,
      244, 248
    of square root, 500–504

Expanded form, 99–105

Exponential decay, 482–487, 492

Exponential function(s)
    comparing to linear functions, 475
    decay, 482–487, 492
    evaluating, 455–461, 490
    graph of, 455–461, 490
    growth, 476–481, 484, 492

Exponential growth, 475–481, 484,
    492

Exponent(s), 9–14, 56, *See also*
    Exponential functions
    division properties of, 462–468,
      490–491
    grouping symbols and, 10–11
    multiplication properties of,
      441–448, 489
    rational, 710–714, 748
    scientific notation and, 469–474
    zero and negative, 449–454,
      464–468, 489–490

Expression(s)
    absolute value, 71–76, 122
    addition, 78–83
    combining like terms in, 107–112,
      124
    describing patterns with, 22–23
    distributive property and, 99–105,
      123
    division, 113–117, 124
    equivalent, 99
    evaluating, 4–8, 55, 381
    exponential, 9–14, 56, 443–454,
      462–468
    with fraction bars, 16, 19

    multiplication, 93–98, 123
    order of operations and, 15–21
    radical, 501–504
    rational
      adding and subtracting,
        658–669, 683–684
      factoring, 647–650, 671–676
      multiplying and dividing,
        652–657, 683
      simplifying, 646–650, 682
      with rational exponents, 710–714
    simplified, 107–112
    square root, 500–504
    subtraction, 86–91, 122
    terms of, 87–91
    translating words into, 30–35, 57
    value of, 4
    variable, 94–98
    variables and, 3–8

**Extension: Inductive and Deductive
    Reasoning,** 119–120

Extension exercises, 120, 199, 385,
    563

Extraneous solution, 705–709

Extra Practice for Chapters, 1–12,
    783–794

Extremes of a proportion, 633

F

Factored cubic equation, 589–593

Factored form of a polynomial,
    588–593, 624

Factoring, rational expressions,
    647–650, 671–676

Factoring a polynomial
    $ax^2 + bx + c$, 602–608, 625
    cubic, 616–622, 626
    special products, 609–615,
      618–620, 626
    $x^2 + bx + c$, 594–601, 625

Factor(s), 761
    prime, 495, 761

FOIL pattern, 576, 578, 603

Formula(s)
    area, 172, 174–175, 192, 516, 772
    Celsius/Fahrenheit temperature,
      171, 174
    compound interest, 477
    density, 173, 175
    distance, 3–4, 7, 8, 38, 129, 173,
      730–735, 750
    falling object, 507
    lateral surface area of a cone, 696
    Continued

Improper fraction, 495, 763
Independent variable, 4–5
Indirect proof, 742, 743, 745
Inductive reasoning, 119–120
    exercises, 234
Inequality, *See also* Linear
        inequality; Quadratic
        inequality
    absolute value, 361–366, 378
        multi-step, 363–365
    checking solutions of, 26–29,
        56–57
    compound
        involving *and*, 342–347, 376
        involving *or*, 348–353, 377
        multi-step, 344–346, 349–352,
        377
    definition of, 26
    equivalent, 324
    graphing
        absolute value, 361–366
        compound, 342–347, 348–353
        one variable, 323–328, 330–335,
        336–341
    properties of, 324–328, 330–335
    solution of, 26
    solving
        using addition or subtraction,
        323–328, 375
        using multiplication and
        division, 330–335, 375
        multi-step, 336–341, 376
    systems of, 423–429, 434
    words for, 31–35, 57, 323, 326
    writing, 325, 327, 342, 345, 348,
        351, 357, 359
        systems of, 426–429
Inequality symbols, 26, 66
Input, 48
Input-output table, 48–54, 58, 195,
        252, 255
    definition of, 48
Integer(s)
    addition of, 77–83, 381
    changing decimals to, 167
    comparing, 66
    definition of, 65
    graphing on a number line, 65–70
    multiplication of, 92–98
    subtraction of, 84–91
Intercepts, 222–227, 260
Interest, compound, 477, 479, 480
Internet Connections
    Application Links, 1, 63, 129, 161,

201, 214, 226, 237, 267, 271,
274, 321, 327, 365, 372, 387,
398, 413, 439, 457, 497, 513,
524, 537, 565, 631, 635, 689
    Career Links, 38, 44, 97, 136, 173,
187, 207, 340, 359, 371, 391,
421, 428, 447, 466, 486, 509,
544, 598, 675, 696, 734, 742
    Data Updates, 42, 46, 67, 91, 182,
205, 227, 273, 298, 347, 413,
473
    Homework Help, 7, 19, 34, 40, 46,
52, 69, 75, 90, 104, 117, 136,
142, 148, 155, 162, 167, 181,
187, 215, 256, 273, 282, 289,
295, 303, 310, 327, 346, 359,
365, 400, 421, 429, 447, 480,
487, 503, 525, 538, 579, 586,
592, 607, 643, 656, 661, 675,
702, 708, 720, 728, 744
    Keystroke Help, 250, 374, 395,
461, 532, 645
    More Examples, 10, 25, 50, 61, 67,
73, 80, 95, 101, 108, 115, 127,
133, 139, 145, 153, 159, 164,
172, 179, 185, 195, 204, 217,
224, 232, 237, 245, 265, 280,
287, 306, 319, 332, 337, 349,
369, 381, 389, 404, 411, 437,
450, 457, 464, 470, 495, 506,
512, 527, 534, 542, 549, 559,
569, 576, 583, 589, 598, 605,
612, 618, 629, 641, 647, 654,
659, 665, 672, 687, 693, 705,
712, 725, 732, 737, 739, 743
    Software Help, 170
Inverse operations
    addition and subtraction, 133
    multiplication and division, 138
    square and square root, 499
Inverse property
    of real number multiplication, 113,
        740
    of real number addition, 79–83,
        740
Inverse proportion, *See* Inverse
        variation
Inverse variation, 639–645,
        681–682
    rational functions and, 678–680
Investigations, *See* Reasoning;
        Technology Activities
Irrational number, 500

J

Jones, Brian, 650
Justification of steps, 23, 75, 84, 85,
        89, 111, 120, 131, 135, 137,
        148, 150, 155, 161, 167, 168,
        176, 187, 337, 339, 405, 407,
        420, 427, 428, 448, 458, 475,
        514, 515, 516, 538, 545, 546,
        560, 561, 563, 642, 644, 650,
        689, 691, 718–720, 728, 729,
        744, 749, 751, 753

K

Keystroke Help, *See* Calculator,
        Student Help, Internet
        Connections
Kuhn, Jon, 13

L

Leading coefficient, 505
Least common denominator
        (LCD), 629, 663–669,
        671–762, 674–676
Least common multiple (LCM),
        761
Left-to-right rule, 16–19
Like denominators, 658
Like terms
    arranging in columns, 403, 404
    combining, 107–112, 124,
        145–149, 559
Linear combinations, 402–407,
        432–433
Linear equation(s)
    checking solutions of, 210
    decimal, 163–169, 191
    definition of, 134
    direct variation, 236–240, 261
    forms of, 210, 211, 216, 217, 236,
        243, 269, 278, 291
    formulas, 171–176
    function form of, 211
    graphing
        direct variation, 237–240
        horizontal lines, 216–220, 260
        using intercepts, 222–227, 260
        parallel lines, 245, 247, 248
        using slope-intercept form,
        243–248, 262
        using a table of values, 211–215
        vertical lines, 216–220
    for horizontal lines, 293, 295
    Continued

Multiplication, *cont.*
  of rational expressions, 652–657,
      683
  real number, 93–98, 123
  by a reciprocal, 139–143,
      146–149, 763
  to solve an inequality, 330–335,
      375
  to solve a linear equation,
      138–143, 189
**Multiplication property of
    inequality,** 330–335, 375

N

Negative number(s), 65
  adding, 78–83
  dividing by, 331–335
  as exponents, 449–454, 464–468,
      489–490
  multiplying by, 331–335
  square root and, 500
Negative one, property of, 94
Negative slope, 231
Negative square root, 499
Number line
  absolute value and, 71
  absolute value equations and, 354,
      357–359
  absolute value inequalities and,
      361–362, 364–365
  adding real numbers on, 78, 81
  comparing and ordering numbers
      with, 770–771
  drawing, 319
  graphing inequalities on, 323–328,
      330–335, 336–339, 341,
      342–347, 348–353, 375
  graphing opposites on, 71
  graphing real numbers on, 65–70,
      121
  plotting fractions and decimals on,
      61
Number(s)
  absolute value of, 71–76, 121–122
  integer, 65–66
  irrational, 500
  negative, 65
  opposites, 71
  perfect square, 500
  positive, 65
  prime, 761
  rational, 646
  real, 62–118
    comparing, 67–70

  ordering, 67–70, 121
  whole, 65

O

Opposite
  adding to subtract, 86–91
  of a polynomial, 570
  of a real number, 71
Ordered pair
  definition of, 203
  as solution of an equation, 210
Ordering
  rational numbers, 770–771
  real numbers, 67–70, 121
Order of operations, 15–21, 56, 265
  grouping symbols and, 10–11
  left-to-right rule, 16–19
Origin, coordinate plane, 203
Output, 48

P

Parabola, 53, 520
Parallel lines
  graphing, 245, 247, 248, 280–282
  slope and, 245
Patterns
  algebraic expressions and, 22–23
  difference of two cubes, 618–621
  difference of two squares, 609–615
  exponential, 453
  FOIL, 576, 578, 603
  geometric, 781
  graphs of equations, 242
  for multiplying integers, 92
  perfect square trinomial, 609–615
  special product, 581, 624
  square of a binomial, 581–587
  sum of two cubes, 618–621
  in tables, 1, 42
Percent, 183–188, 192
  decay functions and, 482–483,
      485–487
  decimals and, 165, 437, 768–796
  definition, 183
  discount, 183, 185
  fractions and, 768–769
  growth functions and, 475–481
Perfect square, 500
Perfect square trinomial, 609–615,
      687
  completing the square and,
      716–721
Perimeter, 5, 6, 7, 22–23, 772–773

Perpendicular lines
  definition of, 306
  equations of, 306–311, 316
  slope of, 305, 316
Piccard, Bertrand, 650
Plot
  points from a table of values,
      211–215
  scatter plot, 205, 207, 259
**Point of intersection, of the graphs
    of linear equations,** 389
Point-slope form, 276–283, 314
  general formula, 276–278
  for writing equations given two
      points, 286–290, 314
Polygon(s), perimeter and area of,
      772–773
Polynomial equation, *See also*
      Quadratic equation
  factored form of, 588–593
  solving
    by factoring, 598, 599, 600–601,
        605–607, 612–615
    by graphing, 526–532, 555
    by the quadratic formula,
        533–539, 555
  summary of, 619
Polynomial(s)
  addition of, 567–573, 623
  classifying, 569
  cubic, 616–622, 626
  definition of, 569
  degree of, 569
  factored form, 588–593, 624
  factoring
    $ax^2 + bx + c$, 602–608, 625–626
    cubic, 616–622
    $x^2 + bx + c$, 594–601, 625
  multiplication of, 574–580,
      623–624
  special products, 581–587, 624
  subtraction of, 567, 570–573, 623
Positive number(s), 65
Positive slope, 230
Positive square root, 499
Postulate, 740
Power of a power property,
      444–448
Power of a product property,
      444–448
Power of a quotient property,
      463–468
Powers, 441–448, *See also* Exponents
  coefficients and, 107

INDEX

Credits

Cover Photography

Ralph Mercer

Photography

i, ii Ralph Mercer; **iii** RMIP/Richard Haynes (all); **iv** Kevin Horan/Tony Stone Images; **v** Stuart Westmorland/Photo Researchers, Inc.; **vi** Baron Wolman/Tony Stone Images; **vii** Darrell Gulin/Tony Stone Images; **viii** Dennis Hallinan/FPG International; **ix** Melissa Farlow/National Geographic Image Collection; **x** Bob Daemmrich/The Image Works; **xi** Billy Hustace/Tony Stone Images; **xii** Dean Abramson/Stock Boston/PNI/PictureQuest; **xiii** Vincent Laforet/Allsport; **xiv** Roger Ressmeyer/CORBIS; **xv** CORBIS/Phillip Gould; **xvi** Rex A. Butcher/Tony Stone Images; **xxvi** Stuart Westmorland/Photo Researchers, Inc.; **1** Stuart Westmorland/Photo Researchers, Inc.; **3** Lewis Portnoy/The Stock Market; **4** CORBIS/AFP; **9** Gibbs, M. QSF/Animals Animals; **13** John Kuhn; **15** David Young-Wolff/Tony Stone Images; **17** Eric R. Berndt/Unicorn Stock Photo; **19** RMIP/Richard Haynes; **20** Mark Gibson; **23** RMIP/Richard Haynes (all); **24** Zane Williams/Tony Stone Images; **25** CORBIS **26** Zigy Kaluzny/Tony Stone Images; **28** Hurlin-Saola/Liaison Agency; **30** Martha Granger/EDGE Productions; **34** John Feingersh/Stock Boston; **36** Ted Streshinsky/Photo 20-20; **38** David H. Frazier/Tony Stone Images; **40** Robert Ginn/PhotoEdit; **42** Mark Stouffer/Bruce Coleman Inc.; **44** Tom McHugh/Photo Researchers, Inc.; **46** Stephen R. Swinburne/Stock Boston; **48** Mark Wagner/Tony Stone Images; **52** Courtesy of the Archives Division of the Oklahoma Historical Society, negative number 1757.; **53** Stephen Frink/The Stock Market; **62** Baron Wolman/Tony Stone Images; **63** George Hall/Woodfin Camp and Associates; **67** Charles Krebs/The Stock Market; **69** Jay M. Pasachoff/Visuals Unlimited; **71** courtesy, NASA; **75** courtesy, NASA; **78** Bert Sagara/Tony Stone Images; **82** AP Photo/Osamu Honda; **86** Alan Schein/The Stock Market; **88** Hulton-Deutsch Collection/CORBIS; **93** Marty Stouffer/Animals Animals; **95** Nick Bergkessel/Photo Researchers, Inc.; **97** Galen Rowell/CORBIS; **100** Bob Daemmrich/The Image Works; **102** Phil Degginger/Animals Animals; **105** David Joel/Tony Stone Images; **107** Richard T. Nowitz/Corbis; **109** Alan Schein/The Stock Market; **111** Phil Degginger/Bruce Coleman Inc.; **113** James Handkley/Tony Stone Images; **128** Darrell Gulin/Tony Stone Images; **129** Tom & Pat Leeson/DRK Photo; **132** Bobbi Lane/Tony Stone Images (background); Deborah Davis/Tony Stone Images (inset); **134** Tom Bean Photography; **136** Robert Brenner/PhotoEdit; **138** Antman/The Image Works; **140** Mel Traxel/Motion Picture and Television Photo Archive; **142** Rob Matheson/ The Stock Market; **144** Photri/The Stock Market; **151** Tom Brakefield/DRK Photo; **157** Bob Daemmrich Photography; **161** Don Mason/The Stock Market; **163** Shahn Kermani/Liaison Agency, Inc.; **167** Aaron Haupt/Photo Researchers, Inc.; **171** National Geographic Image Collection (r); Mike Brown/Florida Today/Liaison Agency, Inc. (l); **173** AP Photo/Kevork Djansezian; **175** Flip Nicklin/Minden Pictures; **177** Dave G. Houser; **179** School Division, Houghton Mifflin Company; **183** Martha Granger/EDGE Productions; **187** David Young Wolff-PhotoEdit; **198** Stephen Frisch/Stock Boston; **199** Paul Barton/The Stock Market; **200, 201** Dennis Hallinan/FPG International; **203** CC Lockwood/Animals Animals; **207** Eastcott/The Image Works; **210** Bongarts Photography/Sportschrome; **214** Thomas Zimmerman/Tony Stone Images; **216** Pat and Tom Lesson/Photo Researchers, Inc. (background); Calvin Larsen/Photo Researchers, Inc. (inset); **220** Kent & Donna Dannen; **222** Bob Rowan; Progressive Image/CORBIS; **226** Frank Fournier/The Stock Market; **228** RMIP/Richard Haynes (all); **229** Kevin Horan/Tony Stone Images; **233** Frank Siteman/Stock Boston; **234** James Lemass/Index Stock Photography, Inc.; **235** Mark Antman/Stock Boston; **236** Michael Nelson/FPG International; **237** Adam Tanner/The Image Works; **240** Bob Daemmrich Photography (l); Artville, LLC. (r); **243** Tony Freeman/PhotoEdit; **247** CORBIS; **248** Matthew J. Atanian/Tony Stone Images; **252** Stephen Dalton/Animals Animals; **257** Tim Mosenfelder/CORBIS; **266** Melissa Farlow/National Geographic Image Collection; **267** Mastrorillo/The Stock Market; **269** Simon Bruty/Allsport; **271** courtesy, NASA; **274** Barbara Filet/Tony Stone Images; **278** CORBIS/The Purcell Team; **282** Peter David/Photo Researchers, Inc.; **285** Andrew Hourmont/Tony Stone Images; **291** Wayne Lankinen/DRK Photo; **296** Len Rue Jr./Photo Researchers, Inc.; **298** Bob Daemmrich Photography; **302** Bob Daemmrich Photos; **303** Werner Forman Archive, Maxwell Museum of Anthropology, Albuquerque, NM, USA/Art Resource; **304** Ken Frick; **305** RMIP/Richard Haynes; **306** CORBIS/Douglas Peebles; **308** John Darling/Tony Stone Images; **311** Stock Montage; **320, 321** Bob Daemmrich/The Image Works; **323** Roger Ressmeyer/CORBIS; **327** James Sugar/Black Star/PNI (l); Kevin Scola (r); **330** Catherine Karnow/Woodfin Camp and Associates; **334** Paul S. Howell/Liaison Agency, Inc.; **336** David J. Sams/Stock Boston; **338** Charles Thatcher/Tony Stone Images; **340** Courtesy of Chance Rides, Inc.; **342** Chuck Pefley/Tony Stone Images; **343** W. Perry Conway/CORBIS (l); Rich Iwaski/Tony Stone Images (r); **346** Stock Montage (l); Frederica Georgia/Photo Researchers, Inc. (r); **348** RMIP/Richard Haynes (inset); **352** Willie Hill/Stock Boston; **355** Walter Chandoha; **359** Paul Souders/Tony Stone Images; **361** Bachmann/PhotoEdit; **365** J. F. Towers/The Stock Market; **367** Michael Newman/PhotoEdit; **371** Yoav Levy/Phototake; **372** Al Giddings Images; **384** RMIP/Richard Haynes (all); **385** Jon Riley/Tony Stone Images; **386** Billy Hustace/Tony Stone Images; **387** Bob Daemmrich/Uniphoto; **391** Bob Daemmrich Photography; **393** Hulton-Deutsh Collection/CORBIS; **396** RMIP/Richard Haynes; **398** Associated Press AP; **400** Bob Daemmrich Photos; **402** Tom Evans/Photo Researchers, Inc.; **406** North Wind Picture Archives; **407** Reproduced by Permission of the Commercial Press (Hong Kong) Limited from the publication of *Chinese Mathematics: A Concise History*; **409** Don Smetzer/Tony Stone Images; **410** Doug Martin/Photo Researchers, Inc.; **413** Kevin R. Morris/CORBIS; **417** Mary Kate Denny/PhotoEdit; **421** Bill Varie/CORBIS; **424** Charlie Westerman/International Stock Photo; **428** M. Granitsas/The Image Works; **438** Dean Abramson/Stock Boston/PNI; **439** David Madison; **443** Mark Wagner/Tony Stone Images; **447** Keith Wood/Tony Stone Images; **449** Archive Photos; **457** Texas Historical Commission; **459** Nancy Sheehan/PhotoEdit; **462** Jonathan Daniel/Allsport; **466** Tim Flach/Tony Stone Images; **469** Hulton Getty Collection/Tony Stone Images; **473** The Granger Collection (l); North Wind Picture Archives (r); **476** Tom McHugh/Photo Researchers, Inc.; **482** James Wilson/Woodfin Camp and Associates; **486** Owen Franken/CORBIS; **496, 497** Vincent Laforet/Allsport; **499** Catherine Karnow/CORBIS; **503** Gianni Dagli Orti/CORBIS; **505** Richard B. Levine; **509** Ken M. Johns/Photo Researchers, Inc. (tl); Photo Researchers, Inc. (cl); Charles D. Winters/Photo Researchers, Inc.(tc); E.R. Degginger/Photo Researchers, Inc. (cr, bl); Tom McHugh/Photo Researchers, Inc. (bc); Biophoto Associates/Photo Researchers, Inc. (br); **511** Stephen Munday/Allsport; **513** Mike Hewitt/Allsport; **520** Chris Cole/Allsport; **524** Tim Davis/Photo Researchers, Inc. (l); Michel Hans/Vandystadt/Allsport (r); **526** Susan Van Etten/PhotoEdit; **530** courtesy, NASA; **533** Mike Powell/Allsport; **537** Gordon & Cathy Illg/Animals Animals (l); **540** Bob Gurr/DRK Photo; **544** Gary A. Conner/PhotoEdit; **547** Amos Nachoum/CORBIS; **562** Stephen Frisch/Stock Boston; **563** Phillip Bailey/The Stock Market (tr); G. Brad Lewis/Tony Stone Images (bl); **564, 565** Roger Ressmeyer/CORBIS; **568** Tony Freeman/PhotoEdit; **572** David Lissy/Index Stock Photography; **575** Photodisc, Inc.; **579** Jeff Greenberg/PhotoEdit; **581** Ron Kimball Studios; **584** Mark E. Gibson/The Stock Market; **586** Michael Schimpf; **588** Dave G.

Selected Answers

Pre-Course Practice

DECIMALS (p. xx) **1.** 21.1 **3.** 67.95 **5.** 15.105 **7.** 66.3
9. 76.304 **11.** 729.008 **13.** 3.7 **15.** 0.35

FACTORS AND MULTIPLES (p. xx) **1.** 1, 2, 3, 4, 6, 12
3. 1, 2, 3, 6, 9, 18, 27, 54 **5.** $2 \cdot 3^3$ **7.** $5 \cdot 7$ **9.** 1, 2, 4
11. 1, 2, 7, 14 **13.** 4 **15.** 3 **17.** 6 **19.** 2 **21.** 36
23. 42 **25.** 48 **27.** 900 **29.** 24 **31.** 60 **33.** 28 **35.** 54

FRACTIONS (p. xxi) **1.** $\frac{1}{8}$ **3.** $\frac{5}{9}$ **5.** $\frac{1}{2}$ **7.** $1\frac{1}{5}$ **9.** $\frac{5}{9}$
11. $\frac{19}{24}$ **13.** $\frac{3}{10}$ **15.** $\frac{9}{10}$ **17.** $\frac{1}{2}$ **19.** 6 **21.** $1\frac{1}{2}$ **23.** $13\frac{31}{40}$
25. $1\frac{1}{3}$ **27.** $1\frac{1}{4}$

FRACTIONS, DECIMALS, AND PERCENTS (p. xxi) **1.** 0.08,
$\frac{2}{25}$ **3.** 0.38, $\frac{19}{50}$ **5.** 1.35, $1\frac{7}{20}$ **7.** 0.064, $\frac{8}{125}$ **9.** 44%,
$\frac{11}{25}$ **11.** 13%, $\frac{13}{100}$ **13.** 160%, $1\frac{3}{5}$ **15.** 660%, $6\frac{3}{5}$
17. 0.6, 60% **19.** 0.68, 68% **21.** 5.2, 520% **23.** 3.063,
306.3%

COMPARING AND ORDERING NUMBERS (p. xxii)
1. $13{,}458 < 14{,}455$ **3.** $-8344 > -8434$ **5.** $0.58 > 0.578$
7. $\frac{15}{16} > \frac{9}{10}$ **9.** $\frac{9}{24} = \frac{3}{8}$ **11.** $-2\frac{11}{16} > -3\frac{2}{9}$ **13.** 1075,
1507, 1705, 1775 **15.** $-0.205, -0.035, -0.019, -0.013$
17. $\frac{2}{7}, \frac{5}{11}, \frac{1}{2}, \frac{5}{8}$ **19.** $-\frac{4}{2}, -\frac{3}{2}, -\frac{4}{3}, -\frac{2}{3}$ **21.** $\frac{7}{5}, 1\frac{3}{5}, \frac{5}{3}, 1\frac{4}{5}$

PERIMETER, AREA, AND VOLUME (p. xxii) **1.** 10 m
3. 22.6 km **5.** 95 ft **7.** 3.92 in.^{2} **9.** 39,304 ft^3
11. 78.65 mm^3

DATA DISPLAYS (p. xxiii) **1.** *Sample answer:* 0 to 60 by
tens: 0, 10, 20, 30, 40, 50, 60 **3.** *Sample answer:* 0 to
25 by fives: 0, 5, 10, 15, 20, 25
5. *Sample answer:* bar graph

MEASURES OF CENTRAL TENDENCY (p. xxiii) **1.** 4.9; 5; 7
3. 52.1; 53; no mode

Chapter 1

STUDY GUIDE (p. 2) **1.** B **2.** A **3.** B **4.** A

1.1 GUIDED PRACTICE (p. 6) **7.** p minus 4, subtraction
9. 8 times x, multiplication **11.** 1 **13.** $\frac{1}{11}$ **15.** 54

1.1 PRACTICE AND APPLICATIONS (pp. 6–8) **21.** 20
23. 2 **25.** 20 **27.** 9 **29.** 70 **31.** 6 **33.** 260 mi
35. 40 ft **37.** 340 mi **39.** 240 ft **41.** 64 m **43.** 10 m^2
45. 6 yd^2 **49.** 4 h **53.** 9.48 **55.** 15 **57.** $\frac{1}{6}$ **59.** 23.9
61. 11.1508 **63.** 53.55 **65.** 13.405

1.2 GUIDED PRACTICE (p. 12) **5.** B **7.** A **9.** 9 **11.** 36

1.2 PRACTICE AND APPLICATIONS (pp. 12–14) **13.** 2^3
15. 9^5 **17.** 3^4 **19.** 5^2; 25 **21.** 16 **23.** 64 **25.** 1 **27.** 0
29. 729 **31.** 32 **33.** 125 **35.** 371,293 **37.** 35,831,808
39. 531,441 **41.** 29 **43.** 9 **45.** 20 **47.** 6 **49.** 15,625
51. 100,000 **53.** 8 ft^3 **55.** 2^3, 8 cubic units **57.** 4^3,
64 cubic units **65.** 18 **67.** 45 **69.** 9 **71.** 28 **73.** 3
75. 9 **77.** 5 **79.** $\frac{3}{10}$ **81.** $\frac{6}{7}$ **83.** 9 **85.** 3 **87.** 7
89, 91, and 93. Estimates may vary. **89.** about 0.3; 0.27
91. about 5; 4.764 **93.** about 6; 6.325

1.3 GUIDED PRACTICE (p. 18) **3.** 60 **5.** 12 **7.** 17
9. 23 **11.** 4 **13.** 246 **15.** 3

1.3 PRACTICE AND APPLICATIONS (pp. 18–21) **17.** 34
19. 1 **21.** 82 **23.** 300 **25.** 42 **27.** 11 **29.** 16 **31.** 48
33. 14 **35.** 46 **37.** 3 **39.** $\frac{1}{2}$ **41.** 128 **47.** 35($230 +
$300 + $40 + $15 + $100 + $200) − $2000 **49.** $\frac{3}{4}x^2$
51. 2($7) + $5 + 2($4) **59.** 8 **61.** 162 **63.** 11 **65.** z^6
67. 81 **69.** 900 **71.** composite; 1, 3, 9 **73.** composite;
1, 2, 19, 38 **75.** composite; 1, 2, 5, 10, 25, 50 **77.** prime

QUIZ 1 (p. 21) **1.** 18 **2.** 14 **3.** 32 **4.** 9 **5.** 5 **6.** 16
7. 6 **8.** 54 **9.** 216 **10.** 200 mi **11.** 2000 mi **12.** 20 mi
13. 6^3 **14.** 4^5 **15.** $(5y)^3$ **16.** 3^3 **17.** $(2x)^4$ **18.** 8^2
19. 64 ft^3 **20.** 2 **21.** $\frac{1}{3}$ **22.** $\frac{1}{2}$

1.4 GUIDED PRACTICE (p. 27) **9.** not a solution
11. solution **13.** not a solution **15.** solution **17.** not a
solution **19.** solution **21.** not a solution **23.** solution
25. solution

1.4 PRACTICE AND APPLICATIONS (pp. 27–29) **27.** not a
solution **29.** solution **31.** solution **33.** solution **35.** 5
37. 8 **39.** 9 **41.** 21 **43.** 2 **45.** 5 **47.** 6 **51.** solution
53. not a solution **55.** solution **57.** 34 boxes or more
59. 7, 2, 1 **65.** 16 **67.** 2 **69.** 7^2 **71.** 9^6 **73.** $(8d)^3$
75. 12 **77.** 3 **79.** 9 **81.** 9 **83.** 5.6 **85.** 0.457
87. 758.95 **89.** 0.3 **91.** 4.10

1.5 GUIDED PRACTICE (p. 33) 3. B 5. A

7. $x + 10 = 24$ 9. $\dfrac{20}{n} \le 2$

1.5 PRACTICE AND APPLICATIONS (pp. 33–35)

11. $10 - x$ 13. $x + 9$ 15. $\dfrac{x}{50}$ 17. $x + 18$ 19. $x - 7$
25. $x + 10 \ge 44$ 27. $35 < 21 - x$ 29. $7x = 56$
31. $\dfrac{35}{x} = 7$ 33. $28 - x = 18; 10$ 35. $\dfrac{49}{x} = 7; 7$
37. $110 = 55t; 2$ h   43. solution   45. not a solution
47. 0.28 49. 0.4 51. 0.45 53. 0.174

QUIZ 2 (p. 35) 1. solution   2. not a solution   3. solution
4. solution   5. not a solution   6. solution   7. solution
8. not a solution   9. solution   10. $8x = 32$; 4 units
11. $\dfrac{x}{9} < 17$ 12. $10x = 50$ 13. $y + 10 \ge 57$
14. $y - 6 = 15$

1.6 PRACTICE AND APPLICATIONS (pp. 39–41) 5. 20 min
7. walking speed $= 4$ (mi/h), time to walk home $= t$,
distance to home $= 1$ (mi)   9. $t = \dfrac{1}{4}$ h or 15 min
11. original length $+$ number of days $\cdot$ growth rate $=$
total length   17. number of weeks worked $= 8$,
amount saved each week $= m$ ($), price of stereo with
CD $= 480$ ($)   19. $60   25. 1000   27. 14   29. 12
31. solution   33. $0.25l + 0.50(100) = 100; 200$ 35. $1\dfrac{3}{4}$
37. $2\dfrac{1}{6}$ 39. $2\dfrac{1}{3}$ 41. $2\dfrac{1}{7}$ 43. $4\dfrac{1}{2}$ 45. $6\dfrac{2}{3}$

1.7 GUIDED PRACTICE (p. 45) 3. false   5. false

1.7 PRACTICE AND APPLICATIONS (pp. 45–47) 7. Player 4;
Player 1   9. 1990; 2000   11. about 150 ft   13. The
braking distance at that speed is about 300 ft. You need
to have time to react to any emergency and still allow
time for your car to travel that distance while stopping.
15. the 6 years from 1991 to 1996   17. 1998

19. *Sample answer:*
I chose a line graph
because line graphs are
useful in showing
changes over time.
23. 42 in., 98 in.^{2}
25. 56 ft, 84 ft^2
27. solution
29. not a solution
31. solution
33. not a solution
35. $<$ 37. $>$
39. $=$ 41. $>$
43. $=$

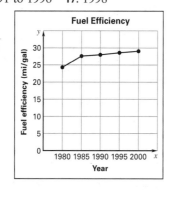

1.8 GUIDED PRACTICE (p. 51)

5.

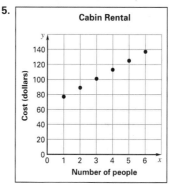

1.8 PRACTICE AND APPLICATIONS (pp. 51–54)

7.

Input x	0	1	2	3	4	5
Output y	5	11	17	23	29	35

9.

Input x	0	1	2	3	4	5
Output y	21	28	35	42	49	56

11.

Input x	0	1	2	3	4	5
Output y	75	70	65	60	55	50

13.

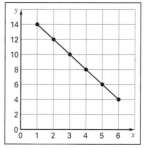

15.

Input t	0	5	10	15	20	25	30
Output d	0	1	2	3	4	5	6

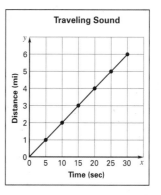

17. no   19. no

21.

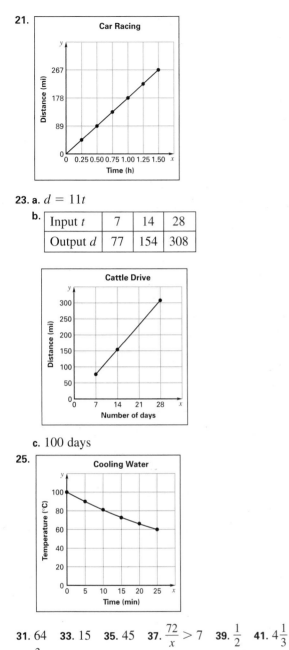

Car Racing

23. a. $d = 11t$

b.

Input t	7	14	28
Output d	77	154	308

Cattle Drive

c. 100 days

25.

Cooling Water

31. 64   **33.** 15   **35.** 45   **37.** $\dfrac{72}{x} > 7$ **39.** $\dfrac{1}{2}$ **41.** $4\dfrac{1}{3}$

43. $\dfrac{3}{8}$ **45.** 3

QUIZ 3 (p. 54) **1.** 6 bottles

2.

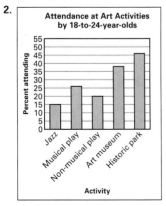

Attendance at Art Activities by 18-to-24-year-olds

3. *Sample answer:* Attending historic parks was most popular; attending a jazz concert is about a third as popular as attending a historic park. Since the percents total more than 100%, some 18-to-24-year-olds attend more than one kind of arts activity.

4. *Sample table:*

Input t	0	1	2	3	4
Output h	200	225	250	275	300

5.

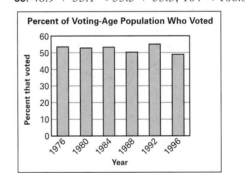

Altitude of Balloon

6. $h \geq 200$ and $h \leq 300$

CHAPTER SUMMARY AND REVIEW (pp. 55–58) **1.** 20   **3.** 6
5. 10   **7.** 6 miles   **9.** 525 miles   **11.** 26 m   **13.** 6^3
15. 16   **17.** 33   **19.** 54   **21.** 3   **23.** $\dfrac{17}{4}$ **25.** solution
27. solution   **29.** 3   **31.** 16   **33.** 10   **35.** $x + 30$
37. $x - 9$
39. $48.9 + 55.1 < 53.5 + 53.3$; $104 < 106.8$; yes

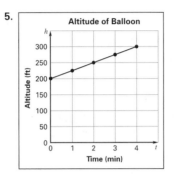

Percent of Voting-Age Population Who Voted

MAINTAINING SKILLS (p. 61) **1.** 2.7   **3.** 12.1   **5.** 5.806
7. 4.244   **9.** 155.8   **11.** 0.99
13–20.

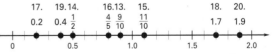

17. 0.2   19. 0.4   14. $\dfrac{1}{2}$ 16. $\dfrac{4}{5}$ 13. $\dfrac{9}{10}$ 15. $\dfrac{11}{10}$ 18. 1.7   20. 1.9

Chapter 2

STUDY GUIDE (p. 64) **1.** B **2.** A **3.** D **4.** C

2.1 GUIDED PRACTICE (p. 68)

3.

5.

7. > **9.** > **11.** $-8, -3, -2, 1, 2$ **13.** $-9, -7, -\frac{1}{5}, \frac{5}{4}, 2$

2.1 PRACTICE AND APPLICATIONS (pp. 68–70)

15.

19.

23. $-2 < 3, 3 > -2$ **25.** $-6 < -1, -1 > -6$
27. $-4 < 0, 0 > -4$ **29.** $10 < 11, 11 > 10$

35.

39.

43.

45. $-3.0, -0.3, -0.2, 0, 0.2, 2.0$ **47.** $-5.2, -5.1, -\frac{10}{4},$
$3.4, 4.1, \frac{9}{2}$ **49.** $-\frac{7}{2}, -2.6, -\frac{1}{2}, 0, \frac{1}{2}, 4.8$ **51.** > **53.** -8

55.

57. Pollux, Altair, Spica, Regulus, Deneb **59.** Regulus
63. 4 ft^2 **65.** 81 cm^2 **67.** 4 **69.** 5 **71.** 3 **73.** $65.9°,$
$67.5°, 69.1°, 69.9°, 72.3°$ **75.** $64.3 \le T \le 72.3$
77. $5 \cdot 7$ **79.** 2^6 **81.** prime **83.** $2^4 \cdot 3^2$

2.2 GUIDED PRACTICE (p. 74) **3.** -1 **5.** 2.4 **7.** 12
9. -5.1 **11.** $8, -8$ **13.** $5.5, -5.5$ **15.** False. *Sample
counterexample:* if $a = -2$, then $-a = -(-2) = 2$,
which is greater than -2.

2.2 PRACTICE AND APPLICATIONS (p. 74–76) **17.** -8
19. 10 **21.** 3.8 **23.** $\frac{1}{9}$ **25.** 7 **27.** -3 **29.** 0.8 **31.** $\frac{2}{3}$
33. $4, -4$ **35.** no solution **37.** $3.7, -3.7$ **39.** $\frac{11}{2}, -\frac{11}{2}$
41. Mercury: 1080; Mars: 288 **43.** negative
45. positive **47.** -6 ft/sec **49.** 400 ft/min **51.** False:
Sample counterexample: The opposite of $-a$ is a.
If $-a = 5$, then $a = -5$, which is negative. **53.** true

61. 3 **63.** 75 **65.** 3 **67.** $x + 8 = 17$ **69.** $9y < 6$
71. $-6 < -2, -2 > -6$ **73.** $-3 < 0.4, 0.4 > -3$
75. $-10 < -\frac{1}{10}, -\frac{1}{10} > -10$ **77.** $\frac{5}{9}$ **79.** $\frac{2}{3}$ **81.** $\frac{1}{2}$

2.3 GUIDED PRACTICE (p. 81) **5.** $-5 + 9 = 4$ **7.** -10
9. 7 **11.** -10 **13.** 7

2.3 PRACTICE AND APPLICATIONS (pp. 81–83) **19.** -6
21. -11 **23.** -4 **25.** 6 **27.** 7 **29.** -11 **31.** 3
33. -31 **35.** -35 **37.** commutative property
39. property of opposites **41.** 10 **43.** 0 **45.** 5 **47.** 4
49. $-2\frac{4}{7}$ **51.** -81.14 **53.** 356.773 **55.** two strokes
under par **59.** 4^2 **61.** x^3 **63.** 33 **65.** 4 **67.** 24
69. solution **71.** not a solution **73.** not a solution
75. 9300 **77.** 100 **79.** 2900

QUIZ 1 (p. 83) **1.** $-2 < 7, 7 > -2$ **2.** $-3 < -2,$
$-2 > -3$ **3.** $-6 < 1, 1 > -6$ **4.** $-10, -8, -3, 2, 9$
5. $-7, -5.2, 3.3, 5, 7.1$ **6.** $-1, -\frac{2}{5}, 0, \frac{1}{10}, 2$ **7.** 5
8. 13 **9.** -0.56 **10.** no solution **11.** $2.7, -2.7$
12. $-\frac{3}{5}, \frac{3}{5}$ **13.** -13 **14.** -6 **15.** 4 **16.** -7 **17.** -2
18. 0 **19.** yes

2.4 GUIDED PRACTICE (p. 89) **3.** -7 **5.** 7 **7.** -1
9. $3\frac{1}{2}$ **11.** $12, -5x$ **13.** $-12y, 6$

2.4 PRACTICE AND APPLICATIONS (pp. 89–91)
15. 9 **17.** -11 **19.** 39 **21.** 36 **23.** 9.2 **25.** -1.2
27. 3 **29.** $-4\frac{1}{2}$ **31.** -1 **33.** 31 **35.** -43
37. 10.2 **39.** 1 **41.** $1\frac{1}{10}$ **43.** 14, 13, 12, 11
45. $-6.5, -7.5, -8.5, -9.5$ **47.** $-2\frac{1}{2}, -1\frac{1}{2}, -\frac{1}{2}, \frac{1}{2}$
49. $-x, -7$ **51.** $9, -28x$ **53.** $a, -5$ **55.** up 275 ft
57. $-7301 - 662 - 1883 + 77 - 1311 + 8021; -3059$
65. 35 **67.** 41 **69.** 64 **71.** true
73.

75.

79. 0.04 **81.** 0.0338 **83.** 19.176

2.5 GUIDED PRACTICE (p. 96) **7.** -35 **9.** -1 **11.** $5t^4$
13. 40

2.5 PRACTICE AND APPLICATIONS (pp. 96–98) **15.** yes
17. -28 **19.** -12.6 **21.** $-\frac{4}{3}$ **23.** -216 **25.** -49
27. -54 **29.** 97.2 **31.** $-\frac{3}{2}$ **33.** $-7x$ **35.** $-5a^3$
37. $-10r^2$ **39.** $-2x^2$ **41.** -48 **43.** -147 **45.** 41
47. true **49.** False. *Sample counterexample:* $3 > 2$,
but $3 \cdot 0 = 2 \cdot 0$ **51.** -20 ft **53.** $d \approx -300t$
55. about 150 ft **63.** 2 **65.** 4 **67.** 12

69.

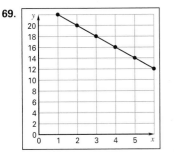

71. 2 **73.** −9 **75.** 7.2 **77.** 10.43 **79.** 12, −z
81. 4w, −11 **83.** −7x, 4x **85.** 20 **87.** 150 **89.** 10,920

2.6 GUIDED PRACTICE (p. 103) **5.** 12(x + 5); 12x + 60
7. D **9.** B **11.** 4(1) + 4(0.15); 4 + 0.6; 4.6

2.6 PRACTICE AND APPLICATIONS (pp. 103–106)
13. 3(4 + x) = 12 + 3x **15.** (x + 5)(11) = 11x + 55
17. 3x + 12 **19.** 7 + 7t **21.** 12 + 6u **23.** 4y + 2
25. 12 + 18a **27.** 1.3x + 2.6 **29.** 5y − 10 **31.** 63 − 9a
33. 28 − 4m **35.** 10 − 30t **37.** 18x − 18
39. −9.3u − 2.4 **41.** −3r − 24 **43.** −1 − s
45. −y − 9 **47.** −24a − 18 **49.** −6y + 5
51. −13.8 + 42w **53.** forgot to distribute 9(3) − 9(5);
−18 **55.** 24.44 **57.** 27.60 **59.** 5.80 **61.** −12.30
63. −22.10 **65.** −54.95 **67.** $19.96 **69.** $10.45
71. 200(x + 225); 200x + 45,000 **73.** 60,000 **79.** $\frac{12}{5}$
81. 3 **83.** 5 **85.** identity property of addition
87. associative property of addition **89.** 12 **91.** 3
93. $-1\frac{1}{3}$ **95.** $\frac{1}{4}$ **97.** $\frac{1}{2}$ **99.** $\frac{41}{50}$ **101.** $\frac{24}{25}$

QUIZ 2 (p. 106) **1.** −15, −13, −11, −9 **2.** 30, 28, 26, 24
3. $-3\frac{1}{4}, -1\frac{1}{4}, \frac{3}{4}, 2\frac{3}{4}$ **4.** 2x, −9 **5.** 8, −x **6.** −10x, 4
7. −0.25, 0.12, −0.12, −0.13 **8.** −63 **9.** 30
10. −2800 **11.** 10.8 **12.** −3 **13.** 270 **14.** 11x + 22
15. 60 − 5y **16.** −12a + 16 **17.** $49.90

2.7 GUIDED PRACTICE (p. 110) **3.** 6r **5.** −8
7. 4a² + 3a − 5 **9.** 18f + 4 **11.** −11m − 20
13. 9x − 27

2.7 PRACTICE AND APPLICATIONS (pp. 110–112) **15.** 3a, 5a
17. m, 6m **19.** −6w, −3w **21.** −7m **23.** 2c − 5
25. 6r − 7 **27.** already simplified **29.** 6p² + 4p − 2
31. −27 − 4y **33.** −11 − 6r **35.** 10m + 19
37. 2c + 48 **39.** 7 is not a like term with 3x and −2x;
x + 7 = 16 **41.** x + (x − 7) + x + (x − 7); 4x − 14
43. 2(x + 2) + (x + 4) + 2(x + 2) + (x + 4); 6x + 16
47. 15,675 tons **49.** T = −45c + 480 **51.** 1.06x + 21.2
59. about 35% **61.** 9 **63.** −6 **65.** −14.1 **67.** −180
69. −3 **71.** 29.88 **73.** $\frac{2}{10}, \frac{4}{10}, \frac{5}{10}, \frac{6}{10}, \frac{9}{10}$
75. $\frac{1}{4}, \frac{3}{8}, \frac{4}{8}, \frac{3}{4}, \frac{7}{8}$ **77.** $\frac{2}{6}, \frac{4}{6}, \frac{3}{4}, \frac{2}{2}, \frac{5}{2}$
79. $\frac{3}{8}, \frac{8}{8}, 1\frac{2}{8}, \frac{12}{8}, 2\frac{1}{8}$ **81.** $\frac{11}{15}, \frac{4}{5}, \frac{5}{6}, 2\frac{2}{3}, 2\frac{7}{10}$

2.8 GUIDED PRACTICE (p. 116) **3.** $\frac{1}{32}$ **5.** $-\frac{5}{1}$ or −5
7. −4 **9.** −2 **11.** 2 **13.** all real numbers except x = 4
15. all real numbers except x = 0

2.8 PRACTICE AND APPLICATIONS (pp. 116–118)
17. multiply by reciprocal; −27 **19.** −3 **21.** −1
23. −5 **25.** 2 **27.** −12 **29.** $-\frac{5}{6}$ **31.** 12 **33.** −48
35. $-\frac{1}{9}$ **37.** $-\frac{3}{2}$ **39.** $-\frac{1}{3}$ **41.** 4 **43.** 6x − 3
45. already simplified **47.** 11 + 2t **49.** all real numbers
except x = −2 **51.** all real numbers **53.** −10.5 m/sec
57. 24 **59.** 5 **61.** 10 **63.** 2n ≥ 7 **65.** −21 **67.** −19.9
69. $4\frac{1}{4}$ or $\frac{17}{4}$ **71.** < **73.** < **75.** > **77.** <

QUIZ 3 (p. 118) **1.** 3x, −7x **2.** 6a and 9a, −5 and 10
3. −5p, −p **4.** −26t **5.** 7 + 2d **6.** g² − 8g **7.** 3a − 4
8. 3p − 9 **9.** 5 − 3w **10.** −5 **11.** 16 **12.** −32
13. $\frac{98}{9}$ **14.** −54 **15.** $\frac{1}{8}$ **16.** 5 − 2x **17.** already
simplified **18.** 3x − 2 **19.** all real numbers except
x = −2 **20.** all real numbers **21.** all real numbers
except x = 0

CH. 2 EXTENSION (pp. 119–120)

EXERCISES (p. 120) **1.** inductive reasoning **3.** inductive
reasoning **5.** 64, 128, 256

CHAPTER SUMMARY AND REVIEW (pp. 121–124) **1.** −6,
−4, −3, 1, 2, 5 **3.** −2, −1, $-\frac{1}{2}, \frac{2}{3}$, 1, 4, 6 **5.** 5
7. −45 **9.** −9.1 **11.** $3\frac{1}{2}$ **13.** −12 **15.** 5 **17.** −8
19. 19 **21.** −11.2 **23.** $-3\frac{1}{4}$ **25.** 600 **27.** 4.2
29. −14 **31.** −3f **33.** −12t² **35.** −81b² **37.** 9y + 54
39. 6 − 2w **41.** −3t − 33 **43.** −6x + 60 **45.** 9a
47. 3 + f **49.** 4t + 2 **51.** −4 **53.** 10 **55.** $-\frac{2}{3}$ **57.** −9

MAINTAINING SKILLS (p. 127) **1.** 25 **3.** 100
5.

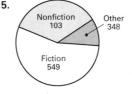

Chapter 3

STUDY GUIDE (p. 130) **1.** D **2.** D **3.** C **4.** B **5.** C

3.1 GUIDED PRACTICE (p. 135) **7.** −1 **9.** −17 **11.** 4
13. 3 **15.** −3 **17.** Check equation **17.** *Sample answer:*
addition

3.1 PRACTICE AND APPLICATIONS (pp. 135–137)
19. subtract 28 **21.** add 3 **23.** subtract −12 **25.** 9
27. −5 **29.** 10 **31.** 8 **33.** −4 **35.** 24 **37.** −15
39. −24 **41.** $\frac{3}{5}$ **43.** 0 **45.** 5 **47.** 6 **49.** 3 **51.** 1

53. 20 cm   **55.** B; 8   **57.** 6463 seats   **59.** 10,534 acres; $4218 + 3800 + 2764 - 248 = x$ **61.** Simplify with subtraction rule; subtract 2 from both sides.   **65.** $5x = 160$ **67.** $36 - k = 15$ **69.** $4x + 8$ **71.** $-5y - 20$ **73.** $-2x + 12$ **75.** $\frac{4}{7}$ **77.** $\frac{3}{32}$ **79.** $\frac{4}{7}$ **81.** 1

3.2 GUIDED PRACTICE (p. 141) **7.** -1 **9.** 32   **11.** 28   **13.** -6 **15.** 60 mph

3.2 PRACTICE AND APPLICATIONS (pp. 141–143)
17. divide by 5   **19.** divide by -4 **21.** multiply by 7   **23.** -8 **25.** -6 **27.** 11   **29.** $\frac{9}{10}$ **31.** -10 **33.** 30   **35.** 84   **37.** $\frac{4}{3}$ **39.** 0   **41.** 12   **43.** 18   **45.** -45 **47.** multiply by $-\frac{4}{3}$; -8 **49.** $\frac{3}{8} \cdot p = 3.30$; $8.80   **51.** 13   **57.** $27 - 8x$ **59.** $-2x + 6$ **61.** $12y + 15$ **63.** 8   **65.** -19 **67.** 2   **69.** A; 18   **71.** 10   **73.** 5   **75.** 9   **77.** 3

3.3 GUIDED PRACTICE (p. 147) **7.** 2   **9.** -1 **11.** 2   **13.** 25   **15.** -9 **17.** 19

3.3 PRACTICE AND APPLICATIONS (pp. 147–149) **19.** 2   **21.** 14   **23.** 2   **25.** 3   **27.** 5   **29.** -3 **31.** 3   **33.** 9   **35.** 14   **37.** 11   **39.** 6   **41.** 5 and $3x$ are not like terms, so $3x$ cannot be subtracted from 5; $-\frac{5}{3}$ **43.** Subtract 3 from each side; multiply each side by 2; divide each side by 5.   **45.** 14 months   **55.** a^6 **57.** 4^3 **59.** t^3 **61.** 10   **63.** 47   **65.** 14   **67.** $<$ **69.** $<$ **71.** $<$ **73.** $<$

QUIZ 1 (p. 149) **1.** 21   **2.** -17 **3.** -7 **4.** -1 **5.** 282   **6.** 5   **7.** B   **8.** $6x = 72$; $12   **9.** 9   **10.** 2   **11.** 2   **12.** 1   **13.** -25 **14.** 14   **15.** 9 min

3.4 GUIDED PRACTICE (p. 154) **9.** one solution, -1 **11.** one solution, 7   **13.** identity   **15.** B

3.4 PRACTICE AND APPLICATIONS (pp. 154–156)
17. subtract x from each side   **19.** add $8x$ to each side   **21.** 3   **23.** 3   **25.** 2   **27.** $\frac{3}{7}$ **29.** -8 **31.** 4   **33.** -2 **35.** $3x - 12x = -9x$; $x = -5$ **37.** one solution, 2   **39.** one solution, -1 **41.** one solution, -5 **43.** no solution   **45.** one solution   **47.** 121 hours   **49.** 25 sec; the gazelle would probably be safe since the cheetah begins to tire after 20 seconds.   **57.** 144 miles   **59.** 8   **61.** 216   **63.** 144   **65.** 10   **67.** yes   **69.** -4 **71.** 12   **73.** -23 **75.** 0   **77.** 90   **79.** 2000   **81.** 9   **83.** 8   **85.** 3910

3.5 GUIDED PRACTICE (p. 160) **11.** -5 **13.** -2 **15.** -6 **17.** 2

3.5 PRACTICE AND APPLICATIONS (pp. 160–162) **19.** 19   **21.** 14   **23.** 3   **25.** 21   **27.** -1 **29.** -4 **31.** -1 **33.** $\frac{1}{2}$ **35.** 1   **37.** $3x - 12 + 2x = 6 - x$, $6x - 12 = 6$, $6x = 18$, $x = 3$ **39.** $-4(3 - n) = -12 + 4n$, $8(4n - 3) = 32n - 24$; $n = \frac{3}{7}$ **43.** C, $x = 25$; you will need to use the gym more than 25 times to justify the cost of the yearly fee.   **51.** 400,000 km; 700,000 km; 1,100,000 km; 1,900,000 km   **55.** 36   **57.** -77 **59.** $3w^2 - w$ **61.** $s + 11t$ **63.** $-6m - m^2$ **65.** 11.5   **67.** 6.42   **69.** 22.49

3.6 GUIDED PRACTICE (p. 166) **7.** 23.4   **9.** -13.9 **11.** 56.1   **13.** 8.8   **15.** 6.82   **17.** 4.22   **19.** $12

3.6 PRACTICE AND APPLICATIONS (pp. 166–169) **21.** 5.78   **23.** 7.57   **25.** 4.33   **27.** 0.77   **29.** 2.22   **31.** 0.94   **33.** 0.42   **35.** -2.63 **37.** $M = 150 + 0.38x$ **39.** 1.0   **41.** 1.9   **43.** $162 + 30 = 71n$, where n is the number of buses needed   **45.** Round up to 3 buses; you need enough buses to seat all the students.   **51.** $697.45   **52.** -234.87 **53.**

Input t	2	3	4	5	6
Output A	18	23	28	33	38

55. 3   **57.** $-\frac{4}{5}$ **59.** -5.6 **61.** 16   **63.** 14   **65.** $13\frac{6}{7}$ **67.** $25\frac{9}{16}$ **69.** 11

QUIZ 2 (p. 169) **1.** no solution   **2.** one solution   **3.** identity   **4.** no solution   **5.** -3 **6.** -7 **7.** 10   **8.** 1   **9.** 5   **10.** 4   **11.** -1 **12.** 19   **13.** 8   **14.** 13   **15.** You need to use the bike for at least 10 hours to justify the cost of the helmet.   **16.** -1.14 **17.** -0.68 **18.** 1.63   **19.** 0.36   **20.** -5.03 **21.** -2.23 **22.** 7

3.6 TECHNOLOGY (p. 170) **1.** 12.3   **3.** 5.3

3.7 GUIDED PRACTICE (p. 174) **3.** $r = s + t$ **5.** $y = \frac{x}{3}$ **7.** $y = 2x - 4$ **9.** $w = \frac{A}{l}$

3.7 PRACTICE AND APPLICATIONS (pp. 174–176) **11.** $C = \frac{5}{9}(F - 32)$ **13.** $w = \frac{A}{l}$; $w = 4$ **15.** $l = \frac{A}{w}$; $l = 16$ **17.** 18 cm^2 **19.** 16.67 cm^3 **21.** 6 min   **23.** 30 ft   **27.** solution   **29.** not a solution   **31.** not a solution   **33.** not a solution   **35.** solution   **37.** 28%   **39.** $\frac{3}{7}$ **41.** $\frac{2}{9}$ **43.** $\frac{1}{2}$ **45.** $\frac{7}{8}$

3.8 GUIDED PRACTICE (p. 180) **5.** $\frac{4}{5}$ **7.** $\frac{2}{3}$ **9.** 0.05 mi/min   **11.** 231 miles

3.8 PRACTICE AND APPLICATIONS (pp. 180–182) **13.** $\frac{1}{4}$ **15.** $\frac{3}{5}$ **17.** $\frac{11}{3}$ **19.** $\frac{4}{5}$ **21.** $\frac{5}{8}$ **23.** 15 mi/day   **25.** $.40/can   **27.** 8 oz/serving   **29.** miles   **33.** 24 months   **35.** 21.2 hours   **37.** 2 km   **39.** 21 mi/hr   **41.** 12 min   **43.** $91   **49.** $4 > -3$; $-3 < 4$ **51.** $-6 < 3$; $3 > -6$ **53.** 1.43   **55.** 75 ft   **57.** 18   **59.** 21   **61.** 162   **63.** 490

3.9 GUIDED PRACTICE (p. 186) **7.** 175%   **9.** 72   **11.** $a = 0.06(10)$

3.9 PRACTICE AND APPLICATIONS (pp. 186–188)

17. 20   **19.** 30.8 ft   **21.** 10   **23.** 84 ft   **25.** $1000
27. 200   **29.** 480%   **31.** 30%   **33.** 20%
35. no; A: 30%(60) = $18 discount, cost = $42;
B: 20%(60) = $12, cost = $48, 10%(48) = 4.8,
final cost = $48 − $4.80 = $43.20   **37.** 21%   **39.** 27%
41. $a = 3b$; *Sample answer:* $a = 30$, $b = 10$, $p = 300$
45. $21x = 105$; $x = 5$ **47.** 32   **49.** −16   **51.** 217, 270,
2017, 2170, 2701   **53.** 5.09, 5.1, 5.19, 5.9, 5.91

QUIZ 3 (p. 188)
1. $t = \dfrac{d}{r}$ **2.** $h = \dfrac{2A}{b}$ **3.** $v = \dfrac{m}{d}$
4. $\dfrac{7 \text{ days}}{1 \text{ week}}$ **5.** $\dfrac{1 \text{ ft}}{12 \text{ in.}}$ **6.** 300 students/school   **7.** 240 hours
8. 25%   **9.** $23 - 17.25 = p(23)$; $p = 0.25$ or 25%

CHAPTER SUMMARY AND REVIEW (pp. 189–192)
1. 11   **3.** −8   **5.** −9   **7.** −3   **9.** 1   **11.** 2   **13.** one
solution; 2   **15.** one solution; 5   **17.** one solution, −2
19. $12 + n = 6 + 2n$; $n = 6$; the plants will be the
same height after 6 weeks.   **21.** 1.08   **23.** $l = \dfrac{v}{wh}$
25. $b = P - a - c$ **27.** 85 mi

MAINTAINING SKILLS (p. 195)
1.
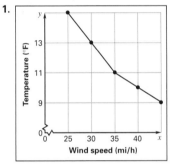

CUMULATIVE PRACTICE (pp. 196–197)
1. 8   **3.** 41   **5.** 216
7. 5   **9.** 7   **11.** 57   **13.** not a solution   **15.** solution
17. not a solution   **19.** $x^3 - 8$ **21.** $-3x < 12$
23.
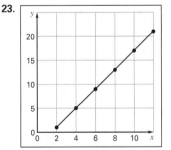

25. <   **27.** >   **29.** <   **31.** <   **33.** $-5y^3$ **35.** $-4 + 2t$
37. $4x - 6$ **39.** $43x + 25$ **41.** −30 ft; negative; downward
velocity is negative.   **43.** $15(x + 6) = 15x + 90$
45. −9   **47.** 18   **49.** 0   **51.** $\dfrac{3}{2}$ **53.** $3(50) + 2n = 750$;
300 rolls   **55.** −20.33   **57.** −2.30   **59.** −1.22
61. 10 cm   **63.** $45.50

Chapter 4

STUDY GUIDE (p. 202)
1. B   **2.** B   **3.** D

4.1 GUIDED PRACTICE (p. 206)
5.
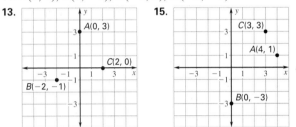

7. always   **9.** always

4.1 PRACTICE AND APPLICATIONS (pp. 206–208)
11. $A(2, 4)$, $B(0, -1)$, $C(-1, 0)$, $D(-2, -1)$
13.   **15.**

19. IV   **21.** I   **23.** III   **25.** III   **27.** pounds; inches
31. Gas mileage decreases as weight increases.
33.
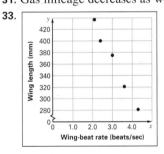

35. As wing-beat rate increases, the wing length
decreases.   **41.** 7   **43.** 3   **45.** 39   **47.** −13   **49.** 1.07
51. $\dfrac{2}{3}$ **53.** 5   **55.** 1   **57.** 5   **59.** $2\dfrac{1}{3}$ **61.** $7\dfrac{4}{15}$ **63.** $\dfrac{5}{11}$
65. $5\dfrac{5}{7}$

4.2 GUIDED PRACTICE (p. 213)
3. solution   **5.** solution
7. $y = -x - 2$ **9.** $y = -2x + 4$ **11.** *Sample answer:*
$(0, 7)$, $(-1, 2)$, $(1, 12)$
13.   **15.**
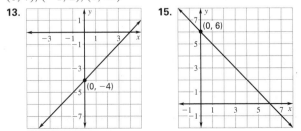

4.2 PRACTICE AND APPLICATIONS (pp. 213–215)

17. not solution **19.** solution **21.** not solution

23. $y = -\frac{2}{3}x + 2$ **25.** $y = -x + \frac{19}{5}$ **27.** $y = -x - 5$

29. $y = -\frac{3}{2}x - \frac{3}{2}$ *Sample answers given for 31–39*

31. $(0, -5), (1, -2), (-1, -8)$ **33.** $(0, -6), (1, -8),$ $(-1, -4)$ **35.** $(0, 3), (3, 1), (-3, 5)$ **37.** $(0, 5), (2, 0),$ $(4, -5)$ **39.** $(0, -4), \left(1, -\frac{17}{3}\right), (3, -9)$

43. 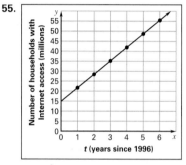 **47.**

49. $7.1x + 10.1y = 800$ **51.** about 48 minutes **53.** The boiling temperature of water decreases as altitude increases.

55.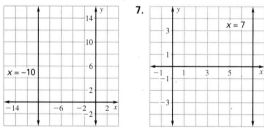

61. -12 **63.** 6 **65.** $-14x + 6y$ **67.** $-5t^3 - 9r$ **69.** $-3k^3 + h$ **71.** -15 **73.** 63 **75.** 63% **77.** 2% **79.** 127% **81.** 860%

4.3 GUIDED PRACTICE (p. 219)

5. **7.**

9. $x = 3$ **11.** sometimes **13.** always

4.3 PRACTICE AND APPLICATIONS (pp. 219–221) **15.** not solution **17.** not solution **19.** $\left(\frac{1}{2}, 0\right), \left(\frac{1}{2}, 2\right), \left(\frac{1}{2}, -2\right)$ **21.** $(0, -5), (3, -5), (-3, -5)$ **23.** $(0, 7), (-2, 7),$ $(-3, 7)$

25. 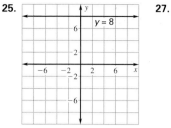 **27.**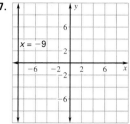

31. $x = -4$ **33. a.** $H = 110$; domain: 0–5; range: 110 **b.** $H = 160$; domain: 0–10; range: 160 **37.** 7 **39.** 8 **41.** 10 **43.** 5 **45.** 15 **47.** $21; \frac{15}{21}, \frac{14}{21}$ **49.** $21; \frac{15}{21}, \frac{4}{21}$ **51.** $26; \frac{24}{26}, \frac{5}{26}$ **53.** $60; \frac{9}{60}, \frac{28}{60}$

QUIZ 1 (p. 221)

1. 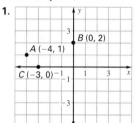 **2.**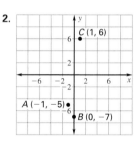

3. 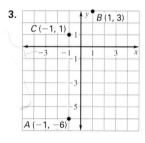 **4.**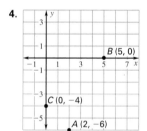

5. I **6.** III **7.** IV **8.** II **9.** $y = -2x$ **10.** $y = \frac{5}{2}x - 10$ **11.** $y = -\frac{1}{2}x - 4$ **12.** *Sample answer:* $(0, -6),$ $(1, -4), (2, -2)$

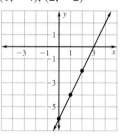

13. *Sample answer:* $(0, 1), (1, 5), (-1, -3)$

14. *Sample answer:* $(0, 2), (1, -4), (-1, 8)$

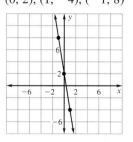

15. *Sample answer:*
(0, 12), (3, 3), (6, −6)

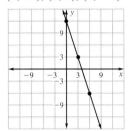

16. *Sample answer:*
(0, 5), (1, −5), (2, −15)

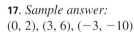

17. *Sample answer:*
(0, 2), (3, 6), (−3, −10)

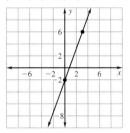

18.

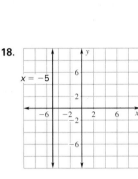

19.

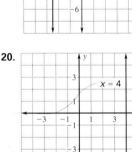

20.

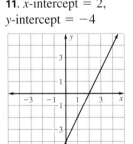

4.4 GUIDED PRACTICE (p. 225) **3.** 6 **5.** −3 **7.** −2
9. *x*-intercept = −2,   **11.** *x*-intercept = 2,
y-intercept = 2   *y*-intercept = −4

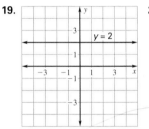

13. *x*-intercept = −3, *y*-intercept = 3

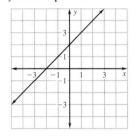

4.4 PRACTICE AND APPLICATIONS (pp. 225–227)
15. *x*-intercept = 2, *y*-intercept = 3
17. *x*-intercept = −4, *y*-intercept = −1   **19.** −2   **21.** 19
23. 6   **25.** −12   **27.** −2   **29.** 26   **31.** −4

33.

35.

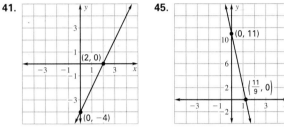

41.

45.

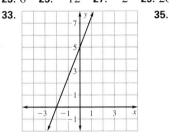

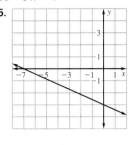

49. 7.5; if students get in free, the adult ticket price needs
to be $7.50.   **53.** about 189,000   **57.** −4   **59.** −5
61. $\frac{5}{3}$ **63.** −17   **65.** 6   **67.** −2   **69.** −60   **71.** $\frac{1}{4}$
75. $1.65   **77.** $8.36   **79.** $3.15   **81.** $5.11

4.5 GUIDED PRACTICE (p. 233) **5.** positive   **7.** negative
9. zero   **11.** undefined

4.5 PRACTICE AND APPLICATIONS (pp. 233–235)
13. $-\frac{3}{2}$ **15.** $\frac{1}{2}$ **17.** $\frac{3}{4}$ **19.** −1   **21.** 1   **23.** $\frac{1}{2}$ **25.** $-\frac{1}{4}$
27. $-\frac{3}{2}$ **29.** neither   **31.** zero   **33.** neither   **35.** $\frac{3}{2}$
39. $\frac{1}{5}$; it represents how the rise changes with respect to
the run.   **41.** 6%   **45.** 5   **47.** 4   **49.** $y = 2x + 9$
51. $y = 4x + 5$ **53.** $y = -\frac{5}{2}x - \frac{5}{2}$ **55.** true   **57.** false
59. true

4.6 GUIDED PRACTICE (p. 239) **3.** $\frac{1}{9}$ **5.** $\frac{1}{7}$ **7.** $y = 5x$
9.

11.

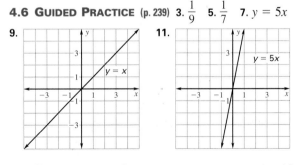

4.6 PRACTICE AND APPLICATIONS (pp. 239–241) **13.** 12
15. 25   **17.** $y = 5x$ **19.** $y = 6x$ **21.** $y = -\frac{1}{3}x$
23. $y = -10x$ **25.** yes, direct variation

27.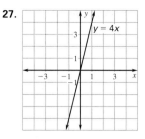

29.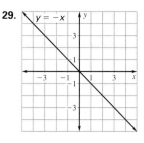

18.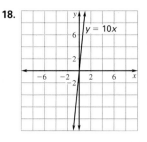

31. yes; line through origin   **33.** no; line does not pass through origin   **35.** 17 min   **37.** about 16 in.   **41.** 2
43. -5 **45.** -3 **47.** $y = -\dfrac{2}{5}x + \dfrac{12}{5}$ **49.** solution
51. solution   **53.** solution   **55.** 66   **57.** 56   **59.** 3570

19. 10,500 bolts

4.7 GUIDED PRACTICE (p. 246) **3.** $m = 2, b = 1$
5. $m = 5, b = -3$ **7.** $m = -1, b = 15$ **9.** B

4.7 PRACTICE AND APPLICATIONS (pp. 246–249)
11. $y = x + 9$ **13.** $y = 2x - 10$ **15.** $y = \dfrac{1}{2}x - 6$
17. $m = 6, b = 4$ **19.** $m = 2, b = -9$ **21.** $m = 9,$ $b = 0$ **23.** $m = -3, b = 6$ **25.** $m = 2, b = 4$

27.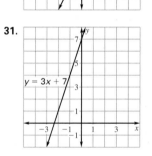

29.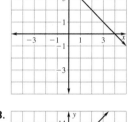

QUIZ 2 (p. 241)

1.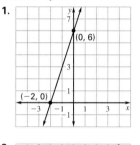

2.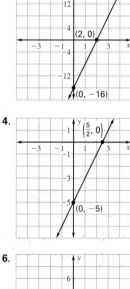

3.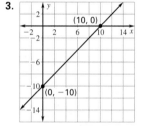

4.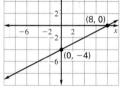

31.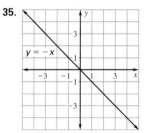

33.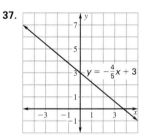

5.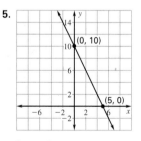

6.

35.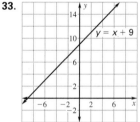

37.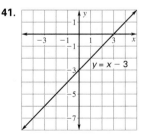

7. $\dfrac{2}{5}$ **8.** $\dfrac{2}{5}$ **9.** $\dfrac{7}{9}$ **10.** 2   **11.** 0   **12.** -1 **13.** $y = 3x$
14. $y = 8x$ **15.** $y = 4x$

16.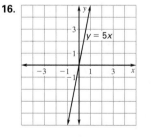

17.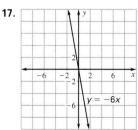

39.

41.

47. $m = -\frac{4}{3}$, $b = 4$ **49.** parallel; same slope, $m = -3$
51. parallel; same slope, $m = 1$ **53.** not parallel;
different slopes **55.** (1) $\frac{9}{70}$ (2) $\frac{1}{7}$ **63.** line a and
line b **71.** 5 **73.** 12 **75.** 6 **77.** -5
79. Atomic weight $\approx 2 \times$ Atomic number **81.** $\frac{13}{40}$
83. $1\frac{23}{36}$ **85.** $1\frac{13}{56}$ **87.** $1\frac{1}{21}$

4.8 GUIDED PRACTICE (p. 255) **3.** -22 **5.** 8
7. function; domain: 10, 20, 30, 40, 50; range: 100, 200, 300, 400, 500 **9.** not a function **11.** not a function

4.8 PRACTICE AND APPLICATIONS (pp. 255–258)
13. function; domain: 1, 2, 3, 4; range: 2, 3, 4, 5
15. not a function **17.** function; domain: 0, 2, 3, 4;
range: 1, 2, 3, 4 **19.** function **21.** function **23.** function
25. 6, 0, -6 **27.** 1, -5, -11 **29.** 11, 1, -9
31. 23, 7, -9 **33.** 4, -6, -16

37. 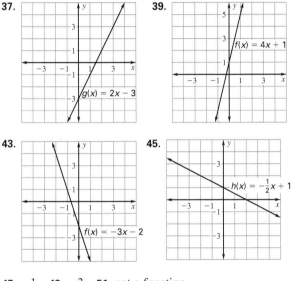 **39.**

43. **45.**

47. -1 **49.** -3 **51.** not a function
53. function; domain: -2, 0, 1, 2; range: -2, 0, 1, 2

55.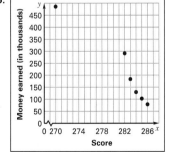

Yes. *Sample explanation:* For each input, there is exactly one output. (The score 285 occurs twice, but the prize money is the same each time.) Domain: 270, 282, 283, 284, 285, 286; range: 486,000, 291,600, 183,600, 129,600, 102,600, 78,570

57. 1500 miles **59.** $f(t) \approx 5.88t$ **63.** 6 **65.** $\frac{1}{3}$
67. no solution **69.** -1 **71.** -4 **73.** 0 **75.** $-\frac{3}{5}$
77. $\frac{1}{2}$ **79.** $\frac{2}{3}$

QUIZ 3 (p. 258) **1.** $y = 3x + 4$; $m = 3$, $b = 4$
2. $y = -x + 2$; $m = -1$, $b = 2$ **3.** $y = -2x + 6$;
$m = -2$, $b = 6$ **4.** $y = -\frac{5}{8}x + 4$; $m = -\frac{5}{8}$, $b = 4$
5. $y = \left(\frac{4}{3}\right)x - 8$; $m = \frac{4}{3}$, $b = -8$
6. $y = 1$; $m = 0$, $b = 1$
7. 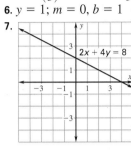 **8.**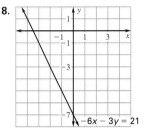

9.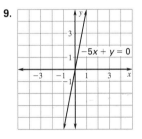

10. not parallel **11.** not parallel **12.** -24, 0, 32
13. 6, -9, -29 **14.** -9, 3, 19 **15.** -21, -12, 0
16. 4.2, 0, -5.6 **17.** $\frac{3}{4}$, 0, -1
18. 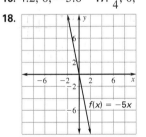 **19.**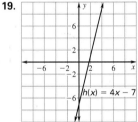

20.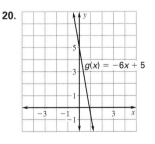

1. Quadrant I   **3.** Quadrant II

Graph for Ex. 1 and 3   **5.**

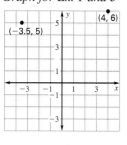

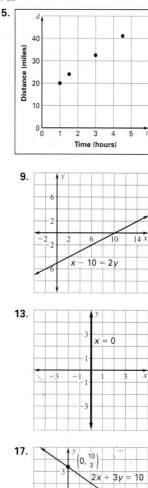

7.

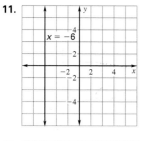

9.

11.

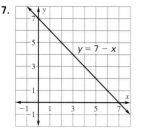

13.

15.

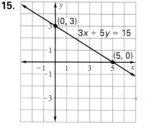

17.

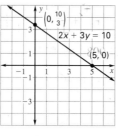

19. 0   **21.** undefined   **23.** $y = -\frac{1}{3}x$ **25.** $y = 3.5x$

27. $y = -2x + 6$ **29.** $y = \frac{2}{3}x - 4$

31.

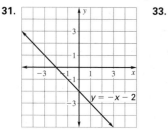

33.

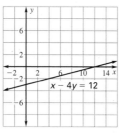

35. -9

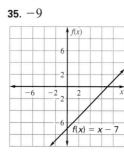

$f(x) = x - 7$

37. 11

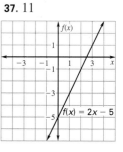

$f(x) = 2x - 5$

39. function; domain: $-1, 0, 1$; range: $2, 4, 6$

41. function; domain: $-2, 0, 2$; range: 6

MAINTAINING SKILLS (p. 265)   **1.** $\frac{1}{2}$ **3.** $\frac{1}{9}$ **5.** $\frac{5}{4}$ **7.** $\frac{1}{10}$ **9.** 0   **11.** -11 **13.** -11

Chapter 5

STUDY GUIDE (p. 268)   **1.** C   **2.** C   **3.** B

5.1 GUIDED PRACTICE (p. 272)   **5.** no   **7.** $y = x$ **9.** $y = -x + 3$ **11.** $y = 5x + 5$

5.1 PRACTICE AND APPLICATIONS (pp. 272–275)

13. $y = 3x + 2$ **15.** $y = 6$ **17.** $y = \frac{2}{5}x + 7$

19. $y = -x - \frac{2}{5}$ **21.** $y = -\frac{1}{5}x + \frac{2}{3}$ **23.** $m = -\frac{1}{2}$; $b = 1$ **25.** $m = \frac{3}{2}$; $b = 2$ **27.** $m = -\frac{2}{3}$; $b = -1$

29. $y = -3x - 1$ **31.** $y = -x + 1$ **33.** $y = 2x - 1$

41. 13.16 sec   **43.** *Sample answer:* The prediction may be unrealistic because athletes may be unable to continue the downward trend.   **45.** All three lines have the same slope, $\frac{1}{2}$.   **47.** $y = x + 63.64$, $y = -x - 63.64$, $y = x - 63.64$ **49.** $y = -x + 63.64$ **53.** 92 min

57. 3   **59.** -1 **61.** -1 **63.** *Sample answer:* $(-1, -3)$, $(0, -4)$, $(1, -5)$ **65.** *Sample answer:* $(0, 7)$, $(-1, 12)$, $(1, 2)$ **67.** *Sample answer:* $(-3, 4)$, $(0, 3)$, $(3, 2)$

69. 3; 5

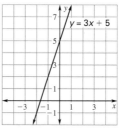

$y = 3x + 5$

71. -2; 3

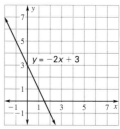

$y = -2x + 3$

73. 5; -6

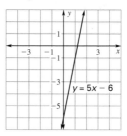

$y = 5x - 6$

75. $\frac{3}{4}$ **77.** $\frac{31}{50}$ **79.** $\frac{1}{200}$ **81.** $1\frac{7}{25}$ **83.** $\frac{3}{50}$

5.2 GUIDED PRACTICE (p. 281) **3.** $y - 4 = 4(x - 3)$
5. $y - 4 = \frac{1}{2}(x - 3)$ **7.** $y - 2 = 3(x - 2)$
9. $y = \frac{1}{2}x - \frac{5}{2}$ **11.** $y = x$ **13.** $y = \frac{1}{4}x + \frac{9}{4}$

5.2 PRACTICE AND APPLICATIONS (pp. 281–284)
15. $y - 2 = \frac{1}{2}(x - 1)$ **17.** $y + 3 = \frac{1}{3}(x + 1)$
19. $y + 4 = -(x - 4)$ **21.** $y - 2 = -5(x + 6)$
23. $y + 2 = 2(x + 8)$ **25.** $y - 4 = 6(x + 3)$
27. $y + 1 = 0(x - 8)$; $y = -1$ **29.** $y - 4 = 2(x - 1)$;
$y = 2x + 2$ **31.** $y + 5 = -2(x + 5)$; $y = -2x - 15$
33. $y - 1 = -\frac{1}{3}(x + 1)$; $y = -\frac{1}{3}x + \frac{2}{3}$ **35.** $y = 2x - 2$
37. $y = \frac{1}{3}x - \frac{8}{3}$ **39.** $y = -9x - 5$ **41.** $y = 2x - 1$
43. $y = -x - 4$ **45.** 55.25 psi **53.** yes **55.** yes **57.** no
61.

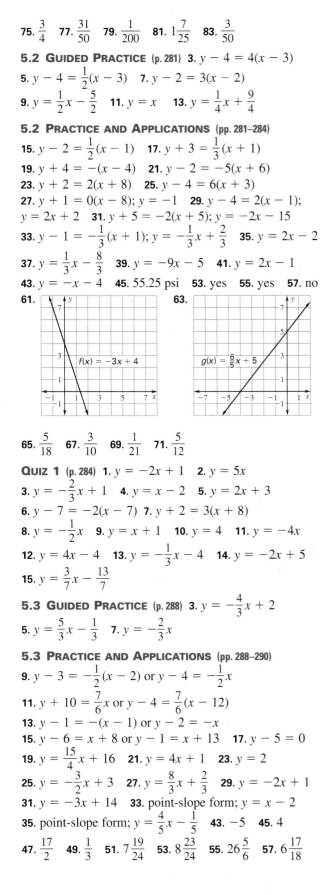

65. $\frac{5}{18}$ **67.** $\frac{3}{10}$ **69.** $\frac{1}{21}$ **71.** $\frac{5}{12}$

QUIZ 1 (p. 284) **1.** $y = -2x + 1$ **2.** $y = 5x$
3. $y = -\frac{2}{3}x + 1$ **4.** $y = x - 2$ **5.** $y = 2x + 3$
6. $y - 7 = -2(x - 7)$ **7.** $y + 2 = 3(x + 8)$
8. $y = -\frac{1}{2}x$ **9.** $y = x + 1$ **10.** $y = 4$ **11.** $y = -4x$
12. $y = 4x - 4$ **13.** $y = -\frac{1}{3}x - 4$ **14.** $y = -2x + 5$
15. $y = \frac{3}{7}x - \frac{13}{7}$

5.3 GUIDED PRACTICE (p. 288) **3.** $y = -\frac{4}{3}x + 2$
5. $y = \frac{5}{3}x - \frac{1}{3}$ **7.** $y = -\frac{2}{3}x$

5.3 PRACTICE AND APPLICATIONS (pp. 288–290)
9. $y - 3 = -\frac{1}{2}(x - 2)$ or $y - 4 = -\frac{1}{2}x$
11. $y + 10 = \frac{7}{6}x$ or $y - 4 = \frac{7}{6}(x - 12)$
13. $y - 1 = -(x - 1)$ or $y - 2 = -x$
15. $y - 6 = x + 8$ or $y - 1 = x + 13$ **17.** $y - 5 = 0$
19. $y = \frac{15}{4}x + 16$ **21.** $y = 4x + 1$ **23.** $y = 2$
25. $y = -\frac{3}{2}x + 3$ **27.** $y = \frac{8}{3}x + \frac{2}{3}$ **29.** $y = -2x + 1$
31. $y = -3x + 14$ **33.** point-slope form; $y = x - 2$
35. point-slope form; $y = \frac{4}{5}x - \frac{1}{5}$ **43.** -5 **45.** 4
47. $\frac{17}{2}$ **49.** $\frac{1}{3}$ **51.** $7\frac{19}{24}$ **53.** $8\frac{23}{24}$ **55.** $26\frac{5}{6}$ **57.** $6\frac{17}{18}$

5.4 GUIDED PRACTICE (p. 294) **3.** $2x - y = 9$ or
$-2x + y = -9$ **5.** $3x - 4y = 0$ **7.** $5x - y = 7$
9. $3x + y = 10$ **11.** $3x + 5y = 15$ **13.** $x = -2$

5.4 PRACTICE AND APPLICATIONS (pp. 294–297)
15. $5x + y = 2$ **17.** $-4x + y = -9$ or $4x - y = 9$
19. $3x + 8y = 0$ **21.** $2x - y = -19$ **23.** $3x + y = 1$
25. $5x - y = 17$ **27.** $2x - 5y = -41$ **29.** $x + 3y = 16$
31. $2x - 3y = -6$ **33.** $2x + y = 1$ **35.** $x + y = -3$
37. $x + 10y = 27$ **39.** $y = -2$ **41.** $x = 4$ **43.** $x = -3\frac{1}{2}$
45. $x = 9$ **47.** $y = 10$ **49.** $-x + y = 4$ **51.** $x + y = 7$
53. $4x + 3y = -8$ **55.** Only the right side was
multiplied by 3.
57.

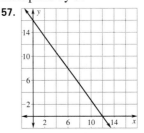

63. -5 **65.** -42 **67.** $\frac{21}{2}$ or 10.5

69.

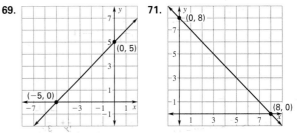

73. $908 **75.** $14,098 **77.** $0 **79.** $12,346

QUIZ 2 (p. 297) **1.** $y = -\frac{1}{5}x - 1$ **2.** $y = 3x - 16$
3. $y = 4$ **4.** $y = -4x + 3$ **5.** $y = \frac{1}{3}x - \frac{1}{3}$
6. $3x + y = 9$ **7.** $-x + 2y = 8$ **8.** $-2x + 5y = -5$
9. $2x - y = 4$ **10.** $x + 2y = 6$ **11.** $2x - 5y = -23$
12. $2x - y = -2$ **13.** $x + 2y = 2$ **14.** $y = 3$

5.5 GUIDED PRACTICE (p. 301) **3.** C; the slope, 1.5,
represents the amount paid for each unit produced per
hour. **5.** B; the slope, 0.32, represents the amount paid
per day for each mile driven.

5.5 PRACTICE AND APPLICATIONS (pp. 301–304) **7.** 124
9. $y = 124t$ **11.** about 3.2 hours **13.** 10
15.

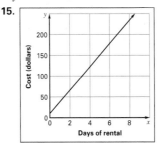

17. 2 days   **19.** (1, 48.9)   **21.** about 67 cents
23. *Sample answer:* about 51 cents   **25.** $5x + 7y = 315$
27. $2x + y = 102$ **29.** 62; 52; 42; 32; 22
31. $2C + 1.25B = 10$ **33.** *Sample answer:* 4500 years
37. 0   **39.** -50 **41.** 3 feet   **43.** $\frac{3}{7}$; *Sample answer:* The slope is the rise divided by the run of the ramp.
45. $y = -2x + 3$ **47.** $y = \frac{4}{3}x - 3$ **49.** $y = 2$ **51.** $>$
53. $<$ **55.** $=$ **57.** $=$

5.6 GUIDED PRACTICE (p. 309)   **3.** yes   **5.** no
7. $y = x + 3$; the product of the slopes of the lines is $(1)(-1) = -1$, so the lines are perpendicular.
9. $y = 2x - 8$

5.6 PRACTICE AND APPLICATIONS (pp. 309–312)   **11.** no
13. yes   **15.** yes   **17.** $y = -x - 2$, $y = x - 3$; yes
19. $y = -3$, $x = -2$; yes   **21.** $y = -\frac{1}{3}x - \frac{8}{3}$; the
product of the slopes of the lines is $\left(-\frac{1}{3}\right)(3) = -1$, so
the lines are perpendicular.   **23.** $y = 4x - 23$; the
product of the slopes of the lines is $(4)\left(-\frac{1}{4}\right) = -1$, so
the lines are perpendicular.   **25.** $y = \frac{2}{3}x$; the product of
the slopes of the lines is $\left(\frac{2}{3}\right)\left(-\frac{3}{2}\right) = -1$, so the lines
are perpendicular.   **27.** $y = -x - 2$ **29.** $y = x - 1$
31. $y = -2x + 5$ **33.** $y = -\frac{8}{7}x + 3$ **35.** $x = -2$
37. $y = -\frac{3}{2}x + 2$ **39.** $y = \frac{1}{4}x - 6$ **41.** always
43. always   **45.** $y = \frac{4}{3}x + 3$, $y = -\frac{3}{4}x + \frac{3}{2}$ **49.** $-6k - 8$
51. $6x + 12y + 2$ **53.** $\frac{13}{3}$
55. horizontal   **57.** vertical

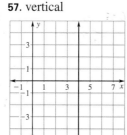

59. $\frac{7}{10}$ **61.** $\frac{2}{3}$ **63.** $\frac{8}{27}$ **65.** 7   **67.** $\frac{7}{13}$ **69.** $\frac{2}{21}$

QUIZ 3 (p. 312)   **1.** $7x + 3y = 42$ **2.** $y = -\frac{7}{3}x + 14$;
14, 7, 0
3.

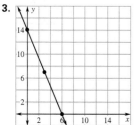

4. yes   **5.** yes   **6.** $y = x + 1$; The product of the slopes of
the lines is $(1)(-1) = -1$, so the lines are perpendicular.
7. $y = -\frac{4}{3}x - 4$; The product of the slopes of the lines is
$\left(-\frac{4}{3}\right)\left(\frac{3}{4}\right) = -1$, so the lines are perpendicular.
8. $y = -2x + 11$

CHAPTER SUMMARY AND REVIEW (pp. 313–316)
1. $y = 6x - 4$ **3.** $y = -8x + 8$ **5.** $y = \frac{3}{2}x$
7. $y = 2x - 2$ **9.** $y = -x - 4$ **11.** $y + 1 = \frac{5}{2}(x + 3)$;
$y = \frac{5}{2}x + \frac{13}{2}$ **13.** $y - 3 = 5(x + 2)$ or $y = 5x + 13$
15. $y = 3x + 5$ **17.** $y = -8x + 12$ **19.** $y = \frac{16}{9}x$
21. $y = -1$ **23.** $y = 7, x = -1$ **25.** $y = -6, x = -8$
27. $2x + y = 7$ **29.** \$1,489,200   **31.** 6; 4; 2; 0   **33.** yes
35. $y = -2x$

MAINTAINING SKILLS (p. 319)
1.
-21 -14 -7 0 7 14 21 28

3.
0 30 60 90 120 150

5. $<$ **7.** $>$ **9.** $>$ **11.** $>$ **13.** $>$

Chapter 6

STUDY GUIDE (p. 322)   **1.** C   **2.** B   **3.** C   **4.** B

6.1 GUIDED PRACTICE (p. 326)   **3.** open   **5.** solid
7. solid   **9.** left   **11.** left   **13.** left

6.1 PRACTICE AND APPLICATIONS (pp. 326–328)
15. all real numbers less than 8   **17.** all real numbers
greater than or equal to 21   **19.** solution   **21.** solution
29. subtract 11   **31.** subtract 6   **33.** add 3
41. $x < 2$ **45.** $p \geq 11$

-4 -2 0 2 4   4 6 8 10 12

49. $-2 > c$ **55.** $c < 14$

-4 -2 0 2 4   8 10 12 14 16

57. $r > 0.11$
59. $d > 16.3$
0 5 10 15 20

61. subtract 4 from each side; $x < -3$ **65.** 6   **67.** 14
69. 32   **71.** 3   **73.** -1 **75.** $y = -x + 3$ **77.** $y = -x + 2$
79. $y = 2x - 1$ **81.** $y = -\frac{1}{3}x + \frac{10}{3}$ **83.** $y = \frac{2}{5}x + \frac{36}{5}$
85. -3 **87.** $-\frac{32}{7}$ **89.** $-\frac{15}{8}$ **91.** -1 **93.** $\frac{1}{9}$ **95.** $\frac{8}{5}$

6.2 GUIDED PRACTICE (p. 333)   **3.** multiply by 5; do not
reverse   **5.** divide by 4; do not reverse   **7.** multiply
by -6; reverse   **9.** not equivalent   **11.** equivalent
13. not equivalent

6.2 PRACTICE AND APPLICATIONS (pp. 333–335)

15. multiply by 3; do not reverse   **17.** multiply by 2; do not reverse   **19.** divide by -7; reverse   **21.** divide by -3; reverse   **23.** solution   **25.** solution   **27.** Not equivalent; $12y > -24$ is equivalent to $y > -2$.
29. equivalent   **31.** equivalent   **33.** Reverse the inequality sign when dividing by -3; $x \le -5$.
35. $p < 4$

-4 -2 0 2 4

37. $j \le -18$

-20 -18 -16 -14 -12

39. $n > -60$

-60 -40 -20 0 20

43. $a \ge 20$

-10 0 10 20 30

47. $d < 5$; $1.999 \approx 2$

-8 -6 -4 -2 0 2 4 6 8

49. $a \le -18$; $5.91 \approx 6$

-25 -20 -15 -10 -5

51. always   **53.** never   **55.** $20n \ge 25{,}000$; $n \ge 1250$
57. 31 or fewer rides   **63.** -14 **65.** 0   **67.** 2   **69.** -4
71. -27 **73.** 9   **75.** -1 **77.** -2 **79.** $b = \dfrac{2A}{h}$
81. $A(4, -2)$, $B(2, 1)$, $C(-3, -3)$, $D(0, 0)$ **83.** 1, 2, 4, 5, 7, 10, 14, 20, 28, 35, 70, 140   **85.** 1, 2, 3, 4, 6, 8, 9, 12, 16, 18, 24, 36, 48, 72, 144   **87.** 1, 5, 17, 25, 85, 425
89. 1, 3, 9, 13, 19, 39, 57, 117, 171, 247, 741, 2223

6.3 GUIDED PRACTICE (p. 339)

3. not multistep; subtract 2   **5.** not multistep; divide by -4 **7.** multistep; subtract 12, divide by 5   **9.** multistep; subtract 2, multiply by 2   **11.** multistep; subtract $2w$, subtract 2, divide by 4

6.3 PRACTICE AND APPLICATIONS (pp. 339–341)

13. 14, 14; -7; -7; 7   **15.** subtract 11, divide by -2 and reverse inequality   **17.** subtract 22, divide by 3
19. divide by 6, add 2; or distribute 6, add 12, divide by 6
21. $x < 5$ **23.** $\dfrac{7}{6} \le x$ **25.** $x \ge -8$ **27.** $x \ge -3$
33. $x < 12$ **35.** $6 \le x$ **37.** $x \le -1$ **39.** $x > \dfrac{1}{2}$
41. $x > -\dfrac{14}{3}$ **43.** In line 2, distribute the 4 over -1 and distribute 3 over 1; $f > -\dfrac{7}{2}$.   **45.** $n \le 16$; you may purchase up to 16 tickets.   **47.** $0.75t + 14 \le 18.50$
49. $2x + 18 > 26$; $x > 4$ m   **51.** $\dfrac{1}{2}(8x) < 12$, $x < 3$ ft
55. 3   **57.** 3   **59.** $h = 4 + a$ **61.** $77.48   **63.** $\dfrac{9}{7}$ **65.** $\dfrac{15}{4}$

QUIZ 1 (p. 341)

1.

6 8 10 12 14

2.

-10 -8 -6 -4 -2

3.

-10 -8 -6 -4 -2

4. $a < 5$

0 2 4 6 8

5. $m \le -8$

-10 -8 -6 -4 -2

6. $-12 > b$

-16 -14 -12 -10 -8

7. $z \ge -21$

-22 -20 -18 -16 -14

8. $x \ge 36$

33 34 35 36 37

9. $-7 < k$

-10 -8 -6 -4 -2

10. $h \ge 52$ **11.** 8 or fewer plays   **12.** $-2 \ge x$
13. $x \le -3$ **14.** $x < 2$ **15.** $x > -2$ **16.** $7 \ge x$
17. $17 \le x$

6.4 GUIDED PRACTICE (p. 345)

3. A   **5.** $(4 + x)$ is greater than 7 and less than 8.   **7.** $(8 - x)$ is greater than or equal to 4 and less than 7.   **9.** $-4 \le x \le 4$

6.4 PRACTICE AND APPLICATIONS (pp. 345–347)

11. x is greater than or equal to -23 and less than or equal to -7.   **13.** x is greater than or equal to -4 and less than 19.   **15.** $2 < x < 3$ **17.** $-2 \le x < 2$
19. $0 \le x < 5$

-2 0 2 4 6

21. $-4 < x \le -2$

-6 -4 -2 0 2

23. $85 \le s \le 1100$ **25.** $15 \le s \le 50{,}000$
27. $85{,}000 \le c \le 2{,}600{,}000$
29. $12 < x \le 14$

8 10 12 14 16

35. $-4 \le x \le 3$

-4 -2 0 2 4

37. $4 < x < 7$

0 2 4 6 8

39. $-2 < x \le 10$

-2 0 2 4 6 8 10

41. $-16 \le x < -14$

-18 -16 -14 -12 -10

43. $2 < x \le 4$

-4 -2 0 2 4

51. 24   **53.** 2   **55.** 20   **57.** -6 **59.** -8 **61.** 16
63. -12 **65.** -7 **67.** more than 25 times
69. 262 million   **71.** 37.5%   **73.** $33\dfrac{1}{3}\%$ **75.** 75%
77. 84%

6.5 GUIDED PRACTICE (p. 351)

3. B   **5.** A   **7.** all real numbers less than 10 or greater than 13
9. $x < -6 \text{ or } x > -1$

-6 -4 -2 0 2

6.5 PRACTICE AND APPLICATIONS (pp. 351–353)

11. all real numbers less than or equal to 15 or greater than or equal to 31   **13.** all real numbers less than or equal to -7 or greater than 11   **15.** $x \le -3 \text{ or } x > 0$
17. $x \le 7 \text{ or } x \ge 8$
19. $x > 7 \text{ or } x < 0$ **21.** $x \le -2 \text{ or } x > 5$

0 2 4 6 8   -2 0 2 4 6

23. $x \geq -1$ or $x \leq -4$

25. $x < -6$ or $x \geq -2$

29. $x < 10$ or $x > 12$; solution **31.** $x \leq -3$ or $x > 2$; not a solution

33. $x < -2$ or $x \geq 4$

35. $x > 6$ or $x < -3$

37. $x < -2$ or $x \geq 1$

39. $x < -8$ or $x \geq -2$

41.

Input x	0	0.5	1	1.5	2
Output y	-4	-2	0	2	4

The velocity of the yo-yo decreases until it reaches the bottom of the string and then as the yo-yo ascends, the velocity increases. At 1 second, the yo-yo has reached the bottom and has a velocity of 0. From then, it rises and gains speed.

43. $t \leq 32$ or $t \geq 212$ **45.** $y < 11$ or $y \geq 65$

49.

Input x	0	1	2	3	4
Output y	2	5	8	11	14

51.

Input x	0	1	2	3	4
Output y	5	4	3	2	1

53.

Input x	0	1	2	3	4
Output y	-4	-2	0	2	4

55.

57.

59. 1.20 **61.** 6.65 **63.** -0.29

65. $9 < x$

67. $x \geq 25$

71. $x < -8$

73. 28 **75.** 221 **77.** 28,000 **79.** 5400 **81.** 11,000

6.6 GUIDED PRACTICE (p. 358) **3.** A, C **5.** none
7. $x - 4 = 10$, $x - 4 = -10$
9. $3x + 2 = 6$, $3x + 2 = -6$

6.6 PRACTICE AND APPLICATIONS (pp. 358–360)
11. 9, -9 **13.** no solution **15.** 100, -100 **17.** 7, -3
19. 12, -12 **21.** 10, -2 **23.** 3.5, -3.5 **25.** 10, -4
27. 18, -18 **29.** always **31.** always **33.** 6, -5
35. -1, -4 **37.** 8, -1 **39.** 11, -7 **45.** $|x - 2| = 8$
47. midpoint: 92.95 million miles; distance: 1.55 million miles

53.

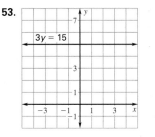

55. $y = -5x + 20$ **57.** $y = 4x - 12$ **59.** $y = -2x - 1$
61. 48,000 **63.** 47,500 **65.** 47,503.13

QUIZ 2 (p. 360)
1. $3 < x < 12$

2. $-9 < x \leq 7$

3. $-4 \leq x \leq -2$

4. $x > 5$ or $x < -5$

5. $x < -9$ or $x > -4$

6. $x < -1$ or $x > 5$

7. $-128.6 \leq T \leq 136$ **8.** 14, -14 **9.** no solution
10. 33, -15 **11.** -9, -21 **12.** 18, -6 **13.** 7, -11
14. $|x - 7.5| = 10.5$ or $|2x - 15| = 21$

6.7 GUIDED PRACTICE (p. 364) **5.** not a solution
7. solution

6.7 PRACTICE AND APPLICATIONS (pp. 364–366)
9. $x > 1$, $x < -1$; or **11.** $x - 1 \leq 9$, $x - 1 \geq -9$; and
13. $10 + 7x \geq 11$, $10 + 7x \leq -11$; or
15. $-15 < x < 15$ **19.** $x \geq 30$ or $x \leq -10$

21. $x > 12$ or $x < -4$

25. $-16 \leq x \leq -2$

27. never **29.** always
31. $-2 < x < 1$

37. $x > 1$ or $x < -\dfrac{7}{2}$

39. $x \geq 8$ or $x \leq -2$

41. $0 \leq x \leq 6$

43. $t < 3$ or $t > 7$ **45.** orange **51.** all real numbers except 4 **53.** \$38 **55.** *Sample answers:* $(-12, 0)$, $(-12, 3)$, $(-12, -4)$ **57.** *Sample answers:* $\left(\dfrac{2}{3}, 0\right)$, $\left(\dfrac{2}{3}, 1\right)$, $\left(\dfrac{2}{3}, 5\right)$ **59.** function **61.** not a function

63. $5\dfrac{11}{18}$ **65.** $11\dfrac{5}{18}$ **67.** $19\dfrac{3}{8}$

6.8 GUIDED PRACTICE (p. 370) **5.** B **7.** to the right
9. solution **11.** not a solution **13.** not a solution

6.8 PRACTICE AND APPLICATIONS (pp. 370–373)
15. Both $(0, 0)$ and $(-1, -1)$ are solutions. **17.** $(0, 0)$ is a solution; $(2, 0)$ is not a solution. **19.** Neither $(0, 0)$ nor $(2, -4)$ are solutions. **23.** solid **25.** dashed **27.** $y = x$; solid **29.** $y = \frac{1}{2}x - 8$; solid **31.** $y = -2x - 3$; dashed
33. solid **35.** yes

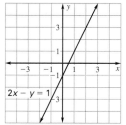

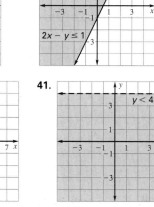

37. **41.**

45. **49.**

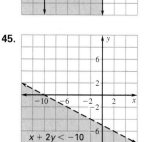

51. *Sample answer:* $(1, 3), (2, 2), (3, 1)$
53. $y \le -2x + 3200$

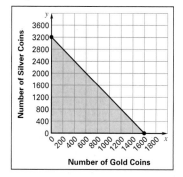
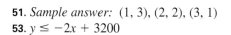

57. 15 **59.** 69 **61.** 30°C **63.** $m = \frac{1}{2}, b = -2$
65. $m = -3, b = 7$ **67.** $m = 0, b = 5$ **69.** 52%

QUIZ 3 (p. 373)
1. $x \ge 18$ or $x \le -18$ **2.** $x > 5$ or $x < 3$

3. $-9 < x < -5$ **4.** $1 \le x \le 7$

5. $-16 \le x \le 9$ **6.** $x > 5$ or $x < -6$

7. $t < 0.75$ or $t > 2.25$ **8.** Both $(0, -1)$ and $(2, 2)$ are solutions. **9.** $(0, 0)$ is not a solution; $(-4, 1)$ is a solution. **10.** $(2, 1)$ is not a solution; $(-1, 2)$ is a solution. **11.** $(1, -1)$ is a solution; $(2, -3)$ is not a solution.

12. **13.**

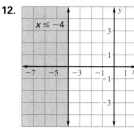

14. **15.**

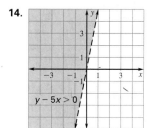

16. **17.**

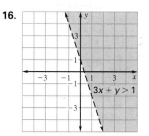
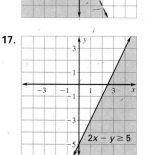

6.8 TECHNOLOGY (p. 374)
1. **3.**

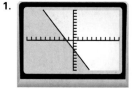

5.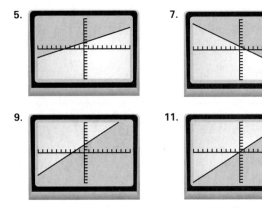

7.

9.

11.

13. $y > x$

CHAPTER SUMMARY AND REVIEW (pp. 375–378)

1. $x \leq 2$

3. $2 < x$

5. $8 < x$

7. $27 \leq p$

9. $n \leq -6$

11. $t \leq 56$

13. $x \geq 2$ **15.** $x \geq 5$ **17.** $x < -\frac{1}{3}$ **19.** $x \geq 1$

21. $x \leq 13$

23. $-1 \leq x \leq 5$

25. $2 < x < 4$

27. $8 \leq x < 40$

29. $x \leq -5 \text{ or } x > -2$

31. $x \leq 1 \text{ or } x > 7$

33. $x < 2 \text{ or } x > 10$

35. no solution **37.** $9, -9$ **39.** no solution

41. $-2 \leq x \leq 2$

43. $2 \leq x \leq 18$

45. $-3 < x < 5$

47. $-2 < x < 10$

49. $x < -\frac{13}{2} \text{ or } x > \frac{11}{2}$

51.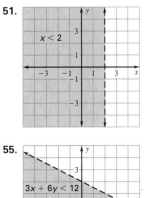

53.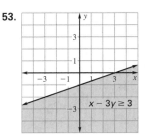

55.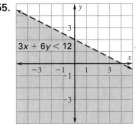

MAINTAINING SKILLS (p. 381) **1.** 70 **3.** 37 **5.** 69 **7.** 51
9. -17 **11.** 7 **13.** 3 **15.** 7

CUMULATIVE PRACTICE (pp. 382–383) **1.** 7 **3.** 45 **5.** 3
7.

Input n	0	1	2	3	4	5	6
Output C	65	66	67	68	69	70	71

9. 2.5 **11.** -18 **13.** 4.6 **15.** $83°F$ **17.** $18 + 3x$
19. $-15 + 5t$ **21.** $11b + 7$ **23.** $6y + 6$ **25.** -18
27. 24 **29.** -4 **31.** 10 **33.** 75 **35.** 1 **37.** 12.5 cm^3
39. 52 mi/h **41.** 25 ft/sec

43.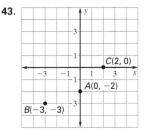

45.

47. The sales of catfish have increased since 1990, although not consistently. There are points clustered around sales of \$370 to \$380 million.

49.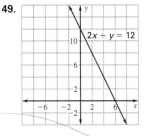

51.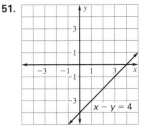

53.

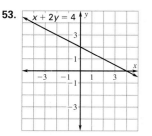

55. $y = -2x + 5$ **57.** $y = 4x + 1$ **59.** $y = x + 1$
61. $y = \frac{1}{4}x - \frac{7}{4}$ **63.** $y = -3x - 4$
65. $y - 4 = x - 1$ or $y - 6 = x - 3$
67. $y + 7 = -8(x + 1)$ or $y - 1 = -8(x + 2)$
69. $y - 7 = \frac{3}{4}(x - 4)$ or $y - 10 = \frac{3}{4}(x - 8)$
71. $x < 2$ **73.** $x \ge -7$ **75.** $x > 4$ **77.** $-5 \le x \le 2$
79. $x > 4$ or $x \le -2$ **81.** $-6 \le x \le 1$

Chapter 7

STUDY GUIDE (p. 388) **1.** B   **2.** B   **3.** A   **4.** D

7.1 GUIDED PRACTICE (p. 392) **3.** $y = x - 2$;
$y = -2x + 10$ **5.** (4, 2)

7.1 PRACTICE AND APPLICATIONS (pp. 392–394)
7. solution   **9.** not a solution   **11.** not a solution   **13.** (4, 5)
15. (3, 0)   **17.** (6, −6)   **19.** (−3, −5)   **21.** (−4, −5)
23. (1, 4)   **25.** 125,000 miles   **27.** 14 years   **33.** 4
35. 5   **37.** −2   **39.** $y = x + 7$ **41.** $y = -2x - 9$
43. $y = -3x + 2$ **45.** 4.764   **47.** 2   **49.** 10

7.1 TECHNOLOGY (p. 395) **1.** (−3.5, 2.5)
3. (−0.8, −2.05)

7.2 GUIDED PRACTICE (p. 399) **3.** Equation 2; y has a
coefficient of −1   **5.** $x = 1$ **7.** (−5, 18)   **9.** (1, 3)

7.2 PRACTICE AND APPLICATIONS (pp. 399–401)
11. Equation 2; m has a coefficient of 1, no constant.
13. Equation 2; x and y have coefficients of 1.
15. Equation 2; x has a coefficient of 1.   **17.** (9, 5)
19. (4, −2)   **21.** (−1, 5)   **23.** (0, 0)   **25.** (−7, 4)
27. $\left(-\frac{7}{2}, -\frac{13}{2}\right)$ **29.** 30 11-inch softballs and 50 12-inch
softballs   **31.** $3375 in ABC and $1125 in XYZ
33. 1200 meters uphill, 1000 meters downhill   **39.** $-2x$
41. 26

43. 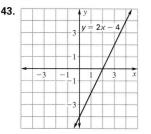   **45.**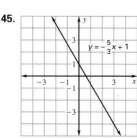

47.

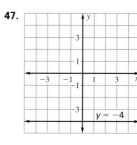

49. $-19 \le x \le 9$

51. $x < 1$ or $x > 3$

53. 1, 3   **55.** 1, 3   **57.** 1, 2, 3, 6   **59.** 1, 3

7.3 GUIDED PRACTICE (p. 405) **3.** $9x + 7x = 16x$;
$24 + 8 = 32$; Solution: (2, 2)   **5.** *Sample answer:*
multiply equation 2 by −4, then add and solve for x.
Solution: (1, −1)

7.3 PRACTICE AND APPLICATIONS (pp. 405–408)
7. (−3, 7)   **9.** (2, 0)   **11.** (3, 5)   **13.** (−8, 6)   **15.** (3, 0)
17. (3, 2)   **19.** (2, 0)   **21.** $\left(\frac{7}{2}, 5\right)$ **23.** (21, −3)
25. (8, −1)   **27.** (3, −4)   **29.** $\left(-79, -\frac{61}{5}\right)$ **31.** (1, 2)
33. (1, 0)   **35.** (2, 1)   **37.** (2, 0)   **39.** (3, 2)   **41.** (2, 0)
43. about 3 cubic centimeters   **45.** There are 15,120 men
and 20,000 rolls of cotton.   **49.** $y = 3x + 10$
51. $y = -3x + 30$ **53.** $y = x - 1$ **55.** (1, 3) is a
solution; (2, 0) is not a solution.   **57.** (−3, −2)
59. (10, −2)   **61.** true   **63.** true   **65.** false

QUIZ 1 (p. 408) **1.** (3, −4)   **2.** (0, 0)
3. (6, 8)   **4.** (1, 9)   **5.** (−1, 3)   **6.** (−6, 10)   **7.** (6, 8)
8. (5, 1)   **9.** $\left(-\frac{1}{2}, \frac{1}{2}\right)$ **10.** (2, −1)   **11.** (0, 1)   **12.** (2, 1)
13. Four compact discs were bought at $10.50 each and
6 were bought at $8.50 each.

7.4 GUIDED PRACTICE (p. 412) **3.** (7.5, 1.5)
5. You would have to sell $600,000 of merchandise.
7. $10d$

7.4 PRACTICE AND APPLICATIONS (pp. 412–414)
9. (0, 2)   **11.** (3, 6)

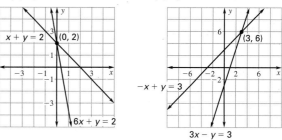

13. *Sample answer:* Multiplication and addition. No variable can be easily isolated. **15.** *Sample answer:* Substitution. Equation 2 can be solved for x or y.
17. *Sample answer:* Substitution. Equations 1 or 2 can be solved for x. **19.** $(3, 3)$ **21.** $\left(\dfrac{4}{15}, \dfrac{6}{5}\right)$ **23.** $(-2, 1)$
25. $(-3, 2)$ **31.** 6 pea plants, 7 broccoli plants
33. about $(1.6, 6474)$ **39.** parallel; $m = 4$ for both lines
41. not parallel; different slopes

43. 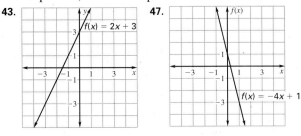 **47.**

49. $1\dfrac{1}{5}$ **51.** $1\dfrac{11}{72}$ **53.** $\dfrac{23}{30}$ **55.** $\dfrac{25}{32}$

7.5 GUIDED PRACTICE (p. 420)
5. No solution; the two equations represent parallel lines.

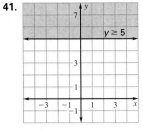

7. no solution **9.** one solution; $(5, 12)$

7.5 PRACTICE AND APPLICATIONS (pp. 420–422)
17. no solution **19.** no solution **21.** one solution
23. Infinitely many solutions; multiplying Equation 1 by 4 yields Equation 2. **25.** infinitely many solutions; one line **27.** infinitely many solutions; one line
29. no solution; parallel lines **31.** No; there are infinitely many solutions for the system. **33.** Yes, $14.98. *Sample explanation:* The solution of the system $4x + 2y = 99.62$ and $8x + y = 139.62$ is $(14.98, 19.78)$.
39. about 4:27 P.M.

41. 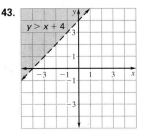 **43.**

45.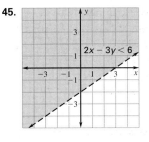

47. 20 **49.** 20; 20

7.6 GUIDED PRACTICE (p. 427)
3.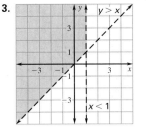

5. The student graphed $y \geq 1$, instead of $y > -1$; graphed $x \leq 2$, instead of $x \geq 2$; graphed $y \leq x - 4$, instead of $y > x - 4$. **7.** $y \leq -x$, $y > -2$

7.6 PRACTICE AND APPLICATIONS (pp. 427–430)
13. **15.**

19. **21.**

25. *Sample answer:* $2y - x \leq 4$, $2y - x \geq -4$
27. *Sample answer:* $y \geq 0$, $y \leq -x + 2$, $y \leq x + 2$
29. *Sample answer:* $y \geq 0$, $3y \leq -5x$, $4y \leq 5x + 35$
31. $b + c \geq 240$; $b < c$; $5b + 3c \leq 1200$
35.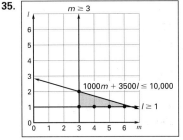

37. $b + c \le 20$, $5b + 6c \ge 90$ **39.** *Sample answer:*
5 hours babysitting and 15 hours as a cashier; 15 hours
babysitting and 5 hours as a cashier **41.** $y \ge 0$, $x \ge 0$,
$y \le -x + 4$ **45.** 243 **47.** 137 **49.** 62 **51.** 49
53. -60 **55.** 38 5-point questions and 30 2-point
questions **57.** 9.25 **59.** 2.8 **61.** 3.8 **63.** 6.875

QUIZ 2 (p. 430) **1.** $l = 8$ ft, $w = 3$ ft **2.** premium gas costs
$1.57/gallon, regular gas costs $1.35/gallon **3.** no
solution **4.** one solution; $(0, 1)$ **5.** infinitely many
solutions

6.
7.

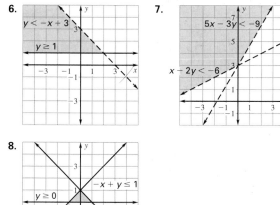

8.

9. $x + 2y \le 4$, $-x + y \ge -1$

CHAPTER SUMMARY AND REVIEW (pp. 431–434)
1. $(9, -3)$ **3.** $(0, 1)$ **5.** $\left(4, -\frac{1}{2}\right)$ **7.** $(0, 3)$ **9.** $\left(\frac{5}{8}, \frac{3}{2}\right)$
11. $\left(\frac{1}{2}, 0\right)$ **13.** $\left(-\frac{83}{14}, \frac{39}{14}\right)$ **15.** $(3, -5)$ **17.** $(-1, 1)$
19. 2 regular movies; 3 new releases **21.** no solution

23.
25.

27.

MAINTAINING SKILLS (p. 437) **1.** 125 **3.** 9 **5.** 0.47
7. 0.035 **9.** 61% **11.** 200%

Chapter 8

STUDY GUIDE (p. 440) **1.** A **2.** C **3.** D **4.** D **5.** A
8.1 GUIDED PRACTICE (p. 446) **5.** $(-5)^6$ **7.** 2^{12} **9.** y^{20}
11. $16n^4$

8.1 PRACTICE AND APPLICATIONS (pp. 446–448) **13.** 5
15. 18 **17.** 7 **19.** 4^9 **21.** $(-2)^6$ **23.** x^9 **25.** 3 **27.** 12
29. 9 **31.** 2^6 **33.** $(-4)^{15}$ **35.** c^{80} **37.** 441 **39.** 576
41. $64d^6$ **43.** $64m^6n^6$ **45.** $-r^5s^5t^5$ **47.** $<$ **49.** $<$
51. $>$ **53.** $-4x^7$ **55.** r^8s^{12} **57.** $18x^5$ **59.** $a^4b^4c^6$
61. $V = 36\pi a^3 \approx 113.1a^3$ **63.** 8, or 8 to 1 **65.** $2^1 = 2$,
$2^2 = 4$, $2^3 = 8$ **67.** $2^{30} = 1{,}073{,}741{,}824$ pennies
75. 10,000 **77.** $\frac{1}{25}$ **79.** $\frac{45}{4}$

83.

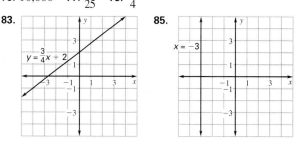

85.

87. $x < 7$ **89.** $x \le 1$ **91.** $x \ge \frac{7}{4}$ **93.** true **95.** false; 10
97. false; 1

8.2 GUIDED PRACTICE (p. 452) **3.** 1 **5.** 64 **7.** 2
9. $\frac{1}{16}$ **11.** 0.0016 **13.** 0.0156 **15.** $\frac{1}{m^2}$ **17.** $3c^5$

8.2 PRACTICE AND APPLICATIONS (pp. 452–454) **19.** $\frac{1}{2}$, $\frac{1}{5}$,
$\frac{1}{6}$ **21.** 1 **23.** $\frac{1}{16}$ **25.** $-\frac{1}{343}$ **27.** 256 **29.** $\frac{1}{8}$ **31.** $\frac{1}{36}$
33. 64 **35.** $\frac{1}{9}$ **37.** $\frac{1}{400}$ **39.** $\frac{1}{16}$ **41.** 0.0313 **43.** 0.0016
45. 0.0625 **47.** 0.0714 **49.** The 5 should not be raised
to a negative power; $\frac{5}{x^3}$. **51.** $\frac{1}{x^5}$ **53.** $\frac{y^4}{x^2}$ **55.** x^2
57. $x^{10}y^4$ **59.** $\frac{1}{64x^3}$ **61.** $\frac{216}{x^9}$ **63.** about 5.31 million
people **73.** 4 **75.** 2 **77.** $\frac{27}{2} = 13.5$ **79.** -9
81. 15 **83.** -15
85. $-13 < x < -5$
87. $-6 \le x \le 1$

89. $x > 2$ or $x < -\frac{20}{3}$

91. $\left(-\frac{5}{3}, -1\right)$ **93.** $(5, 0)$ **95.** $(2, 3)$ **97.** *Sample
answer:* $\frac{6}{10}$, $\frac{9}{15}$, $\frac{12}{20}$ **99.** *Sample answer:* $\frac{2}{16}$, $\frac{3}{24}$, $\frac{4}{32}$
101. *Sample answer:* $\frac{30}{32}$, $\frac{45}{48}$, $\frac{60}{64}$
103. *Sample answer:* $\frac{50}{64}$, $\frac{75}{96}$, $\frac{100}{128}$

8.3 GUIDED PRACTICE (p. 458)

3.

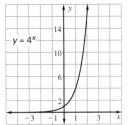

5. domain: all real numbers; range: all positive real numbers

8.3 PRACTICE AND APPLICATIONS (pp. 458–460)
7. yes; $2^0 = 1$ **9.** no; $2(3)^0 = 2$ **11.** yes; $\left(\dfrac{1}{8}\right)^0 = 1$ **13.** no; $7\left(\dfrac{1}{5}\right)^0 = 7$

15.

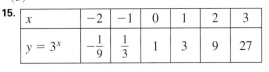

x	-2	-1	0	1	2	3
$y = 3^x$	$-\dfrac{1}{9}$	$\dfrac{1}{3}$	1	3	9	27

17.

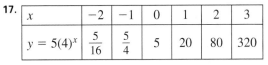

x	-2	-1	0	1	2	3
$y = 5(4)^x$	$\dfrac{5}{16}$	$\dfrac{5}{4}$	5	20	80	320

19.

x	-2	-1	0	1	2	3
$y = \left(\dfrac{1}{6}\right)^x$	36	6	1	$\dfrac{1}{6}$	$\dfrac{1}{36}$	$\dfrac{1}{216}$

21.

x	-2	-1	0	1	2	3
$y = 2\left(\dfrac{1}{7}\right)^x$	98	14	2	$\dfrac{2}{7}$	$\dfrac{2}{49}$	$\dfrac{2}{343}$

23. 55.90 **25.** 45.25 **27.** 0 **29.** 1.06

35.

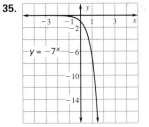

37.

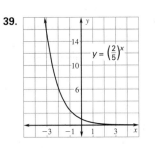

39.

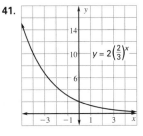

41.

43. domain: all real numbers; range: all negative real numbers **45.** domain: all real numbers; range: all negative real numbers **47.** domain: all real numbers; range: all positive real numbers **49.** domain: all real numbers; range: all positive real numbers

51.

Year	1995	2000	2005	2010
t	-5	0	5	10
U (in millions)	17.8	135	1025.2	7784.8

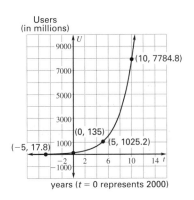

55. 0.38 **57.** -0.46 **59.** -1.91 **61.** $8x + y = 4$ **63.** $7x - 8y = 0$ **65.** $3x + 16y = 9$ **67.** 1 solution **69.** no solution **71.** infinitely many solutions **73.** $-5, -4, 6$ **75.** $-3\dfrac{4}{5}, -2\dfrac{3}{4}, -2\dfrac{1}{5}$ **77.** 3.001, 3.01, 3.25

QUIZ 1 (p. 460) **1.** 59,049 **2.** 64 **3.** 1600 **4.** 36 **5.** $\dfrac{1}{25}$ **6.** 1 **7.** r^{13} **8.** k^8 **9.** $9d^2$ **10.** $\dfrac{2}{x^3 y^9}$ **11.** $\dfrac{a^{10} b^{12}}{5}$ **12.** $\dfrac{1}{m^7 n^7}$ **13.** about \$1008; about \$2177

14.

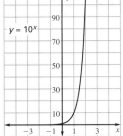

15.

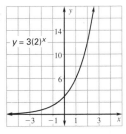

16.

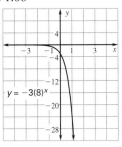

8.3 TECHNOLOGY (p. 461)

1.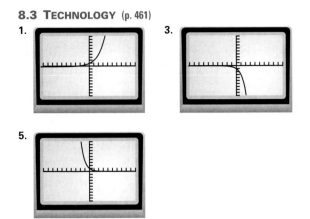
3.
5.

7. *Sample answer:* For $a > 1$, the graph of $y = a^x$ is a curve that passes through $(0, 1)$ and increases to the right. The graph of $y = -a^x$ passes through $(0, -1)$ and decreases to the right. Both graphs approach the x-axis to the left.

8.4 GUIDED PRACTICE (p. 465)
3. 125   5. -32 7. x^3
9. $\frac{1}{m^6}$ 11. $\frac{1}{32}$ 13. $\frac{256}{81}$ 15. $\frac{25}{m^2}$ 17. $\frac{m^6}{n^{10}}$

8.4 PRACTICE AND APPLICATIONS (pp. 465–468)
19. 4
21. 11   23. 6   25. 125   27. 1   29. $\frac{1}{x}$ 31. $\frac{1}{x^3}$ 33. 1296
35. 3   37. 10   39. $\frac{1}{625}$ 41. $-\frac{8}{27}$ 43. $\frac{81}{x^4}$ 45. $\frac{x^5}{y^5}$
47. $\left(\frac{6a}{b^2}\right)^3 = \frac{6^3 a^3}{b^6} = \frac{216 a^3}{b^6}$ 49. $5x^3 y^3$ 51. $6a^8 b^3$
53. $\frac{96x^4}{y}$ 55. $\frac{2y^9}{3x^3}$ 57. $\frac{9x^2 y^2}{2}$ 59. ≈ 0.437 61. 200,
160, 128, 102, 82, 66, 52   63. product of powers property; quotient of powers property; product of powers property; canceling a common factor   69. 100,000   71. 1
73. $y = \frac{1}{2}x + 4$ 75. $y = -x - 8$ 77. $y = -x + 3$
79. solution   81. not a solution   83. $(8, 4)$ 85. $(4, 3)$
87. $(9, -1)$ 89–93. Estimates may vary.   89. 450
91. 80.5   93. 1750

8.5 GUIDED PRACTICE (p. 472)
3. 430   5. 0.05
7. 0.245   9. 6.9×10^6 11. 9.9×10^{-1}
13. 2.05×10^{-2} 15. 2×10^{-11}

8.5 PRACTICE AND APPLICATIONS (pp. 472–474)
17. right, 2   19. left, 7   21. 8000   23. 21,000
25. 433,000,000   27. 0.009   29. 0.098
31. 0.00000000011   33. in scientific notation
35. 9×10^2 37. 8.8×10^7 39. 9.52×10^1
41. 1×10^{-1} 43. 6×10^{-6} 45. 8.5×10^{-3}
47. 1.23×10^9 49. 1.5×10^5 51. 7.0×10^{-4}
53. 2.7×10^7 55. $\approx 4.44 \times 10^{-3}$ 57. 1.09926×10^6;
1,099,260   59. 1.5×10^{-11}; 0.000000000015
61. $\approx 7.9626 \times 10^{-19}$; $\approx 0.00000000000000000079626$

63. 0.00098   65. 2×10^{-23} 67. about \$18.12 per square mile   69. about $(4.87 \times 10^{14})\pi$ km^3 or about 1.53×10^{15} km^3 73. no solution
75. 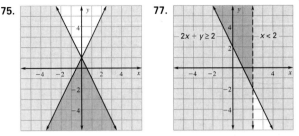   77.

79. 212%   81. 67.4%   83. 7.567

QUIZ 2 (p. 474)
1. 7776   2. $\frac{1}{x^2}$ 3. $-\frac{343}{8}$ 4. $\frac{b^5}{a^5}$ 5. $\frac{4}{3y^9}$
6. $30x^2$ 7. $-\frac{25b^6}{a^3}$ 8. $\frac{16m^4}{81n^4}$ 9. $\frac{4x^3 y^7}{5}$ 10. $\frac{243}{w^2 z^{11}}$
11. 5,000,000,000   12. 4,800   13. 33,500   14. 0.000007
15. 0.011   16. 0.0000208   17. 1.05×10^2
18. 9.9×10^4 19. 3.07×10^7 20. 2.5×10^{-1}
21. 4×10^{-4} 22. 6.7×10^{-6}

8.6 GUIDED PRACTICE (p. 479)
3. 0.04   5. about \$608

8.6 PRACTICE AND APPLICATIONS (pp. 479–481)
7. $C = 100$, $r = 0.5$ 9. $C = 7.5$, $r = 0.75$
11. $y = 310,000(1.15)^t$; y = salary, t = number of years
13. $y = 10,000(1.25)^{10}$; y = population, t = number of years   15. $y = 15,000(1.3)^{15}$; y = concert attendance, t = number of years   17. \$2231.39   19. \$4489.99
21. \$382.88   23. \$510.51   25. \$1466.01   27. \$1770.44
29. 3, 4   31. 2   33. 3   35. about 13.2 L/min, 46.3 L/min, 86.5 L/min   45. 5   47. -2 49. -7
51. 4   53. 2^4 55. 3^7 57. r^6 59. $\frac{1}{4}$ 61. $\frac{1}{8}$

8.7 GUIDED PRACTICE (p. 485)
3. \$6185.20   5. \$4266.98
7. C   9. exponential decay   11. exponential decay

8.7 PRACTICE AND APPLICATIONS (pp. 485–488)
13. 18; 0.11   15. 0.5; 0.625   17. $y = 100,000(0.98)^t$
19. $y = 100(0.91)^t$ 21. $y = 70(0.99)^t$ 23. about \$11,192
25. about \$8372   27. about 229 mg   29. $y = 64(0.5)^t$
31. 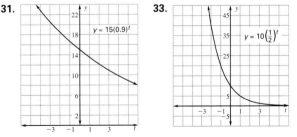   33.

35. $y = 22,000(0.91)^t$; about \$10,300
37. $y = 10,500(0.9)^t$; about \$3700
39. 302, 239, 189, 150, 119   41. about 106 miles

45. exponential decay; 0.98 **47.** exponential decay; $\dfrac{2}{3}$

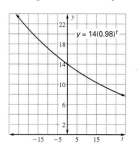

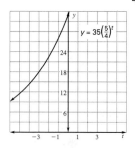

49. exponential growth; $\dfrac{5}{4}$

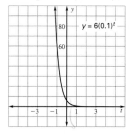

51. *Sample answer:* As b increases, the curve becomes steeper or more vertical. **57.** 24 **59.** 72 **61.** -0.92
63. -0.64 **65.** $y - 5 = 3(x - 2)$ **67.** $y + 4 = 4(x + 1)$
69. $y - 7 = -6(x + 1)$ **71.** 2.5 **73.** 0.2 **75.** 5.5

QUIZ 3 (p. 488) **1.** $270 **2.** $314.93 **3.** $367.33
4. $462.73 **5.** 1600 raccoons **6.** about $12,422
7. about $10,286 **8.** about $9360 **9.** about $5841
10. $y = 20{,}000(0.92)^t$; about $13,200
11. exponential decay; 0.1 **12.** exponential growth; 1.2

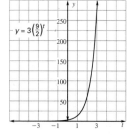

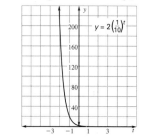

13. exponential growth; 4.5 **14.** exponential decay; 0.1

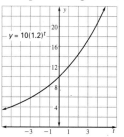

CHAPTER SUMMARY AND REVIEW (pp. 489–492) **1.** 128
3. 40% **5.** $81x^4$ **7.** $8p^4$ **9.** 1 **11.** $\dfrac{1}{49}$ **13.** $\dfrac{x^6}{y^6}$ **15.** $\dfrac{b^5}{a^2}$

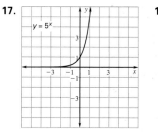

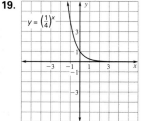

21. $\dfrac{1}{3}$ **23.** $\dfrac{16}{81}$ **25.** $9y$ **27.** $\dfrac{8a^6b^{12}}{125}$ **29.** 70 **31.** 0.0002
33. 5.2×10^7 **35.** 9×10^{-3} **37.** 1.5×10^7
39. 1.44×10^7 **41.** 7×10^8 **43.** $y = 2(1.05)^t$
45. $y = 125(0.97)^t$

MAINTAINING SKILLS (p. 495) **1.** 2^3 **3.** $3 \cdot 5 \cdot 7$ **5.** $2\dfrac{5}{8}$
7. $1\dfrac{12}{15}$

Chapter 9

STUDY GUIDE (p. 498) **1.** B **2.** D **3.** C

9.1 GUIDED PRACTICE (p. 502) **5.** ± 11 **7.** -2
9. irrational **11.** rational **13.** 14.66, -2.66
15. 13.31, -9.31

9.1 PRACTICE AND APPLICATIONS (pp. 502–504) **17.** The positive and negative square roots of 16 are 4 and -4.
19. The positive square root of 225 is 15. **21.** The negative square root of 289 is -17. **23.** The positive square root of 1 is 1. **25.** 12 **27.** 14 **29.** ± 7 **31.** -16
33. 20 **35.** 11 **37.** -1 **39.** 13 **41.** no **43.** no
45. yes **47.** no **49.** no **51.** no **53.** 2.24 **55.** 3.61
57. -7 **59.** ± 1 **61.** ± 3.87 **63.** -4.47 **65.** 3 **67.** 0
69. 6 **71.** 7 **73.** 7 **75.** 10.24, 5.76 **77.** -0.34, -11.66
79. -11.24, -2.76 **81.** 5.13, -1.80 **83.** -2.90, 0.57
85. m is a perfect square **87.** False. *Sample counterexample:* the square root of 0 is 0. **95.** $(2, -2)$
97. 116 adult tickets and 208 student tickets
99. $(-4, -19)$ **101.** $(5, -6)$ **103.** $0.5\overline{3}$ **105.** 0.875
107. 0.3125 **109.** 0.4 **111.** $0.\overline{8}$ **113.** 0.9

9.2 GUIDED PRACTICE (p. 508) **3.** 2 **5.** 0 **7.** 2 **9.** ± 7
11. $\pm\sqrt{7}$ **13.** no real solution **15.** 1.7 sec **17.** 3.5 sec

9.2 PRACTICE AND APPLICATIONS (pp. 508–510) **19.** ± 1
21. no real solution **23.** ± 15 **25.** ± 11 **27.** ± 16
29. ± 7 **31.** ± 8 **33.** ± 4 **35.** $\pm\sqrt{2}$ **37.** ± 3 **39.** no real solution **41.** ± 5 **43.** $\pm\sqrt{3}$ **45.** ± 6 **47.** $\pm\sqrt{14}$
49. The equation has no real solution. **51.** ± 1.41
53. ± 2.83 **55.** ± 1.84 **57.** True; the solutions of $x^2 = 9$ are 3 and -3. **59.** $h = -16t^2 + 96$ **61.** 0.40 mm
63. 0.15 mm **65.** 0.12 mm **67.** 5,500,400; 22,582,900; 73,830,400 **71.** -18 **73.** 12 **75.** 5; 6 **77.** 8; 2
79. $x \geq -2$ **81.** $x < 2$ **83.** 8×10^{-7} **85.** 8.721×10^3
87. $\dfrac{2}{3}$ **89.** $\dfrac{1}{3}$ **91.** $\dfrac{5}{6}$ **93.** $\dfrac{3}{4}$

9.3 GUIDED PRACTICE (p. 514)   **5.** D   **7.** B   **9.** 6
11. $2\sqrt{15}$ **13.** $\dfrac{\sqrt{15}}{4}$ **15.** $\dfrac{\sqrt{10}}{5}$

9.3 PRACTICE AND APPLICATIONS (pp. 514–517)
17. no; radical in the denominator   **19.** yes   **21.** $2\sqrt{11}$
23. $3\sqrt{2}$ **25.** $3\sqrt{3}$ **27.** $10\sqrt{2}$ **29.** $5\sqrt{5}$ **31.** 12   **33.** $\dfrac{1}{2}$

35. $\dfrac{2}{5}$ **37.** $\dfrac{6}{5}$ **39.** $\dfrac{\sqrt{11}}{9}$ **41.** $\dfrac{3}{4}$ **43.** $\dfrac{\sqrt{5}}{9}$

45. $\sqrt{20} = \sqrt{4 \cdot 5} = 2\sqrt{5}$ **47.** $\dfrac{\sqrt{5}}{5}$ **49.** $\dfrac{\sqrt{2}}{2}$ **51.** $\dfrac{\sqrt{3}}{3}$

53. $\dfrac{\sqrt{10}}{5}$ **55.** $\dfrac{\sqrt{11}}{11}$ **57.** $\dfrac{5\sqrt{3}}{3}$ **59.** 20   **61.** $-6\sqrt{3}$

63. -12 **65.** -1 **67.** $3\sqrt{6}$ **69.** $-3\sqrt{10}$ **71.** $\dfrac{\sqrt{15}}{5}$

73. $2\sqrt{5}$ **75.** $70\sqrt{2}$ m/sec   **77.** No; ratio of speeds is
the square root of the ratio of depths.   **79.** 98
81. Multiplication; square

93. 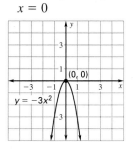   **95.**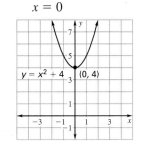

97. $81x^4$ **99.** 144   **101.** $64x^2y^2$ **103.** $-a^3b^3c^3$
105. domain: all real numbers; range: all negative real
numbers   **107.** $\dfrac{1}{4}$ **109.** $\dfrac{3}{8}$ **111.** $\dfrac{2}{189}$ **113.** $\dfrac{1}{10}$

QUIZ 1 (p. 517)   **1.** 9   **2.** -5 **3.** 4   **4.** -2 **5.** ±1 **6.** 10
7. ±7 **8.** 11   **9.** ±8 **10.** $\pm\sqrt{63}$ or $\pm3\sqrt{7}$ **11.** $\pm\sqrt{6}$
12. no real solution   **13.** ±4 **14.** ±5 **15.** $3\sqrt{2}$
16. $2\sqrt{15}$ **17.** $\sqrt{3}$ **18.** -9 **19.** $4\sqrt{30}$ **20.** $\dfrac{2\sqrt{3}}{3}$

21. $\dfrac{\sqrt{5}}{3}$ **22.** $\dfrac{1}{2}$ **23.** $\dfrac{\sqrt{5}}{4}$ **24.** $2\sqrt{2}$ **25.** $\dfrac{\sqrt{6}}{3}$ **26.** $\dfrac{6\sqrt{5}}{5}$

9.4 GUIDED PRACTICE (p. 523)   **3.** up   **5.** down   **7.** up
9. axis of symmetry: **11.** axis of symmetry:
   $x = 0$ $x = 0$

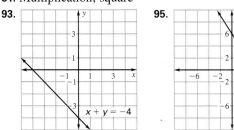

13. axis of symmetry:
   $x = 1$

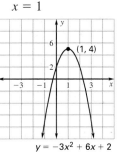

$$y = -3x^2 + 6x + 2$$

9.4 PRACTICE AND APPLICATIONS (pp. 523–525)   **15.** up
17. down   **19.** down   **21.** down   **23.** down

25.
$(0, 0)$

x	-2	-1	0	1	2	3
y	24	6	0	6	24	54

27.
$\left(\dfrac{5}{2}, -\dfrac{25}{2}\right)$

x	0	1	2	$\dfrac{5}{2}$	3	4	5
y	0	-8	-12	$-\dfrac{25}{2}$	-12	-8	0

29.
$\left(-\dfrac{1}{6}, 3\dfrac{5}{6}\right)$

x	-2	-1	$-\dfrac{1}{6}$	0	1	2
y	24	8	$3\dfrac{5}{6}$	4	12	32

31.
$\left(-\dfrac{1}{2}, 9\right)$

x	-3	-2	-1	$-\dfrac{1}{2}$	0	1	2
y	-16	0	8	9	8	0	-16

37.   **39.**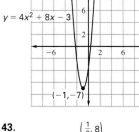

41.   **43.**

45. $\left(\dfrac{15}{32}, \dfrac{609}{64}\right)$; this point represents the highest point on the path of the basketball. At $\dfrac{15}{32} \approx 0.47$ sec the ball reaches its high point of $\dfrac{609}{64} \approx 9.52$ ft. **47.** 10 ft

55. 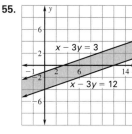 **57.**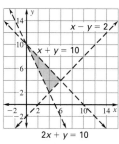

59. $(-5)^9$ **61.** x^8 **63.** m^8 **65.** 2^5 **67.** $\dfrac{4}{15}, \dfrac{1}{3}, \dfrac{2}{5}$

69. $\dfrac{3}{4}, \dfrac{7}{8}, \dfrac{9}{10}$

9.5 GUIDED PRACTICE (p. 529) **3.** B **5.** A **7.** ± 1
9. ± 4 **11.** 2, 5

9.5 PRACTICE AND APPLICATIONS (pp. 529–531)
13. $x^2 - 6x + 6 = 0$ **15.** $3x^2 - x - 5 = 0$
17. $6x^2 - 12x = 0$ **19.** $-3, 1$ **23.** $-3, 1$ **25.** $-3, 1$
27. $-1, 5$ **29.** $-5, 1$ **31.** $-3, 2$ **33.** $-1, 2$ **35.** ± 5
37. ± 5 **39.** ± 4 **41.** ± 9 **43.** ± 2 **45.** ± 3 **47.** $-4, 1$
49. $-4, 8$ **51.** 10 sec **55.** pasta: \$5.95; salad: \$1.95

57. (3, 2); one solution **59.** $\left(-\dfrac{7}{2}, 6\right)$; one solution

61. no solution **63.** 4 **65.** 0 **67.** 2 **69.** -9 **71.** 6

73. $10\sqrt{2}$ **75.** $\sqrt{3}$ **77.** $\dfrac{20\sqrt{3}}{3}$ **79.** $>$ **81.** $>$ **83.** $<$ **85.** $<$

9.5 TECHNOLOGY (p. 532) **1.** $-1, 2$ **3.** $-0.77, 2.27$ **5.** 2

9.6 GUIDED PRACTICE (p. 536) **5.** $2x^2 - 16x + 32 = 0$; $a = 2, b = -16, c = 32$ **7.** $-7, 1$ **9.** -6

11. $\dfrac{-1 \pm \sqrt{13}}{6}$ **13.** $2x^2 + x - 6 = 0; -2, \dfrac{3}{2}$

15. $x^2 - x - 2 = 0; -1, 2$ **17.** $x^2 - 4x + 3 = 0; 1, 3$

9.6 PRACTICE AND APPLICATIONS (pp. 536–539)
19. $3x^2 - 3x - 6 = 0; a = 3, b = -3, c = -6$
21. $x^2 - 5x + 6 = 0; a = 1, b = -5, c = 6$
23. $3x^2 - 24x + 45 = 0; a = 3, b = -24, c = 45$
25. $k^2 - \dfrac{1}{4} = 0; a = 1, b = 0, c = \dfrac{1}{4}$
27. $\dfrac{2}{3}x^2 + 2x - \dfrac{1}{3} = 0; a = \dfrac{2}{3}, b = 2, c = -\dfrac{1}{3}$ **29.** 9
31. 1 **33.** 169 **35.** 148 **37.** 21 **39.** 39 **41.** $-1, -10$
43. $-\dfrac{4}{3}, 2$ **45.** $-1.30, -0.26$ **47.** $-1.87, 13.87$
49. $2x^2 - 4x - 30 = 0; -3, 5$ **51.** $x^2 + 6x - 5 = 0$;
$-3 \pm \sqrt{14}$ **53.** $2x^2 - 5x - 7 = 0; -1, \dfrac{7}{2}$
55. $x^2 - 2x - 3 = 0; -1, 3$ **57.** $2x^2 - 2x - 12 = 0$;
$-2, 3$ **59.** $-2, -3$ **61.** $-2, -8$ **63.** $-1, 4$ **65.** $-3, 1$
67. 2.30 sec **69.** 2.21 sec **71.** 0.92 sec **73.** 0.4 sec

75. 1.4 sec **77.** 5.7 sec **79.** about 5.04 sec **81.** $-2, -\dfrac{3}{2}$

83. $-\dfrac{3}{4}, 3$ **85.** $-4, -\dfrac{3}{2}$ **91.** -20 **93.** -54

94.

96.

97. $x \le -\dfrac{1}{3}$ **99.** $x > 16$ **101.** $>$ **103.** $>$ **105.** $<$

QUIZ 2 (p. 539) **1.** up **2.** up **3.** down **4.** up **5.** down
6. down

7.

8.

9.

10. $-2, 5$ **11.** 6 **12.** $-1, -3$ **13.** -3 **14.** $-6, -\dfrac{1}{2}$

15. $-2, 8$ **16.** $\dfrac{3}{2}, 2$ **17.** $1.17, -2.84$ **18.** $1.55, -0.22$

9.7 GUIDED PRACTICE (p. 543) **5.** one solution **7.** B
9. A **11.** 2

9.7 PRACTICE AND APPLICATIONS (pp. 543–545)
13. 49 **15.** -40 **17.** 0 **19.** -111 **21.** -40
23. no solution **25.** two solutions **27.** no solution
29. two solutions **31.** two solutions **33.** one solution
35. 60 **37.** It crosses the x-axis at two distinct points.
39. 0 **41.** 0 **43.** 1 **47.** domain: $0 \le t \le 5$;
range: $9.29 \le P \le 161.49$ **49.** about 8.3 years
53. $1 < x < 4$ **55.** $-3 < x < 5$

57.

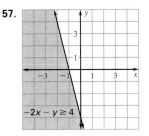

59. 0.06 **61.** 0.01 **63.** 0.0018

9.8 GUIDED PRACTICE (p. 550) **3.** inside **5.** outside
7. $(0, 0)$, yes; $(1, -2)$, no

9.

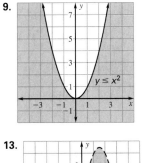

11.

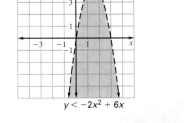

$y < -x^2 + 2x$

13.

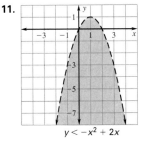

$y < -2x^2 + 6x$

9.8 PRACTICE AND APPLICATIONS (pp. 550–552) **15.** yes
17. no **19.** no **21.** outside **23.** inside **25.** sometimes
27. sometimes

33.

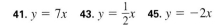

$y < x^2 - 4$

35.

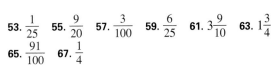

$y > -x^2 - 3x - 2$

37.

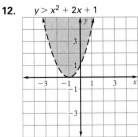

$y > -3x^2 - 5x - 1$

41. $y = 7x$ **43.** $y = \frac{1}{2}x$ **45.** $y = -2x$

48.

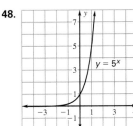

$y = 5^x$

50.

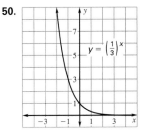

$y = \left(\frac{1}{3}\right)^x$

52.

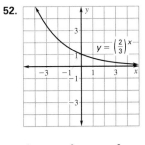

$y = \left(\frac{2}{3}\right)^x$

53. $\frac{1}{25}$ **55.** $\frac{9}{20}$ **57.** $\frac{3}{100}$ **59.** $\frac{6}{25}$ **61.** $3\frac{9}{10}$ **63.** $1\frac{3}{4}$
65. $\frac{91}{100}$ **67.** $\frac{1}{4}$

QUIZ 3 (p. 552) **1.** two solutions **2.** one solution **3.** no
solution **4.** No. *Sample answer:* the vertical motion
model is $h(t) = -16t^2 + 50t + 5$. If you let $h(t) = 45$
and solve for t, you have the quadratic equation
$8t^2 - 25t + 20 = 0$. The discriminant has a value of
$625 - 640 = -15$, so there are no solutions. **5.** A **7.** B

8.

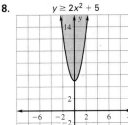

$y \geq 2x^2 + 5$

9.

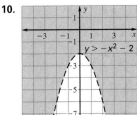

$y < x^2 + 3x$

10.

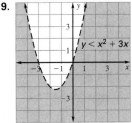

$y > -x^2 - 2$

11.

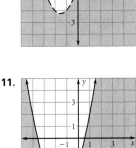

$y \leq x^2 + 3x - 2$

12.

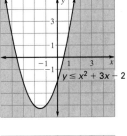

$y > x^2 + 2x + 1$

13.

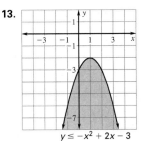

$y \leq -x^2 + 2x - 3$

Summary and Review (pp. 553–556) 1. −2 3. 10

5. ±12 7. ±4 9. $3\sqrt{5}$ 11. $\dfrac{\sqrt{6}}{2}$

13.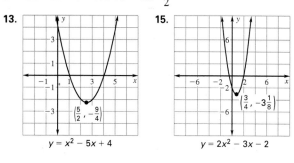

$y = x^2 - 5x + 4$

15.

$y = 2x^2 - 3x - 2$

17. 5, 1 19. $1, \dfrac{1}{3}$ 21. $\dfrac{1}{2}, \dfrac{3}{5}$ 23. two solutions 25. 2 27. 1

29.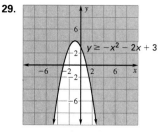

$y \geq -x^2 - 2x + 3$

Maintaining Skills (p. 559) 1. $16x - 96$ 3. $5m - 65$
5. $30a + 80$ 7. $21m + 6n$ 9. $2x + 10$

Chapters 1–9 Cumulative Practice (p. 560–561)
1. No. Each input value can only have one output value.
5 has two. 3. $3x - 6$ 5. $9 + 2h$ 7. $1.25x = 60$;
48 pretzels 9. 360 11. 400% 13. $-3; \dfrac{1}{2}$ 15. $\dfrac{14}{5}$; 14

17. $(-2; -28)$ 19. Yes; slope of both lines is 4.

21. $y = -x + 10$ 23. $y = -2x - 2$ 25. $y = -\dfrac{1}{2}x + \dfrac{9}{2}$

27. $3x - 5y = -6$ 29. $-2x + 7y = 15$ 31. $x + 4y = 24$

33. $m \leq -9$ 35. $t \leq -8$ 37. $y \geq 14$ 39. $y > -4$

41. $k \geq 7$ 43. $(2, 6)$ 45. $(-5, -4)$ 47. $\left(1, -\dfrac{1}{2}\right)$

49.

51.

53. x^9 55. $64t^2$ 57. 243 59. $\dfrac{1}{16}$ 61. $\dfrac{x^4 y^8}{4}$ 63. $\dfrac{9x^3}{y}$

65. 1.5×10^3 67. 6×10^{10} 69. 8×10^0 71. $2\sqrt{10}$

73. $6\sqrt{2}$ 75. $\dfrac{\sqrt{21}}{2}$ 77. $3\sqrt{2}$ 79. $\dfrac{\sqrt{10}}{10}$ 81. $\dfrac{2\sqrt{3}}{3}$

83.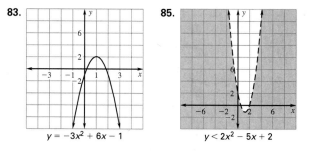

$y = -3x^2 + 6x - 1$

85.

$y < 2x^2 - 5x + 2$

87. No. Discriminant for $-16t^2 + 100t - 180 = 0$ is -1520, so there is no real solution.

Chapter 10

Study Guide (p. 566) 1. B 2. C 3. D

10.1 Guided Practice (p. 571) 3. linear binomial
5. quadratic binomial 7. cubic trinomial 9. $-3x^2$
and $-5x$ are not like terms; $9x^3 - 3x^2 - 5x - 2$
11. $3x - 16$ 13. $4x^2 - 7x - 2$

10.1 Practice and Applications (pp. 571–573)
15. always 17. sometimes 19. always 21. 4
23. 4 25. $20m^3$; cubic monomial 27. -16; constant
monomial 29. $11y^3 - 14$; cubic binomial
31. $7b^3 - 4b^2$; cubic binomial 33. $-6x^3 + 4x^2 - 6$
35. $-7m^2 + 7m - 3$ 37. -6 39. $3x^2 - 5$
41. $z^3 + 1$ 43. $-n^3 + 3n^2 + 3n - 5$
45. $25x^3 + 8x + 2$ 47. $x^2 + 2x + 2$ 49. $-3x^2 + 6$
51. $1.5x^2 + 60x$ 53. $A = 1.381t^2 + 3.494t + 235.325$
59. $5x - 2$ 61. $-15x + 9$ 63. $-7x - 55$ 65. 32
67. 256 69. 256 71. 1.295; 1.053 73. 4 75. $1\dfrac{5}{8}$

77. $3\dfrac{7}{10}$ 79. $12\dfrac{19}{28}$ 81. $3\dfrac{3}{14}$ 83. $15\dfrac{31}{72}$

10.2 Guided Practice (p. 578) 3. $(x + 3), (x + 3)$
5. 3 7. 20 9. $-8x^2 - 14x$ 11. $-12x^4 - 8x^3 + 24x^2$
13. $y^2 + 6y - 16$ 15. $w^2 + 2w - 15$
17. $8x^2 - 29x - 12$ 19. $x^2 + x - 56$

10.2 Practice and Applications (pp. 578–580)
21. $-8x^2 + 20x$ 23. $2x^3 - 16x^2 + 2x$
25. $12w^5 - 8w^4 - 4w^3$ 27. $t^2 + 13t + 40$
29. $d^2 - 2d - 15$ 31. $2y^2 + 5y + 2$ 33. $3s^2 + 5s - 2$
35. $8y^2 - 18y + 7$ 37. $y^2 - 3y - 40$
39. $2w^2 + 5w - 25$ 41. $2x^2 - 3x - 135$
43. $6z^2 + 25z + 14$ 45. $10t^2 + 9t - 9$
47. $63w^2 - 143w + 60$ 49. $d^3 - 7d^2 + 4d + 30$
51. $6x^3 + x^2 - 8x + 6$ 53. $a^3 + 4a^2 - 19a + 14$
55. $4y^3 + 45y^2 - 38y - 24$ 57. $21x^2 + 100x + 100$
59. $R = -3.15t^2 - 6.21t + 989.12$, in millions of dollars
61. $2x^2 + 7x + 3$ 65. $49x^2$ 67. $\dfrac{4}{25}y^2$ 69. 9^8 71. b^7
73. $432t^4$ 75. $-108x^3 y^5$ 77. two solutions 79. two
solutions 81. one solution 83. two solutions 85. two
solutions

87.

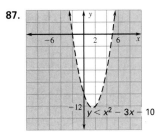

$y < x^2 - 3x - 10$

89. $0.0\overline{3}$ **91.** 2   **93.** $\dfrac{27}{8}$ **95.** $\dfrac{87}{92}$ **97.** 2

10.3 GUIDED PRACTICE (p. 585) **3.** $x^2 - 12x + 36$
5. $p^2 + 12p + 36$ **7.** $t^2 - 36$ **9.** sometimes
11. sometimes

10.3 PRACTICE AND APPLICATIONS (pp. 585–587) **13.** yes
15. no   **17.** yes   **19.** yes   **21.** yes   **23.** $x^2 - 25$
25. $4m^2 - 4$ **27.** $9 - 4x^2$ **29.** $x^2 + 10x + 25$
31. $9x^2 + 6x + 1$ **33.** $16b^2 - 24b + 9$ **35.** $x^2 - 16$
37. $9x^2 - 6x + 1$ **39.** $4y^2 - 25$ **41.** $a^2 - 4b^2$
43. $9x^2 - 16y^2$ **45.** $81 - 16t^2$ **47.** false;
$a^2 + 4ab + 4b^2$ **49.** true   **51.** $(x + 3)^2 = x^2 + 6x + 9$;
square of a binomial   **53.** $(2x + 4)^2 = 4x^2 + 16x + 16$;
square of a binomial   **55.** $9x^2 - 24x + 16$ in.^{2}
57. 25% normal feathers; 50% mildly frizzled;
25% extremely frizzled   **61.** x **63.** $\dfrac{15x^2}{y}$

65.

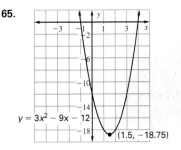

$y = 3x^2 - 9x - 12$

$(1.5, -18.75)$

67. $\dfrac{1}{4}$ **69.** $\dfrac{4}{9}$ **71.** $\dfrac{1}{27}$ **73.** $\dfrac{27}{64}$

QUIZ 1 (p. 587) **1.** 2   **2.** 0   **3.** 3   **4.** 5   **5.** $3x^2 + 5x + 9$
6. $-6x^3 - 14x^2 + 2x - 2$ **7.** $3t^2 - 13t + 14$
8. $6x^3 + 3x^2 + 4x + 3$ **9.** $x^2 + 7x - 8$
10. $y^2 + 11y + 18$ **11.** $-12x^5 + 11x^4 - 3x^2$
12. $4x^2 - 49y^2$ **13.** $16n^2 - 49$ **14.** $2x^3 - 3x^2 - 6x + 8$
15. $x^2 - 36$ **16.** $16x^2 - 9$ **17.** $25 - 9b^2$
18. $4x^2 - 49y^2$ **19.** $9x^2 + 36x + 36$
20. $64x^2 + 96x + 36$

10.4 GUIDED PRACTICE (p. 591) **3.** No; 2 and -5 are
solutions, 3 is not.   **5.** no   **7.** yes   **9.** $-1, -3$ **11.** 7

13.

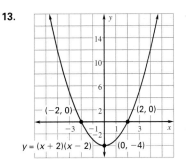

$y = (x + 2)(x - 2)$

$(-2, 0)$ $(2, 0)$ $(0, -4)$

10.4 PRACTICE AND APPLICATIONS (pp. 591–593)
15. $-8, 6$ **17.** -3 **19.** -7 **21.** $-2, -3$ **23.** 17
25. -9 **27.** $20, -15$ **29.** $-1, -2, 4$ **31.** $-5, 6$
33. $-8, -9, 12$ **35.** $8, -\dfrac{1}{2}, -2$

41. x-intercepts: $(-5, -3)$;   **45.** x-intercepts: $(-4, -3)$;
vertex: $(-4, -1)$ vertex: $(-3.5, -0.25)$

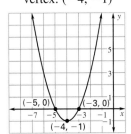

$(-5, 0)$ $(-3, 0)$ $(-4, -1)$

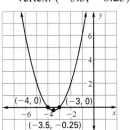

$(-4, 0)$ $(-3, 0)$ $(-3.5, -0.25)$

47. $(0, -14)$ **49.** 630 ft   **51.** 200 m   **55.** 0.04443
57. 1,250,000   **59.** 9,960,000   **61.** 81,700,000
63. $x^2 - 64$ **65.** $6x^2 + 19x - 7$ **67.** $24x^2 - x - 3$
69. $x^2 + 20x + 100$ **71.** exponential decay;
$y = P(0.84)^t$ where $P =$ the average price of the computer
in 1996, and t is the number of years since 1996.
73. exponential decay; $y = N(0.97)^t$ where N is the
number of members in 1996 and t is the number of years
since 1996.   **75.** 1, 2, 3, 4, 6, 12   **77.** 1, 2, 3, 6, 9, 18
79. 1, 3, 17, 51   **81.** 1, 2, 3, 4, 6, 9, 12, 18, 36
83. 1, 2, 4, 8, 16, 32, 64   **85.** 1, 2, 3, 4, 6, 7, 12, 14, 21,
28, 42, 84

10.5 GUIDED PRACTICE (p. 599) **3.** A   **5.** C   **7.** 5, -1
9. always   **11.** never

10.5 PRACTICE AND APPLICATIONS (pp. 599–601)
15. $(z + 1)(z + 5)$ **17.** $(b + 8)(b - 3)$ **19.** $(r + 4)(r + 4)$
21. $(m - 10)(m + 3)$ **23.** $(b + 8)(b - 5)$ **25.** $2, -7$
27. $-1, -15$ **29.** $6, -9$ **31.** $4, 11$ **33.** $5, -13$
35. $8, -7$ **37.** $-4, -8$ **39.** $2, 15$ **41.** $3, -6$
43. base: 8 ft, height: 5 ft   **45.** 305 m by 550 m   **51.** 15
53. 1   **55.** 18   **57.** $y^2 + 5y - 36$ **59.** $-3w^2 + 3w + 60$
61. $20t^2 - 62t + 30$ **63.** $-2, -3$ **65.** 6, 9   **67.** 1, $-\dfrac{1}{2}$
69. $-4, 3, \dfrac{1}{2}$ **71.** 11.056   **73.** 11.86   **75.** 20.9204
77. 114.8106

10.6 GUIDED PRACTICE (p. 606) **3.** -6 **5.** $10x^2$ **7.** D
9. C **11.** $(2x + 1)(x - 2)$ **13.** $(3x - 4)(4x - 1)$
15. $(3x - 4)(x + 2)$ **17.** $\frac{1}{2}, -8$

10.6 PRACTICE AND APPLICATIONS (pp. 606–608)
23. $(3t + 1)(t + 5)$ **25.** $(2a + 1)(3a + 1)$
27. $(6b + 1)(b - 2)$ **29.** $3(x + 1)(2x - 5)$
31. $(2z - 1)(z + 10)$ **33.** $(4x + 7)(x + 5)$
35. $(3c - 4)(c - 11)$ **37.** $(2t + 7)(3t - 10)$
39. $(2y - 5)(4y - 3)$ **41.** Incorrectly factored:
$3y^2 - 16y - 35 = (3y + 5)(y - 7)$; solutions are $-\frac{5}{3}$, 7.
43. $\frac{3}{7}, 1$ **45.** $\frac{1}{4}, 5$ **47.** $\frac{13}{5}, -2$ **49.** $\frac{1}{2}, \frac{3}{2}$ **51.** $\frac{5}{2}, \frac{7}{4}$
53. $\frac{3}{7}, -\frac{1}{4}$ **55. a.** $h = -16t^2 + 8t + 8$ **b.** 1 sec
57. 2 sec; the other solution of $\frac{3}{4}$ second is the time it takes for the T-shirt to leave the cannon and go up to a height of 30 feet. You would probably catch the T-shirt as it fell. **61.** $\left(-\frac{49}{12}, -\frac{11}{2}\right)$ **63.** $16t^2 - 8t + 1$
65. $9x^2 + 30x + 25$ **67.** $121 - 132x + 36x^2$ **69.** $\frac{4}{33}$
71. $\frac{5}{27}$ **73.** $\frac{16}{35}$ **75.** $\frac{5}{4}$

QUIZ 2 (p. 608) **1.** -5 **2.** -4 **3.** $-\frac{7}{2}, 4$ **4.** $0, \frac{2}{5}$
5. $5, -\frac{1}{2}$ **6.** $0, -4, 7$

7. x-intercepts: 2, -2; **8.** x-intercepts: $-3, -5$;
  vertex: $(0, -4)$ vertex: $(-4, -1)$

9. x-intercepts: 1, -3; vertex: $(-1, -4)$

10. $(y + 4)(y - 1)$ **11.** $(w + 11)(w + 2)$
12. $(n + 19)(n - 3)$ **13.** cannot be factored
14. $(b - 8)(b + 2)$ **15.** $(r - 7)(r + 4)$
16. $(m - 9)(m + 5)$ **17.** $(x + 6)(x + 11)$
18. $(r - 43)(r + 2)$ **19.** $1, -6$ **20.** $-1, -25$ **21.** $5, 9$

22. $-9, -2$ **23.** $-\frac{1}{2}, -5$ **24.** $\frac{1}{3}, 1$ **25.** $-\frac{2}{3}, 4$
26. $-\frac{3}{2}$ **27.** $-\frac{7}{3}, -\frac{2}{5}$

10.7 GUIDED PRACTICE (p. 613) **3.** $(b + 5)^2$
5. $(w - 8)^2$ **7.** $6(y - 2)(y + 2)$ **9.** $(2x - 1)^2$ **11.** -3
13. 7 **15.** 3 **17.** 3 sec

10.7 PRACTICE AND APPLICATIONS (pp. 613–615)
19. $(q - 8)(q + 8)$ **21.** $(3c - 1)(3c + 1)$
23. $(9 - x)(9 + x)$ **25.** $(w - 3y)(w + 3y)$ **27.** $(x + 4)^2$
29. $(b - 7)^2$ **31.** $(3x + 1)^2$ **33.** $(5n - 2)^2$
35. $4(2w - 5)^2$ **37.** $(a - 2b)^2$ **39.** $4(n - 3)(n + 3)$
41. $5(c + 2)^2$ **43.** $9(3t^2 + 2t + 1)$ **45.** $3(k - 10)(k - 3)$
47. $4(b - 5)^2$ **49.** $4(2w + 5)^2$ **51.** $-\frac{1}{2}$ **53.** 4 **55.** 6
57. $\frac{7}{4}$ **59.** 5 sec **61.** $S = 2D^2$; about 2.12 in.
63. 1 sec **65.** 16 ft **69.** solution **71.** not a solution
73. $(1, -1)$ **75.** $(0, 0)$ **77.** $(2, 2)$ **79.** $6\sqrt{6}$ **81.** $10\sqrt{2}$
83. $\frac{2\sqrt{7}}{7}$ **85.** 8 **87.** $\frac{7 \pm 4\sqrt{7}}{9}$ **89.** $\frac{9 \pm \sqrt{557}}{14}$
91. $2^2 \cdot 5$ **93.** $3 \cdot 19$ **95.** $2^4 \cdot 5$ **97.** $2^3 \cdot 3 \cdot 5$
99. $3 \cdot 5 \cdot 23$ **101.** $2^3 \cdot 3 \cdot 5^2$

10.8 GUIDED PRACTICE (p. 620) **3.** When factoring out $-2b$, the remaining factor is $(b^2 - 6b + 7)$; answer is $-2b(b - 7)(b + 1)$. **5.** $3x^2(x^2 + 2)$
7. $(x - 1)(x^2 + x + 1)$ **9.** $(3x + 1)(9x^2 - 3x + 1)$
11. $2b(b - 3)(b + 3)$ **13.** $3t(t + 3)^2$ **15.** $x(x - 4)(x + 4)$

10.8 PRACTICE AND APPLICATIONS (pp. 620–622)
17. $6v(v^2 - 3)$ **19.** $3x(1 - 3x)$ **21.** $4a^2(1 - 2a^3)$
23. $5x(3x + 2)(x - 1)$ **25.** $3d(6d^5 - 2d + 1)$
27. $(a + b)(a + 3)$ **29.** $(5x + 1)(2x - 3)$
31. $(10x - 7)(x - 1)$ **33.** $(c - 2)(c^2 + 2c + 4)$
35. $(m - 5)(m^2 + 5m + 25)$ **37.** $2y(y - 6)(y + 1)$
39. $4t(t - 6)(t + 6)$ **41.** $(c^3 - 12)(c + 1)$
43. $3(x + 10)(x^2 - 10x + 100)$ **45.** $-3, -4$ **47.** $9, -3$
49. $0, \frac{1}{2}, -\frac{1}{2}$ **51.** $-\frac{3}{4}, 3$ **53.** $\frac{-5 \pm \sqrt{17}}{4}$ **55.** $\frac{2 \pm 2\sqrt{43}}{12}$
57. 3 sec **59.** $h, l = h - 3, w = h - 9$ **61.** $h = 12$ in., $l = 9$ in., $w = 3$ in. **65.** $x < 1$ **67.** $-3, 3$ **69.** $7, -19$
72. $y = 3x + 2$

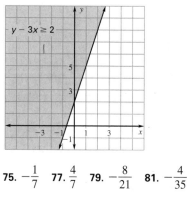

75. $-\frac{1}{7}$ **77.** $\frac{4}{7}$ **79.** $-\frac{8}{21}$ **81.** $-\frac{4}{35}$

1. $(7x - 8)(7x + 8)$; difference of squares
2. $(11 - 3x)(11 + 3x)$; difference of squares
3. $(2t + 5)^2$; perfect square trinomial
4. $2(6 - 5y)(6 + 5y)$; difference of squares
5. $(3y + 7)^2$; perfect square trinomial **6.** $3(n - 6)^2$;
perfect square trinomial **7.** 4 **8.** -4 **9.** $0, 3, -12$
10. $3x^2(x + 4)$ **11.** $3x(2x + 1)$ **12.** $9x^3(2x - 1)$
13. $2x(4x^4 + 2x - 1)$ **14.** $2x(x - 2)(x - 1)$
15. $(x^2 + 4)(x + 3)$ **16.** $4(x - 5)(x^2 + 5x + 25)$
17. $0, \dfrac{5}{6}, -\dfrac{5}{6}$ **18.** 2

CHAPTER SUMMARY AND REVIEW (pp. 623–626)
1. $3x - 5$ **3.** $2x^2 + 5x + 7$ **5.** $x^3 + 2x^2 + 2x - 2$
7. $6a^3 - 15a^2 + 3a$ **9.** $a^2 + 3a - 40$
11. $d^3 - d^2 - 16d - 20$ **13.** $x^2 - 225$
15. $x^2 + 4x + 4$ **17.** $(2x + 2)^2 = 4x^2 + 8x + 4$; square
of a binomial **19.** $2, 3$ **21.** $0, \dfrac{3}{5}$ **23.** $0, -9, 12$
25. $-\dfrac{1}{3}, 4$ **27.** $(x + 6)(x + 4)$ **29.** $(m - 10)(m + 2)$
31. $-8, 4$ **33.** $(3x + 1)(4x + 1)$ **35.** $(4r - 3)(r + 2)$
37. $-\dfrac{1}{2}, 1$ **39.** $\dfrac{1}{2}, -4$ **41.** $\dfrac{1}{4}, -\dfrac{1}{4}$ **43.** $10, -10$
45. $-\dfrac{2}{5}$ **47.** $5y^2(y^2 - 4y + 2)$ **49.** $(y^2 - 2)(3y - 4)$
51. $(3b + 1)(9b^2 - 3b + 1)$ **53.** $5, -5$

MAINTAINING SKILLS (p. 629) **1.** $\dfrac{1}{4}, \dfrac{2}{5}$ **3.** $\dfrac{1}{3}, \dfrac{1}{2}, \dfrac{5}{6}$ **5.** $\dfrac{3}{10}$,
$\dfrac{13}{20}, \dfrac{3}{4}$ **7.** $\dfrac{5}{6}, \dfrac{5}{4}, 1\dfrac{1}{3}$ **9.** $1\dfrac{1}{12}$ **11.** $\dfrac{29}{35}$ **13.** $\dfrac{11}{30}$ **15.** $5\dfrac{1}{3}$

Chapter 11

STUDY GUIDE (p. 632) **1.** B **2.** B **3.** D

11.1 GUIDED PRACTICE (p. 636) **3.** 3 **5.** $\dfrac{1}{7}$ **7.** 6 **9.** no
11. yes (assuming $a, c \neq 0$)

11.1 PRACTICE AND APPLICATIONS (pp. 636–638)
13. $\dfrac{32}{9}$ **15.** 35 **17.** 3 **19.** $\dfrac{45}{8}$ **21.** $\dfrac{5}{2}$ **23.** $\dfrac{1}{3}$ **25.** ± 8
27. 10 **29.** $-\dfrac{5}{3}$ **31.** $-5, 2$ **33.** $2, 5$ **35.** $4, \dfrac{5}{2}$
37. about 7.5 ft high and 5.4 ft wide **39.** 6.875 in.
45. $y + 3 = -4(x - 5)$ **47.** $2x + y = 26$
49. $3x - 4y = -29$ **51.** $12x + y = 84$ **53.** 8 **55.** 100
57. $3\sqrt{2}$ **59.** $4\sqrt{5}$ **61.** 54 **63.** $\sqrt{7}$
65.

Decimal	0.78	0.2	$0.\overline{6}$	0.073	0.03	0.48
Percent	78%	20%	$66\dfrac{2}{3}\%$	7.3%	3%	48%
Fraction	$\dfrac{39}{50}$	$\dfrac{1}{5}$	$\dfrac{2}{3}$	$\dfrac{73}{1000}$	$\dfrac{3}{100}$	$\dfrac{12}{25}$

11.2 GUIDED PRACTICE (p. 642) **3.** Direct variation; the
graph is a line passing through the origin. **5.** Inverse
variation; the graph represents $y = \dfrac{4}{x}$. **7.** neither
9. inverse variation **11.** $y = \dfrac{24}{x}$

11.2 PRACTICE AND APPLICATIONS (pp. 642–644)
13. $y = 4x$ **15.** $y = 3x$ **17.** $y = \dfrac{1}{9}x$ **19.** $y = \dfrac{21}{x}$
21. $y = \dfrac{22}{x}$ **23.** $y = \dfrac{13}{x}$ **25.** $y = \dfrac{27}{x}$
27. inversely **29.** directly

31. inverse variation **33.** inverse variation **35.** 116 lb
37. about 0.36 pounds per square inch **39.** 2.2° **45.** 4.5
47. 1 **49.** 5.5 **51.** yes **53.** yes **55.** $(x + 7)(x - 2)$
57. $(5x - 6)(x - 9)$ **59.** $5x^2(3x + 2)(x - 4)$
61. about 1.36 to 1 **63.** $\dfrac{2}{3}$ **65.** 2 **67.** $9\dfrac{7}{15}$ **69.** $1\dfrac{28}{55}$

11.2 TECHNOLOGY (p. 645) **1.** directly; 0.825; $y = 0.825x$

11.3 GUIDED PRACTICE (p. 649) **5.** $\dfrac{1}{8c}$ **7.** already in
simplest form **9.** $\dfrac{2n}{3n^2 + 10}$ **11.** $y^4 - 1$ **13.** $3y + 1$
15. $x + 1$

11.3 PRACTICE AND APPLICATIONS (pp. 649–651) **17.** $3x$
19. $\dfrac{7}{25x^2}$ **21.** $\dfrac{-4}{3}$ **23.** $\dfrac{t^2}{t + 2}$ **25.** $\dfrac{7}{12 + x}$ **27.** $\dfrac{7 - x^2}{6}$
29. -1 **31.** $\dfrac{x - 4}{x - 3}$ **33.** $\dfrac{x + 1}{x + 6}$ **35.** $2x - 1$ **37.** $-\dfrac{1}{x}$
39. $-\dfrac{1}{2y}$ **41.** $-\dfrac{1}{y + 3}$ **43.** $a - 2$ **45.** $x - 8$
47. $-\dfrac{4(11x - 738)}{5(x + 40)}$; 3.6 lb per in.^{2} **51.** $-\dfrac{1}{3}$ **53.** $\dfrac{24}{49}$
55. $\dfrac{9y}{20}$ **57.** $4m^3$ **59.** $\dfrac{8c^2}{3}$

61. **63.**

65.

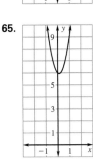

67. 2.387 **69.** 111.4 **71.** 0.02

QUIZ 1 (p. 651) **1.** 8 **2.** $\frac{27}{7}$ **3.** 4 **4.** 1, $-\frac{5}{3}$ **5.** $y = 4x$

6. $y = \frac{3}{5}x$ **7.** $y = \frac{3}{2}x$ **8.** $y = \frac{24}{x}$ **9.** $y = \frac{16}{x}$ **10.** $y = \frac{7.5}{x}$

11. $\frac{3x}{2}$ **12.** $\frac{x-4}{x+6}$ **13.** $-\frac{1}{x+4}$ **14.** $\frac{5}{11+x}$ **15.** $x + 4$

16. $2x + 3$

11.4 GUIDED PRACTICE (p. 655) **3.** $\frac{1}{2x^2}$ **5.** $\frac{x}{(x+5)^2}$

7. $\frac{1}{4}$ **9.** The solver should have multiplied the first
expression by the reciprocal of the second expression;

$\frac{x+3}{x-3} \div \frac{4x}{x^2-9} = \frac{x+3}{x-3} \cdot \frac{x^2-9}{4x} =$

$\frac{(x+3)(x+3)(x-3)}{(x-3)(4x)} = \frac{(x+3)^2}{4x}$.

11.4 PRACTICE AND APPLICATIONS (pp. 655–657) **11.** x

13. $\frac{6}{35x}$ **15.** $-\frac{1}{4(x-7)}$ **17.** $\frac{z(z+1)}{10(z-7)}$ **19.** 3 **21.** x

23. $\frac{c-8}{4c^2(c+1)}$ **25.** $9x$ **27.** $2(y-3)$ **29.** $x + 3$ **31.** $5x$

33. $\frac{5}{6x}$ **35.** $\frac{x+2}{2(x-2)}$ **37.** $\frac{x(x-6)}{x+3}$ **39.** $\frac{x(2x+1)}{2(x-1)^2}$

41. $-\frac{x+6}{5x^2}$ **43.** $\frac{1}{(2y+3)(y-2)}$

45. $\frac{4x+3}{(x-1)(4x-3)(x+1)}$ **47.** $\frac{x+3}{x+1}$ **49.** The ratio
approaches 1.

55.

Input x	2	3	4	5	6
Output y	11	12	13	14	15

57. $-19 < x < 5$ **59.** $x \le -46$ or $x \ge 20$

61. $x < -22$ or $x > 12$ **63.** $-3 \pm 2\sqrt{3}$ **65.** $-\frac{5}{3}$, -2

67. $\frac{1}{2}$, $-\frac{5}{3}$ **69.** $2x^2 + 11x - 18$

71. $16p^3 + 11p^2 - 8p + 8$ **73.** 0.85 **75.** 1.74

77. 1.125 **79.** 1.12

11.5 GUIDED PRACTICE (p. 660) **3.** $\frac{5(y+2)}{y+3}$ **5.** $\frac{7}{3r}$

7. $-\frac{5}{c^2-4}$ **9.** $-\frac{12}{y-2}$ **11.** $\frac{2}{r+4}$

11.5 PRACTICE AND APPLICATIONS (pp. 660–662)

13. $\frac{7}{x+7}$ **15.** 2 **17.** $\frac{1}{2}$ **19.** $\frac{t+14}{3t}$ **21.** $\frac{2-5x}{3x-1}$ **23.** 2

25. $\frac{a-1}{a-5}$ **27.** $\frac{x+5}{x+2}$ **29.** $\frac{2x+3}{x+1}$ **31.** $\frac{y-3}{y-7}$ **33.** The
solver multiplied the rational expressions rather than
adding them; $\frac{y+2}{y+3} + \frac{y-4}{y+3} = \frac{2y-2}{y+3}$. **35.** $\frac{3x+9}{x-9}$

37. $-\frac{2}{x-3}$ **39.** $\frac{2(3x-4)^2}{x^2}$ **41.** $\frac{14x}{x+1}$ **43.** 1 joule

45. $\frac{x}{x-10}$ joules **49.** $\frac{x^5}{y^6}$ **51.** $\frac{y^5}{2x^8}$ **53.** $\frac{1}{1296c^4}$ **55.** c^2d

57. $\frac{1}{p^2}$ **59.** $\frac{1}{a^5}$ **61.** m^{16} **63.** $-\frac{v^9}{8u^3}$ **65.** 1.6×10^2

67. 8.1×10^{-7} **69.** 1.6×10^{-3} **71.** 9, 11, 13 **73.** 42,
35, 27 **75.** 8, $\frac{19}{2}$, 11

11.6 GUIDED PRACTICE (p. 667) **3.** $\frac{x}{3}$ **5.** $\frac{(x+2)(2x+7)}{(x+1)(2x+3)}$

7. -1

11.6 PRACTICE AND APPLICATIONS (pp. 667–669) **9.** 15

11. $7c^5$ **13.** $5b$ **15.** $90x^3$ **17.** $24y^2$ **19.** $21a^7 + 7a^6$

21. $8a^4 - 12a^3$ **23.** $\frac{155}{78x}$ **25.** $\frac{4x+5}{4}$ **27.** $\frac{7n^2+1}{30n}$

29. $\frac{63x-4}{14x^2}$ **31.** $-\frac{3x+1}{6x^2}$ **33.** $\frac{19x-11}{33x}$

35. $\frac{2(x^2-20)}{(x-10)(x+6)}$ **37.** $\frac{4x^2+17x+5}{(3x-1)(x+1)}$

39. $-\frac{x^2+14x-2}{(3x-1)(x-2)}$ **41.** $-\frac{5x(x-3)}{(x-1)(x+4)}$

43. $T = \frac{x}{10} + \frac{8-x}{20}$, where x is the number of miles in
the woods.

45.

Distance (woods), x	0	2	4	6	8
Total time, T	0.4	0.5	0.6	0.7	0.8

47. $T = \frac{48x}{(x-2)(x+2)}$ **49.** $\frac{2(2x^2+x+1)}{(2x+1)(2x-1)}$ **51.** $\frac{3}{35}$

55. $y + 2 = 2(x + 3)$ **57.** $y - 6 = \frac{1}{2}(x + 3)$

59. $y = \frac{3}{7}(x-7)$ **61.** $\frac{1}{2x}$ **63.** $\frac{1}{2x^4}$ **65.** $\frac{1}{12x}$ **67.** $\frac{3p^2}{4q}$

69. $6x^2 - 5x + 7 = 0$ **71.** $3y^2 - y - 4 = 0$

73. $12x^2 + 5x - 7 = 0$ **75.** $|x - 8500| \le 1000$

77. 0.315 **79.** 0.296 **81.** -0.708 **83.** -0.545 **85.** 0.104

87. -0.514

11.7 GUIDED PRACTICE (p. 674) **3.** $3x$ **5.** $3x^3$ **7.** 6, -1

9. 7 **11.** 2

11.7 PRACTICE AND APPLICATIONS (pp. 674–677) **13.** 28

15. 13 **17.** $\frac{1}{2}$ **19.** -7 **21.** 10, -2 **23.** 0, 16 **25.** $\frac{1}{3}$

27. 2 **29.** 2 **31.** $-\frac{6}{7}$ **33.** $\frac{2}{3}$ **35.** 3, $-\frac{1}{4}$ **37.** 0, 3

39. -12 **41.** 3, -2 **43.** 7, -6 **45.** -4 **47.** 3, 6

49. about 6.43 hours, or 6 hours 26 minutes; about
128.57 hours, or 128 hours 34 minutes **51.** $1.00 per
pound **53.** 7 dimes, 5 quarters **61.** 9, 8, 7, 6, 5

63. 0, -1, -4, -9, -16 **65.** 0, $\frac{1}{2}$, 2, $\frac{9}{2}$, 8 **67.** 36 **69.** 1

71. 125 **73.** $6\sqrt{2}$ **75.** $\sqrt{13}$ **77.** $\frac{3\sqrt{10}}{4}$ **79.** $\frac{21\sqrt{17}}{8}$

81. $3\sqrt{3}$ **83.** $3\sqrt{3}$ **85.** $\frac{7}{8}$ **87.** $\frac{31}{45}$ **89.** 1 **91.** $-\frac{7}{24}$

93. 1 **95.** $\frac{89}{220}$

QUIZ 2 (p. 677) **1.** $\frac{7x^2}{2}$ **2.** 10 **3.** $\frac{3}{2}$ **4.** $\frac{x-3}{x+2}$ **5.** $\frac{1}{x-7}$

6. $\frac{1}{x+1}$ **7.** $\frac{7x^2-7x+6}{(x+1)(x-1)}$ **8.** $\frac{x(x^2+2x-2)}{(x-3)(x+2)}$ **9.** 4

10. -2 **11.** 3 **12.** 130 **13.** $\frac{15}{x+2}$; $\frac{15}{x-2}$

14. $\frac{15}{x+2} + \frac{15}{x-2} = \frac{30x}{(x+2)(x-2)}$ **15.** 18 hours

16. about 1.71 hours, or 1 hour 43 minutes

SELECTED ANSWERS

1. $\dfrac{10}{x-9}$ **3.** $\dfrac{2x-1}{x^2}$

5. $\dfrac{x(11x+7)}{(x-7)(x+7)}$ **7.** $\dfrac{3x+5}{3x+7}$ **9.** $-\dfrac{x+3}{x^2}$

11. $-\dfrac{18}{(x+9)(x-9)}$ **13.** $\dfrac{3}{x(x+15)}$ **15.** $\dfrac{3(x-2)^2}{2x}$

17. $(x-2)^2$ **19.** $\dfrac{x(x+3)}{x+1}$ **21.** $\dfrac{x^2}{(2x+1)^2}$ **23.** $\dfrac{(x+5)^2}{(x+2)^2}$

25. $f(x) = \dfrac{1}{x-9}$ **27.** $g(x) = \dfrac{x}{2x+3}$

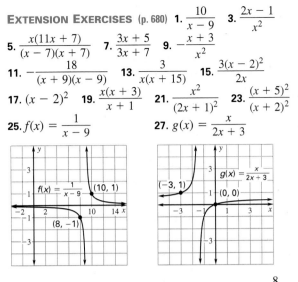

CHAPTER SUMMARY AND REVIEW (pp. 681–684) **1.** $\dfrac{8}{7}$

3. 4 **5.** $y = 5x$ **7.** $y = \dfrac{4}{5}x$ **9.** $y = 14x$ **11.** $y = \dfrac{36}{x}$

13. $y = \dfrac{450}{x}$ **15.** $y = \dfrac{22}{x}$ **17.** $\dfrac{x}{3x^2+1}$ **19.** $\dfrac{7x(x-2)}{3x+2}$

21. $\dfrac{x+2}{x+7}$ **23.** $\dfrac{x+7}{x-1}$ **25.** $\dfrac{y-8}{2y-3}$ **27.** $20x^2$

29. $\dfrac{8(2x+7)}{x-1}$ **31.** $9x$ **33.** $\dfrac{x+2}{x}$ **35.** 1 **37.** $\dfrac{x+2}{4}$

39. $\dfrac{4x-5}{x-2}$ **41.** $\dfrac{1}{6}$ **43.** $-4, 2$ **45.** no solution

MAINTAINING SKILLS (p. 687) **1.** $\dfrac{4\sqrt{2}}{7}$ **3.** $\dfrac{\sqrt{5}}{3}$ **5.** $\dfrac{11\sqrt{3}}{12}$

7. $2\sqrt{2}$ **9.** $(a-9)^2$ **11.** $(y-11)^2$ **13.** $(15+r)^2$ or $(r+15)^2$ **15.** $(2x+5)^2$ **17.** $(4-7x)^2$ or $(7x-4)^2$

Chapter 12

STUDY GUIDE (p. 690) **1.** D **2.** A **3.** B

12.1 GUIDED PRACTICE (p. 695) **3.** 0, 4, 5.7, 6.9, 8
5. 4, 7, 8.2, 9.2, 10 **7.** 1.4, 1.7, 2, 2.2, 2.4 **9.** domain: all nonnegative real numbers; range: all nonnegative real numbers **11.** domain: all nonnegative real numbers; range: all real numbers ≥ -10 **13.** domain: all real numbers ≥ -5; range: all nonnegative real numbers **15.** all nonnegative real numbers

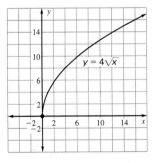

17. all real numbers ≥ -1

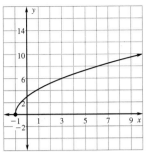

19. 1200 gal/min

12.1 PRACTICE AND APPLICATIONS (pp. 695–697)
21. -10 **23.** 6 **25.** 6 **27.** 4
29. All nonnegative real numbers. *Sample table:*

x	0	1	4	9
$y = 6\sqrt{x}$	0	6	12	18

31. All real numbers $\geq \dfrac{10}{3}$. *Sample table:*

x	$\dfrac{10}{3}$	$\dfrac{11}{3}$	4	5	6
$y = \sqrt{(3x-10)}$	0	1	≈ 1.4	≈ 2.2	≈ 2.8

33. All nonnegative real numbers. *Sample table:*

x	0	1	4	9	16
$y = 4 + \sqrt{x}$	4	5	6	7	8

35. All real numbers ≥ -9. *Sample table:*

x	-9	-8	-5	0	7
$y = \sqrt{x+9}$	0	1	2	3	4

37. All nonnegative real numbers. *Sample table:*

x	0	1	4	9
$y = x\sqrt{x}$	0	1	8	27

39. incorrect statement; $S = 42$ mph
41. domain: all nonnegative real numbers; range: all nonnegative real numbers
47. domain: all nonnegative real numbers; range: all real numbers ≥ -3

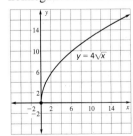

49. domain: all nonnegative real numbers; range: all real numbers ≤ 6

55. domain: all real numbers $\ge -\dfrac{5}{2}$; range: all nonnegative real numbers

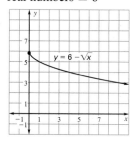

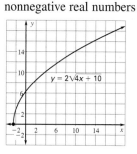

57. twice as fast **63.** $2\sqrt{15}$ **65.** $6\sqrt{10}$ **67.** $2\sqrt{5}$
69. $\sqrt{11}$ **71.** $-1.24, 3.24$ **73.** $-3.30, 0.30$
75. $0.19, 1.31$ **77.** $3x^2 + 5x - 28$
79. $10x^2 - 33x + 27$ **81.** $2x^3 + x^2 + x - 1$ **83.** $\dfrac{8}{3}$
85. $\dfrac{x}{x+1}$ **87.** $\dfrac{1}{2}$ **89.** 24 **91.** 35 **93.** 0.2635

12.2 GUIDED PRACTICE (p. 701) **3.** $4 + 6\sqrt{5}$ **5.** $5\sqrt{6}$
7. $16 + 6\sqrt{7}$ **9.** $\dfrac{4\sqrt{13}}{13}$ **11.** $\dfrac{3\sqrt{10}}{5}$

12.2 PRACTICE AND APPLICATIONS (pp. 701–703)
13. $7\sqrt{7}$ **15.** $-\sqrt{3}$ **17.** $\sqrt{3} + 5\sqrt{5}$ **19.** $5\sqrt{2}$
21. $\sqrt{5}$ **23.** $12\sqrt{5}$ **25.** 6 **27.** $3\sqrt{10}$ **29.** $6 - \sqrt{6}$
31. $4\sqrt{5} + 5$ **33.** $5\sqrt{6} + 3$ **35.** -12 **37.** 5 **39.** 33
41. $\dfrac{5\sqrt{7}}{7}$ **43.** $\dfrac{\sqrt{3}}{4}$ **45.** $\dfrac{\sqrt{30}}{3}$ **47.** $\dfrac{12 - 2\sqrt{3}}{11}$
49. $\dfrac{2 - \sqrt{2}}{2}$ **51.** $\dfrac{3\sqrt{5} + 5}{4}$ **53.** $\sqrt{12}$ and $\sqrt{13}$ are not like terms; $\sqrt{12} + \sqrt{13} = 2\sqrt{3} + \sqrt{13}$ **55.** You ran $16\sqrt{5} - 32 \approx 3.78$ ft/sec faster. **61.** 43.75% **63.** 147
65. $-5, 3$ **67.** $13, -2$ **69.** $-\dfrac{2}{3}, -1$ **71.** -30
73. All nonnegative real numbers. *Sample table:*

x	0	1	4	9	16
$y = \sqrt{x} - 3$	-3	-2	-1	0	1

75. All nonnegative real numbers. *Sample table:*

x	0	1	4	9	16
$y = 6\sqrt{x}$	0	6	12	18	24

77. All real numbers ≥ -3. *Sample table:*

x	-3	-2	1	6	13
$y = \sqrt{x+3}$	0	1	2	3	4

79. $>$ **81.** $=$ **83.** $>$ **85.** $<$ **87.** $<$ **89.** $=$ **91.** $<$
93. $>$ **95.** $<$

12.3 GUIDED PRACTICE (p. 707) **3.** 64 **5.** 196 **7.** 36
9. no solution **11.** 4 **13.** 25 **15.** 3 **17.** 3

12.3 PRACTICE AND APPLICATIONS (pp. 707–709)
19. 1 **21.** 100 **23.** 256 **25.** 6 **27.** 3 **29.** $\dfrac{1}{3}$ **31.** 48
33. Line 2 should be $(\sqrt{x})^2 = 7^2$; $x = 49$. **35.** 75
37. about 28.4 lb/in.^{2} **39.** *Sample answer:* $\sqrt{2x - 20} = 4$
41. no solution **43.** no solution **45.** no solution **47.** 3
49. no solution **51.** 3 **53.** 4 **55.** 270 m/sec^2
57. false; $\sqrt{36} \ne -6$ **61.** $\pm\sqrt{11}$ **63.** ± 2 **65.** $\pm\sqrt{3}$
67. $4x^2 - 12x + 9$ **69.** $9x^2 - 25y^2$
71. $4a^2 - 36ab + 81b^2$ **73.** $(x - 6)^2$ **75.** $\dfrac{9}{19}$ **77.** $\dfrac{10}{13}$
79. $\dfrac{50}{57}$ **81.** $\dfrac{9}{34}$

QUIZ 1 (p. 709)
1. domain: all nonnegative real numbers; range: all nonnegative real numbers

2. domain: all real numbers ≥ 9; range: all nonnegative real numbers

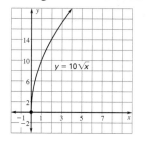

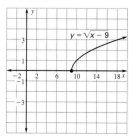

3. domain: all real numbers $\ge \dfrac{1}{2}$; range: all nonnegative real numbers

4. domain: all nonnegative real numbers; range: all real numbers ≥ -2

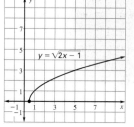

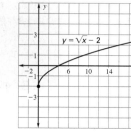

5. $18\sqrt{10}$ **6.** $3\sqrt{6} + 3$ **7.** $4\sqrt{7} + \sqrt{5}$ **8.** 4 **9.** 64
10. $-\dfrac{1}{3}$ **11.** 6 **12.** 7 **13.** 3 **14.** 1.78 lb/in.^{2}

12.4 GUIDED PRACTICE (p. 713) **3.** 7 **5.** 125 **7.** 27
9. 729

12.4 PRACTICE AND APPLICATIONS (pp. 713–714)
11. $11^{1/3}$ **13.** $16^{5/2}$ **15.** $\sqrt{7}$ **17.** $\left(\sqrt[3]{8}\right)^7$ **19.** 100 **21.** 2
23. 16 **25.** 81 **27.** 25 **29.** 256 **31.** 16 **33.** 36 **35.** 20
37. 64 **39.** $x^{5/6}$ or $\left(\sqrt[6]{x}\right)^5$ **41.** $x^{1/2}y^{1/2}$ or $\sqrt{xy}$ **43.** y^2
45. sometimes **49.** $\pm 2\sqrt{14}$ **51.** ± 6 **53.** $\pm\dfrac{2\sqrt{5}}{5}$
55. $-4, 8$ **57.** prime **59.** composite; $3 \cdot 5^2$
61. composite; $2 \cdot 3^2$ **63.** composite; $3 \cdot 23$

12.5 GUIDED PRACTICE (p. 719)   **3.** 100   **5.** 25   **7.** 121

9. $\dfrac{3 \pm \sqrt{41}}{2}$ **11.** $-5 \pm \sqrt{35}$ **13.** $-13, -1$

15. $-\dfrac{2}{3}, -5$ **17.** $\dfrac{5 \pm \sqrt{85}}{6}$ **19.** $\pm\dfrac{\sqrt{6}}{3}$

12.5 PRACTICE AND APPLICATIONS (pp. 719–721)

21. 16   **23.** 121   **25.** 400   **27.** 9   **29.** 2, 6   **31.** 2, −8
33. $-5 \pm \sqrt{37}$ **35.** 3, −13   **37.** 2, 22   **39.** $1 \pm \sqrt{6}$
41. $2 \pm \sqrt{5}$ **43.** $-7 \pm \sqrt{51}$ **45.** $-5 \pm 2\sqrt{7}$
47. $-11 \pm 2\sqrt{30}$ **49.** $-4 \pm \sqrt{22}$ **51.** $-10 \pm 7\sqrt{2}$
53. $6 \pm \sqrt{39}$ **55.** $1 \pm \sqrt{5}$ **57.** about 12.25 ft by 12.25 ft
59. Base is about 6.8 ft; height is about 17.6 ft.   **61.** ± 3
63. −7, 2   **65.** $-3, \dfrac{4}{3}$ **67.** $3 \pm \sqrt{2}$ **69.** $-\dfrac{1}{2}, -3$
71. $12 \pm 5\sqrt{6}$ **73.** no solution   **75.** about 8.6 ft
81. (4, 0)   **83.** ± 7 **85.** ± 9 **87.** $\pm 4\sqrt{10}$ **89.** no
solution   **91.** no solution   **93.** 3, −1   **95.** −4, 8
97. −5, −6   **99.** 3   **101.** $(x + 5)(x - 4)$ **103.** $(x + 2)^2$
105. $(2x - 3)(x + 1)$ **107.** $\dfrac{3}{5}$ **109.** $\dfrac{11}{100}$ **111.** $\dfrac{1}{100}$
113. $\dfrac{3}{100}$ **115.** $\dfrac{3}{8}$

12.6 GUIDED PRACTICE (p. 727)   **3.** $c = 25$ **5.** $a = 8$
7. $a = 60$ **9.** $b = 16$ **11.** 6, 8

12.6 PRACTICE AND APPLICATIONS (pp. 727–729)

13. $b = \sqrt{7} \approx 2.65$ **15.** $a = 2\sqrt{10} \approx 6.32$
17. $b = 5\sqrt{3} \approx 8.66$ **19.** $c = 2\sqrt{17} \approx 8.25$
21. $a = \sqrt{91} \approx 9.54$ **23.** $b = \sqrt{33} \approx 5.74$
25. $x - 6 = 18, x = 24$ **27.** $x = 5, x + 5 = 10$
29. $x = 1, \sqrt{2}x = \sqrt{2}$ **31.** about 127.3 ft
33. about 12.2 in.   **35.** about 4.9 ft   **37.** right triangle;
$5^2 + 12^2 = 13^2$ **39.** right triangle; $11^2 + 60^2 = 61^2$
41. not a right triangle   **43.** not a right triangle;
$6^2 + 9^2 \neq 11^2$

47. **49.**

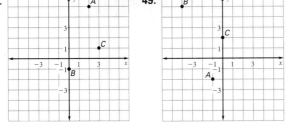

51. zero   **53.** two   **55.** two   **57.** 35   **59.** 50   **61.** 51

QUIZ 2 (p. 729)   **1.** 2   **2.** 42   **3.** 9   **4.** $3 \pm \sqrt{2}$
5. $-2 \pm \sqrt{5}$ **6.** $-1 \pm \sqrt{3}$ **7.** not a right triangle;
$6^2 + 9^2 \neq 11^2$ **8.** right triangle; $12^2 + 35^2 = 37^2$
9. right triangle; $1^2 + 1^2 = \left(\sqrt{2}\right)^2$ **10.** 2000 ft

12.7 GUIDED PRACTICE (p. 733)   **3.** 7.62   **5.** right
triangle   **7.** not a right triangle   **9.** 25 yd

12.7 PRACTICE AND APPLICATIONS (pp. 733–735)
11. 12.08   **13.** 8.60   **15.** 4.24   **17.** 9   **19.** 21.26

21. 16.16   **23.** 12.73   **25.** right triangle   **27.** not a right
triangle   **29.** right triangle   **31.** $AB = 4\sqrt{2} \approx 5.66$,
$BC = \sqrt{17} \approx 4.12, CA = 5$ **33.** 269 mi
35. about 670 mi   **37.** about 457 mi
43. $9(3x - 4)(3x + 4)$ **45.** $(x + 6)^2$
47. $(3x + 1)^2$ **49.** $2(6 - 5p)(6 + 5p)$
51. $3y(y + 6)(y - 1)$ **53.** $2x^2(x - 2)(x + 2)$
55. $\dfrac{x}{7}$ **57.** $4x$ **59.** $\dfrac{7 - x}{4x}$ **61.** $x + 6$ **63.** $9a - 36$
65. $\dfrac{x + 12}{x}$ **67.** $\dfrac{13}{x}$ **69.** $\dfrac{43}{12x}$ **71.** 40%   **73.** $33.\overline{3}\%$
75. 62.5%   **77.** 4%

12.8 GUIDED PRACTICE (p. 738)   **3.** $\left(\dfrac{3}{2}, 3\right)$ **5.** $(-4, 0)$

7. $(0, 5)$ **9.** $(2, 1); d = \sqrt{17} \approx 4.12$ **11.** $(3, 4)$;
$d = \sqrt{5} \approx 2.24$ **13.** $(-1, 7); d = \sqrt{5} \approx 2.24$

12.8 PRACTICE AND APPLICATIONS (pp. 738–739)

15. (3, 3)   **17.** (3, 3)   **19.** $\left(-\dfrac{1}{2}, \dfrac{1}{2}\right)$ **21.** $\left(-\dfrac{5}{2}, -\dfrac{3}{2}\right)$
23. $\left(-\dfrac{5}{2}, -4\right)$ **25.** $\left(\dfrac{1}{2}, 1\right); d = \dfrac{\sqrt{5}}{2} \approx 1.12$ **27.** $(3, -2)$;
$d = \sqrt{13} \approx 3.61$ **29.** $\left(-1, \dfrac{5}{2}\right); d = \dfrac{\sqrt{97}}{2} \approx 4.92$

31. $(-2, 5); d = \sqrt{193} \approx 13.89$ **33.** $\left(\dfrac{5}{2}, 8\right), (7, 1)$,
$\left(-\dfrac{17}{2}, 1\right)$ **35.** (39.95° N, 115.35° W)   **37.** (1, 1)
or 1 mi east and 1 mi north of the starting point
39. $\left(\dfrac{1}{3}, -\dfrac{1}{9}\right)$ **41.** (2, −1)   **43.** $\left(\dfrac{3}{2}, 0\right)$; one   **45.** =   **47.** <

12.9 GUIDED PRACTICE (p. 743)   **3.** identity property
of multiplication   **5.** distributive property   **7.** identity
property of addition

12.9 PRACTICE AND APPLICATIONS (p. 744–746)
9. inverse property of addition; identity property of
addition   **13.** *Sample answer: $a = 3, b = 2$*
15. *Sample answer: $a = 3, b = 2$*   **17.** Yes; the map
cannot be colored with three different colors so that no
two countries that share a border have the same color.
27. 10,000   **29.** 20   **31.** 2 solutions   **33.** 1 solution
35. no real solution   **37.** not a solution   **39.** solution
41. $2\dfrac{3}{4}$ **43.** $\dfrac{11}{12}$ **45.** $-\dfrac{7}{8}$

QUIZ 3 (p. 746)   **1.** right triangle   **2.** right triangle
3. 13.42; (4, −3)   **4.** 7.21; (4, −8)   **5.** 16.12; (4, −7)
6. 16; (−8, 0)   **7.** 6; (0, 4)   **8.** 10.30; $\left(-\dfrac{3}{2}, \dfrac{5}{2}\right)$
9. *Sample answer: $a = 2, b = 3, c = -5$*   **10.** *Sample
answer: $a = 2, b = 3$*

CHAPTER SUMMARY AND REVIEW (pp. 747–750)

1. domain: all nonnegative real numbers; range: all nonnegative real numbers

3. domain: all nonnegative real numbers; range: all real numbers ≥ 3

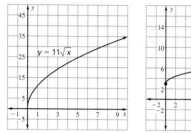

5. $3\sqrt{5} - \sqrt{3}$ **7.** $6\sqrt{2} - 8\sqrt{3}$ **9.** $\dfrac{48 + 8\sqrt{7}}{27}$

11. no solution **13.** 26 **15.** 9 **17.** 16 **19.** 16 **21.** 22

23. $2 \pm 2\sqrt{3}$ **25.** $8 \pm 2\sqrt{14}$ **27.** $\dfrac{1 \pm \sqrt{13}}{2}$

29. $c = 2\sqrt{13}$ **31.** $b = 5, 2b + 2 = 12$ **33.** not a right triangle; $10^2 + 14^2 \neq 17^2$ **35.** 9.49 **37.** 10.77

39. $(2, -1)$ **41.** $\left(-\dfrac{1}{2}, -\dfrac{13}{2}\right)$

43. Sample answer:

$(c)(-b) = (c)[(-1)(b)]$ Multiplication property of -1

$= [(c)(-1)](b)$ Associative property of multiplication

$= [(-1)(c)](b)$ Commutative property of multiplication

$= (-1)[(c)(b)]$ Associative property of multiplication

$= -cb$ Multiplication property of -1

CHAPTERS 1–12 CUMULATIVE PRACTICE (pp. 754–755)

1. $\dfrac{m}{7} \geq 16; m \geq 112$ **3.** $t = 3d; t = 9$ mi **5.** 25

7. -63 **9.** -27 **11.** $\dfrac{34}{3}$ **13.** -49 **15.** -1.64

17. -5.56 **19.** Sample answer: $y = \dfrac{2}{3}x - \dfrac{10}{3}$

21. function; domain: $-1, 1, 3, 5$; range: $-1, 1, 3$

23. function; domain: $-2, -1, 0, 1, 2$; range: $-2, -1, 0, 1$ **25.** $4x - 5y = 15$

27. $-\dfrac{5}{4} \leq x < 3$

29. $x > 3$ or $x < 2$

31. $(24, 21)$ **33.** $b^6; 64$ **35.** $-8a^3b^6; -512$ **37.** $\dfrac{4b^5}{a^4};$

128 **39.** 2 solutions; $\pm\dfrac{\sqrt{39}}{3}$ **41.** 1 solution; -1

43. $(x - 28)(x + 4)$ **45.** $(2x + 3)^2$ **47.** $(x - 7)^2$

49. $-\dfrac{3}{2}, \dfrac{5}{3}$ **51.** -2 **53.** $0, -3, -6$ **55.** $\dfrac{2}{x - 3}$

57. $\dfrac{1}{3x}$ **59.** $\dfrac{2x^2 - 7x}{(x + 4)(x - 1)}$ **61.** $-15\sqrt{2}$ **63.** $\dfrac{77 + 11\sqrt{3}}{46}$

65. $6 \pm \sqrt{55}$ **67.** $3 \pm \sqrt{22}$ **69.** $-11 \pm 2\sqrt{29}$

71. 4.47; $(3, 5)$ **73.** 9.43; $\left(2, -\dfrac{1}{2}\right)$ **75.** 12.21; $\left(5, 7\dfrac{1}{2}\right)$

77. 11.18; $\left(2, 4\dfrac{1}{2}\right)$

Skills Review Handbook

DECIMALS (p. 760) **1.** 14.42 **3.** 122.312 **5.** 25.72

7. 1.02 **9.** 2.458 **11.** 7.07 **13.** 40.625 **15.** 3.6

17. 520.37908 **19.** 16.7 **21.** 18.4 **23.** 4220

25. $62.44; $7.56

FACTORS AND MULTIPLES (p. 762) **1.** 1, 2, 3, 6, 9, 18

3. 1, 7, 11, 77 **5.** 1, 3, 9, 27 **7.** 1, 2, 3, 6, 7, 14, 21, 42

9. 3^3 **11.** 2^5 **13.** $5 \cdot 11$ **15.** $2^2 \cdot 37$ **17.** 1 **19.** 1, 5

21. 1, 3, 9 **23.** 1, 5 **25.** 5 **27.** 1 **29.** 14 **31.** 51

33. 35 **35.** 208 **37.** 45 **39.** 42 **41.** 12 **43.** 30

45. 140 **47.** 51

FRACTIONS (p. 766) **1.** $\dfrac{1}{7}$ **3.** $\dfrac{12}{7}$, or $1\dfrac{5}{7}$ **5.** 20 **7.** $\dfrac{13}{5}$, or

$2\dfrac{3}{5}$ **9.** $\dfrac{5}{6}$ **11.** 3 **13.** $\dfrac{5}{32}$ **15.** $\dfrac{7}{2}$, or $3\dfrac{1}{2}$ **17.** $\dfrac{5}{6}$ **19.** $\dfrac{1}{3}$

21. $\dfrac{5}{8}$ **23.** $1\dfrac{1}{30}$ **25.** $2\dfrac{3}{8}$ **27.** $1\dfrac{13}{24}$ **29.** $8\dfrac{1}{5}$ **31.** $3\dfrac{7}{16}$

33. $\dfrac{1}{4}$ **35.** $\dfrac{1}{6}$ **37.** $\dfrac{2}{3}$ **39.** $7\dfrac{2}{3}$ **41.** $1\dfrac{1}{6}$ **43.** $1\dfrac{1}{5}$ **45.** 6

47. $\dfrac{17}{20}$ **49.** $\dfrac{13}{16}$ **51.** 1 **53.** $5\dfrac{3}{8}$ **55.** $\dfrac{7}{18}$ **57.** $2\dfrac{5}{6}$ **59.** $1\dfrac{3}{5}$

61. $1\dfrac{11}{40}$ **63.** $\dfrac{11}{40}$

WRITING FRACTIONS AND DECIMALS (p. 768) **1.** 0.25

3. 0.08 **5.** $0.\overline{3}$ **7.** $0.\overline{90}$ **9.** $\dfrac{1}{2}$ **11.** $\dfrac{289}{1000}$ **13.** $\dfrac{7}{9}$ **15.** $\dfrac{613}{999}$

FRACTIONS, DECIMALS, AND PERCENTS (p. 769) **1.** 0.63;

$\dfrac{63}{100}$ **3.** 0.24; $\dfrac{6}{25}$ **5.** 0.17; $\dfrac{17}{100}$ **7.** 0.45; $\dfrac{9}{20}$ **9.** $0.\overline{3}; \dfrac{1}{3}$

11. 0.625; $\dfrac{5}{8}$ **13.** 0.052; $\dfrac{13}{250}$ **15.** 0.0012; $\dfrac{3}{2500}$ **17.** 8%;

$\dfrac{2}{25}$ **19.** 150%; $\dfrac{3}{2}$ **21.** 5%; $\dfrac{1}{20}$ **23.** 480%; $4\dfrac{4}{5}$

25. 375%; $3\dfrac{3}{4}$ **27.** 52%; $\dfrac{13}{25}$ **29.** 0.5%; $\dfrac{1}{200}$ **31.** 0.7;

70% **33.** 0.44; 44% **35.** 0.375; 37.5% **37.** 5.125;

512.5% **39.** 0.875; 87.5%

COMPARING AND ORDERING NUMBERS (p. 771)

1. $12,428 < 15,116$ **3.** $-140,999 > -142,109$

5. $0.40506 > 0.000456$ **7.** $1005.2 < 1050.7$

9. $-0.058 > -0.102$ **11.** $17\dfrac{1}{4} = 17\dfrac{2}{8}$ **13.** $-\dfrac{5}{9} = -\dfrac{15}{27}$

15. $\dfrac{1}{8} > \dfrac{1}{9}$ **17.** $42\dfrac{1}{5} > 41\dfrac{7}{8}$ **19.** $32,227 > 32,226.5$

21. $-17\dfrac{5}{6} < -17\dfrac{5}{7}$ **23.** $-45,617; -45,242; -40,099;$

$-40,071$ **25.** 9.003, 9.027, 9.10, 9.27, 9.3 **27.** $\dfrac{1}{3}, \dfrac{3}{8},$

$\dfrac{5}{6}, \dfrac{5}{4}$ **29.** $\dfrac{15}{16}, 1\dfrac{1}{8}, 1\dfrac{2}{5}, \dfrac{5}{3}, \dfrac{7}{4}$ **31.** $-1\dfrac{1}{3}, -\dfrac{5}{4}, -\dfrac{7}{8}, -\dfrac{5}{12}$

PERIMETER, AREA, AND VOLUME (p. 773) **1.** 34
3. 84 ft **5.** 72 ft **7.** 841 yd^2 **9.** 12.25 in.^{2} **11.** 20 in.^{2}
13. 15,625 ft^3 **15.** 420 yd^3 **17.** 212 in.^{3}

ESTIMATION (p. 776) **1–53.** Estimates may vary. **1.** 50
3. 2400 **5.** 500 **7.** 20 **9.** 1600 **11.** 800 **13.** 22.5
15. 481 **17.** 1340 **19.** 41 **21.** 209 **23.** 267 **25.** 2500
27. 30,000 **29.** 30 **31.** 3 **33.** 40 **35.** 4 **37.** 750
39. 80,000 **41.** 7000 **43.** 23 **45.** 10 **47.** 50 **49.** 16
51. 17 **53.** 18

DATA DISPLAYS (p. 779) **1–10.** Sample answers are given.
1. 0 to 25 by fives **3.** 0 to 20 by fives

5.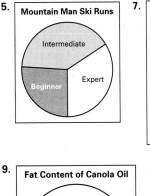

7.

9.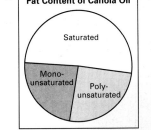

MEASURES OF CENTRAL TENDENCY (p. 780) **1.** 1.3; 0.5;
0, 2, 4 **3.** 30; 30; no mode **5.** ≈550.1; 487; 376

PROBLEM SOLVING (p. 782) **1.** 5 salads, 3 cartons of milk
3. $26.25 **5.** no later than 6:25 A.M. **7.** 10 groups
9. The problem cannot be solved; not enough information
is given.

Extra Practice

CHAPTER 1 (p. 783) **1.** 105 **3.** 8 **5.** 512 **7.** 76 **9.** 49
11. 31 **13.** 3 **15.** 1 **17.** 7 **19.** 12 **21.** 24 **23.** solution
25. not a solution **27.** solution **29.** $16 > 20 - x$

31.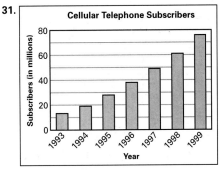

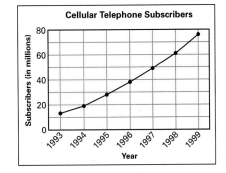

33.

Input x	0	1	2	3	4	5
Output y	1	8	15	22	29	36

CHAPTER 2 (p. 784)
1. $-7 < 8, 8 > -7$ **3.** $-4 > -7, -7 < -4$

5. 3 **7.** 8.5 **9.** 5 **11.** -2 **13.** 3 **15.** -3 **17.** -13
19. -2.2 **21.** -7 **23.** -6.5 **25.** -7 **27.** 15
29. -450 **31.** 6 **33.** -81 **35.** 48 **37.** -90 ft
39. $4a - 24$ **41.** $8x + 6$ **43.** $-2 - t$ **45.** $1.5y - 4.5$
47. $7r$ **49.** $7w - 4$ **51.** $-m^2 + 2m$ **53.** -4 **55.** 66

CHAPTER 3 (p. 785) **1.** 14 **3.** 17 **5.** 7 **7.** 3 **9.** 5
11. $\frac{1}{2}$ **13.** -20 **15.** 84 **17.** 4 **19.** 2 **21.** $-\frac{37}{3}$ **23.** 1
25. 2 **27.** -2 **29.** 3 **31.** $-\frac{3}{2}$ **33.** -7.46 **35.** -0.25
37. 12 mi/hr **39.** $7.25/hr **41.** 2 g/bar **43.** 51.2 m
45. 45

CHAPTER 4 (p. 786)

1.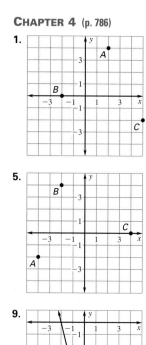

3.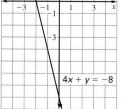

5.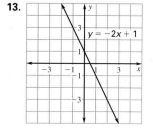

7.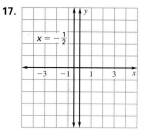

9.

$$4x + y = -8$$

11.

$$y - 2x = -5$$

13. $y = -2x + 1$

15. $y = -2$

17. $x = -\frac{1}{2}$

19. -1 **21.** 6 **23.** -5 **25.** 6 **27.** 0 **29.** -7
31. undefined   **33.** $y = 3x$ **35.** $y = -\frac{7}{8}x$ **37.** $y = x$
39. $y = -3x$

41.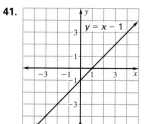

$$y = x - 1$$

43.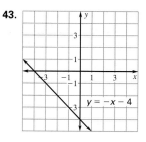

$$y = -x - 4$$

45.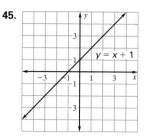

$$y = x + 1$$

47. function; domain is 1, 3, 5, 7 and range is 1, 2, 3
49. not a function

CHAPTER 5 (p. 787)

1. $y = 2x + 1$ **3.** $y = \frac{1}{2}x - 3$
5. $y = 3(x + 1)$ **7.** $y - 6 = 0(x - 3)$
9. $y + 1 = 4(x + 3)$ **11.** $y + 1 = \frac{1}{2}(x - 2)$
13. $y = 3x - 11$ **15.** $y = -\frac{1}{2}x - 2$ **17.** $y = -x + 2$
19. $3x - y = 17$ **21.** $5x + 6y = -2$ **23.** $7x + y = 8$
25. $2x + y = 12$ **27.** $4A + 5R = 50$

29.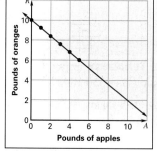

31. not perpendicular   **33.** not perpendicular
35. $y = -\frac{4}{3}x + \frac{8}{3}$

CHAPTER 6 (p. 788)

1. $x < 1$

3. $7 \geq y$

5. $x \geq 4$

7. $k \leq 18$

9. $x > -1$ **11.** $x \geq -2\frac{1}{2}$ **13.** $x \leq 9$
15. $-5 < x < 2$ **17.** $-3 < x \leq 5$

19. $-1 \le x < 4$

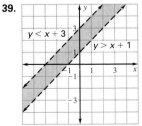

21. $1 < x \le 7$

23. $x \le 1 \text{ or } x > 4$

25. $x < 3 \text{ or } x > 4$

27. $-14, 14$ **29.** $-12, 12$ **31.** $-14, -6$ **33.** $\frac{1}{5}, 1$

35. $1, 7$

37. $-8 \le x \le 8$

39. $-5 \le x \le 5$

41. $x \le -2 \text{ or } x \ge -\frac{1}{2}$

43. $-\frac{1}{3} < x < 2$

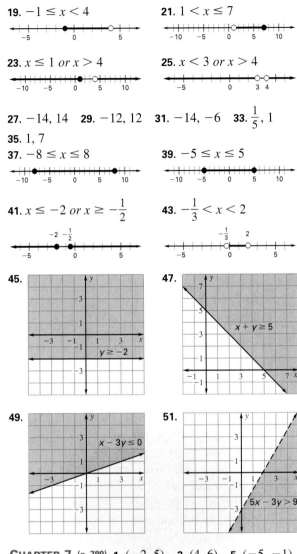

45.

47. $x + y \ge 5$

49. $x - 3y \le 0$

51. $5x - 3y > 9$

CHAPTER 7 (p. 789)   **1.** $(-2, 5)$ **3.** $(4, 6)$ **5.** $(-5, -1)$

7. $(6, 3)$ **9.** $(-36, 31)$ **11.** $\left(\frac{31}{2}, -24\right)$ **13.** $(4, 2)$

15. $(0, -2)$ **17.** $(13, -2)$ **19.** $(2, 1)$ **21.** *Sample answer:* substitution, because it is easy to solve for x; $(0, 5)$
23. *Sample answer:* substitution, because the equations are already solved for y; $(-1, -4)$ **25.** *Sample answer:* linear combinations, because it is easy to eliminate y; $(3, 0)$ **27.** *Sample answer:* linear combinations, because it is easy to eliminate y; $(2, 0)$ **29.** 12 adult tickets and 8 student tickets   **31.** none   **33.** one   **35.** infinitely many   **37.** none

39. $y < x + 3$, $y > x + 1$

41. $2y - 4 > 3x$, $y + 2 < -x$

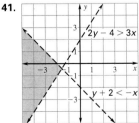

43.

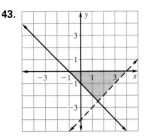

45.

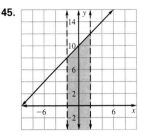

CHAPTER 8 (p. 790)   **1.** $16{,}807$ **3.** $1728x^3$ **5.** m^6 **7.** $98x^7$
9. $\frac{1}{x^4}$ **11.** $\frac{1}{x^3 y^2}$ **13.** $4xy^5$ **15.** $\frac{16}{y^4}$

17.

19.

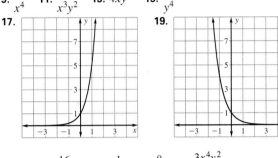

21. 8 **23.** $\frac{16}{81}$ **25.** $-\frac{1}{64}$ **27.** $\frac{8}{3}$ **29.** $\frac{3x^4 y^2}{2}$
31. $\frac{27x^3 z^9}{8}$ **33.** $\frac{4b^7}{9a^5}$ **35.** 0.000004813 **37.** 0.084162
39. $50{,}645{,}000{,}000$ **41.** 0.0000000234 **43.** 5.28×10^3
45. 1.138×10^1 **47.** 8.2766×10^2 **49.** 1.6354×10^1
51. 3.95×10^0 **53.** 8×10^{-3} **55.** $\$1155$ **57.** $\$2286.82$
59. $y = 120{,}000(0.90)^t$

CHAPTER 9 (p. 791)   **1.** 1.73 **3.** -10 **5.** 3.87 **7.** 14.83
9. ± 5 **11.** no real solution   **13.** ± 4 **15.** $\pm\sqrt{3}$
17. 2.2 sec   **19.** $2\sqrt{22}$ **21.** $4\sqrt{7}$ **23.** 2 **25.** $\sqrt{3}$

27.

29.

31.

33. $(2, 11)$

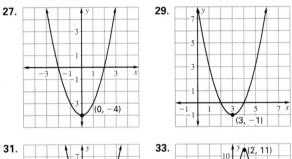

35. $-3, -2$ **37.** $-5, 2$ **39.** $-1, 3$
41. $3x^2 + 8x + 32 = 0$; no real solution
43. $x^2 - 5x + 4 = 0$; $1, 4$ **45.** $2x^2 - 6x - 5 = 0$; $\frac{3 \pm \sqrt{19}}{2}$ **47.** $2x^2 - 6x - 10 = 0$; $-2, \frac{5}{2}$ **49.** one solution
51. one solution   **53.** no real solution   **55.** no real solution

57.

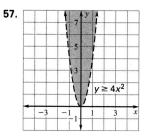

$y \geq 4x^2$

59.

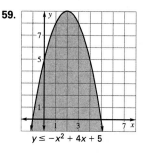

$y \leq -x^2 + 4x + 5$

CHAPTER 10 (p. 792) **1.** $8x^2 + 1$ **3.** $14x^2 - 7x + 8$
5. $x^2 + 9x - 4$ **7.** $4x^3 - 8x^2 + 7x$
9. $15b^5 - 10b^4 + 5b^2$ **11.** $d^2 + 4d - 5$
13. $x^3 + x^2 + 18$ **15.** $x^2 + 18x + 81$ **17.** $a^2 - 4$
19. $16x^2 + 40x + 25$ **21.** $4a^2 - 9b^2$ **23.** $-6, -3$
25. $-5, 1$ **27.** $\frac{3}{2}, 7$ **29.** $1, 2$

31. $6, 8; (7, -1)$

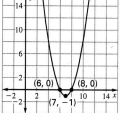

33. $5, 7; (6, -1)$

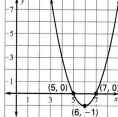

35. $5, 9; (7, 4)$

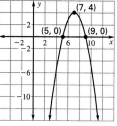

37. $-1, 3; (1, -4)$

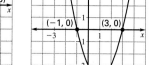

39. -3 **41.** 6 **43.** $6, 9$ **45.** $-4, 6$ **47.** $-2, \frac{3}{2}$ **49.** $-\frac{4}{3}$
51. $-\frac{3}{4}, 2$ **53.** $-\frac{7}{3}, 8$ **55.** $(x + 1)(x - 1)$ **57.** $(11 + x)$
$(11 - x)$ **59.** $(t + 1)^2$ **61.** $(8y + 3)^2$ **63.** $x^2(x + 3)$
$(x - 3)$ **65.** $x^2(x + 9)(x - 5)$ **67.** $-3y(y + 1)(y + 4)$
69. $7x^4(x^2 - 3)$ **71.** 4 ft by 2 ft by 12 ft

CHAPTER 11 (p. 793) **1.** 6 **3.** $1\frac{3}{5}$ **5.** 4 **7.** $y = 3x$
9. $y = \frac{1}{4}x$ **11.** $y = \frac{15}{x}$ **13.** $y = \frac{2}{x}$ **15.** $\frac{2x^3}{7}$ **17.** $\frac{1}{x+1}$
19. $\frac{2}{3x}$ **21.** $-\frac{1}{y+4}$ **23.** $\frac{1}{2}$ **25.** $\frac{10x^2}{x+5}$ **27.** $\frac{5}{x-3}$ **29.** $\frac{1}{x}$
31. $-\frac{2(x+1)}{x-1}$ **33.** $\frac{5-3x}{x^2}$ **35.** $\frac{x^2+35}{(x-3)(x+8)}$
37. $\frac{2(5x+14)}{(x+5)(x-5)}$ **39.** $33\frac{1}{3}$ **41.** -2 **43.** 4

CHAPTER 12 (p. 794)
1. domain: all nonnegative real numbers; range: all nonnegative real numbers **3.** domain: all nonnegative real numbers; range: all real numbers ≥ -5

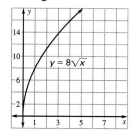

$y = 8\sqrt{x}$

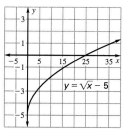

$y = \sqrt{x} - 5$

5. domain: all real numbers ≥ 2; range: all nonnegative real numbers **7.** domain: all real numbers $\geq -\frac{2}{3}$; range: all nonnegative real numbers

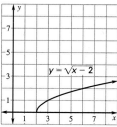

$y = \sqrt{x - 2}$

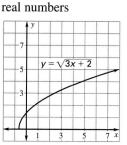

$y = \sqrt{3x + 2}$

9. $5\sqrt{5}$ **11.** $16\sqrt{2}$ **13.** $7\sqrt{3} - 3\sqrt{2}$ **15.** $\frac{6}{3}$ **17.** 121
19. no solution **21.** $1, 3$ **23.** 16 **25.** 64 **27.** $x^{3/4}$
29. $x^6 y^{5/2}$ **31.** $-14, 4$ **33.** $2, 5$ **35.** $-2, 8$ **37.** $\sqrt{2}$
39. 8 **41.** 20 **43.** 8 **45.** 18.36 **47.** 12.08 **49.** 4.47
51. $(2, 4.5); d = \sqrt{4.25}$ **53.** $(2.5, -2); d = 2.5$
55. $(0, 4); d = 2\sqrt{5}$ **57.** $(5, 6); d = \sqrt{17}$ **59.** *Sample answer:* Assume $xy = 0$ and both $x \neq 0$ and $y \neq 0$. If $xy = 0$ and $x \neq 0$, then $y = \frac{0}{x} = 0$, but this is impossible since $y \neq 0$. Therefore if $xy = 0$, either $x = 0$ or $y = 0$.

7051 2